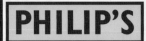

PHILIP'S

RO

C000173632

2021
EASY TO READ
BRITAIN

CONTENTS

Inside front cover: **Key to map pages**

II	**Route planning maps**
XII	**Distances and journey times**
XIII	**Key to map symbols**
2	**Road maps of Britain**
289	**Index to road maps of Britain**

Inside back cover: **County and unitary authority boundaries**

www.philips-maps.co.uk

First published in 2020 by Philip's
a division of Octopus Publishing Group Ltd
www.octopusbooks.co.uk
Carmelite House, 50 Victoria Embankment
London EC4Y 0DZ
An Hachette UK Company
www.hachette.co.uk

First edition 2020
First impression 2020

ISBN 978-1-84907-535-0

Cartography by Philip's
Copyright © 2020 Philip's

Map data

This product includes mapping data licensed from Ordnance Survey®, with the permission of the Controller of Her Majesty's Stationery Office. © Crown copyright 2020. All rights reserved. Licence number 100011710.

Information for National Parks, Areas of Outstanding Natural Beauty, National Trails and Country Parks in Wales supplied by the Countryside Council for Wales.

Information for National Parks, Areas of Outstanding Natural Beauty, National Trails and Country Parks in England supplied by Natural England. Data for Regional Parks, Long Distance Footpaths and Country Parks in Scotland provided by Scottish Natural Heritage.

Gaelic name forms used in the Western Isles provided by Comhairle nan Eilean.

Data for the National Nature Reserves in England provided by Natural England. Data for the National Nature Reserves in Wales provided by Countryside Council for Wales. Darparwyd data'n ymwneud â Gwarchodfeydd Natur Cenedlaethol Cymru gan Gyngor Cefn Gwlad Cymru.

Information on the location of National Nature Reserves in Scotland was provided by Scottish Natural Heritage.

Data for National Scenic Areas in Scotland provided by the Scottish Executive Office. Crown copyright material is reproduced with the permission of the Controller of HMSO and the Queen's Printer for Scotland. Licence number C02W0003960.

Printed in China

*Data from Nielsen Total Consumer Market 2016 weeks 1–52

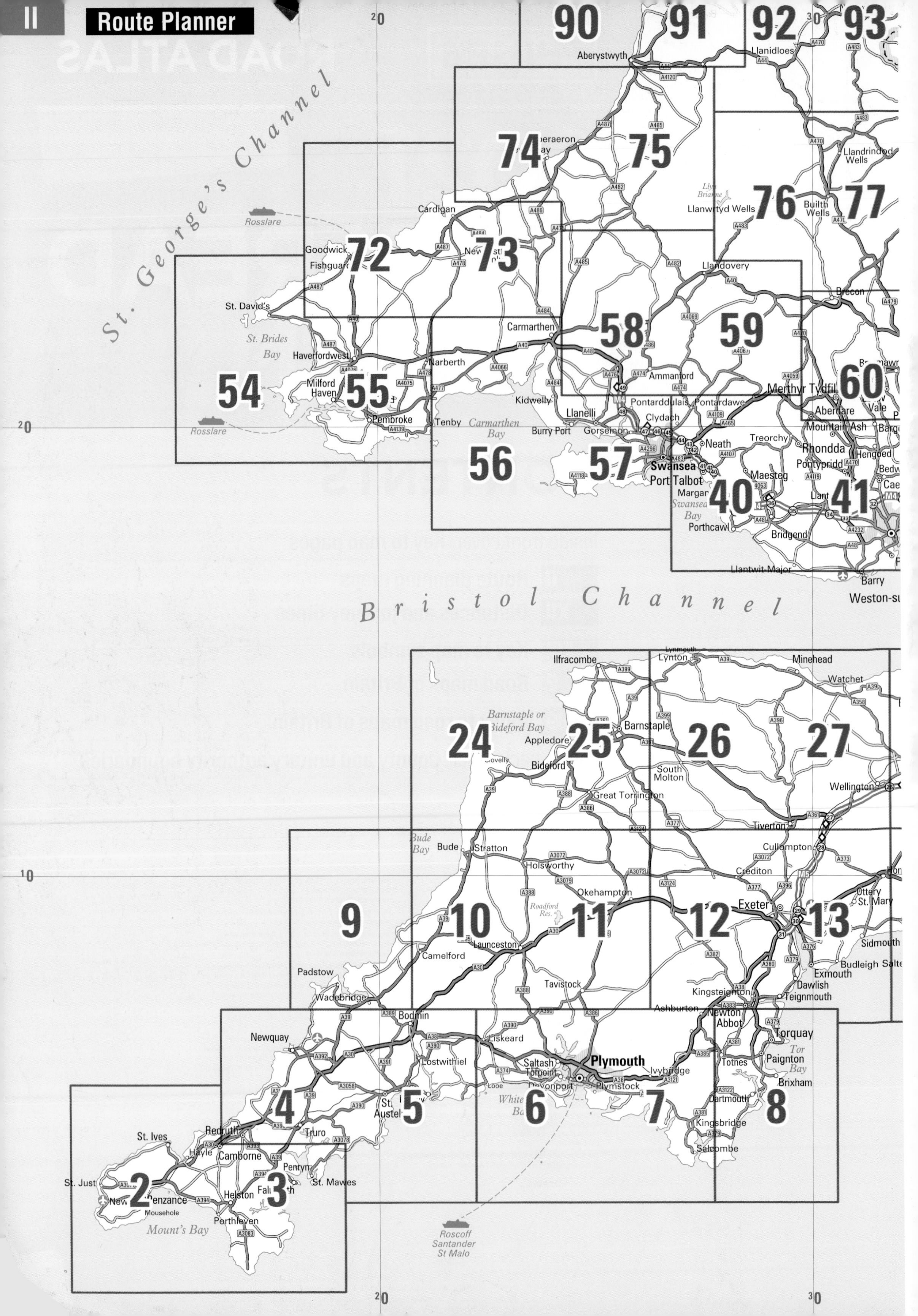

St. George's Channel
Bristol Channel
Rosslare
Aberystwyth
Llanidloes
Cardigan
Goodwick
Fishguard
St. David's
St. Brides Bay
Haverfordwest
Milford Haven
Pembroke
Narberth
Tenby
Carmarthen
Carmarthen Bay
Kidwelly
Llanelli
Burry Port
Gorseinon
Pontarddulais
Pontardawe
Clydach
Ammanford
Llandovery
Llanwrtyd Wells
Builth Wells
Llandrindod Wells
Brecon
Merthyr Tydfil
Aberdare
Mountain Ash
Treorchy
Rhondda
Pontypridd
Hengoed
Neath
Swansea
Port Talbot
Maesteg
Swansea Bay
Porthcawl
Bridgend
Llantwit Major
Barry
Weston-su
Ilfracombe
Lynmouth
Lynton
Minehead
Watchet
Barnstaple or Bideford Bay
Barnstaple
Appledore
Bideford
South Molton
Great Torrington
Wellington
Tiverton
Bude Bay
Bude
Stratton
Holsworthy
Okehampton
Roadford Res.
Cullompton
Crediton
Exeter
Ottery St. Mary
Sidmouth
Budleigh Salterton
Exmouth
Dawlish
Teignmouth
Kingsteignton
Ashburton
Newton Abbot
Torquay
Paignton
Tor Bay
Brixham
Totnes
Dartmouth
Kingsbridge
Salcombe
Launceston
Camelford
Tavistock
Padstow
Wadebridge
Bodmin
Newquay
Liskeard
Lostwithiel
Saltash
Torpoint
Devonport
Plymouth
Plymstock
Ivybridge
Looe
St. Austell
Truro
Redruth
Camborne
Hayle
St. Ives
St. Just
Penzance
Mousehole
Mount's Bay
Helston
Porthleven
Penryn
St. Mawes
Roscoff
Santander
St Malo
2
3
4
5
6
7
8
9
10
11
12
13
24
25
26
27
40
41
54
55
56
57
58
59
60
72
73
74
75
76
77
90
91
92
93

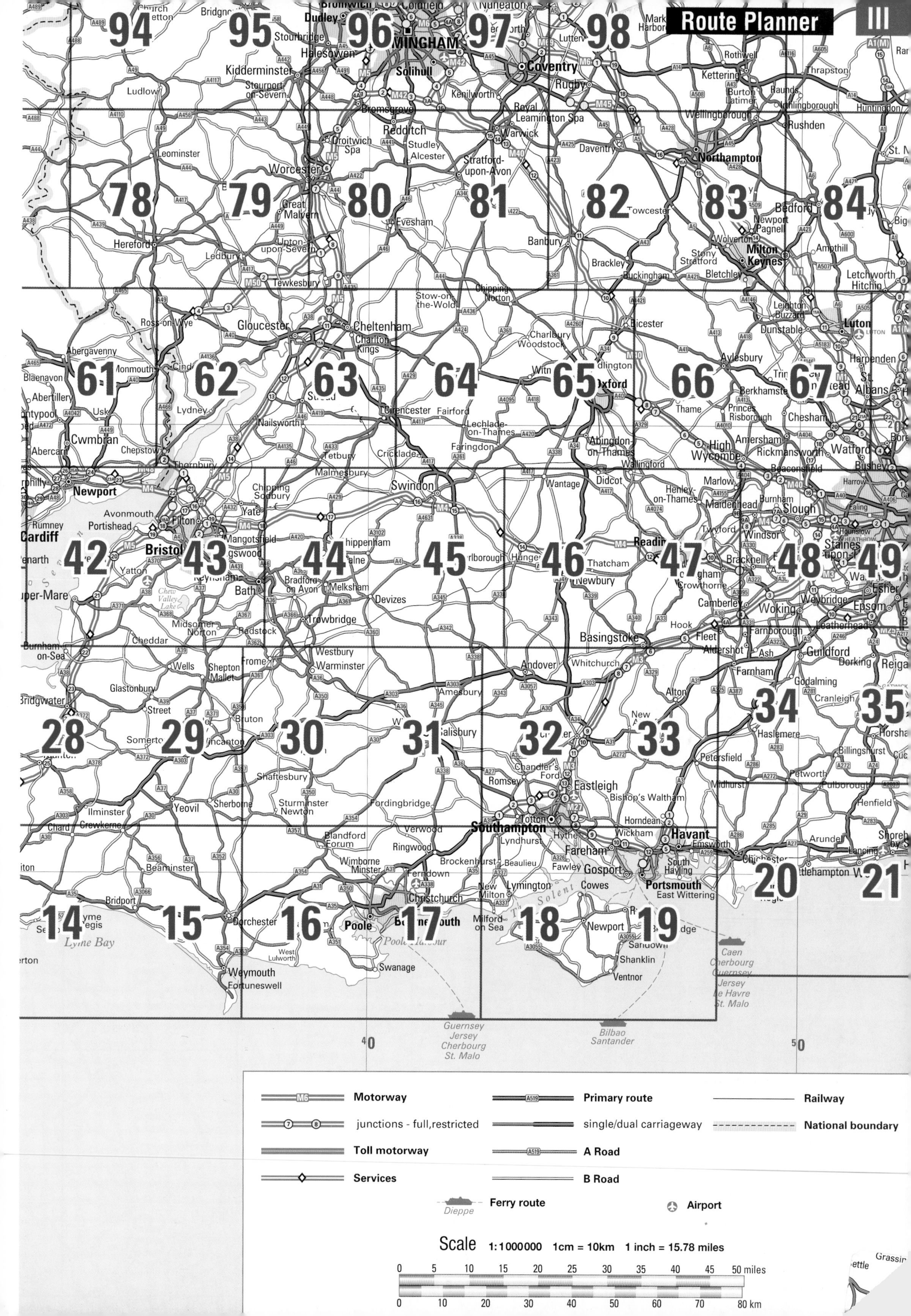

Scale

1:1 000 000   1cm = 10km   1 inch = 15.78 miles

	Motorway		Primary route		Railway
	junctions - full, restricted		single/dual carriageway		National boundary
	Toll motorway		A Road		
	Services		B Road		
	Ferry route		Airport		

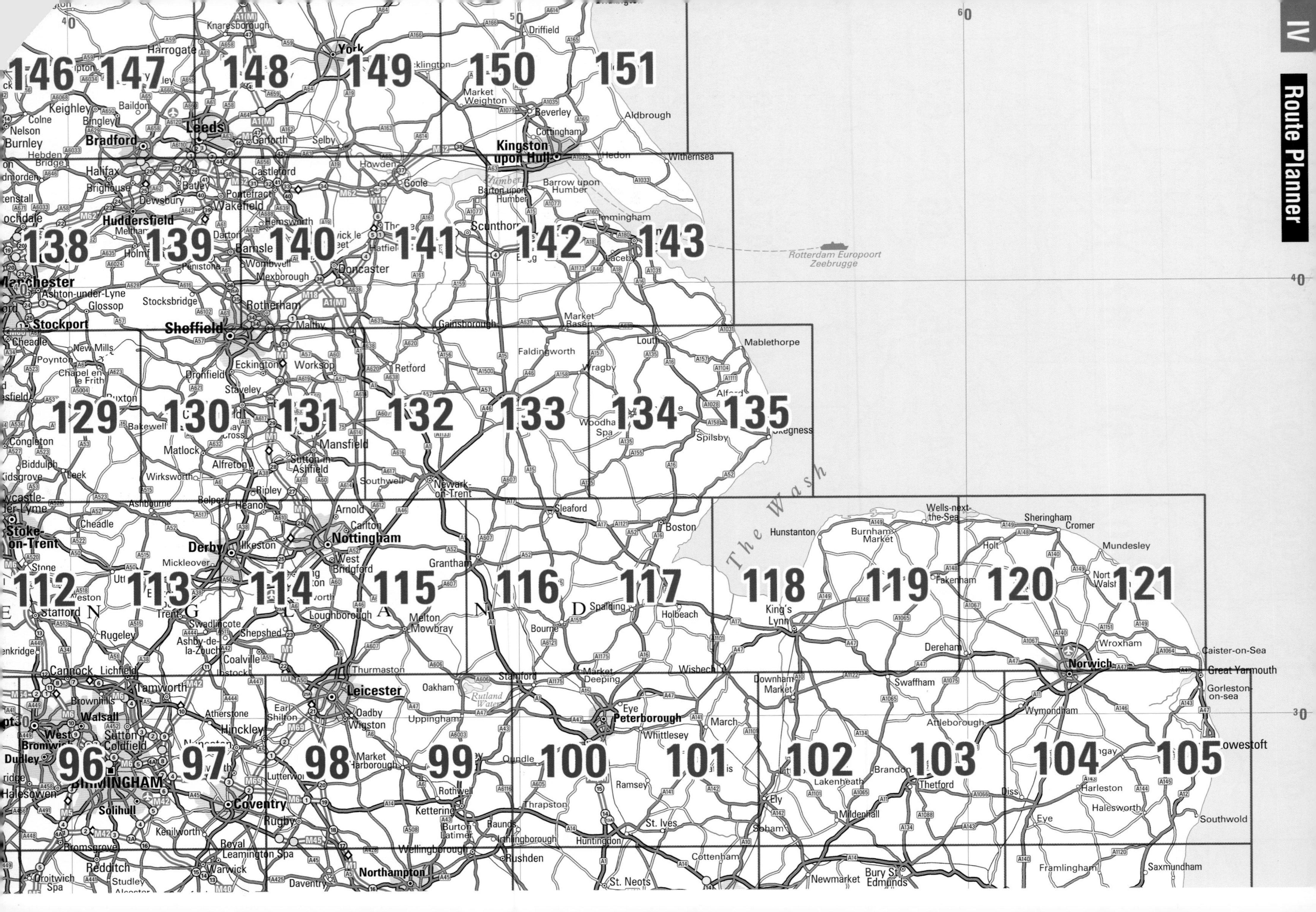
146
147
148
149
150
151
138
139
140
141
142
143
129
130
131
132
133
134
135
112
113
114
115
116
117
118
119
120
121
96
97
98
99
100
101
102
103
104
105
York
Leeds
Bradford
Harrogate
Knaresborough
Keighley
Bingley
Baildon
Halifax
Huddersfield
Wakefield
Pontefract
Castleford
Selby
Goole
Howden
Doncaster
Barnsley
Rotherham
Sheffield
Stockport
Glossop
Kingston upon Hull
Beverley
Cottingham
Driffield
Market Weighton
Withernsea
Aldbrough
Immingham
Scunthorpe
Barton-upon-Humber
Gainsborough
Market Rasen
Louth
Mablethorpe
Spilsby
Alford
Wragby
Boston
Sleaford
Newark-on-Trent
Retford
Worksop
Mansfield
Sutton-in-Ashfield
Bakewell
Matlock
Alfreton
Ripley
Belper
Heanor
Ilkeston
Derby
Nottingham
West Bridgford
Arnold
Carlton
Southwell
Grantham
Melton Mowbray
Loughborough
Leicester
Oakham
Uppingham
Stamford
Peterborough
Spalding
Holbeach
Wisbech
King's Lynn
Hunstanton
Burnham Market
Wells-next-the-Sea
Sheringham
Cromer
Mundesley
Holt
Fakenham
Dereham
Norwich
Wroxham
Great Yarmouth
Caister-on-Sea
Gorleston-on-sea
Southwold
Wymondham
Attleborough
Swaffham
Thetford
Brandon
Diss
Eye
Harleston
Halesworth
Framlingham
Saxmundham
Downham Market
Ely
Soham
Mildenhall
Lakenheath
Newmarket
Bury St. Edmunds
March
Whittlesey
Ramsey
St. Ives
Huntingdon
St. Neots
Cottenham
Oundle
Thrapston
Kettering
Rothwell
Market Harborough
Wellingborough
Rushden
Northampton
Daventry
Rugby
Coventry
Hinckley
Atherstone
Tamworth
Lichfield
Sutton Coldfield
Solihull
Walsall
Dudley
Halesowen
Redditch
Kenilworth
Warwick
Royal Leamington Spa
Cannock
Rugeley
Stafford
Stone
Leek
Biddulph
Congleton
Cheadle
Ashbourne
Wirksworth
Swadlincote
Ashby-de-la-Zouch
Coalville
Shepshed
Ashton-under-Lyne
Stocksbridge
Penistone
Wombwell
Mexborough
Hemsworth
Nelson
Colne
Burnley
The Wash
Rotterdam Europoort
Zeebrugge
Rutland Water

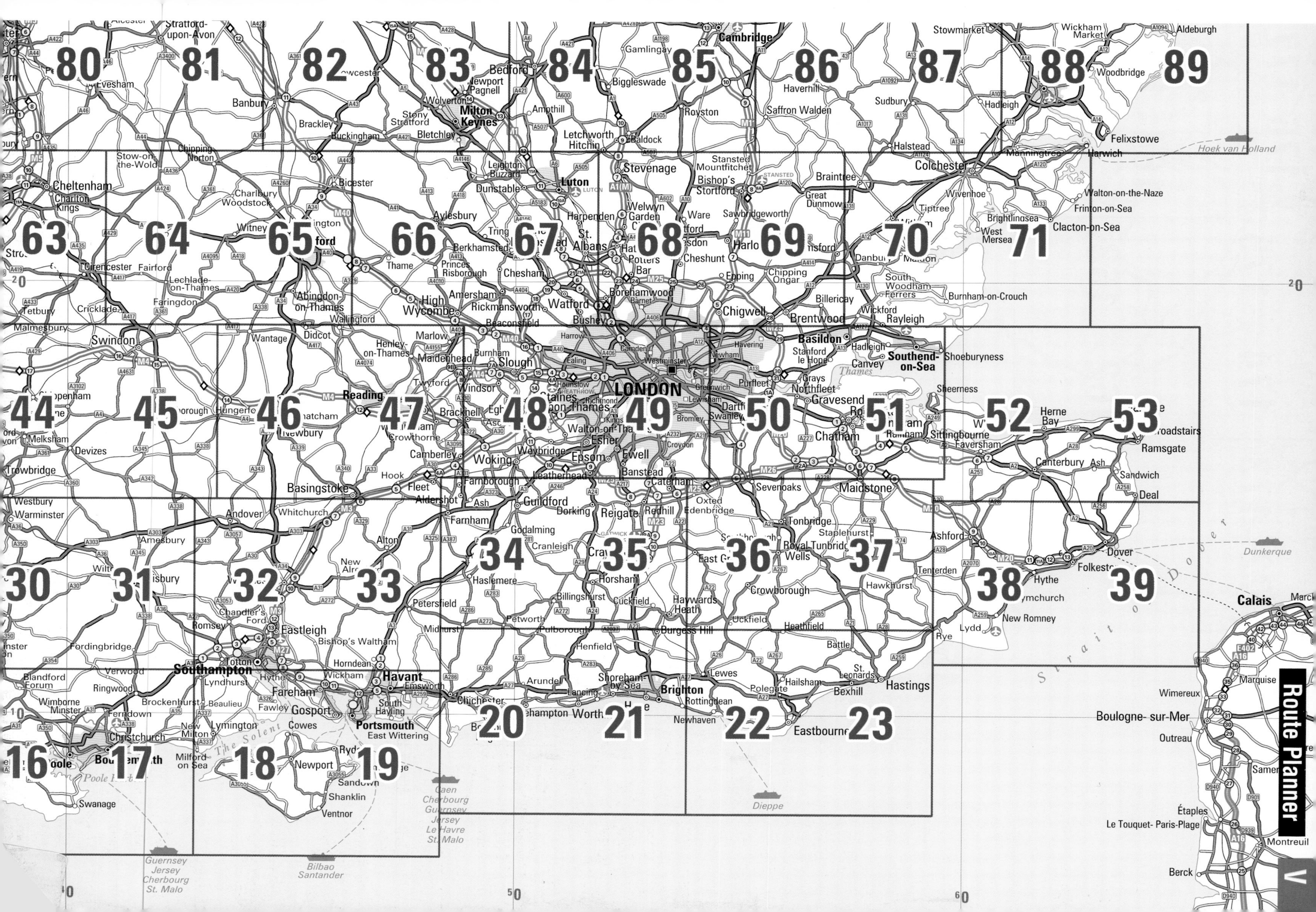
80 81 82 83 84 85 86 87 88 89
63 64 65 66 67 68 69 70 71
44 45 46 47 48 49 50 51 52 53
30 31 32 33 34 35 36 37 38 39
16 17 18 19 20 21 22 23
LONDON
Cambridge
Stratford-upon-Avon
Evesham
Banbury
Brackley
Buckingham
Bedford
Newport Pagnell
Milton Keynes
Bletchley
Stony Stratford
Biggleswade
Royston
Haverhill
Saffron Walden
Sudbury
Halstead
Stowmarket
Hadleigh
Wickham Market
Woodbridge
Aldeburgh
Felixstowe
Harwich
Hoek van Holland
Cheltenham
Charlton Kings
Stow-on-the-Wold
Chipping Norton
Charlbury
Woodstock
Bicester
Aylesbury
Luton
Dunstable
Leighton Buzzard
Letchworth
Hitchin
Baldock
Stevenage
Stansted Mountfitchet
Bishop's Stortford
Braintree
Great Dunmow
Colchester
Wivenhoe
Tiptree
Brightlingsea
West Mersea
Walton-on-the-Naze
Frinton-on-Sea
Clacton-on-Sea
Witney
Thame
Tring
Berkhamsted
Princes Risborough
Harpenden
St. Albans
Welwyn Garden City
Ware
Sawbridgeworth
Harlow
Cheshunt
Potters Bar
Epping
Chipping Ongar
Danbury
South Woodham Ferrers
Burnham-on-Crouch
Cirencester
Fairford
Lechlade-on-Thames
Faringdon
Cricklade
Tetbury
Malmesbury
Abingdon-on-Thames
Wallingford
Didcot
Wantage
High Wycombe
Amersham
Chesham
Rickmansworth
Watford
Borehamwood
Barnet
Bushey
Chigwell
Billericay
Brentwood
Wickford
Rayleigh
Swindon
Chippenham
Melksham
Devizes
Trowbridge
Hungerford
Newbury
Reading
Twyford
Henley-on-Thames
Marlow
Maidenhead
Burnham
Beaconsfield
Slough
Windsor
Bracknell
Crowthorne
Camberley
Staines
Hounslow
Harrow
Ealing
Camden
Westminster
Newham
Havering
Basildon
Stanford le Hope
Canvey
Hadleigh
Southend-on-Sea
Shoeburyness
Thames
Grays
Purfleet
Greenwich
Lewisham
Northfleet
Gravesend
Chatham
Sheerness
Sittingbourne
Faversham
Herne Bay
Ramsgate
Canterbury
Sandwich
Deal
Walton-on-Thames
Esher
Epsom
Ewell
Bromley
Croydon
Swanley
Woking
Weybridge
Leatherhead
Banstead
Caterham
Sevenoaks
Maidstone
Westbury
Warminster
Andover
Whitchurch
Basingstoke
Hook
Fleet
Farnborough
Aldershot
Ash
Guildford
Dorking
Reigate
Redhill
Oxted
Edenbridge
Tonbridge
Ashford
Amesbury
Farnham
Godalming
Cranleigh
Alton
Haslemere
Horsham
Royal Tunbridge Wells
Staplehurst
Tenterden
Hythe
Folkestone
Dover
Dunkerque
Petersfield
Billingshurst
Cuckfield
Haywards Heath
Crowborough
Hawkhurst
New Romney
Lydd
Rye
Calais
Fordingbridge
Romsey
Chandler's Ford
Eastleigh
Bishop's Waltham
Midhurst
Petworth
Pulborough
Henfield
Burgess Hill
Uckfield
Heathfield
Battle
Verwood
Ringwood
Southampton
Totton
Lyndhurst
Hythe
Fareham
Wickham
Horndean
Havant
Emsworth
Chichester
Arundel
Lancing
Shoreham-by-Sea
Brighton
Lewes
Polegate
Hailsham
St. Leonards
Hastings
Bexhill
Blandford Forum
Wimborne Minster
Ferndown
Christchurch
Brockenhurst
Beaulieu
Fawley
Gosport
New Milton
Lymington
Milford on Sea
The Solent
Cowes
Portsmouth
South Hayling
East Wittering
Rottingdean
Newhaven
Eastbourne
Wimereux
Boulogne-sur-Mer
Outreau
Marquise
Samer
Étaples
Le Touquet-Paris-Plage
Montreuil
Berck
Poole
Swanage
Newport
Ryde
Sandown
Shanklin
Ventnor
Caen
Cherbourg
Guernsey
Jersey
Le Havre
St. Malo
Dieppe
Bilbao
Santander
Strait of Dover

Route Planner

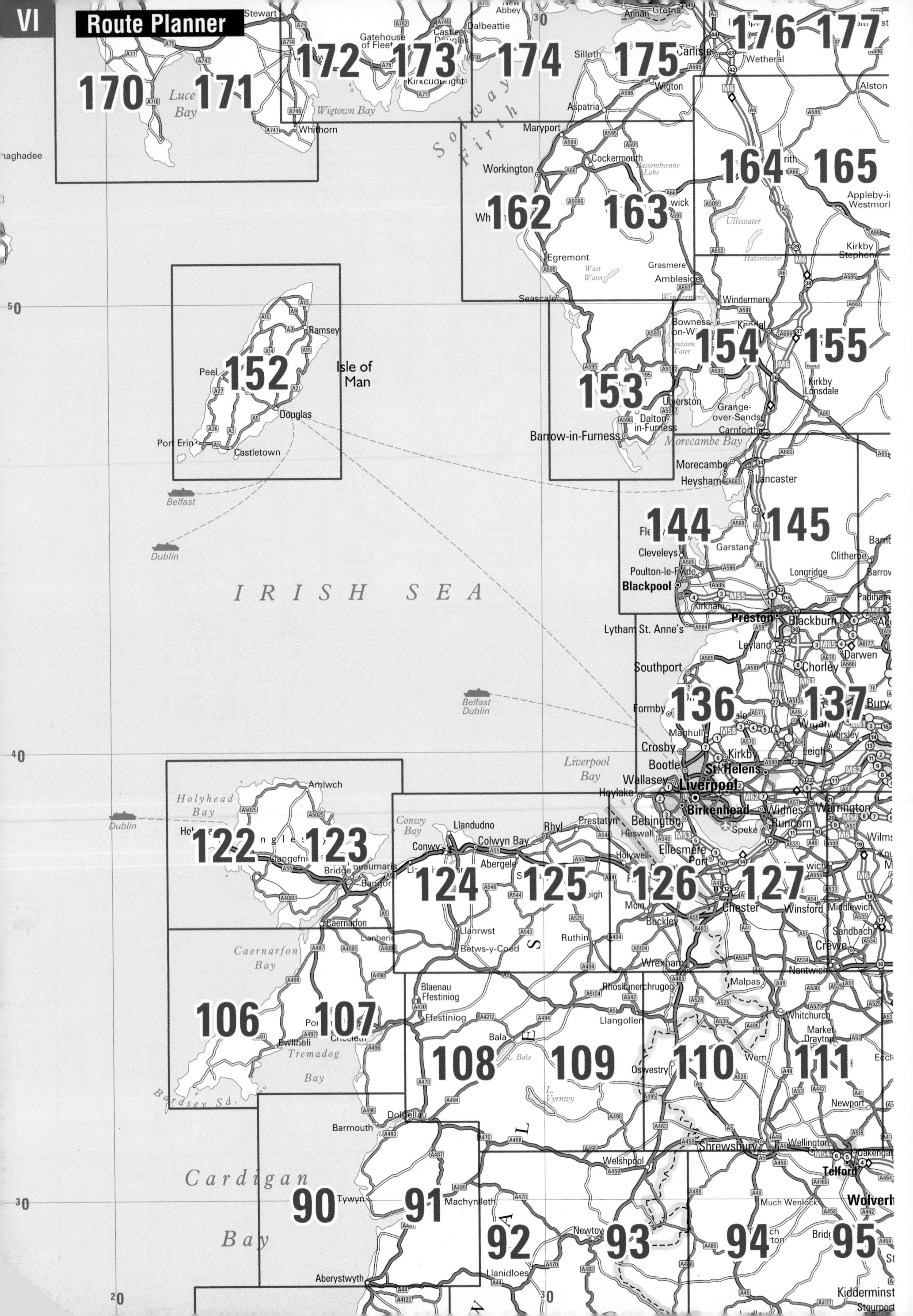

170
171
172
173
174
175
176
177
Stewart
Gatehouse of Fleet
Castle Douglas
Dalbeattie
Kirkcudbright
Luce Bay
Wigtown Bay
Whithorn
Annan
Gretna
Silloth
Carlisle
Wetheral
Wigton
Aspatria
Alston
Solway Firth
Maryport
Workington
Cockermouth
Bassenthwaite Lake
164
165
162
163
Appleby-in-Westmorland
Ullswater
Egremont
Wast Water
Grasmere
Ambleside
Haweswater
Kirkby Stephen
Seascale
Windermere
Bowness-on-Windermere
Kendal
Coniston Water
154
155
152
Ramsey
Peel
Isle of Man
Douglas
Port Erin
Castletown
153
Kirkby Lonsdale
Ulverston
Dalton-in-Furness
Grange-over-Sands
Carnforth
Barrow-in-Furness
Morecambe Bay
Morecambe
Heysham
Lancaster
Belfast
Dublin
144
145
Garstang
Cleveleys
Clitheroe
Poulton-le-Fylde
Longridge
Blackpool
IRISH SEA
Kirkham
Preston
Blackburn
Lytham St. Anne's
Leyland
Darwen
Chorley
Southport
Belfast
Dublin
Formby
136
137
Maghull
Wigan
Worsley
Crosby
Kirkby
Leigh
Liverpool Bay
Bootle
St. Helens
Wallasey
Liverpool
Hoylake
Birkenhead
Widnes
Warrington
Holyhead Bay
Amlwch
Bebington
Speke
Runcorn
Dublin
122
123
Llandudno
Prestatyn
Rhyl
Heswall
Conwy Bay
Conwy
Colwyn Bay
Holywell
Ellesmere Port
Llangefni
Beaumaris
Abergele
Bangor
124
125
126
127
Chester
Winsford
Middlewich
Mold
Buckley
Caernarfon
Llanberis
Llanrwst
Ruthin
Sandbach
Crewe
Caernarfon Bay
Betws-y-Coed
Wrexham
Nantwich
Blaenau Ffestiniog
Rhosllanerchrugog
Malpas
106
107
Ffestiniog
Llangollen
Whitchurch
Pwllheli
Tremadog Bay
Bala
L. Bala
Market Drayton
108
109
110
111
Oswestry
Wem
L. Vyrnwy
Newport
Bardsey Sd.
Dolgellau
Barmouth
Shrewsbury
Wellington
Telford
Welshpool
Cardigan Bay
90
91
Tywyn
Machynlleth
Much Wenlock
Wolverhampton
92
93
94
95
Newtown
Llanidloes
Aberystwyth
Kidderminster
Stourport
WALES

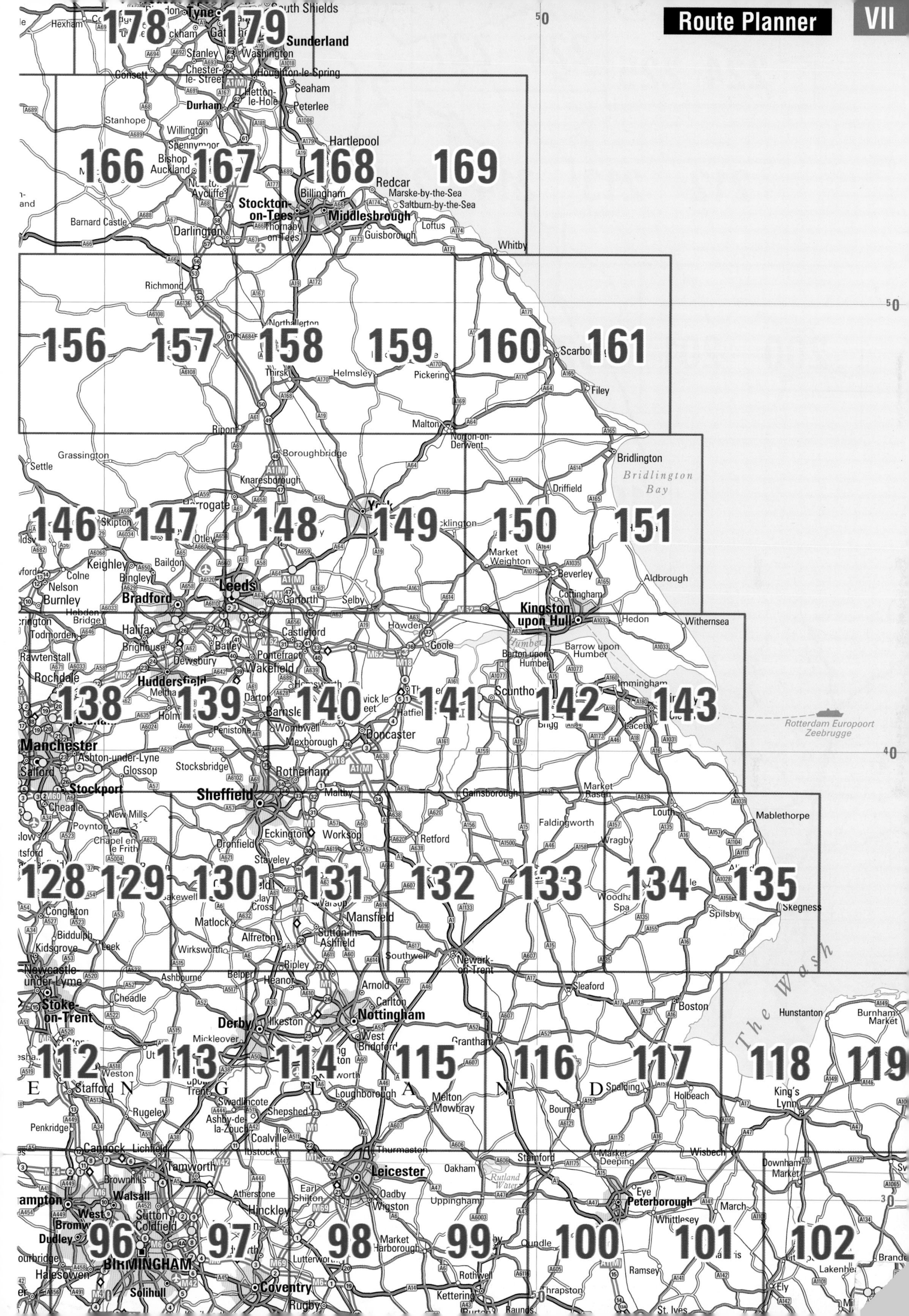
178
179
Sunderland
South Shields
Hexham
Stanley
Washington
Chester-le-Street
Consett
Houghton-le-Spring
Seaham
Durham
Hetton-le-Hole
Peterlee
Stanhope
Willington
Spennymoor
Hartlepool
166
167
168
169
Bishop Auckland
Newton Aycliffe
Redcar
Marske-by-the-Sea
Saltburn-by-the-Sea
Billingham
Stockton-on-Tees
Middlesbrough
Barnard Castle
Darlington
Thornaby-on-Tees
Guisborough
Loftus
Whitby
Richmond
Northallerton
156
157
158
159
160
161
Scarborough
Thirsk
Helmsley
Pickering
Filey
Ripon
Malton
Norton-on-Derwent
Settle
Grassington
Boroughbridge
Knaresborough
Bridlington
Bridlington Bay
Driffield
Harrogate
York
146
147
148
149
150
151
Skipton
Otley
Market Weighton
Keighley
Baildon
Colne
Bingley
Nelson
Burnley
Bradford
Leeds
Garforth
Selby
Beverley
Aldbrough
Cottingham
Kingston upon Hull
Hedon
Withernsea
Hebden Bridge
Todmorden
Halifax
Castleford
Howden
Goole
Brighouse
Batley
Pontefract
Barton upon Humber
Barrow upon Humber
Rawtenstall
Dewsbury
Wakefield
Rochdale
Huddersfield
Immingham
138
139
140
141
142
143
Darton
Barnsley
Hatfield
Scunthorpe
Brigg
Laceby
Rotterdam Europoort
Zeebrugge
Penistone
Wombwell
Doncaster
Manchester
Mexborough
Salford
Ashton-under-Lyne
Stocksbridge
Glossop
Rotherham
Stockport
Sheffield
Maltby
Gainsborough
Market Rasen
Cheadle
New Mills
Louth
Mablethorpe
Poynton
Eckington
Worksop
Faldingworth
Chapel en le Frith
Dronfield
Retford
Wragby
Staveley
128
129
130
131
132
133
134
135
Congleton
Clay Cross
Mansfield
Woodhall Spa
Spilsby
Skegness
Matlock
Biddulph
Alfreton
Sutton-in-Ashfield
Kidsgrove
Leek
Wirksworth
Southwell
Newark-on-Trent
The Wash
Newcastle-under-Lyme
Ashbourne
Belper
Heanor
Ripley
Arnold
Sleaford
Cheadle
Carlton
Boston
Stoke-on-Trent
Derby
Ilkeston
Nottingham
Hunstanton
Burnham Market
Mickleover
West Bridgford
Grantham
112
113
114
115
116
117
118
119
Stafford
Weston
E
N
G
L
A
N
D
Loughborough
Melton Mowbray
Spalding
Holbeach
King's Lynn
Swadlincote
Shepshed
Bourne
Rugeley
Ashby-de-la-Zouch
Penkridge
Coalville
Cannock
Lichfield
Thurmaston
Stamford
Market Deeping
Wisbech
Downham Market
Tamworth
Leicester
Oakham
Rutland Water
Brownhills
Walsall
Atherstone
Earl Shilton
Oadby
Wigston
Uppingham
Eye
Peterborough
Hinckley
March
Sutton Coldfield
Whittlesey
96
97
98
99
100
101
102
Dudley
Market Harborough
Oundle
BIRMINGHAM
Halesowen
Lutterworth
Rothwell
Ramsey
Lakenheath
Coventry
Solihull
Kettering
Thrapston
Ely
Rugby
St. Ives
Humber

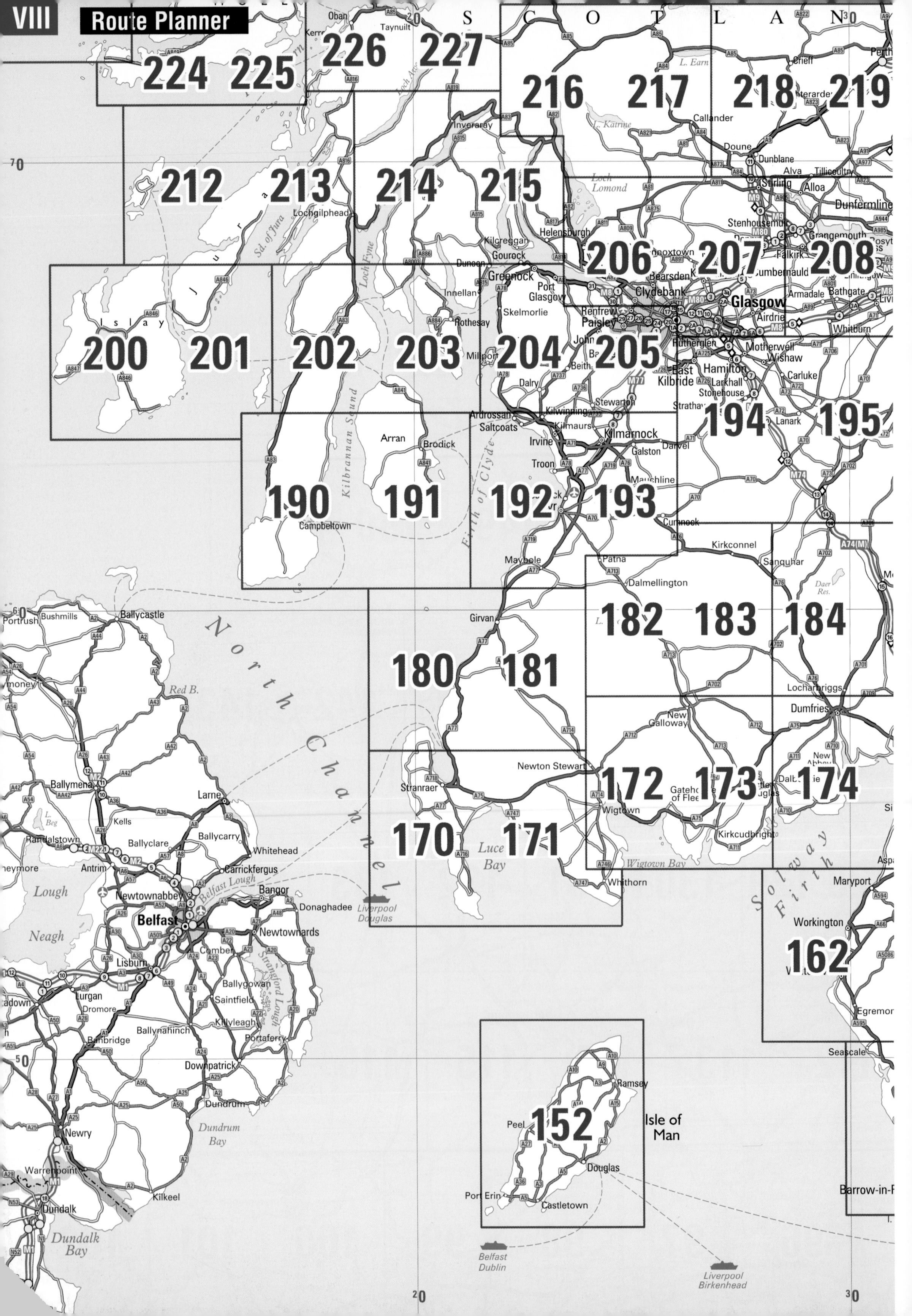
SCOTLAND
224
225
226
227
216
217
218
219
212
213
214
215
206
207
208
200
201
202
203
204
205
194
195
190
191
192
193
182
183
184
180
181
172
173
174
170
171
162
152
Oban
Taynuilt
Crieff
Perth
L. Earn
Callander
L. Katrine
Doune
Dunblane
Inveraray
Loch Lomond
Alva
Tillicoultry
Stirling
Alloa
Dunfermline
Lochgilphead
Sd. of Jura
Jura
Helensburgh
Kilcreggan
Gourock
Stenhousemuir
Grangemouth
Falkirk
Cumbernauld
Dunoon
Greenock
Port Glasgow
Clydebank
Bearsden
Glasgow
Armadale
Bathgate
Innellan
Islay
Skelmorlie
Renfrew
Paisley
Airdrie
Whitburn
Rothesay
Millport
Rutherglen
Motherwell
Wishaw
Beith
East Kilbride
Hamilton
Larkhall
Stonehouse
Carluke
Dalry
Stewarton
Kilbrannan Sound
Ardrossan
Saltcoats
Kilwinning
Kilmaurs
Kilmarnock
Lanark
Arran
Brodick
Irvine
Galston
Darvel
Troon
Mauchline
Firth of Clyde
Campbeltown
Cumnock
Maybole
Patna
Kirkconnel
Sanquhar
Dalmellington
Daer Res.
Girvan
Locharbriggs
Dumfries
New Galloway
Newton Stewart
New Abbey
Stranraer
Wigtown
Gatehouse of Fleet
Luce Bay
Kirkcudbright
Wigtown Bay
Whithorn
Solway Firth
Maryport
Workington
Egremont
Seascale
North Channel
Liverpool
Douglas
Portrush
Bushmills
Ballycastle
Red B.
Ballymena
Larne
Kells
Randalstown
Ballyclare
Ballycarry
Whitehead
Antrim
Carrickfergus
Lough Neagh
Newtownabbey
Belfast Lough
Bangor
Donaghadee
Belfast
Newtownards
Comber
Lisburn
Lurgan
Dromore
Ballygowan
Saintfield
Strangford Lough
Killyleagh
Ballynahinch
Banbridge
Portaferry
Downpatrick
Dundrum
Dundrum Bay
Newry
Warrenpoint
Kilkeel
Dundalk
Dundalk Bay
Isle of Man
Ramsey
Peel
Douglas
Port Erin
Castletown
Barrow-in-F
Belfast
Dublin
Liverpool
Birkenhead

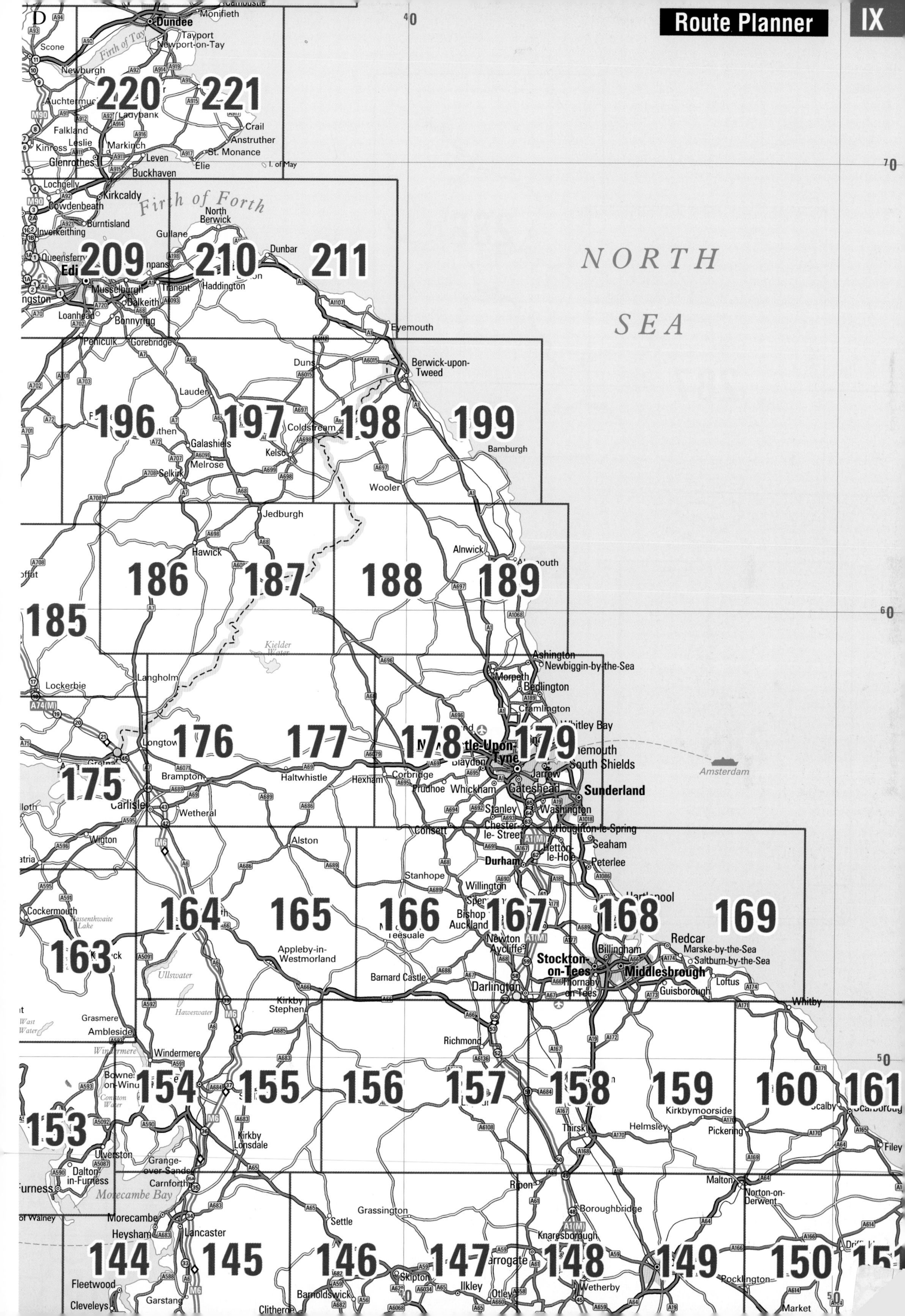

Route Planner
IX
NORTH SEA
Amsterdam
Firth of Forth
Firth of Tay
Dundee
Monifieth
Tayport
Newport-on-Tay
Scone
Newburgh
Ladybank
Crail
Anstruther
St. Monance
Elie
Falkland
Leslie
Kinross
Markinch
Leven
Glenrothes
Buckhaven
I. of May
Lochgelly
Kirkcaldy
Cowdenbeath
Burntisland
Inverkeithing
North Berwick
Gullane
Dunbar
Queensferry
Musselburgh
Tranent
Haddington
Dalkeith
Loanhead
Bonnyrigg
Eyemouth
Penicuik
Gorebridge
Duns
Berwick-upon-Tweed
Lauder
Coldstream
Galashiels
Kelso
Melrose
Selkirk
Bamburgh
Wooler
Jedburgh
Hawick
Alnwick
Kielder Water
Ashington
Newbiggin-by-the-Sea
Morpeth
Bedlington
Lockerbie
Langholm
Cramlington
Whitley Bay
Longtown
South Shields
Brampton
Haltwhistle
Hexham
Corbridge
Blaydon
Prudhoe
Whickham
Gateshead
Jarrow
Sunderland
Carlisle
Wetheral
Stanley
Washington
Wigton
Alston
Consett
Chester-le-Street
Houghton-le-Spring
Seaham
Durham
Hetton-le-Hole
Peterlee
Stanhope
Willington
Cockermouth
Bassenthwaite Lake
Bishop Auckland
Newton Aycliffe
Redcar
Billingham
Marske-by-the-Sea
Saltburn-by-the-Sea
Appleby-in-Westmorland
Ullswater
Stockton-on-Tees
Middlesbrough
Barnard Castle
Thornaby on Tees
Loftus
Darlington
Guisborough
Haweswater
Kirkby Stephen
Whitby
Grasmere
Ambleside
Richmond
Windermere
Kirkbymoorside
Helmsley
Pickering
Thirsk
Scalby
Ulverston
Grange-over-Sands
Kirkby Lonsdale
Dalton-in-Furness
Furness
Carnforth
Morecambe Bay
Malton
Norton-on-Derwent
Ripon
Boroughbridge
Filey
Morecambe
Heysham
Lancaster
Settle
Grassington
Knaresborough
Harrogate
Fleetwood
Cleveleys
Garstang
Skipton
Ilkley
Otley
Wetherby
Barnoldswick
Clitheroe
Pocklington
Market
220
221
209
210
211
196
197
198
199
186
187
188
189
185
176
177
178
179
175
164
165
166
167
168
169
163
154
155
156
157
158
159
160
161
153
144
145
146
147
148
149
150
40
70
60
50

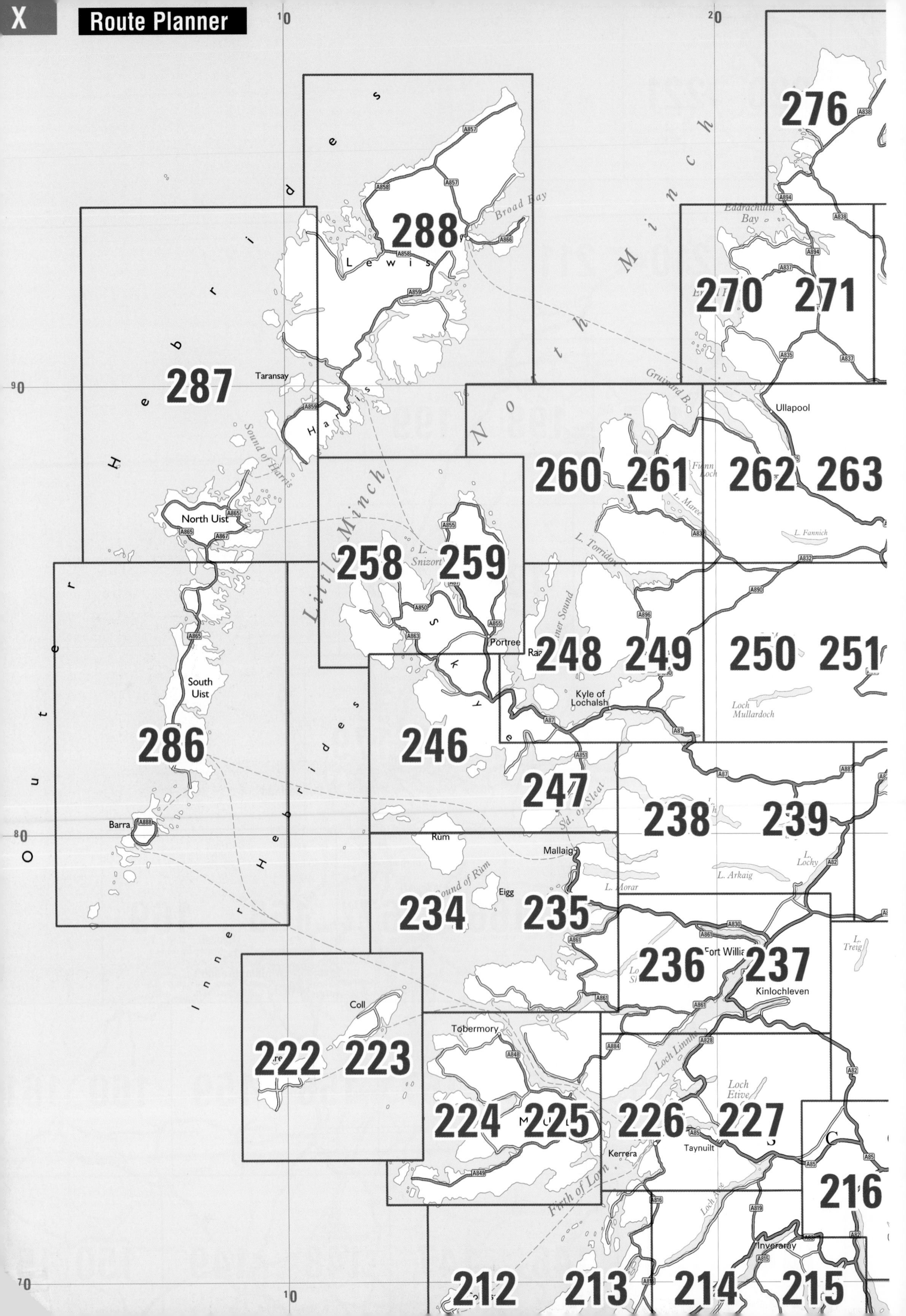
276
288
Lewis
Broad Bay
270
271
Eddrachillis Bay
287
Taransay
Harris
Sound of Harris
Outer Hebrides
North Minch
Gruinard B.
Ullapool
260
261
262
263
L. Fannich
North Uist
258
259
L. Snizort
Little Minch
L. Torridon
Skye
Portree
248
249
250
251
Kyle of Lochalsh
Loch Mullardoch
South Uist
286
246
247
Sd. of Sleat
238
239
Barra
Rum
Mallaig
L. Lochy
L. Arkaig
L. Morar
Sound of Rum
Eigg
234
235
Inner Hebrides
236
237
Fort William
Kinlochleven
L. Treig
Coll
Tobermory
222
223
224
225
226
227
Mull
Loch Linnhe
Loch Etive
Kerrera
Taynuilt
Firth of Lorn
216
Inverarary
212
213
214
215

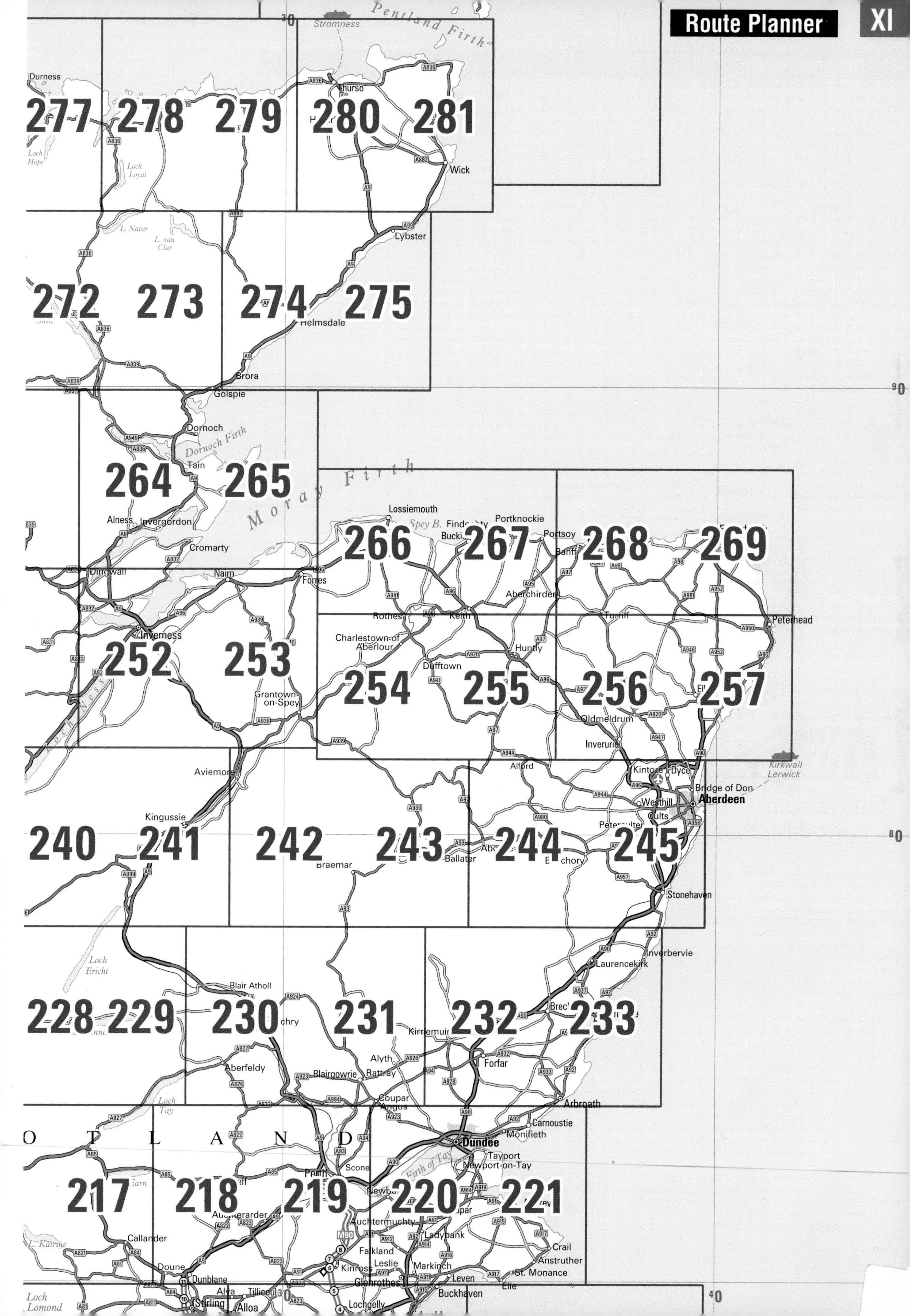
277 278 279 280 281
272 273 274 275
264 265
266 267 268 269
252 253
254 255 256 257
240 241 242 243 244 245
228 229 230 231 232 233
217 218 219 220 221
Pentland Firth
Stromness
Durness
Thurso
Wick
Loch Hope
Loch Loyal
L. Naver
L. nan Clar
Lybster
Helmsdale
Brora
Golspie
Dornoch
Dornoch Firth
Tain
Moray Firth
Alness
Invergordon
Cromarty
Dingwall
Nairn
Forres
Inverness
Lossiemouth
Spey B.
Portknockie
Portsoy
Banff
Aberchirder
Rothes
Keith
Turriff
Peterhead
Charlestown-of-Aberlour
Huntly
Dufftown
Grantown-on-Spey
Oldmeldrum
Inverurie
Kintore
Dyce
Kirkwall
Lerwick
Alford
Bridge of Don
Aberdeen
Westhill
Cults
Aviemore
Kingussie
Braemar
Ballater
Stonehaven
Loch Ericht
Blair Atholl
Inverbervie
Laurencekirk
Kirriemuir
Alyth
Forfar
Aberfeldy
Blairgowrie
Rattray
Coupar Angus
Arbroath
Loch Tay
Carnoustie
Monifieth
Dundee
Tayport
Newport-on-Tay
Firth of Tay
Perth
Scone
Auchterarder
Auchtermuchty
Ladybank
Crail
Anstruther
St. Monance
Callander
L. Katrine
Falkland
Leslie
Markinch
Kinross
Glenrothes
Leven
Elie
Buckhaven
Doune
Dunblane
Alva
Tillicoultry
Stirling
Alloa
Lochgelly
Loch Lomond
90
80
40
30

Distance table

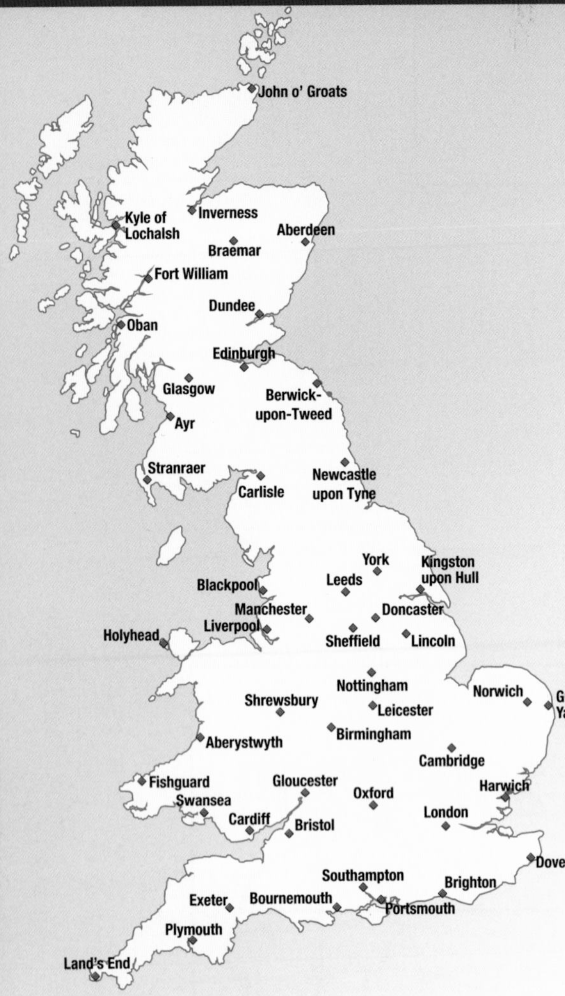

How to use this table

Distances are shown in miles and kilometres with estimated journey times in hours and minutes.

For example: the distance between Dover and Fishguard is 331 miles or 533 kilometres with an estimated journey time of 6 hours, 20 minutes.

Estimated driving times are based on an average speed of 60mph on Motorways and 40mph on other roads. Drivers should allow extra time when driving at peak periods or through areas likely to be congested.

London																																																
Aberdeen																																																517 832 11:20
Aberystwyth																																															445 716 8:40	211 340 4:40
Ayr																																														317 510 6:10	183 295 4:20	394 634 7:20
Berwick-upon-Tweed																																													134 216 3:00	311 501 6:20	182 293 4:40	352 567 7:30
Birmingham																																												274 441 5:30	289 465 5:30	114 183 2:50	420 676 8:30	117 188 2:50
Blackpool																																											123 198 2:40	181 291 3:50	180 290 3:30	153 246 3:20	308 496 6:20	226 364 4:30
Bournemouth																																										270 435 5:00	147 237 3:10	412 663 7:50	436 702 8:00	207 333 4:30	564 908 10:20	107 172 2:40
Braemar																																									524 843 9:30	281 452 5:20	385 620 7:10	148 238 3:20	143 230 3:00	405 652 7:50	59 95 1:30	482 776 10:30
Brighton																																								534 859 9:40	92 148 2:10	286 460 5:20	163 262 3:20	409 658 7:40	446 718 8:00	253 407 5:10	573 922 10:30	52 84 1:50
Bristol																																							147 237 4:10	477 768 8:40	82 132 2:30	204 328 3:50	81 130 2:00	362 583 6:50	370 595 6:40	125 201 3:00	493 793 9:10	122 196 2:50
Cambridge																																						169 272 3:10	116 187 2:20	438 705 7:50	154 248 3:00	208 335 3:50	100 161 2:10	306 493 5:40	357 575 6:20	214 344 4:20	471 758 10:00	54 87 1:30
Cardiff																																					190 306 3:30	45 72 1:20	182 293 3:40	483 778 8:40	117 188 3:00	209 336 4:00	103 166 2:20	368 592 7:00	382 615 7:00	105 169 2:40	505 813 9:20	157 253 3:20
Carlisle																																				289 465 5:20	264 425 4:40	277 446 5:00	370 596 6:40	196 316 3:50	343 552 6:20	87 140 1:50	196 315 3:50	87 140 2:10	93 150 2:00	224 360 4:30	221 356 4:30	301 484 5:40
Doncaster																																			142 229 3:00	209 336 4:00	116 187 2:10	175 282 3:20	236 380 4:30	310 499 5:40	235 378 4:20	94 151 1:50	94 151 2:00	184 296 3:50	235 378 4:20	176 283 3:40	344 554 6:50	171 275 3:30
Dover																																		242 390 4:30	389 626 7:00	238 383 4:30	125 201 2:30	202 325 3:50	82 132 2:20	553 890 9:50	174 280 4:30	312 502 5:40	194 312 3:50	424 683 7:50	478 769 8:30	297 478 5:50	588 947 10:40	71 114 2:00
Dundee																																	523 842 9:10	275 443 5:00	152 245 3:00	441 710 8:00	406 654 7:10	430 692 7:40	517 832 9:10	52 84 1:20	495 797 8:50	239 385 4:30	349 562 6:20	113 182 2:40	117 188 2:30	376 605 7:10	67 108 1:50	448 721 8:40
Edinburgh																																56 90 1:30	462 744 8:10	219 352 4:00	96 154 2:00	385 620 7:00	345 555 6:10	373 600 6:50	456 734 8:20	91 146 2:10	439 707 8:00	183 295 3:30	292 470 5:30	57 92 1:40	73 117 1:50	320 515 6:20	125 201 3:10	390 628 7:20
Exeter																															450 724 8:00	518 834 9:10	248 399 4:40	251 404 4:30	353 568 6:20	121 195 2:30	249 401 4:30	76 122 1:40	184 296 5:00	550 885 9:40	82 132 2:20	282 454 5:10	157 253 3:10	428 689 7:50	446 718 7:50	201 323 4:10	569 916 10:20	181 291 3:40
Fishguard																														230 370 4:30	399 642 7:30	460 740 8:30	331 533 6:20	247 398 4:50	297 478 5:40	112 180 2:40	270 435 5:10	154 248 3:20	291 468 5:40	493 794 9:10	222 357 4:40	209 336 4:10	170 274 3:40	371 597 7:20	373 600 7:00	56 90 1:30	504 811 10:10	260 418 5:20
Fort William																													486 782 9:30	560 901 10:20	144 232 3:30	127 204 3:10	596 959 11:00	357 575 7:00	206 332 4:30	485 781 9:10	479 771 9:00	486 782 9:10	575 926 10:50	125 201 3:10	539 867 10:10	296 476 6:00	392 631 7:40	190 306 4:40	133 214 3:20	430 692 8:40	149 240 3:50	510 821 9:50
Glasgow																												101 163 2:50	376 605 7:10	449 723 8:00	44 71 1:20	83 134 2:00	488 786 8:40	249 401 4:40	96 154 2:10	385 620 7:00	372 599 6:40	373 600 6:50	468 753 8:30	110 177 2:30	439 707 8:00	183 295 3:40	292 470 5:30	101 163 2:40	33 53 1:10	320 515 6:20	145 233 3:30	397 639 7:30
Gloucester																											346 557 6:10	454 731 8:30	153 246 3:10	111 179 2:10	349 562 6:10	410 660 7:10	191 307 3:30	150 241 2:50	247 398 4:20	56 90 1:20	123 198 2:20	35 56 1:00	159 256 3:10	443 713 8:00	99 159 2:40	174 280 3:10	56 90 1:20	318 512 6:00	330 531 5:50	102 164 2:30	468 753 8:30	109 175 2:30
Great Yarmouth																										225 362 4:40	419 674 8:00	527 848 10:20	366 589 7:20	335 539 6:30	386 621 7:30	484 779 9:00	185 298 4:00	167 269 3:40	320 515 6:20	284 457 5:50	82 132 2:10	275 443 5:40	180 290 4:10	477 768 9:10	240 386 5:00	252 406 5:10	180 290 4:10	345 555 7:00	402 647 7:40	294 473 6:20	517 832 10:50	128 206 3:40
Harwich																									82 132 2:10	196 316 4:00	432 695 8:10	543 874 10:30	337 542 6:40	279 449 5:20	413 665 7:40	469 755 8:40	125 201 2:50	194 312 4:00	336 541 6:20	246 396 5:00	67 108 1:50	217 349 4:30	128 206 3:00	504 811 9:20	187 301 4:00	275 443 5:20	167 269 3:40	372 599 7:20	425 684 8:00	281 452 5:50	535 861 11:20	76 122 2:20
Holyhead																								349 562 7:10	334 538 7:00	191 307 4:00	330 531 6:40	438 705 8:50	167 269 4:00	282 454 5:40	333 536 6:40	394 634 7:30	360 580 7:00	181 291 3:50	231 372 4:50	216 348 5:40	270 435 5:20	206 332 4:30	334 538 6:40	426 686 8:20	288 463 5:50	141 227 3:20	148 238 3:30	311 501 6:30	305 491 6:10	111 179 2:50	439 707 8:40	269 433 5:40
Inverness																							474 763 9:40	569 916 11:00	553 890 11:00	504 811 9:30	166 267 4:00	66 106 1:40	542 872 10:30	618 995 11:30	158 254 3:50	132 212 3:20	622 1001 11:30	383 617 7:30	262 422 5:30	549 884 10:20	505 813 9:30	539 867 10:10	617 993 11:30	75 121 2:00	597 961 11:20	348 560 7:00	458 737 9:00	215 346 5:10	199 320 4:30	486 782 9:40	105 169 2:50	550 885 10:40
John o' Groats																						129 208 3:20	603 970 12:40	693 1116 14:00	677 1090 14:00	628 1011 12:30	295 475 7:10	195 314 5:00	671 1080 13:40	744 1197 14:30	285 459 7:00	259 417 6:30	746 1201 14:40	507 816 10:30	391 629 8:40	680 1094 13:30	630 1014 12:30	668 1075 13:20	741 1193 14:40	202 325 5:00	724 1165 14:20	478 769 10:00	574 924 11:50	342 550 8:10	328 528 7:40	601 967 12:40	232 373 5:50	663 1067 13:30
Kingston upon Hull																					518 834 10:50	394 634 7:50	231 372 4:50	196 316 4:10	207 333 5:20	169 272 3:10	254 409 4:50	369 594 7:20	280 451 5:30	309 497 5:40	234 377 4:30	295 475 5:30	256 412 4:50	47 76 1:10	158 254 3:00	244 393 4:40	139 224 3:10	233 375 4:20	245 394 4:40	327 526 6:10	264 425 5:00	127 204 2:30	134 216 2:50	185 298 3:50	251 404 4:40	223 359 4:40	364 586 7:20	184 296 3:50
Kyle of Lochalsh																				445 716 9:00	189 304 4:40	84 135 2:10	514 827 10:40	611 983 12:10	602 969 12:10	528 850 10:20	179 288 4:40	76 122 1:50	567 913 11:20	628 1011 12:00	216 348 5:20	186 299 4:40	671 1080 12:50	432 695 8:40	275 443 6:10	564 908 11:10	555 893 10:50	552 888 10:50	651 1048 12:40	159 256 4:00	618 995 12:10	372 599 7:50	471 758 9:40	263 423 6:20	212 341 5:10	499 803 10:20	189 304 4:50	586 943 11:40
Land's End																			763 1228 15:10	421 678 8:20	868 1397 17:20	741 1193 14:20	405 652 8:30	390 628 8:00	446 718 9:10	235 378 5:00	573 922 10:50	686 1104 13:20	353 568 7:20	123 198 3:20	574 924 10:50	642 1033 12:00	381 613 7:40	374 602 7:20	477 768 9:10	245 394 5:20	374 602 7:20	200 322 4:40	308 496 7:50	665 1070 12:30	205 330 5:20	405 652 8:00	281 452 6:00	552 888 10:40	570 917 10:50	313 504 6:50	692 1114 13:10	297 478 6:30
Leeds																		405 652 8:00	394 634 8:20	55 89 1:30	487 784 10:20	360 579 7:10	176 283 4:00	223 359 4:30	196 315 4:20	174 280 3:20	215 346 4:10	329 530 6:40	237 381 4:40	270 435 5:00	202 325 4:00	258 415 4:50	260 418 4:50	29 47 0:50	119 192 2:30	232 373 4:20	145 233 2:50	194 312 3:50	260 419 5:00	293 472 5:30	255 410 4:50	72 116 1:40	113 182 2:30	156 251 3:20	212 341 4:00	169 272 3:40	327 526 6:50	189 304 3:50
Leicester																	95 153 2:00	320 515 6:30	500 805 9:50	102 164 2:10	588 947 11:50	461 742 8:50	190 306 4:00	147 237 3:10	140 225 3:20	85 137 1:40	314 505 5:40	422 679 8:00	209 336 4:10	196 315 3:40	296 476 5:20	349 562 6:20	185 298 3:30	74 119 1:30	206 332 3:50	154 248 3:00	68 109 1:20	120 193 2:30	166 267 3:20	389 626 7:00	158 254 3:10	140 225 2:40	39 63 1:10	252 406 5:00	299 481 5:20	153 246 3:20	414 666 7:40	97 156 2:20
Lincoln																51 82 1:20	68 109 1:50	371 597 7:30	476 766 9:40	44 71 1:20	554 892 11:30	427 687 8:30	216 348 4:40	155 249 3:30	128 206 3:20	159 256 3:10	291 468 5:30	399 642 7:50	272 438 5:30	247 398 4:40	258 415 5:00	314 505 5:50	202 325 4:00	39 63 1:10	191 307 3:40	208 335 4:10	85 137 2:20	183 295 3:40	197 317 4:00	357 575 6:40	209 336 4:10	128 206 2:40	90 145 2:10	224 360 4:40	274 441 5:10	199 320 4:20	383 616 7:20	131 211 3:10
Liverpool															129 208 2:50	130 209 2:40	75 121 1:50	361 581 7:20	407 655 8:30	130 209 2:40	511 822 10:40	382 615 7:40	102 164 2:40	265 427 5:20	240 386 5:00	140 225 2:40	216 348 4:10	329 530 6:40	160 257 3:30	237 381 4:30	216 348 4:10	286 460 5:20	299 481 5:30	86 138 1:50	120 193 2:30	169 272 3:20	194 312 3:40	161 259 3:10	272 438 5:10	318 512 6:00	234 377 4:30	49 79 1:20	93 150 2:10	219 352 4:30	213 343 4:10	104 167 2:40	341 549 6:40	202 325 4:10
Manchester														35 56 1:10	84 135 2:00	92 148 2:00	40 64 1:10	361 581 7:20	406 654 8:30	95 153 2:10	500 805 10:30	373 600 7:30	124 200 3:00	228 367 4:40	212 341 4:30	126 203 2:30	215 346 4:10	329 530 6:40	197 317 4:00	236 380 4:20	215 346 4:10	285 459 5:20	276 444 5:10	61 98 1:30	119 192 2:30	183 295 3:40	165 266 3:10	161 259 3:10	257 414 4:50	318 512 6:00	227 365 4:20	48 77 1:20	80 129 2:00	196 315 4:00	212 341 4:00	129 208 3:00	340 547 6:30	185 298 3:50
Newcastle upon Tyne													132 212 2:50	168 270 3:20	159 256 3:20	187 301 3:40	92 148 2:10	498 802 9:40	318 512 7:00	132 212 2:50	395 636 8:50	268 431 5:40	272 438 5:40	308 496 6:00	281 452 5:40	266 428 4:50	148 238 3:10	253 407 5:20	329 529 6:20	364 586 6:30	110 177 2:20	166 267 3:20	358 576 6:30	114 183 2:20	57 92 1:50	325 523 6:00	241 388 4:20	299 481 5:30	352 567 6:30	201 323 4:00	347 558 6:30	129 208 2:40	207 333 4:10	64 103 1:50	149 240 3:00	257 414 5:20	235 378 4:50	286 460 5:40
Norwich												264 425 5:20	185 298 4:30	220 354 4:40	105 169 2:50	119 192 3:20	176 283 3:50	421 678 8:40	582 937 11:50	149 240 4:00	654 1053 13:30	529 852 10:30	311 501 6:40	73 117 2:00	20 32 0:40	204 328 4:10	385 620 9:00	504 811 10:00	343 552 7:00	308 496 6:00	366 589 7:00	422 679 8:00	174 280 3:50	147 237 3:20	289 465 5:40	262 422 5:20	62 100 1:50	252 406 5:10	175 282 4:00	457 735 8:40	214 344 4:40	232 373 4:50	166 267 3:50	328 528 6:40	382 615 7:20	276 444 6:00	496 798 9:40	114 183 3:30
Nottingham											130 209 3:40	157 253 3:10	73 118 1:40	98 158 2:10	35 56 1:10	25 40 0:50	70 113 1:40	345 555 7:00	479 771 9:40	90 145 2:00	557 896 11:30	430 692 8:20	185 298 4:00	150 241 3:20	153 246 3:30	110 177 2:10	293 472 5:30	401 646 7:50	220 354 4:30	221 356 4:10	262 422 4:50	328 528 6:00	205 330 3:50	43 69 1:10	194 312 3:40	172 277 3:20	83 134 1:40	145 233 3:00	193 311 3:50	353 568 6:30	183 295 3:40	111 179 2:20	50 80 1:20	221 356 4:30	274 441 5:10	164 264 3:40	393 633 7:30	122 196 2:40
Oban										390 628 7:30	492 792 9:40	233 375 4:50	307 494 6:00	308 496 6:10	387 623 7:30	419 674 7:50	307 494 6:00	665 1070 12:50	128 206 3:10	346 557 6:40	244 393 6:10	117 188 3:00	427 687 8:30	524 843 10:00	515 829 10:00	441 710 8:10	92 148 2:30	49 79 1:20	481 774 9:10	549 884 10:00	123 198 3:00	117 188 2:50	585 942 10:40	346 557 6:40	188 303 4:00	477 768 9:00	468 753 8:40	465 748 8:40	565 910 10:30	141 227 3:30	530 853 9:50	285 459 5:40	384 618 7:30	180 290 4:20	94 151 2:20	412 663 8:10	178 286 4:20	499 803 9:30
Oxford									462 744 8:30	109 175 2:10	145 233 3:50	260 418 4:50	144 232 2:50	172 277 3:20	137 221 2:50	73 117 1:30	168 270 3:10	274 441 5:40	550 885 10:40	192 309 3:40	656 1056 13:00	532 856 10:00	238 383 4:50	145 233 3:10	200 322 4:20	52 84 1:30	356 573 6:30	472 760 9:00	205 330 4:10	156 251 3:00	372 599 6:40	433 697 7:40	141 227 2:50	145 233 2:40	260 418 4:40	108 174 2:20	83 134 1:40	74 119 1:40	108 174 2:20	465 749 8:20	90 145 2:00	187 301 3:30	64 103 1:30	324 521 6:10	353 568 6:20	154 248 3:20	483 777 8:50	57 92 1:40
Plymouth								199 320 4:00	587 945 11:00	267 430 5:10	343 552 7:00	410 660 7:40	283 455 5:30	283 455 5:30	293 472 5:50	242 389 4:40	316 509 6:00	89 143 2:20	674 1085 13:10	355 571 6:40	790 1271 15:40	664 1069 12:30	328 528 6:40	309 497 6:10	365 588 7:20	157 253 3:20	495 797 9:10	595 958 11:20	264 425 5:30	46 74 1:30	496 798 9:00	552 888 10:00	300 483 5:50	297 478 5:40	399 642 7:20	167 269 3:40	293 472 5:30	122 196 2:50	224 361 6:00	587 945 10:40	128 206 3:30	328 528 6:10	203 327 4:20	474 763 9:00	492 792 9:00	237 382 5:10	615 990 11:20	218 351 4:40
Portsmouth							176 283 4:50	77 124 1:40	545 877 10:00	191 307 3:40	207 333 4:20	337 542 6:10	236 380 4:30	254 409 4:50	201 323 4:00	162 261 3:10	257 414 4:50	259 417 5:40	633 1019 12:10	269 433 5:00	737 1186 14:30	613 987 11:30	311 501 6:10	166 267 3:40	221 356 4:40	119 192 3:00	448 721 8:10	555 893 10:20	251 404 5:00	135 217 2:40	453 729 8:10	514 827 9:00	130 209 2:50	234 377 4:20	348 560 6:10	142 229 3:00	144 232 2:50	97 156 2:10	48 77 1:40	547 881 9:50	52 84 1:30	264 425 4:50	141 227 3:00	401 645 7:30	430 692 7:40	222 357 4:40	560 901 10:10	70 113 2:00
Sheffield						230 370 4:20	283 455 5:30	135 217 2:40	339 546 6:30	37 60 1:00	146 235 3:20	125 201 2:40	38 61 1:00	72 116 1:40	46 74 1:20	62 100 1:20	33 53 1:00	361 581 7:10	427 687 8:40	65 105 1:30	520 837 10:50	393 632 7:40	168 270 3:40	187 301 3:50	166 267 3:40	126 203 2:20	248 399 4:40	348 560 6:50	215 346 4:20	237 381 4:20	235 378 4:20	291 468 5:20	245 394 4:30	18 29 0:40	152 245 3:00	194 312 3:40	120 193 2:20	161 259 3:10	226 364 4:20	320 515 6:00	216 348 4:10	86 138 1:50	76 122 1:50	190 306 4:00	245 394 4:30	159 256 3:30	360 579 6:50	159 256 3:20
Shrewsbury					82 132 2:10	207 333 3:50	225 362 4:40	106 171 2:10	364 586 7:00	93 150 2:00	205 330 4:20	201 323 3:50	69 111 1:40	58 93 1:50	133 214 2:50	84 135 1:40	109 175 2:20	303 488 6:10	451 726 9:00	169 272 3:10	567 912 11:30	438 705 8:20	113 182 2:50	240 386 4:40	225 362 4:40	77 124 1:30	272 438 5:00	382 615 7:20	145 233 3:10	179 288 3:20	274 441 5:00	330 531 6:00	251 404 4:30	109 175 2:10	176 283 3:20	111 179 2:20	159 256 3:00	103 166 2:50	226 364 4:20	371 597 6:50	185 298 3:40	98 158 2:00	45 72 1:20	265 426 5:10	269 433 5:00	77 124 2:10	399 642 7:30	160 258 3:20
Southampton				185 298 4:10	199 320 3:40	21 34 0:50	151 243 4:10	64 103 1:30	530 853 9:40	176 283 3:20	206 332 4:20	324 521 5:50	221 356 4:10	239 385 4:30	204 328 4:00	137 220 2:40	232 373 4:20	228 367 5:00	618 995 12:00	256 412 4:40	723 1164 14:10	598 963 11:10	293 472 5:50	164 264 3:30	220 354 4:40	105 169 2:40	433 697 7:40	541 871 10:00	233 375 4:40	105 169 3:00	438 705 7:50	500 805 8:50	143 230 2:50	209 336 3:50	324 521 5:50	121 195 2:30	148 238 2:50	76 122 2:20	61 98 1:50	532 856 9:30	31 50 1:00	251 404 4:40	128 206 2:40	388 624 7:10	417 671 7:30	201 323 4:10	547 880 10:00	77 124 2:00
Stranraer			445 716 8:20	277 446 5:30	263 423 5:20	461 742 8:40	500 805 9:40	379 610 7:10	148 238 3:40	290 467 5:50	403 649 8:10	158 254 3:40	220 354 4:40	221 356 4:40	298 480 6:00	330 531 6:20	220 354 4:40	585 942 11:30	263 423 6:30	259 417 5:20	379 610 9:00	262 422 6:00	338 544 7:00	410 660 8:10	426 686 8:40	343 552 6:30	84 135 2:30	195 314 4:50	392 631 7:50	454 731 8:30	124 200 3:00	167 269 3:40	496 798 9:10	257 414 5:10	101 163 2:40	390 628 7:30	379 610 7:10	378 608 7:20	475 765 9:00	194 312 4:20	444 715 8:30	188 303 4:00	297 478 6:00	170 274 4:10	51 82 1:20	325 523 6:50	228 367 5:10	402 647 7:50
Swansea		417 671 7:50	161 259 3:00	118 190 2:20	217 349 4:00	182 293 3:30	206 332 4:10	141 227 2:40	506 815 9:20	192 309 3:40	301 485 6:00	347 559 6:20	187 301 3:30	195 314 3:40	233 375 4:30	177 285 3:20	248 399 4:40	285 459 6:00	594 956 11:30	264 425 4:50	696 1120 13:40	572 921 10:40	184 296 4:50	267 430 5:10	329 530 6:30	89 143 1:50	409 658 7:20	496 798 9:20	67 108 1:50	161 259 3:00	412 663 7:20	473 761 8:20	274 441 5:00	232 373 4:10	309 497 5:30	41 66 1:10	227 365 4:10	85 137 1:50	222 357 4:20	505 813 9:00	167 269 3:20	216 348 4:00	119 192 2:30	383 616 7:10	379 610 6:50	73 117 2:00	507 816 9:20	194 312 4:00
York	272 438 5:10	222 357 4:40	258 415 5:10	133 214 2:40	52 84 1:20	278 448 5:10	333 536 6:20	181 291 3:20	309 497 6:00	77 124 1:40	181 291 4:20	84 135 2:20	64 103 1:30	99 159 2:10	75 121 1:50	108 174 2:10	24 39 0:50	411 661 8:00	407 655 8:20	37 60 1:10	479 771 10:10	352 566 7:00	204 328 4:20	228 367 4:40	201 323 4:20	189 304 3:30	217 349 4:10	330 531 6:30	261 420 5:10	287 462 5:10	194 312 3:40	250 402 4:40	282 454 5:10	34 55 1:00	121 195 2:30	244 393 4:40	165 266 3:10	222 357 4:10	275 443 5:10	285 459 5:20	269 433 5:00	96 154 2:00	130 209 2:40	148 238 3:10	214 344 4:00	195 314 4:10	319 513 6:10	207 333 4:10

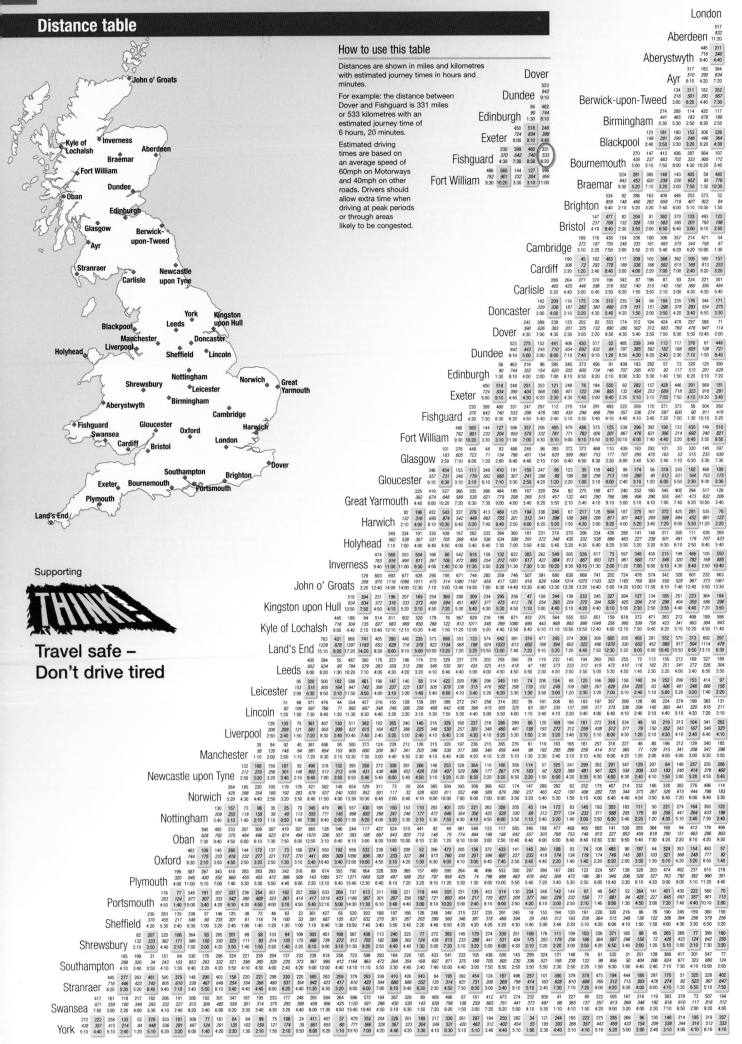

Supporting

THINK!

Travel safe – Don't drive tired

Road map symbols

Motorway, toll motorway
Motorway junction – full, restricted access
Motorway service area – full, restricted access
Motorway under construction

Primary route – dual, single carriageway
Service area, roundabout, multi-level junction
Numbered junction – full, restricted access
Primary route under construction
Narrow primary route
Primary destination

A road – dual, single carriageway
A road under construction, narrow A road

B road – dual, single carriageway
B road under construction, narrow B road

Minor road – over 4 metres, under 4 metres wide
Minor road with restricted access

Distance in miles
Scenic route
Toll, steep gradient – arrow points downhill
Tunnel

National trail – England and Wales
Long distance footpath – Scotland

Railway with station
Level crossing, tunnel
Preserved railway with station

National boundary
County / unitary authority boundary

Car ferry, catamaran
Passenger ferry, catamaran
Hovercraft
Ferry destination
Car ferry – river crossing
Principal airport, other airport

National Park, Area of Outstanding Natural Beauty – England and Wales **National Scenic Area** – Scotland
forest park / regional park / national forest

Beach
Linear antiquity
Roman road
Hillfort, battlefield – with date
Viewpoint, nature reserve, spot height – in metres
Golf course, youth hostel, sporting venue
Camp site, caravan site, camping and caravan site
Shopping village, park and ride

Adjoining page number – road maps

Tourist information

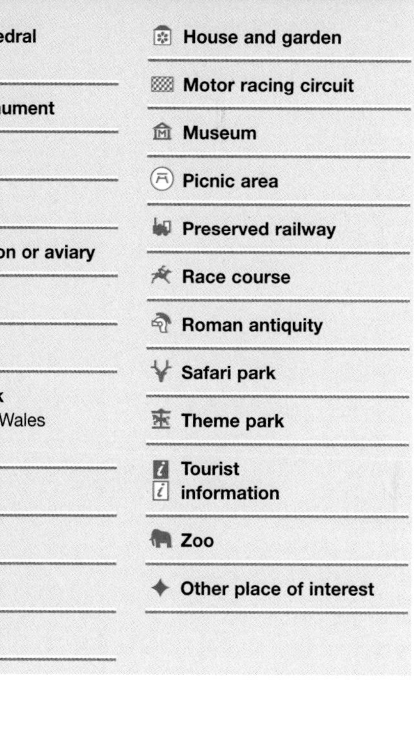

† **Abbey, cathedral or priory**
Ancient monument
Aquarium
Art gallery
Bird collection or aviary
Castle
Church
Country park England and Wales Scotland
Farm park
Garden
Historic ship
House

House and garden
Motor racing circuit
Museum
Picnic area
Preserved railway
Race course
Roman antiquity
Safari park
Theme park
Tourist information
Zoo
Other place of interest

Road map scale
1: 150 000 • 1 cm = 1.5 km • 1 inch = 2·37 miles

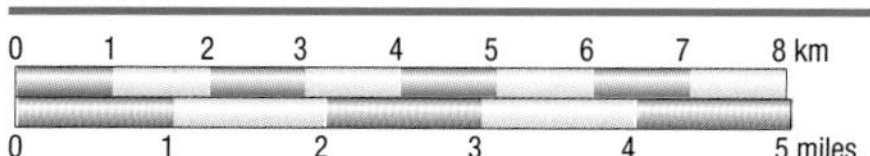

Outer Hebrides, Orkney and Shetland:
1: 303 000 • 1 cm = 3.0 km • 1 inch = 4.78 miles

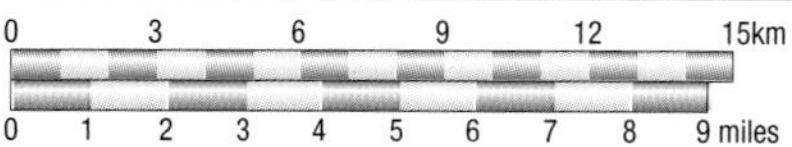

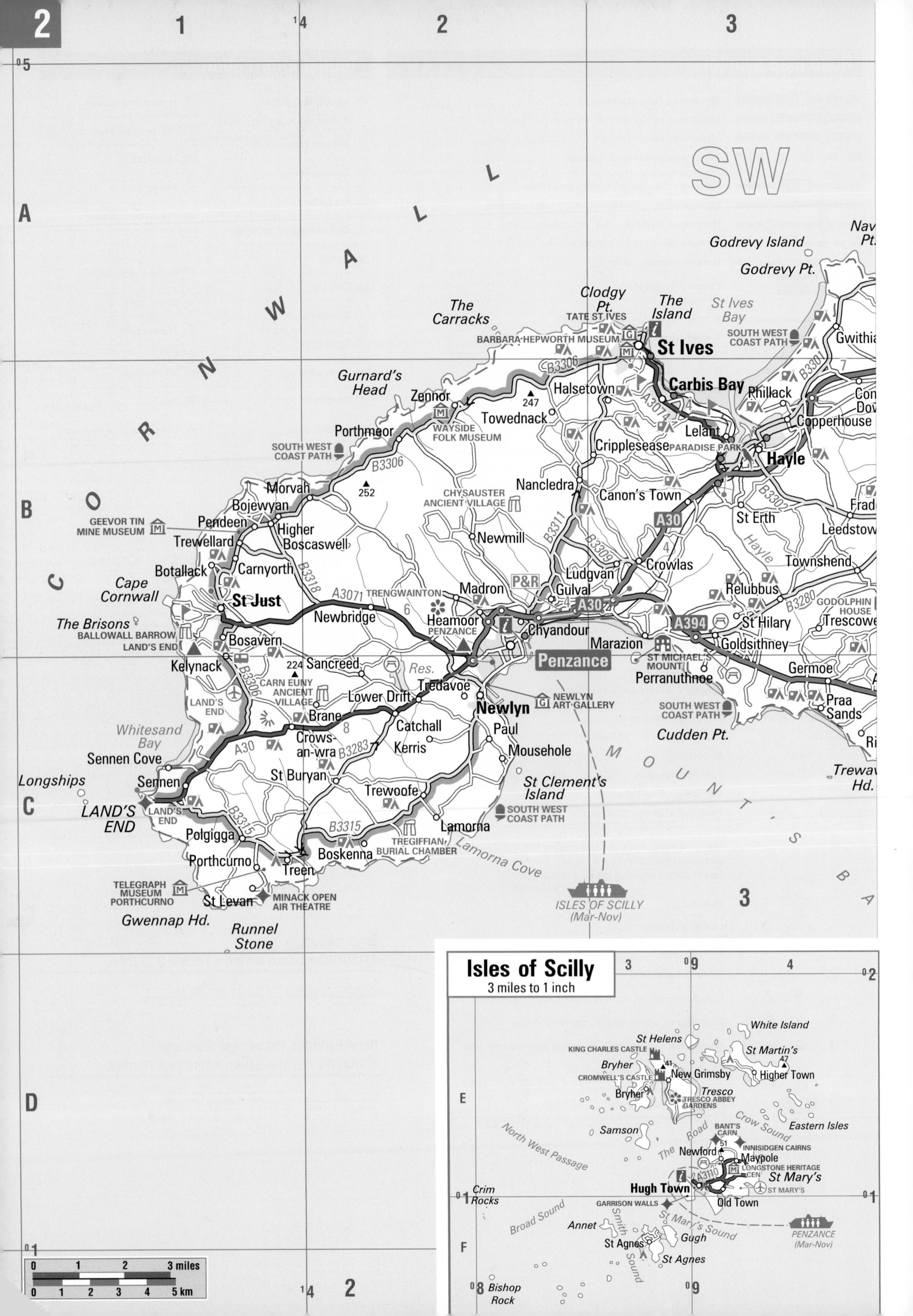

2

1 ·4 2 3

5

CORNWALL

SW

A

Godrevy Island
Godrevy Pt.
Nav Pt.

The Carracks

Clodgy Pt.
TATE ST IVES
The Island
St Ives Bay
SOUTH WEST COAST PATH
Gwithia

BARBARA HEPWORTH MUSEUM
St Ives
B3306
Carbis Bay
Phillack
Con Dov
B3301

Gurnard's Head
Zennor
Halsetown
Lelant
Copperhouse

Porthmeor
WAYSIDE FOLK MUSEUM
247
Towednack
A3074
Cripplesease
PARADISE PARK
Hayle

SOUTH WEST COAST PATH
B3306

252
Nancledra
Canon's Town
B3302
Frad

B
GEEVOR TIN MINE MUSEUM
Morvah
Bojewyan
CHYSAUSTER ANCIENT VILLAGE
Newmill
B3311
Canon's Town
St Erth
Leedstow

Pendeen
Higher Boscaswell
B3309
A30
St Ives Bay

C
Trewellard
Crowlas
Townshend

Botallack
Carnyorth
B3318
Madron
Ludgvan
Relubbus
B3280
GODOLPHIN HOUSE
Trescowe

Cape Cornwall
St Just
A3071 TRENGWAINTON
6
Gulval
A30
A394
St Hilary

The Brisons
BALLOWALL BARROW
LAND'S END
Newbridge
Heamoor
PENZANCE
Chyandour
Marazion
ST MICHAEL'S MOUNT
Goldsithney
Germoe

Bosavern
224
Sancreed
CARN EUNY ANCIENT VILLAGE
Tredavoe
Penzance
Perranuthnoe
Praa Sands

Kelynack
B3306
LAND'S END
Res.
Lower Drift
Brane
NEWLYN ART GALLERY
SOUTH WEST COAST PATH
Cudden Pt.

Whitesand Bay
A30
Crows-an-wra
B3283
Catchall
Kerris
Newlyn
Paul
Mousehole
Ri
Trewa Hd.

Sennen Cove
St Buryan
St Clement's Island

Longships
Sennen
LAND'S END
Trewoofe
SOUTH WEST COAST PATH

C
LAND'S END
B3315
Boskenna
TREGIFFIAN BURIAL CHAMBER
Lamorna
Lamorna Cove

Polgigga
B3315

Porthcurno
Treen
ISLES OF SCILLY (Mar-Nov)
3

TELEGRAPH MUSEUM PORTHCURNO
St Levan
MINACK OPEN AIR THEATRE

Gwennap Hd.
Runnel Stone

Isles of Scilly
3 miles to 1 inch

3 ·9 4 ·2

White Island

E
St Helens
St Martin's
KING CHARLES CASTLE
Bryher
41
47
Higher Town
CROMWELL'S CASTLE
New Grimsby
Bryher
Tresco
TRESCO ABBEY GARDENS
Crow Sound

North West Passage
Samson
BANT'S CARN
Eastern Isles

The Road
Newford
51
INNISIDGEN CAIRNS
LONGSTONE HERITAGE CEN
Maypole
St Mary's

Hugh Town
A3110
ST MARY'S

Crim Rocks
GARRISON WALLS
Old Town
1

Broad Sound
Annet
Gugh
St Mary's Sound
St Mary's Sound
PENZANCE (Mar-Nov)

F
St Agnes
St Agnes

8 9
Bishop Rock

D

0 1 2 3 miles
0 1 2 3 4 5 km

·4 2 ·4 9

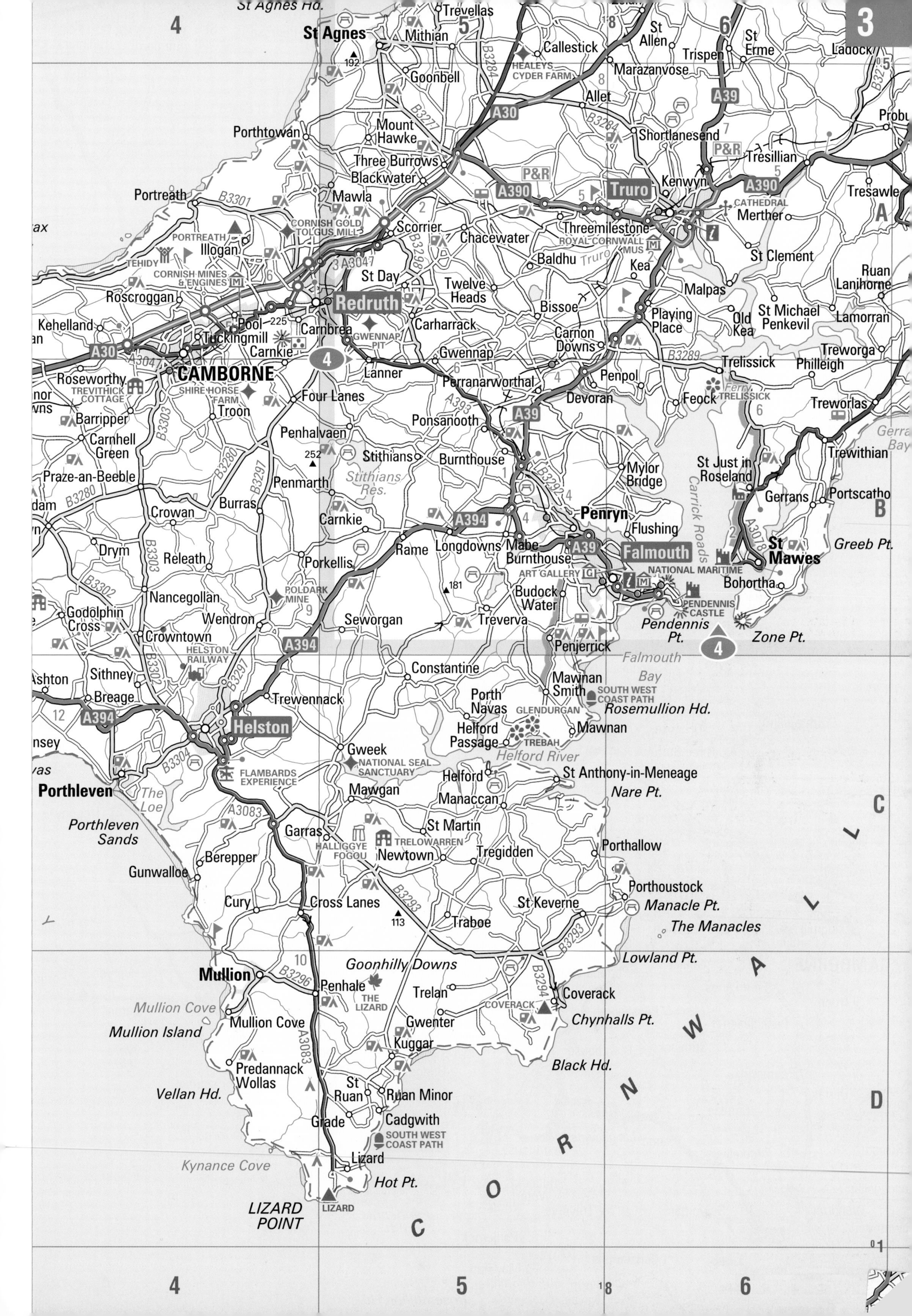
3
4
5
6
St Agnes Hd.
St Agnes
Trevellas
Mithian
Callestick
St Allen
Trispen
St Erme
Ladock
HEALEYS CYDER FARM
Goonbell
Marazanvose
Allet
A30
A39
Porthtowan
Mount Hawke
Shortlanesend
Tresillian
Probus
Three Burrows
Blackwater
P&R
Kenwyn
Truro
A390
Tresawle
Portreath
Mawla
CATHEDRAL
Merther
CORNISH GOLD TOLGUS MILL
Scorrier
Chacewater
Threemilestone
ROYAL CORNWALL MUS
PORTREATH
Illogan
TEHIDY
CORNISH MINES & ENGINES
St Day
Baldhu
Kea
St Clement
Ruan Lanihorne
Roscroggan
Redruth
Twelve Heads
Malpas
Bissoe
Playing Place
Old Kea
St Michael Penkevil
Lamorran
Kehelland
Pool
Tuckingmill
Carnbrea
GWENNAP PIT
Carharrack
Carnon Downs
Treworga
Carnkie
Gwennap
Trelissick
Philleigh
Roseworthy
CAMBORNE
Lanner
Perranarworthal
Penpol
TREVITHICK COTTAGE
SHIRE HORSE FARM
Four Lanes
Devoran
Feock
TRELISSICK
Treworlas
Troon
Ponsanooth
Barripper
Penhalvaen
Carnhell Green
Stithians
Burnthouse
Mylor Bridge
St Just in Roseland
Trewithian
Gerrans Bay
Stithians Res.
Carrick Roads
Praze-an-Beeble
Penmarth
Gerrans
Portscatho
Crowan
Burras
Penryn
Flushing
Carnkie
A394
St Mawes
Greeb Pt.
Drym
Rame
Longdowns
Mabe Burnthouse
Falmouth
Releath
Porkellis
ART GALLERY
NATIONAL MARITIME
Bohortha
Godolphin Cross
Nancegollan
POLDARK MINE
Budock Water
PENDENNIS CASTLE
Wendron
Seworgan
Treverva
Pendennis Pt.
Crowntown
Zone Pt.
HELSTON RAILWAY
Penjerrick
Falmouth Bay
Ashton
Sithney
Constantine
Mawnan Smith
SOUTH WEST COAST PATH
Breage
Trewennack
Porth Navas
GLENDURGAN
Rosemullion Hd.
Helston
Helford Passage
Mawnan
TREBAH
Gweek
Helford River
NATIONAL SEAL SANCTUARY
FLAMBARDS EXPERIENCE
Helford
St Anthony-in-Meneage
Porthleven
The Loe
Mawgan
Manaccan
Nare Pt.
Porthleven Sands
Garras
St Martin
HALLIGGYE FOGOU
TRELOWARREN
Newtown
Tregidden
Porthallow
Berepper
Gunwalloe
Porthoustock
Cury
Cross Lanes
St Keverne
Manacle Pt.
Traboe
The Manacles
Lowland Pt.
Goonhilly Downs
Mullion
Penhale
THE LIZARD
Trelan
Coverack
Mullion Cove
COVERACK
Gwenter
Chynhalls Pt.
Mullion Island
Kuggar
Black Hd.
Predannack Wollas
Vellan Hd.
St Ruan
Ruan Minor
Grade
Cadgwith
SOUTH WEST COAST PATH
Kynance Cove
Lizard
Hot Pt.
LIZARD POINT
LIZARD
C O R N W A L L
A
B
C
D

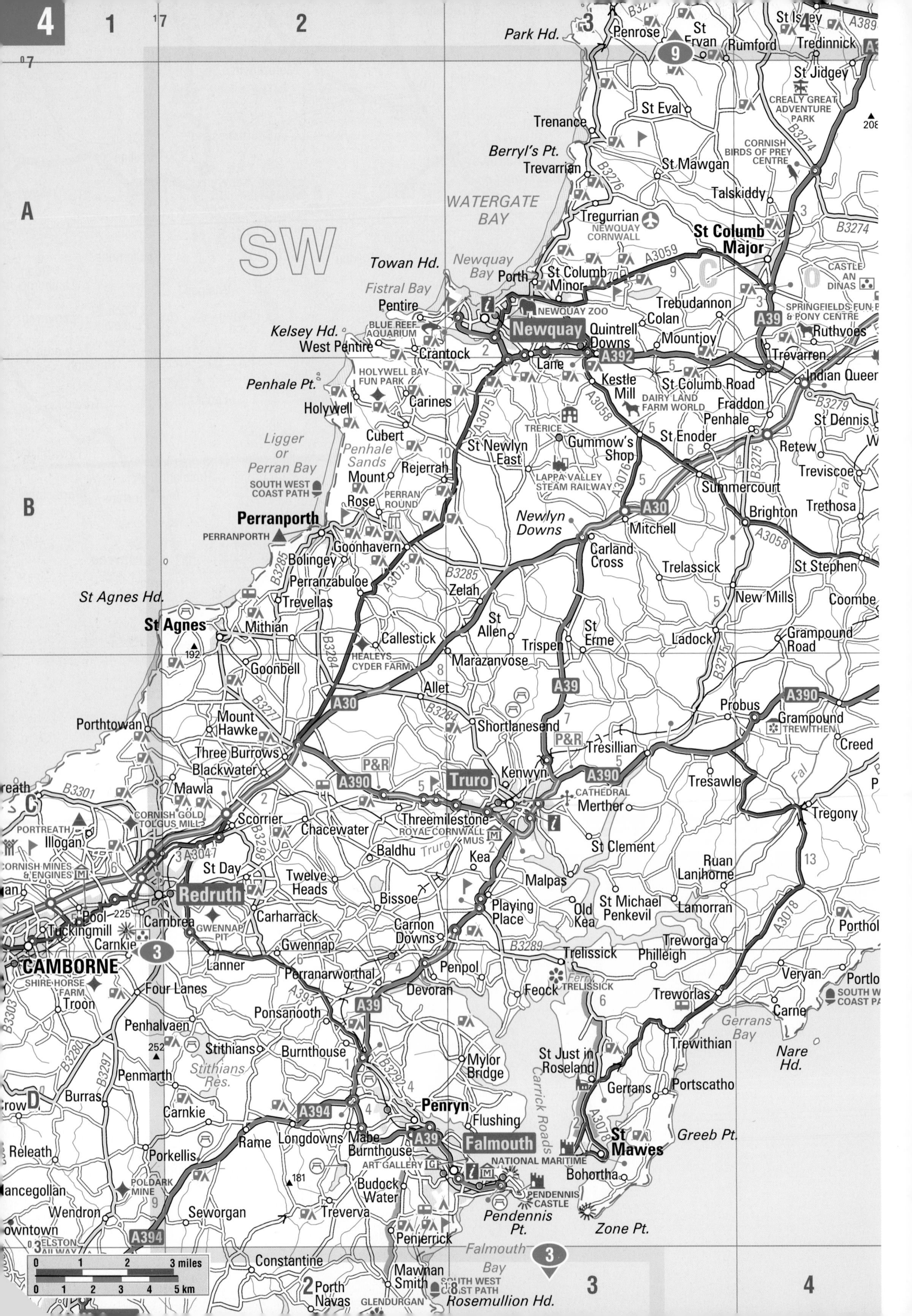
4
1
2
3
4
A
B
C
D
SW
Park Hd.
Penrose
St Ervan
Rumford
St Issey
Tredinnick
St Jidgey
CREALY GREAT ADVENTURE PARK
St Eval
Trenance
Berryl's Pt.
Trevarrian
St Mawgan
CORNISH BIRDS OF PREY CENTRE
Talskiddy
WATERGATE BAY
Tregurrian
NEWQUAY CORNWALL
St Columb Major
B3274
B3276
A3059
Towan Hd.
Newquay Bay
Porth
St Columb Minor
CASTLE AN DINAS
Fistral Bay
Pentire
NEWQUAY ZOO
Trebudannon
Colan
SPRINGFIELDS FUN & PONY CENTRE
Kelsey Hd.
BLUE REEF AQUARIUM
Newquay
Quintrell Downs
Mountjoy
Ruthvoes
West Pentire
Crantock
Lane
A392
Trevarren
Indian Queens
Penhale Pt.
HOLYWELL BAY FUN PARK
Kestle Mill
St Columb Road
Holywell
Carines
DAIRY LAND FARM WORLD
Fraddon
Penhale
B3279
St Dennis
A3075
A3058
TRERICE
Ligger or Perran Bay
Cubert
St Newlyn East
Gummow's Shop
St Enoder
Retew
Penhale Sands
Mount
Rejerrah
LAPPA VALLEY STEAM RAILWAY
A3076
B3275
Treviscoe
SOUTH WEST COAST PATH
PERRAN ROUND
Summercourt
Rose
A30
Trethosa
Perranporth
PERRANPORTH
Newlyn Downs
Mitchell
Brighton
Goonhavern
Carland Cross
Bolingey
B3285
Trelassick
St Stephen
St Agnes Hd.
Perranzabuloe
Zelah
Trevellas
New Mills
Coombe
St Agnes
Mithian
St Allen
St Erme
Ladock
Grampound Road
192
Callestick
Trispen
HEALEYS CYDER FARM
Marazanvose
Goonbell
B3284
A39
Allet
A390
Probus
Grampound
TREWITHEN
Porthtowan
Mount Hawke
Shortlanesend
Creed
B3277
Three Burrows
Tresillian
P&R
Blackwater
Truro
Kenwyn
Tresawle
Fal
B3301
Mawla
CATHEDRAL
Merther
Tregony
PORTREATH
CORNISH GOLD TOLGUS MILL
Scorrier
Chacewater
Threemilestone
ROYAL CORNWALL MUS
Illogan
St Clement
CORNISH MINES & ENGINES
A3047
Baldhu
Kea
Ruan Lanihorne
St Day
B3298
Twelve Heads
Malpas
Redruth
Bissoe
Playing Place
Old Kea
St Michael Penkevil
Lamorran
Pool
225
Carnbrea
Carharrack
GWENNAP PIT
Tuckingmill
Carnon Downs
A3078
Portholland
Carnkie
Gwennap
B3289
Treworga
CAMBORNE
Lanner
Trelissick
Philleigh
Perranarworthal
Penpol
Veryan
Portloe
SHIRE HORSE FARM
Troon
Four Lanes
Ferry
TRELISSICK
Feock
Devoran
Treworlas
SOUTH WEST COAST PATH
Carne
B3303
Ponsanooth
A393
Gerrans Bay
Penhalvaen
Trewithian
252
Stithians
Burnthouse
Mylor Bridge
St Just in Roseland
Nare Hd.
B3280
B3297
Stithians Res.
Carrick Roads
Penmarth
B3292
Gerrans
Portscatho
Burras
Crowan
A394
Penryn
Flushing
Carnkie
Rame
Longdowns
Mabe Burnthouse
Falmouth
St Mawes
Greeb Pt.
Releath
Porkellis
ART GALLERY
NATIONAL MARITIME
Bohortha
181
POLDARK MINE
Budock Water
Trenance
Wendron
Seworgan
Treverva
PENDENNIS CASTLE
Pendennis Pt.
Zone Pt.
Polwithen
Penjerrick
Constantine
Falmouth Bay
Porth Navas
Mawnan Smith
SOUTH WEST COAST PATH
GLENDURGAN
Rosemullion Hd.
0 1 2 3 miles
0 1 2 3 4 5 km

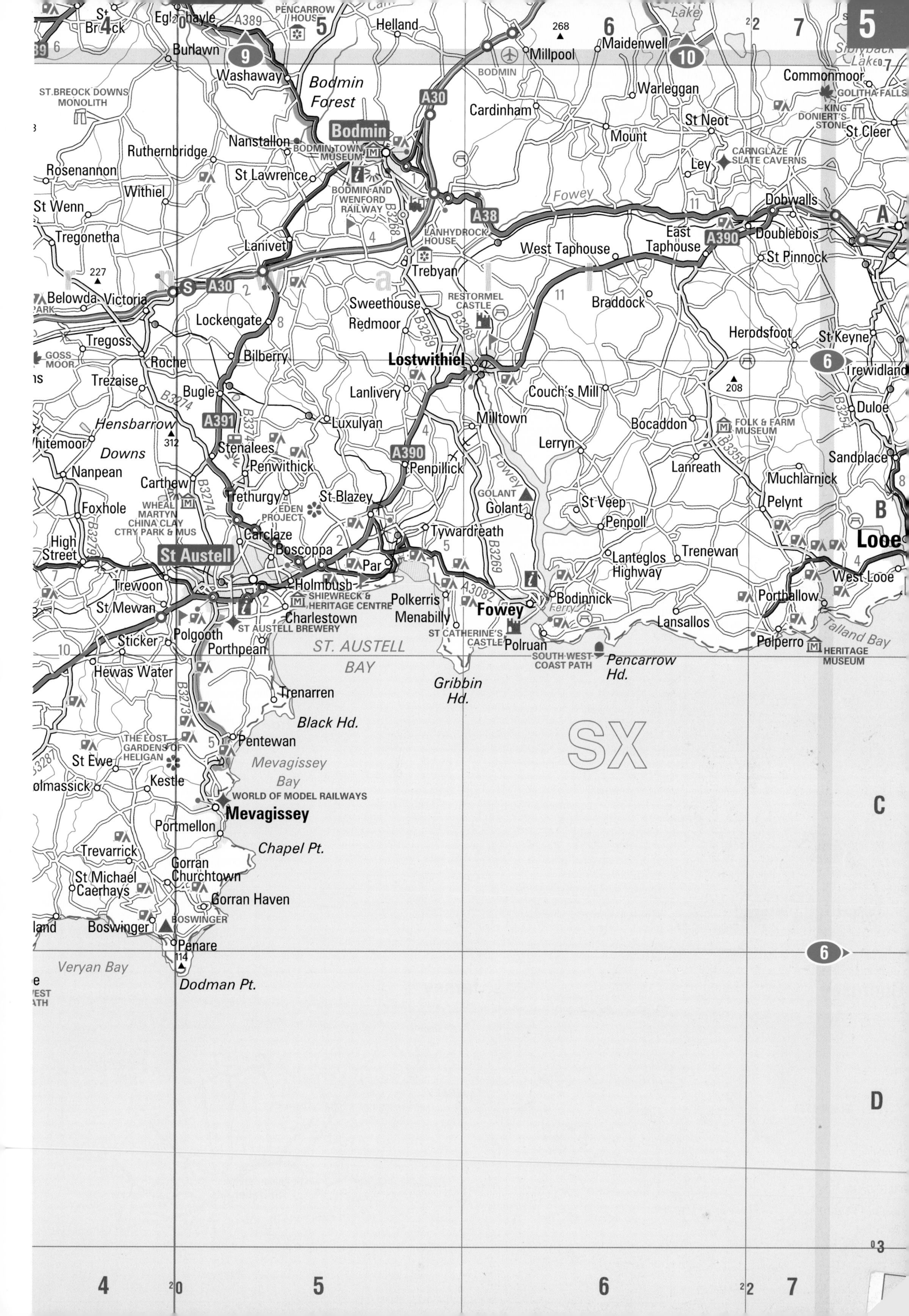

5
Bodmin
Bodmin Forest
Helland
Washaway
Burlawn
Millpool
Maidenwell
Warleggan
Cardinham
Commonmoor
Mount
St Neot
St Cleer
Nanstallon
Ruthernbridge
Rosenannon
St Lawrence
Withiel
St Wenn
Tregonetha
Lanivet
Lanhydrock House
Trebyan
Dobwalls
Doublebois
East Taphouse
West Taphouse
St Pinnock
Belowda
Victoria
Lockengate
Sweethouse
Redmoor
Restormel Castle
Braddock
Herodsfoot
St Keyne
Tregoss
Roche
Bilberry
Lostwithiel
Trewidland
Trezaise
Bugle
Lanlivery
Couch's Mill
Duloe
Hensbarrow Downs
Luxulyan
Milltown
Bocaddon
Lerryn
Nanpean
Stenalees
Penwithick
Penpillick
Lanreath
Sandplace
Muchlarnick
Carthew
Trethurgy
St Blazey
Golant
St Veep
Pelynt
Foxhole
Eden Project
Penpoll
High Street
Carclaze
Tywardreath
Boscoppa
Par
Lanteglos Highway
Trenewan
Looe
St Austell
West Looe
Trewoon
Holmbush
Polkerris
Menabilly
Fowey
Bodinnick
Porthallow
St Mewan
Charlestown
Lansallos
Polgooth
Sticker
Porthpean
Polruan
Polperro
St Catherine's Castle
St Austell Bay
Talland Bay
Heritage Museum
Hewas Water
Pencarrow Hd.
Gribbin Hd.
South West Coast Path
Trenarren
Black Hd.
Pentewan
St Ewe
The Lost Gardens of Heligan
Mevagissey Bay
Kestle
World of Model Railways
Mevagissey
Portmellon
Chapel Pt.
Trevarrick
St Michael Caerhays
Gorran Churchtown
Gorran Haven
Boswinger
Penare
Veryan Bay
Dodman Pt.
SX
Bodmin Town Museum
Bodmin and Wenford Railway
St Breock Downs Monolith
Golitha Falls
King Doniert's Stone
Carnglaze Slate Caverns
Folk & Farm Museum
Wheal Martyn China Clay Ctry Park & Mus
Shipwreck & Heritage Centre
St Austell Brewery
Goss Moor
Golant
Pencarrow House
Siblyback Lake
A30
A38
A390
A391
A389
A3082
B3268
B3269
B3274
B3374
B3359
B3254
B3273
B3279
4
6
7
A
B
C
D

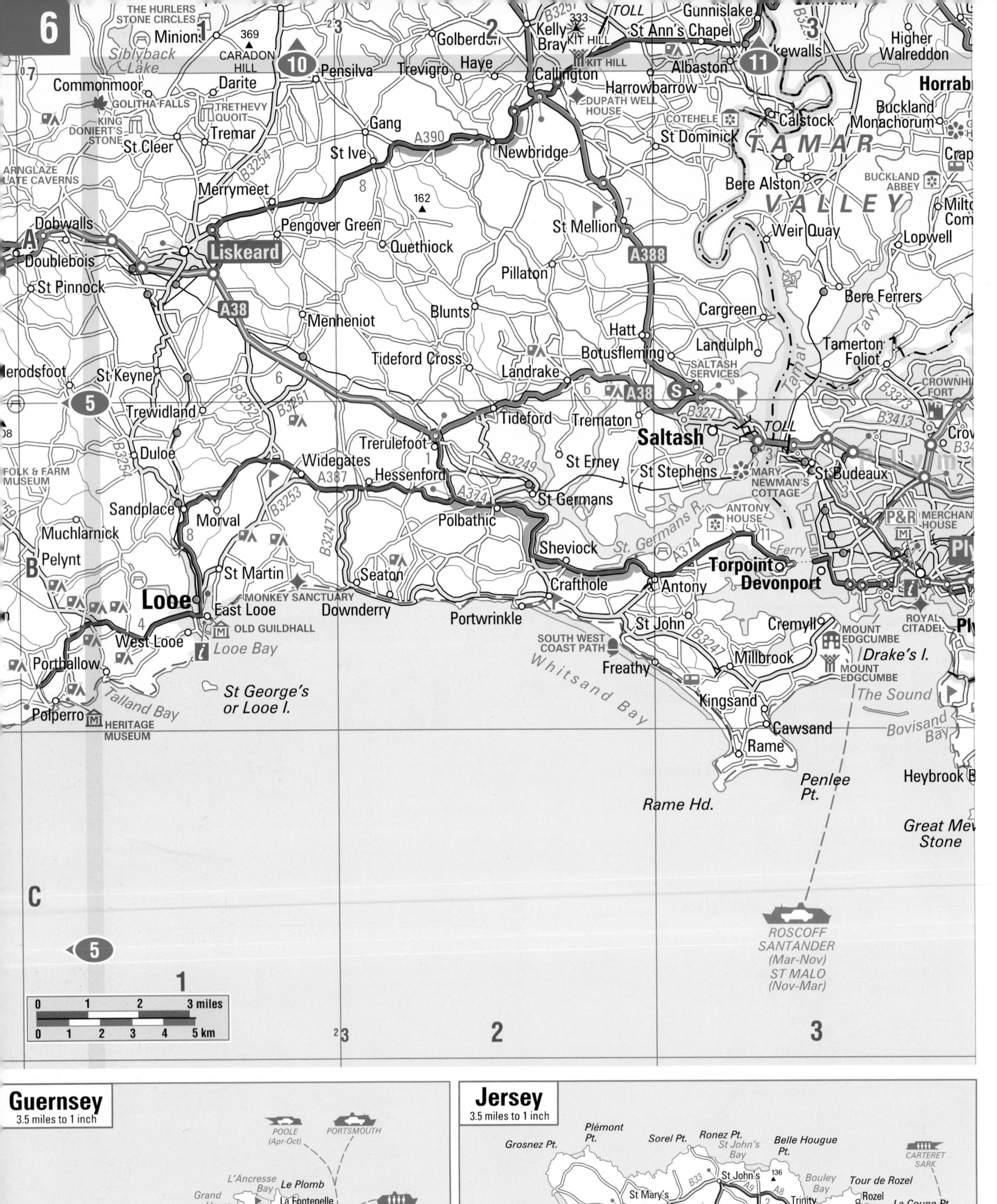

6

THE HURLERS STONE CIRCLES
Siblyback Lake
Minions
369
CARADON HILL
10
Pensilva
Commonmoor
Darite
GOLITHA FALLS
KING DONIERT'S STONE
TRETHEVY QUOIT
Tremar
ARNGLAZE SLATE CAVERNS
St Cleer
Merrymeet
Golberdon
Haye
Kelly Bray
KIT HILL
333
St Ann's Chapel
TOLL
Gunnislake
Higher Walreddon
kewalls
Albaston
11
Callington
Harrowbarrow
DUPATH WELL HOUSE
COTEHELE
St Dominick
Calstock
Buckland Monachorum
BUCKLAND ABBEY
Horrab
Crap
TAMAR
VALLEY

Gang
A390
Newbridge
St Ive
8
Bere Alston
Weir Quay
Milto
Com
Lopwell

Dobwalls
Doublebois
A38
Liskeard
Pengover Green
162
Quethiock
St Mellion
A388
Pillaton
Bere Ferrers
St Pinnock

Menheniot
Blunts
Hatt
Cargreen
Landulph
Tamerton Foliot

Herodsfoot
St Keyne
5
Trewidland
Tideford Cross
Landrake
Botusfleming
6
A38
SALTASH SERVICES
S
B3271
CROWNHI FORT

Duloe
6
Tideford
Trematon
Saltash
TOLL
3
B3273
Crow
B34

FOLK & FARM MUSEUM
Trerulefoot
St Erney
Trematon
B3271
MARY NEWMAN'S COTTAGE
St Budeaux
Sandplace
Widegates
A387
Hessenford
1
B3249
St Germans
ANTONY HOUSE
11
Ferry
P&R
MERCHANT HOUSE
PI

Muchlarnick
Morval
B3253
A374
Polbathic
Sheviock
St. Germans R.
A374
Torpoint
Devonport
Pl
Pelynt
B3247
St Martin
Seaton
Crafthole
Antony
Cremyll
MOUNT EDGCUMBE
Drake's I.
ROYAL CITADEL

Looe
MONKEY SANCTUARY
Downderry
Portwrinkle
St John
B3247
Millbrook
MOUNT EDGCUMBE
THE SOUND

East Looe
OLD GUILDHALL
SOUTH WEST COAST PATH
Freathy
Kingsand
Cawsand
Bovisand Bay

West Looe
Looe Bay
Whitsand Bay
Rame
Heybrook B

Porthallow
Talland Bay
St George's or Looe I.
Rame Hd.
Penlee Pt.
Great Mev Stone

Polperro
HERITAGE MUSEUM

C

ROSCOFF SANTANDER (Mar-Nov) ST MALO (Nov-Mar)

5

| 0 | 1 | 2 | 3 miles |
| 0 | 1 | 2 | 3 | 4 | 5 km |

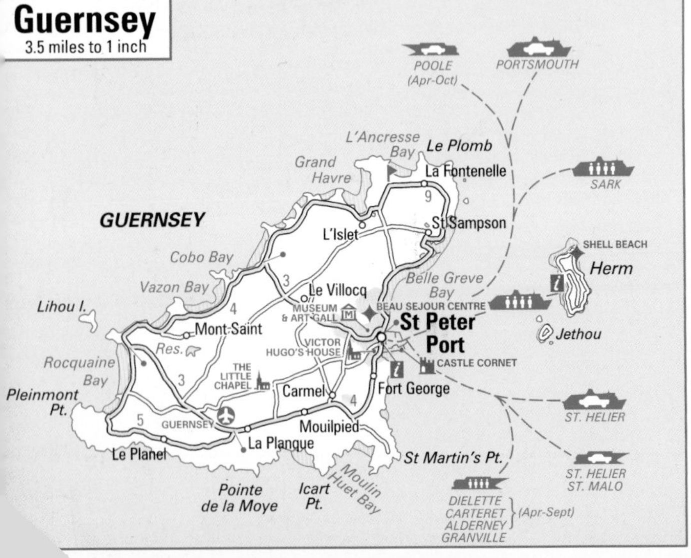

Guernsey
3.5 miles to 1 inch

POOLE (Apr-Oct)
PORTSMOUTH
L'Ancresse Bay
Le Plomb
La Fontenelle
SARK
Grand Havre
St Sampson
GUERNSEY
L'Islet
SHELL BEACH
Cobo Bay
Herm
Vazon Bay
Le Villocq
MUSEUM & ART GALL
BEAU SEJOUR CENTRE
Belle Greve Bay
Jethou
Lihou I.
Mont Saint
Res.
VICTOR HUGO'S HOUSE
St Peter Port
Rocquaine Bay
THE LITTLE CHAPEL
Carmel
Castle Cornet
Pleinmont Pt.
Le Planel
Mouilpied
Fort George
La Planque
Pointe de la Moye
Icart Pt.
St Martin's Pt.
Moulin Huet Bay
DIELETTE CARTERET ALDERNEY GRANVILLE (Apr-Sept)
ST HELIER
ST HELIER ST MALO

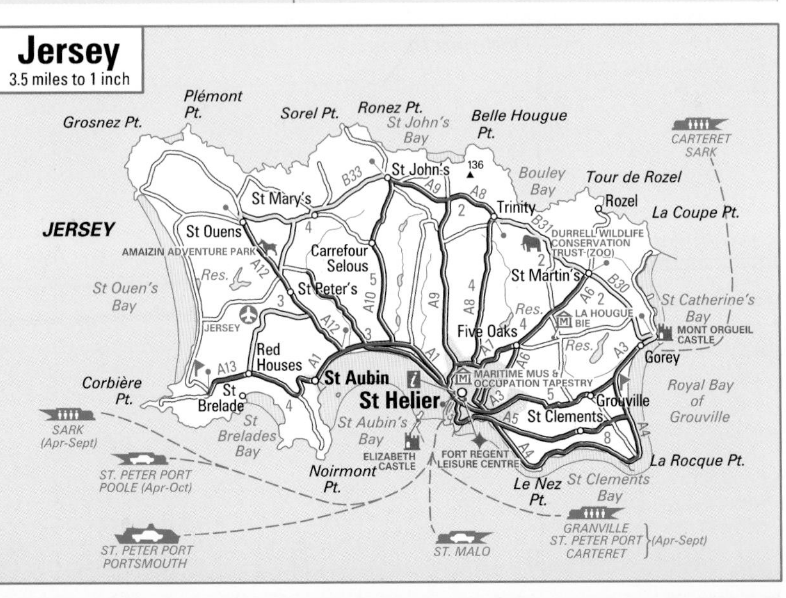

Jersey
3.5 miles to 1 inch

Plémont Pt.
Sorel Pt.
Ronez Pt.
Belle Hougue Pt.
Grosnez Pt.
St John's Bay
CARTERET SARK
136
B33
St John's
Bouley Bay
Tour de Rozel
La Coupe Pt.
St Mary's
Trinity
Rozel
JERSEY
St Ouens
A9
A8
DURRELL WILDLIFE CONSERVATION TRUST (ZOO)
AMAIZIN ADVENTURE PARK
Carrefour Selous
A10
St Peter's
St Martin's
St Catherine's Bay
St Ouen's Bay
JERSEY
A12
A9
Five Oaks
LA HOUGUE BIE
MONT ORGUEIL CASTLE
A1
Red Houses
MARITIME MUS & OCCUPATION TAPESTRY
Gorey
Corbière Pt.
A13
St Brelade
St Aubin
St Helier
A5
St Clements
Royal Bay of Grouville
SARK (Apr-Sept)
St Brelade's Bay
St Aubin's Bay
FORT REGENT LEISURE CENTRE
Grouville
La Rocque Pt.
ELIZABETH CASTLE
Noirmont Pt.
Le Nez Pt.
St Clements Bay
ST PETER PORT POOLE (Apr-Oct)
ST PETER PORT PORTSMOUTH
Le Nez Pt.
ST MALO
GRANVILLE ST PETER PORT CARTERET (Apr-Sept)

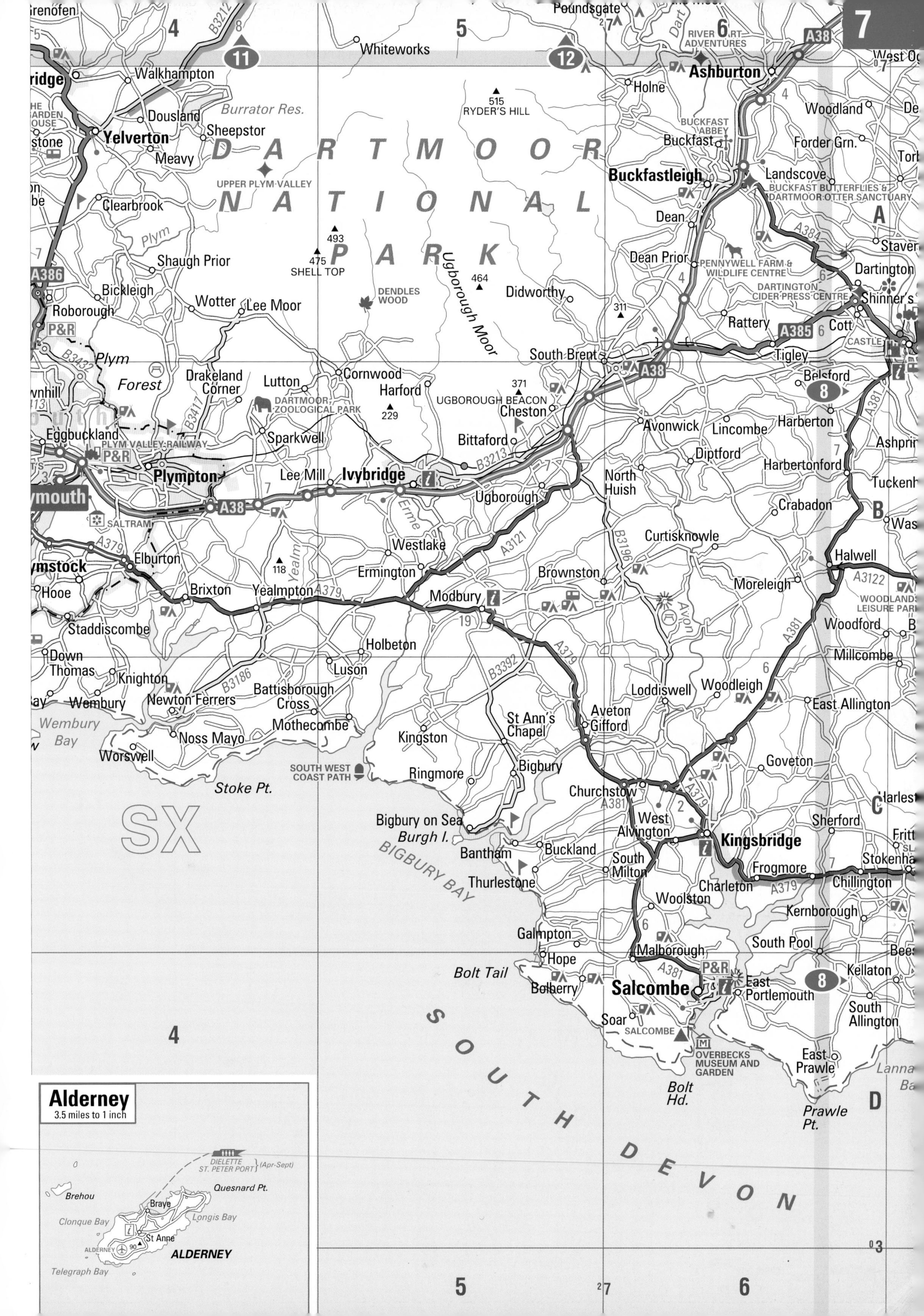

DARTMOOR NATIONAL PARK

Alderney
3.5 miles to 1 inch

ALDERNEY

SOUTH DEVON

SX

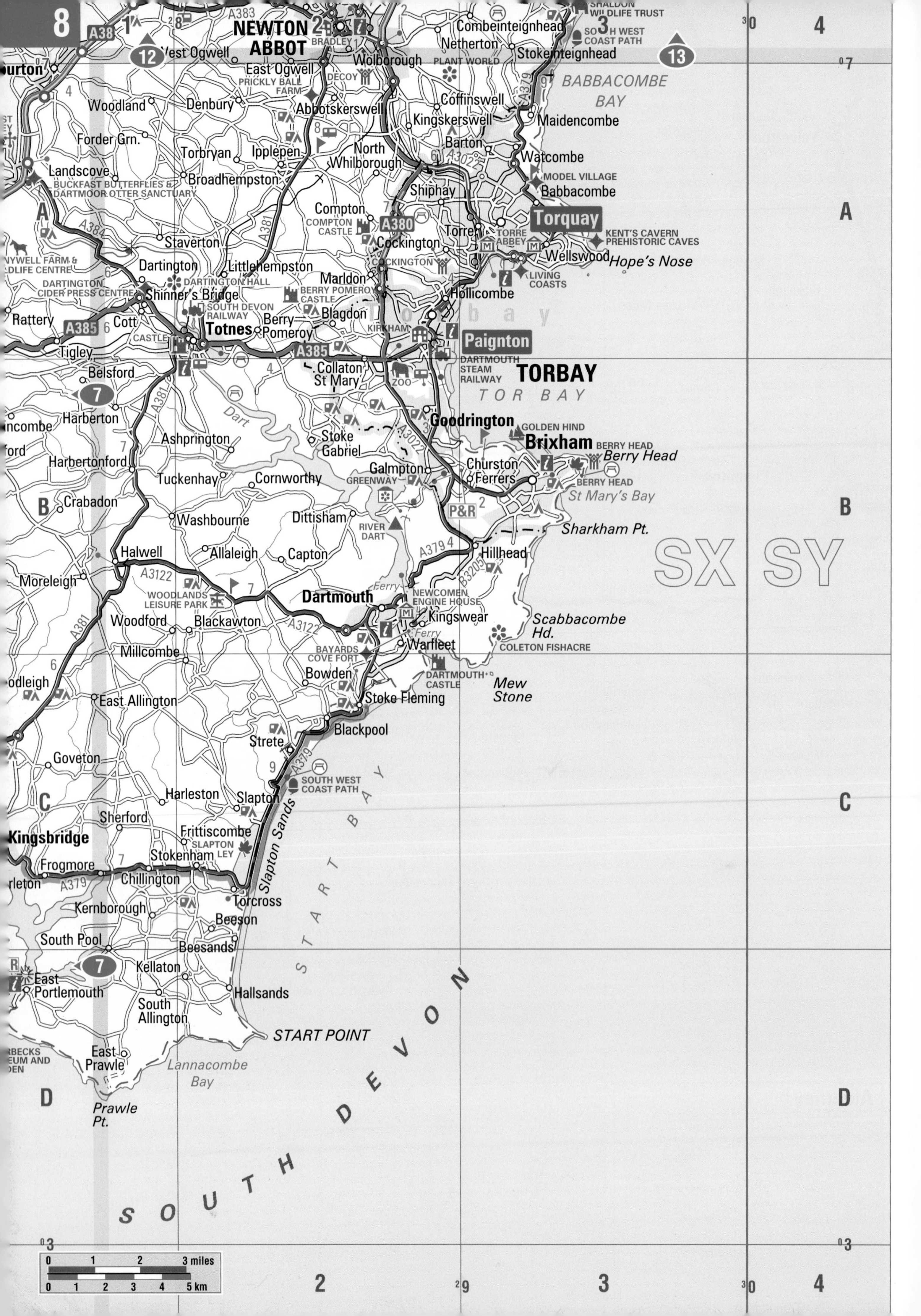
NEWTON ABBOT
Combeinteignhead
Netherton
Stokeinteignhead
Wolborough
West Ogwell
East Ogwell
PRICKLY BALL FARM
DECOY
PLANT WORLD
BABBACOMBE BAY
Woodland
Denbury
Abbotskerswell
Coffinswell
Kingskerswell
Maidencombe
Forder Grn.
Barton
Torbryan
Ipplepen
North Whilborough
Watcombe
Landscove
BUCKFAST BUTTERFLIES & DARTMOOR OTTER SANCTUARY
Broadhempston
Shiphay
MODEL VILLAGE
Babbacombe
Compton
COMPTON CASTLE
A380
Torquay
Torre
TORRE ABBEY
KENT'S CAVERN PREHISTORIC CAVES
Staverton
Cockington
COCKINGTON
Wellswood
Hope's Nose
Dartington
Littlehempston
LIVING COASTS
DARTINGTON HALL
Marldon
DARTINGTON CIDER PRESS CENTRE
Shinner's Bridge
BERRY POMEROY CASTLE
Hollicombe
SOUTH DEVON RAILWAY
Berry Pomeroy
Blagdon
Rattery
Cott
Totnes
KIRKHAM
Paignton
Tigley
CASTLE
A385
Collaton St Mary
DARTMOUTH STEAM RAILWAY
TORBAY
Belsford
ZOO
TOR BAY
Harberton
Dart
Goodrington
GOLDEN HIND
Ashprington
Stoke Gabriel
Brixham
BERRY HEAD
Berry Head
Harbertonford
Galmpton
Churston Ferrers
Tuckenhay
Cornworthy
GREENWAY
BERRY HEAD
St Mary's Bay
Crabadon
P&R
Washbourne
Dittisham
RIVER DART
Sharkham Pt.
Halwell
Allaleigh
Capton
Hillhead
SX
SY
Moreleigh
A3122
WOODLANDS LEISURE PARK
Dartmouth
Ferry
NEWCOMEN ENGINE HOUSE
Woodford
Blackawton
Kingswear
Scabbacombe Hd.
BAYARDS COVE FORT
Warfleet
COLETON FISHACRE
Millcombe
Bowden
DARTMOUTH CASTLE
Mew Stone
East Allington
Stoke Fleming
Blackpool
Strete
Goveton
SOUTH WEST COAST PATH
Harleston
Slapton
Sherford
Kingsbridge
Frittiscombe
SLAPTON LEY
Stokenham
Slapton Sands
START BAY
Frogmore
Chillington
A379
Torcross
Kernborough
Beeson
South Pool
Beesands
Kellaton
East Portlemouth
Hallsands
South Allington
START POINT
East Prawle
Lannacombe Bay
Prawle Pt.
SOUTH DEVON
0 1 2 3 miles
0 1 2 3 4 5 km

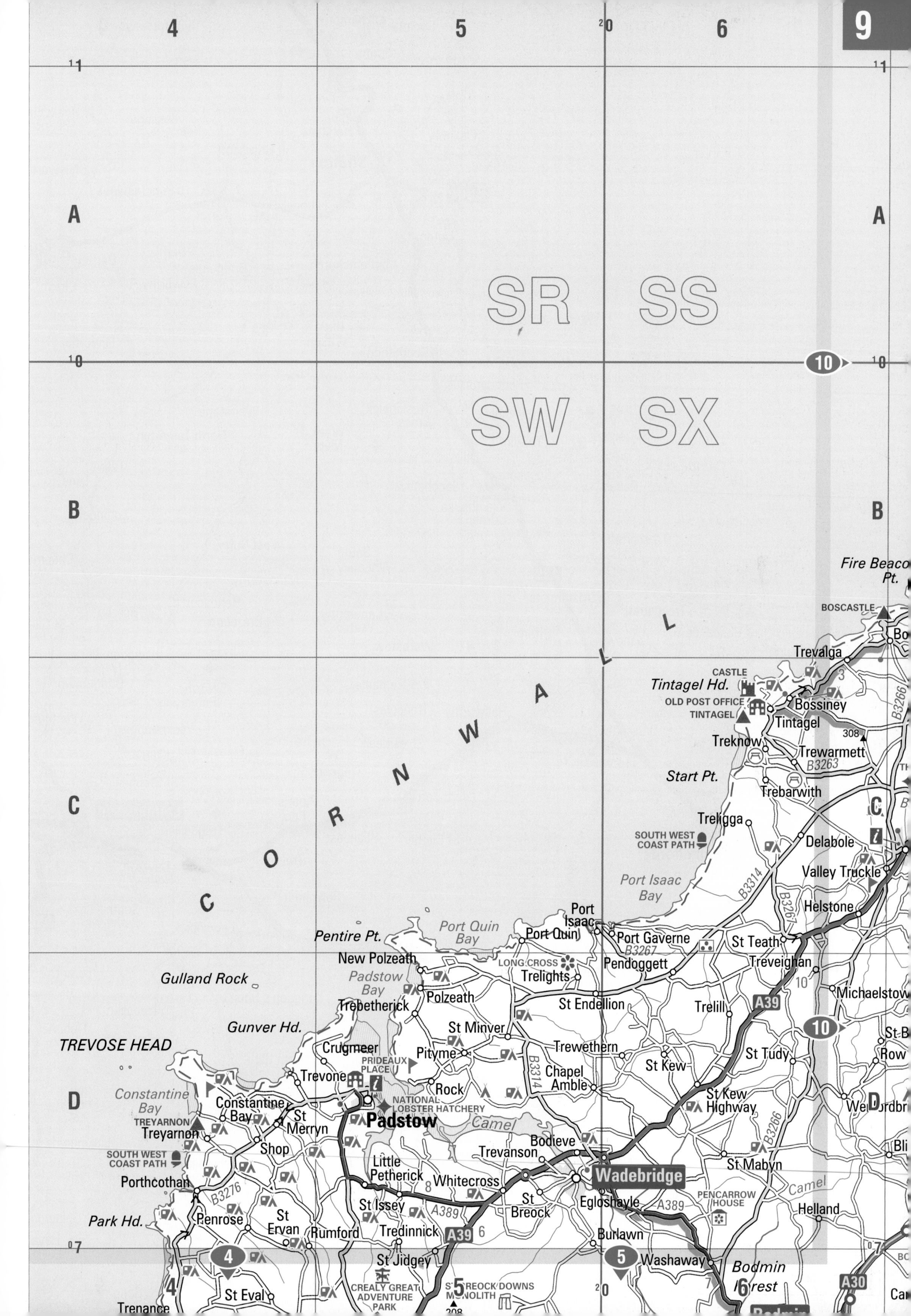

4
5
6
A
B
C
D
SR
SS
SW
SX
10
C O R N W A L L
Fire Beacon Pt.
BOSCASTLE
Trevalga
CASTLE
Tintagel Hd.
OLD POST OFFICE
TINTAGEL
Bossiney
Tintagel
B3266
308
Treknow
Trewarmett
B3263
Start Pt.
Trebarwith
Treligga
SOUTH WEST COAST PATH
Delabole
Valley Truckle
Port Isaac Bay
B3314
Helstone
Port Isaac
Port Quin
Port Quin Bay
Pentire Pt.
Port Gaverne
B3267
St Teath
New Polzeath
LONG CROSS
Trelights
Pendoggett
Treveighan
Gulland Rock
Padstow Bay
Polzeath
Trebetherick
St Endellion
Trelill
A39
Michaelstow
Gunver Hd.
St Minver
TREVOSE HEAD
Crugmeer
Pityme
Trewethern
St Kew
St Tudy
B3314
PRIDEAUX PLACE
Chapel Amble
Trevone
Rock
St Kew Highway
Constantine Bay
Constantine Bay
NATIONAL LOBSTER HATCHERY
St Merryn
TREYARNON
Treyarnon
Padstow
Camel
Bodieve
B3266
Shop
Trevanson
SOUTH WEST COAST PATH
St Mabyn
Little Petherick
Wadebridge
Porthcothan
Whitecross
B3276
St Breock
Egloshayle
PENCARROW HOUSE
Camel
Park Hd.
Penrose
St Issey
A389
A389
Helland
St Ervan
Rumford
Tredinnick
A39
Burlawn
St Jidgey
Washaway
Bodmin Forest
St Eval
CREALY GREAT ADVENTURE PARK
ST BREOCK DOWNS MONOLITH
208
A30
Trenance

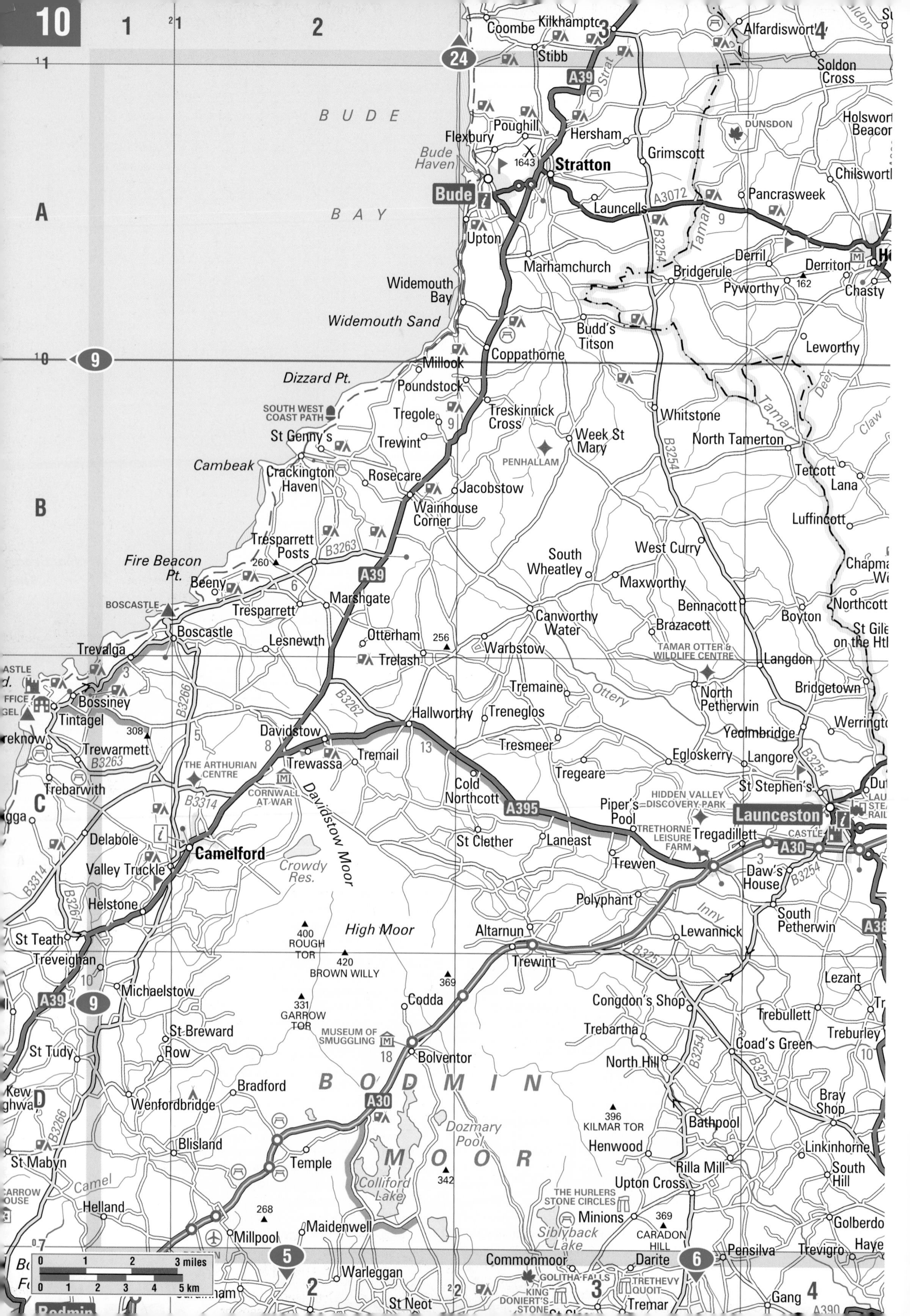

1
2
3
4
A
B
C
D
24
9
5
6
BUDE
BAY
Coombe
Kilkhampton
Stibb
Alfardisworthy
Soldon Cross
Holsworthy Beacon
Chilsworthy
A39
Strat
Poughill
Flexbury
Hersham
DUNSDON
Bude Haven
1643
Stratton
Grimscott
Bude
Launcells
A3072
Pancrasweek
Tamar
B3254
Upton
Marhamchurch
Derril
Bridgerule
Derriton
Pyworthy
162
Chasty
Widemouth Bay
Widemouth Sand
Budd's Titson
Coppathorne
Leworthy
Millook
Dizzard Pt.
Poundstock
SOUTH WEST COAST PATH
Tregole
Treskinnick Cross
Whitstone
St Gennys
Trewint
Week St Mary
North Tamerton
PENHALLAM
Deer
Claw
Cambeak
Crackington Haven
Rosecare
Jacobstow
Tetcott
Lana
Wainhouse Corner
Luffincott
Tresparrett Posts
B3263
West Curry
Fire Beacon Pt.
260
South Wheatley
Maxworthy
Beeny
A39
Marshgate
Bennacott
Northcott
BOSCASTLE
Tresparrett
Canworthy Water
Boyton
Boscastle
Otterham
256
Brazacott
Lesnewth
Warbstow
St Giles on the Heath
Trevalga
Trelash
TAMAR OTTER & WILDLIFE CENTRE
Langdon
Tremaine
Ottery
Bridgetown
Bossiney
Tintagel
B3266
B3262
North Petherwin
Hallworthy
Treneglos
Werrington
308
Davidstow
Yeolmbridge
Trewarmett
Tresmeer
B3263
Tremail
Egloskerry
Langore
Trewassa
THE ARTHURIAN CENTRE
Tregeare
Trebarwith
CORNWALL AT WAR
Cold Northcott
St Stephen's
Davidstow Moor
B3314
A395
Piper's Pool
HIDDEN VALLEY DISCOVERY PARK
Launceston
Delabole
St Clether
Laneast
TRETHORNE LEISURE FARM
Tregadillett
CASTLE
Camelford
A30
Valley Truckle
Trewen
Crowdy Res.
Daw's House
B3314
B3254
B3267
Helstone
Polyphant
South Petherwin
Inny
St Teath
400 ROUGH TOR
High Moor
Altarnun
Lewannick
420 BROWN WILLY
Treveighan
Trewint
B3257
Lezant
369
Michaelstow
Codda
Congdon's Shop
A39
331 GARROW TOR
Trebullett
St Breward
Trebartha
Treburley
MUSEUM OF SMUGGLING
Coad's Green
St Tudy
Row
18
Bolventor
North Hill
B3254
B3257
BODMIN MOOR
Bradford
396 KILMAR TOR
Bray Shop
Wenfordbridge
A30
B3266
Dozmary Pool
Bathpool
Blisland
Henwood
Linkinhorne
St Mabyn
Temple
Rilla Mill
South Hill
Camel
Colliford Lake
342
Upton Cross
THE HURLERS STONE CIRCLES
Helland
268
Minions
Golberdon
Maidenwell
369 CARADON HILL
Siblyback Lake
Millpool
Pensilva
Trevigro
Commonmoor
Darite
Warleggan
GOLITHA FALLS
TRETHEVY QUOIT
KING DONIERT'S STONE
St Neot
Tremar
Gang
A390
0 1 2 3 miles
0 1 2 3 4 5 km
Bodmin

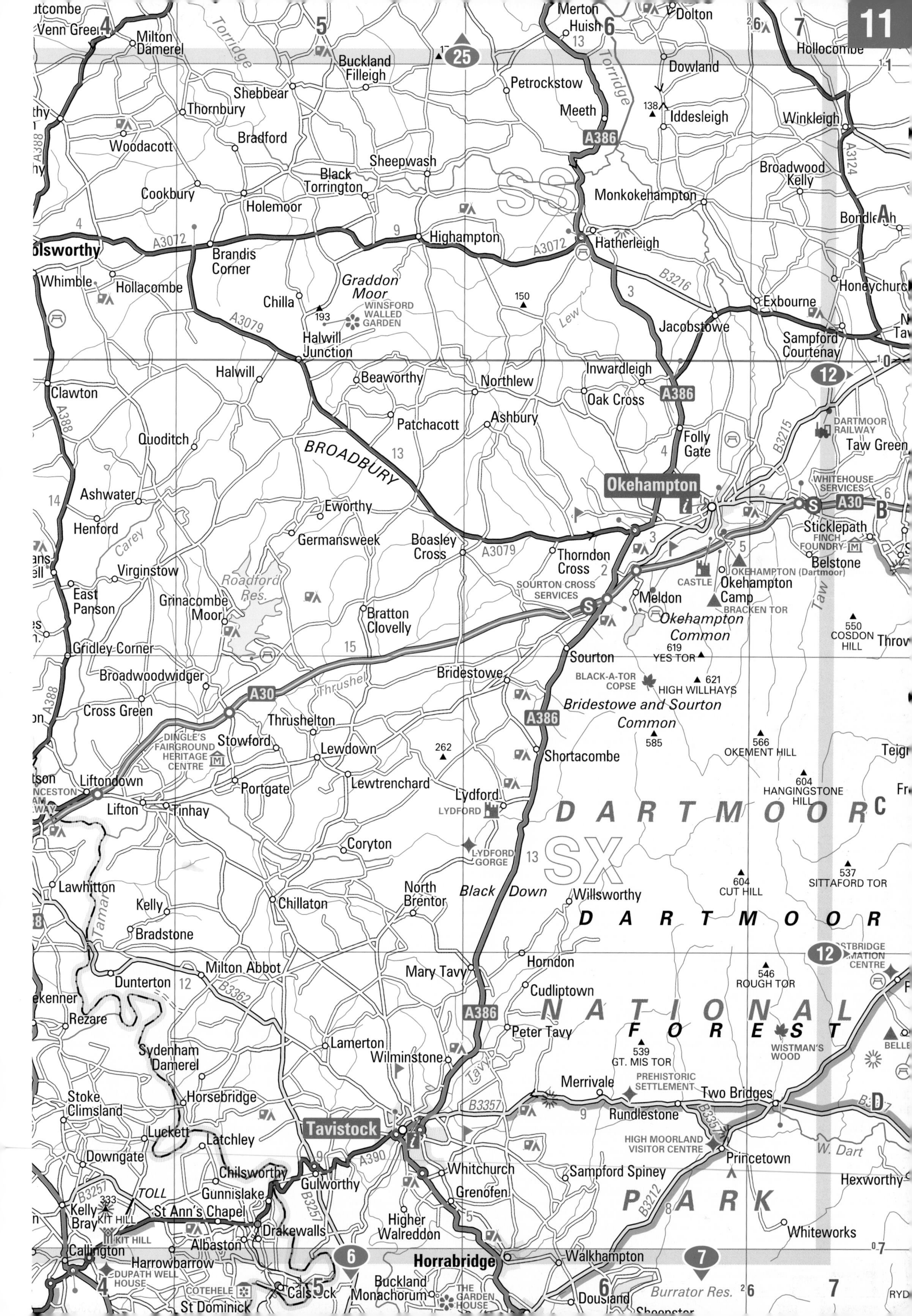
Milton Damerel
Buckland Filleigh
Shebbear
Thornbury
Woodacott
Bradford
Sheepwash
Black Torrington
Cookbury
Holemoor
Highampton
Brandis Corner
Whimble
Hollacombe
Chilla
Graddon Moor
WINSFORD WALLED GARDEN
Halwill Junction
Halwill
Clawton
Beaworthy
Patchacott
BROADBURY
Quoditch
Ashwater
Henford
Eworthy
Germansweek
Boasley Cross
Virginstow
East Panson
Grinacombe Moor
Roadford Res.
Bratton Clovelly
Gridley Corner
Broadwoodwidger
Cross Green
Thrushelton
Stowford
DINGLE'S FAIRGROUND HERITAGE CENTRE
Lewdown
Lewtrenchard
Portgate
Liftondown
Lifton
Tinhay
Coryton
Lawhitton
Kelly
Bradstone
Chillaton
Dunterton
Milton Abbot
Rezare
Sydenham Damerel
Lamerton
Stoke Climsland
Horsebridge
Luckett
Latchley
Downgate
Chilsworthy
Gunnislake
Gulworthy
Kelly Bray
St Ann's Chapel
Drakewalls
Albaston
Callington
Harrowbarrow
DUPATH WELL HOUSE
COTEHELE
Calstock
St Dominick
Tavistock
Whitchurch
Grenofen
Higher Walreddon
Horrabridge
Buckland Monachorum
THE GARDEN HOUSE
Merton
Huish
Dolton
Dowland
Petrockstow
Meeth
Iddesleigh
Winkleigh
Hollocombe
Broadwood Kelly
Monkokehampton
Hatherleigh
Bondleigh
Honeychurch
Exbourne
Jacobstowe
Sampford Courtenay
Inwardleigh
Northlew
Oak Cross
Ashbury
Folly Gate
DARTMOOR RAILWAY
Taw Green
Okehampton
WHITEHOUSE SERVICES
Sticklepath
FINCH FOUNDRY
Belstone
Thorndon Cross
SOURTON CROSS SERVICES
Meldon
CASTLE
OKEHAMPTON (Dartmoor)
Okehampton Camp
BRACKEN TOR
Okehampton Common
COSDON HILL
YES TOR
Sourton
BLACK-A-TOR COPSE
HIGH WILLHAYS
Bridestowe
Bridestowe and Sourton Common
Shortacombe
OKEMENT HILL
HANGINGSTONE HILL
Lydford
LYDFORD
LYDFORD GORGE
DARTMOOR
SX
CUT HILL
SITTAFORD TOR
North Brentor
Black Down
Willsworthy
Horndon
Mary Tavy
Cudliptown
ROUGH TOR
NATIONAL
FOREST
Peter Tavy
Wilminstone
GT. MIS TOR
WISTMAN'S WOOD
Merrivale
PREHISTORIC SETTLEMENT
Two Bridges
Rundlestone
HIGH MOORLAND VISITOR CENTRE
Princetown
Hexworthy
Sampford Spiney
PARK
Whiteworks
Walkhampton
Dousland
Burrator Res.
A386
A3072
A3079
A30
A388
A390
A3124
B3216
B3215
B3362
B3357
B3257
B3212
Torridge
Tamar
Tavy
W. Dart
Taw
Lew
Carey
Thrushel
TOLL
KIT HILL

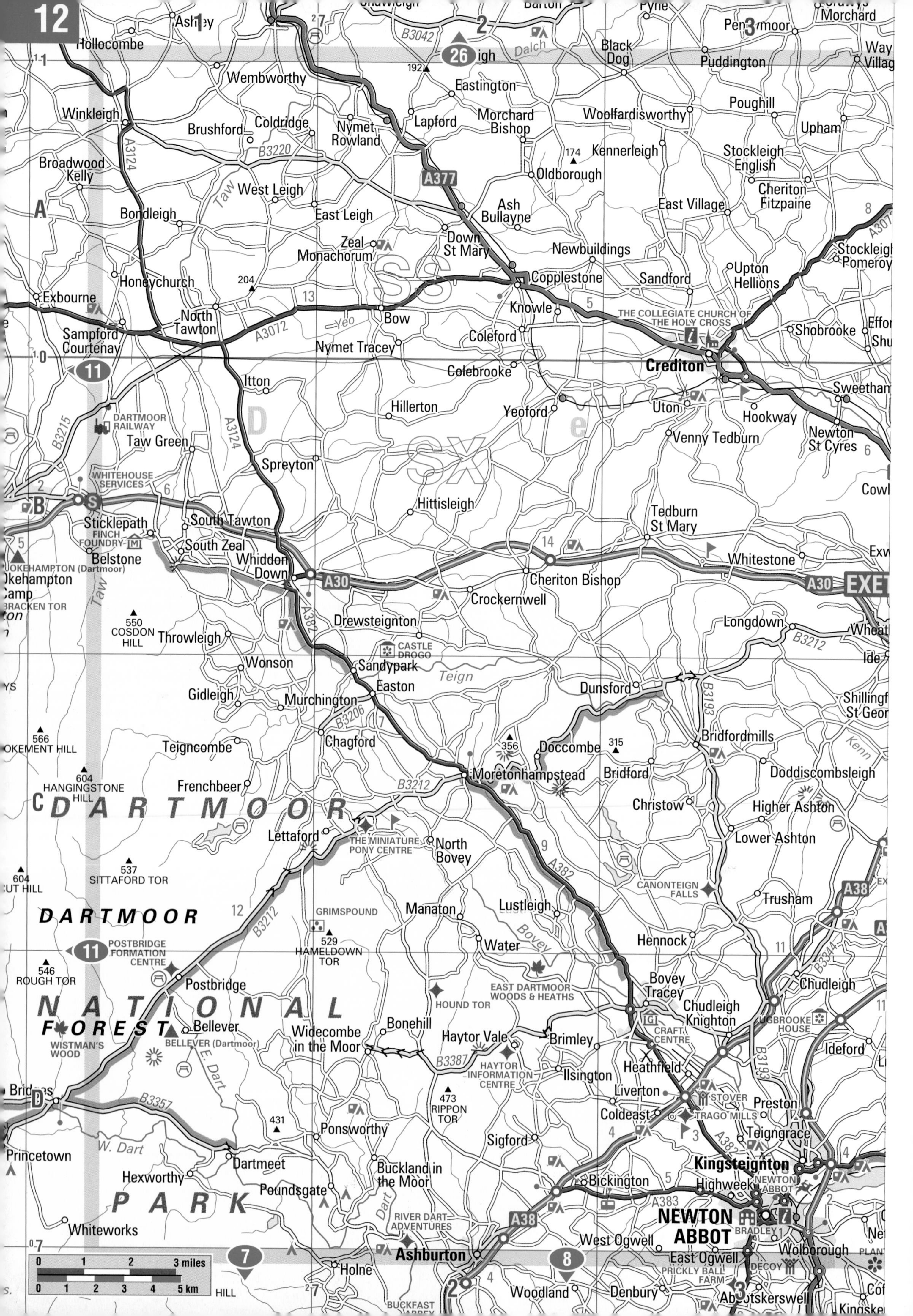
Hollocombe
Ashley
Wembworthy
Eastington
Black Dog
Puddington
Pennymoor
Winkleigh
Brushford
Coldridge
Nymet Rowland
Lapford
Morchard Bishop
Woolfardisworthy
Poughill
Upham
Broadwood Kelly
Kennerleigh
Stockleigh English
Oldborough
West Leigh
Cheriton Fitzpaine
Bondleigh
East Leigh
Ash Bullayne
East Village
Zeal Monachorum
Down St Mary
Newbuildings
Honeychurch
Copplestone
Sandford
Upton Hellions
Exbourne
Knowle
Bow
North Tawton
Sampford Courtenay
Nymet Tracey
Coleford
THE COLLEGIATE CHURCH OF THE HOLY CROSS
Shobrooke
Colebrooke
Crediton
Itton
DARTMOOR RAILWAY
Hillerton
Yeoford
Uton
Hookway
Sweetham
Taw Green
Venny Tedburn
Newton St Cyres
Spreyton
WHITEHOUSE SERVICES
Hittisleigh
Tedburn St Mary
Sticklepath
South Tawton
FINCH FOUNDRY
South Zeal
Belstone
Whiddon Down
Cheriton Bishop
Whitestone
OKEHAMPTON (Dartmoor)
Okehampton Camp
BRACKEN TOR
Crockernwell
550 COSDON HILL
Throwleigh
Drewsteignton
Longdown
CASTLE DROGO
Wonson
Sandypark
Easton
Teign
Dunsford
Ide
Gidleigh
Murchington
566 OKEMENT HILL
Chagford
Bridfordmills
Teigncombe
356
Doccombe
315
Bridford
604 HANGINGSTONE HILL
Moretonhampstead
Doddiscombsleigh
Frenchbeer
Christow
Higher Ashton
DARTMOOR
Lettaford
THE MINIATURE PONY CENTRE
North Bovey
Lower Ashton
604
537 SITTAFORD TOR
CANONTEIGN FALLS
Trusham
GRIMSPOUND
Manaton
Lustleigh
DARTMOOR
529 HAMELDOWN TOR
Water
Hennock
POSTBRIDGE FORMATION CENTRE
546 ROUGH TOR
Postbridge
EAST DARTMOOR WOODS & HEATHS
Bovey Tracey
Chudleigh
HOUND TOR
NATIONAL
Chudleigh Knighton
UGBROOKE HOUSE
FOREST
Bellever
BELLEVER (Dartmoor)
Bonehill
Haytor Vale
Brimley
CRAFT CENTRE
WISTMAN'S WOOD
Widecombe in the Moor
HAYTOR INFORMATION CENTRE
Ilsington
Heathfield
Ideford
Liverton
STOVER
Preston
473 RIPPON TOR
Coldeast
TRAGO MILLS
431
Ponsworthy
Sigford
Teigngrace
Princetown
Dartmeet
Kingsteignton
Hexworthy
Buckland in the Moor
Bickington
Highweek
NEWTON ABBOT
Poundsgate
PARK
A383
Whiteworks
RIVER DART ADVENTURES
NEWTON ABBOT
BRADLEY
West Ogwell
Wolborough
Ashburton
East Ogwell
DECOY
PRICKLY BALL FARM
Holne
Woodland
Denbury
Abbotskerswell
BUCKFAST ABBEY
0 1 2 3 miles
0 1 2 3 4 5 km
A30
A38
A382
A3124
A3072
A377
B3220
B3215
B3212
B3206
B3193
B3344
B3387
B3357
B3042
Taw
Yeo
Bovey
W. Dart
E. Dart
Dart
Kenn
26
11
7
8

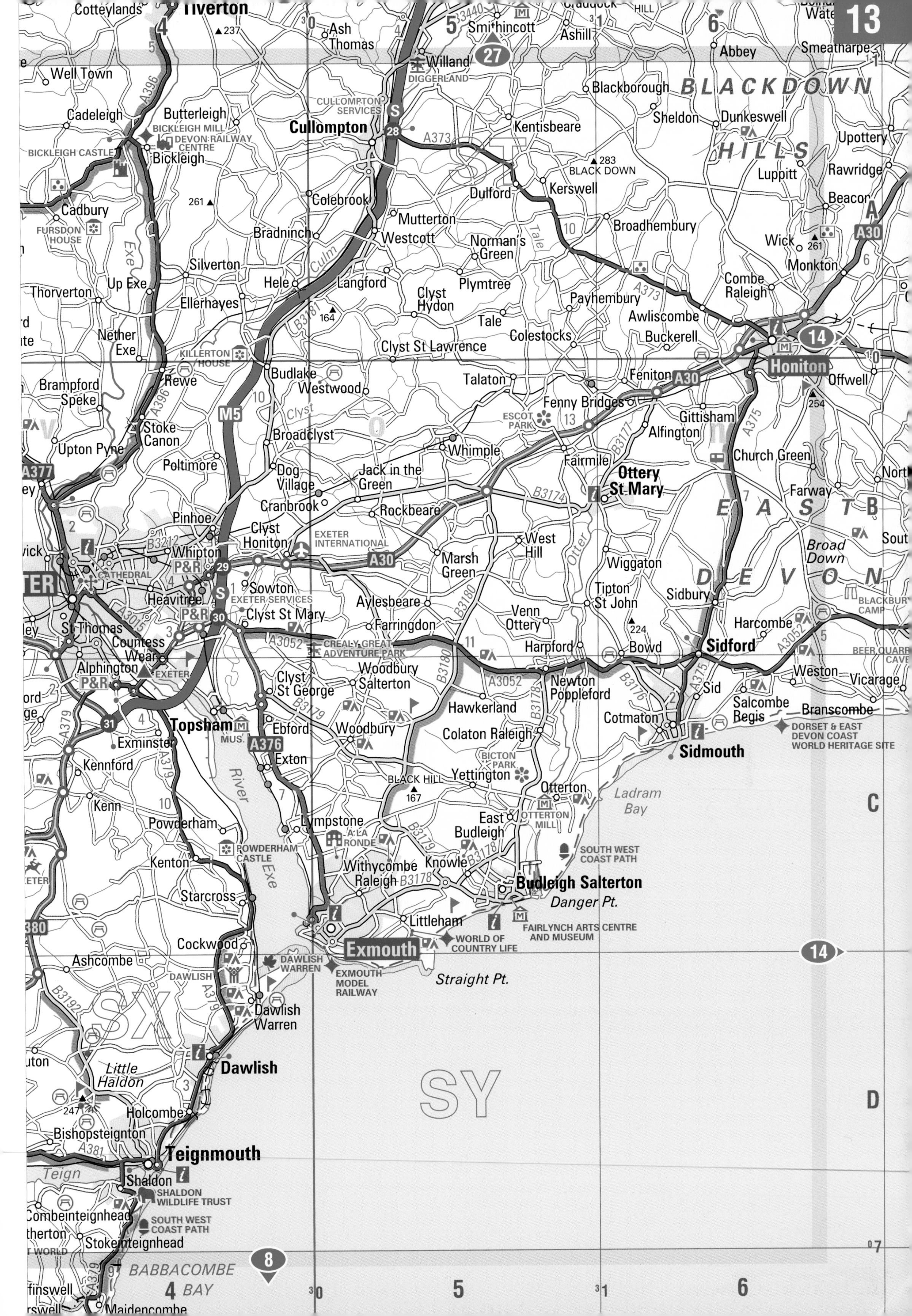
Cotteylands
Tiverton
Ash Thomas
Smithincott
Ashill
Abbey
Smeatharpe
Willand
DIGGERLAND
27
Well Town
Blackborough
BLACKDOWN
HILLS
CULLOMPTON SERVICES
Cullompton
Cadeleigh
Butterleigh
BICKLEIGH MILL
DEVON RAILWAY CENTRE
BICKLEIGH CASTLE
Bickleigh
Kentisbeare
Sheldon
Dunkeswell
Upottery
BLACK DOWN
Luppitt
Rawridge
Kerswell
Dulford
Colebrook
Cadbury
FURSDON HOUSE
Mutterton
Broadhembury
Beacon
Bradninch
Westcott
Norman's Green
Wick
Silverton
Monkton
Up Exe
Hele
Langford
Plymtree
Combe Raleigh
Thorverton
Ellerhayes
Clyst Hydon
Payhembury
Awliscombe
Nether Exe
Tale
Colestocks
Buckerell
Clyst St Lawrence
KILLERTON HOUSE
Budlake
Talaton
Feniton
Honiton
Offwell
Brampford Speke
Rewe
Westwood
Fenny Bridges
Gittisham
ESCOT PARK
Alfington
Stoke Canon
Upton Pyne
Broadclyst
Whimple
Church Green
Poltimore
Dog Village
Jack in the Green
Fairmile
Ottery St Mary
Farway
Cranbrook
Rockbeare
EAST
Pinhoe
Clyst Honiton
EXETER INTERNATIONAL
West Hill
Broad Down
Whipton
CATHEDRAL
Marsh Green
Wiggaton
DEVON
Sowton
EXETER SERVICES
Heavitree
Aylesbeare
Tipton St John
Sidbury
BLACKBURY CAMP
Clyst St Mary
St Thomas
Farringdon
Venn Ottery
Harcombe
Countess Wear
CREALY GREAT ADVENTURE PARK
Harpford
Bowd
Sidford
BEER QUARRY CAVES
Alphington
EXETER
Woodbury Salterton
Clyst St George
Newton Poppleford
Weston
Vicarage
Hawkerland
Sid
Salcombe Regis
Branscombe
Topsham
MUS.
Ebford
Woodbury
Colaton Raleigh
Cotmaton
Exminster
Sidmouth
DORSET & EAST DEVON COAST WORLD HERITAGE SITE
Kennford
Exton
BICTON PARK
Yettington
BLACK HILL
River Exe
Kenn
Otterton
Ladram Bay
Powderham
Lympstone
A LA RONDE
East Budleigh
OTTERTON MILL
POWDERHAM CASTLE
SOUTH WEST COAST PATH
Kenton
Withycombe Raleigh
Knowle
Budleigh Salterton
Starcross
Danger Pt.
Littleham
FAIRLYNCH ARTS CENTRE AND MUSEUM
Cockwood
Exmouth
WORLD OF COUNTRY LIFE
Ashcombe
DAWLISH WARREN
EXMOUTH MODEL RAILWAY
Straight Pt.
DAWLISH
Dawlish Warren
SX
SY
Dawlish
Little Haldon
Holcombe
Bishopsteignton
Teignmouth
Teign
Shaldon
SHALDON WILDLIFE TRUST
Combeinteignhead
SOUTH WEST COAST PATH
Stokeinteignhead
BABBACOMBE BAY
Maidencombe
M5
A30
A373
A396
A377
A376
A3052
A3015
A379
A380
A381
A375
B3181
B3174
B3177
B3180
B3178
B3179
B3176
B3192
B3212
14
8

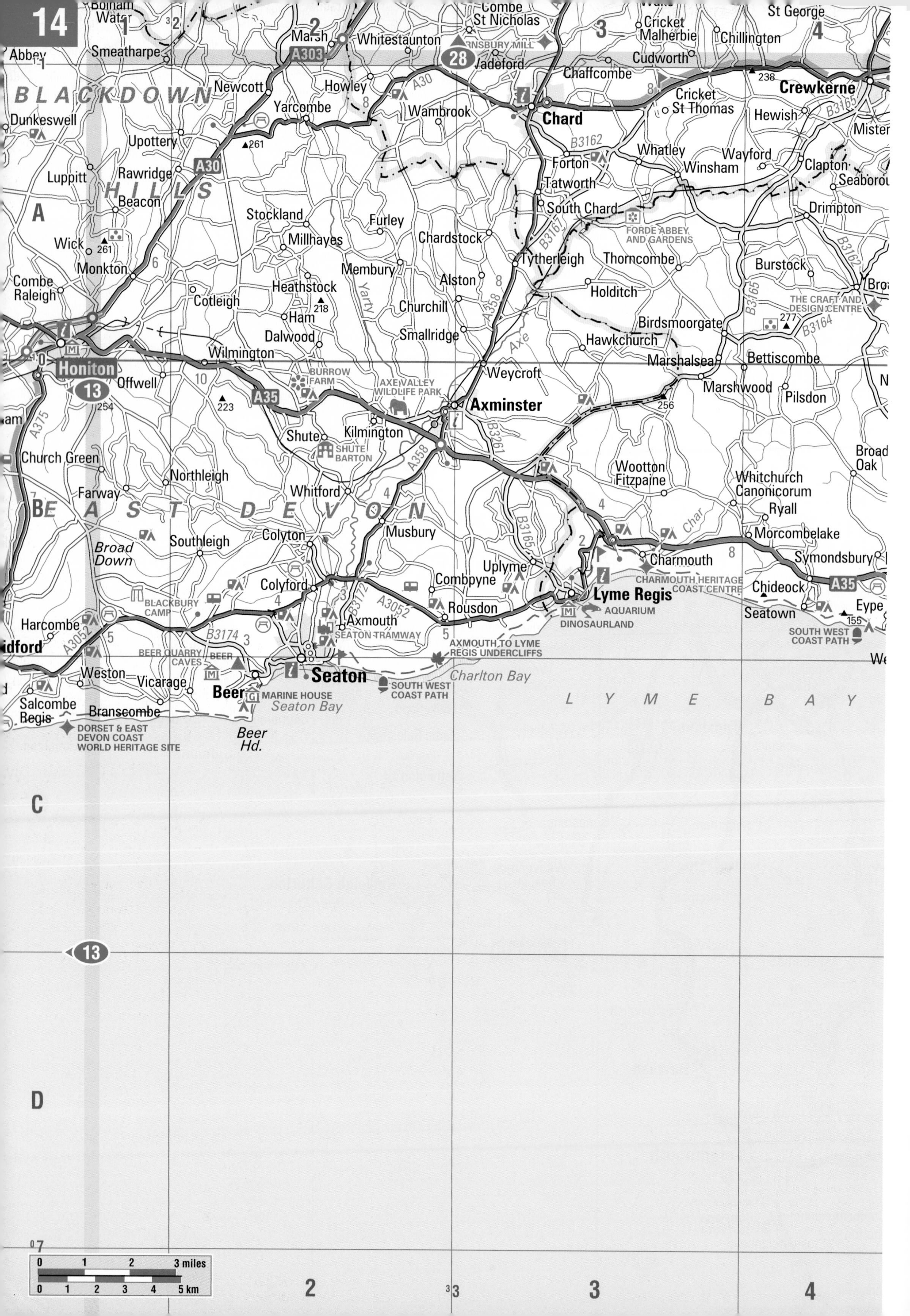
Smeatharpe
Whitestaunton
Combe St Nicholas
Cricket Malherbie
Chillington
St George
Cudworth
Chaffcombe
Crewkerne
Wadeford
A303
28
A30
BLACKDOWN HILLS
Newcott
Howley
Yarcombe
Wambrook
Chard
Cricket St Thomas
Hewish
B3165
Misterton
Dunkeswell
Upottery
261
B3162
Whatley
Wayford
Forton
Winsham
Clapton
Luppitt
Rawridge
Tatworth
Seaborough
Beacon
South Chard
Drimpton
FORDE ABBEY AND GARDENS
Stockland
Furley
Millhayes
Chardstock
Wick
Tytherleigh
Thorncombe
Burstock
B3167
Monkton
Membury
Alston
Combe Raleigh
Heathstock
Holditch
218
Cotleigh
Churchill
THE CRAFT AND DESIGN CENTRE
Ham
Birdsmoorgate
277
B3164
Dalwood
Smallridge
Hawkchurch
Wilmington
Marshalsea
Bettiscombe
Honiton
13
Offwell
BURROW FARM
AXE VALLEY WILDLIFE PARK
Weycroft
Marshwood
Pilsdon
254
223
A35
Axminster
256
A375
Shute
Kilmington
SHUTE BARTON
B3261
Church Green
Broad Oak
Northleigh
Wootton Fitzpaine
Whitchurch Canonicorum
Farway
Whitford
EAST DEVON
Ryall
Musbury
Colyton
Southleigh
Morcombelake
Broad Down
Charmouth
Symondsbury
Uplyme
Colyford
Combpyne
CHARMOUTH HERITAGE COAST CENTRE
Chideock
Lyme Regis
BLACKBURY CAMP
Rousdon
AQUARIUM
Eype
Axmouth
DINOSAURLAND
Seatown
Harcombe
155
B3174
SEATON TRAMWAY
SOUTH WEST COAST PATH
A3052
B3172
AXMOUTH TO LYME REGIS UNDERCLIFFS
Sidford
BEER QUARRY CAVES
BEER
Weston
Seaton
Charlton Bay
Vicarage
Beer
MARINE HOUSE
Salcombe Regis
Branscombe
Seaton Bay
LYME BAY
DORSET & EAST DEVON COAST WORLD HERITAGE SITE
Beer Hd.
A
B
C
D
1
2
3
4
13
0 1 2 3 miles
0 1 2 3 4 5 km

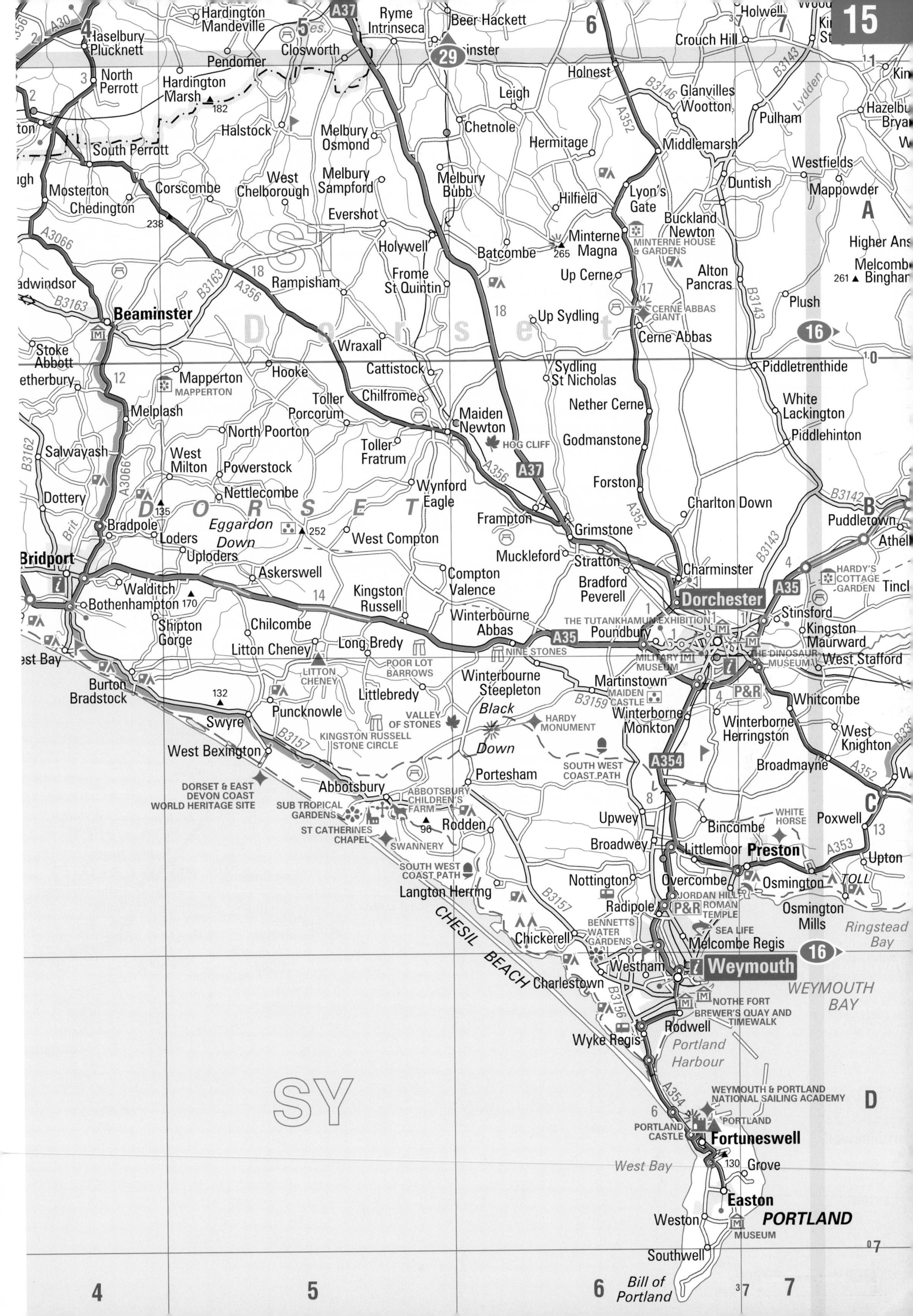

Haselbury Plucknett
Hardington Mandeville
Pendomer
Closworth
Ryme Intrinseca
Beer Hackett
Yetminster
Holwell
Crouch Hill
North Perrott
Hardington Marsh
182
Halstock
Melbury Osmond
Chetnole
Holnest
Leigh
Glanvilles Wootton
Pulham
Lydden
South Perrott
Hermitage
Middlemarsh
Westfields
Mosterton
Chedington
Corscombe
West Chelborough
Melbury Sampford
Melbury Bubb
Hilfield
Lyon's Gate
Duntish
Mappowder
Evershot
Buckland Newton
238
Holywell
Batcombe
Minterne Magna
265
MINTERNE HOUSE & GARDENS
Higher Ansty
Melcombe Bingham
261
Broadwindsor
Rampisham
Frome St Quintin
Up Cerne
Alton Pancras
Plush
Beaminster
Up Sydling
CERNE ABBAS GIANT
Cerne Abbas
Dorset
Stoke Abbott
Wraxall
Cattistock
Sydling St Nicholas
Piddletrenthide
Netherbury
Mapperton
MAPPERTON
Hooke
Chilfrome
Toller Porcorum
White Lackington
Melplash
Maiden Newton
Nether Cerne
North Poorton
Piddlehinton
Salwayash
Toller Fratrum
HOG CLIFF
Godmanstone
West Milton
Powerstock
Wynford Eagle
Forston
Dottery
Nettlecombe
Charlton Down
DORSET
135
Frampton
Puddletown
Athelhampton
Bradpole
Eggardon Down
252
West Compton
Grimstone
Loders
Uploders
Muckleford
Stratton
Bridport
Askerswell
Compton Valence
Charminster
HARDY'S COTTAGE GARDEN
Tincleton
Walditch
170
Bradford Peverell
Dorchester
Bothenhampton
Kingston Russell
Winterbourne Abbas
Stinsford
Shipton Gorge
Chilcombe
THE TUTANKHAMUN EXHIBITION
Kingston Maurward
Poundbury
West Bay
Litton Cheney
Long Bredy
NINE STONES
MILITARY MUSEUM
THE DINOSAUR MUSEUM
West Stafford
LITTON CHENEY
POOR LOT BARROWS
Burton Bradstock
132
Littlebredy
Winterbourne Steepleton
Martinstown
MAIDEN CASTLE
Whitcombe
Swyre
Puncknowle
VALLEY OF STONES
Black Down
HARDY MONUMENT
Winterborne Monkton
Winterborne Herrington
West Knighton
KINGSTON RUSSELL STONE CIRCLE
West Bexington
Portesham
SOUTH WEST COAST PATH
Broadmayne
DORSET & EAST DEVON COAST WORLD HERITAGE SITE
Abbotsbury
ABBOTSBURY CHILDREN'S FARM
SUB TROPICAL GARDENS
WHITE HORSE
Poxwell
Upwey
96
Rodden
Bincombe
ST CATHERINES CHAPEL
SWANNERY
Broadwey
Littlemoor
Preston
Upton
SOUTH WEST COAST PATH
Nottington
Overcombe
Osmington
TOLL
Langton Herring
JORDAN HILL ROMAN TEMPLE
Radipole
Osmington Mills
CHESIL BEACH
Ringstead Bay
BENNETTS WATER GARDENS
SEA LIFE
Chickerell
Melcombe Regis
Westham
Weymouth
Charlestown
WEYMOUTH BAY
NOTHE FORT
BREWER'S QUAY AND TIMEWALK
Rodwell
Wyke Regis
Portland Harbour
SY
WEYMOUTH & PORTLAND NATIONAL SAILING ACADEMY
PORTLAND
PORTLAND CASTLE
Fortuneswell
West Bay
130
Grove
Easton
Weston
PORTLAND
MUSEUM
Southwell
Bill of Portland
A37
A30
A3066
A356
B3163
B3162
B3146
B3143
A352
B3142
A35
B3159
B3157
A354
A353
B3156
29
16
A
B
C
D
4
5
6
7

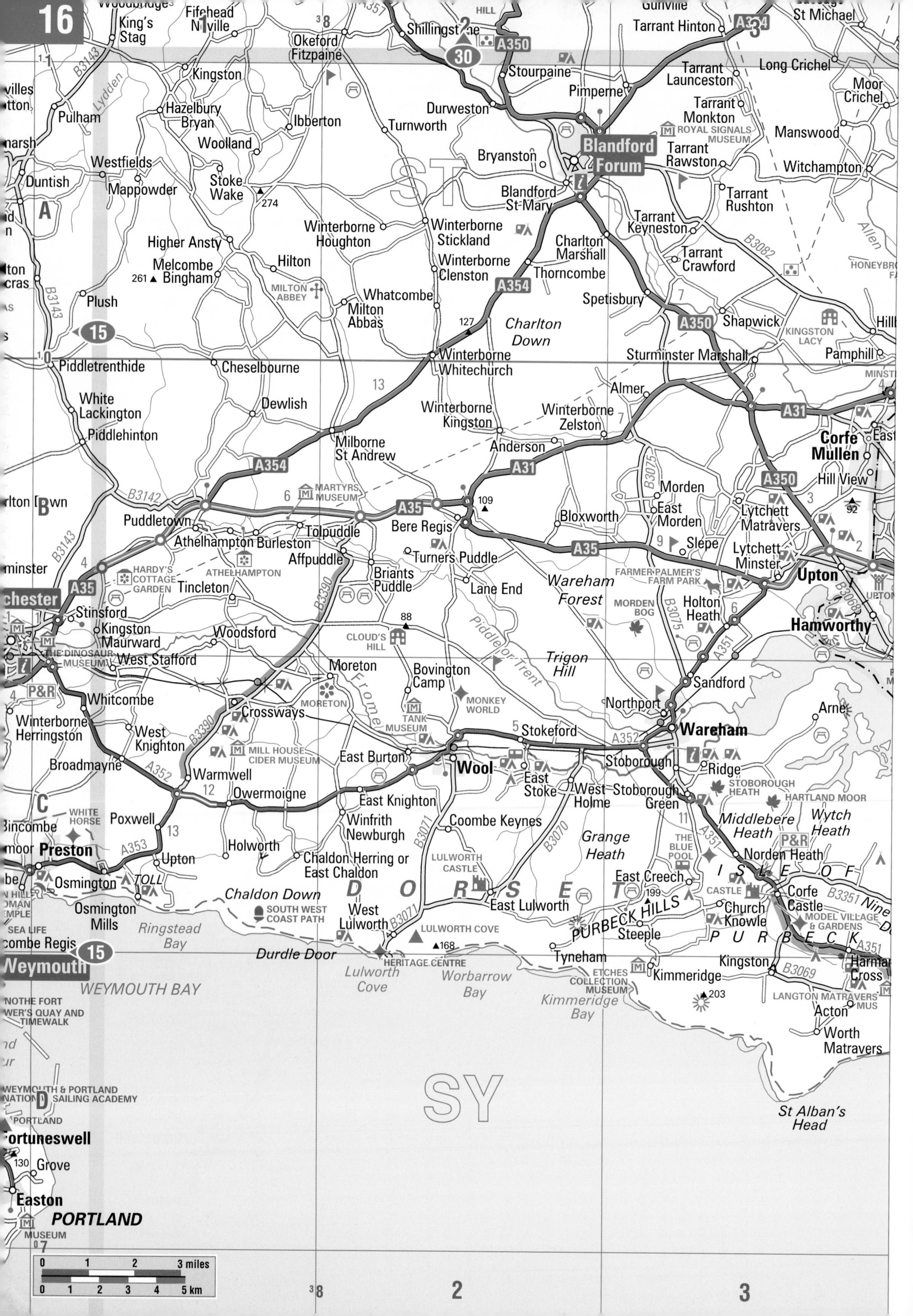
King's Stag
Fifehead Neville
Okeford Fitzpaine
Shillingstone
HILL
A350
30
Gunville
Tarrant Hinton
A354
St Michael
Kingston
Stourpaine
Pimperne
Tarrant Launceston
Long Crichel
Moor Crichel
Pulham
Hazelbury Bryan
Ibberton
Durweston
Turnworth
Tarrant Monkton
Manswood
Woolland
ROYAL SIGNALS MUSEUM
Blandford Forum
Tarrant Rawston
Westfields
Mappowder
Duntish
Stoke Wake
274
Bryanston
Blandford St Mary
Witchampton
Tarrant Rushton
A
Winterborne Houghton
Winterborne Stickland
Tarrant Keyneston
Higher Ansty
Hilton
Charlton Marshall
Tarrant Crawford
Melcombe Bingham
261
Winterborne Clenston
Thorncombe
B3082
Allen
HONEYBROOK
B3143
Plush
MILTON ABBEY
Whatcombe
Milton Abbas
A354
Spetisbury
127
Charlton Down
A350
Shapwick
KINGSTON LACY
15
Piddletrenthide
Cheselbourne
Winterborne Whitechurch
Sturminster Marshall
Pamphill
13
White Lackington
Dewlish
Winterborne Kingston
Almer
Winterborne Zelston
A31
Piddlehinton
Milborne St Andrew
Anderson
Corfe Mullen
A354
A31
B3075
Morden
A350
Hill View
B3142
B
6
MARTYRS MUSEUM
109
East Morden
Lytchett Matravers
92
A35
Bloxworth
Puddletown
Tolpuddle
Bere Regis
Athelhampton
Burleston
9
Slepe
Lytchett Minster
A35
Affpuddle
Turners Puddle
Upton
4
HARDY'S COTTAGE GARDEN
ATHELHAMPTON
Tincleton
Briants Puddle
Lane End
Wareham Forest
FARMER PALMER'S FARM PARK
B3068
A35
B3390
MORDEN BOG
Holton Heath
Stinsford
Kingston Maurward
88
Piddle or Trent
6
Hamworthy
Woodsford
CLOUD'S HILL
THE DINOSAUR MUSEUM
West Stafford
Moreton
Bovington Camp
Trigon Hill
A351
P&R
Frome
Sandford
Whitcombe
MORETON
MONKEY WORLD
Northport
Arne
Winterborne Herringston
Crossways
TANK MUSEUM
5
Stokeford
A352
Wareham
West Knighton
B3390
MILL HOUSE CIDER MUSEUM
East Burton
Broadmayne
Stoborough
Ridge
Wool
East Stoke
A352
Warmwell
12
Owermoigne
East Knighton
West Holme
Stoborough Green
STOBOROUGH HEATH
HARTLAND MOOR
C
WHITE HORSE
Poxwell
Winfrith Newburgh
Coombe Keynes
11
Middlebere Heath
Wytch Heath
13
B3071
B3070
Grange Heath
THE BLUE POOL
P&R
Preston
A353
Holworth
Upton
Chaldon Herring or East Chaldon
A351
Norden Heath
LULWORTH CASTLE
Osmington
TOLL
East Creech
ISLE OF
Corfe Castle
Chaldon Down
DORSET
199
CASTLE
B3351
Osmington Mills
SOUTH WEST COAST PATH
West Lulworth
East Lulworth
Church Knowle
MODEL VILLAGE & GARDENS
SEA LIFE
Ringstead Bay
B3071
LULWORTH COVE
PURBECK HILLS
Steeple
PURBECK
A351
Weymouth
15
Durdle Door
168
HERITAGE CENTRE
Tyneham
Kingston
Harmans Cross
Lulworth Cove
Worbarrow Bay
ETCHES COLLECTION MUSEUM
Kimmeridge
B3069
WEYMOUTH BAY
Kimmeridge Bay
203
LANGTON MATRAVERS MUS
NOTHE FORT
WER'S QUAY AND TIMEWALK
Acton
Worth Matravers
SY
ST
WEYMOUTH & PORTLAND NATIONAL SAILING ACADEMY
D
PORTLAND
St Alban's Head
Fortuneswell
130
Grove
Easton
PORTLAND
MUSEUM
0 1 2 3 miles
0 1 2 3 4 5 km
38
2
3

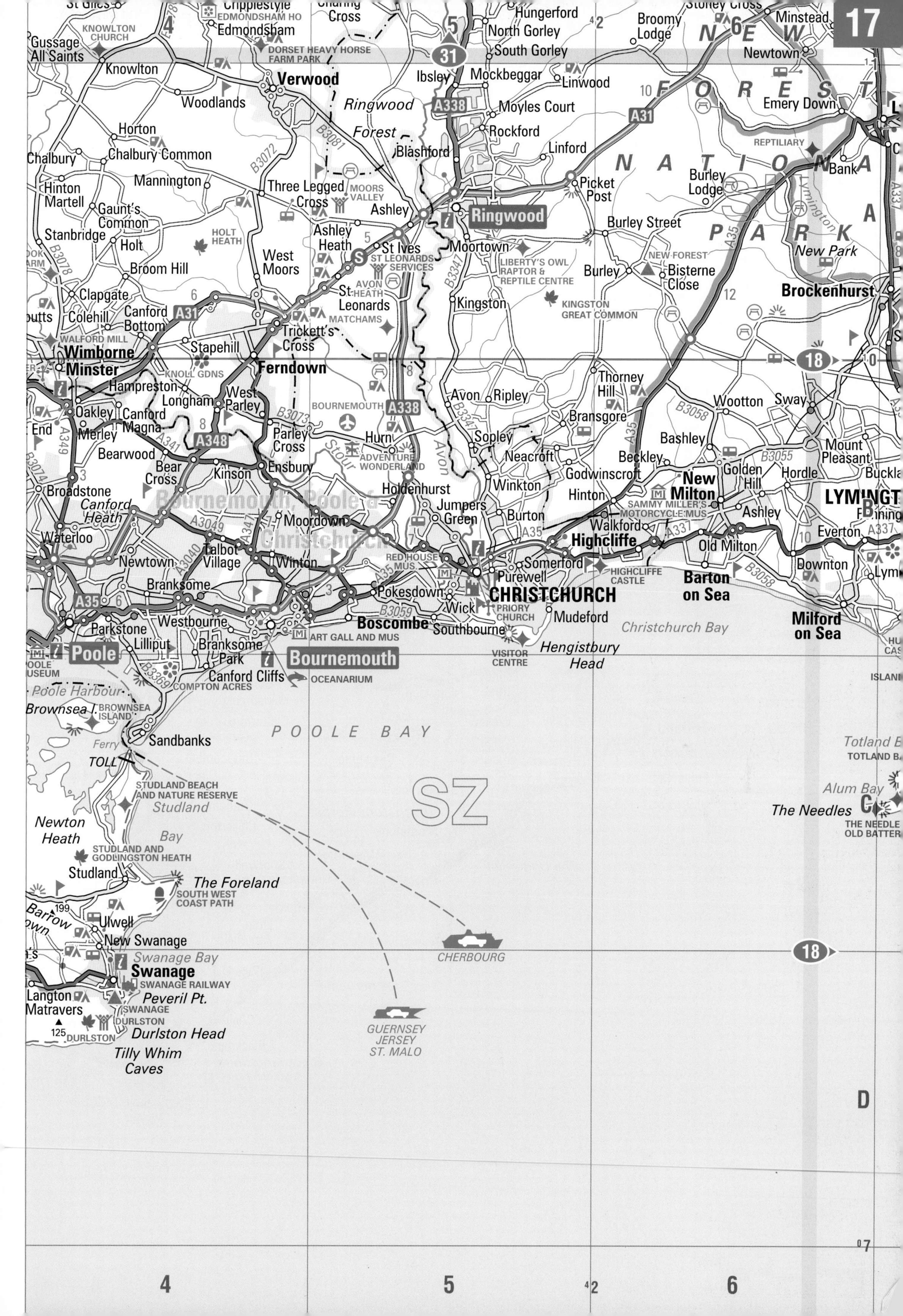
Gussage All Saints
KNOWLTON CHURCH
Knowlton
Edmondsham
EDMONDSHAM HO
DORSET HEAVY HORSE FARM PARK
Verwood
Woodlands
Horton
Chalbury
Chalbury Common
Mannington
Hinton Martell
Gaunt's Common
Stanbridge
Holt
HOLT HEATH
Broom Hill
Clapgate
Colehill
Canford Bottom
WALFORD MILL
Wimborne Minster
Stapehill
KNOLL GDNS
Hampreston
Longham
West Parley
Oakley
Canford Magna
Merley
Bearwood
Bear Cross
Kinson
Ensbury
Broadstone
Canford Heath
Waterloo
Newtown
Talbot Village
Winton
Branksome
Parkstone
Westbourne
Lilliput
Branksome Park
Canford Cliffs
COMPTON ACRES
Poole
POOLE MUSEUM
Bournemouth
ART GALL AND MUS
OCEANARIUM
Boscombe
Southbourne
Pokesdown
RED HOUSE MUS
Wick
Bournemouth, Poole & Christchurch
Moordown
Holdenhurst
Jumpers Green
Hurn
ADVENTURE WONDERLAND
BOURNEMOUTH
Parley Cross
Ferndown
Trickett's Cross
MATCHAMS
St Leonards
AVON HEATH
St Ives
ST LEONARDS SERVICES
Ashley Heath
West Moors
Three Legged Cross
MOORS VALLEY
Ashley
Ringwood Forest
Blashford
Ibsley
Mockbeggar
Moyles Court
Rockford
Linford
Ringwood
Moortown
Kingston
LIBERTY'S OWL RAPTOR & REPTILE CENTRE
KINGSTON GREAT COMMON
Burley
Burley Street
Picket Post
Linwood
Hungerford
North Gorley
South Gorley
Broomy Lodge
Minstead
Newtown
Emery Down
REPTILIARY
Bank
Burley Lodge
NEW FOREST
Bisterne Close
New Park
Brockenhurst
NEW FOREST NATIONAL PARK
Thorney Hill
Avon
Ripley
Bransgore
Sopley
Neacroft
Godwinscroft
Winkton
Hinton
Burton
Wootton
Sway
Bashley
Beckley
New Milton
SAMMY MILLER'S MOTORCYCLE MUS
Golden Hill
Mount Pleasant
Hordle
Walkford
Highcliffe
Somerford
HIGHCLIFFE CASTLE
Purewell
CHRISTCHURCH
PRIORY CHURCH
Mudeford
Ashley
Old Milton
Barton on Sea
Everton
Downton
Milford on Sea
LYMINGTON
Christchurch Bay
VISITOR CENTRE
Hengistbury Head
Poole Harbour
Brownsea I.
BROWNSEA ISLAND
Sandbanks
Ferry
TOLL
POOLE BAY
SZ
STUDLAND BEACH AND NATURE RESERVE
Studland Bay
Newton Heath
STUDLAND AND GODLINGSTON HEATH
Studland
The Foreland
SOUTH WEST COAST PATH
Ulwell
New Swanage
Swanage Bay
Swanage
SWANAGE RAILWAY
Peveril Pt.
SWANAGE
DURLSTON
Langton Matravers
Durlston Head
Tilly Whim Caves
CHERBOURG
GUERNSEY JERSEY ST. MALO
Totland Bay
TOTLAND BAY
Alum Bay
The Needles
THE NEEDLES OLD BATTERY
D
4
5
6

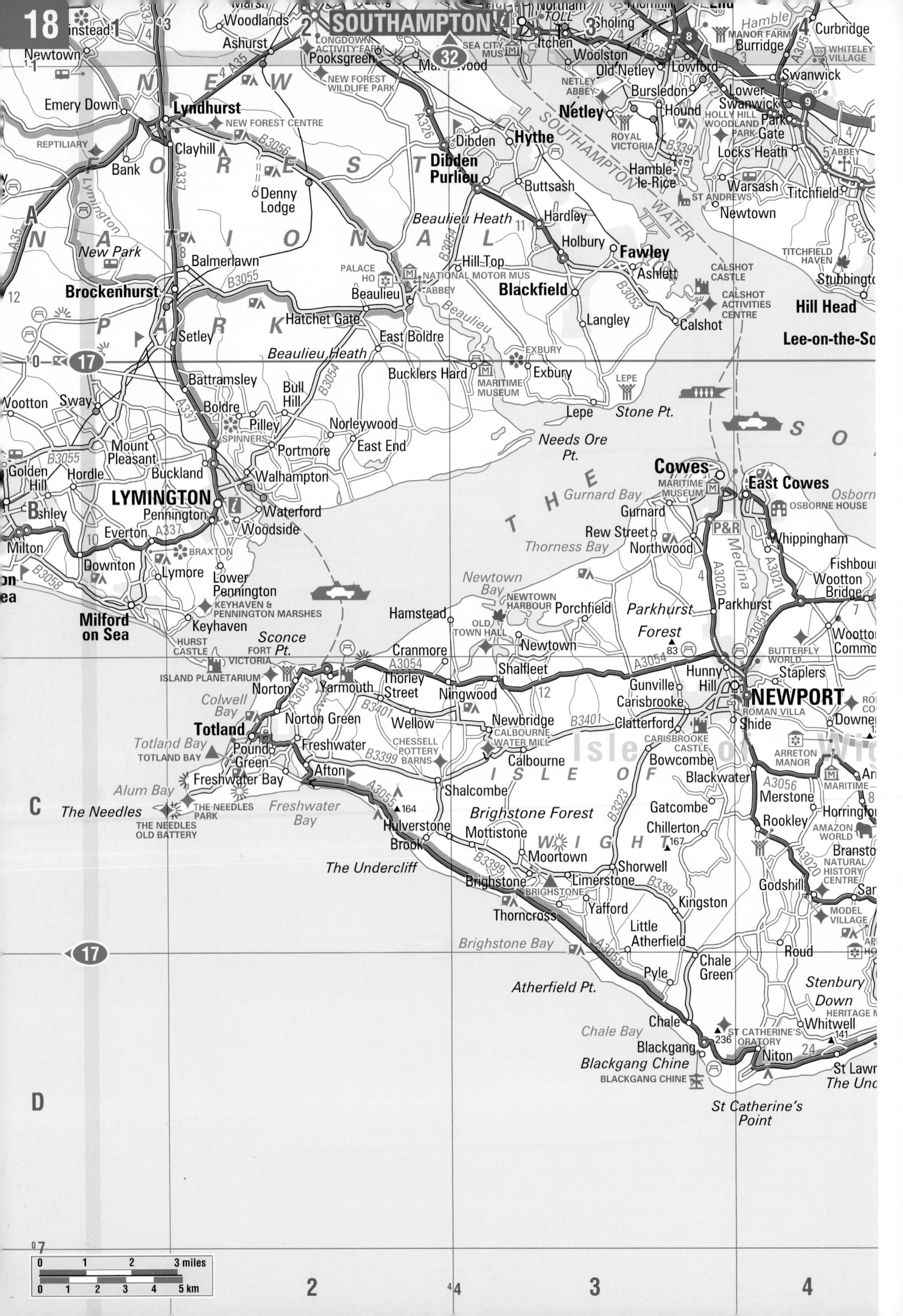
SOUTHAMPTON
Woodlands
Ashurst
Newtown
LONGDOWN ACTIVITY FARM
Pooksgreen
NEW FOREST WILDLIFE PARK
SEA CITY MUS
32
Itchen
Sholing
Woolston
Old Netley
Lowford
Hamble
MANOR FARM
Burridge
Curbridge
WHITELEY VILLAGE
Swanwick
Lower Swanwick
Park Gate
Bursledon
Hound
NETLEY ABBEY
Netley
ROYAL VICTORIA
HOLLY HILL WOODLAND PARK
Locks Heath
ABBEY
Titchfield
Warsash
ST ANDREWS
Newtown
Hamble-le-Rice
SOUTHAMPTON WATER
Emery Down
Lyndhurst
NEW FOREST CENTRE
REPTILIARY
Clayhill
Bank
Denny Lodge
Dibden
Hythe
Dibden Purlieu
Buttsash
Beaulieu Heath
Hardley
Holbury
Fawley
Ashlett
CALSHOT CASTLE
CALSHOT ACTIVITIES CENTRE
Calshot
TITCHFIELD HAVEN
Stubbington
Hill Head
Lee-on-the-So
NEW FOREST NATIONAL PARK
New Park
Balmerlawn
Brockenhurst
PALACE HO
NATIONAL MOTOR MUS
ABBEY
Hill Top
Beaulieu
Blackfield
Langley
Hatchet Gate
Setley
East Boldre
Beaulieu Heath
Bucklers Hard
MARITIME MUSEUM
EXBURY
Exbury
LEPE
Lepe
Stone Pt.
Battramsley
Wootton
Sway
Bull Hill
Boldre
Pilley
SPINNERS
Norleywood
East End
Mount Pleasant
Portmore
Needs Ore Pt.
Golden Hill
Hordle
Buckland
Walhampton
LYMINGTON
Pennington
Waterford
Woodside
Ashley
Everton
Milton
Downton
BRAXTON
Lymore
Lower Pennington
KEYHAVEN & PENNINGTON MARSHES
Keyhaven
Milford on Sea
HURST CASTLE
Cowes
MARITIME MUSEUM
East Cowes
OSBORNE HOUSE
Gurnard Bay
Gurnard
Rew Street
Northwood
Thorness Bay
Whippingham
Fishbou
Wootton Bridge
Newtown Bay
NEWTOWN HARBOUR
Porchfield
Parkhurst
Parkhurst Forest
Hamstead
OLD TOWN HALL
Newtown
Sconce Pt.
FORT VICTORIA
Cranmore
ISLAND PLANETARIUM
Norton
Yarmouth
Thorley Street
Ningwood
Shalfleet
Gunville
Hunny Hill
NEWPORT
BUTTERFLY WORLD
Staplers
Wootton Common
Colwell Bay
Carisbrooke
ROMAN VILLA
Shide
Downe
Totland
Norton Green
Wellow
Newbridge
CALBOURNE WATER MILL
Clatterford
CARISBROOKE CASTLE
Totland Bay
TOTLAND BAY
Freshwater
CHESSELL POTTERY BARNS
Calbourne
Bowcombe
ARRETON MANOR
Pound Green
Freshwater Bay
Afton
Shalcombe
ISLE OF WIGHT
Blackwater
MARITIME
Alum Bay
A3056
Merstone
Horringfo
THE NEEDLES PARK
The Needles
THE NEEDLES OLD BATTERY
Freshwater Bay
Brighstone Forest
Gatcombe
Rookley
AMAZON WORLD
Hulverstone
Mottistone
Chillerton
Bransto
Brook
Moortown
NATURAL HISTORY CENTRE
The Undercliff
Shorwell
Brighstone
Limerstone
BRIGHSTONE
Godshill
Thorncross
Yafford
Kingston
MODEL VILLAGE
Little Atherfield
Brighstone Bay
Roud
Chale Green
Pyle
Atherfield Pt.
Stenbury Down
HERITAGE
Chale
Whitwell
Chale Bay
Blackgang
ST CATHERINE'S ORATORY
Niton
Blackgang Chine
BLACKGANG CHINE
St Lawr
The Und
St Catherine's Point
THE SOLENT
A35
A337
A326
A3025
A27
B3056
B3055
B3054
B3053
B3397
B3334
A3054
A3020
A3021
B3401
B3399
A3055
B3058
B3323
17
0 1 2 3 miles
0 1 2 3 4 5 km
A
B
C
D
1
2
3
4

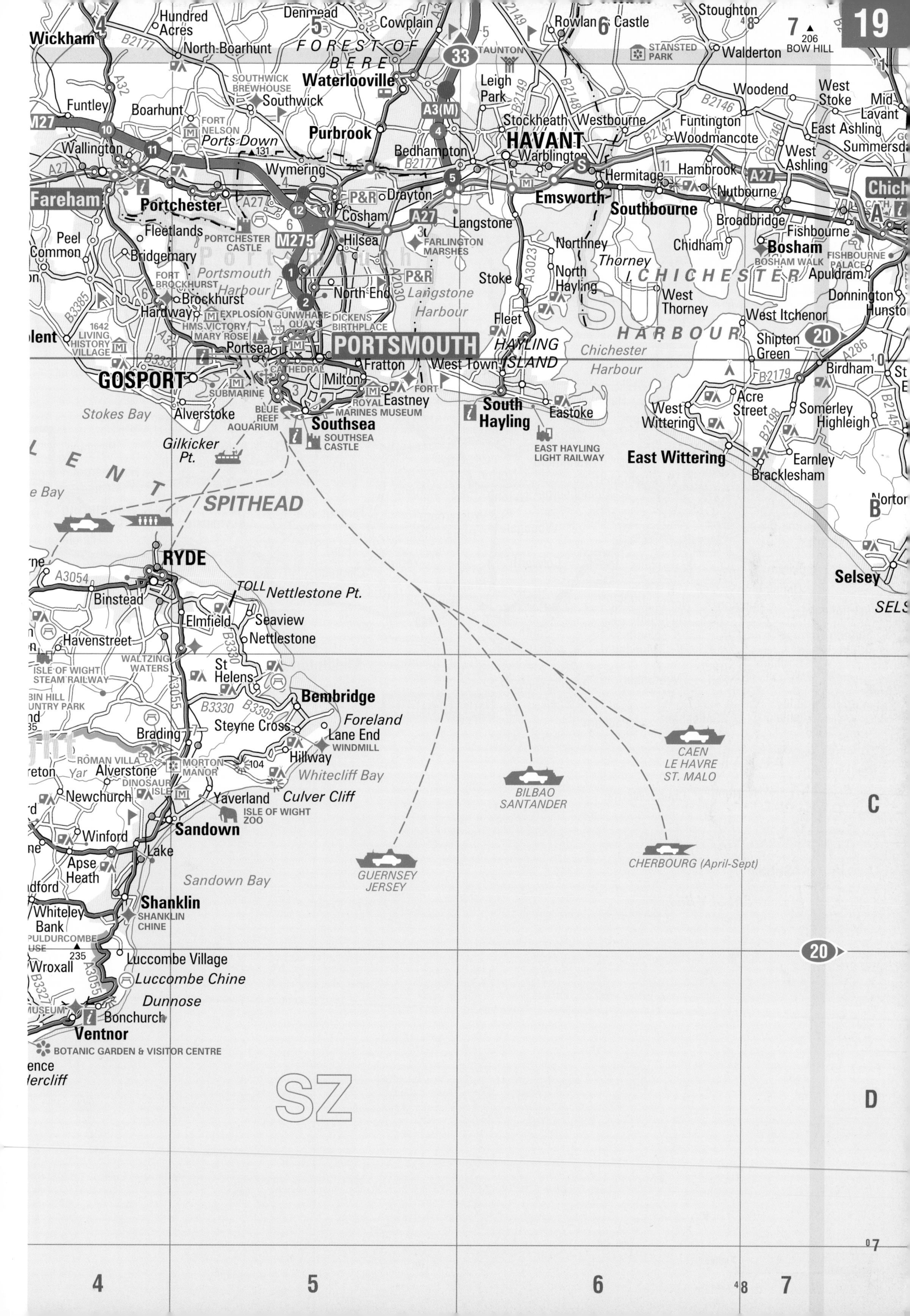
Wickham
Hundred Acres
North Boarhunt
Denmead
Cowplain
FOREST OF BERE
Waterlooville
Rowlan
Castle
Stoughton
BOW HILL
Walderton
STANSTED PARK
TAUNTON
Leigh Park
SOUTHWICK BREWHOUSE
Southwick
Funtley
Boarhunt
FORT NELSON
Ports Down
Purbrook
Woodend
West Stoke
Mid Lavant
East Ashling
Summersdale
West Ashling
Stockheath
Westbourne
Funtington
Woodmancote
HAVANT
Warblington
Bedhampton
Wallington
Wymering
Hermitage
Hambrook
Nutbourne
Fareham
Portchester
Drayton
Cosham
Emsworth
Southbourne
Langstone
Broadbridge
Fishbourne
Peel Common
Fleetlands
PORTCHESTER CASTLE
Hilsea
FARLINGTON MARSHES
Northney
Chidham
Bosham
Bridgemary
Portsmouth Harbour
Thorney
BOSHAM WALK
FISHBOURNE PALACE
Apuldram
FORT BROCKHURST
North End
Stoke
North Hayling
CHICHESTER
Brockhurst
Langstone Harbour
West Thorney
Donnington
Hardway
EXPLOSION
GUNWHARF QUAYS
DICKENS BIRTHPLACE
Fleet
West Itchenor
HMS VICTORY
MARY ROSE
HARBOUR
Shipton Green
1642 LIVING HISTORY VILLAGE
Portsea
PORTSMOUTH
HAYLING ISLAND
Chichester Harbour
Fratton
West Town
Birdham
GOSPORT
CATHEDRAL
Milton
FORT
SUBMARINE
Eastney
ROYAL MARINES MUSEUM
Acre Street
Stokes Bay
Alverstoke
BLUE REEF AQUARIUM
Southsea
South Hayling
Eastoke
West Wittering
Somerley
Highleigh
SOUTHSEA CASTLE
EAST HAYLING LIGHT RAILWAY
Gilkicker Pt.
East Wittering
Earnley
Bracklesham
SOLENT
SPITHEAD
Norton
Selsey
RYDE
Binstead
TOLL
Nettlestone Pt.
Elmfield
Seaview
Nettlestone
Havenstreet
WALTZING WATERS
ISLE OF WIGHT STEAM RAILWAY
St Helens
Bembridge
Foreland
Lane End
WINDMILL
Brading
Steyne Cross
Hillway
ROMAN VILLA
MORTON MANOR
Whitecliff Bay
Alverstone
DINOSAUR ISLE
Culver Cliff
Newchurch
Yaverland
ISLE OF WIGHT ZOO
Sandown
Winford
Lake
Apse Heath
Sandown Bay
Shanklin
SHANKLIN CHINE
Whiteley Bank
Luccombe Village
Wroxall
Luccombe Chine
Dunnose
Bonchurch
Ventnor
BOTANIC GARDEN & VISITOR CENTRE
CAEN
LE HAVRE
ST. MALO
BILBAO
SANTANDER
GUERNSEY
JERSEY
CHERBOURG (April-Sept)
SZ
C
D
4
5
6
7

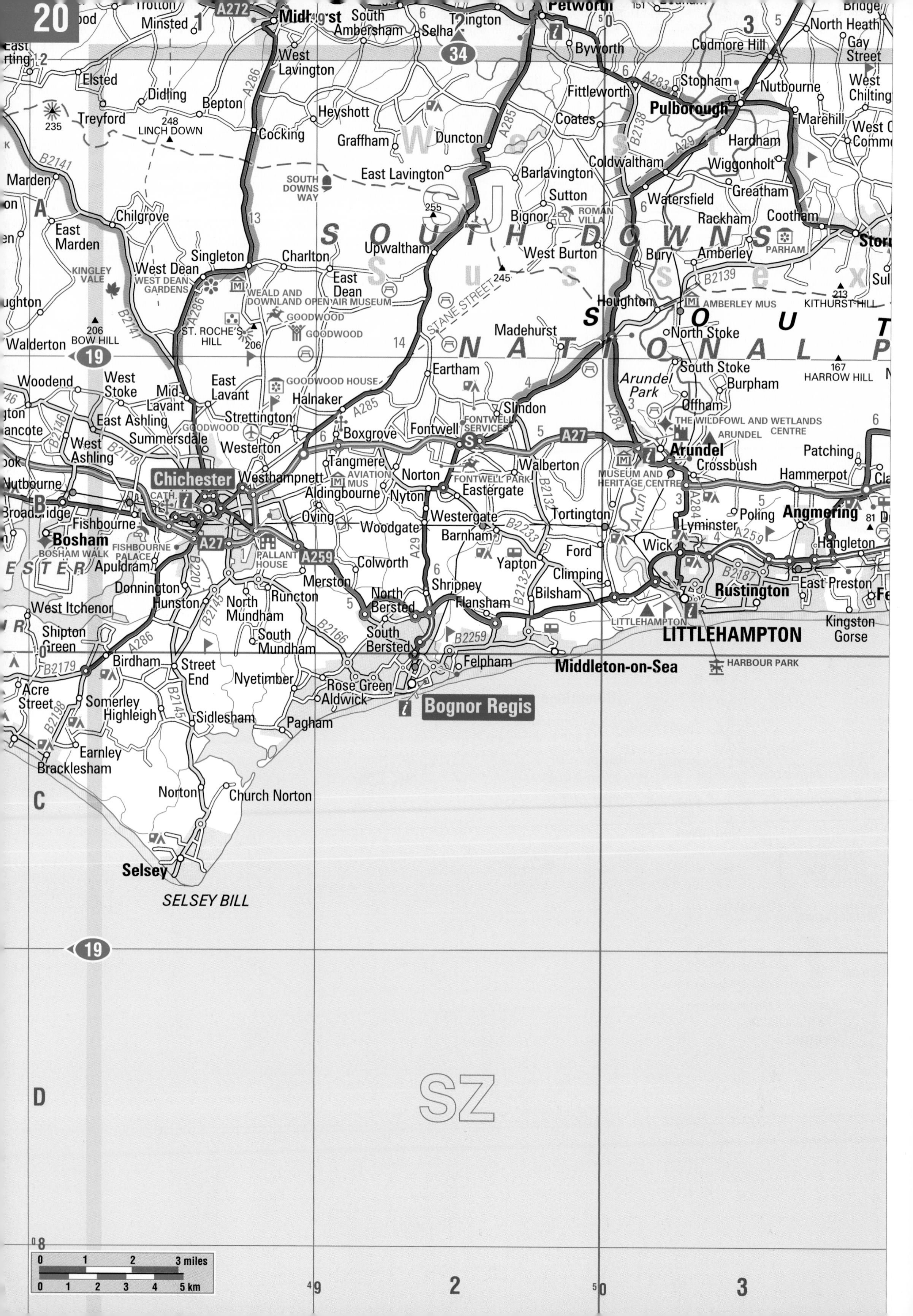
Minsted
Midhurst
South Ambersham
Selham
Tillington
Petworth
34
Byworth
Codmore Hill
North Heath
Gay Street
West Chiltington
Elsted
Didling
Bepton
West Lavington
Stopham
Nutbourne
Fittleworth
Pulborough
Treyford
235
248
LINCH DOWN
Cocking
Heyshott
Graffham
Duncton
Coates
Marehill
Hardham
Marden
Coldwaltham
Wiggonholt
East Lavington
Barlavington
SOUTH DOWNS WAY
Greatham
Watersfield
Sutton
255
Chilgrove
East Marden
Bignor
ROMAN VILLA
Rackham
Cootham
SOUTH DOWNS
West Sussex
Upwaltham
Charlton
Singleton
West Burton
Bury
Amberley
PARHAM
KINGLEY VALE
West Dean
WEST DEAN GARDENS
East Dean
WEALD AND DOWNLAND OPEN AIR MUSEUM
245
STANE STREET
Houghton
AMBERLEY MUS
213
KITHURST HILL
206
BOW HILL
ST. ROCHE'S HILL
GOODWOOD
Madehurst
SOUTH DOWNS NATIONAL PARK
North Stoke
Walderton
19
South Stoke
Burpham
167
HARROW HILL
Woodend
West Stoke
Mid Lavant
East Lavant
GOODWOOD HOUSE
Eartham
Arundel Park
Halnaker
Slindon
Offham
East Ashling
Strettington
THE WILDFOWL AND WETLANDS CENTRE
ARUNDEL
West Ashling
Summersdale
GOODWOOD
Westerton
Boxgrove
Fontwell
FONTWELL SERVICES
A27
Arundel
Patching
Walberton
Crossbush
Tangmere
AVIATION MUS
Norton
FONTWELL PARK
MUSEUM AND HERITAGE CENTRE
Hammerpot
Nutbourne
Chichester
Westhampnett
Aldingbourne
Nyton
Eastergate
Broadbridge
CATH.
Tortington
Poling
Angmering
Fishbourne
Oving
Westergate
Woodgate
Lyminster
Bosham
Barnham
Hangleton
BOSHAM WALK
FISHBOURNE PALACE
PALLANT HOUSE
A259
Colworth
Wick
Ford
Yapton
Apuldram
Climping
Donnington
Merston
Shripney
East Preston
Rustington
Runcton
North Bersted
Bilsham
Hunston
West Itchenor
North Mundham
Flansham
LITTLEHAMPTON
Kingston Gorse
Shipton Green
South Mundham
South Bersted
LITTLEHAMPTON
Birdham
Street End
Felpham
Middleton-on-Sea
HARBOUR PARK
Nyetimber
Rose Green
Acre Street
Somerley
Aldwick
Highleigh
Sidlesham
Bognor Regis
Pagham
Earnley
Bracklesham
Norton
Church Norton
Selsey
SELSEY BILL
19
SZ
A
B
C
D
0 1 2 3 miles
0 1 2 3 4 5 km

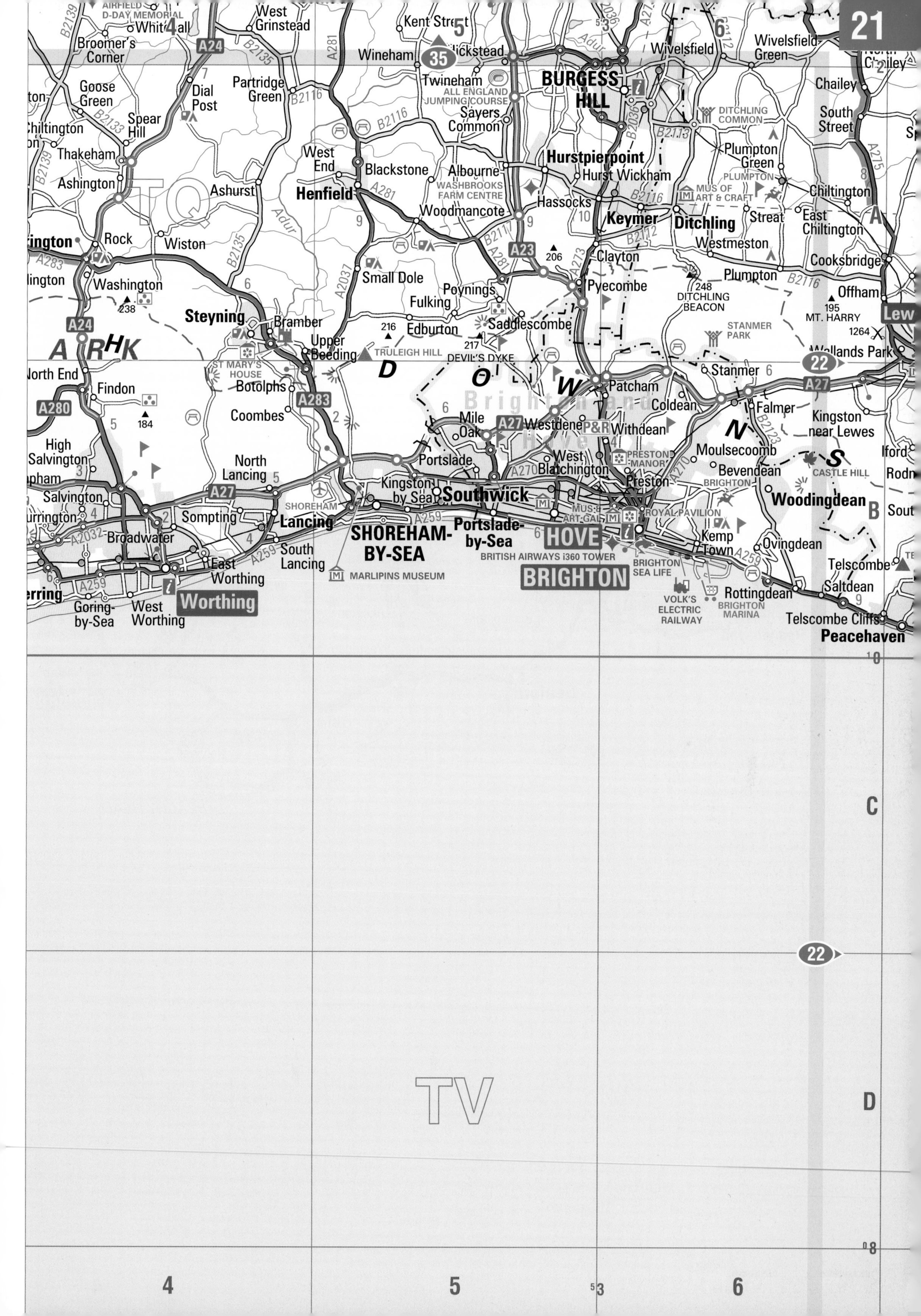
West Grinstead
Kent Street
Wineham
Twineham
ALL ENGLAND JUMPING COURSE
Sayers Common
BURGESS HILL
Wivelsfield
Wivelsfield Green
Chailey
South Street
Broomer's Corner
Goose Green
Dial Post
Partridge Green
Spear Hill
Thakeham
Ashington
West End
Blackstone
Albourne
WASHBROOKS FARM CENTRE
Hurstpierpoint
Hurst Wickham
DITCHLING COMMON
Plumpton Green
PLUMPTON
MUS OF ART & CRAFT
Chiltington
East Chiltington
Ashurst
Henfield
Woodmancote
Hassocks
Keymer
Ditchling
Streat
Westmeston
Cooksbridge
Rock
Wiston
Clayton
Pyecombe
Plumpton
Offham
Washington
Small Dole
Poynings
Fulking
DITCHLING BEACON
STANMER PARK
MT. HARRY
Steyning
Bramber
Upper Beeding
Edburton
Saddlescombe
TRULEIGH HILL
DEVIL'S DYKE
Wallands Park
Stanmer
North End
Findon
ST MARY'S HOUSE
Botolphs
Patcham
Coldean
Falmer
Kingston near Lewes
Coombes
Mile Oak
Westdene
Withdean
High Salvington
North Lancing
Portslade
West Blatchington
PRESTON MANOR
Moulsecoomb
Bevendean
CASTLE HILL
Iford
Rodmell
Salvington
Kingston by Sea
Southwick
Preston
BRIGHTON
Woodingdean
Sompting
SHOREHAM
Lancing
Broadwater
East Worthing
South Lancing
SHOREHAM-BY-SEA
Portslade-by-Sea
HOVE
MUS & ART GAL
ROYAL PAVILION
Kemp Town
Ovingdean
BRITISH AIRWAYS i360 TOWER
BRIGHTON
BRIGHTON SEA LIFE
Telscombe
Saltdean
MARLIPINS MUSEUM
Worthing
Goring-by-Sea
West Worthing
VOLK'S ELECTRIC RAILWAY
Rottingdean
BRIGHTON MARINA
Telscombe Cliffs
Peacehaven
TQ
TV
SOUTH DOWNS
A24
A27
A23
A283
A280
A259
A270
A281
A2037
22

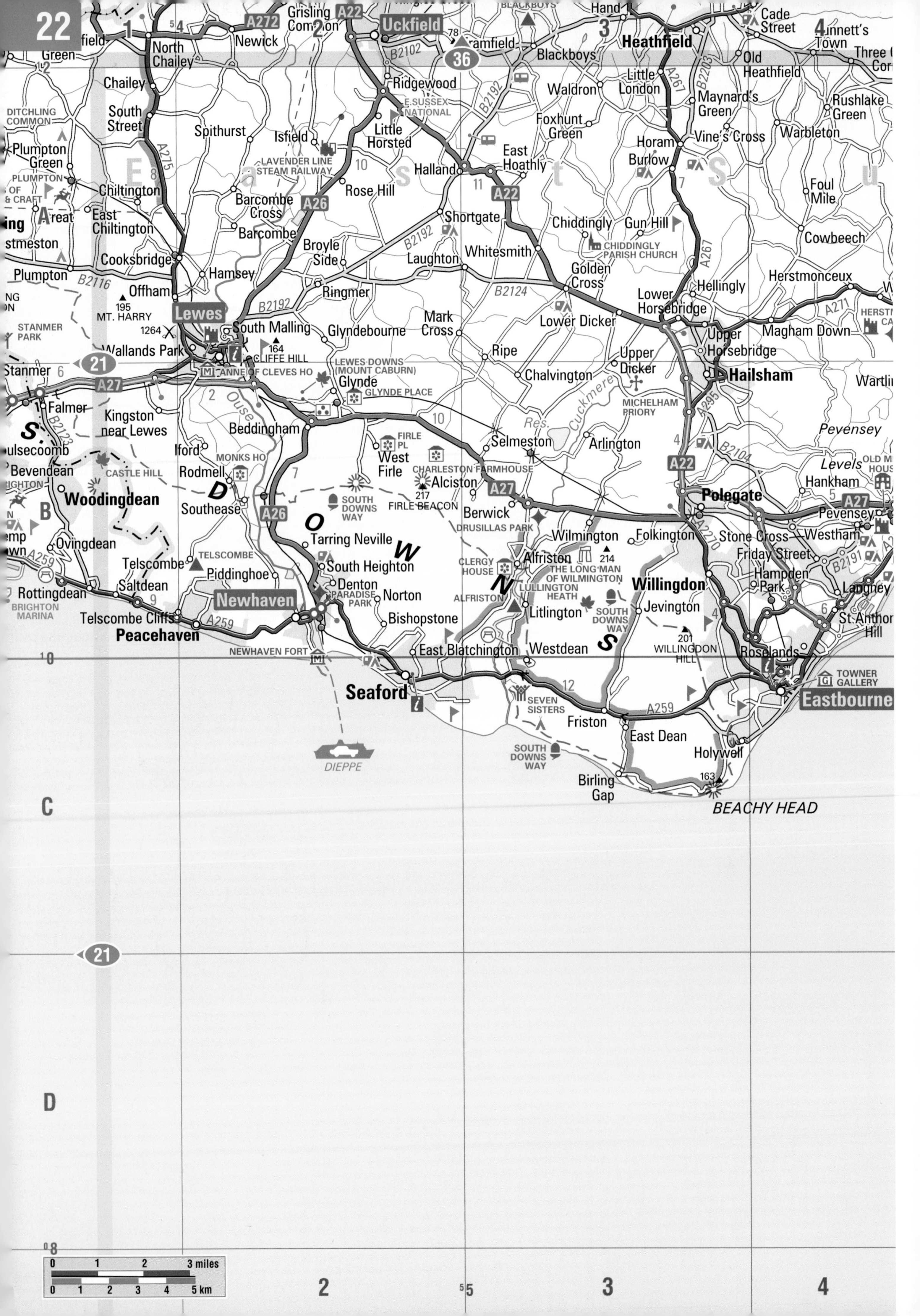
North Chailey
Newick
Grisling Common
Uckfield
Framfield
Blackboys
Heathfield
Cade Street
Punnett's Town
Old Heathfield
Chailey
South Street
Ridgewood
E.SUSSEX NATIONAL
Little London
Waldron
Maynard's Green
Rushlake Green
Foxhunt Green
Warbleton
Spithurst
Isfield
Little Horsted
East Hoathly
Horam
Vine's Cross
Burlow
Plumpton Green
LAVENDER LINE STEAM RAILWAY
Halland
Foul Mile
Chiltington
Rose Hill
Barcombe Cross
East Chiltington
Shortgate
Chiddingly
Gun Hill
Barcombe
Cowbeech
CHIDDINGLY PARISH CHURCH
Broyle Side
Laughton
Whitesmith
Golden Cross
Cooksbridge
Hamsey
Herstmonceux
Plumpton
Offham
Ringmer
Lower Horsebridge
Hellingly
MT. HARRY
Lewes
South Malling
Glyndebourne
Mark Cross
Lower Dicker
STANMER PARK
Wallands Park
CLIFFE HILL
Ripe
Upper Horsebridge
Magham Down
Upper Dicker
Stanmer
LEWES DOWNS (MOUNT CABURN)
Chalvington
Hailsham
ANNE OF CLEVES HO
Glynde
GLYNDE PLACE
MICHELHAM PRIORY
Falmer
Kingston near Lewes
Beddingham
Selmeston
Arlington
Pevensey
FIRLE PL
West Firle
Iford
MONKS HO
Rodmell
Bevendean
CASTLE HILL
CHARLESTON FARMHOUSE
Alciston
Pevensey Levels
Hankham
Woodingdean
Southease
SOUTH DOWNS WAY
FIRLE BEACON
Berwick
Polegate
DRUSILLAS PARK
Tarring Neville
Wilmington
Folkington
Stone Cross
Westham
Ovingdean
Alfriston
THE LONG MAN OF WILMINGTON
Friday Street
Telscombe
TELSCOMBE
South Heighton
CLERGY HOUSE
LULLINGTON HEATH
Willingdon
Hampden Park
Piddinghoe
Saltdean
Denton
PARADISE PARK
Norton
ALFRISTON
Litlington
Jevington
Langney
Rottingdean
BRIGHTON MARINA
Newhaven
Telscombe Cliffs
Peacehaven
Bishopstone
St Anthony's Hill
WILLINGDON HILL
Roselands
NEWHAVEN FORT
East Blatchington
Westdean
TOWNER GALLERY
Seaford
Eastbourne
SEVEN SISTERS
Friston
East Dean
Holywell
DIEPPE
Birling Gap
BEACHY HEAD
A22
A272
A26
A27
A275
A267
A271
A295
A2270
A259
B2102
B2192
B2116
B2124
B2123
B2104
B2191
B2203
Ouse
Cuckmere
Res.
SOUTH DOWNS
EAST SUSSEX
0 1 2 3 miles
0 1 2 3 4 5 km

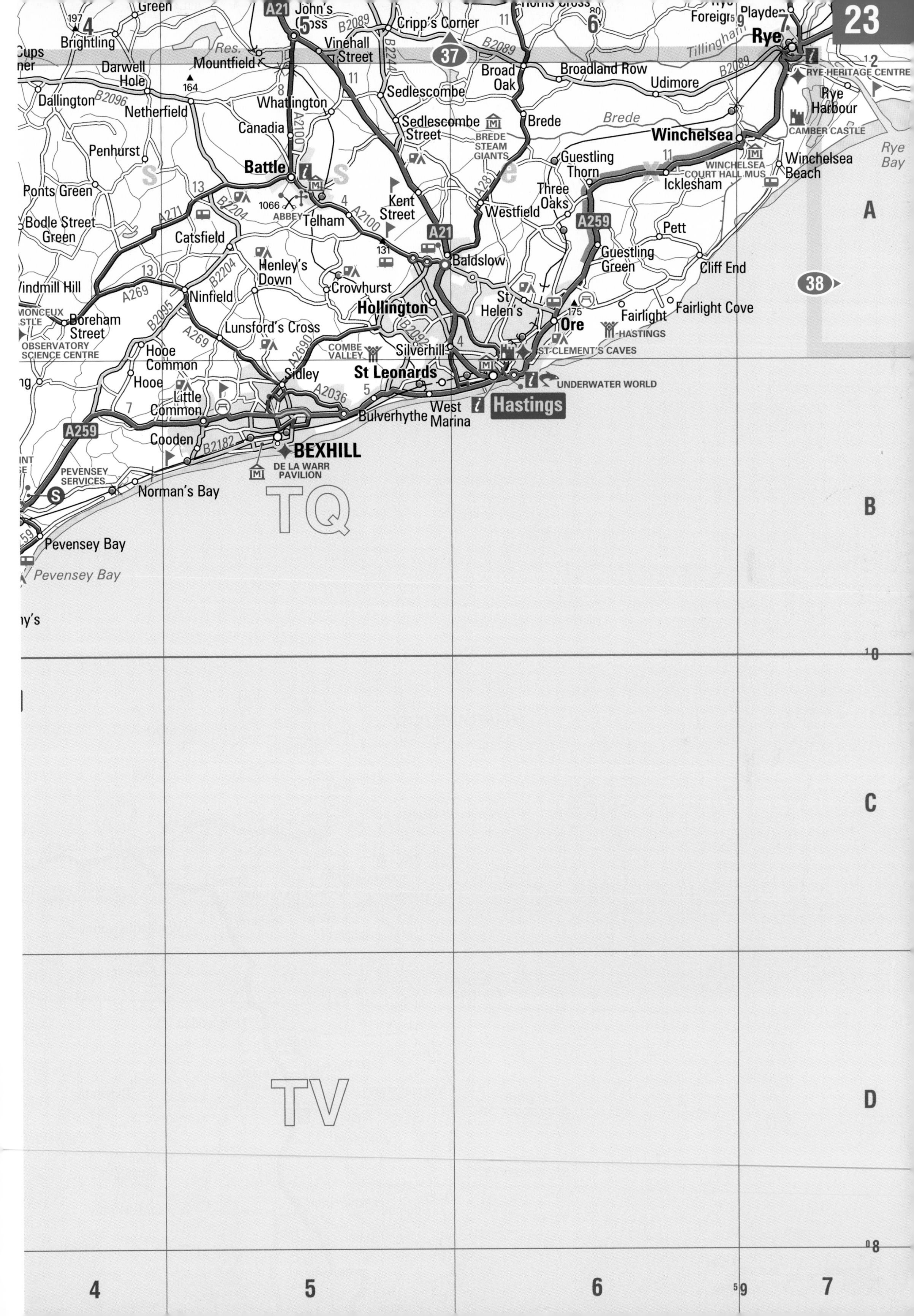

Brightling
Darwell Hole
Dallington
Netherfield
Mountfield
Whatlington
Canadia
Penhurst
Battle
Ponts Green
Bodle Street Green
Catsfield
Windmill Hill
Ninfield
Boreham Street
OBSERVATORY SCIENCE CENTRE
Hooe Common
Hooe
Little Common
Cooden
PEVENSEY SERVICES
Norman's Bay
Pevensey Bay
BEXHILL
DE LA WARR PAVILION
Sidley
Lunsford's Cross
Henley's Down
Telham
ABBEY
Crowhurst
Hollington
COMBE VALLEY
Silverhill
St Leonards
Bulverhythe
West Marina
Hastings
UNDERWATER WORLD
ST CLEMENT'S CAVES
HASTINGS
Ore
St Helen's
Baldslow
Kent Street
Westfield
Three Oaks
Guestling Thorn
Guestling Green
Fairlight
Fairlight Cove
Cliff End
Pett
Icklesham
WINCHELSEA COURT HALL MUS
Winchelsea
Winchelsea Beach
Rye Bay
CAMBER CASTLE
Rye Harbour
RYE HERITAGE CENTRE
Rye
Playden
Udimore
Broadland Row
Broad Oak
Brede
BREDE STEAM GIANTS
Sedlescombe
Sedlescombe Street
Vinehall Street
Cripp's Corner
John's Cross
Tillingham
TQ
TV
A
B
C
D
4
5
6
7

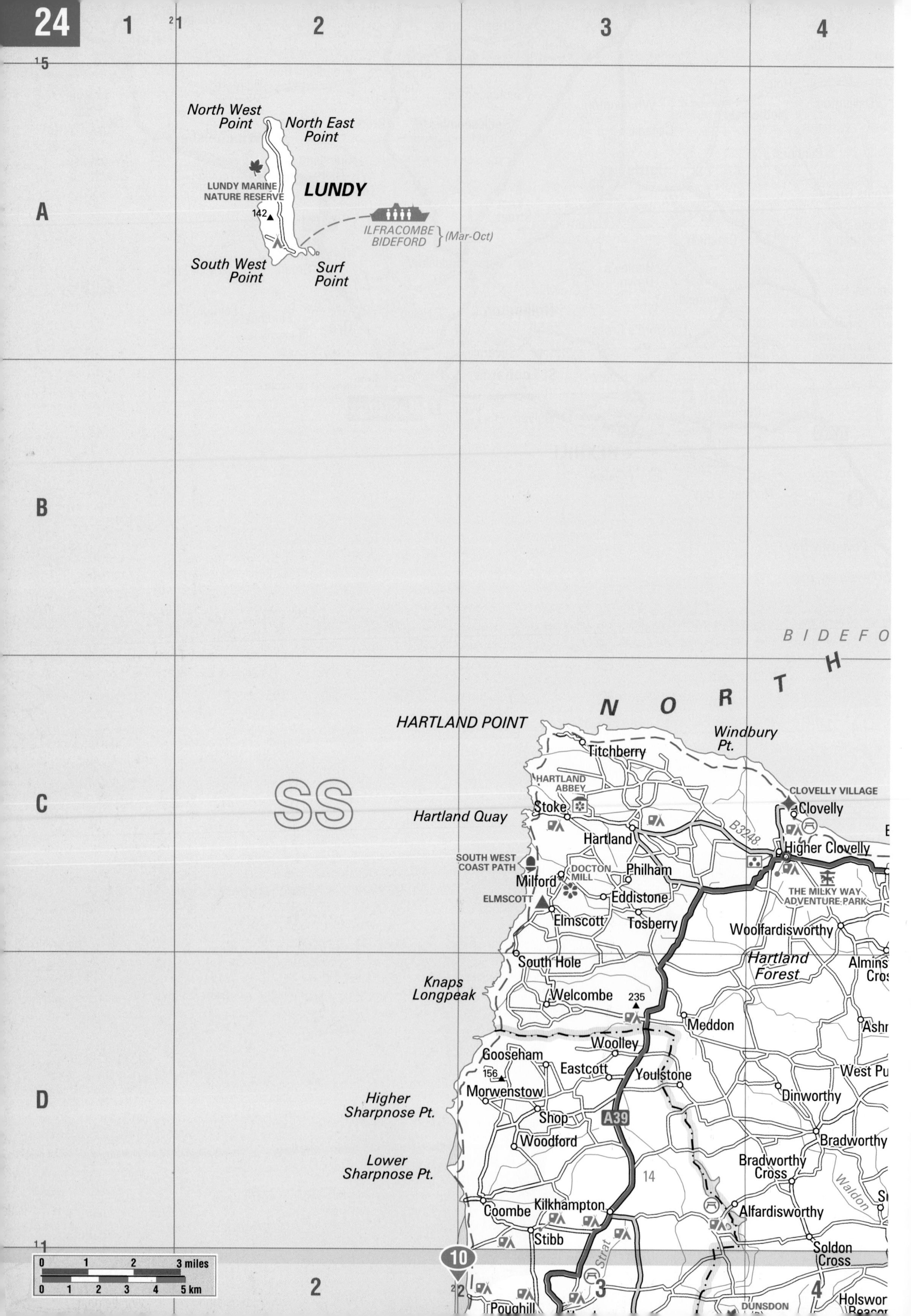

A

North West Point   North East Point

LUNDY MARINE NATURE RESERVE

142 ▲

LUNDY

ILFRACOMBE BIDEFORD } (Mar-Oct)

South West Point   Surf Point

B

B I D E F O

N   O   R   T   H

HARTLAND POINT

Titchberry

Windbury Pt.

CLOVELLY VILLAGE

C

SS

Hartland Quay

HARTLAND ABBEY

Stoke ✚

Clovelly

B3248

Higher Clovelly

Hartland

SOUTH WEST COAST PATH

DOCTON MILL

Philham

THE MILKY WAY ADVENTURE PARK

Milford

ELMSCOTT ▲

Eddistone

Elmscott

Tosberry

Woolfardisworthy

Hartland Forest

Almins Cros

South Hole

Knaps Longpeak

Welcombe   235 ▲

Meddon

Ashr

Woolley

Gooseham

156 ▲

Eastcott

Youlstone

West Pu

D

Higher Sharpnose Pt.

Morwenstow

Shop

A39

Dinworthy

Woodford

Bradworthy

Lower Sharpnose Pt.

14

Bradworthy Cross

Waldon

Coombe   Kilkhampton

Alfardisworthy

Stibb

Soldon Cross

10

Strat

S

Poughill

DUNSDON

Holswor Beaco

0   1   2   3 miles
0   1   2   3   4   5 km
2   2 2   3   4

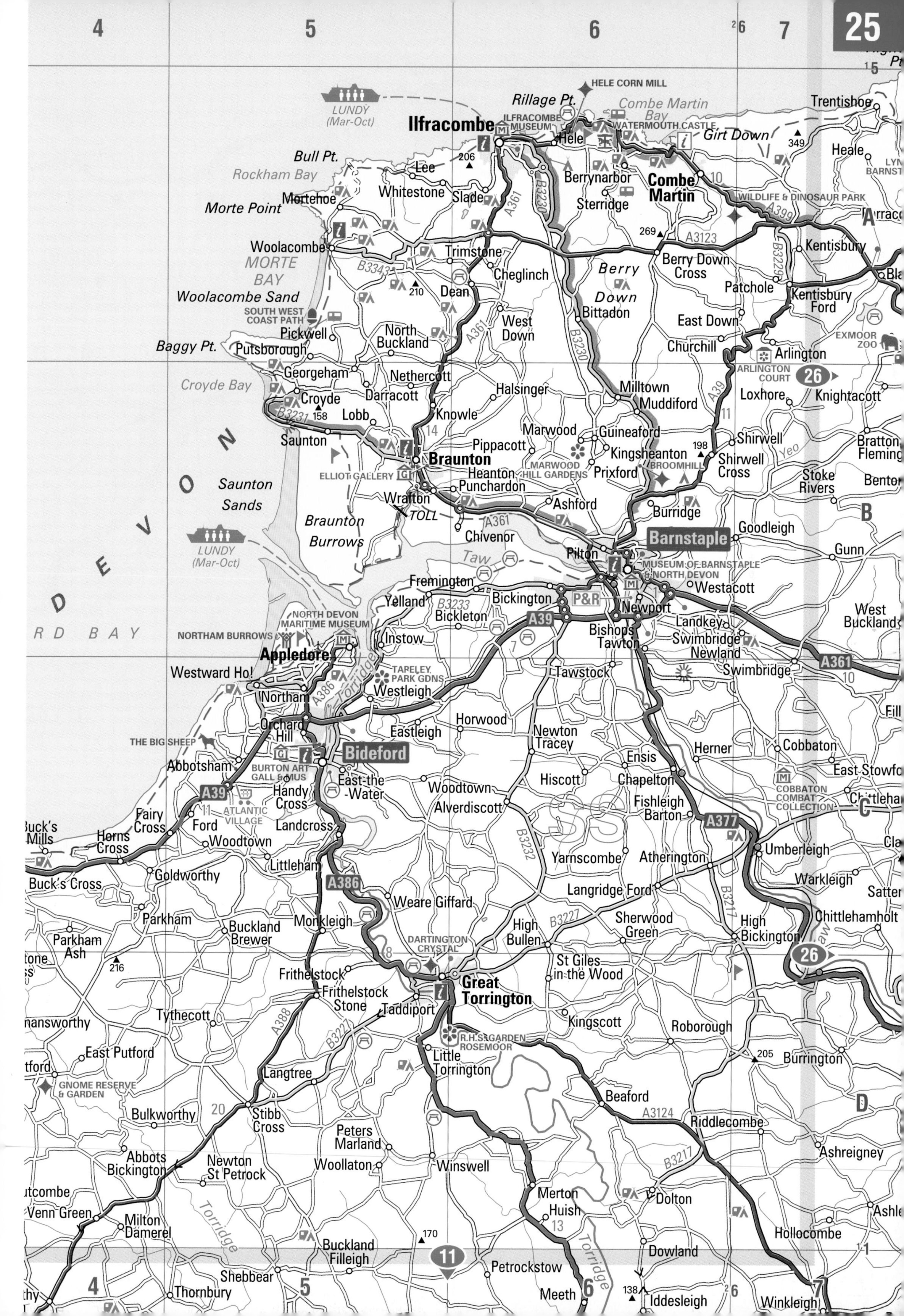
4
5
6
7
LUNDY (Mar-Oct)
HELE CORN MILL
Rillage Pt.
Combe Martin Bay
Ilfracombe
ILFRACOMBE MUSEUM
WATERMOUTH CASTLE
Hele
Girt Down
Trentishoe
349
Heale
Bull Pt.
206
Lee
Rockham Bay
Berrynarbor
Combe Martin
10
Whitestone
Slade
Sterridge
WILDLIFE & DINOSAUR PARK
Mortehoe
Morte Point
A361
B3230
A399
269
A3123
Woolacombe
MORTE BAY
Trimstone
Berry Down Cross
B3229
Kentisbury
B3343
Cheglinch
Berry Down
Patchole
Kentisbury Ford
Woolacombe Sand
210
Dean
SOUTH WEST COAST PATH
Bittadon
West Down
East Down
Pickwell
North Buckland
EXMOOR ZOO
Baggy Pt.
Putsborough
Churchill
Arlington
Georgeham
ARLINGTON COURT
26
Croyde Bay
Nethercott
Halsinger
Milltown
Loxhore
Knightacott
Croyde
Darracott
Muddiford
B3231
158
Lobb
Knowle
A39
11
14
Saunton
Marwood
Guineaford
Shirwell
Bratton Fleming
Pippacott
198
Kingsheanton
DEVON
Braunton
MARWOOD HILL GARDENS
BROOMHILL
Shirwell Cross
Yeo
Saunton Sands
ELLIOT GALLERY
Heanton Punchardon
Prixford
Stoke Rivers
Bentor
Wrafton
Ashford
Braunton Burrows
TOLL
Burridge
B
Chivenor
Goodleigh
LUNDY (Mar-Oct)
Barnstaple
Taw
Pilton
Gunn
MUSEUM OF BARNSTAPLE & NORTH DEVON
Fremington
Westacott
Yelland
B3233
Bickington
P&R
Newport
West Buckland
BIDEFORD BAY
NORTH DEVON MARITIME MUSEUM
Bickleton
A39
Bishops Tawton
Landkey
NORTHAM BURROWS
Instow
7
Swimbridge Newland
Appledore
Westward Ho!
TAPELEY PARK GDNS
Tawstock
Swimbridge
A361
10
Torridge
Northam
A386
Westleigh
Orchard Hill
Horwood
Eastleigh
Newton Tracey
THE BIG SHEEP
Bideford
Herner
Cobbaton
Ensis
East Stowford
Abbotsham
BURTON ART GALL & MUS
East-the-Water
Hiscott
Chapelton
COBBATON COMBAT COLLECTION
Chittlehampton
A39
Handy Cross
Woodtown
Alverdiscott
Fishleigh Barton
C
ATLANTIC VILLAGE
11
Fairy Cross
Ford
Landcross
A377
Buck's Mills
Horns Cross
Woodtown
B3232
Umberleigh
SS
Yarnscombe
Atherington
Goldworthy
Littleham
Buck's Cross
A386
Warkleigh
Satter
Langridge Ford
Weare Giffard
B3217
Parkham
Sherwood Green
Chittlehamholt
Monkleigh
High Bullen
High Bickington
B3227
Buckland Brewer
Parkham Ash
DARTINGTON CRYSTAL
26
216
8
St Giles in the Wood
Frithelstock
Great Torrington
Frithelstock Stone
Tythecott
Taddiport
A388
Kingscott
Roborough
B3227
R.H.S. GARDEN ROSEMOOR
East Putford
Little Torrington
205
Burrington
GNOME RESERVE & GARDEN
Langtree
Beaford
D
Bulkworthy
20
Stibb Cross
A3124
Riddlecombe
Peters Marland
Ashreigney
Abbots Bickington
Newton St Petrock
B3217
Woollaton
Winswell
Merton
Dolton
Venn Green
Milton Damerel
Huish
13
Torridge
170
Hollacombe
Buckland Filleigh
Dowland
11
Petrockstow
Shebbear
4
5
6
Torridge
Thornbury
Meeth
138
Iddesleigh
6
Winkleigh
7

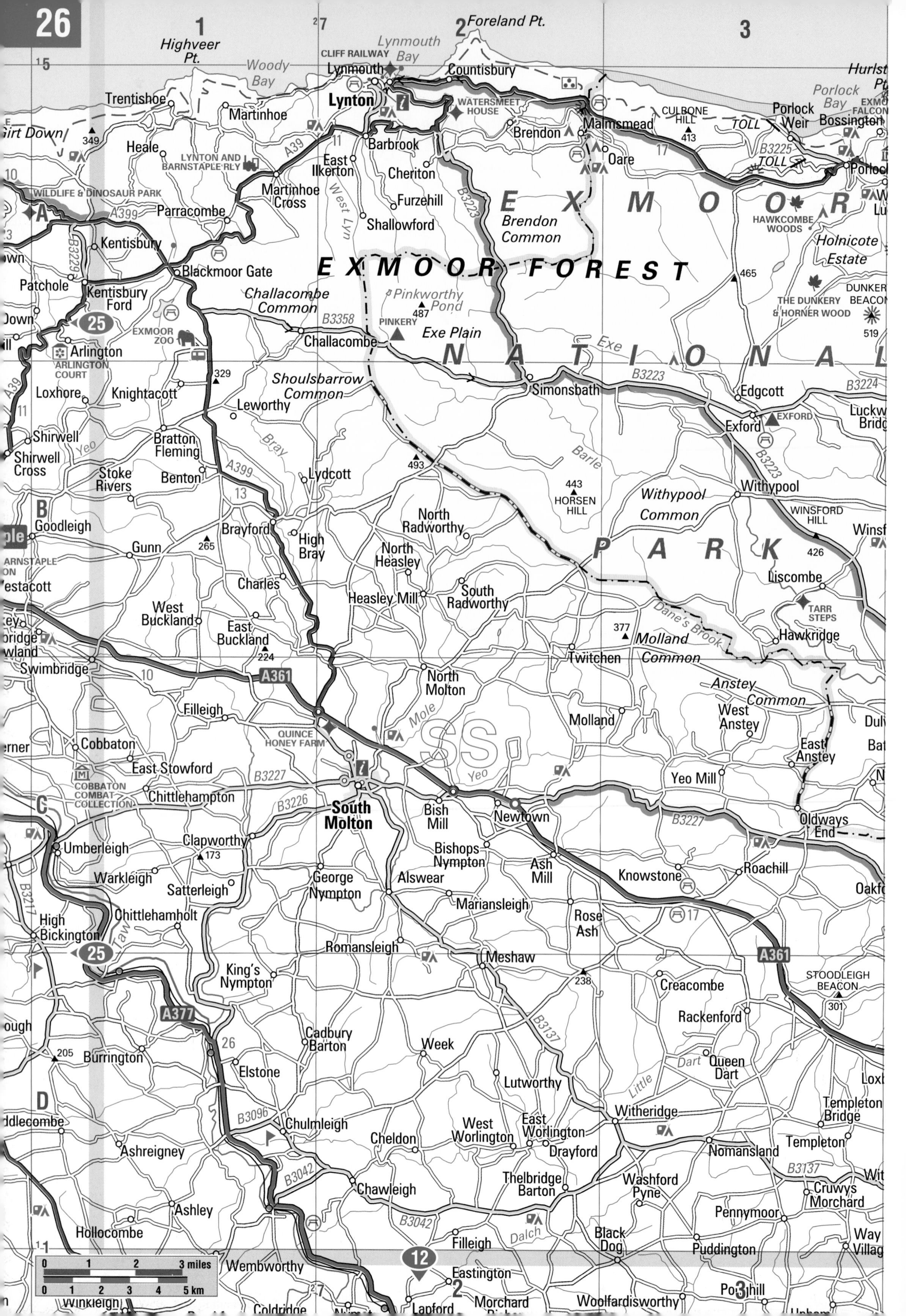

Foreland Pt.
Highveer Pt.
Lynmouth Bay
Woody Bay
CLIFF RAILWAY
Lynmouth
Countisbury
Hurlstone Pt.
Porlock Bay
Trentishoe
Lynton
WATERSMEET HOUSE
CULBONE HILL
Porlock Weir
Bossington
Martinhoe
Brendon
Malmsmead
TOLL
413
Girt Down
349
Barbrook
Oare
B3225
Heale
LYNTON AND BARNSTAPLE RLY
A39
East Ilkerton
Cheriton
Porlock
WILDLIFE & DINOSAUR PARK
Martinhoe Cross
B3223
E X M O O R
A399
Parracombe
Furzehill
Brendon Common
HAWKCOMBE WOODS
B3229
Kentisbury
West Lyn
Shallowford
Holnicote Estate
Patchole
Blackmoor Gate
E X M O O R F O R E S T
465
Kentisbury Ford
Challacombe Common
Pinkworthy Pond
487
THE DUNKERY & HORNER WOOD
DUNKERY BEACON
25
EXMOOR ZOO
B3358
PINKERY
Exe Plain
519
Arlington
ARLINGTON COURT
Challacombe
Exe
N A T I O N A L
329
Shoulsbarrow Common
Simonsbath
B3223
B3224
Loxhore
Knightacott
Edgcott
Leworthy
Exford
EXFORD
Shirwell
Bratton Fleming
Bray
Barle
Shirwell Cross
Yeo
A399
493
Stoke Rivers
Benton
Lydcott
443
HORSEN HILL
Withypool
Withypool Common
B
13
North Radworthy
WINSFORD HILL
Goodleigh
Brayford
High Bray
265
Gunn
North Heasley
P A R K
426
Liscombe
Charles
South Radworthy
Heasley Mill
TARR STEPS
West Buckland
Dane's Brook
East Buckland
377
Molland Common
Hawkridge
224
Twitchen
Swimbridge
10
A361
North Molton
Anstey Common
Filleigh
West Anstey
Molland
QUINCE HONEY FARM
Mole
SS
Cobbaton
East Anstey
East Stowford
B3227
Yeo
Yeo Mill
COBBATON COMBAT COLLECTION
Chittlehampton
B3226
South Molton
Bish Mill
Newtown
C
B3227
Oldways End
Umberleigh
Clapworthy
Bishops Nympton
173
Ash Mill
Warkleigh
George Nympton
Alswear
Knowstone
Roachill
Satterleigh
Mariansleigh
B3217
Chittlehamholt
Rose Ash
17
High Bickington
Taw
25
Romansleigh
Meshaw
A361
King's Nympton
238
Creacombe
STOODLEIGH BEACON
A377
301
Rackenford
Cadbury Barton
B3137
26
Week
205
Burrington
Dart
Queen Dart
Elstone
Lutworthy
Little
D
Templeton Bridge
Witheridge
B3096
West Worlington
East Worlington
Chulmleigh
Cheldon
Drayford
Nomansland
Templeton
Ashreigney
B3042
B3137
Thelbridge Barton
Washford Pyne
Cruwys Morchard
Chawleigh
Ashley
Pennymoor
B3042
Hollocombe
Dalch
Black Dog
Filleigh
Puddington
Way Village
12
Wembworthy
Eastington
0 1 2 3 miles
0 1 2 3 4 5 km
Winkleigh
Coldridge
Lapford
Morchard
Woolfardisworthy
Poughill

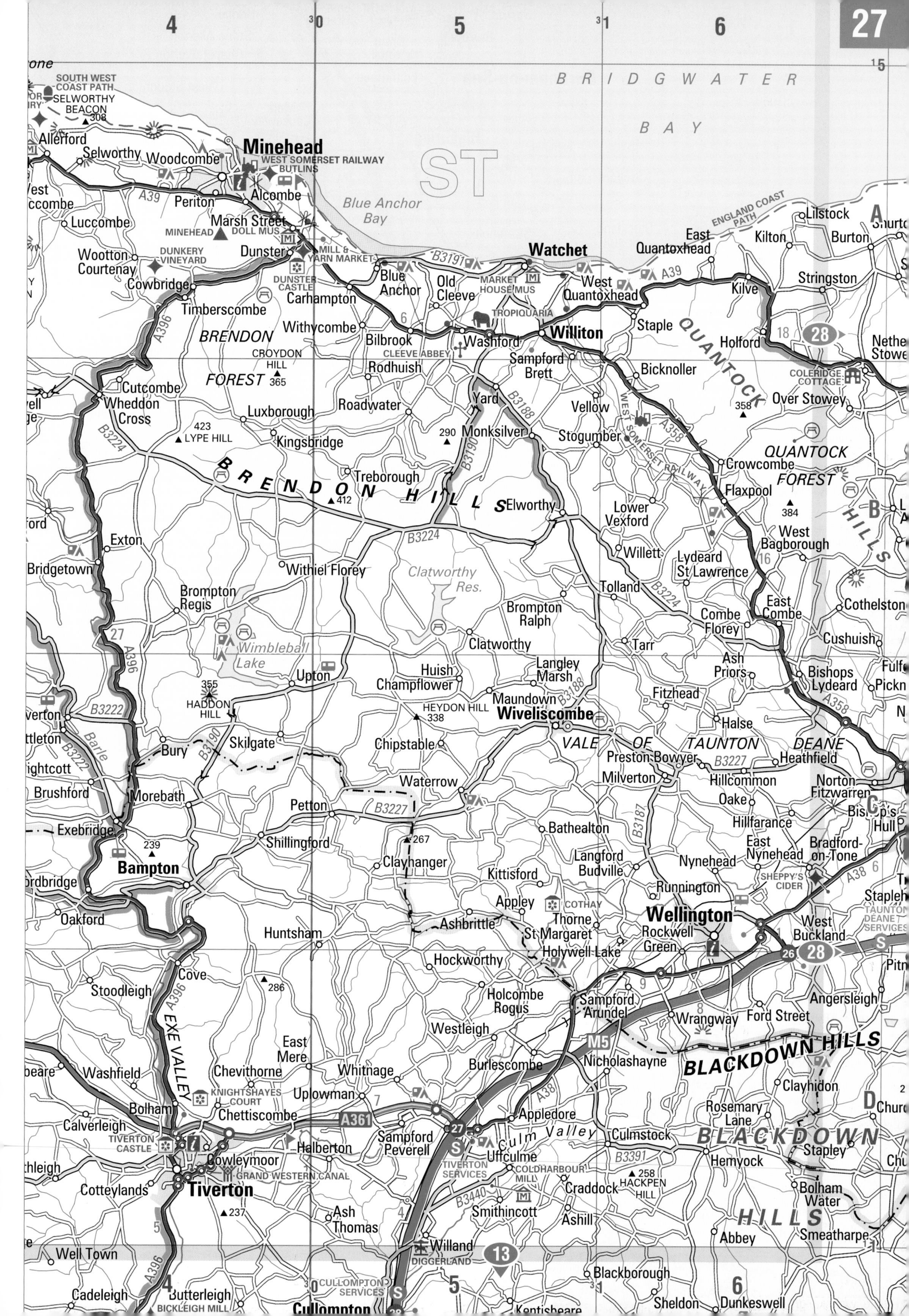
BRIDGWATER BAY
ST
Blue Anchor Bay
Minehead
WEST SOMERSET RAILWAY
BUTLINS
SOUTH WEST COAST PATH
SELWORTHY BEACON
308
Allerford
Selworthy
Woodcombe
Periton
Alcombe
Luccombe
Marsh Street
MINEHEAD
DOLL MUS
Dunster
MILL & YARN MARKET
Wootton Courtenay
DUNKERY VINEYARD
DUNSTER CASTLE
Cowbridge
Carhampton
Timberscombe
BRENDON
Withycombe
Blue Anchor
Old Cleeve
Watchet
MARKET HOUSE MUS
West Quantoxhead
East Quantoxhead
ENGLAND COAST PATH
Lilstock
Kilton
Burton
Kilve
Stringston
Staple
QUANTOCK
Holford
Williton
TROPIQUARIA
Washford
Bilbrook
CLEEVE ABBEY
CROYDON HILL
365
FOREST
Rodhuish
Sampford Brett
Bicknoller
COLERIDGE COTTAGE
Over Stowey
Cutcombe
Wheddon Cross
Luxborough
Roadwater
Yard
Vellow
Monksilver
Stogumber
WEST SOMERSET RAILWAY
423
LYPE HILL
Kingsbridge
290
Treborough
BRENDON HILLS
412
Elworthy
Crowcombe
QUANTOCK FOREST
Flaxpool
384
Lower Vexford
West Bagborough
Exton
B3224
Willett
Lydeard St Lawrence
Bridgetown
Withiel Florey
Clatworthy Res.
Tolland
Brompton Regis
Brompton Ralph
Combe Florey
East Combe
Cothelston
Cushuish
Clatworthy
Tarr
Wimbleball Lake
Ash Priors
Bishops Lydeard
Upton
Huish Champflower
Langley Marsh
355
HADDON HILL
Maundown
HEYDON HILL
338
Wiveliscombe
Fitzhead
Halse
B3222
Barle
Bury
Skilgate
Chipstable
VALE OF TAUNTON DEANE
Preston Bowyer
Heathfield
Milverton
Hillcommon
Norton Fitzwarren
Waterrow
Oake
Brushford
Morebath
Petton
B3227
Exebridge
Shillingford
267
Bathealton
Hillfarance
Bradford-on-Tone
East Nynehead
239
Bampton
Clayhanger
Langford Budville
Nynehead
SHEPPY'S CIDER
Kittisford
Runnington
Oakford
Appley
COTHAY
Thorne St Margaret
Wellington
West Buckland
TAUNTON DEANE SERVICES
Ashbrittle
Huntsham
Rockwell Green
Holywell Lake
Hockworthy
Cove
Stoodleigh
286
Holcombe Rogus
Sampford Arundel
Angersleigh
Wrangway
Ford Street
EXE VALLEY
Westleigh
East Mere
BLACKDOWN HILLS
Nicholashayne
Burlescombe
Washfield
Chevithorne
Whitnage
Clayhidon
KNIGHTSHAYES COURT
Uplowman
Bolham
Chettiscombe
Appledore
Rosemary Lane
Calverleigh
A361
Culm Valley
Culmstock
TIVERTON CASTLE
Halberton
Sampford Peverell
BLACKDOWN
Stapley
Cowleymoor
Uffculme
Hemyock
GRAND WESTERN CANAL
TIVERTON SERVICES
COLDHARBOUR MILL
258
HACKPEN HILL
Cotteylands
Tiverton
Craddock
Bolham Water
237
Ash Thomas
Smithincott
Ashill
HILLS
Abbey
Smeatharpe
Well Town
Willand
DIGGERLAND
Blackborough
CULLOMPTON SERVICES
Cadeleigh
Butterleigh
BICKLEIGH MILL
Cullompton
Sheldon
Dunkeswell
Kentisbeare
Nether Stowey
Fulford
Pickney
Bishop's Hull
Staplehay
Churchinford
A39
A396
A358
A38
M5
B3191
B3188
B3190
B3187
B3391
B3440
28
13

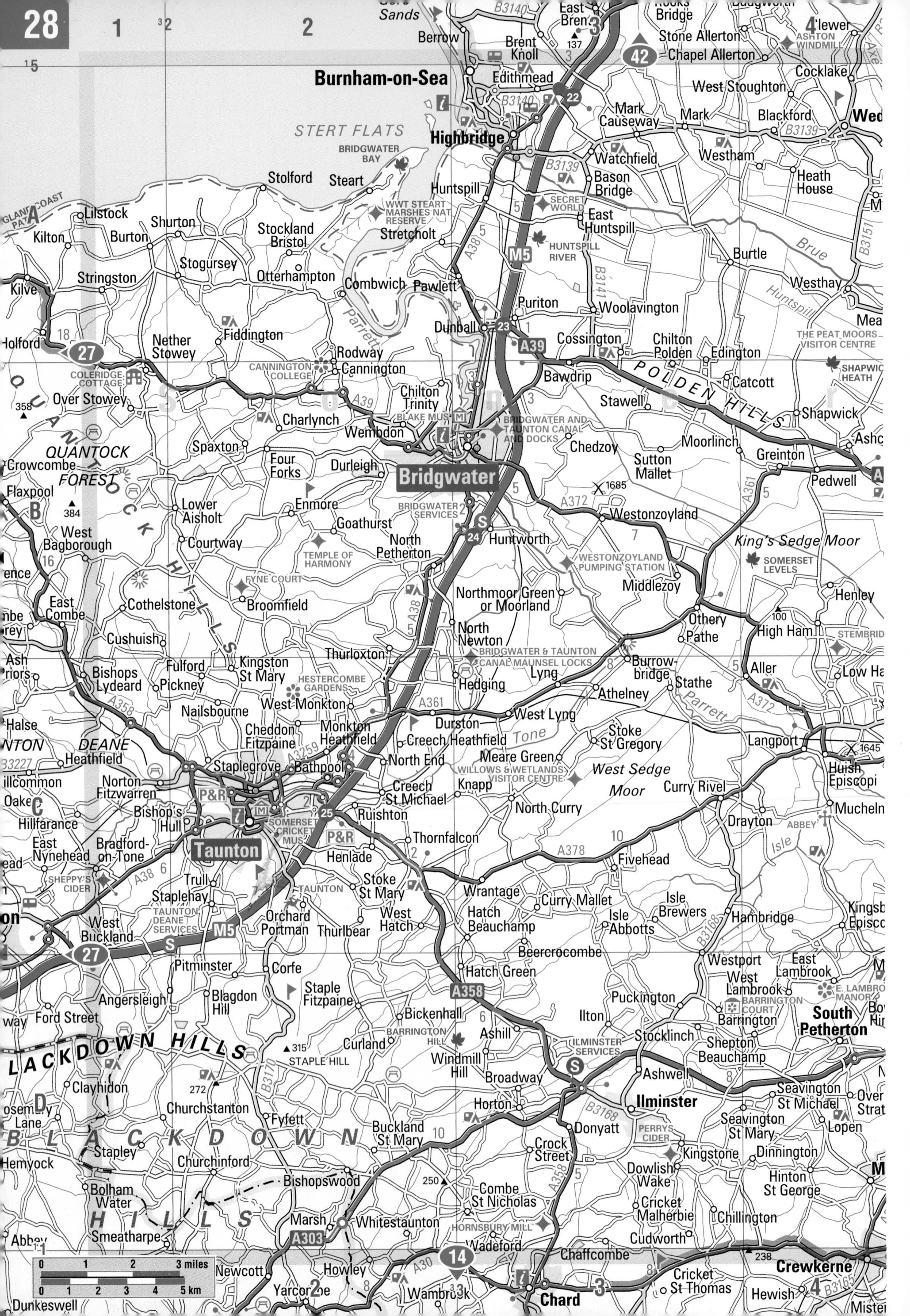

Burnham-on-Sea
Berrow
Brent Knoll
East Brent
Edithmead
Highbridge
STERT FLATS
BRIDGWATER BAY
Stolford
Steart
Huntspill
Lilstock
Kilton
Burton
Shurton
Stockland Bristol
Stretcholt
WWT STEART MARSHES NAT RESERVE
Stogursey
Otterhampton
Combwich
Pawlett
Stringston
Kilve
Holford
Nether Stowey
Fiddington
Rodway
Cannington
CANNINGTON COLLEGE
COLERIDGE COTTAGE
Over Stowey
Chilton Trinity
Charlynch
Wembdon
BLAKE MUS
Spaxton
Four Forks
Durleigh
Bridgwater
QUANTOCK FOREST
QUANTOCK HILLS
Crowcombe
Flaxpool
Lower Aisholt
Enmore
Goathurst
North Petherton
BRIDGWATER SERVICES
West Bagborough
Courtway
TEMPLE OF HARMONY
FYNE COURT
Broomfield
Cothelstone
East Combe
Cushuish
Bishops Lydeard
Fulford
Kingston St Mary
Pickney
HESTERCOMBE GARDENS
Thurloxton
Nailsbourne
West Monkton
Cheddon Fitzpaine
Monkton Heathfield
DEANE
Heathfield
Staplegrove
Bathpool
Norton Fitzwarren
Bishop's Hull
Taunton
SOMERSET CRICKET MUS
Hillfarance
East Nynehead
Bradford-on-Tone
SHEPPY'S CIDER
Trull
Staplehay
TAUNTON DEANE SERVICES
West Buckland
Orchard Portman
Thurlbear
Henlade
Ruishton
Thornfalcon
Stoke St Mary
West Hatch
Pitminster
Corfe
Angersleigh
Blagdon Hill
Staple Fitzpaine
Ford Street
BLACKDOWN HILLS
STAPLE HILL
Clayhidon
Churchstanton
Fyfett
Stapley
Hemyock
Churchinford
Bishopswood
Bolham Water
Smeatharpe
Marsh
Whitestaunton
Abbey
Newcott
Howley
Yarcombe
Wambrook
Dunkeswell
Chard
Rooks Bridge
Stone Allerton
Chapel Allerton
Cocklake
West Stoughton
Mark Causeway
Mark
Blackford
ASHTON WINDMILL
Watchfield
Westham
Bason Bridge
Heath House
SECRET WORLD
East Huntspill
HUNTSPILL RIVER
Burtle
Westhay
Puriton
Woolavington
Dunball
Cossington
Chilton Polden
Edington
Catcott
THE PEAT MOORS VISITOR CENTRE
SHAPWICK HEATH
POLDEN HILLS
Bawdrip
Stawell
Shapwick
BRIDGWATER AND TAUNTON CANAL AND DOCKS
Chedzoy
Sutton Mallet
Moorlinch
Greinton
Ashcott
Pedwell
Westonzoyland
Huntworth
King's Sedge Moor
SOMERSET LEVELS
WESTONZOYLAND PUMPING STATION
Middlezoy
Northmoor Green or Moorland
Othery
Pathe
Henley
High Ham
North Newton
BRIDGWATER & TAUNTON CANAL MAUNSEL LOCKS
Burrowbridge
Lyng
Hedging
Stathe
Aller
Athelney
Durston
West Lyng
Creech Heathfield
Stoke St Gregory
Langport
Low Ham
North End
Meare Green
WILLOWS & WETLANDS VISITOR CENTRE
West Sedge Moor
Huish Episcopi
Creech St Michael
Knapp
Curry Rivel
North Curry
Drayton
ABBEY
Muchelney
Fivehead
Wrantage
Curry Mallet
Hatch Beauchamp
Isle Abbotts
Isle Brewers
Hambridge
Beercrocombe
Hatch Green
Westport
West Lambrook
East Lambrook
E. LAMBROOK MANOR
BARRINGTON COURT
Barrington
Puckington
Ilton
Bickenhall
Ashill
BARRINGTON HILL
Curland
Windmill Hill
ILMINSTER SERVICES
Stocklinch
Shepton Beauchamp
South Petherton
Broadway
Ashwell
Ilminster
Horton
Buckland St Mary
Donyatt
PERRYS CIDER
Seavington St Michael
Seavington St Mary
Lopen
Crock Street
Kingstone
Dinnington
Dowlish Wake
Hinton St George
Combe St Nicholas
Cricket Malherbie
Chillington
HORNSBURY MILL
Wadeford
Cudworth
Chaffcombe
Cricket St Thomas
Crewkerne
Hewish
0 1 2 3 miles
0 1 2 3 4 5 km

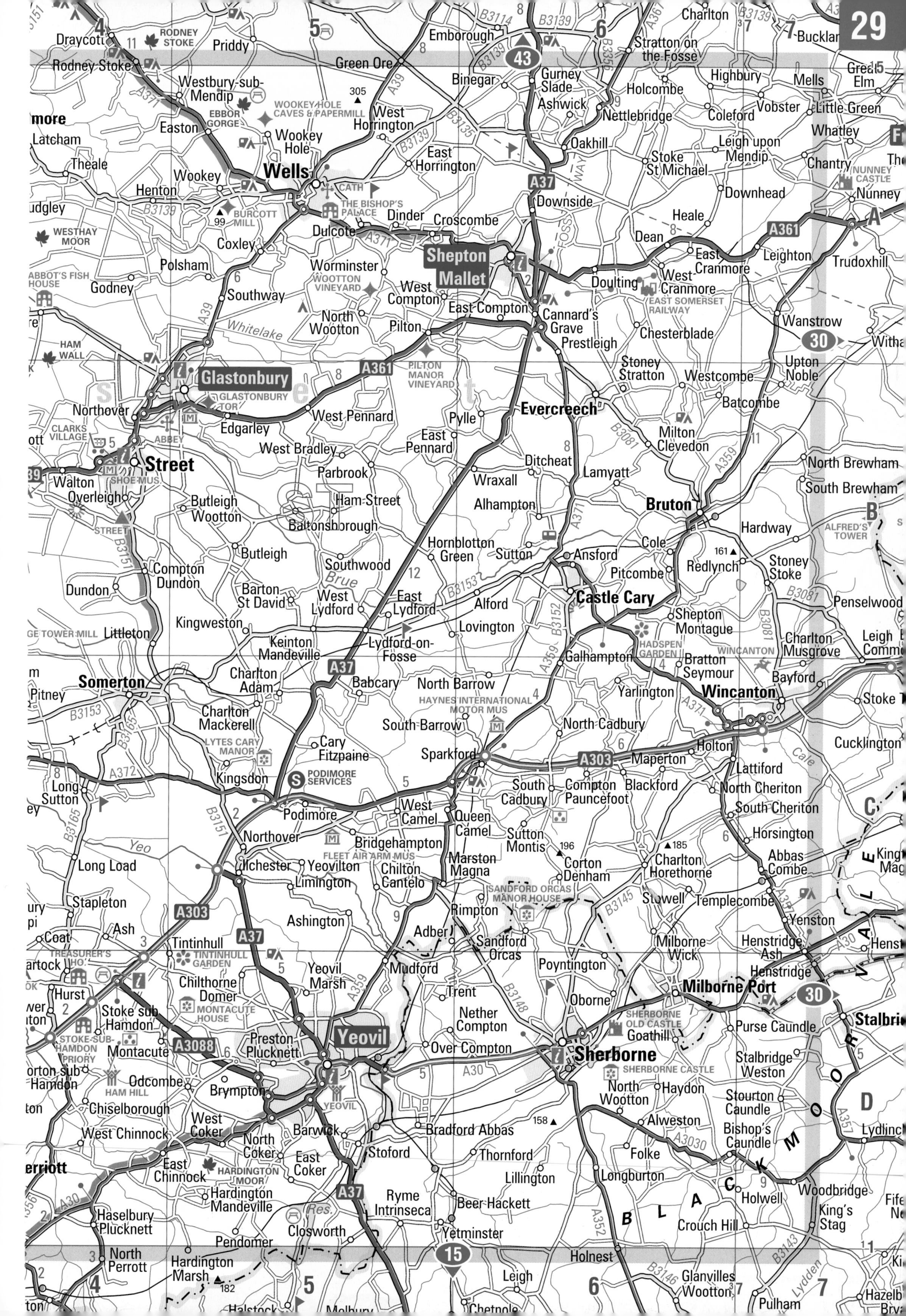
Draycott
Rodney Stoke
RODNEY STOKE
Priddy
Emborough
Charlton
Stratton on the Fosse
Buckland
43
Green Ore
Binegar
Gurney Slade
Highbury
Mells
Great Elm
Westbury-sub-Mendip
EBBOR GORGE
WOOKEY HOLE CAVES & PAPERMILL
West Horrington
Holcombe
Ashwick
Nettlebridge
Coleford
Vobster
Little Green
Easton
Wookey Hole
Whatley
Latcham
Theale
Wells
East Horrington
Oakhill
Stoke St Michael
Leigh upon Mendip
Chantry
NUNNEY CASTLE
Nunney
Henton
Wookey
CATH
THE BISHOP'S PALACE
Downside
Downhead
Mudgley
BURCOTT MILL
Dinder
Croscombe
Heale
WESTHAY MOOR
Dulcote
Dean
A361
Coxley
Shepton Mallet
East Cranmore
Leighton
Trudoxhill
ABBOT'S FISH HOUSE
Polsham
Worminster
WOOTTON VINEYARD
West Cranmore
Doulting
Godney
Southway
West Compton
EAST SOMERSET RAILWAY
East Compton
Cannard's Grave
North Wootton
Pilton
Whitelake
Chesterblade
Wanstrow
Prestleigh
30
Witham
HAM WALL
Glastonbury
GLASTONBURY TOR
PILTON MANOR VINEYARD
Stoney Stratton
Westcombe
Upton Noble
Batcombe
Northover
West Pennard
Evercreech
CLARKS VILLAGE
ABBEY
Edgarley
Pylle
Milton Clevedon
East Pennard
West Bradley
Walton
Street
SHOE MUS
Ditcheat
Lamyatt
North Brewham
South Brewham
Parbrook
Wraxall
Overleigh
Butleigh Wootton
Ham Street
Alhampton
Bruton
STREET
Baltonsborough
Hardway
ALFRED'S TOWER
Hornblotton Green
Sutton
Cole
Butleigh
Ansford
Redlynch
Stoney Stoke
Compton Dundon
Southwood
Brue
Pitcombe
Dundon
Barton St David
West Lydford
East Lydford
Alford
Castle Cary
Penselwood
Kingweston
Shepton Montague
TOWER MILL
Littleton
Lovington
Charlton Musgrove
Leigh Common
Keinton Mandeville
Lydford-on-Fosse
HADSPEN GARDEN
Galhampton
Bratton Seymour
WINCANTON
Somerton
Charlton Adam
A37
Babcary
North Barrow
Bayford
Pitney
Yarlington
Wincanton
HAYNES INTERNATIONAL MOTOR MUS
Stoke Trister
Charlton Mackerell
South Barrow
North Cadbury
LYTES CARY MANOR
Cary Fitzpaine
Sparkford
Holton
Cucklington
Maperton
Kingsdon
PODIMORE SERVICES
A303
Cale
Lattiford
Long Sutton
South Cadbury
Compton Pauncefoot
Blackford
North Cheriton
West Camel
Podimore
Queen Camel
South Cheriton
Northover
Sutton Montis
Horsington
Bridgehampton
Yeo
FLEET AIR ARM MUS
Marston Magna
Corton Denham
Charlton Horethorne
Abbas Combe
Long Load
Ilchester
Yeovilton
Chilton Cantelo
Limington
SANDFORD ORCAS MANOR HOUSE
Stowell
Templecombe
Stapleton
Ashington
Rimpton
Yenston
A303
Ash
Tintinhull
Adber
Sandford Orcas
Milborne Wick
Henstridge Ash
Henstridge
TREASURER'S HO.
TINTINHULL GARDEN
Yeovil Marsh
Mudford
Poyntington
Milborne Port
Chilthorne Domer
Trent
Hurst
Stoke sub Hamdon
MONTACUTE HOUSE
Nether Compton
Oborne
SHERBORNE OLD CASTLE
Purse Caundle
Stalbridge
STOKE-SUB-HAMDON PRIORY
A3088
Preston Plucknett
Yeovil
Goathill
Montacute
Over Compton
Sherborne
Stalbridge Weston
Norton-sub-Hamdon
Odcombe
HAM HILL
Brympton
A30
SHERBORNE CASTLE
North Wootton
Haydon
Stourton Caundle
Chiselborough
YEOVIL
West Coker
West Chinnock
Barwick
Bradford Abbas
Alweston
Bishop's Caundle
Lydlinch
North Coker
A3030
Stoford
Folke
East Coker
Thornford
Merriott
East Chinnock
HARDINGTON MOOR
Lillington
Longburton
Woodbridge
Hardington Mandeville
Ryme Intrinseca
Beer Hackett
Holwell
Haselbury Plucknett
Res.
King's Stag
Closworth
Crouch Hill
BLACKMORE VALE
Yetminster
Pendomer
North Perrott
15
Holnest
Hardington Marsh
Leigh
Glanvilles Wootton
Lydden
Pulham
Hazelbury Bryan
Halstock
Melbury
Chetnole

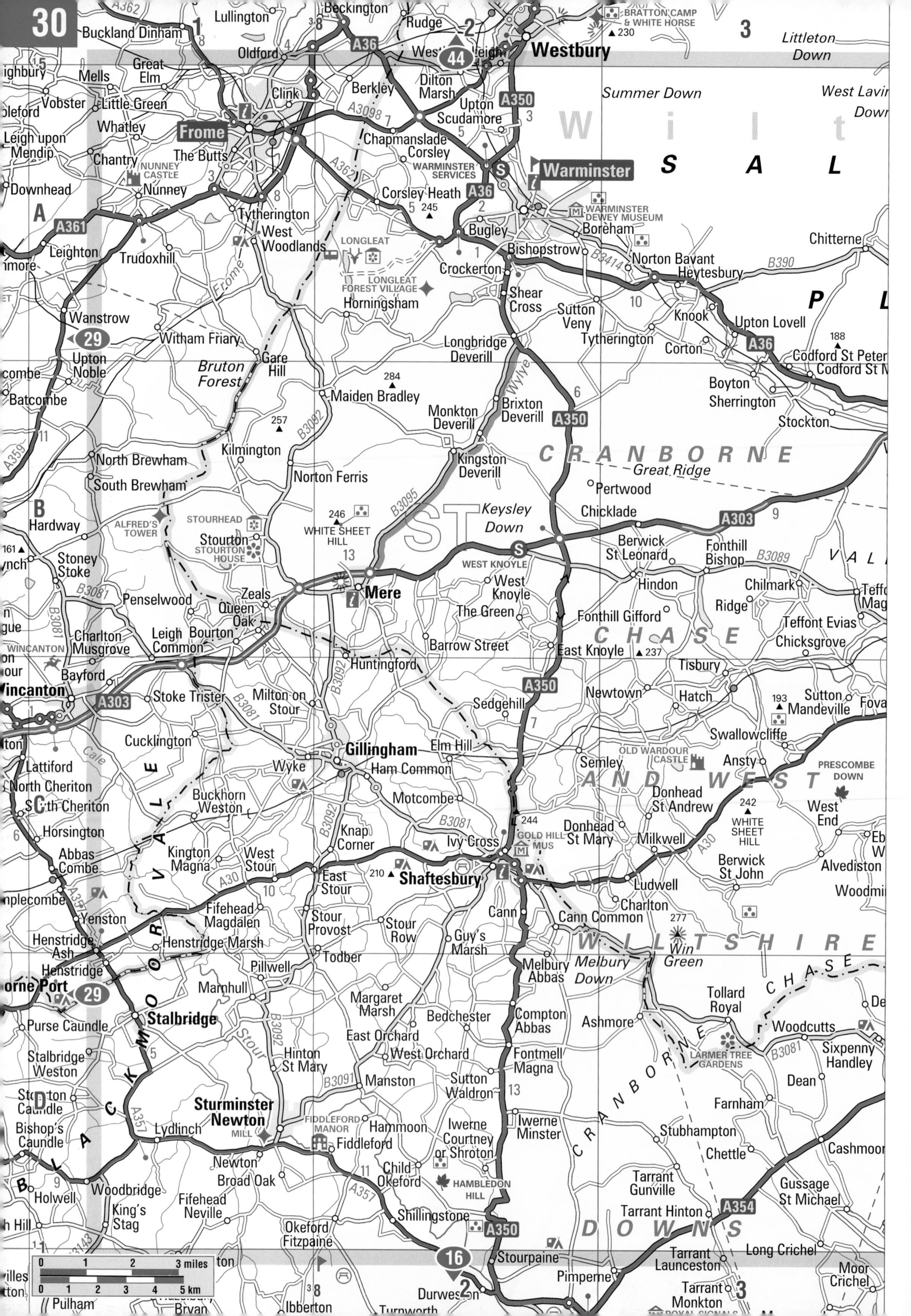
Buckland Dinham
Lullington
Beckington
Rudge
BRATTON CAMP & WHITE HORSE
230
Westbury
Littleton Down
Oldford
Great Elm
Mells
Vobster
Little Green
Clink
Berkley
Dilton Marsh
Upton Scudamore
Summer Down
West Lavington Down
Frome
Whatley
Leigh upon Mendip
Chantry
NUNNEY CASTLE
The Butts
Nunney
Downhead
Chapmanslade
Corsley
WARMINSTER SERVICES
Corsley Heath
245
Warminster
W i l t
S A L
Tytherington
West Woodlands
LONGLEAT
LONGLEAT FOREST VILLAGE
Horningsham
Bugley
Crockerton
Bishopstrow
WARMINSTER DEWEY MUSEUM
Boreham
Norton Bavant
Heytesbury
Chitterne
Leighton
Trudoxhill
Shear Cross
Sutton Veny
Tytherington
Knook
Upton Lovell
Corton
188
Codford St Peter
Codford St Mary
P L
Wanstrow
Witham Friary
Upton Noble
Gare Hill
Bruton Forest
Longbridge Deverill
Boyton
Sherrington
Stockton
Batcombe
284
Maiden Bradley
Monkton Deverill
Brixton Deverill
257
Kilmington
North Brewham
South Brewham
Norton Ferris
Kingston Deverill
CRANBORNE
Great Ridge
Pertwood
Keysley Down
Chicklade
Hardway
ALFRED'S TOWER
STOURHEAD
Stourton
STOURTON HOUSE
246
WHITE SHEET HILL
Berwick St Leonard
Fonthill Bishop
161
Stoney Stoke
WEST KNOYLE
Hindon
Chilmark
Teffont Magna
Penselwood
Zeals
Queen Oak
Mere
West Knoyle
The Green
Fonthill Gifford
Ridge
Teffont Evias
Chicksgrove
WINCANTON
Charlton Musgrove
Leigh Common
Bourton
Barrow Street
East Knoyle
237
CHASE
Bayford
Huntingford
Tisbury
Wincanton
Stoke Trister
Milton on Stour
Sedgehill
Newtown
Hatch
193
Sutton Mandeville
Fovant
Cucklington
Gillingham
Elm Hill
Swallowcliffe
Lattiford
Wyke
Ham Common
Semley
OLD WARDOUR CASTLE
Ansty
PRESCOMBE DOWN
North Cheriton
South Cheriton
Buckhorn Weston
Motcombe
AND WEST
Donhead St Andrew
242
WHITE SHEET HILL
West End
Horsington
244
Donhead St Mary
Milkwell
GOLD HILL MUS
Ivy Cross
Abbas Combe
Kington Magna
West Stour
East Stour
210
Shaftesbury
Berwick St John
Alvediston
Ludwell
Templecombe
Fifehead Magdalen
Stour Provost
Stour Row
Guy's Marsh
Cann
Charlton
Cann Common
Woodminton
Yenston
Henstridge Ash
Henstridge Marsh
277
Win Green
WILTSHIRE
Henstridge
Todber
Pillwell
Melbury Abbas
Melbury Down
Milborne Port
Marnhull
Margaret Marsh
Tollard Royal
CHASE
Purse Caundle
Stalbridge
Bedchester
Compton Abbas
Ashmore
Woodcutts
Sixpenny Handley
Stalbridge Weston
Hinton St Mary
East Orchard
West Orchard
Fontmell Magna
LARMER TREE GARDENS
Stourton Caundle
Manston
Sutton Waldron
Dean
BLACKMORE VALE
Sturminster Newton
MILL
FIDDLEFORD MANOR
Hammoon
Fiddleford
Iwerne Courtney or Shroton
Iwerne Minster
CRANBORNE
Farnham
Bishop's Caundle
Lydlinch
Stubhampton
Chettle
Cashmoor
Newton
Broad Oak
Child Okeford
Holwell
Woodbridge
Fifehead Neville
HAMBLEDON HILL
Tarrant Gunville
Gussage St Michael
King's Stag
Shillingstone
Tarrant Hinton
DOWNS
Okeford Fitzpaine
Long Crichel
Stourpaine
Tarrant Launceston
Moor Crichel
Pimperne
Tarrant Monkton
Durweston
Pulham
Ibberton
0 1 2 3 miles
0 1 2 3 4 5 km
A36 A350 A3098 A362 A361 A359 A303 A30 A357 A354 A3081 B3092 B3095 B3081 B3089 B3414 B390 B3091
1 2 3 A B C D 29 44 16

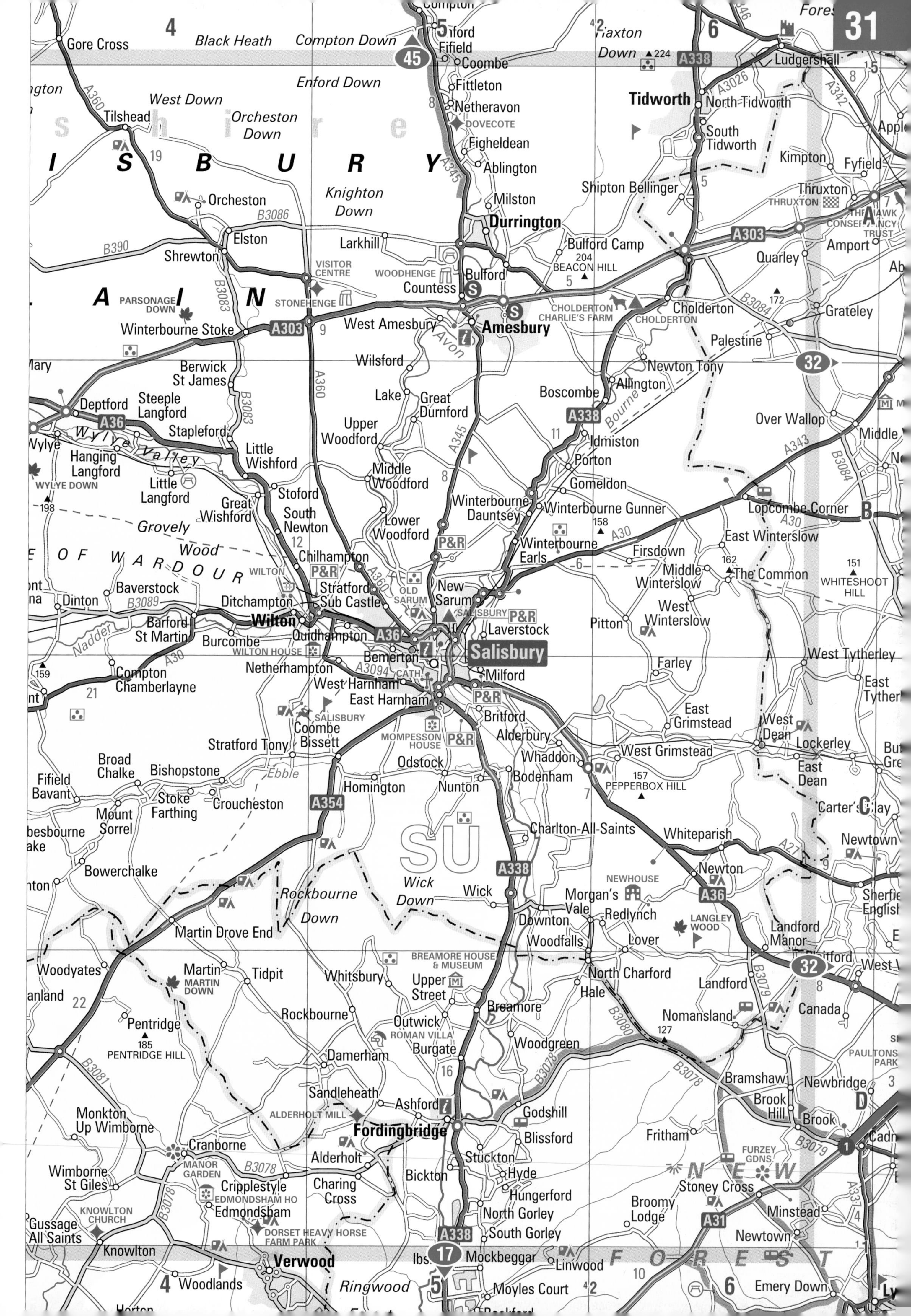
Gore Cross
Black Heath
Compton Down
Enford Down
West Down
Tilshead
Orcheston Down
S A L I S B U R Y
P L A I N
Orcheston
Knighton Down
Elston
Shrewton
Larkhill
Durrington
Bulford Camp
BEACON HILL
Bulford
Countess
WOODHENGE
VISITOR CENTRE
STONEHENGE
PARSONAGE DOWN
Winterbourne Stoke
West Amesbury
Amesbury
CHOLDERTON CHARLIE'S FARM
Cholderton
Wilsford
Berwick St James
Lake
Great Durnford
Deptford
Steeple Langford
Stapleford
Upper Woodford
Wylye Valley
Hanging Langford
Little Langford
WYLYE DOWN
Little Wishford
Great Wishford
Stoford
South Newton
Middle Woodford
Lower Woodford
Grovely Wood
Winterbourne Dauntsey
Winterbourne Gunner
Winterbourne Earls
Chilhampton
VALE OF WARDOUR
WILTON
Baverstock
Dinton
Ditchampton
Stratford Sub Castle
OLD SARUM
New Sarum
Wilton
Barford St Martin
Burcombe
WILTON HOUSE
Quidhampton
Bemerton
Salisbury
Laverstock
Netherhampton
Compton Chamberlayne
West Harnham
East Harnham
Milford
Britford
Coombe Bissett
MOMPESSON HOUSE
Stratford Tony
Broad Chalke
Bishopstone
Fifield Bavant
Stoke Farthing
Croucheston
Mount Sorrel
Homington
Odstock
Nunton
Alderbury
Whaddon
Bodenham
Charlton-All-Saints
Bowerchalke
Rockbourne Down
Wick Down
Wick
Martin Drove End
Woodyates
Martin
MARTIN DOWN
Tidpit
Whitsbury
Pentridge
PENTRIDGE HILL
Rockbourne
BREAMORE HOUSE & MUSEUM
Upper Street
Outwick
ROMAN VILLA
Burgate
Breamore
Damerham
Sandleheath
Ashford
ALDERHOLT MILL
Fordingbridge
Monkton Up Wimborne
Cranborne
MANOR GARDEN
Wimborne St Giles
Alderholt
Cripplestyle
EDMONDSHAM HO
Edmondsham
Charing Cross
Bickton
KNOWLTON CHURCH
Gussage All Saints
DORSET HEAVY HORSE FARM PARK
Knowlton
Verwood
Woodlands
Ringwood
Ibsley
Mockbeggar
Moyles Court
Stuckton
Hyde
Hungerford
North Gorley
South Gorley
Godshill
Blissford
Woodgreen
Hale
North Charford
Woodfalls
Downton
Morgan's Vale
Redlynch
Lover
NEWHOUSE
LANGLEY WOOD
Newton
Whiteparish
PEPPERBOX HILL
West Grimstead
East Grimstead
Farley
Pitton
West Winterslow
Middle Winterslow
The Common
East Winterslow
Firsdown
Lopcombe Corner
WHITESHOOT HILL
West Tytherley
East Tytherley
West Dean
Lockerley
East Dean
Carter's Clay
Newtown
Landford Manor
Landford
Nomansland
Canada
Bramshaw
Newbridge
Brook Hill
Brook
Fritham
FURZEY GDNS
NEW FOREST
Stoney Cross
Broomy Lodge
Minstead
Newtown
Linwood
Emery Down
PAULTONS PARK
Boscombe
Newton Tony
Allington
Idmiston
Porton
Gomeldon
Over Wallop
Middle Wallop
Palestine
Grateley
Quarley
Amport
Thruxton
THRUXTON
HAWK CONSERVANCY TRUST
Kimpton
Fyfield
Shipton Bellinger
Tidworth
North Tidworth
South Tidworth
Ludgershall
Haxton Down
Fittleton
Netheravon
DOVECOTE
Figheldean
Ablington
Milston
Fifield
Coombe
SU
A303
A36
A30
A338
A345
A360
A354
A27
A31
A342
A343
A3026
B3086
B390
B3083
B3089
B3094
B3078
B3080
B3079
B3081
B3084
Avon
Bourne
Nadder
Ebble

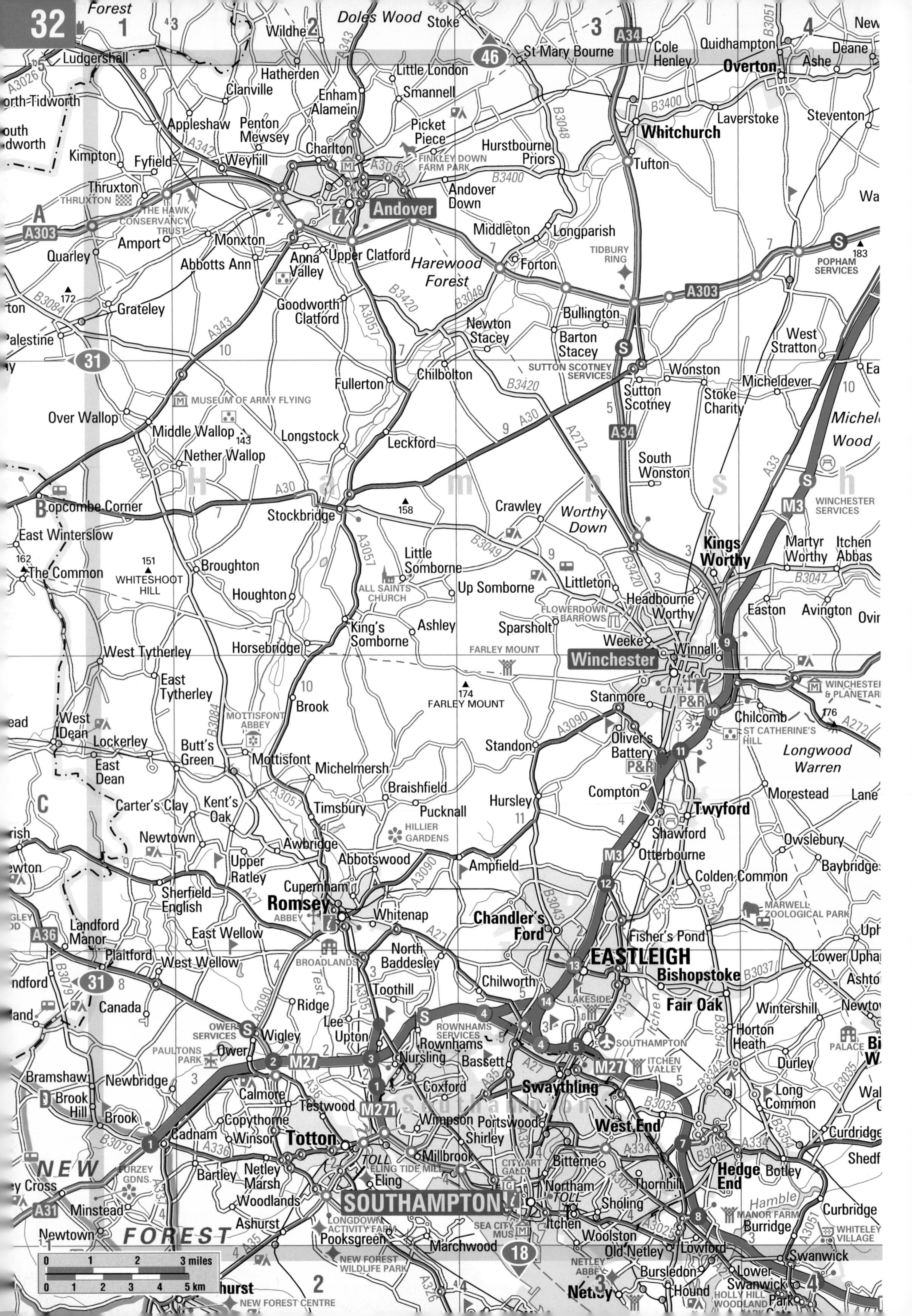

Forest
Doles Wood
Stoke
46
St Mary Bourne
A34
Cole Henley
Quidhampton
Deane
Overton
Ashe
Ludgershall
Hatherden
Little London
Smannell
Enham Alamein
Clanville
North Tidworth
Appleshaw
Penton Mewsey
Picket Piece
Hurstbourne Priors
Whitchurch
Laverstoke
Steventon
B3400
Kimpton
Fyfield
Weyhill
Charlton
FINKLEY DOWN FARM PARK
Tufton
Thruxton
THRUXTON
A3093
Andover Down
THE HAWK CONSERVANCY TRUST
Andover
A303
Amport
Monxton
Middleton
Longparish
Quarley
Abbotts Ann
Anna Valley
Upper Clatford
Harewood Forest
Forton
TIDBURY RING
POPHAM SERVICES
183
172
B3084
Grateley
Goodworth Clatford
A3057
B3420
B3048
Bullington
Newton Stacey
Barton Stacey
West Stratton
Palestine
31
A343
SUTTON SCOTNEY SERVICES
Wonston
Fullerton
Chilbolton
Sutton Scotney
Micheldever
Stoke Charity
MUSEUM OF ARMY FLYING
Over Wallop
Middle Wallop
143
Longstock
Leckford
A30
A272
Micheldever Wood
Nether Wallop
South Wonston
A33
Hampshire
Lopcombe Corner
Stockbridge
158
Crawley
Worthy Down
M3
WINCHESTER SERVICES
East Winterslow
162
The Common
151
WHITESHOOT HILL
Broughton
Little Somborne
B3049
Littleton
Kings Worthy
Martyr Worthy
Itchen Abbas
B3047
ALL SAINTS CHURCH
Up Somborne
FLOWERDOWN BARROWS
Headbourne Worthy
Easton
Avington
Houghton
B3420
King's Somborne
Ashley
Sparsholt
Weeke
Winnall
West Tytherley
Horsebridge
FARLEY MOUNT
Winchester
East Tytherley
174
FARLEY MOUNT
Stanmore
CATH.
P&R
WINCHESTER & PLANETARIUM
Brook
Chilcomb
176
West Dean
MOTTISFONT ABBEY
B3084
A3090
Oliver's Battery
ST CATHERINE'S HILL
A272
Lockerley
Butt's Green
Mottisfont
Standon
Longwood Warren
East Dean
Michelmersh
Braishfield
Compton
Morestead
C
Carter's Clay
Kent's Oak
Timsbury
Pucknall
Hursley
Twyford
HILLIER GARDENS
Shawford
Owslebury
Newtown
Awbridge
Abbotswood
Ampfield
Otterbourne
Upper Ratley
Colden Common
Baybridge
Sherfield English
Cupernham
Romsey
ABBEY
Whitenap
Chandler's Ford
MARWELL ZOOLOGICAL PARK
Landford Manor
East Wellow
A27
B3043
Fisher's Pond
A36
BROADLANDS
North Baddesley
EASTLEIGH
Lower Upham
Plaitford
West Wellow
Chilworth
Bishopstoke
B3037
Canada
Toothill
Fair Oak
Ridge
LAKESIDE
Wintershill
Lee
Upton
ROWNHAMS SERVICES
Rownhams
SOUTHAMPTON
Horton Heath
OWER SERVICES
Wigley
Ower
PAULTONS PARK
M27
Nursling
Bassett
ITCHEN VALLEY
Durley
Bramshaw
Newbridge
Calmore
Coxford
Swaythling
Long Common
Brook Hill
Brook
Testwood
M271
Wimpson
Portswood
B3035
Copythorne
Cadnam
Winsor
Totton
Shirley
West End
Curdridge
B3079
Millbrook
A334
NEW
FURZEY GDNS.
Bartley
Netley Marsh
TOLL
ELING TIDE MILL
Eling
CITY ART GALL.
Bitterne
Thornhill
Hedge End
Botley
Shedfield
Cross
Woodlands
Northam
TOLL
A31
Minstead
SOUTHAMPTON
Sholing
MANOR FARM
Curbridge
Ashurst
LONGDOWN ACTIVITY FARM
SEA CITY MUS.
Itchen
Burridge
WHITELEY VILLAGE
Newtown
FOREST
Pooksgreen
Woolston
Marchwood
Old Netley
Lowford
Swanwick
18
NETLEY ABBEY
Bursledon
NEW FOREST WILDLIFE PARK
Lower Swanwick
Hound
Park
HOLLY HILL WOODLAND PARK
Netley
Lyndhurst
NEW FOREST CENTRE
0 1 2 3 miles
0 1 2 3 4 5 km

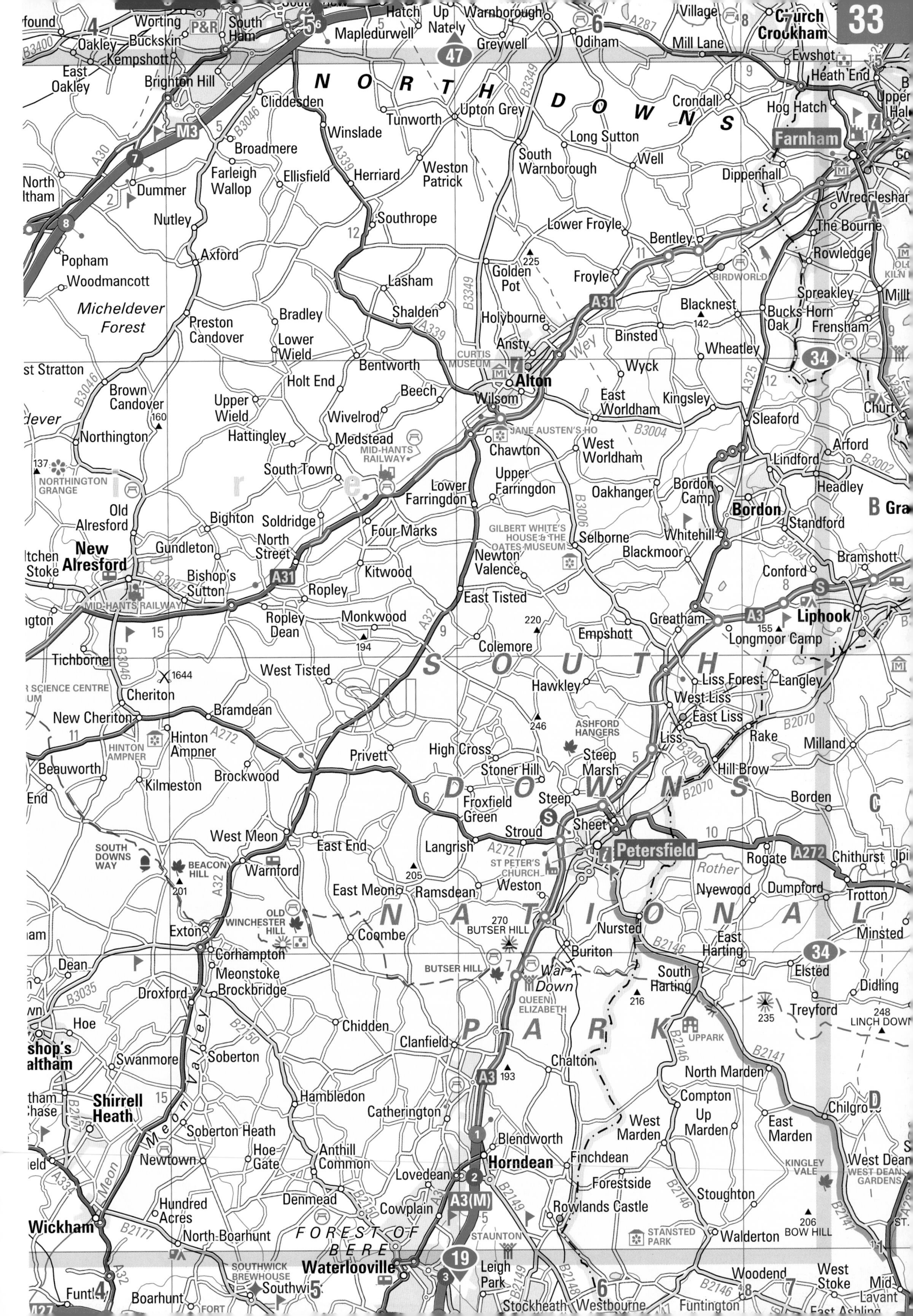

Worting
South Ham
P&R
Hatch
Up Nately
Warnborough
Mapledurwell
Greywell
47
Odiham
A287
Village
Church Crookham
Mill Lane
Ewshot
Heath End
Upper Hale
Oakley
Buckskin
Kempshott
East Oakley
Brighton Hill
B3400
M3
N O R T H   D O W N S
Cliddesden
Tunworth
Upton Grey
B3349
Crondall
Hog Hatch
Farnham
Long Sutton
Winslade
Broadmere
B3046
A30
Dummer
Farleigh Wallop
Ellisfield
A339
Herriard
Weston Patrick
South Warnborough
Well
Dippenhall
Wrecclesham
North Waltham
Nutley
Southrope
Lower Froyle
Bentley
The Bourne
Rowledge
Popham
Axford
Golden Pot
Froyle
BIRDWORLD
Woodmancott
Lasham
Micheldever Forest
Shalden
Holybourne
A31
Blacknest
Spreakley
Bucks Horn Oak
Frensham
Preston Candover
Bradley
Lower Wield
Ansty
Binsted
Wey
Wheatley
Bentworth
CURTIS MUSEUM
Alton
Wyck
East Stratton
Holt End
Beech
Brown Candover
Upper Wield
Wilson
East Worldham
Kingsley
A325
Sleaford
Churt
Micheldever
Northington
Hattingley
Wivelrod
Medstead
MID-HANTS RAILWAY
JANE AUSTEN'S HO
Chawton
B3004
West Worldham
Arford
NORTHINGTON GRANGE
South Town
Lower Farringdon
Upper Farringdon
Oakhanger
Lindford
B3002
Headley
Bordon Camp
Bordon
Old Alresford
Bighton
Soldridge
Four Marks
GILBERT WHITE'S HOUSE & THE OATES MUSEUM
B3006
Selborne
Whitehill
Standford
Grayshott
Itchen Stoke
New Alresford
Gundleton
North Street
Newton Valence
Blackmoor
Bramshott
Bishop's Sutton
Kitwood
Conford
Liphook
MID-HANTS RAILWAY
Ropley
East Tisted
Ropley Dean
Monkwood
A32
Greatham
A3
Longmoor Camp
Tichborne
Colemore
Empshott
West Tisted
S O U T H
Liss Forest
Langley
Cheriton
Hawkley
West Liss
East Liss
New Cheriton
Bramdean
SU
ASHFORD HANGERS
B2070
Hinton Ampner
HINTON AMPNER
A272
Privett
High Cross
Steep Marsh
Rake
Milland
Beauworth
Brockwood
Stoner Hill
Hill Brow
Kilmeston
Froxfield Green
D O W N S
Steep
Borden
Sheet
Stroud
West Meon
East End
Langrish
Petersfield
Rogate
Chithurst
SOUTH DOWNS WAY
BEACON HILL
Warnford
ST PETER'S CHURCH
Weston
Rother
Nyewood
Dumpford
Trotton
East Meon
Ramsdean
N A T I O N A L
Exton
OLD WINCHESTER HILL
Coombe
BUTSER HILL
Nursted
Buriton
East Harting
Minsted
Corhampton
Dean
Meonstoke
South Harting
Elsted
Brockbridge
Droxford
War Down
QUEEN ELIZABETH
Didling
Treyford
LINCH DOWN
B3035
B2150
Chidden
P A R K
UPPARK
Hoe
Bishop's Waltham
Swanmore
Soberton
Clanfield
Chalton
B2146
B2141
North Marden
Shirrell Heath
Hambledon
Catherington
Compton
Up Marden
West Marden
East Marden
Chilgrove
Soberton Heath
Meon Valley
Blendworth
Hoe Gate
Anthill Common
Horndean
Finchdean
KINGLEY VALE
West Dean
WEST DEAN GARDENS
Newtown
Lovedean
Forestside
Hundred Acres
Denmead
Cowplain
A3(M)
B2149
Rowlands Castle
Stoughton
Wickham
B2177
North Boarhunt
FOREST OF BERE
STAUNTON
STANSTED PARK
Walderton
BOW HILL
Waterlooville
Leigh Park
SOUTHWICK BREWHOUSE
Southwick
Woodend
West Stoke
Mid Lavant
Funtley
Boarhunt
FORT
Stockheath
Westbourne
Funtington
East Ashling
B2148
M27

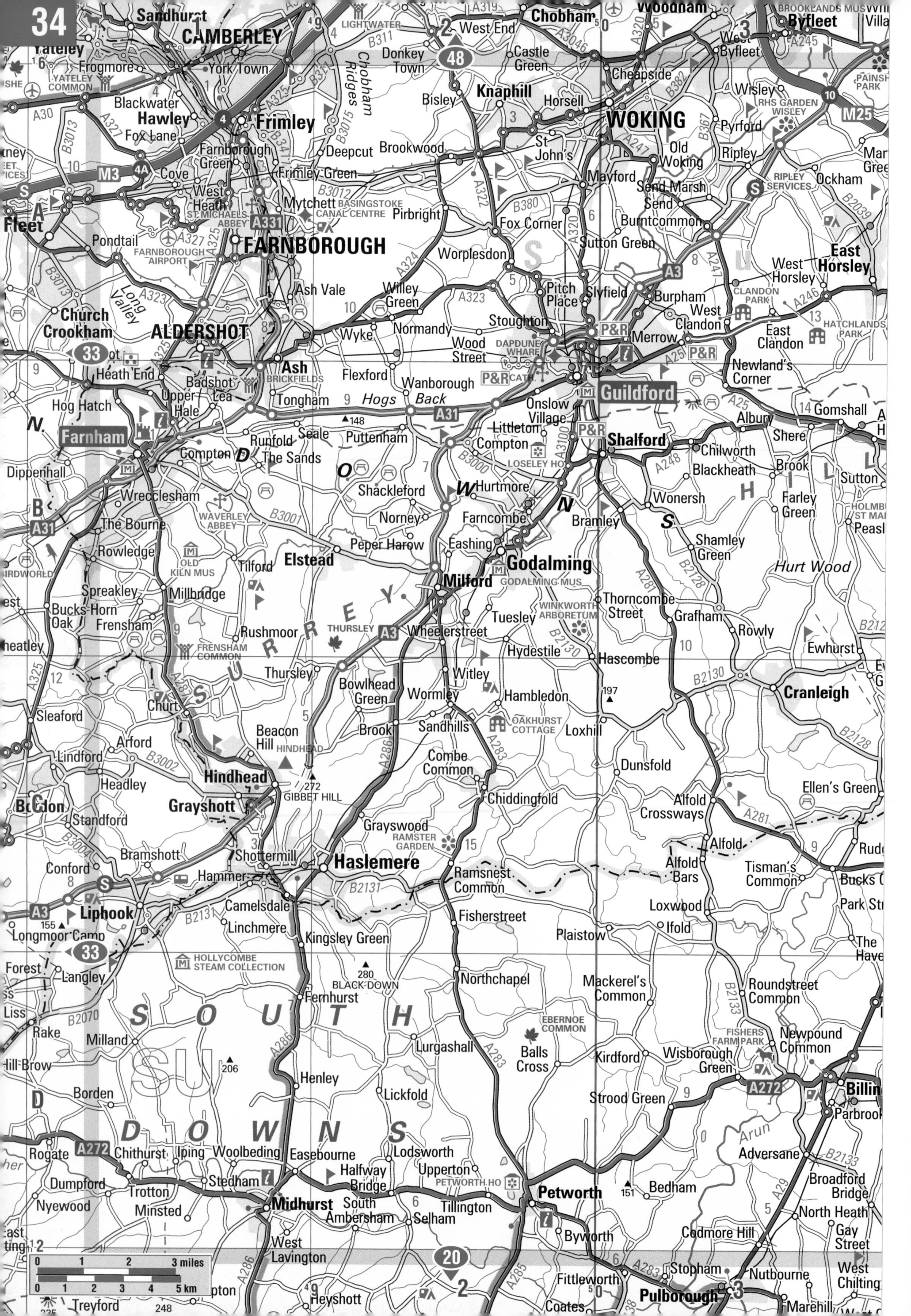
Sandhurst
CAMBERLEY
Yateley
Frogmore
York Town
YATELEY COMMON
LIGHTWATER
West End
Chobham
Woodham
BROOKLANDS MUS
Byfleet
West Byfleet
Donkey Town
Castle Green
Chobham Ridges
48
Cheapside
Knaphill
Bisley
Horsell
WOKING
Wisley
RHS GARDEN WISLEY
PAINSHILL PARK
Blackwater
Hawley
Frimley
Fox Lane
Farnborough Green
Deepcut
Brookwood
St John's
Old Woking
Pyrford
Ripley
M25
M3
Cove
Frimley Green
Mayford
Send Marsh
RIPLEY SERVICES
Ockham
West Heath
Mytchett
BASINGSTOKE CANAL CENTRE
Pirbright
Send
Burntcommon
ST MICHAEL'S ABBEY
Fleet
Pondtail
FARNBOROUGH AIRPORT
FARNBOROUGH
Fox Corner
Sutton Green
Worplesdon
East Horsley
West Horsley
Long Valley
Ash Vale
Willey Green
Pitch Place
Slyfield
Burpham
CLANDON PARK
West Clandon
Church Crookham
ALDERSHOT
Wyke
Normandy
Stoughton
Merrow
East Clandon
HATCHLANDS PARK
33
Ash
Wood Street
DAPDUNE WHARF
Newland's Corner
Heath End
BRICKFIELDS
Flexford
Badshot Lea
Upper Hale
Tongham
Wanborough
Hogs Back
CATH
Guildford
P&R
Hog Hatch
Onslow Village
Gomshall
Farnham
Runfold
Seale
Puttenham
148
Littleton
Compton
Albury
Shere
Shalford
Chilworth
Dippenhall
Compton
The Sands
LOSELEY HO
Blackheath
Brook
Sutton
Wrecclesham
Shackleford
Hurtmore
Wonersh
Farley Green
The Bourne
WAVERLEY ABBEY
Norney
Farncombe
Bramley
Rowledge
OLD KILN MUS
Peper Harow
Eashing
Shamley Green
Tilford
Elstead
Godalming
GODALMING MUS
Hurt Wood
Spreakley
Millbridge
Milford
Bucks Horn Oak
Frensham
Thorncombe Street
WINKWORTH ARBORETUM
Tuesley
Grafham
Rowly
Rushmoor
THURSLEY
Wheelerstreet
FRENSHAM COMMON
Hydestile
Hascombe
Ewhurst
Thursley
Witley
Cranleigh
Bowlhead Green
Wormley
197
Hambledon
Churt
Sleaford
Beacon Hill
HINDHEAD
Brook
Sandhills
OAKHURST COTTAGE
Loxhill
Arford
Lindford
Combe Common
Dunsfold
Headley
Hindhead
272
GIBBET HILL
Chiddingfold
Ellen's Green
Grayshott
Alfold Crossways
Standford
Grayswood
RAMSTER GARDEN
Alfold
Bramshott
Shottermill
Haslemere
Alfold Bars
Conford
Hammer
Ramsnest Common
Tisman's Common
Bucks
Liphook
Camelsdale
Loxwood
Park St
155
Longmoor Camp
Linchmere
Fisherstreet
Ifold
Kingsley Green
Plaistow
The Have
Forest
Langley
HOLLYCOMBE STEAM COLLECTION
280
BLACK DOWN
Northchapel
Mackerel's Common
Roundstreet Common
Fernhurst
Liss
EBERNOE COMMON
Rake
Milland
Lurgashall
Balls Cross
FISHERS FARM PARK
Newpound Common
Hill Brow
206
Kirdford
Wisborough Green
Henley
Borden
Lickfold
Strood Green
Parbrook
SOUTH DOWNS
Rogate
Chithurst
Iping
Woolbeding
Easebourne
Lodsworth
Adversane
Dumpford
Stedham
Halfway Bridge
Upperton
PETWORTH HO
Broadford Bridge
Trotton
Petworth
Bedham
151
Nyewood
Minsted
Midhurst
South Ambersham
Selham
Tillington
North Heath
Gay Street
Byworth
Codmore Hill
West Lavington
20
Stopham
Nutbourne
West Chilting
Fittleworth
Heyshott
Pulborough
Treyford
248
Coates
Marehill
0 1 2 3 miles
0 1 2 3 4 5 km

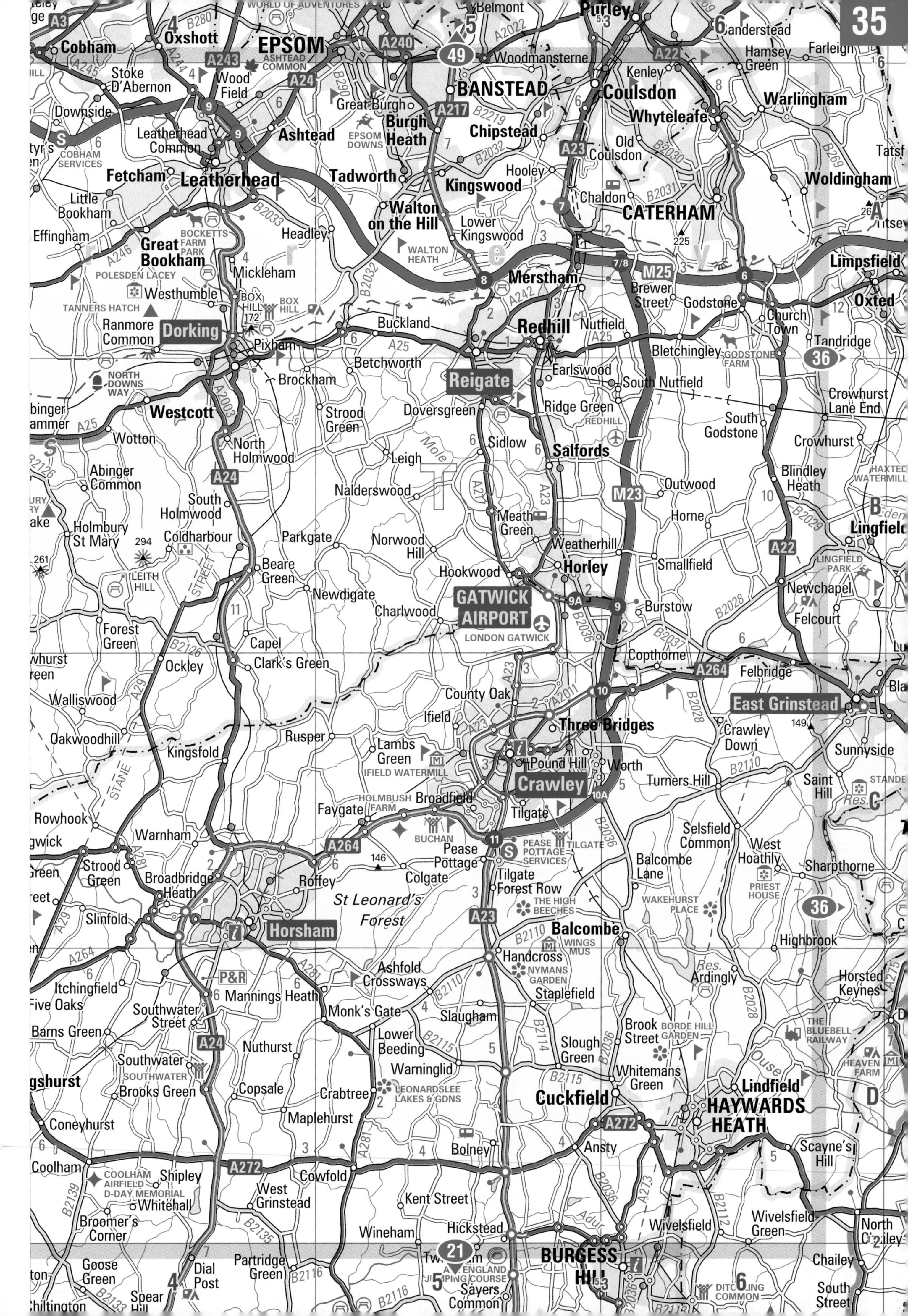
Cobham
Oxshott
EPSOM
Belmont
Purley
Sanderstead
Hamsey Green
Farleigh
Stoke D'Abernon
Wood Field
ASHTEAD COMMON
Woodmansterne
BANSTEAD
Kenley
Coulsdon
Warlingham
Downside
Great Burgh
Burgh Heath
Chipstead
Whyteleafe
Leatherhead Common
Ashtead
EPSOM DOWNS
Old Coulsdon
Tatsfield
COBHAM SERVICES
Fetcham
Leatherhead
Tadworth
Kingswood
Hooley
Woldingham
Little Bookham
Walton on the Hill
Chaldon
CATERHAM
Effingham
BOCKETTS FARM PARK
Headley
Lower Kingswood
Great Bookham
Mickleham
WALTON HEATH
Limpsfield
POLESDEN LACEY
Merstham
Brewer Street
Godstone
Oxted
Westhumble
BOX HILL
TANNERS HATCH
Buckland
Redhill
Nutfield
Church Town
Ranmore Common
Dorking
Pixham
Bletchingley
GODSTONE FARM
Tandridge
Betchworth
Earlswood
NORTH DOWNS WAY
Brockham
Reigate
South Nutfield
Crowhurst Lane End
Strood Green
Doversgreen
Ridge Green
Westcott
REDHILL
South Godstone
Wotton
Sidlow
Salfords
Crowhurst
North Holmwood
Leigh
Mole
Abinger Common
Blindley Heath
HAXTED WATERMILL
Nalderswood
Outwood
South Holmwood
Meath Green
Horne
Lingfield
Holmbury St Mary
Coldharbour
Parkgate
Norwood Hill
Weatherhill
Smallfield
LEITH HILL
Beare Green
Hookwood
Horley
LINGFIELD PARK
Newdigate
GATWICK AIRPORT
Burstow
Newchapel
Charlwood
LONDON GATWICK
Felcourt
Forest Green
Capel
Copthorne
Ockley
Clark's Green
Felbridge
Walliswood
County Oak
Ifield
East Grinstead
Three Bridges
Oakwoodhill
Rusper
Crawley Down
Kingsfold
Lambs Green
Pound Hill
Worth
Sunnyside
IFIELD WATERMILL
Crawley
Turners Hill
Saint Hill
STANE STREET
HOLMBUSH FARM
Broadfield
Rowhook
Faygate
Tilgate
Selsfield Common
Warnham
BUCHAN
PEASE POTTAGE SERVICES
West Hoathly
Pease Pottage
TILGATE
Strood Green
Colgate
Balcombe Lane
Sharpthorne
Broadbridge Heath
Roffey
Tilgate Forest Row
PRIEST HOUSE
St Leonard's Forest
THE HIGH BEECHES
WAKEHURST PLACE
Slinfold
Horsham
Balcombe
WINGS MUS
Highbrook
Handcross
NYMANS GARDEN
Res.
Ardingly
Horsted Keynes
Itchingfield
P&R
Ashfold Crossways
Staplefield
Five Oaks
Mannings Heath
Southwater Street
Monk's Gate
Slaugham
Barns Green
Lower Beeding
Brook Street
BORDE HILL GARDEN
THE BLUEBELL RAILWAY
Nuthurst
Slough Green
Southwater
SOUTHWATER
Warninglid
Whitemans Green
HEAVEN FARM
Ouse
Brooks Green
Copsale
LEONARDSLEE LAKES & GDNS
Crabtree
Cuckfield
Lindfield
HAYWARDS HEATH
Coneyhurst
Maplehurst
Bolney
Ansty
Scayne's Hill
Coolham
COOLHAM AIRFIELD D-DAY MEMORIAL
Shipley
Cowfold
Whitehall
West Grinstead
Kent Street
Broomer's Corner
Wivelsfield
Wivelsfield Green
North Chailey
Wineham
Hickstead
Adur
Twineham
BURGESS HILL
Chailey
Goose Green
Partridge Green
Dial Post
ALL ENGLAND JUMPING COURSE
Sayers Common
DITCHLING COMMON
South Street
Spear Hill
Thakeham
Ashington
M25
M23
A24
A23
A22
A25
A264
A272
A243
A217
A240
A29
A281
49
21
36

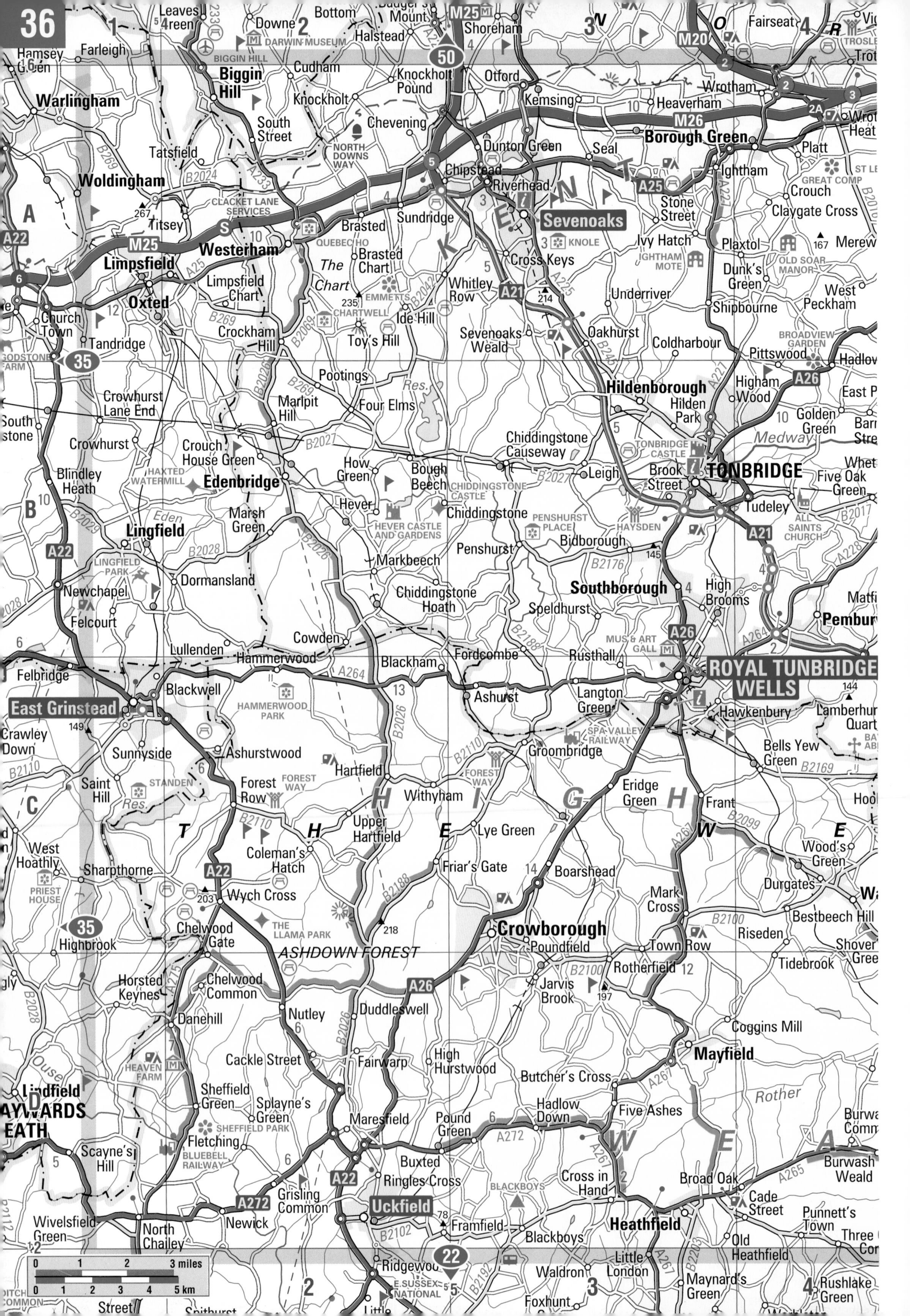

Leaves Green
Downe
Bottom
Badgers Mount
M25
Shoreham
Fairseat
Hamsey Green
Farleigh
DARWIN MUSEUM
Halstead
BIGGIN HILL
50
M20
Trosley
Biggin Hill
Cudham
Knockholt Pound
Otford
Wrotham
Warlingham
Knockholt
Kemsing
Heaverham
South Street
Chevening
M26
Borough Green
Tatsfield
NORTH DOWNS WAY
Dunton Green
Seal
Platt
Woldingham
B2024
Chipstead
Riverhead
Ightham
A25
GREAT COMP
A
CLACKET LANE SERVICES
Sundridge
Stone Street
Crouch
Titsey
Brasted
Sevenoaks
Claygate Cross
M25
QUEBEC HO
KNOLE
Ivy Hatch
Plaxtol
Merewor
Westerham
Brasted Chart
IGHTHAM MOTE
Limpsfield
The Chart
Cross Keys
Dunk's Green
OLD SOAR MANOR
Limpsfield Chart
Whitley Row
A21
Underriver
West Peckham
Oxted
EMMETTS
Church Town
CHARTWELL
Ide Hill
Shipbourne
Tandridge
Crockham Hill
Toy's Hill
Sevenoaks Weald
Oakhurst
Coldharbour
BROADVIEW GARDEN
GODSTONE FARM
35
Pittswood
Hadlow
Pootings
Res.
Hildenborough
Higham Wood
A26
Crowhurst Lane End
Marlpit Hill
Four Elms
Hilden Park
East Peckham
Golden Green
South Godstone
Medway
Crowhurst
B2027
Chiddingstone Causeway
TONBRIDGE CASTLE
Crouch House Green
How Green
Bough Beech
Leigh
Brook Street
TONBRIDGE
Five Oak Green
Blindley Heath
HAXTED WATERMILL
Edenbridge
CHIDDINGSTONE CASTLE
Tudeley
B
Hever
Chiddingstone
PENSHURST PLACE
HAYSDEN
ALL SAINTS CHURCH
Eden
Marsh Green
HEVER CASTLE AND GARDENS
Lingfield
Bidborough
A21
A22
B2028
B2026
Penshurst
LINGFIELD PARK
Markbeech
B2176
Dormansland
Southborough
High Brooms
Matfield
Newchapel
Chiddingstone Hoath
Pembury
Felcourt
Speldhurst
A264
Cowden
MUS & ART GALL
Lullenden
Hammerwood
Blackham
Fordcombe
Rusthall
Felbridge
ROYAL TUNBRIDGE WELLS
Blackwell
Ashurst
Langton Green
East Grinstead
HAMMERWOOD PARK
Hawkenbury
Lamberhurst Quarter
Crawley Down
SPA VALLEY RAILWAY
Sunnyside
Ashurstwood
Groombridge
Bells Yew Green
B2110
B2169
Saint Hill
STANDEN
Forest Row
FOREST WAY
Hartfield
Eridge Green
C
Res.
Withyham
Frant
T
H
I
G
H
W
E
Upper Hartfield
Lye Green
West Hoathly
Coleman's Hatch
Friar's Gate
Boarshead
Wood's Green
Sharpthorne
A22
Mark Cross
Durgates
PRIEST HOUSE
Wych Cross
Crowborough
Bestbeech Hill
35
Chelwood Gate
THE LLAMA PARK
Riseden
Highbrook
ASHDOWN FOREST
Poundfield
Town Row
Tidebrook
Horsted Keynes
Chelwood Common
A26
Rotherfield
Jarvis Brook
Danehill
Nutley
Duddleswell
Coggins Mill
Cackle Street
High Hurstwood
Fairwarp
Mayfield
HEAVEN FARM
Butcher's Cross
Ouse
Lindfield
Sheffield Green
Splayne's Green
Rother
HAYWARDS HEATH
Hadlow Down
Five Ashes
SHEFFIELD PARK
Maresfield
Pound Green
Burwash Common
Fletching
A272
W
E
A
BLUEBELL RAILWAY
Scayne's Hill
Buxted
Burwash Weald
Ringles Cross
Cross in Hand
Broad Oak
Grisling Common
BLACKBOYS
Cade Street
A272
Uckfield
Punnett's Town
Wivelsfield Green
Newick
Framfield
Heathfield
North Chailey
B2102
Blackboys
Three Cups Corner
Old Heathfield
22
Little London
Ridgewood
Waldron
Maynard's Green
Rushlake Green
E.SUSSEX NATIONAL
Foxhunt
0 1 2 3 miles
0 1 2 3 4 5 km

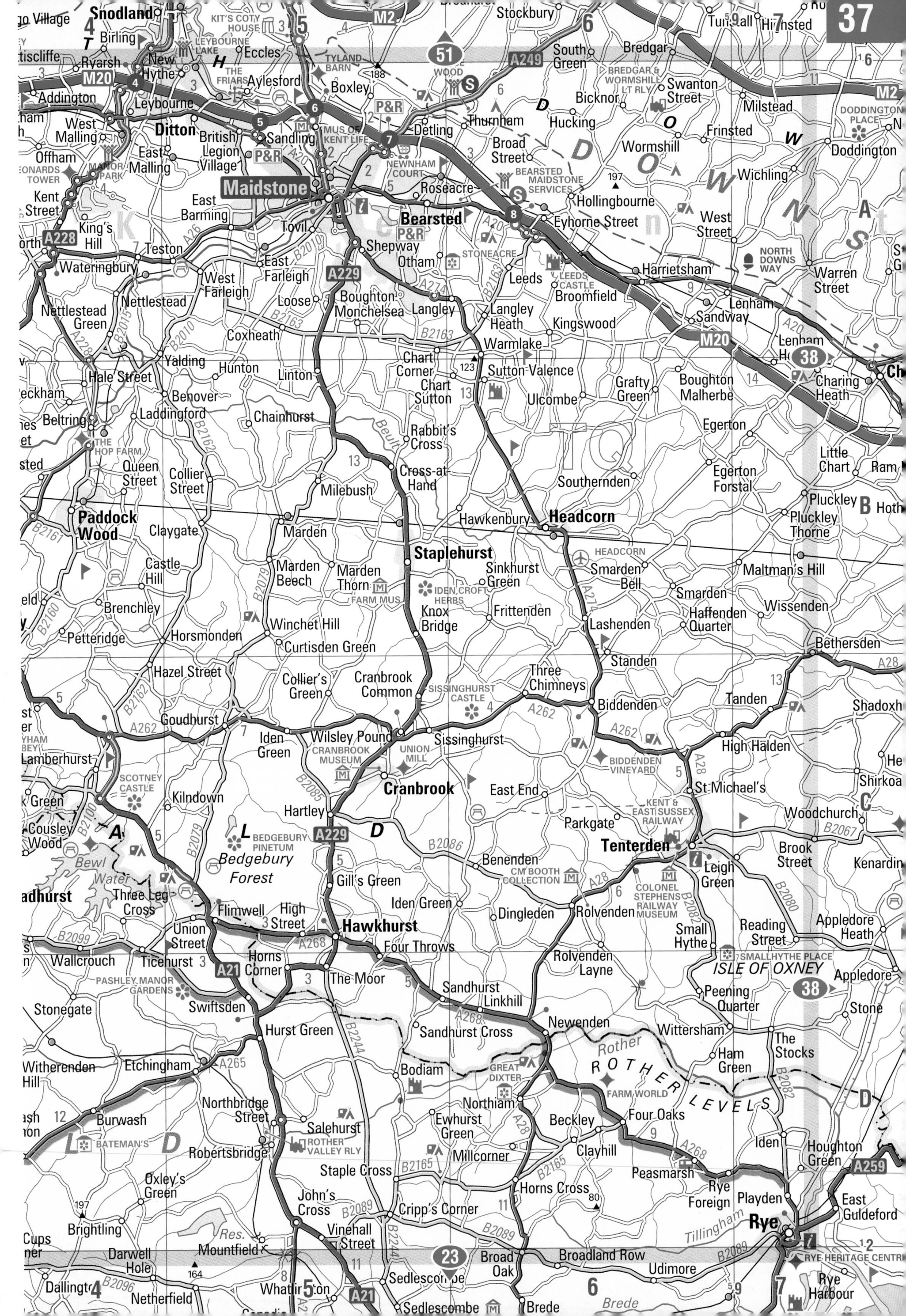
Snodland
Stockbury
Tunstall
Hinsted
Birling
Kit's Coty House
Leybourne Lake
Eccles
Ryarsh
New Hythe
The Friars
Aylesford
Tyland Barn
Boxley
M2
M20
M2
A249
South Green
Bredgar
Bredgar & Wormshill Lt Rly
Swanton Street
Bicknor
Milstead
Doddington Place
Addington
Leybourne
West Malling
Ditton
Sandling
Mus of Kent Life
Detling
Thurnham
Hucking
Wormshill
Frinsted
Doddington
Offham
East Malling
British Legion Village
Broad Street
Manor Park
St Leonards Tower
Maidstone
Newnham Court
Roseacre
Bearsted Maidstone Services
Hollingbourne
Wichling
Kent Street
East Barming
Bearsted
Eyhorne Street
West Street
King's Hill
Tovil
Stoneacre
A228
Teston
Shepway
Otham
Leeds
Leeds Castle
Harrietsham
North Downs Way
Warren Street
Wateringbury
East Farleigh
West Farleigh
A229
Broomfield
Lenham
Nettlestead
Loose
Boughton Monchelsea
Langley
Langley Heath
Sandway
Nettlestead Green
Kingswood
Coxheath
Warmlake
Lenham Heath
Yalding
Chart Corner
Sutton Valence
Charing Heath
Hunton
Linton
Chart Sutton
Grafty Green
Boughton Malherbe
Hale Street
Benover
Ulcombe
Laddingford
Chainhurst
Beltring
Egerton
Rabbit's Cross
The Hop Farm
TQ
Little Chart
Queen Street
Collier Street
Cross-at-Hand
Egerton Forstal
Milebush
Southernden
Pluckley
Paddock Wood
Claygate
Marden
Hawkenbury
Headcorn
Pluckley Thorne
Staplehurst
Castle Hill
Marden Beech
Marden Thorn
Farm Mus
Sinkhurst Green
Headcorn
Smarden Bell
Maltman's Hill
Iden Croft Herbs
Smarden
Brenchley
Knox Bridge
Frittenden
Haffenden Quarter
Wissenden
Petteridge
Winchet Hill
Lashenden
Horsmonden
Curtisden Green
Bethersden
Standen
Hazel Street
Collier's Green
Cranbrook Common
Three Chimneys
Sissinghurst Castle
Biddenden
Tanden
Shadoxhurst
Goudhurst
A262
Iden Green
Wilsley Pound
Sissinghurst
Lamberhurst
Cranbrook Museum
Union Mill
High Halden
Biddenden Vineyard
Scotney Castle
Shirkoak
Kilndown
Cranbrook
East End
St Michael's
Hartley
Kent & East Sussex Railway
Woodchurch
Cousley Wood
Parkgate
Bedgebury Pinetum
Bedgebury Forest
Tenterden
Brook Street
Bewl Water
Benenden
CM Booth Collection
Leigh Green
Kenardington
Gill's Green
Colonel Stephens Railway Museum
Three Leg Cross
Iden Green
Flimwell
High Street
Dingleden
Rolvenden
Small Hythe
Reading Street
Appledore Heath
Union Street
Hawkhurst
Wallcrouch
Ticehurst
Horns Corner
Four Throws
Rolvenden Layne
Smallhythe Place
Isle of Oxney
Appledore
The Moor
Pashley Manor Gardens
Sandhurst
Linkhill
Peening Quarter
Stonegate
Swiftsden
Stone
Hurst Green
Sandhurst Cross
Newenden
Wittersham
Rother
Witherenden Hill
Etchingham
The Stocks
Bodiam
Great Dixter
Ham Green
Rother Levels
Farm World
Northbridge Street
Northiam
Burwash
Salehurst
Ewhurst Green
Beckley
Four Oaks
Bateman's
Rother Valley Rly
Iden
Robertsbridge
Clayhill
Houghton Green
Millcorner
Staple Cross
Peasmarsh
Oxley's Green
Horns Cross
Rye Foreign
Playden
East Guldeford
John's Cross
Cripp's Corner
Brightling
Rye
Vinehall Street
Tillingham
Mountfield
Darwell Hole
Broad Oak
Broadland Row
Udimore
Rye Heritage Centre
Dallington
Sedlescombe
Whatlington
Netherfield
Brede
Rye Harbour
Sedlescombe
A21
A268
A28
A259
A265
A274
A20
B2163
B2010
B2015
B2162
B2161
B2160
B2079
B2085
B2086
B2082
B2080
B2067
B2099
B2100
B2244
B2165
B2089
B2096
51
38
23

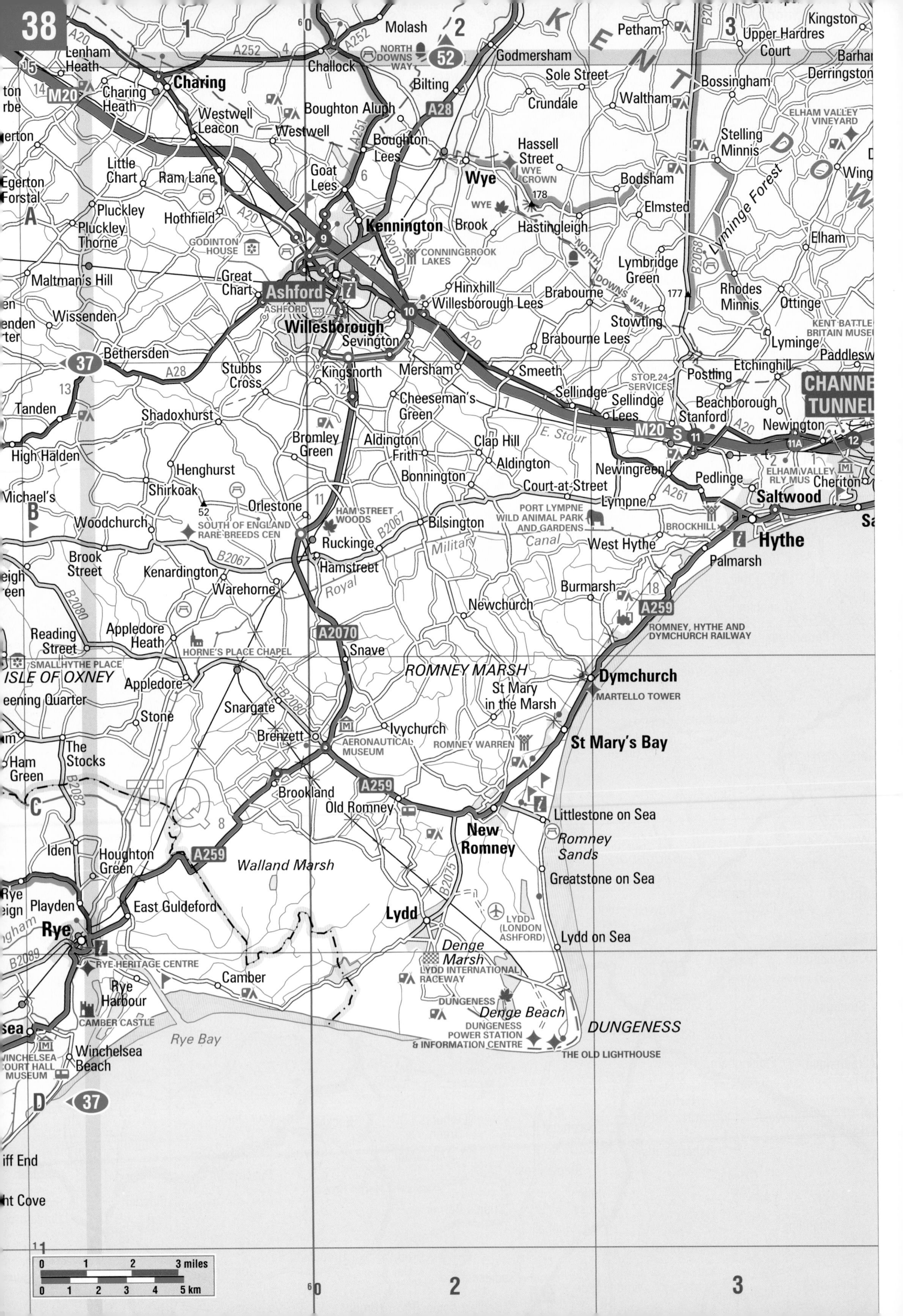

KENT DOWNS
Molash
Petham
Kingston
Upper Hardres Court
Barham
Lenham Heath
Charing
Charing Heath
Challock
NORTH DOWNS WAY
Godmersham
Sole Street
Derringston
Bilting
Bossingham
Crundale
Waltham
ELHAM VALLEY VINEYARD
Boughton Aluph
Westwell Leacon
Westwell
Boughton Lees
Hassell Street
Stelling Minnis
Little Chart
Ram Lane
Goat Lees
Wye
WYE CROWN
Bodsham
Egerton Forstal
Lyminge Forest
Pluckley
Hothfield
WYE
Elmsted
Pluckley Thorne
Kennington
Brook
Hastingleigh
Elham
GODINTON HOUSE
CONNINGBROOK LAKES
Lymbridge Green
Maltman's Hill
Great Chart
Ashford
Hinxhill
Brabourne
Rhodes Minnis
Ottinge
ASHFORD
Willesborough Lees
Stowting
Wissenden
Willesborough
Sevington
KENT BATTLE OF BRITAIN MUSEUM
Brabourne Lees
Lyminge
Bethersden
Stubbs Cross
Kingsnorth
Mersham
Smeeth
Postling
Etchinghill
Paddlesworth
STOP 24 SERVICES
CHANNEL TUNNEL
Sellindge
Sellindge Lees
Beachborough
Tanden
Shadoxhurst
Cheeseman's Green
Stanford
Newington
Bromley Green
Aldington Frith
Clap Hill
E. Stour
High Halden
Aldington
Henghurst
Newingreen
Pedlinge
ELHAM VALLEY RLY MUS
Cheriton
Bonnington
Shirkoak
Court-at-Street
Michael's
Orlestone
Lympne
Saltwood
PORT LYMPNE WILD ANIMAL PARK AND GARDENS
HAM STREET WOODS
Woodchurch
SOUTH OF ENGLAND RARE BREEDS CEN
Bilsington
BROCKHILL
Hythe
Ruckinge
Military Canal
West Hythe
Brook Street
Hamstreet
Palmarsh
Kenardington
Warehorne
Royal
Burmarsh
Newchurch
Reading Street
Appledore Heath
ROMNEY, HYTHE AND DYMCHURCH RAILWAY
HORNE'S PLACE CHAPEL
Snave
SMALLHYTHE PLACE
ISLE OF OXNEY
Appledore
ROMNEY MARSH
Dymchurch
MARTELLO TOWER
St Mary in the Marsh
Snargate
Stone
Ivychurch
Brenzett
St Mary's Bay
The Stocks
AERONAUTICAL MUSEUM
ROMNEY WARREN
Ham Green
Brookland
Old Romney
Littlestone on Sea
New Romney
Romney Sands
Iden
Houghton Green
Walland Marsh
Greatstone on Sea
Rye
Playden
East Guldeford
Lydd
LYDD (LONDON ASHFORD)
Lydd on Sea
Denge Marsh
RYE HERITAGE CENTRE
LYDD INTERNATIONAL RACEWAY
Camber
Rye Harbour
DUNGENESS
Denge Beach
CAMBER CASTLE
DUNGENESS POWER STATION & INFORMATION CENTRE
DUNGENESS
Rye Bay
THE OLD LIGHTHOUSE
WINCHELSEA COURT HALL MUSEUM
Winchelsea Beach
M20
A20
A28
A252
A251
A2070
A259
A261
B2067
B2068
B2080
B2082
B2075
B2089
TQ
37
52
0 1 2 3 miles
0 1 2 3 4 5 km

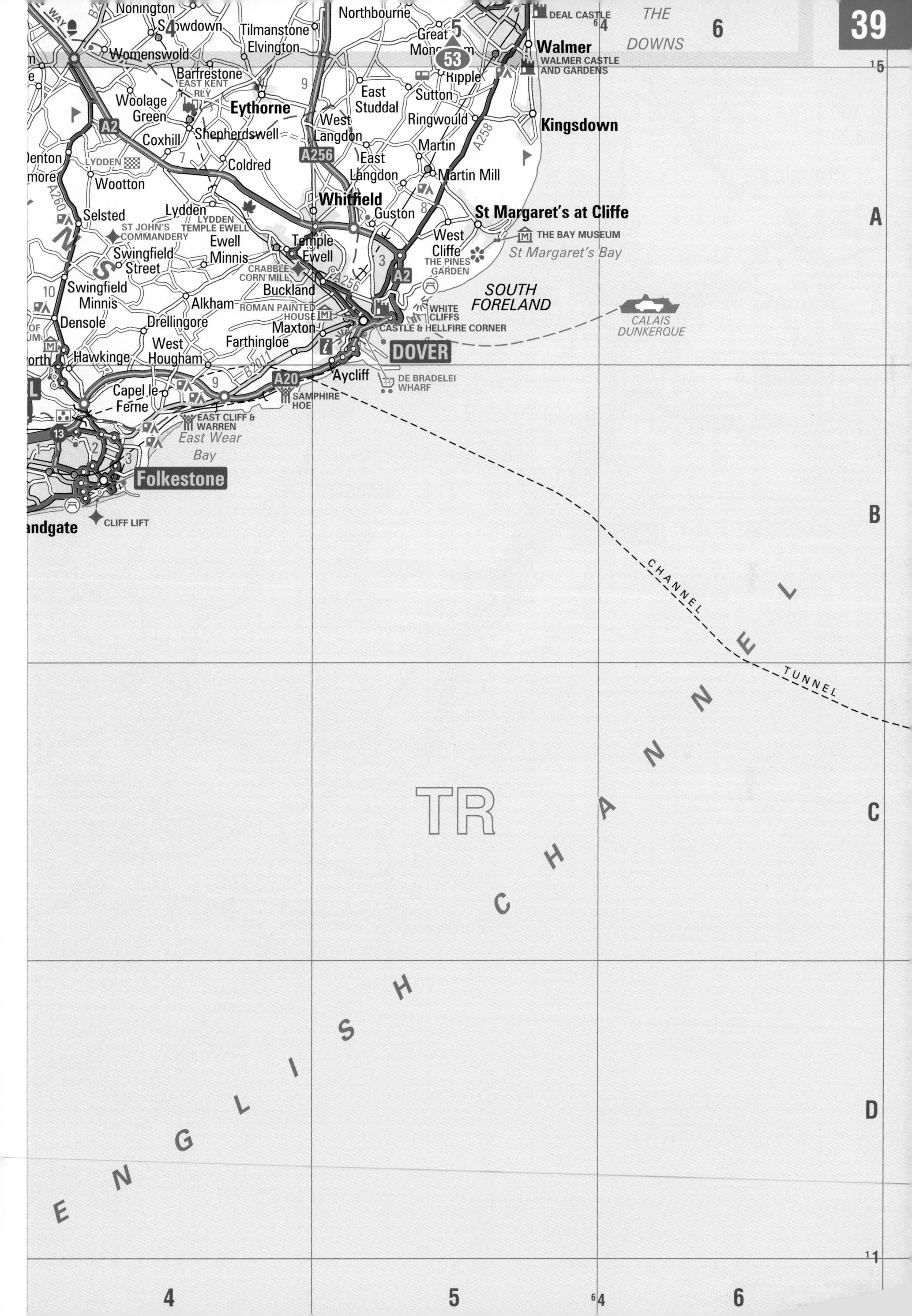

THE DOWNS

DEAL CASTLE

Walmer

WALMER CASTLE
AND GARDENS

Ripple

Kingsdown

Northbourne

Great
Mongeham

53

Nonington

Snowdown

Tilmanstone

Elvington

East Kent Rly

Eythorne

East
Studdal

Sutton

Ringwould

Martin

Barfrestone

Woolage
Green

Coxhill

Shepherdswell

West
Langdon

East
Langdon

Martin Mill

Coldred

A256

Whitfield

Guston

St Margaret's at Cliffe

A2

Wootton

Lydden

West
Cliffe

THE BAY MUSEUM

St Margaret's Bay

Selsted

ST JOHN'S
COMMANDERY

Ewell
Minnis

LYDDEN
TEMPLE EWELL

Temple
Ewell

THE PINES
GARDEN

Swingfield
Street

CRABBLE
CORN MILL

A256

Swingfield
Minnis

Alkham

ROMAN PAINTED
HOUSE

Buckland

WHITE
CLIFFS

SOUTH
FORELAND

CALAIS
DUNKERQUE

Densole

Drellingore

Maxton

CASTLE & HELLFIRE CORNER

Denton

LYDDEN

Hawkinge

West
Hougham

Farthingloe

DOVER

DE BRADELEI
WHARF

Capel le
Ferne

EAST CLIFF &
WARREN

A20

Aycliff

SAMPHIRE
HOE

13

East Wear
Bay

Folkestone

CLIFF LIFT

Sandgate

CHANNEL TUNNEL

A2

A260

B2011

TR

ENGLISH CHANNEL

A

B

C

D

4

5

6

15

11

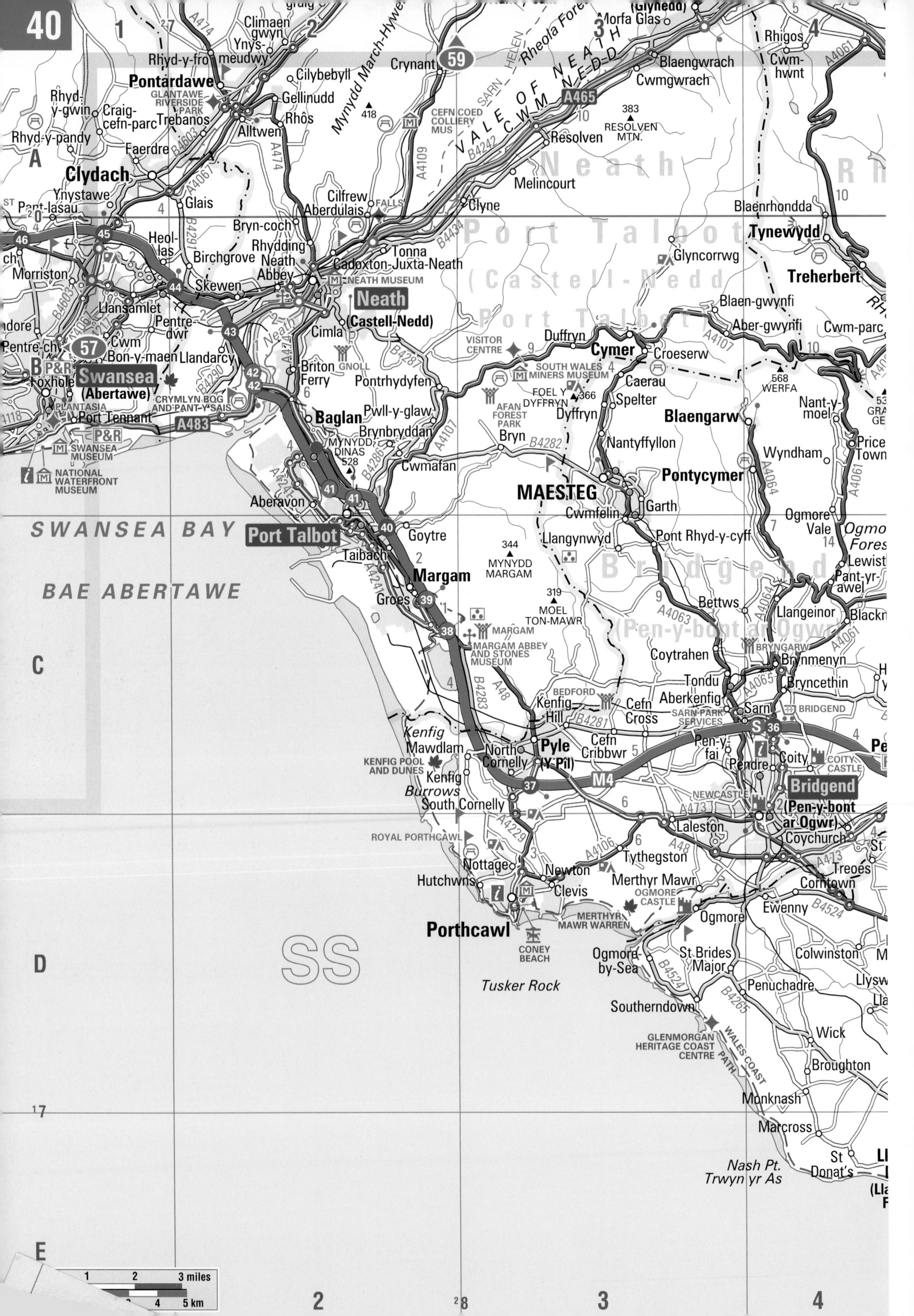
Climaen gwyn
Ynys-meudwy
Rhyd-y-fro
Pontardawe
GLANTAWE RIVERSIDE PARK
Rhyd-y-gwin
Craig-cefn-parc
Trebanos
Rhyd-y-pandy
Faerdre
Clydach
Ynystawe
Pant-lasau
Glais
Gellinudd
Rhôs
Alltwen
Cilybebyll
Mynydd March-Hywel
Crynant
Rheola Forest
Morfa Glas
Blaengwrach
Cwmgwrach
Rhigos
Cwm-hwnt
VALE OF NEATH
CWM NEDD
CEFN COED COLLIERY MUS
Resolven
383
RESOLVEN MTN.
Neath
Melincourt
Clyne
Cilfrew
Aberdulais
FALLS
Bryn-coch
Heol-las
Rhydding
Birchgrove
Neath Abbey
Tonna
Cadoxton-Juxta-Neath
NEATH MUSEUM
Neath
(Castell-Nedd)
Port Talbot
(Castell-Nedd Port Talbot)
Blaenrhondda
Tynewydd
Glyncorrwg
Treherbert
Morriston
Skewen
Llansamlet
Pentre-dwr
Cwm
Bon-y-maen
Llandarcy
Cimla
Swansea
(Abertawe)
Foxhole
CRYMLYN BOG AND PANT-Y-SAIS
PLANTASIA
Port Tennant
SWANSEA MUSEUM
NATIONAL WATERFRONT MUSEUM
Briton Ferry
GNOLL
Pontrhydyfen
Baglan
Pwll-y-glaw
Brynbryddan
MYNYDD DINAS
528
Cwmafan
Aberavon
Port Talbot
Taibach
Goytre
Margam
Groes
SWANSEA BAY
BAE ABERTAWE
VISITOR CENTRE
Duffryn
Cymer
Croeserw
Blaen-gwynfi
Aber-gwynfi
Cwm-parc
SOUTH WALES MINERS MUSEUM
Caerau
FOEL Y DYFFRYN
366
Dyffryn
Spelter
AFAN FOREST PARK
Bryn
Nantyffyllon
Blaengarw
568
WERFA
Nant-y-moel
Wyndham
Price Town
MAESTEG
Pontycymer
Garth
Cwmfelin
Llangynwyd
Pont Rhyd-y-cyff
Ogmore Vale
344
MYNYDD MARGAM
319
MOEL TON-MAWR
MARGAM
MARGAM ABBEY AND STONES MUSEUM
Bridgend
(Pen-y-bont ar Ogwr)
Bettws
Llangeinor
Coytrahen
BRYNGARW
Brynmenyn
Tondu
Bryncethin
Aberkenfig
BEDFORD
Kenfig Hill
Cefn Cross
SARN PARK SERVICES
Sarn
BRIDGEND
Kenfig
Mawdlam
KENFIG POOL AND DUNES
Kenfig Burrows
North Cornelly
Pyle
(Y Pil)
Cefn Cribbwr
Pen-y-fai
Pendre
Coity
COITY CASTLE
Bridgend
(Pen-y-bont ar Ogwr)
South Cornelly
NEWCASTLE
Laleston
Coychurch
ROYAL PORTHCAWL
Nottage
Tythegston
Hutchwns
Newton
Clevis
Merthyr Mawr
OGMORE CASTLE
Treoes
Corntown
Ewenny
Porthcawl
CONEY BEACH
MERTHYR MAWR WARREN
Ogmore
Ogmore-by-Sea
St Brides Major
Colwinston
SS
Tusker Rock
Southerndown
Penuchadre
GLENMORGAN HERITAGE COAST CENTRE
WALES COAST PATH
Wick
Broughton
Monknash
Marcross
St Donat's
Nash Pt.
Trwyn yr As
A
B
C
D
E
1
2
3
4
1
2
3 miles
4
5 km
M4
A465
A483
A4107
A4061
A4063
A48
A473
B4283
B4282
B4281
B4524
B4265

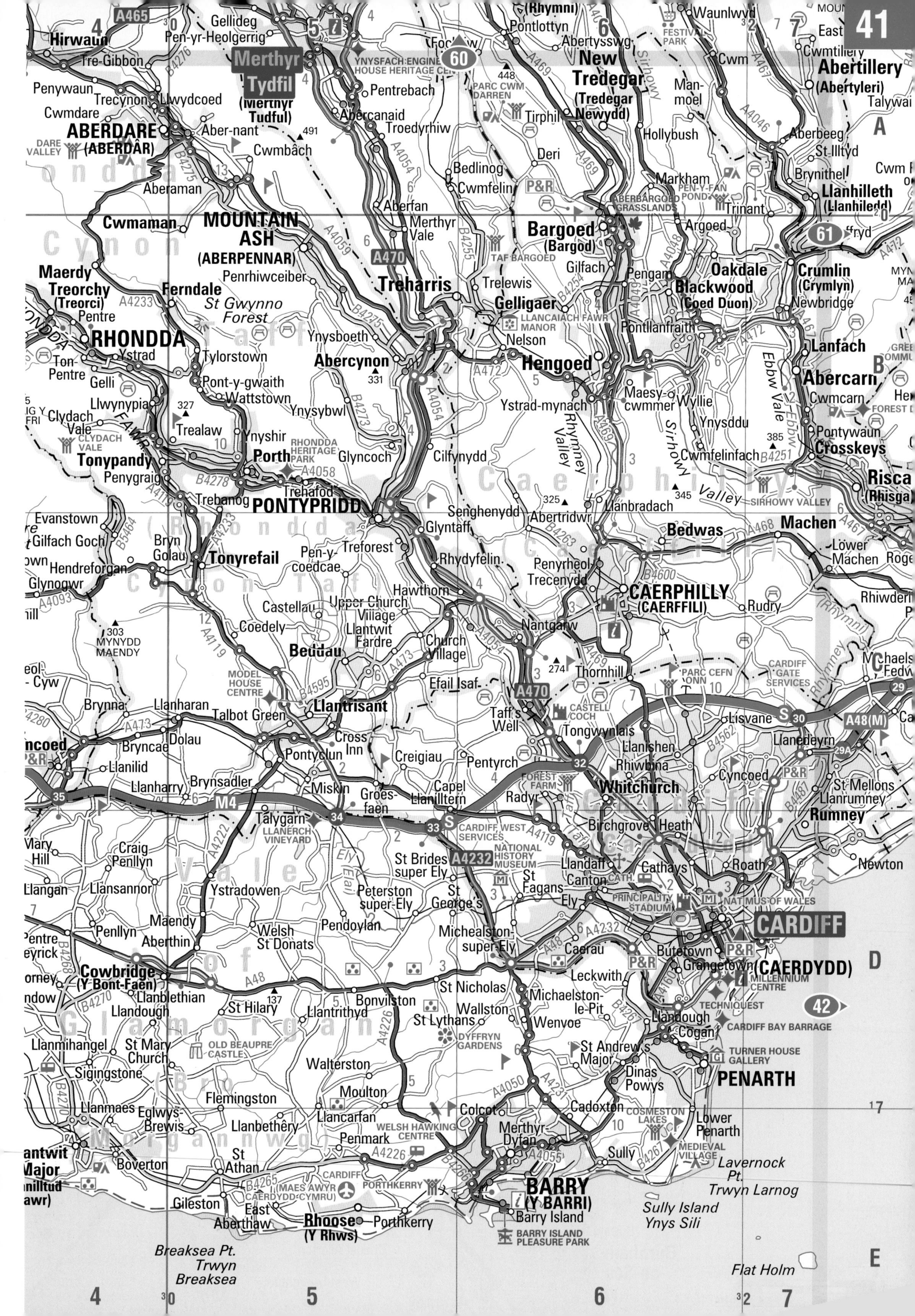

4
A465
Hirwaun
Gellideg
Pen-yr-Heolgerrig
5
Merthyr Tydfil
(Merthyr Tudful)
YNYSFACH ENGINE HOUSE HERITAGE CENTRE
60
(Rhymni)
Pontlottyn
6
Abertysswg
Waunlwyd
FESTIVAL PARK
7
East
Cwmtillery
Abertillery
(Abertyleri)
Talywain
Tre-Gibbon
Penywaun
Trecynon
Llwydcoed
Cwmdare
ABERDARE
(ABERDÂR)
DARE VALLEY
Aber-nant
491
Cwmbâch
Pentrebach
Abercanaid
Troedyrhiw
A4054
448
PARC CWM DARREN
Tirphil
New Tredegar
(Tredegar Newydd)
Man-moel
Hollybush
Cwm
A4046
Aberbeeg
St Illtyd
A
B4275
13
Aberaman
Bedlinog
Cwmfelin
P&R
Deri
A469
Markham
PEN-Y-FAN POND
ABERBARGOED GRASSLANDS
Trinant
Brynithel
Llanhilleth
(Llanhiledd)
Cwm
Cwmaman
MOUNTAIN ASH
(ABERPENNAR)
A4059
Aberfan
Merthyr Vale
Bargoed
(Bargod)
TAF BARGOED
Argoed
A4048
61
A472
Maerdy
Treorchy
(Treorci)
Pentre
A4233
Ferndale
Penrhiwceiber
St Gwynno Forest
A470
Treharris
Trelewis
Gelligaer
Gilfach
B4254
Pengam
A4049
Oakdale
Blackwood
(Coed Duon)
Crumlin
(Crymlyn)
Newbridge
A467
RHONDDA
Ystrad
Ton-Pentre
Gelli
Tylorstown
Ynysboeth
B4275
Abercynon
331
LLANCAIACH FAWR MANOR
Nelson
Hengoed
A472
Pontllanfraith
Ebbw Vale
Lanfach
Abercarn
Cwmcarn
FOREST DRIVE
B
Llwynypia
327
Pont-y-gwaith
Wattstown
Ynysybwl
B4273
A4054
Ystrad-mynach
Maesy-cwmmer
Wyllie
Rhymney Valley
Sirhowy
Ynysddu
385
Pontywaun
Crosskeys
Clydach Vale
CLYDACH VALE
Trealaw
Ynyshir
RHONDDA HERITAGE PARK
Porth
Glyncoch
Cilfynydd
Caerphilly
Cwmfelinfach
B4251
Risca
(Rhisga)
Tonypandy
Penygraig
B4278
A4058
Trehafod
A4119
Trebanog
PONTYPRIDD
Senghenydd
325
Abertridwr
Llanbradach
345
Sirhowy Valley
SIRHOWY VALLEY
Evanstown
Gilfach Goch
B5464
Bryn Golau
A4233
Tonyrefail
Rhondda
Pen-y-coedcae
Treforest
Glyntaff
Rhydyfelin
B4263
Penyrheol
Trecenydd
Bedwas
A468
Machen
Lower Machen
Hendreforgan
Glynogwr
A4093
Cynon Taf
Castellau
Upper Church Village
Llantwit Fardre
Hawthorn
4
CAERPHILLY
(CAERFFILI)
B4600
Rudry
Rhiwderin
Rhymni
303
MYNYDD MAENDY
12
A4119
Coedely
Beddau
A473
Church Village
A4054
Nantgarw
A469
274
Thornhill
Michaelston-y-Fedw
MODEL HOUSE CENTRE
Efail Isaf
A470
PARC CEFN ONN
10
CARDIFF GATE SERVICES
29
Brynna
Llanharan
Talbot Green
B4595
Llantrisant
Taff's Well
CASTELL COCH
Lisvane
30
A48(M)
A473
Dolau
Bryncae
Cross Inn
Tongwynlais
Llanishen
B4562
Llanedeyrn
29A
Pontyclun
Creigiau
Pentyrch
32
Rhiwbina
Cyncoed
P&R
Llanilid
Llanharry
Brynsadler
Miskin
Groes-faen
Capel Llanilltern
FOREST FARM
Radyr
Whitchurch
St Mellons
Llanrumney
B4487
35
M4
Talygarn
LLANERCH VINEYARD
34
33
S
CARDIFF WEST SERVICES
A4119
Birchgrove
Heath
Rumney
A4222
Craig Penllyn
St Brides super Ely
A4232
NATIONAL HISTORY MUSEUM
Llandaff
Cathays
Roath
Newton
Llangan
Llansannor
Ystradowen
Peterston super-Ely
St George's
St Fagans
Canton
CATH.
PRINCIPALITY STADIUM
NAT MUS OF WALES
Ely
Maendy
Penllyn
Welsh St Donats
Pendoylan
Michaelston-super-Ely
A4232
CARDIFF
Aberthin
B4268
Caerau
Butetown
P&R
D
Cowbridge
(Y Bont-Faen)
Llanblethian
A48
3
St Nicholas
Leckwith
Grangetown
(CAERDYDD)
MILLENNIUM CENTRE
B4270
Llandough
137
St Hilary
Bonvilston
Llantrithyd
A4226
Wallston
St Lythans
Michaelston-le-Pit
Wenvoe
TECHNIQUEST
Llandough
Cogan
CARDIFF BAY BARRAGE
42
Llanmihangel
St Mary Church
OLD BEAUPRE CASTLE
DYFFRYN GARDENS
St Andrews Major
TURNER HOUSE GALLERY
PENARTH
Sigingstone
Walterston
Dinas Powys
A4050
A4231
Flemingston
Moulton
Cadoxton
COSMESTON LAKES
Lower Penarth
Llanmaes
Eglwys-Brewis
Llanbethery
Llancarfan
WELSH HAWKING CENTRE
Colcot
Merthyr Dyfan
10
Penmark
A4226
A4055
Sully
B4267
MEDIEVAL VILLAGE
Lavernock Pt.
Trwyn Larnog
Llantwit Major
(Llanilltud Fawr)
Boverton
St Athan
B4265
CARDIFF (MAES AWYR CAERDYDD-CYMRU)
PORTHKERRY
B4266
BARRY
(Y BARRI)
Barry Island
BARRY ISLAND PLEASURE PARK
Sully Island
Ynys Sili
Gileston
East Aberthaw
Rhoose
(Y Rhws)
Porthkerry
Breaksea Pt.
Trwyn Breaksea
Flat Holm
E
Vale of Glamorgan
(Bro Morgannwg)
Cardiff
4
30
5
6
32
7
17

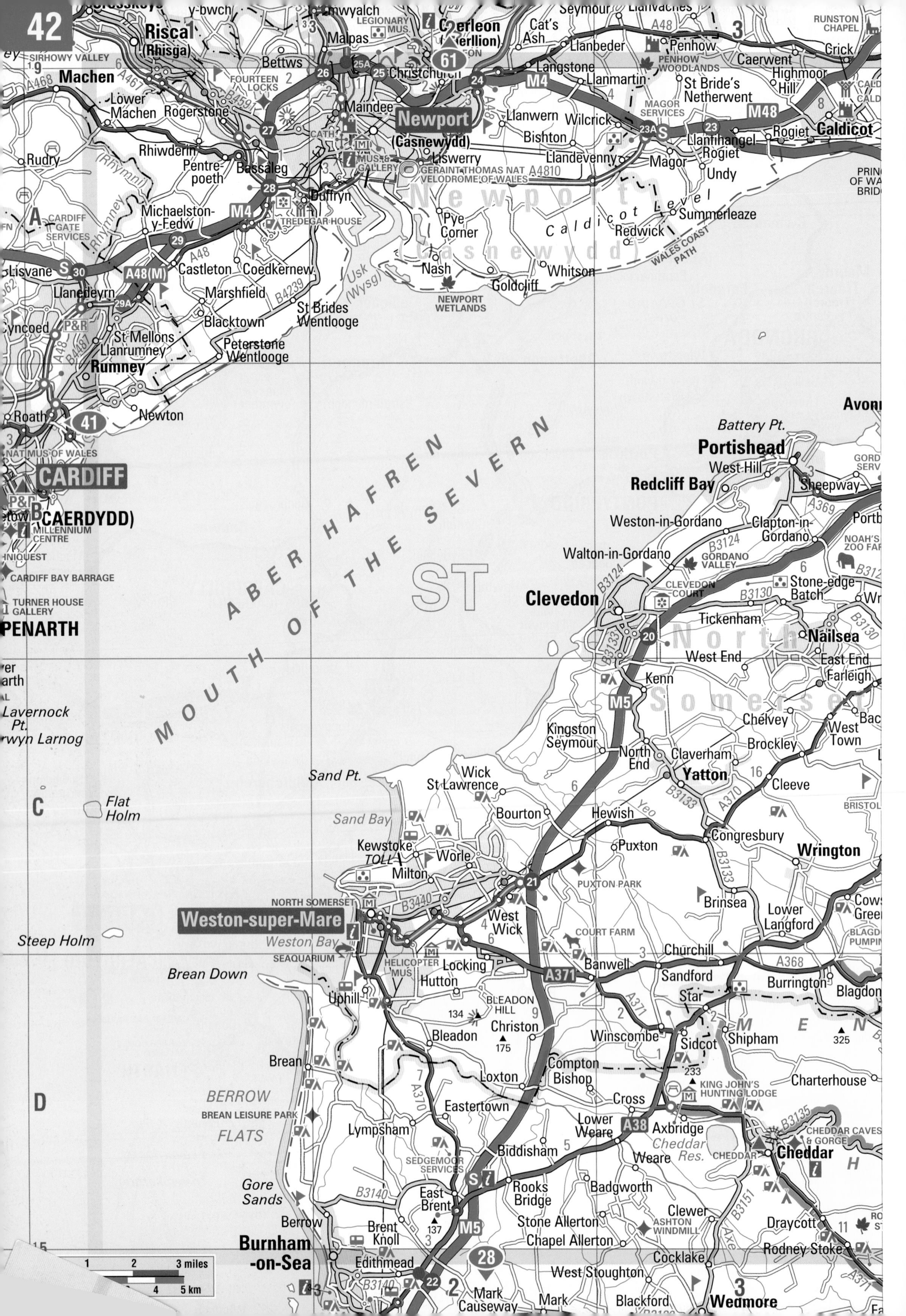
Risca (Rhisga)
SIRHOWY VALLEY
Machen
Lower Machen
Rogerstone
FOURTEEN LOCKS
Bettws
Malpas
LEGIONARY MUS.
Caerleon
61
Cat's Ash
Llanbeder
Penhow
PENHOW WOODLANDS
Caerwent
RUNSTON CHAPEL
Crick
Highmoor Hill
Langstone
Llanmartin
St Bride's Netherwent
MAGOR SERVICES
M4
M48
Caldicot
Christchurch
Maindee
Newport
(Casnewydd)
Llanwern
Wilcrick
Bishton
Llandevenny
Magor
Llanfihangel-Rogiet
Rogiet
Undy
Rudry
Rhiwderin
Pentre-poeth
Bassaleg
Liswerry
MUS & GALLERY
GERAINT THOMAS NAT VELODROME OF WALES
A4810
Duffryn
Michaelston-y-Fedw
CARDIFF GATE SERVICES
TREDEGAR HOUSE
Pye Corner
Newport
Caldicot Level
Summerleaze
Redwick
WALES COAST PATH
(Casnewydd)
Lisvane
A48(M)
Castleton
Coedkernew
Nash
Goldcliff
Whitson
NEWPORT WETLANDS
Usk (Wysg)
Llanedeyrn
Marshfield
B4239
St Brides Wentlooge
Blacktown
St Mellons
Llanrumney
Peterstone Wentlooge
Rumney
Roath
41
Newton
NAT MUS OF WALES
CARDIFF
(CAERDYDD)
MILLENNIUM CENTRE
CARDIFF BAY BARRAGE
TURNER HOUSE GALLERY
PENARTH
Lavernock Pt.
ABER HAFREN
MOUTH OF THE SEVERN
ST
Flat Holm
Steep Holm
Battery Pt.
Portishead
West Hill
Redcliff Bay
Sheepway
Weston-in-Gordano
Clapton-in-Gordano
Walton-in-Gordano
GORDANO VALLEY
NOAH'S ZOO FARM
Clevedon
CLEVEDON COURT
Stone-edge Batch
Tickenham
Nailsea
North Somerset
West End
East End
Farleigh
Kenn
M5
Kingston Seymour
Chelvey
Brockley
West Town
North End
Claverham
Yatton
Cleeve
Sand Pt.
Wick St Lawrence
Bourton
Hewish
Yeo
Congresbury
Sand Bay
Kewstoke
TOLL
Worle
Puxton
Wrington
Milton
PUXTON PARK
21
NORTH SOMERSET MUS
Weston-super-Mare
West Wick
Brinsea
Lower Langford
Weston Bay
SEAQUARIUM
HELICOPTER MUS
Locking
COURT FARM
Churchill
A368
Brean Down
Hutton
A371
Banwell
Sandford
Burrington
Blagdon
Uphill
BLEADON HILL
134
Star
Christon
175
Winscombe
Sidcot
Shipham
325
Bleadon
Brean
Compton Bishop
233
KING JOHN'S HUNTING LODGE
Loxton
Charterhouse
BERROW
BREAN LEISURE PARK
FLATS
Cross
Eastertown
Lower Weare
A38
Axbridge
Cheddar Res.
CHEDDAR CAVES & GORGE
Lympsham
Weare
CHEDDAR
Cheddar
Biddisham
SEDGEMOOR SERVICES
Gore Sands
B3140
East Brent
Rooks Bridge
Badgworth
Clewer
ASHTON WINDMILL
Berrow
Brent Knoll
137
Stone Allerton
Chapel Allerton
Draycott
Rodney Stoke
Burnham-on-Sea
28
Cocklake
Edithmead
West Stoughton
22
Mark Causeway
Mark
Blackford
Wedmore
1 2 3 miles
4 5 km

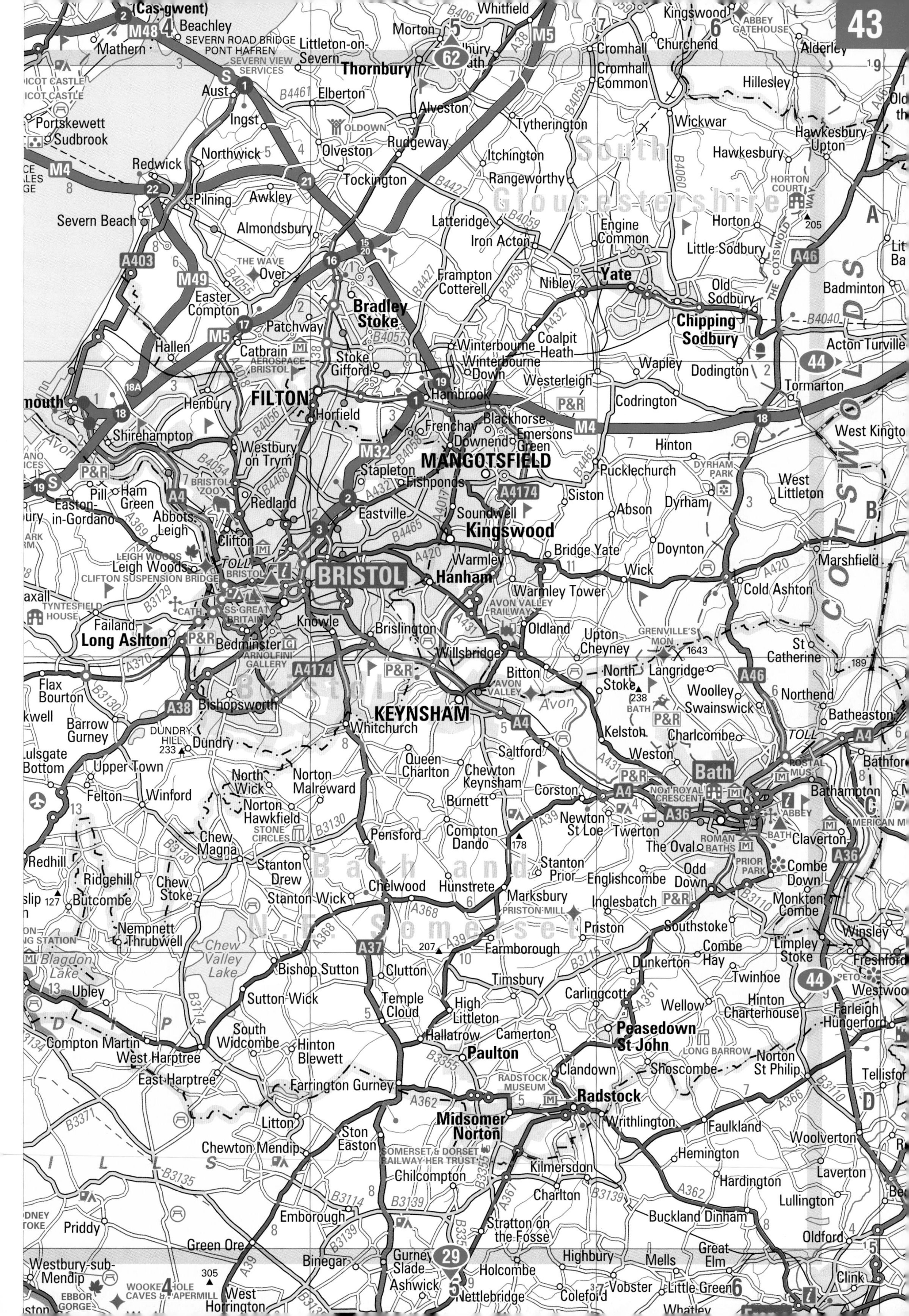
(Cas-gwent)
Beachley
Mathern
SEVERN ROAD BRIDGE
PONT HAFREN
SEVERN VIEW SERVICES
Littleton-on-Severn
Whitfield
Morton
Thornbury
Kingswood
ABBEY GATEHOUSE
Cromhall
Churchend
Alderley
Cromhall Common
Hillesley
Aust
Elberton
Alveston
Ingst
OLDOWN
Tytherington
Wickwar
Hawkesbury Upton
Portskewett
Sudbrook
Redwick
Northwick
Olveston
Rudgeway
Itchington
Hawkesbury
South Gloucestershire
Tockington
Rangeworthy
HORTON COURT
Pilning
Awkley
Severn Beach
Almondsbury
Latteridge
Iron Acton
Engine Common
Horton
Little Sodbury
THE COTSWOLD WAY
THE WAVE
Over
Easter Compton
Frampton Cotterell
Nibley
Yate
Old Sodbury
Chipping Sodbury
Badminton
Bradley Stoke
Patchway
Hallen
Catbrain
AEROSPACE BRISTOL
Stoke Gifford
Winterbourne
Coalpit Heath
Winterbourne Down
Wapley
Dodington
Acton Turville
Tormarton
Henbury
FILTON
Horfield
Hambrook
Westerleigh
Codrington
Shirehampton
Frenchay
Blackhorse
Emersons Green
Downend
Westbury on Trym
Stapleton
MANGOTSFIELD
Pucklechurch
Hinton
DYRHAM PARK
West Kington
West Littleton
Pill
Ham Green
Easton-in-Gordano
Abbots Leigh
BRISTOL ZOO
Redland
Fishponds
Eastville
Soundwell
Siston
Abson
Dyrham
Kingswood
Clifton
LEIGH WOODS
Leigh Woods
CLIFTON SUSPENSION BRIDGE
BRISTOL
Warmley
Hanham
Bridge Yate
Doynton
Wick
Marshfield
Cold Ashton
Warmley Tower
AVON VALLEY RAILWAY
TYNTESFIELD HOUSE
CATH.
SS GREAT BRITAIN
Failand
Long Ashton
Knowle
Brislington
Oldland
Upton Cheyney
GRENVILLE'S MON
Bedminster
ARNOLFINI GALLERY
Willsbridge
Langridge
St Catherine
Flax Bourton
Bitton
North Stoke
AVON VALLEY
Woolley
Swainswick
Northend
Batheaston
Bishopsworth
Bristol
KEYNSHAM
BATH
Avon
Barrow Gurney
DUNDRY HILL
Dundry
Whitchurch
Kelston
Charlcombe
Lulsgate Bottom
Upper Town
Saltford
Weston
Bathford
North Wick
Norton Malreward
Queen Charlton
Chewton Keynsham
Bath
ROYAL CRESCENT
POSTAL MUS.
Felton
Winford
Norton Hawkfield
Burnett
Corston
Bathampton
STONE CIRCLES
Compton Dando
Newton St Loe
Twerton
ABBEY
AMERICAN M
Redhill
Chew Magna
Pensford
The Oval
ROMAN BATHS
Claverton
Ridgehill
Chew Stoke
Stanton Drew
Stanton Prior
Englishcombe
Odd Down
PRIOR PARK
Combe Down
Butcombe
Stanton Wick
Chelwood
Hunstrete
Marksbury
Inglesbatch
Monkton Combe
PRISTON MILL
Bath and N.E. Somerset
Nempnett Thrubwell
Priston
Southstoke
Winsley
Chew Valley Lake
Blagdon Lake
Farmborough
Combe Hay
Limpley Stoke
Freshford
Bishop Sutton
Clutton
Dunkerton
Timsbury
Twinhoe
PETO
Ubley
Sutton Wick
Temple Cloud
High Littleton
Carlingcott
Wellow
Hinton Charterhouse
Westwood
Farleigh Hungerford
South Widcombe
Hallatrow
Camerton
Peasedown St John
Compton Martin
Hinton Blewett
LONG BARROW
West Harptree
Paulton
Clandown
Shoscombe
Norton St Philip
East Harptree
RADSTOCK MUSEUM
Tellisford
Farrington Gurney
Radstock
Midsomer Norton
Writhlington
Faulkland
Litton
Ston Easton
Woolverton
Chewton Mendip
SOMERSET & DORSET RAILWAY HER TRUST
Hemington
Kilmersdon
Chilcompton
Laverton
Charlton
Hardington
Lullington
Emborough
Buckland Dinham
Priddy
Stratton on the Fosse
Oldford
Green Ore
Highbury
Great Elm
Binegar
Gurney Slade
Mells
Westbury-sub-Mendip
Holcombe
Clink
WOOKEY HOLE CAVES & PAPERMILL
EBBOR GORGE
West Horrington
Ashwick
Nettlebridge
Vobster
Coleford
Little Green
Whatley
COTSWOLDS
MENDIP

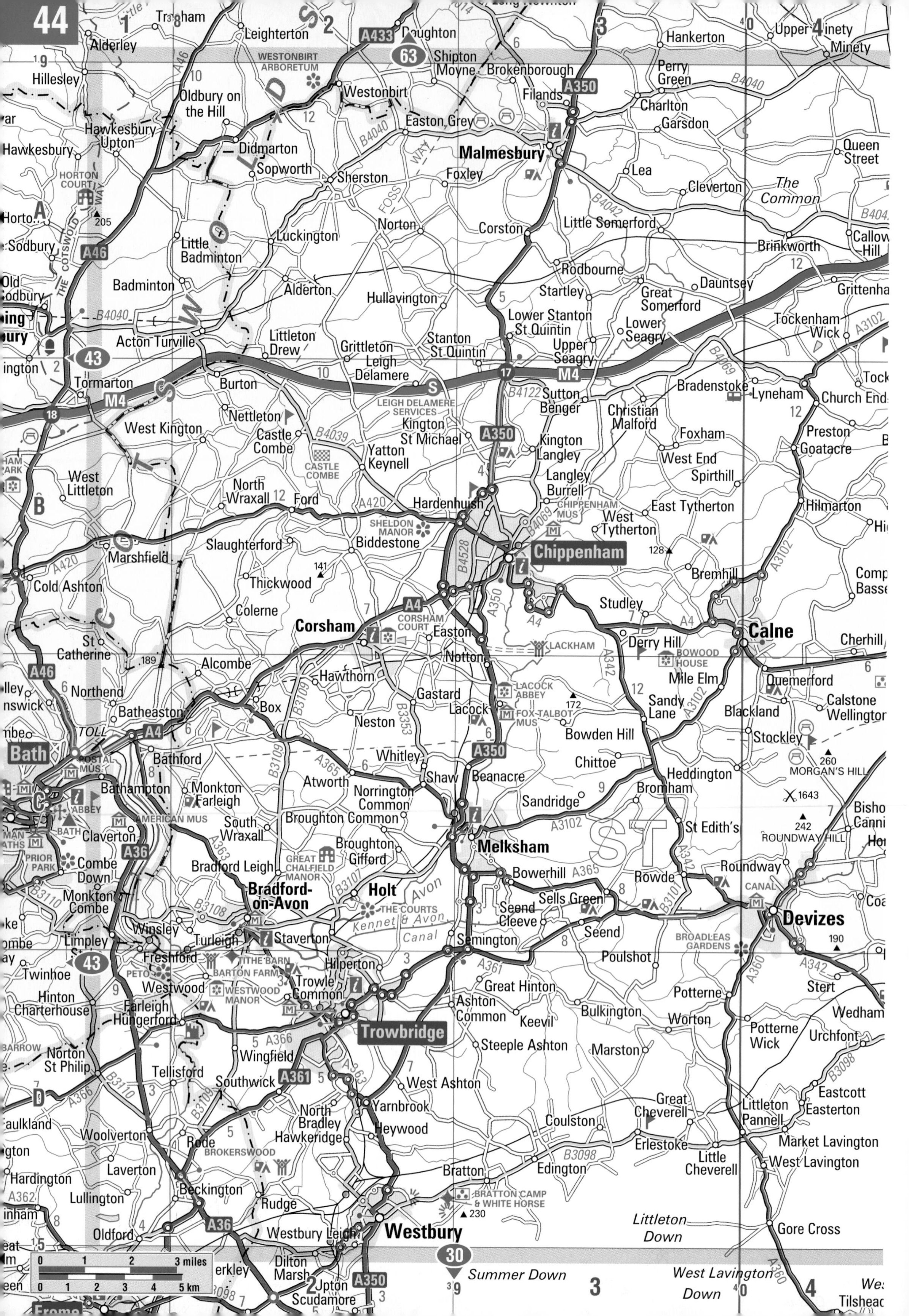
Alderley
Tresham
Leighterton
A433
Doughton
63
Shipton Moyne
Brokenborough
Hankerton
Upper Minety
Minety
Hillesley
WESTONBIRT ARBORETUM
Perry Green
B4040
Filands
A350
Charlton
Oldbury on the Hill
Westonbirt
Hawkesbury Upton
Easton Grey
Garsdon
Hawkesbury
Didmarton
B4040
Malmesbury
Queen Street
Sopworth
Sherston
Foxley
Lea
HORTON COURT
Cleverton
The Common
FOSS WAY
COTSWOLD WAY
205
Norton
Corston
Little Somerford
B4042
Horton
Luckington
Brinkworth
Callow Hill
Sodbury
A46
Little Badminton
Rodbourne
Badminton
Alderton
Dauntsey
Grittenham
Old Sodbury
Hullavington
Startley
Great Somerford
Lower Stanton St Quintin
Tockenham Wick
A3102
B4040
Lower Seagry
Acton Turville
Littleton Drew
Grittleton
Stanton St Quintin
Upper Seagry
B4069
43
Leigh Delamere
M4
Tormarton
Burton
17
Sutton Benger
Bradenstoke
Lyneham
Church End
M4
B4122
18
Nettleton
LEIGH DELAMERE SERVICES
Christian Malford
Kington St Michael
West Kington
Castle Combe
B4039
A350
Kington Langley
Foxham
Preston
Goatacre
Yatton Keynell
CASTLE COMBE
West End
West Littleton
Langley Burrell
Spirthill
North Wraxall
Ford
A420
Hardenhuish
CHIPPENHAM MUS
East Tytherton
Hilmarton
SHELDON MANOR
West Tytherton
Biddestone
Slaughterford
Marshfield
B4528
B4069
Chippenham
A420
128
Bremhill
A3102
Thickwood
141
Cold Ashton
A350
Studley
A4
Colerne
CORSHAM COURT
Corsham
Easton
A4
Calne
Cherhill
St Catherine
LACKHAM
Derry Hill
Notton
BOWOOD HOUSE
189
Alcombe
A46
Hawthorn
A342
Mile Elm
Quemerford
Northend
B3109
Gastard
LACOCK ABBEY
172
Sandy Lane
Calstone Wellington
Batheaston
Box
Lacock
FOX TALBOT MUS
Blackland
A3102
Neston
B3353
Bowden Hill
Stockley
TOLL
A4
A350
Bath
Bathford
POSTAL MUS
A365
Whitley
Chittoe
260
MORGAN'S HILL
Heddington
Shaw
Beanacre
Atworth
Norrington Common
Bathampton
Monkton Farleigh
Bromham
1643
Sandridge
Broughton Common
ABBEY
South Wraxall
AMERICAN MUS
242
ROUNDWAY HILL
A3102
St Edith's
BATH
Claverton
Melksham
Broughton Gifford
A36
A363
GREAT CHALFIELD MANOR
PRIOR PARK
Combe Down
Bradford Leigh
Bowerhill
A365
Roundway
Rowde
Bradford-on-Avon
Holt
Avon
CANAL
B3107
Sells Green
B3101
Monkton Combe
B3110
B3108
THE COURTS
Seend Cleeve
Devizes
Kennet & Avon Canal
Winsley
Seend
Limpley Stoke
Turleigh
Staverton
BROADLEAS GARDENS
190
Semington
43
Freshford
TITHE BARN
Hilperton
Poulshot
A342
BARTON FARM
PETO
A361
Twinhoe
Stert
A360
Westwood
Trowle Common
Great Hinton
WESTWOOD MANOR
Potterne
Hinton Charterhouse
Farleigh Hungerford
Ashton Common
Keevil
Bulkington
Worton
Wedham
Trowbridge
Potterne Wick
Urchfont
A366
Steeple Ashton
Marston
Norton St Philip
Wingfield
B3098
A361
Tellisford
Southwick
West Ashton
B3110
A363
Eastcott
A366
B3109
Yarnbrook
Great Cheverell
Littleton Pannell
Easterton
Faulkland
North Bradley
Woolverton
Heywood
Coulston
Hawkeridge
Rode
Erlestoke
Market Lavington
BROKERSWOOD
B3098
Little Cheverell
West Lavington
Hardington
Laverton
Edington
Bratton
A362
Lullington
Beckington
BRATTON CAMP & WHITE HORSE
Rudge
230
Littleton Down
Gore Cross
A36
Oldford
Westbury Leigh
Westbury
30
0 1 2 3 miles
0 1 2 3 4 5 km
Dilton Marsh
Summer Down
West Lavington Down
A360
A350
Upton Scudamore
Tilshead
Frome

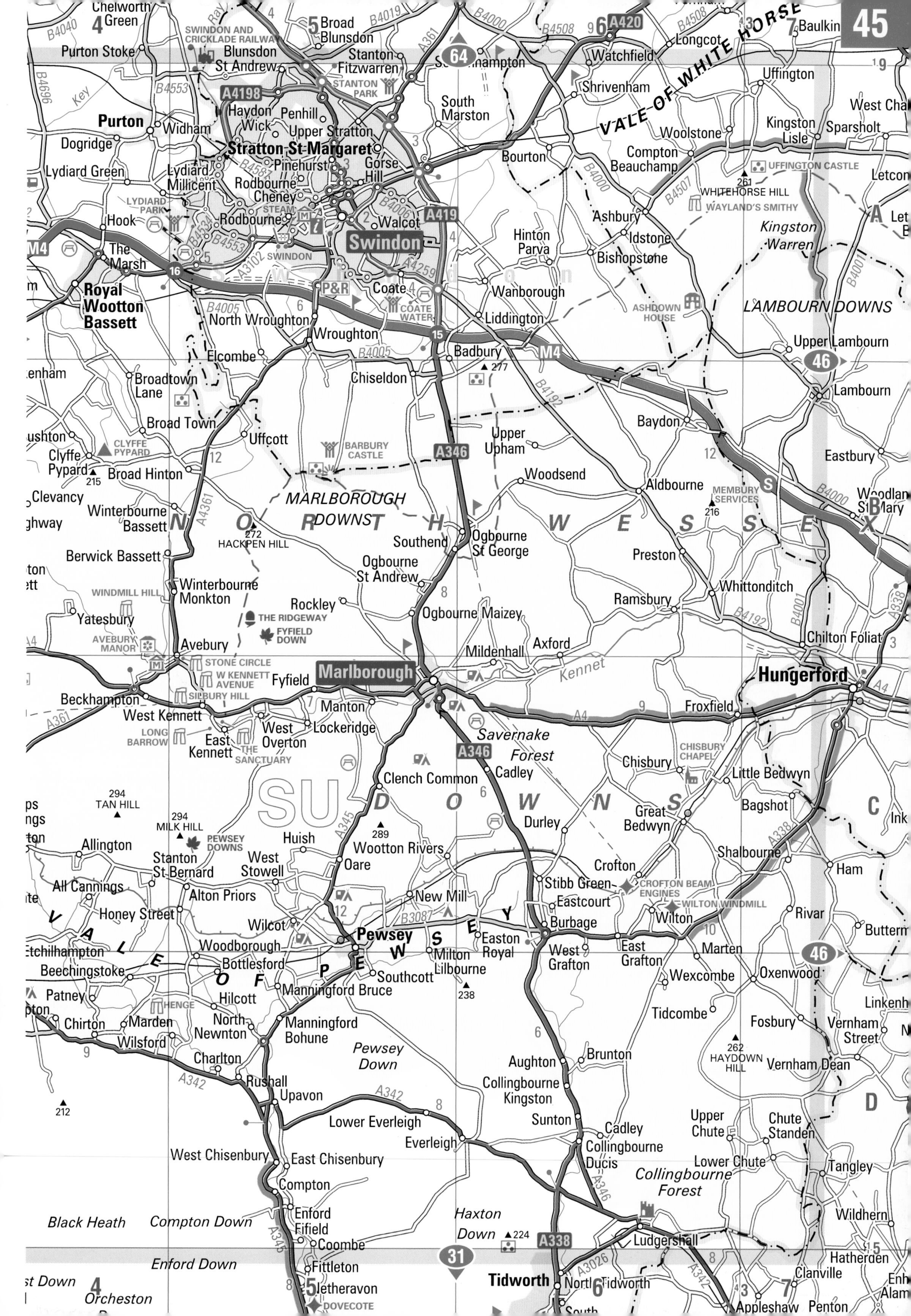

Swindon
Marlborough
Hungerford
Royal Wootton Bassett
Purton
Stratton St Margaret
Pewsey
Tidworth
Ludgershall
VALE OF WHITE HORSE
LAMBOURN DOWNS
MARLBOROUGH DOWNS
NORTH WESSEX DOWNS
Savernake Forest
Pewsey Down
Collingbourne Forest
VALE OF PEWSEY
Kennet
M4
A346
A419
A4
A338
A345
A342
A361
A4361
Avebury
Wroughton
Chiseldon
Aldbourne
Ramsbury
Lambourn
Upper Lambourn
Great Bedwyn
Burbage
Upavon
Ogbourne St George
Ogbourne St Andrew
Uffington
Shrivenham
Highworth
Lydiard Green
Broad Town
Yatesbury
Wilton
Oare
64
46
31

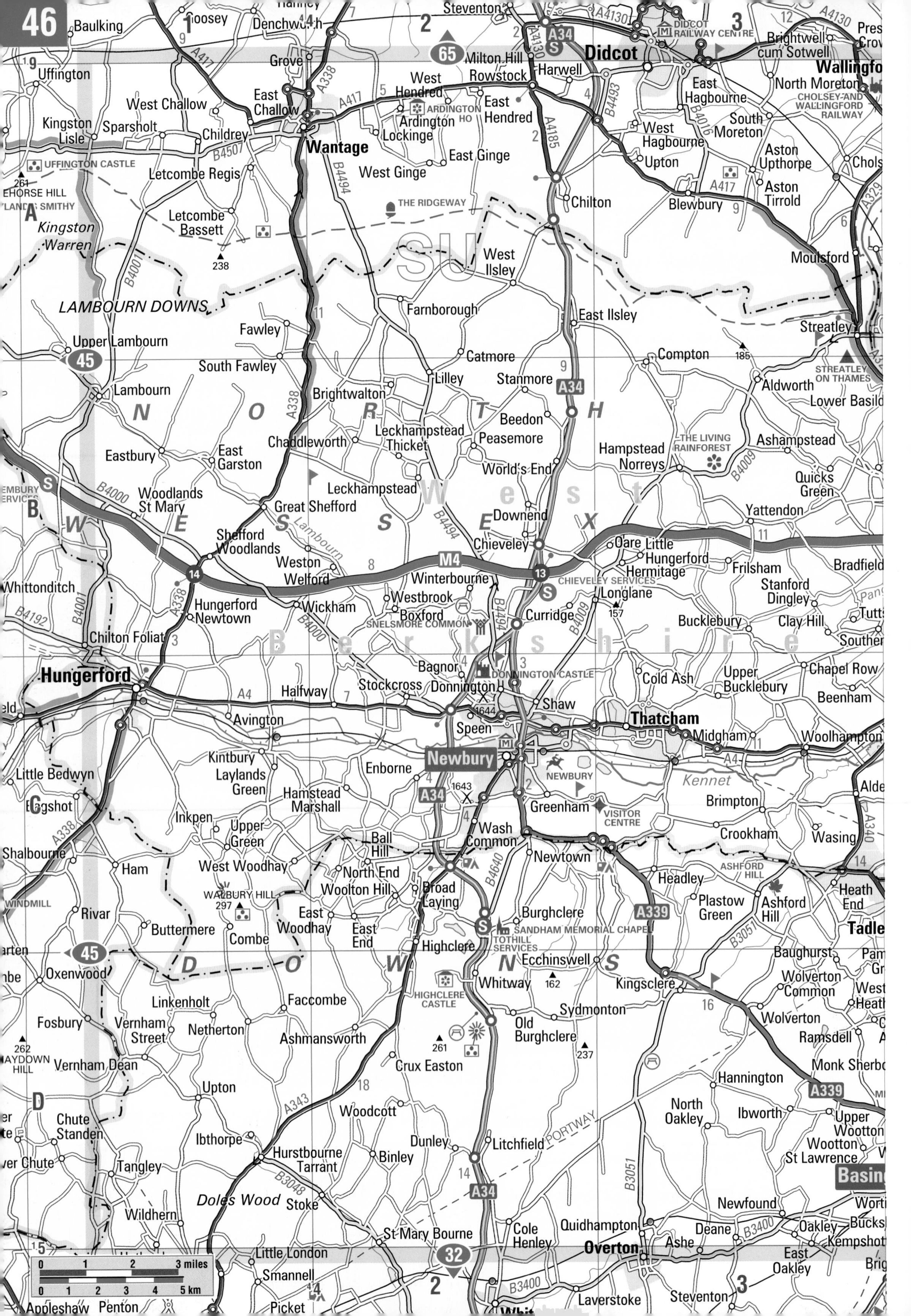

Baulking
Goosey
Denchworth
Steventon
Didcot
DIDCOT RAILWAY CENTRE
Brightwell-cum-Sotwell
Wallingford
Uffington
Grove
Milton Hill
Rowstock
Harwell
North Moreton
CHOLSEY AND WALLINGFORD RAILWAY
West Challow
East Challow
West Hendred
East Hendred
ARDINGTON HO
Ardington
East Hagbourne
South Moreton
Kingston Lisle
Sparsholt
Childrey
Wantage
Lockinge
West Hagbourne
Upton
Aston Upthorpe
Cholsey
UFFINGTON CASTLE
Letcombe Regis
East Ginge
West Ginge
Aston Tirrold
WHITE HORSE HILL
WAYLAND'S SMITHY
THE RIDGEWAY
Chilton
Blewbury
Kingston Warren
Letcombe Bassett
SU
West Ilsley
Moulsford
LAMBOURN DOWNS
Farnborough
East Ilsley
Streatley
Upper Lambourn
Fawley
Catmore
Compton
STREATLEY ON THAMES
South Fawley
Lilley
Stanmore
Aldworth
Lambourn
Brightwalton
Lower Basildon
Beedon
Leckhampstead Thicket
Peasemore
Hampstead Norreys
THE LIVING RAINFOREST
Ashampstead
Chaddleworth
Eastbury
East Garston
World's End
Quicks Green
Leckhampstead
Woodlands St Mary
Great Shefford
Downend
Yattendon
NORTH
WEST
ESSEX
West Berkshire
Shefford Woodlands
Chieveley
Oare
Little Hungerford
Hermitage
Frilsham
Bradfield
Weston
Welford
Lambourn
Winterbourne
CHIEVELEY SERVICES
Stanford Dingley
Whittonditch
Hungerford Newtown
Westbrook
Longlane
Wickham
Boxford
Curridge
Bucklebury
Clay Hill
Tutts Clump
SNELSMORE COMMON
Chilton Foliat
Southend
Bagnor
DONNINGTON CASTLE
Cold Ash
Upper Bucklebury
Chapel Row
Hungerford
Halfway
Stockcross
Donnington
Shaw
Beenham
Avington
Speen
Thatcham
Midgham
Woolhampton
Kintbury
Newbury
Laylands Green
Enborne
NEWBURY
Kennet
Little Bedwyn
Hamstead Marshall
Brimpton
Aldermaston
Froxfield
Bagshot
Inkpen
Upper Green
Greenham
VISITOR CENTRE
Wash Common
Crookham
Wasing
Ball Hill
Shalbourne
Ham
West Woodhay
North End
Newtown
Headley
ASHFORD HILL
Heath End
Woolton Hill
Broad Laying
WALBURY HILL
WINDMILL
Rivar
Buttermere
East Woodhay
Burghclere
Plastow Green
Ashford Hill
East End
SANDHAM MEMORIAL CHAPEL
Tadley
Combe
Highclere
TOTHILL SERVICES
Baughurst
Oxenwood
HAMPSHIRE
DOWNS
Ecchinswell
Kingsclere
Whitway
Wolverton Common
HIGHCLERE CASTLE
Linkenholt
Faccombe
Sydmonton
Wolverton
Fosbury
Vernham Street
Netherton
Old Burghclere
Ramsdell
Ashmansworth
HAYDOWN HILL
Vernham Dean
Crux Easton
Monk Sherborne
Upton
Hannington
North Oakley
Ibworth
Upper Wootton
Woodcott
Chute Standen
Ibthorpe
Dunley
Litchfield
PORTWAY
Wootton St Lawrence
Hurstbourne Tarrant
Binley
Basingstoke
Tangley
Doles Wood
Stoke
Newfound
Wildhern
St Mary Bourne
Cole Henley
Quidhampton
Deane
Ashe
Oakley
Kempshott
Little London
Overton
East Oakley
Smannell
Appleshaw
Penton
Picket
Laverstoke
Steventon
A417
A338
A34
A4130
A4185
B4493
B4016
B4507
B4494
B4001
A329
B4009
B4000
M4
A4
B4192
A340
B4640
A339
B3051
A343
B3048
B3400
65
45
32
3 miles
5 km

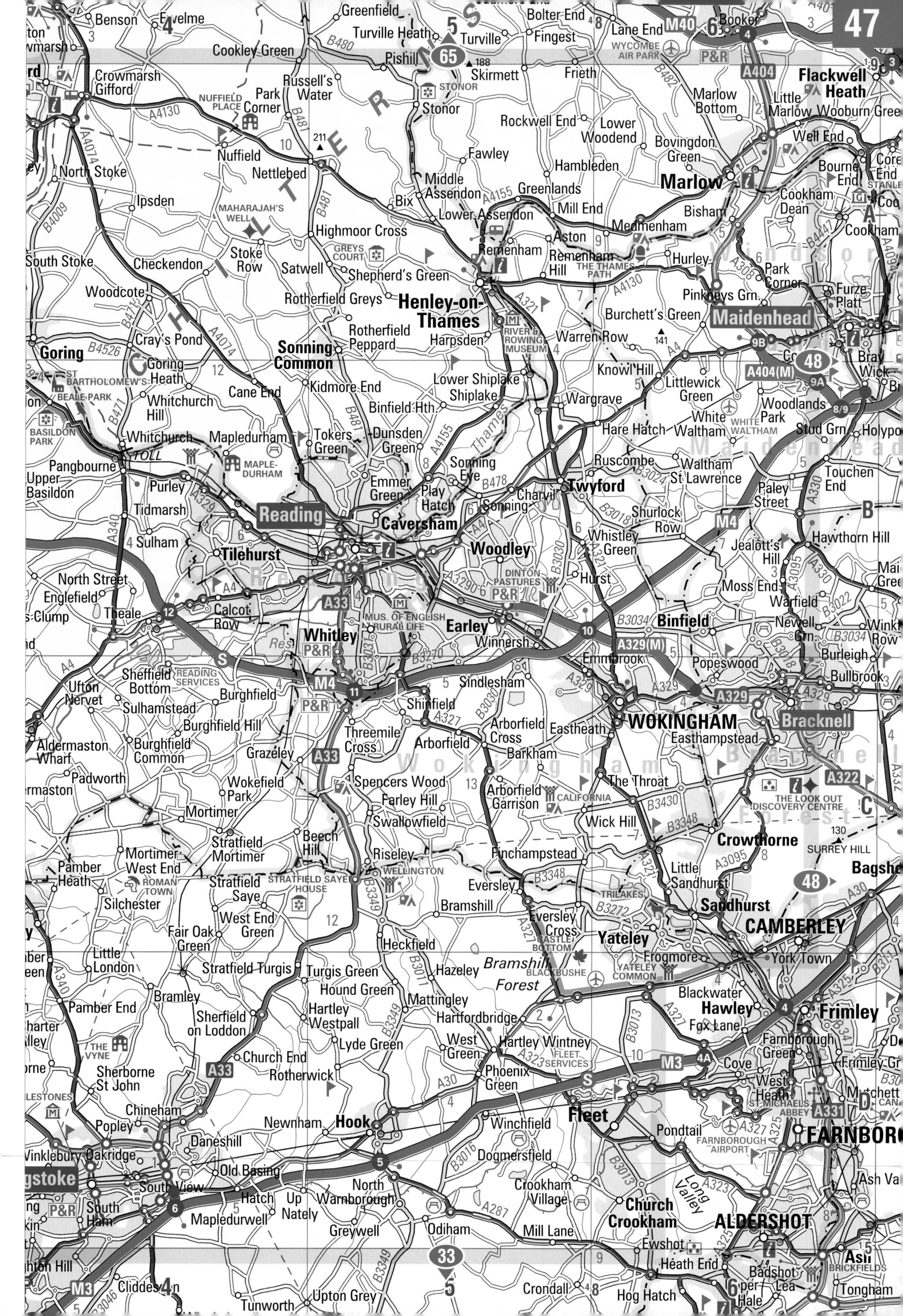
Benson
Ewelme
Greenfield
Turville Heath
Turville
Bolter End
Fingest
Lane End
Booker
WYCOMBE AIR PARK
Cookley Green
Pishill
65
Skirmett
Frieth
Crowmarsh Gifford
Russell's Water
STONOR
Stonor
Flackwell Heath
Little Marlow
Marlow Bottom
Wooburn Green
NUFFIELD PLACE
Park Corner
Rockwell End
Lower Woodend
Bovingdon Green
Well End
Nuffield
Nettlebed
Fawley
Hambleden
Marlow
Bourne End
North Stoke
Middle Assendon
Greenlands
Cookham Dean
Ipsden
Bix
Lower Assendon
Mill End
Bisham
Cookham
MAHARAJAH'S WELL
Highmoor Cross
Aston
Medmenham
South Stoke
Checkendon
Stoke Row
GREYS COURT
Remenham
Remenham Hill
THE THAMES PATH
Hurley
Park Corner
Satwell
Shepherd's Green
Woodcote
Rotherfield Greys
Henley-on-Thames
Pinkneys Grn.
Furze Platt
Burchett's Green
Maidenhead
Goring
Cray's Pond
Rotherfield Peppard
Harpsden
RIVER & ROWING MUSEUM
Warren Row
Sonning Common
Goring Heath
Knowl Hill
Bray Wick
48
BEALE PARK
ST BARTHOLOMEW'S
Cane End
Kidmore End
Lower Shiplake
Shiplake
Littlewick Green
Whitchurch Hill
Binfield Hth.
Wargrave
Woodlands Park
BASILDON PARK
White Waltham
WHITE WALTHAM
Hare Hatch
Stud Grn.
Holyport
Whitchurch
Mapledurham
Tokers Green
Dunsden Green
MAPLE-DURHAM
Ruscombe
Waltham St Lawrence
Pangbourne
Upper Basildon
Purley
Sonning Eye
Emmer Green
Play Hatch
Charvil
Twyford
Touchen End
Paley Street
Tidmarsh
Reading
Sonning
Caversham
Shurlock Row
Sulham
Tilehurst
Woodley
Whistley Green
Hawthorn Hill
Jealott's Hill
North Street
DINTON PASTURES
Hurst
Englefield
Theale
Calcot Row
MUS. OF ENGLISH RURAL LIFE
Earley
Moss End
Warfield
Binfield
Newell Grn.
Winkfield Row
Whitley
Winnersh
Emmbrook
Burleigh
Popeswood
Bullbrook
Sheffield Bottom
READING SERVICES
Ufton Nervet
Burghfield
Sindlesham
Shinfield
Sulhamstead
Burghfield Hill
WOKINGHAM
Bracknell
Arborfield Cross
Eastheath
Aldermaston Wharf
Burghfield Common
Threemile Cross
Arborfield
Easthampstead
Grazeley
Barkham
Padworth
Wokefield Park
Spencers Wood
Arborfield Garrison
CALIFORNIA
The Throat
THE LOOK OUT DISCOVERY CENTRE
Farley Hill
Mortimer
Swallowfield
Wick Hill
Beech Hill
Stratfield Mortimer
Crowthorne
SURREY HILL
Mortimer West End
Riseley
Finchampstead
Pamber Heath
WELLINGTON
ROMAN TOWN
Stratfield Saye
STRATFIELD SAYE HOUSE
Eversley
Little Sandhurst
Silchester
TRILAKES
Sandhurst
Bramshill
West End Green
Eversley Cross
CASTLE BOTTOM
CAMBERLEY
Fair Oak Green
Yateley
Heckfield
Little London
Frogmore
York Town
Stratfield Turgis
Turgis Green
Hazeley
Bramshill Forest
BLACKBUSHE
YATELEY COMMON
Hound Green
Bramley
Blackwater
Mattingley
Pamber End
Hartley Westpall
Hawley
Frimley
Sherfield on Loddon
Hartfordbridge
Fox Lane
THE VYNE
Lyde Green
West Green
Hartley Wintney
Farnborough Green
FLEET SERVICES
Church End
Cove
Frimley Gr
Sherborne St John
Rotherwick
Phoenix Green
West Heath
ST MICHAEL'S ABBEY
Chineham
Fleet
Popley
Newnham
Hook
Winchfield
Pondtail
FARNBOROUGH AIRPORT
FARNBOROUGH
Daneshill
Oakridge
Winklebury
Dogmersfield
Old Basing
South View
North Warnborough
Crookham Village
Long Valley
Ash Vale
Hatch
Up Nately
South Ham
Mapledurwell
Church Crookham
ALDERSHOT
Greywell
Odiham
Mill Lane
Ewshot
Heath End
Ash
33
BRICKFIELDS
Badshot Lea
Cliddesden
Upton Grey
Crondall
Hog Hatch
Tongham
Tunworth
Hale
M40
M4
M3
A404
A404(M)
A4130
A4074
A4155
A321
A329
A329(M)
A33
A327
A323
A30
A340
A322
A331
A4
B480
B481
B482
B4009
B4526
B471
B3030
B3034
B3018
B3024
B3270
B3031
B3349
B3011
B3348
B3430
B3272
B3013
B3016
B3046
A287
A325
A3095
B478
B3022
A308
CHILTERNS
Windsor
Maidenhead
Reading
Wokingham
Bracknell Forest
Thames

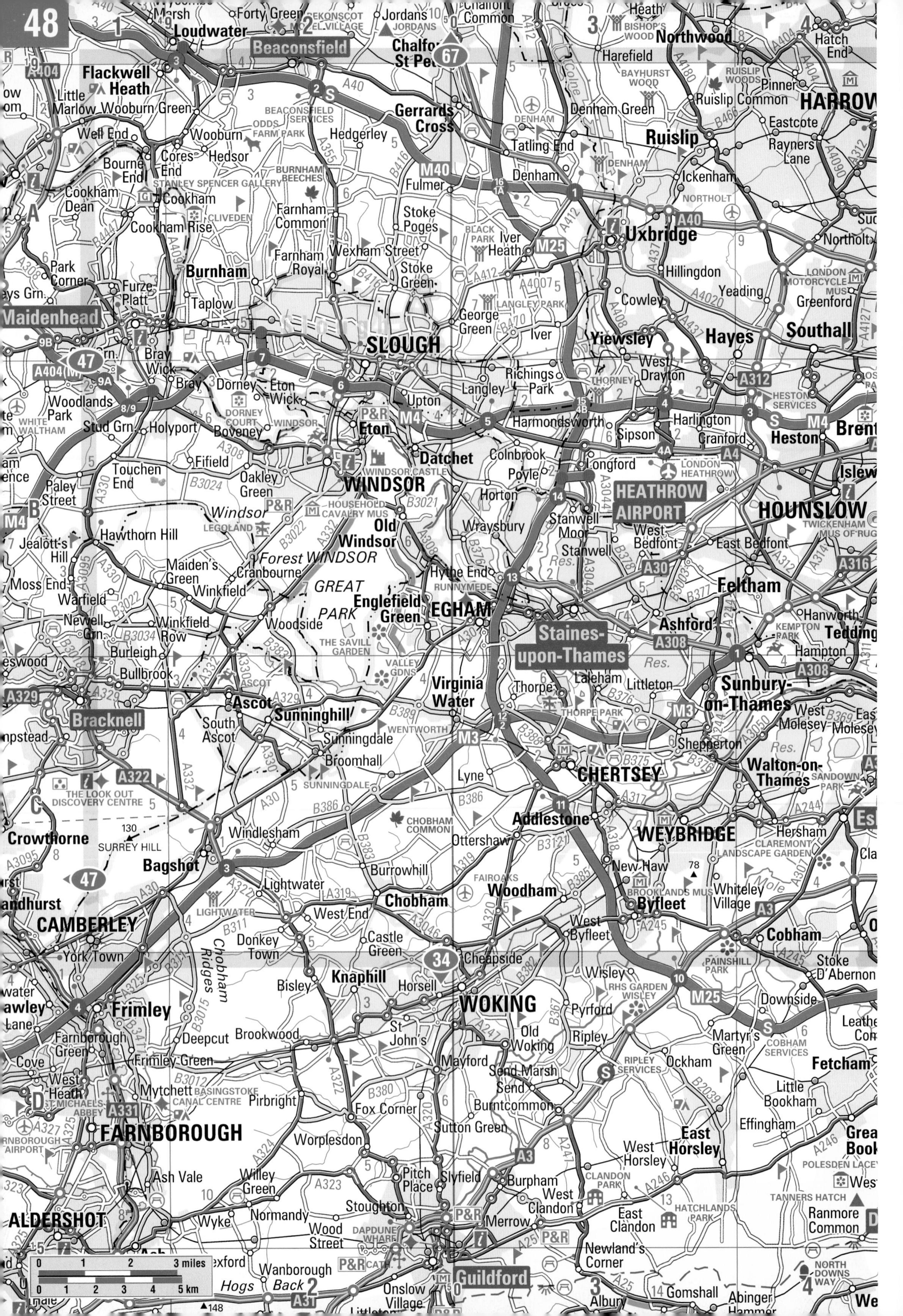
Loudwater
Forty Green
BEKONSCOT MODEL VILLAGE
Jordans
JORDANS
Chalfont Common
Heath
BISHOP'S WOOD
Northwood
Hatch End
Beaconsfield
Chalfont St Peter
67
Harefield
BAYHURST WOOD
RUISLIP WOODS
Pinner
HARROW
Flackwell Heath
Little Marlow
Wooburn Green
BEACONSFIELD SERVICES
ODDS FARM PARK
Gerrards Cross
Hedgerley
Denham Green
Ruislip Common
Eastcote
Rayners Lane
Well End
Wooburn
Cores End
Hedsor
Bourne End
DENHAM
Tatling End
Ruislip
BURNHAM BEECHES
STANLEY SPENCER GALLERY
M40
Fulmer
Denham
Ickenham
Cookham Dean
Cookham
CLIVEDEN
Farnham Common
Stoke Poges
BLACK PARK
Iver Heath
NORTHOLT
A40
Uxbridge
Northolt
Cookham Rise
Farnham Royal
Wexham Street
M25
Park Corner
Burnham
Stoke Green
Hillingdon
LONDON MOTORCYCLE MUS
Furze Platt
Taplow
LANGLEY PARK
Cowley
Yeading
Greenford
Maidenhead
George Green
Iver
Yiewsley
Hayes
Southall
SLOUGH
47
Bray Wick
Richings Park
West Drayton
A404(M)
Bray
Dorney
Eton Wick
Langley
THORNEY
A312
HESTON SERVICES
Woodlands Park
Upton
P&R
M4
Harmondsworth
Harlington
WHITE WALTHAM
Stud Grn.
Holyport
DORNEY COURT
WINDSOR
Eton
Sipson
Cranford
Heston
Brent
Boveney
Datchet
Colnbrook
A4
Fifield
WINDSOR CASTLE
Longford
LONDON HEATHROW
Touchen End
Paley Street
Oakley Green
WINDSOR
Poyle
HEATHROW AIRPORT
HOUNSLOW
Horton
HOUSEHOLD CAVALRY MUS
Windsor
Old Windsor
Stanwell Moor
TWICKENHAM MUS OF RUGBY
Hawthorn Hill
LEGOLAND
Wraysbury
West Bedfont
Jealott's Hill
Forest WINDSOR
Stanwell
East Bedfont
Maiden's Green
Cranbourne
GREAT PARK
Res.
A30
Moss End
Warfield
Winkfield
Hythe End
RUNNYMEDE
Feltham
Englefield Green
EGHAM
Newell Grn.
Winkfield Row
Woodside
Ashford
Hanworth
KEMPTON PARK
Tedding
Staines-upon-Thames
Burleigh
THE SAVILL GARDEN
A308
Hampton
Bullbrook
VALLEY GDNS
Laleham
Littleton
ASCOT
Virginia Water
Thorpe
Sunbury-on-Thames
Bracknell
Ascot
Sunninghill
WENTWORTH
THORPE PARK
M3
West Molesey
East Molesey
South Ascot
Sunningdale
Shepperton
Broomhall
Lyne
CHERTSEY
Walton-on-Thames
SUNNINGDALE
SANDOWN PARK
A322
THE LOOK OUT DISCOVERY CENTRE
CHOBHAM COMMON
Addlestone
Crowthorne
Windlesham
Ottershaw
WEYBRIDGE
Hersham
SURREY HILL
CLAREMONT LANDSCAPE GARDEN
Bagshot
Burrowhill
New Haw
Lightwater
FAIROAKS
Woodham
BROOKLANDS MUS
Whiteley Village
Sandhurst
Chobham
Byfleet
LIGHTWATER
West End
CAMBERLEY
West Byfleet
Cobham
Donkey Town
Castle Green
York Town
Chobham Ridges
34
Cheapside
Stoke D'Abernon
Wisley
PAINSHILL PARK
Bisley
Knaphill
Horsell
RHS GARDEN WISLEY
Frimley
WOKING
Pyrford
Downside
Farnborough Green
Deepcut
Brookwood
St John's
Old Woking
Ripley
Martyr's Green
COBHAM SERVICES
Cove
Frimley Green
Mayford
Send Marsh
RIPLEY SERVICES
Ockham
Fetcham
West Heath
Mytchett
BASINGSTOKE CANAL CENTRE
Send
Little Bookham
ST MICHAEL'S ABBEY
Pirbright
Fox Corner
Burntcommon
A331
FARNBOROUGH
Sutton Green
Effingham
FARNBOROUGH AIRPORT
Worplesdon
East Horsley
West Horsley
A3
Ash Vale
Willey Green
Pitch Place
Slyfield
Burpham
CLANDON PARK
POLESDEN LACEY
West Clandon
HATCHLANDS PARK
TANNERS HATCH
ALDERSHOT
Wyke
Normandy
Stoughton
East Clandon
Ranmore Common
Wood Street
DAPDUNE WHARF
Merrow
Newland's Corner
Wanborough
Hogs Back
Guildford
Onslow Village
NORTH DOWNS WAY
Gomshall
Abinger Hammer
Albury
0 1 2 3 miles
0 1 2 3 4 5 km

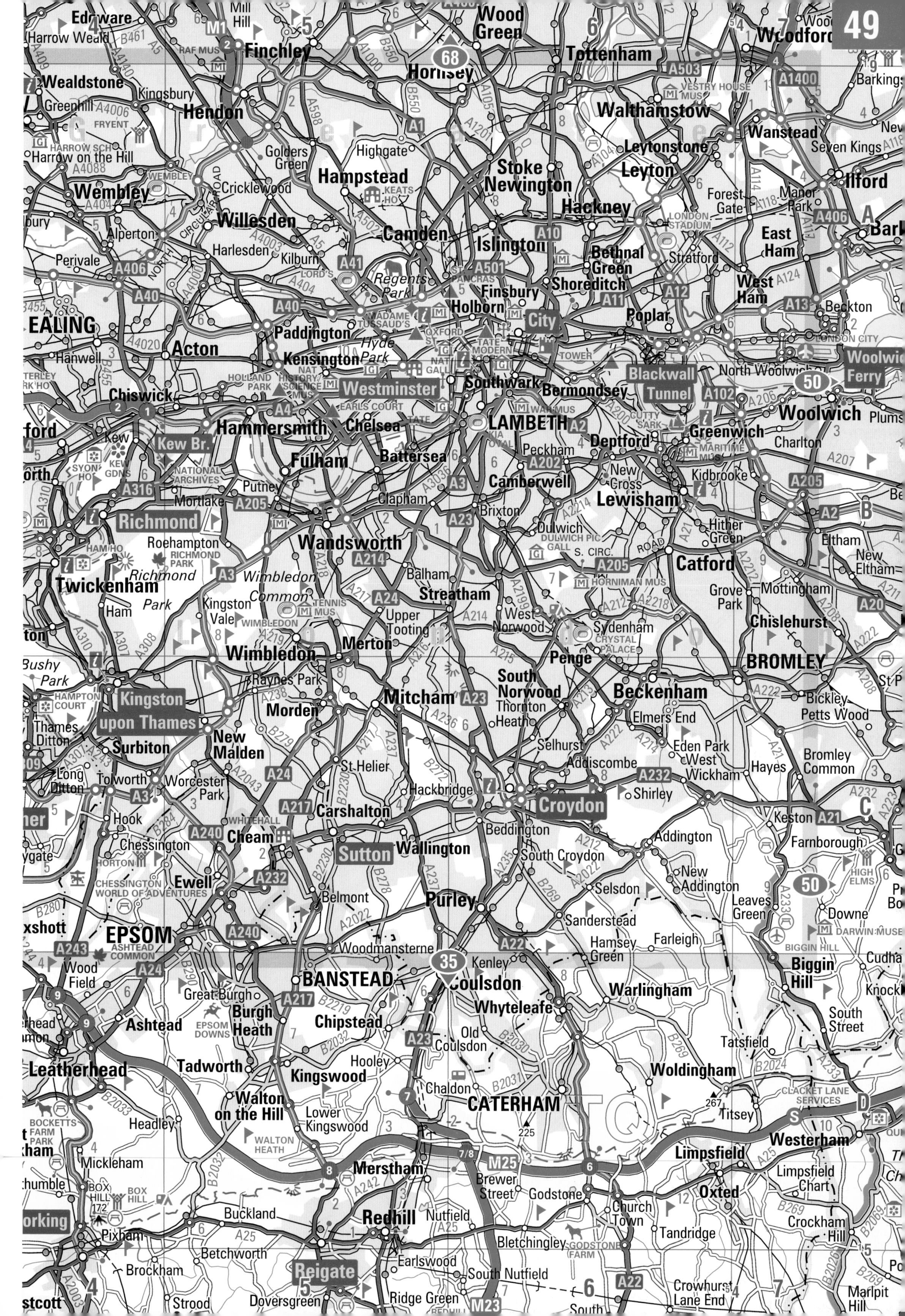
Edgware
Harrow Weald
Mill Hill
Finchley
Wood Green
Tottenham
Woodford
Hornsey
Wealdstone
Kingsbury
Hendon
Walthamstow
Barking
Greenhill
Harrow on the Hill
Golders Green
Highgate
Leytonstone
Wanstead
Seven Kings
Wembley
Cricklewood
Hampstead
Stoke Newington
Leyton
Ilford
Willesden
Hackney
Forest Gate
Manor Park
Alperton
Perivale
Harlesden
Kilburn
Camden
Islington
Bethnal Green
Stratford
East Ham
Regents Park
Shoreditch
Finsbury
West Ham
Holborn
City
Poplar
Beckton
EALING
Acton
Paddington
Hyde Park
Hanwell
Kensington
Westminster
Southwark
Bermondsey
Blackwall Tunnel
North Woolwich
Woolwich Ferry
Chiswick
Hammersmith
Chelsea
LAMBETH
Deptford
Greenwich
Woolwich
Charlton
Kew
Kew Br.
Fulham
Battersea
Peckham
New Cross
Kidbrooke
Camberwell
Putney
Mortlake
Clapham
Brixton
Lewisham
Richmond
Roehampton
Wandsworth
Dulwich
Hither Green
Eltham
New Eltham
Catford
Twickenham
Richmond Park
Wimbledon Common
Balham
Streatham
Grove Park
Mottingham
Ham
Kingston Vale
Upper Tooting
West Norwood
Sydenham
Chislehurst
Wimbledon
Merton
Penge
BROMLEY
Bushy Park
Raynes Park
South Norwood
Beckenham
Kingston upon Thames
Morden
Mitcham
Thornton Heath
Elmers End
Bickley
Petts Wood
Thames Ditton
Surbiton
New Malden
Selhurst
Eden Park
West Wickham
Hayes
Bromley Common
Long Ditton
Tolworth
Worcester Park
St Helier
Addiscombe
Hackbridge
Shirley
Croydon
Carshalton
Hook
Cheam
Beddington
Keston
Addington
Farnborough
Chessington
Sutton
Wallington
South Croydon
New Addington
Ewell
Belmont
Selsdon
Leaves Green
Purley
Sanderstead
Downe
EPSOM
Woodmansterne
Hamsey Green
Farleigh
Biggin Hill
Wood Field
BANSTEAD
Kenley
Coulsdon
Warlingham
Great Burgh
Burgh Heath
Chipstead
Whyteleafe
Ashtead
Old Coulsdon
South Street
Tatsfield
Leatherhead
Tadworth
Kingswood
Hooley
Woldingham
Chaldon
CATERHAM
Titsey
Walton on the Hill
Lower Kingswood
Headley
Westerham
Mickleham
Merstham
Limpsfield
Limpsfield Chart
Brewer Street
Godstone
Oxted
Church Town
Tandridge
Buckland
Redhill
Nutfield
Crockham Hill
Pixham
Betchworth
Bletchingley
Brockham
Reigate
Earlswood
South Nutfield
Crowhurst Lane End
Strood
Doversgreen
Ridge Green
Marlpit Hill
M1
M25
M23
A406
A40
A4
A3
A23
A24
A22
A21
A20
A2
A13
A12
A11
A10
A1
A41
A501
A205
A214
A217
A232
A240
A243
68
50
35

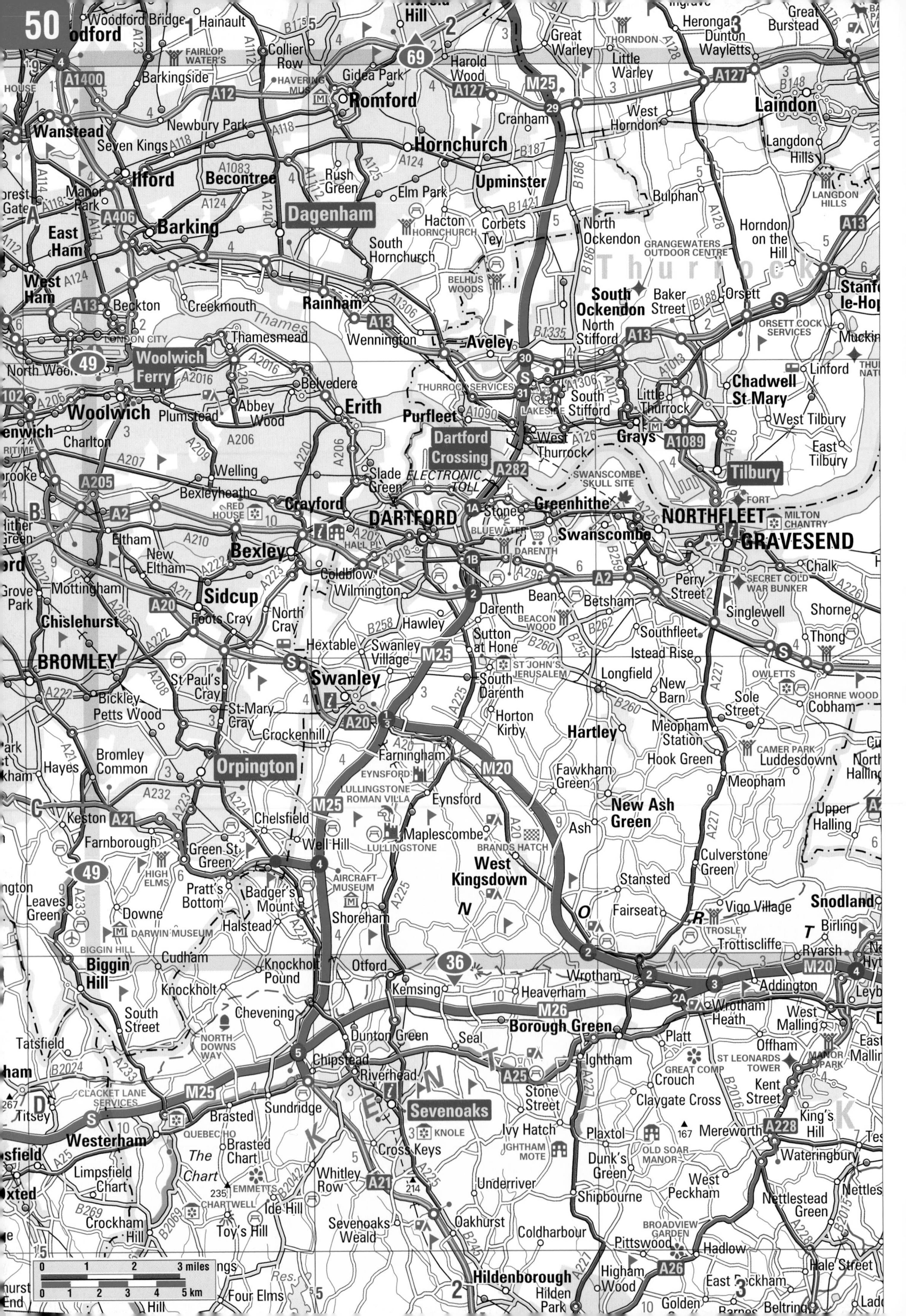
Woodford Bridge
Hainault
Woodford
FAIRLOP WATER'S
Collier Row
Harold Hill
Harold Wood
Gidea Park
HAVERING MUS
Romford
Great Warley
THORNDON
Little Warley
Herongate
Dunton Wayletts
Great Burstead
Barkingside
Newbury Park
Seven Kings
Wanstead
Ilford
Becontree
Rush Green
Dagenham
Hornchurch
Elm Park
Cranham
Upminster
West Horndon
Laindon
Langdon Hills
LANGDON HILLS
Forest Gate
Manor Park
Barking
East Ham
West Ham
Beckton
Creekmouth
Rainham
Hacton
HORNCHURCH
South Hornchurch
Corbets Tey
North Ockendon
GRANGEWATERS OUTDOOR CENTRE
Bulphan
Horndon on the Hill
Thurrock
BELHUS WOODS
South Ockendon
Baker Street
Orsett
Stanford-le-Hope
North Stifford
Wennington
Aveley
LONDON CITY
Thames
Thamesmead
Woolwich Ferry
North Woolwich
Woolwich
Plumstead
Abbey Wood
Belvedere
Erith
Purfleet
THURROCK SERVICES
LAKESIDE
South Stifford
Little Thurrock
Grays
ORSETT COCK SERVICES
Mucking
Linford
Chadwell St Mary
West Tilbury
East Tilbury
Tilbury
Greenwich
Charlton
Welling
Bexleyheath
Slade Green
ELECTRONIC TOLL
Dartford Crossing
West Thurrock
SWANSCOMBE SKULL SITE
FORT
RED HOUSE
Crayford
DARTFORD
Stone
Greenhithe
BLUEWATER
Swanscombe
NORTHFLEET
MILTON CHANTRY
GRAVESEND
Hither Green
Eltham
New Eltham
Bexley
HALL PL
Coldblow
Wilmington
DARENTH
Chalk
Grove Park
Mottingham
Sidcup
Foots Cray
North Cray
Bean
Betsham
Perry Street
SECRET COLD WAR BUNKER
Shorne
Singlewell
Chislehurst
Hawley
Darenth
BEACON WOOD
Sutton at Hone
Southfleet
Thong
Istead Rise
BROMLEY
Hextable
Swanley Village
Swanley
ST JOHN'S JERUSALEM
South Darenth
Longfield
New Barn
OWLETTS
SHORNE WOOD
St Paul's Cray
Bickley
Petts Wood
St Mary Cray
Crockenhill
Horton Kirby
Hartley
Sole Street
Cobham
Meopham Station
CAMER PARK
Luddesdown
Hayes
Bromley Common
Orpington
Farningham
EYNSFORD
LULLINGSTONE ROMAN VILLA
Eynsford
Fawkham Green
Hook Green
Meopham
North Halling
Keston
Chelsfield
Maplescombe
New Ash Green
Ash
Upper Halling
Farnborough
Well Hill
LULLINGSTONE
BRANDS HATCH
HIGH ELMS
Green St Green
AIRCRAFT MUSEUM
West Kingsdown
Culverstone Green
Stansted
Pratt's Bottom
Badger's Mount
Shoreham
Fairseat
Vigo Village
Snodland
Leaves Green
Downe
DARWIN MUSEUM
Halstead
TROSLEY
Trottiscliffe
Birling
BIGGIN HILL
Ryarsh
Biggin Hill
Cudham
Knockholt Pound
Otford
Kemsing
Wrotham
Heaverham
Addington
Knockholt
South Street
Chevening
Borough Green
Wrotham Heath
West Malling
Tatsfield
NORTH DOWNS WAY
Dunton Green
Seal
Platt
Offham
East Malling
Chipstead
Riverhead
Ightham
GREAT COMP
Crouch
ST LEONARDS TOWER
MANOR PARK
CLACKET LANE SERVICES
Titsey
Sundridge
Brasted
Sevenoaks
Stone Street
Claygate Cross
Kent Street
KENT
Westerham
QUEBEC HO
KNOLE
Ivy Hatch
Plaxtol
Mereworth
King's Hill
Limpsfield
Brasted Chart
The Chart
Cross Keys
IGHTHAM MOTE
OLD SOAR MANOR
Wateringbury
Limpsfield Chart
EMMETTS
Whitley Row
Dunk's Green
West Peckham
Oxted
CHARTWELL
Ide Hill
Underriver
Shipbourne
Nettlestead Green
Crockham Hill
Toy's Hill
Sevenoaks Weald
Oakhurst
Coldharbour
BROADVIEW GARDEN
Pittswood
Hadlow
Hale Street
Higham Wood
Hildenborough
East Peckham
Four Elms
Hilden Park
Golden Green
Beltring
0 1 2 3 miles
0 1 2 3 4 5 km
M25
M20
M26
A2
A20
A13
A12
A127
A21
A25
A26
A282
A1089
A205
A228
A406
A1400
69
49
36
N
O
R
T

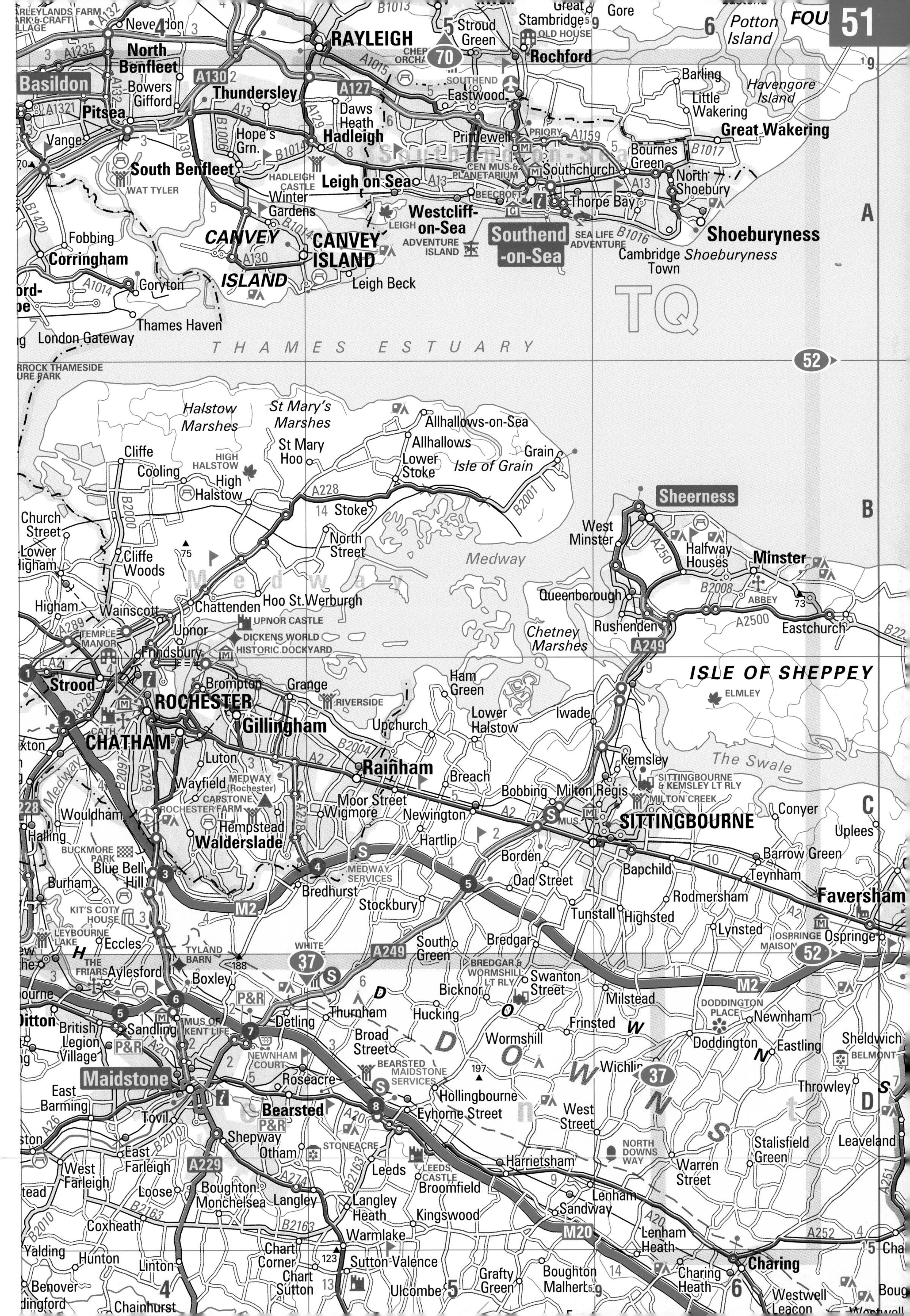

RAYLEIGH
Stroud Green
Stambridge
Gore
Potton Island
Rochford
Neveudon
North Benfleet
Basildon
Bowers Gifford
Pitsea
Thundersley
Vange
Hope's Grn.
Hadleigh
Daws Heath
Eastwood
Prittlewell
Barling
Little Wakering
Havengore Island
Great Wakering
Bournes Green
North Shoebury
South Benfleet
WAT TYLER
HADLEIGH CASTLE
Leigh on Sea
Winter Gardens
Southchurch
Thorpe Bay
Fobbing
Corringham
CANVEY ISLAND
Westcliff-on-Sea
Southend-on-Sea
SEA LIFE ADVENTURE
ADVENTURE ISLAND
Shoeburyness
Cambridge Town
Goryton
Leigh Beck
Thames Haven
London Gateway
TQ
THAMES ESTUARY
Halstow Marshes
St Mary's Marshes
Allhallows-on-Sea
Allhallows
St Mary Hoo
Lower Stoke
Isle of Grain
Grain
Cliffe
Cooling
HIGH HALSTOW
High Halstow
Stoke
Sheerness
Church Street
Lower Higham
Cliffe Woods
North Street
Medway
West Minster
Halfway Houses
Minster
Higham
Wainscott
Chattenden
Hoo St.Werburgh
Queenborough
ABBEY
UPNOR CASTLE
Upnor
DICKENS WORLD
HISTORIC DOCKYARD
TEMPLE MANOR
Frindsbury
Rushenden
Eastchurch
Chetney Marshes
Strood
Brompton
Grange
Ham Green
ISLE OF SHEPPEY
ELMLEY
ROCHESTER
RIVERSIDE
Gillingham
Lower Halstow
Iwade
CHATHAM
Upchurch
Luton
Kemsley
The Swale
Rainham
Breach
SITTINGBOURNE & KEMSLEY LT RLY
MILTON CREEK
Wayfield
MEDWAY (Rochester)
CAPSTONE
ROCHESTER FARM
Bobbing
Milton Regis
Moor Street
Wigmore
Newington
Conyer
Wouldham
Hempstead
SITTINGBOURNE
Uplees
Halling
Walderslade
Hartlip
Borden
Barrow Green
BUCKMORE PARK
Blue Bell Hill
MEDWAY SERVICES
Bapchild
Teynham
Burham
Bredhurst
Oad Street
KIT'S COTY HOUSE
Stockbury
Tunstall
Highsted
Rodmersham
Faversham
LEYBOURNE LAKE
Eccles
South Green
Bredgar
Lynsted
OSPRINGE MAISON
Ospringe
THE FRIARS
Aylesford
TYLAND BARN
WHITE
BREDGAR & WORMSHILL LT RLY
Swanton Street
Boxley
Bicknor
Milstead
DODDINGTON PLACE
Newnham
Ditton
British Legion Village
Sandling
MUS OF KENT LIFE
Detling
Thurnham
Hucking
Frinsted
Doddington
Sheldwich
Eastling
BELMONT
Maidstone
NEWNHAM COURT
Broad Street
Wormshill
BEARSTED MAIDSTONE SERVICES
Wichling
East Barming
Roseacre
Hollingbourne
Throwley
Tovil
Bearsted
Eyhorne Street
West Street
NORTH DOWNS WAY
Stalisfield Green
Leaveland
Shepway
East Farleigh
Otham
STONEACRE
Harrietsham
Warren Street
West Farleigh
Leeds
LEEDS CASTLE
Broomfield
Lenham
Loose
Boughton Monchelsea
Langley
Langley Heath
Kingswood
Sandway
Coxheath
Warmlake
Lenham Heath
Yalding
Hunton
Chart Corner
Linton
Sutton Valence
Charing
Grafty Green
Boughton Malherbe
Charing Heath
Benover
Chart Sutton
Ulcombe
Westwell Leacon
Chainhurst

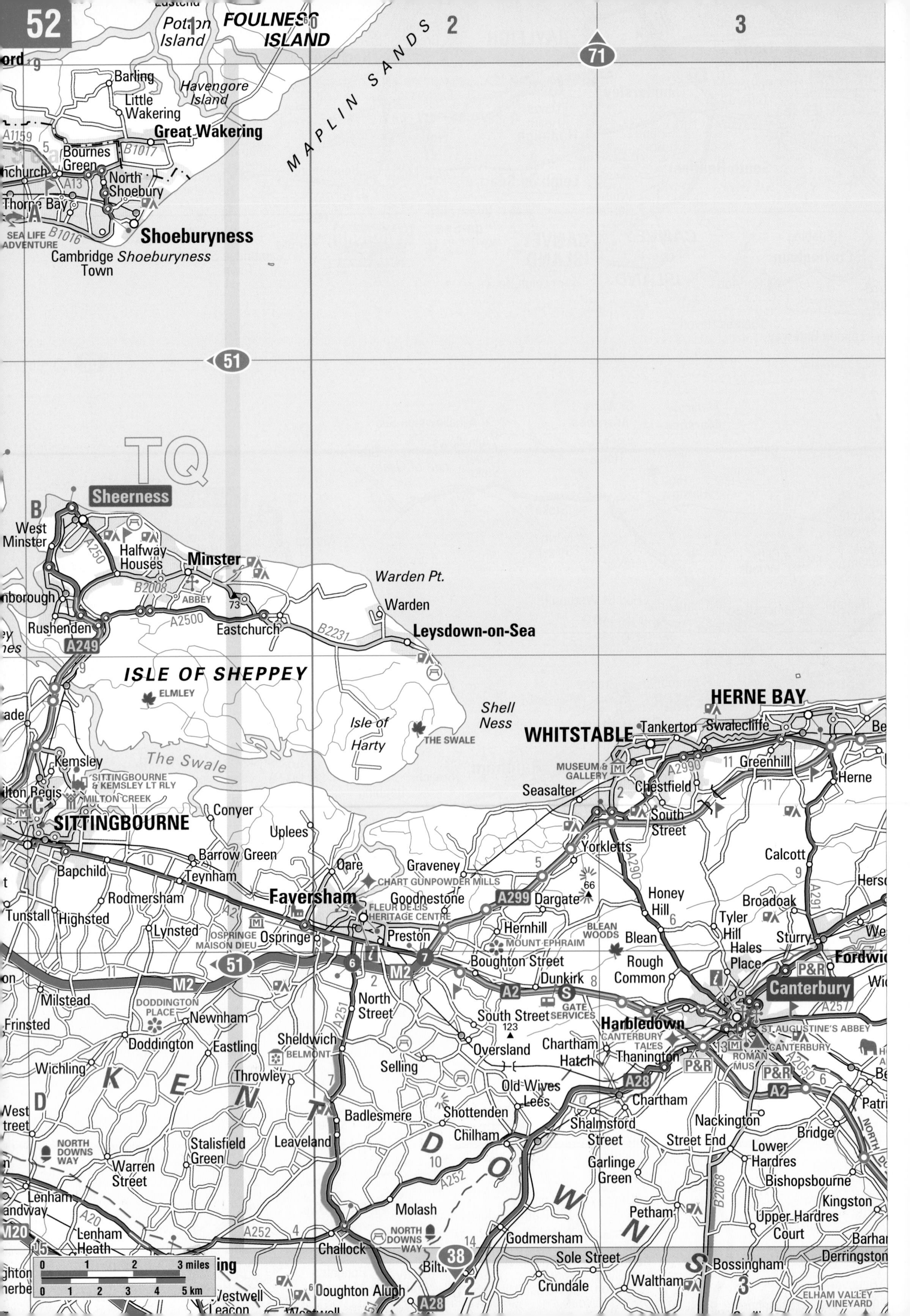

FOULNESS ISLAND

Potton Island

MAPLIN SANDS

71

Barling
Little Wakering
Great Wakering
Havengore Island

A1159

Bournes Green
B1017
North Shoebury
A13
Thorpe Bay

Shoeburyness

SEA LIFE ADVENTURE
B1016

Cambridge *Shoeburyness* Town

51

TQ

Sheerness

West Minster

A250

Halfway Houses
Minster
Warden Pt.

nborough
B2008
ABBEY
73
Warden

Rushenden
A2500
Eastchurch
B2231
Leysdown-on-Sea

A249

ISLE OF SHEPPEY

ELMLEY

Isle of Harty

Shell Ness

THE SWALE

The Swale

Kemsley
SITTINGBOURNE & KEMSLEY LT RLY
MILTON CREEK
lton Regis

HERNE BAY

Tankerton
Swalecliffe
Be

WHITSTABLE
MUSEUM & GALLERY
11 Greenhill
Herne

Seasalter
Chestfield

C

SITTINGBOURNE

Conyer
Uplees
Barrow Green
Teynham
Bapchild
Rodmersham
Tunstall Highsted
Lynsted
Ospringe

A2
MAISON DIEU

Faversham
FLEUR DE LIS HERITAGE CENTRE
Preston
Goodnestone
CHART GUNPOWDER MILLS
Oare
Graveney
A299
Dargate
66

Yorkletts
A290
South Street
Calcott
9

Honey Hill
6
Broadoak
Tyler Hill
A291
Herso
Sturry

Hernhill
MOUNT EPHRAIM
BLEAN WOODS
Blean
Rough Common
Hales Place
Fordwi

51
M2
7
M2
Boughton Street
Dunkirk
8
A2

Canterbury
A257

i
P&R

DODDINGTON PLACE
Newnham
North Street
A251
2
South Street
123
S
GATE SERVICES

Milstead
Frinsted
Doddington
Eastling
Sheldwich
BELMONT
Selling
Oversland
Chartham Hatch
CANTERBURY TALES
Thanington
ROMAN MUS
i
M
CANTERBURY
P&R
ST. AUGUSTINE'S ABBEY
A2050
Be
Wichling
Throwley
7
Old Wives Lees
A28
Chartham
A2
6
Patri

D
K
Stalisfield Green
Leaveland
Badlesmere
Shottenden
Chilham
Shalmsford Street
Street End
Nackington
Bridge
Lower Hardres
Bishopsbourne

NORTH DOWNS WAY
Warren Street
E
N
Garlinge Green
B2068
Kingston
Upper Hardres Court

West treet
A20
Lenham Heath
A252
4
Molash
NORTH DOWNS WAY
Challock
Bilti
38
Godmersham
Sole Street
Petham
Crundale
Waltham
Bossingham
Derrington

M20
 J5

0   1   2   3 miles
0 1 2 3 4 5 km

ng

A252
Westwell
eacon
oughton Aluph
A28
2
3

ELHAM VALLEY VINEYARD

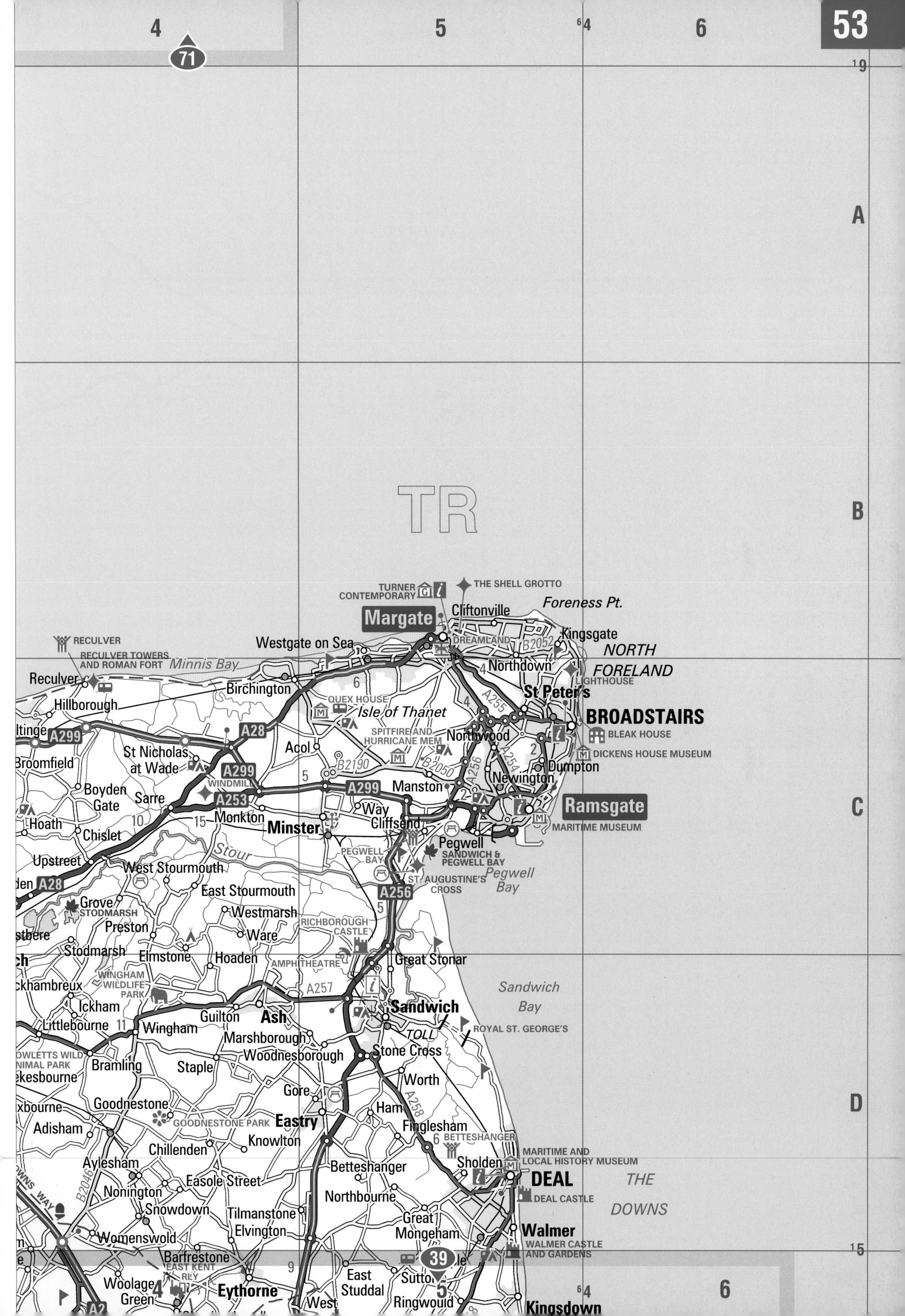

A

B

TR

TURNER
CONTEMPORARY   THE SHELL GROTTO

Foreness Pt.

Margate   Cliftonville

Kingsgate

Westgate on Sea   DREAMLAND   B2052   **NORTH**

RECULVER   Minnis Bay   Northdown   **FORELAND**

RECULVER TOWERS
AND ROMAN FORT   Birchington   A255   LIGHTHOUSE

Reculver   QUEX HOUSE   **St Peter's**

Hillborough   Isle of Thanet   **BROADSTAIRS**

ltinge   **A299**   **A28**   SPITFIRE AND   Northwood   BLEAK HOUSE

Broomfield   Acol   HURRICANE MEM   A256   A254   DICKENS HOUSE MUSEUM

St Nicholas   B2190   B2050   2   Dumpton

at Wade   **A299**   Manston   Newington

Boyden   **A253**   Way   **Ramsgate**   C

Gate   Sarre   10   15   Monkton   Cliffsend   MARITIME MUSEUM

Hoath   **Minster**   PEGWELL   Pegwell

Chislet   Stour   BAY   SANDWICH &
PEGWELL BAY

Upstreet   **A28**   West Stourmouth   ST. AUGUSTINE'S   Pegwell

den   Grove   East Stourmouth   CROSS   Bay

STODMARSH   Westmarsh   **A256**

stbere   Preston   Ware   5

Stodmarsh   RICHBOROUGH
CASTLE

ckhambreux   Elmstone   Hoaden   AMPHITHEATRE   Great Stonar   Sandwich

WINGHAM   A257   Bay

WILDLIFE
PARK

Ickham   Guilton   **Sandwich**

Littlebourne   11   Wingham   **Ash**   ROYAL ST. GEORGE'S

kesbourne   Marshborough   TOLL

OWLETTS WILD   Bramling   Woodnesborough   Stone Cross

ANIMAL PARK   Staple

ekesbourne   Gore   Worth

xbourne   Goodnestone   Ham   A258   D

Adisham   GOODNESTONE PARK   **Eastry**   Finglesham

Knowlton   6   BETTESHANGER   MARITIME AND
LOCAL HISTORY MUSEUM

Chillenden   Betteshanger   Sholden

Aylesham   Easole Street   Northbourne   **DEAL**

Nonington   B2046   Tilmanstone   DEAL CASTLE   *THE*

Snowdown   Elvington   Great   *DOWNS*

OWNS WAY   Womenswold   Mongeham   **Walmer**

WALMER CASTLE
AND GARDENS   15

Barfrestone   EAST KENT   **39**   le

Woolage   RLY   East   Sutton

Green   **4**   **Eythorne**   Studdal   **5**   West   6 4   **6**

A2   West   Ringwould   **Kingsdown**

71

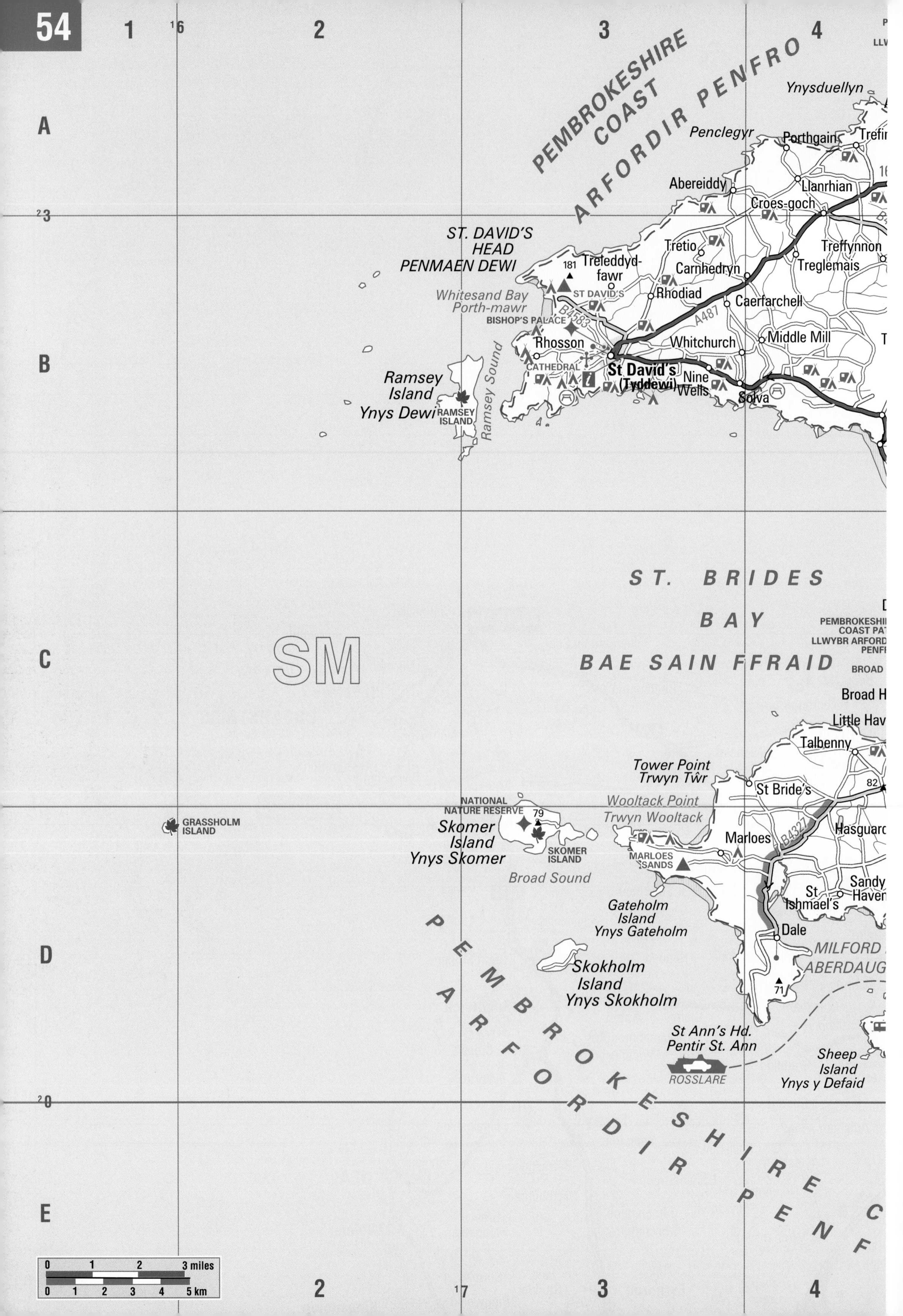

1   16   2   3   PEMBROKESHIRE   4
                          COAST
A   ARFORDIR PENFRO   Ynysduellyn

                                          Penclegyr   Porthgain   Trefin
                                          Abereiddy   Llanrhian
                                          Croes-goch

3

        ST. DAVID'S   Tretio   Treffynnon
        HEAD   Treleddyd-   Treglemais
        PENMAEN DEWI   fawr   Carnhedryn
                          181   ST DAVID'S   Rhodiad   Caerfarchell
        Whitesand Bay
        Porth-mawr   BISHOP'S PALACE   A487
                                          Whitchurch   Middle Mill
B   Ramsey   Rhosson   Nine
        Island   CATHEDRAL   St David's   Wells   Solva
        Ynys Dewi   RAMSEY   (Tyddewi)
                      ISLAND

                                    ST. BRIDES

                                         BAY
                                                      PEMBROKESHIRE
                                                      COAST PAT
                                                      LLWYBR ARFORD
                                    BAE SAIN FFRAID   PENF
                                                      BROAD
C   SM
                                                      Broad H

                                                      Little Hav
                                                      Talbenny
                                    Tower Point
                                    Trwyn Twr   St Bride's   82
                                    Wooltack Point
        GRASSHOLM   NATIONAL   Trwyn Wooltack
        ISLAND   NATURE RESERVE 79
                     Skomer   Marloes   Hasguard
                     Island   SKOMER
                     Ynys Skomer ISLAND
                                  MARLOES   Sandy
                                  SANDS   St   Haven
                     Broad Sound   Ishmael's
                          Gateholm
                          Island   Dale
                          Ynys Gateholm   MILFORD
D   Skokholm   ABERDAUG
                     Island
                     Ynys Skokholm   71
                          St Ann's Hd.
                          Pentir St. Ann   Sheep
                     ROSSLARE   Island
                                                      Ynys y Defaid
2 0

                          PEMBROKESHIRE
                          PARFORDIR
                          PEN   C

E

0   1   2   3 miles
0   1   2   3   4   5 km   2   17   3   4

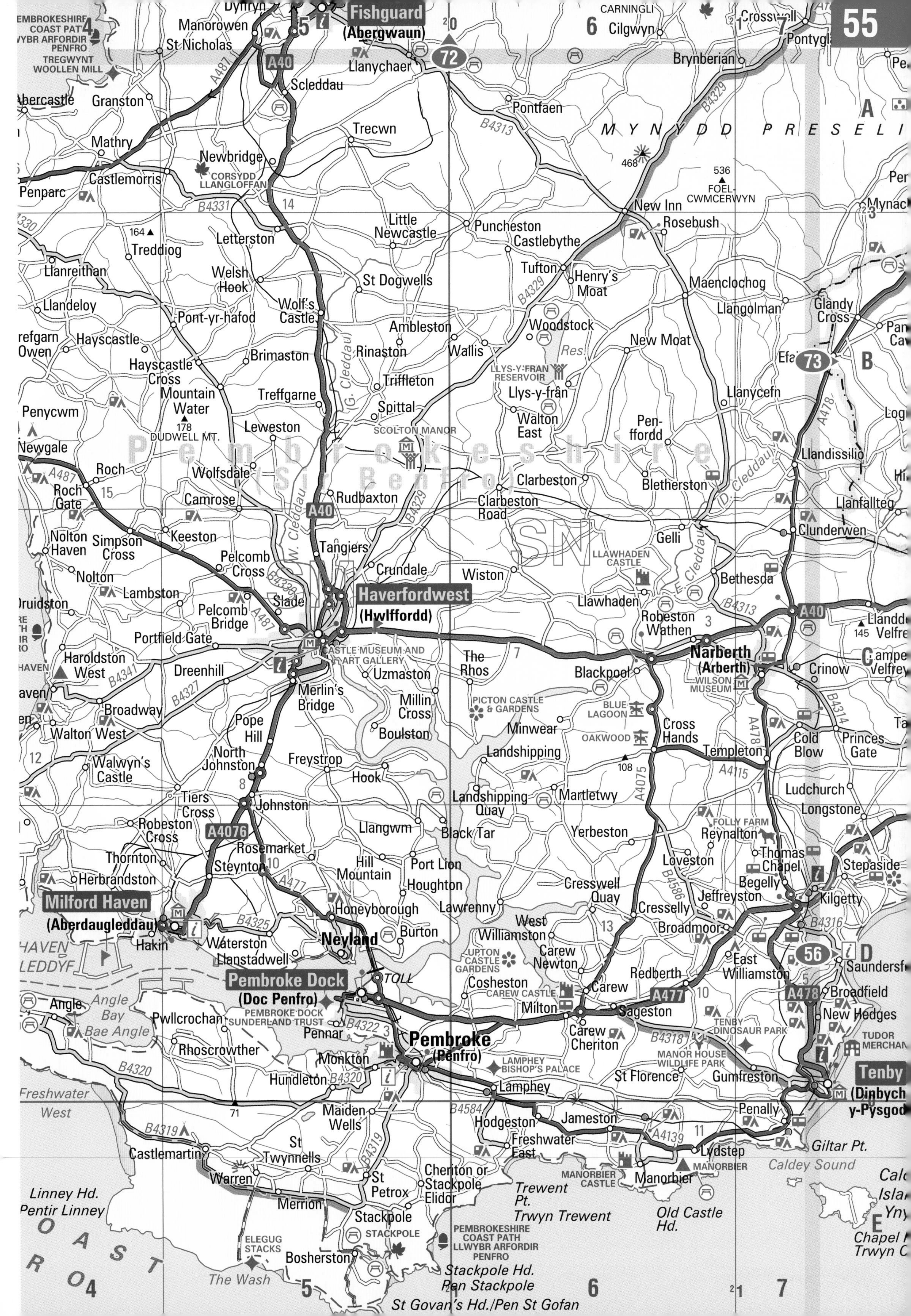
Fishguard
(Abergwaun)
Manorowen
St Nicholas
PEMBROKESHIRE COAST PATH
LLWYBR ARFORDIR PENFRO
TREGWYNT WOOLLEN MILL
Abercastle
Granston
Scleddau
Llanychaer
72
CARNINGLI
Cilgwyn
Crosswell
Pontygl
Brynberian
Pontfaen
MYNYDD PRESELI
Trecwn
Mathry
Newbridge
CORSYDD LLANGLOFFAN
Castlemorris
Penparc
468
536
FOEL-CWMCERWYN
New Inn
Rosebush
Mynac
B4331
B4313
B4329
A40
A487
Letterston
Little Newcastle
Puncheston
Castlebythe
164
Treddiog
Llanreithan
Welsh Hook
St Dogwells
Tufton
Henry's Moat
Maenclochog
Llandeloy
Wolf's Castle
Pont-yr-hafod
Llangolman
Glandy Cross
Trefgarn Owen
Hayscastle
Brimaston
Ambleston
Woodstock
Rinaston
Wallis
New Moat
Res.
73
Hayscastle Cross
Mountain Water
LLYS-Y-FRAN RESERVOIR
Llys-y-frân
Treffgarne
Triffleton
Llanycefn
Penycwm
Spittal
Walton East
178
DUDWELL MT.
Leweston
SCOLTON MANOR
Pen-ffordd
Newgale
Pembrokeshire (Sir Benfro)
Llandissilio
Roch
Wolfsdale
Clarbeston
Bletherston
Roch Gate
Camrose
Rudbaxton
Clarbeston Road
Llanfallteg
Nolton Haven
Simpson Cross
Keeston
Tangiers
SN
Gelli
Clunderwen
Nolton
Pelcomb Cross
Crundale
Wiston
LLAWHADEN CASTLE
Bethesda
Lambston
Druidston
Pelcomb Bridge
Slade
Haverfordwest
(Hwlffordd)
Llawhaden
Robeston Wathen
B4313
Llanddewi Velfrey
145
Portfield Gate
Haroldston West
Dreenhill
CASTLE MUSEUM AND ART GALLERY
Uzmaston
The Rhos
Blackpool
Narberth
(Arberth)
WILSON MUSEUM
Crinow
Campeter Velfrey
Broadway
B4341
B4327
Merlin's Bridge
Millin Cross
PICTON CASTLE & GARDENS
BLUE LAGOON
Walton West
Pope Hill
Boulston
Minwear
OAKWOOD
Cross Hands
Cold Blow
Princes Gate
Walwyn's Castle
North Johnston
Freystrop
Landshipping
108
Templeton
A4115
A4075
A478
Tiers Cross
Hook
Landshipping Quay
Martletwy
Ludchurch
Johnston
Longstone
Robeston Cross
A4076
Llangwm
Black Tar
Yerbeston
FOLLY FARM
Reynalton
Thornton
Rosemarket
Hill Mountain
Port Lion
Loveston
Thomas Chapel
Stepaside
Herbrandston
Steynton
Houghton
Cresswell Quay
Begelly
Milford Haven
(Aberdaugleddau)
A477
Honeyborough
Lawrenny
Jeffreyston
Kilgetty
Cresselly
B4586
Hakin
B4325
Waterston
Llanstadwell
Neyland
Burton
West Williamston
Broadmoor
B4316
Carew Newton
East Williamston
56
Saundersfoot
TOLL
UPTON CASTLE GARDENS
Redberth
Pembroke Dock
(Doc Penfro)
Cosheston
Carew
Broadfield
PEMBROKE DOCK SUNDERLAND TRUST
CAREW CASTLE
Milton
Sageston
A478
New Hedges
Angle
Angle Bay
Bae Angle
Pwllcrochan
Pennar
B4322
Carew Cheriton
TENBY DINOSAUR PARK
TUDOR MERCHANT
Rhoscrowther
Pembroke
(Penfro)
B4318
MANOR HOUSE WILDLIFE PARK
Monkton
LAMPHEY BISHOP'S PALACE
St Florence
Gumfreston
Tenby
(Dinbych-y-Pysgod)
B4320
Hundleton
Lamphey
Freshwater West
71
Maiden Wells
B4584
Jameston
Penally
Hodgeston
A4139
B4319
St Twynnells
Freshwater East
Lydstep
Giltar Pt.
Castlemartin
MANORBIER
Caldey Sound
Warren
St Petrox
Cheriton or Stackpole Elidor
MANORBIER CASTLE
Manorbier
Trewent Pt.
Trwyn Trewent
Caldey Island
Linney Hd.
Pentir Linney
Merrion
Stackpole
Old Castle Hd.
Chapel Pt.
ELEGUG STACKS
STACKPOLE
PEMBROKESHIRE COAST PATH
LLWYBR ARFORDIR PENFRO
Bosherston
Stackpole Hd.
Pen Stackpole
The Wash
St Govan's Hd./Pen St Gofan
COAST
A
B
C
D
E
4
5
6
7

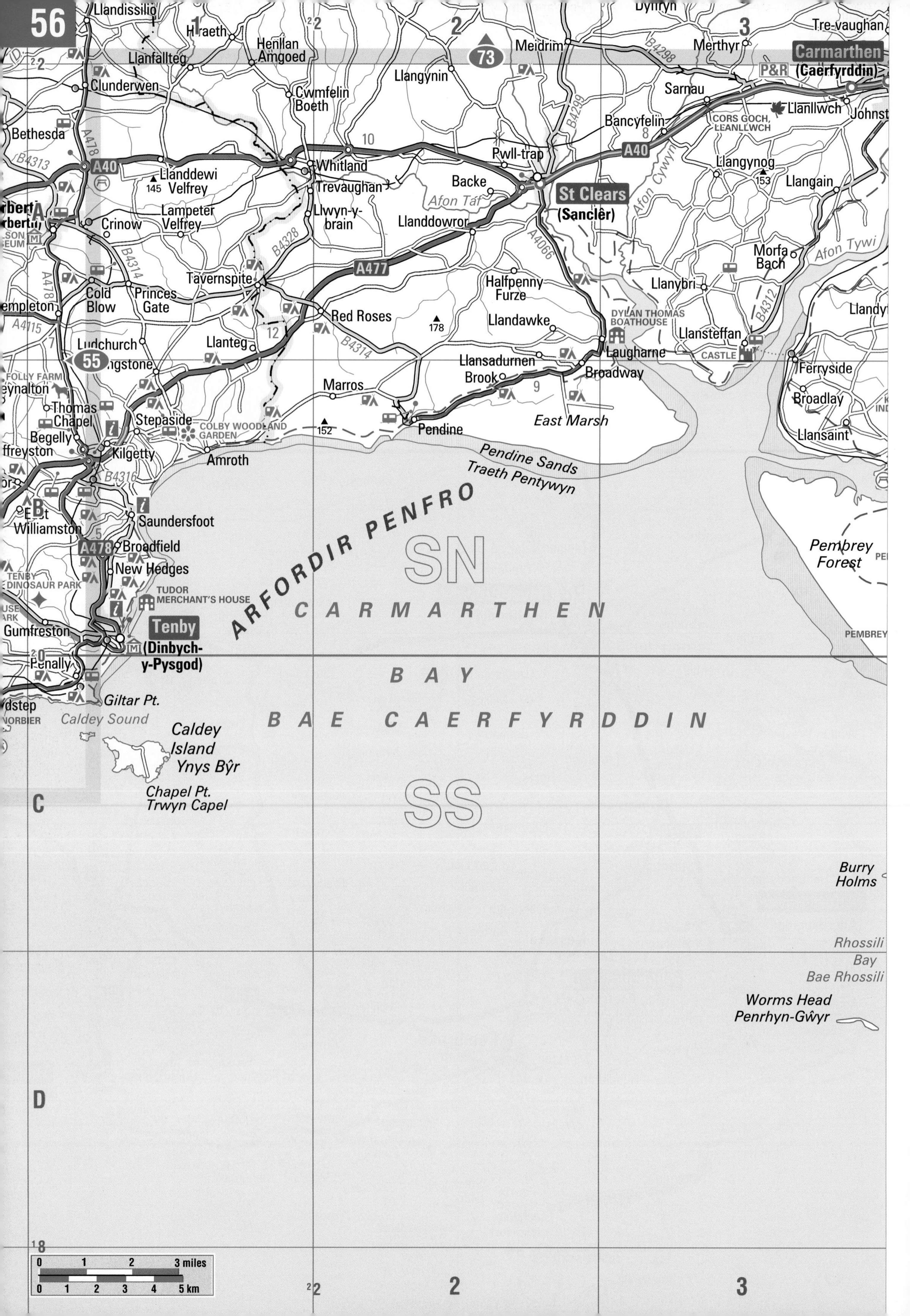

Llandissilio
H raeth
Henllan
Amgoed
Llangynin
Dyffryn
Meidrim
Merthyr
Tre-vaughan
**Carmarthen
(Caerfyrddin)**
Llanfallteg
73
B4298
Clunderwen
Cwmfelin
Boeth
Sarnau
Llanllwch
Johnst
Bethesda
B4299
Bancyfelin
CORS GOCH,
LEANLLWCH
B4313
A40
Whitland
Backe
A40
Llangynog
Llangain
Llanddewi
Velfrey
Trevaughan
Pwll-trap
St Clears
(Sanclêr)
153
145
Llwyn-y-
brain
Afon Tâf
Llanddowror
Afon Tywi
rberti
Lampeter
Velfrey
Morfa
Bach
Crinow
B4328
A4066
Llanybri
Llandy
A477
Halfpenny
Furze
DYLAN THOMAS
BOATHOUSE
Tavernspite
Cold
Blow
Princes
Gate
B4314
Red Roses
178
Llandawke
Llansteffan
empleton
A4115
B4314
Laugharne
CASTLE
Ferryside
7
Ludchurch
55
Llanteg
12
Llansadurnen
Brook
Broadway
Broadlay
ngstone
Marros
9
FOLLY FARM
eynalton
East Marsh
Llansaint
Thomas
Chapel
Stepaside
COLBY WOODLAND
GARDEN
152
Pendine
Begelly
ffreyston
Kilgetty
Amroth
Pendine Sands
Traeth Pentywyn
Pembrey
Forest
B4316
ARFORDIR PENFRO
t
Williamston
Saundersfoot
SN
PEMBREY
A478
Broadfield
C A R M A R T H E N
TENBY
DINOSAUR PARK
New Hedges
Gumfreston
TUDOR
MERCHANT'S HOUSE
B A Y
USE
ARK
**Tenby
(Dinbych-
y-Pysgod)**
Penally
B A E   C A E R F Y R D D I N
Giltar Pt.
dstep
ORBIER
Caldey Sound
*Caldey
Island
Ynys Bŷr*
SS
*Chapel Pt.
Trwyn Capel*
C
*Burry
Holms*
*Rhossili
Bay
Bae Rhossili*
*Worms Head
Penrhyn-Gŵyr*
D

| 0 | | 1 | | 2 | | 3 miles |
| 0 | 1 | 2 | 3 | 4 | | 5 km |

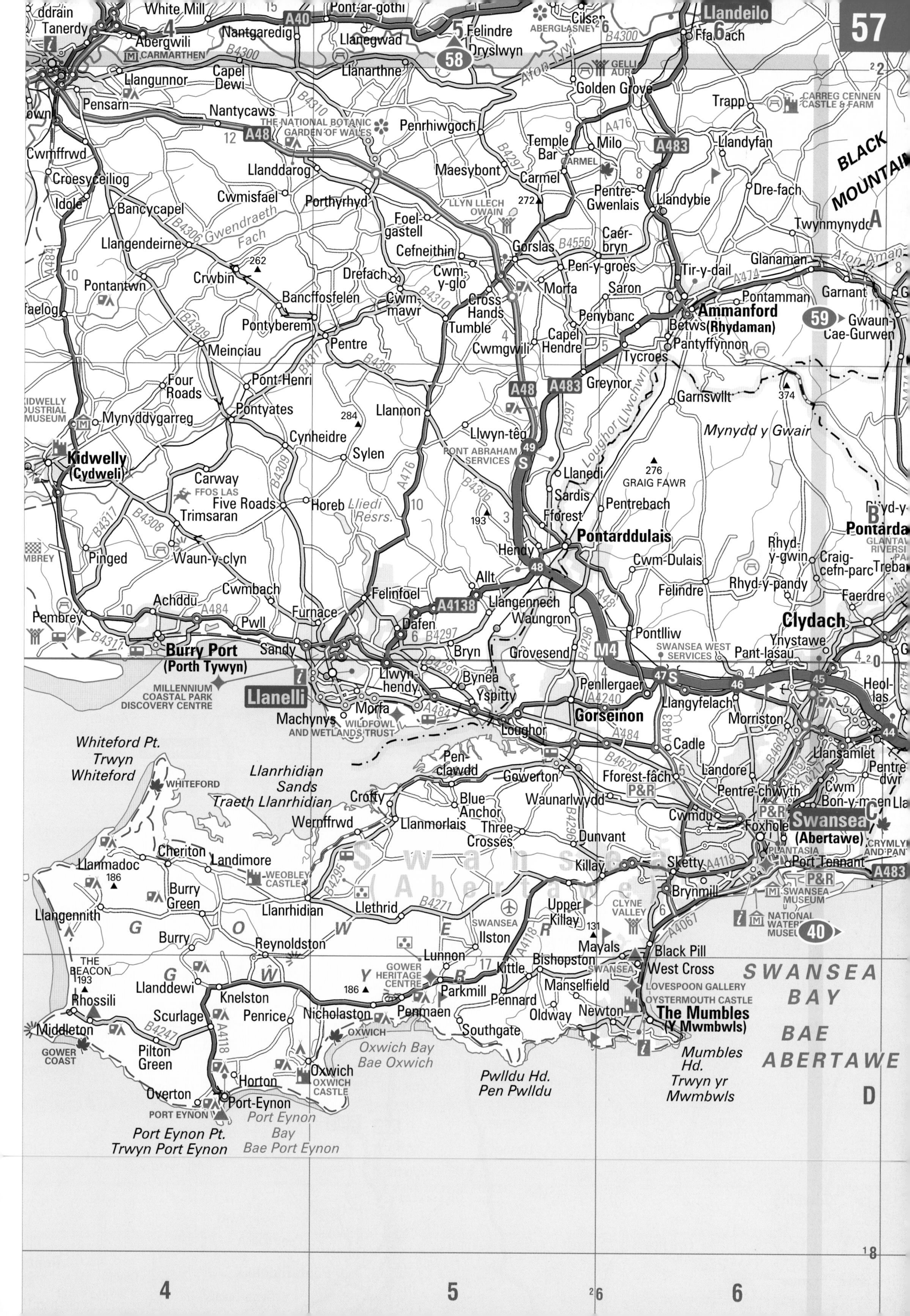
White Mill
Pont-ar-gothi
Llandeilo
Tanerdy
Abergwili
Nantgaredig
Llanegwad
Felindre
ABERGLASNEY
Cilsan
Ffairfach
CARMARTHEN
Dryslwyn
58
Llangunnor
Capel Dewi
Llanarthne
Afon Tywi
GELLI AUR
Golden Grove
Trapp
CARREG CENNEN CASTLE & FARM
Pensarn
Nantycaws
THE NATIONAL BOTANIC GARDEN OF WALES
Penrhiwgoch
Temple Bar
Milo
Llandyfan
BLACK MOUNTAIN
Cwmffrwd
A48
A483
A476
A40
B4300
B4310
B4297
B4306
B4309
B4317
B4308
B4311
B4556
A474
A484
B4295
B4271
B4247
A4118
A4138
A4240
B4296
B4620
A4067
B4603
A4217
A4118
M4
Llanddarog
Maesybont
CARMEL
Carmel
Croesyceiliog
Pentre-Gwenlais
Dre-fach
Idole
Bancycapel
Cwmisfael
Porthyrhyd
LLYN LLECH OWAIN
Llandybie
Twynmynydd
Gwendraeth Fach
Foel-gastell
Caer-bryn
Llangendeirne
Cefneithin
Gorslas
Glanaman
Afon Aman
Pen-y-groes
Tir-y-dail
Crwbin
Drefach
Cwm-y-glo
Morfa
Saron
Garnant
Pontantwn
Bancffosfelen
Cwm-mawr
Cross Hands
Pontamman
Ammanford
(Rhydaman)
Penybanc
Betws
59
Gwaun-Cae-Gurwen
Pontyberem
Tumble
Capel Hendre
Pantyffynnon
Meinciau
Pentre
Cwmgwili
Tycroes
Four Roads
Pont-Henri
Greynor
Garnswllt
KIDWELLY INDUSTRIAL MUSEUM
Pontyates
Llannon
Mynyddygarreg
Loughor (Llwchwr)
Mynydd y Gwair
Cynheidre
Llwyn-têg
Kidwelly
(Cydweli)
Sylen
PONT ABRAHAM SERVICES
Llanedi
GRAIG FAWR
Carway
FFOS LAS
Five Roads
Horeb
Lliedi Resrs.
Sardis
Pentrebach
Trimsaran
Fforest
Pontarddulais
Pontardawe
Hendy
Rhyd-y-gwin
Craig-cefn-parc
Pinged
Waun-y-clyn
Cwm-Dulais
Allt
Felindre
Rhyd-y-pandy
Cwmbach
Felinfoel
Llangennech
Faerdre
Achddu
Waungron
Clydach
Pembrey
Pwll
Furnace
Dafen
Pontlliw
Ynystawe
Burry Port
(Porth Tywyn)
Sandy
Bryn
Grovesend
SWANSEA WEST SERVICES
Pant-lasau
MILLENNIUM COASTAL PARK DISCOVERY CENTRE
Llwyn-hendy
Bynea
Penllergaer
Heol-las
Llanelli
Yspitty
Llangyfelach
Morriston
Machynys
Morfa
WILDFOWL AND WETLANDS TRUST
Loughor
Gorseinon
Llansamlet
Cadle
Whiteford Pt.
Trwyn Whiteford
WHITEFORD
Llanrhidian Sands
Traeth Llanrhidian
Pen-clawdd
Gowerton
Fforest-fach
Landore
P&R
Pentre-chwyth
Crofty
Blue Anchor
Waunarlwydd
Cwm
Bon-y-maen
Wernffrwd
Llanmorlais
Three Crosses
Cwmdu
Foxhole
Swansea
(Abertawe)
Dunvant
CRYMLYN AND PANT
Cheriton
Landimore
Swansea (Abertawe)
Killay
Sketty
PLANTASIA
Port Tennant
Llanmadoc
WEOBLEY CASTLE
Brynmill
Burry Green
SWANSEA MUSEUM
Llangennith
Llanrhidian
Llethrid
Upper Killay
CLYNE VALLEY
NATIONAL WATERFRONT MUSEUM
40
GOWER
SWANSEA
Ilston
Burry
Reynoldston
Mayals
THE BEACON
Lunnon
Black Pill
GOWER HERITAGE CENTRE
Kittle
Bishopston
West Cross
SWANSEA BAY
Llanddewi
Parkmill
Mansefield
LOVESPOON GALLERY
Knelston
OYSTERMOUTH CASTLE
BAE ABERTAWE
Rhossili
Pennard
Scurlage
Penrice
Nicholaston
Penmaen
Oldway
Newton
The Mumbles
(Y Mwmbwls)
Middleton
OXWICH
Southgate
GOWER COAST
Pilton Green
Oxwich Bay
Bae Oxwich
Mumbles Hd.
Trwyn yr Mwmbwls
Oxwich
OXWICH CASTLE
Horton
Pwlldu Hd.
Pen Pwlldu
Overton
Port-Eynon
PORT EYNON
Port Eynon Bay
Bae Port Eynon
Port Eynon Pt.
Trwyn Port Eynon
A
B
C
D
4
5
6

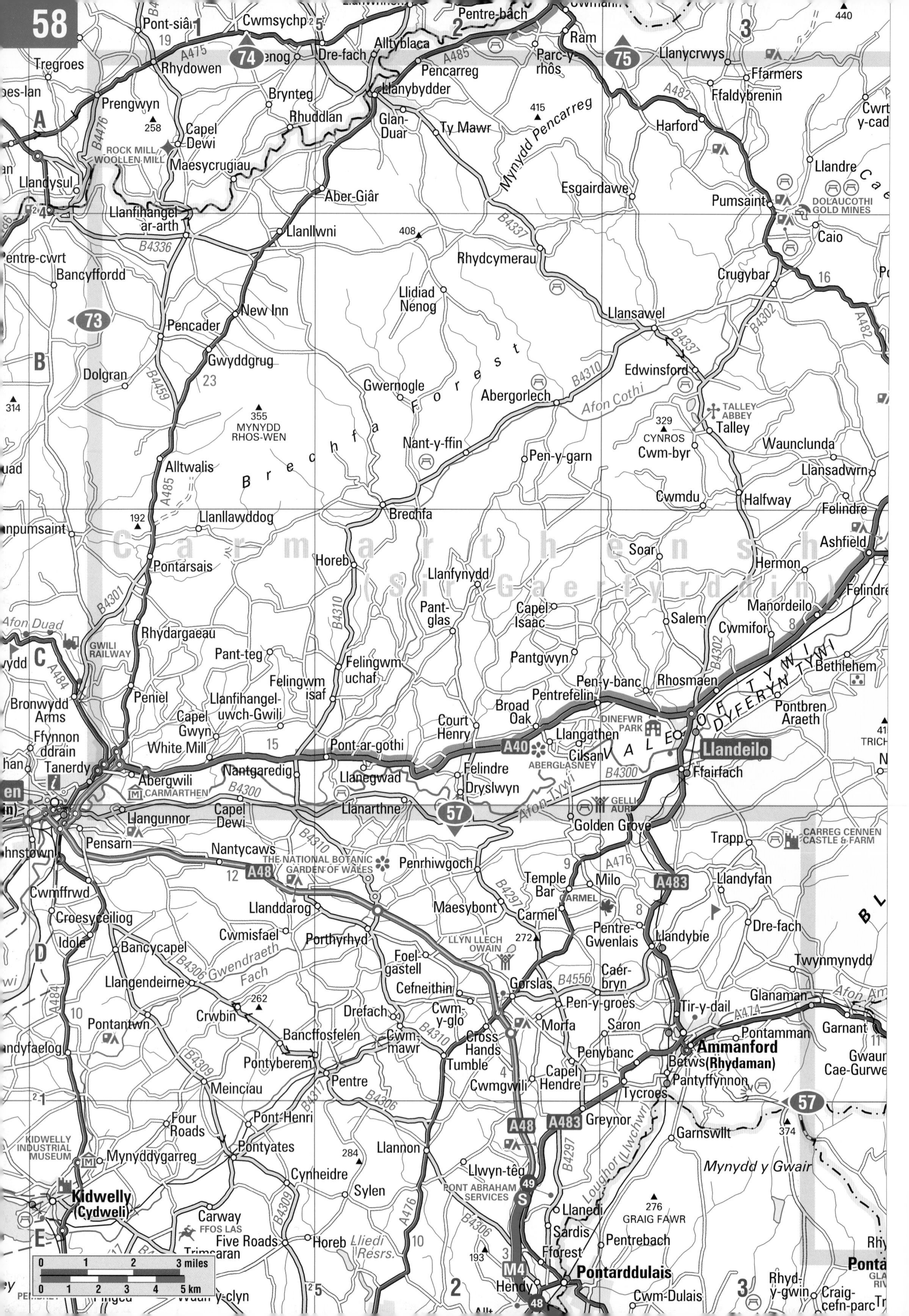

Pont-siân
Cwmsychpant
Pentre-bach
Ram
Tregroes
Rhydowen
Dre-fach
Alltyblaca
Pencarreg
Parc-y-rhôs
Llanycrwys
Ffarmers
Ffaldybrenin
Prengwyn
Brynteg
Llanybydder
Rhuddlan
Glan-Duar
Ty Mawr
Mynydd Pencarreg
Harford
Capel Dewi
ROCK MILL WOOLLEN MILL
Maesycrugiau
Llandysul
Aber-Giâr
Esgairdawe
Llandre
Pumsaint
DOLAUCOTHI GOLD MINES
Caio
Llanfihangel-ar-arth
Llanllwni
Rhydcymerau
Crugybar
Pentre-cwrt
Bancyffordd
Llidiad Nenog
New Inn
Pencader
Llansawel
Gwyddgrug
Dolgran
Gwernogle
Brechfa Forest
Abergorlech
Edwinsford
Afon Cothi
MYNYDD RHOS-WEN
Nant-y-ffin
TALLEY ABBEY
Talley
CYNROS
Cwm-byr
Pen-y-garn
Waunclunda
Llansadwrn
Alltwalis
Brechfa
Cwmdu
Halfway
Felindre
Llanllawddog
Carmarthenshire (Sir Gaerfyrddin)
Horeb
Soar
Hermon
Ashfield
Pontarsais
Llanfynydd
Pant-glas
Capel Isaac
Salem
Manordeilo
Cwmifor
Rhydargaeau
GWILI RAILWAY
Pant-teg
Pantgwyn
Felingwm uchaf
Felingwm isaf
Rhosmaen
Bethlehem
Bronwydd Arms
Peniel
Llanfihangel-uwch-Gwili
Capel Gwyn
Pen-y-banc
Pentrefelin
Broad Oak
DINEFWR PARK
Pontbren Araeth
VALE OF TYWI
DYFFRYN TYWI
Ffynnon ddrain
White Mill
Court Henry
Pont-ar-gothi
Llangathen
Cilsan
Llandeilo
Tanerdy
Abergwili
Nantgaredig
Llanegwad
Felindre
Dryslwyn
ABERGLASNEY
Ffairfach
CARMARTHEN
Llangunnor
Capel Dewi
Llanarthne
Afon Tywi
GELLI AUR
Golden Grove
Trapp
CARREG CENNEN CASTLE & FARM
Pensarn
Nantycaws
THE NATIONAL BOTANIC GARDEN OF WALES
Penrhiwgoch
Temple Bar
Milo
Llandyfan
Cwmffrwd
Llanddarog
Maesybont
Carmel
Croesyceiliog
Pentre-Gwenlais
Dre-fach
Cwmisfael
Porthyrhyd
LLYN LLECH OWAIN
Llandybie
Idole
Bancycapel
Gwendraeth Fach
Foel-gastell
Caer-bryn
Twynmynydd
Llangendeirne
Gorslas
Cefneithin
Pen-y-groes
Glanaman
Afon Aman
Crwbin
Drefach
Cwm-y-glo
Morfa
Tir-y-dail
Pontantwn
Saron
Pontamman
Garnant
Llandyfaelog
Bancffosfelen
Cwm-mawr
Cross Hands
Penybanc
Ammanford (Rhydaman)
Gwaun Cae-Gurwen
Pontyberem
Tumble
Betws
Pentre
Capel Hendre
Pantyffynnon
Meinciau
Cwmgwili
Tycroes
Four Roads
Pont-Henri
Greynor
Garnswllt
Pontyates
KIDWELLY INDUSTRIAL MUSEUM
Mynyddygarreg
Llannon
Mynydd y Gwair
Cynheidre
Llwyn-têg
Kidwelly (Cydweli)
Sylen
PONT ABRAHAM SERVICES
Llanedi
GRAIG FAWR
Carway
FFOS LAS
Sardis
Pentrebach
Five Roads
Horeb
Lliedi Resrs.
Trimsaran
Fforest
Pontarddulais
Hendy
Cwm-Dulais
Rhyd-y-gwin
Craig-cefn-parc
0 1 2 3 miles
0 1 2 3 4 5 km

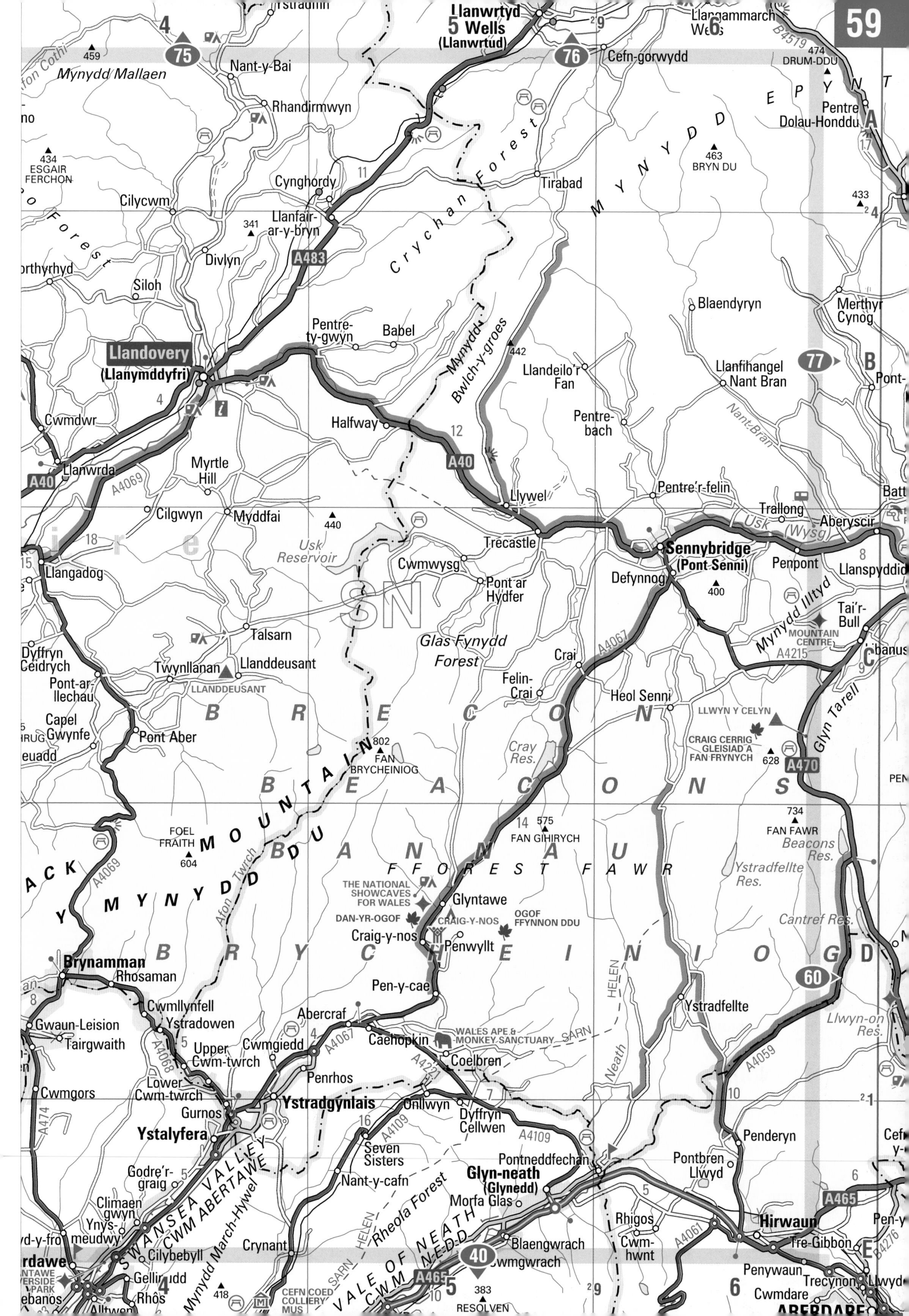
Llanwrtyd
Wells
(Llanwrtud)
Llangammarch
Wells
Cefn-gorwydd
DRUM-DDU
Mynydd Mallaen
Nant-y-Bai
Rhandirmwyn
ESGAIR
FERCHON
Cynghordy
Cilycwm
Llanfair-
ar-y-bryn
Divlyn
Siloh
Crychan Forest
Tirabad
MYNYDD EPYNT
BRYN DU
Pentre
Dolau-Honddu
Blaendyryn
Merthyr
Cynog
Pentre-
ty-gwyn
Babel
Llandovery
(Llanymddyfri)
Mynydd
Bwlch-y-groes
Llandeilo'r
Fan
Llanfihangel
Nant Bran
Pont-
Pentre-
bach
Nant Bran
Cwmdwr
Halfway
Llanwrda
Myrtle
Hill
Llywel
Pentre'r-felin
Trallong
Cilgwyn
Myddfai
Trecastle
Aberyscir
Usk
(Wysg)
Usk
Reservoir
Cwmwysg
Sennybridge
(Pont Senni)
Penpont
Llanspyddid
Llangadog
Defynnog
Pont ar
Hydfer
Mynydd Illtyd
Tai'r-
Bull
MOUNTAIN
CENTRE
Talsarn
Dyffryn
Ceidrych
Glas Fynydd
Forest
Crai
Libanus
Twynllanan
Llanddeusant
LLANDDEUSANT
Pont-ar-
llechau
Felin-
Crai
Heol Senni
LLWYN Y CELYN
Capel
Gwynfe
Pont Aber
BRECON BEACONS
CRAIG CERRIG
GLEISIAD A
FAN FRYNYCH
Glyn Tarell
FAN
BRYCHEINIOG
Cray
Res.
FAN FAWR
FOEL
FRAITH
BLACK MOUNTAIN
FAN GIHIRYCH
Beacons
Res.
FFOREST FAWR
Ystradfellte
Res.
Y MYNYDD DU
FFOREST FAWR
THE NATIONAL
SHOWCAVES
FOR WALES
Glyntawe
DAN-YR-OGOF
CRAIG-Y-NOS
OGOF
FFYNNON DDU
Cantref Res.
Afon Twrch
Craig-y-nos
Penwyllt
BRYCHEINIOG
Brynamman
Rhosaman
HELEN
Pen-y-cae
Cwmllynfell
Ystradowen
Abercraf
Ystradfellte
Llwyn-on
Res.
Gwaun-Leision
Tairgwaith
Upper
Cwm-twrch
Cwmgiedd
Caehopkin
WALES APE &
MONKEY SANCTUARY
SARN
Coelbren
Lower
Cwm-twrch
Penrhos
Neath
Cwmgors
Gurnos
Ystradgynlais
Onllwyn
Dyffryn
Cellwen
Ystalyfera
Seven
Sisters
Penderyn
SWANSEA VALLEY
CWM ABERTAWE
Pontneddfechan
Pontbren
Llwyd
Godre'r-
graig
Nant-y-cafn
Glyn-neath
(Glynedd)
Climaen
gwyn
Rheola Forest
Morfa Glas
Ynys-
meudwy
Mynydd March-Hywel
Rhigos
Hirwaun
Cilybebyll
Crynant
Blaengwrach
Cwm-
hwnt
Tre-Gibbon
Gellinudd
Cwmgwrach
VALE OF NEATH
CWM NEDD
Penywaun
Trecynon
Llwyd
Rhôs
CEFN COED
COLLIERY
MUS
RESOLVEN
Cwmdare
ABERDARE
Alltwen
Pontardawe

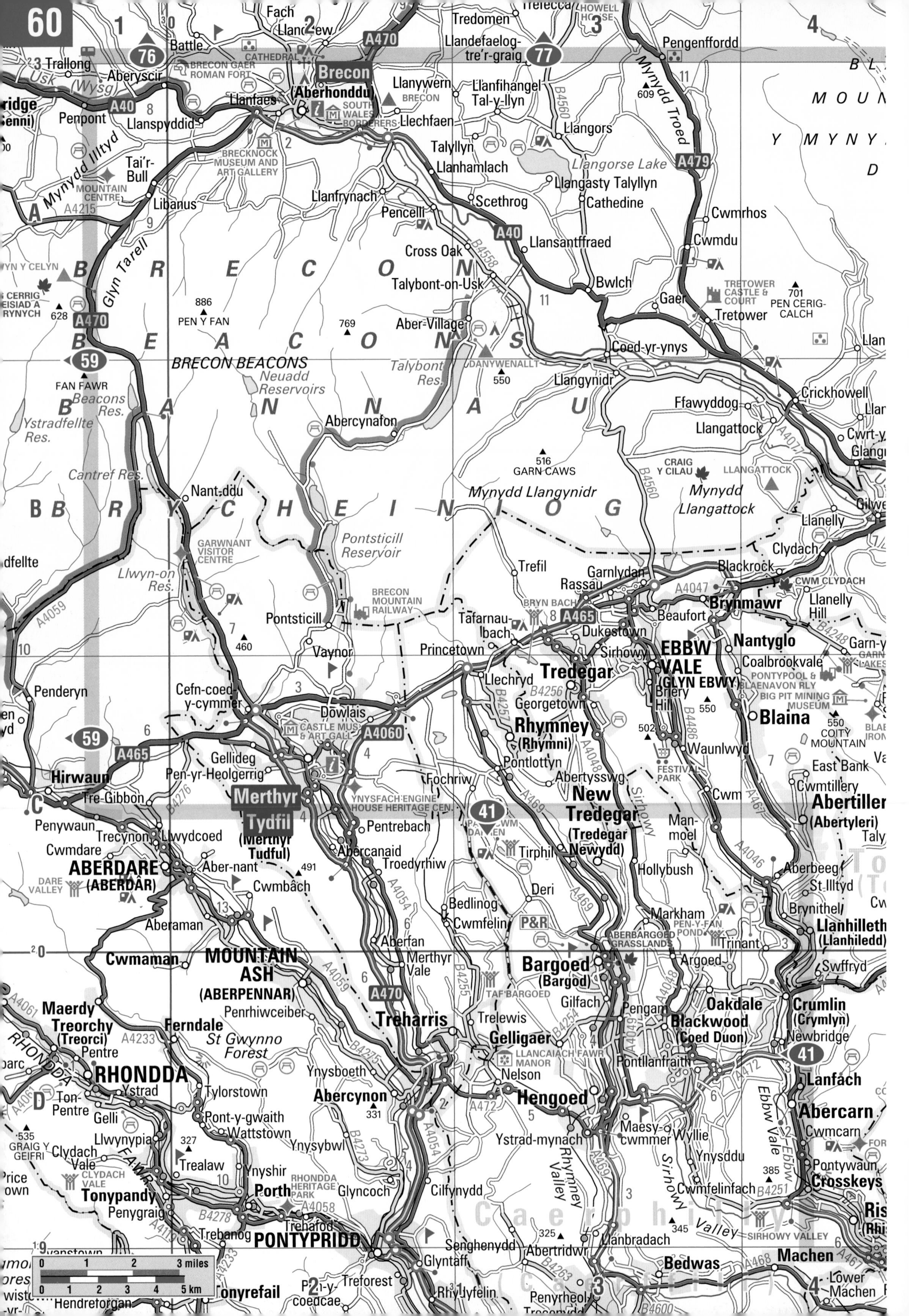

Fach
Llanddew
Tredomen
Trefecca
HOWELL HOUSE
Battle
Trallong
Aberyscir
BRECON GAER ROMAN FORT
CATHEDRAL
Brecon
(Aberhonddu)
Llandefaelog-tre'r-graig
Pengenffordd
76
77
Usk
(Wysg)
A470
A40
Penpont
Llanspyddid
Llanfaes
SOUTH WALES BORDERERS
Llanywern
BRECON
Llanfihangel Tal-y-llyn
Llechfaen
Llangors
Talyllyn
Llanhamlach
Llangorse Lake
A479
Mynydd Troed
609
BLACK MOUNTAINS
Y MYNYDD DU
BRECKNOCK MUSEUM AND ART GALLERY
Mynydd Illtyd
Tai'r-Bull
MOUNTAIN CENTRE
Libanus
A4215
Llanfrynach
Pencelli
Scethrog
Llangasty Talyllyn
Cathedine
Cwmrhos
Cwmdu
Llansantffraed
Cross Oak
Talybont-on-Usk
B4558
B4560
Bwlch
Gaer
Tretower
TRETOWER CASTLE & COURT
701
PEN CERIG-CALCH
Glyn Tarell
BRECON BEACONS
886
PEN Y FAN
628
769
Aber-Village
DANYWENALLT
550
Coed-yr-ynys
Llangynidr
59
FAN FAWR
Beacons Res.
Ystradfellte Res.
Neuadd Reservoirs
Talybont Res.
Abercynafon
Crickhowell
Ffawyddog
Llangattock
Glangrwyney
516
GARN CAWS
CRAIG Y CILAU
LLANGATTOCK
Mynydd Llangynidr
Mynydd Llangattock
Cantref Res.
Nant-ddu
BRYCHEINIOG
Pontsticill Reservoir
Llanelly
Clydach
GARWNANT VISITOR CENTRE
Llwyn-on Res.
Trefil
Garnlydan
Rassau
Blackrock
CWM CLYDACH
A4047
Brynmawr
Llanelly Hill
BRECON MOUNTAIN RAILWAY
Pontsticill
BRYN BACH
A465
Tafarnau-bach
Beaufort
Dukestown
Nantyglo
Garn-yr-erw
A4059
460
Vaynor
Princetown
Sirhowy
EBBW VALE
(GLYN EBWY)
Coalbrookvale
PONTYPOOL & BLAENAVON RLY
BIG PIT MINING MUSEUM
Tredegar
Llechryd
Briery Hill
550
Blaina
COITY MOUNTAIN
Penderyn
Cefn-coed-y-cymmer
Dowlais
B4256
Georgetown
Rhymney
(Rhymni)
502
Waunlwyd
CASTLE MUS. & ART GALL.
A4060
B4257
A4048
B4486
FESTIVAL PARK
East Bank
A465
Gellideg
Pen-yr-Heolgerrig
Pontlottyn
Fochriw
Abertysswg
Cwm
Cwmtillery
Hirwaun
Tre-Gibbon
B4276
Merthyr Tydfil
(Merthyr Tudful)
YNYSFACH ENGINE HOUSE HERITAGE CEN.
41
A469
New Tredegar
(Tredegar Newydd)
Sirhowy
Man-moel
A467
Abertillery
(Abertyleri)
Penywaun
Trecynon
Llwydcoed
Pentrebach
Cwmdare
Abercanaid
Troedyrhiw
Tirphil
Hollybush
A4046
Aberbeeg
St Illtyd
ABERDARE
(ABERDÂR)
DARE VALLEY
Aber-nant
491
Cwmbach
A4054
Deri
Bedlinog
Cwmfelin
P&R
Markham
PEN-Y-FAN POND
Brynithel
Llanhilleth
(Llanhiledd)
Aberaman
Aberfan
ABERBARGOED GRASSLANDS
Trinant
Cwmaman
MOUNTAIN ASH
(ABERPENNAR)
A4059
Merthyr Vale
Bargoed
(Bargod)
Argoed
Swffryd
A4061
Maerdy
Treorchy
(Treorci)
Pentre
RHONDDA
Ferndale
A4233
Penrhiwceiber
St Gwynno Forest
A470
Treharris
TAF BARGOED
B4255
Trelewis
Gelligaer
B4254
Gilfach
Pengam
A4049
Oakdale
Blackwood
(Coed Duon)
A4048
Crumlin
(Crymlyn)
Newbridge
B4275
LLANCAIACH FAWR MANOR
Nelson
Pontllanfraith
A472
Ynysboeth
Ystrad
Tylorstown
Abercynon
331
A472
Hengoed
Lanfach
Abercarn
Ton-Pentre
Gelli
Pont-y-gwaith
Wattstown
Ynysybwl
B4273
Ystrad-mynach
Maesycwmmer
Wyllie
Ebbw Vale
Cwmcarn
Llwynypia
327
Ynysddu
Rhymney Valley
Sirhowy
A469
Pontywaun
Crosskeys
385
535
GRAIG Y GEIFRI
Clydach Vale
CLYDACH VALE
Trealaw
Ynyshir
RHONDDA HERITAGE PARK
Glyncoch
Cilfynydd
Cwmfelinfach
B4251
Tonypandy
Penygraig
Porth
A4058
B4278
A4119
Trehafod
Trebanog
PONTYPRIDD
Caerphilly
(Caerffili)
345
Sirhowy Valley
SIRHOWY VALLEY
Senghenydd
325
Abertridwr
Llanbradach
A4233
Glyntaff
Bedwas
A468
Machen
A4263
B4263
Treforest
Pant-y-coedcae
Rhydyfelin
Penyrheol
B4600
Lower Machen
Tonyrefail
Hendreforgan
0 1 2 3 miles
0 1 2 3 4 5 km

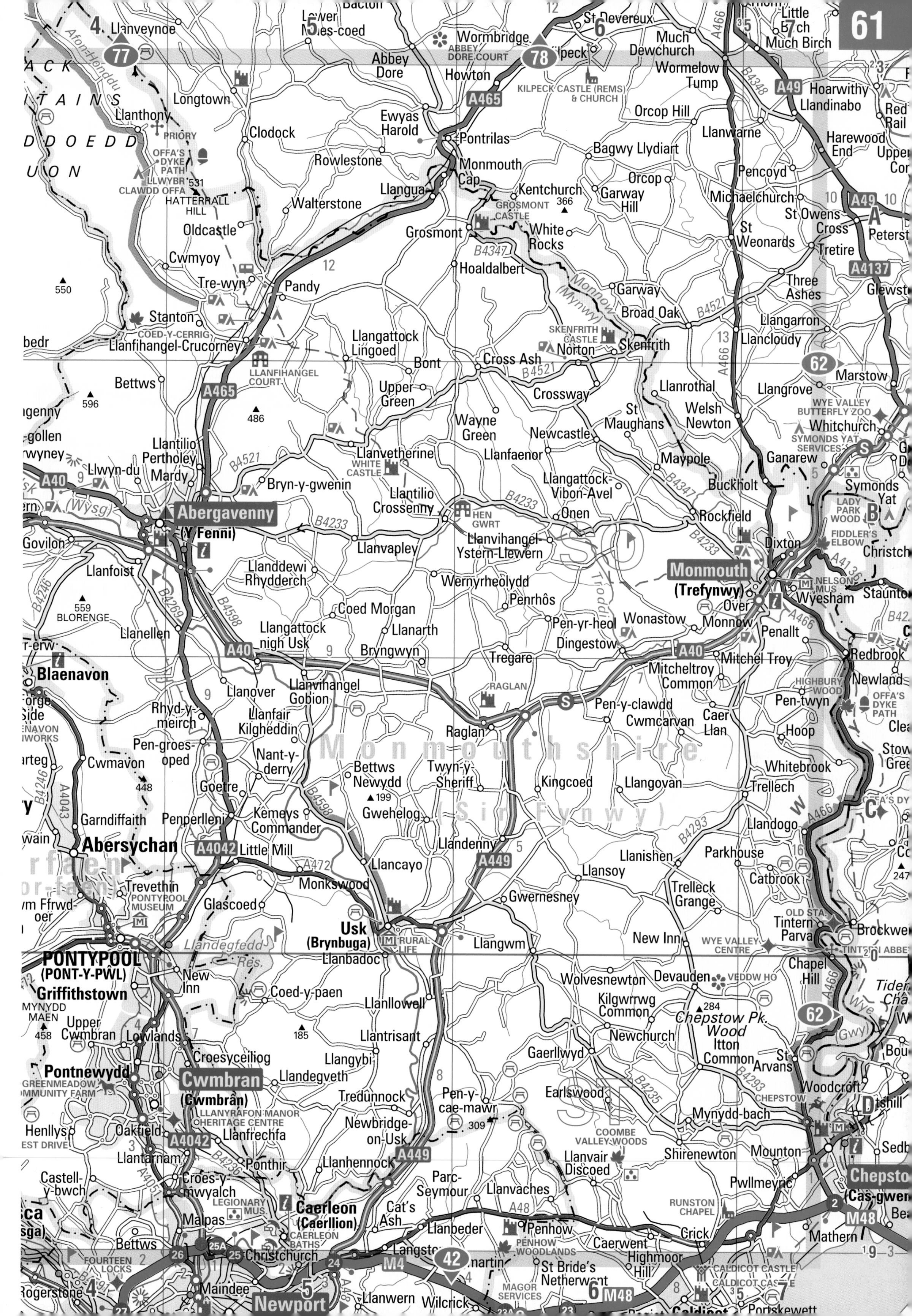

Llanveynoe
Lower Maes-coed
Bacton
Wormbridge
ABBEY DORE COURT
Abbey Dore
Howton
Kilpeck
St Devereux
Much Dewchurch
Wormelow Tump
Little Birch
Much Birch
A466
B4348
A49
Hoarwithy
Llandinabo
Red Rail
KILPECK CASTLE (REMS) & CHURCH
A465
Afon Honddu
Longtown
Llanthony
PRIORY
Clodock
Ewyas Harold
Pontrilas
Orcop Hill
Llanwarne
Harewood End
OFFA'S DYKE PATH
LLWYBR CLAWDD OFFA
HATTERRALL HILL
531
Rowlestone
Monmouth Cap
Bagwy Llydiart
Orcop
Pencoyd
Llangua
Kentchurch
Garway Hill
366
Michaelchurch
Walterstone
GROSMONT CASTLE
St Owens Cross
Oldcastle
Grosmont
White Rocks
St Weonards
Tretire
A4137
B4347
Hoaldalbert
Cwmyoy
550
Tre-wyn
Pandy
Monnow (Mynwy)
Garway
Three Ashes
Broad Oak
B4521
Stanton
COED-Y-CERRIG
Llangattock Lingoed
SKENFRITH CASTLE
Norton
Skenfrith
Llangarron
Llancloudy
Llanfihangel-Crucorney
LLANFIHANGEL COURT
Bont
Cross Ash
Marstow
Bettws
596
Upper Green
Crossway
Llanrothal
Llangrove
WYE VALLEY BUTTERFLY ZOO
486
Wayne Green
St Maughans
Welsh Newton
Whitchurch
SYMONDS YAT SERVICES
Llantilio Pertholey
Llwyn-du
Mardy
Llanvetherine
WHITE CASTLE
Newcastle
Llanfaenor
Maypole
Ganarew
A40
Bryn-y-gwenin
Llantilio Crossenny
HEN GWRT
Llangattock-Vibon-Avel
Onen
Buckholt
Symonds Yat
Abergavenny (Y Fenni)
Goviton
B4233
Llanvapley
Llanvihangel-Ystern-Llewern
Rockfield
LADY PARK WOOD
FIDDLER'S ELBOW
Dixton
Christchurch
Llanfoist
Llanddewi Rhydderch
Wernyrheolydd
Monmouth (Trefynwy)
NELSON MUS
Wyesham
Staunton
559
BLORENGE
B4246
B4269
B4598
Coed Morgan
Penrhôs
Over Monnow
Llangattock nigh Usk
Llanarth
Pen-yr-heol
Wonastow
A466
Penallt
Llanellen
Bryngwyn
Tregare
Dingestow
Mitchel Troy
Redbrook
Blaenavon
Llanover
Llanvihangel Gobion
RAGLAN
Mitcheltroy Common
HIGHBURY WOOD
Newland
Rhyd-y-meirch
Llanfair Kilgheddin
Raglan
Pen-y-clawdd
Cwmcarvan
Caer Llan
Pen-twyn
OFFA'S DYKE PATH
Pen-groes-oped
Cwmavon
Nant-y-derry
Monmouthshire (Sir Fynwy)
Hoop
Whitebrook
Bettws Newydd
199
Twyn-y-Sheriff
Kingcoed
Llangovan
Trellech
448
Goetre
B4598
A4043
Garndiffaith
Penperlleni
Kemeys Commander
Gwehelog
Llandenny
B4293
Llandogo
Abersychan
A4042
Little Mill
A472
Llancayo
A449
Llanishen
Parkhouse
Catbrook
Trevethin
PONTYPOOL MUSEUM
Glascoed
Monkswood
Llansoy
Gwernesney
Trelleck Grange
Tintern Parva
OLD STA.
Brockweir
Usk (Brynbuga)
RURAL LIFE
Llangwm
New Inn
WYE VALLEY CENTRE
TINTERN ABBEY
Llandegfedd Res.
Pontypool (PONT-Y-PŴL)
Llanbadoc
Chapel Hill
Wolvesnewton
Devauden
VEDDW HO
New Inn
Griffithstown
Coed-y-paen
Kilgwrrwg Common
284
Chepstow Pk. Wood
MYNYDD MAEN
458
Upper Cwmbran
Lowlands
Llanllowell
185
Llantrisant
Newchurch
Itton Common
Wye (Gwy)
Croesyceiliog
Gaerllwyd
St Arvans
Pontnewydd
Llangybi
GREENMEADOW COMMUNITY FARM
Cwmbran (Cwmbrân)
Llandegveth
B4235
Earlswood
Woodcroft
Tredunnock
Pen-y-cae-mawr
CHEPSTOW
LLANYRAFON MANOR HERITAGE CENTRE
Mynydd-bach
309
Henllys
Oakfield
Llanfrechfa
Newbridge-on-Usk
COOMBE VALLEY WOODS
Shirenewton
Mounton
Sedbury
Llantarnam
B4236
A4051
Ponthir
Llanhennock
Llanvair Discoed
Chepstow (Cas-gwent)
Castell-y-bwch
Croes-y-mwyalch
Parc-Seymour
Llanvaches
Pwllmeyric
Malpas
LEGIONARY MUS.
Caerleon (Caerllion)
Cat's Ash
A48
RUNSTON CHAPEL
Llanbeder
Penhow
Mathern
M48
Bettws
CAERLEON BATHS
PENHOW WOODLANDS
Caerwent
Crick
FOURTEEN LOCKS
Christchurch
Langstone
M4
Highmoor Hill
CALDICOT CASTLE
Rogerstone
Maindee
Newport
Llanwern
Wilcrick
MAGOR SERVICES
St Bride's Netherwent
Portskewett
62
77
78
42

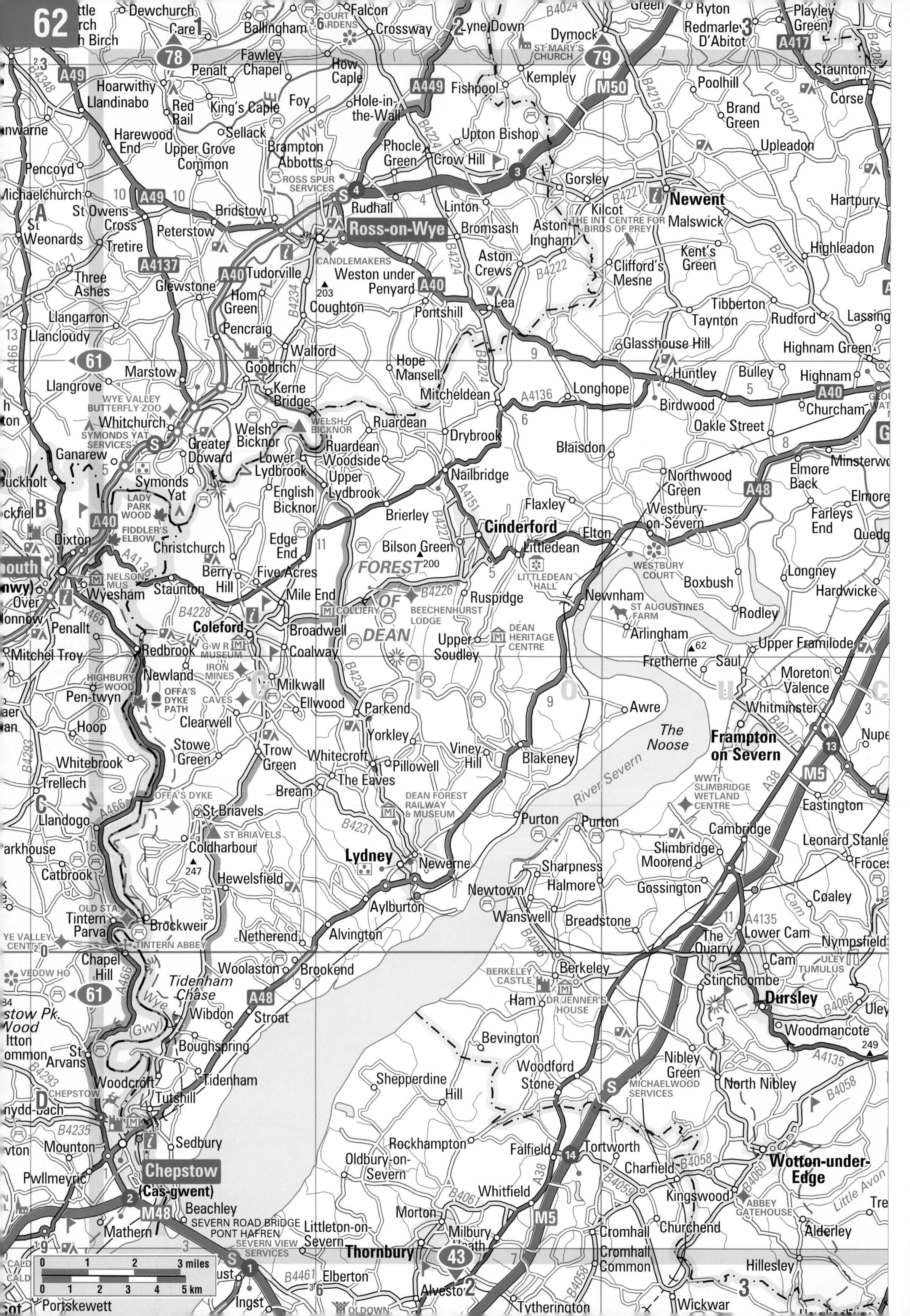
Dewchurch
Care
Ballingham
Court Gardens
Falcon
Crossway
Lyne Down
Dymock
St Mary's Church
Ryton
Redmarley D'Abitot
Playley Green
Staunton
Corse
78
Fawley Chapel
Penalt
How Caple
Hoarwithy
Llandinabo
Red Rail
King's Caple
Foy
Hole-in-the-Wall
Fishpool
Kempley
79
M50
Poolhill
Brand Green
Leadon
Harewood End
Sellack
Upper Grove Common
Brampton Abbotts
Wye
Phocle Green
Crow Hill
Upton Bishop
Upleadon
Pencoyd
Michaelchurch
Ross Spur Services
Rudhall
Linton
Gorsley
Kilcot
Newent
Hartpury
St Owens Cross
St Weonards
Bridstow
Peterstow
Tretire
Ross-on-Wye
Bromsash
Aston Ingham
The Int Centre for Birds of Prey
Malswick
Highleadon
Three Ashes
Candlemakers
Weston under Penyard
Aston Crews
Clifford's Mesne
Kent's Green
Glewstone
Tudorville
Hom Green
Coughton
Pontshill
Lea
Tibberton
Taynton
Rudford
Lassington
Llangarron
Llancloudy
Pencraig
Walford
Glasshouse Hill
Highnam Green
61
Marstow
Goodrich
Hope Mansell
Huntley
Bulley
Highnam
Llangrove
Kerne Bridge
Mitcheldean
Longhope
Birdwood
Churcham
Wye Valley Butterfly Zoo
Whitchurch
Symonds Yat Services
Welsh Bicknor
Greater Doward
Ruardean
Drybrook
Oakle Street
Ruardean Woodside
Blaisdon
Minsterworth
Ganarew
Lower Lydbrook
Upper Lydbrook
Nailbridge
Northwood Green
Elmore Back
Buckholt
Symonds Yat
English Bicknor
Lady Park Wood
Brierley
Flaxley
Westbury-on-Severn
Elmore
Farleys End
Fiddler's Elbow
Dixton
Christchurch
Edge End
Bilson Green
Cinderford
Elton
Quedgeley
Littledean
Monmouth
Nelson Mus
Berry Hill
Five Acres
Forest of Dean
Westbury Court
Longney
Hardwicke
Over Monnow
Wyesham
Staunton
Mile End
Colliery
Littledean Hall
Newnham
Boxbush
Penallt
Coleford
Broadwell
Beechenhurst Lodge
Ruspidge
St Augustines Farm
Rodley
Mitchel Troy
Redbrook
G W R Museum
Coalway
Upper Soudley
Dean Heritage Centre
Arlingham
Upper Framilode
Highbury Wood
Newland
Iron Mines
Fretherne
Saul
Moreton Valence
Pen-twyn
Offa's Dyke Path
Caves
Milkwall
Ellwood
Parkend
Whitminster
Hoop
Clearwell
Awre
The Noose
Frampton on Severn
Nupend
Stowe Green
Trow Green
Yorkley
Whitebrook
Whitecroft
Pillowell
Viney Hill
Blakeney
Trellech
Bream
The Eaves
River Severn
WWT Slimbridge Wetland Centre
Eastington
Offa's Dyke
Dean Forest Railway & Museum
St Briavels
Llandogo
St Briavels
Purton
Cambridge
Leonard Stanley
Parkhouse
Coldharbour
Lydney
Newerne
Slimbridge
Moorend
Frocester
Catbrook
Hewelsfield
Sharpness
Halmore
Gossington
Newtown
Coaley
Old Sta.
Tintern Parva
Brockweir
Aylburton
Wanswell
Breadstone
Lower Cam
Wye Valley Centre
Tintern Abbey
Netherend
Alvington
The Quarry
Nympsfield
Chapel Hill
Cam
Uley Tumulus
Woolaston
Brookend
Berkeley
Berkeley Castle
Stinchcombe
Tidenham Chase
Dursley
Ham
Dr Jenner's House
Uley
Wibdon
Stroat
Woodmancote
Boughspring
Bevington
St Arvans
Nibley Green
Woodford
Woodcroft
Tidenham
Shepperdine
Stone
North Nibley
Michaelwood Services
Tutshill
Hill
Chepstow
Mounton
Sedbury
Rockhampton
Falfield
Tortworth
Wotton-under-Edge
Oldbury-on-Severn
Charfield
Pwllmeyric
Chepstow (Cas-gwent)
Whitfield
Kingswood
Abbey Gatehouse
Little Avon
Beachley
Morton
Mathern
Severn Road Bridge Pont Hafren
Littleton-on-Severn
Milbury Heath
Cromhall
Churchend
Alderley
Severn View Services
Thornbury
43
Cromhall Common
Hillesley
Elberton
Alveston
Portskewett
Ingst
Oldown
Tytherington
Wickwar
0 1 2 3 miles
0 1 2 3 4 5 km

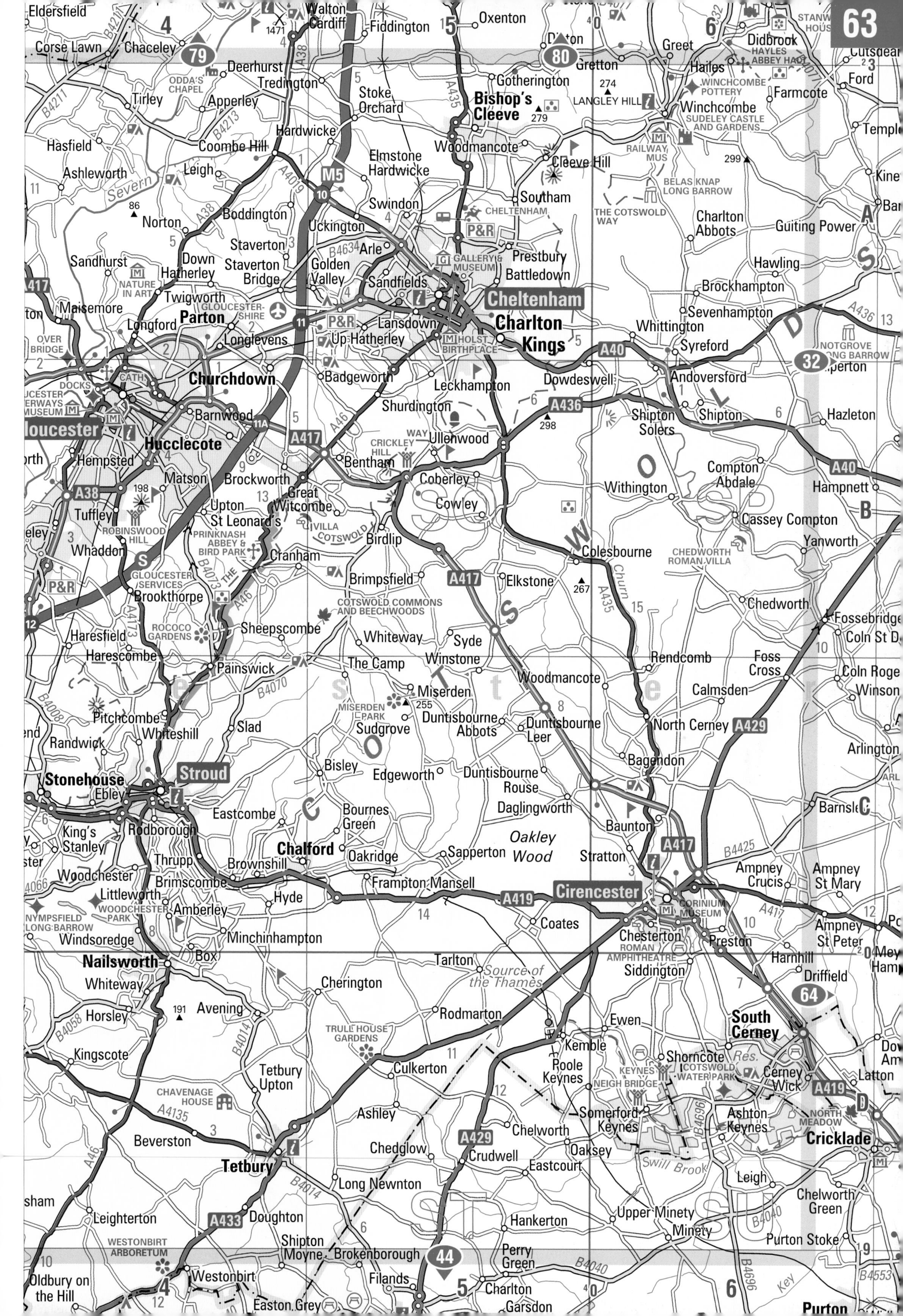
Eldersfield
Corse Lawn
Chaceley
Walton Cardiff
Fiddington
Oxenton
Dixton
Greet
Didbrook
Hayles Abbey
Hailes
Deerhurst
Odda's Chapel
Tredington
Gotherington
Langley Hill
Winchcombe Pottery
Farmcote
Ford
Tirley
Apperley
Stoke Orchard
Bishop's Cleeve
Winchcombe
Sudeley Castle and Gardens
Hasfield
Coombe Hill
Hardwicke
Elmstone Hardwicke
Woodmancote
Cleeve Hill
Railway Mus
Ashleworth
Leigh
Severn
M5
Swindon
Southam
Belas Knap Long Barrow
Norton
Boddington
Uckington
Cheltenham
The Cotswold Way
Charlton Abbots
Guiting Power
Staverton
Arle
Prestbury
Sandhurst
Down Hatherley
Staverton Bridge
Golden Valley
Gallery & Museum
Hawling
Nature in Art
Sandfields
Battledown
Brockhampton
Twigworth
Gloucestershire
Maisemore
Longford
Parton
Lansdown
Charlton Kings
Sevenhampton
Whittington
Over Bridge
Longlevens
Up Hatherley
Holst Birthplace
Syreford
Notgrove Long Barrow
Cath
Docks
Gloucester Waterways Museum
Churchdown
Badgeworth
Leckhampton
Dowdeswell
Andoversford
Gloucester
Barnwood
Shurdington
Shipton Solers
Shipton
Hazleton
Hucclecote
Crickley Hill
Ullenwood
Hempsted
Matson
Brockworth
Bentham
Coberley
Compton Abdale
Withington
Hampnett
Tuffley
Upton St Leonard's
Great Witcombe
Cowley
Cassey Compton
Robinswood Hill
Prinknash Abbey & Bird Park
Villa
Birdlip
Whaddon
Cranham
Colesbourne
Chedworth Roman Villa
Yanworth
Gloucester Services
Brimpsfield
Elkstone
Brookthorpe
Cotswold Commons and Beechwoods
Chedworth
Fossebridge
Coln St Dennis
Rococo Gardens
Sheepscombe
Haresfield
Whiteway
Syde
Harescombe
Painswick
The Camp
Winstone
Rendcomb
Foss Cross
Coln Rogers
Woodmancote
Calmsden
Winson
Miserden
Miserden Park
Pitchcombe
Whiteshill
Slad
Sudgrove
Duntisbourne Abbots
Duntisbourne Leer
North Cerney
Randwick
Arlington
Bagendon
Bisley
Edgeworth
Duntisbourne Rouse
Stonehouse
Stroud
Ebley
Eastcombe
Bournes Green
Daglingworth
Baunton
Barnsley
King's Stanley
Rodborough
Oakley Wood
Chalford
Oakridge
Sapperton
Stratton
Ampney Crucis
Ampney St Mary
Thrupp
Brownshill
Woodchester
Brimscombe
Frampton Mansell
Littleworth
Hyde
Cirencester
Corinium Museum
Nympsfield Long Barrow
Woodchester Park
Amberley
Coates
Chesterton
Roman Amphitheatre
Ampney St Peter
Preston
Windsoredge
Minchinhampton
Nailsworth
Box
Tarlton
Source of the Thames
Siddington
Harnhill
Driffield
Whiteway
Cherington
Horsley
Avening
Rodmarton
Ewen
South Cerney
Kingscote
Trull House Gardens
Kemble
Poole Keynes
Shorncote
Keynes
Cotswold Water Park
Cerney Wick
Latton
Tetbury Upton
Culkerton
Neigh Bridge
Chavenage House
Ashley
Somerford Keynes
Ashton Keynes
North Meadow
Beverston
Chelworth
Cricklade
Tetbury
Chedglow
Crudwell
Oaksey
Eastcourt
Swill Brook
Long Newnton
Leigh
Leighterton
Doughton
Hankerton
Upper Minety
Minety
Chelworth Green
Westonbirt Arboretum
Shipton Moyne
Brokenborough
Perry Green
Purton Stoke
Oldbury on the Hill
Westonbirt
Filands
Charlton
Easton Grey
Garsdon
Purton
Cotswolds
A38
A40
A46
A417
A419
A429
A433
A435
A436
A4135
A4173
A4019
B4008
B4014
B4040
B4058
B4066
B4070
B4073
B4211
B4213
B4425
B4553
B4634
B4696
79
80
32
64
44

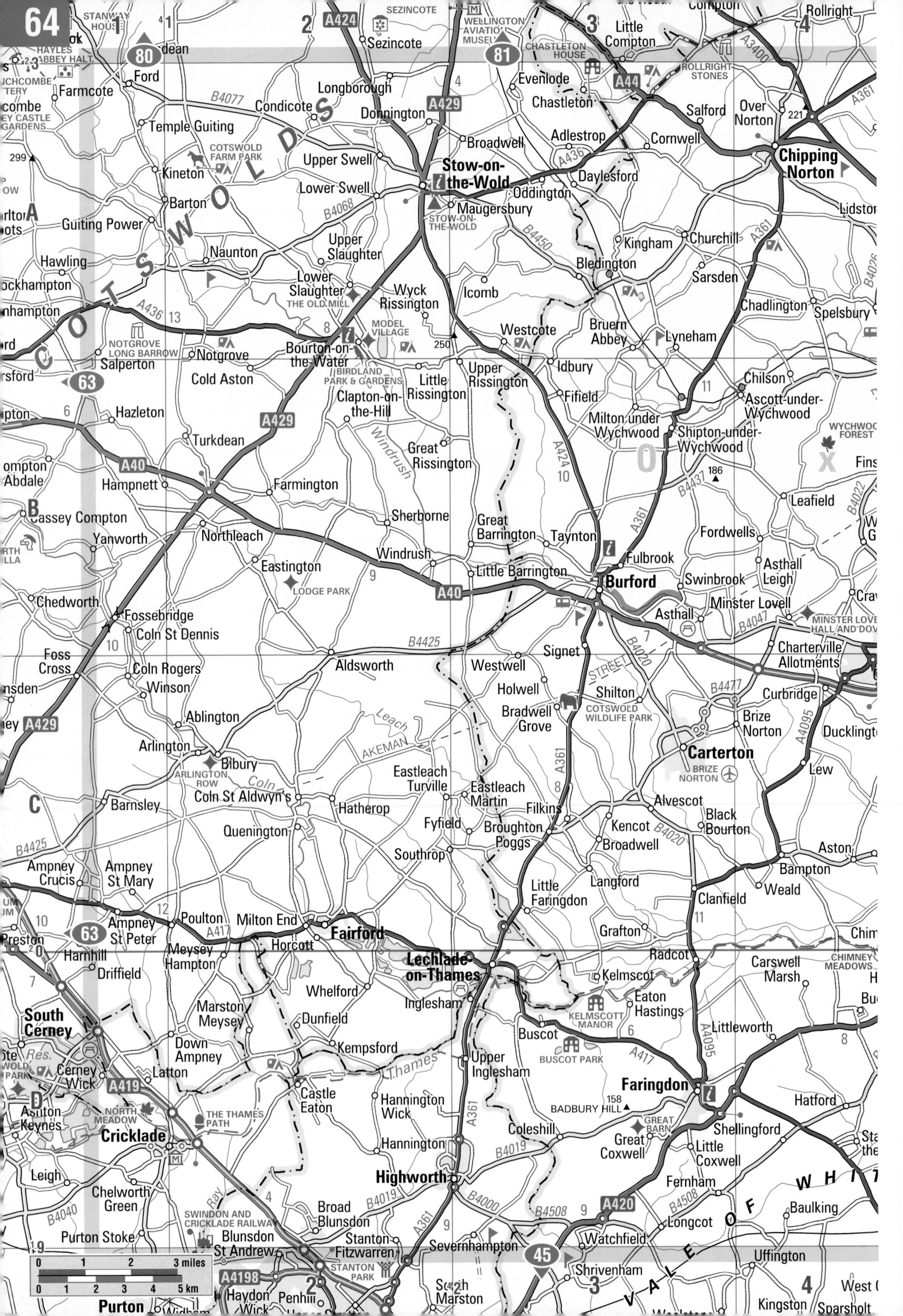

64
Sezincote
Wellington Aviation Museum
Chastleton House
Little Compton
Rollright
Rollright Stones
Hayles Abbey Halt
Ford
Farmcote
Temple Guiting
Condicote
Longborough
Donnington
Evenlode
Chastleton
Salford
Over Norton
Chipping Norton
Cotswold Farm Park
Kineton
Upper Swell
Lower Swell
Broadwell
Adlestrop
Cornwell
Stow-on-the-Wold
Oddington
Daylesford
Maugersbury
Barton
Guiting Power
Naunton
Upper Slaughter
Lower Slaughter
The Old Mill
Wyck Rissington
Icomb
Kingham
Churchill
Bledington
Sarsden
Hawling
Chadlington
Spelsbury
Cotswolds
Notgrove Long Barrow
Notgrove
Salperton
Cold Aston
Model Village
Bourton-on-the-Water
Birdland Park & Gardens
Westcote
Bruern Abbey
Lyneham
Little Rissington
Upper Rissington
Idbury
Fifield
Chilson
Ascott-under-Wychwood
Clapton-on-the-Hill
Milton under Wychwood
Shipton-under-Wychwood
Wychwood Forest
Hazleton
Turkdean
Windrush
Great Rissington
Hampnett
Farmington
Leafield
Cassey Compton
Yanworth
Northleach
Sherborne
Great Barrington
Taynton
Fordwells
Eastington
Lodge Park
Little Barrington
Fulbrook
Burford
Swinbrook
Asthall Leigh
Chedworth
Fossebridge
Coln St Dennis
Minster Lovell
Asthall
Minster Lovell Hall and Dovecote
Foss Cross
Coln Rogers
Winson
Aldsworth
Westwell
Signet
Charterville Allotments
Holwell
Shilton
Cotswold Wildlife Park
Bradwell Grove
Curbridge
Brize Norton
Ablington
Leach
Akeman Street
Arlington
Bibury
Arlington Row
Eastleach Turville
Eastleach Martin
Carterton
Brize Norton
Ducklington
Lew
Coln
Coln St Aldwyn's
Barnsley
Hatherop
Filkins
Alvescot
Black Bourton
Fyfield
Broughton Poggs
Kencot
Quenington
Broadwell
Southrop
Aston
Bampton
Ampney Crucis
Ampney St Mary
Little Faringdon
Langford
Weald
Clanfield
Ampney St Peter
Poulton
Milton End
Fairford
Grafton
Preston
Harnhill
Meysey Hampton
Horcott
Radcot
Driffield
Lechlade-on-Thames
Kelmscott
Carswell Marsh
Chimney Meadows
Whelford
Inglesham
Eaton Hastings
Kelmscott Manor
South Cerney
Marston Meysey
Dunfield
Littleworth
Buscot
Down Ampney
Kempsford
Buscot Park
Cerney Wick
Latton
Thames
Upper Inglesham
Faringdon
Castle Eaton
Hannington Wick
Badbury Hill
Hatford
Ashton Keynes
North Meadow
The Thames Path
Cricklade
Coleshill
Great Barn
Great Coxwell
Shellingford
Little Coxwell
Hannington
Leigh
Highworth
Fernham
Chelworth Green
Ray
Swindon and Cricklade Railway
Broad Blunsdon
Longcot
Baulking
Purton Stoke
Blunsdon St Andrew
Stanton Fitzwarren
Stanton Park
Severnhampton
Watchfield
Shrivenham
Uffington
Haydon Wick
Penhill
South Marston
Purton
Kingston
Sparsholt
Vale of White Horse
0 1 2 3 miles
0 1 2 3 4 5 km
A424
A429
A44
A436
A361
A3400
B4077
B4068
B4450
B4437
B4047
B4020
B4477
A4095
B4022
B4026
A40
B4425
A417
A419
B4019
B4000
B4508
A420
B4040
A4198

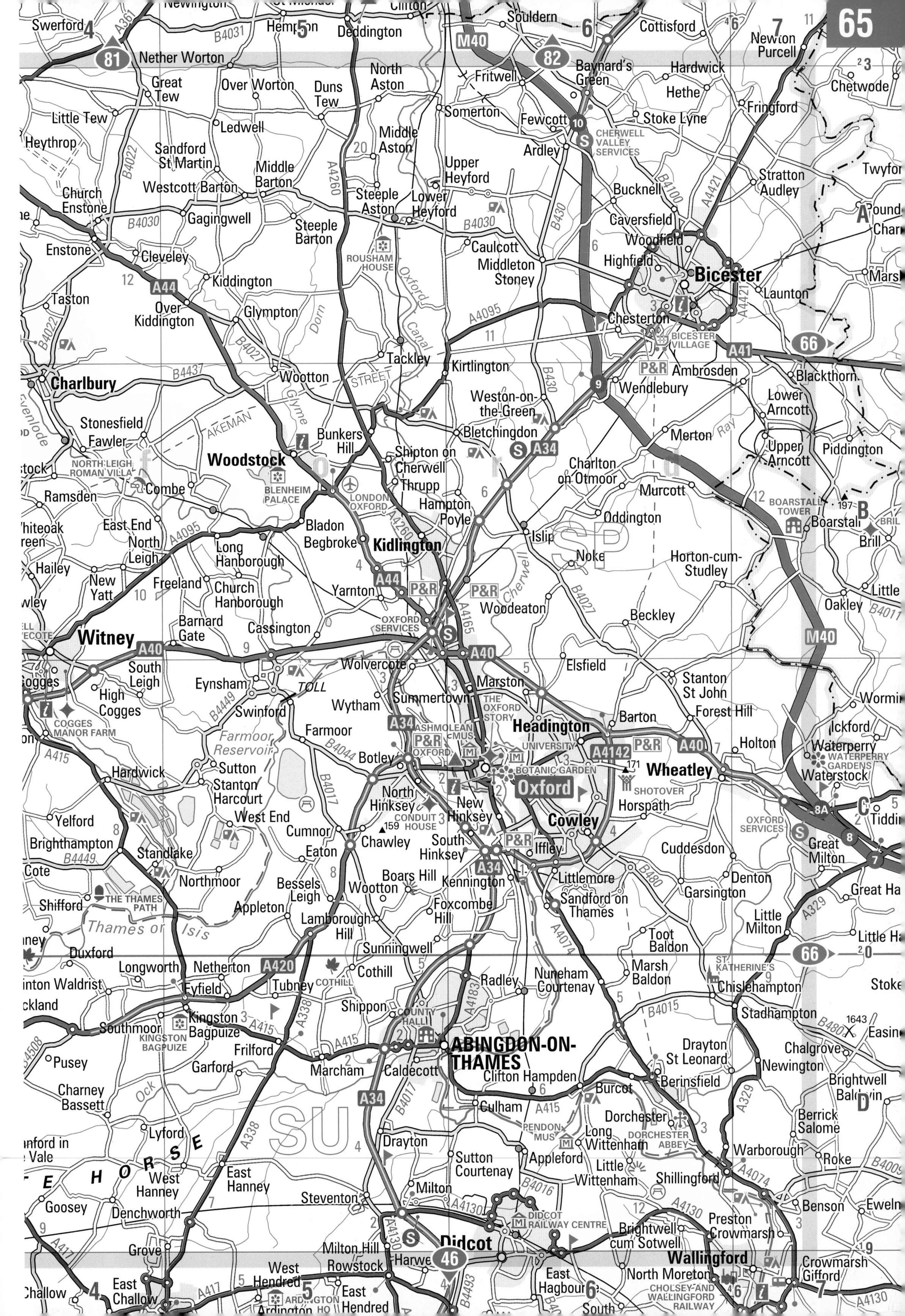
Swerford
Hempton
Deddington
Souldern
Cottisford
Newton Purcell
Nether Worton
Fritwell
Baynard's Green
Hardwick
Hethe
Chetwode
Great Tew
Over Worton
Duns Tew
North Aston
Somerton
Fewcott
Stoke Lyne
Fringford
Little Tew
Ledwell
Middle Aston
Ardley
CHERWELL VALLEY SERVICES
Heythrop
Sandford St Martin
Middle Barton
Upper Heyford
Bucknell
Stratton Audley
Twyford
Church Enstone
Westcott Barton
Steeple Aston
Lower Heyford
Caversfield
Pound
Gagingwell
Steeple Barton
Woodfield
Enstone
Cleveley
ROUSHAM HOUSE
Caulcott
Middleton Stoney
Highfield
Bicester
Kiddington
Oxford Canal
Launton
Taston
Over Kiddington
Glympton
Chesterton
BICESTER VILLAGE
Tackley
Kirtlington
Ambrosden
Blackthorn
Charlbury
Wootton
STREET
Weston-on-the-Green
Wendlebury
Lower Arncott
AKEMAN
Stonesfield
Fawler
Bunkers Hill
Bletchingdon
Merton
Upper Arncott
Piddington
NORTH LEIGH ROMAN VILLA
Woodstock
Shipton on Cherwell
Charlton on Otmoor
Thrupp
Combe
BLENHEIM PALACE
LONDON OXFORD
Hampton Poyle
Murcott
Ramsden
Oddington
BOARSTALL TOWER
Boarstall
Brill
East End
Bladon
Begbroke
Kidlington
Islip
Noke
North Leigh
Long Hanborough
Horton-cum-Studley
Hailey
New Yatt
Freeland
Church Hanborough
Yarnton
P&R
Woodeaton
Little
Oakley
Witney
Barnard Gate
Cassington
OXFORD SERVICES
Beckley
South Leigh
Wolvercote
Elsfield
Eynsham
TOLL
Marston
Stanton St John
High Cogges
Swinford
Wytham
Summertown
THE OXFORD STORY
Forest Hill
COGGES MANOR FARM
Farmoor
ASHMOLEAN MUS
Headington
Barton
Ickford
Farmoor Reservoir
Botley
UNIVERSITY
Holton
Waterperry
WATERPERRY GARDENS
Hardwick
Sutton
BOTANIC GARDEN
Oxford
Wheatley
Waterstock
Stanton Harcourt
North Hinksey
New Hinksey
SHOTOVER
Horspath
CONDUIT HOUSE
Cowley
OXFORD SERVICES
Yelford
West End
Cumnor
Chawley
South Hinksey
Iffley
Cuddesdon
Great Milton
Brighthampton
Eaton
Standlake
Boars Hill
Kennington
Littlemore
Denton
Cote
Northmoor
Bessels Leigh
Wootton
Sandford on Thames
Garsington
Great Ha
Shifford
THE THAMES PATH
Appleton
Foxcombe Hill
Little Milton
Thames or Isis
Lamborough Hill
Toot Baldon
Little Ha
Sunningwell
Duxford
Cothill
Radley
Marsh Baldon
ST KATHERINE'S
Longworth
Netherton
Nuneham Courtenay
Chislehampton
Stoke
Fyfield
Tubney
COTHILL
Kingston Bagpuize
Shippon
COUNTY HALL
Stadhampton
Southmoor
KINGSTON BAGPUIZE
ABINGDON-ON-THAMES
Drayton St Leonard
Chalgrove
Easing
Pusey
Frilford
Marcham
Caldecott
Newington
Garford
Clifton Hampden
Berinsfield
Brightwell Baldwin
Charney Bassett
Burcot
Culham
Dorchester
Berrick Salome
Ock
SU
PENDON MUS
Long Wittenham
DORCHESTER ABBEY
Lyford
Drayton
Stanford in the Vale
Sutton Courtenay
Appleford
Warborough
Roke
WHITE HORSE
West Hanney
East Hanney
Little Wittenham
Shillingford
Milton
Benson
Goosey
Denchworth
Steventon
Preston Crowmarsh
Ewelme
DIDCOT RAILWAY CENTRE
Brightwell cum Sotwell
Grove
Milton Hill
Didcot
Wallingford
Crowmarsh Gifford
West Hendred
Rowstock
Harwell
East Hagbourne
North Moreton
East Challow
Challow
ARDINGTON HO
East Hendred
Ardington
CHOLSEY AND WALLINGFORD RAILWAY
South
M40
A361
A4260
A44
A4095
A41
A34
A40
A4165
A4142
A415
A420
A338
A4183
A4074
A329
A4130
A417
A4421
B4031
B4022
B4030
B430
B4100
B4027
B4437
B4449
B4044
B4017
B4480
B4015
B480
B4016
B4493
B4009
B4011
B4508
Cherwell
Glyme
Dorn
Evenlode
Ray
81
82
66
46
SP
1643
197
171
159

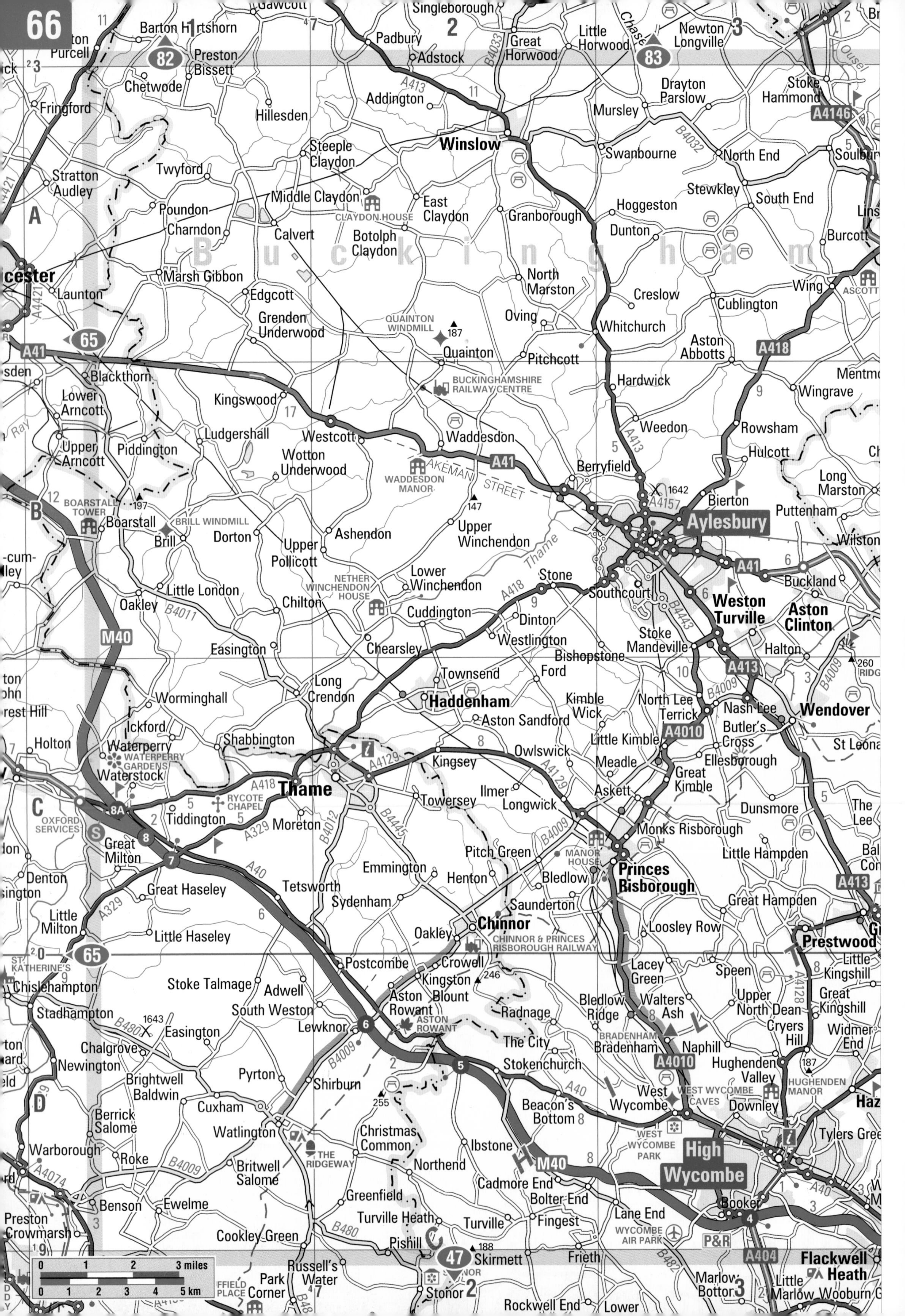

Singleborough
Padbury
Adstock
Great Horwood
Little Horwood
Newton Longville
Barton Hartshorn
Preston Bissett
82
83
Chetwode
Fringford
Addington
Hillesden
Drayton Parslow
Stoke Hammond
Mursley
A4146
Winslow
Swanbourne
North End
Soulbury
Steeple Claydon
Twyford
Stratton Audley
Middle Claydon
Claydon House
East Claydon
Stewkley
South End
Poundon
Charndon
Calvert
Botolph Claydon
Granborough
Hoggeston
Dunton
Burcott
Buckingham
Marsh Gibbon
North Marston
Launton
Edgcott
Creslow
Wing
Ascott
Cublington
Grendon Underwood
Quainton Windmill
187
Oving
Whitchurch
Aston Abbotts
65
A41
A418
Quainton
Pitchcott
Blackthorn
Buckinghamshire Railway Centre
Hardwick
Wingrave
Lower Arncott
Kingswood
Upper Arncott
Piddington
Ludgershall
Westcott
Waddesdon
Weedon
Rowsham
Wotton Underwood
Hulcott
Waddesdon Manor
Akeman Street
Berryfield
Long Marston
A413
1642
A4157
Bierton
Puttenham
Boarstall Tower
197
Boarstall
Brill Windmill
Brill
Dorton
Ashendon
147
Upper Winchendon
Aylesbury
Upper Pollicott
Thame
Wilstone
Buckland
Nether Winchendon House
Lower Winchendon
Stone
Southcourt
Weston Turville
Aston Clinton
Oakley
Little London
B4011
Chilton
Cuddington
Dinton
B4443
M40
Easington
Chearsley
Westlington
Stoke Mandeville
Halton
Bishopstone
260
Townsend
Ford
Worminghall
Long Crendon
Haddenham
Kimble Wick
North Lee
Terrick
Nash Lee
Wendover
Aston Sandford
B4009
A4010
Ickford
Holton
Waterperry
Waterperry Gardens
Shabbington
Owlswick
Little Kimble
Butler's Cross
St Leonards
Meadle
Ellesborough
Kingsey
A4129
Waterstock
Great Kimble
Thame
Towersey
Ilmer
Longwick
Askett
Dunsmore
The Lee
8A
Oxford Services
Tiddington
Rycote Chapel
A329
Moreton
B4012
B4445
Monks Risborough
Little Hampden
Great Milton
Pitch Green
Manor House
Denton
Emmington
Henton
Princes Risborough
Bledlow
A40
Great Haseley
Tetsworth
Sydenham
Great Hampden
Saunderton
Little Milton
Little Haseley
Oakley
Chinnor
Loosley Row
Prestwood
Chinnor & Princes Risborough Railway
St Katherine's
Chiselhampton
Postcombe
Crowell
Lacey Green
Speen
Little Kingshill
Stoke Talmage
Adwell
Kingston Blount
246
Stadhampton
South Weston
Aston Rowant
Bledlow Ridge
Walters Ash
Upper North Dean
Great Kingshill
A4128
1643
Easington
B480
Radnage
Lewknor
Aston Rowant
Cryers Hill
Widmer End
Chalgrove
The City
Bradenham
Naphill
Newington
Stokenchurch
Hughenden Valley
187
Brightwell Baldwin
Pyrton
Shirburn
Hughenden Manor
Berrick Salome
Cuxham
255
Beacon's Bottom
West Wycombe
West Wycombe Caves
Downley
Watlington
Christmas Common
West Wycombe Park
Tylers Green
Warborough
Roke
The Ridgeway
Ibstone
High Wycombe
Britwell Salome
Northend
A4074
B4009
Greenfield
Cadmore End
Bolter End
Benson
Ewelme
Turville Heath
Turville
Fingest
Lane End
Booker
Preston Crowmarsh
Cookley Green
Wycombe Air Park
P&R
A404
Pishill
47
188
Skirmett
Frieth
Flackwell Heath
Russell's Water
B482
Park Corner
Stonor
Marlow Bottom
Little Marlow
Wooburn Green
Rockwell End
Lower
0 1 2 3 miles
0 1 2 3 4 5 km

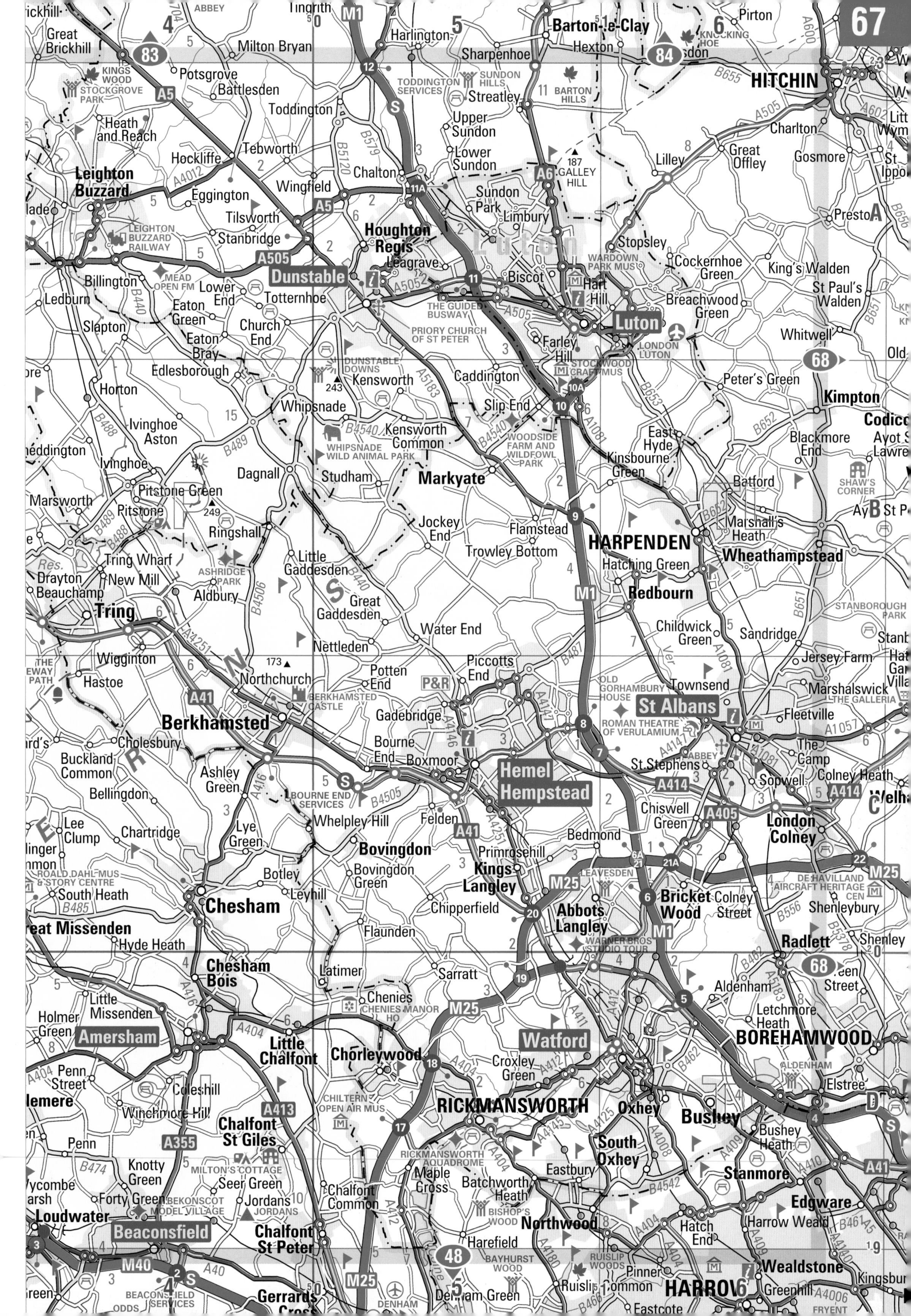
Great Brickhill
Milton Bryan
Harlington
Barton-le-Clay
Pirton
Sharpenhoe
Hexton
HITCHIN
Potsgrove
Battlesden
Toddington
TODDINGTON SERVICES
SUNDON HILLS
Streatley
BARTON HILLS
KINGS WOOD
STOCKGROVE PARK
Heath and Reach
Upper Sundon
Lower Sundon
Charlton
Great Offley
Lilley
Gosmore
Hockliffe
Tebworth
Chalton
Leighton Buzzard
Eggington
Wingfield
GALLEY HILL
Sundon Park
Limbury
Tilsworth
Stanbridge
Houghton Regis
Luton
Stopsley
Preston
LEIGHTON BUZZARD RAILWAY
Dunstable
Leagrave
Biscot
WARDOWN PARK MUS
Cockernhoe Green
King's Walden
Billington
MEAD OPEN FM
Lower End
Totternhoe
Hart Hill
Breachwood Green
St Paul's Walden
Ledburn
Eaton Green
THE GUIDED BUSWAY
Slapton
Church End
Eaton Bray
PRIORY CHURCH OF ST PETER
Farley Hill
LONDON LUTON
Whitwell
Edlesborough
DUNSTABLE DOWNS
STOCKWOOD CRAFT MUS
Kensworth
Caddington
Peter's Green
Horton
Whipsnade
Slip End
Kimpton
Ivinghoe Aston
Kensworth Common
East Hyde
Blackmore End
WHIPSNADE WILD ANIMAL PARK
WOODSIDE FARM AND WILDFOWL PARK
Kinsbourne Green
Ivinghoe
Dagnall
Studham
Markyate
Batford
SHAW'S CORNER
Marsworth
Pitstone Green
Pitstone
Jockey End
Flamstead
HARPENDEN
Marshall's Heath
Ringshall
Trowley Bottom
Wheathampstead
Tring Wharf
Little Gaddesden
Hatching Green
Drayton Beauchamp
New Mill
ASHRIDGE PARK
Redbourn
Aldbury
Great Gaddesden
Tring
STANBOROUGH PARK
Childwick Green
Sandridge
Water End
Wigginton
Nettleden
Jersey Farm
Piccotts End
Potten End
Hastoe
Northchurch
OLD GORHAMBURY HOUSE
Townsend
Marshalswick
BERKHAMSTED CASTLE
St Albans
THE GALLERIA
Gadebridge
Berkhamsted
ROMAN THEATRE OF VERULAMIUM
Fleetville
Cholesbury
Bourne End
Boxmoor
Hemel Hempstead
The Camp
Buckland Common
St Stephens
Colney Heath
Ashley Green
Sopwell
Bellingdon
BOURNE END SERVICES
Chiswell Green
London Colney
Lee Clump
Whelpley Hill
Felden
Bedmond
Chartridge
Lye Green
Bovingdon
Primrosehill
ROALD DAHL MUS & STORY CENTRE
Botley
Bovingdon Green
Kings Langley
LEAVESDEN
DE HAVILLAND AIRCRAFT HERITAGE CEN
South Heath
Leyhill
Bricket Wood
Colney Street
Chesham
Chipperfield
Abbots Langley
Shenleybury
Great Missenden
Hyde Heath
Flaunden
WARNER BROS STUDIO TOUR
Radlett
Shenley
Chesham Bois
Latimer
Sarratt
Aldenham
Little Missenden
Chenies
CHENIES MANOR HO
Letchmore Heath
Holmer Green
Amersham
Little Chalfont
Chorleywood
Watford
BOREHAMWOOD
Penn Street
Coleshill
Croxley Green
ALDENHAM
Elstree
CHILTERN OPEN AIR MUS
RICKMANSWORTH
Oxhey
Bushey
Winchmore Hill
Chalfont St Giles
Bushey Heath
Penn
South Oxhey
Knotty Green
MILTON'S COTTAGE
Seer Green
RICKMANSWORTH AQUADROME
Maple Cross
Eastbury
Stanmore
Forty Green
Jordans
Chalfont Common
Batchworth Heath
BEKONSCOT MODEL VILLAGE
Edgware
Loudwater
Beaconsfield
Chalfont St Peter
BISHOP'S WOOD
Northwood
Hatch End
Harrow Weald
Harefield
BAYHURST WOOD
RUISLIP WOODS
Pinner
Wealdstone
BEACONSFIELD SERVICES
Gerrards Cross
Denham Green
DENHAM
Ruislip Common
HARROW
Greenhill
Kingsbury
Eastcote
83
84
68
48

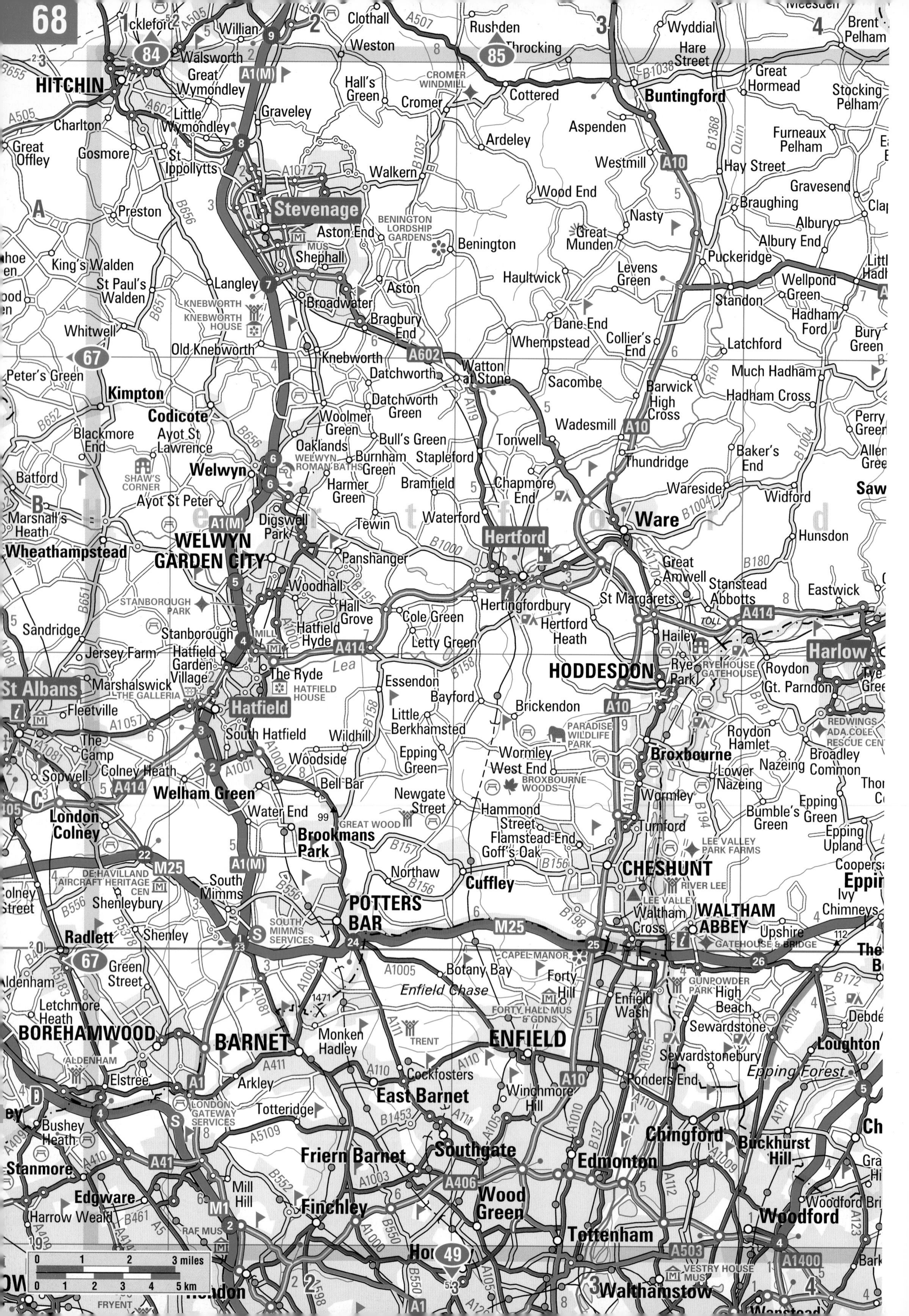

Ickleford
Willian
Clothall
Rushden
Wyddial
Brent Pelham
84
Walsworth
Weston
85
Throcking
Hare Street
HITCHIN
Great Wymondley
Hall's Green
CROMER WINDMILL
Cromer
Cottered
Great Hormead
Buntingford
Stocking Pelham
Charlton
Little Wymondley
Graveley
Aspenden
Furneaux Pelham
Great Offley
Gosmore
St Ippollytts
Ardeley
Westmill
Walkern
Hay Street
Wood End
Gravesend
Stevenage
Preston
Braughing
Nasty
BENINGTON LORDSHIP GARDENS
Aston End
Albury
Great Munden
Albury End
King's Walden
Shephall
Benington
Puckeridge
Levens Green
St Paul's Walden
Langley
Haultwick
Wellpond Green
Aston
Standon
KNEBWORTH HOUSE
Broadwater
Hadham Ford
Bragbury End
Dane End
Whitwell
Whempstead
Collier's End
Bury Green
67
Old Knebworth
Latchford
Knebworth
Watton at Stone
Peter's Green
Datchworth
Sacombe
Much Hadham
Kimpton
Barwick
Datchworth Green
High Cross
Hadham Cross
Codicote
Woolmer Green
Wadesmill
Perry Green
Blackmore End
Ayot St Lawrence
Oaklands
Bull's Green
Tonwell
Baker's End
Allen's Green
Welwyn
WELWYN ROMAN BATHS
Burnham Green
Stapleford
Thundridge
Batford
SHAW'S CORNER
Harmer Green
Bramfield
Chapmore End
Wareside
Widford
Ayot St Peter
Marshall's Heath
Digswell Park
Tewin
Waterford
Ware
Hunsdon
WELWYN GARDEN CITY
Wheathampstead
Hertford
Panshanger
Great Amwell
STANBOROUGH PARK
Woodhall
Hertingfordbury
St Margarets
Stanstead Abbotts
Eastwick
Hall Grove
Cole Green
Hertford Heath
Hailey
Harlow
Sandridge
Stanborough
Hatfield Hyde
Letty Green
Jersey Farm
Hatfield Garden Village
HODDESDON
Rye Park
RYE HOUSE GATEHOUSE
Roydon
Marshalswick
The Ryde
Essendon
Gt. Parndon
St Albans
THE GALLERIA
HATFIELD HOUSE
Bayford
Fleetville
Hatfield
Brickendon
Little Berkhamsted
PARADISE WILDLIFE PARK
REDWINGS ADA COLE RESCUE CENTRE
The Camp
South Hatfield
Wildhill
Roydon Hamlet
Woodside
Epping Green
Wormley West End
Broxbourne
Broadley Common
Nazeing
Sopwell
Colney Heath
BROXBOURNE WOODS
Lower Nazeing
Bell Bar
Wormley
London Colney
Welham Green
Newgate Street
Hammond Street
Bumble's Green
Epping Green
Water End
Brookmans Park
GREAT WOOD
Turnford
Flamstead End
Goff's Oak
LEE VALLEY PARK FARMS
Epping Upland
DE HAVILLAND AIRCRAFT HERITAGE CEN
South Mimms
Northaw
Cuffley
CHESHUNT
Coopersale
Epping
Colney Street
Shenleybury
POTTERS BAR
RIVER LEE
LEE VALLEY
Ivy Chimneys
Radlett
SOUTH MIMMS SERVICES
Shenley
Waltham Cross
WALTHAM ABBEY
Upshire
GATEHOUSE & BRIDGE
CAPEL MANOR
Aldenham
Green Street
Botany Bay
Forty Hill
GUNPOWDER PARK
Enfield Chase
Letchmore Heath
FORTY HALL MUS & GDNS
Enfield Wash
High Beach
BOREHAMWOOD
BARNET
Monken Hadley
TRENT
ENFIELD
Sewardstone
Loughton
ALDENHAM
Sewardstonebury
Elstree
Arkley
Cockfosters
Ponders End
Epping Forest
LONDON GATEWAY SERVICES
East Barnet
Winchmore Hill
Bushey Heath
Totteridge
Chingford
Buckhurst Hill
Southgate
Friern Barnet
Edmonton
Stanmore
Edgware
Mill Hill
Wood Green
Woodford Bridge
Finchley
Woodford
Harrow Weald
RAF MUS
Tottenham
VESTRY HOUSE MUS
Walthamstow
FRYENT
49
0 1 2 3 miles
0 1 2 3 4 5 km

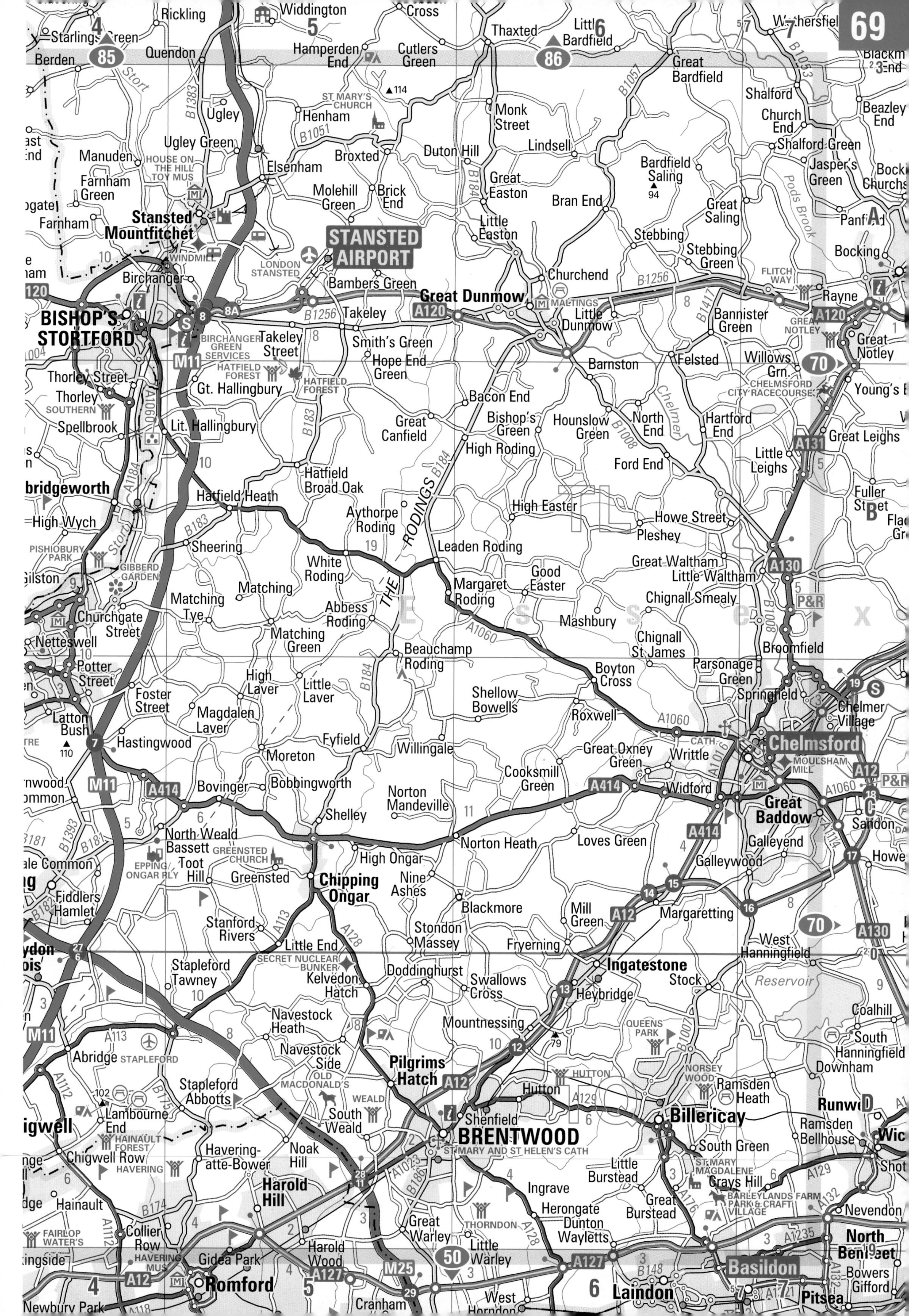
Rickling
Widdington
Cross
Thaxted
Little Bardfield
Wethersfield
Starlings Green
Berden
Quendon
Hamperden End
Cutlers Green
85
86
Great Bardfield
Blackmore End
ST MARY'S CHURCH
Henham
Ugley
Monk Street
Shalford
Church End
Beazley End
Ugley Green
Broxted
Duton Hill
Lindsell
Shalford Green
Manuden
HOUSE ON THE HILL TOY MUS
Elsenham
Bardfield Saling
Jasper's Green
Farnham Green
Molehill Green
Brick End
Great Easton
Bran End
Great Saling
Farnham
Stansted Mountfitchet
STANSTED AIRPORT
Little Easton
Stebbing
Stebbing Green
Bocking
WINDMILL
LONDON STANSTED
Churchend
FLITCH WAY
Birchanger
Bambers Green
Rayne
Great Dunmow
MALTINGS
Little Dunmow
Bannister Green
GREAT NOTLEY
Great Notley
BISHOP'S STORTFORD
Takeley
A120
Takeley Street
BIRCHANGER GREEN SERVICES
Smith's Green
Hope End Green
Barnston
Felsted
Willows Grn.
70
HATFIELD FOREST
Thorley Street
Gt. Hallingbury
Thorley
SOUTHERN
Bacon End
CHELMSFORD CITY RACECOURSE
Young's End
Spellbrook
Lit. Hallingbury
Great Canfield
Bishop's Green
Hounslow Green
North End
Hartford End
Great Leighs
High Roding
Ford End
Little Leighs
A131
Sawbridgeworth
Hatfield Heath
Hatfield Broad Oak
THE RODINGS
High Easter
Fuller Street
High Wych
Aythorpe Roding
Howe Street
Pleshey
PISHIOBURY PARK
Sheering
Leaden Roding
White Roding
GIBBERD GARDEN
Great Waltham
Little Waltham
Good Easter
A130
Matching
Matching Tye
Margaret Roding
Chignall Smealy
P&R
Churchgate Street
Abbess Roding
Mashbury
Essex
Matching Green
Chignall St James
Netteswell
Beauchamp Roding
Broomfield
Potter Street
Boyton Cross
Parsonage Green
High Laver
Little Laver
Foster Street
Shellow Bowells
Springfield
Chelmer Village
Magdalen Laver
Roxwell
Latton Bush
Fyfield
Hastingwood
Moreton
Willingale
Great Oxney Green
Writtle
Chelmsford
MOULSHAM MILL
Cooksmill Green
A414
Bovinger
Bobbingworth
Norton Mandeville
Widford
Great Baddow
Sandon
Shelley
North Weald Bassett
GREENSTED CHURCH
Norton Heath
Loves Green
Galleyend
Howe Green
EPPING ONGAR RLY
Toot Hill
Greensted
High Ongar
Galleywood
Fiddlers Hamlet
Chipping Ongar
Nine Ashes
Blackmore
Mill Green
Margaretting
Stanford Rivers
Stondon Massey
Fryerning
West Hanningfield
Little End
SECRET NUCLEAR BUNKER
Stapleford Tawney
Kelvedon Hatch
Doddinghurst
Swallows Cross
Ingatestone
Stock
Heybridge
Reservoir
Navestock Heath
Mountnessing
QUEENS PARK
Coalhill
South Hanningfield
Abridge
STAPLEFORD
Navestock Side
Pilgrims Hatch
HUTTON
NORSEY WOOD
Ramsden Heath
Downham
OLD MACDONALD'S
Stapleford Abbotts
WEALD
Hutton
Runwell
Lambourne End
South Weald
Shenfield
Billericay
Ramsden Bellhouse
Chigwell
HAINAULT FOREST
BRENTWOOD
ST MARY AND ST HELEN'S CATH
South Green
Havering-atte-Bower
Noak Hill
Chigwell Row
HAVERING
Little Burstead
ST MARY MAGDALENE
Crays Hill
Hainault
Harold Hill
Ingrave
BARLEYLANDS FARM PARK & CRAFT VILLAGE
Herongate
Great Burstead
Nevendon
FAIRLOP WATER'S
Collier Row
THORNDON
Dunton Wayletts
North Benfleet
Great Warley
Little Warley
Harold Wood
Gidea Park
HAVERING MUS
50
Basildon
Bowers Gifford
Romford
Laindon
Pitsea
Newbury Park
Cranham
West Horndon
M11
M25
A12
A127
A1060
A414
A113
A128
A129
A130
A131
A132
A1016
A1114
A176
A1235
B1256
B184
B183
B1008
B1007
B148
B186
B1383
B1051
B1057
B1053
B1417
B1393
B175
B174
B181

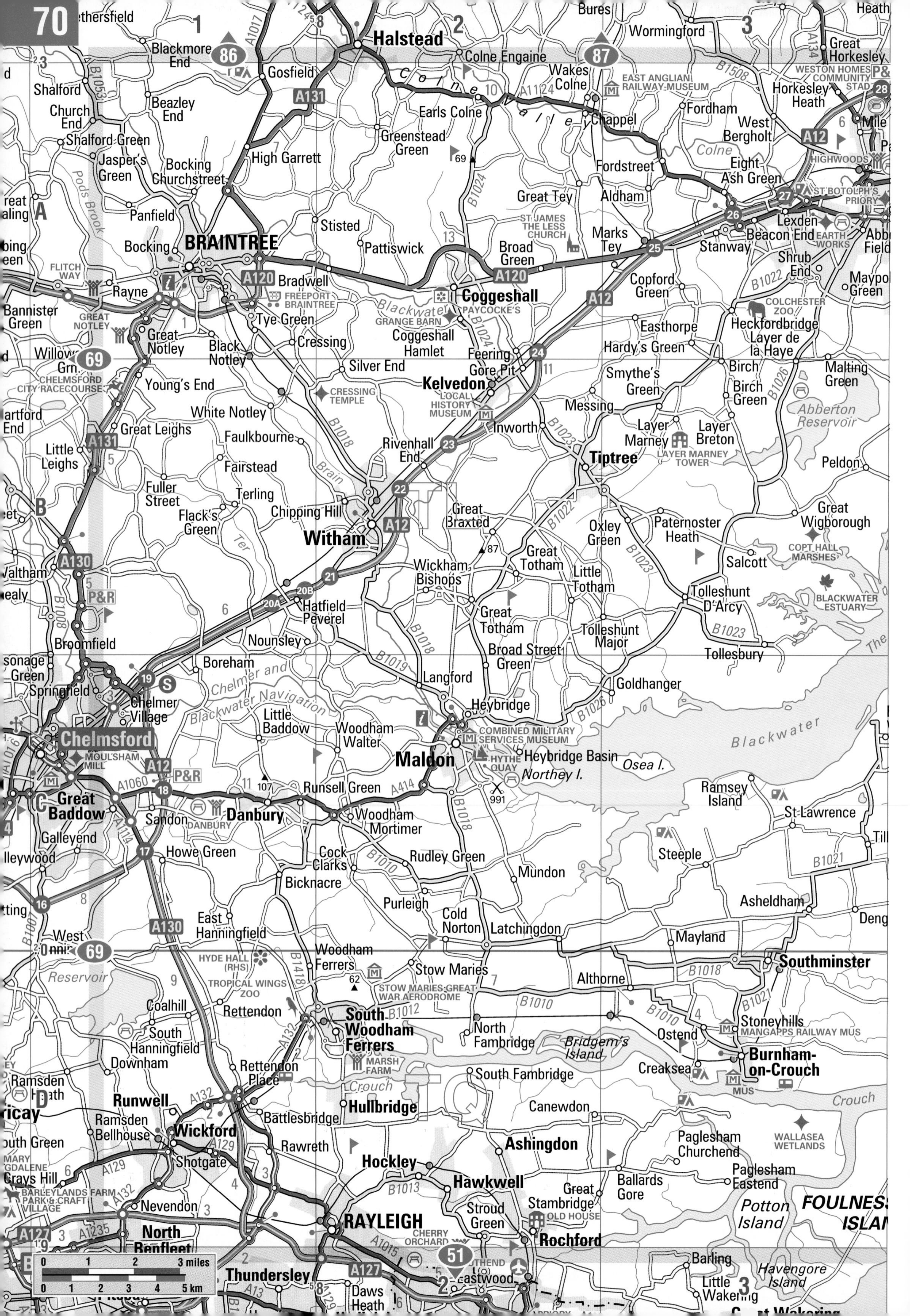
Halstead
Bures
Wormingford
Heath
Great Horkesley
Blackmore End
86
87
Gosfield
Colne Engaine
Wakes Colne
EAST ANGLIAN RAILWAY MUSEUM
WESTON HOMES COMMUNITY STAD
Horkesley Heath
Shalford
Church End
Beazley End
A131
Colne Valley
Earls Colne
Chappel
Fordham
West Bergholt
Mile
Shalford Green
Greenstead Green
High Garrett
Jasper's Green
Bocking Churchstreet
Colne
Eight Ash Green
HIGHWOODS
Fordstreet
Great Tey
Aldham
ST BOTOLPH'S PRIORY
Panfield
Pods Brook
Stisted
ST JAMES THE LESS CHURCH
Lexden
Marks Tey
Beacon End
EARTH WORKS
Bocking
BRAINTREE
Pattiswick
Broad Green
Stanway
Shrub End
FLITCH WAY
Rayne
A120
Bradwell
Coggeshall
Copford Green
Maypole Green
FREEPORT BRAINTREE
A12
COLCHESTER ZOO
Bannister Green
GREAT NOTLEY
Tye Green
Blackwater
PAYCOCKE'S
GRANGE BARN
Easthorpe
Heckfordbridge
Great Notley
Black Notley
Cressing
Coggeshall Hamlet
Feering
Hardy's Green
Layer de la Haye
Willow Grn
69
Silver End
Gore Pit
Birch
Malting Green
CHELMSFORD CITY RACECOURSE
Young's End
Kelvedon
Smythe's Green
Birch Green
CRESSING TEMPLE
LOCAL HISTORY MUSEUM
Messing
Abberton Reservoir
White Notley
Inworth
Layer Marney
Layer Breton
Great Leighs
Faulkbourne
Rivenhall End
B1018
LAYER MARNEY TOWER
Little Leighs
Tiptree
Peldon
Fairstead
Brain
Fuller Street
Terling
Great Braxted
Oxley Green
Paternoster Heath
Great Wigborough
Flack's Green
Chipping Hill
Witham
Ter
Great Totham
COPT HALL MARSHES
A130
Salcott
Wickham Bishops
Little Totham
Tolleshunt D'Arcy
Hatfield Peverel
BLACKWATER ESTUARY
Great Totham
Tolleshunt Major
Broomfield
Nounsley
B1023
Tollesbury
Boreham
Broad Street Green
Langford
Goldhanger
Springfield
Chelmer and Blackwater Navigation
Chelmer Village
Heybridge
Little Baddow
Woodham Walter
Chelmsford
COMBINED MILITARY SERVICES MUSEUM
MOULSHAM MILL
Maldon
HYTHE QUAY
Heybridge Basin
Blackwater
Osea I.
Northey I.
P&R
Runsell Green
A414
Ramsey Island
Great Baddow
Danbury
Sandon
Woodham Mortimer
St Lawrence
Galleyend
Howe Green
Cock Clarks
Rudley Green
Steeple
B1021
Bicknacre
Mundon
Purleigh
Asheldham
Cold Norton
Latchingdon
Deng
East Hanningfield
Mayland
West Hanningfield
Woodham Ferrers
HYDE HALL (RHS)
Stow Maries
Southminster
Reservoir
TROPICAL WINGS ZOO
STOW MARIES GREAT WAR AERODROME
Althorne
Coalhill
Rettendon
South Woodham Ferrers
B1010
Stoneyhills
MANGAPPS RAILWAY MUS
South Hanningfield
North Fambridge
Bridgemarsh Island
Ostend
Downham
Rettendon Place
MARSH FARM
Burnham-on-Crouch
Ramsden Heath
Crouch
South Fambridge
Creeksea
Runwell
Hullbridge
Canewdon
Crouch
Ramsden Bellhouse
Battlesbridge
Wickford
WALLASEA WETLANDS
Rawreth
Ashingdon
Paglesham Churchend
Shotgate
Crays Hill
Hockley
Hawkwell
BARLEYLANDS FARM PARK & CRAFT VILLAGE
Great Stambridge
Ballards Gore
Paglesham Eastend
Nevendon
Stroud Green
Potton Island
FOULNESS ISLAND
North Benfleet
RAYLEIGH
CHERRY ORCHARD
OLD HOUSE
Rochford
51
Barling
Havengore Island
Thundersley
Eastwood
Daws Heath
Little Wakering
0 1 2 3 miles
0 1 2 3 4 5 km

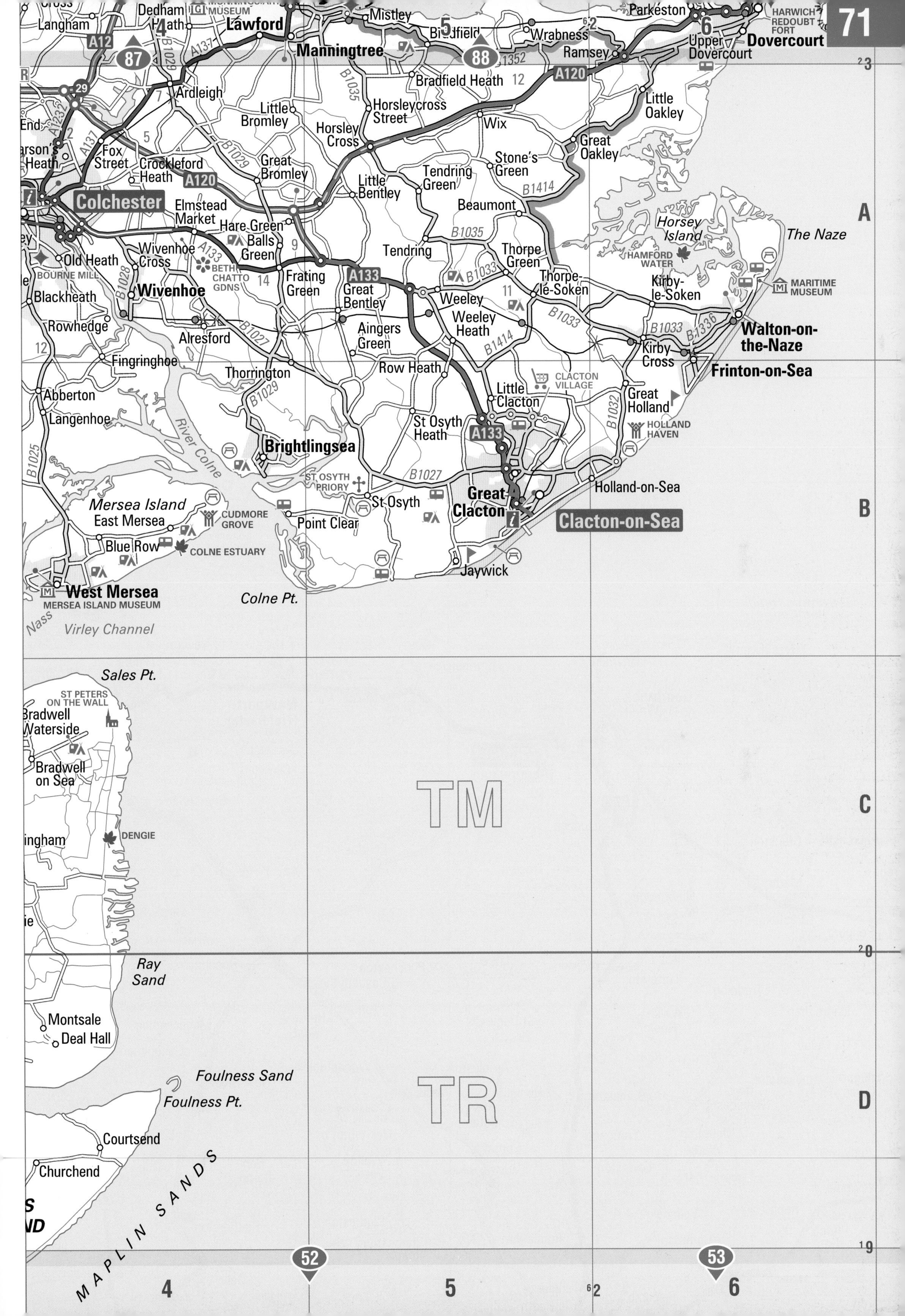

Langham
Dedham Heath
Lawford
Mistley
Manningtree
Bradfield
Wrabness
Parkeston
Ramsey
Upper Dovercourt
Dovercourt
HARWICH REDOUBT FORT
87
88
A12
A120
A133
Ardleigh
Bradfield Heath
Little Bromley
Horsleycross Street
Horsley Cross
Wix
Little Oakley
Great Oakley
Fox Street
Crockleford Heath
Great Bromley
Tendring Green
Stone's Green
Little Bentley
Colchester
Elmstead Market
Beaumont
Hare Green
Balls Green
Horsey Island
The Naze
Tendring
Thorpe Green
HAMFORD WATER
Wivenhoe Cross
Old Heath
BOURNE MILL
BETH CHATTO GDNS
Frating Green
Great Bentley
Thorpe-le-Soken
Kirby-le-Soken
MARITIME MUSEUM
Wivenhoe
Blackheath
Weeley
Weeley Heath
Rowhedge
Alresford
Aingers Green
Walton-on-the-Naze
Kirby Cross
Fingringhoe
Frinton-on-Sea
Thorrington
Row Heath
CLACTON VILLAGE
Abberton
Little Clacton
Great Holland
Langenhoe
St Osyth Heath
HOLLAND HAVEN
River Colne
Brightlingsea
ST OSYTH PRIORY
Holland-on-Sea
Mersea Island
East Mersea
CUDMORE GROVE
St Osyth
Great Clacton
Clacton-on-Sea
Point Clear
Blue Row
COLNE ESTUARY
Jaywick
West Mersea
MERSEA ISLAND MUSEUM
Colne Pt.
Nass
Virley Channel
Sales Pt.
ST PETERS ON THE WALL
Bradwell Waterside
Bradwell on Sea
TM
DENGIE
Ray Sand
Montsale
Deal Hall
Foulness Sand
Foulness Pt.
TR
Courtsend
Churchend
MAPLIN SANDS
52
53
4
5
6
A
B
C
D

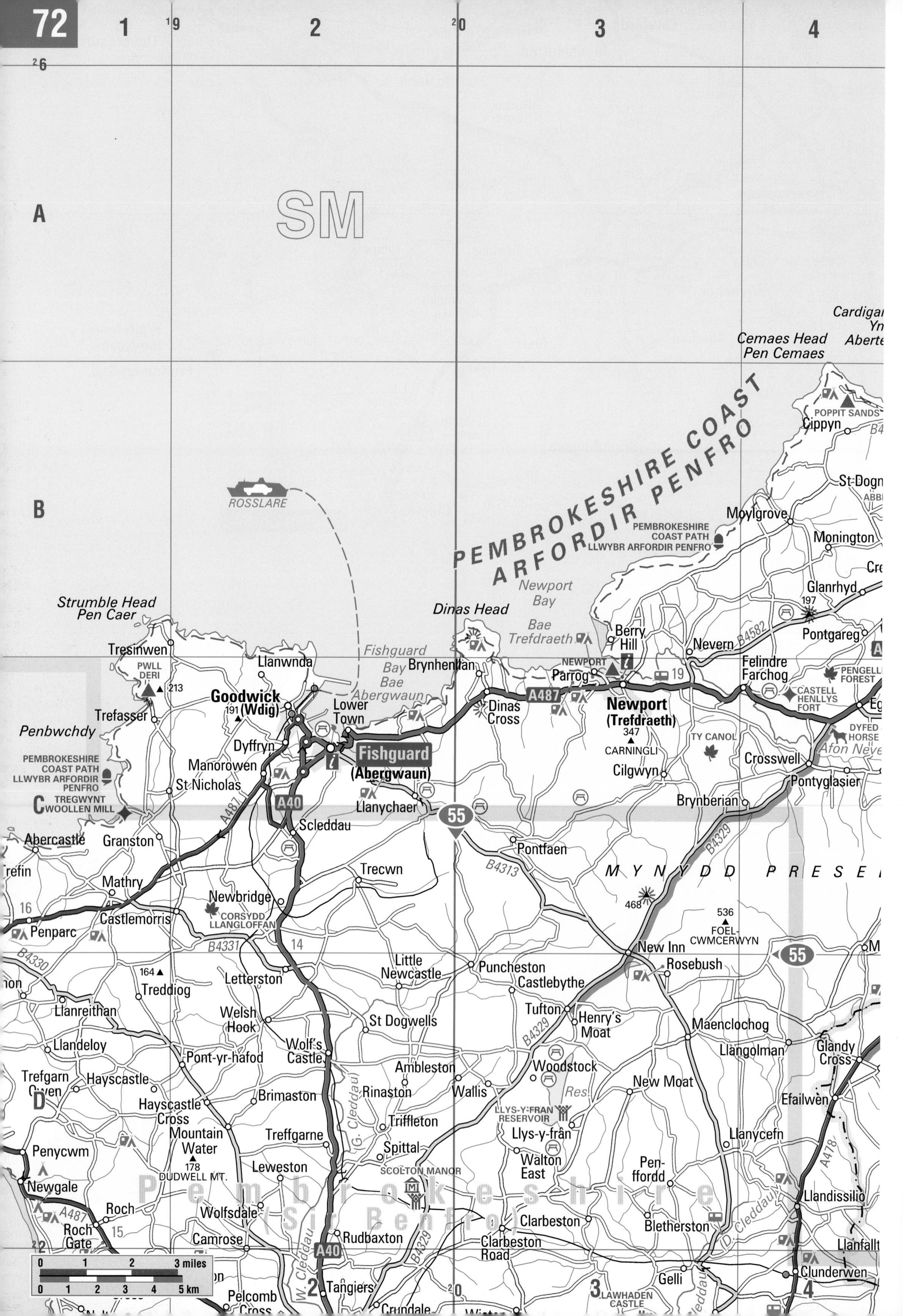

SM
ROSSLARE
PEMBROKESHIRE COAST
ARFORDIR PENFRO
Cemaes Head
Pen Cemaes
POPPIT SANDS
Cippyn
St Dogm
Moylgrove
PEMBROKESHIRE COAST PATH
LLWYBR ARFORDIR PENFRO
Monington
Glanrhyd
Newport Bay
Bae Trefdraeth
Dinas Head
Strumble Head
Pen Caer
Tresinwen
PWLL DERI
Llanwnda
Fishguard Bay
Bae Abergwaun
Brynhenllan
Berry Hill
Nevern
Pontgareg
Felindre Farchog
PENGELLI FOREST
CASTELL HENLLYS FORT
Goodwick (Wdig)
Lower Town
Dinas Cross
NEWPORT
Parrog
Newport (Trefdraeth)
Trefasser
Penbwchdy
Dyffryn
Fishguard (Abergwaun)
CARNINGLI
TY CANOL
Crosswell
DYFED HORSE
Afon Nevern
PEMBROKESHIRE COAST PATH
LLWYBR ARFORDIR PENFRO
Manorowen
St Nicholas
Cilgwyn
Pontyglasier
TREGWYNT WOOLLEN MILL
Llanychaer
Brynberian
Abercastle
Granston
Scleddau
Pontfaen
Trefin
Mathry
Trecwn
MYNYDD PRESELI
Newbridge
Castlemorris
CORSYDD LLANGLOFFAN
FOEL-CWMCERWYN
Penparc
New Inn
Rosebush
Letterston
Little Newcastle
Puncheston
Castlebythe
Treddiog
Llanreithan
Welsh Hook
Tufton
Henry's Moat
St Dogwells
Maenclochog
Llandeloy
Wolf's Castle
Llangolman
Glandy Cross
Pont-yr-hafod
Ambleston
Woodstock
Trefgarn Owen
Hayscastle
New Moat
Hayscastle Cross
Brimaston
Rinaston
Wallis
Efailwen
LLYS-Y-FRAN RESERVOIR
Res.
Mountain Water
Triffleton
Llys-y-frân
Treffgarne
Llanycefn
Penycwm
Spittal
Walton East
DUDWELL MT.
Leweston
SCOLTON MANOR
Pen-ffordd
Newgale
Pembrokeshire (Sir Benfro)
Roch
Wolfsdale
Clarbeston
Llandissilio
Roch Gate
Bletherston
Camrose
Rudbaxton
Clarbeston Road
Llanfallteg
W. Cleddau
G. Cleddau
E. Cleddau
Gelli
Clunderwen
Tangiers
Pelcomb Cross
Crundale
LAWHADEN CASTLE
A40
A487
B4313
B4329
B4331
B4330
B4582
A478
0 1 2 3 miles
0 1 2 3 4 5 km

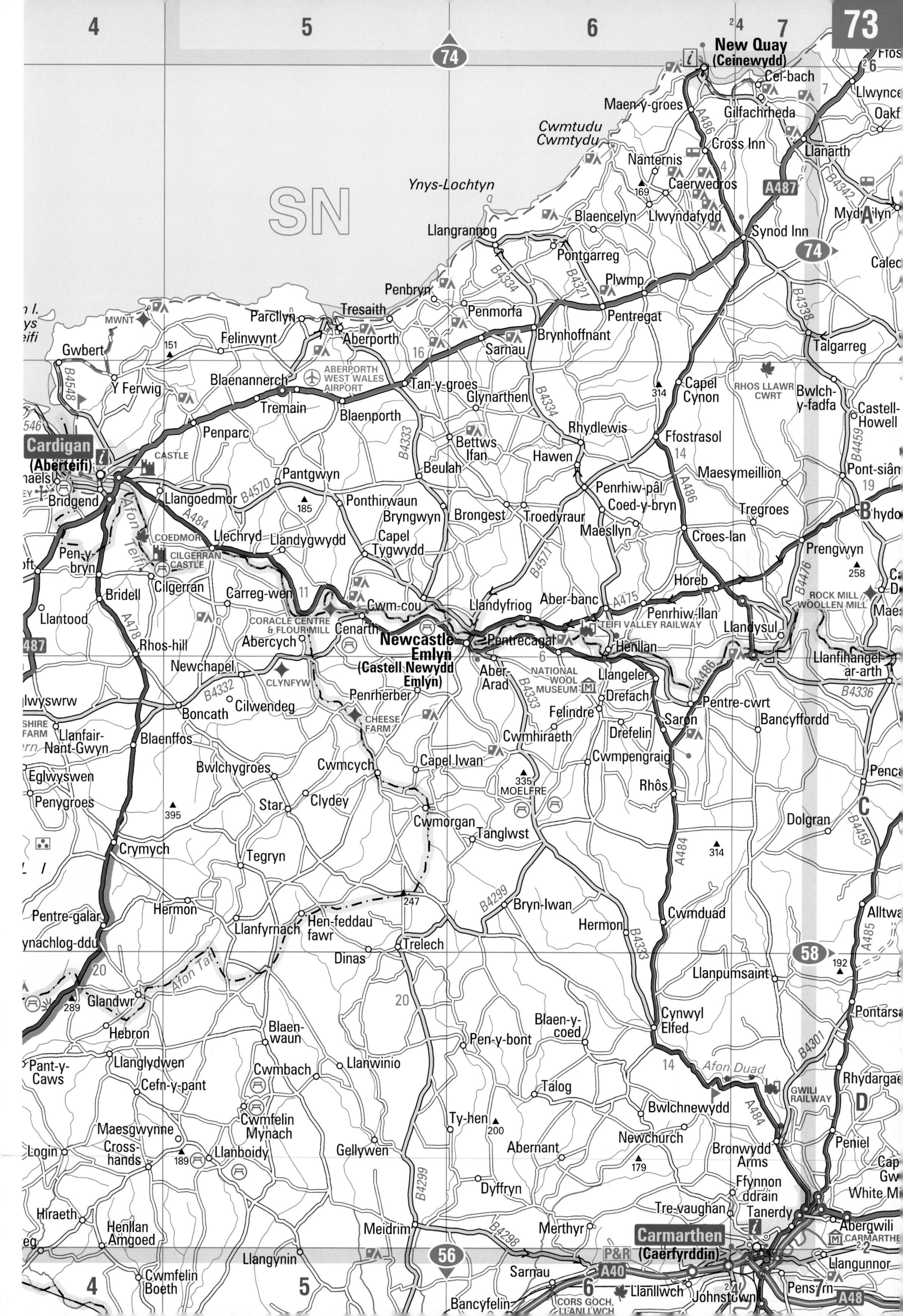
4
5
6
7
74
New Quay
(Ceinewydd)
Cei-bach
Maen-y-groes
Gilfachrheda
Cwmtudu
Cwmtydu
Cross Inn
Llanarth
Nanternis
Caerwedros
A487
Ynys-Lochtyn
SN
169
Blaencelyn
Llwyndafydd
Synod Inn
Llangrannog
Pontgarreg
B4334
B4321
Plwmp
Penbryn
Pentregat
B4338
Penmorfa
Tresaith
Parcllyn
MWNT
Aberporth
Brynhoffnant
Talgarreg
Felinwynt
151
Sarnau
Gwbert
16
B4548
Y Ferwig
Blaenannerch
ABERPORTH WEST WALES AIRPORT
Tan-y-groes
Capel Cynon
RHOS LLAWR CWRT
Bwlch-y-fadfa
Glynarthen
314
Castell-Howell
Tremain
Blaenporth
Penparc
B4333
Bettws Ifan
Rhydlewis
Ffostrasol
B4459
Cardigan
(Aberteifi)
CASTLE
Hawen
14
Pont-siân
Beulah
Maesymeillion
19
Pantgwyn
Bridgend
Llangoedmor
B4570
Penrhiw-pâl
Ponthirwaun
Coed-y-bryn
A486
185
Tregroes
Bryngwyn
Brongest
Troedyraur
Maesllyn
A484
COEDMOR
Llechryd
Llandygwydd
Capel Tygwydd
Croes-lan
Pen-y-bryn
Afon Teifi
CILGERRAN CASTLE
Prengwyn
B4571
258
Cilgerran
Horeb
B4476
Bridell
Carreg-wen
11
Aber-banc
A475
ROCK MILL WOOLLEN MILL
Llantood
Cwm-cou
Llandyfriog
Penrhiw-llan
A478
CORACLE CENTRE & FLOUR MILL
Cenarth
TEIFI VALLEY RAILWAY
Llandysul
Abercych
Newcastle Emlyn
(Castell Newydd Emlyn)
Pentrecagal
Henllan
Rhos-hill
Llanfihangel-ar-arth
Newchapel
Aber-Arad
NATIONAL WOOL MUSEUM
Llangeler
CLYNFYW
B4332
B4333
B4336
Drefach
Penrherber
Cilwendeg
Boncath
Felindre
Pentre-cwrt
CHEESE FARM
Saron
Bancyffordd
Llanfair-Nant-Gwyn
Drefelin
Blaenffos
Cwmhiraeth
Cwmpengraig
Capel Iwan
Bwlchygroes
Cwmcych
335
MOELFRE
Eglwyswen
Rhôs
Star
Clydey
Penygroes
395
Dolgran
Cwmorgan
B4459
Tanglwst
A484
314
Crymych
Tegryn
247
B4299
Bryn-Iwan
Hermon
Pentre-galar
Cwmduad
Hen-feddau fawr
Llanfyrnach
Hermon
B4333
A485
Trelech
Dinas
58
192
20
Afon Taf
Llanpumsaint
Glandwr
289
20
Hebron
Blaen-y-coed
Cynwyl Elfed
Pontarsais
Blaen-waun
Pen-y-bont
Pant-y-Caws
Llanglydwen
Cwmbach
Llanwinio
14
Afon Duad
B4301
Rhydargaeau
Cefn-y-pant
Talog
GWILI RAILWAY
Ty-hen
200
Bwlchnewydd
Cwmfelin Mynach
Maesgwynne
A484
Abernant
Newchurch
Peniel
Login
Cross-hands
189
Llanboidy
Gellywen
Bronwydd Arms
179
B4299
Dyffryn
Ffynnon ddrain
Hiraeth
Tre-vaughan
Tanerdy
Henllan Amgoed
Meidrim
B4298
Merthyr
Carmarthen
(Caerfyrddin)
Abergwili
CARMARTHEN
Llangynin
56
P&R
A40
Llangunnor
Cwmfelin Boeth
Sarnau
Llanllwch
Johnstown
Pensarn
A48
Bancyfelin
CORS GOCH, LLANLLWCH

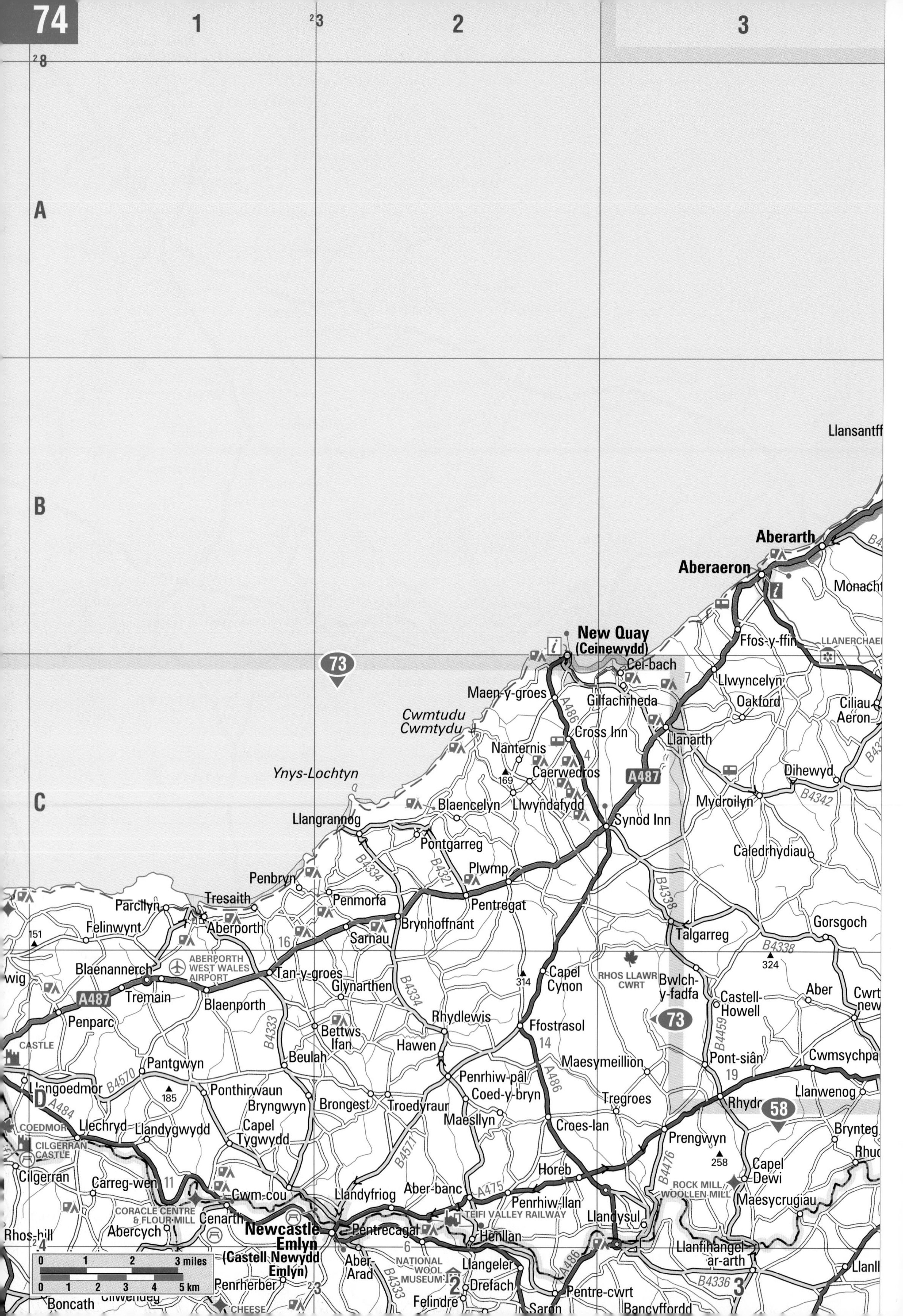
1
2
3
A
B
C
D
Llansantff
Aberarth
Aberaeron
Monacht
New Quay
(Ceinewydd)
Cei-bach
Ffos-y-ffin
LLANERCHAE
Maen-y-groes
Gilfachrheda
Llwyncelyn
Oakford
Ciliau Aeron
Cwmtudu
Cwmtydu
Cross Inn
Llanarth
Nanternis
Caerwedros
169
A487
Dihewyd
Ynys-Lochtyn
Mydroilyn
B4342
Blaencelyn
Llwyndafydd
Synod Inn
Llangrannog
Pontgarreg
Caledrhydiau
B4334
B4321
Plwmp
Penbryn
B4338
Tresaith
Penmorfa
Pentregat
Parcllyn
Aberporth
Brynhoffnant
Talgarreg
Gorsgoch
Felinwynt
151
16
Sarnau
B4338
324
ABERPORTH WEST WALES AIRPORT
Blaenannerch
Tan-y-groes
Glynarthen
314
Capel Cynon
RHOS LLAWR CWRT
Bwlch-y-fadfa
Castell-Howell
Aber
Cwrt new
A487
Tremain
Blaenporth
B4334
73
Penparc
B4333
Bettws Ifan
Rhydlewis
Hawen
Ffostrasol
B4459
CASTLE
14
Beulah
Maesymeillion
Pont-siân
Cwmsychpa
Pantgwyn
B4570
Penrhiw-pâl
A486
19
Llangoedmor
185
Ponthirwaun
Coed-y-bryn
Llanwenog
A484
Bryngwyn
Brongest
Troedyraur
Tregroes
Rhydc
58
Maesllyn
Croes-lan
COEDMOR
Llechryd
Llandygwydd
Capel Tygwydd
B4571
Prengwyn
Brynteg
CILGERRAN CASTLE
B4476
258
Capel Dewi
Rhuc
Horeb
Cilgerran
Carreg-wen
11
Cwm-cou
Aber-banc
A475
ROCK MILL WOOLLEN MILL
Maesycrugiau
Llandyfriog
Penrhiw-llan
CORACLE CENTRE & FLOUR MILL
Cenarth
TEIFI VALLEY RAILWAY
Llandysul
Rhos-hill
Abercych
Newcastle Emlyn
(Castell Newydd Emlyn)
Pentrecagal
Henllan
Llanfihangel-ar-arth
6
Aber-Arad
NATIONAL WOOL MUSEUM
Llangeler
A486
B4333
Llanll
0 1 2 3 miles
0 1 2 3 4 5 km
Penrherber
Drefach
B4336
Boncath
Cilwendeg
CHEESE
Felindre
Pentre-cwrt
Saron
Bancyffordd
wig

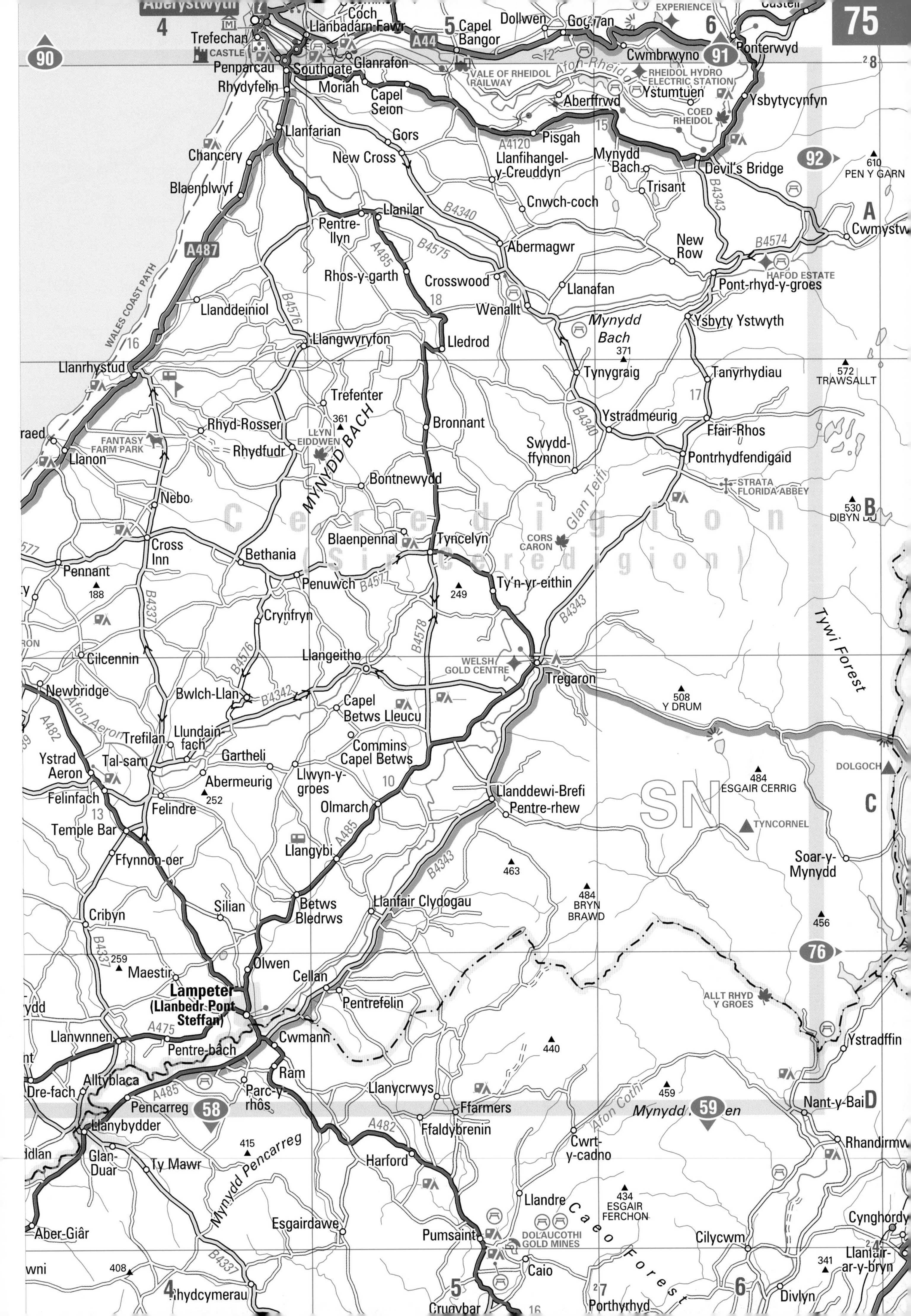
Aberystwyth
Coch
Llanbadarn Fawr
Capel Bangor
Dollwen
Goginan
EXPERIENCE
Trefechan
CASTLE
Penparcau
Southgate
Glanrafon
Rhydyfelin
Moriah
Capel Seion
A44
Cwmbrwyno
Ponterwyd
VALE OF RHEIDOL RAILWAY
Afon Rheidol
RHEIDOL HYDRO ELECTRIC STATION
Ystumtuen
Aberffrwd
Ysbytycynfyn
COED RHEIDOL
Llanfarian
Gors
Pisgah
A4120
Chancery
New Cross
Llanfihangel-y-Creuddyn
Mynydd Bach
Devil's Bridge
610
PEN Y GARN
Blaenplwyf
Trisant
B4343
Cnwch-coch
Llanilar
Pentre-llyn
B4340
A
Cwmystwyth
A487
Abermagwr
New Row
B4574
HAFOD ESTATE
A485
B4575
Rhos-y-garth
Crosswood
Pont-rhyd-y-groes
Llanafan
WALES COAST PATH
Llanddeiniol
Wenallt
B4576
Mynydd Bach
Ysbyty Ystwyth
Llangwyryfon
Lledrod
371
Llanrhystud
Tynygraig
Tanyrhydiau
572
TRAWSALLT
Trefenter
361
Ystradmeurig
Ffair-Rhos
Rhyd-Rosser
LLYN EIDDWEN
MYNYDD BACH
Bronnant
FANTASY FARM PARK
Rhydfudr
Swydd-ffynnon
Pontrhydfendigaid
Llanon
STRATA FLORIDA ABBEY
Bontnewydd
Nebo
Glan Teifi
530
DIBYN DU
B
Ceredigion (Sir Ceredigion)
Blaenpennal
Tyncelyn
CORS CARON
Cross Inn
Bethania
Pennant
Penuwch
B4577
Ty'n-yr-eithin
188
249
B4337
B4343
Crynfryn
Tywi Forest
B4578
Cilcennin
Llangeitho
WELSH GOLD CENTRE
Tregaron
Newbridge
Bwlch-Llan
B4342
Capel Betws Lleucu
508
Y DRUM
Afon Aeron
A482
Trefilan
Llundain-fach
Ystrad Aeron
Tal-sarn
Gartheli
Commins Capel Betws
DOLGOCH
Abermeurig
Llwyn-y-groes
484
ESGAIR CERRIG
Felinfach
252
Llanddewi-Brefi
Pentre-rhew
SN
C
Felindre
Olmarch
13
Temple Bar
TYNCORNEL
Llangybi
Ffynnon-oer
463
Soar-y-Mynydd
B4343
484
BRYN BRAWD
Cribyn
Silian
Betws Bledrws
Llanfair Clydogau
456
259
76
Maestir
Olwen
Cellan
Lampeter (Llanbedr Pont Steffan)
Pentrefelin
ALLT RHYD Y GROES
A475
Llanwnnen
Pentre-bach
Cwmann
440
Ystradffin
Ram
Alltyblaca
Dre-fach
Parc-y-rhôs
Llanycrwys
459
A485
Pencarreg
58
Ffarmers
Afon Cothi
Mynydd 59 en
Nant-y-Bai
D
Llanybydder
A482
Ffaldybrenin
415
Cwrt-y-cadno
Rhandirmwyn
Glan-Duar
Ty Mawr
Mynydd Pencarreg
Harford
434
ESGAIR FERCHON
Llandre
Caeo Forest
Cynghordy
Aber-Giâr
Esgairdawe
Pumsaint
DOLAUCOTHI GOLD MINES
Cilycwm
Llanfair-ar-y-bryn
408
B4337
Caio
341
Rhydcymerau
Crugybar
Porthyrhyd
Divlyn
4
5
6
90
91
92

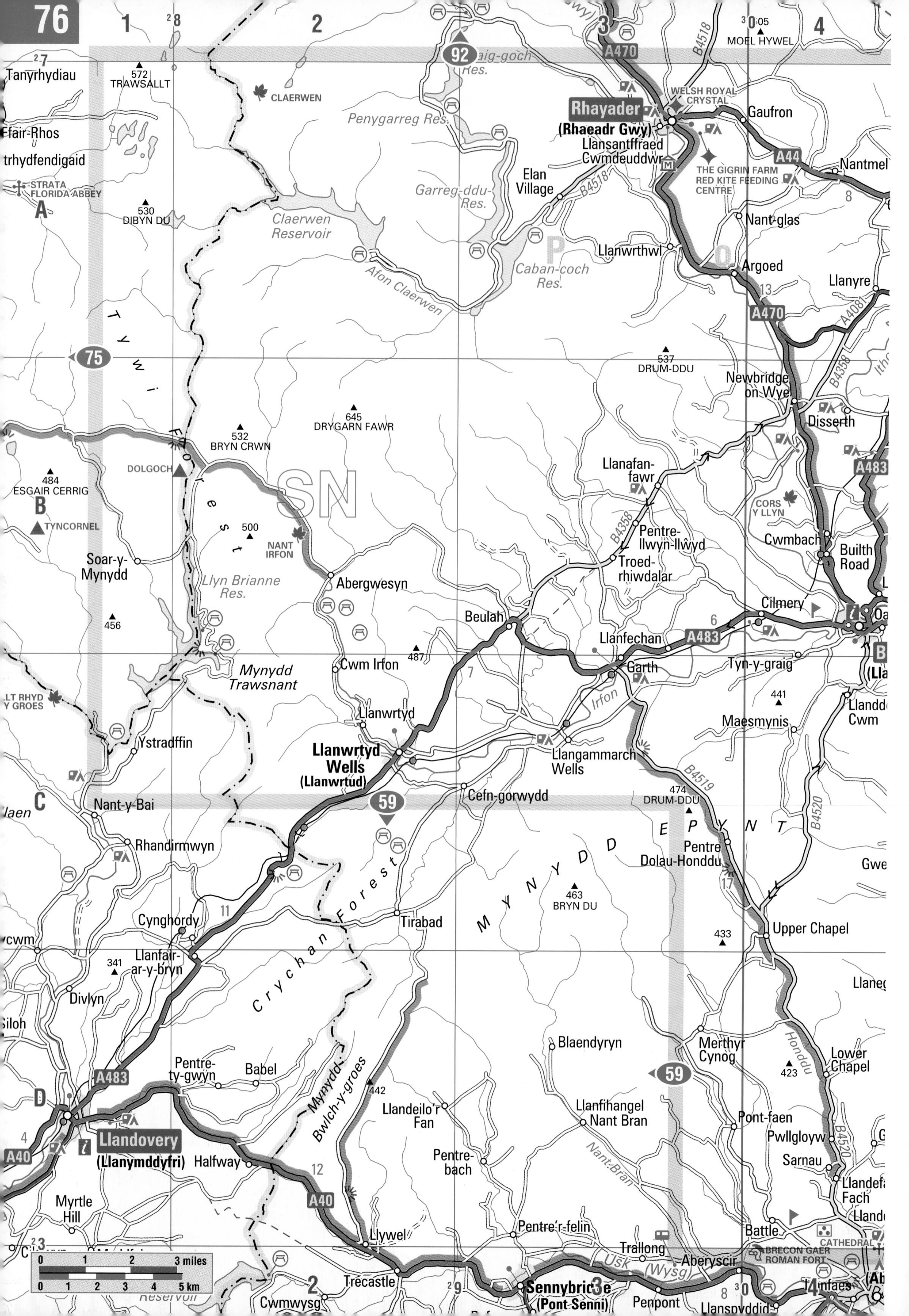
Tanyrhydiau
572 TRAWSALLT
CLAERWEN
Penygarreg Res.
Rhayader
(Rhaeadr Gwy)
Llansantffraed Cwmdeuddwr
WELSH ROYAL CRYSTAL
Gaufron
MOEL HYWEL
Nantmel
Ffair-Rhos
trhydfendigaid
STRATA FLORIDA ABBEY
530 DIBYN DU
Claerwen Reservoir
Garreg-ddu Res.
Elan Village
THE GIGRIN FARM RED KITE FEEDING CENTRE
Nant-glas
Llanwrthwl
Caban-coch Res.
Afon Claerwen
Argoed
Llanyre
537 DRUM-DDU
Newbridge on Wye
Disserth
645 DRYGARN FAWR
532 BRYN CRWN
Tywi Forest
DOLGOCH
484 ESGAIR CERRIG
TYNCORNEL
SN
500
NANT IRFON
Llanafan-fawr
CORS Y LLYN
Pentre-llwyn-llŵyd
Troed-rhiwdalar
Cwmbach
Builth Road
Soar-y-Mynydd
Llyn Brianne Res.
Abergwesyn
Beulah
Cilmery
456
Llanfechan
Garth
Tyn-y-graig
Mynydd Trawsnant
Cwm Irfon
487
LT RHYD Y GROES
Irfon
441
Llanwrtyd
Maesmynis
Ystradffin
Llanwrtyd Wells
(Llanwrtud)
Llangammarch Wells
Cefn-gorwydd
474 DRUM-DDU
Nant-y-Bai
Rhandirmwyn
MYNYDD EPYNT
Pentre Dolau-Honddu
463 BRYN DU
Crychan Forest
Tirabad
Cynghordy
Upper Chapel
433
Llanfair-ar-y-bryn
341
Divlyn
Blaendyryn
Merthyr Cynog
Lower Chapel
423
Honddu
Pentre-ty-gwyn
Babel
Mynydd Bwlch-y-groes
442
Llandeilo'r Fan
Llanfihangel Nant Bran
Pont-faen
Pwllgloyw
Llandovery
(Llanymddyfri)
Halfway
Pentre-bach
Nant Brân
Sarnau
Myrtle Hill
Pentre'r-felin
Llywel
Battle
CATHEDRAL
Trallong
BRECON GAER ROMAN FORT
Aberyscir
Usk (Wysg)
Trecastle
Sennybridge
(Pont-Senni)
Penpont
Cwmwysg
Llanspyddid
A470
A44
A483
A4081
B4358
B4518
B4519
B4520
A40
92
75
59
0 1 2 3 miles
0 1 2 3 4 5 km

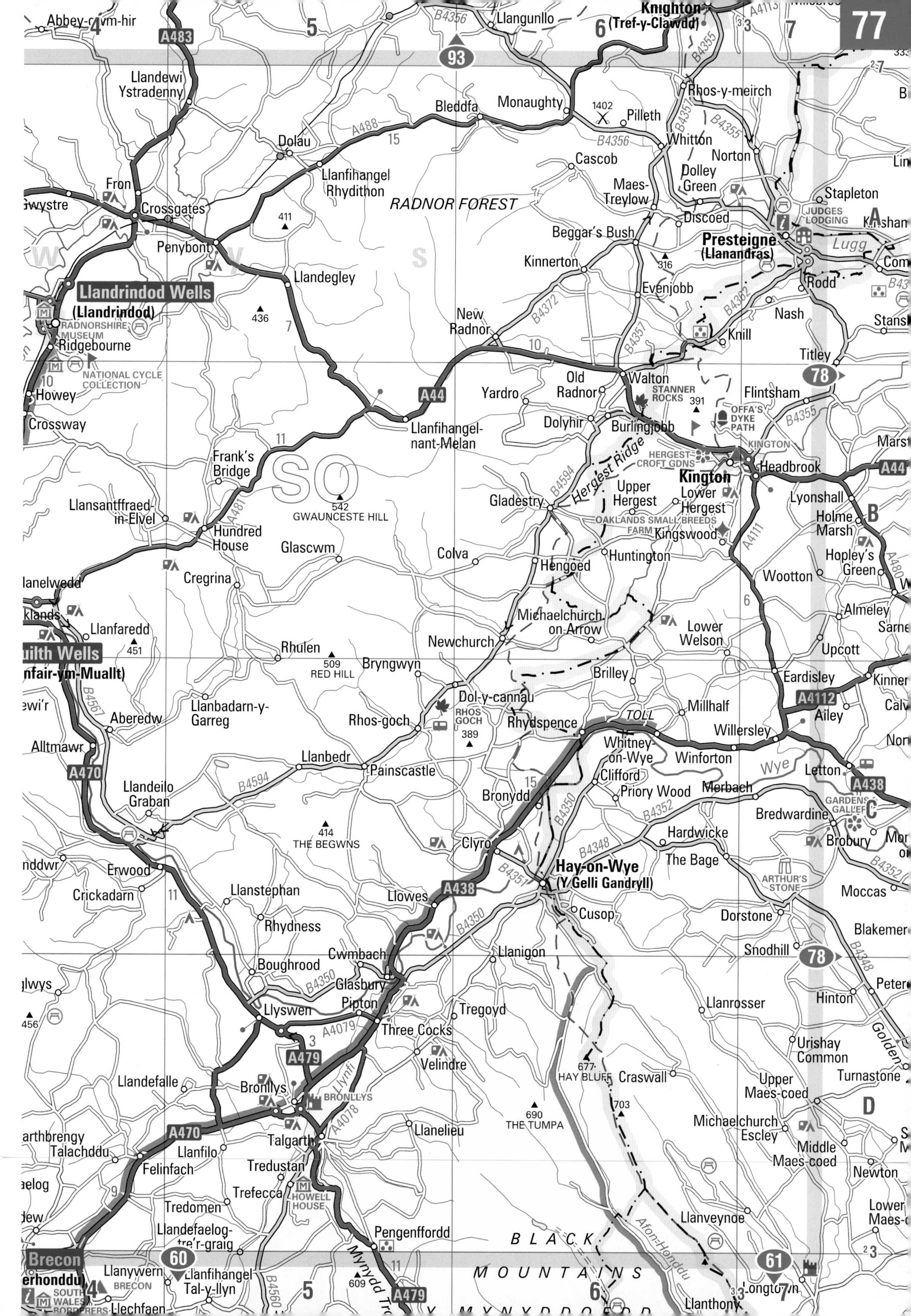

Abbey-cwm-hir
A483
5
B4356
Llangunllo
93
6
Knighton
(Tref-y-Clawdd)
B4355
A4113
7
Llandewi
Ystradenny
Bleddfa
Monaughty
1402
Pilleth
Rhos-y-meirch
B4357
B4355
A488
15
Dolau
B4356
Whitton
Norton
Cascob
Llanfihangel
Rhydithon
Dolley
Green
Fron
Maes-
Treylow
Stapleton
Crossgates
RADNOR FOREST
Discoed
JUDGES
LODGING
411
Penybont
Beggar's Bush
Presteigne
(Llanandras)
Lugg
Kinnerton
316
Llandegley
Rodd
Llandrindod Wells
(Llandrindod)
Evenjobb
B4362
RADNORSHIRE
MUSEUM
436
7
New
Radnor
B4372
Nash
Ridgebourne
Knill
B4357
10
Titley
NATIONAL CYCLE
COLLECTION
10
Old
Radnor
Walton
78
Howey
Yardro
STANNER
ROCKS
391
Flintsham
A44
OFFA'S
DYKE
PATH
B4355
Crossway
Dolyhir
Burlingjobb
Llanfihangel-
nant-Melan
KINGTON
11
HERGEST
CROFT GDNS
Frank's
Bridge
Hergest Ridge
Kington
Headbrook
A44
SO
B4594
Upper
Hergest
Lower
Hergest
Lyonshall
542
GWAUNCESTE HILL
Gladestry
Llansantffraed-
in-Elvel
A481
OAKLANDS SMALL BREEDS
FARM
Kingswood
Holme
Marsh
B
Hundred
House
Glascwm
Colva
Hengoed
Huntington
A4111
Hopley's
Green
A480
Cregrina
Wootton
6
Almeley
Michaelchurch-
on-Arrow
Llanfaredd
Lower
Welson
451
Newchurch
Builth Wells
(Llanfair-ym-Muallt)
Rhulen
509
RED HILL
Bryngwyn
Upcott
Brilley
Eardisley
B4567
Dol-y-cannau
Millhalf
A4112
Llanbadarn-y-
Garreg
Aberedw
Rhos-goch
RHOS
GOCH
389
Rhydspence
TOLL
Ailey
Willersley
Alltmawr
Whitney-
on-Wye
Winforton
A470
Llanbedr
Painscastle
Clifford
Wye
Letton
Llandeilo
Graban
B4594
15
Bronydd
Priory Wood
Merbach
A438
B4352
GARDENS
GALLERY
C
B4350
Bredwardine
414
THE BEGWNS
Clyro
Hardwicke
B4348
Brobury
Erwood
B4351
Hay-on-Wye
(Y Gelli Gandryll)
The Bage
ARTHUR'S
STONE
B4352
Crickadarn
11
Llanstephan
Llowes
A438
Cusop
Moccas
Dorstone
Rhydness
B4350
Blakemere
Cwmbach
Llanigon
Snodhill
78
B4348
Boughrood
B4350
Glasbury
Pipton
Llanrosser
Hinton
Llyswen
Tregoyd
456
3
A4079
Three Cocks
Urishay
Common
A479
Velindre
677
HAY BLUFF
Craswall
Turnastone
Llandefalle
Bronllys
Llynfi
BRONLLYS
Upper
Maes-coed
703
D
690
THE TUMPA
A4078
Llanelieu
Michaelchurch
Escley
Talachddu
A470
Llanfilo
Talgarth
Middle
Maes-coed
Felinfach
Tredustan
Newton
HOWELL
HOUSE
Trefecca
9
Tredomen
Llanveynoe
Afon-Honddu
Llandefaelog-
tre'r-graig
Pengenffordd
BLACK
MOUNTAINS
Brecon
60
Llanywern
Llanfihangel
Tal-y-llyn
BRECON
Mynydd Troed
609
11
B4560
5
A479
6
61
3
Longtown
7
SOUTH
WALES
BORDERERS
Llechfaen
Llanthony

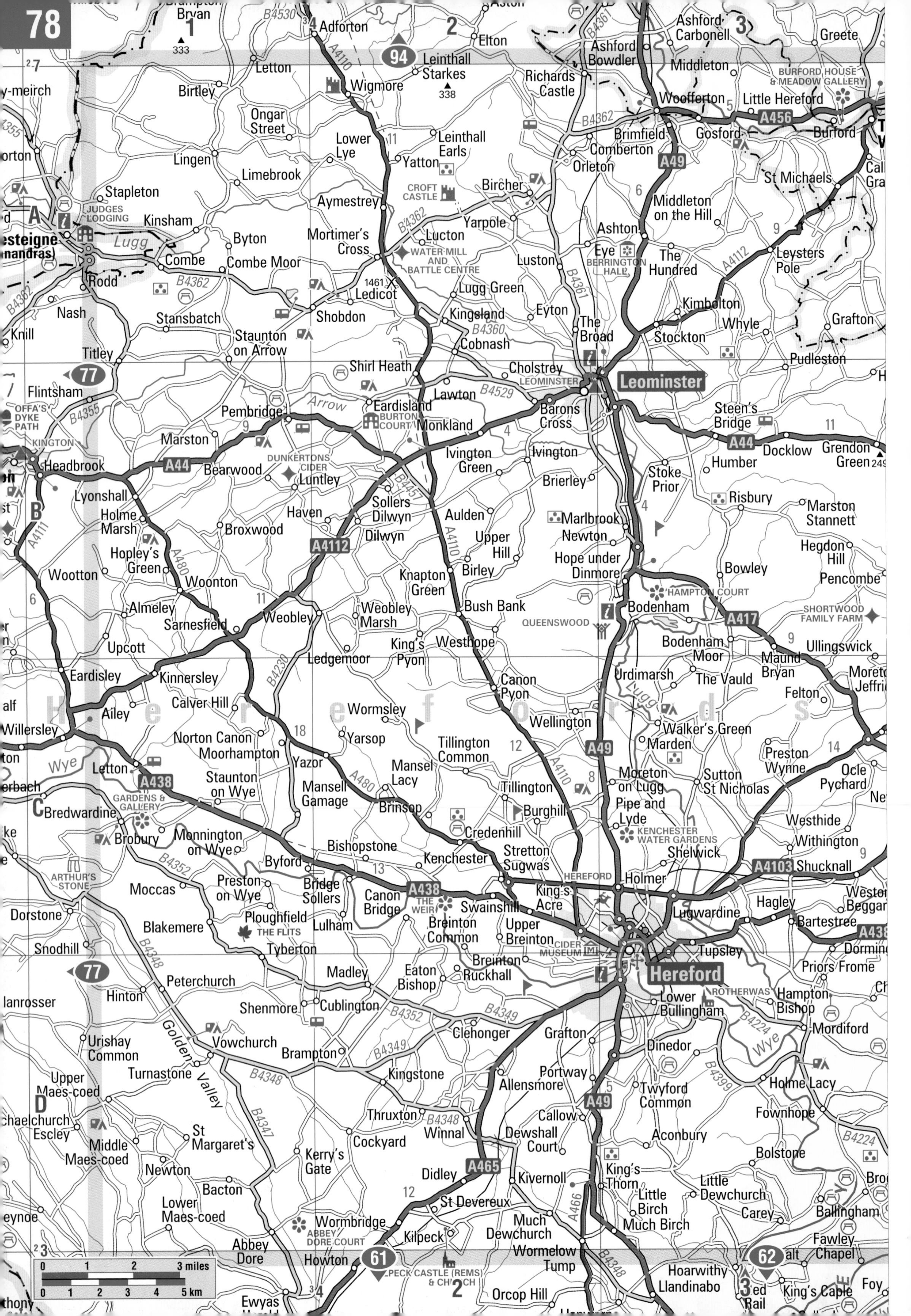
Brampton Bryan
Adforton
Aston
Elton
Ashford Carbonell
Greete
Ashford Bowdler
94
Leinthall Starkes
Letton
Middleton
Burford House & Meadow Gallery
Birtley
Wigmore
Richards Castle
Woofferton
Little Hereford
Ongar Street
Lower Lye
Leinthall Earls
Brimfield
Gosford
Burford
Comberton
Lingen
Yatton
Orleton
St Michaels
Limebrook
Croft Castle
Bircher
Stapleton
Aymestrey
Middleton on the Hill
Judges Lodging
Kinsham
Yarpole
Ashton
Presteigne (Llanandras)
Byton
Mortimer's Cross
Lucton
Eye
Berrington Hall
The Hundred
Leysters Pole
Lugg
Combe
Combe Moor
Water Mill and Battle Centre
Luston
Rodd
Ledicot
Lugg Green
Kimbolton
Nash
Shobdon
Kingsland
Eyton
Whyle
Grafton
Stansbatch
Staunton on Arrow
Cobnash
The Broad
Stockton
Knill
Titley
Shirl Heath
Cholstrey
Pudleston
77
Leominster
Flintsham
Lawton
Eardisland
Barons Cross
Steen's Bridge
Offa's Dyke Path
Pembridge
Arrow
Burton Court
Monkland
Kington
Marston
Ivington Green
Ivington
Docklow
Grendon Green
Headbrook
Dunkertons Cider
Bearwood
Luntley
Brierley
Stoke Prior
Humber
Lyonshall
Sollers Dilwyn
Risbury
Marston Stannett
Holme Marsh
Haven
Aulden
Marlbrook
Broxwood
Dilwyn
Newton
Upper Hill
Hegdon Hill
Hopley's Green
Hope under Dinmore
Bowley
Wootton
Knapton Green
Birley
Pencombe
Woonton
Hampton Court
Almeley
Weobley Marsh
Bush Bank
Bodenham
Shortwood Family Farm
Sarnesfield
Weobley
Queenswood
Upcott
King's Pyon
Westhope
Bodenham Moor
Ullingswick
Ledgemoor
Maund Bryan
Eardisley
Kinnersley
Urdimarsh
The Vault
Moreton Jeffries
Canon Pyon
Felton
Calver Hill
Wormsley
Ailey
Wellington
Willersley
Walker's Green
Norton Canon
Yarsop
Marden
Preston Wynne
Moorhampton
Tillington Common
Ocle Pychard
Letton
Wye
Yazor
Mansel Lacy
Moreton on Lugg
Staunton on Wye
Sutton St Nicholas
Mansell Gamage
Tillington
Bredwardine
Gardens & Gallery
Brinsop
Burghill
Pipe and Lyde
Westhide
Kenchester Water Gardens
Withington
Brobury
Monnington on Wye
Credenhill
Bishopstone
Stretton Sugwas
Shelwick
Arthur's Stone
Byford
Kenchester
Hereford
Holmer
Shucknall
Moccas
Preston on Wye
Bridge Sollers
Canon Bridge
The Weir
Swainshill
King's Acre
Hagley
Weston Beggard
Dorstone
Ploughfield
Breinton Common
Upper Breinton
Lugwardine
Bartestree
Blakemere
The Flits
Lulham
Cider Museum
Tupsley
Dormington
Snodhill
Tyberton
Breinton
Priors Frome
Madley
Eaton Bishop
Ruckhall
Peterchurch
Rotherwas
Hampton Bishop
Llanrosser
Hinton
Shenmore
Cublington
Lower Bullingham
Mordiford
Vowchurch
Clehonger
Grafton
Urishay Common
Brampton
Dinedor
Golden Valley
Turnastone
Kingstone
Portway
Allensmore
Twyford Common
Holme Lacy
Upper Maes-coed
Thruxton
Callow
Fownhope
Michaelchurch Escley
Winnal
Dewshall Court
Middle Maes-coed
St Margaret's
Cockyard
Aconbury
Bolstone
Kerry's Gate
Didley
Kivernoll
Newton
King's Thorn
Little Birch
Little Dewchurch
Bacton
Much Birch
Carey
Ballingham
Lower Maes-coed
St Devereux
Much Dewchurch
Wormbridge
Abbey Dore Court
Kilpeck
Fawley Chapel
Abbey Dore
Wormelow Tump
Howton
61
Kilpeck Castle (Rems) & Church
62
Hoarwithy
Llandinabo
King's Caple
Foy
Orcop Hill
Ewyas Harold
Red Rail
A4110
A456
A49
A4112
B4362
B4361
B4360
B4529
B4355
A44
B4457
A4112
A480
B4230
A417
A438
B4352
A4103
B4224
B4349
B4348
B4347
B4399
A465
A466
0 1 2 3 miles
0 1 2 3 4 5 km

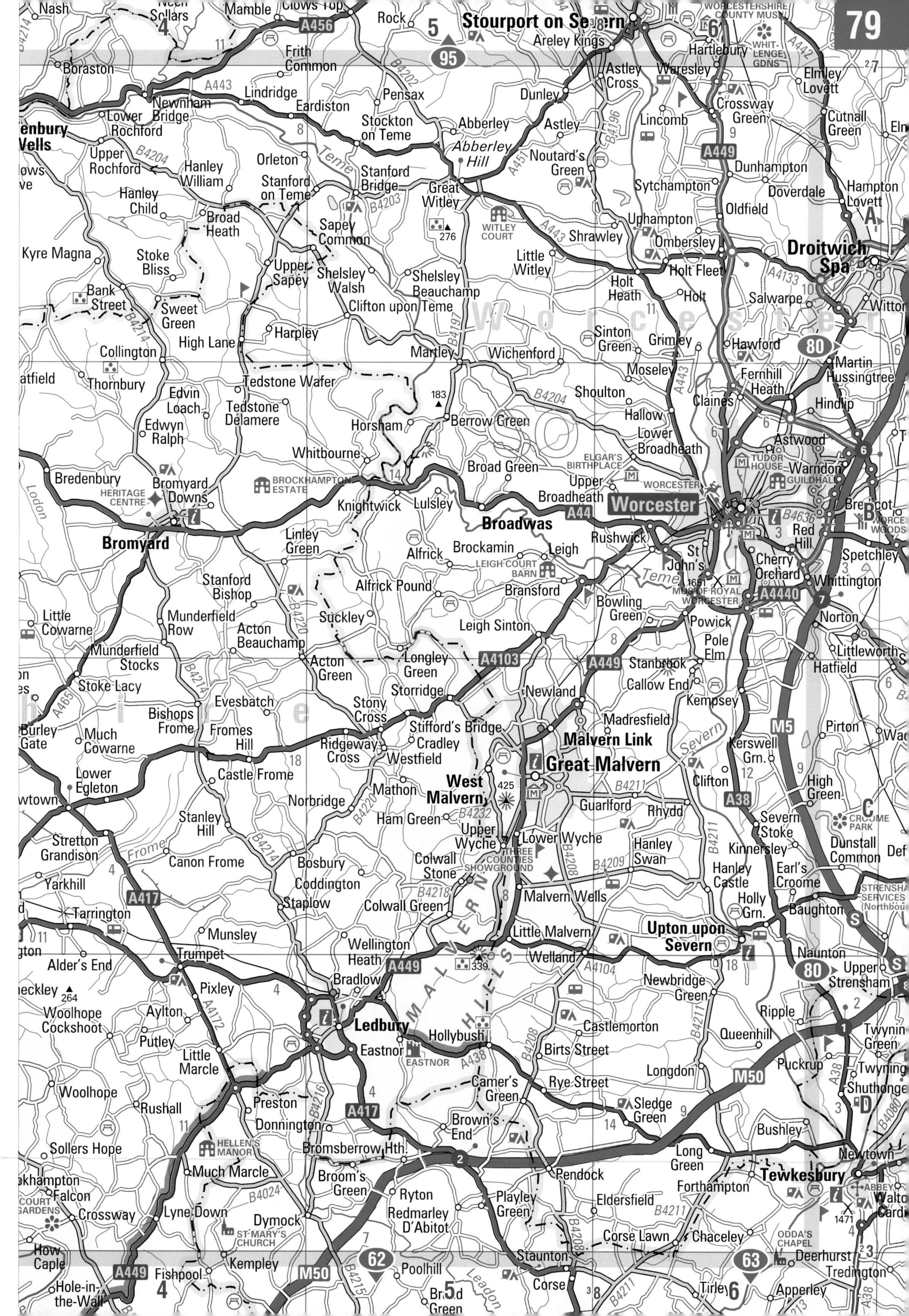
Nash
Neen Sollars
Mamble
Clows Top
Rock
Stourport on Severn
Areley Kings
Hartlebury
WORCESTERSHIRE COUNTY MUS.
WHITLENGE GDNS
A456
A442
95
Boraston
Frith Common
Astley Cross
Waresley
Elmley Lovett
A443
Lindridge
Pensax
Dunley
Newnham Bridge
Lower Rochford
Eardiston
Stockton on Teme
Abberley
Astley
Crossway Green
Cutnall Green
Tenbury Wells
B4196
Lincomb
Upper Rochford
B4204
Orleton
Abberley Hill
Noutard's Green
A449
Dunhampton
Hanley William
Teme
Stanford Bridge
Stanford on Teme
Great Witley
A451
Sytchampton
Doverdale
Hampton Lovett
Hanley Child
B4203
Oldfield
Broad Heath
Sapey Common
276
WITLEY COURT
Uphampton
A443
Shrawley
Ombersley
Droitwich Spa
Kyre Magna
Stoke Bliss
Upper Sapey
Shelsley Walsh
Little Witley
Holt Heath
Holt Fleet
A4133
Bank Street
Shelsley Beauchamp
Holt
Salwarpe
Sweet Green
B4214
Clifton upon Teme
Worcester
High Lane
Harpley
B4197
Sinton Green
Grimley
Hawford
80
Collington
Martley
Wichenford
Martin Hussingtree
Thornbury
Tedstone Wafer
Moseley
Fernhill Heath
Edvin Loach
Tedstone Delamere
183
Shoulton
A443
Claines
Hindlip
Edwyn Ralph
Horsham
Berrow Green
Hallow
Lower Broadheath
Astwood
Whitbourne
ELGAR'S BIRTHPLACE
TUDOR HOUSE
Warndon
Bredenbury
BROCKHAMPTON ESTATE
Broad Green
GUILDHALL
Loden
HERITAGE CENTRE
Bromyard Downs
Upper Broadheath
WORCESTER
Knightwick
Lulsley
Broadwas
Worcester
A44
Brockamin
Bromyard
Linley Green
Alfrick
Leigh
Rushwick
B4636
Red Hill
Spetchley
LEIGH COURT BARN
St John's
Cherry Orchard
Stanford Bishop
Alfrick Pound
Bransford
1651
MUS. OF ROYAL WORCESTER
Whittington
A4440
Little Cowarne
Munderfield Row
B4220
Suckley
Bowling Green
Powick
Norton
Acton Beauchamp
Leigh Sinton
Pole Elm
Munderfield Stocks
Longley Green
A4103
A449
Stanbrook
Littleworth
Acton Green
Hatfield
Stoke Lacy
B4214
Callow End
Storridge
Newland
Kempsey
A465
Evesbatch
Bishops Frome
Stony Cross
Madresfield
Burley Gate
Much Cowarne
Fromes Hill
Stifford's Bridge
Malvern Link
M5
Pirton
Ridgeway Cross
Cradley
Kerswell Grn.
Westfield
Great Malvern
Severn
Lower Egleton
Castle Frome
West Malvern
425
Clifton
High Green
Mathon
Norbridge
B4232
Guarlford
B4211
Rhydd
A38
Stanley Hill
Ham Green
Stretton Grandison
Upper Wyche
Lower Wyche
Hanley Swan
Severn Stoke
CROOME PARK
Frome
Kinnersley
Dunstall Common
Canon Frome
Bosbury
THREE COUNTIES SHOWGROUND
B4208
Colwall Stone
B4209
Hanley Castle
Earl's Croome
Yarkhill
Coddington
B4218
Malvern Wells
A417
Staplow
Colwall Green
Holly Grn.
Baughton
Tarrington
MALVERN HILLS
Little Malvern
Upton upon Severn
Munsley
Wellington Heath
Welland
Naunton
Trumpet
A4104
Upper Strensham
Alder's End
A449
339
Bradlow
Newbridge Green
Pixley
264
A4172
Ripple
Woolhope Cockshoot
Aylton
Ledbury
Hollybush
Castlemorton
Queenhill
Twyning Green
Putley
Eastnor
EASTNOR
Birts Street
Little Marcle
A438
Longdon
Puckrup
Camer's Green
Rye Street
M50
Twyning
Shuthonger
Woolhope
Preston
Sledge Green
Rushall
B4216
A417
Donnington
Brown's End
Bushley
Sollers Hope
HELLEN'S MANOR
Bromsberrow Hth.
Long Green
Newtown
Much Marcle
Pendock
Tewkesbury
Falcon
Broom's Green
Ryton
Forthampton
ABBEY
B4024
Playley Green
Eldersfield
Crossway
Lyne Down
Redmarley D'Abitot
B4211
1471
Dymock
ST MARY'S CHURCH
Corse Lawn
Chaceley
ODDA'S CHAPEL
How Caple
Kempley
62
Staunton
63
Deerhurst
Tredington
A449
Fishpool
M50
Poolhill
Corse
Hole-in-the-Wall
B4215
Bro'd Green
Leadon
Tirley
Apperley
Lower Broadheath
Worcester
Droitwich Spa

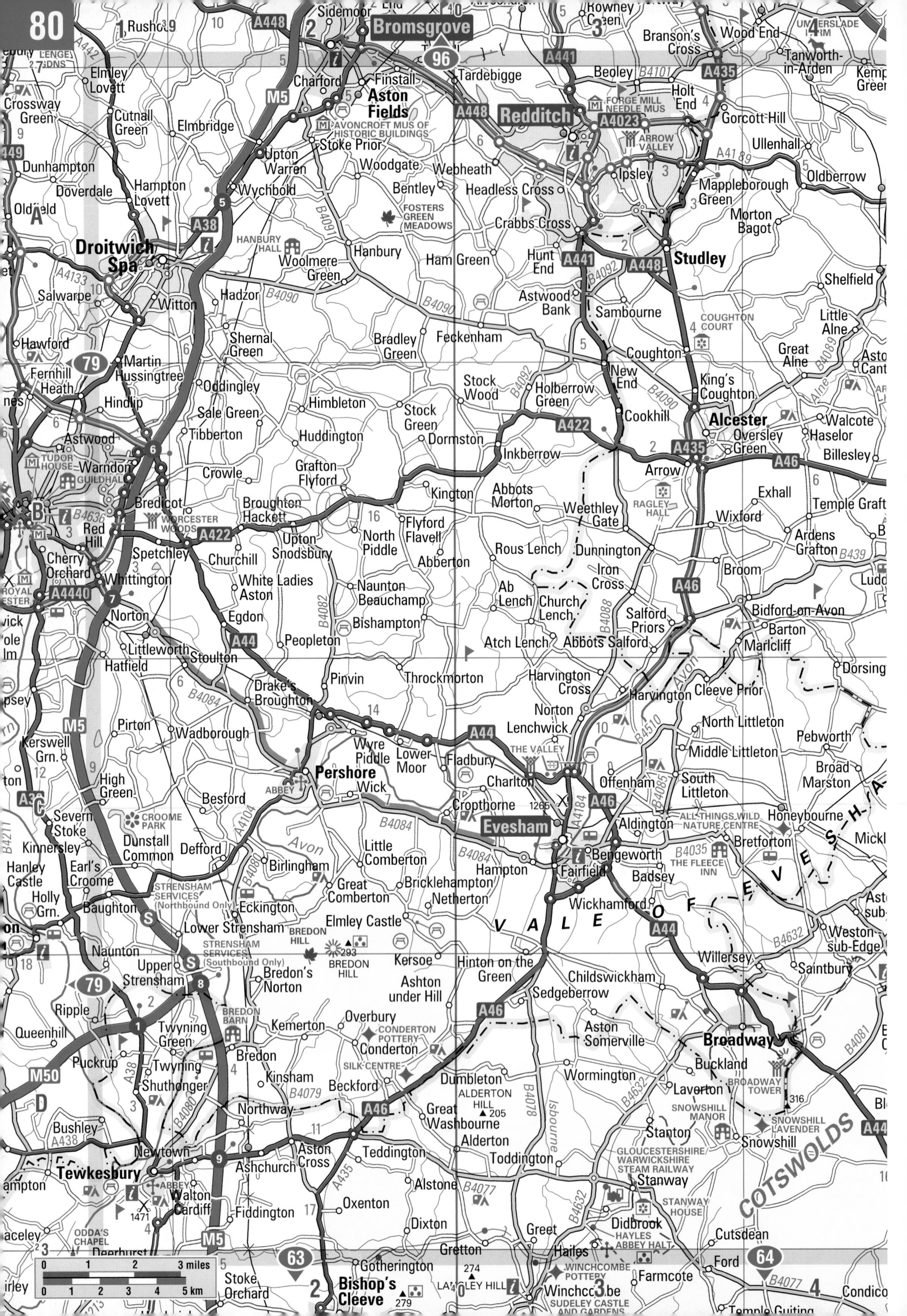

Rushock
Sidemoor
Bromsgrove
96
Rowney Green
Branson's Cross
Wood End
Umberslade Farm
Tanworth-in-Arden
Elmley Lovett
Charford
Finstall
Aston Fields
Tardebigge
Beoley
Holt End
Kemp Green
Crossway Green
Cutnall Green
Elmbridge
Avoncroft Mus of Historic Buildings
Redditch
Forge Mill Needle Mus
Gorcott Hill
Stoke Prior
Arrow Valley
Ullenhall
Dunhampton
Upton Warren
Woodgate
Webheath
Ipsley
Oldberrow
Doverdale
Hampton Lovett
Wychbold
Bentley
Headless Cross
Mappleborough Green
Oldfield
Fosters Green Meadows
Crabbs Cross
Morton Bagot
Droitwich Spa
Hanbury Hall
Hanbury
Ham Green
Hunt End
Studley
Woolmere Green
Salwarpe
Witton
Hadzor
Astwood Bank
Sambourne
Shelfield
Coughton Court
Little Alne
Hawford
Shernal Green
Bradley Green
Feckenham
Coughton
Great Alne
Aston Cantlow
Fernhill Heath
79
Martin Hussingtree
Oddingley
Stock Wood
Holberrow Green
New End
King's Coughton
Hindlip
Sale Green
Himbleton
Stock Green
Cookhill
Alcester
Walcote
Astwood
Tibberton
Huddington
Dormston
Oversley Green
Haselor
Tudor House
Warndon
Guildhall
Crowle
Grafton Flyford
Inkberrow
Arrow
Billesley
Kington
Abbots Morton
Exhall
Bredicot
Worcester Woods
Broughton Hackett
Weethley Gate
Ragley Hall
Wixford
Temple Grafton
Red Hill
Upton Snodsbury
North Piddle
Flyford Flavell
Ardens Grafton
Spetchley
Churchill
Abberton
Rous Lench
Dunnington
Cherry Orchard
Whittington
White Ladies Aston
Naunton Beauchamp
Iron Cross
Broom
Royal
Ab Lench
Church Lench
Salford Priors
Bidford-on-Avon
Norton
Egdon
Bishampton
Barton
Littleworth
Stoulton
Peopleton
Atch Lench
Abbots Salford
Marlcliff
Hatfield
Harvington Cross
Harvington
Cleeve Prior
Dorsington
Drake's Broughton
Pinvin
Throckmorton
Norton
North Littleton
Pirton
Wadborough
Wyre Piddle
Lower Moor
Lenchwick
Middle Littleton
Pebworth
Kerswell Grn.
Fladbury
The Valley
Offenham
South Littleton
Broad Marston
High Green
Pershore
Abbey
Wick
Charlton
Besford
Cropthorne
Evesham
Aldington
All Things Wild Nature Centre
Honeybourne
Croome Park
Severn Stoke
Bretforton
Mickleton
Kinnersley
Dunstall Common
Defford
Avon
Little Comberton
Bengeworth
The Fleece Inn
Hanley Castle
Earl's Croome
Birlingham
Great Comberton
Hampton
Bricklehampton
Fairfield
Badsey
Holly Grn.
Strensham Services (Northbound Only)
Baughton
Eckington
Netherton
Wickhamford
Vale of Evesham
Lower Strensham
Bredon Hill
Elmley Castle
Weston-sub-Edge
Naunton
Strensham Services (Southbound Only)
Kersoe
Hinton on the Green
Willersey
Upper Strensham
Bredon's Norton
Ashton under Hill
Childswickham
Saintbury
Sedgeberrow
Ripple
Bredon Barn
Overbury
Queenhill
Kemerton
Twyning Green
Conderton Pottery
Conderton
Aston Somerville
Broadway
Puckrup
Twyning
Bredon
Silk Centre
Buckland
Shuthonger
Kinsham
Beckford
Dumbleton
Wormington
Broadway Tower
Laverton
Alderton Hill
Northway
Great Washbourne
Snowshill Manor
Snowshill Lavender
Bushley
Stanton
Alderton
Snowshill
Cotswolds
Newtown
Aston Cross
Teddington
Toddington
Gloucestershire Warwickshire Steam Railway
Tewkesbury
Ashchurch
Stanway
Abbey
Walton Cardiff
Alstone
Stanway House
Fiddington
Oxenton
Dixton
Didbrook
Hayles Abbey Halt
Cutsdean
Odda's Chapel
Deerhurst
Greet
Gretton
Hailes
63
64
Ford
Gotherington
Winchcombe Pottery
Farmcote
Stoke Orchard
Bishop's Cleeve
Langley Hill
Winchcombe
Sudeley Castle and Gardens
Temple Guiting
Condicote
M5
M50
A38
A44
A46
A422
A435
A441
A448
A4023
A4440
B4084
B4090
B4092
B4077
B4632
0 1 2 3 miles
0 1 2 3 4 5 km

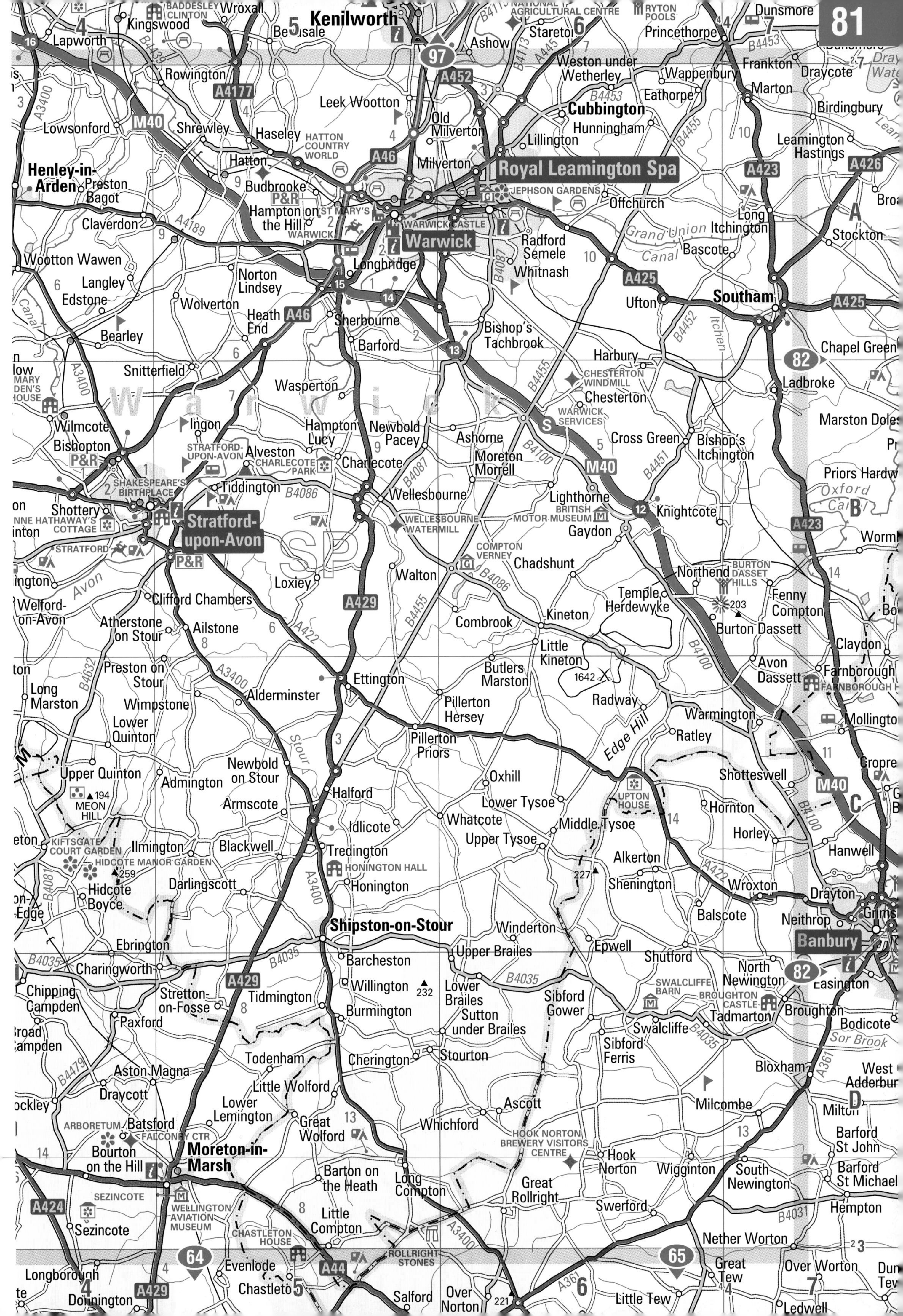

Kenilworth
Royal Leamington Spa
Warwick
Stratford-upon-Avon
Southam
Shipston-on-Stour
Moreton-in-Marsh
Banbury
Henley-in-Arden
Cubbington
Warwick
SP
M40
A46
A429
A3400
A422
A423
A425
A452
A4177
A44
A424
A361
B4100
B4035
B4455
B4086
B4087
Grand Union Canal
Oxford Canal
Edge Hill
Kineton
Wellesbourne
Gaydon
Ettington
Charlecote
Barford
Bishop's Tachbrook
Harbury
Ladbroke
Fenny Compton
Farnborough
Warmington
Ratley
Hornton
Shenington
Wroxton
Drayton
Brailes
Long Compton
Hook Norton
Chipping Campden
Ilmington
Tredington
Halford
Alderminster
Lighthorne
Chesterton
Radway
Tysoe
Epwell
Swalcliffe
Bloxham
Milcombe
Wigginton
Todenham
Evenlode
Chastleton
Little Compton
Barton on the Heath
Great Wolford
Little Wolford
Whichford
Ascott
Cherington
Stourton
Burmington
Barcheston
Willington
Tidmington
Blackwell
Armscote
Admington
Upper Quinton
Lower Quinton
Long Marston
Welford-on-Avon
Clifford Chambers
Atherstone on Stour
Preston on Stour
Wimpstone
Newbold on Stour
Loxley
Walton
Combrook
Butlers Marston
Pillerton Hersey
Pillerton Priors
Oxhill
Whatcote
Idlicote
Honington
Darlingscott
Ebrington
Hidcote Boyce
Paxford
Aston Magna
Draycott
Batsford
Bourton on the Hill
Sezincote
Longborough
Donnington
Salford
Over Norton
Little Tew
Great Tew
Swerford
Great Rollright
Nether Worton
Over Worton
Ledwell
Hempton
Barford St John
Barford St Michael
South Newington
Milton
West Adderbury
Bodicote
Broughton
Tadmarton
Sibford Gower
Sibford Ferris
North Newington
Shutford
Balscote
Alkerton
Horley
Hanwell
Shotteswell
Mollington
Cropredy
Claydon
Avon Dassett
Burton Dassett
Northend
Knightcote
Bishop's Itchington
Cross Green
Marston Doles
Priors Hardwick
Chapel Green
Ufton
Long Itchington
Bascote
Stockton
Birdingbury
Leamington Hastings
Marton
Eathorpe
Frankton
Draycote
Wappenbury
Weston under Wetherley
Hunningham
Offchurch
Radford Semele
Whitnash
Lillington
Old Milverton
Milverton
Leek Wootton
Ashow
Stareton
Princethorpe
Dunsmore
Kingswood
Lapworth
Rowington
Lowsonford
Shrewley
Haseley
Hatton
Budbrooke
Hampton on the Hill
Claverdon
Preston Bagot
Wootton Wawen
Langley
Edstone
Wolverton
Norton Lindsey
Heath End
Sherbourne
Longbridge
Bearley
Snitterfield
Wasperton
Hampton Lucy
Newbold Pacey
Ashorne
Moreton Morrell
Ingon
Wilmcote
Bishopton
Alveston
Tiddington
Shottery
Chadshunt
Temple Herdewyke
Little Kineton
Middle Tysoe
Upper Tysoe
Lower Tysoe
Winderton
Upper Brailes
Lower Brailes
Sutton under Brailes
Stretton-on-Fosse
Upton House
Compton Verney
Charlecote Park
Wellesbourne Watermill
British Motor Museum
Chesterton Windmill
Warwick Services
Burton Dassett Hills
Farnborough Hall
Honington Hall
Hidcote Manor Garden
Kiftsgate Court Garden
Meon Hill
Swalcliffe Barn
Broughton Castle
Hook Norton Brewery Visitors Centre
Rollright Stones
Chastleton House
Wellington Aviation Museum
Sezincote
Arboretum
Falconry Ctr
Shakespeare's Birthplace
Anne Hathaway's Cottage
Stratford
Hatton Country World
Jephson Gardens
Warwick Castle
St Mary's
National Agricultural Centre
Ryton Pools
Baddesley Clinton
Wroxall
Beausale
97
82
64
65

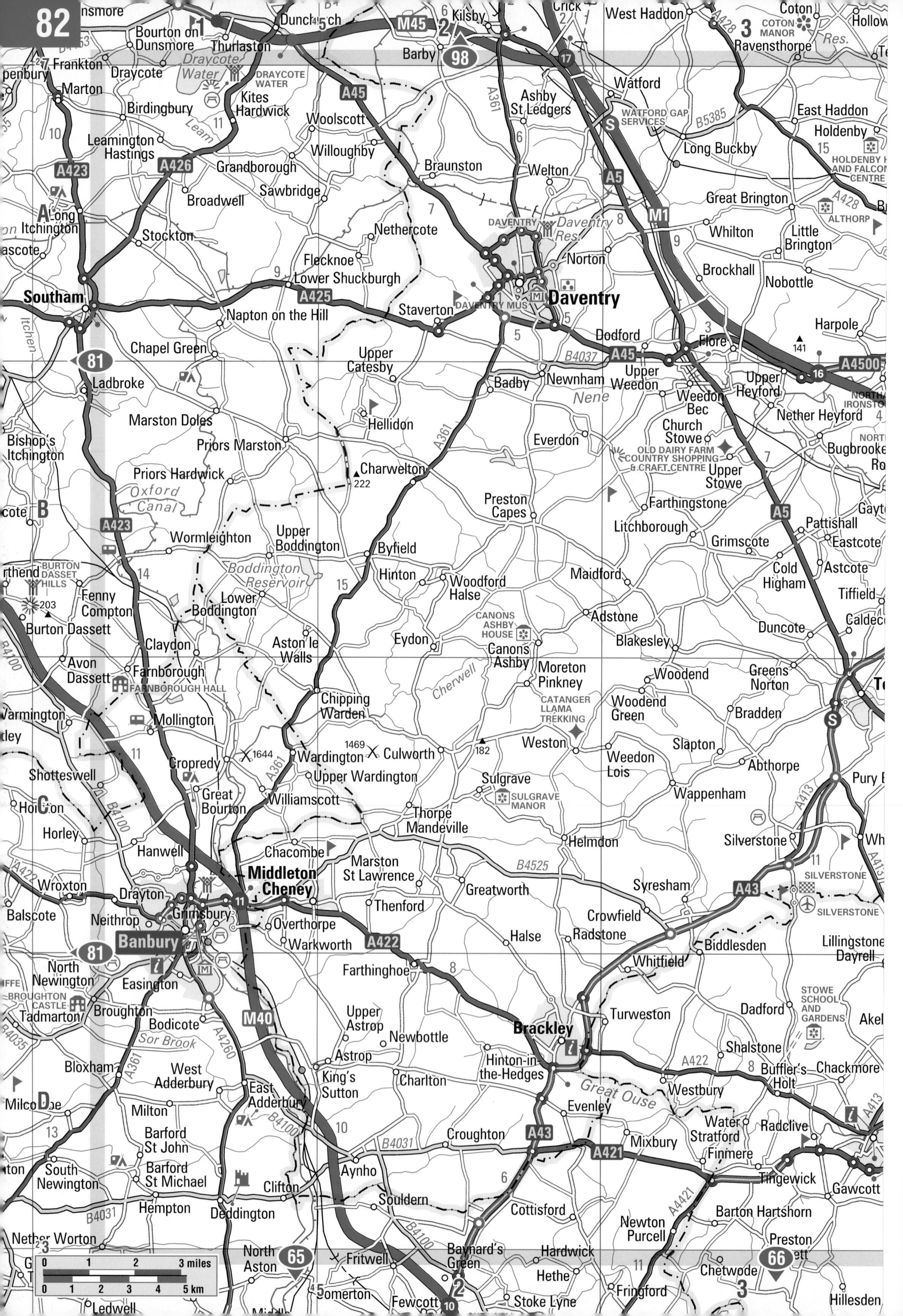
Southam
Daventry
Banbury
Middleton Cheney
Brackley
Long Itchington
Ladbroke
Napton on the Hill
Staverton
Braunston
Welton
Norton
Dodford
Flore
Badby
Newnham
Upper Weedon
Weedon Bec
Byfield
Woodford Halse
Chipping Warden
Wardington
Culworth
Sulgrave
Thorpe Mandeville
Cropredy
Great Bourton
Mollington
Farnborough
Fenny Compton
Wormleighton
Priors Marston
Priors Hardwick
Marston Doles
Hellidon
Charwelton
Preston Capes
Everdon
Litchborough
Maidford
Adstone
Blakesley
Canons Ashby
Moreton Pinkney
Eydon
Weston
Weedon Lois
Wappenham
Slapton
Abthorpe
Silverstone
Helmdon
Syresham
Greatworth
Thenford
Farthinghoe
Warkworth
Overthorpe
Grimsbury
Neithrop
Drayton
Wroxton
Hanwell
Horley
Bodicote
Bloxham
Adderbury
Aynho
Croughton
Evenley
Turweston
Whitfield
Biddlesden
Westbury
Water Stratford
Finmere
Mixbury
Souldern
Deddington
Clifton
Hempton
Fritwell
Somerton
Fewcott
Hethe
Fringford
Cottisford
Hardwick
Stoke Lyne
Bainard's Green
Newton Purcell
Tingewick
Barton Hartshorn
Chetwode
Gawcott
Radclive
Buckingham
Dadford
Shalstone
Biddlesden
Lillingstone Dayrell
Pury End
Bradden
Greens Norton
Towcester
Duncote
Tiffield
Cold Higham
Pattishall
Eastcote
Astcote
Grimscote
Farthingstone
Upper Stowe
Church Stowe
Nether Heyford
Upper Heyford
Harpole
Nobottle
Brockhall
Whilton
Little Brington
Great Brington
Long Buckby
East Haddon
Holdenby
Ravensthorpe
Coton
Watford
West Haddon
Crick
Kilsby
Barby
Dunchurch
Thurlaston
Bourton on Dunsmore
Frankton
Draycote
Marton
Birdingbury
Leamington Hastings
Kites Hardwick
Woolscott
Willoughby
Grandborough
Sawbridge
Broadwell
Stockton
Nethercote
Flecknoe
Lower Shuckburgh
Upper Catesby
Chapel Green
Ashby St Ledgers
Bishop's Itchington
Burton Dassett
Avon Dassett
Claydon
Lower Boddington
Upper Boddington
Aston le Walls
Hinton
Williamscott
Upper Wardington
Chacombe
Marston St Lawrence
Halse
Radstone
Crowfield
Upper Astrop
Astrop
Newbottle
King's Sutton
Charlton
Hinton-in-the-Hedges
North Newington
Easington
Broughton
Tadmarton
West Adderbury
Milton
Barford St John
Barford St Michael
South Newington
Nether Worton
North Aston
Ledwell
Shotteswell
Warmington
Hornton
Balscote
Milcombe
Hillesden
Preston Bissett
Chackmore
Akeley
Buffler's Holt
Whittlebury
Caldecote
Bugbrooke
Nene
Cherwell
Great Ouse
Leam
Itchen
Sor Brook
Oxford Canal
Draycote Water
Boddington Reservoir
Daventry Res.
DRAYCOTE WATER
WATFORD GAP SERVICES
HOLDENBY HOUSE AND FALCONRY CENTRE
ALTHORP
COTON MANOR
DAVENTRY MUS
OLD DAIRY FARM COUNTRY SHOPPING & CRAFT CENTRE
CANONS ASHBY HOUSE
CATANGER LLAMA TREKKING
SULGRAVE MANOR
FARNBOROUGH HALL
BURTON DASSETT HILLS
BROUGHTON CASTLE
STOWE SCHOOL AND GARDENS
SILVERSTONE
M1
M40
M45
A5
A43
A45
A361
A422
A423
A425
A426
A421
A428
A4500
A413
A4260
A4421
B4100
B4525
B4031
B4037
B5385
B4035
B4453
222
203
182
141
1469
1644
98
81
65
66
A
B
C
D
0 1 2 3 miles
0 1 2 3 4 5 km

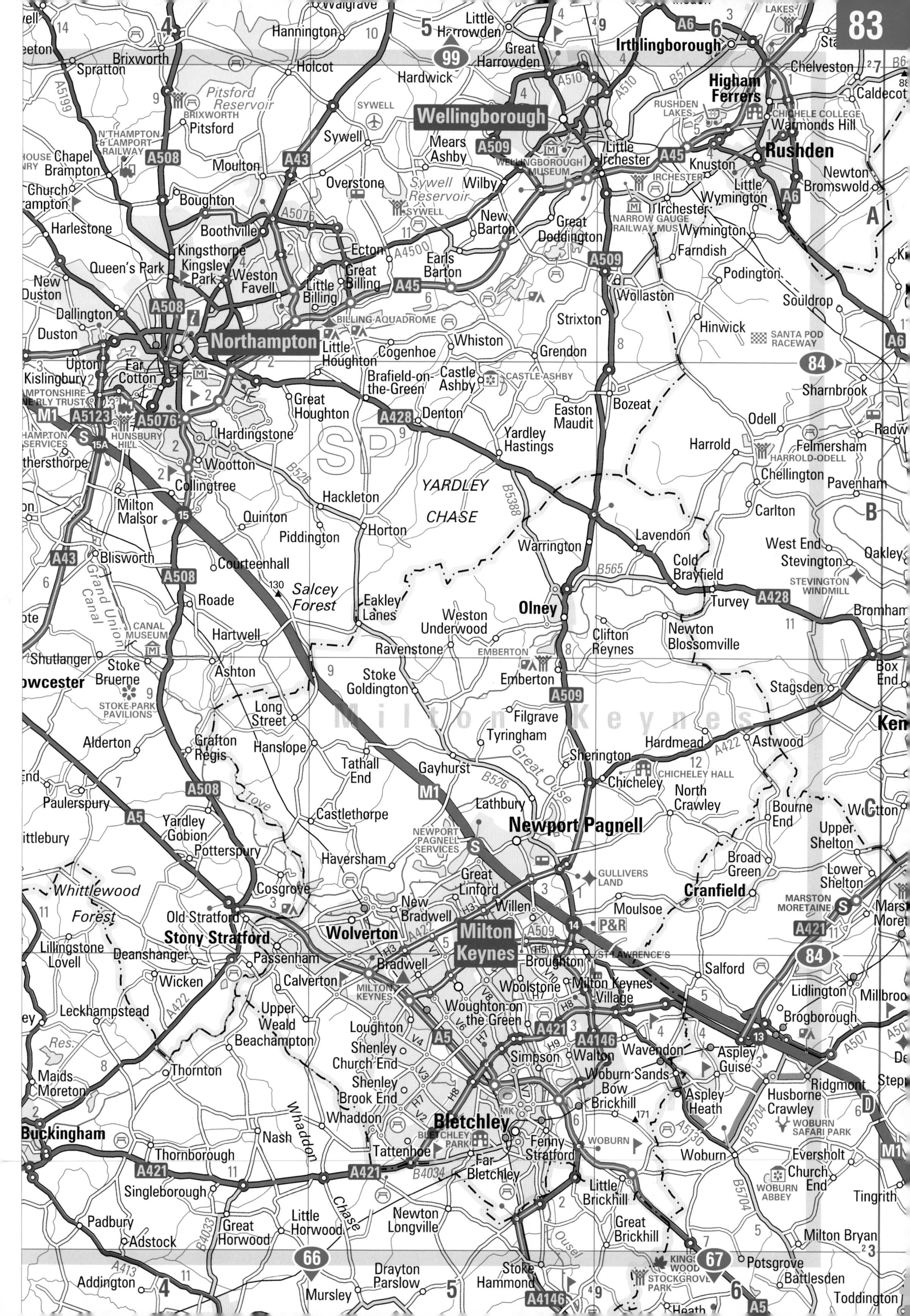

Walgrave
Hannington
Little Harrowden
Great Harrowden
Irthlingborough
Brixworth
Spratton
Holcot
Hardwick
Higham Ferrers
Chelveston
Caldecott
Pitsford Reservoir
Pitsford
Sywell
Wellingborough
Chichele College
Wymonds Hill
Rushden Lakes
Mears Ashby
Little Irchester
Knuston
Rushden
Chapel Brampton
Church Brampton
Moulton
Overstone
Sywell Reservoir
Wilby
Wellingborough Museum
Irchester
Newton Bromswold
Little Irchester
Wymington
Boughton
Harlestone
Boothville
New Barton
Great Doddington
Narrow Gauge Railway Mus
Farndish
Podington
Kingsthorpe
Ecton
Earls Barton
Queen's Park
Kingsley Park
Weston Favell
Great Billing
Little Billing
Wollaston
Souldrop
New Duston
Dallington
Duston
Billing Aquadrome
Strixton
Hinwick
Santa Pod Raceway
Northampton
Little Houghton
Cogenhoe
Whiston
Grendon
Upton
Kislingbury
Far Cotton
Brafield-on-the-Green
Castle Ashby
Bozeat
Sharnbrook
Great Houghton
Denton
Easton Maudit
Odell
Hunsbury Hill
Hardingstone
Yardley Hastings
Harrold
Felmersham
Harrold-Odell
Wootton
Chellington
Pavenham
Collingtree
Yardley Chase
Hackleton
Carlton
Milton Malsor
Quinton
Horton
Lavendon
West End
Piddington
Warrington
Stevington
Oakley
Blisworth
Cold Brayfield
Courteenhall
Salcey Forest
Stevington Windmill
Grand Union Canal
Roade
Eakley Lanes
Olney
Turvey
Bromham
Weston Underwood
Hartwell
Canal Museum
Clifton Reynes
Newton Blossomville
Shutlanger
Stoke Bruerne
Ravenstone
Emberton
Ashton
Towcester
Stoke Goldington
Box End
Stoke Park Pavilions
Stagsden
Long Street
Filgrave
Milton Keynes
Tyringham
Alderton
Grafton Regis
Hanslope
Tathall End
Hardmead
Astwood
Sherington
Gayhurst
Great Ouse
Chicheley Hall
Chicheley
Paulerspury
North Crawley
Lathbury
Castlethorpe
Bourne End
Yardley Gobion
Newport Pagnell
Upper Shelton
Potterspury
Newport Pagnell Services
Haversham
Broad Green
Whittlewood Forest
Great Linford
Gullivers Land
Lower Shelton
Cosgrove
Cranfield
Marston Moretaine
New Bradwell
Willen
Moulsoe
Old Stratford
Stony Stratford
Wolverton
Milton Keynes
Lillingstone Lovell
Deanshanger
Passenham
Bradwell
Broughton
St Lawrence's
Salford
Wicken
Calverton
Woolstone
Milton Keynes Village
Lidlington
Millbrook
Leckhampstead
Upper Weald
Woughton-on-the-Green
Brogborough
Loughton
Beachampton
Shenley Church End
Wavendon
Aspley Guise
Thornton
Simpson
Walton
Woburn Sands
Ridgmont
Maids Moreton
Shenley Brook End
Bow Brickhill
Aspley Heath
Husborne Crawley
Woburn Safari Park
Whaddon
Bletchley
Buckingham
Nash
Tattenhoe
Bletchley Park
Fenny Stratford
Woburn
Woburn
Eversholt
Thornborough
Far Bletchley
Church End
Woburn Abbey
Singleborough
Little Brickhill
Tingrith
Padbury
Great Horwood
Little Horwood
Newton Longville
Great Brickhill
Adstock
Milton Bryan
Drayton Parslow
Stoke Hammond
King's Wood
Potsgrove
Stockgrove Park
Battlesden
Addington
Mursley
Toddington

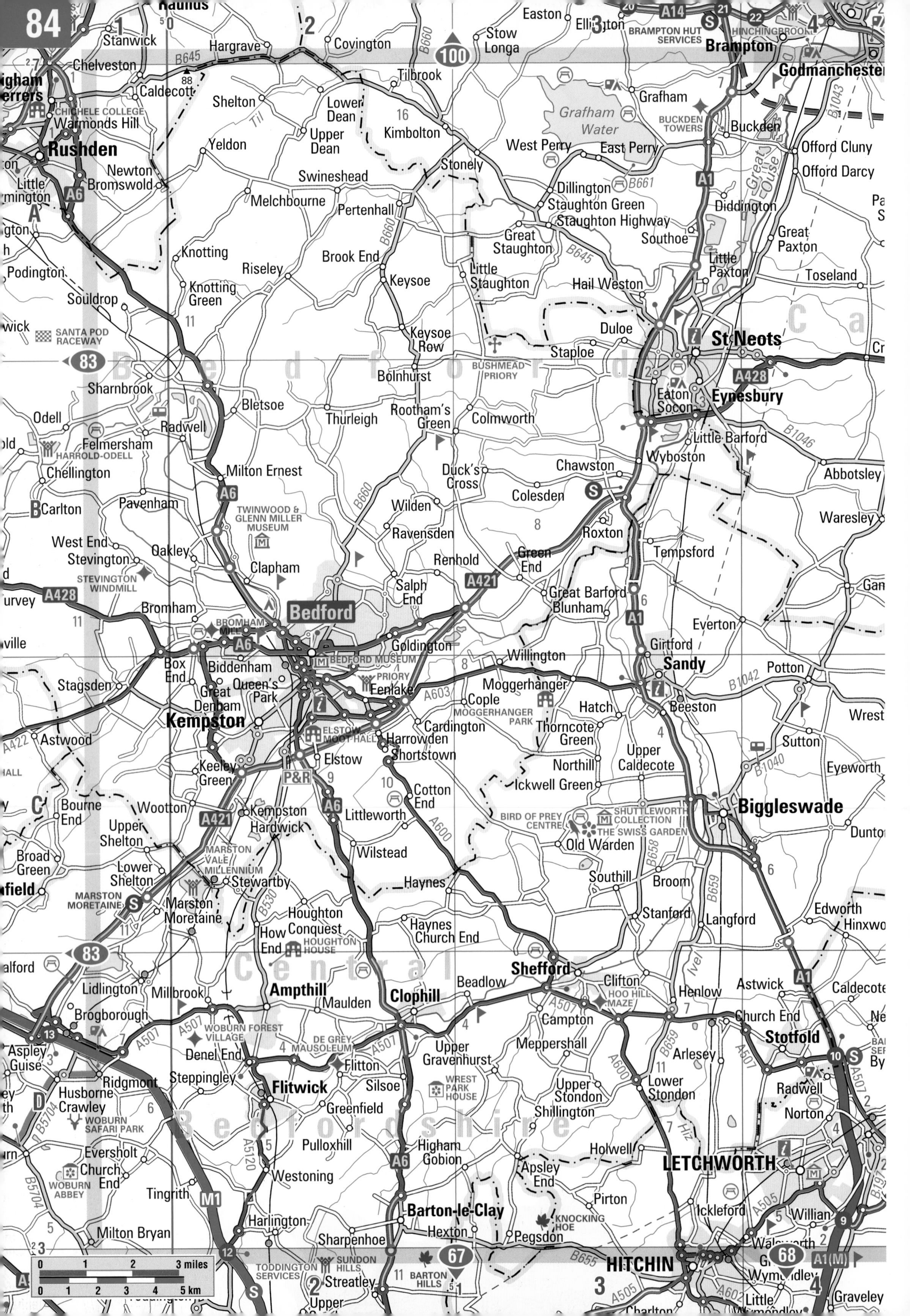
Raunds
Stanwick
Hargrave
Covington
Easton
Ellington
A14
BRAMPTON HUT SERVICES
Brampton
HINCHINGBROOKE
Godmanchester
100
Stow Longa
Chelveston
Caldecott
Tilbrook
B645
Higham Ferrers
CHICHELE COLLEGE
Warmonds Hill
Shelton
Lower Dean
Upper Dean
Kimbolton
Grafham
Grafham Water
BUCKDEN TOWERS
Buckden
Rushden
Yeldon
West Perry
East Perry
Offord Cluny
Offord Darcy
Newton Bromswold
Swineshead
Stonely
Dillington
B661
A1
Great Ouse
Little Irchester
A6
Melchbourne
Pertenhall
Staughton Green
Staughton Highway
Diddington
Great Staughton
Southoe
Great Paxton
Podington
Knotting
Riseley
Brook End
B660
Keysoe
Little Staughton
Hail Weston
Little Paxton
Toseland
Souldrop
Knotting Green
SANTA POD RACEWAY
Keysoe Row
Duloe
St Neots
Staploe
83
Bedford
BUSHMEAD PRIORY
Bolnhurst
Sharnbrook
A428
Eaton Socon
Eynesbury
Odell
Bletsoe
Thurleigh
Rootham's Green
Colmworth
Radwell
Felmersham
HARROLD-ODELL
Little Barford
B1046
Wyboston
Chellington
Milton Ernest
Duck's Cross
Chawston
Abbotsley
Carlton
Pavenham
Colesden
Wilden
TWINWOOD & GLENN MILLER MUSEUM
West End
Stevington
Oakley
Ravensden
Roxton
Waresley
Clapham
Tempsford
STEVINGTON WINDMILL
Renhold
Green End
Salph End
A421
Great Barford
Blunham
Bromham
Everton
BROMHAM MILL
Goldington
Girtford
Willington
Sandy
Potton
B1042
BEDFORD MUSEUM
Box End
Biddenham
PRIORY
Stagsden
Queen's Park
Fenlake
Moggerhanger
A603
Cople
MOGGERHANGER PARK
Great Denham
Kempston
Hatch
Beeston
Wrest
Cardington
Astwood
ELSTOW MOOT HALL
Harrowden
Thorncote Green
Shortstown
Elstow
Upper Caldecote
Sutton
A422
Keeley Green
Northill
B1040
Eyeworth
P&R
Ickwell Green
Cotton End
Bourne End
Wootton
Kempston Hardwick
Littleworth
BIRD OF PREY CENTRE
SHUTTLEWORTH COLLECTION
THE SWISS GARDEN
Biggleswade
Upper Shelton
A600
Old Warden
Dunton
Broad Green
MARSTON VALE MILLENNIUM
Wilstead
B658
Lower Shelton
Stewartby
Southill
Broom
MARSTON MORETAINE
Haynes
B659
Marston Moretaine
B530
Houghton Conquest
Stanford
Langford
Edworth
Hinxworth
How End
HOUGHTON HOUSE
Haynes Church End
Salford
Central Bedfordshire
Lidlington
Millbrook
Ampthill
Maulden
Clophill
Beadlow
Shefford
Clifton
HOO HILL MAZE
Henlow
Astwick
Caldecote
Brogborough
A507
WOBURN FOREST VILLAGE
Campton
Church End
Stotfold
Aspley Guise
DE GREY MAUSOLEUM
Upper Gravenhurst
Meppershall
Denel End
Flitton
Arlesey
Ridgmont
Steppingley
Flitwick
Silsoe
WREST PARK HOUSE
Lower Stondon
Upper Stondon
Radwell
Husborne Crawley
Greenfield
Shillington
Norton
WOBURN SAFARI PARK
B5704
Eversholt
Pulloxhill
Higham Gobion
Holwell
Hiz
LETCHWORTH
Church End
WOBURN ABBEY
A5120
Westoning
Apsley End
Tingrith
M1
Pirton
A505
Willian
Barton-le-Clay
KNOCKING HOE
Ickleford
Harlington
Milton Bryan
Hexton
Pegsdon
Walsworth
Sharpenhoe
TODDINGTON SERVICES
SUNDON HILLS
67
B655
HITCHIN
68
A1(M)
Wymondley
BARTON HILLS
Streatley
A505
A602
Little Wymondley
Graveley
Upper
0 1 2 3 miles
0 1 2 3 4 5 km

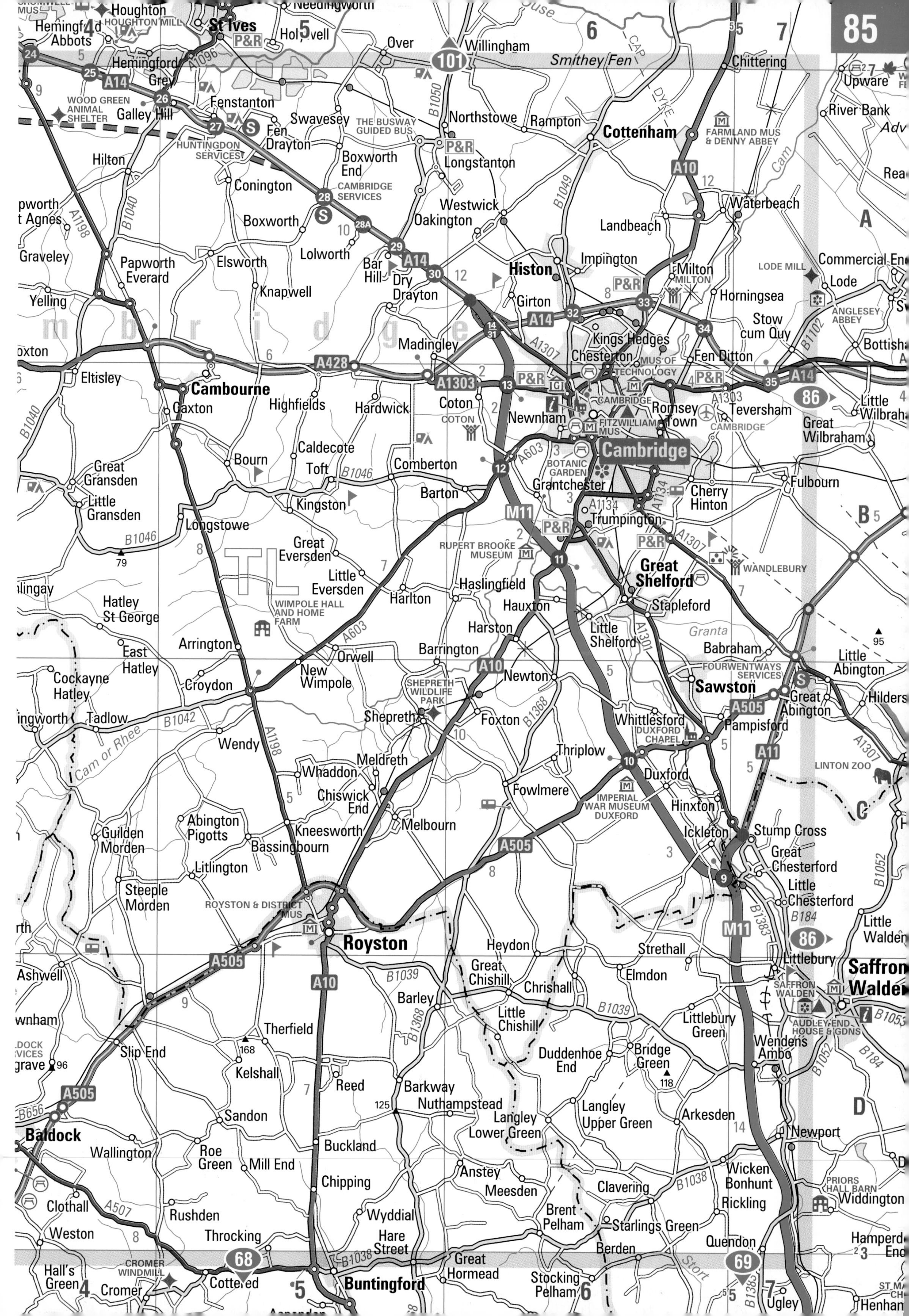
Houghton
Hemingford Abbots
HOUGHTON MILL
St Ives
P&R
Holywell
Needingworth
Over
Willingham
101
Smithey Fen
Chittering
Upware
River Bank
Hemingford Grey
A1096
A14
WOOD GREEN ANIMAL SHELTER
Galley Hill
Fenstanton
Fen Drayton
Swavesey
THE BUSWAY GUIDED BUS
B1050
Northstowe
Rampton
Cottenham
FARMLAND MUS & DENNY ABBEY
HUNTINGDON SERVICES
Hilton
Boxworth End
Longstanton
A10
Conington
CAMBRIDGE SERVICES
Westwick
Oakington
B1049
Waterbeach
Papworth St Agnes
A1198
B1040
Boxworth
Landbeach
Graveley
Papworth Everard
Elsworth
Lolworth
Bar Hill
Dry Drayton
Histon
Impington
Milton
MILTON
LODE MILL
Commercial End
Lode
Yelling
Knapwell
Girton
Horningsea
Stow cum Quy
ANGLESEY ABBEY
Kings Hedges
Fen Ditton
Bottisham
Madingley
Chesterton
MUS OF TECHNOLOGY
A428
A1303
A1307
Eltisley
Cambourne
Caxton
Highfields
Hardwick
Coton
COTON
Newnham
CAMBRIDGE
FITZWILLIAM MUS
Romsey Town
Teversham
CAMBRIDGE
Little Wilbraham
Great Wilbraham
86
Cambridge
Caldecote
Toft
B1046
Comberton
Barton
BOTANIC GARDEN
Grantchester
Cherry Hinton
Fulbourn
Great Gransden
Little Gransden
Bourn
Kingston
A603
A1134
Trumpington
M11
Longstowe
B1046
79
Great Eversden
RUPERT BROOKE MUSEUM
Great Shelford
WANDLEBURY
Little Eversden
Harlton
Haslingfield
Hauxton
Stapleford
Gamlingay
Hatley St George
WIMPOLE HALL AND HOME FARM
TL
Harston
Little Shelford
Granta
Babraham
95
East Hatley
Arrington
Orwell
Barrington
A1301
FOURWENTWAYS SERVICES
Little Abington
Cockayne Hatley
New Wimpole
A10
Newton
Sawston
Croydon
SHEPRETH WILDLIFE PARK
Great Abington
Hildersham
Wrestlingworth
Tadlow
B1042
Shepreth
Foxton
B1368
Whittlesford
DUXFORD CHAPEL
A505
Pampisford
Wendy
Cam or Rhee
A1198
Thriplow
A11
LINTON ZOO
Whaddon
Meldreth
Duxford
Fowlmere
Chiswick End
IMPERIAL WAR MUSEUM DUXFORD
Hinxton
Guilden Morden
Abington Pigotts
Kneesworth
Melbourn
Ickleton
Stump Cross
Bassingbourn
Great Chesterford
Litlington
A505
Little Chesterford
Steeple Morden
ROYSTON & DISTRICT MUS
B1383
B184
B1052
Little Walden
Royston
Heydon
Strethall
Ashwell
A505
Great Chishill
Elmdon
Littlebury
Saffron Walden
A10
B1039
Chrishall
SAFFRON WALDEN
Barley
B1039
AUDLEY END HOUSE & GDNS
B1053
Newnham
Little Chishill
Littlebury Green
Wendens Ambo
Therfield
B1368
Bridge Green
Slip End
168
Duddenhoe End
Kelshall
118
Baldock
Reed
Barkway
A505
Nuthampstead
125
Langley Upper Green
Langley Lower Green
Arkesden
B656
Sandon
Newport
Wallington
Roe Green
Mill End
Buckland
Anstey
Wicken Bonhunt
Chipping
Meesden
Clavering
B1038
PRIORS HALL BARN
Widdington
Clothall
A507
Rushden
Wyddial
Brent Pelham
Starlings Green
Rickling
Weston
Throcking
Hare Street
Berden
Quendon
Hamperden End
68
B1038
Great Hormead
Stort
69
CROMER WINDMILL
Hall's Green
Cromer
Cottered
Buntingford
Stocking Pelham
B1383
Ugley
Henham

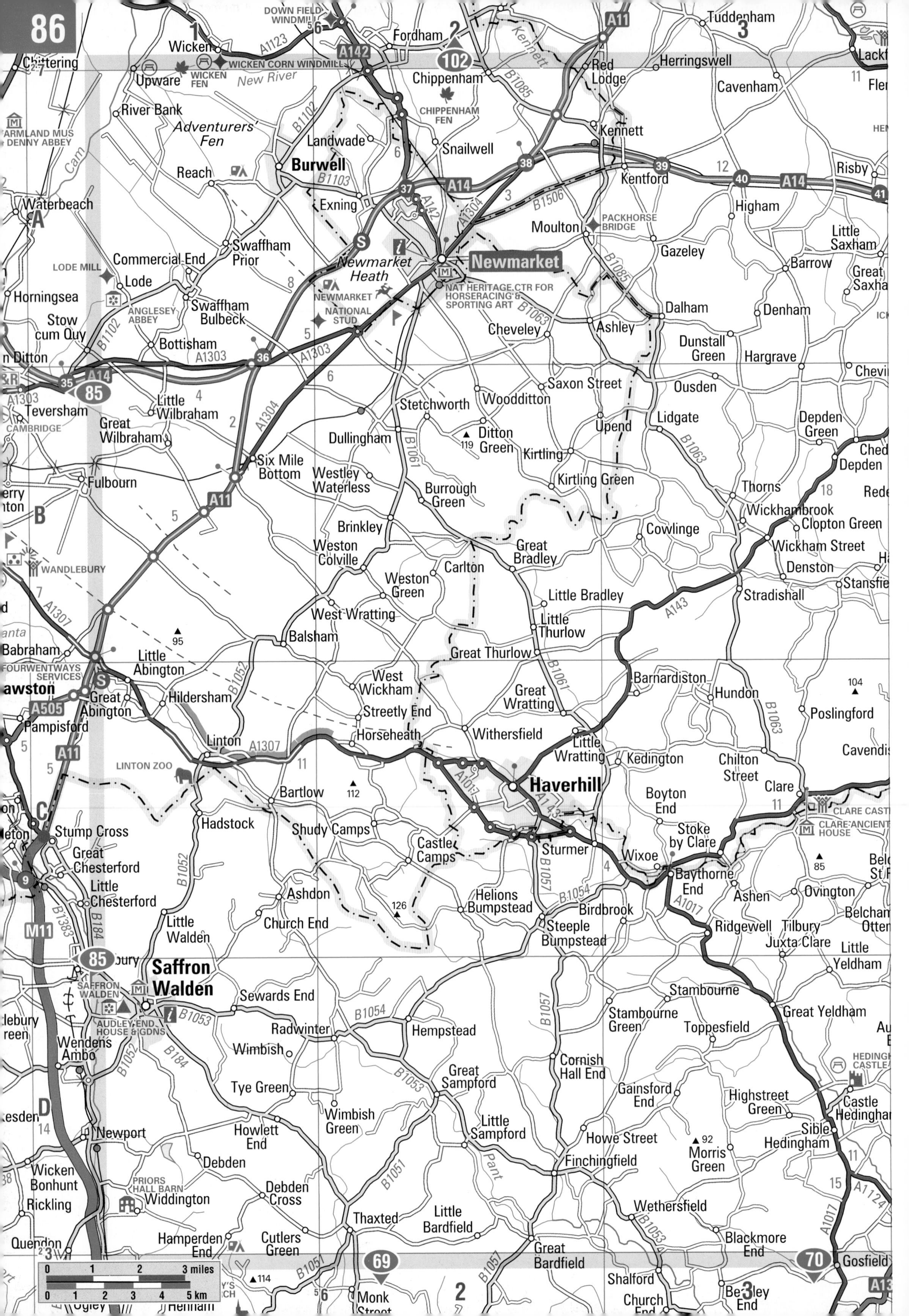
DOWN FIELD WINDMILL
Wicken
Fordham
Tuddenham
Chittering
WICKEN CORN WINDMILL
Upware
WICKEN FEN
New River
Chippenham
CHIPPENHAM FEN
Red Lodge
Herringswell
Cavenham
Lackford
Kennett
River Bank
Adventurers' Fen
FARMLAND MUS
DENNY ABBEY
Landwade
Snailwell
Kentford
Risby
Burwell
Reach
Exning
Higham
Waterbeach
Moulton
PACKHORSE BRIDGE
Little Saxham
Swaffham Prior
Newmarket Heath
Newmarket
Gazeley
Barrow
LODE MILL
Commercial End
Lode
NAT HERITAGE CTR FOR HORSERACING & SPORTING ART
Great Saxham
Horningsea
NEWMARKET
NATIONAL STUD
Dalham
Denham
Stow cum Quy
ANGLESEY ABBEY
Swaffham Bulbeck
Cheveley
Ashley
Bottisham
Dunstall Green
Hargrave
Ditton
Saxon Street
Ousden
Teversham
Little Wilbraham
Stetchworth
Woodditton
Lidgate
Depden Green
CAMBRIDGE
Great Wilbraham
Dullingham
Ditton Green
Upend
Kirtling
Chedburgh
Depden
Six Mile Bottom
Westley Waterless
Kirtling Green
Fulbourn
Burrough Green
Thorns
Wickhambrook
Clopton Green
Brinkley
Cowlinge
Weston Colville
Great Bradley
Wickham Street
Carlton
Denston
WANDLEBURY
Weston Green
Little Bradley
Stradishall
Stansfield
West Wratting
Little Thurlow
Balsham
Great Thurlow
Babraham
Little Abington
FOURWENTWAYS SERVICES
West Wickham
Barnardiston
Hundon
Sawston
Great Abington
Hildersham
Great Wratting
Poslingford
Pampisford
Streetly End
Linton
Horseheath
Withersfield
Little Wratting
Kedington
Chilton Street
Cavendish
LINTON ZOO
Haverhill
Clare
Bartlow
Boyton End
CLARE CASTLE
CLARE ANCIENT HOUSE
Hadstock
Shudy Camps
Castle Camps
Stoke by Clare
Stump Cross
Great Chesterford
Sturmer
Wixoe
Baythorne End
Little Chesterford
Helions Bumpstead
Ashdon
Birdbrook
Ashen
Ovington
Belchamp Otten
Church End
Steeple Bumpstead
Ridgewell
Tilbury Juxta Clare
Little Walden
Little Yeldham
Saffron Walden
SAFFRON WALDEN
AUDLEY END HOUSE & GDNS
Sewards End
Stambourne
Great Yeldham
Radwinter
Hempstead
Stambourne Green
Toppesfield
Wendens Ambo
Wimbish
Cornish Hall End
HEDINGHAM CASTLE
Great Sampford
Tye Green
Gainsford End
Highstreet Green
Castle Hedingham
Wimbish Green
Newport
Howlett End
Little Sampford
Howe Street
Morris Green
Sible Hedingham
Debden
Finchingfield
Wicken Bonhunt
PRIORS HALL BARN
Widdington
Debden Cross
Rickling
Thaxted
Little Bardfield
Wethersfield
Quendon
Hamperden End
Cutlers Green
Great Bardfield
Blackmore End
Gosfield
Monk Street
Shalford
Church End
Beazley End
0 1 2 3 miles
0 1 2 3 4 5 km

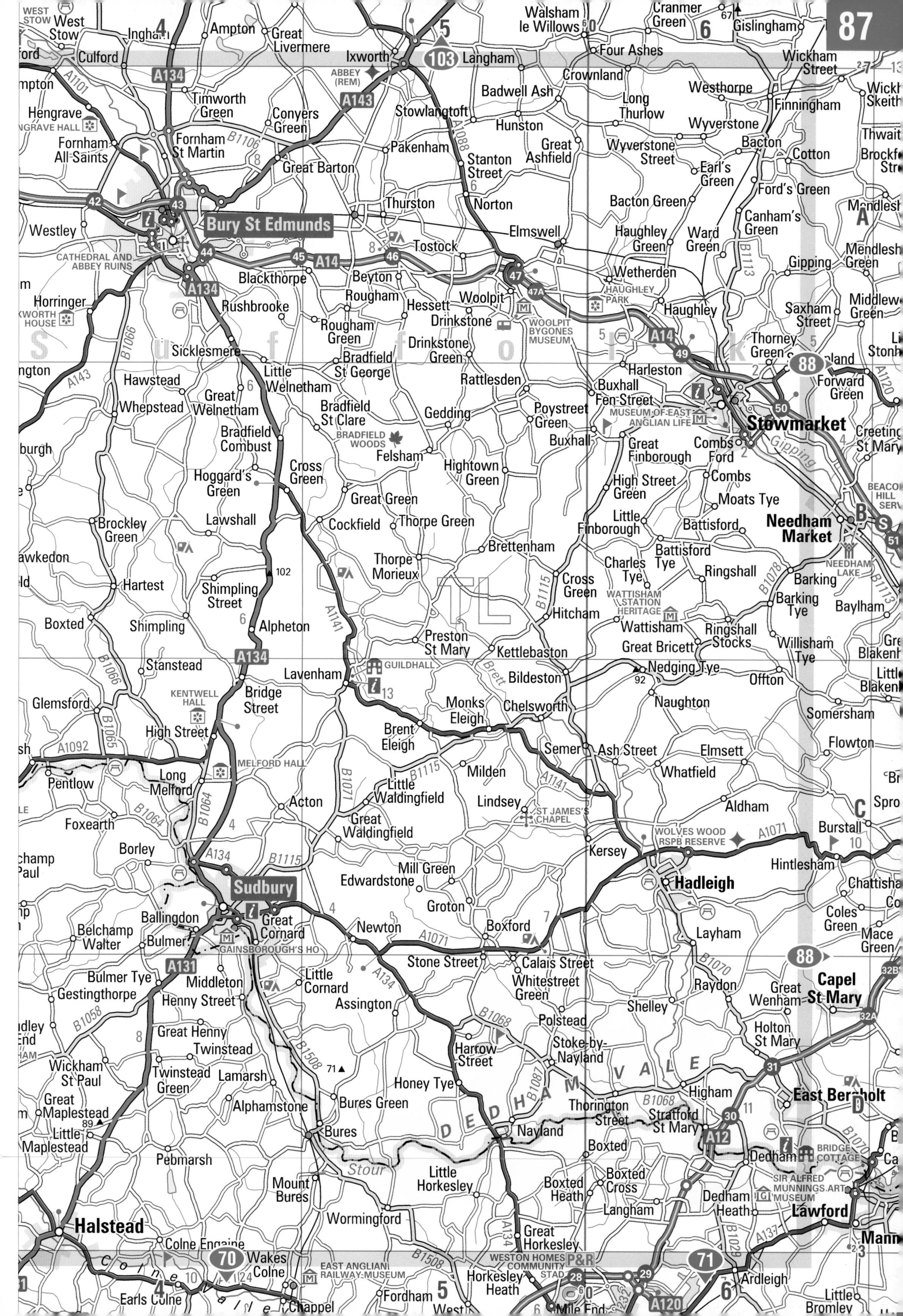

West Stow
West Stow
Ingham
Ampton
Great Livermere
Walsham le Willows
Cranmer Green
Gislingham
Culford
Ixworth
Abbey (rem)
103
Langham
Four Ashes
Wickham Street
A134
A143
A1101
Hengrave
Hengrave Hall
Timworth Green
Conyers Green
Stowlangtoft
Badwell Ash
Crownland
Long Thurlow
Westhorpe
Finningham
Wickham Skeith
Fornham All Saints
Fornham St Martin
B1106
Pakenham
A1088
Hunston
Great Ashfield
Wyverstone
Wyverstone Street
Bacton
Cotton
Thwaite
Great Barton
Stanton Street
Earl's Green
Ford's Green
Brockford Street
42
43
Westley
Bury St Edmunds
Thurston
Norton
Bacton Green
Canham's Green
Mendlesham
Cathedral and Abbey Ruins
44
45
A14
46
Tostock
Elmswell
Haughley Green
Ward Green
B1113
Mendlesham Green
Blackthorpe
Beyton
47
47A
Wetherden
Gipping
Horringer
Ickworth House
Rushbrooke
Rougham
Hessett
Woolpit
Drinkstone
Woolpit Bygones Museum
Haughley Park
Haughley
Saxham Street
Middlewood Green
B1066
Rougham Green
Drinkstone Green
Thorney Green
Suffolk
Sicklesmere
Bradfield St George
49
88
Forward Green
A1120
A143
Hawstead
Little Welnetham
Rattlesden
Harleston
Great Welnetham
Buxhall Fen Street
50
Whepstead
Bradfield St Clare
Gedding
Poystreet Green
Museum of East Anglian Life
Stowmarket
Creeting St Mary
Bradfield Combust
Bradfield Woods
Felsham
Buxhall
Great Finborough
Combs Ford
Gipping
Cross Green
Hoggard's Green
Hightown Green
High Street Green
Combs
Beacon Hill Serv
Great Green
Moats Tye
Brockley Green
Lawshall
Cockfield
Thorpe Green
Little Finborough
Battisford
Needham Market
51
Brettenham
Battisford Tye
Hawkedon
102
Thorpe Morieux
Charles Tye
Ringshall
Needham Lake
Hartest
Shimpling Street
B1115
Cross Green
Wattisham Station Heritage
Barking
B1078
TL
Barking Tye
Baylham
A1141
Hitcham
Boxted
Shimpling
Alpheton
Preston St Mary
Wattisham
Ringshall Stocks
Willisham Tye
Great Bricett
Kettlebaston
B1066
Stanstead
A134
Guildhall
Brett
Nedging Tye
92
Lavenham
Bildeston
Offton
Kentwell Hall
Bridge Street
13
Glemsford
Monks Eleigh
Chelsworth
Naughton
B1065
Brent Eleigh
High Street
Somersham
A1092
Semer
Ash Street
Elmsett
Flowton
Melford Hall
Long Melford
Pentlow
B1115
Little Waldingfield
Milden
Whatfield
B1064
B1071
A1141
Acton
Lindsey
Aldham
St James's Chapel
Foxearth
Great Waldingfield
Wolves Wood RSPB Reserve
A1071
Burstall
Borley
A134
B1115
Kersey
Belchamp St Paul
Mill Green
Hintlesham
Edwardstone
Sudbury
Hadleigh
Groton
Ballingdon
Great Cornard
Newton
Boxford
Coles Green
Belchamp Walter
Bulmer
Gainsborough's Ho
A1071
Layham
Mace Green
Stone Street
Calais Street
88
A131
Bulmer Tye
Middleton
Little Cornard
Whitestreet Green
B1070
Capel St Mary
Great Wenham
Raydon
Gestingthorpe
Henny Street
Assington
A134
Shelley
Polstead
B1068
B1058
Great Henny
Harrow Street
Stoke-by-Nayland
Holton St Mary
Wickham St Paul
Twinstead
B1508
71
Twinstead Green
Lamarsh
Dedham Vale
Honey Tye
B1087
Higham
31
East Bergholt
Great Maplestead
89
Alphamstone
Bures Green
Thorington Street
B1068
Stratford St Mary
30
11
Little Maplestead
Bures
Nayland
A12
Dedham
Bridge Cottage
Pebmarsh
Stour
Boxted
B1070
Little Horkesley
Boxted Cross
Sir Alfred Munnings Art Museum
Mount Bures
Boxted Heath
Dedham Heath
Lawford
Halstead
Wormingford
Langham
B1029
A137
A134
Great Horkesley
Colne Engaine
Colne
70
Wakes Colne
East Anglian Railway Museum
B1508
Weston Homes Community Stad
P&R
29
71
Horkesley Heath
28
Ardleigh
Earls Colne
Chappel
Fordham
A120
Mile End
Little Bromley

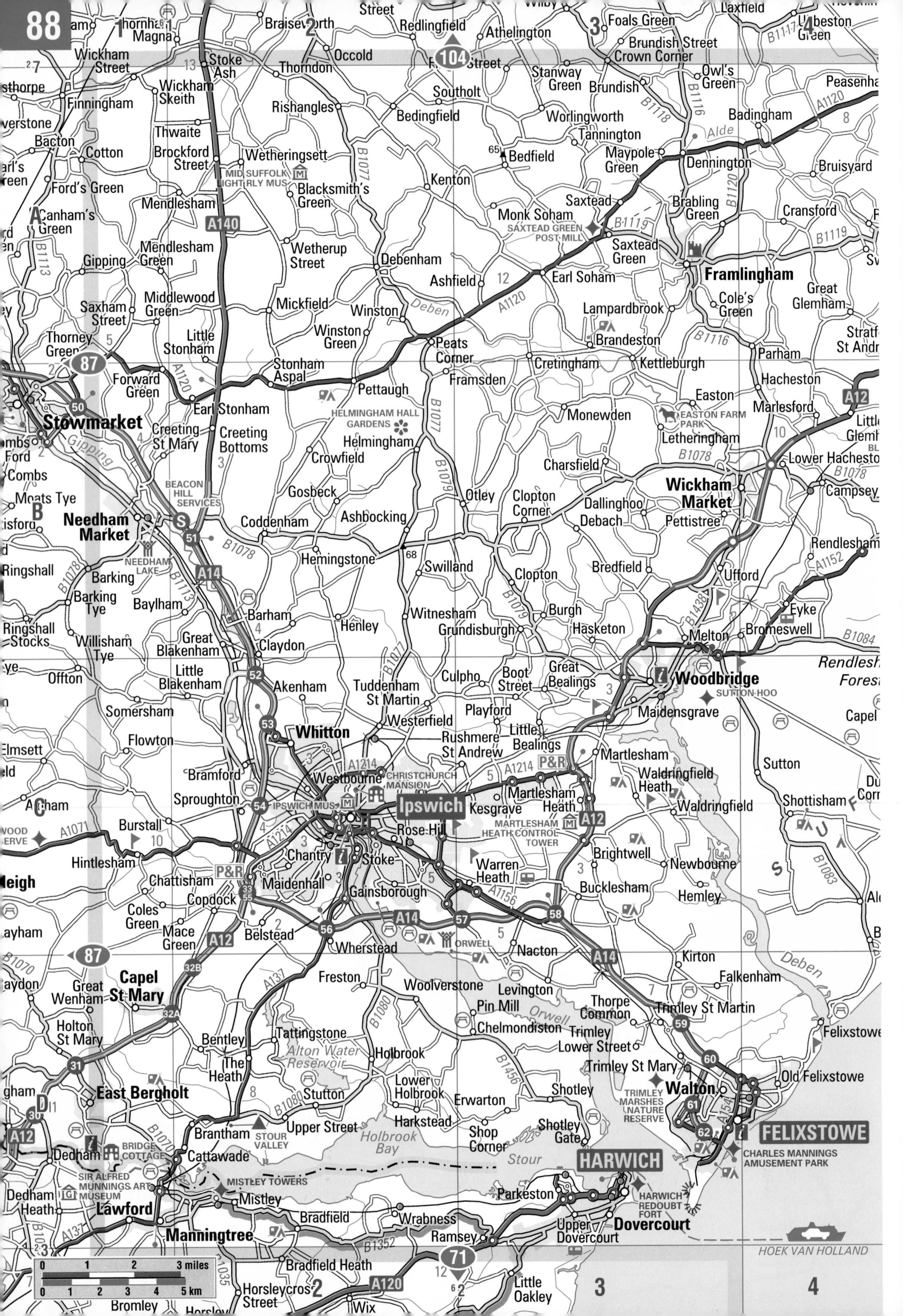
Braiseworth
Redlingfield
Athelington
Foals Green
Laxfield
Ubbeston Green
Thornham Magna
Occold
Brundish Street
Crown Corner
Wickham Street
Stoke Ash
Thorndon
Stanway Green
Owl's Green
Finningham
Wickham Skeith
Southolt
Brundish
Peasenhall
Rishangles
Bedingfield
Worlingworth
Badingham
Thwaite
Tannington
Alde
Bacton
Cotton
Brockford Street
Wetheringsett
Bedfield
Maypole Green
Dennington
Bruisyard
Ford's Green
MID SUFFOLK LIGHT RLY MUS
Blacksmith's Green
Kenton
Saxtead
Brabling Green
Cransford
Mendlesham
Monk Soham
SAXTEAD GREEN POST MILL
Canham's Green
Saxtead Green
Mendlesham Green
Wetherup Street
Framlingham
Gipping
Debenham
Ashfield
Earl Soham
Great Glemham
Saxham Street
Middlewood Green
Mickfield
Winston
Deben
Lampardbrook
Cole's Green
Thorney Green
Little Stonham
Winston Green
Brandeston
Stratford St Andrew
Peats Corner
Cretingham
Kettleburgh
Parham
Stonham Aspal
Framsden
Hacheston
Forward Green
Pettaugh
Easton
Earl Stonham
HELMINGHAM HALL GARDENS
Monewden
EASTON FARM PARK
Marlesford
Stowmarket
Creeting St Mary
Creeting Bottoms
Helmingham
Letheringham
Little Glemham
Gipping
Crowfield
Charsfield
Lower Hacheston
Combs Ford
Combs
BEACON HILL SERVICES
Gosbeck
Otley
Clopton Corner
Dallinghoo
Wickham Market
Campsey Ash
Moats Tye
Needham Market
Coddenham
Ashbocking
Debach
Pettistree
NEEDHAM LAKE
Hemingstone
Swilland
Clopton
Bredfield
Rendlesham
Ringshall
Barking
Ufford
Barking Tye
Baylham
Barham
Burgh
Eyke
Ringshall Stocks
Willisham Tye
Great Blakenham
Henley
Witnesham
Grundisburgh
Hasketon
Melton
Bromeswell
Claydon
Offton
Little Blakenham
Akenham
Tuddenham St Martin
Culpho
Boot Street
Great Bealings
Woodbridge
Rendlesham Forest
SUTTON HOO
Somersham
Whitton
Westerfield
Playford
Little Bealings
Maidensgrave
Capel
Flowton
Rushmere St Andrew
Martlesham
Sutton
Elmsett
Bramford
Westbourne
CHRISTCHURCH MANSION
Waldringfield Heath
Sproughton
IPSWICH MUS
Ipswich
Kesgrave
Martlesham Heath
Waldringfield
Shottisham
Burstall
MARTLESHAM HEATH CONTROL TOWER
Rose Hill
Hintlesham
Chantry
Stoke
Warren Heath
Brightwell
Newbourne
Chattisham
Maidenhall
Bucklesham
Hemley
Copdock
Gainsborough
Coles Green
Mace Green
Belstead
Wherstead
ORWELL
Nacton
Kirton
Deben
Capel St Mary
Great Wenham
Freston
Woolverstone
Levington
Falkenham
Thorpe Common
Trimley St Martin
Holton St Mary
Pin Mill
Orwell
Tattingstone
Chelmondiston
Trimley Lower Street
Felixstowe Ferry
Bentley
Alton Water Reservoir
Holbrook
Trimley St Mary
The Heath
Lower Holbrook
Old Felixstowe
East Bergholt
Stutton
Erwarton
Shotley
Walton
TRIMLEY MARSHES NATURE RESERVE
Harkstead
Shotley Gate
Brantham
STOUR VALLEY
Upper Street
Holbrook Bay
Shop Corner
FELIXSTOWE
Dedham
BRIDGE COTTAGE
Cattawade
Stour
HARWICH
CHARLES MANNINGS AMUSEMENT PARK
SIR ALFRED MUNNINGS ART MUSEUM
MISTLEY TOWERS
Mistley
Parkeston
HARWICH REDOUBT FORT
Dedham Heath
Lawford
Bradfield
Wrabness
Manningtree
Ramsey
Upper Dovercourt
Dovercourt
HOEK VAN HOLLAND
Bradfield Heath
Horsleycross Street
Little Oakley
Bromley
Wix
0 1 2 3 miles
0 1 2 3 4 5 km

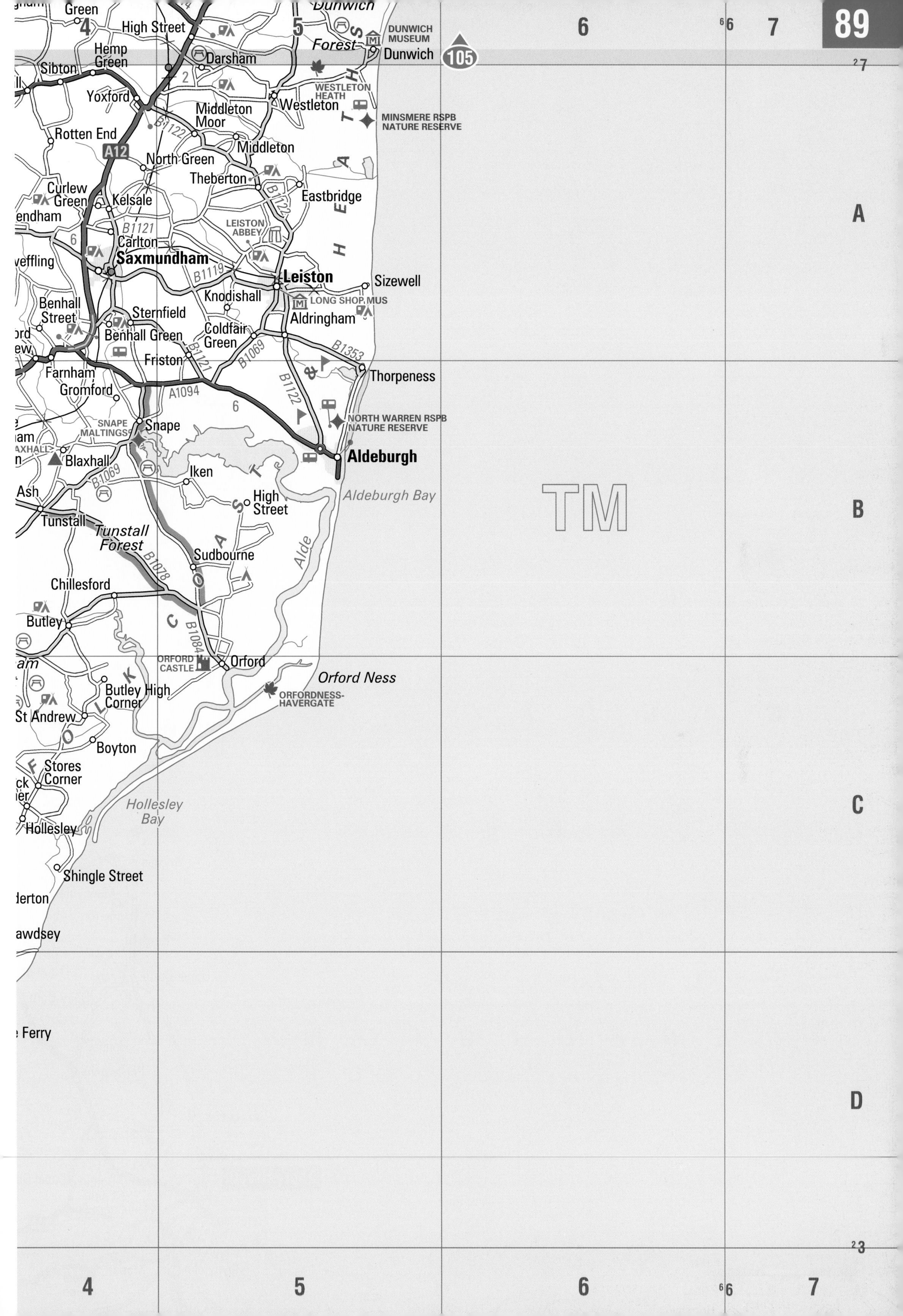

Green
High Street
Hemp Green
Sibton
Darsham
Dunwich
Forest
DUNWICH MUSEUM
Dunwich 105
Yoxford
WESTLETON HEATH
Westleton
Middleton Moor
Rotten End
A12
B1122
North Green
Middleton
Theberton
Eastbridge
MINSMERE RSPB NATURE RESERVE
Curlew Green
endham
Kelsale
B1121
LEISTON ABBEY
B1122
6
Carlton
Saxmundham
veffling
B1119
Leiston
Sizewell
Knodishall
LONG SHOP MUS
Benhall Street
Sternfield
Aldringham
ord
ew
Benhall Green
Coldfair Green
B1069
B1353
Friston
B1121
Farnham
Gromford
A1094
6
B1122
Thorpeness
SNAPE MALTINGS
Snape
NORTH WARREN RSPB NATURE RESERVE
am
AXHALL
Blaxhall
B1069
Iken
Aldeburgh
Aldeburgh Bay
Ash
High Street
Tunstall
Tunstall Forest
B1078
Sudbourne
Alde
Chillesford
Butley
B1084
ORFORD CASTLE
Orford
Orford Ness
ORFORDNESS-HAVERGATE
am
Butley High Corner
St Andrew
Boyton
Stores Corner
ck
er
Hollesley Bay
Hollesley
Shingle Street
lerton
awdsey
e Ferry

A

B

TM

C

D

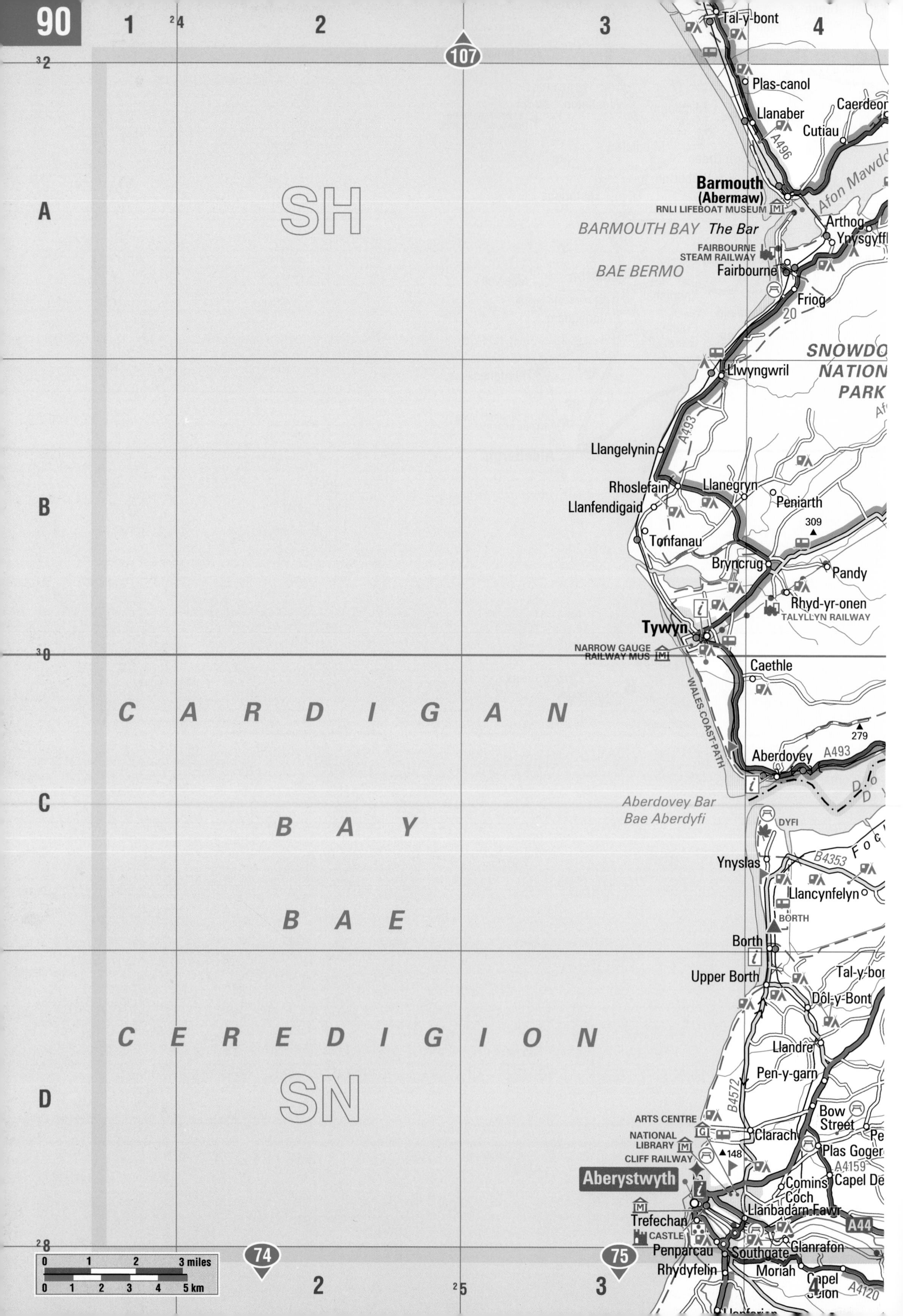

SH

Tal-y-bont

Plas-canol

Llanaber
Caerdeon

Cutiau

A496

**Barmouth
(Abermaw)**
RNLI LIFEBOAT MUSEUM

Afon Mawdd

Arthog

Ynysgyff

BARMOUTH BAY   The Bar

BARMOUTH BAY

FAIRBOURNE
STEAM RAILWAY

Fairbourne

BAE BERMO

Friog
20

SNOWDO
NATION
PARK

Llwyngwril

Af

Llangelynin

A493

Rhoslefain
Llanegryn

Llanfendigaid

Peniarth

Tonfanau
309

Bryncrug
Pandy

Rhyd-yr-onen

i

TALYLLYN RAILWAY

Tywyn

NARROW GAUGE
RAILWAY MUS

Caethle

C A R D I G A N

WALES COAST PATH

279

Aberdovey
A493

D

B A Y

Aberdovey Bar
Bae Aberdyfi

DYFI

Fo

B4353

Ynyslas

Llancynfelyn

B A E

BORTH

Borth

Upper Borth

Tal-y-bo

Dôl-y-Bont

C E R E D I G I O N

Llandre

Pen-y-garn

SN

Bow
Street

ARTS CENTRE

NATIONAL
LIBRARY

Clarach

CLIFF RAILWAY

Plas Goger

148

Aberystwyth
i

Comins
Coch
Capel De

A4159

Llanbadarn-Fawr

A44

Trefechan
CASTLE

Penparcau
Southgate
Glanrafon

Rhydyfelin
Moriah
Capel
Seion

A4120

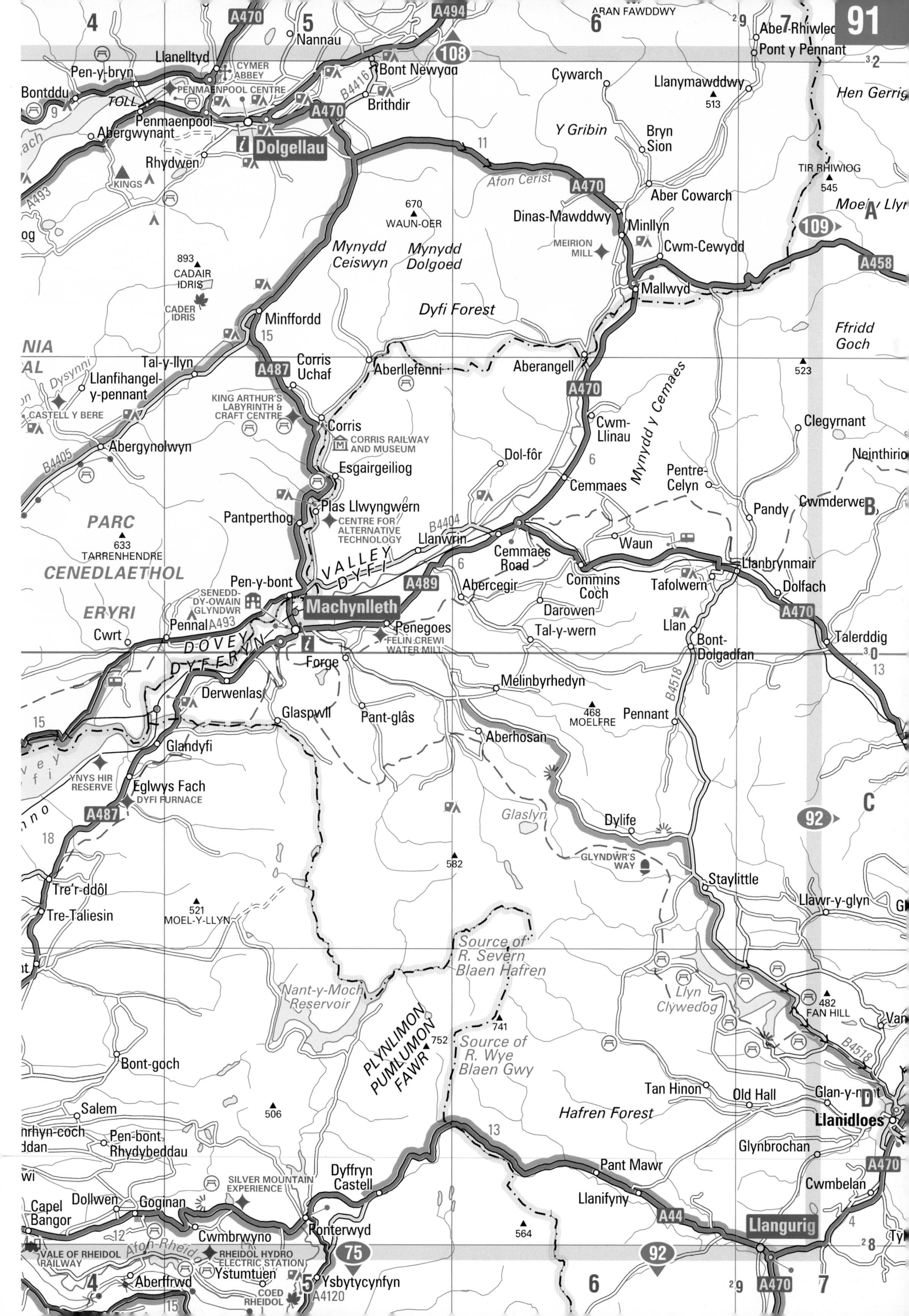

A470
A494
108
Nannau
ARAN FAWDDWY
Aber-Rhiwlech
Pont y Pennant
Llanelltyd
CYMER ABBEY
Pen-y-bryn
Bont Newydd
Cywarch
Llanymawddwy
513
Hen Gerrig
Bontddu
TOLL
PENMAENPOOL CENTRE
B4416
Brithdir
Penmaenpool
Abergwynant
Dolgellau
Y Gribin
Bryn Sion
Rhydwen
KINGS
TIR RHIWIOG
545
Afon Cerist
Aber Cowarch
670
WAUN-OER
Dinas-Mawddwy
Minllyn
109
MEIRION MILL
Cwm-Cewydd
Mynydd Ceiswyn
Mynydd Dolgoed
893
CADAIR IDRIS
A458
Mallwyd
CADER IDRIS
Dyfi Forest
Minffordd
Ffridd Goch
Tal-y-llyn
Corris Uchaf
Aberllefenni
Aberangell
523
Llanfihangel-y-pennant
Dysynni
CASTELL Y BERE
KING ARTHUR'S LABYRINTH & CRAFT CENTRE
A487
Mynydd y Cemaes
Corris
Cwm-Llinau
Clegyrnant
CORRIS RAILWAY AND MUSEUM
Abergynolwyn
B4405
Dol-fôr
Neinthirion
Esgairgeiliog
Pentre-Celyn
Cemmaes
Plas Llwyngwern
Pandy
Cwmderwen
PARC
Pantperthog
CENTRE FOR ALTERNATIVE TECHNOLOGY
B4404
633
TARRENHENDRE
Llanwrin
Waun
Cemmaes Road
VALLEY DYFI
CENEDLAETHOL
Llanbrynmair
Pen-y-bont
Commins Coch
Tafolwern
Dolfach
SENEDD-DY-OWAIN GLYNDWR
A489
Abercegir
Machynlleth
ERYRI
Darowen
A470
Cwrt
Pennal
A493
Penegoes
Tal-y-wern
Llan
Talerddig
DOVEY
DYFFRYN
FELIN CREWI WATER MILL
Bont-Dolgadfan
Forge
B4518
Melinbyrhedyn
Derwenlas
468
MOELFRE
Glaspwll
Pant-glâs
Pennant
Aberhosan
Glandyfi
YNYS HIR RESERVE
Eglwys Fach
DYFI FURNACE
Glaslyn
92
Dylife
582
GLYNDWR'S WAY
Tre'r-ddôl
Staylittle
521
MOEL-Y-LLYN
Tre-Taliesin
Llawr-y-glyn
Source of R. Severn
Blaen Hafren
Nant-y-Moch Reservoir
Llyn Clywedog
482
FAN HILL
741
PLYNLIMON PUMLUMON FAWR
752
Source of R. Wye
Blaen Gwy
Bont-goch
B4518
Tan Hinon
Old Hall
Glan-y-nant
Salem
506
Hafren Forest
Llanidloes
Pen-bont Rhydybeddau
Glynbrochan
Pant Mawr
SILVER MOUNTAIN EXPERIENCE
Dyffryn Castell
Cwmbelan
Capel Bangor
Dollwen
Goginan
Llanifyny
A44
Ponterwyd
Llangurig
564
Cwmbrwyno
VALE OF RHEIDOL RAILWAY
Afon Rheidol
RHEIDOL HYDRO ELECTRIC STATION
75
Ystumtuen
Aberffrwd
COED RHEIDOL
Ysbytycynfyn
A4120

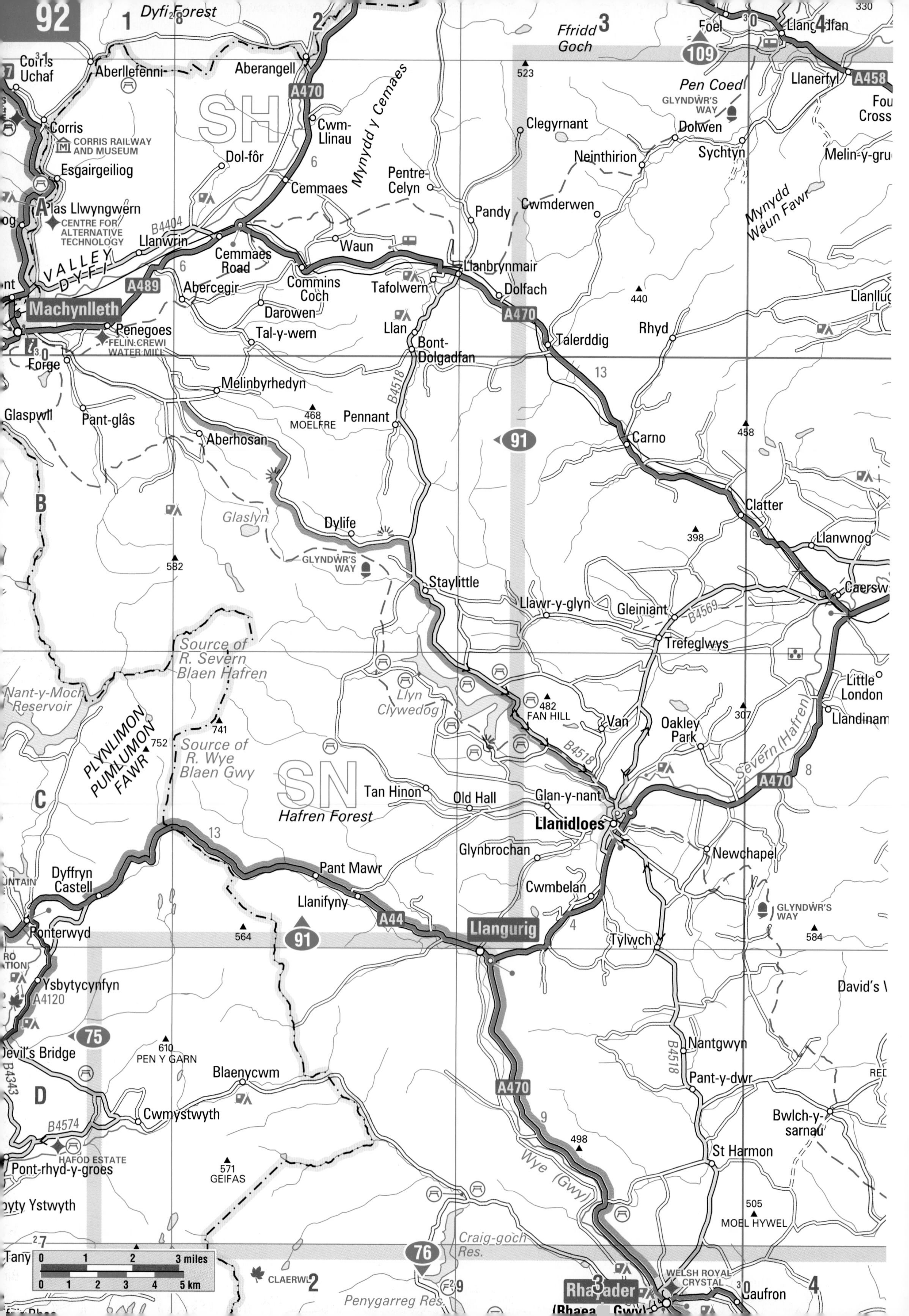
Dyfi Forest
Corris Uchaf
Aberllefenni
Aberangell
A470
SH
Cwm-Llinau
Mynydd y Cemaes
Corris
CORRIS RAILWAY AND MUSEUM
Dol-fôr
Esgairgeiliog
Cemmaes
Pentre-Celyn
Plas Llwyngwern
CENTRE FOR ALTERNATIVE TECHNOLOGY
B4404
Llanwrin
Cemmaes Road
Waun
DYFI VALLEY
A489
Abercegir
Commins Coch
Tafolwern
Llanbrynmair
Machynlleth
Darowen
Llan
Penegoes
FELIN CREWI WATER MILL
Tal-y-wern
Bont-Dolgadfan
Forge
Melinbyrhedyn
B4518
Glaspwll
Pant-glâs
468 MOELFRE
Pennant
Aberhosan
Glaslyn
Dylife
GLYNDŴR'S WAY
582
Staylittle
Source of R. Severn Blaen Hafren
Nant-y-Moch Reservoir
Llyn Clywedog
741
PLYNLIMON PUMLUMON FAWR
752
Source of R. Wye Blaen Gwy
SN
Tan Hinon
Old Hall
Hafren Forest
13
Dyffryn Castell
Pant Mawr
Llanifyny
Ponterwyd
A44
564
91
Ysbytycynfyn
A4120
75
Devil's Bridge
610 PEN Y GARN
B4343
Blaenycwm
D
Cwmystwyth
B4574
HAFOD ESTATE
571 GEIFAS
Pont-rhyd-y-groes
Ysbyty Ystwyth
Tany
0 1 2 3 miles
0 1 2 3 4 5 km
CLAERWEN
76
Penygarreg Res.
Craig-goch Res.
Ffridd Goch
523
Foel
109
Llangadfan
Llanerfyl
A458
Pen Coed
GLYNDŴR'S WAY
Four Crosses
Clegyrnant
Dolwen
Sychtyn
Melin-y-grug
Neinthirion
Mynydd Waun Fawr
Pandy
Cwmderwen
Dolfach
440
Llanllugan
A470
Talerddig
Rhyd
13
Carno
458
91
Clatter
398
Llanwnog
Caersws
Llawr-y-glyn
Gleiniant
B4569
Trefeglwys
Little London
482 FAN HILL
Van
Oakley Park
307
Llandinam
B4518
Severn (Hafren)
Glan-y-nant
Llanidloes
Glynbrochan
Newchapel
Cwmbelan
GLYNDŴR'S WAY
Llangurig
Tylwch
584
David's Well
Nantgwyn
B4518
Pant-y-dwr
A470
Bwlch-y-sarnau
498
Wye (Gwy)
St Harmon
505 MOEL HYWEL
WELSH ROYAL CRYSTAL
Rhayader (Rhaeadr Gwy)
Gaufron

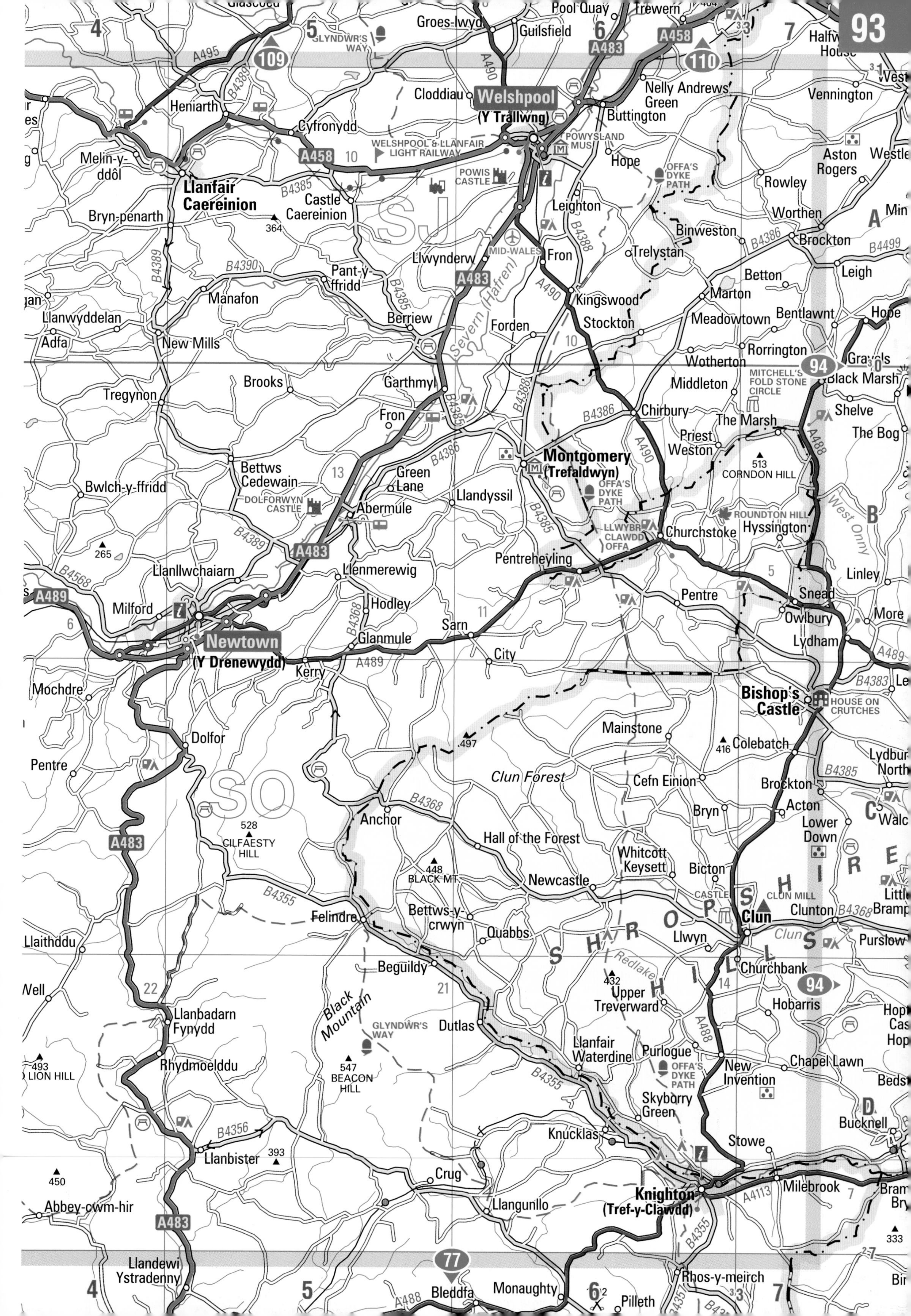
Welshpool
(Y Trallwng)
Llanfair
Caereinion
Montgomery
(Trefaldwyn)
Newtown
(Y Drenewydd)
Bishop's
Castle
Clun
Knighton
(Tref-y-Clawdd)
Groes-lwyd
Guilsfield
Pool Quay
Trewern
Halfway
House
Heniarth
Cyfronydd
Cloddiau
Nelly Andrews
Green
Buttington
Vennington
Melin-y-
ddôl
WELSHPOOL & LLANFAIR
LIGHT RAILWAY
POWYSLAND
MUS
Hope
Aston
Rogers
Westley
POWIS
CASTLE
OFFA'S
DYKE
PATH
Rowley
Castle
Caereinion
Bryn-penarth
364
Leighton
Worthen
Binweston
Brockton
MID-WALES
Fron
Trelystan
Llwynderw
Pant-y-
ffridd
Severn (Hafren)
Betton
Leigh
Manafon
Kingswood
Marton
Llanwyddelan
Adfa
New Mills
Berriew
Forden
Stockton
Meadowtown
Bentlawnt
Hope
Rorrington
Wotherton
Gravels
Black Marsh
Brooks
Garthmyl
Middleton
MITCHELL'S
FOLD STONE
CIRCLE
Tregynon
Fron
Chirbury
The Marsh
Shelve
The Bog
Priest
Weston
Bettws
Cedewain
Green
Lane
Llandyssil
513
CORNDON HILL
Bwlch-y-ffridd
DOLFORWYN
CASTLE
Abermule
ROUNDTON HILL
Hyssington
West Onny
Churchstoke
LLWYBR
CLAWDD
OFFA
265
Llanllwchaiarn
Llanmerewig
Pentreheyling
Linley
Hodley
Pentre
Snead
Milford
Sarn
Owlbury
More
Glanmule
Lydham
City
Kerry
Mochdre
HOUSE ON
CRUTCHES
Mainstone
Dolfor
497
416
Colebatch
Lydbury
North
Pentre
SO
Clun Forest
Cefn Einion
Brockton
Anchor
Bryn
Acton
Lower
Down
528
CILFAESTY
HILL
Hall of the Forest
Whitcott
Keysett
448
BLACK MT.
Newcastle
Bicton
CASTLE
CLUN MILL
Clunton
Felindre
Bettws-y-
crwyn
Quabbs
Llwyn
Clun
Purslow
Llaithddu
Beguildy
SHROPSHIRE
Churchbank
Redlake
432
Upper
Treverward
Hobarris
Well
Llanbadarn
Fynydd
Black
Mountain
GLYNDWR'S
WAY
Dutlas
Llanfair
Waterdine
Purlogue
New
Invention
Chapel Lawn
493
LION HILL
Rhydmoelddu
547
BEACON
HILL
Skyborry
Green
Bucknell
Knucklas
Stowe
Llanbister
393
450
Crug
Milebrook
Abbey-cwm-hir
Llangunllo
333
Llandewi
Ystradenny
Bleddfa
Monaughty
Rhos-y-meirch
Pilleth
A495
A458
A483
A490
A489
A488
A4113
B4389
B4385
B4390
B4388
B4386
B4499
B4568
B4368
B4355
B4356
B4383
109
110
94
77
4
5
6
7
A
B
C
D
SJ
10
11
13
14
21
22

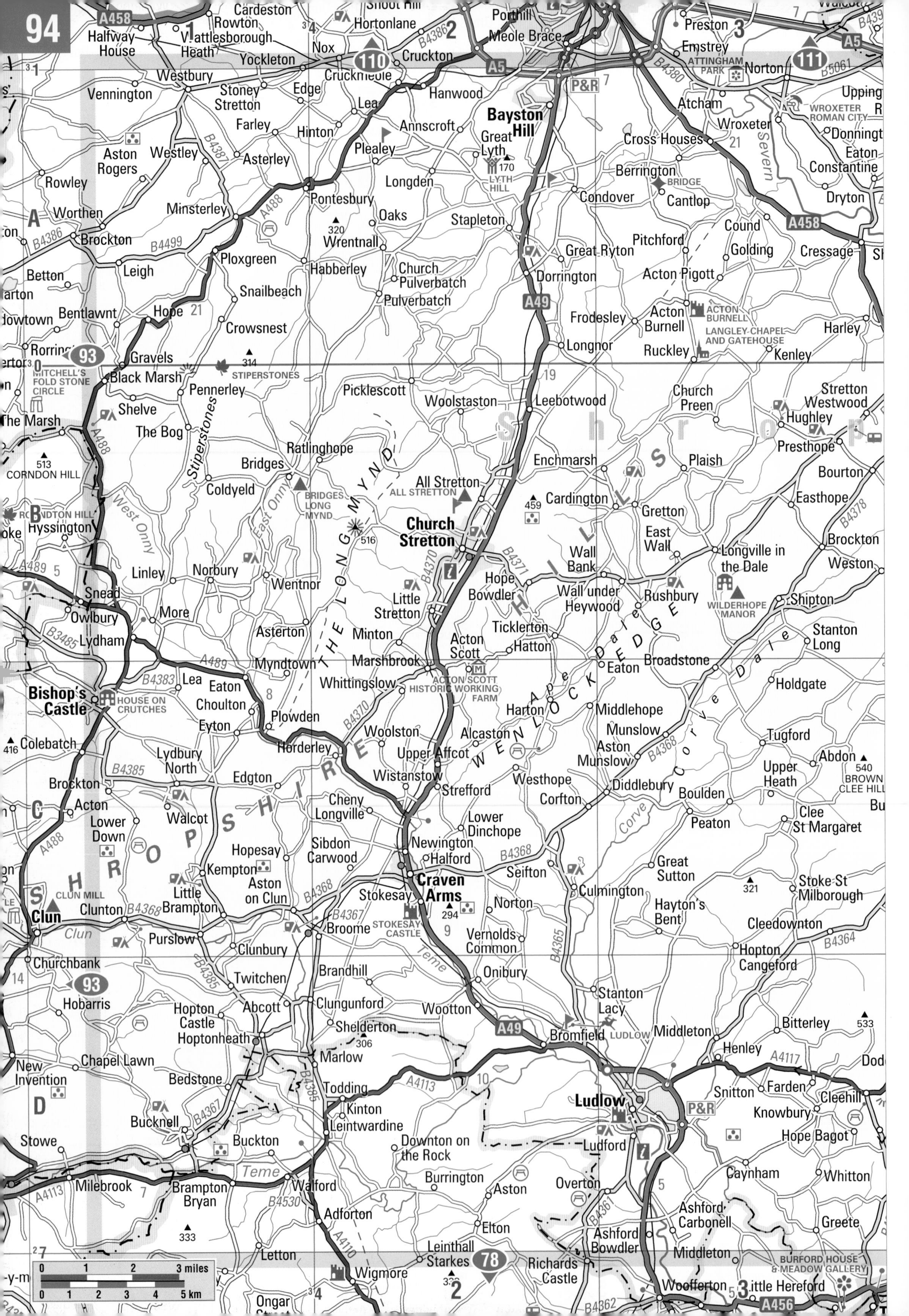
A458
Halfway House
Cardeston
Rowton
Vennington
Wattlesborough Heath
Yockleton
Westbury
Nox
Hortonlane
110
Cruckton
Cruckmeole
Edge
Stoney Stretton
Farley
Hinton
Lea
Hanwood
B4386
Porthill
Meole Brace
A5
P&R
Bayston Hill
Great Lyth
Annscroft
Pleaely
Longden
LYTH HILL
170
Preston
Emstrey
ATTINGHAM PARK
Norton
111
B5061
B4380
Atcham
Uppington
WROXETER ROMAN CITY
Wroxeter
Donnington
Eaton Constantine
Cross Houses
Severn
Berrington
BRIDGE
Cantlop
Dryton
Condover
Cound
A458
Cressage
Golding
Pitchford
Acton Pigott
Great Ryton
Dorrington
Stapleton
Aston Rogers
Westley
B4387
Asterley
Rowley
Pontesbury
Oaks
Minsterley
A488
A
Worthen
Brockton
B4386
B4499
320
Wrentnall
Habberley
Church Pulverbatch
Pulverbatch
Ploxgreen
Leigh
Betton
Snailbeach
Bentlawnt
Hope
21
Crowsnest
Rorrington
93
Gravels
314
STIPERSTONES
MITCHELL'S FOLD STONE CIRCLE
Black Marsh
Pennerley
Shelve
The Bog
The Marsh
A488
Stiperstones
513
CORNDON HILL
Frodesley
Acton Burnell
ACTON BURNELL
LANGLEY CHAPEL AND GATEHOUSE
Ruckley
Kenley
Harley
Longnor
A49
19
Leebotwood
Woolstaston
Picklescott
Church Preen
Stretton Westwood
Hughley
Presthope
Shropshire
Ratlinghope
Bridges
Coldyeld
Enchmarsh
Plaish
Bourton
Easthope
All Stretton
ALL STRETTON
BRIDGES LONG MYND
459
Cardington
Gretton
B4378
West Onny
East Onny
THE LONG MYND
516
Church Stretton
East Wall
Wall Bank
Longville in the Dale
Brockton
Weston
RONDTON HILL
B
Hyssington
A489
Linley
Norbury
Wentnor
B4370
Little Stretton
B4371
Hope Bowdler
Wall under Heywood
Rushbury
WILDERHOPE MANOR
Shipton
Snead
Owlbury
More
Lydham
B3485
Asterton
Minton
Tickerton
Hatton
Acton Scott
ACTON SCOTT HISTORIC WORKING FARM
WENLOCK EDGE
Ape Dale
Eaton
Broadstone
Stanton Long
Corve Dale
Holdgate
A489
Myndtown
Marshbrook
Whittingslow
B4383
Lea
Eaton
8
Bishop's Castle
HOUSE ON CRUTCHES
Choulton
Eyton
Plowden
Harton
Middlehope
Munslow
Aston Munslow
B4368
Tugford
Abdon
540
BROWN CLEE HILL
416
Colebatch
Lydbury North
Horderley
B4370
Woolston
Alcaston
Upper Affcot
Wistanstow
Westhope
Strefford
Corfton
Diddlebury
Boulden
Upper Heath
Brockton
B4385
Edgton
C
Acton
Lower Down
Walcot
A488
SHROPSHIRE
Cheny Longville
Lower Dinchope
Peaton
Corve
Clee St Margaret
Hopesay
Kempton
Aston on Clun
Sibdon Carwood
Newington
Halford
B4368
Craven Arms
Seifton
Culmington
Great Sutton
321
Stoke St Milborough
CLUN MILL
Clun
Clunton
B4368
Little Brampton
Stokesay
294
Norton
Hayton's Bent
Clun
Purslow
B4367
Broome
STOKESAY CASTLE
9
Vernolds Common
B4365
Cleedownton
Hopton Cangeford
B4364
Churchbank
Clunbury
B4385
Teme
14
93
Hobarris
Twitchen
Brandhill
Onibury
Stanton Lacy
Hopton Castle
Hoptonheath
Abcott
Clungunford
Wootton
Shelderton
306
A49
Bromfield
LUDLOW
Middleton
Bitterley
533
New Invention
Chapel Lawn
Bedstone
Marlow
Henley
A4117
D
B4385
Todding
A4113
10
Ludlow
P&R
Snitton
Farden
Cleehill
Knowbury
Bucknell
B4367
Kinton
Leintwardine
Stowe
Buckton
Downton on the Rock
Ludford
Hope Bagot
Teme
A4113
Milebrook
7
Brampton Bryan
Walford
B4530
Burrington
Aston
Overton
5
Caynham
Whitton
333
Adforton
A4110
Elton
B4361
Ashford Bowdler
Ashford Carbonell
Greete
Letton
Leinthall Starkes
78
Richards Castle
Middleton
BURFORD HOUSE & MEADOW GALLERY
Wigmore
336
Ongar Street
B4362
Woofferton
Little Hereford
A456
0 1 2 3 miles
0 1 2 3 4 5 km

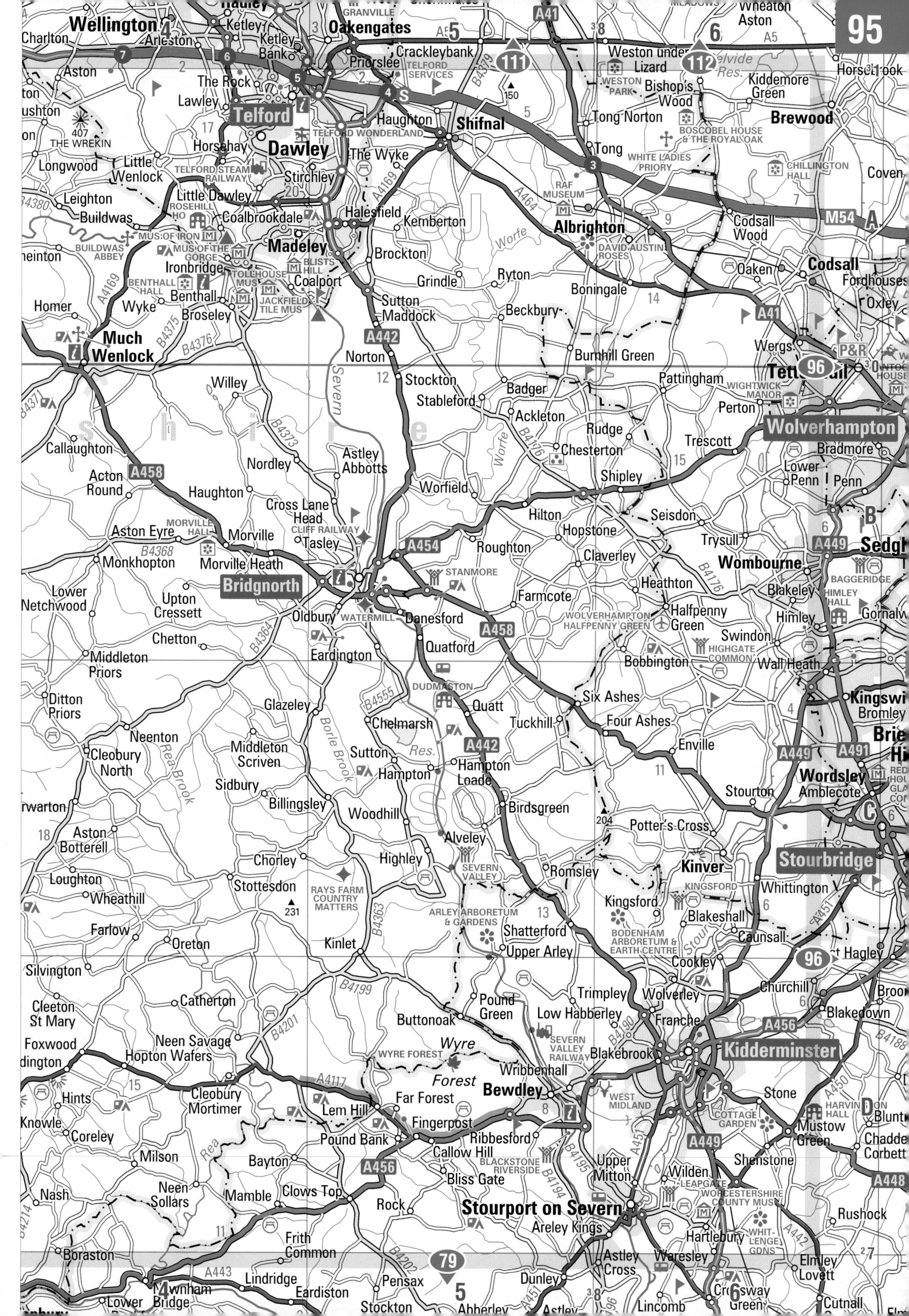
Wellington
Charlton
Arleston
Ketley
Ketley Bank
Oakengates
GRANVILLE
Crackleybank
Priorslee
TELFORD SERVICES
Weston under Lizard
WESTON PARK
Wheaton Aston
A5
A41
111
112
Kiddemore Green
Horsebrook
Aston
The Rock
Lawley
Telford
Haughton
Shifnal
Bishop's Wood
Tong Norton
Brewood
BOSCOBEL HOUSE & THE ROYAL OAK
407
THE WREKIN
Horsehay
Dawley
TELFORD WONDERLAND
The Wyke
Tong
WHITE LADIES PRIORY
CHILLINGTON HALL
Coven
Longwood
Little Wenlock
TELFORD STEAM RAILWAY
Stirchley
A4169
RAF MUSEUM
Little Dawley
ROSEHILL HO
Leighton
Buildwas
Coalbrookdale
Halesfield
Kemberton
A464
Albrighton
Codsall Wood
M54
MUS OF IRON
MUS OF THE GORGE
Madeley
BUILDWAS ABBEY
Ironbridge
BLISTS HILL
Brockton
Worfe
DAVID AUSTIN ROSES
Oaken
Codsall
BENTHALL HALL
Benthall
TOLLHOUSE MUS
Coalport
Grindle
Ryton
Boningale
Fordhouses
Homer
Wyke
Broseley
JACKFIELD TILE MUS
Sutton Maddock
Oxley
A4169
Beckbury
A41
Much Wenlock
B4375
B4376
A442
Wergs
Norton
Burnhill Green
P&R
Tettenhall
96
Willey
Severn
Stockton
Stableford
Badger
Pattingham
WIGHTWICK MANOR
Perton
B4371
Ackleton
Rudge
Wolverhampton
B4373
B4176
Chesterton
Trescott
Callaughton
Astley Abbotts
Bradmore
Nordley
Worfe
Lower Penn
Penn
Acton Round
A458
Haughton
Worfield
Shipley
Cross Lane Head
Hilton
Seisdon
MORVILLE HALL
Aston Eyre
Morville
CLIFF RAILWAY
Tasley
Hopstone
Trysull
A454
Roughton
A449
Sedgley
B4368
Monkhopton
Morville Heath
Claverley
Wombourne
STANMORE
BAGGERIDGE
Bridgnorth
B4176
Heathton
Blakeley
Lower Netchwood
Upton Cressett
Farmcote
HIMLEY HALL
Oldbury
WATERMILL
Danesford
WOLVERHAMPTON HALFPENNY GREEN
Halfpenny Green
Himley
Gornal
Chetton
A458
Swindon
B4364
Eardington
Quatford
HIGHGATE COMMON
Middleton Priors
Bobbington
Wall Heath
DUDMASTON
Ditton Priors
Glazeley
B4555
Quatt
Six Ashes
Kingswinford
Bromley
Neenton
Chelmarsh
Tuckhill
Four Ashes
Cleobury North
Middleton Scriven
Borle Brook
Rea Brook
A442
Enville
Brierley Hill
Sutton
Res.
Hampton Loade
A449
A491
Hampton
Sidbury
Billingsley
11
Wordsley
Amblecote
Stourton
Burwarton
Woodhill
Birdsgreen
Aston Botterell
204
Potter's Cross
Alveley
Stourbridge
Chorley
Highley
SEVERN VALLEY
Romsley
Kinver
Loughton
Stottesdon
RAYS FARM COUNTRY MATTERS
Whittington
Wheathill
231
KINGSFORD
Kingsford
ARLEY ARBORETUM & GARDENS
13
Blakeshall
B4363
A451
Farlow
Kinlet
Shatterford
BODENHAM ARBORETUM & EARTH CENTRE
Caunsall
Oreton
Upper Arley
Stour
Hagley
Silvington
Cookley
B4199
Churchill
Cleeton St Mary
Catherton
Pound Green
Trimpley
Wolverley
Broome
Buttonoak
Low Habberley
Franche
Blakedown
Foxwood
B4201
Wyre
B4190
A456
Neen Savage
Hopton Wafers
WYRE FOREST
SEVERN VALLEY RAILWAY
Blakebrook
Kidderminster
B4188
Forest
Wribbenhall
15
Cleobury Mortimer
A4117
Bewdley
Hints
Lem Hill
Far Forest
WEST MIDLAND
Stone
A450
Knowle
HARVINGTON HALL
Blunt
Fingerpost
COTTAGE GARDEN
Mustow Green
Coreley
Pound Bank
Ribbesford
A449
Chaddesley Corbett
Milson
Callow Hill
BLACKSTONE RIVERSIDE
B4195
Upper Mitton
Shenstone
Rea
Bayton
A456
Bliss Gate
B4194
Wilden
LEAPGATE
A448
Neen Sollars
Nash
Mamble
Clows Top
Rock
Stourport on Severn
WORCESTERSHIRE COUNTY MUS
Rushock
B4214
11
Areley Kings
Frith Common
Hartlebury
WHITLENGE GDNS
A442
Boraston
79
B4202
Astley Cross
Waresley
Elmley Lovett
A443
Lindridge
Pensax
Dunley
A451
Newnham Bridge
Eardiston
Lower
Stockton
Abberley
Astley
Lincomb
Crossway Green
Cutnall

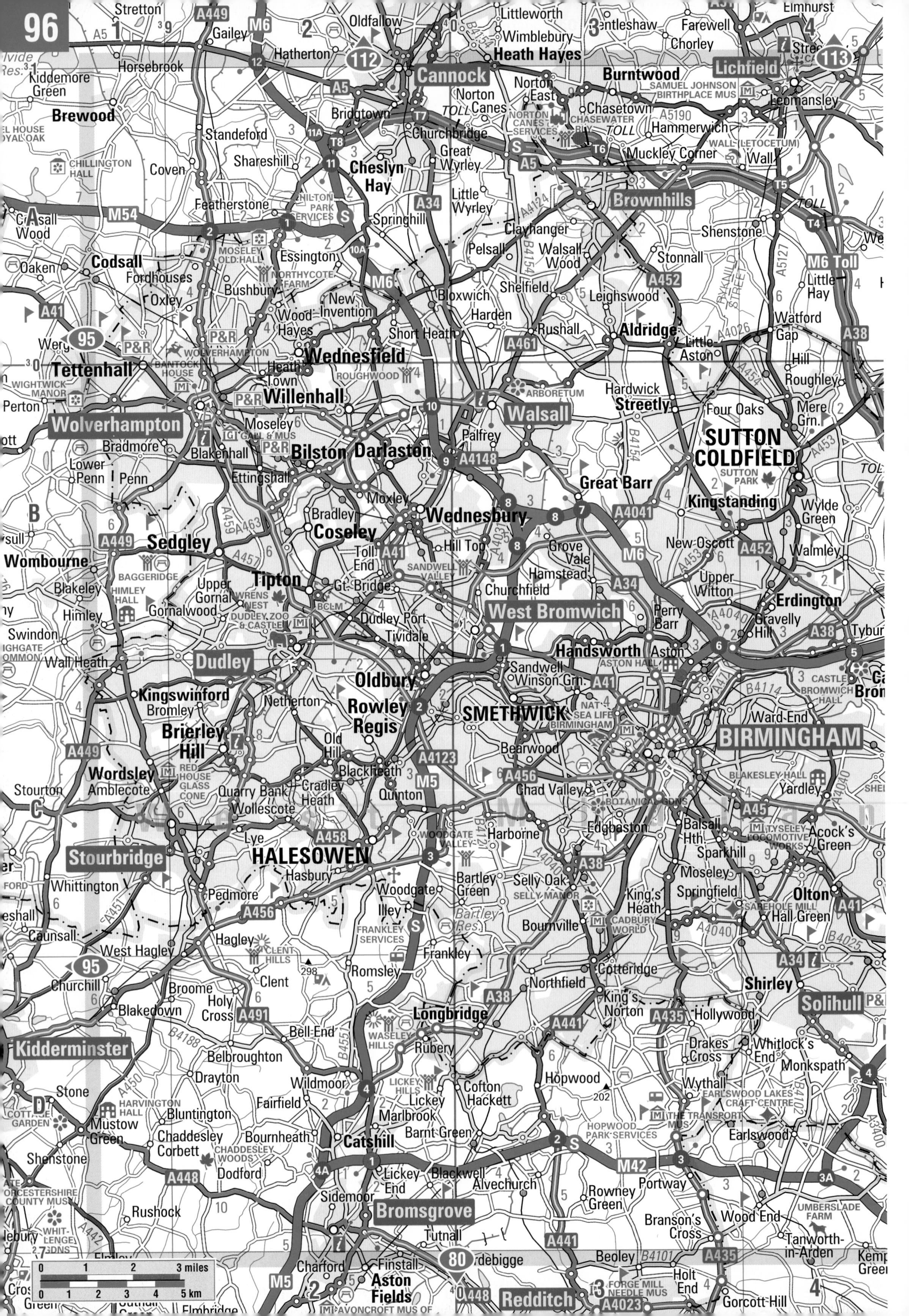
Stretton
Gailey
Oldfallow
Littleworth
Wimblebury
Farewell
Chorley
Elmhurst
Lichfield
Kiddemore Green
Horsebrook
Hatherton
Cannock
Heath Hayes
Burntwood
Samuel Johnson Birthplace Mus
Brewood
Bridgtown
Norton Canes
Norton East
Chasetown
Leomansley
Standeford
Churchbridge
Norton Canes Services
Chasewater
Hammerwich
Chillington Hall
Coven
Shareshill
Cheslyn Hay
Great Wyrley
Muckley Corner
Wall (Letocetum)
Wall
Hilton Park Services
Little Wyrley
Brownhills
Featherstone
M54
Springhill
Clayhanger
Shenstone
Wood
Codsall
Oaken
Moseley Old Hall
Essington
Pelsall
Walsall Wood
Stonnall
M6 Toll
Fordhouses
Northycote Farm
Bushbury
Oxley
New Invention
Bloxwich
Shelfield
Leighswood
Little Hay
Wood Hayes
Harden
Rushall
Aldridge
Watford Gap
Wolverhampton
Short Heath
Wednesfield
Little Aston
Tettenhall
Bantock House
Heath Town
Roughwood
Hill
Roughley
Wightwick Manor
Perton
Willenhall
Arboretum
Hardwick
Streetly
Four Oaks
Mere Grn.
Walsall
Moseley
Gall & Mus
Palfrey
Bradmore
Bilston
Darlaston
Sutton Coldfield
Blakenhall
Lower Penn
Penn
Ettingshall
Great Barr
Sutton Park
Kingstanding
Wylde Green
Moxley
Bradley
Wednesbury
Coseley
Sedgley
Hill Top
Grove Vale
New Oscott
Walmley
Wombourne
Toll End
Sandwell Valley
Hamstead
Baggeridge
Tipton
Upper Gornal
Gt. Bridge
Churchfield
Upper Witton
Blakeley
Himley Hall
Wrens Nest
BCLM
Erdington
Himley
Gornalwood
Dudley Zoo & Castle
Dudley Port
West Bromwich
Perry Barr
Gravelly Hill
Swindon
Tividale
Tyburn
Wall Heath
Dudley
Handsworth
Aston
Aston Hall
Sandwell
Winson Grn.
Castle Bromwich Hall
Oldbury
Kingswinford
Bromley
Netherton
Rowley Regis
Smethwick
Nat. Sea Life Birmingham
Ward End
Birmingham
Brierley Hill
Old Hill
Bearwood
Wordsley
Red House Glass Cone
Blackheath
Blakesley Hall
Yardley
Stourton
Amblecote
Quarry Bank
Cradley Heath
Quinton
Chad Valley
Botanical Gdns
Wollescote
Edgbaston
Balsall Hth.
Tyseley Locomotive Works
Acock's Green
Lye
Woodgate Valley
Harborne
Sparkhill
Stourbridge
Halesowen
Moseley
Whittington
Hasbury
Bartley Green
Selly Oak
Selly Manor
King's Heath
Springfield
Olton
Pedmore
Woodgate
Illey
Bournville
Cadbury World
Sarehole Mill
Hall Green
Caunsall
Bartley Res.
Frankley Services
Hagley
Clent Hills
West Hagley
Frankley
Churchill
Romsley
Clent
Cotteridge
Northfield
Shirley
Solihull
Broome
Holy Cross
Blakedown
King's Norton
Longbridge
Hollywood
Bell End
Waseley Hills
Rubery
Kidderminster
Drakes Cross
Whitlock's End
Monkspath
Belbroughton
Drayton
Wildmoor
Cofton Hackett
Hopwood
Lickey Hills
Lickey
Wythall
Earlswood Lakes Craft Centre
Stone
Harvington Hall
Bluntington
Fairfield
Marlbrook
The Transport Mus
Cottage Garden
Mustow Green
Barnt Green
Hopwood Park Services
Earlswood
Chaddesley Corbett
Bournheath
Catshill
Chaddesley Woods
Shenstone
Dodford
Lickey End
Blackwell
Alvechurch
M42
Portway
Rowney Green
Worcestershire County Mus
Sidemoor
Bromsgrove
Rushock
Umberslade Farm
Wood End
Branson's Cross
Whitlenge Gdns
Tutnall
Tanworth-in-Arden
Beoley
Charford
Finstall
Holt End
Aston Fields
Forge Mill Needle Mus
Redditch
Gorcott Hill
Avoncroft Mus of
0 1 2 3 miles
0 1 2 3 4 5 km

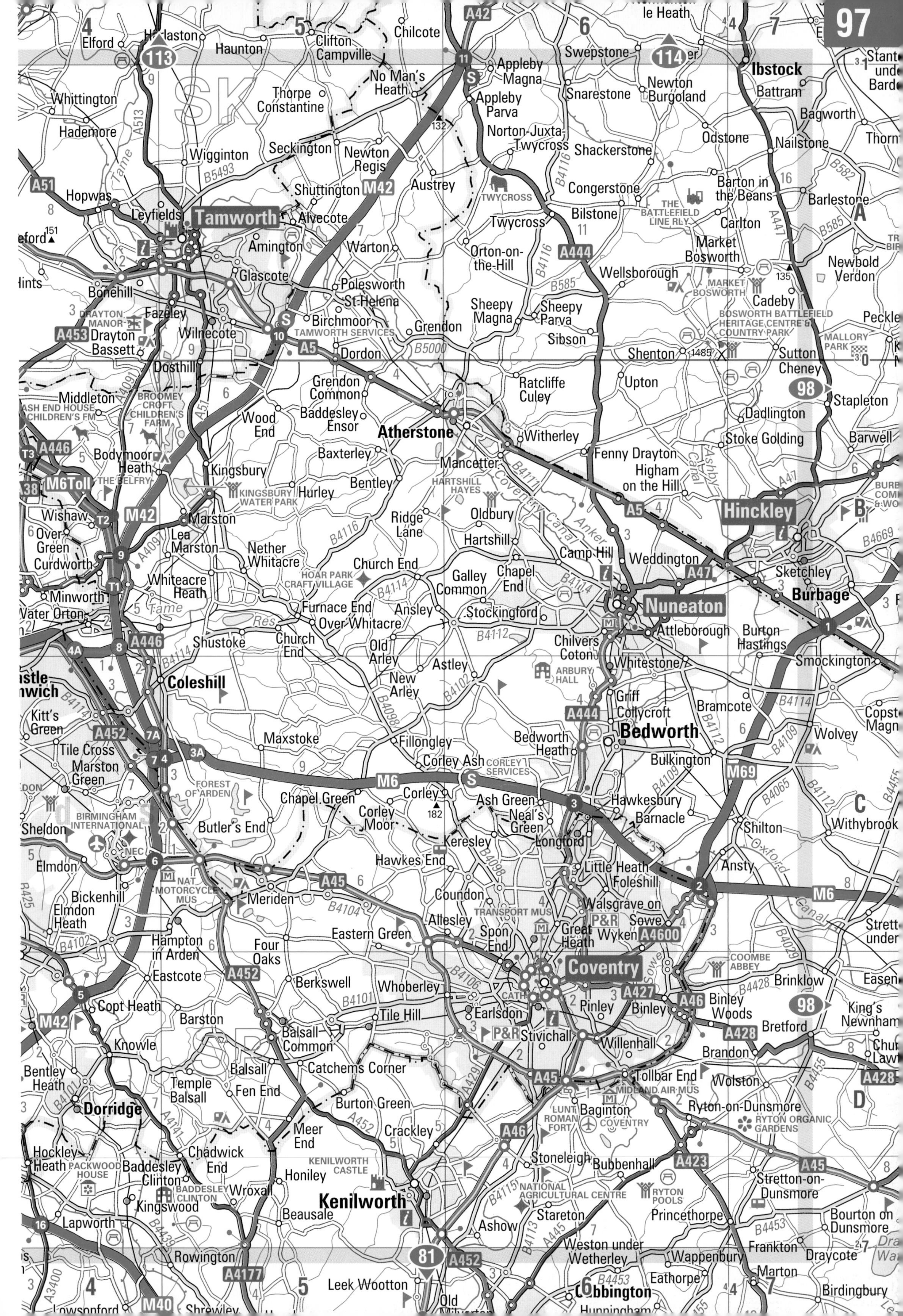
97
Elford
Harlaston
Haunton
Clifton Campville
Chilcote
le Heath
Swepstone
Ibstock
Whittington
Hademore
Thorpe Constantine
No Man's Heath
Appleby Magna
Appleby Parva
Snarestone
Newton Burgoland
Battram
Bagworth
Wigginton
Seckington
Newton Regis
Norton-Juxta-Twycross
Shackerstone
Odstone
Nailstone
Hopwas
Shuttington
Austrey
TWYCROSS
Congerstone
Barton in the Beans
Barlestone
Leyfields
Tamworth
Alvecote
Bilstone
THE BATTLEFIELD LINE RLY
Carlton
Amington
Warton
Twycross
Orton-on-the-Hill
Market Bosworth
Newbold Verdon
Glascote
Bonehill
Polesworth
St Helena
Wellsborough
MARKET BOSWORTH
Cadeby
DRAYTON MANOR
Fazeley
Birchmoor
Sheepy Magna
Sheepy Parva
BOSWORTH BATTLEFIELD HERITAGE CENTRE & COUNTRY PARK
Drayton Bassett
Wilnecote
TAMWORTH SERVICES
Grendon
Sibson
MALLORY PARK
Dosthill
Dordon
Shenton
Sutton Cheney
Grendon Common
Ratcliffe Culey
Upton
Middleton
BROOMEY CROFT CHILDREN'S FARM
ASH END HOUSE CHILDREN'S FM
Wood End
Baddesley Ensor
Atherstone
Dadlington
Stapleton
Witherley
Stoke Golding
Barwell
Bodymoor Heath
Baxterley
Mancetter
Fenny Drayton
Kingsbury
THE BELFRY
Bentley
HARTSHILL HAYES
Higham on the Hill
Ashby Canal
KINGSBURY WATER PARK
Hurley
Coventry Canal
Hinckley
Wishaw
Marston
Ridge Lane
Oldbury
Over Green
Curdworth
Lea Marston
Nether Whitacre
Hartshill
Camp Hill
Weddington
Sketchley
Church End
HOAR PARK CRAFT VILLAGE
Galley Common
Chapel End
Whiteacre Heath
Minworth
Water Orton
Furnace End
Over Whitacre
Ansley
Stockingford
Nuneaton
Burbage
Attleborough
Burton Hastings
Shustoke
Church End
Old Arley
Chilvers Coton
Whitestone
Smockington
Coleshill
Astley
ARBURY HALL
New Arley
Griff
Collycroft
Bramcote
Kitt's Green
Bedworth
Copston Magna
Maxstoke
Tile Cross
Fillongley
Bedworth Heath
Wolvey
Marston Green
Corley Ash
CORLEY SERVICES
Bulkington
FOREST OF ARDEN
Chapel Green
Corley
Ash Green
Hawkesbury
Corley Moor
Neal's Green
Barnacle
Shilton
Withybrook
BIRMINGHAM INTERNATIONAL
Sheldon
Butler's End
Keresley
Longford
NEC
Hawkes End
Little Heath
Ansty
Elmdon
NAT MOTORCYCLE MUS
Foleshill
Meriden
Coundon
Walsgrave on Sowe
Bickenhill
Elmdon Heath
TRANSPORT MUS
Allesley
Eastern Green
Spon End
Great Heath
Wyken
Hampton in Arden
Four Oaks
COOMBE ABBEY
Eastcote
Coventry
Berkswell
Whoberley
Brinklow
Copt Heath
CATH
Earlsdon
Pinley
Binley
Binley Woods
King's Newnham
Barston
Tile Hill
Stivichall
Bretford
Knowle
Balsall Common
Willenhall
Brandon
Bentley Heath
Balsall
Catchems Corner
Tollbar End
Wolston
Temple Balsall
Fen End
MIDLAND AIR MUS
Dorridge
Burton Green
LUNT ROMAN FORT
Baginton
Ryton-on-Dunsmore
RYTON ORGANIC GARDENS
COVENTRY
Meer End
Crackley
Hockley Heath
PACKWOOD HOUSE
Chadwick End
Baddesley Clinton
KENILWORTH CASTLE
Stoneleigh
Bubbenhall
Honiley
Stretton-on-Dunsmore
BADDESLEY CLINTON
Wroxall
Kingswood
NATIONAL AGRICULTURAL CENTRE
RYTON POOLS
Kenilworth
Lapworth
Beausale
Ashow
Stareton
Princethorpe
Bourton on Dunsmore
Frankton
Weston under Wetherley
Wappenbury
Draycote
Rowington
Eathorpe
Marton
Leek Wootton
Birdingbury
Lowsonford
Shrewley
Old Milverton
Hunningham
A42
A51
A513
A453
A5
A446
A4091
M6Toll
M42
M6
M69
A444
A47
A452
A45
A4600
A427
A46
A428
A429
A423
A4177
A452
M40
A3400
B5493
B4116
B585
B5000
B4111
B4114
B4112
B4102
B4098
B4104
B4101
B4106
B4109
B4065
B4029
B4428
B4455
B4113
B4115
B4453
B4439
B4102
B4669
B582
B585
A447
SK
SP
Tame
Anker
Oxford Canal
113
114
98
81

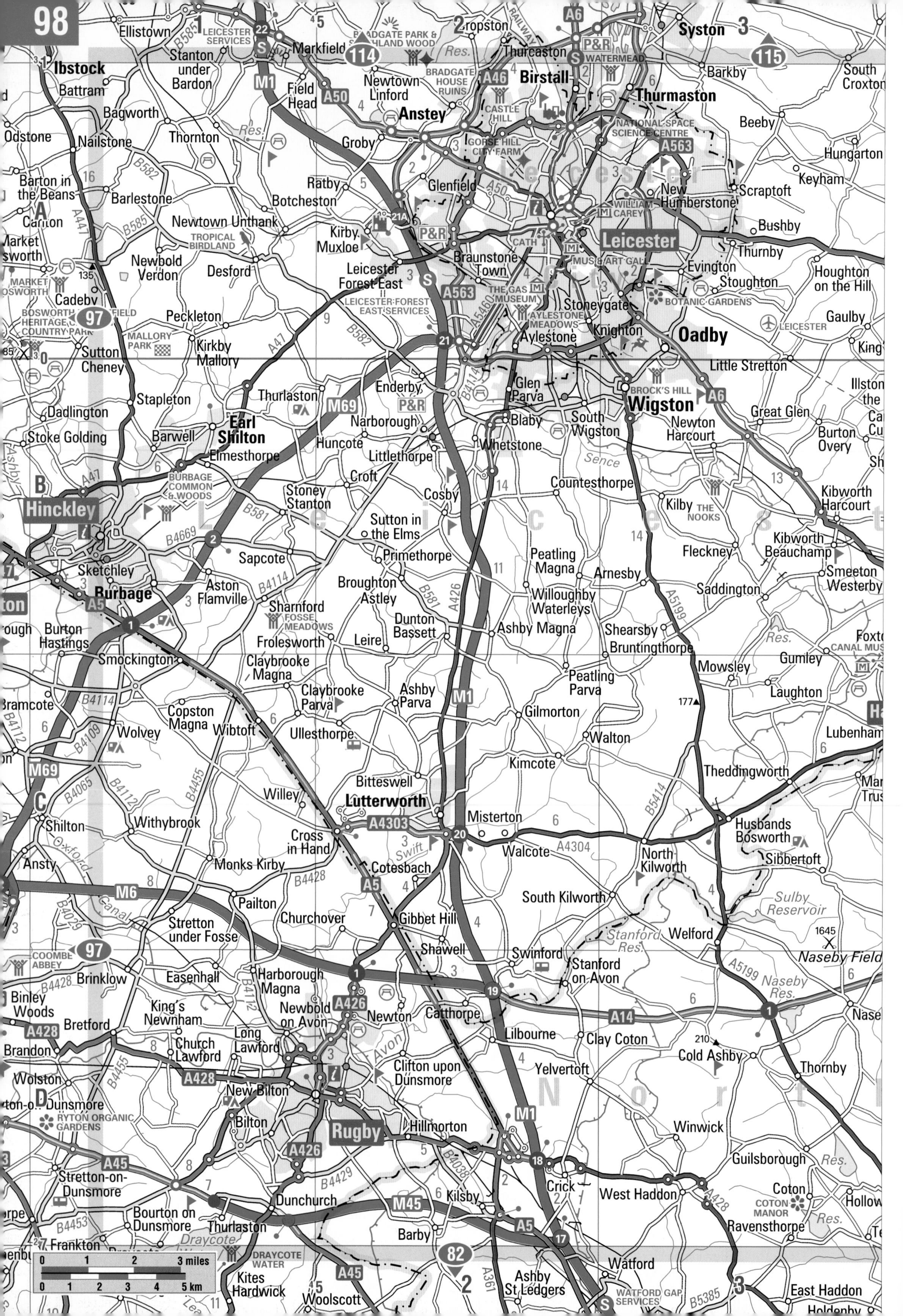
Ellistown
LEICESTER SERVICES
Markfield
BRADGATE PARK & SWITHLAND WOOD
Cropston
Thurcaston
Syston
Ibstock
Stanton under Bardon
Newtown Linford
BRADGATE HOUSE RUINS
Birstall
WATERMEAD
Barkby
South Croxton
Battram
Field Head
Anstey
Thurmaston
Bagworth
CASTLE HILL
NATIONAL SPACE SCIENCE CENTRE
Beeby
Odstone
Nailstone
Thornton
Groby
GORSE HILL CITY FARM
Hungarton
Barton in the Beans
Ratby
Glenfield
New Humberstone
Scraptoft
Keyham
Barlestone
Botcheston
WILLIAM CAREY
Carlton
Newtown Unthank
TROPICAL BIRDLAND
Kirby Muxloe
Bushby
Market Bosworth
Newbold Verdon
Desford
Leicester Forest East
Braunstone Town
CATH
Leicester
MUS & ART GAL
Thurnby
Evington
Houghton on the Hill
Stoughton
MARKET BOSWORTH
Cadeby
LEICESTER FOREST EAST SERVICES
THE GAS MUSEUM
Stoneygate
BOTANIC GARDENS
BOSWORTH HERITAGE & COUNTRY PARK
Peckleton
AYLESTONE MEADOWS
Knighton
Oadby
Gaulby
LEICESTER
MALLORY PARK
Kirkby Mallory
Aylestone
Sutton Cheney
Little Stretton
Enderby
Glen Parva
BROCK'S HILL
Illston on the Hill
Stapleton
Thurlaston
Wigston
Great Glen
Dadlington
Earl Shilton
Narborough
Blaby
South Wigston
Newton Harcourt
Burton Overy
Stoke Golding
Barwell
Huncote
Whetstone
Elmesthorpe
Littlethorpe
BURBAGE COMMON & WOODS
Croft
Countesthorpe
Hinckley
Stoney Stanton
Cosby
Kilby
THE NOOKS
Kibworth Harcourt
Sutton in the Elms
Kibworth Beauchamp
Sapcote
Primethorpe
Peatling Magna
Fleckney
Sketchley
Arnesby
Smeeton Westerby
Burbage
Aston Flamville
Broughton Astley
Willoughby Waterleys
Saddington
Sharnford
FOSSE MEADOWS
Dunton Bassett
Burton Hastings
Ashby Magna
Shearsby
Foxton
CANAL MUS
Frolesworth
Leire
Bruntingthorpe
Smockington
Mowsley
Gumley
Claybrooke Magna
Peatling Parva
Laughton
Claybrooke Parva
Ashby Parva
Bramcote
Copston Magna
Gilmorton
Wolvey
Wibtoft
Ullesthorpe
Walton
Lubenham
Kimcote
Theddingworth
Bitteswell
Willey
Lutterworth
Shilton
Withybrook
Cross in Hand
Misterton
Husbands Bosworth
Walcote
Swift
Ansty
Monks Kirby
Cotesbach
North Kilworth
Sibbertoft
South Kilworth
Pailton
Sulby Reservoir
Churchover
Gibbet Hill
Stretton under Fosse
Stanford Res.
Welford
Shawell
Swinford
COOMBE ABBEY
Naseby Field
Stanford on Avon
Brinklow
Easenhall
Harborough Magna
Naseby Res.
Binley Woods
King's Newnham
Newbold on Avon
Newton
Catthorpe
Bretford
Church Lawford
Long Lawford
Lilbourne
Clay Coton
Brandon
Cold Ashby
Thornby
Clifton upon Dunsmore
Yelvertoft
Wolston
New Bilton
Ryton-on-Dunsmore
RYTON ORGANIC GARDENS
Bilton
Rugby
Hillmorton
Winwick
Guilsborough
Stretton-on-Dunsmore
Crick
West Haddon
Coton
COTON MANOR
Kilsby
Dunchurch
Bourton on Dunsmore
Thurlaston
Barby
Ravensthorpe
Frankton
Draycote
DRAYCOTE WATER
Watford
Kites Hardwick
Ashby St Ledgers
WATFORD GAP SERVICES
East Haddon
Woolscott
Holdenby
0 1 2 3 miles
0 1 2 3 4 5 km
M1
M6
M69
M45
A46
A50
A563
A6
A47
A5
A426
A4303
A4304
A14
A428
A45
A5199
A5460
B5414
B581
B582
B585
B4114
B4669
B4109
B4112
B4065
B4455
B4428
B4029
B4429
B4038
B4453
B5385
114
115
97
82

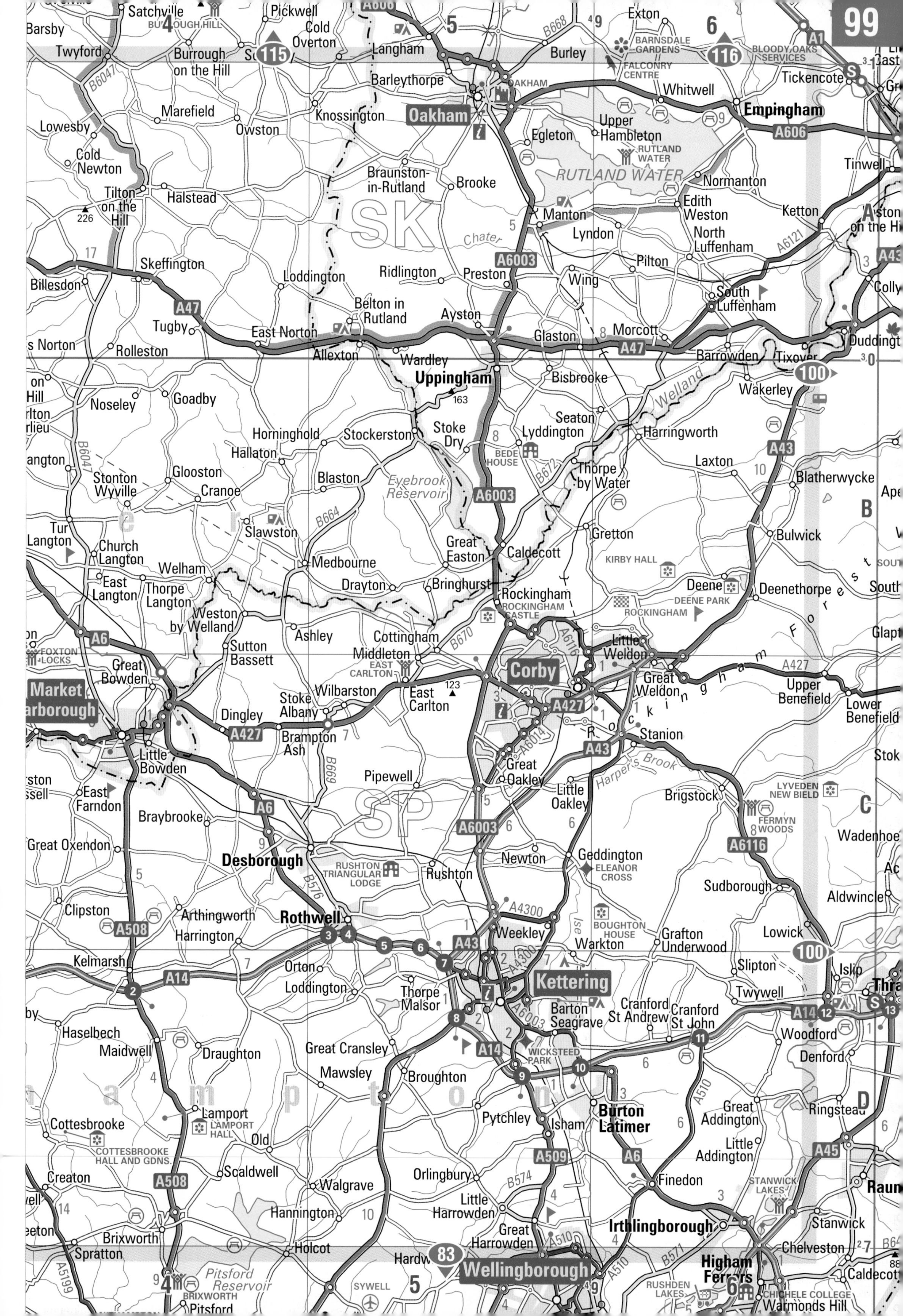
Satchville
Pickwell
Exton
Barsby
Burrough Hill
Cold Overton
Langham
Burley
Barnsdale Gardens
Bloody Oaks Services
Twyford
Burrough on the Hill
115
116
Falconry Centre
Tickencote
Barleythorpe
Oakham
Whitwell
Marefield
Knossington
Empingham
Lowesby
Owston
Egleton
Upper Hambleton
Rutland Water
Cold Newton
Tinwell
Tilton on the Hill
Halstead
Braunston-in-Rutland
Brooke
Normanton
SK
Manton
Edith Weston
Ketton
Lyndon
North Luffenham
Chater
Skeffington
A6003
Pilton
Billesdon
Loddington
Ridlington
Preston
Wing
South Luffenham
A47
Belton in Rutland
Tugby
Ayston
Morcott
East Norton
Glaston
Rolleston
Allexton
Wardley
Barrowden
Tixover
Uppingham
Bisbrooke
100
Noseley
Goadby
Wakerley
Welland
Seaton
Horninghold
Stockerston
Stoke Dry
Lyddington
Harringworth
Hallaton
Bede House
Laxton
Glooston
Blaston
Thorpe by Water
Blatherwycke
Stonton Wyville
Cranoe
Eyebrook Reservoir
A43
Slawston
Gretton
Bulwick
Tur Langton
Church Langton
Great Easton
Caldecott
Medbourne
Kirby Hall
Welham
Deene
Deenethorpe
East Langton
Thorpe Langton
Drayton
Bringhurst
Rockingham
Rockingham Castle
Deene Park
Rockingham
Weston by Welland
Ashley
Cottingham
Little Weldon
Foxton Locks
Sutton Bassett
Middleton
East Carlton
Corby
A427
Great Bowden
Great Weldon
Upper Benefield
Lower Benefield
Market Harborough
Wilbarston
East Carlton
Stoke Albany
Dingley
Brampton Ash
Stanion
Little Bowden
Rockingham Forest
Harper's Brook
Great Oakley
Pipewell
Little Oakley
Brigstock
Lyveden New Bield
East Farndon
Braybrooke
SP
Fermyn Woods
Wadenhoe
Great Oxendon
Desborough
Rushton Triangular Lodge
Rushton
Newton
Geddington
Eleanor Cross
A6116
Sudborough
Aldwincle
Clipston
Arthingworth
Rothwell
A4300
Boughton House
A508
Harrington
Weekley
Grafton Underwood
Lowick
Warkton
Kelmarsh
Orton
Slipton
A14
Loddington
Thorpe Malsor
Kettering
Islip
Barton Seagrave
Cranford St Andrew
Cranford St John
Twywell
Haselbech
Woodford
Maidwell
Draughton
Great Cransley
Wicksteed Park
Denford
Mawsley
Broughton
Lamport
Lamport Hall
Pytchley
Isham
Burton Latimer
Great Addington
Ringstead
Cottesbrooke
Cottesbrooke Hall and Gdns.
Old
A509
Little Addington
A45
Creaton
Scaldwell
Orlingbury
B574
Walgrave
A6
Finedon
Stanwick Lakes
Little Harrowden
Hannington
Irthlingborough
Stanwick
Brixworth
Great Harrowden
Spratton
Holcot
Chelveston
Hardwick
83
Wellingborough
Higham Ferrers
Caldecott
Pitsford Reservoir
Brixworth
Pitsford
Sywell
Rushden Lakes
Chichele College
Warmonds Hill

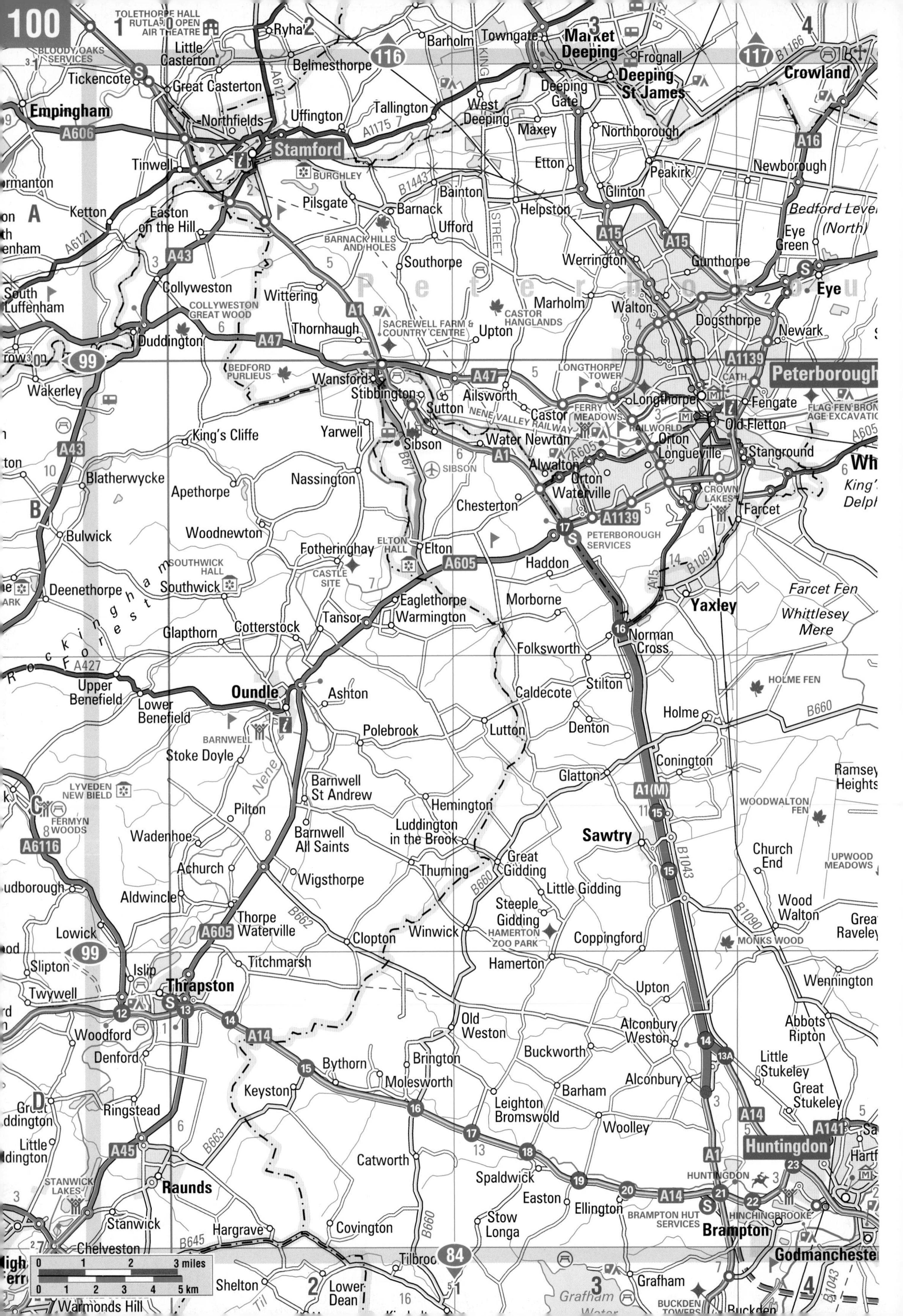

Stamford
Market Deeping
Deeping St James
Crowland
Empingham
Peterborough
Eye
Oundle
Yaxley
Sawtry
Thrapston
Raunds
Huntingdon
Brampton
Godmanchester
Tickencote
Great Casterton
Little Casterton
Tolethorpe Hall Rutland Open Air Theatre
Ryhall
Belmesthorpe
Barholm
Towngate
Frognall
Deeping Gate
West Deeping
Tallington
Uffington
Northfields
Maxey
Northborough
Etton
Peakirk
Glinton
Newborough
Tinwell
Burghley
Bainton
Helpston
Ketton
Easton on the Hill
Pilsgate
Barnack
Ufford
Barnack Hills and Holes
Southorpe
Werrington
Gunthorpe
Eye Green
Bedford Level (North)
Collyweston
Wittering
South Luffenham
Collyweston Great Wood
Marholm
Walton
Dogsthorpe
Newark
Sacrewell Farm & Country Centre
Castor Hanglands
Upton
Thornhaugh
Duddington
Wakerley
Bedford Purlieus
Wansford
Stibbington
Sutton
Ailsworth
Castor
Longthorpe Tower
Longthorpe
Ferry Meadows
Nene Valley Railway
Railworld
Fengate
Flag Fen Bronze Age Excavation
Old Fletton
Orton Longueville
Stanground
King's Cliffe
Yarwell
Sibson
Water Newton
Alwalton
Orton Waterville
Chesterton
Nassington
Apethorpe
Blatherwycke
Bulwick
Woodnewton
Crown Lakes
Farcet
King's Delph
Peterborough Services
Elton Hall
Elton
Fotheringhay
Castle Site
Southwick Hall
Southwick
Haddon
Deenethorpe
Rockingham Forest
Eaglethorpe
Warmington
Tansor
Morborne
Farcet Fen
Whittlesey Mere
Glapthorn
Cotterstock
Folksworth
Norman Cross
Upper Benefield
Lower Benefield
Ashton
Caldecote
Stilton
Holme Fen
Holme
Polebrook
Lutton
Denton
Barnwell
Stoke Doyle
Conington
Glatton
Ramsey Heights
Lyveden New Bield
Barnwell St Andrew
Pilton
Hemington
Woodwalton Fen
Fermyn Woods
Wadenhoe
Barnwell All Saints
Luddington in the Brook
Thurning
Great Gidding
Church End
Upwood Meadows
Achurch
Wigsthorpe
Little Gidding
Aldwincle
Steeple Gidding
Wood Walton
Thorpe Waterville
Winwick
Hamerton Zoo Park
Coppingford
Monks Wood
Great Raveley
Lowick
Clopton
Titchmarsh
Hamerton
Slipton
Islip
Wennington
Twywell
Upton
Old Weston
Alconbury Weston
Abbots Ripton
Woodford
Denford
Bythorn
Brington
Buckworth
Little Stukeley
Molesworth
Keyston
Barham
Alconbury
Great Stukeley
Ringstead
Leighton Bromswold
Woolley
Catworth
Spaldwick
Huntingdon
Stanwick Lakes
Stanwick
Easton
Ellington
Stow Longa
Brampton Hut Services
Hinchingbrooke
Hargrave
Covington
Chelveston
Tilbrook
Shelton
Lower Dean
Grafham
Grafham Water
Buckden Towers
Warmonds Hill
Bloody Oaks Services
A606
A6121
A43
A1
A47
A15
A16
A1139
A605
A427
A6116
A1(M)
A14
A45
A141
B1443
B1091
B1043
B1090
B660
B662
B663
B645
B671
B1166
A1175
116
117
99
84
0 1 2 3 miles
0 1 2 3 4 5 km

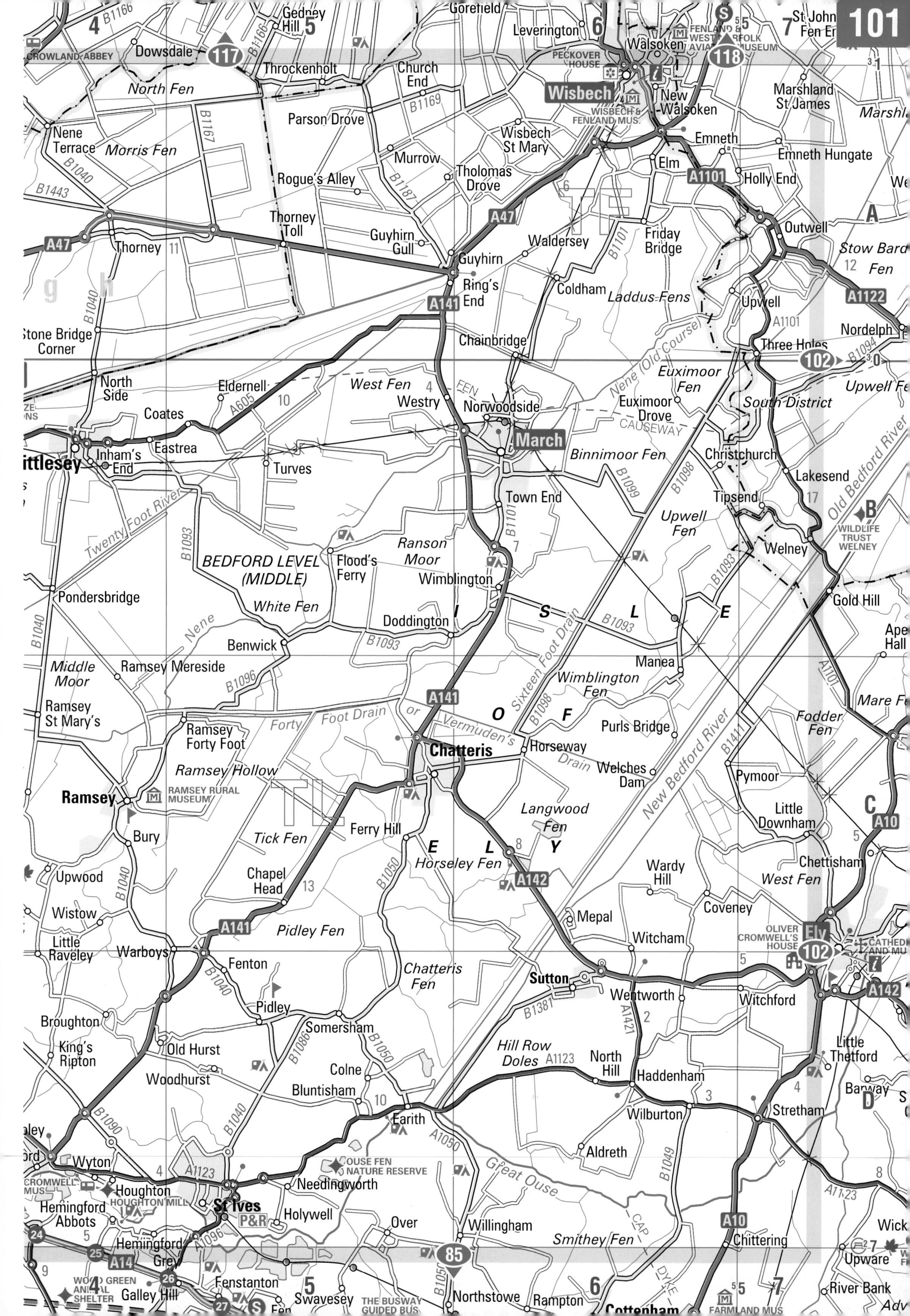
Gedney Hill
Gorefield
Leverington
Walsoken
FENLAND & WEST NORFOLK AVIATION MUSEUM
St John's Fen End
CROWLAND ABBEY
Dowsdale
117
118
PECKOVER HOUSE
Throckenholt
Church End
North Fen
Wisbech
New Walsoken
Marshland St James
WISBECH & FENLAND MUS.
Parson Drove
Nene Terrace
Morris Fen
Wisbech St Mary
Emneth
Murrow
Emneth Hungate
Elm
Rogue's Alley
Tholomas Drove
A1101
Holly End
Thorney Toll
A47
Outwell
Thorney
Guyhirn Gull
Waldersey
Friday Bridge
Stow Bardolph Fen
Guyhirn
Ring's End
Coldham
Laddus Fens
Upwell
A141
A1122
Stone Bridge Corner
Chainbridge
Nordelph
Three Holes
102
Nene (Old Course)
Euximoor Fen
Upwell Fen
North Side
Eldernell
West Fen
Westry
Norwoodside
Euximoor Drove
South District
Coates
A605
CAUSEWAY
Whittlesey
Inham's End
Eastrea
March
Binnimoor Fen
Christchurch
Turves
Town End
Lakesend
Old Bedford River
Twenty Foot River
Tipsend
Upwell Fen
Ranson Moor
WILDLIFE TRUST WELNEY
BEDFORD LEVEL (MIDDLE)
Flood's Ferry
Welney
Wimblington
Pondersbridge
White Fen
Gold Hill
Doddington
ISLE
Nene
Benwick
Sixteen Foot Drain
Apes Hall
Middle Moor
Ramsey Mereside
Manea
Wimblington Fen
Ramsey St Mary's
Forty Foot Drain or Vermuden's Drain
OF
Purls Bridge
Fodder Fen
Mare Fen
Ramsey Forty Foot
Chatteris
Horseway
Welches Dam
Ramsey Hollow
New Bedford River
Pymoor
Ramsey
RAMSEY RURAL MUSEUM
Little Downham
Langwood Fen
Bury
Tick Fen
Ferry Hill
ELY
Chettisham
Upwood
Horseley Fen
Wardy Hill
West Fen
Chapel Head
A142
Wistow
Pidley Fen
Mepal
Coveney
OLIVER CROMWELL'S HOUSE
Ely
CATHEDRAL AND MUSEUM
Little Raveley
Warboys
Witcham
Fenton
Chatteris Fen
Sutton
Wentworth
Witchford
Pidley
Broughton
Somersham
Hill Row Doles
North Hill
Little Thetford
King's Ripton
Old Hurst
Colne
Haddenham
Barway
Woodhurst
Bluntisham
Wilburton
Stretham
Earith
Aldreth
Wyton
OUSE FEN NATURE RESERVE
Great Ouse
Houghton
HOUGHTON MILL
Needingworth
Hemingford Abbots
St Ives
P&R
Holywell
Over
Willingham
A10
Smithey Fen
Chittering
Wicken
Hemingford Grey
A14
85
Upware
WOOD GREEN ANIMAL SHELTER
Galley Hill
Fenstanton
Swavesey
THE BUSWAY GUIDED BUS
Northstowe
Rampton
Cottenham
FARMLAND MUS
River Bank

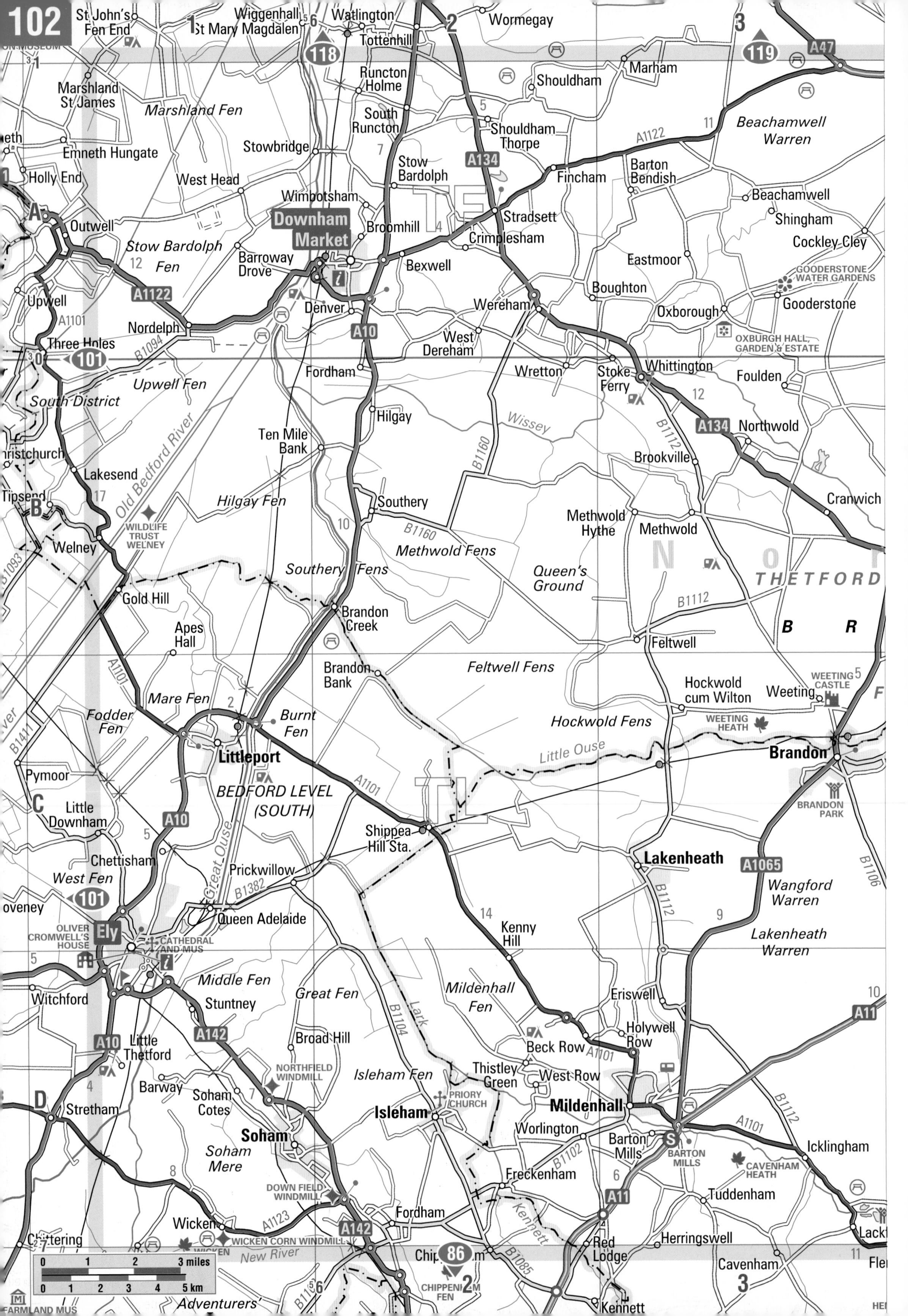
St John's Fen End
Wiggenhall St Mary Magdalen
Watlington
Tottenhill
Wormegay
118
119
A47
Marham
Shouldham
Runcton Holme
Marshland St James
Marshland Fen
South Runcton
Shouldham Thorpe
Beachamwell Warren
A1122
Emneth Hungate
Stowbridge
Stow Bardolph
A134
Fincham
Barton Bendish
Holly End
West Head
Wimbotsham
Beachamwell
Shingham
Outwell
Downham Market
Broomhill
Stradsett
Crimplesham
Cockley Cley
Stow Bardolph Fen
Barroway Drove
Bexwell
Eastmoor
GOODERSTONE WATER GARDENS
A1122
Upwell
Denver
Boughton
Wereham
Gooderstone
Oxborough
A1101
Nordelph
A10
West Dereham
OXBURGH HALL, GARDEN & ESTATE
Three Holes
B1094
101
Fordham
Wretton
Stoke Ferry
Whittington
Foulden
Upwell Fen
South District
Hilgay
Wissey
A134
Northwold
Ten Mile Bank
Old Bedford River
B1160
B1112
Brookville
Lakesend
Tipsend
Hilgay Fen
Southery
Cranwich
WILDLIFE TRUST WELNEY
B1160
Methwold Hythe
Methwold
Welney
Methwold Fens
Southery Fens
Queen's Ground
THETFORD
Gold Hill
B1112
Brandon Creek
Apes Hall
Feltwell
A1101
Brandon Bank
Feltwell Fens
Hockwold cum Wilton
Weeting
WEETING CASTLE
Mare Fen
Burnt Fen
Fodder Fen
Hockwold Fens
WEETING HEATH
B1411
Little Ouse
Littleport
Brandon
Pymoor
BEDFORD LEVEL (SOUTH)
A1101
Little Downham
A10
BRANDON PARK
Shippea Hill Sta.
Great Ouse
Chettisham
Lakenheath
A1065
West Fen
Prickwillow
B1382
Wangford Warren
B1106
Coveney
101
Queen Adelaide
B1112
OLIVER CROMWELL'S HOUSE
Ely
CATHEDRAL AND MUS
Kenny Hill
Lakenheath Warren
Middle Fen
Great Fen
Mildenhall Fen
Witchford
Stuntney
Eriswell
A11
Lark
A142
Broad Hill
B1104
Holywell Row
A10
Little Thetford
Beck Row
A1101
NORTHFIELD WINDMILL
Isleham Fen
Thistley Green
West Row
Barway
PRIORY CHURCH
Soham Cotes
Stretham
Isleham
Mildenhall
B1112
Worlington
A1101
Soham
Barton Mills
Icklingham
Soham Mere
B1102
BARTON MILLS
CAVENHAM HEATH
Freckenham
DOWN FIELD WINDMILL
A11
Tuddenham
Wicken
A1123
Fordham
Kennett
Chittering
WICKEN CORN WINDMILL
A142
Red Lodge
Herringswell
WICKEN
New River
86
B1085
Cavenham
0 1 2 3 miles
0 1 2 3 4 5 km
CHIPPENHAM FEN
FARMLAND MUS
Adventurers'
Kennett

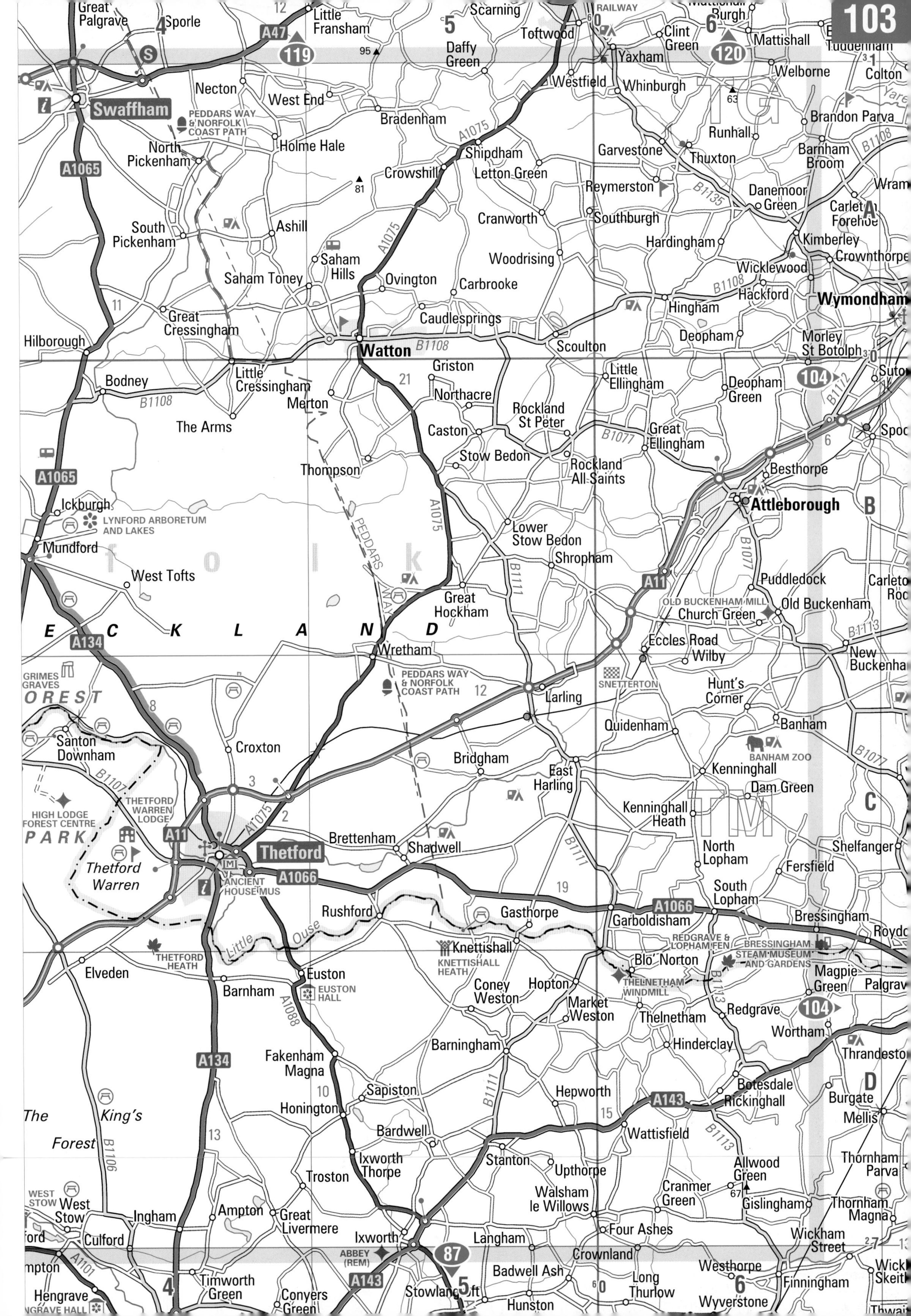

Great Palgrave
Sporle
Little Fransham
Scarning
RAILWAY
Burgh
A47
119
Toftwood
Clint Green
120
Mattishall
Tuddenham
Daffy Green
Yaxham
Welborne
Colton
Necton
Westfield
Whinburgh
Swaffham
West End
Bradenham
TG
Brandon Parva
PEDDARS WAY & NORFOLK COAST PATH
A1075
Runhall
North Pickenham
Holme Hale
Garvestone
Thuxton
Barnham Broom
B1108
A1065
Shipdham
Crowshill
Letton Green
Reymerston
B1135
Danemoor Green
Wramplingham
South Pickenham
Ashill
Cranworth
Southburgh
Carleton Forehoe
Hardingham
Kimberley
Saham Hills
Woodrising
Crownthorpe
Saham Toney
Ovington
Carbrooke
Wicklewood
Hackford
Wymondham
Great Cressingham
Caudlesprings
Hingham
Hilborough
Watton
B1108
Scoulton
Deopham
Morley St Botolph
Griston
Little Ellingham
Deopham Green
104
Bodney
Little Cressingham
Merton
Northacre
Rockland St Peter
B1108
The Arms
Caston
B1077
Great Ellingham
Spooner Row
Stow Bedon
Rockland All Saints
Besthorpe
A1065
Thompson
Attleborough
Ickburgh
LYNFORD ARBORETUM AND LAKES
Lower Stow Bedon
Mundford
PEDDARS WAY
A1075
Shropham
B1077
West Tofts
B1111
A11
Puddledock
Great Hockham
OLD BUCKENHAM MILL
Church Green
Old Buckenham
Carleton Rode
B1113
BRECKLAND
Eccles Road
Wilby
New Buckenham
A134
Wretham
GRIMES GRAVES
PEDDARS WAY & NORFOLK COAST PATH
SNETTERTON
Hunt's Corner
FOREST
Larling
Quidenham
Banham
Santon Downham
Croxton
Bridgham
BANHAM ZOO
B1077
Kenninghall
B1107
East Harling
Dam Green
HIGH LODGE FOREST CENTRE
THETFORD WARREN LODGE
A1075
Kenninghall Heath
TM
PARK
A11
Brettenham
Shadwell
B1111
North Lopham
Shelfanger
Thetford
Thetford Warren
A1066
ANCIENT HOUSE MUS
South Lopham
Fersfield
Rushford
Gasthorpe
A1066
Garboldisham
Bressingham
Roydon
Little Ouse
REDGRAVE & LOPHAM FEN
BRESSINGHAM STEAM MUSEUM AND GARDENS
Knettishall
KNETTISHALL HEATH
Blo' Norton
Elveden
THETFORD HEATH
Euston
EUSTON HALL
THELNETHAM WINDMILL
Magpie Green
Palgrave
Barnham
Coney Weston
Hopton
B1113
A1088
Market Weston
Thelnetham
Redgrave
104
Wortham
Fakenham Magna
Barningham
Hinderclay
Thrandeston
A134
Botesdale
Rickinghall
Sapiston
Hepworth
A143
Burgate
The
King's
Honington
B1111
Mellis
Forest
Bardwell
Wattisfield
B1113
B1106
Ixworth Thorpe
Stanton
Upthorpe
Allwood Green
Thornham Parva
Troston
WEST STOW
West Stow
Walsham le Willows
Cranmer Green
Gislingham
Thornham Magna
Ingham
Ampton
Great Livermere
Four Ashes
Culford
Ixworth
Langham
Wickham Street
ABBEY (REM)
87
Crownland
A1101
Badwell Ash
Westhorpe
Wickham Skeith
A143
Long Thurlow
Finningham
Timworth Green
Hengrave
Conyers Green
Stowlangtoft
Hunston
Wyverstone
HENGRAVE HALL

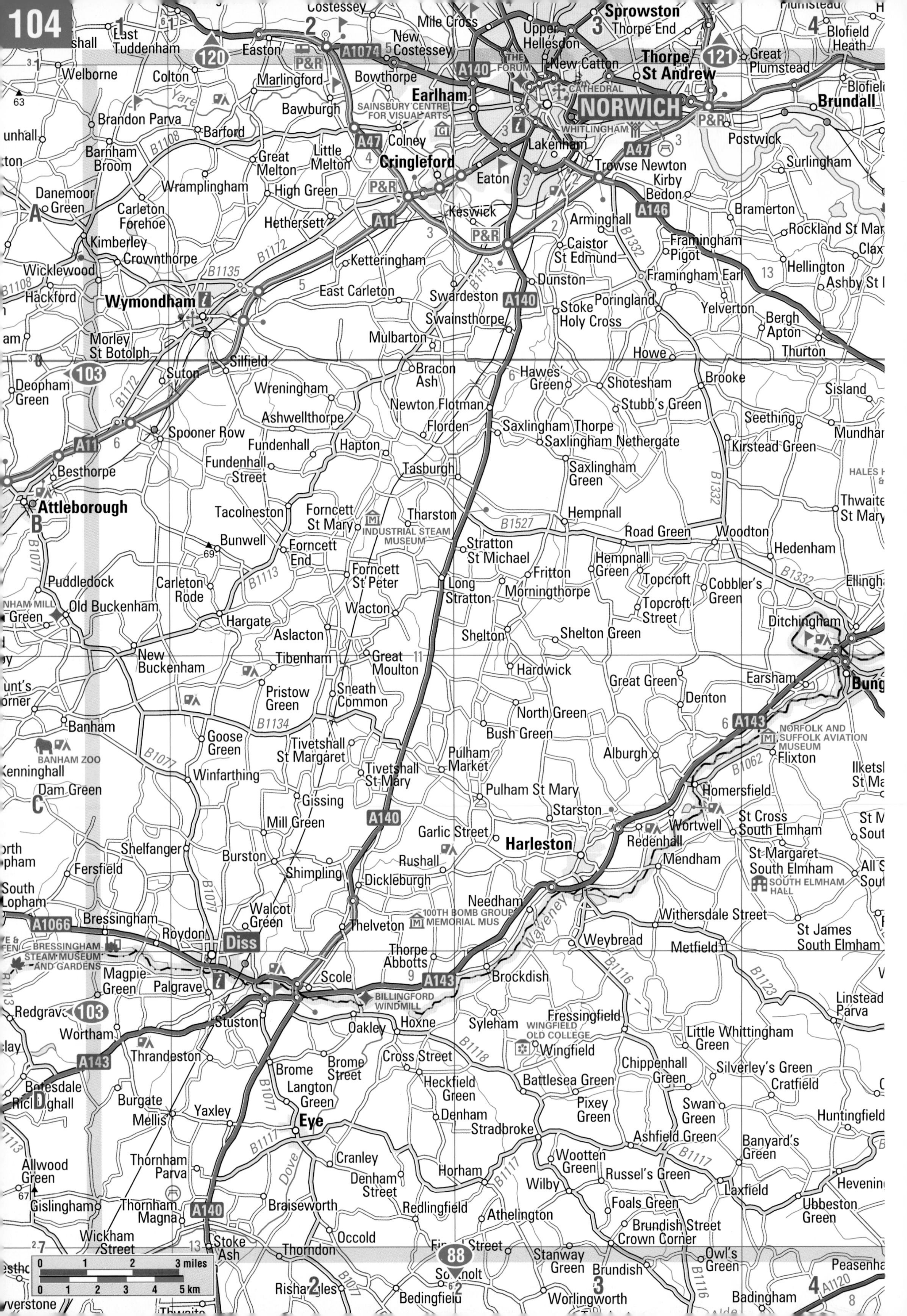
Costessey
Mile Cross
Sprowston
Thorpe End
East Tuddenham
Easton
New Costessey
Upper Hellesdon
New Catton
Thorpe St Andrew
Great Plumstead
Blofield Heath
Welborne
Colton
Marlingford
Bowthorpe
Earlham
THE FORUM
CATHEDRAL
NORWICH
Brundall
Brandon Parva
Barford
Bawburgh
SAINSBURY CENTRE FOR VISUAL ARTS
WHITLINGHAM
Postwick
Barnham Broom
Great Melton
Little Melton
Colney
Cringleford
Lakenham
Trowse Newton
Kirby Bedon
Surlingham
Danemoor Green
Carleton Forehoe
Wramplingham
High Green
Eaton
Keswick
Arminghall
Bramerton
Kimberley
Hethersett
Caistor St Edmund
Framingham Pigot
Rockland St Mary
Crownthorpe
Ketteringham
Framingham Earl
Hellington
Wicklewood
Hackford
Wymondham
East Carleton
Swardeston
Dunston
Stoke Holy Cross
Poringland
Yelverton
Bergh Apton
Morley St Botolph
Swainsthorpe
Mulbarton
Howe
Thurton
Silfield
Suton
Bracon Ash
Hawes' Green
Shotesham
Brooke
Sisland
Deopham Green
Wreningham
Newton Flotman
Stubb's Green
Ashwellthorpe
Florden
Saxlingham Thorpe
Seething
Spooner Row
Fundenhall
Hapton
Saxlingham Nethergate
Kirstead Green
Besthorpe
Fundenhall Street
Tasburgh
Saxlingham Green
Attleborough
Tacolneston
Forncett St Mary
Tharston
Hempnall
INDUSTRIAL STEAM MUSEUM
Bunwell
Forncett End
Stratton St Michael
Road Green
Woodton
Hedenham
Thwaite St Mary
Puddledock
Carleton Rode
Forncett St Peter
Long Stratton
Fritton
Hempnall Green
Topcroft
Cobbler's Green
Old Buckenham
Hargate
Wacton
Morningthorpe
Topcroft Street
Ditchingham
Aslacton
Shelton
Shelton Green
New Buckenham
Tibenham
Great Moulton
Hardwick
Great Green
Earsham
Denton
Pristow Green
Sneath Common
North Green
Banham
Goose Green
Tivetshall St Margaret
Bush Green
Pulham Market
Alburgh
NORFOLK AND SUFFOLK AVIATION MUSEUM
Flixton
BANHAM ZOO
Winfarthing
Tivetshall St Mary
Dam Green
Gissing
Pulham St Mary
Homersfield
Starston
Mill Green
Garlic Street
Harleston
Wortwell
St Cross South Elmham
Shelfanger
Burston
Redenhall
Rushall
Mendham
St Margaret South Elmham
Fersfield
Shimpling
Dickleburgh
SOUTH ELMHAM HALL
South Lopham
Needham
Walcot Green
100TH BOMB GROUP MEMORIAL MUS
Withersdale Street
Bressingham
Roydon
Thelveton
St James South Elmham
BRESSINGHAM STEAM MUSEUM AND GARDENS
Diss
Weybread
Metfield
Thorpe Abbotts
Magpie Green
Palgrave
Scole
Brockdish
BILLINGFORD WINDMILL
Redgrave
Linstead Parva
Wortham
Stuston
Oakley
Hoxne
Syleham
Fressingfield
WINGFIELD OLD COLLEGE
Little Whittingham Green
Thrandeston
Cross Street
Wingfield
Brome
Brome Street
Chippenhall Green
Silverley's Green
Botesdale
Rickinghall
Langton Green
Heckfield Green
Battlesea Green
Cratfield
Burgate
Yaxley
Mellis
Eye
Denham
Pixey Green
Swan Green
Huntingfield
Stradbroke
Ashfield Green
Banyard's Green
Cranley
Wootten Green
Allwood Green
Thornham Parva
Denham Street
Horham
Wilby
Russel's Green
Laxfield
Gislingham
Thornham Magna
Braiseworth
Redlingfield
Athelington
Foals Green
Ubbeston Green
Brundish Street
Crown Corner
Wickham Street
Occold
Stoke Ash
Thorndon
Stanway Green
Brundish
Owl's Green
Risha'gles
Bedingfield
Worlingworth
Badingham
Yare
Waveney
Dove
A1074
A140
A47
A11
A146
A143
A1066
B1108
B1172
B1135
B1113
B1332
B1527
B1077
B1134
B1062
B1116
B1123
B1118
B1117
P&R
120
121
103
88
0 1 2 3 miles
0 1 2 3 4 5 km

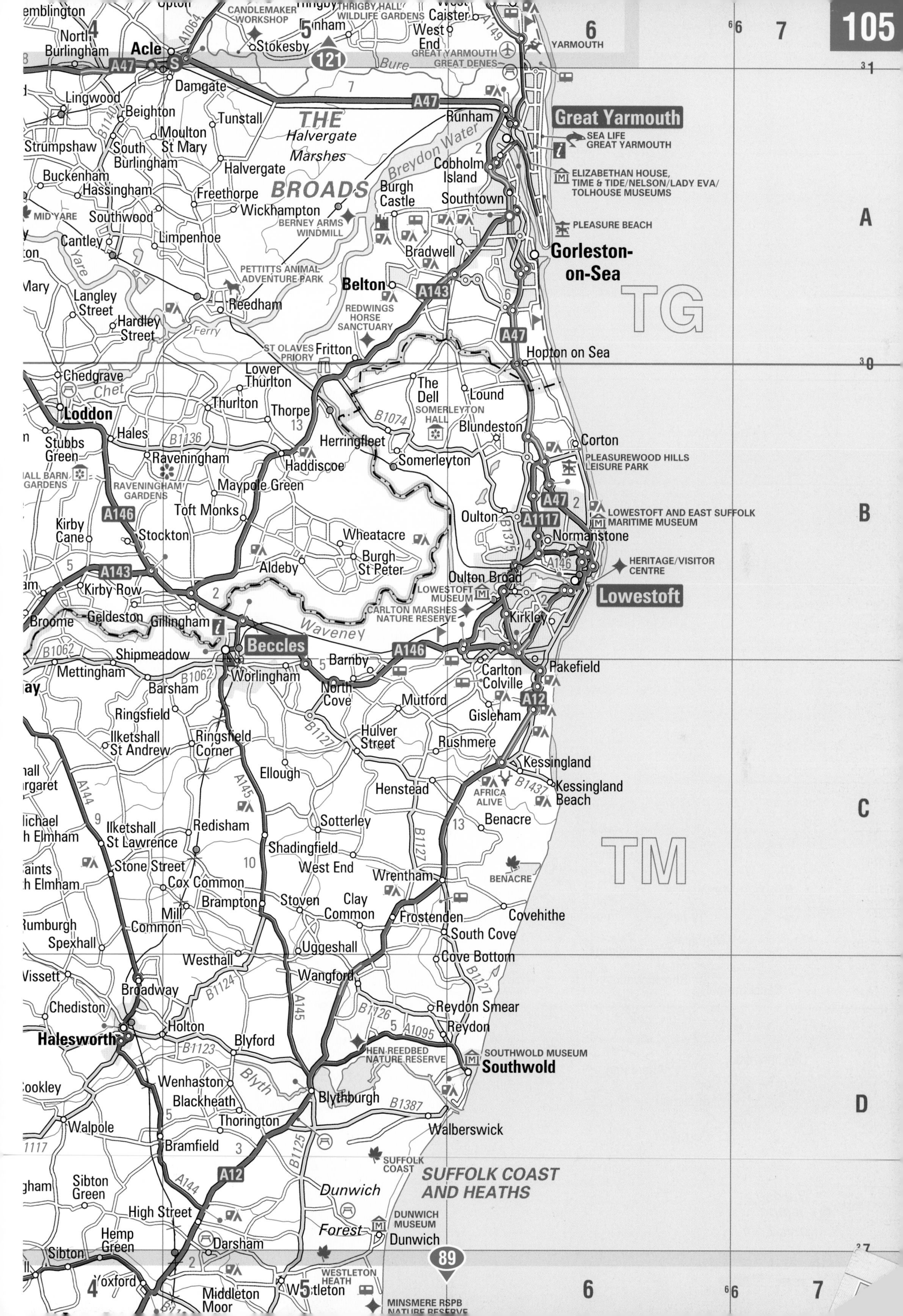

4
5
6
7
North Burlingham
Acle
Stokesby
CANDLEMAKER WORKSHOP
THRIGBY HALL WILDLIFE GARDENS
Caister
West End
YARMOUTH
GREAT YARMOUTH
GREAT DENES
A47
A1064
A149
121
Bure
Damgate
Lingwood
Beighton
Tunstall
THE
Halvergate
Marshes
BROADS
Runham
Breydon Water
Great Yarmouth
SEA LIFE GREAT YARMOUTH
Strumpshaw
South Burlingham
Moulton St Mary
Halvergate
Cobholm Island
ELIZABETHAN HOUSE, TIME & TIDE/NELSON/LADY EVA/ TOLHOUSE MUSEUMS
Buckenham
Hassingham
Freethorpe
Wickhampton
Burgh Castle
Southtown
MID YARE
Southwood
BERNEY ARMS WINDMILL
PLEASURE BEACH
Cantley
Limpenhoe
Bradwell
Gorleston-on-Sea
Yare
PETTITTS ANIMAL ADVENTURE PARK
Belton
A143
Langley Street
Reedham
REDWINGS HORSE SANCTUARY
TG
Hardley Street
Ferry
A47
ST OLAVES PRIORY
Fritton
Hopton on Sea
Chedgrave
Chet
Lower Thurlton
The Dell
Lound
Loddon
Thurlton
Thorpe
SOMERLEYTON HALL
B1074
Blundeston
Hales
B1136
Herringfleet
Corton
Stubbs Green
Raveningham
Haddiscoe
Somerleyton
PLEASUREWOOD HILLS LEISURE PARK
HALL BARN GARDENS
RAVENINGHAM GARDENS
Maypole Green
A47
Toft Monks
Oulton
A1117
LOWESTOFT AND EAST SUFFOLK MARITIME MUSEUM
A146
Kirby Cane
Stockton
Wheatacre
Normanstone
B1375
Burgh St Peter
A146
HERITAGE/VISITOR CENTRE
A143
Aldeby
Oulton Broad
Kirby Row
LOWESTOFT MUSEUM
Lowestoft
Broome
Geldeston
Gillingham
CARLTON MARSHES NATURE RESERVE
Kirkley
Waveney
Beccles
B1062
Shipmeadow
Barnby
A146
Pakefield
Mettingham
Worlingham
Carlton Colville
Barsham
B1062
North Cove
Mutford
A12
Ringsfield
Gisleham
Ilketshall St Andrew
Ringsfield Corner
B1127
Hulver Street
Rushmere
Ellough
Kessingland
A145
A144
Henstead
AFRICA ALIVE
B1437
Kessingland Beach
Benacre
Redisham
Sotterley
Ilketshall St Lawrence
B1127
Shadingfield
Stone Street
West End
BENACRE
TM
Cox Common
Wrentham
Brampton
Stoven
Clay Common
Mill Common
Frostenden
Covehithe
Rumburgh
South Cove
Spexhall
Uggeshall
Westhall
Cove Bottom
Wissett
Wangford
B1124
B1127
Broadway
A145
Chediston
Reydon Smear
B1126
Holton
A1095
Reydon
Halesworth
Blyford
HEN REEDBED NATURE RESERVE
SOUTHWOLD MUSEUM
B1123
Southwold
Blyth
Wenhaston
Cookley
Blackheath
Blythburgh
B1387
Walpole
Thorington
Walberswick
Bramfield
B1125
SUFFOLK COAST
SUFFOLK COAST AND HEATHS
A12
A144
Sibton Green
Dunwich
High Street
DUNWICH MUSEUM
Hemp Green
Forest
Dunwich
Darsham
Sibton
89
WESTLETON HEATH
Yoxford
Westleton
Middleton Moor
MINSMERE RSPB NATURE RESERVE
A
B
C
D

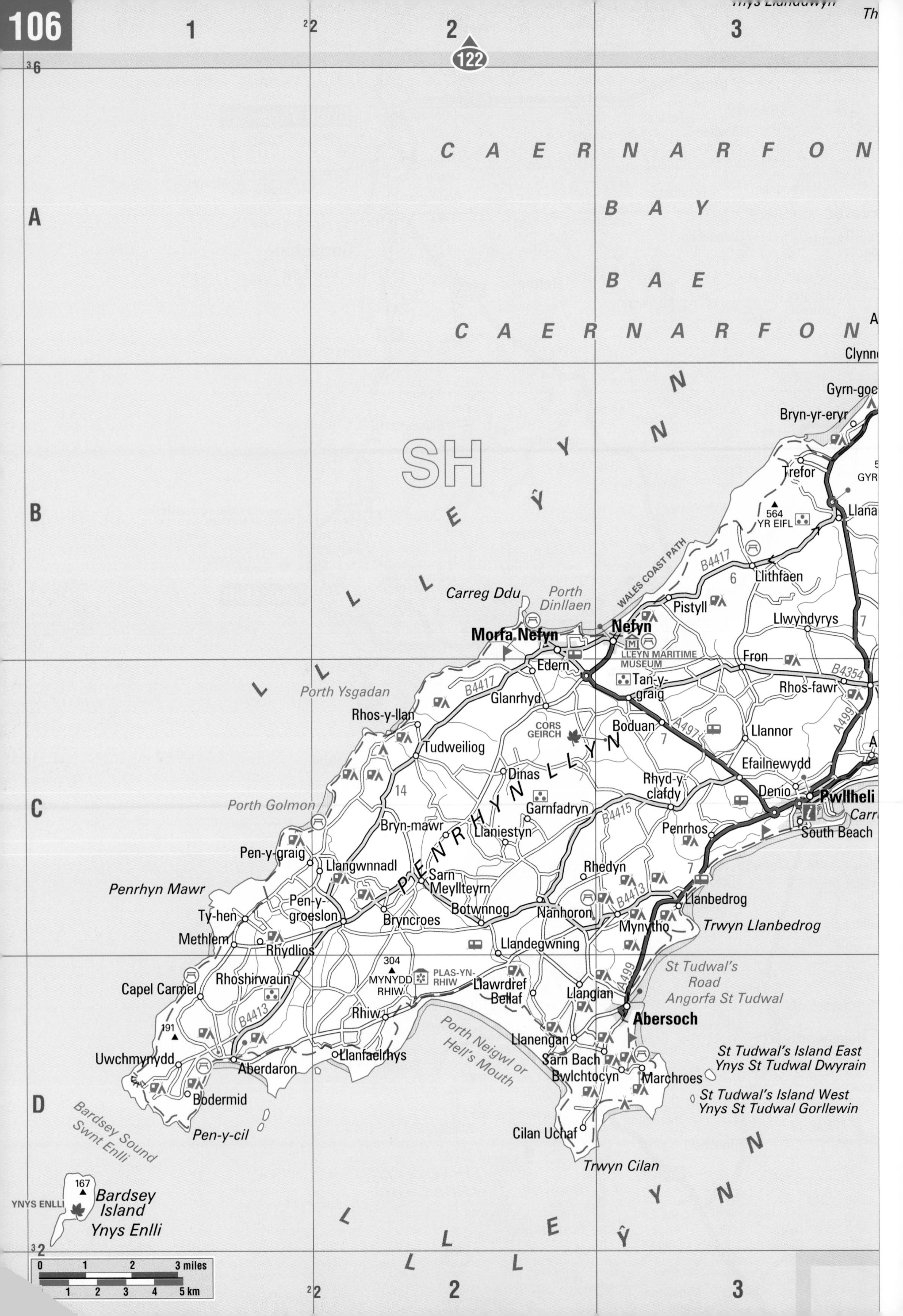
106
1
2
3
122
CAERNARFON BAY
BAE CAERNARFON
A
B
C
D
SH
LLEYN
PENRHYN LLYN
Clynn
Gyrn-goe
Bryn-yr-eryr
Trefor
GYR
564
YR EIFL
Llana
WALES COAST PATH
B4417
Llithfaen
Carreg Ddu
Porth Dinllaen
Pistyll
Llwyndyrys
Morfa Nefyn
Nefyn
LLEYN MARITIME MUSEUM
Edern
Fron
B4354
Tan-y-graig
Rhos-fawr
Porth Ysgadan
Glanrhyd
Rhos-y-llan
CORS GEIRCH
Boduan
A497
Llannor
A499
Tudweiliog
Efailnewydd
Dinas
Rhyd-y-clafdy
Denio
Pwllheli
Porth Golmon
Garnfadryn
B4415
Carr
South Beach
Bryn-mawr
Llaniestyn
Penrhos
Pen-y-graig
Llangwnnadl
Rhedyn
Sarn Meyllteyrn
Penrhyn Mawr
Pen-y-groeslon
B4413
Llanbedrog
Ty-hen
Botwnnog
Nanhoron
Bryncroes
Mynytho
Trwyn Llanbedrog
Methlem
Rhydlios
Llandegwning
304
MYNYDD RHIW
PLAS-YN-RHIW
St Tudwal's Road
Angorfa St Tudwal
Capel Carmel
Rhoshirwaun
Llawrdref Bellaf
Llangian
Rhiw
Abersoch
191
Porth Neigwl or Hell's Mouth
Llanengan
Uwchmynydd
Llanfaelrhys
Sarn Bach
St Tudwal's Island East
Ynys St Tudwal Dwyrain
Aberdaron
Bwlchtocyn
Marchroes
Bodermid
St Tudwal's Island West
Ynys St Tudwal Gorllewin
Bardsey Sound
Swnt Enlli
Pen-y-cil
Cilan Uchaf
Trwyn Cilan
167
YNYS ENLLI
Bardsey Island
Ynys Enlli
0 1 2 3 miles
0 1 2 3 4 5 km

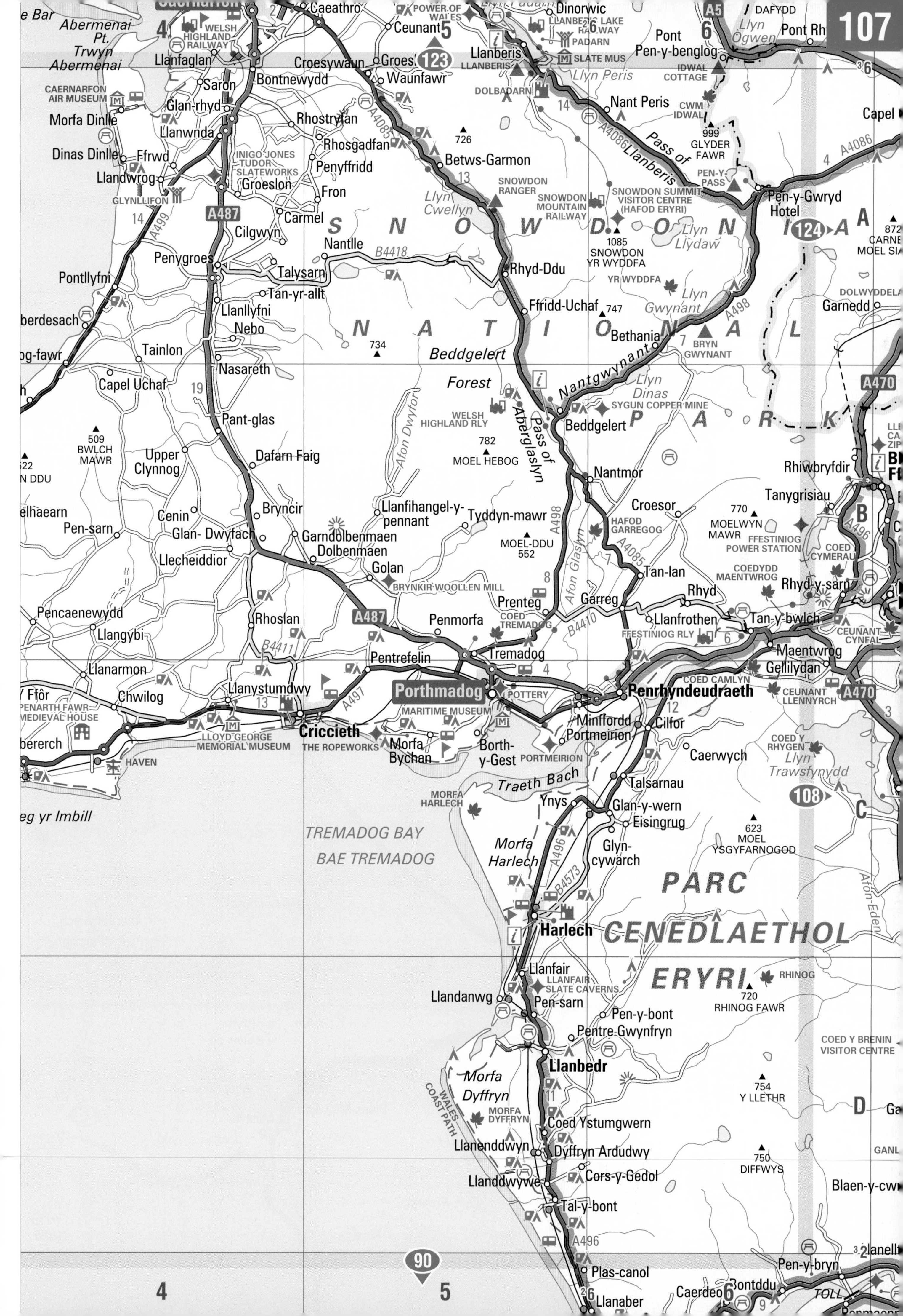
Abermenai Pt.
Trwyn Abermenai
Caeathro
Ceunant
POWER OF WALES
Dinorwic
LLANBERIS LAKE RAILWAY
PADARN
DAFYDD
Llyn Ogwen
Pont Rh
WELSH HIGHLAND RAILWAY
Llanfaglan
Croesywaun
Groes
123
Llanberis
SLATE MUS
Pont Pen-y-benglog
IDWAL COTTAGE
Saron
Bontnewydd
Waunfawr
Llyn Peris
DOLBADARN
CAERNARFON AIR MUSEUM
Glan-rhyd
Nant Peris
CWM IDWAL
Capel
Morfa Dinlle
Rhostryfan
726
A4085
A4086
Pass of Llanberis
999 GLYDER FAWR
Llanwnda
Rhosgadfan
Dinas Dinlle
Ffrwd
INIGO JONES TUDOR SLATEWORKS
Betws-Garmon
A4086
Llandwrog
Penyffridd
PEN-Y-PASS
Groeslon
Fron
SNOWDON RANGER
SNOWDON MOUNTAIN RAILWAY
SNOWDON SUMMIT VISITOR CENTRE (HAFOD ERYRI)
Pen-y-Gwryd Hotel
GLYNLLIFON
Llyn Cwellyn
A487
Carmel
A499
SNOWDONIA
Llyn Llydaw
124
872 CARNE MOEL SI
Cilgwyn
1085 SNOWDON YR WYDDFA
Nantlle
B4418
Penygroes
Rhyd-Ddu
YR WYDDFA
Pontllyfni
Talysarn
Llyn Gwynant
DOLWYDDELA
Tan-yr-allt
Ffridd-Uchaf
747
Garnedd
Llanllyfni
A498
berdesach
Nebo
NATIONAL
Bethania
BRYN GWYNANT
734
og-fawr
Tainlon
Beddgelert
Nasareth
Forest
Nantgwynant
Capel Uchaf
Llyn Dinas
A470
19
WELSH HIGHLAND RLY
SYGUN COPPER MINE
Pant-glas
Pass of Aberglaslyn
Beddgelert
PARK
509 BWLCH MAWR
782 MOEL HEBOG
Upper Clynnog
Dafarn Faig
Afon Dwyfor
N DDU
Rhiwbryfdir
Nantmor
Tanygrisiau
elhaearn
Bryncir
Croesor
770 MOELWYN MAWR
Cenin
Llanfihangel-y-pennant
Tyddyn-mawr
HAFOD GARREGOG
Pen-sarn
Glan-Dwyfach
Garndolbenmaen
MOEL-DDU 552
A498
FFESTINIOG POWER STATION
COED CYMERAU
Dolbenmaen
A4085
A496
Llecheiddior
Golan
Afon Glaslyn
Tan-lan
COEDYDD MAENTWROG
BRYNKIR WOOLLEN MILL
Rhyd
Rhyd-y-sarn
Prenteg
Garreg
Pencaenewydd
A487
Penmorfa
COED TREMADOG
B4410
Llanfrothen
Tan-y-bwlch
Rhoslan
Llangybi
FFESTINIOG RLY
CEUNANT CYNFAL
B4411
Tremadog
Maentwrog
Llanarmon
Pentrefelin
Gellilydan
Ffôr
Chwilog
Llanystumdwy
A497
Porthmadog
POTTERY
Penrhyndeudraeth
COED CAMLYN
CEUNANT LLENNYRCH
A470
PENARTH FAWR MEDIEVAL HOUSE
MARITIME MUSEUM
Minffordd
Cilfor
Criccieth
Portmeirion
bererch
LLOYD GEORGE MEMORIAL MUSEUM
THE ROPEWORKS
Morfa Bychan
Borth-y-Gest
PORTMEIRION
Caerwych
COED Y RHYGEN
Llyn Trawsfynydd
HAVEN
Traeth Bach
Talsarnau
MORFA HARLECH
Ynys
108
Glan-y-wern
eg yr Imbill
Eisingrug
TREMADOG BAY
BAE TREMADOG
Morfa Harlech
A496
Glyn-cywarch
623 MOEL YSGYFARNOGOD
B4573
PARC CENEDLAETHOL ERYRI
Afon Eden
Harlech
Llanfair
LLANFAIR SLATE CAVERNS
RHINOG
720 RHINOG FAWR
Llandanwg
Pen-sarn
Pen-y-bont
Pentre-Gwynfryn
COED Y BRENIN VISITOR CENTRE
Llanbedr
Morfa Dyffryn
WALES COAST PATH
754 Y LLETHR
MORFA DYFFRYN
Coed Ystumgwern
Llanenddwyn
Dyffryn Ardudwy
750 DIFFWYS
Llanddwywe
Cors-y-Gedol
Blaen-y-cw
Tal-y-bont
A496
Llanell
90
Plas-canol
Pen-y-bryn
Caerdeo
Bontddu
TOLL
Llanaber
4
5
6

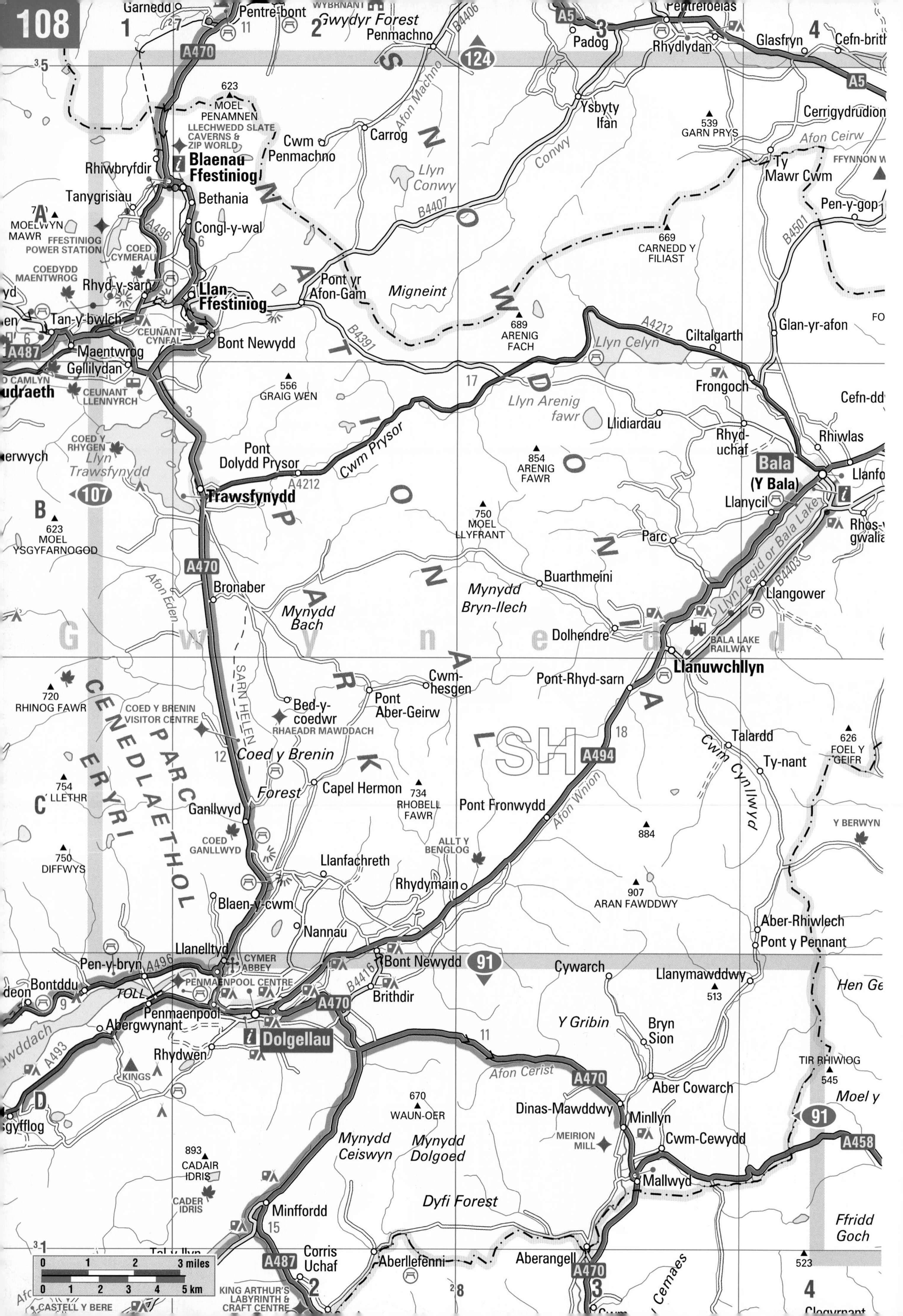

1
2
3
4
A
B
C
D
Garnedd
Pentre-bont
Gwydyr Forest
Penmachno
Pentrefoelas
Padog
Rhydlydan
Glasfryn
Cefn-brith
A5
A470
B4406
124
623
MOEL PENAMNEN
LLECHWEDD SLATE CAVERNS & ZIP WORLD
Blaenau Ffestiniog
Rhiwbryfdir
Tanygrisiau
Bethania
Congl-y-wal
Cwm Penmachno
Carrog
Afon Machno
Llyn Conwy
Ysbyty Ifan
Conwy
539
GARN PRYS
Cerrigydrudion
Afon Ceirw
Ty Mawr Cwm
FFYNNON W
Pen-y-gop
B4501
B4407
MOELWYN MAWR
FFESTINIOG POWER STATION
COED CYMERAU
A496
COEDYDD MAENTWROG
Rhyd-y-sarn
Llan-Ffestiniog
Pont yr Afon-Gam
Migneint
669
CARNEDD Y FILIAST
Tan-y-bwlch
CEUNANT CYNFAL
Bont Newydd
Maentwrog
A487
Gellilydan
CAMLYN
udraeth
CEUNANT LLENNYRCH
B4391
689
ARENIG FACH
A4212
Llyn Celyn
Ciltalgarth
Glan-yr-afon
Frongoch
556
GRAIG WEN
17
Llyn Arenig fawr
Llidiardau
Cefn-dd
Rhyd-uchaf
Rhiwlas
COED Y RHYGEN
Llyn Trawsfynydd
erwych
Pont Dolydd Prysor
Cwm Prysor
854
ARENIG FAWR
Bala
(Y Bala)
Llanfor
Llanycil
107
Trawsfynydd
623
MOEL YSGYFARNOGOD
750
MOEL LLYFRANT
Parc
Llyn Tegid or Bala Lake
Rhos-y-gwalia
B4403
Afon Eden
Bronaber
Buarthmeini
Mynydd Bach
Mynydd Bryn-llech
Llangower
Dolhendre
BALA LAKE RAILWAY
Llanuwchllyn
SNOWDONIA NATIONAL PARK
Gwynedd
720
RHINOG FAWR
COED Y BRENIN VISITOR CENTRE
SARN HELEN
Bed-y-coedwr
RHAEADR MAWDDACH
Pont Aber-Geirw
Cwm-hesgen
Pont-Rhyd-sarn
PARC CENEDLAETHOL ERYRI
Coed y Brenin
12
Forest
Capel Hermon
734
RHOBELL FAWR
SH
18
A494
Talardd
Cwm Cynllwyd
626
FOEL Y GEIFR
Ty-nant
754
LLETHR
Ganllwyd
Pont Fronwydd
Afon Wnion
884
Y BERWYN
COED GANLLWYD
ALLT Y BENGLOG
750
DIFFWYS
Llanfachreth
Rhydymain
907
ARAN FAWDDWY
Blaen-y-cwm
Nannau
Aber-Rhiwlech
Pont y Pennant
Llanelltyd
CYMER ABBEY
Pen-y-bryn
Bont Newydd
91
Cywarch
Llanymawddwy
Hen Ge
Bontddu
deon
TOLL
PENMAENPOOL CENTRE
9
Penmaenpool
B4416
Brithdir
513
Abergwynant
Y Gribin
Dolgellau
11
Bryn Sion
wddach
A493
Rhydwen
KINGS
Afon Cerist
TIR RHIWIOG
545
Aber Cowarch
Moel y
670
WAUN-OER
Dinas-Mawddwy
Minllyn
sgyfflog
MEIRION MILL
Cwm-Cewydd
A458
Mynydd Ceiswyn
Mynydd Dolgoed
893
CADAIR IDRIS
Mallwyd
CADER IDRIS
Dyfi Forest
Minffordd
15
Ffridd Goch
Corris Uchaf
Aberllefenni
Aberangell
523
0 1 2 3 miles
0 1 2 3 4 5 km
KING ARTHUR'S LABYRINTH & CRAFT CENTRE
CASTELL Y BERE
Cemaes
Clogyrnant

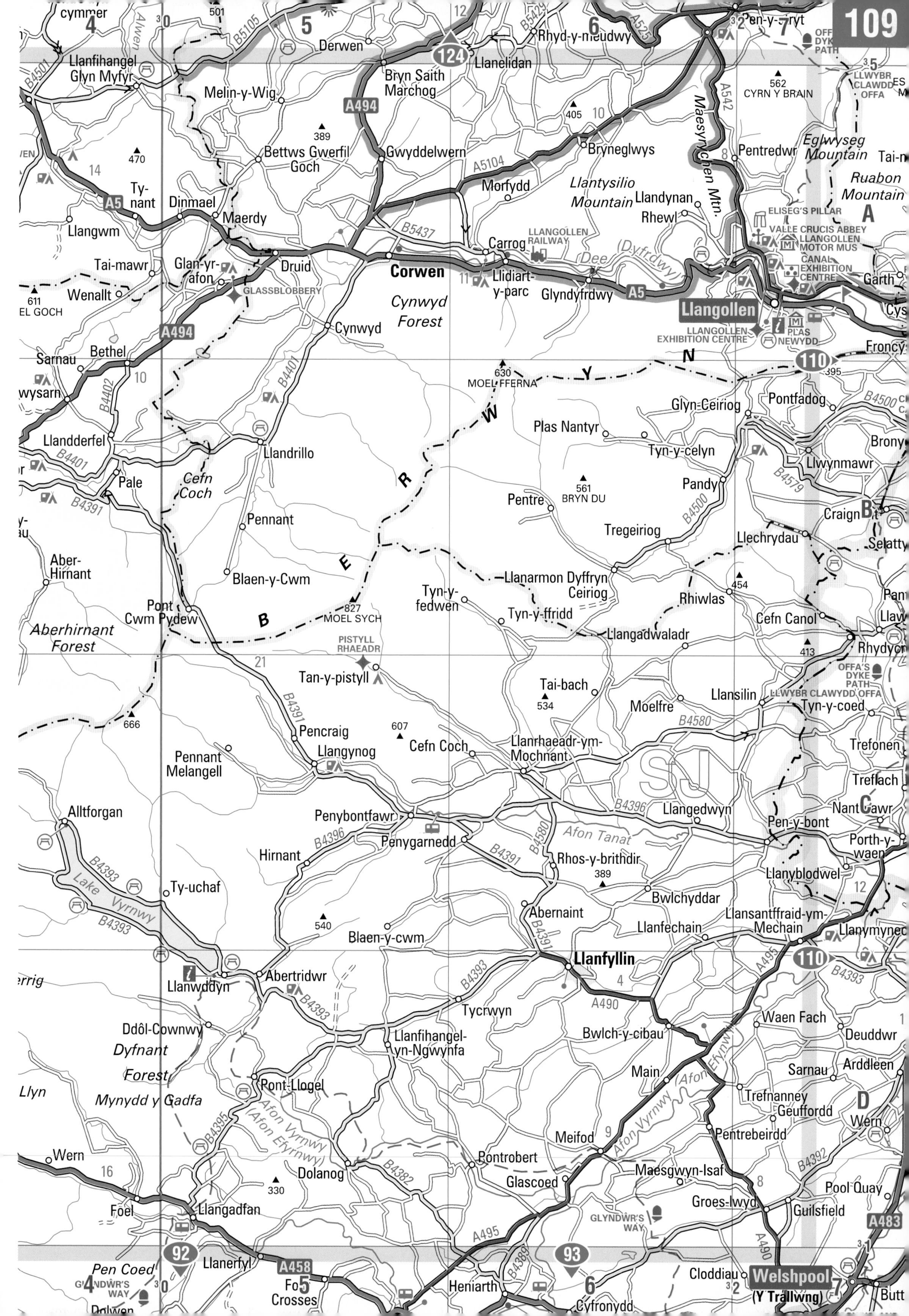

Llanfihangel Glyn Myfyr
Melin-y-Wig
Derwen
Bryn Saith Marchog
Llanelidan
Rhyd-y-meudwy
Pen-y-stryt
CYRN Y BRAIN
LLWYBR CLAWDD OFFA
OFFA'S DYKE PATH
Bettws Gwerfil Goch
Gwyddelwern
Bryneglwys
Maesyrychen Mtn.
Pentredwr
Eglwyseg Mountain
Ruabon Mountain
Ty-nant
Dinmael
Maerdy
Morfydd
Llantysilio Mountain
Llandynan
Rhewl
ELISEG'S PILLAR
VALLE CRUCIS ABBEY
LLANGOLLEN MOTOR MUS
CANAL EXHIBITION CENTRE
Llangwm
Tai-mawr
Glan-yr-afon
Druid
Corwen
Carrog
LLANGOLLEN RAILWAY
Dee (Dyfrdwy)
Llidiart-y-parc
Glyndyfrdwy
Garth
Wenallt
GLASSBLOBBERY
Cynwyd Forest
Llangollen
LLANGOLLEN EXHIBITION CENTRE
PLAS NEWYDD
Cynwyd
Sarnau
Bethel
Froncysyllte
MOEL FFERNA
BERWYN
Glyn-Ceiriog
Pontfadog
Llandderfel
Llandrillo
Plas Nantyr
Tyn-y-celyn
Llwynmawr
Pale
Cefn Coch
Pandy
Pentre
BRYN DU
Craignant
Pennant
Tregeiriog
Llechrydau
Selattyn
Aber-Hirnant
Blaen-y-Cwm
Llanarmon Dyffryn Ceiriog
Pont Cwm Pydew
Tyn-y-fedwen
MOEL SYCH
Tyn-y-ffridd
Rhiwlas
Cefn Canol
Aberhirnant Forest
Llangadwaladr
Rhydycroesau
PISTYLL RHAEADR
Tan-y-pistyll
Tai-bach
Llansilin
Moelfre
Tyn-y-coed
Pencraig
Cefn Coch
Llanrhaeadr-ym-Mochnant
Trefonen
Pennant Melangell
Llangynog
Treflach
Alltforgan
Penybontfawr
Llangedwyn
Nant-y-gawr
Penygarnedd
Afon Tanat
Pen-y-bont
Porth-y-waen
Hirnant
Rhos-y-brithdir
Llanyblodwel
Lake Vyrnwy
Ty-uchaf
Bwlchyddar
Abernaint
Llansantffraid-ym-Mechain
Blaen-y-cwm
Llanfechain
Llanymynech
Llanfyllin
Llanwddyn
Abertridwr
Tycrwyn
Waen Fach
Ddôl-Cownwy
Llanfihangel-yn-Ngwynfa
Bwlch-y-cibau
Deuddwr
Dyfnant Forest
Arddleen
Sarnau
Main
Afon Efyrnwy
Llyn
Mynydd y Gadfa
Pont-Llogel
Trefnanney
Geuffordd
Afon Vyrnwy (Afon Efyrnwy)
Wern
Meifod
Pentrebeirdd
Wern
Pontrobert
Dolanog
Maesgwyn-Isaf
Glascoed
Pool Quay
Groes-lwyd
Guilsfield
Foel
Llangadfan
GLYNDWR'S WAY
Pen Coed
Llanerfyl
Cloddiau
Welshpool (Y Trallwng)
Foel Crosses
Heniarth
Cyfronydd
Butt
A5
A494
A5104
A542
A525
A458
A495
A490
A483
B4401
B4391
B4396
B4580
B4393
B4395
B4382
B4389
B4500
B4579
B4402
B4501
B5105
B5437
B4392
B4580
SJ

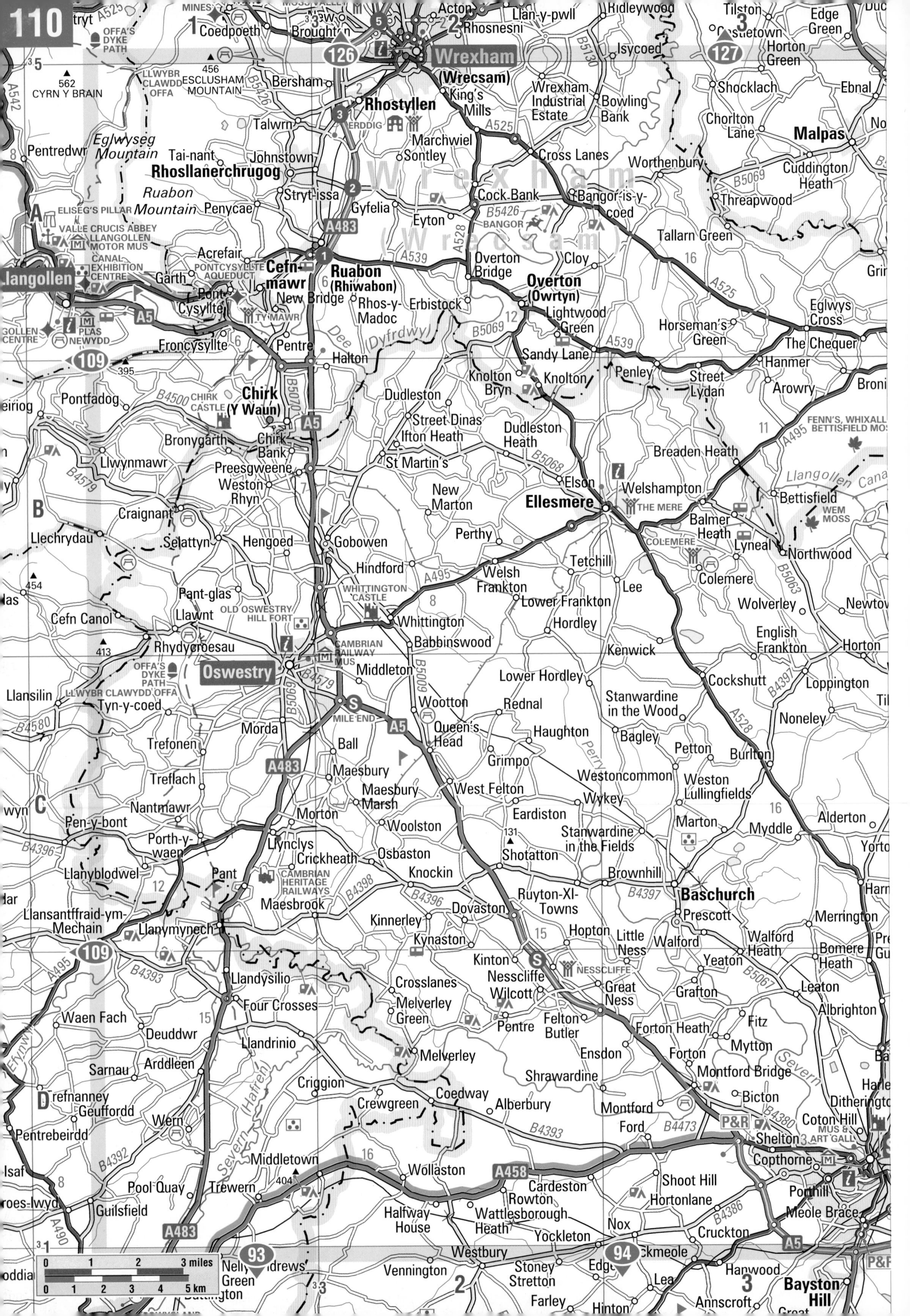

OFFA'S DYKE PATH
Coedpoeth
Broughton
Acton
Llan-y-pwll
Rhosnesni
Ridleywood
Tilston
Edge Green
Castletown
Horton Green
Wrexham
(Wrecsam)
Isycoed
562 CYRN Y BRAIN
456 ESCLUSHAM MOUNTAIN
LLWYBR CLAWDD OFFA
Bersham
Rhostyllen
ERDDIG
King's Mills
Wrexham Industrial Estate
Bowling Bank
Shocklach
Ebnal
Chorlton Lane
Malpas
Talwrn
Marchwiel
Eglwyseg Mountain
Pentredwr
Tai-nant
Johnstown
Sontley
Cross Lanes
Worthenbury
Cuddington Heath
Rhosllanerchrugog
Ruabon Mountain
Stryt-issa
Gyfelia
Cock Bank
Bangor-is-y-coed
Threapwood
Wrexham
(Wrecsam)
ELISEG'S PILLAR
VALLE CRUCIS ABBEY
LLANGOLLEN MOTOR MUS
CANAL EXHIBITION CENTRE
Penycae
Eyton
BANGOR
Tallarn Green
Acrefair
PONTCYSYLLTE AQUEDUCT
Cefn-mawr
Ruabon
(Rhiwabon)
Overton Bridge
Cloy
Llangollen
Garth
Pont Cysyllte
TY MAWR
New Bridge
Rhos-y-Madoc
Erbistock
Overton
(Owrtyn)
Lightwood Green
Horseman's Green
Eglwys Cross
The Chequer
PLAS NEWYDD
Froncysyllte
Pentre
Dee (Dyfrdwy)
Halton
Sandy Lane
Knolton Bryn
Knolton
Penley
Hanmer
Street Lydan
Arowry
Bronington
395
Pontfadog
CHIRK CASTLE
Chirk
(Y Waun)
Dudleston
Dudleston Heath
Street Dinas
Ifton Heath
FENN'S, WHIXALL, BETTISFIELD MOSSES
Bronygarth
Chirk Bank
Llwynmawr
Preesgweene
St Martin's
Breaden Heath
Weston Rhyn
New Marton
Elson
Welshampton
Llangollen Canal
Bettisfield
Craignant
Ellesmere
THE MERE
Balmer Heath
WEM MOSS
Llechrydau
Selattyn
Hengoed
Gobowen
Perthy
COLEMERE
Lyneal
Northwood
454
Hindford
Welsh Frankton
Tetchill
Colemere
Lee
WHITTINGTON CASTLE
Pant-glas
OLD OSWESTRY HILL FORT
Lower Frankton
Wolverley
Cefn Canol
Llawnt
Whittington
Hordley
English Frankton
Horton
413
Rhydycroesau
CAMBRIAN RAILWAY MUS
Babbinswood
Kenwick
OFFA'S DYKE PATH
Oswestry
Middleton
Lower Hordley
Cockshutt
Loppington
Llansilin
LLWYBR CLAWDD OFFA
Tyn-y-coed
MILE END
Wootton
Rednal
Stanwardine in the Wood
Noneley
Morda
Queen's Head
Haughton
Bagley
Trefonen
Ball
Petton
Burlton
Grimpo
Maesbury
Weston Lullingfields
Treflach
Westoncommon
Maesbury Marsh
West Felton
Nantmawr
Wykey
Eardiston
Alderton
Morton
Pen-y-bont
Woolston
Marton
Myddle
Porth-y-waen
Llynclys
131
Stanwardine in the Fields
Shotatton
Crickheath
Osbaston
Llanyblodwel
CAMBRIAN HERITAGE RAILWAYS
Knockin
Brownhill
Pant
Baschurch
Maesbrook
Ruyton-XI-Towns
Dovaston
Prescott
Llansantffraid-ym-Mechain
Kinnerley
Merrington
Llanymynech
Kynaston
Hopton
Little Ness
Walford
Walford Heath
Kinton
NESSCLIFFE
Yeaton
Bomere Heath
Nesscliffe
Llandysilio
Crosslanes
Great Ness
Wilcott
Grafton
Leaton
Four Crosses
Melverley Green
Felton Butler
Pentre
Fitz
Albrighton
Waen Fach
Deuddwr
Forton Heath
Llandrinio
Melverley
Ensdon
Forton
Mytton
Sarnau
Arddleen
Shrawardine
Montford Bridge
Severn
Criggion
Drefnanney
Geuffordd
Crewgreen
Coedway
Alberbury
Montford
Bicton
Dithering
Severn (Hafren)
Wern
Coton Hill
MUS & ART GALL
Pentrebeirdd
Ford
P&R
Shelton
Middletown
Copthorne
Wollaston
Shoot Hill
404
Cardeston
Pool Quay
Trewern
Rowton
Hortonlane
Porthill
Guilsfield
Halfway House
Wattlesborough Heath
Nox
Meole Brace
Cruckton
Yockleton
Westbury
Nelly Andrews Green
Vennington
Stoney Stretton
Hanwood
Bayston Hill
Lea
Farley
Hinton
Annscroft
0 1 2 3 miles
0 1 2 3 4 5 km

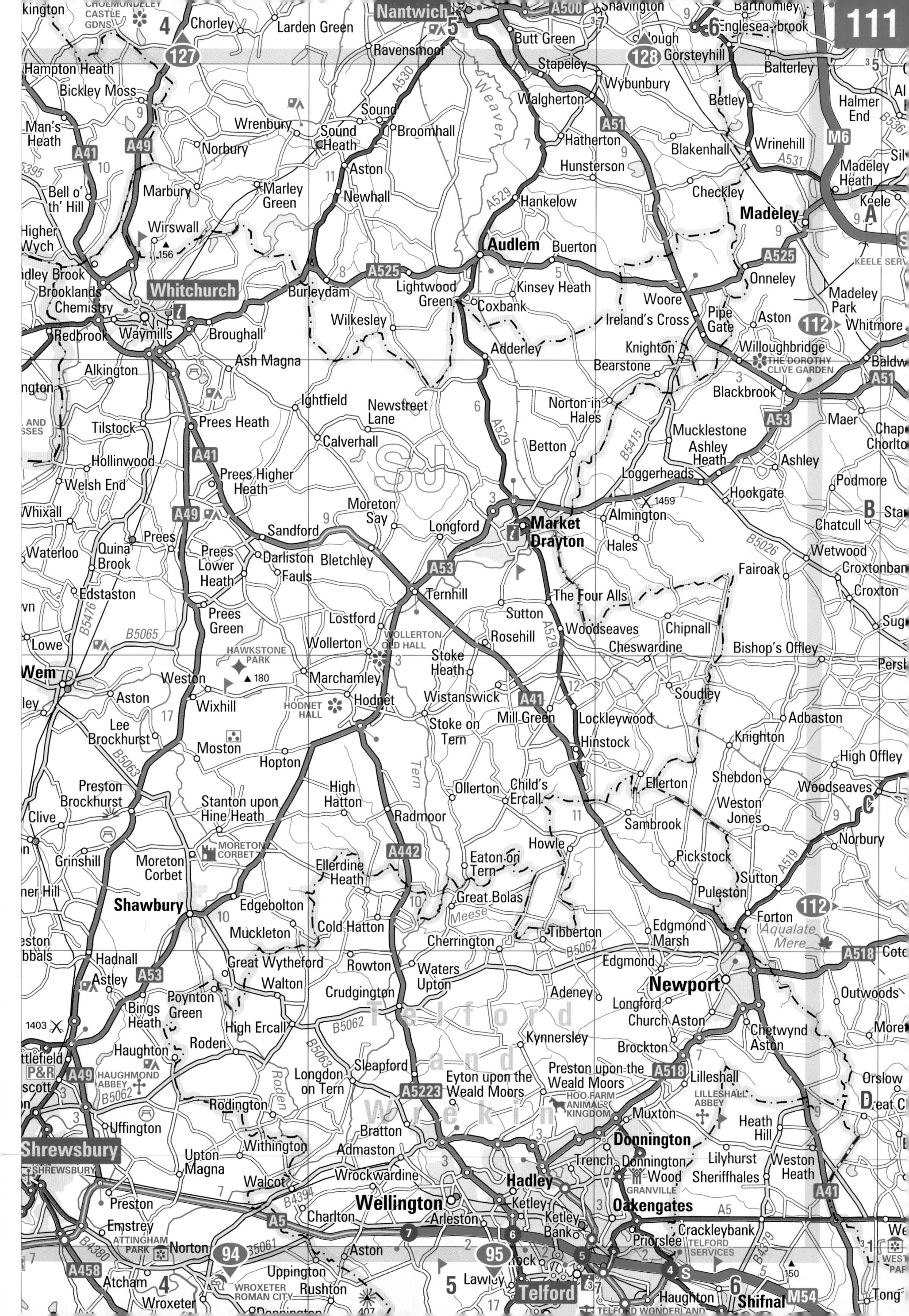
111
Nantwich
Chorley
Larden Green
Ravensmoor
Shavington
Barthomley
Englesea-brook
Butt Green
Stapeley
Wybunbury
Gorsteyhill
Balterley
Hampton Heath
Bickley Moss
Man's Heath
Wrenbury
Sound
Sound Heath
Broomhall
Walgherton
Hatherton
Betley
Halmer End
Wrinehill
Blakenhall
Norbury
Aston
Newhall
Hunsterson
Madeley Heath
Bell o' th' Hill
Marbury
Marley Green
Hankelow
Checkley
Madeley
Keele
Higher Wych
Wirswall
Audlem
Buerton
Whitchurch
Brooklands
Chemistry
Burleydam
Lightwood Green
Kinsey Heath
Woore
Onneley
Madeley Park
Redbrook
Waymills
Broughall
Wilkesley
Coxbank
Ireland's Cross
Pipe Gate
Whitmore
Adderley
Knighton
Willoughbridge
THE DOROTHY CLIVE GARDEN
Ash Magna
Alkington
Bearstone
Blackbrook
Ightfield
Newstreet Lane
Norton in Hales
Tilstock
Prees Heath
Calverhall
Mucklestone
Ashley Heath
Maer
Betton
Ashley
Hollinwood
Prees Higher Heath
Loggerheads
Welsh End
SJ
Hookgate
Podmore
Whixall
Moreton Say
Almington
Market Drayton
Chatcull
Sandford
Longford
Prees
Hales
Waterloo
Quina Brook
Prees Lower Heath
Darliston
Bletchley
Fauls
Wetwood
Fairoak
Croxton
Edstaston
Ternhill
The Four Alls
Prees Green
Lostford
Sutton
Woodseaves
Chipnall
Lowe
Wollerton
WOLLERTON OLD HALL
Rosehill
Cheswardine
Bishop's Offley
HAWKSTONE PARK
Stoke Heath
Wem
Weston
Marchamley
Aston
Wixhill
HODNET HALL
Hodnet
Wistanswick
Mill Green
Soudley
Lee Brockhurst
Stoke on Tern
Lockleywood
Adbaston
Moston
Hinstock
Knighton
Hopton
High Offley
Preston Brockhurst
High Hatton
Ollerton
Child's Ercall
Shebdon
Ellerton
Woodseaves
Clive
Stanton upon Hine Heath
Radmoor
Weston Jones
Sambrook
Howle
Norbury
Grinshill
Moreton Corbet
MORETON CORBET
Ellerdine Heath
Eaton on Tern
Pickstock
Sutton
Shawbury
Edgebolton
Great Bolas
Puleston
Muckleton
Cold Hatton
Meese
Forton
Cherrington
Tibberton
Edgmond Marsh
Aqualate Mere
Hadnall
Great Wytheford
Rowton
Waters Upton
Edgmond
Astley
Walton
Newport
Crudgington
Adeney
Outwoods
Poynton Green
Bings Heath
Longford
Church Aston
Telford and Wrekin
High Ercall
Roden
Kynnersley
Chetwynd Aston
Brockton
Haughton
Preston upon the Weald Moors
Sleapford
Longdon on Tern
Eyton upon the Weald Moors
Lilleshall
Orslow
HAUGHMOND ABBEY
Rodington
HOO FARM ANIMAL KINGDOM
LILLESHALL ABBEY
Uffington
Muxton
Heath Hill
Bratton
Shrewsbury
Withington
Admaston
Donnington
Upton Magna
Trench
Donnington Wood
Lilyhurst
Weston Heath
Wrockwardine
Hadley
GRANVILLE
Sheriffhales
Walcot
Preston
Wellington
Ketley
Oakengates
Charlton
Arleston
Ketley Bank
Crackleybank
Emstrey
Priorslee
ATTINGHAM PARK
Norton
TELFORD SERVICES
Aston
Atcham
Uppington
Lawley
Rushton
Wroxeter
WROXETER ROMAN CITY
Telford
Haughton
Shifnal
Tong
TELFORD WONDERLAND
A500
A530
A51
A531
M6
A49
A41
A525
A529
B5415
A53
B5026
A442
A519
A518
B5062
B5063
A5223
B5062
A458
A5
B4394
B4380
B5061
B4379
M54
B5476
B5065
B5063
127
128
112
94
95

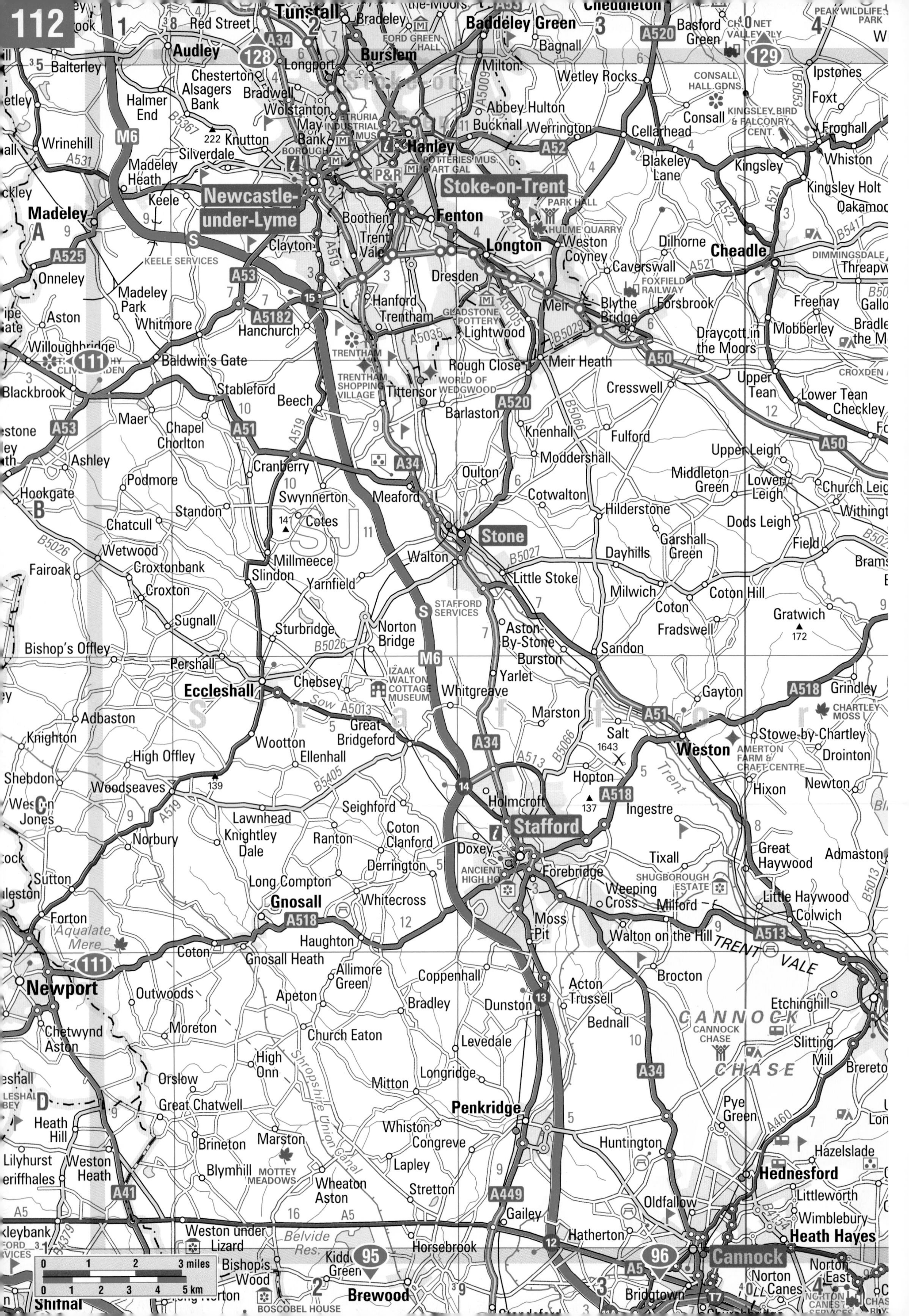

Tunstall
Red Street
Audley
Balterley
Bradeley
Burslem
Longport
Baddeley Green
Bagnall
Cheddleton
Basford Green
Milton
Wetley Rocks
Ipstones
Foxt
Chesterton
Alsagers Bank
Bradwell
Wolstanton
Halmer End
Abbey Hulton
Bucknall
Werrington
Cellarhead
Consall
Froghall
Whiston
Wrinehill
May Bank
Hanley
Knutton
Silverdale
Madeley Heath
Keele
Newcastle-under-Lyme
Stoke-on-Trent
Blakeley Lane
Kingsley
Kingsley Holt
Madeley
Boothen
Fenton
Trent Vale
Clayton
Longton
Weston Coyney
Dilhorne
Cheadle
Caverswall
Onneley
Keele Services
Madeley Park
Whitmore
Hanford
Trentham
Dresden
Meir
Blythe Bridge
Forsbrook
Freehay
Aston
Hanchurch
Lightwood
Draycott in the Moors
Mobberley
Willoughbridge
Baldwin's Gate
Rough Close
Meir Heath
Blackbrook
Stableford
Beech
Tittensor
Barlaston
Cresswell
Upper Tean
Lower Tean
Checkley
Maer
Chapel Chorlton
Knenhall
Fulford
Ashley
Cranberry
Moddershall
Upper Leigh
Podmore
Oulton
Middleton Green
Lower Leigh
Church Leigh
Hookgate
Swynnerton
Meaford
Cotwalton
Hilderstone
Standon
Cotes
Stone
Dods Leigh
Chatcull
Garshall Green
Wetwood
Millmeece
Walton
Dayhills
Field
Fairoak
Croxtonbank
Slindon
Little Stoke
Milwich
Coton Hill
Croxton
Yarnfield
Coton
Sugnall
Stafford Services
Gratwich
Sturbridge
Norton Bridge
Aston-By-Stone
Fradswell
Bishop's Offley
Pershall
Burston
Sandon
Eccleshall
Chebsey
Izaak Walton Cottage Museum
Yarlet
Whitgreave
Gayton
Grindley
Adbaston
Great Bridgeford
Marston
Salt
Weston
Stowe-by-Chartley
Knighton
Wootton
Ellenhall
Drointon
High Offley
Hopton
Shebdon
Woodseaves
Holmcroft
Hixon
Newton
Ingestre
Seighford
Lawnhead
Coton Clanford
Stafford
Norbury
Knightley Dale
Ranton
Doxey
Tixall
Great Haywood
Admaston
Derrington
Forebridge
Shugborough Estate
Long Compton
Sutton
Weeping Cross
Milford
Little Haywood
Gnosall
Whitecross
Forton
Colwich
Moss Pit
Aqualate Mere
Haughton
Walton on the Hill
Trent Vale
Coton
Gnosall Heath
Newport
Allimore Green
Coppenhall
Brocton
Outwoods
Apeton
Acton Trussell
Etchinghill
Bradley
Dunston
Chetwynd Aston
Moreton
Bednall
Cannock Chase
Church Eaton
Levedale
Slitting Mill
High Onn
Longridge
Orslow
Mitton
Great Chatwell
Penkridge
Pye Green
Heath Hill
Whiston
Congreve
Lilyhurst
Weston Heath
Brineton
Marston
Huntington
Hazelslade
Blymhill
Mottey Meadows
Lapley
Wheaton Aston
Hednesford
Stretton
Littleworth
Oldfallow
Gailey
Wimblebury
Weston under Lizard
Belvide Res.
Horsebrook
Hatherton
Heath Hayes
Bishop's Wood
Kiddemore Green
Cannock
Norton East
Brewood
Bridgtown
Norton Canes
Shifnal
Boscobel House
Shropshire Union Canal
M6
A34
A53
A50
A51
A518
A520
A519
A5
A41
A449
A513
A525
A5182
A52
A521
A522
A460
A5013
B5026
B5027
B5066
B5405
0 1 2 3 miles
0 1 2 3 4 5 km

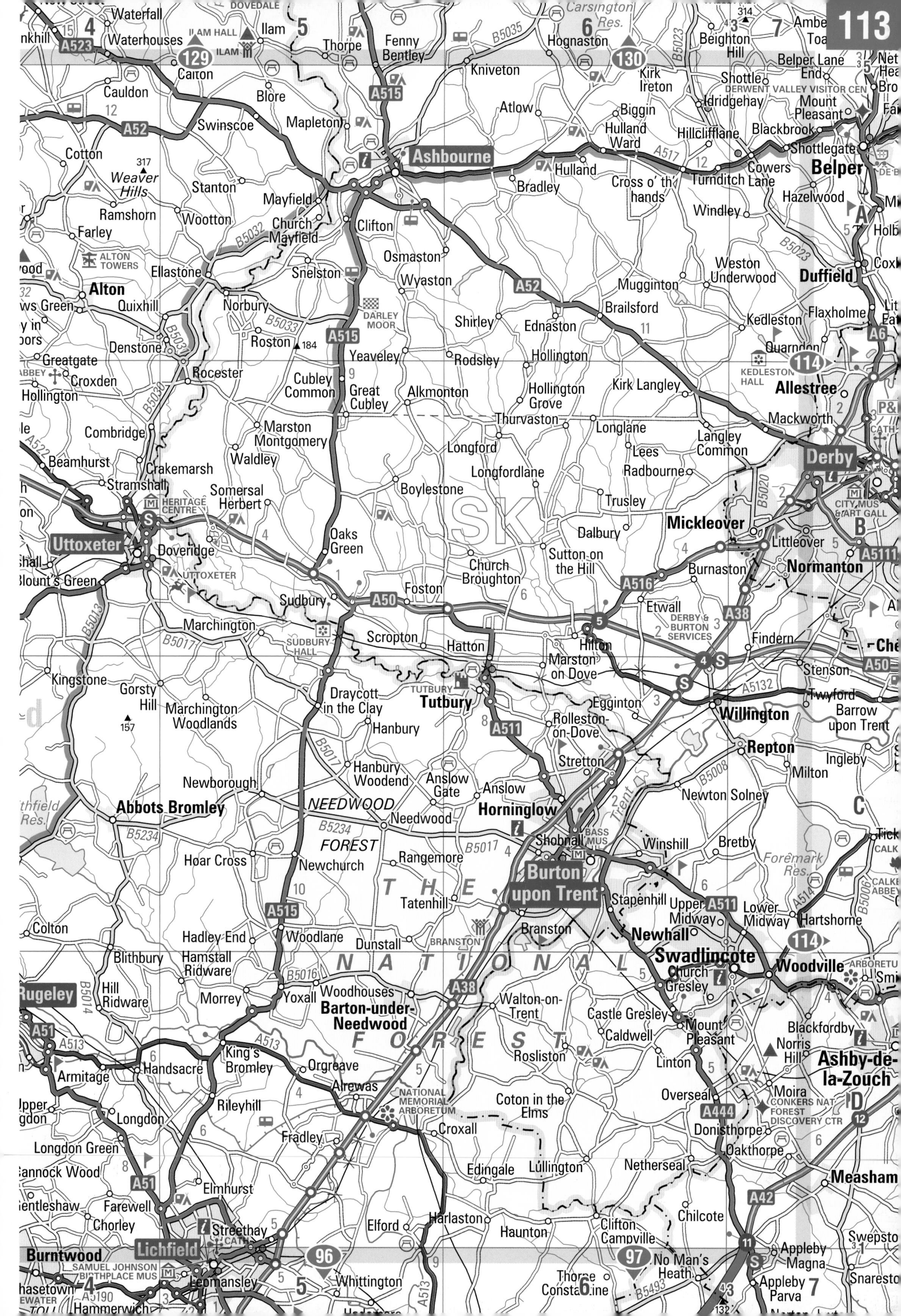
Waterfall
Waterhouses
ILAM HALL
Ilam
Thorpe
Fenny Bentley
Carsington Res.
Hognaston
Beighton Hill
Ambe
Belper Lane End
Calton
Cauldon
Blore
Kniveton
Kirk Ireton
Shottle
DERWENT VALLEY VISITOR CEN
Idridgehay
Mount Pleasant
Swinscoe
Mapleton
Atlow
Biggin
Hulland Ward
Hillcliffiane
Blackbrook
Shottlegate
Cotton
Weaver Hills
Ashbourne
Hulland
Cowers
Belper
Stanton
Bradley
Cross o' th' hands
Turnditch Lane
Hazelwood
Mayfield
Ramshorn
Wootton
Church Mayfield
Clifton
Windley
Farley
ALTON TOWERS
Osmaston
Weston Underwood
Duffield
Ellastone
Snelston
Wyaston
Mugginton
Alton
Quixhill
Norbury
DARLEY MOOR
Shirley
Ednaston
Brailsford
Kedleston
Flaxholme
Denstone
Roston
Yeaveley
Rodsley
Hollington
Quarndon
Greatgate
Croxden
Rocester
Cubley Common
Great Cubley
Alkmonton
Hollington Grove
Kirk Langley
KEDLESTON HALL
Allestree
Hollington
Marston Montgomery
Thurvaston
Longlane
Langley Common
Mackworth
Combridge
Longford
Lees
Radbourne
Derby
Beamhurst
Crakemarsh
Waldley
Longfordlane
Stramshall
Somersal Herbert
Boylestone
Trusley
HERITAGE CENTRE
CITY MUS & ART GALL
Uttoxeter
Doveridge
Oaks Green
SK
Dalbury
Mickleover
Littleover
UTTOXETER
Church Broughton
Sutton on the Hill
Burnaston
Normanton
Blount's Green
Foston
Etwall
DERBY & BURTON SERVICES
Sudbury
Marchington
SUDBURY HALL
Scropton
Hatton
Hilton
Findern
Marston on Dove
Stenson
Kingstone
Gorsty Hill
Draycott in the Clay
TUTBURY
Tutbury
Egginton
Willington
Twyford
Barrow upon Trent
Marchington Woodlands
Hanbury
Rolleston-on-Dove
Repton
Ingleby
Stretton
Milton
Newborough
Hanbury Woodend
Anslow Gate
Anslow
Newton Solney
Abbots Bromley
NEEDWOOD
Needwood
Horninglow
FOREST
Shobnall
BASS MUS
Winshill
Bretby
Hoar Cross
Newchurch
Rangemore
Foremark Res.
Burton upon Trent
THE
Tatenhill
Stapenhill
Upper Midway
Lower Midway
Hartshorne
Colton
Hadley End
Woodlane
Dunstall
BRANSTON
Branston
Newhall
Swadlincote
Woodville
NATIONAL
Blithbury
Hamstall Ridware
Church Gresley
Hill Ridware
Morrey
Yoxall
Woodhouses
Barton-under-Needwood
Walton-on-Trent
Castle Gresley
Rugeley
Caldwell
Mount Pleasant
Blackfordby
FOREST
Norris Hill
Ashby-de-la-Zouch
Armitage
Handsacre
King's Bromley
Orgreave
Rosliston
Linton
Alrewas
Overseal
Moira
NATIONAL MEMORIAL ARBORETUM
Coton in the Elms
CONKERS NAT FOREST DISCOVERY CTR
Longdon
Rileyhill
Donisthorpe
Fradley
Croxall
Oakthorpe
Longdon Green
Edingale
Lullington
Netherseal
Cannock Wood
Measham
Elmhurst
Gentleshaw
Farewell
Chorley
Streethay
Elford
Harlaston
Haunton
Chilcote
Clifton Campville
Swepsto
Burntwood
Lichfield
CATH
No Man's Heath
Appleby Magna
SAMUEL JOHNSON BIRTHPLACE MUS
Leomansley
Whittington
Thorpe Constantine
Appleby Parva
Snarestone
Chasetown
Hammerwich

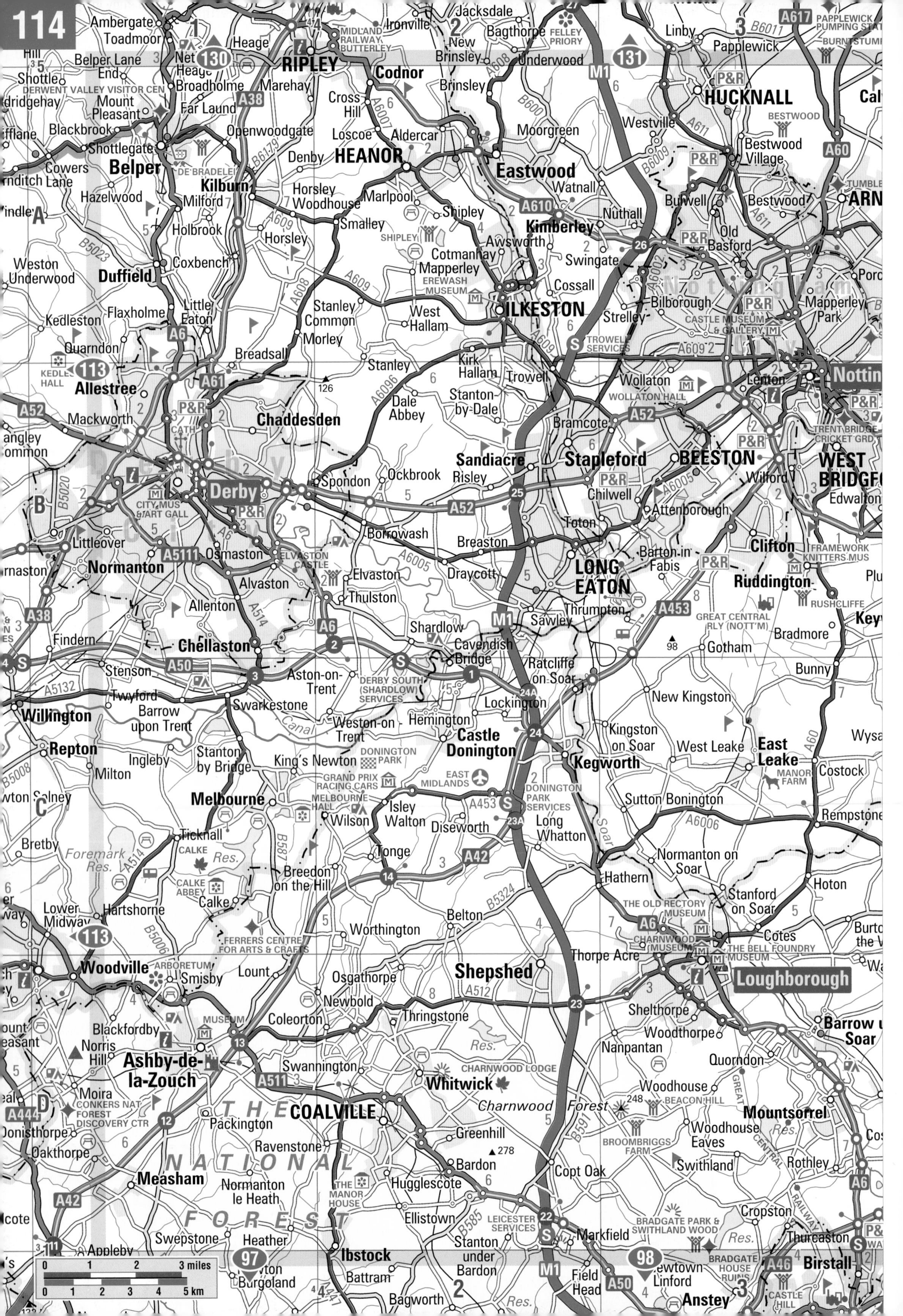

Ambergate
Toadmoor
Heage
Jacksdale
Ironville
Bagthorpe
FELLEY PRIORY
Linby
Papplewick
A617
PAPPLEWICK PUMPING STATION
Belper Lane End
Net Heage
130
RIPLEY
MIDLAND RAILWAY BUTTERLEY
New Brinsley
Underwood
131
Shottle
DERWENT VALLEY VISITOR CENTRE
Broadholme
Marehay
Codnor
Brinsley
M1
HUCKNALL
Mount Pleasant
Far Laund
A38
Cross Hill
A6007
B600
Moorgreen
Westville
BESTWOOD
Blackbrook
Openwoodgate
Loscoe
Aldercar
Bestwood Village
Shottlegate
A611
A60
Cowers Lane
Belper
DE BRADELEI
B6179
Denby
HEANOR
Eastwood
B6009
P&R
Kilburn
Watnall
Hazelwood
Milford
Horsley Woodhouse
Marlpool
A610
Bulwell
Bestwood
ARN
Shipley
Nuthall
Holbrook
A609
Smalley
SHIPLEY
Kimberley
Old Basford
Horsley
Awsworth
26
Weston Underwood
B5023
Coxbench
Cotmanhay
Mapperley
Swingate
Duffield
EREWASH MUSEUM
Cossall
A6002
Nottingham
Porc
Little Eaton
Flaxholme
A608
Stanley Common
West Hallam
ILKESTON
Strelley
Bilborough
Mapperley Park
Kedleston
A6
CASTLE MUSEUM & GALLERY
Quarndon
Morley
TROWELL SERVICES
City
KEDLESTON HALL
113
Breadsall
Stanley
Kirk Hallam
Trowell
Wollaton
Lenton
Nottingham
Allestree
A61
126
A6096
Stanton-by-Dale
WOLLATON HALL
A52
Mackworth
Chaddesden
Dale Abbey
Bramcote
Langley Common
CATH
TRENT BRIDGE CRICKET GRD
Derby
Sandiacre
Stapleford
BEESTON
WEST BRIDGFORD
Risley
Wilford
B5020
Spondon
Ockbrook
Chilwell
Derby
CITY MUS & ART GALL
A6005
Attenborough
Edwalton
Toton
Littleover
Borrowash
Breaston
Clifton
A5111
Osmaston
ELVASTON CASTLE
Barton in Fabis
FRAMEWORK KNITTERS MUS
Normanton
LONG EATON
Elvaston
Draycott
Ruddington
Alvaston
Thulston
EATON
A514
Allenton
Thrumpton
RUSHCLIFFE
A38
Sawley
A453
GREAT CENTRAL RLY (NOTT'M)
Findern
Shardlow
Bradmore
Chellaston
Cavendish Bridge
98
Gotham
Stenson
A50
Ratcliffe on Soar
Bunny
A5132
Aston-on-Trent
DERBY SOUTH (SHARDLOW) SERVICES
24A
Twyford
Lockington
New Kingston
Willington
Barrow upon Trent
Swarkestone
Canal
Weston-on-Trent
Hemington
Kingston on Soar
Castle Donington
24
West Leake
East Leake
Repton
Ingleby
Stanton by Bridge
King's Newton
DONINGTON PARK
Kegworth
Milton
GRAND PRIX RACING CARS
EAST MIDLANDS
Costock
B5008
MANOR FARM
DONINGTON PARK SERVICES
Melbourne
MELBOURNE HALL
Sutton Bonington
Isley Walton
Wilson
Long Whatton
Rempstone
Diseworth
A6006
Ticknall
23A
Soar
Bretby
Foremark Res.
CALKE
Tonge
A42
Normanton on Soar
Res.
Breedon on the Hill
Hathern
Hoton
14
CALKE ABBEY
Calke
B5324
Lower Midway
Hartshorne
Stanford on Soar
THE OLD RECTORY MUSEUM
Belton
Worthington
Cotes
113
FERRERS CENTRE FOR ARTS & CRAFTS
CHARNWOOD MUSEUM
THE BELL FOUNDRY MUSEUM
Woodville
ARBORETUM
Lount
Smisby
Thorpe Acre
Osgathorpe
Shepshed
Loughborough
Newbold
A512
Coleorton
Thringstone
23
Shelthorpe
Barrow upon Soar
Blackfordby
MUSEUM
Woodthorpe
Norris Hill
Nanpantan
Ashby-de-la-Zouch
13
Swannington
CHARNWOOD LODGE
Quorndon
A511
Whitwick
Moira
Woodhouse
CONKERS NAT FOREST DISCOVERY CTR
THE
COALVILLE
Charnwood Forest
248
BEACON HILL
Mountsorrel
A444
12
Packington
Woodhouse Eaves
Donisthorpe
Greenhill
BROOMBRIGGS FARM
Oakthorpe
Ravenstone
NATIONAL
278
Swithland
Rothley
Res.
Measham
Normanton le Heath
Bardon
Copt Oak
THE MANOR HOUSE
Hugglescote
GREAT CENTRAL RAILWAY
A42
FOREST
Ellistown
Cropston
LEICESTER FOREST SERVICES
BRADGATE PARK & SWITHLAND WOOD
B585
22
Swepstone
Heather
Markfield
Thurcaston
Appleby
Stanton under Bardon
11
97
Ibstock
98
BRADGATE HOUSE RUINS
Birstall
A46
Newton Burgoland
Battram
Field Head
Newtown Linford
A50
CASTLE HILL
Bagworth
Res.
Anstey
0 1 2 3 miles
0 1 2 3 4 5 km

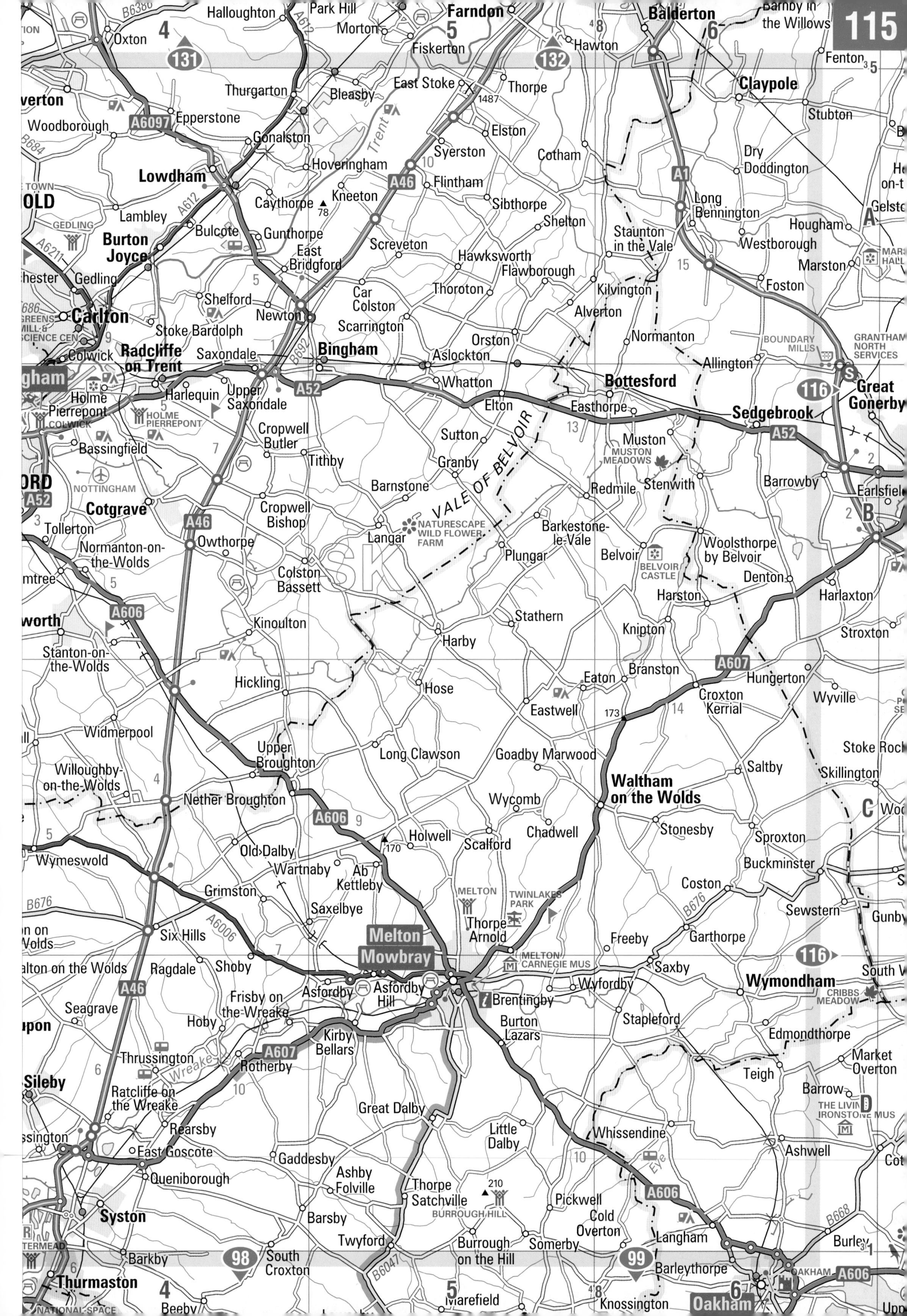
Halloughton
Park Hill
Farndon
Balderton
Barnby in the Willows
Oxton
Morton
Fiskerton
Hawton
Fenton
131
132
Thurgarton
Bleasby
East Stoke
Thorpe
Claypole
Woodborough
Epperstone
Elston
Stubton
Gonalston
Syerston
Cotham
Dry Doddington
Hoveringham
Lowdham
Flintham
Lambley
Caythorpe
Kneeton
Sibthorpe
Long Bennington
Shelton
Gedling
Bulcote
Gunthorpe
Screveton
Staunton in the Vale
Hougham
Westborough
Burton Joyce
East Bridgford
Hawksworth
Flawborough
Marston
Gedling
Thoroton
Kilvington
Foston
Shelford
Car Colston
Carlton
Newton
Alverton
Stoke Bardolph
Scarrington
Orston
Normanton
Boundary Mills
Grantham North Services
Colwick
Radcliffe on Trent
Saxondale
Bingham
Aslockton
Allington
Whatton
Bottesford
Great Gonerby
Holme Pierrepont
Harlequin
Upper Saxondale
Elton
Easthorpe
Sedgebrook
Colwick
Holme Pierrepont
Cropwell Butler
Sutton
Muston
Muston Meadows
Bassingfield
Tithby
Granby
Barrowby
Nottingham
Barnstone
Redmile
Stenwith
Earlsfield
Cotgrave
Cropwell Bishop
Vale of Belvoir
Tollerton
Naturescape Wild Flower Farm
Langar
Barkestone-le-Vale
Woolsthorpe by Belvoir
Owthorpe
Normanton-on-the-Wolds
Plungar
Belvoir
Belvoir Castle
Colston Bassett
Denton
Harston
Harlaxton
Stathern
Kinoulton
Knipton
Stroxton
Harby
Stanton-on-the-Wolds
Hickling
Hose
Eaton
Branston
Hungerton
Croxton Kerrial
Wyville
Eastwell
Widmerpool
Upper Broughton
Long Clawson
Goadby Marwood
Saltby
Stoke Rochford
Willoughby-on-the-Wolds
Skillington
Waltham on the Wolds
Nether Broughton
Wycomb
Stonesby
Chadwell
Holwell
Scalford
Sproxton
Old Dalby
Wymeswold
Wartnaby
Ab Kettleby
Buckminster
Coston
Grimston
Melton
Twinlakes Park
Saxelbye
Sewstern
Thorpe Arnold
Six Hills
Melton Mowbray
Freeby
Garthorpe
Melton Carnegie Mus
Ragdale
Shoby
Saxby
Wymondham
Asfordby
Asfordby Hill
Wyfordby
Cribbs Meadow
Frisby on the Wreake
Brentingby
Stapleford
Seagrave
Hoby
Kirby Bellars
Burton Lazars
Edmondthorpe
Thrussington
Rotherby
Market Overton
Teigh
Sileby
Ratcliffe on the Wreake
Barrow
The Living Ironstone Mus
Great Dalby
Rearsby
Little Dalby
Whissendine
Ashwell
East Goscote
Gaddesby
Queniborough
Ashby Folville
Thorpe Satchville
Pickwell
Cold Overton
Syston
Barsby
Burrough Hill
Langham
Burley
Twyford
Burrough on the Hill
Somerby
Barkby
South Croxton
Barleythorpe
Oakham
Thurmaston
Beeby
Marefield
Knossington
National Space
98
99
116

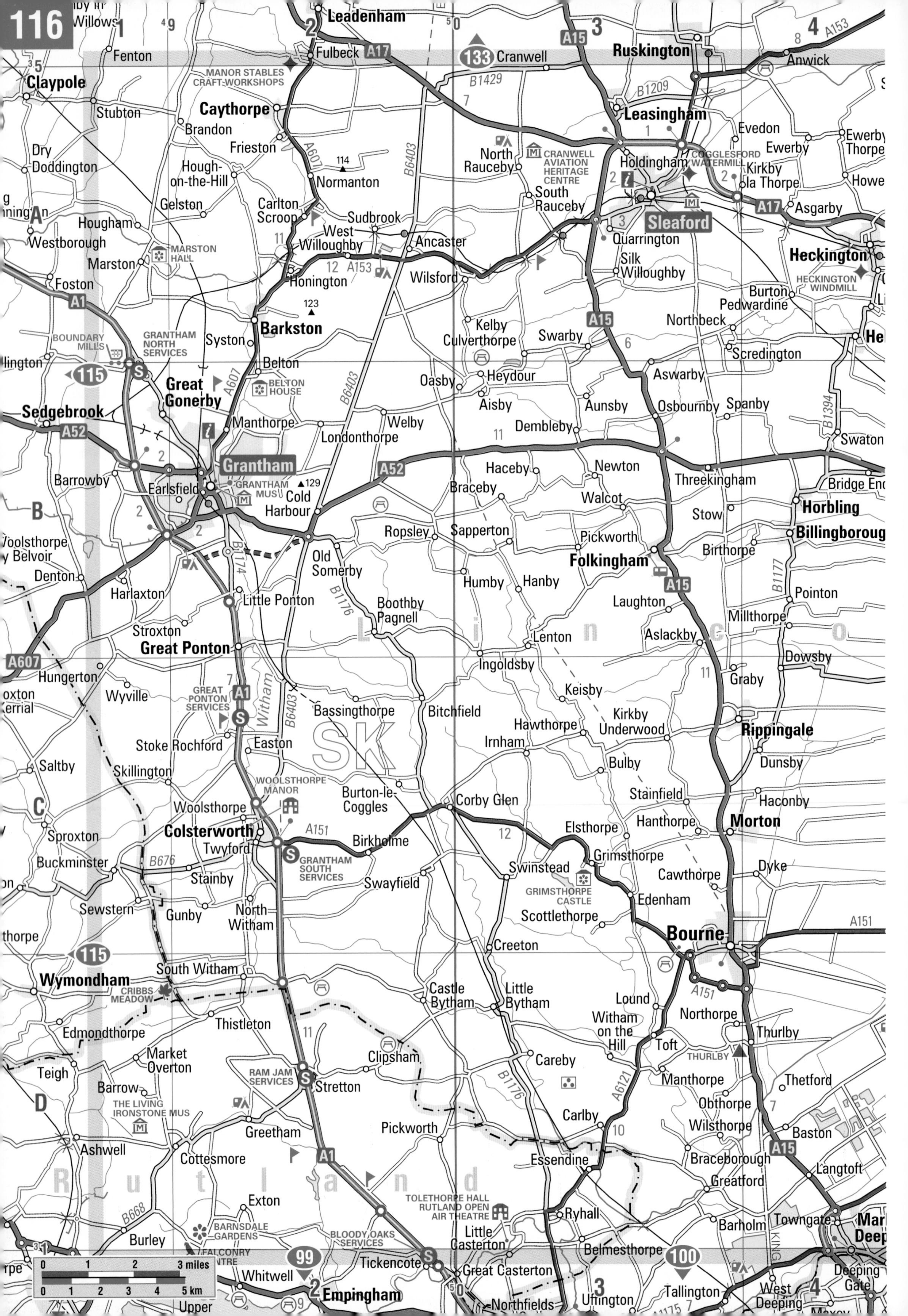
Leadenham
Fulbeck
Fenton
Claypole
MANOR STABLES CRAFT WORKSHOPS
Stubton
Caythorpe
Brandon
Frieston
Dry Doddington
Hough-on-the-Hill
Normanton
Gelston
Carlton Scroop
Hougham
Westborough
Sudbrook
West Willoughby
Ancaster
MARSTON HALL
Marston
Honington
Wilsford
Foston
Barkston
Syston
BOUNDARY MILLS
GRANTHAM NORTH SERVICES
Belton
BELTON HOUSE
Great Gonerby
Sedgebrook
Manthorpe
Londonthorpe
Welby
Barrowby
Grantham
Earlsfield
GRANTHAM MUS
Cold Harbour
Woolsthorpe by Belvoir
Denton
Harlaxton
Little Ponton
Old Somerby
Ropsley
Stroxton
Great Ponton
Boothby Pagnell
Hungerton
Wyville
GREAT PONTON SERVICES
Witham
Bassingthorpe
Bitchfield
Stoke Rochford
Easton
Saltby
Skillington
WOOLSTHORPE MANOR
Burton-le-Coggles
Corby Glen
Woolsthorpe
Colsterworth
Sproxton
Twyford
Birkholme
Buckminster
Stainby
GRANTHAM SOUTH SERVICES
Swayfield
Sewstern
Gunby
North Witham
Wymondham
CRIBBS MEADOW
South Witham
Castle Bytham
Little Bytham
Edmondthorpe
Thistleton
Market Overton
Clipsham
Teigh
Barrow
RAM JAM SERVICES
Stretton
THE LIVING IRONSTONE MUS
Greetham
Pickworth
Ashwell
Cottesmore
Exton
Burley
BARNSDALE GARDENS
FALCONRY CENTRE
BLOODY OAKS SERVICES
Whitwell
Tickencote
Empingham
Upper
Rutland
Cranwell
Ruskington
Anwick
Leasingham
North Rauceby
CRANWELL AVIATION HERITAGE CENTRE
South Rauceby
Holdingham
COGGLESFORD WATERMILL
Evedon
Ewerby
Ewerby Thorpe
Kirkby la Thorpe
Howell
Asgarby
Sleaford
Quarrington
Silk Willoughby
Heckington
HECKINGTON WINDMILL
Burton Pedwardine
Northbeck
Kelby
Culverthorpe
Swarby
Scredington
Heydour
Oasby
Aisby
Aswarby
Aunsby
Osbournby
Spanby
Dembleby
Swaton
Haceby
Newton
Threekingham
Braceby
Walcot
Bridge End
Horbling
Billingborough
Stow
Sapperton
Pickworth
Folkingham
Birthorpe
Humby
Hanby
Laughton
Pointon
Millthorpe
Lenton
Aslackby
Ingoldsby
Dowsby
Graby
Keisby
Kirkby Underwood
Hawthorpe
Irnham
Rippingale
Bulby
Dunsby
Stainfield
Haconby
Hanthorpe
Morton
Elsthorpe
Grimsthorpe
Swinstead
Cawthorpe
Dyke
GRIMSTHORPE CASTLE
Edenham
Scottlethorpe
Bourne
Creeton
Lound
Northorpe
Witham on the Hill
Thurlby
Toft
THURLBY
Careby
Manthorpe
Thetford
Obthorpe
Carlby
Wilsthorpe
Baston
Essendine
Braceborough
Langtoft
Greatford
TOLETHORPE HALL RUTLAND OPEN AIR THEATRE
Ryhall
Barholm
Towngate
Little Casterton
Belmesthorpe
Great Casterton
Tallington
West Deeping
Deeping Gate
Northfields
Uffington
0 1 2 3 miles
0 1 2 3 4 5 km

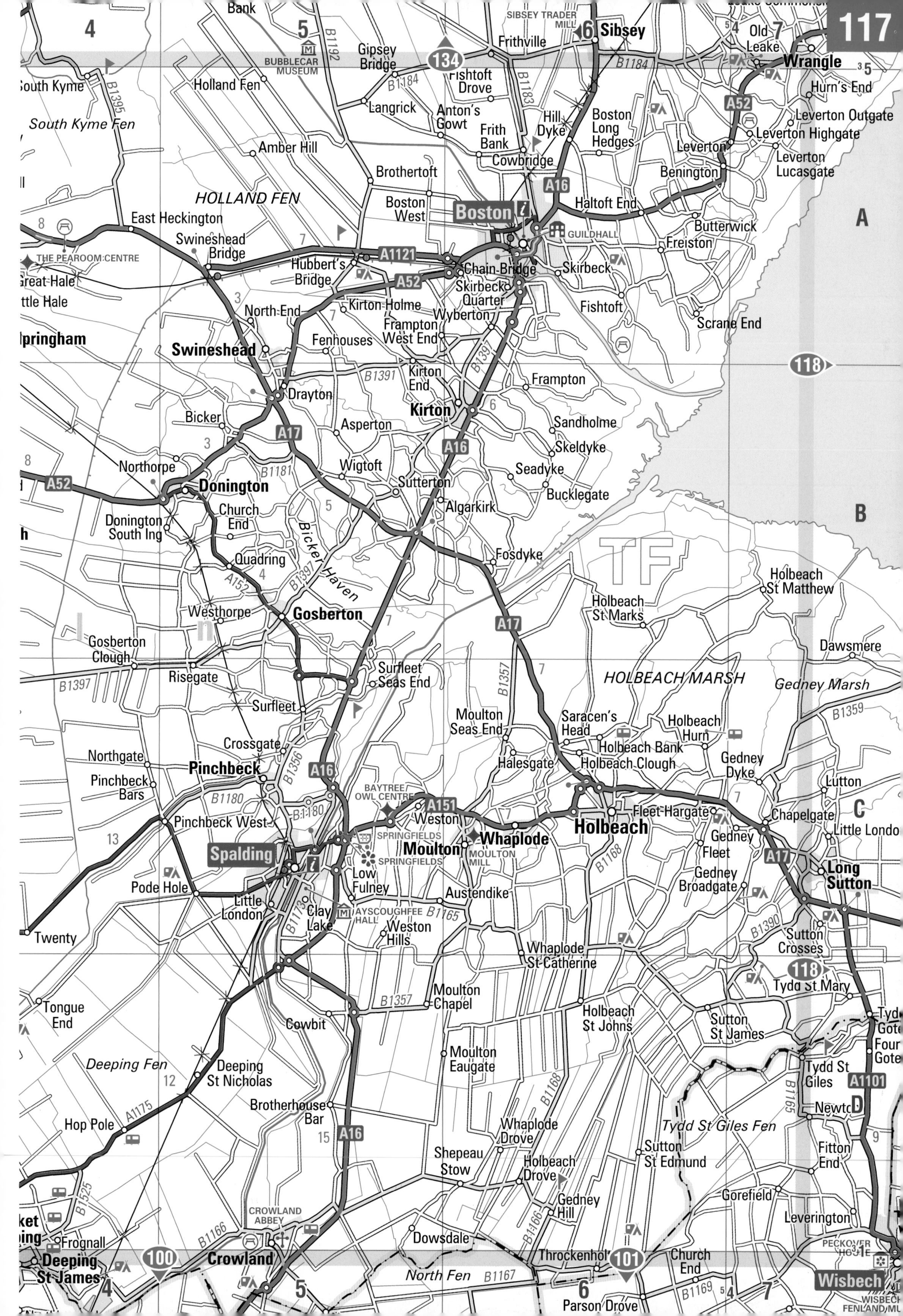

Sibsey
Frithville
Gipsey Bridge
Fishtoft Drove
Langrick
Anton's Gowt
Frith Bank
Hill Dyke
Boston Long Hedges
Wrangle
Old Leake
Hurn's End
Leverton Outgate
Leverton Highgate
Leverton
Leverton Lucasgate
Benington
South Kyme
South Kyme Fen
Holland Fen
Amber Hill
Brothertoft
Cowbridge
HOLLAND FEN
Boston West
Boston
Haltoft End
Butterwick
Freiston
East Heckington
Swineshead Bridge
THE PEAROOM CENTRE
GUILDHALL
BUBBLECAR MUSEUM
SIBSEY TRADER MILL
Hubbert's Bridge
Chain Bridge
Skirbeck
Skirbeck Quarter
Fishtoft
Scrane End
Great Hale
Little Hale
Kirton Holme
North End
Wyberton
Frampton West End
Fenhouses
Swineshead
Kirton End
Frampton
Drayton
Kirton
Bicker
Asperton
Sandholme
Skeldyke
Northorpe
Wigtoft
Seadyke
Donington
Sutterton
Bucklegate
Church End
Algarkirk
Donington South Ing
Quadring
Bicker Haven
Fosdyke
Holbeach St Matthew
Holbeach St Marks
Westhorpe
Gosberton
Gosberton Clough
Dawsmere
Risegate
Surfleet Seas End
HOLBEACH MARSH
Gedney Marsh
Surfleet
Moulton Seas End
Saracen's Head
Holbeach Hurn
Holbeach Bank
Crossgate
Northgate
Halesgate
Holbeach Clough
Gedney Dyke
Pinchbeck
Pinchbeck Bars
Lutton
BAYTREE OWL CENTRE
Weston
Fleet Hargate
Chapelgate
Pinchbeck West
Whaplode
Holbeach
Gedney
Little London
SPRINGFIELDS
Spalding
Moulton
MOULTON MILL
Fleet
Long Sutton
Pode Hole
Low Fulney
Gedney Broadgate
Austendike
Little London
Clay Lake
AYSCOUGHFEE HALL
Weston Hills
Twenty
Sutton Crosses
Whaplode St Catherine
Tydd St Mary
Moulton Chapel
Tongue End
Holbeach St Johns
Cowbit
Sutton St James
Moulton Eaugate
Deeping Fen
Deeping St Nicholas
Tydd St Giles
Brotherhouse Bar
Newton
Hop Pole
Whaplode Drove
Tydd St Giles Fen
Shepeau Stow
Sutton St Edmund
Fitton End
Holbeach Drove
Gedney Hill
Gorefield
Leverington
CROWLAND ABBEY
Frognall
Dowsdale
Deeping St James
Crowland
Throckenholt
Church End
PECKOVER HOUSE
Wisbech
North Fen
Parson Drove
TF
A
B
C
D
A16
A17
A52
A1121
A151
A1101
A1175
B1184
B1183
B1192
B1395
B1391
B1397
B1181
A152
B1357
B1359
B1356
B1180
B1168
B1165
B1173
B1390
B1166
B1525
B1167
B1169

134
118
118
100
101

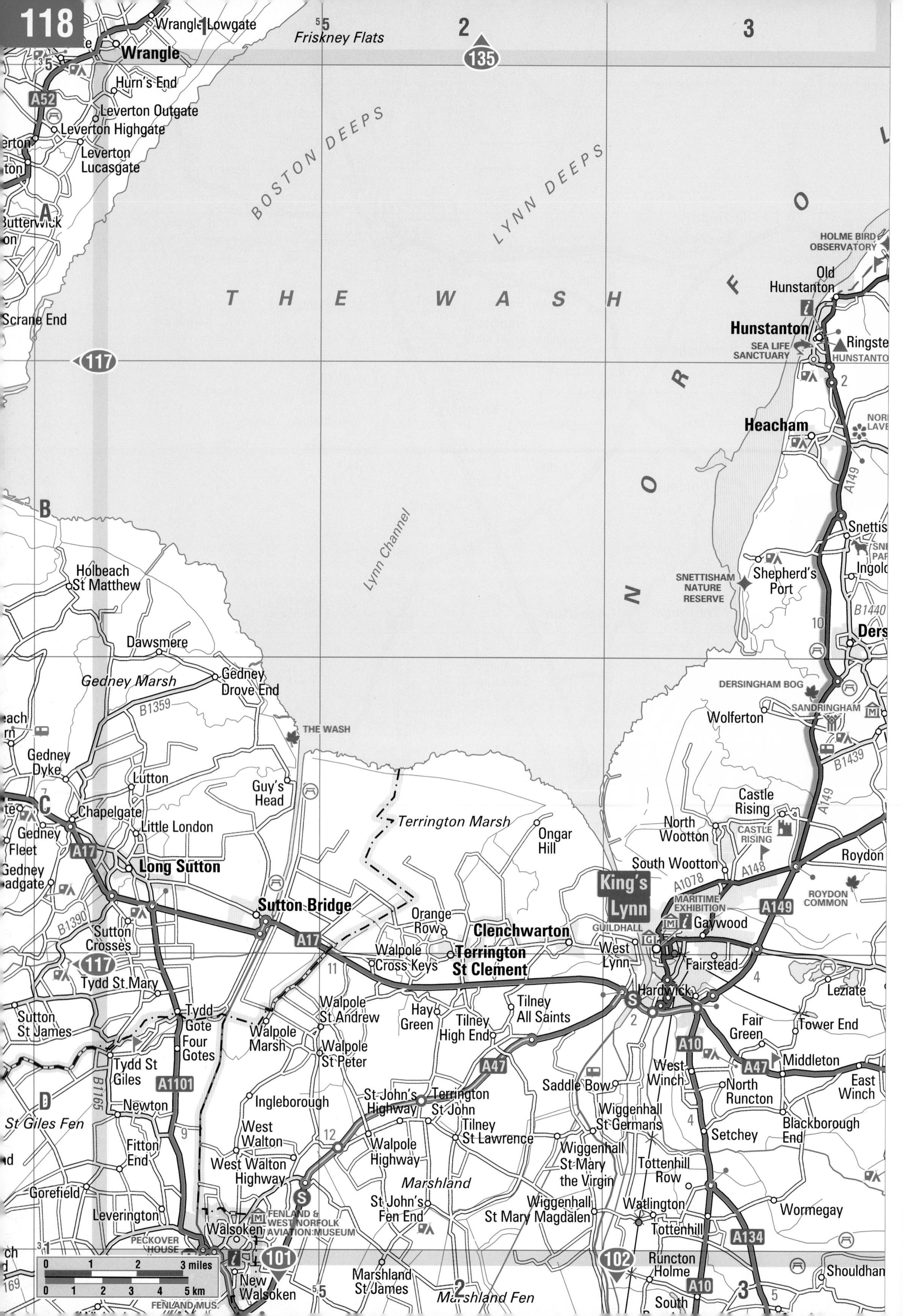

1   5 Friskney Flats   2   3

Wrangle Lowgate
Wrangle
Hurn's End
Leverton Outgate
Leverton Highgate
Leverton Lucasgate
A52
Butterwick
Scrane End

135

BOSTON DEEPS

LYNN DEEPS

A

T H E   W A S H

N O R F O

HOLME BIRD OBSERVATORY
Old Hunstanton
Hunstanton
SEA LIFE SANCTUARY
Ringste
HUNSTANTO

117

B

Lynn Channel

Heacham

NOR
LAVE

A149

Snettis
SNE
PAR
Ingold

Snettisham Port
Shepherd's Port
SNETTISHAM NATURE RESERVE

B1440

Ders

10

Holbeach St Matthew

Dawsmere

Gedney Marsh
Gedney Drove End
B1359

DERSINGHAM BOG
SANDRINGHAM

Wolferton

Gedney Dyke
Lutton

THE WASH

Guy's Head

Terrington Marsh

Ongar Hill

North Wootton

Castle Rising
CASTLE RISING

B1439

A149

C
Chapelgate
Gedney Fleet
A17
Gedney adgate

Little London
Long Sutton

Sutton Bridge

South Wootton

King's Lynn
MARITIME EXHIBITION
GUILDHALL

Roydon

ROYDON COMMON

A1078
A148

A149

B1390
Sutton Crosses

A17
Orange Row

11

Walpole Cross Keys

Clenchwarton
Terrington St Clement

West Lynn

GH
Gaywood

Hardwick
Fairstead

4

Leziate

117
Tydd St Mary

Sutton St James

Tydd Gote Four Gotes

Walpole St Andrew
Walpole Marsh

Hay Green

Walpole St Peter

Tilney High End

Tilney All Saints

S
2

Fair Green

West Winch

Tower End

Tydd St Giles

A1101

Newton

Ingleborough

St John's Highway

Terrington St John

Tilney St Lawrence

Saddle Bow

A47

North Runcton

Middleton

East Winch

D
St Giles Fen

Fitton End

B165

9

West Walton

12

Walpole Highway

Wiggenhall St Germans

Setchey

Blackborough End

Gorefield
Leverington

West Walton Highway

S

Marshland

St John's Fen End

Wiggenhall St Mary the Virgin

Wiggenhall St Mary Magdalen

Tottenhill Row

Watlington

Tottenhill

Wormegay

A134

PECKOVER HOUSE

FENLAND & WEST NORFOLK AVIATION MUSEUM

Walsoken

101

New Walsoken

Marshland St James

5

Marshland Fen

2

St Mary South

102

Runcton Holme

A10

3

5

Shouldha

169

0   1   2   3 miles
0   1   2   3   4   5 km

FENLAND MUS.

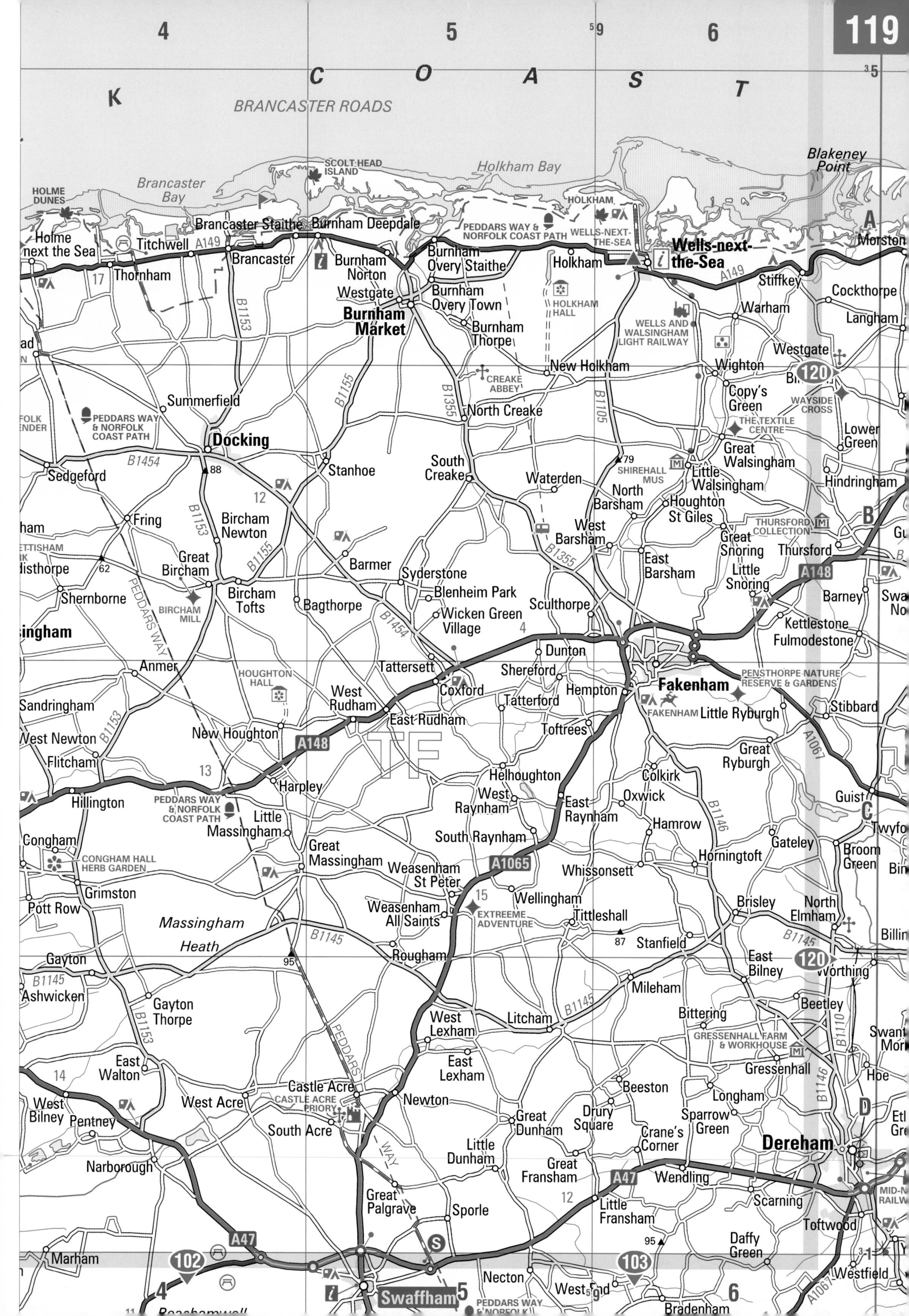

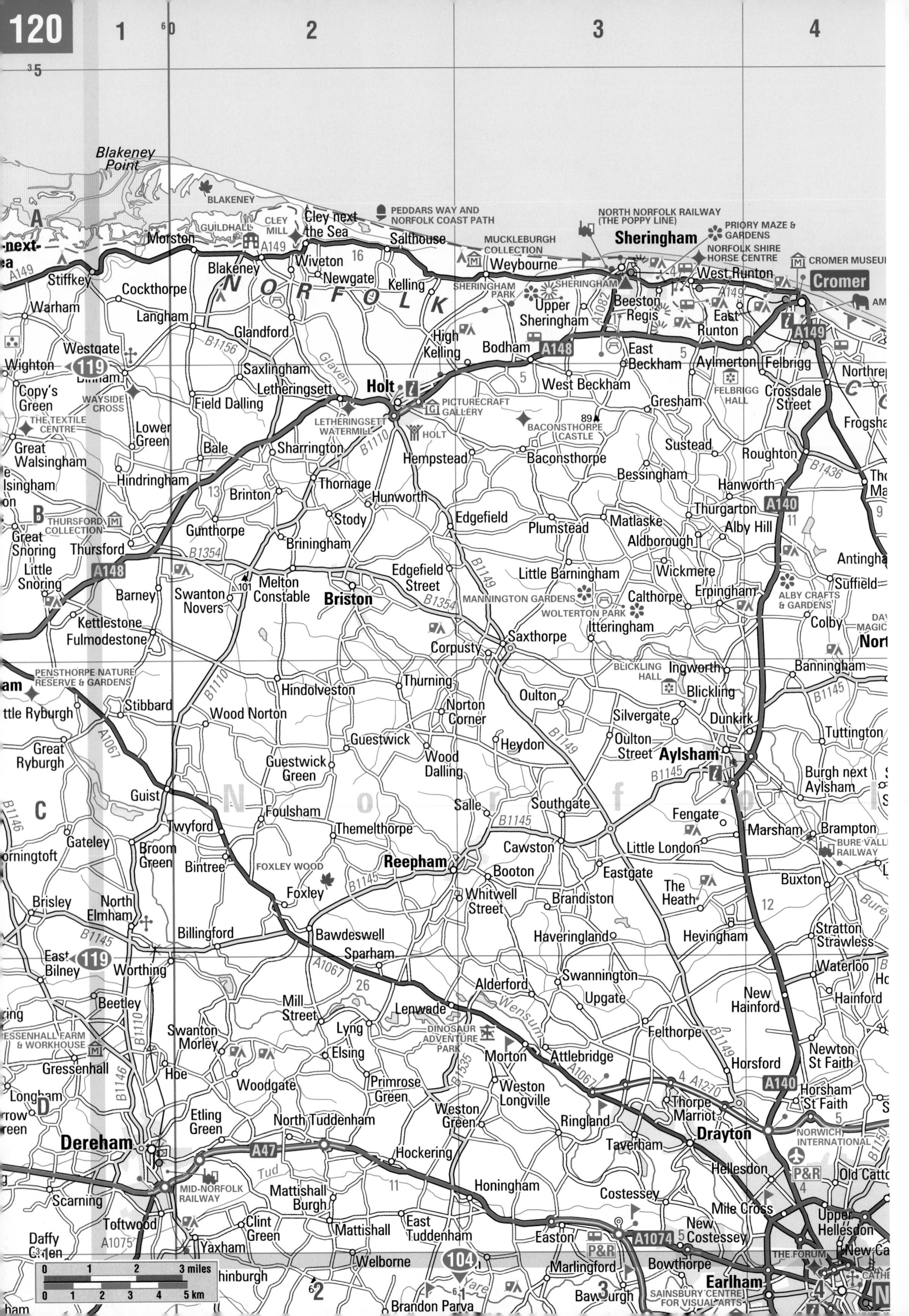
1
2
3
4
A
B
C
D
Blakeney Point
BLAKENEY
GUILDHALL
CLEY MILL
Cley next the Sea
PEDDARS WAY AND NORFOLK COAST PATH
Salthouse
NORTH NORFOLK RAILWAY (THE POPPY LINE)
MUCKLEBURGH COLLECTION
Sheringham
PRIORY MAZE & GARDENS
NORFOLK SHIRE HORSE CENTRE
CROMER MUSEUM
Cromer
Morston
Blakeney
Wiveton
Newgate
Kelling
Weybourne
SHERINGHAM PARK
SHERINGHAM
Beeston Regis
West Runton
East Runton
Upper Sheringham
Stiffkey
Cockthorpe
Warham
Langham
NORFOLK
Glandford
High Kelling
Bodham
East Beckham
Aylmerton
Felbrigg
Northrepps
Westgate
Wighton
Binham
Saxlingham
Glaven
Holt
Letheringsett
PICTURECRAFT GALLERY
West Beckham
Gresham
FELBRIGG HALL
Crossdale Street
Copy's Green
WAYSIDE CROSS
Field Dalling
LETHERINGSETT WATERMILL
HOLT
BACONSTHORPE CASTLE
Frogshall
THE TEXTILE CENTRE
Lower Green
Great Walsingham
Bale
Sharrington
Hempstead
Baconsthorpe
Sustead
Roughton
Hindringham
Thornage
Bessingham
Hanworth
Brinton
Hunworth
Thurgarton
Stody
Edgefield
Plumstead
Matlaske
Alby Hill
THURSFORD COLLECTION
Gunthorpe
Briningham
Aldborough
Great Snoring
Thursford
Antingham
Little Snoring
Barney
Melton Constable
Edgefield Street
Little Barningham
Wickmere
Swanton Novers
Briston
MANNINGTON GARDENS
Calthorpe
Erpingham
Suffield
ALBY CRAFTS & GARDENS
Kettlestone
WOLTERTON PARK
Itteringham
Colby
Fulmodestone
Saxthorpe
Corpusty
North Walsham
PENSTHORPE NATURE RESERVE & GARDENS
BLICKLING HALL
Ingworth
Banningham
Hindolveston
Thurning
Stibbard
Oulton
Blickling
Little Ryburgh
Wood Norton
Norton Corner
Silvergate
Dunkirk
Tuttington
Great Ryburgh
Guestwick
Heydon
Oulton Street
Aylsham
Guestwick Green
Wood Dalling
Burgh next Aylsham
Guist
Norfolk
Salle
Southgate
Fengate
Foulsham
Twyford
Themelthorpe
Marsham
Brampton
BURE VALLEY RAILWAY
Gateley
Cawston
Little London
Broom Green
Bintree
FOXLEY WOOD
Reepham
Booton
Eastgate
Buxton
Whitwell Street
The Heath
Brandiston
Brisley
North Elmham
Foxley
Billingford
Bawdeswell
Haveringland
Hevingham
Stratton Strawless
East Bilney
Worthing
Sparham
Swannington
Waterloo
Alderford
Upgate
New Hainford
Hainford
Beetley
Mill Street
Lenwade
Wensum
GRESSENHALL FARM & WORKHOUSE
Swanton Morley
Lyng
DINOSAUR ADVENTURE PARK
Felthorpe
Elsing
Morton
Attlebridge
Newton St Faith
Gressenhall
Hoe
Horsford
Woodgate
Primrose Green
Weston Longville
Horsham St Faith
Longham
Thorpe Marriott
Etling Green
North Tuddenham
Weston Green
Ringland
NORWICH INTERNATIONAL
Dereham
Drayton
Taverham
Hockering
Hellesdon
Old Catton
MID-NORFOLK RAILWAY
Tud
Mattishall Burgh
Honingham
Costessey
Scarning
Mile Cross
Toftwood
Clint Green
Mattishall
East Tuddenham
New Costessey
Upper Hellesdon
Daffy Green
Yaxham
Easton
THE FORUM
Welborne
Marlingford
Bowthorpe
Whinburgh
Earlham
SAINSBURY CENTRE FOR VISUAL ARTS
Yare
Brandon Parva
Bawburgh
0 1 2 3 miles
0 1 2 3 4 5 km
A149
A148
A1067
A140
A47
A1074
A1270
A1082
A1075
B1156
B1110
B1354
B1149
B1145
B1436
B1146
B1535
P&R
119
104

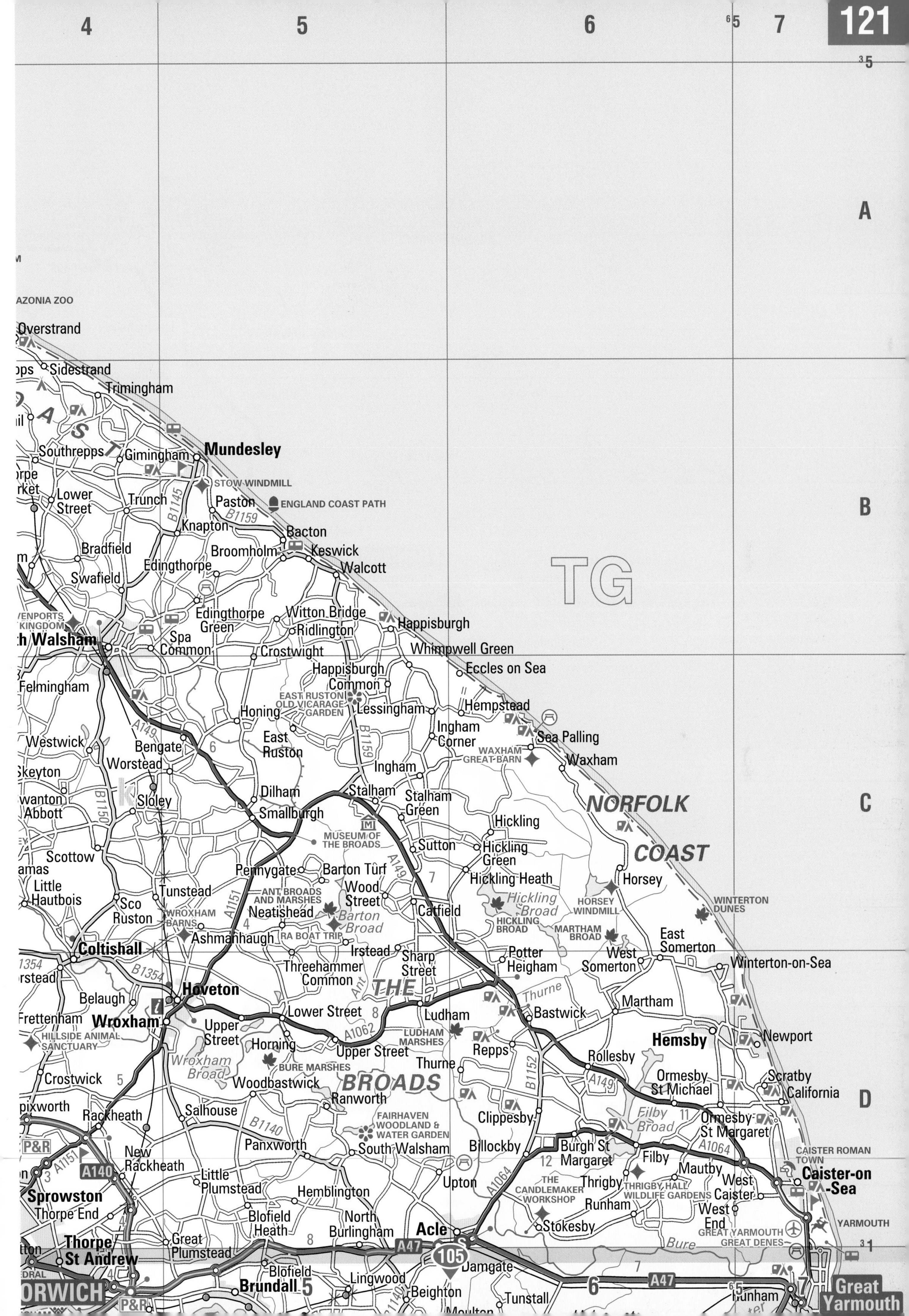

4
5
6
7
A
B
C
D
TG
Overstrand
Sidestrand
Trimingham
Southrepps
Gimingham
Mundesley
STOW WINDMILL
ENGLAND COAST PATH
Lower Street
Trunch
Paston
Knapton
Bacton
Bradfield
Broomholm
Keswick
Walcott
Swafield
Edingthorpe
Edingthorpe Green
Witton Bridge
Ridlington
Happisburgh
Spa Common
Crostwight
Whimpwell Green
Eccles on Sea
Felmingham
Happisburgh Common
EAST RUSTON OLD VICARAGE GARDEN
Honing
Lessingham
Hempstead
Sea Palling
Westwick
Bengate
Worstead
East Ruston
Ingham Corner
WAXHAM GREAT BARN
Waxham
Sloley
Dilham
Ingham
Stalham
Stalham Green
Smallburgh
NORFOLK
MUSEUM OF THE BROADS
Hickling
Scottow
Sutton
Hickling Green
COAST
Little Hautbois
Pennygate
Barton Turf
Hickling Heath
Horsey
Tunstead
Wood Street
Hickling Broad
HORSEY WINDMILL
WINTERTON DUNES
Sco Ruston
ANT BROADS AND MARSHES
Neatishead
Catfield
HICKLING BROAD
WROXHAM BARNS
Barton Broad
MARTHAM BROAD
East Somerton
Ashmanhaugh
RA BOAT TRIP
Coltishall
Irstead
Sharp Street
Potter Heigham
West Somerton
Winterton-on-Sea
Threehammer Common
THE
Hoveton
Belaugh
Thurne
Martham
Frettenham
Wroxham
Upper Street
Lower Street
Ludham
Bastwick
Newport
HILLSIDE ANIMAL SANCTUARY
Horning
Upper Street
LUDHAM MARSHES
Repps
Hemsby
Wroxham Broad
Thurne
Rollesby
Crostwick
Woodbastwick
BURE MARSHES
BROADS
Ormesby St Michael
Scratby
California
Ranworth
Rackheath
Salhouse
FAIRHAVEN WOODLAND & WATER GARDEN
Clippesby
Filby Broad
Ormesby St Margaret
Panxworth
South Walsham
Billockby
Burgh St Margaret
Filby
CAISTER ROMAN TOWN
New Rackheath
Mautby
Caister-on-Sea
Little Plumstead
Upton
THE CANDLEMAKER WORKSHOP
Thrigby
THRIGBY HALL WILDLIFE GARDENS
West Caister
Sprowston
Hemblington
Runham
Thorpe End
Blofield Heath
North Burlingham
Acle
Stokesby
West End
YARMOUTH
Thorpe St Andrew
Great Plumstead
GREAT YARMOUTH GREAT DENES
Bure
Blofield
Damgate
Brundall
Lingwood
Beighton
Tunstall
Runham
NORWICH
Great Yarmouth
B1145
B1159
A149
B1150
A1151
B1354
A1062
B1152
B1140
A1064
A140
A47
105

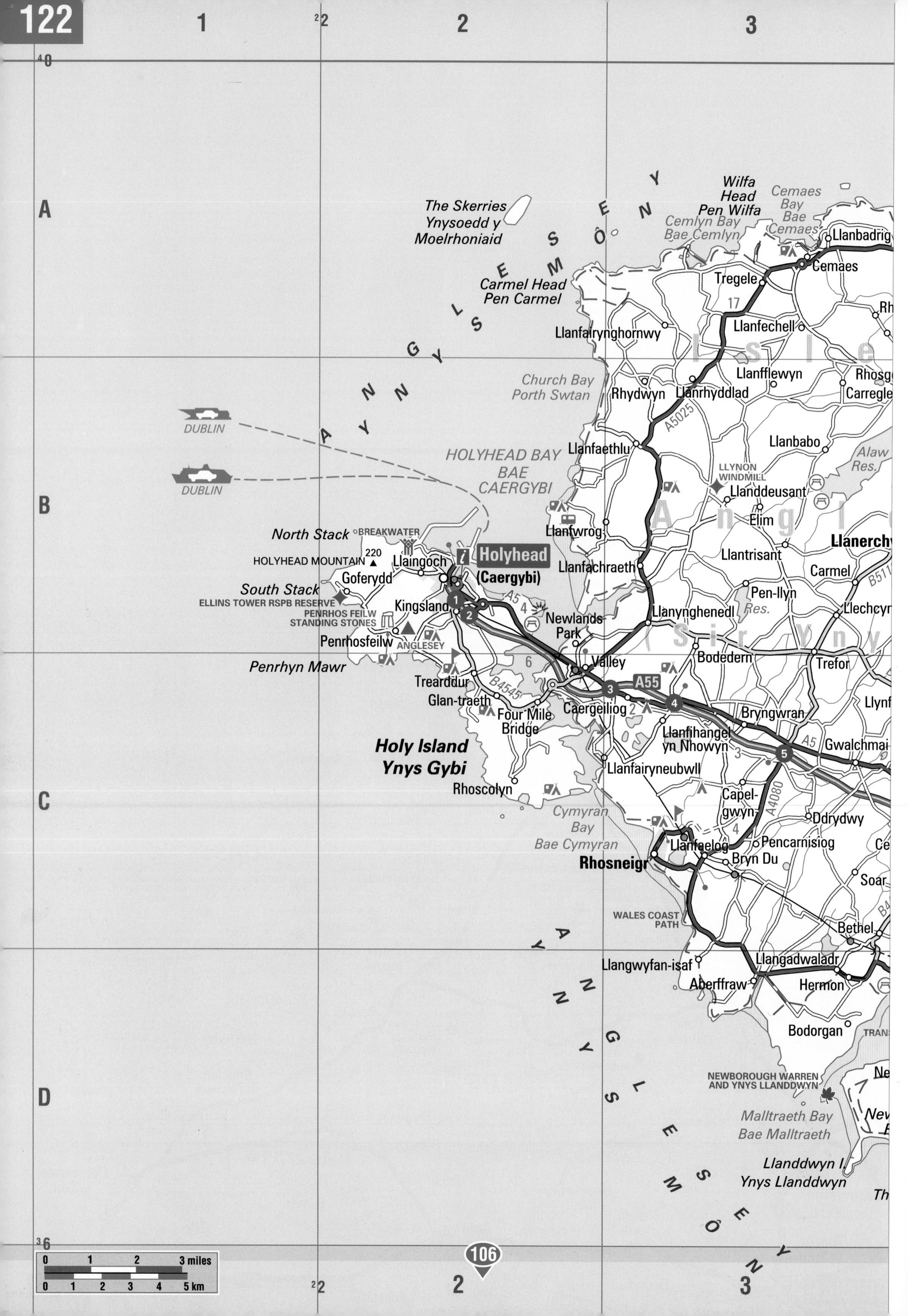
1
2
3
A
B
C
D
The Skerries
Ynysoedd y
Moelrhoniaid
Carmel Head
Pen Carmel
Wilfa
Head
Pen Wilfa
Cemaes
Bay
Bae
Cemaes
Cemlyn Bay
Bae Cemlyn
Llanbadrig
Cemaes
Tregele
Llanfechell
Llanfairynghornwy
Church Bay
Porth Swtan
Rhydwyn
Llanrhyddlad
Llanfflewyn
Rhosgo
Carregle
A5025
Llanbabo
Alaw
Res.
Llanfaethlu
LLYNON
WINDMILL
Llanddeusant
Elim
DUBLIN
DUBLIN
HOLYHEAD BAY
BAE
CAERGYBI
Llanfwrog
North Stack
BREAKWATER
HOLYHEAD MOUNTAIN
220
Llaingoch
Holyhead
(Caergybi)
Llanfachraeth
Llantrisant
Llanerchy
Carmel
Pen-llyn
Res.
South Stack
ELLINS TOWER RSPB RESERVE
Goferydd
Kingsland
A5
Newlands
Park
Llanynghenedl
Llechcyn
PENRHOS FEILW
STANDING STONES
ANGLESEY
Penrhosfeilw
Penrhyn Mawr
Valley
Bodedern
Trefor
Trearddur
B4545
A55
Glan-traeth
Four Mile
Bridge
Caergeiliog
Bryngwran
Llynf
Llanfihangel
yn Nhowyn
Gwalchmai
Holy Island
Ynys Gybi
Llanfairyneubwll
Rhoscolyn
Capel-
gwyn
A4080
Ddrydwy
Cymyran
Bay
Bae Cymyran
Llanfaelog
Pencarnisiog
Bryn Du
Rhosneigr
Soar
WALES COAST
PATH
Bethel
Llangwyfan-isaf
Llangadwaladr
Aberffraw
Hermon
Bodorgan
NEWBOROUGH WARREN
AND YNYS LLANDDWYN
Malltraeth Bay
Bae Malltraeth
Llanddwyn I.
Ynys Llanddwyn
ANGLESEY
YNYS MÔN
0
1
2
3 miles
0
1
2
3
4
5 km

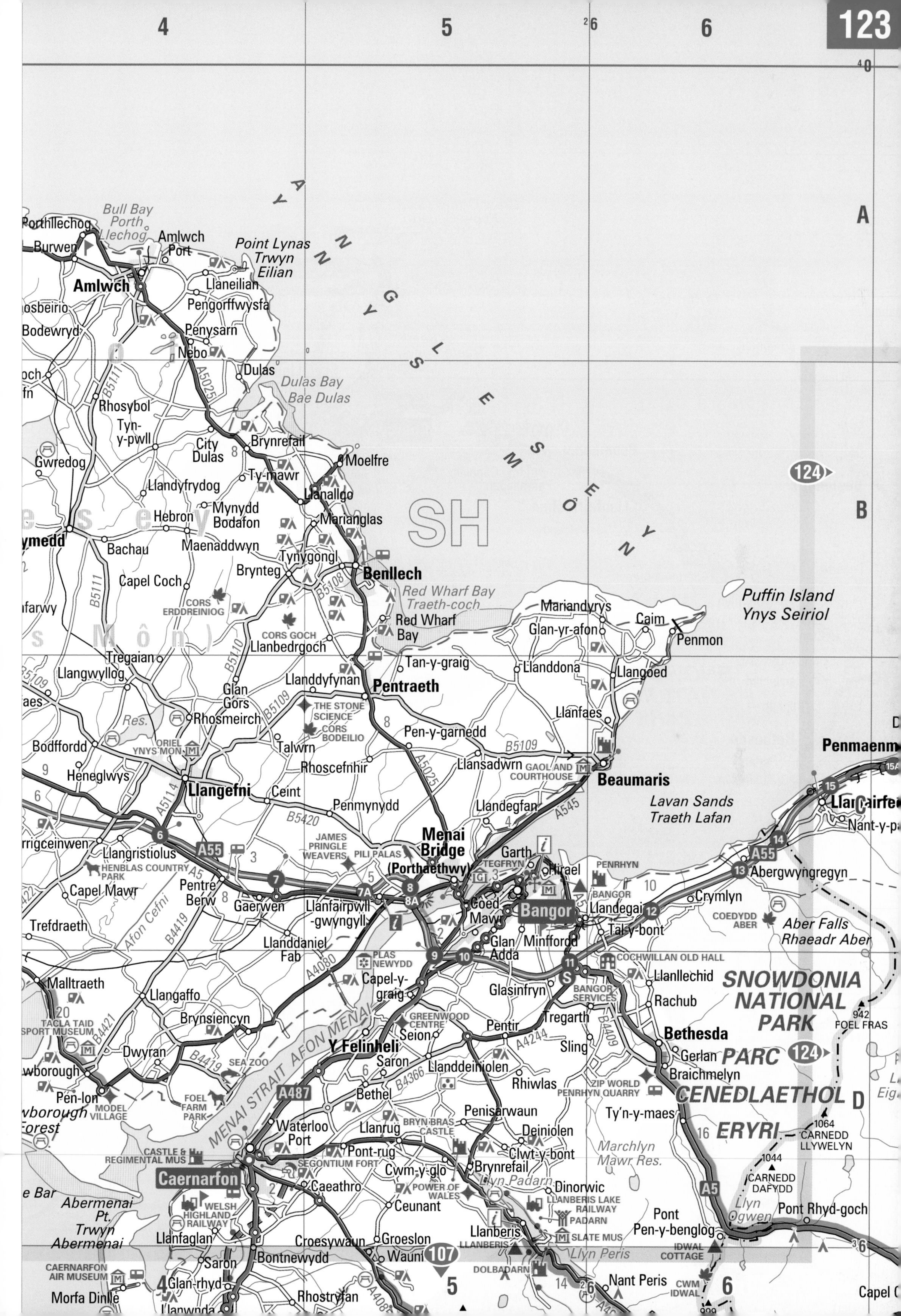
4
5
6
A
B
C
D
Bull Bay
Porth Llechog
Porthllechog
Burwen
Amlwch Port
Amlwch
Point Lynas
Trwyn Eilian
Llaneilian
Pengorffwysfa
Bodewryd
Penysarn
Nebo
Dulas
Dulas Bay
Bae Dulas
A5025
B5111
Rhosybol
Tyn-y-pwll
City Dulas
Brynrefail
Moelfre
Gwredog
Ty-mawr
Llandyfrydog
Llanallgo
Mynydd Bodafon
Hebron
Marianglas
SH
Bachau
Maenaddwyn
Tynygongl
Benllech
Brynteg
Capel Coch
B5108
Red Wharf Bay
Traeth-coch
CORS ERDDREINIOG
CORS GOCH
Red Wharf Bay
Llanbedrgoch
B5110
Tregaian
Llangwyllog
Llanddyfnan
Tan-y-graig
Pentraeth
Glan Gors
Rhosmeirch
B5109
Res.
THE STONE SCIENCE
CORS BODEILIO
Pen-y-garnedd
Bodffordd
ORIEL YNYS MON
Talwrn
Rhoscefnhir
Heneglwys
A5114
Llangefni
Ceint
Penmynydd
B5420
A55
Llangristiolus
HENBLAS COUNTRY PARK
JAMES PRINGLE WEAVERS
PILI PALAS
Menai Bridge
(Porthaethwy)
Capel Mawr
Pentre Berw
Gaerwen
Llanfairpwll -gwyngyll
Trefdraeth
Afon Cefni
B4419
Llanddaniel Fab
A4080
PLAS NEWYDD
Malltraeth
Llangaffo
Capel-y-graig
Brynsiencyn
TACLA TAID SPORT MUSEUM
B4421
Dwyran
B4419
SEA ZOO
MENAI STRAIT AFON MENAI
Y Felinheli
Pen-lon
MODEL VILLAGE
FOEL FARM PARK
A487
Waterloo Port
CASTLE & REGIMENTAL MUS
Caernarfon
SEGONTIUM FORT
WELSH HIGHLAND RAILWAY
Abermenai Pt.
Trwyn Abermenai
Llanfaglan
Caeathro
Croesywaun
Groeslon
Waun
Bontnewydd
Saron
CAERNARFON AIR MUSEUM
Glan-rhyd
Morfa Dinlle
Rhostryfan
Llanwnda
Mariandyrys
Caim
Glan-yr-afon
Penmon
Puffin Island
Ynys Seiriol
Llanddona
Llangoed
Llanfaes
B5109
Llansadwrn
GAOL AND COURTHOUSE
Beaumaris
Llandegfan
A545
Lavan Sands
Traeth Lafan
Garth
TEGFRYN
Hirael
PENRHYN
Coed Mawr
Bangor
BANGOR
Llandegai
Glan Adda
Minffordd
Tal-y-bont
Crymlyn
Abergwyngregyn
COEDYDD ABER
Aber Falls
Rhaeadr Aber
COCHWILLAN OLD HALL
Llanllechid
Glasinfryn
BANGOR SERVICES
Rachub
Tregarth
B4409
Pentir
A4244
GREENWOOD CENTRE
Seion
Sling
Bethesda
Saron
Llanddeiniolen
Gerlan
Rhiwlas
Braichmelyn
B4366
Bethel
ZIP WORLD PENRHYN QUARRY
Penisarwaun
Ty'n-y-maes
Deiniolen
Llanrug
BRYN BRAS CASTLE
Marchlyn Mawr Res.
Clwt-y-bont
Pont-rug
Cwm-y-glo
Brynrefail
Llyn Padarn
Dinorwic
POWER OF WALES
LLANBERIS LAKE RAILWAY
Ceunant
PADARN
Llanberis
SLATE MUS
LLANBERIS
Llyn Peris
DOLBADARN
Nant Peris
CWM IDWAL
IDWAL COTTAGE
Pen-y-benglog
Pont
Llyn Ogwen
Pont Rhyd-goch
SNOWDONIA NATIONAL PARK
PARC CENEDLAETHOL ERYRI
942 FOEL FRAS
1064 CARNEDD LLYWELYN
1044 CARNEDD DAFYDD
A5
Penmaenmawr
Llanfairfechan
Nant-y-pandy
Capel Curig
124
107

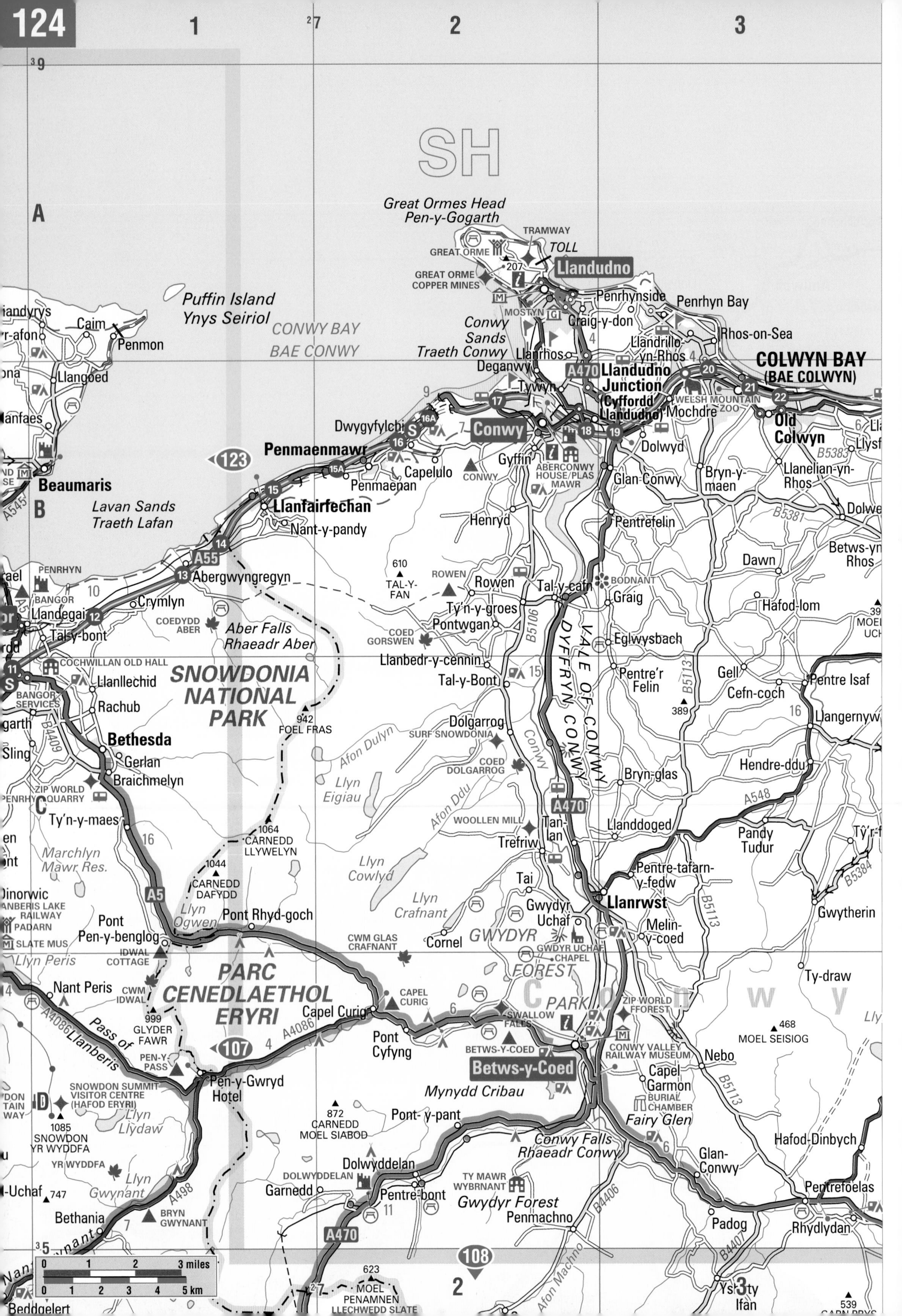

SH
Great Ormes Head
Pen-y-Gogarth
TRAMWAY
GREAT ORME
TOLL
Llandudno
GREAT ORME COPPER MINES
MOSTYN
Puffin Island
Ynys Seiriol
CONWY BAY
BAE CONWY
Conwy Sands
Traeth Conwy
Penrhynside
Penrhyn Bay
Craig-y-don
Rhos-on-Sea
Llandrillo-yn-Rhos
Llanrhos
Deganwy
COLWYN BAY
(BAE COLWYN)
Llandudno Junction
(Cyffordd Llandudno)
Tywyn
WELSH MOUNTAIN ZOO
Mochdre
Old Colwyn
Llysfaen
Caim
Penmon
Llangoed
Beaumaris
Lavan Sands
Traeth Lafan
Dwygyfylchi
Conwy
Penmaenmawr
Capelulo
Penmaenan
Gyffin
CONWY
ABERCONWY HOUSE/PLAS MAWR
Dolwyd
Glan-Conwy
Bryn-y-maen
Llanelian-yn-Rhos
B5383
B5381
Llanfairfechan
Nant-y-pandy
Henryd
Pentrefelin
Dawn
Betws-yn-Rhos
A55
Abergwyngregyn
PENRHYN
BANGOR
Llandegai
Crymlyn
610
TAL-Y-FAN
ROWEN
Rowen
Tal-y-cafn
BODNANT
Graig
Hafod-lom
Ty'n-y-groes
Pontwgan
COEDYDD ABER
Aber Falls
Rhaeadr Aber
Tal-y-bont
COED GORSWEN
Eglwysbach
B5106
VALE OF CONWY
DYFFRYN CONWY
COCHWILLAN OLD HALL
Llanbedr-y-cennin
Tal-y-Bont
Pentre'r Felin
Gell
Pentre Isaf
SNOWDONIA NATIONAL PARK
Llanllechid
BANGOR SERVICES
Rachub
Bethesda
942
FOEL FRAS
B5113
389
Cefn-coch
Llangernyw
Dolgarrog
SURF SNOWDONIA
COED DOLGARROG
Afon Dulyn
Gerlan
Braichmelyn
Llyn Eigiau
Bryn-glas
Hendre-ddu
ZIP WORLD QUARRY
Ty'n-y-maes
A470
Afon Ddu
WOOLLEN MILL
Tan-lan
Llanddoged
A548
Pandy Tudur
Marchlyn Mawr Res.
1064
CARNEDD LLYWELYN
Trefriw
Llyn Cowlyd
Pentre-tafarn-y-fedw
B5384
1044
CARNEDD DAFYDD
Tai
A5
Dinorwic
LLANBERIS LAKE RAILWAY
PADARN
SLATE MUS
Llyn Peris
Pont Pen-y-benglog
Llyn Ogwen
Pont Rhyd-goch
Llyn Crafnant
Gwydyr Uchaf
Llanrwst
B5113
Melin-y-coed
Gwytherin
IDWAL COTTAGE
CWM GLAS CRAFNANT
Cornel
GWYDYR FOREST PARK
GWYDYR UCHAF CHAPEL
Nant Peris
CWM IDWAL
PARC CENEDLAETHOL ERYRI
CAPEL CURIG
Capel Curig
SWALLOW FALLS
ZIP WORLD FFOREST
Conwy
Ty-draw
468
MOEL SEISIOG
A4086
Pass of Llanberis
999
GLYDER FAWR
Pont Cyfyng
BETWS-Y-COED
CONWY VALLEY RAILWAY MUSEUM
Nebo
PEN-Y-PASS
Betws-y-Coed
Capel Garmon
Pen-y-Gwryd Hotel
SNOWDON SUMMIT VISITOR CENTRE (HAFOD ERYRI)
1085
SNOWDON
YR WYDDFA
Llyn Llydaw
Mynydd Cribau
BURIAL CHAMBER
872
CARNEDD MOEL SIABOD
Pont-y-pant
Fairy Glen
Conwy Falls
Rhaeadr Conwy
Hafod-Dinbych
Glan-Conwy
YR WYDDFA
Llyn Gwynant
747
Dolwyddelan
DOLWYDDELAN
Garnedd
TY MAWR WYBRNANT
Pentre-bont
Gwydyr Forest
Penmachno
Pentrefoelas
A498
BRYN GWYNANT
Bethania
B4406
Padog
Rhydlydan
B4407
Afon Machno
623
MOEL PENAMNEN
LLECHWEDD SLATE
Ysbyty Ifan
539
Beddgelert
0 1 2 3 miles
0 1 2 3 4 5 km

123
107
108

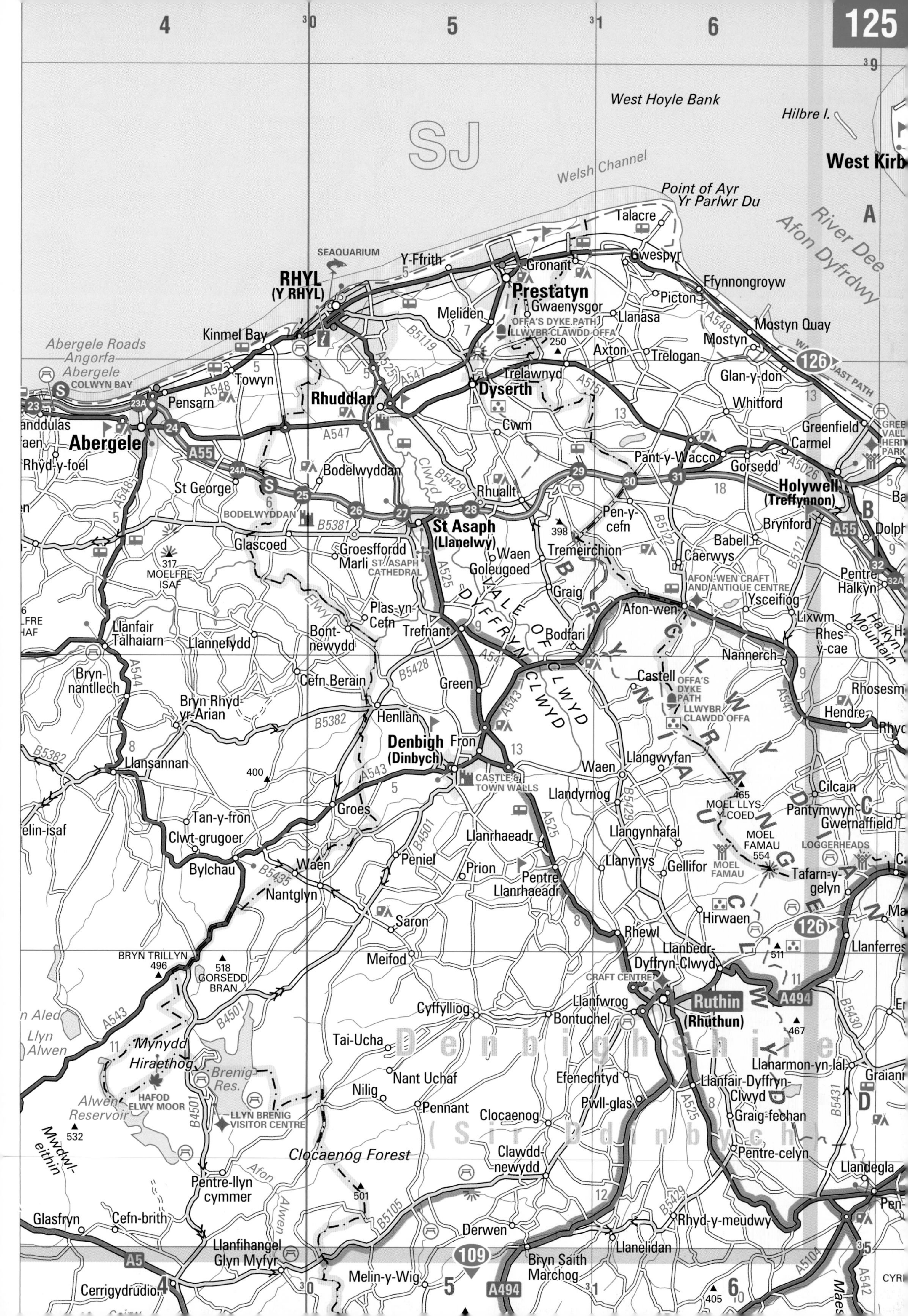

4
5
6
SJ
West Hoyle Bank
Hilbre I.
West Kirb
Welsh Channel
Point of Ayr
Yr Parlwr Du
River Dee
Afon Dyfrdwy
Talacre
Gwespyr
Ffynnongroyw
Picton
Mostyn Quay
Mostyn
SEAQUARIUM
Y-Ffrith
Gronant
Prestatyn
Gwaenysgor
Llanasa
RHYL
(Y RHYL)
Meliden
OFFA'S DYKE PATH
LLWYBR CLAWDD OFFA
250
Axton
Trelogan
126
Glan-y-don
Kinmel Bay
Abergele Roads
Angorfa
Abergele
COLWYN BAY
Towyn
Rhuddlan
Trelawnyd
Dyserth
Whitford
Pensarn
A548
A547
A525
B5119
A5151
Greenfield
Carmel
Abergele
Cwm
Pant-y-Wacco
Gorsedd
Holywell
(Treffynnon)
Rhyd-y-foel
Bodelwyddan
St George
A55
Rhuallt
Pen-y-cefn
BODELWYDDAN
B5381
St Asaph
(Llanelwy)
398
Brynford
Babell
Glascoed
Groesffordd
Marli
ST. ASAPH CATHEDRAL
Waen
Goleugoed
Tremeirchion
Caerwys
317
MOELFRE ISAF
Graig
AFON-WEN CRAFT AND ANTIQUE CENTRE
Ysceifiog
Pentre Halkyn
Plas-yn-Cefn
VALE OF CLWYD
DYFFRYN CLWYD
Afon-wen
Lixwm
Llanfair Talhaiarn
Llannefydd
Bont-newydd
Trefnant
Bodfari
Rhes-y-cae
Halkyn Mountain
Nannerch
Bryn-nantllech
Cefn Berain
B5428
Green
Castell
OFFA'S DYKE PATH
LLWYBR CLAWDD OFFA
CLWYDIAN RANGE
BRYNIAU CLWYD
Rhosesm
Hendre
Bryn Rhyd-yr-Arian
Henllan
B5382
A543
A541
A544
Denbigh
(Dinbych)
Fron
13
Llansannan
400
Waen
Llangwyfan
CASTLE & TOWN WALLS
Llandyrnog
465
MOEL LLYS-Y-COED
Cilcain
Pantymwyn
Gwernaffield
Tan-y-fron
Groes
Clwt-grugoer
Llanrhaeadr
Llangynhafal
MOEL FAMAU
554
LOGGERHEADS
Bylchau
Peniel
Prion
Llanynys
Gellifor
Tafarn-y-gelyn
Nantglyn
Pentre Llanrhaeadr
B5435
B4501
A525
B5429
Saron
Hirwaen
Rhewl
Llanferres
BRYN TRILLYN
496
518
GORSEDD BRAN
Meifod
Llanbedr-Dyffryn-Clwyd
511
CRAFT CENTRE
Cyffylliog
Llanfwrog
Bontuchel
Ruthin
(Rhuthun)
A494
467
B5430
Llyn Alwen
Mynydd Hiraethog
Tai-Ucha
Denbighshire
(Sir Ddinbych)
Llanarmon-yn-Ial
Graianr
Brenig Res.
Nant Uchaf
Efenechtyd
Llanfair-Dyffryn-Clwyd
Alwen Reservoir
HAFOD ELWY MOOR
Nilig
Pwll-glas
LLYN BRENIG VISITOR CENTRE
Pennant
Clocaenog
Graig-fechan
532
Mwdwl-eithin
Clocaenog Forest
Clawdd-newydd
Pentre-celyn
Llandegla
Pentre-llyn cymmer
Afon Alwen
501
B5105
Glasfryn
Cefn-brith
Derwen
Rhyd-y-meudwy
Llanfihangel Glyn Myfyr
Llanelidan
A5
109
Bryn Saith Marchog
Melin-y-Wig
Cerrigydrudion
A494
405
A5104
A542
CYR

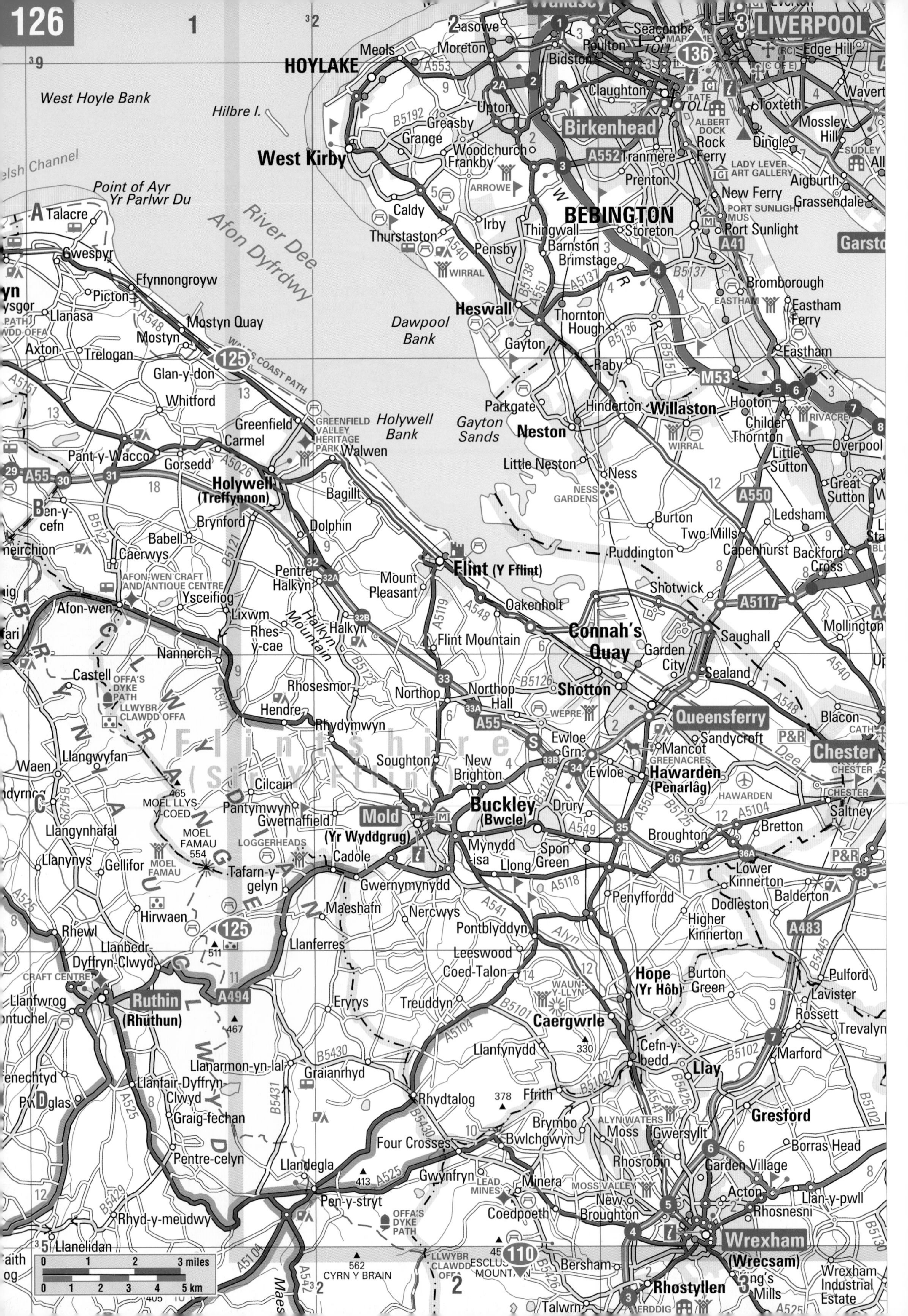

LIVERPOOL
Seacombe
Poulton
Bidston
Edge Hill
Leasowe
Moreton
Meols
HOYLAKE
West Hoyle Bank
Hilbre I.
West Kirby
Upton
Greasby
Grange
Woodchurch
Frankby
Claughton
Birkenhead
Tranmere
Rock Ferry
Prenton
Toxteth
Mossley Hill
Dingle
Aigburth
Grassendale
New Ferry
Port Sunlight
BEBINGTON
Storeton
Caldy
Thurstaston
Irby
Thingwall
Barnston
Brimstage
Pensby
Heswall
Thornton Hough
Gayton
Bromborough
Eastham
Eastham Ferry
Raby
Dawpool Bank
Point of Ayr
Yr Parlwr Du
River Dee
Afon Dyfrdwy
Talacre
Gwespyr
Ffynnongroyw
Picton
Llanasa
Mostyn Quay
Mostyn
Axton
Trelogan
Glan-y-don
Whitford
WALES COAST PATH
Greenfield
Carmel
Holywell Bank
Gayton Sands
Parkgate
Neston
Hinderton
Willaston
Hooton
Childer Thornton
Overpool
Little Sutton
Great Sutton
Little Neston
Ness
NESS GARDENS
Pant-y-Wacco
Gorsedd
Holywell
(Treffynnon)
Walwen
Bagillt
Brynford
Dolphin
Babell
Caerwys
Ben-y-cefn
Burton
Two Mills
Puddington
Capenhurst
Backford Cross
Ledsham
Flint (Y Fflint)
Pentre Halkyn
Mount Pleasant
AFON-WEN CRAFT AND ANTIQUE CENTRE
Afon-wen
Ysceifiog
Lixwm
Halkyn
Halkyn Mountain
Rhes-y-cae
Flint Mountain
Oakenholt
Connah's Quay
Shotwick
Saughall
Mollington
Garden City
Sealand
Nannerch
Castell
OFFA'S DYKE PATH
LLWYBR CLAWDD OFFA
Rhosesmor
Northop
Northop Hall
Shotton
Hendre
Rhydymwyn
Flintshire
(Sir y Fflint)
Queensferry
Blacon
Chester
Ewloe
Mancot
Sandycroft
Soughton
New Brighton
Ewloe Grn.
Hawarden
(Penarlâg)
Llangwyfan
Waen
Cilcain
Pantymwyn
Gwernaffield
Mold
(Yr Wyddgrug)
Buckley
(Bwcle)
Drury
Saltney
Bretton
Broughton
Llangynhafal
MOEL LLYS-Y-COED
MOEL FAMAU
LOGGERHEADS
Llanynys
Gellifor
Tafarn-y-gelyn
Cadole
Mynydd-isa
Llong
Spon Green
Lower Kinnerton
Balderton
Gwernymynydd
Penyffordd
Dodleston
Higher Kinnerton
Hirwaen
Maeshafn
Nercwys
Pontblyddyn
Rhewl
Llanbedr-Dyffryn-Clwyd
Llanferres
Leeswood
Coed-Talon
CRAFT CENTRE
Ruthin
(Rhuthun)
Llanfwrog
Eryrys
Treuddyn
Caergwrle
Hope
(Yr Hôb)
Burton Green
Pulford
Lavister
Rossett
Trevalyn
Llanfynydd
Cefn-y-bedd
Llay
Marford
Llanarmon-yn-Ial
Graianrhyd
Llanfair-Dyffryn-Clwyd
Rhydtalog
Ffrith
Brymbo
Moss
Gwersyllt
Gresford
Graig-fechan
Four Crosses
Bwlchgwyn
Rhosrobin
Borras Head
Garden Village
Pentre-celyn
Llandegla
Gwynfryn
Minera
MOSS VALLEY
New Broughton
Acton
Llan-y-pwll
Rhosnesni
Pen-y-stryt
Coedpoeth
Rhyd-y-meudwy
Llanelidan
Wrexham
(Wrecsam)
Bersham
Rhostyllen
Wrexham Industrial Estate
CYRN Y BRAIN
ESCLUSHAM MOUNTAIN
Talwrn
3 miles
5 km

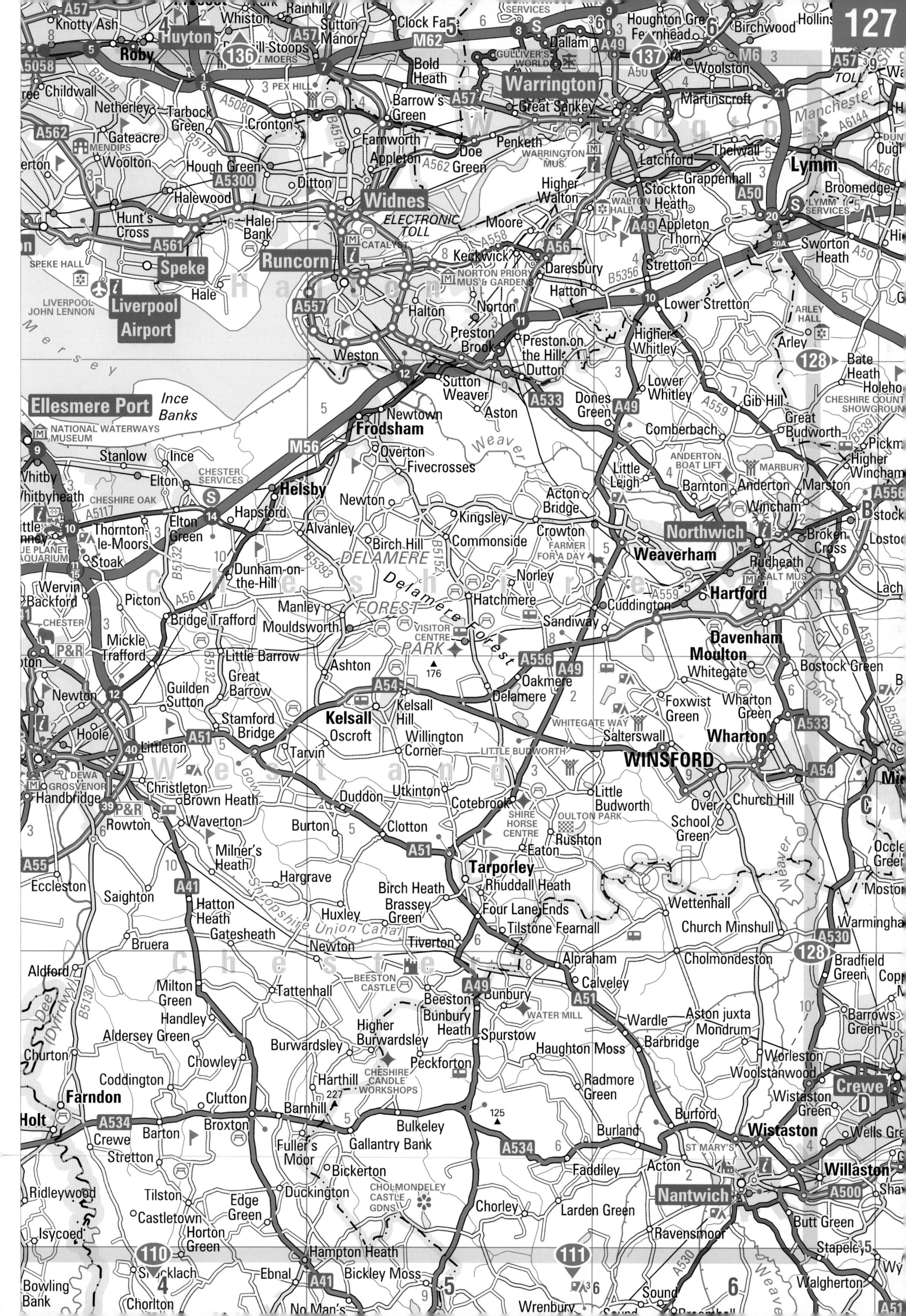
Knotty Ash
Huyton
Roby
Whiston
Rainhill
Sutton Manor
Clock Face
Houghton Green
Fearnhead
Birchwood
Hollins
Dallam
Gulliver's World
Warrington
Woolston
Martinscroft
Bold Heath
Pex Hill
Barrow's Green
Great Sankey
Childwall
Netherley
Tarbock Green
Cronton
Farnworth
Appleton
Penketh
Doe Green
Gateacre
Mendips
Woolton
Hough Green
Ditton
Warrington Mus.
Latchford
Thelwall
Grappenhall
Lymm
Broomedge
Halewood
Widnes
Electronic Toll
Higher Walton
Stockton Heath
Walton Hall
Appleton Thorn
Lymm Services
Hunt's Cross
Hale Bank
Moore
Swarton Heath
Speke Hall
Speke
Runcorn
Catalyst
Keckwick
Daresbury
Stretton
Norton Priory Mus & Gardens
Hatton
Liverpool John Lennon
Liverpool Airport
Hale
Halton
Norton
Lower Stretton
Arley Hall
Preston Brook
Preston on the Hill
Higher Whitley
Arley
Mersey
Weston
Dutton
Sutton Weaver
Bate Heath
Holeho
Lower Whitley
Dones Green
Gib Hill
Cheshire County Showground
Ellesmere Port
Ince Banks
Newtown
Aston
Frodsham
National Waterways Museum
Comberbach
Great Budworth
Overton
Fivecrosses
Weaver
Pickmere
Higher Wincham
Stanlow
Ince
Anderton Boat Lift
Marbury
Little Leigh
Whitby
Elton
Chester Services
Barnton
Anderton
Marston
Whitbyheath
Helsby
Newton
Acton Bridge
Cheshire Oaks
Wincham
Hapsford
Kingsley
Elton Green
Thornton-le-Moors
Alvanley
Crowton
Northwich
Broken Cross
Birch Hill
Commonside
Farmer for a Day
Weaverham
Stoak
Delamere
Dunham-on-the-Hill
Norley
Rudheath
Salt Mus
Wervin
Backford
Picton
Delamere Forest
Hatchmere
Cuddington
Hartford
Manley
Chester
Bridge Trafford
Mouldsworth
Sandiway
Mickle Trafford
Visitor Centre
Park
Davenham
Little Barrow
Moulton
Ashton
Whitegate
Bostock Green
Great Barrow
Oakmere
Newton
Guilden Sutton
Delamere
Foxwist Green
Wharton Green
Kelsall
Kelsall Hill
Whitegate Way
Salterswall
Hoole
Stamford Bridge
Wharton
Littleton
Oscroft
Willington Corner
Tarvin
Little Budworth
Winsford
Dewa
Grosvenor
Christleton
Handbridge
Brown Heath
Duddon
Utkinton
Little Budworth
Over
Church Hill
Rowton
Waverton
Cotebrook
Shire Horse Centre
Oulton Park
School Green
Burton
Clotton
Rushton
Milner's Heath
Eaton
Tarporley
Occle
Eccleston
Saighton
Hargrave
Rhuddall Heath
Birch Heath
Brassey Green
Mostor
Hatton Heath
Shropshire Union Canal
Huxley
Four Lane Ends
Wettenhall
Gatesheath
Tilstone Fearnall
Church Minshull
Warmingha
Bruera
Newton
Tiverton
Aldford
Alpraham
Cholmondeston
Bradfield Green
Calveley
Milton Green
Beeston Castle
Tattenhall
Beeston
Bunbury
Dee (Dyfrdwy)
Handley
Bunbury Heath
Water Mill
Wardle
Aston juxta Mondrum
Barrows Green
Aldersey Green
Higher Burwardsley
Spurstow
Burwardsley
Barbridge
Churton
Chowley
Haughton Moss
Worleston
Peckforton
Cheshire Candle Workshops
Woolstanwood
Coddington
Harthill
Radmore Green
Farndon
Clutton
Wistaston Green
Crewe
Barnhill
Holt
Broxton
Bulkeley
Burford
Wistaston
Wells Green
Crewe
Barton
Fuller's Moor
Gallantry Bank
Burland
Stretton
Bickerton
St Mary's
Faddiley
Acton
Willaston
Ridleywood
Duckington
Cholmondeley Castle Gdns
Nantwich
Tilston
Edge Green
Chorley
Larden Green
Castletown
Horton Green
Butt Green
Isycoed
Ravensmoor
Hampton Heath
Stapeley
Bowling Bank
Stocklach
Ebnal
Bickley Moss
Walgherton
Chorlton
No Man's
Wrenbury
Sound
Lostock
Lach
Bostock
Mi
Hi
Wa
Ough
Warrington
Halton
Cheshire
West and
Chester
Manchester
136
137
128
110
111
M62
M6
M56
A57
A5058
A562
A5300
A561
A557
A56
A49
A50
A533
A559
A556
A54
A51
A41
A55
A534
A530
A500
B5178
A5080
B4519
A562
A558
B5356
B5132
B5393
B5152
B5391
A5117
B5130
B5309
P&R
176
227
125

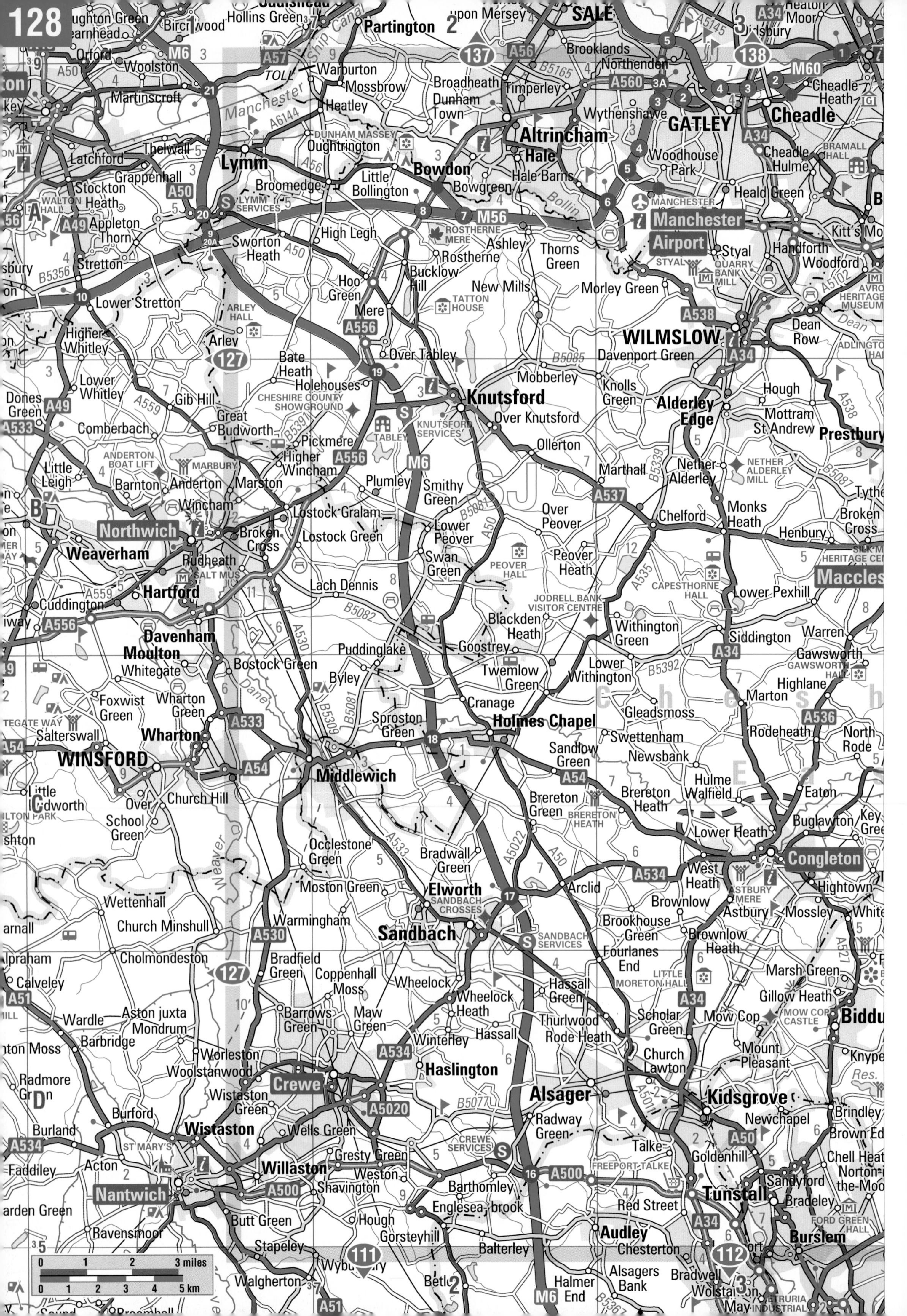
Partington
upon Mersey
SALE
Heaton Moor
Didsbury
137
138
Hollins Green
Birchwood
Orford
Woolston
Martinscroft
Warburton
Mossbrow
Heatley
Manchester Ship Canal
TOLL
Broadheath
Dunham Town
Timperley
Brooklands
Northenden
Wythenshawe
GATLEY
Cheadle
Cheadle Heath
DUNHAM MASSEY
Oughtrington
Altrincham
Hale
Woodhouse Park
Cheadle Hulme
BRAMALL HALL
Latchford
Thelwall
Lymm
Grappenhall
Stockton Heath
WALTON HALL
Appleton Thorn
LYMM SERVICES
Broomedge
Little Bollington
Bowdon
Bowgreen
Hale Barns
Bollin
MANCHESTER
Manchester Airport
Heald Green
Kitt's Moss
Sworton Heath
High Legh
ROSTHERNE MERE
Rostherne
Ashley
Thorns Green
Styal
STYAL
QUARRY BANK MILL
Handforth
Woodford
AVRO HERITAGE MUSEUM
Stretton
Lower Stretton
Bucklow Hill
Hoo Green
Mere
TATTON HOUSE
New Mills
Morley Green
Dean Row
Higher Whitley
ARLEY HALL
Arley
127
WILMSLOW
ADLINGTON HALL
Bate Heath
Over Tabley
Mobberley
Davenport Green
Knolls Green
Hough
Lower Whitley
Holehouses
CHESHIRE COUNTY SHOWGROUND
Knutsford
Alderley Edge
Mottram St Andrew
Prestbury
Dones Green
Gib Hill
Great Budworth
Pickmere
TABLEY
KNUTSFORD SERVICES
Over Knutsford
Comberbach
Higher Wincham
Ollerton
ANDERTON BOAT LIFT
MARBURY
Marthall
Nether Alderley
NETHER ALDERLEY MILL
Little Leigh
Barnton
Anderton
Marston
Plumley
Smithy Green
Wincham
Lostock Gralam
Lower Peover
Over Peover
Chelford
Monks Heath
Broken Cross
Tytherington
Northwich
Broken Cross
Lostock Green
Henbury
Weaverham
Rudheath
SALT MUS
Swan Green
PEOVER HALL
Peover Heath
CAPESTHORNE HALL
SILK MUSEUM
HERITAGE CENTRE
Macclesfield
Cuddington
Hartford
Lach Dennis
JODRELL BANK VISITOR CENTRE
Lower Pexhill
Davenham
Blackden Heath
Withington Green
Siddington
Warren
Moulton
Puddinglake
Goostrey
Gawsworth
GAWSWORTH HALL
Whitegate
Bostock Green
Byley
Twemlow Green
Lower Withington
Highlane
Foxwist Green
Wharton Green
Cranage
Marton
Gleadsmoss
TEGATE WAY
Salterswall
Wharton
Sproston Green
Holmes Chapel
Swettenham
Rodeheath
North Rode
WINSFORD
Middlewich
Sandlow Green
Newsbank
Little Budworth
Over
Church Hill
Brereton Green
BRERETON HEATH
Brereton Heath
Hulme Walfield
Eaton
School Green
Buglawton
Lower Heath
Occlestone Green
Bradwall Green
Congleton
Moston Green
Elworth
SANDBACH CROSSES
Arclid
West Heath
Hightown
Wettenhall
Brownlow
Astbury
ASTBURY MERE
Mossley
Church Minshull
Warmingham
Sandbach
Brookhouse Green
Brownlow Heath
SANDBACH SERVICES
Alpraham
Cholmondeston
Bradfield Green
Coppenhall Moss
Fourlanes End
LITTLE MORETON HALL
Marsh Green
Calveley
Wheelock
Hassall Green
Wheelock Heath
Gillow Heath
Wardle
Aston juxta Mondrum
Barrows Green
Maw Green
Thurlwood
Scholar Green
Mow Cop
MOW COP CASTLE
Biddulph
Barbridge
Hassall
Rode Heath
Winterley
Mount Pleasant
Worleston
Church Lawton
Knypersley
Radmore Green
Woolstanwood
Crewe
Haslington
Alsager
Kidsgrove
Wistaston Green
Brindley
Burford
Newchapel
Burland
Wistaston
Wells Green
Radway Green
Talke
Brown Edge
ST MARY'S
CREWE SERVICES
Goldenhill
Chell Heath
Faddiley
Acton
Gresty Green
Willaston
Weston
FREEPORT TALKE
Sandyford
Norton-in-the-Moors
Nantwich
Shavington
Barthomley
Tunstall
Bradeley
Englesea-brook
Red Street
Marden Green
Butt Green
Ravensmoor
Hough
Gorsteyhill
Audley
FORD GREEN HALL
Burslem
Stapeley
Balterley
Chesterton
111
112
Wybunbury
Walgherton
Betley
Halmer End
Alsagers Bank
Bradwell
Wolstanton
ETRURIA INDUSTRIAL
0 1 2 3 miles
0 1 2 3 4 5 km

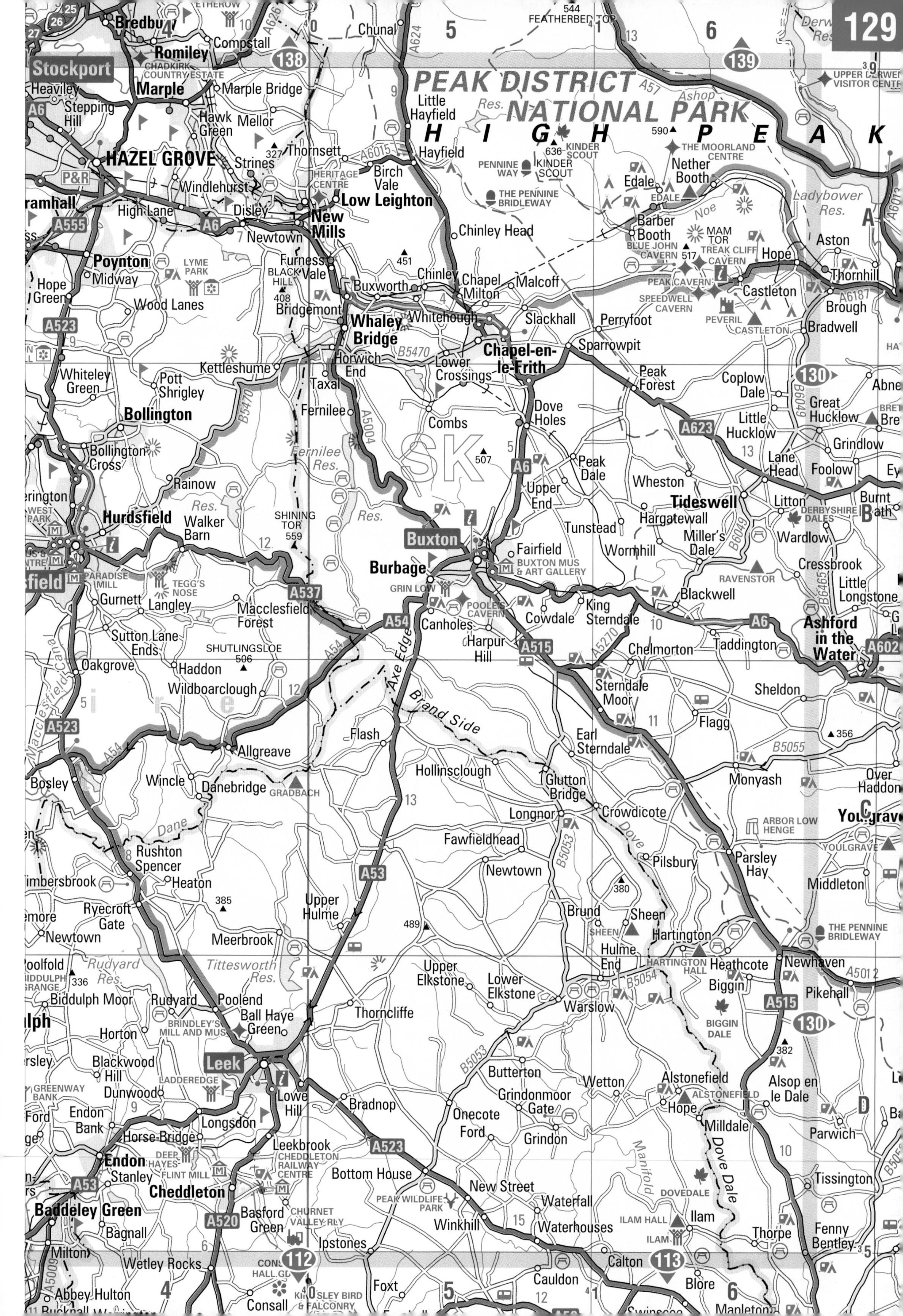
Stockport
Bredbury
Romiley
Compstall
Chunal
FEATHERBED TOP
138
139
PEAK DISTRICT
NATIONAL PARK
H I G H P E A K
UPPER DERWENT VISITOR CENTRE
CHADKIRK COUNTRY ESTATE
Marple
Marple Bridge
Heaviley
Stepping Hill
Hawk Green
Mellor
Little Hayfield
Ashop
HAZEL GROVE
Thornsett
Hayfield
KINDER SCOUT
THE MOORLAND CENTRE
Strines
Birch Vale
PENNINE WAY
Nether Booth
Edale
Windlehurst
HERITAGE CENTRE
THE PENNINE BRIDLEWAY
Ladybower Res.
High Lane
Disley
Low Leighton
New Mills
EDALE
Noe
Newtown
Chinley Head
Barber Booth
MAM TOR
Aston
Poynton
LYME PARK
Furness Vale
BLACK HILL
BLUE JOHN CAVERN
TREAK CLIFF CAVERN
Hope
Midway
Chinley
Chapel Milton
Malcoff
PEAK CAVERN
Thornhill
Hope Green
Buxworth
Castleton
Wood Lanes
Bridgemont
SPEEDWELL CAVERN
Brough
Whaley Bridge
Whitehough
Slackhall
Perryfoot
PEVERIL CASTLE
CASTLETON
Bradwell
A523
Kettleshume
Horwich End
B5470
Lower Crossings
Chapel-en-le-Frith
Sparrowpit
Whiteley Green
Pott Shrigley
Taxal
Peak Forest
Coplow Dale
130
Bollington
Fernilee
Combs
Dove Holes
A623
Little Hucklow
Great Hucklow
Grindlow
Bollington Cross
Fernilee Res.
A5004
SK
Peak Dale
Lane Head
Foolow
Rainow
Upper End
Wheston
Tideswell
Litton
Burnt Bath
Res.
Walker Barn
SHINING TOR
Hargatewall
DERBYSHIRE DALES
Hurdsfield
Tunstead
Miller's Dale
Wardlow
WEST PARK
Buxton
Fairfield
Wormhill
B6049
Burbage
BUXTON MUS & ART GALLERY
Cressbrook
PARADISE MILL
TEGG'S NOSE
GRIN LOW
RAVENSTOR
Little Longstone
Gurnett
Langley
A537
Macclesfield Forest
POOLE'S CAVERN
King Sterndale
Blackwell
Cowdale
A54
Canholes
A6
Ashford in the Water
Sutton Lane Ends
Harpur Hill
A515
Chelmorton
Taddington
A5270
SHUTLINGSLOE
Oakgrove
Haddon
Axe Edge
Macclesfield Canal
Wildboarclough
Sterndale Moor
Sheldon
Brand Side
A523
Flash
Flagg
Earl Sterndale
Allgreave
B5055
Bosley
Wincle
Hollinsclough
Monyash
Over Haddon
Danebridge
GRADBACH
Glutton Bridge
Longnor
Crowdicote
Youlgrave
ARBOR LOW HENGE
Dane
Fawfieldhead
Dove
Rushton Spencer
Parsley Hay
YOULGRAVE
B5053
Pilsbury
Timbersbrook
Heaton
Newtown
A53
Middleton
Ryecroft Gate
Upper Hulme
Brund
Sheen
Newtown
SHEEN
Hartington
THE PENNINE BRIDLEWAY
Meerbrook
Hulme End
Newhaven
Poolfold
Rudyard Res.
Tittesworth Res.
Upper Elkstone
HARTINGTON HALL
Heathcote
A5012
BIDDULPH GRANGE
Lower Elkstone
B5054
Biggin
Biddulph Moor
Rudyard
Poolend
Pikehall
Warslow
Ball Haye Green
Thorncliffe
A515
Horton
BRINDLEY'S MILL AND MUS
BIGGIN DALE
Leek
Blackwood Hill
Butterton
LADDEREDGE
Wetton
Alstonefield
Alsop en le Dale
GREENWAY BANK
Dunwood
Grindonmoor Gate
ALSTONEFIELD
Lowe Hill
Bradnop
Onecote
Hope
Milldale
Endon Bank
Ford
Grindon
Dove Dale
Parwich
Longsdon
Horse Bridge
Manifold
Leekbrook
CHEDDLETON RAILWAY CENTRE
A523
DEEP HAYES
Endon
Stanley
FLINT MILL
Bottom House
Tissington
New Street
Cheddleton
A53
PEAK WILDLIFE PARK
DOVEDALE
Waterfall
Baddeley Green
A520
Basford Green
CHURNET VALLEY RLY
Winkhill
Waterhouses
ILAM HALL
Ilam
Thorpe
Fenny Bentley
Bagnall
ILAM
Ipstones
Milton
Wetley Rocks
CONSALL GD
112
Calton
113
Abbey Hulton
Foxt
Cauldon
Blore
KINGSLEY BIRD & FALCONRY
Consall
Mapleton

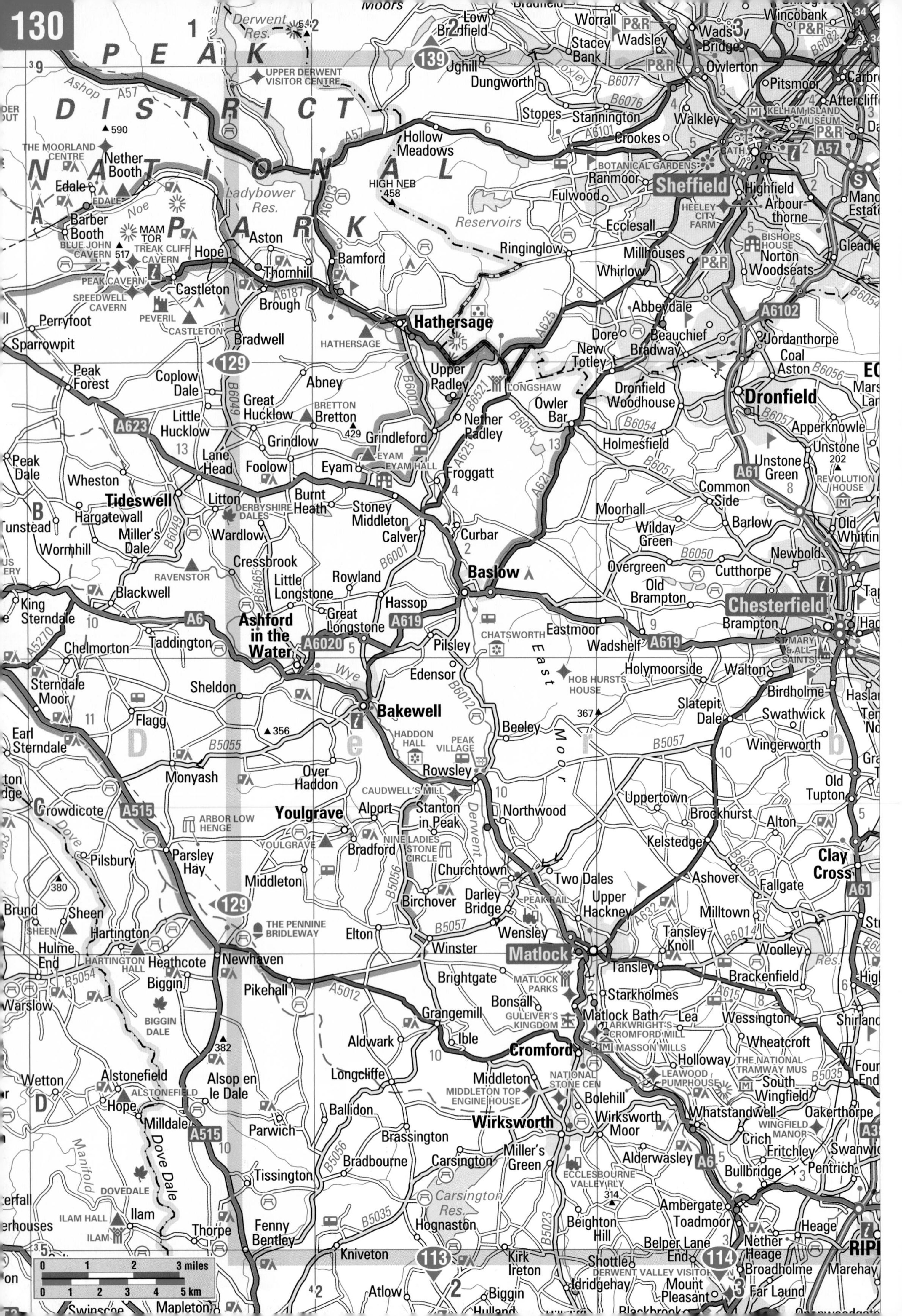
PEAK DISTRICT NATIONAL PARK
Derwent Res.
UPPER DERWENT VISITOR CENTRE
Ladybower Res.
Low Bradfield
Worrall
Stacey Bank
Wadsley
Wadsley Bridge
Wincobank
Owlerton
Pitsmoor
Ughill
Dungworth
Loxley
Stopes
Stannington
Walkley
KELHAM ISLAND MUSEUM
Attercliffe
Crookes
Hollow Meadows
THE MOORLAND CENTRE
Nether Booth
Edale
Barber Booth
MAM TOR
BLUE JOHN CAVERN
TREAK CLIFF CAVERN
PEAK CAVERN
SPEEDWELL CAVERN
PEVERIL CASTLE
Castleton
Hope
Aston
Thornhill
Bamford
HIGH NEB 458
BOTANICAL GARDENS
Ranmoor
Sheffield
Fulwood
Reservoirs
Ecclesall
Highfield
Arbourthorne
HEELEY CITY FARM
BISHOPS HOUSE
Norton
Woodseats
Gleadless
Ringinglow
Millhouses
Whirlow
Abbeydale
Beauchief
Dore
Bradway
Jordanthorpe
Coal Aston
Totley
Brough
Hathersage
HATHERSAGE
Perryfoot
Sparrowpit
Bradwell
Peak Forest
Coplow Dale
Abney
Upper Padley
Nether Padley
LONGSHAW
Owler Bar
Dronfield Woodhouse
Dronfield
Apperknowle
Unstone
Unstone Green
Great Hucklow
Little Hucklow
BRETTON
Bretton
Grindlow
Grindleford
Holmesfield
Peak Dale
Wheston
Lane Head
Foolow
Eyam
EYAM HALL
Froggatt
Tideswell
Litton
Burnt Heath
Stoney Middleton
Common Side
REVOLUTION HOUSE
Tunstead
Hargatewall
DERBYSHIRE DALES
Moorhall
Barlow
Wormhill
Miller's Dale
Wardlow
Calver
Curbar
Wildway Green
Old Whittington
Cressbrook
RAVENSTOR
Little Longstone
Rowland
Baslow
Overgreen
Cutthorpe
Newbold
Blackwell
King Sterndale
Hassop
Old Brampton
Chesterfield
Ashford in the Water
Great Longstone
Eastmoor
Brampton
Chelmorton
Taddington
Pilsley
CHATSWORTH
East Moor
Wadshelf
ST MARY & ALL SAINTS
Sterndale Moor
Sheldon
Wye
Edensor
HOB HURSTS HOUSE
Holymoorside
Walton
Birdholme
Flagg
Bakewell
Slatepit Dale
Swathwick
Earl Sterndale
HADDON HALL
Beeley
PEAK VILLAGE
Wingerworth
Monyash
Over Haddon
Rowsley
Old Tupton
CAUDWELL'S MILL
Crowdicote
ARBOR LOW HENGE
Youlgrave
Alport
Stanton in Peak
Northwood
Uppertown
Brockhurst
Alton
Dove
Pilsbury
Parsley Hay
YOULGRAVE
NINE LADIES STONE CIRCLE
Bradford
Derwent
Kelstedge
Clay Cross
Middleton
Churchtown
Two Dales
Ashover
Fallgate
Brund
Sheen
SHEEN
THE PENNINE BRIDLEWAY
Birchover
Darley Bridge
PEAK RAIL
Upper Hackney
Milltown
Hartington
Elton
Winster
Wensley
Tansley Knoll
Woolley
Hulme End
HARTINGTON HALL
Heathcote
Newhaven
Matlock
Tansley
Brackenfield
Biggin
Pikehall
Brightgate
MATLOCK PARKS
Starkholmes
Warslow
Bonsall
GULLIVER'S KINGDOM
Matlock Bath
Lea
Wessington
Shirland
Grangemill
ARKWRIGHT'S CROMFORD MILL
BIGGIN DALE
Aldwark
Ible
Cromford
MASSON MILLS
Wheatcroft
Holloway
THE NATIONAL TRAMWAY MUS
Wetton
Alstonefield
ALSTONEFIELD
Alsop en le Dale
Longcliffe
Middleton
NATIONAL STONE CEN
LEAWOOD PUMPHOUSE
South Wingfield
Hope
MIDDLETON TOP ENGINE HOUSE
Bolehill
Ballidon
Wirksworth
Wirksworth Moor
Whatstandwell
Oakerthorpe
Milldale
Parwich
Brassington
WINGFIELD MANOR
Crich
Dove Dale
Manifold
Miller's Green
Alderwasley
Fritchley
Bradbourne
Carsington
Bullbridge
Pentrich
Tissington
ECCLESBOURNE VALLEY RLY
DOVEDALE
Carsington Res.
Ambergate
Ilam
ILAM HALL
Toadmoor
Heage
Fenny Bentley
Hognaston
Beighton Hill
Thorpe
Belper Lane End
Nether Heage
Kniveton
Kirk Ireton
Shottle
Broadholme
DERWENT VALLEY VISITOR
Idridgehay
Mount Pleasant
Marehay
Far Laund
Atlow
Biggin
Swinscoe
Mapleton
0 1 2 3 miles
0 1 2 3 4 5 km

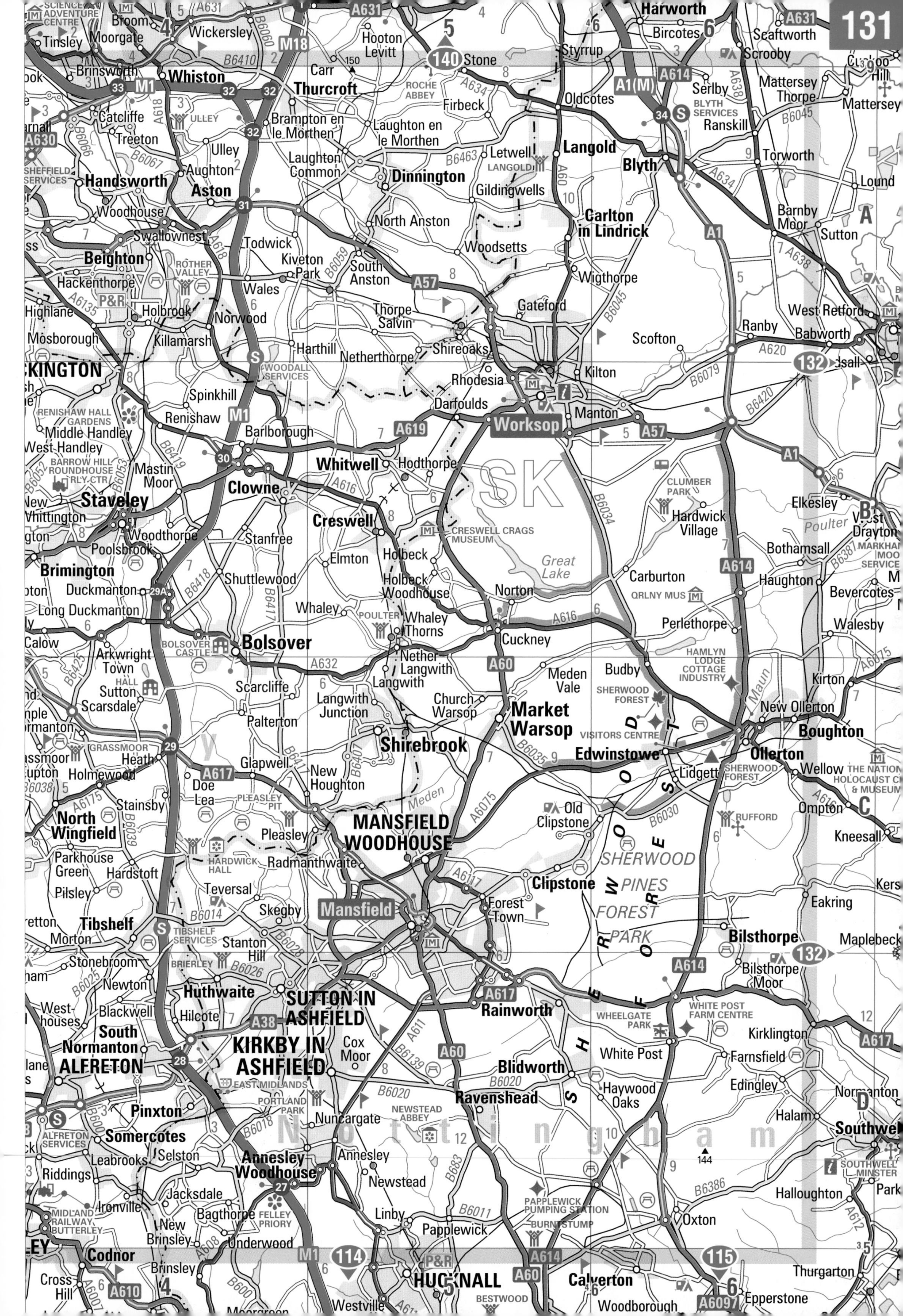
Harworth
Bircotes
Scaftworth
Scrooby
Tinsley
Broom
Wickersley
Moorgate
Hooton Levitt
Stone
Styrrup
Brinsworth
Whiston
Carr
Thurcroft
Roche Abbey
Firbeck
Oldcotes
Serlby
Mattersey Thorpe
Mattersey
Catcliffe
Treeton
Ulley
Brampton en le Morthen
Laughton en le Morthen
Letwell
Langold
Blyth Services
Ranskill
Torworth
Handsworth
Aughton
Aston
Laughton Common
Dinnington
Gildingwells
Blyth
Lound
Woodhouse
Swallownest
North Anston
Carlton in Lindrick
Barnby Moor
Sutton
Beighton
Rother Valley
Todwick
Kiveton Park
South Anston
Woodsetts
Wigthorpe
Hackenthorpe
Wales
Gateford
West Retford
Highlane
Holbrook
Norwood
Thorpe Salvin
Ranby
Babworth
Mosborough
Killamarsh
Harthill
Netherthorpe
Shireoaks
Scofton
Woodall Services
Rhodesia
Kilton
Eckington
Spinkhill
Darfoulds
Manton
Renishaw Hall Gardens
Renishaw
Worksop
Middle Handley
West Handley
Barlborough
Whitwell
Hodthorpe
Barrow Hill Roundhouse Rly Ctr
Mastin Moor
Clowne
Clumber Park
Elkesley
Staveley
New Whittington
Creswell
Hardwick Village
West Drayton
Woodthorpe
Stanfree
Creswell Crags Museum
Poolsbrook
Elmton
Holbeck
Great Lake
Carburton
Bothamsall
Brimington
Shuttlewood
Holbeck Woodhouse
Norton
Haughton
Duckmanton
Long Duckmanton
Whaley
Whaley Thorns
Qrlny Mus
Perlethorpe
Bevercotes
Calow
Bolsover
Bolsover Castle
Cuckney
Walesby
Arkwright Town
Nether Langwith
Langwith
Meden Vale
Budby
Hamlyn Lodge Cottage Industry
Sutton Scarsdale
Scarcliffe
Church Warsop
Market Warsop
Sherwood Forest
Kirton
Langwith Junction
Palterton
Shirebrook
Visitors Centre
Edwinstowe
New Ollerton
Boughton
Grassmoor
Heath
Glapwell
Lidgett
Ollerton
Holmewood
Doe Lea
New Houghton
Wellow
The National Holocaust Centre & Museum
Stainsby
Pleasley Pit
Old Clipstone
Ompton
North Wingfield
Pleasley
Mansfield Woodhouse
Rufford
Kneesall
Parkhouse Green
Hardstoft
Hardwick Hall
Radmanthwaite
Sherwood Pines Forest Park
Pilsley
Teversal
Clipstone
Eakring
Tibshelf
Skegby
Mansfield
Forest Town
Morton
Tibshelf Services
Stanton Hill
Bilsthorpe
Maplebeck
Stonebroom
Brierley
Bilsthorpe Moor
Newton
Huthwaite
Sutton in Ashfield
Blackwell
Hilcote
Rainworth
White Post Farm Centre
Wheelgate Park
Kirklington
South Normanton
Alfreton
Kirkby in Ashfield
Cox Moor
White Post
Farnsfield
Blidworth
East Midlands
Haywood Oaks
Edingley
Portland Park
Ravenshead
Newstead Abbey
Normanton
Pinxton
Halam
Southwell
Somercotes
Alfreton Services
Nuncargate
Nottingham
Selston
Leabrooks
Annesley Woodhouse
Annesley
Southwell Minster
Riddings
Newstead
Halloughton
Jacksdale
Ironville
Felley Priory
Papplewick Pumping Station
Midland Railway Butterley
Bagthorpe
Linby
Oxton
New Brinsley
Papplewick
Burntstump
Underwood
Codnor
Brinsley
Hucknall
Calverton
Thurgarton
Cross Hill
Bestwood
Woodborough
Epperstone
Westville
SK
M1
M18
A1(M)
A1
A57
A60
A614
A616
A617
A619
A620
A630
A631
A632
A38
A610
A611
A609
A6075

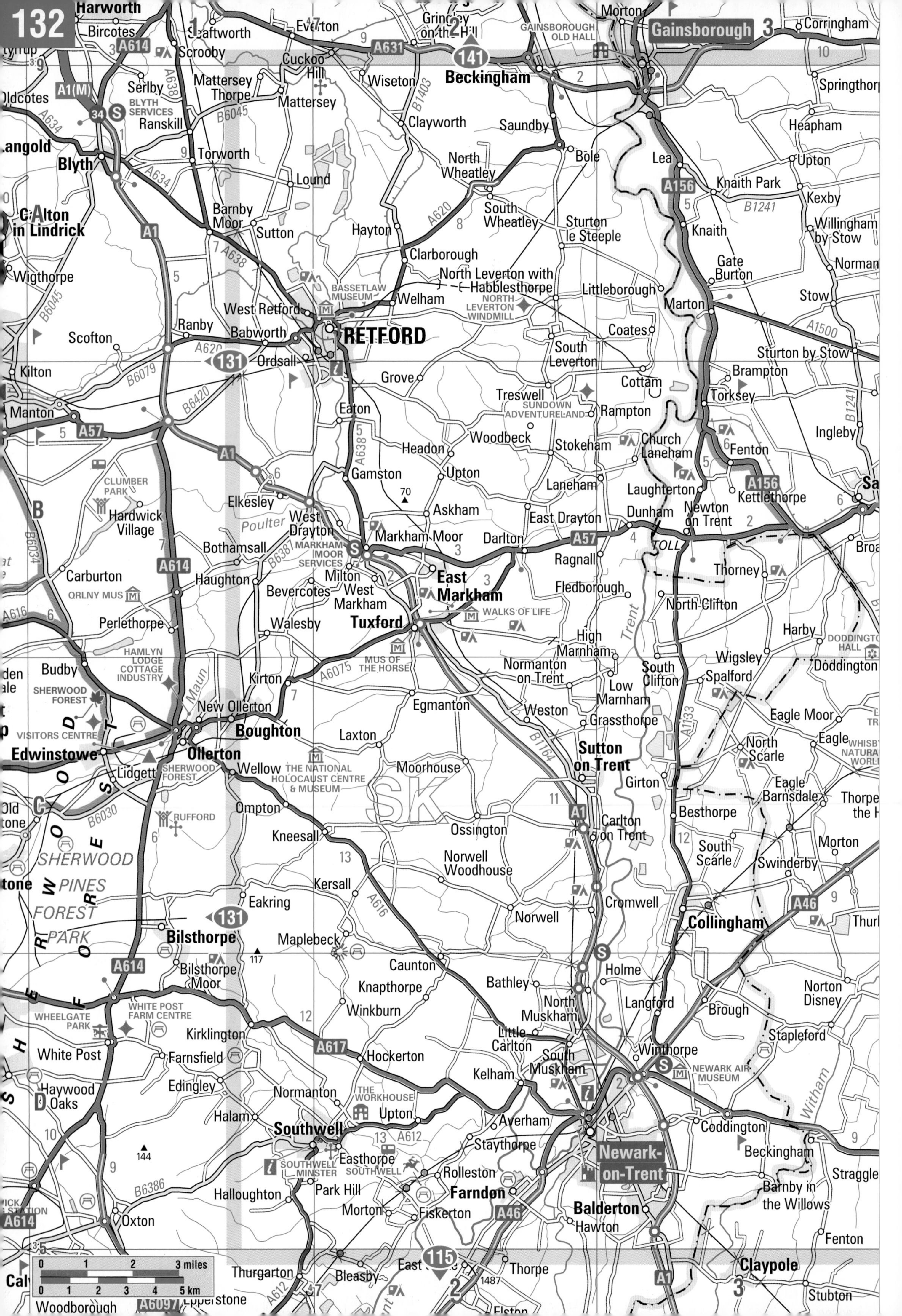

Harworth
Bircotes
Scaftworth
Everton
Gringley on the Hill
Morton
Gainsborough
Corringham
A614
Scrooby
Cuckoo Hill
A631
141
Beckingham
GAINSBOROUGH OLD HALL
Springthorpe
A1(M)
Serlby
Mattersey Thorpe
Wiseton
B1403
Oldcotes
34
BLYTH SERVICES
Ranskill
B6045
Mattersey
Clayworth
Saundby
Heapham
A634
Langold
Torworth
Blyth
Lound
North Wheatley
Bole
Lea
Upton
A156
Knaith Park
Kexby
B1241
Carlton in Lindrick
Barnby Moor
Sutton
Hayton
A620
South Wheatley
Sturton le Steeple
Knaith
Willingham by Stow
A1
A638
Clarborough
Gate Burton
Norman
Wigthorpe
North Leverton with Habblesthorpe
BASSETLAW MUSEUM
Welham
NORTH LEVERTON WINDMILL
Littleborough
Marton
Stow
West Retford
B6045
Scofton
Ranby
Babworth
RETFORD
Coates
A1500
South Leverton
Sturton by Stow
Kilton
131
Ordsall
B6079
Grove
Cottam
Brampton
Treswell
SUNDOWN ADVENTURELAND
Torksey
B6420
Manton
A57
Eaton
Rampton
B1241
Woodbeck
Headon
Stokeham
Church Laneham
Ingleby
Fenton
A1
Gamston
Upton
Laneham
Laughterton
A156
CLUMBER PARK
Hardwick Village
70
Elkesley
Askham
Kettlethorpe
Newton on Trent
Dunham
East Drayton
Poulter
West Drayton
B6034
Markham Moor
Darlton
TOLL
Bothamsall
MARKHAM MOOR SERVICES
Ragnall
Thorney
B6387
East Markham
Carburton
Haughton
Milton
A614
Fledborough
QRLNY MUS
Bevercotes
West Markham
North Clifton
Perlethorpe
Walesby
Tuxford
WALKS OF LIFE
A616
High Marnham
Harby
Trent
DODDINGTON HALL
HAMLYN LODGE COTTAGE INDUSTRY
MUS OF THE HORSE
Normanton on Trent
Wigsley
Budby
Kirton
A6075
South Clifton
Spalford
Doddington
Low Marnham
SHERWOOD FOREST
Maun
Egmanton
VISITORS CENTRE
New Ollerton
Weston
Grassthorpe
Eagle Moor
Boughton
A1133
Laxton
Sutton on Trent
North Scarle
Eagle
Edwinstowe
Ollerton
B1164
Lidgett
SHERWOOD FOREST
Wellow
THE NATIONAL HOLOCAUST CENTRE & MUSEUM
Moorhouse
Girton
Eagle Barnsdale
SK
Thorpe on the Hill
Ompton
A1
Besthorpe
B6030
RUFFORD
Carlton on Trent
Kneesall
Ossington
Morton
South Scarle
SHERWOOD
Norwell Woodhouse
Swinderby
PINES
Kersall
Cromwell
FOREST
Eakring
A46
A616
Norwell
Collingham
PARK
131
Bilsthorpe
Maplebeck
117
Holme
A614
Caunton
Bilsthorpe Moor
Bathley
Knapthorpe
Norton Disney
North Muskham
Langford
WHITE POST FARM CENTRE
Winkburn
Brough
WHEELGATE PARK
Little Carlton
Stapleford
Kirklington
A617
Hockerton
Winthorpe
Witham
White Post
Farnsfield
South Muskham
Kelham
NEWARK AIR MUSEUM
Haywood Oaks
Edingley
Normanton
THE WORKHOUSE
Upton
Halam
Averham
Coddington
Southwell
A612
Staythorpe
Newark-on-Trent
Beckingham
144
SOUTHWELL MINSTER
Easthorpe
SOUTHWELL
Rolleston
Straggle
B6386
Halloughton
Park Hill
Farndon
Barnby in the Willows
Morton
Fiskerton
A46
Balderton
Hawton
Oxton
A614
Fenton
115
Thurgarton
Bleasby
East Stoke
Thorpe
Claypole
1487
A612
A1
Woodborough
A6097
Epperstone
Stubton
0 1 2 3 miles
0 1 2 3 4 5 km

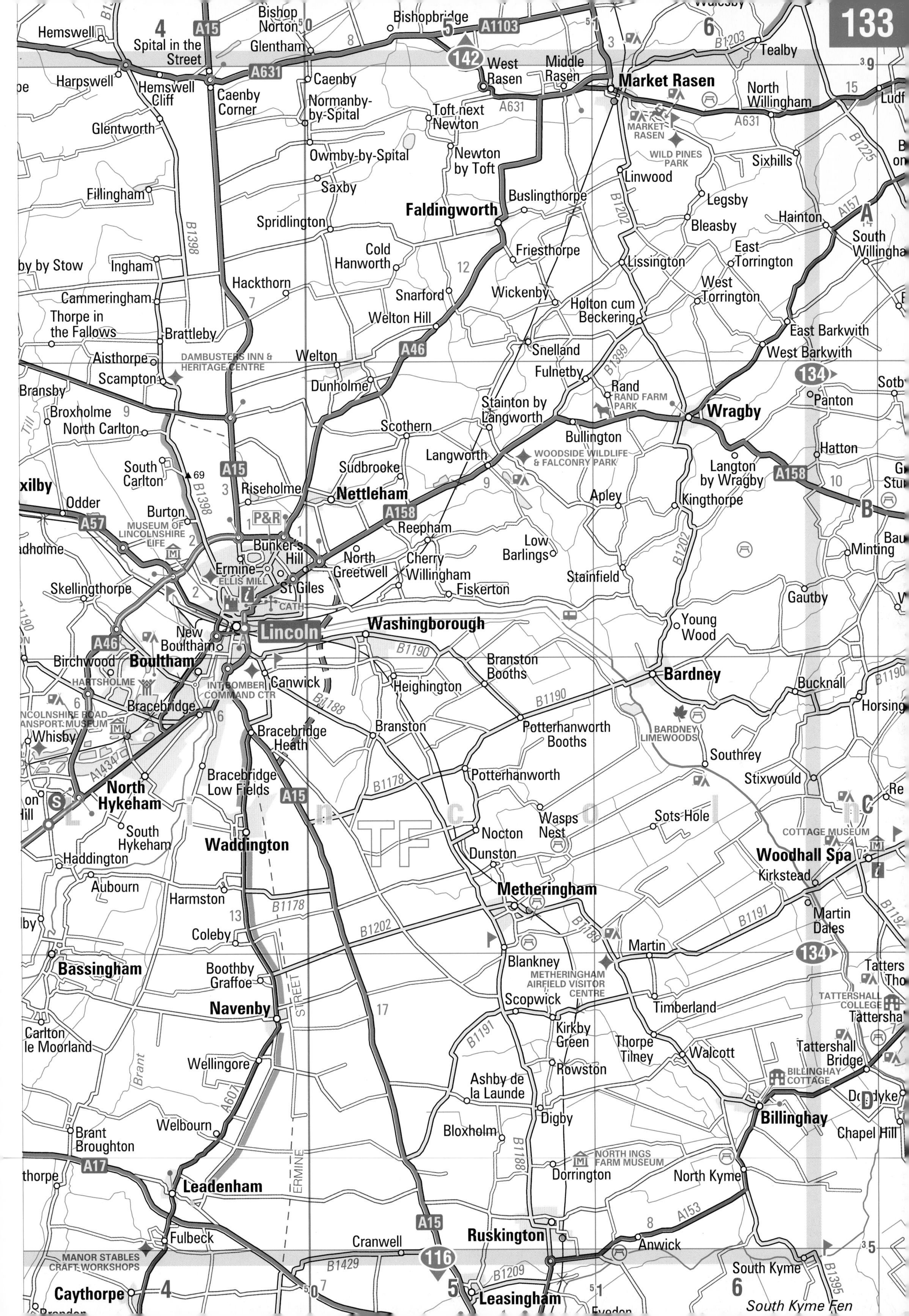
Hemswell
Bishop Norton
Bishopbridge
A1103
Tealby
Spital in the Street
Glentham
A15
142
West Rasen
Middle Rasen
Market Rasen
North Willingham
Harpswell
Hemswell Cliff
A631
Caenby
Caenby Corner
Normanby-by-Spital
Toft next Newton
MARKET RASEN
Glentworth
Owmby-by-Spital
Newton by Toft
WILD PINES PARK
Sixhills
Linwood
Fillingham
Saxby
Buslingthorpe
Legsby
Faldingworth
Hainton
Spridlington
Bleasby
South Willingham
Cold Hanworth
Friesthorpe
East Torrington
Ingham
Lissington
B1398
B1202
Hackthorn
West Torrington
Cammeringham
Snarford
Wickenby
Holton cum Beckering
Thorpe in the Fallows
Welton Hill
East Barkwith
Brattleby
A46
Snelland
West Barkwith
Aisthorpe
DAMBUSTERS INN & HERITAGE CENTRE
Welton
Fulnetby
B1399
134
Scampton
Dunholme
Rand
RAND FARM PARK
Panton
Bransby
Stainton by Langworth
Wragby
Broxholme
North Carlton
Scothern
Bullington
Hatton
South Carlton
Sudbrooke
Langworth
WOODSIDE WILDLIFE & FALCONRY PARK
Langton by Wragby
A158
Riseholme
Nettleham
Apley
Kingthorpe
Odder
Burton
A57
P&R
Reepham
MUSEUM OF LINCOLNSHIRE LIFE
Bunker's Hill
Low Barlings
Minting
Ermine
North Greetwell
Cherry Willingham
Stainfield
ELLIS MILL
Skellingthorpe
St Giles
Fiskerton
Gautby
CATH
Lincoln
Washingborough
Young Wood
New Boultham
B1190
Birchwood
Boultham
Branston Booths
Bardney
HARTSHOLME
INT. BOMBER COMMAND CTR
Canwick
Heighington
Bucknall
Horsington
Bracebridge
B1188
Potterhanworth Booths
BARDNEY LIMEWOODS
Whisby
Bracebridge Heath
Branston
Southrey
A1434
Bracebridge Low Fields
B1178
Potterhanworth
Stixwould
North Hykeham
A15
South Hykeham
Waddington
TF
Nocton
Wasps Nest
Sots Hole
COTTAGE MUSEUM
Haddington
Dunston
Woodhall Spa
Kirkstead
Aubourn
Harmston
Metheringham
Martin Dales
B1191
Coleby
B1202
B1189
Martin
Bassingham
Blankney
Boothby Graffoe
METHERINGHAM AIRFIELD VISITOR CENTRE
Tattershall
STREET
Scopwick
Timberland
TATTERSHALL COLLEGE
Navenby
Carlton le Moorland
Kirkby Green
Thorpe Tilney
Tattershall Bridge
Walcott
Wellingore
Rowston
Brant
BILLINGHAY COTTAGE
Ashby de la Launde
A607
Digby
Billinghay
Dogdyke
Brant Broughton
Welbourn
Bloxholm
Chapel Hill
A17
NORTH INGS FARM MUSEUM
ERMINE
Dorrington
North Kyme
Leadenham
A15
A153
Ruskington
Fulbeck
Cranwell
Anwick
MANOR STABLES CRAFT WORKSHOPS
116
B1429
B1209
South Kyme
B1395
Caythorpe
Leasingham
South Kyme Fen
B1225
A157
B1203

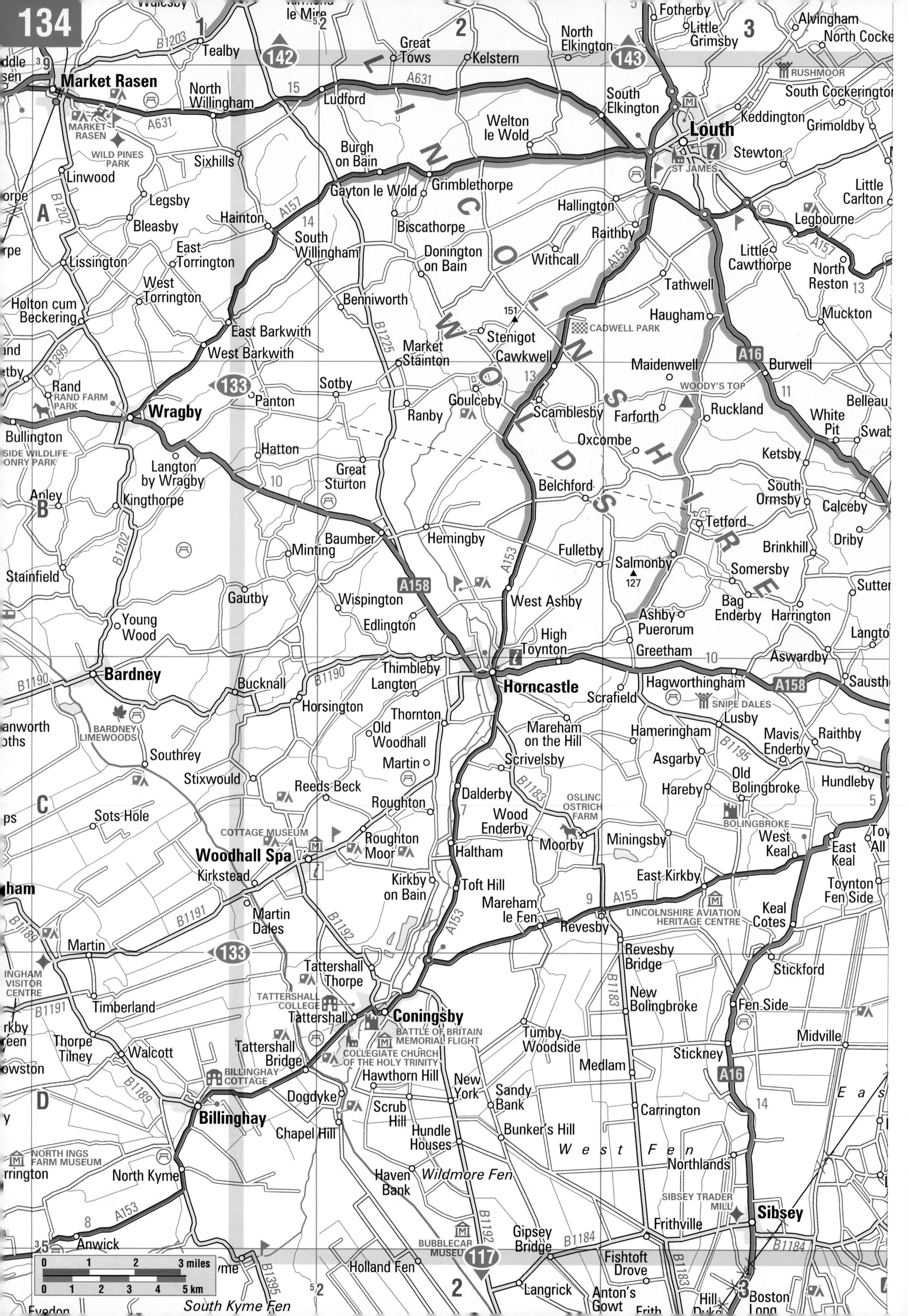
LINCOLNSHIRE WOLDS
Tealby
B1203
142
143
Great Tows
Kelstern
North Elkington
Fotherby
Little Grimsby
Alvingham
North Cockerington
RUSHMOOR
South Cockerington
Market Rasen
North Willingham
Ludford
A631
MARKET RASEN
WILD PINES PARK
A631
South Elkington
Louth
Keddington
Grimoldby
Welton le Wold
Stewton
ST JAMES
Sixhills
Burgh on Bain
Linwood
Gayton le Wold
Grimblethorpe
Little Carlton
Legsby
Hallington
Legbourne
A
B1202
Bleasby
Hainton
A157
South Willingham
Biscathorpe
Raithby
A157
Lissington
East Torrington
Donington on Bain
Withcall
A153
Little Cawthorpe
North Reston
West Torrington
Tathwell
Holton cum Beckering
Benniworth
151
Haugham
Muckton
CADWELL PARK
East Barkwith
West Barkwith
B1225
Market Stainton
Stenigot
Cawkwell
A16
Burwell
B1399
Rand
RAND FARM PARK
133
Panton
Sotby
Maidenwell
Wragby
Ranby
Goulceby
Scamblesby
Farforth
WOODY'S TOP
Ruckland
Belleau
White Pit
Bullington
Hatton
Oxcombe
Ketsby
Langton by Wragby
Great Sturton
Belchford
South Ormsby
Calceby
Apley
B
Kingthorpe
Tetford
Driby
Baumber
Hemingby
Minting
Fulletby
Salmonby
Brinkhill
Somersby
B1202
A153
Stainfield
127
A158
Gautby
Wispington
West Ashby
Bag Enderby
Harrington
Young Wood
Edlington
Ashby Puerorum
High Toynton
Greetham
Aswardby
Bardney
B1190
Bucknall
B1190
Thimbleby
Langton
Horncastle
Scrafield
Hagworthingham
A158
SNIPE DALES
Horsington
Thornton
Lusby
BARDNEY LIMEWOODS
Old Woodhall
Mareham on the Hill
Hameringham
Mavis Enderby
Raithby
Southrey
Martin
Scrivelsby
B1195
Asgarby
Hundleby
Stixwould
Reeds Beck
Dalderby
B1183
OSLINC OSTRICH FARM
Old Bolingbroke
Hareby
C
Sots Hole
Roughton
Wood Enderby
BOLINGBROKE
West Keal
East Keal
COTTAGE MUSEUM
Roughton Moor
Moorby
Miningsby
Woodhall Spa
Kirkstead
Haltham
Kirkby on Bain
Toft Hill
East Kirkby
Toynton Fen Side
Martin Dales
B1191
A153
Mareham le Fen
9
A155
Revesby
LINCOLNSHIRE AVIATION HERITAGE CENTRE
Keal Cotes
B1192
Martin
133
Revesby Bridge
INGHAM VISITOR CENTRE
Tattershall Thorpe
Stickford
TATTERSHALL COLLEGE
Tattershall
Coningsby
B1183
New Bolingbroke
Fen Side
Timberland
B1191
BATTLE OF BRITAIN MEMORIAL FLIGHT
Midville
Thorpe Tilney
Tattershall Bridge
Walcott
COLLEGIATE CHURCH OF THE HOLY TRINITY
Tumby Woodside
Stickney
BILLINGHAY COTTAGE
Hawthorn Hill
Medlam
A16
B1189
New York
D
Dogdyke
Billinghay
Scrub Hill
Sandy Bank
Carrington
Chapel Hill
Hundle Houses
Bunker's Hill
West Fen
NORTH INGS FARM MUSEUM
North Kyme
Haven Bank
Wildmore Fen
Northlands
A153
SIBSEY TRADER MILL
Sibsey
Frithville
B1192
Gipsey Bridge
B1184
Anwick
BUBBLECAR MUSEUM
117
Fishtoft Drove
B1184
B1183
B1395
Holland Fen
Langrick
Anton's Gowt
Boston
South Kyme Fen
0 1 2 3 miles
0 1 2 3 4 5 km

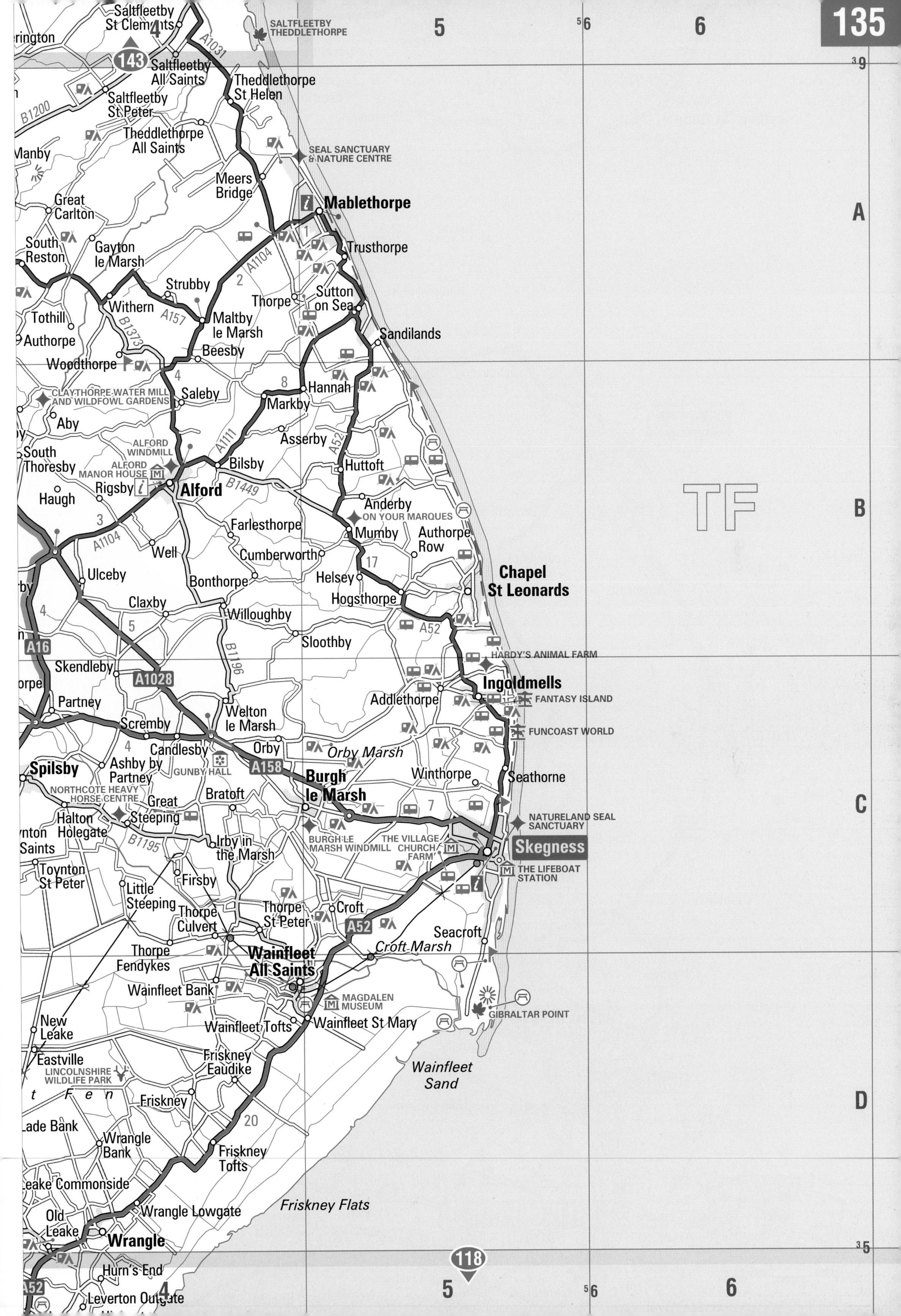
Saltfleetby St Clements
Saltfleetby All Saints
Saltfleetby St Peter
SALTFLEETBY THEDDLETHORPE
Theddlethorpe St Helen
Theddlethorpe All Saints
SEAL SANCTUARY & NATURE CENTRE
Meers Bridge
Mablethorpe
Trusthorpe
Sutton on Sea
Sandilands
Thorpe
Great Carlton
South Reston
Gayton le Marsh
Strubby
Withern
Maltby le Marsh
Tothill
Authorpe
Beesby
Woodthorpe
CLAYTHORPE WATER MILL AND WILDFOWL GARDENS
Saleby
Hannah
Markby
Aby
Asserby
ALFORD WINDMILL
ALFORD MANOR HOUSE
South Thoresby
Bilsby
Huttoft
Rigsby
Alford
Haugh
Anderby
ON YOUR MARQUES
Farlesthorpe
Mumby
Authorpe Row
Well
Cumberworth
Ulceby
Bonthorpe
Helsey
Hogsthorpe
Chapel St Leonards
Claxby
Willoughby
Sloothby
HARDY'S ANIMAL FARM
Skendleby
Ingoldmells
Partney
Addlethorpe
FANTASY ISLAND
Welton le Marsh
Scremby
FUNCOAST WORLD
Candlesby
Orby
Orby Marsh
Spilsby
Ashby by Partney
GUNBY HALL
Burgh le Marsh
Winthorpe
Seathorne
NORTHCOTE HEAVY HORSE CENTRE
Bratoft
Great Steeping
NATURELAND SEAL SANCTUARY
Halton Holegate
Irby in the Marsh
BURGH LE MARSH WINDMILL
THE VILLAGE CHURCH FARM
Skegness
THE LIFEBOAT STATION
Toynton St Peter
Firsby
Little Steeping
Thorpe Culvert
Thorpe St Peter
Croft
Seacroft
Thorpe Fendykes
Wainfleet All Saints
Croft Marsh
Wainfleet Bank
MAGDALEN MUSEUM
GIBRALTAR POINT
New Leake
Wainfleet Tofts
Wainfleet St Mary
Eastville
LINCOLNSHIRE WILDLIFE PARK
Friskney Eaudike
Wainfleet Sand
Friskney
Lade Bank
Wrangle Bank
Friskney Tofts
Leake Commonside
Wrangle Lowgate
Friskney Flats
Old Leake
Wrangle
Hurn's End
Leverton Outgate
TF
A1031
B1200
A1104
A157
B1373
A1111
B1449
A52
A16
A1028
B1196
A158
B1195
143
118
A
B
C
D
4
5
6

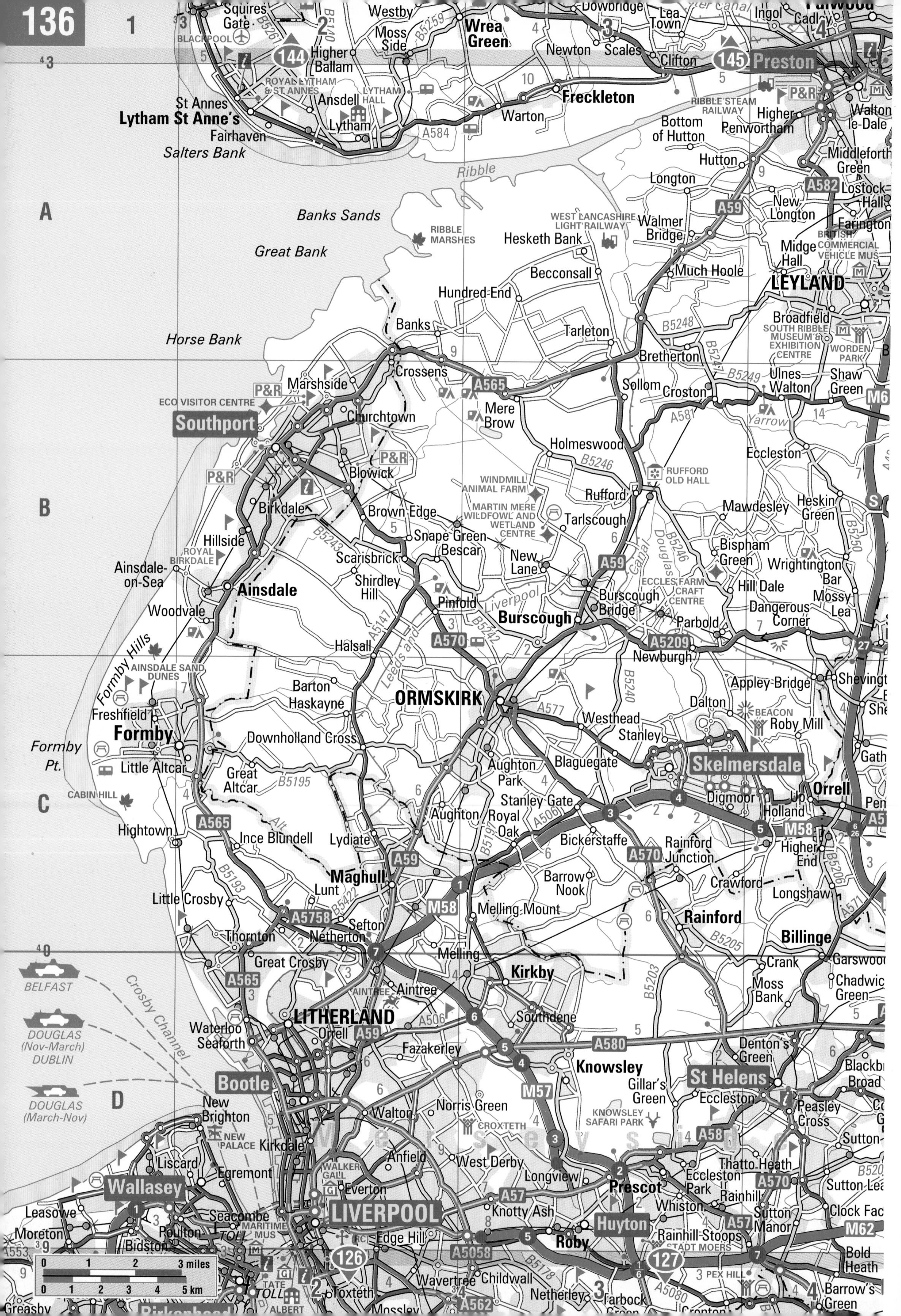
Lytham St Anne's
Southport
Formby
Ainsdale
ORMSKIRK
Burscough
Skelmersdale
LEYLAND
Preston
Freckleton
Maghull
Kirkby
LITHERLAND
Bootle
Wallasey
LIVERPOOL
Knowsley
St Helens
Prescot
Huyton
Rainford
Billinge
Orrell
Ribble
Banks Sands
Great Bank
Horse Bank
Salters Bank
Formby Pt.
Crosby Channel
BELFAST
DOUGLAS (Nov-March) DUBLIN
DOUGLAS (March-Nov)
A565
A570
A59
A580
M58
M57
M62
M6
A57
0 1 2 3 miles
0 1 2 3 4 5 km

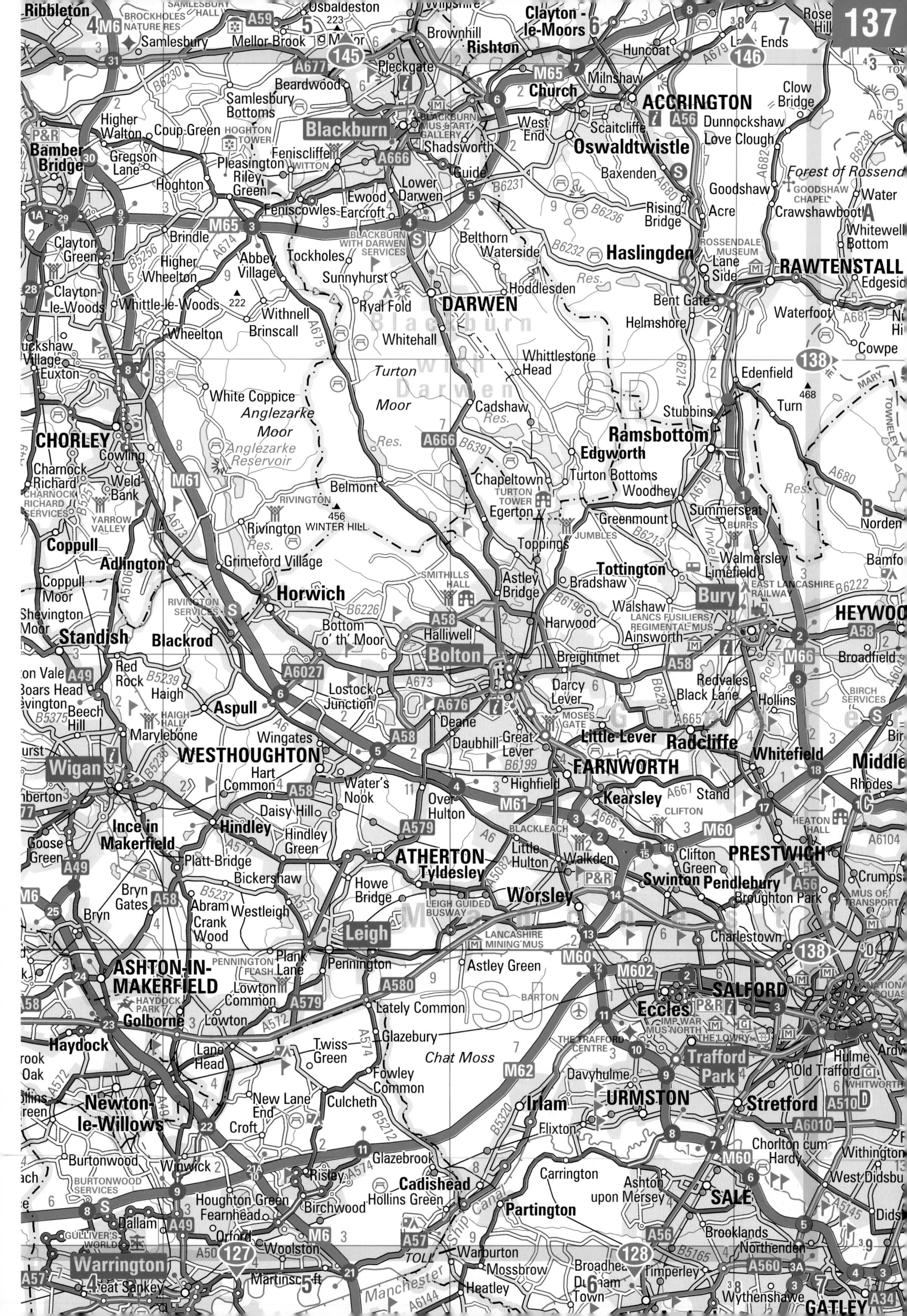
Ribbleton
Samlesbury
Mellor Brook
Osbaldeston
Brownhill
Rishton
Clayton-le-Moors
Huncoat
Rose Hill
Ends
Pleckgate
Beardwood
Samlesbury Bottoms
Church
Milnshaw
ACCRINGTON
Clow Bridge
Dunnockshaw
Love Clough
Higher Walton
Coup Green
Hoghton Tower
Blackburn
West End
Scaitcliffe
Oswaldtwistle
Bamber Bridge
Gregson Lane
Feniscliffe
Witton
Shadsworth
Pleasington
Riley Green
Guide
Baxenden
Forest of Rossend
Hoghton
Lower Darwen
Goodshaw
Goodshaw Chapel
Water
Feniscowles
Ewood
Earcroft
Rising Bridge
Acre
Crawshawbooth
Clayton Green
Brindle
Blackburn with Darwen Services
Tockholes
Belthorn
Waterside
Haslingden
Rossendale Museum
Whitewell Bottom
Higher Wheelton
Abbey Village
Sunnyhurst
Lane Side
RAWTENSTALL
Edgeside
Clayton-le-Woods
Whittle-le-Woods
Withnell
Ryal Fold
DARWEN
Hoddlesden
Bent Gate
Waterfoot
Wheelton
Brinscall
Whitehall
Helmshore
Cowpe
Buckshaw Village
Euxton
Turton Moor
Whittlestone Head
Edenfield
White Coppice
Anglezarke Moor
Cadshaw
Stubbins
Turn
CHORLEY
Cowling
Anglezarke Reservoir
Ramsbottom
Edgworth
Charnock Richard
Charnock Richard Services
Weld Bank
Chapeltown
Turton Tower
Turton Bottoms
Woodhey
Belmont
Rivington
Winter Hill
Egerton
Summerseat
Burrs
Greenmount
Norden
Yarrow Valley
Coppull
Jumbles
Toppings
Adlington
Grimeford Village
Walmersley
Limefield
Bamford
Coppull Moor
Smithills Hall
Tottington
Bradshaw
Astley Bridge
Bury
East Lancashire Railway
Shevington Moor
Horwich
Rivington Services
Walshaw
HEYWOOD
Standish
Blackrod
Bottom o' th' Moor
Halliwell
Harwood
Lancs Fusiliers Regimental Mus
Ainsworth
Bolton
Breightmet
Broadfield
Red Rock
Haigh
Lostock Junction
Darcy Lever
Redvales
Black Lane
Hollins
Birch Services
Beech Hill
Haigh Hall
Aspull
Deane
Daubhill
Great Lever
Moses Gate
Little Lever
Radcliffe
Marylebone
Wingates
WESTHOUGHTON
FARNWORTH
Whitefield
Wigan
Hart Common
Water's Nook
Over Hulton
Highfield
Kearsley
Stand
Clifton
Rhodes
Heaton Hall
Ince in Makerfield
Hindley
Daisy Hill
Hindley Green
Blackleach
Little Hulton
Walkden
PRESTWICH
Goose Green
Platt Bridge
ATHERTON
Tyldesley
Clifton Green
Swinton
Pendlebury
Crumpsall
Bryn Gates
Bickershaw
Howe Bridge
Worsley
Broughton Park
Mus of Transport
Abram
Westleigh
Leigh Guided Busway
Bryn
Crank Wood
Leigh
Lancashire Mining Mus
Charlestown
ASHTON-IN-MAKERFIELD
Pennington Flash
Plank Lane
Pennington
Astley Green
SALFORD
Haydock Park
Lowton Common
Barton
Eccles
Golborne
Lowton
Lately Common
Glazebury
Imp War Mus North
The Lowry
Haydock
Lane Head
Twiss Green
Chat Moss
The Trafford Centre
Trafford Park
Hulme
Old Trafford
Newton-le-Willows
Fowley Common
Davyhulme
New Lane End
Culcheth
Irlam
URMSTON
Stretford
Croft
Flixton
Chorlton cum Hardy
Withington
Burtonwood
Burtonwood Services
Winwick
Glazebrook
Carrington
West Didsbury
Risley
Cadishead
Ashton upon Mersey
SALE
Houghton Green
Fearnhead
Birchwood
Hollins Green
Partington
Dallam
Gulliver's World
Orford
Woolston
Brooklands
Northenden
Warrington
Warburton
Mossbrow
Broadheath
Timperley
Great Sankey
Martinscroft
Heatley
Dunham Town
Wythenshawe
GATLEY
Manchester Ship Canal
Irwell
M6
M61
M62
M65
M66
M60
M602
A59
A677
A666
A56
A58
A49
A6027
A673
A676
A579
A580
A57
A560
A34
A510
A6010
SD
SJ
Greater Manchester
Blackburn with Darwen

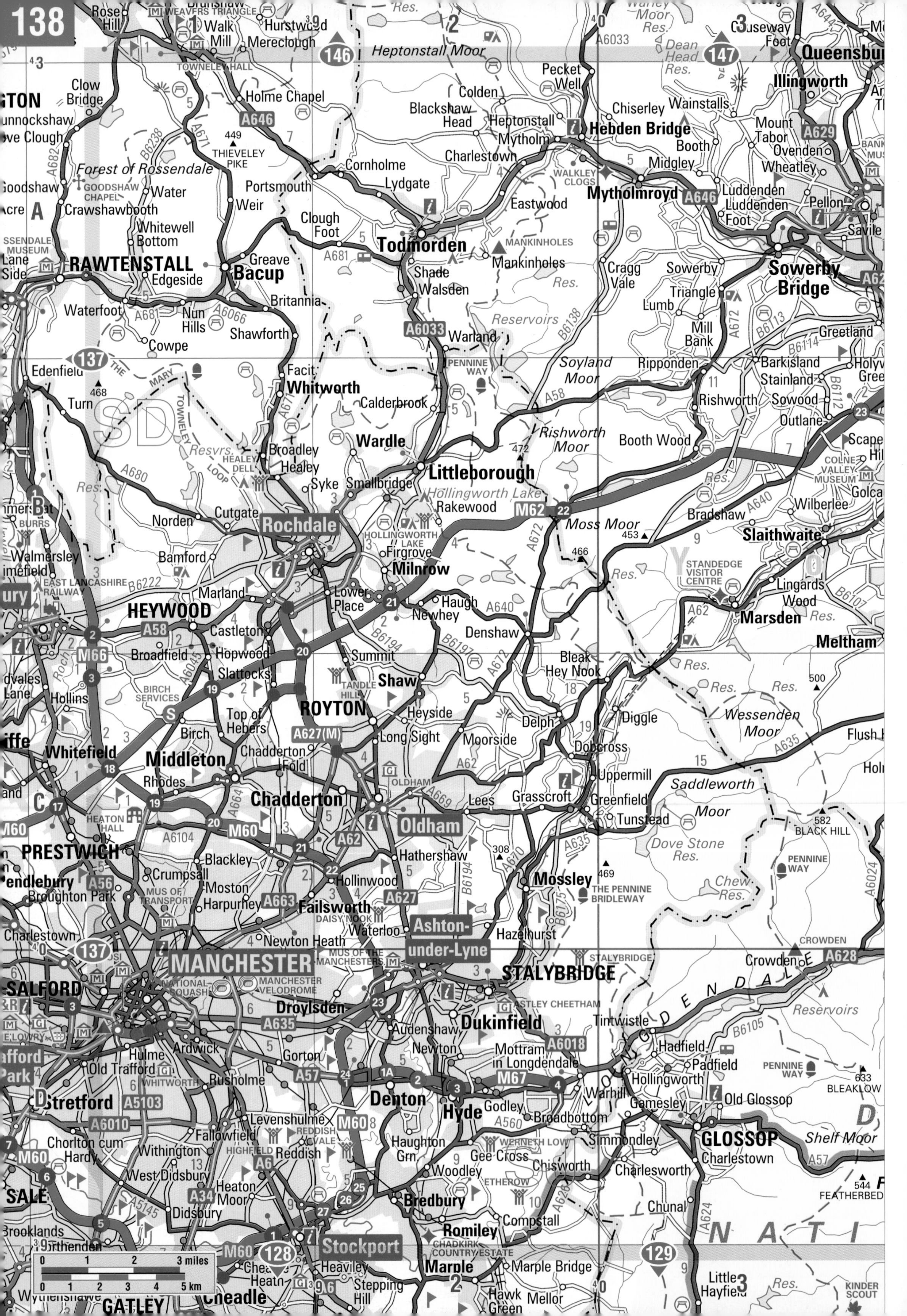
Rose Hill
Walk Mill
Hurstwood
Mereclough
146
Heptonstall Moor
147
Causeway Foot
Queensbury
Dean Head Res.
Moor Res.
TOWNELEY HALL
Clow Bridge
Holme Chapel
A646
Colden
Pecket Well
Illingworth
Blackshaw Head
Heptonstall
Chiserley
Wainstalls
Hebden Bridge
Mount Tabor
A629
Dunnockshaw
Love Clough
449
THIEVELEY PIKE
Mytholm
Booth
Ovenden
Charlestown
Midgley
Wheatley
Forest of Rossendale
Cornholme
WALKLEY CLOGS
Goodshaw
GOODSHAW CHAPEL
Water
Portsmouth
Lydgate
Mytholmroyd
A646
Luddenden
Luddenden Foot
Pellon
Crawshawbooth
Weir
Eastwood
Savile
Whitewell Bottom
Clough Foot
Todmorden
MANKINHOLES
Mankinholes
ROSSENDALE MUSEUM
RAWTENSTALL
Greave
Bacup
A681
Shade
Walsden
Cragg Vale
Sowerby
Sowerby Bridge
Edgeside
Res.
Triangle
Lumb
Waterfoot
A681
Nun Hills
A6066
Britannia
Reservoirs
B6138
Mill Bank
Cowpe
Shawforth
A6033
Warland
A672
B6113
Greetland
B6114
137
Edenfield
THE MARY TOWNELEY LOOP
PENNINE WAY
Soyland Moor
Ripponden
Barkisland
Stainland
Holywell Green
Facit
Whitworth
Turn
468
Calderbrook
A58
Rishworth
Sowood
B6112
Outlane
SD
Rishworth Moor
Booth Wood
Scapegoat Hill
Wardle
472
Resvrs.
HEALEY DELL
Broadley
Healey
Littleborough
A680
Res.
Syke
Smallbridge
Hollingworth Lake
Rakewood
COLNE VALLEY MUSEUM
Golcar
Res.
Wilberlee
Cutgate
Norden
Rochdale
M62
22
Moss Moor
Bradshaw
A640
Slaithwaite
BURRS
HOLLINGWORTH LAKE
453
Walmersley
Bamford
Firgrove
Milnrow
A672
466
Y
STANDEDGE VISITOR CENTRE
Lingards Wood
Limefield
EAST LANCASHIRE RAILWAY
B6222
Marland
Lower Place
21
Haugh
Newhey
A640
Res.
B6107
Marsden
Res.
HEYWOOD
A58
Castleton
Denshaw
A62
Meltham
Broadfield
Hopwood
20
Summit
B6194
B6197
M66
Bleak Hey Nook
Res.
Res.
500
Slattocks
Hollins
BIRCH SERVICES
19
TANDLE HILL
Shaw
Res.
Wessenden Moor
ROYTON
Heyside
18
Diggle
Top of Hebers
A627(M)
Delph
Birch
Long Sight
Moorside
Dobcross
Flush House
Whitefield
Middleton
Chadderton Fold
A635
18
15
Uppermill
A62
Holme
Rhodes
OLDHAM
Saddleworth
Greenfield
Grasscroft
Chadderton
A669
Lees
Tunstead
Moor
HEATON HALL
17
19
A664
20
Oldham
582
BLACK HILL
Dove Stone Res.
A6104
M60
A62
PRESTWICH
21
Hathershaw
308
A635
Blackley
PENNINE WAY
Crumpsall
A670
22
469
Hollinwood
Moston
Mossley
THE PENNINE BRIDLEWAY
Chew Res.
Pendlebury
A56
MUS OF TRANSPORT
Harpurhey
A663
A627
Broughton Park
B6194
A6024
Failsworth
DAISY NOOK
B6175
Waterloo
Ashton-under-Lyne
Hazelhurst
Charlestown
Newton Heath
STALYBRIDGE
CROWDEN
137
MANCHESTER
MUS OF THE MANCHESTERS
STALYBRIDGE
Crowden
A628
SALFORD
NATIONAL SQUASH
MANCHESTER VELODROME
LONGDENDALE
ASTLEY CHEETHAM
Reservoirs
23
Droylsden
Dukinfield
Tintwistle
A635
Audenshaw
B6105
Ardwick
Gorton
Newton
A6018
Hadfield
Hulme
Mottram in Longdendale
Padfield
Trafford Park
Old Trafford
Rusholme
A57
24
1A
2
M67
PENNINE WAY
WHITWORTH
3
4
Hollingworth
633
BLEAKLOW
Stretford
A5103
Denton
Hyde
Godley
Warhill
Gamesley
Old Glossop
Levenshulme
M60
A560
Broadbottom
D
A6010
REDDISH VALE
WERNETH LOW
Simmondley
GLOSSOP
Fallowfield
Shelf Moor
Chorlton cum Hardy
Withington
HIGHFIELD
Reddish
Haughton Grn.
Gee Cross
Charlestown
M60
A6
Chisworth
Charlesworth
A57
West Didsbury
Woodley
ETHEROW
544
FEATHERBED
SALE
Heaton Moor
A34
25
26
A626
A5145
Bredbury
Chunal
Didsbury
27
Compstall
A624
5
Romiley
Brooklands
Northenden
M60
128
Stockport
CHADKIRK COUNTRY ESTATE
129
Cheadle Heath
Heaviley
Marple
Marple Bridge
Stepping Hill
Hawk Green
Mellor
Little Hayfield
Res.
KINDER SCOUT
Wythenshawe
GATLEY
Cheadle
3 miles
5 km

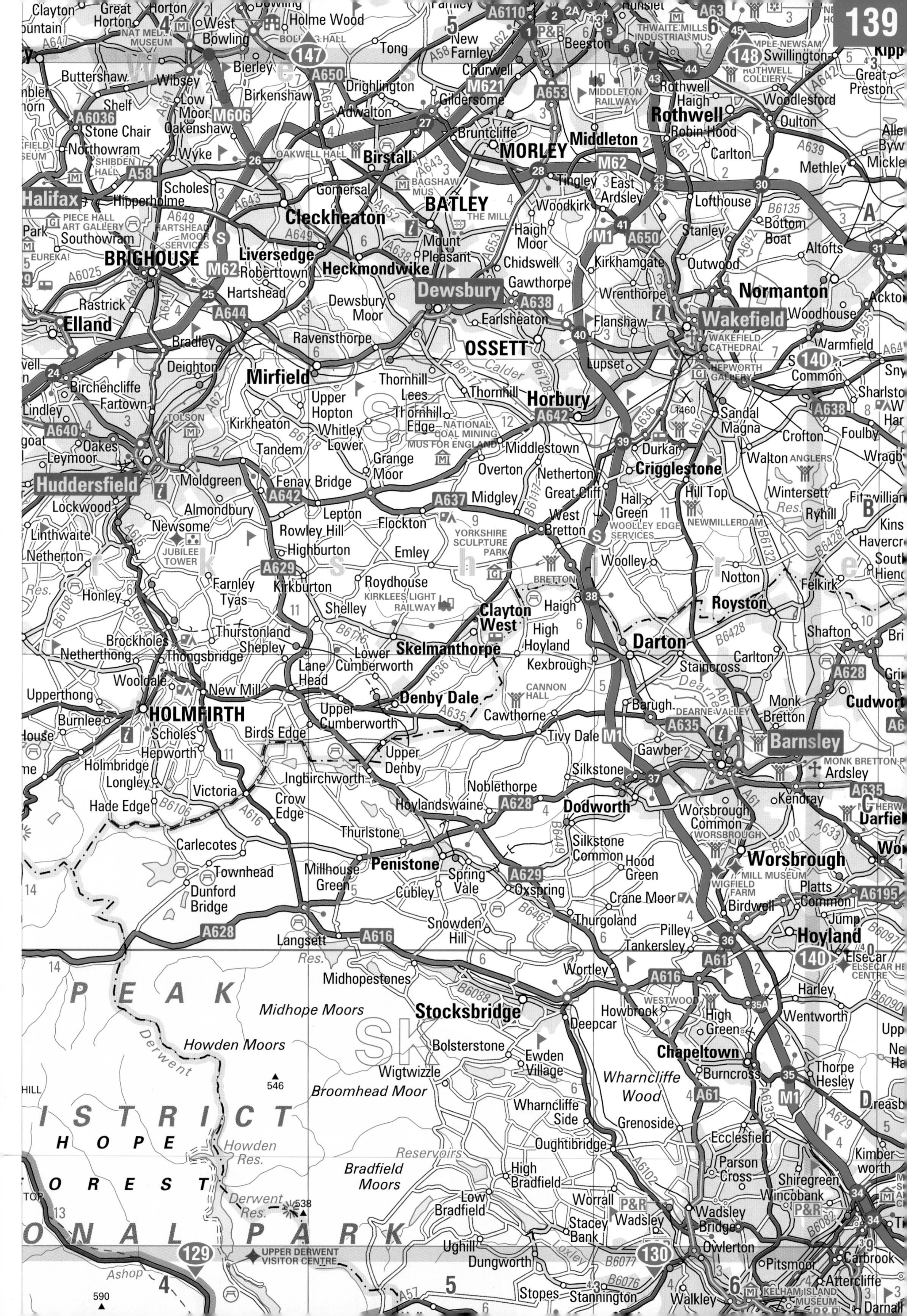
Clayton
Great Horton
Horton
West Bowling
Holme Wood
NAT MEDIA MUSEUM
BOLLING HALL
147
Tong
New Farnley
A6110
Hunslet
THWAITE MILLS INDUSTRIAL MUS
A63
P&R
Beeston
148
TEMPLE NEWSAM
Swillington
A647
Buttershaw
Wibsey
Bierley
A650
Drighlington
Churwell
M621
A653
MIDDLETON RAILWAY
Rothwell
ROTHWELL COLLIERY
Great Preston
Shelf
Low Moor
Birkenshaw
Adwalton
Gildersome
Haigh
Woodlesford
A6036
M606
Stone Chair
Oakenshaw
Bruntcliffe
Middleton
Rothwell
Robin Hood
Oulton
Northowram
SHIBDEN HALL
Wyke
OAKWELL HALL
Birstall
MORLEY
Carlton
A639
Methley
A58
Scholes
Gomersal
BAGSHAW MUS
M62
Tingley
East Ardsley
Halifax
Hipperholme
BATLEY
Woodkirk
Lofthouse
B6135
Bottom Boat
PIECE HALL ART GALLERY
Southowram
A649
HARTSHEAD MOOR SERVICES
Cleckheaton
THE MILL
Haigh Moor
M1
A650
Stanley
Altofts
EUREKA!
BRIGHOUSE
Liversedge
Roberttown
Heckmondwike
Mount Pleasant
Chidswell
Kirkhamgate
Outwood
A6025
Hartshead
Dewsbury
Gawthorpe
Wrenthorpe
Normanton
Rastrick
A644
Dewsbury Moor
A638
Earlsheaton
Flanshaw
Wakefield
Woodhouse
Elland
Bradley
Ravensthorpe
OSSETT
WAKEFIELD CATHEDRAL
Warmfield
Deighton
Mirfield
Calder
Lupset
140
Common
HEPWORTH GALLERY
Birchencliffe
Thornhill Lees
Thornhill
Horbury
Sandal Magna
Sharlston
Fartown
Upper Hopton
Thornhill Edge
A642
A638
Lindley
TOLSON
Kirkheaton
Whitley Lower
NATIONAL COAL MINING MUS FOR ENGLAND
Crofton
Foulby
A640
Oakes
Tandem
Grange Moor
Middlestown
Durkar
Walton
ANGLERS
Leymoor
Overton
Netherton
Crigglestone
Huddersfield
Moldgreen
Fenay Bridge
A642
A637
Midgley
Great Cliff
Hall Green
Hill Top
Wintersett
Lockwood
Almondbury
Lepton
Flockton
West Bretton
WOOLLEY EDGE SERVICES
NEWMILLERDAM
Ryhill
Newsome
Rowley Hill
YORKSHIRE SCULPTURE PARK
Linthwaite
JUBILEE TOWER
Highburton
Emley
Woolley
Notton
Netherton
A629
BRETTON
Felkirk
Farnley Tyas
Kirkburton
Roydhouse
Haigh
Royston
Honley
KIRKLEES LIGHT RAILWAY
Clayton West
Shelley
Thurstonland
High Hoyland
Darton
Shafton
Brockholes
Shepley
Lower Cumberworth
Skelmanthorpe
B6428
Netherthong
Thongsbridge
Kexbrough
Staincross
Carlton
Wooldale
Lane Head
CANNON HALL
A628
New Mill
Denby Dale
Upperthong
Upper Cumberworth
Cawthorne
Barugh
DEARNE VALLEY
Monk Bretton
Cudworth
Burnlee
HOLMFIRTH
A635
A635
Scholes
Birds Edge
Tivy Dale
Gawber
Barnsley
Hepworth
Upper Denby
Silkstone
MONK BRETTON PRIORY
Holmbridge
Ingbirchworth
Ardsley
Longley
Victoria
Noblethorpe
Crow Edge
Hoylandswaine
A628
Dodworth
Kendray
Hade Edge
B6106
A616
Worsbrough Common
WORSBROUGH
Thurlstone
Silkstone Common
B6449
Carlecotes
Penistone
Worsbrough
Millhouse Green
Spring Vale
A629
Hood Green
MILL MUSEUM
Townhead
WIGFIELD FARM
Platts Common
Dunford Bridge
Cubley
Oxspring
Crane Moor
Birdwell
A6195
B6462
Jump
Snowden Hill
Thurgoland
Pilley
Hoyland
A628
Langsett
A616
Tankersley
Res.
140
Elsecar
ELSECAR HERITAGE CENTRE
Wortley
A61
A616
Midhopestones
Harley
PEAK
Midhope Moors
B6088
Stocksbridge
WESTWOOD
Howbrook
High Green
Wentworth
Deepcar
Derwent
Howden Moors
SK
Bolsterstone
Ewden Village
Chapeltown
Thorpe Hesley
Wharncliffe Wood
Wigtwizzle
Burncross
546
Broomhead Moor
M1
Wharncliffe Side
A61
DISTRICT
Grenoside
Ecclesfield
HOPE
Howden Res.
Oughtibridge
Reservoirs
Kimberworth
Bradfield Moors
High Bradfield
Parson Cross
FOREST
Shiregreen
A6102
Worrall
Low Bradfield
Wincobank
P&R
Derwent Res.
538
Wadsley
Wadsley Bridge
Stacey Bank
NATIONAL PARK
Loxley
Ughill
Owlerton
129
130
UPPER DERWENT VISITOR CENTRE
Dungworth
B6077
Pitsmoor
Carbrook
Ashop
B6076
Attercliffe
A57
Stopes
Stannington
Walkley
KELHAM ISLAND MUSEUM
590

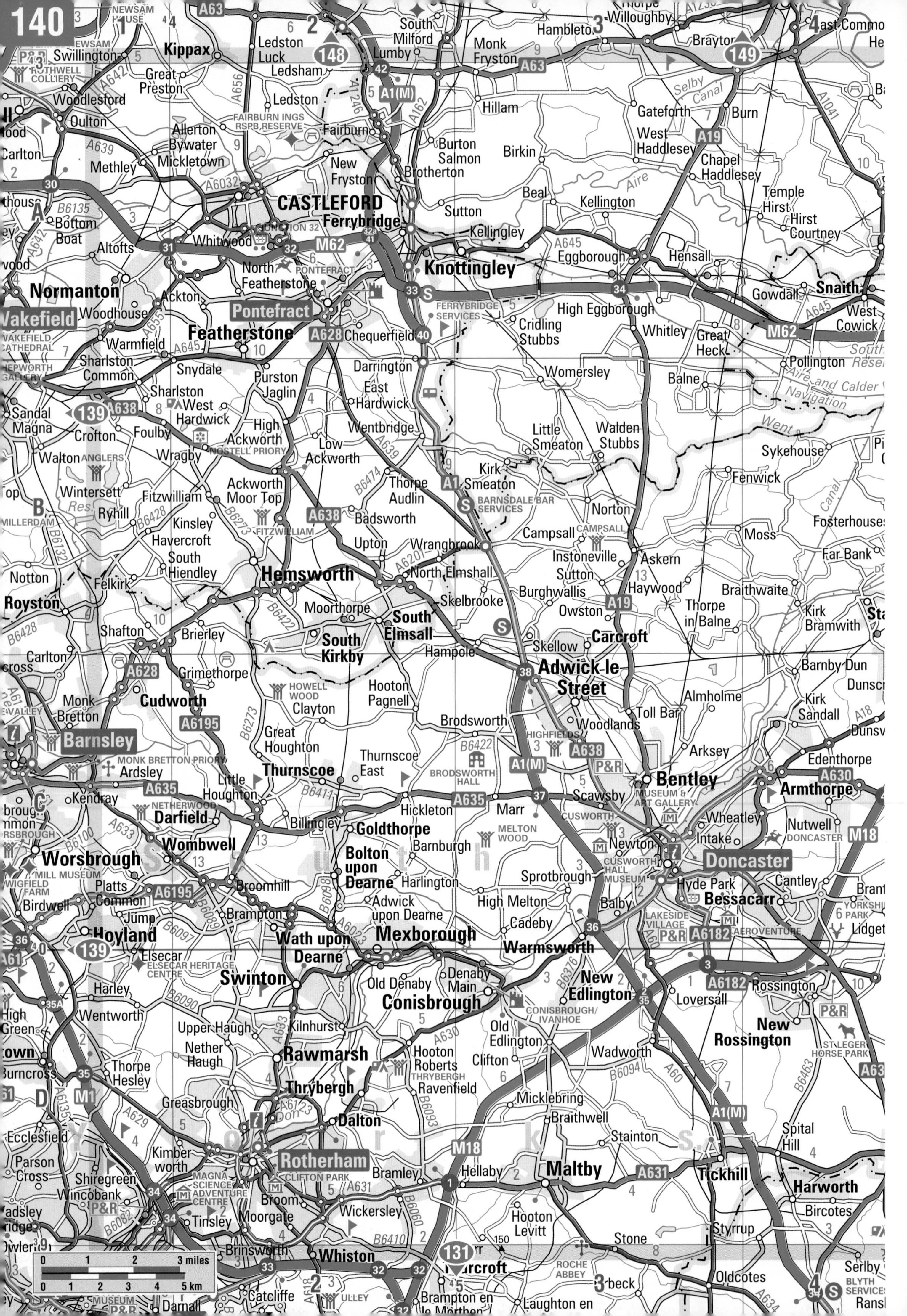

NEWSAM HOUSE
Swillington
Kippax
Ledston Luck
South Milford
Lumby
Hambleton
Willoughby
Monk Fryston
Braytor
Great Preston
Ledsham
Woodlesford
Ledston
Hillam
Gateforth
Selby Canal
Burn
Oulton
FAIRBURN INGS RSPB RESERVE
Fairburn
Burton Salmon
Birkin
West Haddlesey
Allerton Bywater
Mickletown
Methley
Carlton
New Fryston
Brotherton
Chapel Haddlesey
Temple Hirst
CASTLEFORD
Ferrybridge
Beal
Kellington
Sutton
Hirst Courtney
Bottom Boat
Whitwood
JUNCTION 32
Kellingley
Eggborough
Hensall
Altofts
North Featherstone
PONTEFRACT
Knottingley
Normanton
Pontefract
High Eggborough
Gowdall
Snaith
Wakefield
WAKEFIELD CATHEDRAL
Woodhouse
Ackton
Featherstone
Chequerfield
FERRYBRIDGE SERVICES
Cridling Stubbs
Whitley
Great Heck
West Cowick
Warmfield
Sharlston Common
Snydale
Purston Jaglin
Darrington
Womersley
Balne
Pollington
Aire and Calder Navigation
HEPWORTH GALLERY
Sharlston
West Hardwick
East Hardwick
Sandal Magna
Crofton
Foulby
High Ackworth
NOSTELL PRIORY
Wentbridge
Little Smeaton
Walden Stubbs
Walton
ANGLERS
Wragby
Low Ackworth
Sykehouse
Wintersett Res.
Kirk Smeaton
Fenwick
Fitzwilliam
Ackworth Moor Top
Thorpe Audlin
BARNSDALE BAR SERVICES
Norton
Ryhill
Kinsley
Havercroft
FITZWILLIAM
Badsworth
Campsall
CAMPSALL
Fosterhouses
MILLERDAM
South Hiendley
Upton
Wrangbrook
Instoneville
Askern
Moss
Far Bank
Notton
Felkirk
Hemsworth
North Elmshall
Sutton
Haywood
Braithwaite
Royston
Burghwallis
Skelbrooke
Moorthorpe
South Elmsall
Owston
Thorpe in Balne
Kirk Bramwith
Shafton
Brierley
South Kirkby
Hampole
Skellow
Carcroft
Carlton
Grimethorpe
Adwick le Street
Barnby Dun
Monk Bretton
Cudworth
HOWELL WOOD
Clayton
Hooton Pagnell
Almholme
Toll Bar
Kirk Sandall
Barnsley
Great Houghton
Brodsworth
Woodlands
HIGHFIELDS
Arksey
MONK BRETTON PRIORY
Ardsley
Little Houghton
Thurnscoe
Thurnscoe East
BRODSWORTH HALL
Bentley
Edenthorpe
Kendray
NETHERWOOD
Darfield
Hickleton
Marr
Scawsby
MUSEUM & ART GALLERY
Armthorpe
CUSWORTH
Wheatley
Nutwell
DONCASTER
Wombwell
Billingley
Goldthorpe
MELTON WOOD
Newton
Intake
Worsbrough
MILL MUSEUM
Barnburgh
Bolton upon Dearne
Doncaster
CUSWORTH HALL MUSEUM
Sprotbrough
Harlington
Hyde Park
Cantley
Platts Common
Broomhill
Bessacarr
High Melton
Adwick upon Dearne
Birdwell
Jump
Brampton
Balby
LAKESIDE VILLAGE
AEROVENTURE
YORKSHIRE PARK
Lidget
Cadeby
Hoyland
Wath upon Dearne
Mexborough
Warmsworth
Elsecar
ELSECAR HERITAGE CENTRE
Swinton
Denaby Main
New Edlington
Rossington
Harley
Old Denaby
Conisbrough
Loversall
CONISBROUGH/IVANHOE
Wentworth
Upper Haugh
Kilnhurst
Old Edlington
New Rossington
Nether Haugh
Wadworth
ST LEGER HORSE PARK
Thorpe Hesley
Rawmarsh
Hooton Roberts
Clifton
Burncross
THRYBERGH
Thrybergh
Ravenfield
Micklebring
Greasbrough
Braithwell
Dalton
Spital Hill
Ecclesfield
Stainton
Parson Cross
Kimberworth
Rotherham
CLIFTON PARK
Maltby
Tickhill
Bramley
Hellaby
Harworth
Shiregreen
MAGNA SCIENCE ADVENTURE CENTRE
Wincobank
Broom
Bircotes
Tinsley
Moorgate
Wickersley
Hooton Levitt
Styrrup
Brinsworth
Whiston
Stone
Serlby
ROCHE ABBEY
Oldcotes
BLYTH SERVICES
Catcliffe
Darnall
ULLEY
Brampton en le Morthen
Laughton en
South Yorkshire
Aire
Went
Canal
Don
3 miles
5 km

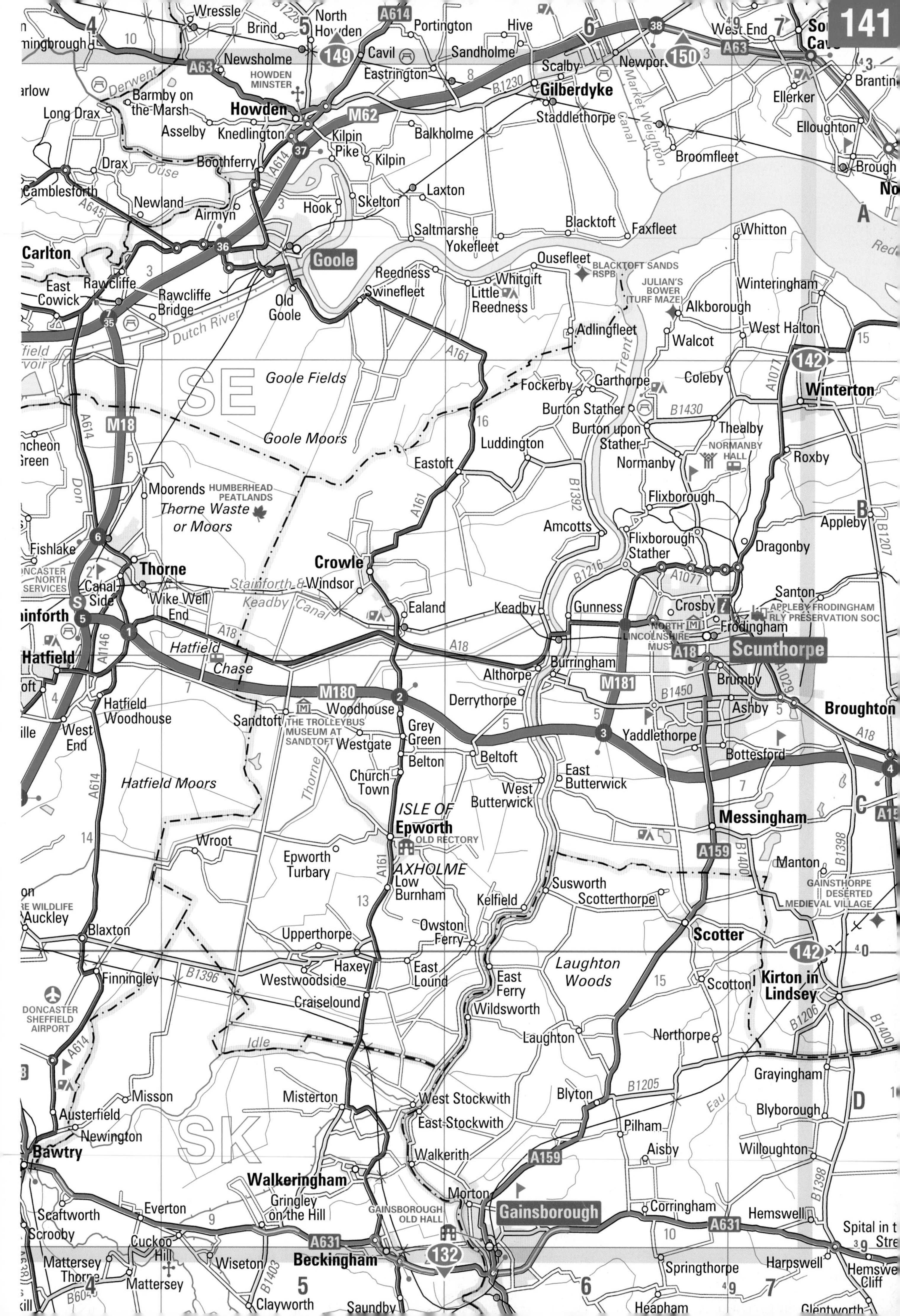
Wressle
Brind
North Howden
A614
Portington
Hive
West End
South Cave
Newsholme
A63
HOWDEN MINSTER
Cavil
Sandholme
Scalby
Newport
Eastrington
B1230
Gilberdyke
Staddlethorpe
Market Weighton Canal
Brantingham
Ellerker
Elloughton
Brough
Broomfleet
Derwent
Barlow
Long Drax
Barmby on the Marsh
Howden
Asselby
Knedlington
M62
Kilpin Pike
Kilpin
Balkholme
Drax
Ouse
Boothferry
Camblesforth
Newland
Airmyn
Hook
Skelton
Laxton
A645
Saltmarshe
Yokefleet
Blacktoft
Faxfleet
Whitton
Carlton
Goole
Ousefleet
BLACKTOFT SANDS RSPB
JULIAN'S BOWER (TURF MAZE)
East Cowick
Rawcliffe
Rawcliffe Bridge
Reedness
Whitgift
Little Reedness
Swinefleet
Old Goole
Winteringham
Alkborough
Dutch River
Adlingfleet
West Halton
Walcot
Trent
A161
SE
Goole Fields
Fockerby
Garthorpe
Coleby
Winterton
Burton Stather
B1430
A1077
Burton upon Stather
Thealby
Goole Moors
Luddington
Normanby
NORMANBY HALL
Roxby
M18
A614
Eastoft
Moorends
HUMBERHEAD PEATLANDS
Thorne Waste or Moors
Flixborough
Don
B1392
Amcotts
Appleby
B1207
Flixborough Stather
Dragonby
Fishlake
Thorne
Crowle
B1216
DONCASTER NORTH SERVICES
Canal Side
Stainforth & Keadby Canal
Windsor
Santon
Wike Well End
Ealand
Keadby
Gunness
Crosby
APPLEBY FRODINGHAM RLY PRESERVATION SOC
Stainforth
A18
NORTH LINCOLNSHIRE MUS
Frodingham
Hatfield
Hatfield Chase
Scunthorpe
A1146
Burringham
Althorpe
M181
Brumby
A1029
M180
Hatfield Woodhouse
Sandtoft
THE TROLLEYBUS MUSEUM AT SANDTOFT
Woodhouse
Derrythorpe
B1450
Ashby
Broughton
West End
Grey Green
Westgate
Yaddlethorpe
Bottesford
Belton
Beltoft
Thorne
Church Town
East Butterwick
Hatfield Moors
West Butterwick
ISLE OF Epworth
OLD RECTORY
Messingham
A159
Wroot
Epworth Turbary
B1400
Manton
B1398
AXHOLME
Low Burnham
Susworth
Scotterthorpe
GAINSTHORPE DESERTED MEDIEVAL VILLAGE
Auckley
Kelfield
Blaxton
Owston Ferry
Upperthorpe
Scotter
Haxey
East Lound
Laughton Woods
Finningley
B1396
Westwoodside
East Ferry
Scotton
Kirton in Lindsey
DONCASTER SHEFFIELD AIRPORT
Craiselound
Wildsworth
B1206
Idle
Laughton
Northorpe
Grayingham
Misson
Misterton
West Stockwith
Blyton
B1205
Austerfield
Eau
Blyborough
SK
East Stockwith
Pilham
Newington
Bawtry
Aisby
Willoughton
Walkerith
Walkeringham
Morton
Gringley on the Hill
Gainsborough
Corringham
Hemswell
Scaftworth
Everton
GAINSBOROUGH OLD HALL
Scrooby
A631
Spital in the Street
Cuckoo Hill
Beckingham
Harpswell
Mattersey Thorpe
Wiseton
B1403
Springthorpe
Hemswell Cliff
Mattersey
B6045
Clayworth
Saundby
Heapham
Glentworth
142
149
150
132

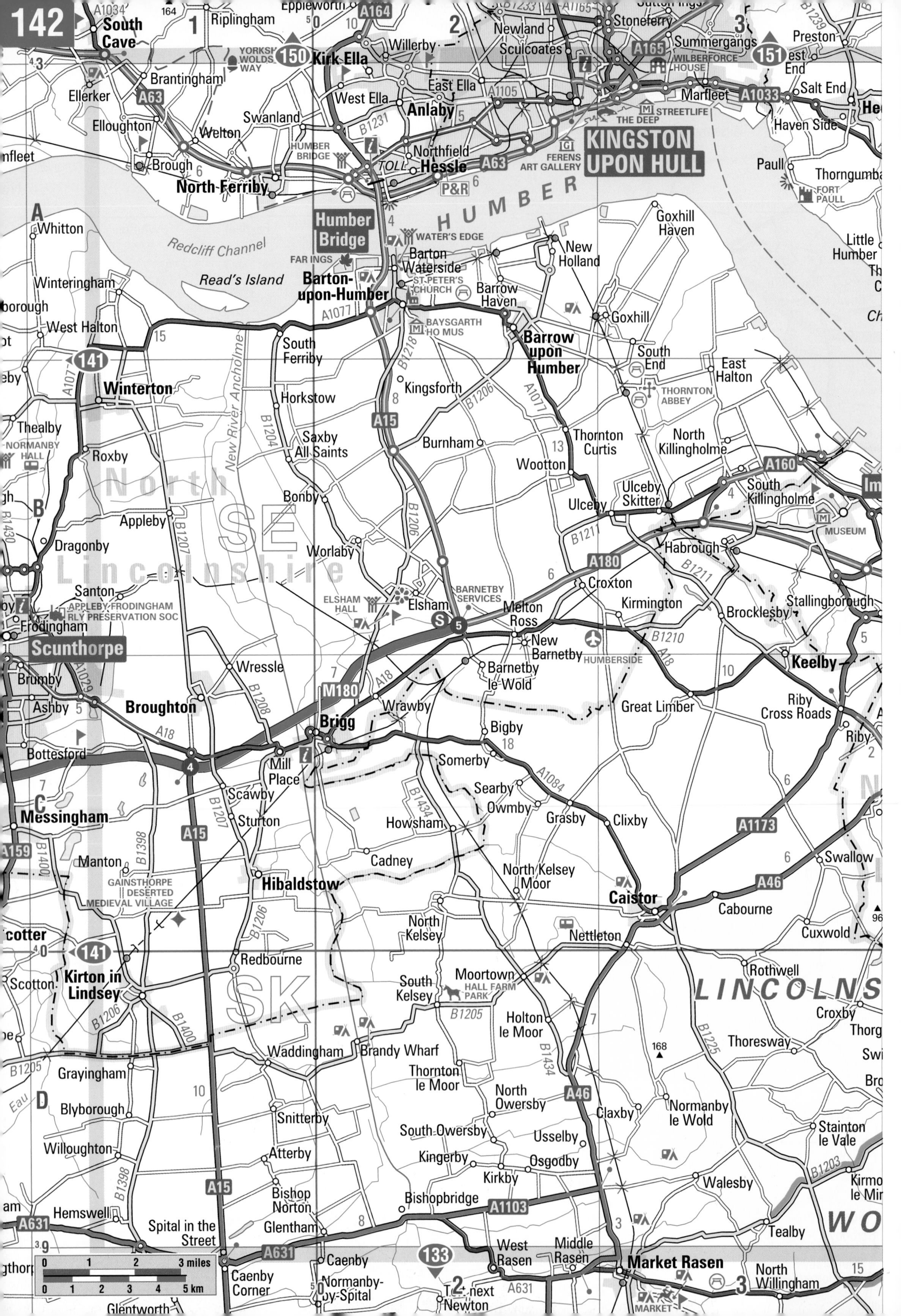
South Cave
Riplingham
Eppleworth
Stoneferry
Newland
Sculcoates
Summergangs
Preston
Kirk Ella
Willerby
YORKSHIRE WOLDS WAY
WILBERFORCE HOUSE
Brantingham
Ellerker
East Ella
Marfleet
Salt End
West Ella
Anlaby
Swanland
Elloughton
Welton
STREETLIFE
THE DEEP
Haven Side
KINGSTON UPON HULL
HUMBER BRIDGE
Northfield
Hessle
FERENS ART GALLERY
Brough
North Ferriby
TOLL
P&R
Paull
Thorngumbald
FORT PAULL
HUMBER
Humber Bridge
WATER'S EDGE
Whitton
Redcliff Channel
FAR INGS
Barton Waterside
New Holland
Goxhill Haven
Little Humber
Read's Island
Winteringham
Barton-upon-Humber
ST PETER'S CHURCH
Barrow Haven
West Halton
BAYSGARTH HO MUS
Goxhill
South Ferriby
Barrow upon Humber
South End
East Halton
Winterton
Horkstow
Kingsforth
THORNTON ABBEY
Thealby
NORMANBY HALL
Saxby All Saints
Burnham
Thornton Curtis
North Killingholme
Roxby
New River Ancholme
Wootton
North
Ulceby Skitter
South Killingholme
Bonby
Ulceby
Appleby
SE
MUSEUM
Dragonby
Worlaby
Habrough
Lincolnshire
Croxton
Santon
ELSHAM HALL
Elsham
BARNETBY SERVICES
Melton Ross
Kirmington
Brocklesby
Stallingborough
APPLEBY-FRODINGHAM RLY PRESERVATION SOC
Frodingham
Scunthorpe
New Barnetby
HUMBERSIDE
Keelby
Brumby
Wressle
Barnetby le Wold
Ashby
Broughton
Wrawby
Great Limber
Riby Cross Roads
Brigg
Riby
Bottesford
Mill Place
Somerby
Bigby
Messingham
Scawby
Searby
Owmby
Grasby
Clixby
Sturton
Howsham
Manton
Cadney
Swallow
GAINSTHORPE DESERTED MEDIEVAL VILLAGE
Hibaldstow
North Kelsey Moor
Caistor
Cabourne
North Kelsey
Nettleton
Cuxwold
Scotter
Redbourne
Rothwell
Scotton
Kirton in Lindsey
Moortown
HALL FARM PARK
South Kelsey
SK
LINCOLNS
Holton le Moor
Croxby
Thoresway
Waddingham
Brandy Wharf
Grayingham
Thornton le Moor
North Owersby
Blyborough
Normanby le Wold
Snitterby
Claxby
Stainton le Vale
South Owersby
Usselby
Willoughton
Atterby
Kingerby
Osgodby
Kirkby
Walesby
Bishop Norton
Bishopbridge
Hemswell
Glentham
Tealby
Spital in the Street
West Rasen
Middle Rasen
Caenby
Market Rasen
North Willingham
Caenby Corner
Normanby-by-Spital
Toft next Newton
MARKET
Glentworth
0 1 2 3 miles
0 1 2 3 4 5 km

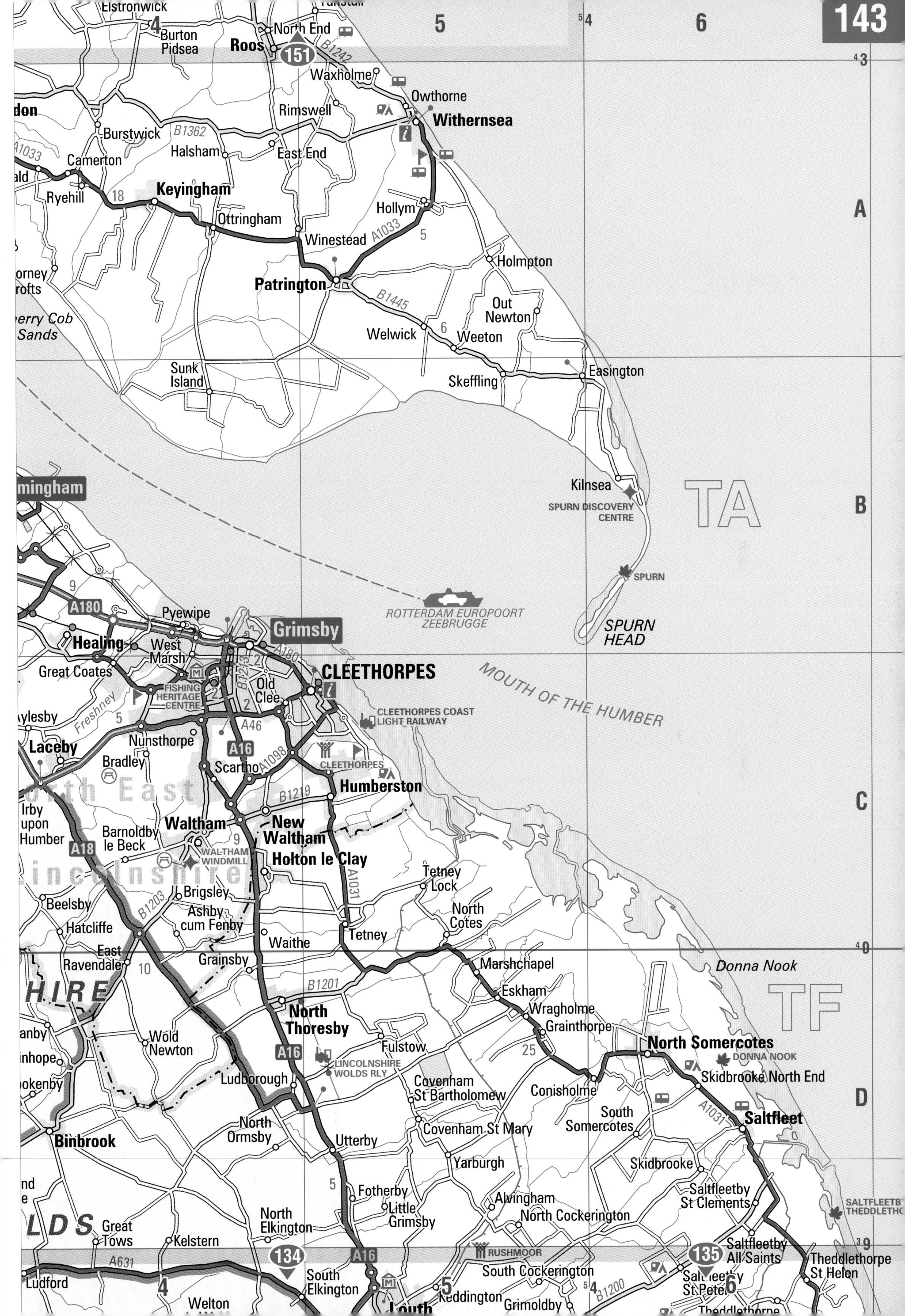

Elstronwick
Burton Pidsea
Roos
North End
151
B1242
Waxholme
Owthorne
Withernsea
Rimswell
Burstwick
B1362
Halsham
East End
Camerton
A1033
Ryehill
18
Keyingham
Ottringham
Hollym
Winestead
A1033
Holmpton
Patrington
B1445
Out Newton
Welwick
Weeton
Sunk Island
Skeffling
Easington
Sands
Kilnsea
SPURN DISCOVERY CENTRE
TA
SPURN
SPURN HEAD
ROTTERDAM EUROPOORT ZEEBRUGGE
MOUTH OF THE HUMBER
A180
Pyewipe
Grimsby
Healing
West Marsh
Great Coates
CLEETHORPES
FISHING HERITAGE CENTRE
Old Clee
CLEETHORPES COAST LIGHT RAILWAY
Freshney
A46
Laceby
Nunsthorpe
A16
Bradley
Scartho
A1098
CLEETHORPES
Humberston
B1219
North East
Irby upon Humber
Waltham
New Waltham
Barnoldby le Beck
A18
WALTHAM WINDMILL
Holton le Clay
Lincolnshire
A1031
Tetney Lock
Beelsby
B1203
Brigsley
Ashby cum Fenby
North Cotes
Hatcliffe
Tetney
Waithe
East Ravendale
Grainsby
Marshchapel
Donna Nook
B1201
Eskham
TF
Wragholme
North Thoresby
Grainthorpe
Wold Newton
Fulstow
North Somercotes
A16
DONNA NOOK
LINCOLNSHIRE WOLDS RLY
Skidbrooke North End
Ludborough
Covenham St Bartholomew
Conisholme
South Somercotes
A1031
Saltfleet
North Ormsby
Binbrook
Covenham St Mary
Utterby
Yarburgh
Skidbrooke
Fotherby
Alvingham
Saltfleetby St Clements
Little Grimsby
North Elkington
North Cockerington
Great Tows
Kelstern
RUSHMOOR
Saltfleetby All Saints
Theddlethorpe St Helen
134
A16
135
A631
South Cockerington
South Elkington
Ludford
Keddington
Grimoldby
B1200
Welton
Louth
Theddlethorpe

1 2 3 4

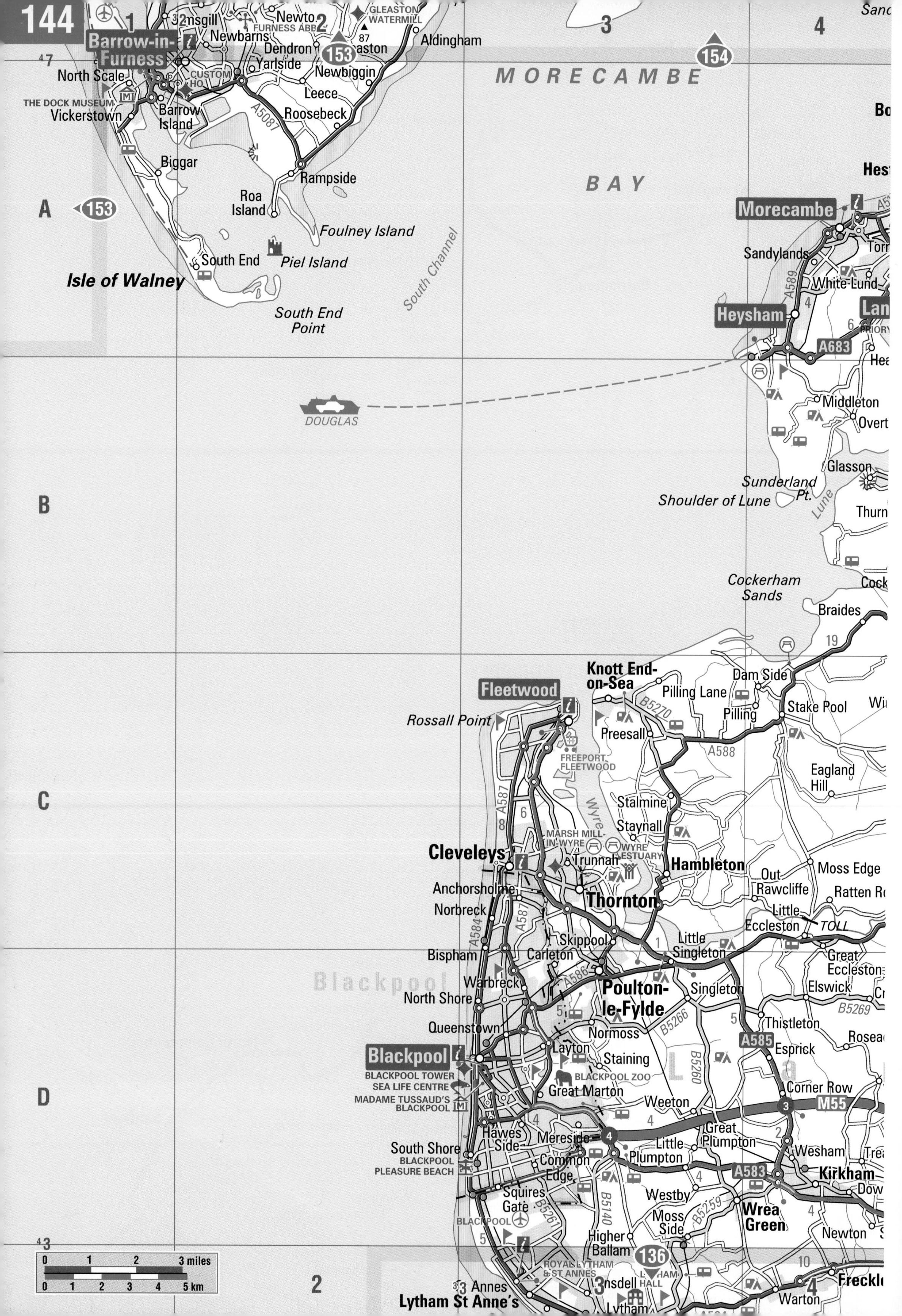

Barrow-in-Furness

North Scale
THE DOCK MUSEUM
Vickerstown
Barrow Island

msgill
Newbarns
Dendron
Yarlside
Newbiggin
Leece
Roosebeck

Newto.
Gleaston
Aston
Aldingham

Newton
GLEASTON WATERMILL
FURNESS ABBEY

87

153

CUSTOM HO.

A5087

Biggar

Rampside

Roa Island

Foulney Island

Piel Island

South Channel

154

A5087

M O R E C A M B E

B A Y

Morecambe

Sandylands

White Lund

A589

Torr

Bo

Hest

A 153

South End

South End Point

Isle of Walney

DOUGLAS

Heysham

Lan

PRIORY

A683

Hea

B

Middleton

Overt

Glasson

Sunderland Pt.

Shoulder of Lune

Lune

Thurn

Cockerham Sands

Cock

Braides

19

C

Knott End-on-Sea

Fleetwood

Rossall Point

FREEPORT FLEETWOOD

Dam Side

Pilling Lane

Pilling

B5270

Preesall

Stake Pool

A588

Wi

Eagland Hill

A587

6

8

Stalmine

Staynall

MARSH MILL-IN-WYRE

Wyre

WYRE ESTUARY

Cleveleys

Anchorsholme

Norbreck

Trunnah

Thornton

Hambleton

Out Rawcliffe

Moss Edge

Ratten R

Little Eccleston

TOLL

A584

A587

Skippool

Carleton

1

Little Singleton

Great Eccleston

Elswick

B5269

Bispham

Warbreck

A586

Singleton

Blackpool

North Shore

Queenstown

Poulton-le-Fylde

B5266

Thistleton

A585

Esprick

Normoss

B5260

Rosea

Blackpool

BLACKPOOL TOWER
SEA LIFE CENTRE
MADAME TUSSAUD'S
BLACKPOOL

Layton

Staining

BLACKPOOL ZOO

Great Marton

L

a

Corner Row

M55

3

A583

D

Weeton

4

Great Plumpton

Kirkham

Dow

Hawes Side

Mereside

Common Edge

Weeton

4

Little Plumpton

Wesham

Tre

South Shore

BLACKPOOL PLEASURE BEACH

Squires Gate

BLACKPOOL

B5261

Westby

Moss Side

B5259

Wrea Green

Newton

Higher Ballam

136

Warton

ROYAL LYTHAM & ST ANNES

L. YTHAM HALL

Freckl

2 3 Annes

Lytham St Anne's

nsdell

3

Lytham

4

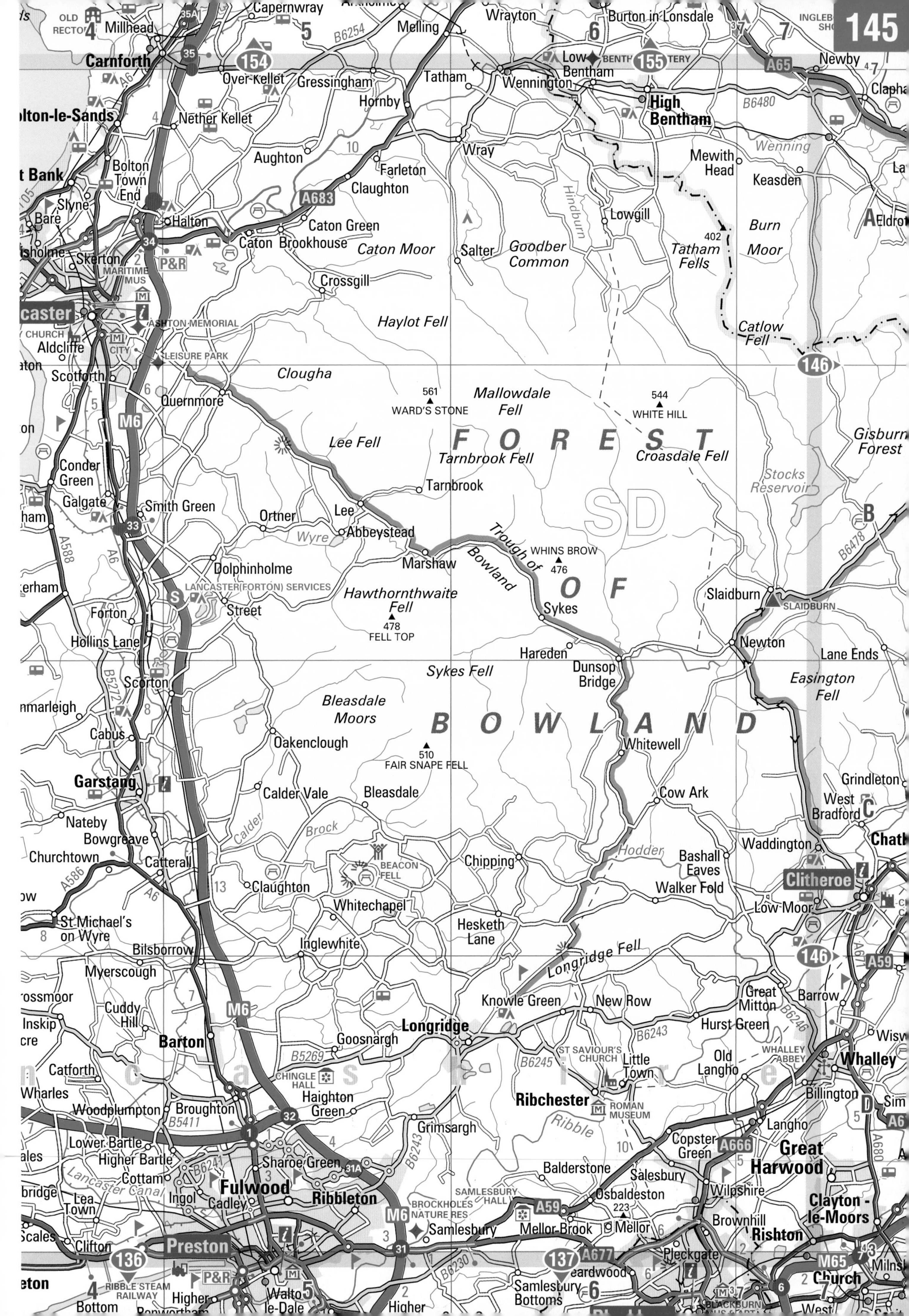
Capernwray
Millhead
Carnforth
154
Over Kellet
Gressingham
Melling
Wrayton
Burton in Lonsdale
Low Bentham
155
Newby
Wennington
Tatham
High Bentham
Hornby
Nether Kellet
Bolton-le-Sands
Aughton
Wray
Mewith Head
Keasden
Farleton
Claughton
A683
Bolton Town End
Slyne
Bare
Halton
Caton Green
Lowgill
Burn Moor
Tatham Fells
402
Caton
Brookhouse
Caton Moor
Salter
Goodber Common
Skerton
Hindburn
Crossgill
Haylot Fell
Catlow Fell
ASHTON MEMORIAL
Aldcliffe
LEISURE PARK
146
Clougha
Scotforth
Quernmore
561
WARD'S STONE
Mallowdale Fell
544
WHITE HILL
Lee Fell
FOREST OF BOWLAND
Tarnbrook Fell
Croasdale Fell
Gisburn Forest
Stocks Reservoir
Conder Green
Tarnbrook
Galgate
Smith Green
SD
Lee
Ortner
Abbeystead
Wyre
Trough of Bowland
WHINS BROW
476
Marshaw
Dolphinholme
LANCASTER(FORTON) SERVICES
Hawthornthwaite Fell
478
FELL TOP
Slaidburn
SLAIDBURN
Sykes
Forton
Street
Hollins Lane
Hareden
Newton
Lane Ends
Dunsop Bridge
Sykes Fell
Easington Fell
Scorton
Bleasdale Moors
Cabus
Oakenclough
510
FAIR SNAPE FELL
Whitewell
Garstang
Calder Vale
Bleasdale
Cow Ark
Grindleton
West Bradford
Nateby
Bowgreave
Calder
Brock
Hodder
Waddington
Bashall Eaves
Churchtown
Catterall
BEACON FELL
Chipping
Clitheroe
Claughton
Walker Fold
Low Moor
Whitechapel
St Michael's on Wyre
Hesketh Lane
Bilsborrow
Inglewhite
Longridge Fell
Myerscough
Knowle Green
New Row
Great Mitton
Barrow
Cuddy Hill
Inskip
Barton
Goosnargh
Longridge
Hurst Green
B5269
ST SAVIOUR'S CHURCH
Little Town
Old Langho
WHALLEY ABBEY
Whalley
Catforth
CHINGLE HALL
Wharles
Haighton Green
Ribchester
ROMAN MUSEUM
Billington
Woodplumpton
Broughton
Ribble
Langho
Grimsargh
Lower Bartle
Higher Bartle
Copster Green
A666
Great Harwood
Cottam
Sharoe Green
Balderstone
Salesbury
Lancaster Canal
Ingol
Fulwood
Ribbleton
SAMLESBURY HALL
Osbaldeston
Wilpshire
Lea Town
Cadley
BROCKHOLES NATURE RES
A59
223
Clayton-le-Moors
Samlesbury
Mellor Brook
Mellor
Brownhill
Rishton
Scales
Clifton
Preston
136
137
A677
Pleckgate
M65
Church
RIBBLE STEAM RAILWAY
P&R
Walton-le-Dale
Samlesbury Bottoms
Bottom
Higher
M6
A6
A588
A586
B5272
B6243
B6245
B6246
B6478
B6480
B6254
B5411
B6241
B6230
A671
A680

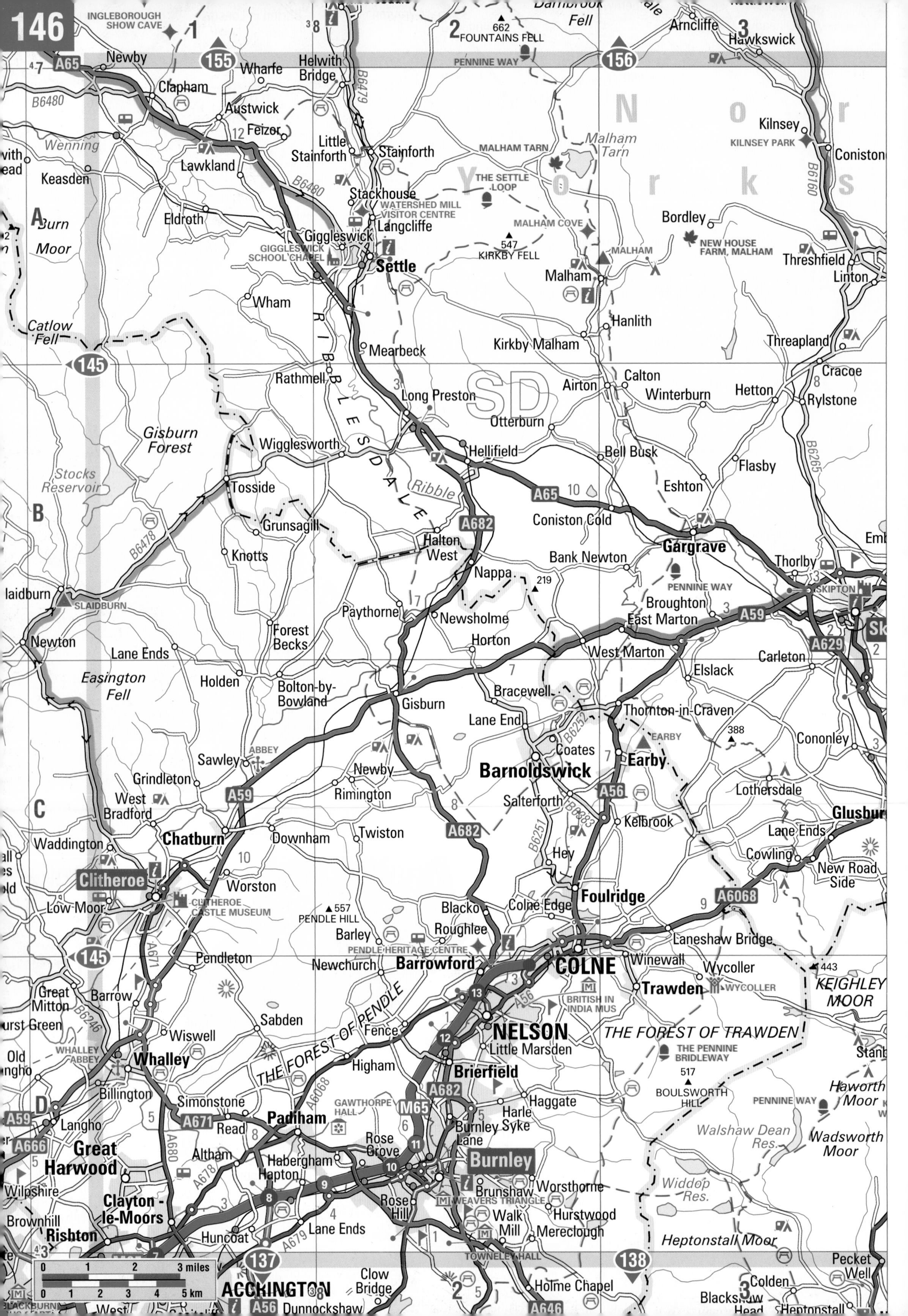
INGLEBOROUGH SHOW CAVE
FOUNTAINS FELL
Arncliffe
Hawkswick
PENNINE WAY
155
156
Newby
Wharfe
Helwith Bridge
Clapham
Austwick
Feizor
Little Stainforth
Stainforth
MALHAM TARN
Malham Tarn
Kilnsey
KILNSEY PARK
Coniston
North Yorks
Wenning
Keasden
Lawkland
Stackhouse
WATERSHED MILL VISITOR CENTRE
THE SETTLE LOOP
Langcliffe
MALHAM COVE
Bordley
NEW HOUSE FARM, MALHAM
Burn Moor
Eldroth
Giggleswick
GIGGLESWICK SCHOOL CHAPEL
Settle
KIRKBY FELL
MALHAM
Malham
Threshfield
Linton
Wham
RIBBLESDALE
Hanlith
Catlow Fell
Mearbeck
Kirkby Malham
Threapland
Cracoe
145
Rathmell
Long Preston
SD
Airton
Calton
Winterburn
Hetton
Rylstone
Otterburn
Gisburn Forest
Wigglesworth
Hellifield
Bell Busk
Flasby
Stocks Reservoir
Tosside
Ribble
Eshton
A65
Coniston Cold
Grunsagill
A682
Halton West
Gargrave
Knotts
Bank Newton
Thorlby
Nappa
SKIPTON
Slaidburn
SLAIDBURN
Paythorne
Newsholme
Broughton
East Marton
A59
Forest Becks
Newton
Horton
West Marton
Carleton
A629
Lane Ends
Easington Fell
Holden
Bolton-by-Bowland
Elslack
Gisburn
Bracewell
Thornton-in-Craven
Lane End
EARBY
Cononley
Coates
Sawley
ABBEY
Earby
Grindleton
Newby
Barnoldswick
Lothersdale
West Bradford
Rimington
Salterforth
Kelbrook
Glusburn
Waddington
Chatburn
Downham
Twiston
Lane Ends
Cowling
Clitheroe
Worston
Hey
New Road Side
Foulridge
A6068
Low Moor
CLITHEROE CASTLE MUSEUM
PENDLE HILL
Blacko
Colne Edge
Barley
Roughlee
Laneshaw Bridge
PENDLE HERITAGE CENTRE
Pendleton
Newchurch
Barrowford
COLNE
Winewall
Wycoller
WYCOLLER
KEIGHLEY MOOR
Great Mitton
Barrow
BRITISH IN INDIA MUS
Trawden
THE FOREST OF PENDLE
Sabden
Fence
NELSON
THE FOREST OF TRAWDEN
Wiswell
Little Marsden
THE PENNINE BRIDLEWAY
WHALLEY ABBEY
Whalley
Higham
Brierfield
BOULSWORTH HILL
Haworth Moor
Billington
Simonstone
Haggate
PENNINE WAY
GAWTHORPE HALL
M65
Harle Syke
Langho
A671
Read
Padiham
Burnley Lane
Walshaw Dean Res.
Wadsworth Moor
Great Harwood
Altham
Rose Grove
Burnley
A666
Habergham
Hapton
Wilpshire
Brunshaw
Worsthorne
Widdop Res.
WEAVERS' TRIANGLE
Clayton-le-Moors
Rose Hill
Walk Mill
Hurstwood
Brownhill
Rishton
Huncoat
Lane Ends
Mereclough
Heptonstall Moor
TOWNELEY HALL
Pecket Well
137
138
Clow Bridge
ACCRINGTON
Holme Chapel
Colden
Blackshaw Head
Heptonstall
Dunnockshaw
A56
A646
BLACKBURN
0 1 2 3 miles
0 1 2 3 4 5 km

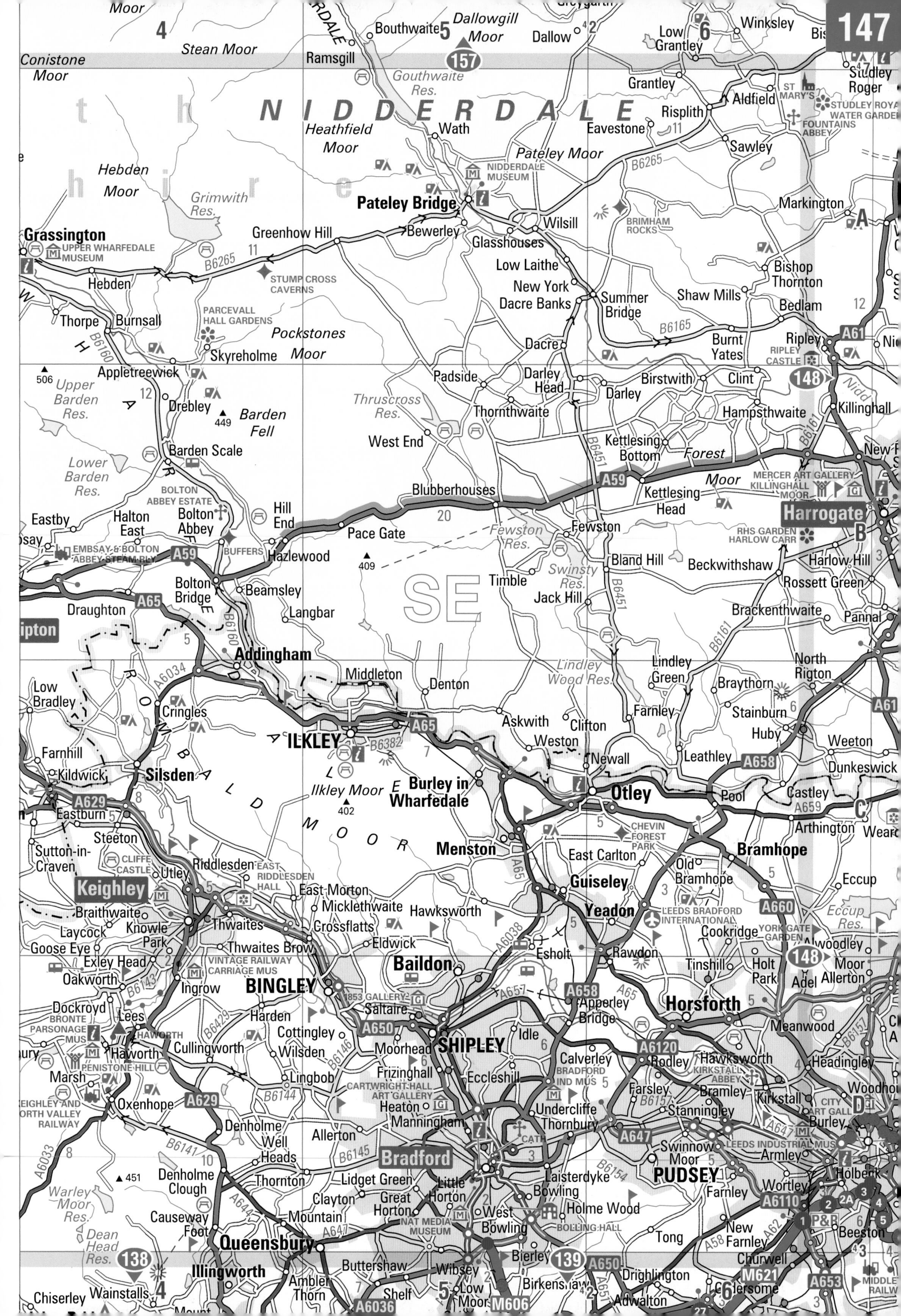
Moor
4
Stean Moor
Bouthwaite
5
Dallowgill Moor
157
Dallow
Low Grantley
6
Winksley
Conistone Moor
Ramsgill
Gouthwaite Res.
Grantley
Studley Roger
ST MARY'S
STUDLEY ROYAL WATER GARDEN
FOUNTAINS ABBEY
Aldfield
NIDDERDALE
Heathfield Moor
Wath
Eavestone
Risplith
Sawley
Hebden Moor
Grimwith Res.
Pateley Moor
B6265
NIDDERDALE MUSEUM
Pateley Bridge
Markington
Grassington
UPPER WHARFEDALE MUSEUM
Greenhow Hill
Bewerley
Wilsill
BRIMHAM ROCKS
Glasshouses
A
B6265
11
Hebden
STUMP CROSS CAVERNS
Low Laithe
Bishop Thornton
New York
Dacre Banks
Summer Bridge
Shaw Mills
Bedlam
12
Thorpe
Burnsall
PARCEVALL HALL GARDENS
Pockstones Moor
B6165
Burnt Yates
Ripley
RIPLEY CASTLE
A61
Skyreholme
Dacre
B6160
Appletreewick
506
Upper Barden Res.
Padside
Darley Head
Darley
Birstwith
Clint
148
Nidd
12
Drebley
449
Barden Fell
Thruscross Res.
Thornthwaite
Hampsthwaite
Killinghall
West End
B6161
Kettlesing Bottom
Forest
New
Lower Barden Res.
Barden Scale
B6451
BOLTON ABBEY ESTATE
Blubberhouses
A59
Moor
MERCER ART GALLERY
KILLINGHALL MOOR
Kettlesing Head
Eastby
Halton East
Bolton Abbey
Hill End
20
Pace Gate
Fewston Res.
Fewston
Harrogate
RHS GARDEN HARLOW CARR
B
EMBSAY & BOLTON ABBEY STEAM RLY
BUFFERS
A59
Hazlewood
409
Bland Hill
Beckwithshaw
Harlow Hill
Swinsty Res.
SE
Timble
Rossett Green
Bolton Bridge
Beamsley
Jack Hill
B6451
Draughton
A65
Langbar
Brackenthwaite
Pannal
B6160
5
Addingham
B6161
North Rigton
Lindley Wood Res.
Lindley Green
Low Bradley
A6034
Middleton
Denton
Braythorn
Stainburn
A61
Cringles
Askwith
Clifton
Farnley
Huby
ILKLEY
A65
B6382
Weston
Weeton
Farnhill
7
Leathley
Newall
A658
Kildwick
Silsden
RUMBALDS MOOR
Burley in Wharfedale
Otley
Pool
Castley
Dunkeswick
A629
Ilkley Moor
402
A659
C
Eastburn
Arthington
Steeton
CHEVIN FOREST PARK
Weardley
Sutton-in-Craven
CLIFFE CASTLE
Menston
Bramhope
Utley
Riddlesden
EAST RIDDLESDEN HALL
East Carlton
Old Bramhope
Eccup
Keighley
East Morton
A65
Guiseley
5
Braithwaite
Micklethwaite
Hawksworth
Yeadon
A660
LEEDS BRADFORD INTERNATIONAL
Eccup Res.
Laycock
Knowle Park
Thwaites
Crossflatts
Cookridge
YORK GATE GARDEN
Goose Eye
Thwaites Brow
Eldwick
A6038
Esholt
Rawdon
Alwoodley
Exley Head
VINTAGE RAILWAY CARRIAGE MUS
Baildon
Tinshill
Holt Park
148
Moor Allerton
Oakworth
B6143
Ingrow
BINGLEY
A657
A658
Adel
Dockroyd
Lees
B6429
1853 GALLERY
Saltaire
Apperley Bridge
A65
Horsforth
BRONTE PARSONAGE MUS
Harden
A650
Cottingley
Meanwood
HAWORTH
Idle
B6157
Haworth
Cullingworth
Wilsden
SHIPLEY
A6120
Calverley
Hawksworth
PENISTONE HILL
Moorhead
Rodley
KIRKSTALL ABBEY
Headingley
Marsh
B6146
Frizinghall
Eccleshill
BRADFORD IND MUS
Farsley
Lingbob
CARTWRIGHT HALL ART GALLERY
Bramley
Kirkstall
KEIGHLEY AND WORTH VALLEY RAILWAY
Oxenhope
A629
B6144
Heaton
Undercliffe
B6157
Stanningley
CITY ART GALL
D
Manningham
Thornbury
Burley
Denholme
A647
A647
Well Heads
Allerton
CATH
Swinnow Moor
LEEDS INDUSTRIAL MUS
B6141
B6145
Bradford
Armley
A6033
8
10
B6154
PUDSEY
Holbeck
451
Denholme Clough
Thornton
Lidget Green
Little Horton
Laisterdyke
Farnley
Wortley
Warley Moor Res.
A644
Clayton
Great Horton
Bowling
Holme Wood
A6110
Causeway Foot
Mountain
NAT MEDIA MUSEUM
West Bowling
BOLLING HALL
New Farnley
Beeston
Dean Head Res.
A647
Tong
A58
A62
Queensbury
138
Bierley
139
A650
Churwell
Illingworth
Buttershaw
Wibsey
Birkenshaw
Drighlington
M621
A653
4
Ambler Thorn
A657
Gildersome
MIDDLETON RAILWAY
Chiserley
Wainstalls
Shelf
Low Moor
M606
Adwalton
A6036
5
6
27

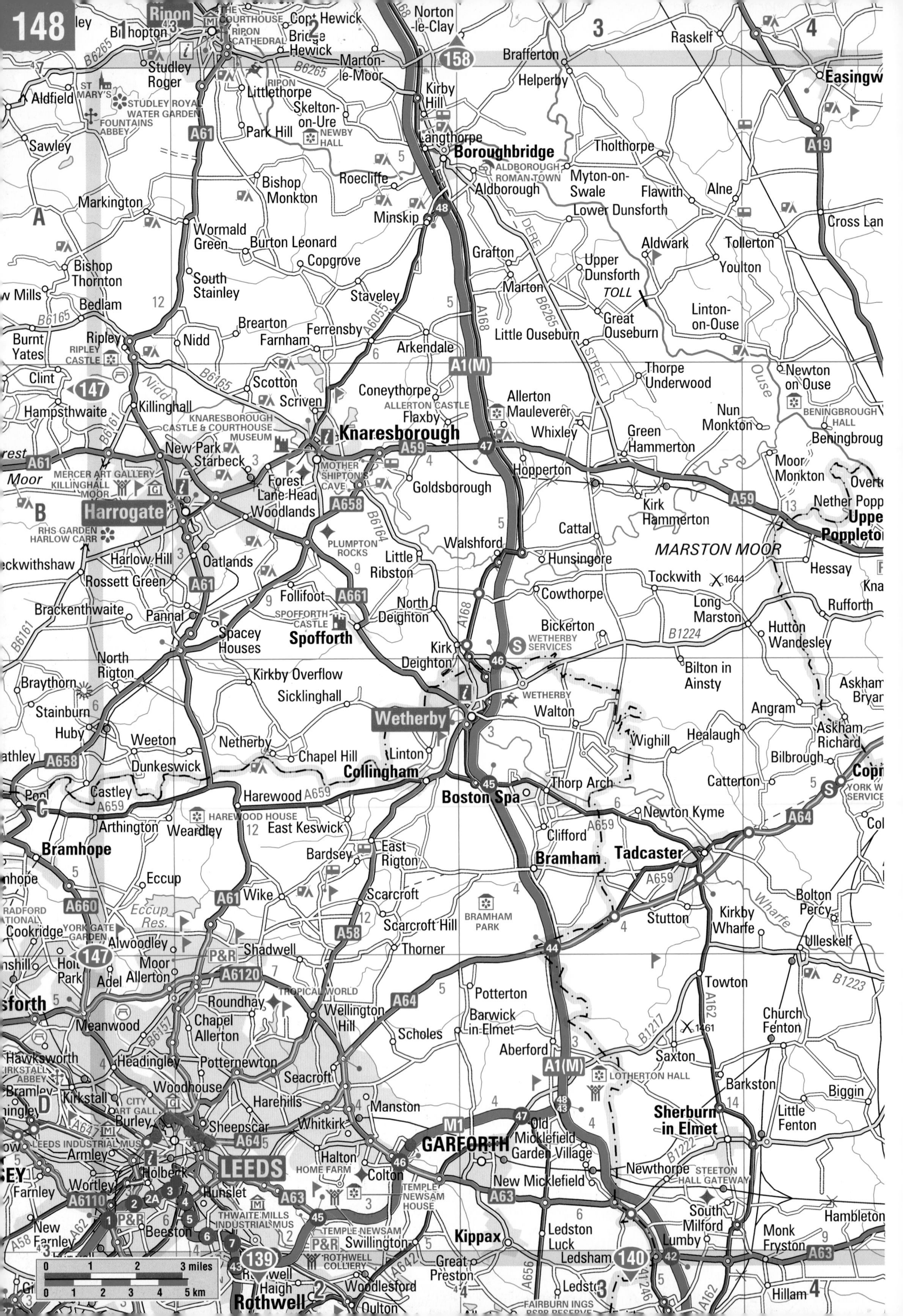
Ripon
Bishopton
Copt Hewick
Bridge Hewick
Norton-le-Clay
Raskelf
Studley Roger
Marton-le-Moor
158
Brafferton
Helperby
Easingwold
Aldfield
St Mary's
Studley Royal Water Garden
Fountains Abbey
Littlethorpe
Skelton-on-Ure
Kirby Hill
Sawley
Park Hill
Newby Hall
Langthorpe
Boroughbridge
Tholthorpe
A19
Bishop Monkton
Roecliffe
Aldborough Roman Town
Aldborough
Myton-on-Swale
Flawith
Alne
Markington
Minskip
Lower Dunsforth
Cross Lane
Wormald Green
Burton Leonard
Grafton
Aldwark
Tollerton
Bishop Thornton
Copgrove
Upper Dunsforth
Youlton
South Stainley
Staveley
Marton
Toll
Bedlam
Great Ouseburn
Linton-on-Ouse
Ripley
Brearton
Ferrensby
Burnt Yates
Nidd
Farnham
Arkendale
Little Ouseburn
Ripley Castle
A1(M)
Clint
147
Scotton
Coneythorpe
Thorpe Underwood
Newton on Ouse
Hampsthwaite
Killinghall
Scriven
Allerton Castle
Allerton Mauleverer
Nun Monkton
Beningbrough Hall
Knaresborough Castle & Courthouse Museum
Flaxby
Knaresborough
Whixley
Green Hammerton
Beningbrough
A61
A59
New Park
Starbeck
Mother Shipton's Cave
Goldsborough
Hopperton
Moor Monkton
Mercer Art Gallery
Killinghall Moor
Forest Lane Head
Kirk Hammerton
Nether Poppleton
Harrogate
Woodlands
A658
Upper Poppleton
RHS Garden Harlow Carr
Plumpton Rocks
Walshford
Cattal
Harlow Hill
Oatlands
Little Ribston
Hunsingore
Marston Moor
Hessay
Beckwithshaw
Rossett Green
Tockwith
1644
Follifoot
A661
Cowthorpe
Long Marston
Brackenthwaite
Pannal
Spofforth Castle
North Deighton
Rufforth
Spacey Houses
Spofforth
Bickerton
Hutton Wandesley
Kirk Deighton
Wetherby Services
B1224
North Rigton
Bilton in Ainsty
Braythorn
Kirkby Overflow
Sicklinghall
Wetherby
Walton
Askham Bryan
Stainburn
Angram
Huby
Weeton
Netherby
Wighill
Healaugh
Askham Richard
Chapel Hill
Linton
Bilbrough
Dunkeswick
Collingham
Catterton
Castley
Harewood
A659
Boston Spa
Thorp Arch
York West Services
Harewood House
Newton Kyme
A64
Arthington
Weardley
East Keswick
Clifford
Bramhope
Bardsey
East Rigton
Bramham
Tadcaster
Eccup
Scarcroft
Bolton Percy
Wike
Stutton
Kirkby Wharfe
Wharfe
Bramham Park
Eccup Res.
Scarcroft Hill
Cookridge
York Gate Garden
Alwoodley
Ulleskelf
Shadwell
Thorner
Moor Allerton
A6120
Towton
B1223
Adel
Tropical World
Potterton
Roundhay
A162
Meanwood
Wellington Hill
Church Fenton
Barwick in Elmet
Chapel Allerton
Scholes
B1217
1461
Hawksworth
Headingley
Potternewton
Aberford
Saxton
Kirkstall Abbey
Seacroft
Lotherton Hall
Barkston
Bramley
Woodhouse
Biggin
Kirkstall
Harehills
Manston
Sherburn in Elmet
City Art Gall.
Burley
M1
Old Micklefield
Little Fenton
Sheepscar
Whitkirk
Garforth
Micklefield Garden Village
Leeds Industrial Mus
Armley
Halton
Leeds
Home Farm
Colton
Newthorpe
Steeton Hall Gateway
Holbeck
B1222
Farnley
Wortley
Hunslet
Temple Newsam House
New Micklefield
A6110
A63
South Milford
Hambleton
Thwaite Mills Industrial Mus
Beeston
Ledston Luck
New Farnley
Temple Newsam
Kippax
Lumby
Monk Fryston
Swillington
Rothwell Colliery
Great Preston
Ledsham
140
139
Rothwell
Haigh
Woodlesford
Ledston
Hillam
Oulton
Fairburn Ings RSPB Reserve
A62
A58
A642
A656
A1246
0 1 2 3 miles
0 1 2 3 4 5 km

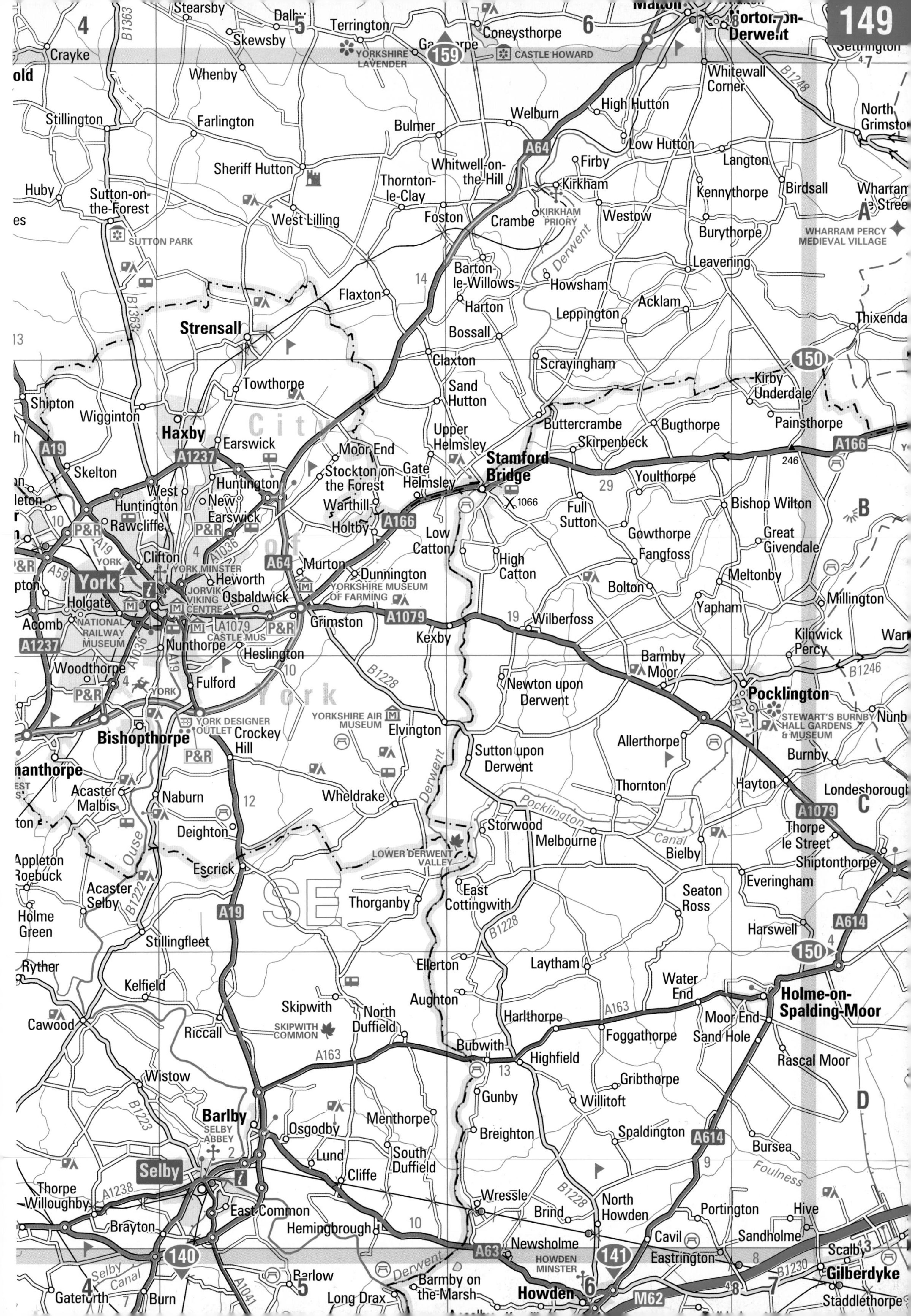

Stearsby
Dalby
Terrington
Coneysthorpe
Malton
Norton-on-Derwent
Skewsby
Crayke
YORKSHIRE LAVENDER
159
CASTLE HOWARD
Settrington
Whenby
Whitewall Corner
B1248
B1363
Stillington
Farlington
Bulmer
Welburn
High Hutton
North Grimston
A64
Low Hutton
Langton
Sheriff Hutton
Whitwell-on-the-Hill
Firby
Huby
Sutton-on-the-Forest
Thornton-le-Clay
Kirkham
Kennythorpe
Birdsall
Wharram le Street
West Lilling
Foston
Crambe
KIRKHAM PRIORY
Westow
Burythorpe
SUTTON PARK
WHARRAM PERCY MEDIEVAL VILLAGE
Derwent
Leavening
Barton-le-Willows
Howsham
Flaxton
Harton
Acklam
Thixendale
Strensall
Leppington
Bossall
Claxton
Scrayingham
150
Kirby Underdale
Towthorpe
Sand Hutton
Shipton
Wigginton
City of York
Buttercrambe
Bugthorpe
Painsthorpe
Haxby
Upper Helmsley
Earswick
Skirpenbeck
A19
A1237
Moor End
Stamford Bridge
A166
Skelton
Stockton on the Forest
Gate Helmsley
Youlthorpe
Huntington
West Huntington
New Earswick
1066
Full Sutton
Bishop Wilton
Warthill
Holtby
Low Catton
Gowthorpe
Great Givendale
Rawcliffe
P&R
Fangfoss
Clifton
A1036
High Catton
YORK MINSTER
A64
Murton
Dunnington
Meltonby
York
Heworth
JORVIK VIKING CENTRE
YORKSHIRE MUSEUM OF FARMING
Bolton
Holgate
Osbaldwick
Millington
Yapham
Acomb
NATIONAL RAILWAY MUSEUM
A1079
Grimston
Kexby
Wilberfoss
Kilnwick Percy
CASTLE MUS
A1237
Nunthorpe
Heslington
Barmby Moor
B1228
B1246
Woodthorpe
Fulford
Newton upon Derwent
Pocklington
Bishopthorpe
YORK DESIGNER OUTLET
Crockey Hill
YORKSHIRE AIR MUSEUM
Elvington
STEWART'S BURNBY HALL GARDENS & MUSEUM
Nunburnholme
B1247
Allerthorpe
Sutton upon Derwent
Burnby
Copmanthorpe
Acaster Malbis
Naburn
Wheldrake
Thornton
Hayton
Londesborough
Pocklington Canal
A1079
Deighton
Storwood
Melbourne
Thorpe le Street
Bielby
Shiptonthorpe
Ouse
LOWER DERWENT VALLEY
Appleton Roebuck
Escrick
Everingham
Acaster Selby
SE
East Cottingwith
Seaton Ross
B1222
Thorganby
A19
Holme Green
Harswell
A614
Stillingfleet
B1228
150
Ryther
Ellerton
Laytham
Kelfield
Water End
Holme-on-Spalding-Moor
Skipwith
Aughton
Cawood
North Duffield
A163
Moor End
Riccall
SKIPWITH COMMON
Harlthorpe
Foggathorpe
Sand Hole
A163
Bubwith
Highfield
Rascal Moor
Wistow
Gunby
Gribthorpe
B1223
Barlby
Willitoft
SELBY ABBEY
Osgodby
Menthorpe
Breighton
Spaldington
A614
Bursea
Lund
South Duffield
Foulness
Selby
Cliffe
Thorpe Willoughby
A1238
Wressle
B1228
North Howden
Portington
Hive
East Common
Brind
Brayton
Hemingbrough
Newsholme
Cavil
Sandholme
A63
HOWDEN MINSTER
141
Eastrington
Scalby
140
B1230
Gilberdyke
Selby Canal
Barlow
Derwent
Barmby on the Marsh
Howden
M62
A1041
Gateforth
Burn
Long Drax
Staddlethorpe

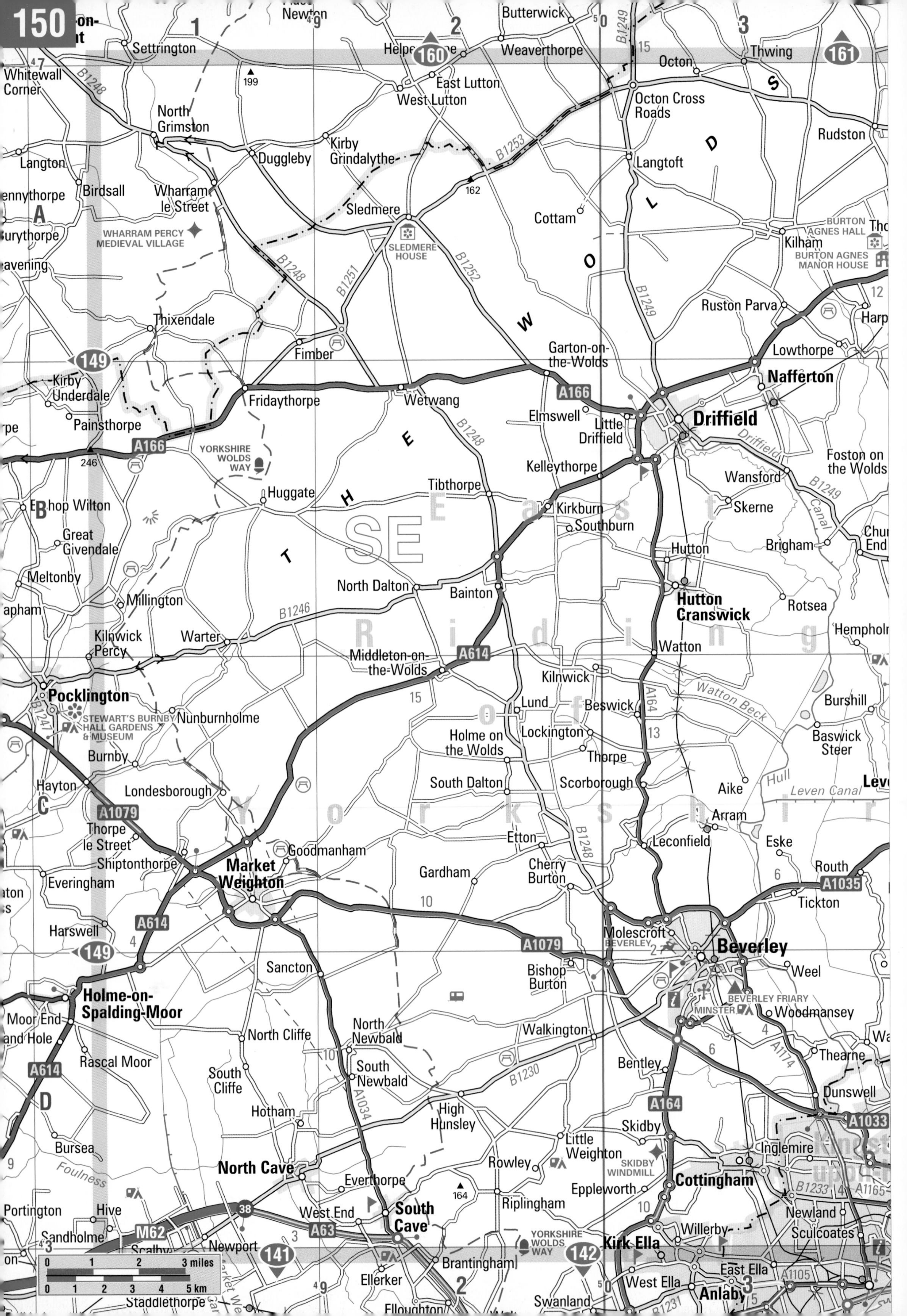
Settrington
Whitewall Corner
B1248
North Grimston
Langton
Birdsall
Wharram le Street
Duggleby
Kirby Grindalythe
WHARRAM PERCY MEDIEVAL VILLAGE
Thixendale
149
Kirby Underdale
Painsthorpe
Fridaythorpe
Fimber
A166
246
YORKSHIRE WOLDS WAY
Huggate
Great Givendale
Meltonby
Millington
Kilnwick Percy
Warter
B1246
Pocklington
STEWART'S BURNBY HALL GARDENS & MUSEUM
Nunburnholme
Burnby
Hayton
Londesborough
A1079
Thorpe le Street
Shiptonthorpe
Everingham
Market Weighton
Goodmanham
A614
Harswell
Holme-on-Spalding-Moor
Moor End
Sancton
North Cliffe
South Cliffe
Rascal Moor
Hotham
Bursea
Foulness
North Cave
Portington
Hive
Sandholme
M62
Scalby
Newport
38
141
A63
West End
South Cave
Everthorpe
Ellerker
Brantingham
Staddlethorpe
Elloughton
North Newbald
South Newbald
A1034
High Hunsley
164
Rowley
Riplingham
Helperthorpe
160
Weaverthorpe
Butterwick
East Lutton
West Lutton
Sledmere
SLEDMERE HOUSE
162
B1253
B1251
B1252
Wetwang
Tibthorpe
North Dalton
Bainton
Middleton-on-the-Wolds
A614
Holme on the Wolds
South Dalton
Lund
Etton
Gardham
Cherry Burton
A1079
Walkington
B1230
Bishop Burton
Bentley
Skidby
SKIDBY WINDMILL
Little Weighton
Eppleworth
Cottingham
Willerby
Kirk Ella
West Ella
Anlaby
East Ella
YORKSHIRE WOLDS WAY
142
Swanland
Octon
Thwing
161
Octon Cross Roads
Langtoft
Cottam
Rudston
BURTON AGNES HALL
Kilham
BURTON AGNES MANOR HOUSE
Ruston Parva
Lowthorpe
Nafferton
Garton-on-the-Wolds
Elmswell
Little Driffield
Driffield
Kelleythorpe
Kirkburn
Southburn
Wansford
Skerne
Foston on the Wolds
Brigham
Hutton
Hutton Cranswick
Rotsea
Watton
Kilnwick
Beswick
A164
Lockington
Thorpe
Scorborough
Leconfield
Arram
Aike
Eske
Watton Beck
Hull
Leven Canal
Burshill
Baswick Steer
Hempholme
Routh
A1035
Tickton
Molescroft
BEVERLEY
Beverley
Weel
BEVERLEY FRIARY
MINSTER
Woodmansey
A1174
Thearne
Dunswell
A1033
Inglemire
B1233
A1165
Newland
Sculcoates
A1105
B1231
THE WOLDS
SE
East Riding of Yorkshire
0 1 2 3 miles
0 1 2 3 4 5 km

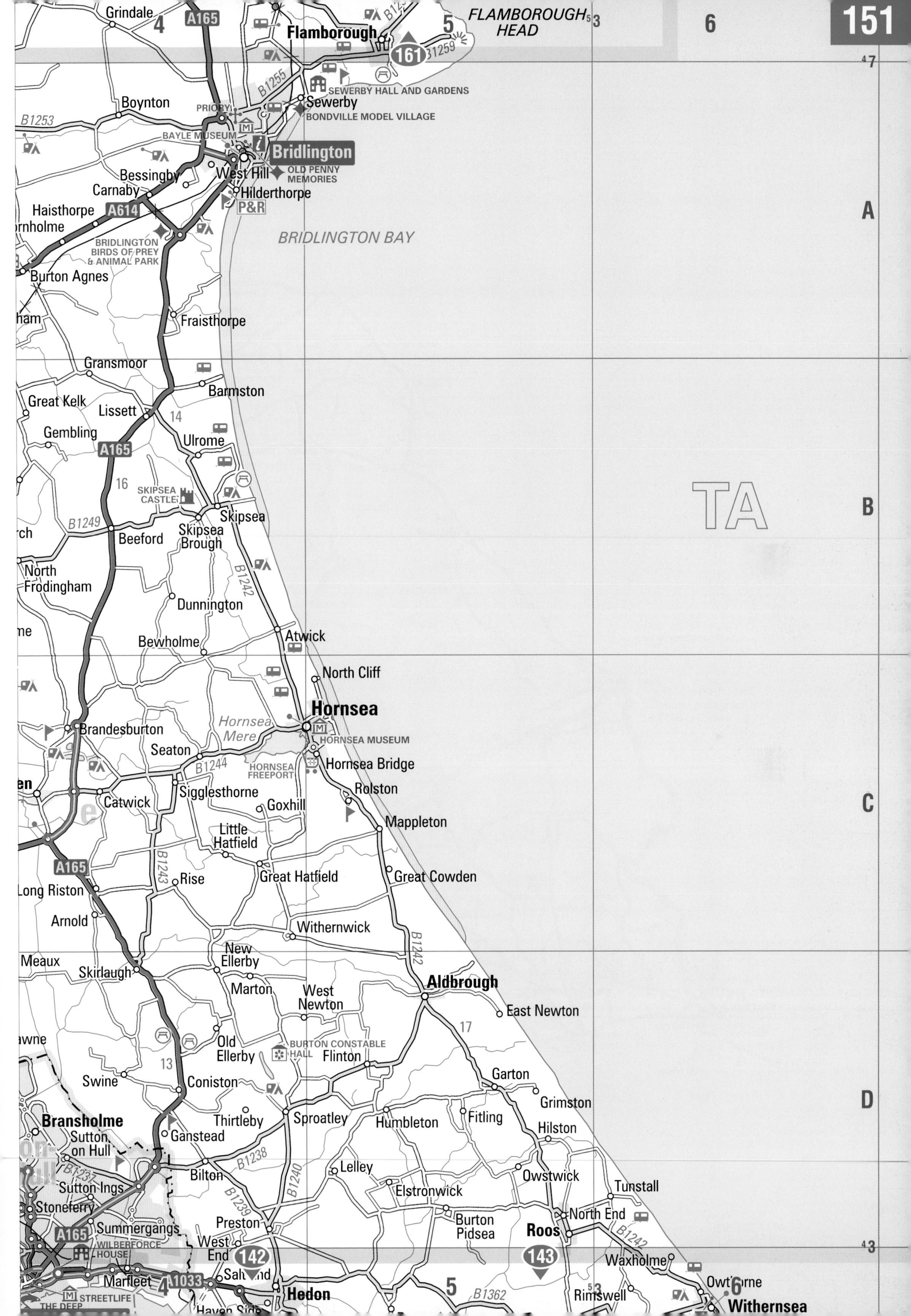

Grindale **A165** 4 3 **Flamborough** 5 **FLAMBOROUGH HEAD** 5 3 6

47

B1255 161 B1259

Boynton SEWERBY HALL AND GARDENS

B1253 PRIORY Sewerby BONDVILLE MODEL VILLAGE

BAYLE MUSEUM

Bessingby *i* **Bridlington** OLD PENNY MEMORIES

Carnaby **West Hill**

Haisthorpe **A614** Hilderthorpe

rnholme P&R

Burton Agnes BRIDLINGTON BIRDS OF PREY & ANIMAL PARK *BRIDLINGTON BAY* A

ham

Fraisthorpe

Gransmoor

Great Kelk Barmston

Lissett 14

Gembling Ulrome

A165

16 SKIPSEA CASTLE

B1249 Skipsea B

Beeford Skipsea Brough

North Frodingham B1242

Dunnington

ne Bewholme Atwick

North Cliff

Brandesburton **Hornsea**

Hornsea Mere HORNSEA MUSEUM

Seaton B1244 HORNSEA FREEPORT Hornsea Bridge

en Sigglesthorne Rolston C

Catwick Goxhill

Little Hatfield Mappleton

A165 B1243 Rise Great Hatfield Great Cowden

Long Riston

Arnold Withernwick

Meaux New Ellerby B1242

Skirlaugh Marton West Newton **Aldbrough**

Old Ellerby East Newton

13 BURTON CONSTABLE HALL Flinton 17 D

Swine Coniston Garton

Bransholme Thirtleby Sproatley Humbleton Fitling Grimston

Sutton on Hull Ganstead Hilston

B1237 B1238

Bilton B1240 Lelley Owstwick Tunstall

Sutton Ings B1239 Elstronwick

Stoneferry North End B1242

A165 Summergangs WILBERFORCE HOUSE Preston West End 142 Burton Pidsea **Roos**

Marfleet A1033 Salt nd 143

THE DEEP STREETLIFE **Hedon** 5 B1362 Waxholme

Haven Side 4 5 3 Rimswell Owt orne 6 **Withernsea**

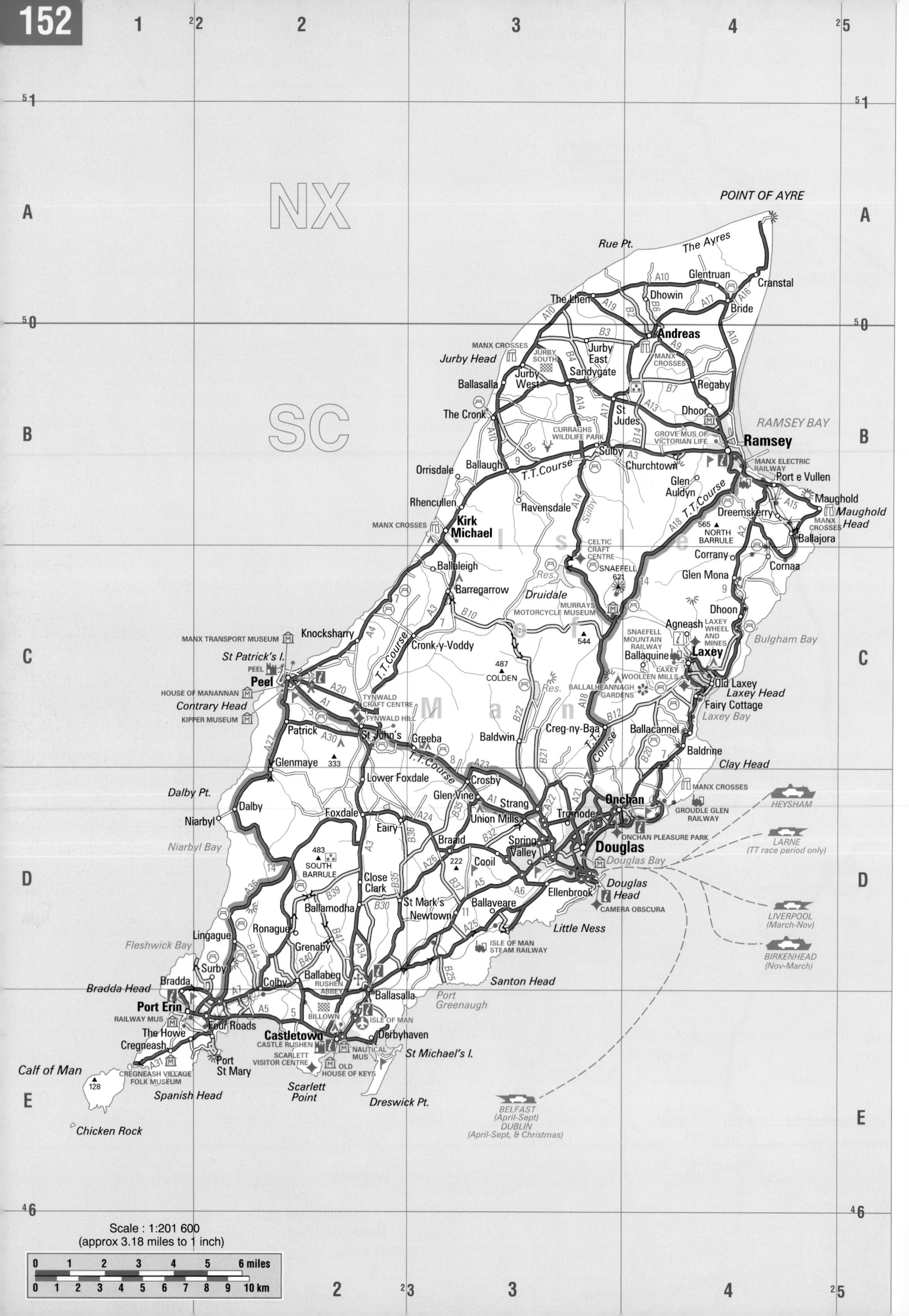
NX
SC
POINT OF AYRE
Rue Pt.
The Ayres
Glentruan
Cranstal
Dhowin
The Lhen
Bride
Andreas
MANX CROSSES
Jurby Head
JURBY SOUTH
Jurby East
Jurby West
Sandygate
Ballasalla
Regaby
The Cronk
St Judes
Dhoor
RAMSEY BAY
CURRAGHS WILDLIFE PARK
GROVE MUS OF VICTORIAN LIFE
Ramsey
Sulby
Churchtown
MANX ELECTRIC RAILWAY
Orrisdale
Ballaugh
T.T.Course
Port e Vullen
Glen Auldyn
Maughold
Maughold Head
Rhencullen
Ravensdale
Dreemskerry
Kirk Michael
565 NORTH BARRULE
Ballajora
CELTIC CRAFT CENTRE
Corrany
Cornaa
Ballaleigh
SNAEFELL 621
Glen Mona
Barregarrow
Druidale
MURRAYS MOTORCYCLE MUSEUM
Dhoon
Isle of Man
Agneash
LAXEY WHEEL AND MINES
Bulgham Bay
MANX TRANSPORT MUSEUM
Knocksharry
SNAEFELL MOUNTAIN RAILWAY
544
St Patrick's I.
Cronk-y-Voddy
Laxey
Ballaquine
PEEL
487 COLDEN
LAXEY WOOLLEN MILLS
Peel
Old Laxey
HOUSE OF MANANNAN
BALLALHEANNAGH GARDENS
Laxey Head
Contrary Head
TYNWALD CRAFT CENTRE
Fairy Cottage
KIPPER MUSEUM
TYNWALD HILL
Laxey Bay
Patrick
St John's
Greeba
Baldwin
Creg-ny-Baa
Ballacannel
Baldrine
Glenmaye
333
Clay Head
Lower Foxdale
Crosby
MANX CROSSES
Dalby Pt.
Glen Vine
Strang
Onchan
HEYSHAM
Dalby
GROUDLE GLEN RAILWAY
Niarbyl
Foxdale
Union Mills
Tromode
Eairy
ONCHAN PLEASURE PARK
LARNE (TT race period only)
Niarbyl Bay
Braaid
Spring Valley
Douglas
483 SOUTH BARRULE
222
Cooil
Douglas Bay
Close Clark
Douglas Head
Ellenbrook
Ballamodha
Ballaveare
CAMERA OBSCURA
LIVERPOOL (March-Nov)
St Mark's
Newtown
Little Ness
Lingague
Ronague
ISLE OF MAN STEAM RAILWAY
BIRKENHEAD (Nov-March)
Fleshwick Bay
Grenaby
Surby
Santon Head
Bradda
Colby
Ballabeg
RUSHEN ABBEY
Bradda Head
Ballasalla
Port Greenaugh
Port Erin
BILLOWN
ISLE OF MAN
RAILWAY MUS
Four Roads
The Howe
Castletown
Derbyhaven
CASTLE RUSHEN
NAUTICAL MUS
Cregneash
St Michael's I.
SCARLETT VISITOR CENTRE
OLD HOUSE OF KEYS
Port St Mary
Calf of Man
CREGNEASH VILLAGE FOLK MUSEUM
128
Spanish Head
Scarlett Point
Dreswick Pt.
BELFAST (April-Sept)
DUBLIN (April-Sept, & Christmas)
Chicken Rock
Scale : 1:201 600
(approx 3.18 miles to 1 inch)
0 1 2 3 4 5 6 miles
0 1 2 3 4 5 6 7 8 9 10 km

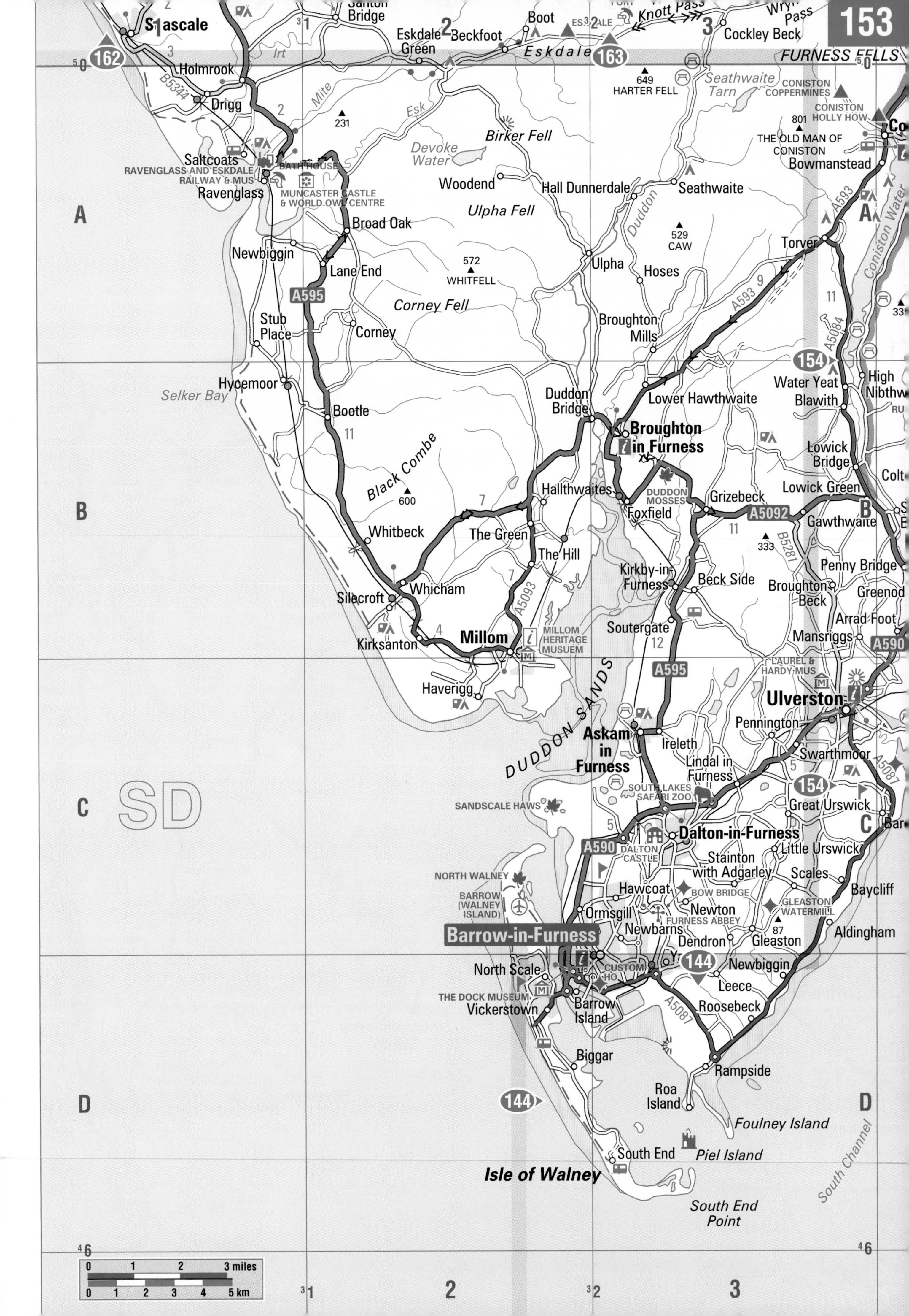
FURNESS FELLS
Seascale
Holmrook
Drigg
Saltcoats
RAVENGLASS AND ESKDALE RAILWAY & MUS
Ravenglass
BATH HOUSE
MUNCASTER CASTLE & WORLD OWL CENTRE
Eskdale Green
Beckfoot
Boot
Eskdale
Knott Pass
Cockley Beck
649 HARTER FELL
Seathwaite Tarn
CONISTON COPPERMINES
CONISTON HOLLY HOW
801 THE OLD MAN OF CONISTON
Bowmanstead
Devoke Water
Birker Fell
Woodend
Hall Dunnerdale
Seathwaite
Ulpha Fell
Broad Oak
Newbiggin
Lane End
572 WHITFELL
Ulpha
Hoses
529 CAW
Torver
Corney Fell
Stub Place
Corney
Broughton Mills
Hycemoor
Selker Bay
Bootle
Duddon Bridge
Lower Hawthwaite
Water Yeat
Blawith
High Nibthwaite
Broughton in Furness
Lowick Bridge
Lowick Green
Black Combe
600
Hallthwaites
DUDDON MOSSES
Foxfield
Grizebeck
Gawthwaite
Whitbeck
The Green
The Hill
Kirkby-in-Furness
Beck Side
333
Penny Bridge
Broughton Beck
Greenodd
Silecroft
Whicham
Millom
MILLOM HERITAGE MUSEUM
Soutergate
Arrad Foot
Mansriggs
Kirksanton
Haverigg
LAUREL & HARDY MUS
Ulverston
DUDDON SANDS
Askam in Furness
Ireleth
Pennington
Swarthmoor
Lindal in Furness
SOUTH LAKES SAFARI ZOO
Great Urswick
SANDSCALE HAWS
Dalton-in-Furness
DALTON CASTLE
Little Urswick
Stainton with Adgarley
Scales
Baycliff
NORTH WALNEY
BARROW (WALNEY ISLAND)
Hawcoat
BOW BRIDGE
Newton
GLEASTON WATERMILL
Ormsgill
FURNESS ABBEY
87
Barrow-in-Furness
Newbarns
Dendron
Gleaston
Aldingham
North Scale
CUSTOM HO
Newbiggin
Leece
THE DOCK MUSEUM
Vickerstown
Barrow Island
Roosebeck
Biggar
Rampside
Roa Island
Foulney Island
South End
Piel Island
Isle of Walney
South End Point
South Channel
Coniston Water
SD
A595
A593
A5084
A5092
B5281
A5093
A590
A5087
B5344
162
163
154
144
0 1 2 3 miles
0 1 2 3 4 5 km

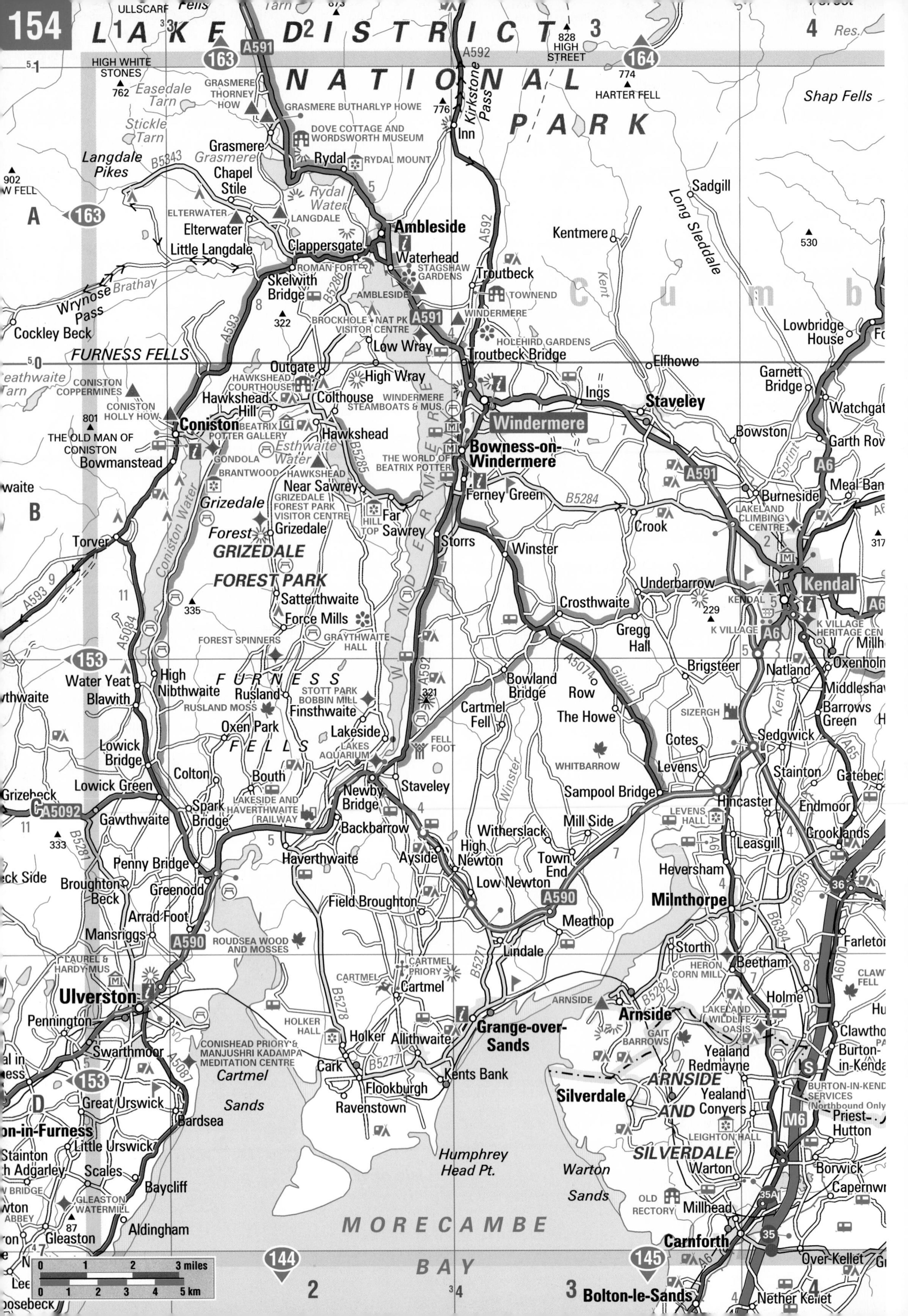
LAKE DISTRICT
NATIONAL
PARK
163
164
A591
A592
ULLSCARF
HIGH WHITE STONES
762
Easedale Tarn
GRASMERE THORNEY HOW
GRASMERE BUTHARLYP HOWE
DOVE COTTAGE AND WORDSWORTH MUSEUM
Stickle Tarn
Grasmere
Rydal
RYDAL MOUNT
Langdale Pikes
B5343
Chapel Stile
Rydal Water
902
776
Kirkstone Pass
Inn
828 HIGH STREET
774
HARTER FELL
Shap Fells
Sadgill
Long Sleddale
Kentmere
530
ELTERWATER
LANGDALE
Elterwater
Ambleside
Little Langdale
Clappersgate
Waterhead
STAGSHAW GARDENS
Troutbeck
TOWNEND
ROMAN FORT
Skelwith Bridge
B5286
AMBLESIDE
Kent
Cumb
Wrynose Pass
Brathay
Cockley Beck
A593
322
BROCKHOLE – NAT PK VISITOR CENTRE
WINDERMERE
HOLEHIRD GARDENS
Lowbridge House
Low Wray
Troutbeck Bridge
Elfhowe
FURNESS FELLS
Outgate
High Wray
HAWKSHEAD COURTHOUSE
Colthouse
WINDERMERE STEAMBOATS & MUS.
Ings
Staveley
Garnett Bridge
Watchgate
CONISTON COPPERMINES
CONISTON HOLLY HOW
Hawkshead Hill
Coniston
BEATRIX POTTER GALLERY
Hawkshead
Windermere
801
THE OLD MAN OF CONISTON
Bowmanstead
GONDOLA
Esthwaite Water
B5285
THE WORLD OF BEATRIX POTTER
Bowness-on-Windermere
Bowston
Garth Row
BRANTWOOD
HAWKSHEAD
Near Sawrey
Ferney Green
A591
A6
Burneside
Meal Bank
Grizedale
GRIZEDALE FOREST PARK VISITOR CENTRE
HILL TOP
Far Sawrey
B5284
Crook
LAKELAND CLIMBING CENTRE
Coniston Water
Forest
Grizedale
Storrs
Torver
GRIZEDALE
Winster
317
WINDERMERE
FOREST PARK
Underbarrow
Kendal
A593
335
Satterthwaite
Crosthwaite
KENDAL
Force Mills
229
Gregg Hall
K VILLAGE
K VILLAGE HERITAGE CENTRE
FOREST SPINNERS
GRAYTHWAITE HALL
A5084
153
A5074
Gilpin
Brigsteer
Natland
Oxenholme
Water Yeat
High Nibthwaite
FURNESS
Bowland Bridge
Row
Blawith
Rusland
STOTT PARK BOBBIN MILL
321
Middleshaw
RUSLAND MOSS
Finsthwaite
Cartmel Fell
The Howe
SIZERGH
Barrows Green
Oxen Park
Lakeside
Cotes
Sedgwick
Lowick Bridge
FELLS
LAKES AQUARIUM
FELL FOOT
WHITBARROW
Levens
A65
Colton
Bouth
Winster
Stainton
Gatebeck
Lowick Green
Newby Bridge
Staveley
Sampool Bridge
Hincaster
Endmoor
Grizebeck
A5092
Spark Bridge
LAKESIDE AND HAVERTHWAITE RAILWAY
LEVENS HALL
Gawthwaite
Backbarrow
Witherslack
Mill Side
Crooklands
333
B5281
Haverthwaite
Ayside
High Newton
Town End
Leasgill
Penny Bridge
Heversham
Broughton Beck
Greenodd
Low Newton
A590
Milnthorpe
36
B6385
Field Broughton
Arrad Foot
Meathop
B6384
Farleton
Mansriggs
A590
ROUDSEA WOOD AND MOSSES
Lindale
Storth
B5271
Beetham
LAUREL & HARDY MUS
CARTMEL PRIORY
HERON CORN MILL
CLAWTHORPE FELL
A6070
CARTMEL
Cartmel
ARNSIDE
B5282
Ulverston
B5278
Arnside
Holme
Pennington
HOLKER HALL
Grange-over-Sands
LAKELAND WILDLIFE OASIS
GAIT BARROWS
Clawthorpe
Holker
Allithwaite
Swarthmoor
CONISHEAD PRIORY & MANJUSHRI KADAMPA MEDITATION CENTRE
A5087
Yealand Redmayne
Burton-in-Kendal
Cark
B5277
Cartmel
153
Kents Bank
ARNSIDE
Flookburgh
Silverdale
Yealand Conyers
BURTON-IN-KENDAL SERVICES (Northbound Only)
Great Urswick
Sands
AND
Ravenstown
Priest Hutton
Bardsea
M6
LEIGHTON HALL
Little Urswick
SILVERDALE
Humphrey Head Pt.
Warton Sands
Warton
Stainton with Adgarley
Scales
Borwick
Baycliff
Capernwray
GLEASTON WATERMILL
OLD RECTORY
Millhead
35A
87
Gleaston
Aldingham
MORECAMBE
Carnforth
35
144
145
BAY
Over Kellet
0 1 2 3 miles
0 1 2 3 4 5 km
2
3
4
Bolton-le-Sands
Nether Kellet

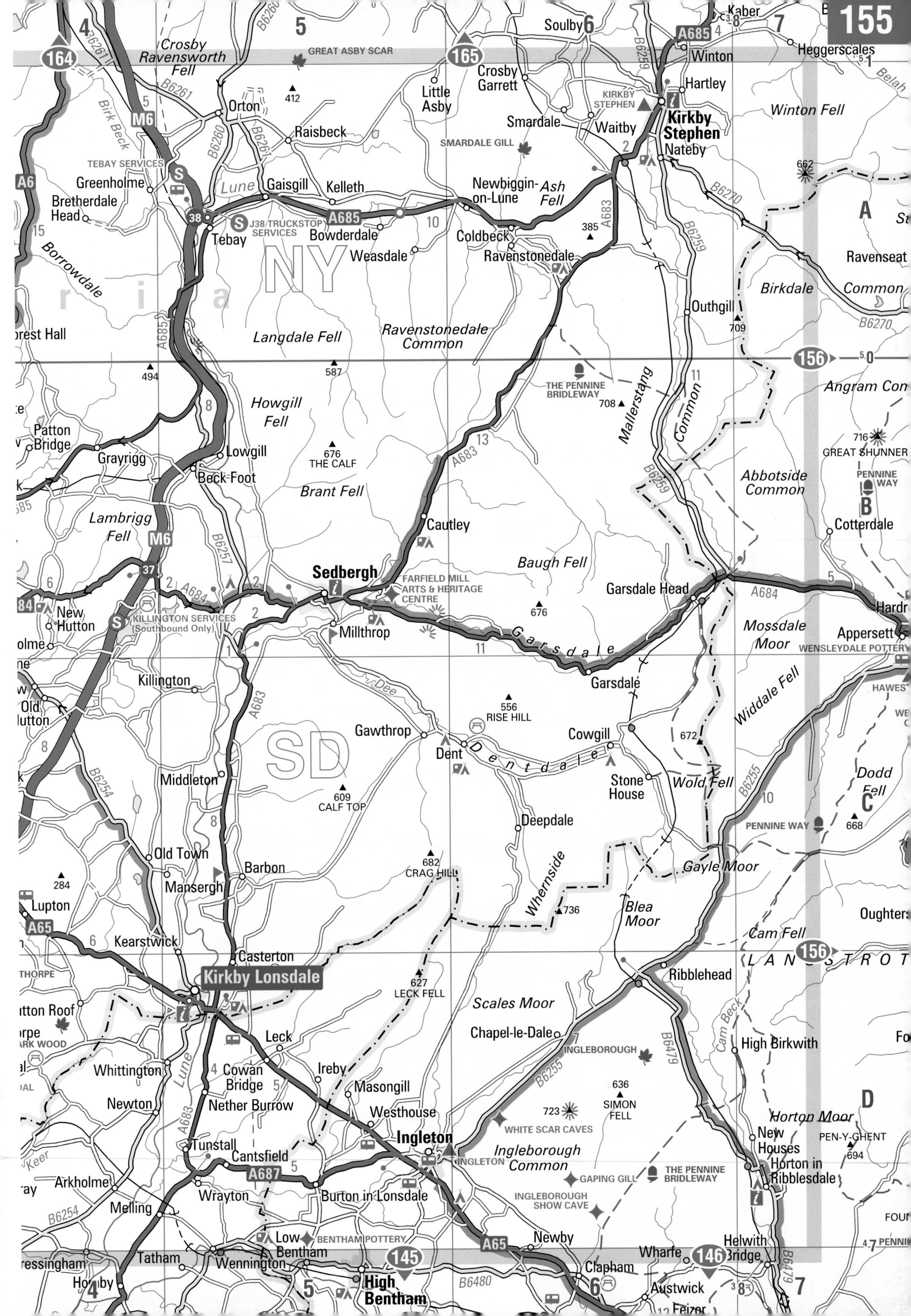

Crosby Ravensworth Fell
GREAT ASBY SCAR
Soulby
Kaber
Winton
Heggerscales
Belah
Little Asby
Crosby Garrett
Hartley
KIRKBY STEPHEN
Kirkby Stephen
Winton Fell
Orton
Raisbeck
Smardale
Waitby
Nateby
SMARDALE GILL
Birk Beck
TEBAY SERVICES
Greenholme
Bretherdale Head
Lune
Gaisgill
Kelleth
Newbiggin-on-Lune
Ash Fell
Tebay
J38 TRUCKSTOP SERVICES
Bowderdale
Weasdale
Coldbeck
Ravenstonedale
Ravenseat
Borrowdale
NY
Birkdale
Common
Outhgill
Langdale Fell
Ravenstonedale Common
Angram Con
THE PENNINE BRIDLEWAY
Mallerstang
Common
Howgill Fell
Patton Bridge
Grayrigg
Lowgill
Beck Foot
THE CALF
GREAT SHUNNER
Abbotside Common
PENNINE WAY
Brant Fell
Lambrigg Fell
Cautley
Cotterdale
Baugh Fell
Sedbergh
FARFIELD MILL ARTS & HERITAGE CENTRE
Garsdale Head
New Hutton
KILLINGTON SERVICES (Southbound Only)
Millthrop
Garsdale
Mossdale Moor
Appersett
WENSLEYDALE POTTERY
HAWES
Killington
Old Hutton
Dee
RISE HILL
Widdale Fell
Gawthrop
Dent
Dentdale
Cowgill
SD
Middleton
Stone House
Wold Fell
Dodd Fell
CALF TOP
Deepdale
PENNINE WAY
Old Town
CRAG HILL
Barbon
Mansergh
Gayle Moor
Whernside
Lupton
Blea Moor
Oughtershaw
Kearstwick
Cam Fell
Casterton
LANGSTROTH
THORPE
Kirkby Lonsdale
Ribblehead
LECK FELL
Scales Moor
Hutton Roof
Chapel-le-Dale
Leck
INGLEBOROUGH
High Birkwith
Cam Beck
Whittington
Cowan Bridge
Ireby
SIMON FELL
Masongill
Newton
Nether Burrow
Westhouse
WHITE SCAR CAVES
Horton Moor
PEN-Y-GHENT
Tunstall
Ingleton
INGLETON
Ingleborough Common
New Houses
Cantsfield
Horton in Ribblesdale
Keer
GAPING GILL
THE PENNINE BRIDLEWAY
Arkholme
Wrayton
Burton in Lonsdale
INGLEBOROUGH SHOW CAVE
Melling
Low Bentham
BENTHAM POTTERY
Newby
Helwith Bridge
Wharfe
Tatham
Wennington
Clapham
Hornby
High Bentham
Austwick
Feizor
M6
A6
A685
A683
A684
A65
A687
B6260
B6261
B6259
B6270
B6257
B6254
B6255
B6479
B6480
164
165
156
145
146

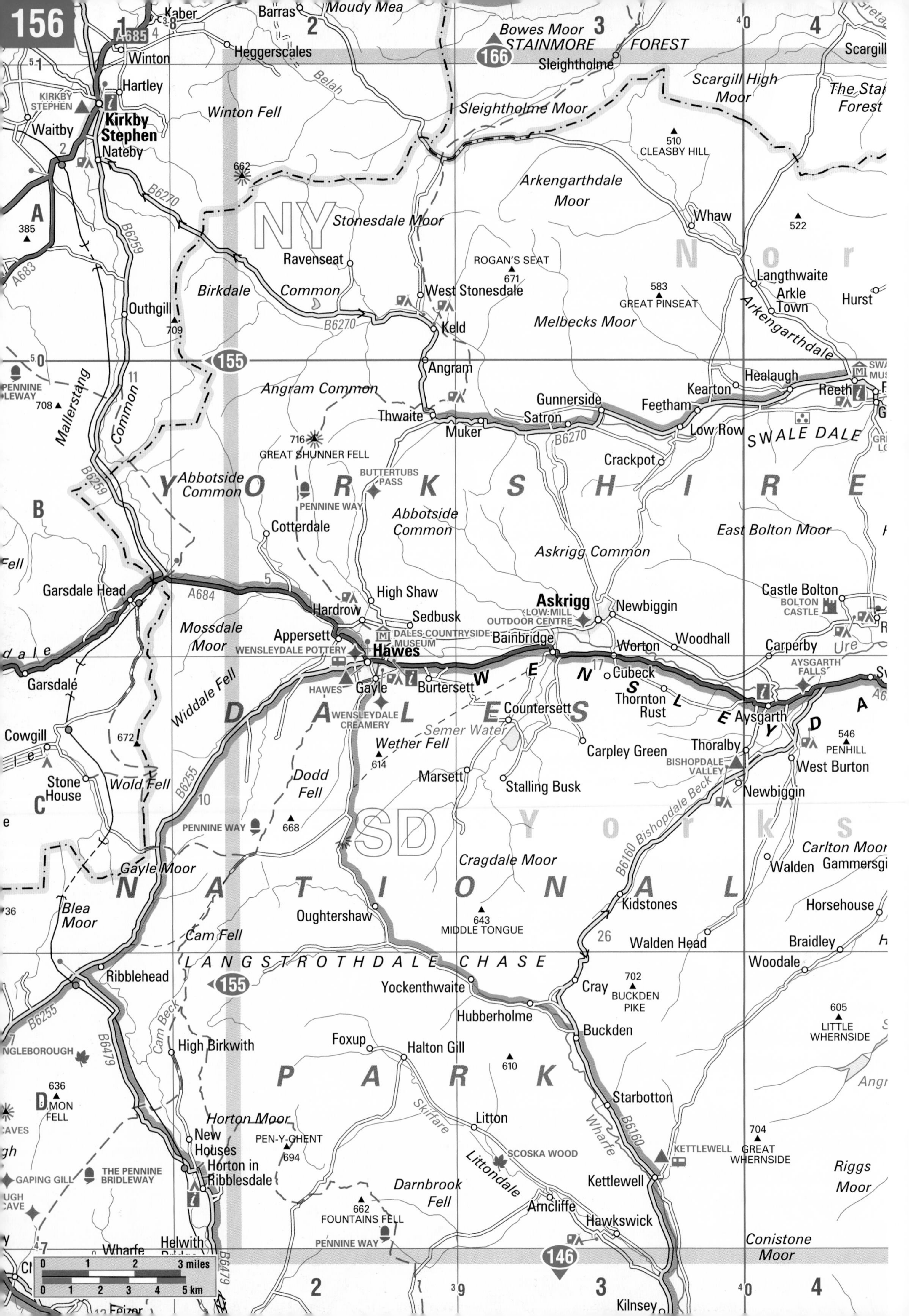

Kaber
Barras
Moudy Mea
Bowes Moor
STAINMORE
FOREST
166
Sleightholme
Scargill
A685
Winton
Heggerscales
Hartley
KIRKBY STEPHEN
Kirkby Stephen
Waitby
Nateby
Belah
Winton Fell
Sleightholme Moor
Scargill High Moor
The Stang Forest
510
CLEASBY HILL
662
B6270
Arkengarthdale Moor
NY
Stonesdale Moor
Whaw
522
385
B6259
Ravenseat
ROGAN'S SEAT
671
Nor
A683
Birkdale
Common
West Stonesdale
583
GREAT PINSEAT
Langthwaite
Arkle Town
Hurst
Outhgill
709
Keld
Melbecks Moor
Arkengarthdale
155
Angram
Healaugh
PENNINE BRIDLEWAY
708
Mallerstang
Common
Angram Common
Kearton
Reeth
Gunnerside
Feetham
Thwaite
Satron
716
Muker
Low Row
SWALE DALE
GREAT SHUNNER FELL
B6270
Crackpot
BUTTERTUBS PASS
Abbotside Common
YORKSHIRE
PENNINE WAY
Abbotside Common
East Bolton Moor
Cotterdale
Askrigg Common
Fell
Garsdale Head
A684
High Shaw
Castle Bolton
BOLTON CASTLE
Askrigg
Newbiggin
Hardrow
Sedbusk
LOW MILL OUTDOOR CENTRE
Mossdale Moor
Appersett
DALES COUNTRYSIDE MUSEUM
Bainbridge
Woodhall
WENSLEYDALE POTTERY
Hawes
Worton
Carperby
Ure
Garsdale
Cubeck
AYSGARTH FALLS
Widdale Fell
HAWES
Gayle
Burtersett
Thornton Rust
Countersett
Aysgarth
WENSLEYDALE
Cowgill
WENSLEYDALE CREAMERY
Semer Water
546
PENHILL
672
Wether Fell
Carpley Green
Thoralby
614
BISHOPDALE VALLEY
West Burton
Dodd Fell
Marsett
Stalling Busk
Stone House
Wold Fell
B6255
Newbiggin
Bishopdale Beck
PENNINE WAY
668
SD
Yorks
B6160
Carlton Moor
Cragdale Moor
Walden
Gammersgill
Gayle Moor
NATIONAL
Kidstones
Horsehouse
Blea Moor
Oughtershaw
643
MIDDLE TONGUE
Cam Fell
Walden Head
Braidley
LANGSTROTHDALE CHASE
Woodale
Ribblehead
702
BUCKDEN PIKE
Cray
Yockenthwaite
Hubberholme
605
LITTLE WHERNSIDE
Buckden
B6255
Cam Beck
INGLEBOROUGH
High Birkwith
Foxup
Halton Gill
610
B6479
PARK
636
SIMON FELL
Starbotton
Skirfare
Horton Moor
Litton
Wharfe
B6160
704
GREAT WHERNSIDE
CAVES
New Houses
PEN-Y-GHENT
694
SCOSKA WOOD
KETTLEWELL
Riggs Moor
GAPING GILL
THE PENNINE BRIDLEWAY
Horton in Ribblesdale
Littondale
Kettlewell
Darnbrook Fell
Arncliffe
662
FOUNTAINS FELL
Hawkswick
PENNINE WAY
Conistone Moor
Wharfe
Helwith Bridge
146
B6479
Kilnsey
Feizor
0 1 2 3 miles
0 1 2 3 4 5 km

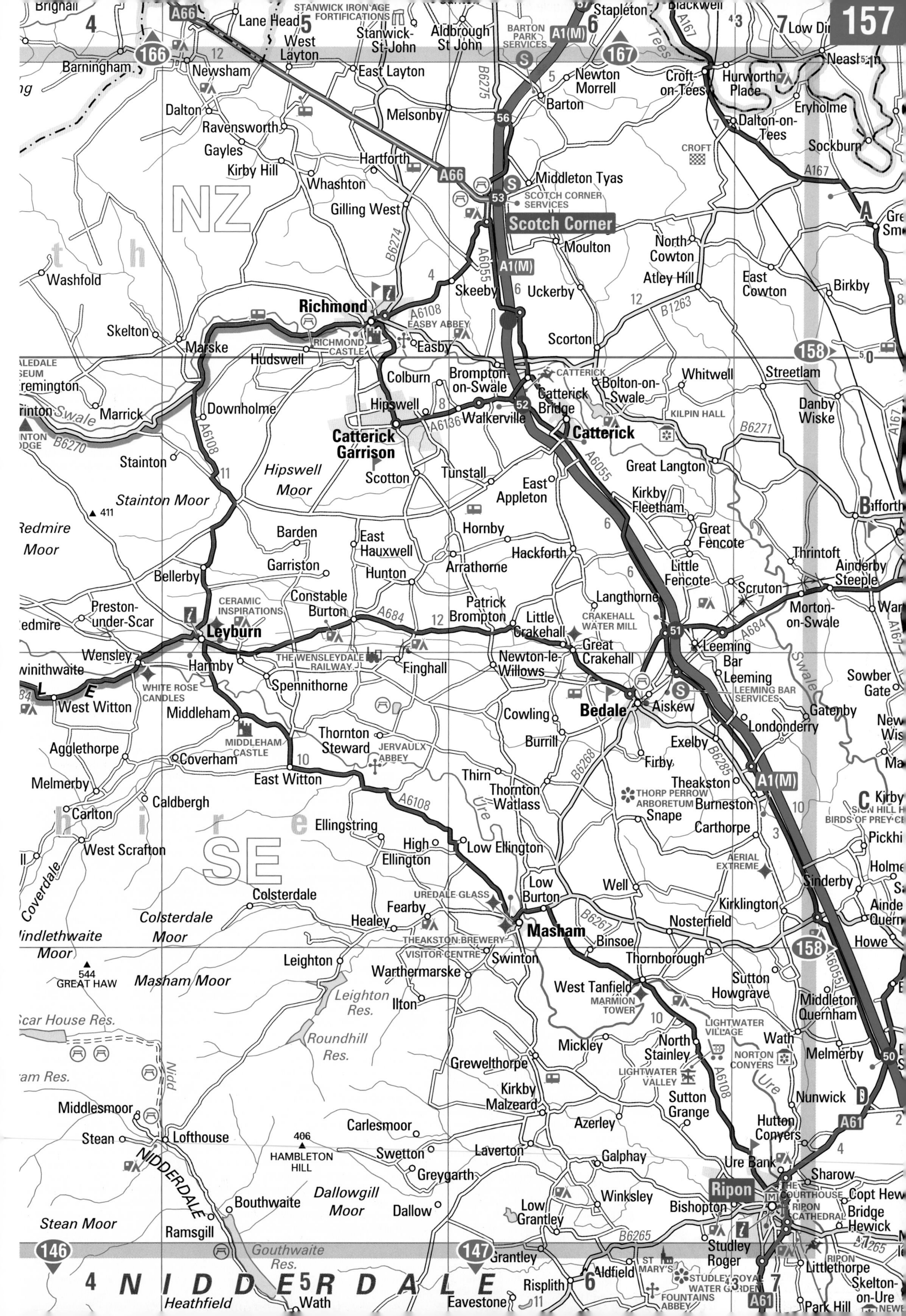
Brignall
Lane Head
STANWICK IRON AGE FORTIFICATIONS
Stanwick-St-John
Aldbrough St John
BARTON PARK SERVICES
Stapleton
Blackwell
Low Dinsdale
West Layton
Barningham
Newsham
East Layton
Newton Morrell
Croft-on-Tees
Hurworth Place
Neasham
Barton
Eryholme
Dalton
Ravensworth
Melsonby
Dalton-on-Tees
Gayles
CROFT
Sockburn
Kirby Hill
Hartforth
Whashton
Middleton Tyas
SCOTCH CORNER SERVICES
Gilling West
Scotch Corner
Moulton
North Cowton
Atley Hill
East Cowton
Birkby
Washfold
Skeeby
Uckerby
Richmond
EASBY ABBEY
Skelton
Marske
RICHMOND CASTLE
Easby
Scorton
Hudswell
Colburn
Brompton-on-Swale
CATTERICK
Bolton-on-Swale
Whitwell
Streetlam
Danby Wiske
Marrick
Downholme
Hipswell
Catterick Bridge
Walkerville
KILPIN HALL
Catterick Garrison
Catterick
Stainton
Swale
Hipswell Moor
Scotton
Tunstall
Great Langton
Stainton Moor
East Appleton
Kirkby Fleetham
Redmire Moor
Barden
Hornby
Great Fencote
East Hauxwell
Hackforth
Thrintoft
Garriston
Arrathorne
Little Fencote
Ainderby Steeple
Bellerby
Hunton
Scruton
Constable Burton
Langthorne
Preston-under-Scar
CERAMIC INSPIRATIONS
Patrick Brompton
Little Crakehall
CRAKEHALL WATER MILL
Morton-on-Swale
Redmire
Leyburn
Great Crakehall
Leeming
Wensley
Harmby
THE WENSLEYDALE RAILWAY
Finghall
Newton-le-Willows
Leeming Bar
Thoralby
Spennithorne
Sowerby Gate
West Witton
WHITE ROSE CANDLES
LEEMING BAR SERVICES
Middleham
Bedale
Aiskew
Cowling
Gatenby
Londonderry
Thornton Steward
Burrill
Exelby
Agglethorpe
MIDDLEHAM CASTLE
JERVAULX ABBEY
Coverham
Firby
East Witton
Thirn
Theakston
Melmerby
Thornton Watlass
THORP PERROW ARBORETUM
Burneston
Kirby Sigston
Carlton
Caldbergh
Snape
Carthorpe
Ellingstring
Ure
High Ellington
Low Ellington
West Scrafton
AERIAL EXTREME
Pickhill
Low Burton
Well
Sinderby
Coverdale
Colsterdale
UREDALE GLASS
Kirklington
Fearby
Colsterdale Moor
Healey
Masham
Nosterfield
Ainderby Quernhow
Dindlethwaite Moor
THEAKSTON BREWERY VISITOR CENTRE
Binsoe
Howe
Leighton
Swinton
Thornborough
Warthermarske
Sutton Howgrave
544 GREAT HAW
Masham Moor
West Tanfield
MARMION TOWER
Leighton Res.
Ilton
Middleton Quernham
LIGHTWATER VILLAGE
Scar House Res.
Roundhill Res.
North Stainley
Wath
Mickley
NORTON CONYERS
Melmerby
Angram Res.
Grewelthorpe
LIGHTWATER VALLEY
Nidd
Kirkby Malzeard
Sutton Grange
Nunwick
Middlesmoor
Carlesmoor
Azerley
Hutton Conyers
Stean
Lofthouse
406 HAMBLETON HILL
Swetton
Laverton
Galphay
Ure Bank
Sharow
NIDDERDALE
Greygarth
Ripon
THE COURTHOUSE
Copt Hewick
RIPON CATHEDRAL
Bridge Hewick
Bouthwaite
Dallowgill Moor
Dallow
Winksley
Bishopton
Stean Moor
Low Grantley
Ramsgill
Studley Roger
Littlethorpe
Gouthwaite Res.
Grantley
ST MARY'S
RIPON RACECOURSE
Aldfield
STUDLEY ROYAL WATER GARDEN
Skelton-on-Ure
NIDDERDALE
Risplith
FOUNTAINS ABBEY
Heathfield
Wath
Eavestone
Park Hill
NZ
SE
A66
A1(M)
A6108
A6136
A684
A6055
A167
A61
B6275
B6274
B1263
B6271
B6270
B6268
B6267
B6285
B6265
166
167
158
146
147

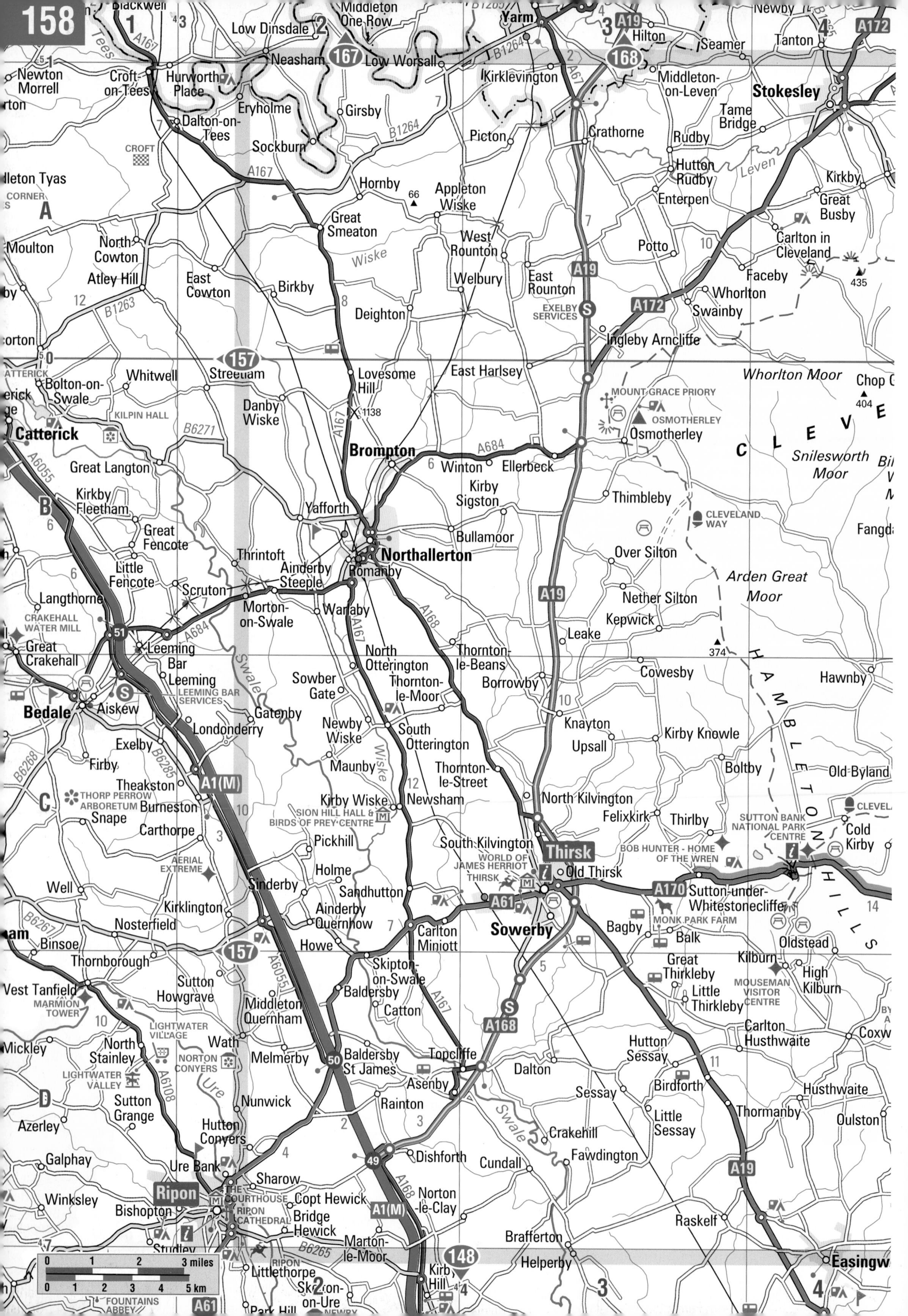

Blackwell
Low Dinsdale
Middleton One Row
Yarm
Newby
Tanton
A172
Hilton
Seamer
Tees
Neasham
167
Low Worsall
168
Newton Morrell
Croft-on-Tees
Hurworth Place
Kirklevington
Middleton-on-Leven
Stokesley
Eryholme
Girsby
Tame Bridge
Dalton-on-Tees
B1264
Picton
Crathorne
Rudby
CROFT
Sockburn
Hutton Rudby
Leven
A167
Hornby
Appleton Wiske
Kirkby
Great Busby
Enterpen
A
Great Smeaton
West Rounton
Potto
Carlton in Cleveland
Moulton
North Cowton
Wiske
Faceby
East Cowton
Welbury
East Rounton
A19
Atley Hill
Birkby
Whorlton
435
B1263
Deighton
EXELBY SERVICES
A172
Swainby
Ingleby Arncliffe
157
Streetlam
Lovesome Hill
East Harlsey
Whitwell
Whorlton Moor
Chop G
Bolton-on-Swale
Danby Wiske
MOUNT GRACE PRIORY
404
KILPIN HALL
1138
OSMOTHERLEY
Catterick
B6271
Osmotherley
C L E V E
A6055
Brompton
A684
Winton
Ellerbeck
Snilesworth Moor
Great Langton
Kirby Sigston
Kirkby Fleetham
Thimbleby
B
Yafforth
CLEVELAND WAY
Great Fencote
Bullamoor
Northallerton
Over Silton
Thrintoft
Ainderby Steeple
Romanby
Little Fencote
Arden Great Moor
Scruton
A19
Langthorne
Morton-on-Swale
Warlaby
Nether Silton
CRAKEHALL WATER MILL
A168
Kepwick
A684
Leake
Great Crakehall
Leeming Bar
North Otterington
Thornton-le-Beans
374
Leeming
Sowber Gate
Thornton-le-Moor
Cowesby
H A M B L E T O N H I L L S
Hawnby
LEEMING BAR SERVICES
Borrowby
Bedale
Aiskew
Gatenby
Newby Wiske
South Otterington
Knayton
Londonderry
Exelby
Upsall
Kirby Knowle
Firby
B6285
Maunby
Wiske
Thornton-le-Street
Boltby
B6268
Old Byland
Theakston
A1(M)
THORP PERROW ARBORETUM
Burneston
Kirby Wiske
Newsham
North Kilvington
C
SION HILL HALL & BIRDS OF PREY CENTRE
Felixkirk
Thirlby
SUTTON BANK NATIONAL PARK CENTRE
Snape
Carthorpe
Cold Kirby
Pickhill
South Kilvington
Thirsk
BOB HUNTER - HOME OF THE WREN
AERIAL EXTREME
WORLD OF JAMES HERRIOT
Holme
Old Thirsk
Well
Sinderby
THIRSK
Sandhutton
A170
Sutton-under-Whitestonecliffe
Kirklington
A61
Ainderby Quernhow
Sowerby
Bagby
MONK PARK FARM
Nosterfield
Carlton Miniott
Balk
Oldstead
B6267
Binsoe
157
Howe
Great Thirkleby
Kilburn
Thornborough
Skipton-on-Swale
High Kilburn
Vest Tanfield
Sutton Howgrave
A6055
Baldersby
MOUSEMAN VISITOR CENTRE
Little Thirkleby
MARMION TOWER
Middleton Quernham
Catton
A167
A168
Carlton Husthwaite
LIGHTWATER VILLAGE
Hutton Sessay
Coxw
Mickley
North Stainley
Wath
Melmerby
Baldersby St James
Topcliffe
Dalton
NORTON CONYERS
LIGHTWATER VALLEY
Ure
Asenby
Birdforth
Husthwaite
D
Sutton Grange
Nunwick
Rainton
Sessay
Thormanby
Azerley
A6108
Little Sessay
Oulston
Hutton Conyers
Swale
Crakehill
Galphay
Dishforth
Fawdington
Ure Bank
Cundall
A19
Sharow
Ripon
Norton-le-Clay
Winksley
Bishopton
THE COURTHOUSE
Copt Hewick
RIPON CATHEDRAL
Bridge Hewick
A1(M)
Raskelf
Studley
B6265
Marton-le-Moor
Brafferton
RIPON
148
Helperby
Easingw
Littlethorpe
Kirby Hill
Skelton-on-Ure
0 1 2 3 miles
0 1 2 3 4 5 km
FOUNTAINS ABBEY
A61
Park Hill
NEWBY

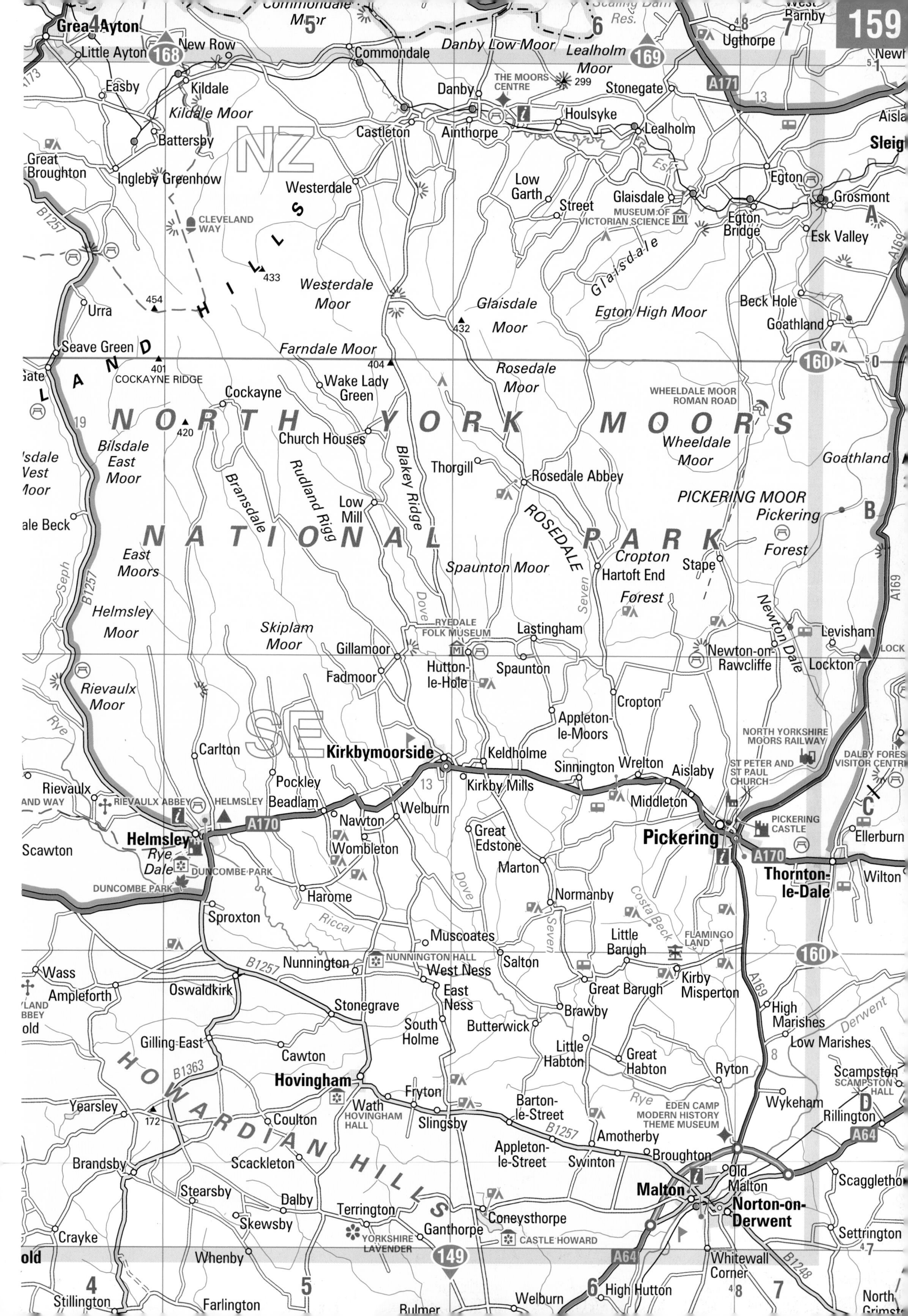
NORTH YORK MOORS NATIONAL PARK
CLEVELAND HILLS
HOWARDIAN HILLS
Great Ayton
Little Ayton
New Row
Commondale
Danby Low Moor
Lealholm Moor
Ugthorpe
Easby
Kildale
Kildale Moor
Battersby
Danby
THE MOORS CENTRE
Stonegate
Castleton
Ainthorpe
Houlsyke
Lealholm
Great Broughton
Ingleby Greenhow
Westerdale
Low Garth
Street
Glaisdale
MUSEUM OF VICTORIAN SCIENCE
Egton
Egton Bridge
Grosmont
Esk Valley
CLEVELAND WAY
Westerdale Moor
Glaisdale Moor
Egton High Moor
Beck Hole
Goathland
Urra
Seave Green
Farndale Moor
Rosedale Moor
COCKAYNE RIDGE
Cockayne
Wake Lady Green
WHEELDALE MOOR ROMAN ROAD
Church Houses
Wheeldale Moor
Bilsdale East Moor
Bransdale
Rudland Rigg
Blakey Ridge
Thorgill
Rosedale Abbey
ROSEDALE
PICKERING MOOR
Pickering Forest
Low Mill
East Moors
Spaunton Moor
Cropton Forest
Hartoft End
Stape
Newton Dale
Helmsley Moor
Skiplam Moor
RYEDALE FOLK MUSEUM
Lastingham
Levisham
Gillamoor
Hutton-le-Hole
Spaunton
Newton-on-Rawcliffe
Lockton
Fadmoor
Rievaulx Moor
Cropton
Appleton-le-Moors
NORTH YORKSHIRE MOORS RAILWAY
Carlton
Kirkbymoorside
Keldholme
Sinnington
Wrelton
Aislaby
ST PETER AND ST PAUL CHURCH
DALBY FOREST VISITOR CENTRE
Pockley
Kirkby Mills
Middleton
Rievaulx
RIEVAULX ABBEY
HELMSLEY
Beadlam
Welburn
Nawton
PICKERING CASTLE
Ellerburn
Helmsley
Great Edstone
Pickering
Scawton
Wombleton
Rye Dale
DUNCOMBE PARK
Marton
Thornton-le-Dale
Wilton
Harome
Normanby
Sproxton
Riccal
Costa Beck
Muscoates
Little Barugh
FLAMINGO LAND
Wass
Nunnington
NUNNINGTON HALL
West Ness
Salton
Kirby Misperton
Great Barugh
Ampleforth
Oswaldkirk
East Ness
Brawby
High Marishes
Stonegrave
South Holme
Butterwick
Low Marishes
Gilling East
Little Habton
Great Habton
Cawton
Ryton
Scampston
SCAMPSTON HALL
Hovingham
Fryton
Barton-le-Street
Wykeham
EDEN CAMP MODERN HISTORY THEME MUSEUM
Rillington
Yearsley
Wath
HOVINGHAM HALL
Coulton
Slingsby
Amotherby
Appleton-le-Street
Broughton
Brandsby
Scackleton
Swinton
Old Malton
Scagglethorpe
Malton
Stearsby
Dalby
Terrington
Coneysthorpe
Norton-on-Derwent
Skewsby
Crayke
Ganthorpe
YORKSHIRE LAVENDER
CASTLE HOWARD
Settrington
Whenby
Whitewall Corner
Stillington
Farlington
Welburn
High Hutton
Bulmer
North Grimston
A170
A169
A171
A64
B1257
B1363
B1248
NZ
SE

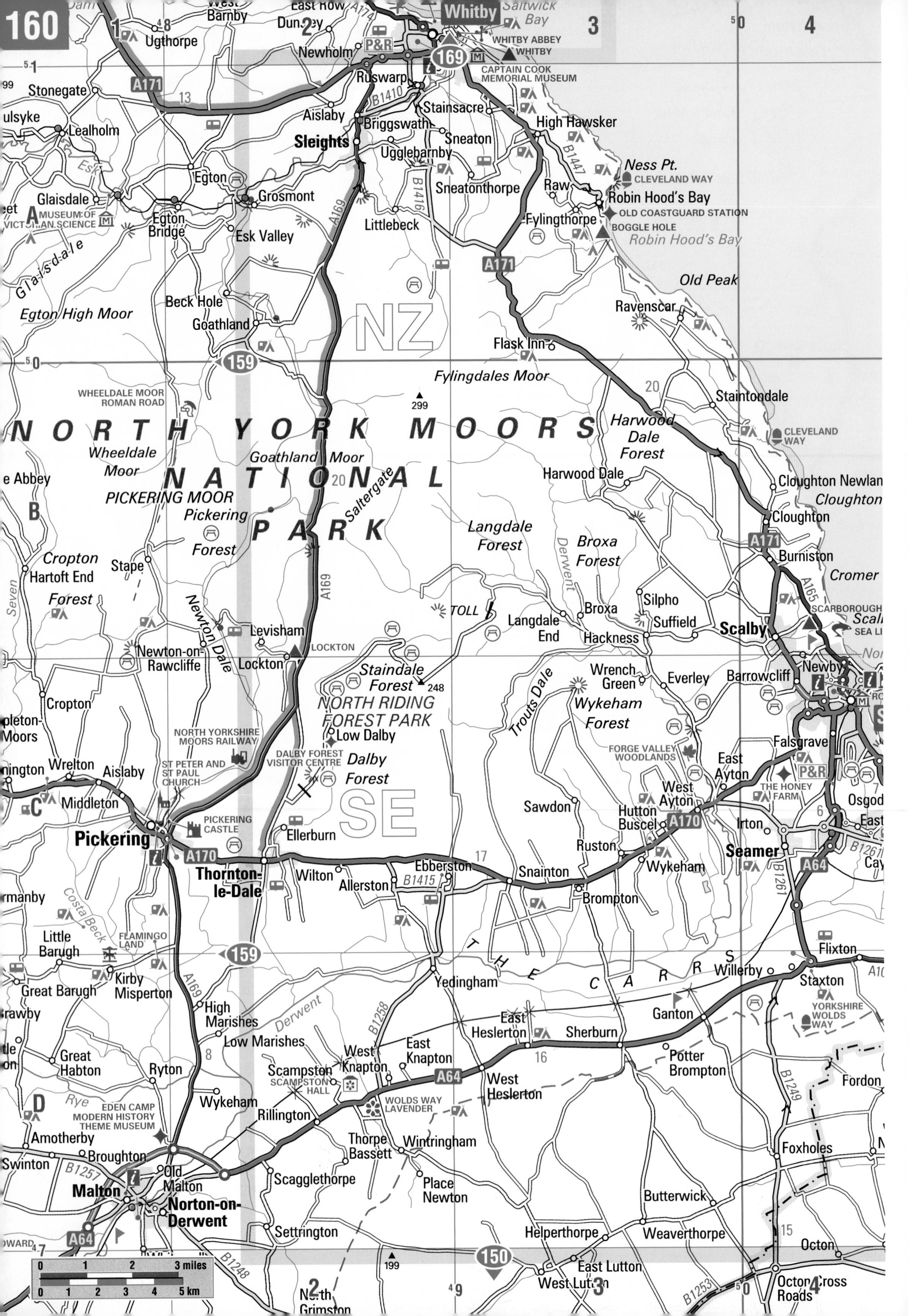
Whitby
Saltwick Bay
WHITBY ABBEY
WHITBY
CAPTAIN COOK MEMORIAL MUSEUM
Barnby
East Row
Dunsley
Ugthorpe
Newholm
P&R
Ruswarp
A171
Stonegate
Aislaby
Briggswath
Stainsacre
High Hawsker
Lealholm
Sleights
Sneaton
Ugglebarnby
B1447
Ness Pt.
CLEVELAND WAY
Egton
Sneatonthorpe
Raw
Robin Hood's Bay
Glaisdale
Grosmont
OLD COASTGUARD STATION
MUSEUM OF VICTORIAN SCIENCE
Egton Bridge
Littlebeck
Fylingthorpe
BOGGLE HOLE
Esk Valley
Robin Hood's Bay
A169
B1416
Glaisdale
Old Peak
Egton High Moor
Beck Hole
Goathland
NZ
Ravenscar
Flask Inn
159
Fylingdales Moor
WHEELDALE MOOR ROMAN ROAD
299
Staintondale
NORTH YORK MOORS NATIONAL PARK
Harwood Dale Forest
CLEVELAND WAY
Wheeldale Moor
Goathland Moor
Harwood Dale
Cloughton Newlands
Cloughton
PICKERING MOOR
Pickering Forest
Saltergate
Langdale Forest
Broxa Forest
Burniston
Cropton
Hartoft End Forest
Stape
Derwent
A165
Cromer
Silpho
Broxa
Suffield
Seven
Newton Dale
TOLL
Langdale End
Hackness
Scalby
SCARBOROUGH
Levisham
LOCKTON
Newton-on-Rawcliffe
Lockton
Staindale Forest
248
Wrench Green
Everley
Barrowcliff
Newby
Cropton
NORTH RIDING FOREST PARK
Trouts Dale
Wykeham Forest
Low Dalby
Appleton-le-Moors
NORTH YORKSHIRE MOORS RAILWAY
FORGE VALLEY WOODLANDS
Falsgrave
Sinnington
Wrelton
Aislaby
ST PETER AND ST PAUL CHURCH
DALBY FOREST VISITOR CENTRE
Dalby Forest
East Ayton
West Ayton
THE HONEY FARM
Osgodby
Middleton
SE
Sawdon
Hutton Buscel
A170
Irton
PICKERING CASTLE
Pickering
Ellerburn
Ruston
Seamer
A170
Thornton-le-Dale
Wilton
Ebberston
17
Snainton
Wykeham
B1261
A64
Allerston
B1415
Brompton
Normanby
Costa Beck
Little Barugh
FLAMINGO LAND
159
THE CARRS
Flixton
Willerby
Staxton
Kirby Misperton
Great Barugh
A169
Yedingham
YORKSHIRE WOLDS WAY
Ganton
High Marishes
East Heslerton
Derwent
B1258
Sherburn
Low Marishes
West Knapton
East Knapton
Potter Brompton
16
Great Habton
Ryton
Scampston
SCAMPSTON HALL
A64
West Heslerton
B1249
Fordon
Wykeham
Rye
EDEN CAMP MODERN HISTORY THEME MUSEUM
Rillington
WOLDS WAY LAVENDER
Amotherby
Thorpe Bassett
Wintringham
Foxholes
Swinton
Broughton
B1257
Old Malton
Scagglethorpe
Malton
Norton-on-Derwent
Place Newton
Butterwick
A64
Settrington
Helperthorpe
Weaverthorpe
Octon
B1248
150
199
East Lutton
West Lutton
B1253
Octon Cross Roads
North Grimston
0 1 2 3 miles
0 1 2 3 4 5 km

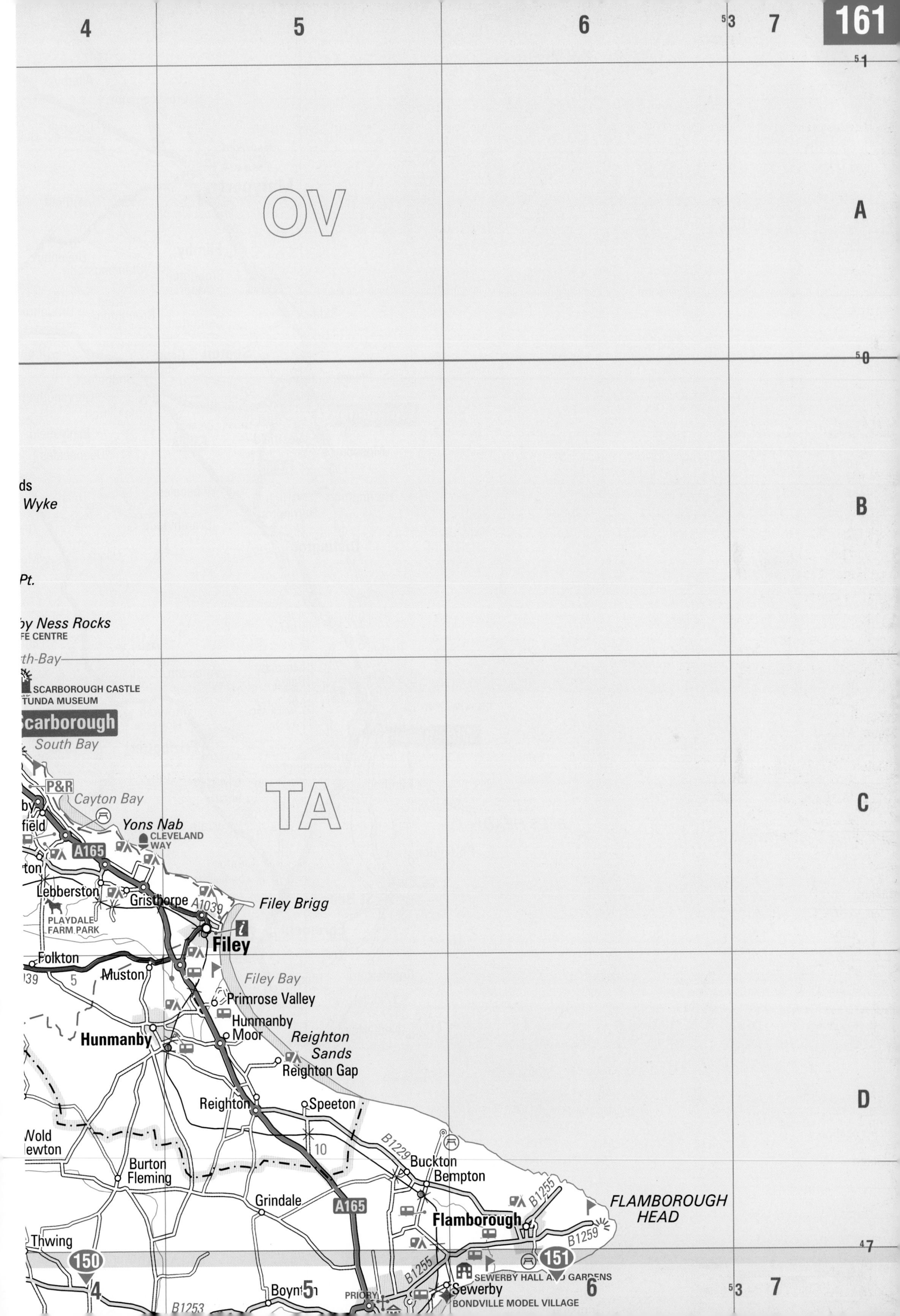

4

5

6

⁵3 7

⁵1

A

B

C

D

⁴7

⁵3 7

OV

Wyke

Pt.

by Ness Rocks
FE CENTRE

th-Bay

SCARBOROUGH CASTLE
TUNDA MUSEUM

Scarborough
South Bay

P&R *Cayton Bay*

by
field

Yons Nab
CLEVELAND
WAY

A165

ton

Lebberston

Gristhorpe *A1039*

Filey Brigg

PLAYDALE
FARM PARK

i

Filey

Folkton

039 5

Muston

Filey Bay

Primrose Valley

Hunmanby
Moor

Hunmanby

Reighton
Sands

Reighton Gap

Reighton

Speeton

Wold
ewton

10

B1229

Buckton

Burton
Fleming

Bempton

Grindale

A165

B1255

Flamborough

FLAMBOROUGH
HEAD

B1259

Thwing

150

151

SEWERBY HALL AND GARDENS

4

Boyn'*5*1

PRIORY

Sewerby

6

B1253

BONDVILLE MODEL VILLAGE

TA

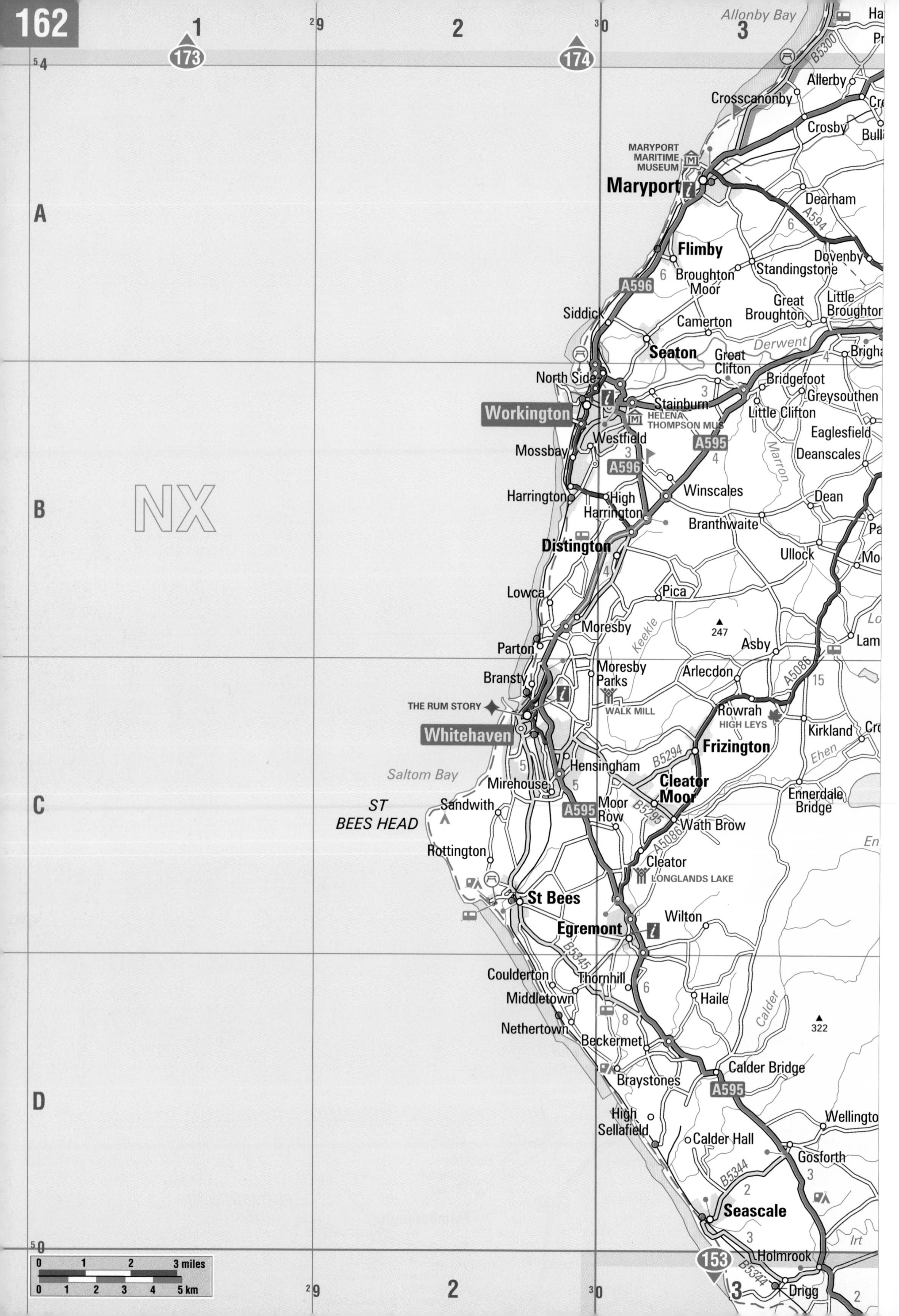

1 ²⁹ **2** ³⁰ **3**

Allonby Bay

173   174

⁵4

A

NX

B

C

ST
BEES HEAD

Saltom Bay

Mirehouse

Sandwith

Rottington

D

⁵0

| 0 | 1 | 2 | 3 miles |

| 0 | 1 | 2 | 3 | 4 | 5 km |

²⁹   **2**   ³⁰

Maryport
MARITIME
MUSEUM

Crosscanonby
Allerby
Crosby
Dearham

Flimby
Broughton
Moor
Standingstone
Dovenby

Siddick
Cameron
Great
Broughton
Great
Broughton
Little
Broughton

A596

Seaton
Great
Clifton
Derwent

North Side
Bridgefoot
Brigh

Workington
Stainburn
Greysouthen
Little Clifton

HELENA
THOMPSON MUS
A595

Westfield
Eaglesfield

Mossbay
A596
Deanscales

Harrington
High
Harrington
Winscales
Dean

Distington
Branthwaite

Ullock

Lowca
Pica

Moresby
247
Asby

Parton
Arlecdon
A5086   15

Bransty
Moresby
Parks
Rowrah

THE RUM STORY
WALK MILL
HIGH LEYS
Kirkland

Whitehaven
B5294
Frizington

Hensingham
**Cleator
Moor**

Moor
Row
Ennerdale
Bridge

A595
Wath Brow

Cleator
LONGLANDS LAKE
En

Wilton

Egremont

Coulderton
Thornhill
Haile

Middletown
6

Nethertown
Beckermet
322

Braystones
Calder Bridge

High
Sellafield
A595
Wellingto

Calder Hall
Gosforth

Seascale
3

153   Holmrook
B5344
Drigg

²⁹   **2**   ³⁰   **3**

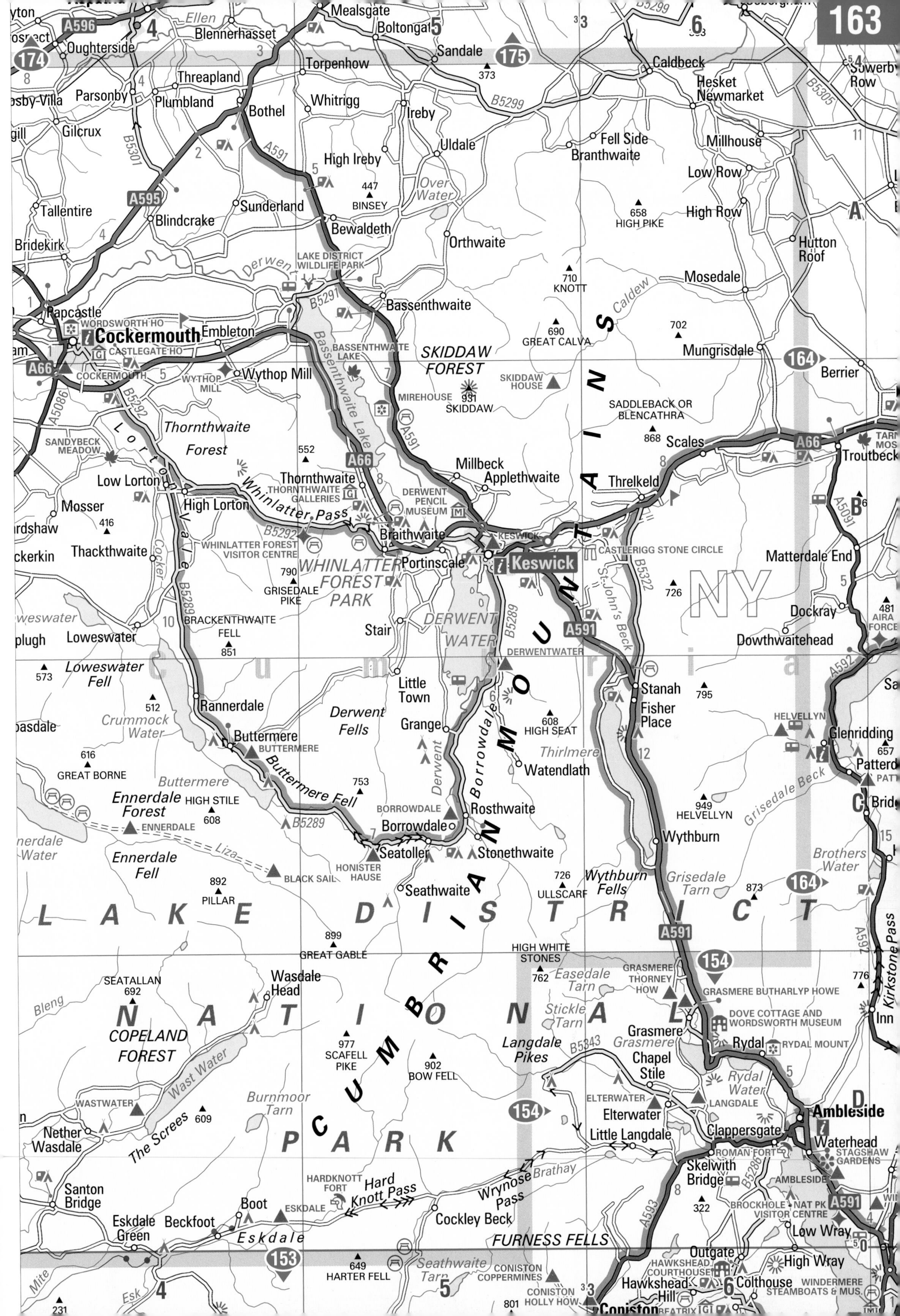
Mealsgate
Boltongate
Sandale
Caldbeck
Hesket Newmarket
Sowerby Row
Oughterside
Blennerhasset
Torpenhow
Threapland
Parsonby
Plumbland
Bothel
Whitrigg
Ireby
Gilcrux
Uldale
Fell Side
Branthwaite
Millhouse
Low Row
High Row
High Ireby
447 BINSEY
Over Water
Tallentire
Blindcrake
Sunderland
Bewaldeth
Orthwaite
658 HIGH PIKE
Hutton Roof
Bridekirk
LAKE DISTRICT WILDLIFE PARK
710 KNOTT
Mosedale
Caldew
Papcastle
WORDSWORTH HO
Cockermouth
Embleton
CASTLEGATE HO
COCKERMOUTH
Bassenthwaite
690 GREAT CALVA
702
Mungrisdale
Berrier
BASSENTHWAITE LAKE
SKIDDAW FOREST
SKIDDAW HOUSE
WYTHOP MILL
Wythop Mill
MIREHOUSE
931 SKIDDAW
SADDLEBACK OR BLENCATHRA
868
Scales
Troutbeck
SANDYBECK MEADOW
Lorton Vale
Thornthwaite Forest
552
Bassenthwaite Lake
Millbeck
Applethwaite
Threlkeld
Low Lorton
High Lorton
Thornthwaite
THORNTHWAITE GALLERIES
DERWENT PENCIL MUSEUM
Mosser
416
Whinlatter Pass
Braithwaite
KESWICK
Thackthwaite
WHINLATTER FOREST VISITOR CENTRE
Portinscale
Keswick
CASTLERIGG STONE CIRCLE
Matterdale End
Cocker
790 GRISEDALE PIKE
WHINLATTER FOREST PARK
726
NY
Dockray
Dowthwaitehead
481 AIRA FORCE
Loweswater
BRACKENTHWAITE FELL 851
Stair
DERWENT WATER
St John's Beck
Loweswater
DERWENTWATER
573
Loweswater Fell
Cumbria
Little Town
Stanah
795
512
Rannerdale
Derwent Fells
Fisher Place
Crummock Water
Grange
608 HIGH SEAT
HELVELLYN
Glenridding
Buttermere
BUTTERMERE
616 GREAT BORNE
Thirlmere
Watendlath
657
Patterdale
Buttermere
Buttermere Fell
753
Borrowdale
Ennerdale Forest
HIGH STILE 608
ENNERDALE
BORROWDALE
Rosthwaite
949 HELVELLYN
Grisedale Beck
Ennerdale Water
Liza
Wythburn
Brothers Water
Ennerdale Fell
Seatoller
HONISTER HAUSE
Stonethwaite
BLACK SAIL
892 PILLAR
Seathwaite
726 ULLSCARF
Wythburn Fells
Grisedale Tarn
873
LAKE DISTRICT
CUMBRIAN MOUNTAINS
899 GREAT GABLE
HIGH WHITE STONES
762
Easedale Tarn
GRASMERE THORNEY HOW
GRASMERE BUTHARLYP HOWE
776
Kirkstone Pass
SEATALLAN 692
Wasdale Head
Bleng
NATIONAL
COPELAND FOREST
Stickle Tarn
DOVE COTTAGE AND WORDSWORTH MUSEUM
Grasmere
Rydal
RYDAL MOUNT
Inn
977 SCAFELL PIKE
902 BOW FELL
Langdale Pikes
Chapel Stile
Rydal Water
Wast Water
Burnmoor Tarn
WASTWATER
609
The Screes
ELTERWATER
Elterwater
LANGDALE
Ambleside
Nether Wasdale
CUMBRIAN
PARK
Little Langdale
Clappersgate
Waterhead
ROMAN FORT
STAGSHAW GARDENS
Skelwith Bridge
AMBLESIDE
Santon Bridge
HARDKNOTT FORT
Hard Knott Pass
Wrynose Pass
Brathay
322
BROCKHOLE NAT PK VISITOR CENTRE
Eskdale Green
Beckfoot
Boot
ESKDALE
Cockley Beck
Low Wray
Eskdale
FURNESS FELLS
Outgate
High Wray
649 HARTER FELL
Seathwaite Tarn
CONISTON COPPERMINES
HAWKSHEAD COURTHOUSE
Hawkshead
Colthouse
Hawkshead Hill
WINDERMERE STEAMBOATS & MUS.
Mite
Esk
231
CONISTON HOLLY HOW
801
Coniston
A596
A595
A591
A66
B5291
B5292
B5289
B5299
B5305
B5301
A5086
A5091
B5322
A592
B5343
B5286
A593
174
175
164
154
153

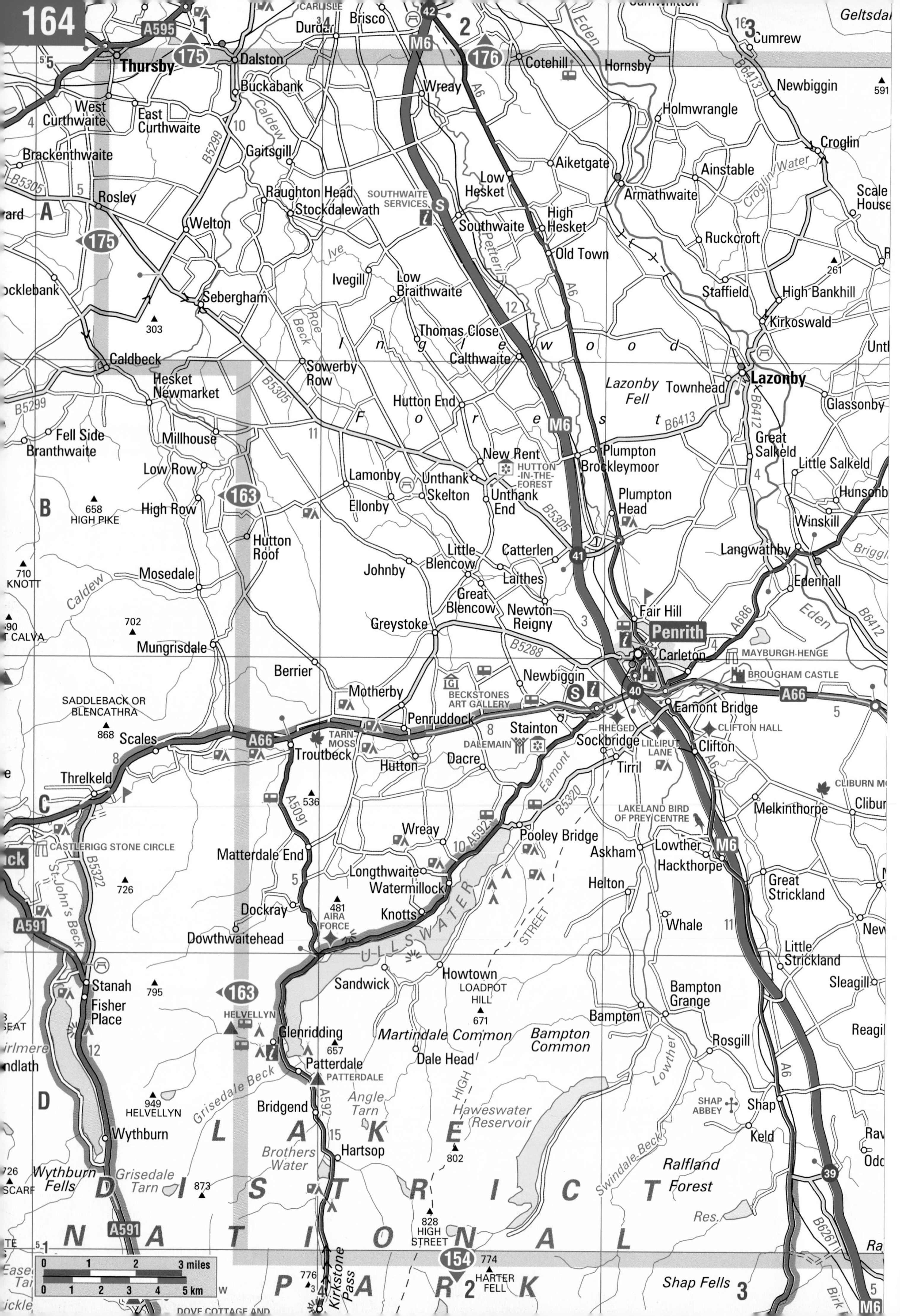

Thursby
Dalston
Cotehill
Hornsby
Cumrew
Geltsdale
Brisco
Durdar
CARLISLE
M6
A595
A6
Eden
Buckabank
Wreay
Newbiggin
West Curthwaite
East Curthwaite
Caldew
Holmwrangle
Croglin
Brackenthwaite
Gaitsgill
Aiketgate
Ainstable
B5305
B5299
Rosley
Raughton Head
Stockdalewath
SOUTHWAITE SERVICES
Low Hesket
Armathwaite
Croglin Water
Scale Houses
Welton
Southwaite
High Hesket
Ruckcroft
Old Town
Petteril
Ive
Ivegill
Low Braithwaite
Staffield
High Bankhill
Kirkoswald
Sebergham
Roe Beck
Thomas Close
Calthwaite
Caldbeck
Sowerby Row
Hesket Newmarket
Inglewood Forest
Lazonby Fell
Townhead
Lazonby
Glassonby
Hutton End
B6413
B6412
Fell Side
Branthwaite
Millhouse
New Rent
Plumpton
Brockleymoor
Great Salkeld
Little Salkeld
Low Row
Lamonby
Unthank
HUTTON-IN-THE-FOREST
Skelton
Unthank End
Plumpton Head
Hunsonby
HIGH PIKE
High Row
Ellonby
Hutton Roof
Winskill
Langwathby
Little Blencow
Catterlen
Mosedale
Johnby
Laithes
KNOTT
Edenhall
Great Blencow
Newton Reigny
Fair Hill
CALVA
Mungrisdale
Greystoke
Penrith
A686
B5288
Carleton
MAYBURGH HENGE
Berrier
Newbiggin
BROUGHAM CASTLE
SADDLEBACK OR BLENCATHRA
Motherby
BECKSTONES ART GALLERY
A66
Eamont Bridge
Penruddock
Stainton
RHEGED
CLIFTON HALL
Scales
TARN MOSS
DALEMAIN
Sockbridge
LILLIPUT LANE
Clifton
Troutbeck
Hutton
Dacre
Tirril
Threlkeld
Eamont
CLIBURN MOSS
Cliburn
B5320
LAKELAND BIRD OF PREY CENTRE
Melkinthorpe
CASTLERIGG STONE CIRCLE
A5091
Wreay
A592
Pooley Bridge
Askham
Lowther
Matterdale End
Hackthorpe
Longthwaite
Watermillock
Helton
Great Strickland
St John's Beck
B5322
Dockray
AIRA FORCE
Knotts
STREET
Whale
A591
Dowthwaitehead
ULLSWATER
Little Strickland
Howtown
Sleagill
Stanah
Sandwick
LOADPOT HILL
Bampton Grange
Fisher Place
HELVELLYN
Bampton
Reagill
Glenridding
Martindale Common
Bampton Common
Rosgill
Thirlmere
Patterdale
PATTERDALE
Dale Head
Lowther
Angle Tarn
HIGH
SHAP ABBEY
Shap
Grisedale Beck
Bridgend
Haweswater Reservoir
Wythburn
Hartsop
Keld
Brothers Water
Swindale Beck
Ralfland Forest
Wythburn Fells
Grisedale Tarn
LAKE DISTRICT NATIONAL PARK
Res.
HIGH STREET
B6261
Kirkstone Pass
HARTER FELL
Shap Fells
DOVE COTTAGE AND
0 1 2 3 miles
0 1 2 3 4 5 km
175
176
163
154

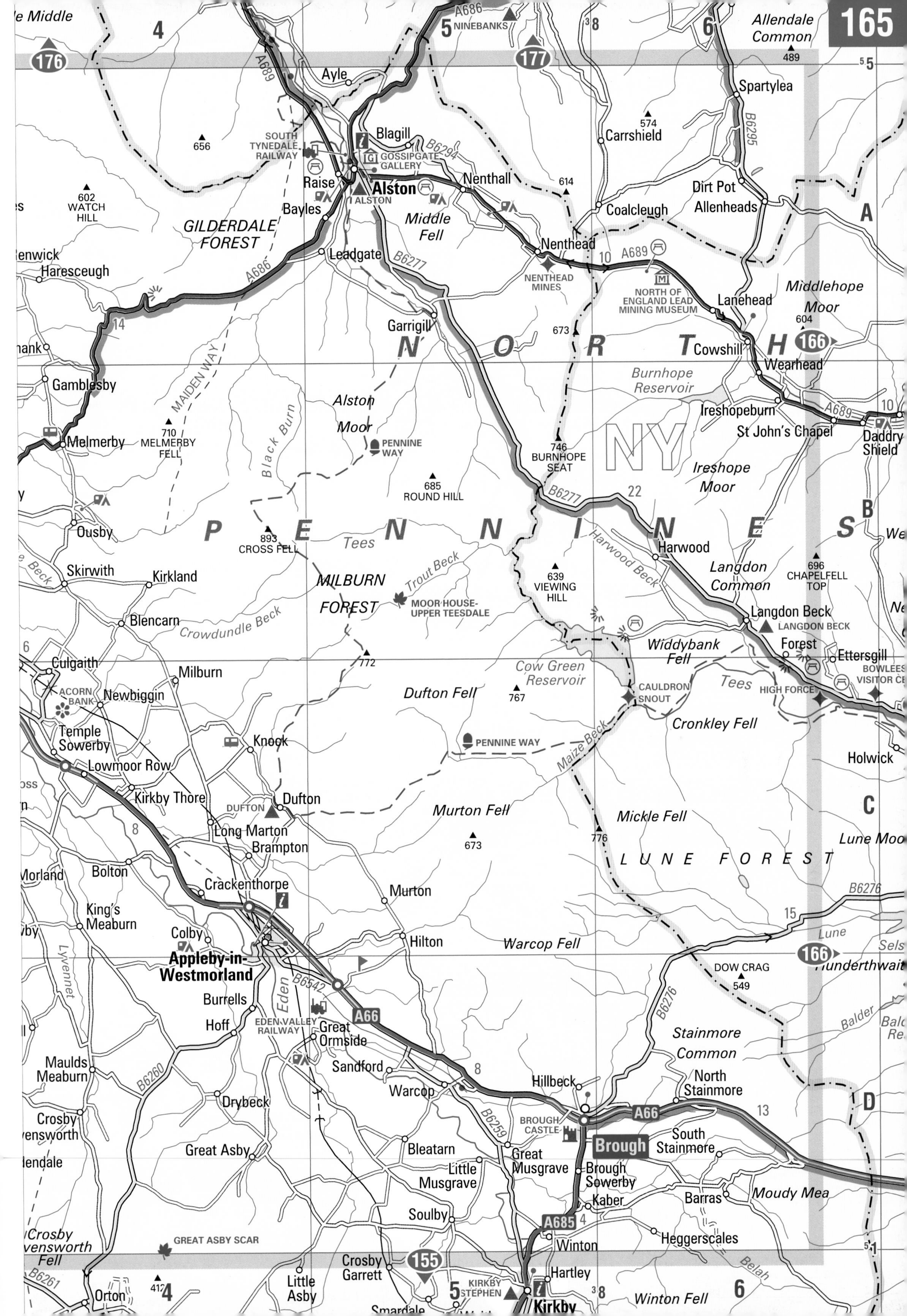
Allendale Common
489
Ninebanks
A686
A689
Ayle
South Tynedale Railway
Blagill
B6294
Gossipgate Gallery
Raise
Alston
Nenthall
Bayles
Middle Fell
Gilderdale Forest
Leadgate
B6277
Nenthead
Nenthead Mines
North of England Lead Mining Museum
Spartylea
B6295
Carrshield
574
614
Coalcleugh
Dirt Pot
Allenheads
Lanehead
Middlehope Moor
604
Cowshill
Wearhead
Burnhope Reservoir
Ireshopeburn
St John's Chapel
Daddry Shield
Ireshope Moor
656
602 Watch Hill
Haresceugh
Gamblesby
Maiden Way
Melmerby
710 Melmerby Fell
Garrigill
North Pennines
Alston Moor
Pennine Way
673
746 Burnhope Seat
685 Round Hill
NY
Black Burn
Ousby
893 Cross Fell
Tees
Milburn Forest
Trout Beck
Moor House-Upper Teesdale
639 Viewing Hill
Harwood Beck
Harwood
Langdon Common
696 Chapelfell Top
Langdon Beck
Skirwith
Kirkland
Blencarn
Crowdundle Beck
772
Widdybank Fell
Forest
Ettersgill
Bowlees Visitor Centre
High Force
Culgaith
Milburn
Cow Green Reservoir
767
Dufton Fell
Cauldron Snout
Tees
Cronkley Fell
Acorn Bank
Newbiggin
Temple Sowerby
Knock
Maize Beck
Holwick
Lowmoor Row
Kirkby Thore
Dufton
Murton Fell
Mickle Fell
776
Lune Moor
Long Marton
Brampton
673
Lune Forest
Morland
Bolton
Crackenthorpe
Murton
B6276
King's Meaburn
Colby
Hilton
Warcop Fell
Lune
Appleby-in-Westmorland
Dow Crag
549
Hunderthwaite
Lyvennet
Eden
B6542
Burrells
A66
Hoff
Eden Valley Railway
Great Ormside
Stainmore Common
Balder
Maulds Meaburn
Sandford
B6260
Warcop
Hillbeck
North Stainmore
Drybeck
Crosby Ravensworth
Brough Castle
B6259
Brough
South Stainmore
Great Asby
Bleatarn
Great Musgrave
Little Musgrave
Brough Sowerby
Kaber
Barras
Moody Mea
Soulby
A685
Winton
Heggerscales
Great Asby Scar
Crosby Garrett
Hartley
Belah
Little Asby
B6261
Orton
Kirkby Stephen
Smardale
Winton Fell
Crosby Ravensworth Fell
176
177
166
155

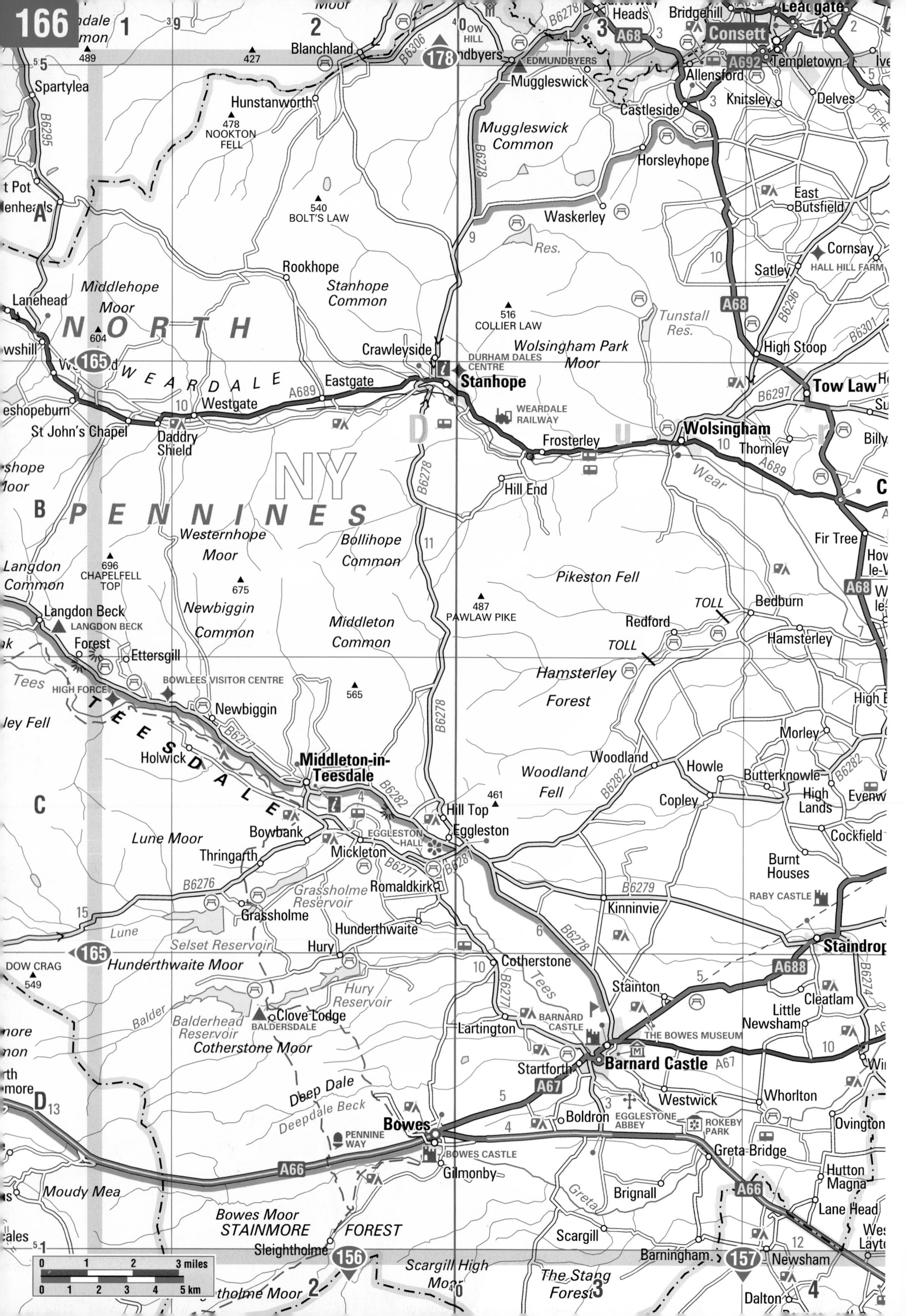
Spartylea
Hunstanworth
NOOKTON FELL
Blanchland
Edmundbyers
EDMUNDBYERS
Muggleswick
Castleside
Muggleswick Common
Horsleyhope
Consett
Templetown
Allensford
Knitsley
Delves
Bridgehill
Leadgate
East Butsfield
Cornsay
HALL HILL FARM
Satley
Waskerley
Res.
BOLT'S LAW
Rookhope
Stanhope Common
Middlehope Moor
Lanehead
NORTH
WEARDALE
Eastgate
Westgate
St John's Chapel
Daddry Shield
Crawleyside
DURHAM DALES CENTRE
Stanhope
COLLIER LAW
Wolsingham Park Moor
Tunstall Res.
High Stoop
Tow Law
WEARDALE RAILWAY
Frosterley
Wolsingham
Thornley
Wear
Hill End
PENNINES
Westernhope Moor
Bollihope Common
Langdon Common
CHAPELFELL TOP
Newbiggin Common
Middleton Common
PAWLAW PIKE
Pikeston Fell
Bedburn
Redford
Hamsterley
TOLL
Hamsterley Forest
Langdon Beck
LANGDON BECK
Forest
Ettersgill
BOWLEES VISITOR CENTRE
HIGH FORCE
Tees
Newbiggin
TEESDALE
Holwick
Middleton-in-Teesdale
Woodland
Woodland Fell
Howle
Copley
Butterknowle
High Lands
Morley
Fir Tree
Hill Top
Eggleston
EGGLESTON HALL
Bowbank
Mickleton
Lune Moor
Thringarth
Romaldkirk
Cockfield
Burnt Houses
RABY CASTLE
Grassholme Reservoir
Grassholme
Kinninvie
Hunderthwaite
Staindrop
Lune
Selset Reservoir
Hury
Cotherstone
DOW CRAG
Hunderthwaite Moor
Hury Reservoir
Stainton
Cleatlam
Little Newsham
Balder
Balderhead Reservoir
Clove Lodge
BALDERSDALE
Cotherstone Moor
Lartington
BARNARD CASTLE
THE BOWES MUSEUM
Barnard Castle
Startforth
Deep Dale
Deepdale Beck
Westwick
Whorlton
Boldron
EGGLESTONE ABBEY
ROKEBY PARK
Ovington
Bowes
PENNINE WAY
BOWES CASTLE
Gilmonby
Greta Bridge
Greta
Brignall
Hutton Magna
Lane Head
Moudy Mea
Bowes Moor
STAINMORE FOREST
Sleightholme
Scargill
Scargill High Moor
The Stang Forest
Barningham
Newsham
Dalton
0 1 2 3 miles
0 1 2 3 4 5 km

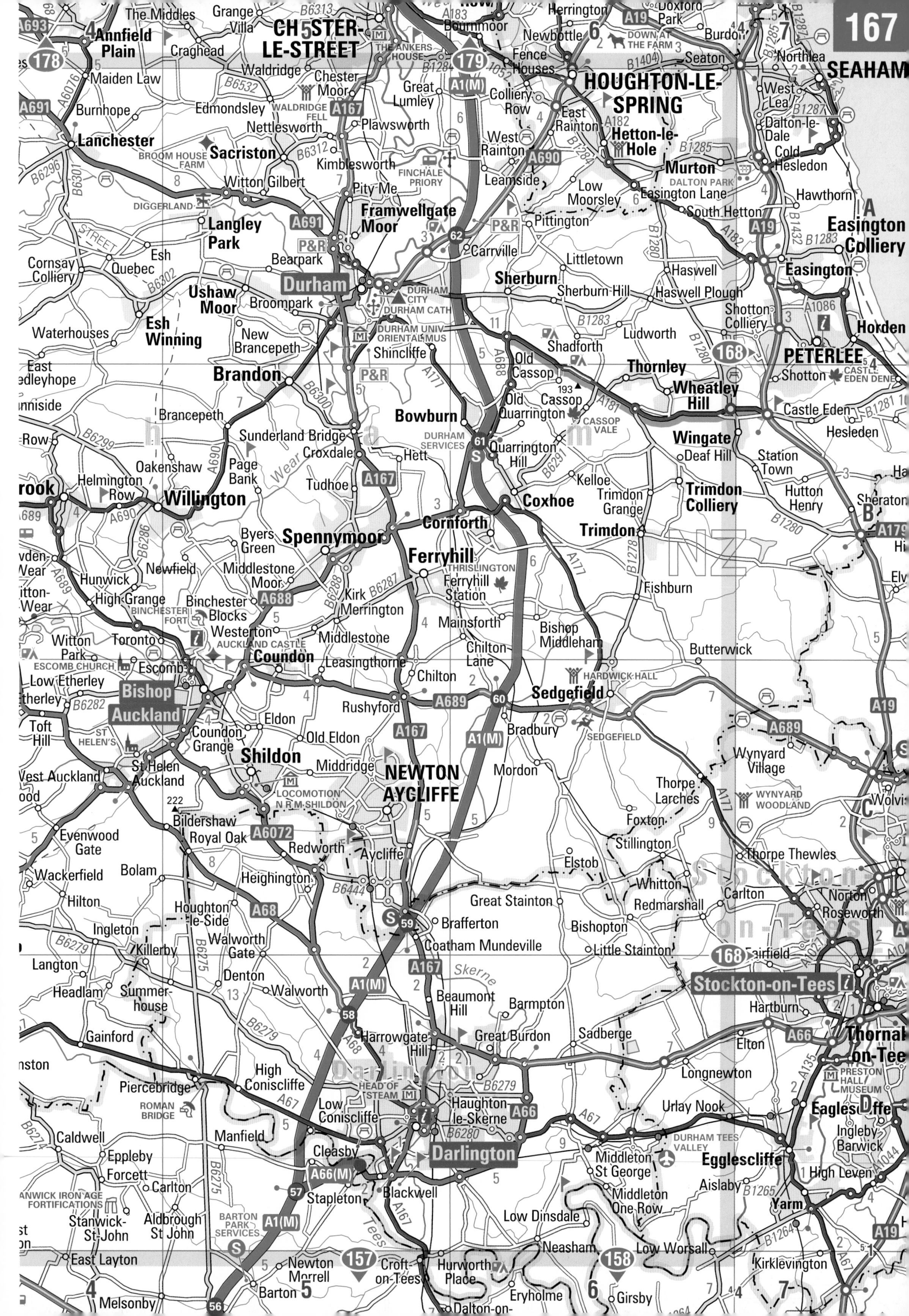
The Middles
Grange Villa
CHESTER-LE-STREET
Herrington
Doxford Park
Annfield Plain
Craghead
THE ANKERS HOUSE
Bournmoor
Newbottle
DOWN AT THE FARM
Burdon
Seaton
Northlea
SEAHAM
Maiden Law
Waldridge
Chester Moor
Great Lumley
Fence Houses
HOUGHTON-LE-SPRING
West Lea
Burnhope
Edmondsley
WALDRIDGE FELL
Colliery Row
East Rainton
Dalton-le-Dale
Nettlesworth
Plawsworth
West Rainton
Hetton-le-Hole
Lanchester
BROOM HOUSE FARM
Sacriston
Kimblesworth
FINCHALE PRIORY
Murton
Cold Hesledon
Witton Gilbert
Pity Me
Leamside
DALTON PARK
Easington Lane
Low Moorsley
Hawthorn
DIGGERLAND
Framwellgate Moor
South Hetton
Langley Park
Pittington
Easington Colliery
Esh
Carrville
Cornsay Colliery
Quebec
Bearpark
Littletown
Haswell
Easington
Durham
Sherburn
Ushaw Moor
Broompark
DURHAM CITY
DURHAM CATH
Sherburn Hill
Haswell Plough
Shotton Colliery
Horden
Esh Winning
Waterhouses
New Brancepeth
DURHAM UNIV ORIENTAL MUS
Shadforth
Ludworth
PETERLEE
East Hedleyhope
Shincliffe
Old Cassop
Thornley
Shotton
CASTLE EDEN DENE
Brandon
Cassop
Wheatley Hill
Castle Eden
Hesleden
Brancepeth
Bowburn
Old Quarrington
CASSOP VALE
Sunderland Bridge
DURHAM SERVICES
Quarrington Hill
Wingate
Deaf Hill
Station Town
Croxdale
Hett
Oakenshaw
Page Bank
Helmington Row
Tudhoe
Kelloe
Trimdon Grange
Trimdon Colliery
Hutton Henry
Sheraton
Willington
Coxhoe
Cornforth
Trimdon
Byers Green
Spennymoor
Ferryhill
THRISLINGTON
Newfield
Middlestone Moor
Hunwick
Ferryhill Station
Fishburn
High Grange
Binchester
Kirk Merrington
BINCHESTER FORT
Blocks
Westerton
Mainsforth
Bishop Middleham
Witton Park
Toronto
AUCKLAND CASTLE
Middlestone
Chilton Lane
Butterwick
ESCOMB CHURCH
Escomb
Coundon
Leasingthorne
HARDWICK HALL
Low Etherley
Bishop Auckland
Chilton
Sedgefield
Rushyford
Eldon
Toft Hill
ST HELEN'S
Coundon Grange
Old Eldon
Bradbury
SEDGEFIELD
Shildon
Wynyard Village
West Auckland
St Helen Auckland
Middridge
NEWTON AYCLIFFE
Mordon
Thorpe Larches
LOCOMOTION N R M SHILDON
WYNYARD WOODLAND
Bildershaw
Foxton
Evenwood Gate
Royal Oak
Stillington
Redworth
Aycliffe
Thorpe Thewles
Wackerfield
Bolam
Elstob
Heighington
Whitton
Carlton
Hilton
Houghton-le-Side
Great Stainton
Redmarshall
Norton
Roseworth
Ingleton
Brafferton
Bishopton
Walworth Gate
Killerby
Coatham Mundeville
Little Stainton
Fairfield
Langton
Denton
Stockton-on-Tees
Headlam
Summerhouse
Walworth
Beaumont Hill
Barmpton
Hartburn
Gainford
Harrowgate Hill
Great Burdon
Sadberge
Elton
Thornaby-on-Tees
High Coniscliffe
Longnewton
Piercebridge
HEAD OF STEAM
Haughton-le-Skerne
PRESTON HALL MUSEUM
ROMAN BRIDGE
Low Coniscliffe
Urlay Nook
Eaglescliffe
Caldwell
Manfield
Ingleby Barwick
DURHAM TEES VALLEY
Cleasby
Darlington
Middleton St George
Egglescliffe
Eppleby
High Leven
Forcett
Carlton
Blackwell
Middleton One Row
Aislaby
STANWICK IRON AGE FORTIFICATIONS
Stapleton
Yarm
Stanwick-St-John
Aldbrough St John
BARTON PARK SERVICES
Low Dinsdale
East Layton
Neasham
Low Worsall
Newton Morrell
Croft-on-Tees
Hurworth Place
Kirklevington
Melsonby
Barton
Eryholme
Girsby
Dalton-on-Tees
A1(M)
A19
A167
A690
A691
A688
A689
A68
A66
A66(M)
A67
A177
A181
A182
A6072
A179
178
179
168
157
158

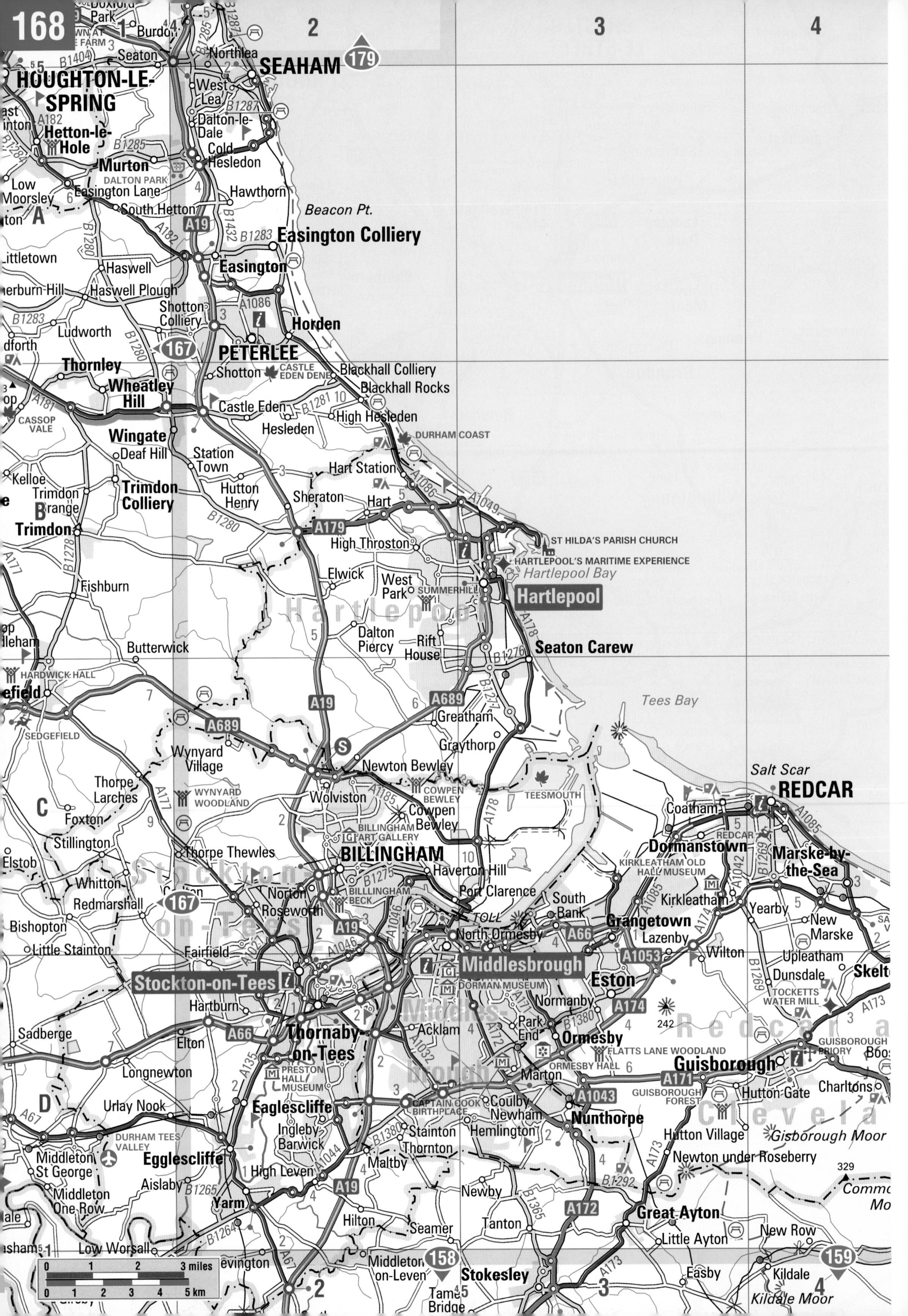
1
2
3
4
A
B
C
D
SEAHAM
179
HOUGHTON-LE-SPRING
Hetton-le-Hole
Murton
Seaton
Northlea
West Lea
Dalton-le-Dale
Cold Hesledon
Hawthorn
Easington Lane
South Hetton
DALTON PARK
Low Moorsley
Beacon Pt.
Easington Colliery
Easington
Haswell
Haswell Plough
Littletown
Shotton Colliery
Horden
PETERLEE
167
Ludworth
Thornley
Wheatley Hill
Shotton
CASTLE EDEN DENE
Blackhall Colliery
Blackhall Rocks
Castle Eden
High Hesleden
Hesleden
CASSOP VALE
Wingate
Deaf Hill
Station Town
DURHAM COAST
Hart Station
Kelloe
Trimdon Grange
Trimdon Colliery
Hutton Henry
Sheraton
Hart
Trimdon
High Throston
ST HILDA'S PARISH CHURCH
HARTLEPOOL'S MARITIME EXPERIENCE
Hartlepool Bay
Elwick
West Park
SUMMERHILL
Hartlepool
Fishburn
Dalton Piercy
Rift House
Seaton Carew
Butterwick
HARDWICK HALL
Sedgefield
SEDGEFIELD
Tees Bay
Greatham
Graythorp
Wynyard Village
Newton Bewley
Salt Scar
REDCAR
Thorpe Larches
WYNYARD WOODLAND
Wolviston
COWPEN BEWLEY
TEESMOUTH
Foxton
Cowpen Bewley
Coatham
BILLINGHAM ART GALLERY
Dormanstown
REDCAR
Stillington
Thorpe Thewles
BILLINGHAM
KIRKLEATHAM OLD HALL MUSEUM
Marske-by-the-Sea
Elstob
Haverton Hill
Whitton
Norton
Port Clarence
South Bank
Kirkleatham
Redmarshall
Roseworth
BILLINGHAM BECK
Yearby
TOLL
Grangetown
New Marske
Bishopton
Lazenby
North Ormesby
Little Stainton
Fairfield
Wilton
Upleatham
Middlesbrough
Dunsdale
Stockton-on-Tees
Eston
DORMAN MUSEUM
TOCKETTS WATER MILL
Hartburn
Normanby
Thornaby-on-Tees
Acklam
Park End
Ormesby
242
Sadberge
Elton
FLATTS LANE WOODLAND
GUISBOROUGH PRIORY
ORMESBY HALL
Guisborough
Longnewton
PRESTON HALL MUSEUM
Marton
Hutton Gate
Charltons
GUISBOROUGH FOREST
Urlay Nook
Eaglescliffe
CAPTAIN COOK BIRTHPLACE
Coulby Newham
Nunthorpe
Stainton
Ingleby Barwick
Hemlington
Hutton Village
Gisborough Moor
DURHAM TEES VALLEY
Thornton
Middleton St George
Egglescliffe
Newton under Roseberry
Maltby
High Leven
329
Middleton One Row
Aislaby
Yarm
Newby
Great Ayton
Tanton
Seamer
Hilton
Little Ayton
New Row
Low Worsall
Middleton-on-Leven
158
Stokesley
Easby
Kildale
159
Kildale Moor
Tame Bridge
A19
A179
A689
A66
A1053
A174
A171
A1043
A172
A173
A67
A1085
A178
A1086
A1049
A181
A182
A177
B1283
B1285
B1287
B1280
B1432
B1281
B1276
B1277
B1275
B1269
B1380
B1365
B1292
B1265
B1264
0 1 2 3 miles
0 1 2 3 4 5 km

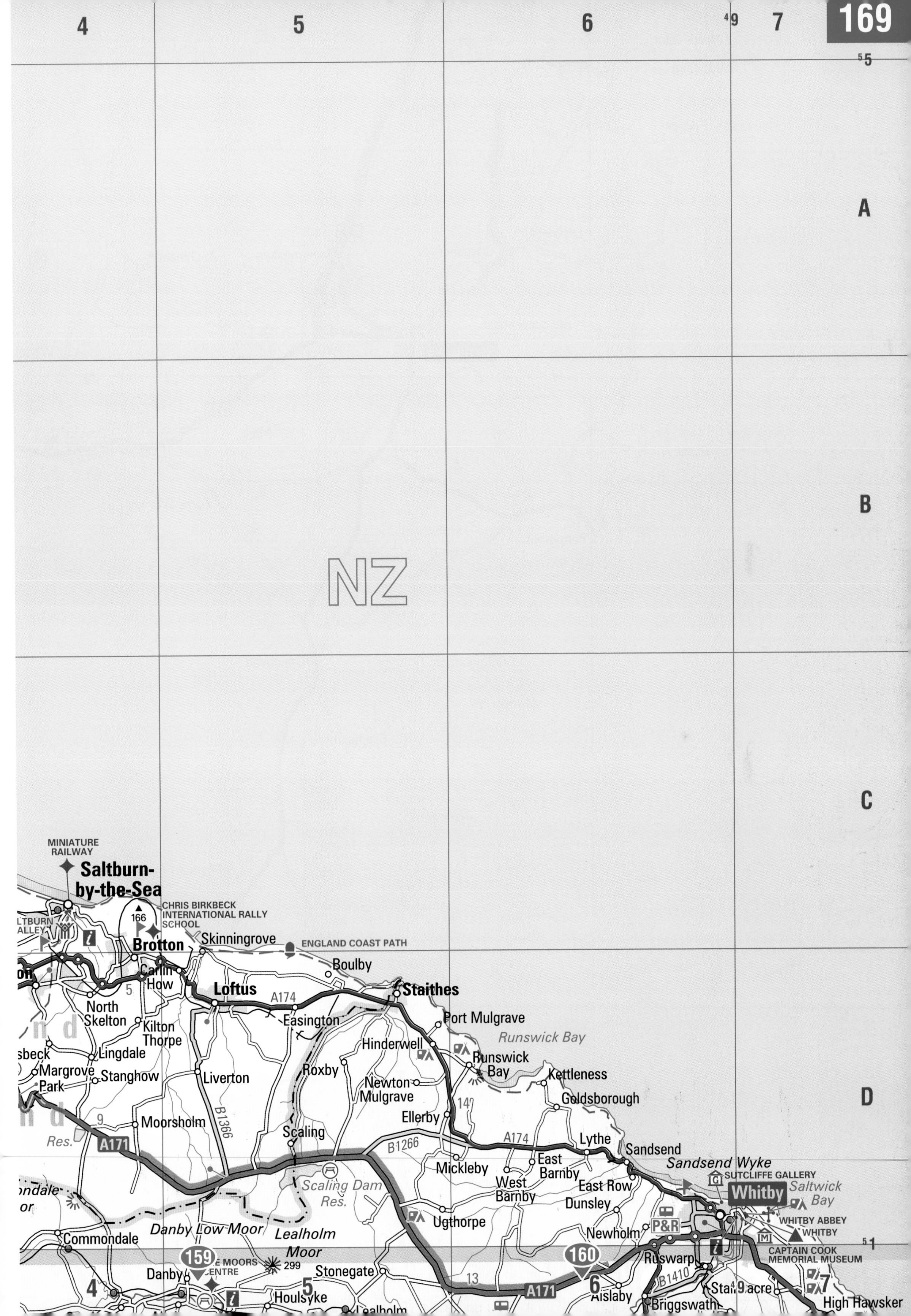

A

B

NZ

C

MINIATURE
RAILWAY

**Saltburn-
by-the-Sea**

CHRIS BIRKBECK
INTERNATIONAL RALLY
SCHOOL

ⓘ

166

SALTBURN
VALLEY

ⓘ

Brotton

Skinningrove

ENGLAND COAST PATH

on

Carlin
How

Boulby

5

Loftus

A174

Staithes

North
Skelton

Easington

Port Mulgrave

Kilton
Thorpe

Runswick Bay

sbeck

Lingdale

Hinderwell

Margrove
Park

Stanghow

Liverton

Roxby

Runswick
Bay

Kettleness

n d

Newton
Mulgrave

Goldsborough

D

Moorsholm

B1366

Ellerby

14

9

Scaling

Lythe

A171

Res.

B1266

A174

Sandsend

Sandsend Wyke

*Scaling Dam
Res.*

Mickleby

East
Barnby

SUTCLIFFE GALLERY

Ⓖ

ondale
or

West
Barnby

East Row

Whitby

*Saltwick
Bay*

Dunsley

Ugthorpe

P&R

Newholm

WHITBY ABBEY

▲ WHITBY

Ⓜ

Commondale

Danby Low Moor

Lealholm

Moor

159

E MOORS
CENTRE

299

Stonegate

160

Ruswarp

ⓘ

CAPTAIN COOK
MEMORIAL MUSEUM

⁵1

Danby

Houlsyke

13

A171

Aislaby

B1410

Stai 9 acre

High Hawsker

Briggswath

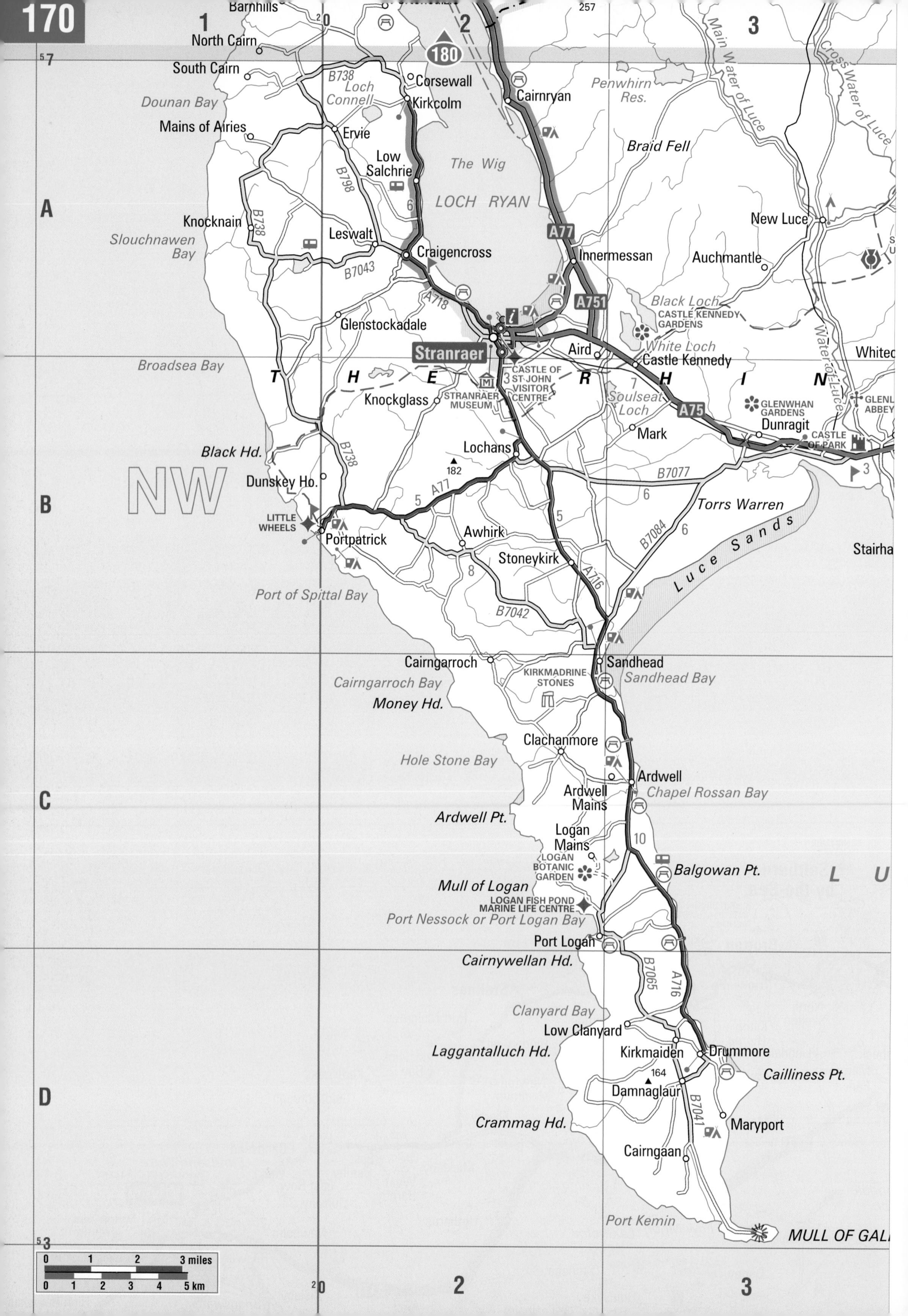

Barnhills
North Cairn
South Cairn
Corsewall
Loch Connell
Kirkcolm
Dounan Bay
Mains of Airies
Ervie
Low Salchrie
The Wig
LOCH RYAN
Knocknain
Slouchnawen Bay
Leswalt
Craigencross
B738
B798
B7043
A718
Glenstockadale
Cairnryan
Penwhirn Res.
Main Water of Luce
Cross Water of Luce
Braid Fell
New Luce
Auchmantle
Innermessan
A77
A751
Black Loch
CASTLE KENNEDY GARDENS
White Loch
Aird
Castle Kennedy
Stranraer
CASTLE OF ST JOHN VISITOR CENTRE
STRANRAER MUSEUM
Broadsea Bay
T H E R H I N
Knockglass
Soulseat Loch
A75
GLENWHAN GARDENS
Dunragit
CASTLE OF PARK
Water of Luce
Mark
Lochans
Black Hd.
Dunskey Ho.
NW
182
B7077
Torrs Warren
LITTLE WHEELS
Portpatrick
Awhirk
Stoneykirk
A716
B7084
Luce Sands
B7042
Port of Spittal Bay
Cairngarroch
Sandhead
Sandhead Bay
Cairngarroch Bay
KIRKMADRINE STONES
Money Hd.
Clachanmore
Hole Stone Bay
Ardwell
Chapel Rossan Bay
Ardwell Mains
Ardwell Pt.
Logan Mains
LOGAN BOTANIC GARDEN
Balgowan Pt.
Mull of Logan
LOGAN FISH POND MARINE LIFE CENTRE
Port Nessock or Port Logan Bay
Port Logan
Cairnywellan Hd.
B7065
Clanyard Bay
Low Clanyard
Kirkmaiden
Drummore
Laggantalluch Hd.
Cailliness Pt.
164
Damnaglaur
B7041
Crammag Hd.
Maryport
Cairngaan
Port Kemin
MULL OF GAL
Stairha
Whitec
GLENL ABBEY
0 1 2 3 miles
0 1 2 3 4 5 km

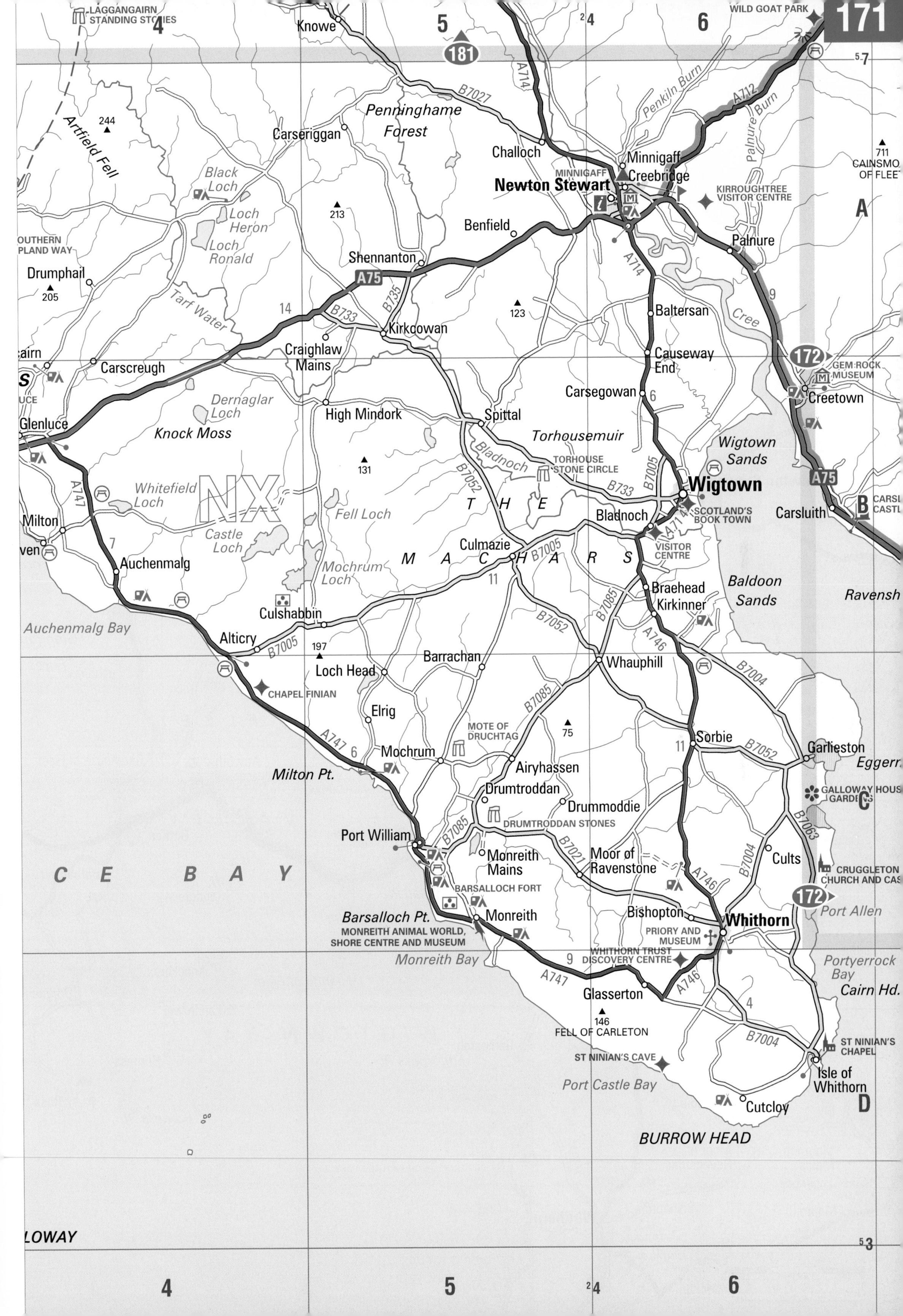
LAGGANGAIRN STANDING STONES
Knowe
181
WILD GOAT PARK
Artfield Fell
Penninghame Forest
Carseriggan
Challoch
Minnigaff
Creebridge
Newton Stewart
KIRROUGHTREE VISITOR CENTRE
Black Loch
Loch Heron
Loch Ronald
SOUTHERN UPLAND WAY
Benfield
Palnure
Penkiln Burn
Palnure Burn
CAIRNSMORE OF FLEET
Drumphail
Shennanton
A75
Tarf Water
Kirkcowan
Baltersan
Cree
Craighlaw Mains
Carscreugh
Causeway End
172
GEM ROCK MUSEUM
Creetown
Carsegowan
Dernaglar Loch
High Mindork
Spittal
Glenluce
Knock Moss
Torhousemuir
Wigtown Sands
TORHOUSE STONE CIRCLE
Bladnoch
Whitefield Loch
NX
Wigtown
SCOTLAND'S BOOK TOWN
Carsluith
CARSLUITH CASTLE
Milton
Castle Loch
Fell Loch
THE MACHARS
Culmazie
VISITOR CENTRE
Auchenmalg
Mochrum Loch
Braehead
Kirkinner
Baldoon Sands
Culshabbin
Auchenmalg Bay
Alticry
Barrachan
Loch Head
Whauphill
CHAPEL FINIAN
Elrig
MOTE OF DRUCHTAG
Sorbie
Mochrum
Garlieston
Airyhassen
Milton Pt.
Drumtroddan
Drummoddie
GALLOWAY HOUSE GARDENS
DRUMTRODDAN STONES
Port William
Monreith Mains
Moor of Ravenstone
Cults
CRUGGLETON CHURCH AND CASTLE
BARSALLOCH FORT
Barsalloch Pt.
Monreith
Bishopton
Whithorn
Port Allen
MONREITH ANIMAL WORLD, SHORE CENTRE AND MUSEUM
PRIORY AND MUSEUM
Monreith Bay
WHITHORN TRUST DISCOVERY CENTRE
Portyerrock Bay
Glasserton
Cairn Hd.
FELL OF CARLETON
ST NINIAN'S CHAPEL
ST NINIAN'S CAVE
Isle of Whithorn
Port Castle Bay
Cutcloy
BURROW HEAD
B7027
A714
A712
B733
B735
B7052
B7005
B7085
A747
A746
B7004
B7021
B7063
4
5
6
A
B
C
D

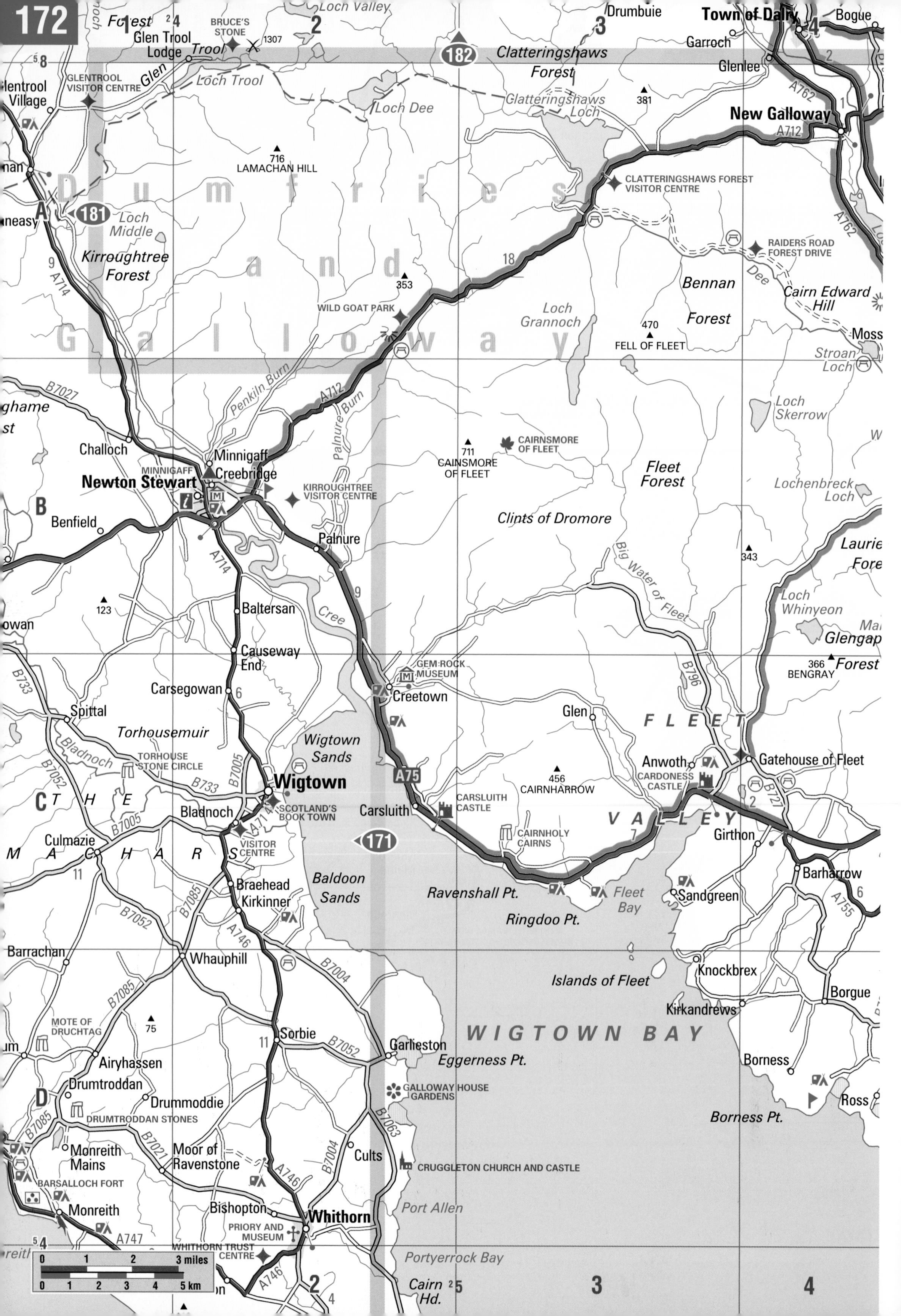

Glen Trool Lodge
BRUCE'S STONE
Loch Trool
GLENTROOL VISITOR CENTRE
Glentrool Village
Loch Dee
182
Clatteringshaws Forest
Clatteringshaws Loch
Drumbuie
Town of Dalry
Bogue
Garroch
Glenlee
New Galloway
A762
A712
716 LAMACHAN HILL
Dumfries and Galloway
181
Loch Middle
Kirroughtree Forest
A714
CLATTERINGSHAWS FOREST VISITOR CENTRE
RAIDERS ROAD FOREST DRIVE
Bennan Forest
Cairn Edward Hill
Loch Grannoch
470 FELL OF FLEET
Stroan Loch
WILD GOAT PARK
353
Penkiln Burn
Palnure Burn
Loch Skerrow
B7027
Challoch
Minnigaff
MINNIGAFF
Creebridge
Newton Stewart
KIRROUGHTREE VISITOR CENTRE
711 CAIRNSMORE OF FLEET
CAIRNSMORE OF FLEET
Fleet Forest
Lochenbreck Loch
Benfield
Clints of Dromore
Palnure
Big Water of Fleet
343
Laurieston Forest
123
Baltersan
Cree
Loch Whinyeon
Glengap Forest
Causeway End
366 BENGRAY
GEM ROCK MUSEUM
Creetown
Carsegowan
B733
B796
Spittal
Glen
Torhousemuir
Wigtown Sands
FLEET VALLEY
Bladnoch
TORHOUSE STONE CIRCLE
B7005
Anwoth
Gatehouse of Fleet
CARDONESS CASTLE
A75
456 CAIRNHARROW
B727
Wigtown
THE MACHARS
Carsluith
CARSLUITH CASTLE
SCOTLAND'S BOOK TOWN
Bladnoch
Girthon
Culmazie
VISITOR CENTRE
171
CAIRNHOLY CAIRNS
Braehead
Baldoon Sands
Barharrow
Kirkinner
Ravenshall Pt.
Fleet Bay
Sandgreen
B7085
Ringdoo Pt.
A755
B7052
A746
Barrachan
Whauphill
B7004
Knockbrex
Islands of Fleet
Borgue
MOTE OF DRUCHTAG
75
Kirkandrews
Sorbie
WIGTOWN BAY
Garlieston
Airyhassen
Eggerness Pt.
Borness
Drumtroddan
GALLOWAY HOUSE GARDENS
Drummoddie
Ross
DRUMTRODDAN STONES
Borness Pt.
B7021
B7063
Monreith Mains
Moor of Ravenstone
Cults
CRUGGLETON CHURCH AND CASTLE
BARSALLOCH FORT
Monreith
Bishopton
Whithorn
Port Allen
A747
PRIORY AND MUSEUM
WHITHORN TRUST CENTRE
Portyerrock Bay
Cairn Hd.
0 1 2 3 miles
0 1 2 3 4 5 km

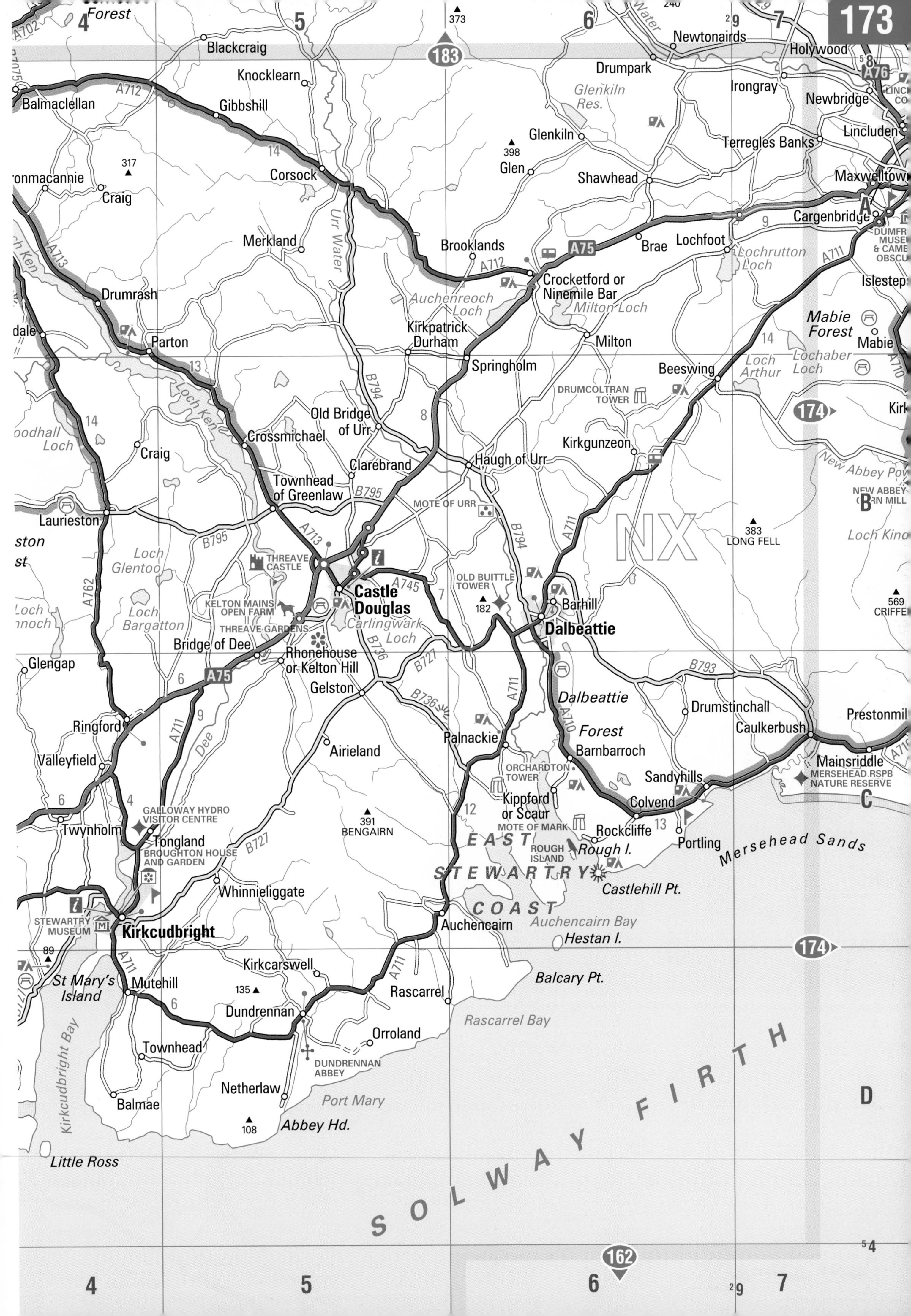
Blackcraig
Knocklearn
Balmaclellan
Gibbshill
Corsock
Craig
Merkland
Drumrash
Parton
Crossmichael
Laurieston
Loch Ken
Loch Glentoo
Loch Bargatton
Glengap
Ringford
Valleyfield
Twynholm
Tongland
GALLOWAY HYDRO VISITOR CENTRE
BROUGHTON HOUSE AND GARDEN
Kirkcudbright
STEWARTRY MUSEUM
St Mary's Island
Mutehill
Townhead
Balmae
Little Ross
Kirkcudbright Bay
Netherlaw
Abbey Hd.
Port Mary
Dundrennan
DUNDRENNAN ABBEY
Orroland
Kirkcarswell
Rascarrel
Rascarrel Bay
Balcary Pt.
Hestan I.
Auchencairn
Auchencairn Bay
Whinnieliggate
BENGAIRN
Airieland
Gelston
Rhonehouse or Kelton Hill
Bridge of Dee
THREAVE GARDENS
KELTON MAINS OPEN FARM
THREAVE CASTLE
Castle Douglas
Carlingwark Loch
Townhead of Greenlaw
Clarebrand
Old Bridge of Urr
Urr Water
Kirkpatrick Durham
Auchenreoch Loch
Brooklands
Springholm
Haugh of Urr
MOTE OF URR
OLD BUITTLE TOWER
Palnackie
Dalbeattie
Barhill
Dalbeattie Forest
Barnbarroch
ORCHARDTON TOWER
Kippford or Scaur
MOTE OF MARK
Rockcliffe
ROUGH ISLAND
Rough I.
Castlehill Pt.
EAST STEWARTRY COAST
Colvend
Portling
Sandyhills
Mersehead Sands
Mainsriddle
MERSEHEAD RSPB NATURE RESERVE
Caulkerbush
Prestonmill
Drumstinchall
Kirkgunzeon
DRUMCOLTRAN TOWER
Milton
Milton Loch
Crocketford or Ninemile Bar
Brae
Lochfoot
Lochrutton Loch
Beeswing
Loch Arthur
Lochaber Loch
Mabie Forest
Mabie
Islesteps
Cargenbridge
Shawhead
Glen
Glenkiln
Glenkiln Res.
Drumpark
Newtonairds
Holywood
Irongray
Newbridge
Terregles Banks
Lincluden
Maxwelltown
LONG FELL
Loch Kind
NEW ABBEY CORN MILL
New Abbey Pow
CRIFFEL
NX
SOLWAY FIRTH
A75
A711
A713
A712
A762
A745
A710
B794
B795
B736
B727
B793
183
174
162

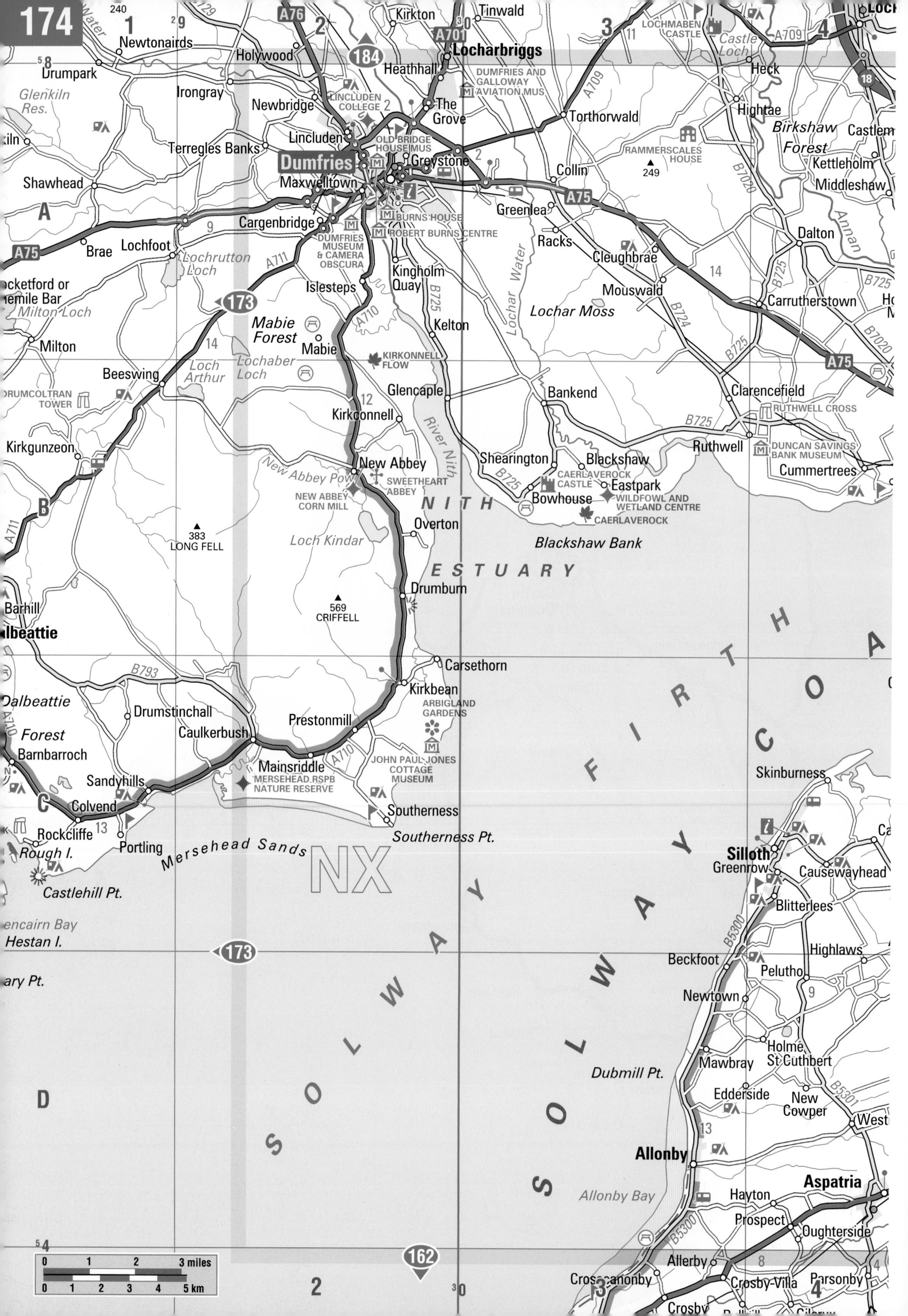

Newtonairds
Holywood
Kirkton
Tinwald
Locharbriggs
LOCHMABEN CASTLE
Castle Loch
Drumpark
Heathhall
DUMFRIES AND GALLOWAY AVIATION MUS
Heck
Glenkiln Res.
Irongray
Newbridge
LINCLUDEN COLLEGE
The Grove
Torthorwald
Hightae
Lincluden
OLD BRIDGE HOUSE MUS
Birkshaw Forest
Terregles Banks
Dumfries
Greystone
RAMMERSCALES HOUSE
249
Kettleholm
Shawhead
Maxwelltown
Collin
Middleshaw
Greenlea
Cargenbridge
BURNS HOUSE
ROBERT BURNS CENTRE
Dalton
Lochfoot
Brae
DUMFRIES MUSEUM & CAMERA OBSCURA
Racks
Cleughbrae
Lochrutton Loch
Kingholm Quay
Islesteps
Mouswald
Carrutherstown
Milton Loch
Lochar Moss
Mabie Forest
Kelton
Mabie
Milton
Loch Arthur
Lochaber Loch
KIRKONNELL FLOW
Beeswing
Glencaple
Bankend
Clarencefield
DRUMCOLTRAN TOWER
Kirkconnell
RUTHWELL CROSS
River Nith
Ruthwell
Kirkgunzeon
DUNCAN SAVINGS BANK MUSEUM
Shearington
Blackshaw
New Abbey
New Abbey Pow
SWEETHEART ABBEY
Cummertrees
CAERLAVEROCK CASTLE
Eastpark
NEW ABBEY CORN MILL
Bowhouse
WILDFOWL AND WETLAND CENTRE
NITH
CAERLAVEROCK
Overton
383 LONG FELL
Loch Kindar
Blackshaw Bank
ESTUARY
Drumburn
Barhill
569 CRIFFELL
Dalbeattie
Carsethorn
Kirkbean
ARBIGLAND GARDENS
Drumstinchall
Dalbeattie Forest
Caulkerbush
Prestonmill
Barnbarroch
Mainsriddle
JOHN PAUL JONES COTTAGE MUSEUM
Skinburness
Sandyhills
MERSEHEAD RSPB NATURE RESERVE
Colvend
Southerness
Rockcliffe
Portling
Southerness Pt.
Rough I.
Mersehead Sands
Silloth
Greenrow
Causewayhead
NX
Castlehill Pt.
Blitterlees
Hestan I.
Beckfoot
Highlaws
Pelutho
Newtown
Holme St Cuthbert
Mawbray
Dubmill Pt.
Edderside
New Cowper
West
Allonby
Aspatria
Allonby Bay
Hayton
Prospect
Oughterside
Allerby
Crosscanonby
Crosby-Villa
Parsonby
Crosby
SOLWAY FIRTH
3 miles
5 km

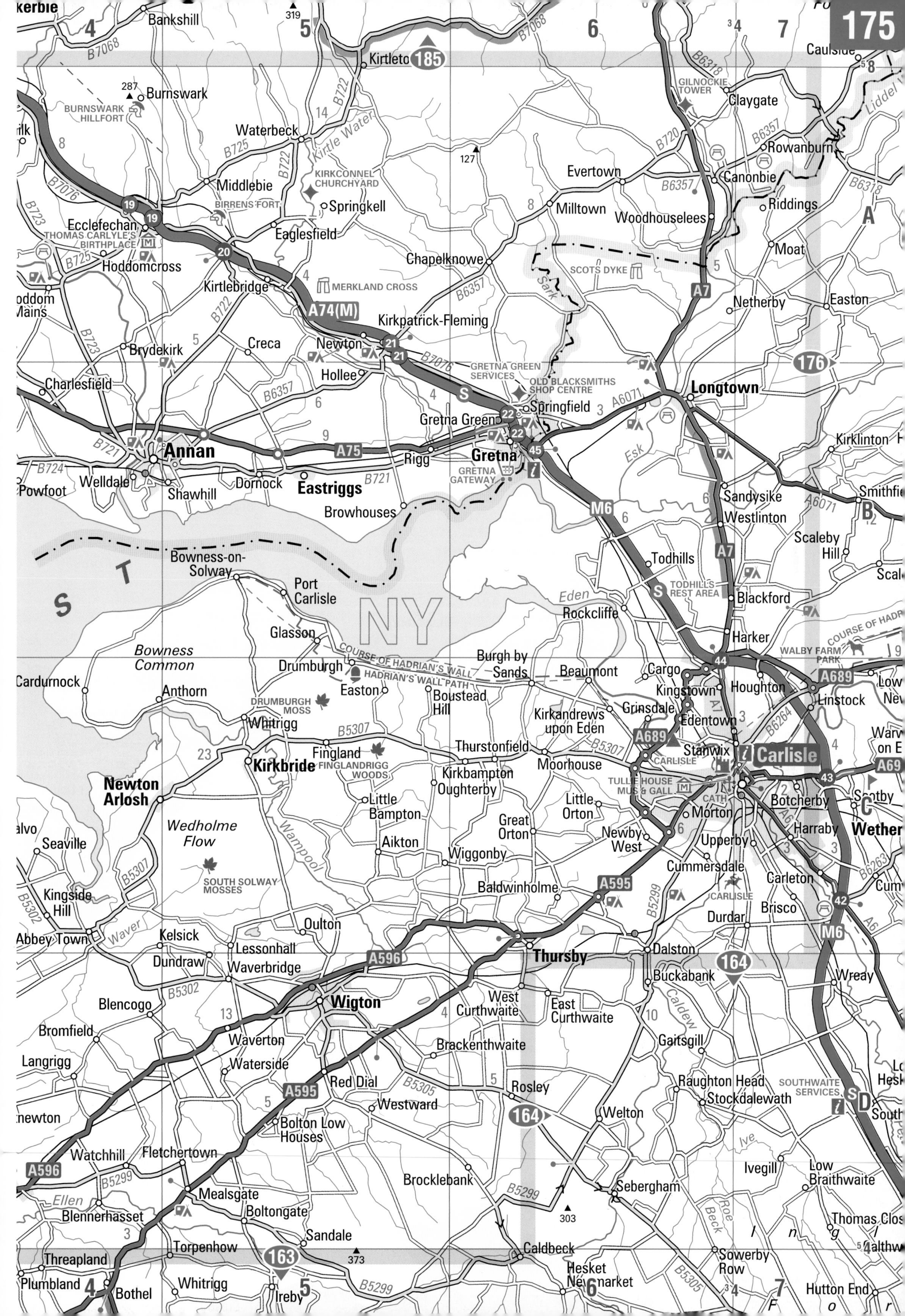
175
Bankshill
Kirtleton
185
Burnswark
BURNSWARK HILLFORT
Waterbeck
Kirtle Water
KIRKCONNEL CHURCHYARD
Middlebie
BIRRENS FORT
Springkell
Ecclefechan
THOMAS CARLYLE'S BIRTHPLACE
Eaglesfield
Hoddomcross
Kirtlebridge
MERKLAND CROSS
A74(M)
Kirkpatrick-Fleming
Brydekirk
Creca
Newton
Charlesfield
Hollee
GRETNA GREEN SERVICES
OLD BLACKSMITHS SHOP CENTRE
Springfield
Gretna Green
Annan
Rigg
Gretna
GRETNA GATEWAY
Welldale
Powfoot
Shawhill
Dornock
Eastriggs
Browhouses
Bowness-on-Solway
Port Carlisle
Glasson
NY
Bowness Common
Cardurnock
Drumburgh
COURSE OF HADRIAN'S WALL
HADRIAN'S WALL PATH
Easton
Burgh by Sands
Anthorn
DRUMBURGH MOSS
Whitrigg
Boustead Hill
Fingland
FINGLANDRIGG WOODS
Kirkbride
Newton Arlosh
Wedholme Flow
SOUTH SOLWAY MOSSES
Wampool
Seaville
Kingside Hill
Abbey Town
Waver
Kelsick
Lessonhall
Oulton
Dundraw
Waverbridge
Wigton
Blencogo
Bromfield
Langrigg
Waverton
Waterside
Red Dial
Westward
Bolton Low Houses
Watchhill
Fletchertown
Mealsgate
Blennerhasset
Ellen
Boltongate
Sandale
Torpenhow
Threapland
Plumbland
Bothel
Whitrigg
Ireby
163
Caldbeck
Hesket Newmarket
Sebergham
Brocklebank
Rosley
164
Welton
Brackenthwaite
West Curthwaite
East Curthwaite
Thursby
Dalston
Buckabank
Caldew
Gaitsgill
Raughton Head
Stockdalewath
Ivegill
Low Braithwaite
Sowerby Row
Roe Beck
Thomas Close
Hutton End
SOUTHWAITE SERVICES
Wreay
Durdar
Brisco
Carleton
Harraby
Upperby
Cummersdale
CARLISLE
Baldwinholme
Wiggonby
Aikton
Little Bampton
Great Orton
Little Orton
Newby West
Morton
Botcherby
Carlisle
TULLIE HOUSE MUS & GALL
CATH
Stanwix
Edentown
Kirkbampton
Oughterby
Thurstonfield
Moorhouse
Kirkandrews upon Eden
Grinsdale
Kingstown
Houghton
Linstock
Cargo
Beaumont
Rockcliffe
Eden
Harker
Blackford
TODHILLS REST AREA
Todhills
Westlinton
Sandysike
Esk
Longtown
176
Kirklinton
Smithfield
Scaleby Hill
WALBY FARM PARK
COURSE OF HADRIAN'S WALL
Netherby
Easton
Moat
Riddings
Canonbie
Rowanburn
Claygate
GILNOCKIE TOWER
Caulside
Liddel Water
Evertown
Milltown
Woodhouselees
Chapelknowe
SCOTS DYKE
Sark
Wetheral
Scotby
Warwick on Eden
Low Hesket
Southwaite
Inglewood Forest
Solway Firth
A7
A75
A6071
A689
A595
A596
A6
M6
B7068
B722
B725
B7076
B723
B6357
B721
B724
B6318
B720
B5307
B5302
B5299
B5305
B6264
B6263
319
287
127
303
373

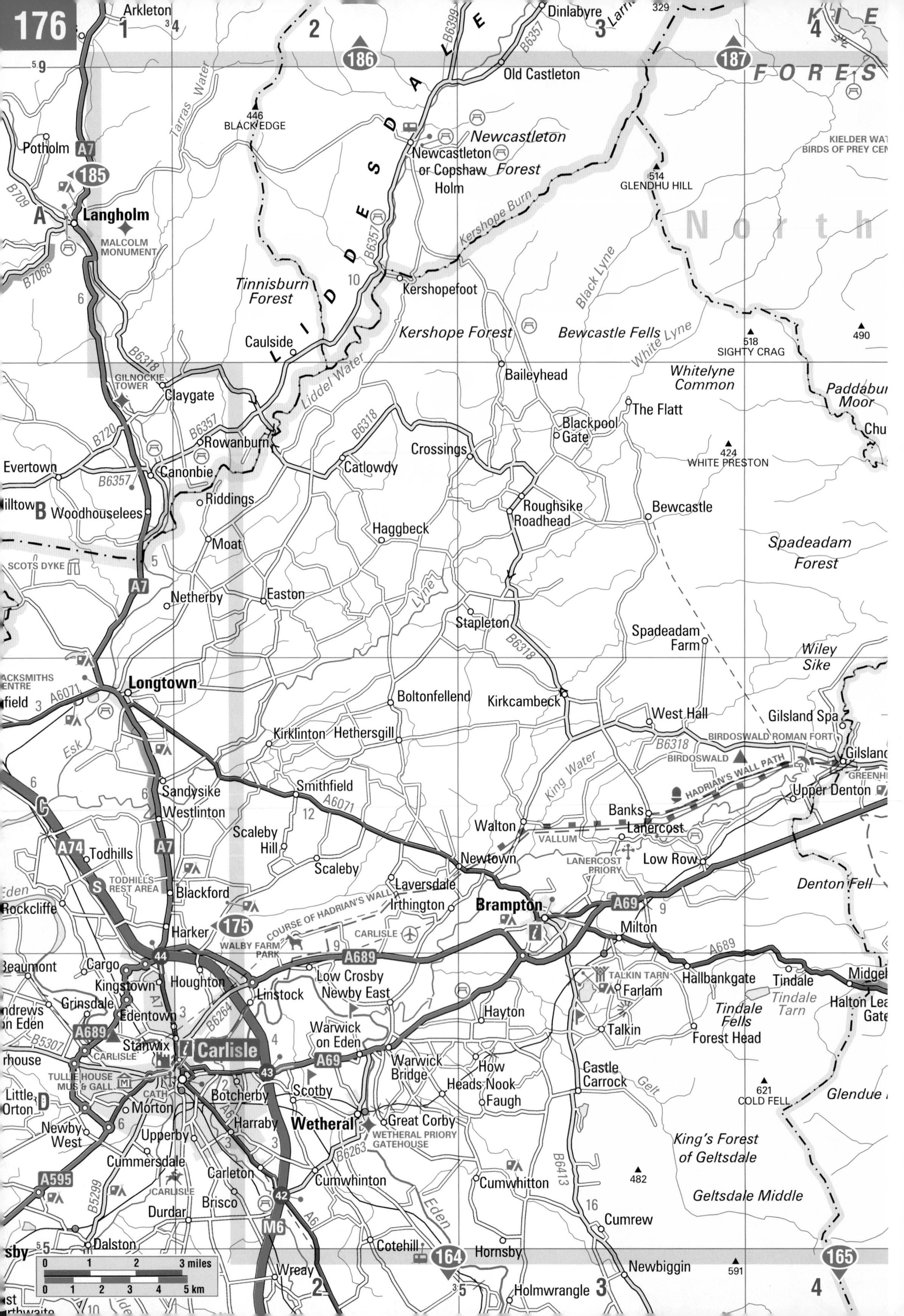
Arkleton
Dinlabyre
Old Castleton
186
187
LIDDESDALE
FORES
Potholm
A7
185
B709
Langholm
MALCOLM MONUMENT
B7068
446
BLACK EDGE
Tarras Water
Newcastleton
Newcastleton or Copshaw Holm
Newcastleton Forest
B6399
B6357
KIELDER WATER BIRDS OF PREY CENTRE
514
GLENDHU HILL
North
Kershope Burn
Tinnisburn Forest
Kershopefoot
Black Lyne
Kershope Forest
Bewcastle Fells
White Lyne
518
SIGHTY CRAG
490
Caulside
B6318
GILNOCKIE TOWER
Claygate
Liddel Water
Baileyhead
Whitelyne Common
Paddaburn Moor
The Flatt
Blackpool Gate
B720
Rowanburn
B6357
Evertown
Canonbie
Catlowdy
Crossings
424
WHITE PRESTON
Riddings
Woodhouselees
Roughsike
Roadhead
Bewcastle
Haggbeck
Moat
Spadeadam Forest
SCOTS DYKE
A7
Netherby
Easton
Lyne
Stapleton
Spadeadam Farm
B6318
Wiley Sike
Longtown
A6071
Boltonfellend
Kirkcambeck
West Hall
Gilsland Spa
Kirklinton
Hethersgill
BIRDOSWALD ROMAN FORT
B6318
BIRDOSWALD
Gilsland
HADRIAN'S WALL PATH
Esk
Sandysike
Smithfield
King Water
Upper Denton
Westlinton
A6071
Banks
Walton
Lanercost
VALLUM
Scaleby Hill
A74
Todhills
A7
Newtown
LANERCOST PRIORY
Low Row
Scaleby
TODHILLS REST AREA
Laversdale
Denton Fell
Blackford
Rockcliffe
COURSE OF HADRIAN'S WALL
Irthington
Brampton
A69
Harker
175
CARLISLE
Milton
WALBY FARM PARK
A689
A689
Beaumont
Cargo
Kingstown
Houghton
Low Crosby
Newby East
TALKIN TARN
Hallbankgate
Tindale
Midgeholme
Farlam
Tindale Tarn
Tindale Fells
Halton Lea Gate
Grinsdale
Linstock
Hayton
Edentown
B6264
Warwick on Eden
Talkin
Forest Head
A689
Stanwix
Carlisle
B5307
CARLISLE
A69
Warwick Bridge
How
Castle Carrock
Gelt
TULLIE HOUSE MUS & GALL.
CATH
Heads Nook
621
COLD FELL
Little Orton
Morton
Botcherby
Scotby
Faugh
Glendue
Newby West
Harraby
Wetheral
Great Corby
Upperby
WETHERAL PRIORY GATEHOUSE
King's Forest of Geltsdale
B6263
Cummersdale
Carleton
A595
Cumwhinton
Cumwhitton
B6413
482
CARLISLE
Brisco
Eden
B5299
Geltsdale Middle
Durdar
M6
Cumrew
Dalston
Cotehill
164
Hornsby
165
Wreay
Newbiggin
591
Holmwrangle
0 1 2 3 miles
0 1 2 3 4 5 km

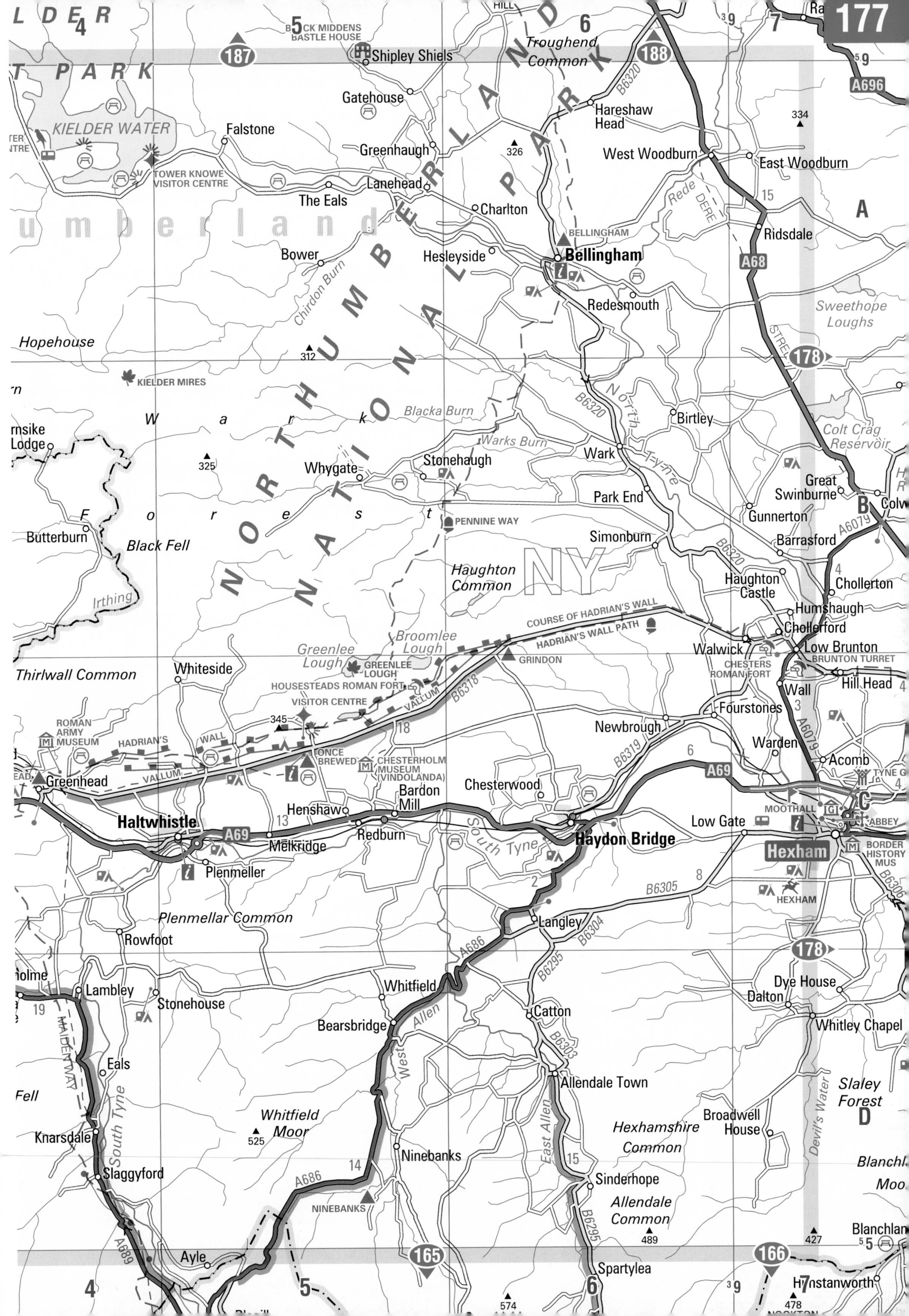

KIELDER WATER
TOWER KNOWE VISITOR CENTRE
Falstone
BLACK MIDDENS BASTLE HOUSE
Shipley Shiels
Gatehouse
Greenhaugh
Lanehead
The Eals
Troughend Common
Hareshaw Head
West Woodburn
East Woodburn
334
326
Charlton
Rede
DERE
Ridsdale
A68
A696
BELLINGHAM
Bellingham
Hesleyside
Bower
Chirdon Burn
Redesmouth
Sweethope Loughs
Hopehouse
312
KIELDER MIRES
NORTHUMBERLAND NATIONAL PARK
Northumberland
Wark Forest
Blacka Burn
Warks Burn
B6320
North Tyne
Birtley
Wark
Colt Crag Reservoir
Lodge
325
Whygate
Stonehaugh
Park End
Great Swinburne
Gunnerton
Colwell
Butterburn
Black Fell
PENNINE WAY
Simonburn
Barrasford
A6079
Haughton Common
NY
Haughton Castle
Chollerton
Irthing
Humshaugh
Chollerford
COURSE OF HADRIAN'S WALL
HADRIAN'S WALL PATH
Broomlee Lough
Greenlee Lough
GREENLEE LOUGH
GRINDON
Walwick
Low Brunton
BRUNTON TURRET
CHESTERS ROMAN FORT
Thirlwall Common
Whiteside
HOUSESTEADS ROMAN FORT
VISITOR CENTRE
VALLUM
B6318
Wall
Hill Head
Fourstones
ROMAN ARMY MUSEUM
345
18
Newbrough
Warden
HADRIAN'S WALL
ONCE BREWED
CHESTERHOLM MUSEUM (VINDOLANDA)
B6319
Acomb
Greenhead
Bardon Mill
Chesterwood
A69
TYNE GREEN
Henshaw
MOOTHALL
ABBEY
Haltwhistle
Melkridge
Redburn
South Tyne
Haydon Bridge
Low Gate
Hexham
BORDER HISTORY MUS
Plenmeller
B6305
HEXHAM
B6306
Plenmellar Common
Langley
B6304
Rowfoot
A686
B6295
Dye House
Lambley
Stonehouse
Whitfield
Dalton
Whitley Chapel
Catton
MAIDEN WAY
Bearsbridge
West Allen
B6303
Eals
Allendale Town
Slaley Forest
Fell
Whitfield Moor
525
South Tyne
Knarsdale
Hexhamshire Common
Broadwell House
Devil's Water
Ninebanks
East Allen
Slaggyford
Sinderhope
Blanchland Moor
Allendale Common
NINEBANKS
489
427
A689
Ayle
Spartylea
Blanchland
Hunstanworth
574
478
187
188
178
165
166
A
B
C
D

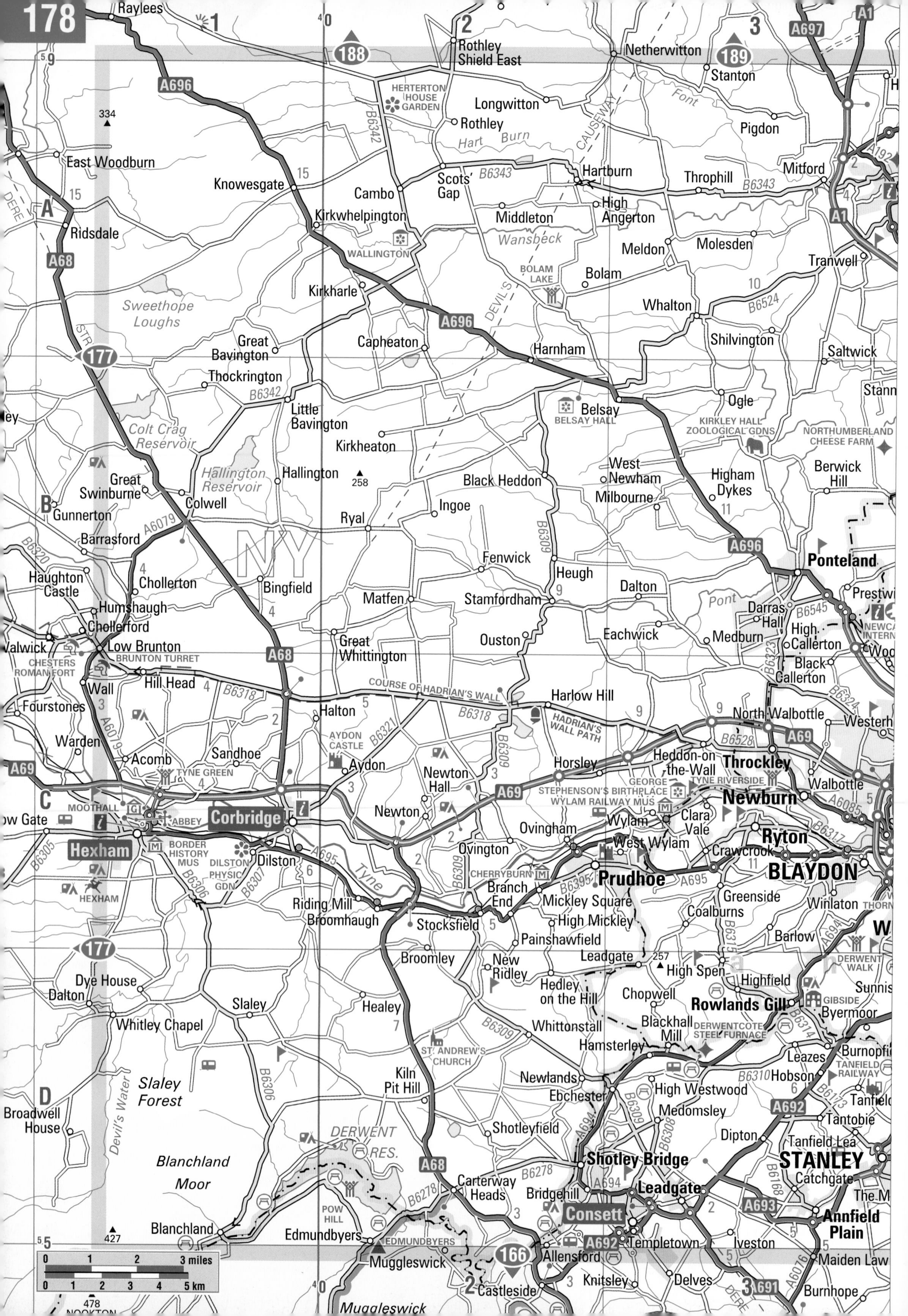
Raylees
188
189
Rothley Shield East
Netherwitton
Stanton
A697
A1
A696
Herterton House Garden
Longwitton
Font
Pigdon
334
B6342
Rothley
Hart Burn
Causeway
East Woodburn
Hartburn
Throphill
Mitford
Knowesgate
Cambo
Scots' Gap
B6343
Dere
A
Ridsdale
Kirkwhelpington
Middleton
High Angerton
Wansbeck
Meldon
Molesden
A68
Wallington
Bolam Lake
Bolam
Tranwell
Sweethope Loughs
Kirkharle
Devil's
Whalton
B6524
Capheaton
Harnham
Shilvington
Saltwick
177
Great Bavington
Thockrington
Little Bavington
Belsay
Belsay Hall
Ogle
Kirkley Hall Zoological Gdns
Northumberland Cheese Farm
Colt Crag Reservoir
Kirkheaton
Hallington Reservoir
Hallington
258
Black Heddon
West Newham
Milbourne
Higham Dykes
Berwick Hill
B
Great Swinburne
Colwell
Gunnerton
Ingoe
Ryal
Barrasford
A6079
B6320
NY
Fenwick
B6309
Heugh
Ponteland
Haughton Castle
Chollerton
Bingfield
Matfen
Stamfordham
Dalton
Pont
Darras Hall
B6545
Humshaugh
Chollerford
Ouston
Eachwick
Medburn
High Callerton
Low Brunton
Brunton Turret
Chesters Roman Fort
Great Whittington
Black Callerton
Wall
Hill Head
B6318
Course of Hadrian's Wall
Harlow Hill
Fourstones
Halton
Hadrian's Wall Path
North Walbottle
Westerhope
Warden
Aydon Castle
B6321
B6528
A69
Acomb
Sandhoe
Aydon
Horsley
Heddon-on-the-Wall
Throckley
Tyne Green
Newton Hall
George Stephenson's Birthplace
Tyne Riverside
Walbottle
C
Moothall
Corbridge
Abbey
Newton
Wylam Railway Mus
Newburn
Wylam
Clara Vale
A6085
Hexham
Border History Mus
Dilston Physic Gdn
Dilston
A695
Ovingham
West Wylam
Ryton
B6317
B6305
Ovington
Crawcrook
Tyne
B6306
B6307
Cherryburn
Prudhoe
Blaydon
Branch End
B6395
Greenside
Riding Mill
Broomhaugh
Mickley Square
Coalburns
Winlaton
Stocksfield
High Mickley
Painshawfield
B6315
Barlow
A694
Broomley
New Ridley
Leadgate
257
High Spen
Derwent Walk
Dye House
Dalton
Hedley on the Hill
Chopwell
Highfield
Slaley
Healey
Rowlands Gill
Gibside
Byermoor
Whitley Chapel
B6309
Whittonstall
Blackhall Mill
Derwentcote Steel Furnace
B6314
St. Andrew's Church
Hamsterley
Leazes
Burnopfield
Slaley Forest
Tanfield Railway
Newlands
Kiln Pit Hill
B6310
Hobson
D
Ebchester
High Westwood
B6173
Tanfield
Broadwell House
Devil's Water
Medomsley
A692
Tantobie
Shotleyfield
B6308
Dipton
Derwent Res.
Tanfield Lea
Blanchland Moor
Shotley Bridge
Stanley
B6168
B6278
Catchgate
Carterway Heads
Bridgehill
Leadgate
Pow Hill
A693
Annfield Plain
Consett
Blanchland
427
Edmundbyers
Templetown
Iveston
Allensford
166
Maiden Law
Muggleswick
A6076
Castleside
Knitsley
Delves
Dere
A691
Burnhope
0 1 2 3 miles
0 1 2 3 4 5 km
478
Nookton
Muggleswick

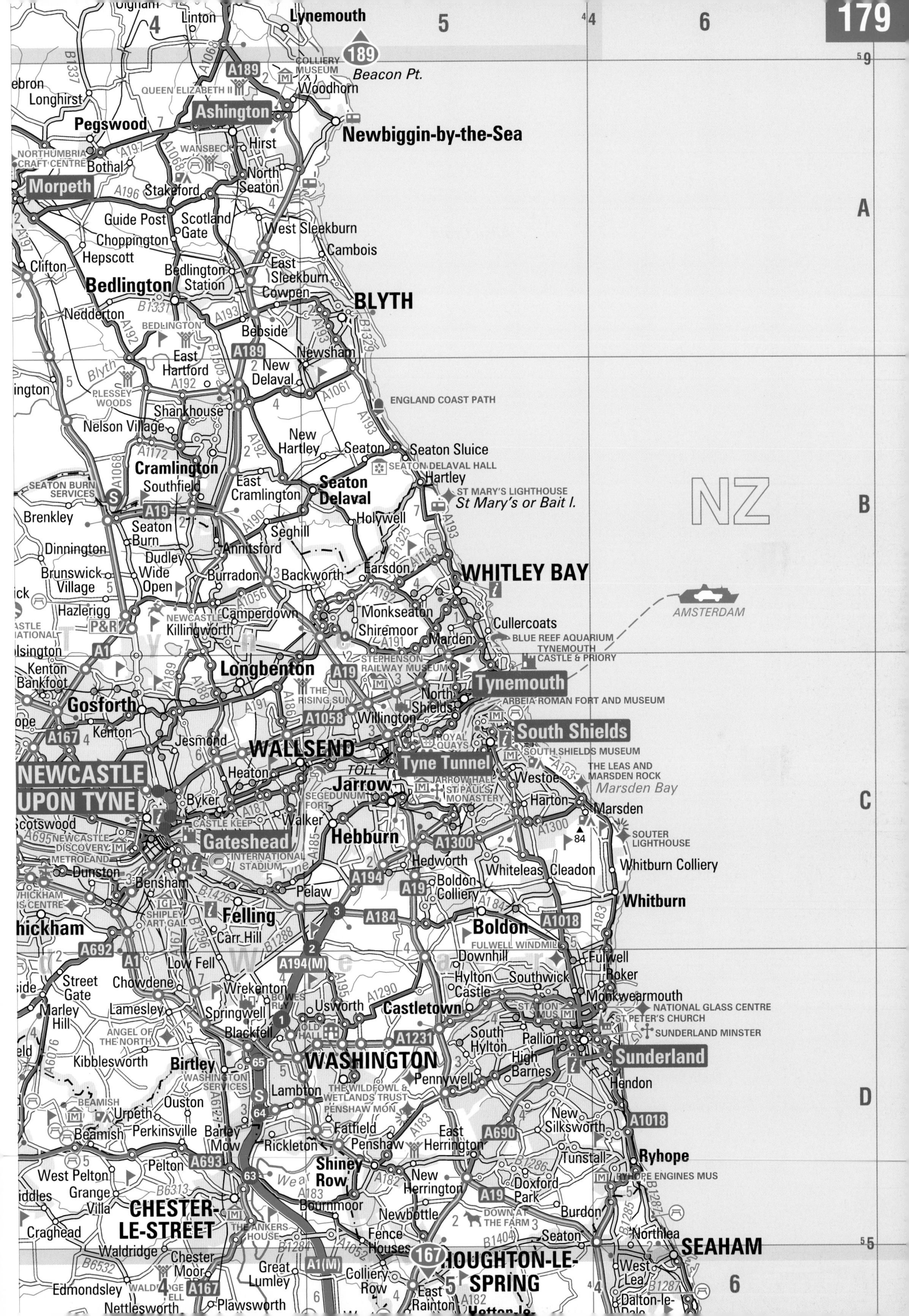

4
5
6
A
B
C
D
NZ
Lynemouth
Linton
189
COLLIERY MUSEUM
Beacon Pt.
Woodhorn
QUEEN ELIZABETH II
Longhirst
Ashington
Pegswood
Newbiggin-by-the-Sea
Hirst
WANSBECK
NORTHUMBRIA CRAFT CENTRE
Bothal
North Seaton
Morpeth
Stakeford
Guide Post
Scotland Gate
West Sleekburn
Choppington
Cambois
Hepscott
Clifton
Bedlington Station
East Sleekburn
Bedlington
Cowpen
BLYTH
Nedderton
BEDLINGTON
Bebside
Newsham
East Hartford
New Delaval
Blyth
PLESSEY WOODS
ENGLAND COAST PATH
Shankhouse
Nelson Village
New Hartley
Seaton
Seaton Sluice
Cramlington
SEATON DELAVAL HALL
Hartley
SEATON BURN SERVICES
Southfield
East Cramlington
Seaton Delaval
ST MARY'S LIGHTHOUSE
St Mary's or Bait I.
Brenkley
Seaton Burn
Holywell
Seghill
Dinnington
Dudley
Annitsford
Earsdon
WHITLEY BAY
Brunswick Village
Wide Open
Burradon
Backworth
Hazlerigg
Camperdown
Monkseaton
AMSTERDAM
NEWCASTLE
Killingworth
Shiremoor
Cullercoats
BLUE REEF AQUARIUM
Marden
TYNEMOUTH CASTLE & PRIORY
Kenton Bankfoot
STEPHENSON RAILWAY MUSEUM
Longbenton
THE RISING SUN
Tynemouth
North Shields
ARBEIA ROMAN FORT AND MUSEUM
Gosforth
Willington
Kenton
South Shields
ROYAL QUAYS
Jesmond
WALLSEND
SOUTH SHIELDS MUSEUM
NEWCASTLE UPON TYNE
Heaton
TOLL
Tyne Tunnel
Westoe
THE LEAS AND MARSDEN ROCK
Marsden Bay
Jarrow
JARROW HALL
ST PAUL'S MONASTERY
SEGEDUNUM FORT
Byker
Harton
Marsden
Walker
Cotswood
CASTLE KEEP
SOUTER LIGHTHOUSE
Hebburn
NEWCASTLE DISCOVERY
Gateshead
Whitburn Colliery
METROLAND
INTERNATIONAL STADIUM
Hedworth
Dunston
Whiteleas
Cleadon
Bensham
Boldon Colliery
Pelaw
Whitburn
SHIPLEY ART GAL
Felling
Boldon
Whickham
Carr Hill
FULWELL WINDMILL
Fulwell
Downhill
Roker
Hylton Castle
Southwick
Street Gate
Chowdene
Low Fell
Monkwearmouth
Wrekenton
NATIONAL GLASS CENTRE
Marley Hill
Lamesley
Usworth
Castletown
ST PETER'S CHURCH
Springwell
SUNDERLAND MINSTER
ANGEL OF THE NORTH
Blackfell
South Hylton
Pallion
Kibblesworth
Birtley
WASHINGTON
Sunderland
WASHINGTON SERVICES
High Barnes
Pennywell
Hendon
BEAMISH
THE WILDFOWL & WETLANDS TRUST
Ouston
Lambton
PENSHAW MON
Urpeth
New Silksworth
Beamish
Perkinsville
Barley Mow
Fatfield
Penshaw
East Herrington
Ryhope
Rickleton
Tunstall
West Pelton
Pelton
Shiney Row
New Herrington
RYHOPE ENGINES MUS
Grange Villa
Doxford Park
CHESTER-LE-STREET
Bournmoor
Craghead
THE ANKERS HOUSE
Newbottle
Burdon
DOWN AT THE FARM
Waldridge
Chester Moor
Fence Houses
Seaton
Northlea
SEAHAM
Great Lumley
167
HOUGHTON-LE-SPRING
Edmondsley
Colliery Row
West Lea
Nettlesworth
Plawsworth
East Rainton
Dalton-le-Dale
A189
A1068
A197
A196
A193
B1331
A192
A189
A1061
A1172
A1068
A19
A190
B1325
A1148
A1056
A191
A1
A189
A188
A19
A186
A1058
A167
A187
A183
A695
A185
A1300
A194
A19
A184
A1018
A183
A692
A1
A194(M)
A195
A1290
A1231
A6076
A167
A183
A690
A1018
A693
B6313
A183
A182
B1286
A19
B1285
B1287
B1404
B1284
A1052
A1(M)
B6532
A167
A182
B1287
84

1 2 3

A

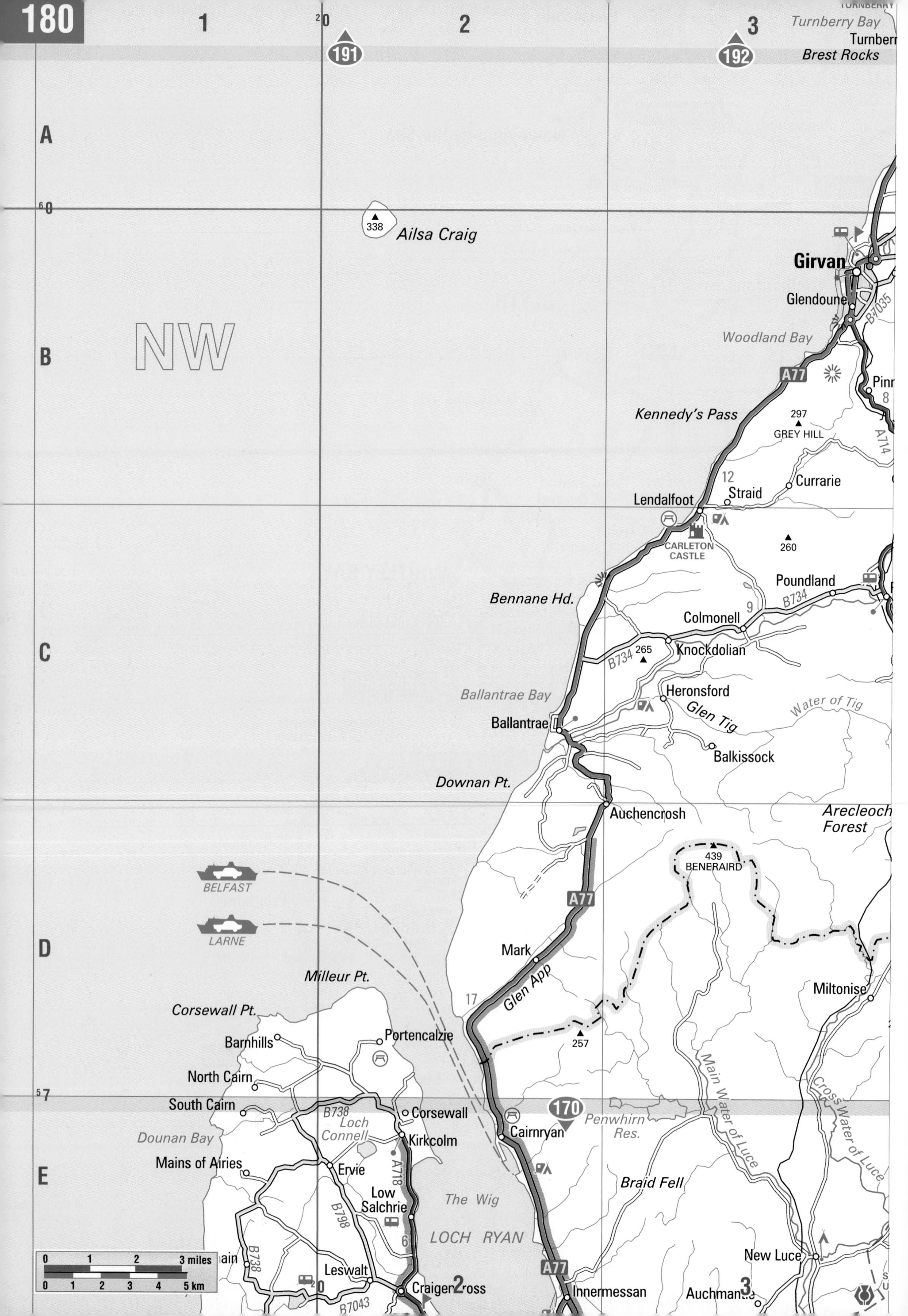

191   **192**   *Turnberry Bay*
TURNBERRY
Turnberr
Brest Rocks

6 0

▲ 338 *Ailsa Craig*

Girvan

Glendoune

B7035

NW

B

Woodland Bay

A77

Kennedy's Pass   ▲ 297
                     GREY HILL

Pinr
8

A714

12
Lendalfoot   Straid   *Currarie*

CARLETON
CASTLE   ▲ 260

Bennane Hd.   Poundland
                                         B734

Colmonell   9

C

B734 ▲ 265
           Knockdolian

Ballantrae Bay   Heronsford
                            Glen Tig   *Water of Tig*
Ballantrae
                          Balkissock

Downan Pt.

Auchencrosh   *Arecleoch*
                        Forest

▲ 439
BENERAIRD

BELFAST

LARNE

D

Milleur Pt.   **A77**

Mark
Corsewall Pt.   *Glen App*   Miltonise

Barnhills   Portencalzie   17
                                      257

North Cairn

5 7
South Cairn   B738   Corsewall   **170**
                   Loch   Cairnryan *Penwhirn*
                   Connell   *Res.*
Dounan Bay   Kirkcolm

Mains of Airies   Ervie   A718
                                              Braid Fell
E   B798   Low
                         Salchrie   *The Wig*

                                 LOCH RYAN

ain   B738
                                                    New Luce
      B738   Leswalt
                                    A77
      B7043   Craiger oss   Innermessan   Auchman

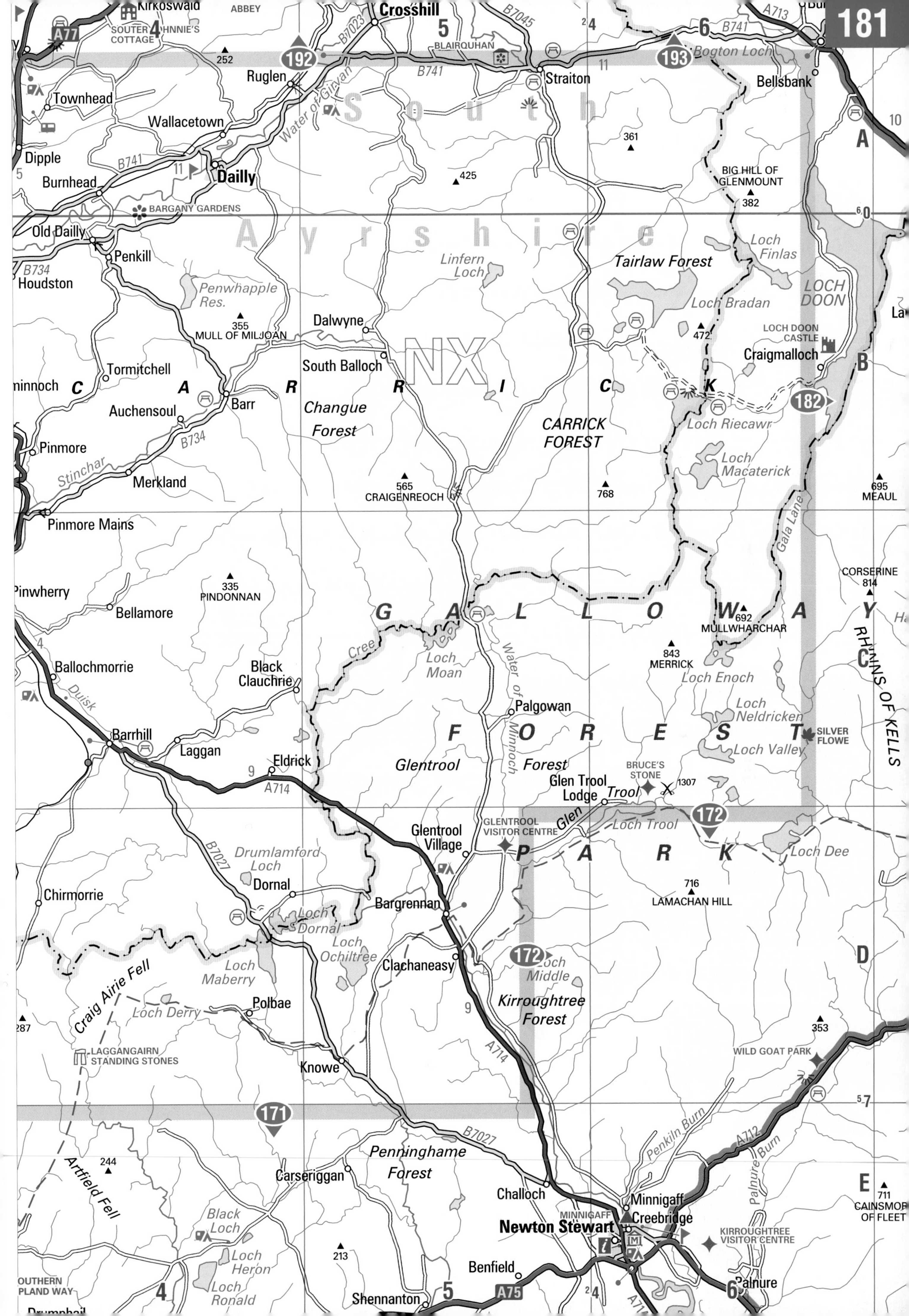
Kirkoswald
ABBEY
SOUTER JOHNNIE'S COTTAGE
A77
Crosshill
B7023
B7045
BLAIRQUHAN
B741
252
192
193
Bogton Loch
Bellsbank
A713
Ruglen
Straiton
Townhead
Wallacetown
Water of Girvan
South
361
Dipple
B741
Dailly
425
Burnhead
BIG HILL OF GLENMOUNT
382
BARGANY GARDENS
Old Dailly
Ayrshire
Loch Finlas
Penkill
Linfern Loch
Tairlaw Forest
B734
Houdston
Penwhapple Res.
LOCH DOON
Loch Bradan
355
MULL OF MILJOAN
Dalwyne
472
LOCH DOON CASTLE
Craigmalloch
South Balloch
NX
Tormitchell
C
A
R
R
I
C
K
Barr
Changue Forest
182
Auchensoul
CARRICK FOREST
Loch Riecawr
Pinmore
B734
Loch Macaterick
Stinchar
Merkland
565
CRAIGENREOCH
768
695
MEAUL
Gala Lane
Pinmore Mains
CORSERINE
814
Pinwherry
335
PINDONNAN
Bellamore
G
A
L
L
O
W
A
Y
692
MULLWHARCHAR
Cree
Loch Moan
Water of Minnoch
843
MERRICK
Loch Enoch
RHINNS OF KELLS
Ballochmorrie
Black Clauchrie
Duisk
Palgowan
Loch Neldricken
Barrhill
F
O
R
E
S
T
SILVER FLOWE
Laggan
Loch Valley
Eldrick
Glentrool
Forest
BRUCE'S STONE
1307
A714
Glen Trool Lodge
Glen Trool
Loch Trool
172
Glentrool Village
GLENTROOL VISITOR CENTRE
P
A
R
K
Loch Dee
Drumlamford Loch
B7027
Dornal
716
LAMACHAN HILL
Chirmorrie
Bargrennan
Loch Dornal
Loch Ochiltree
Clachaneasy
172
Loch Middle
Loch Maberry
Craig Airie Fell
Kirroughtree Forest
Loch Derry
Polbae
287
353
LAGGANGAIRN STANDING STONES
A714
WILD GOAT PARK
Knowe
171
B7027
Penkiln Burn
A712
Palnure Burn
Artfield Fell
244
Penninghame Forest
Carseriggan
Challoch
Minnigaff
711
CAINSMORE OF FLEET
Black Loch
MINNIGAFF
Creebridge
Newton Stewart
KIRROUGHTREE VISITOR CENTRE
213
Loch Heron
Benfield
SOUTHERN UPLAND WAY
Loch Ronald
Shennanton
A75
Palnure

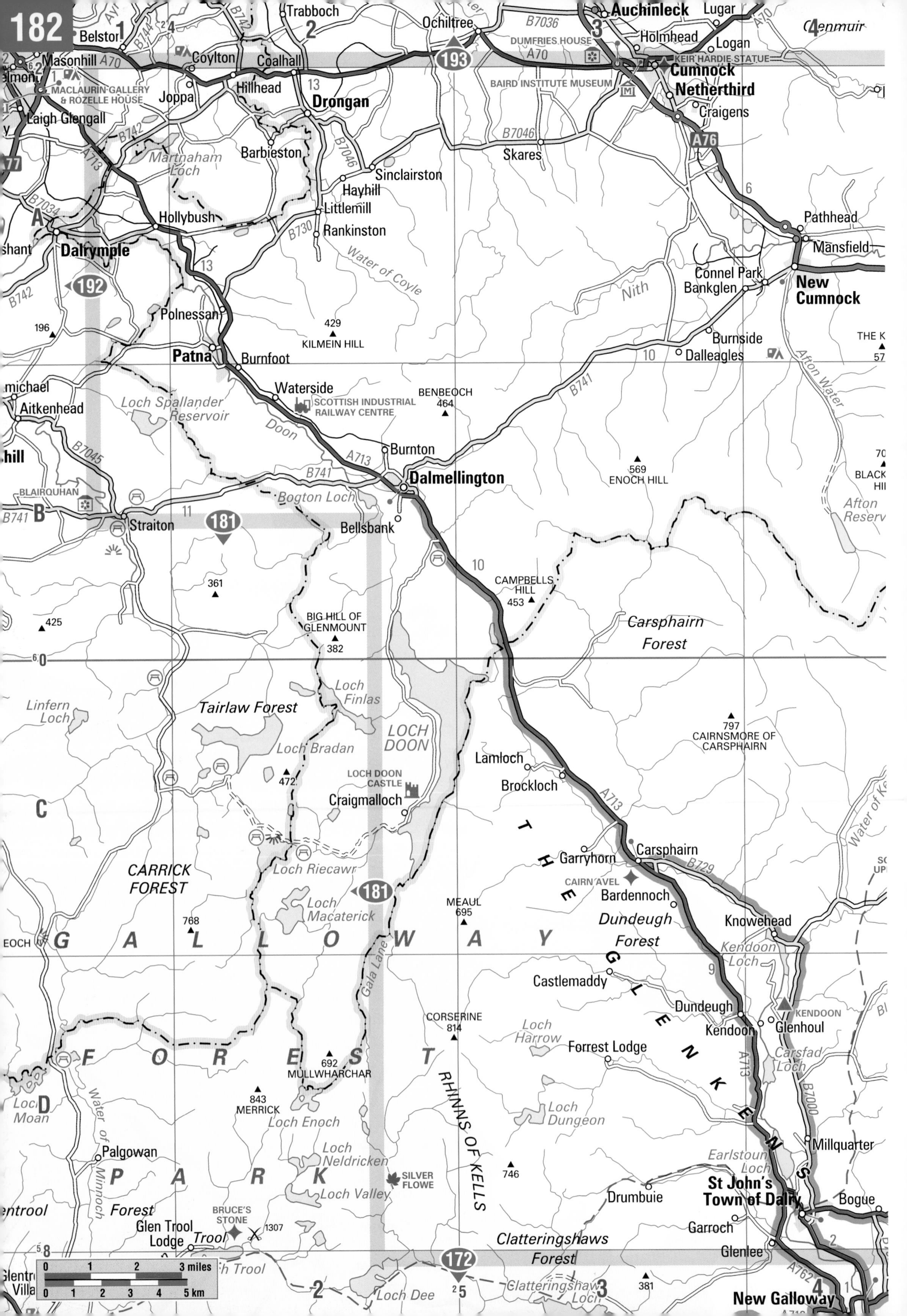
Trabboch
Ochiltree
Auchinleck
Lugar
Belston
Masonhill
Coylton
Coalhall
193
DUMFRIES HOUSE
Holmhead
Logan
KEIR HARDIE STATUE
Cumnock
Netherthird
Craigens
MACLAURIN GALLERY & ROZELLE HOUSE
Joppa
Hillhead
Drongan
BAIRD INSTITUTE MUSEUM
Laigh Glengall
Martnaham Loch
Barbieston
Sinclairston
Hayhill
Littlemill
Rankinston
Skares
Hollybush
Dalrymple
Water of Coyle
Pathhead
Mansfield
Connel Park
Bankglen
New Cumnock
Nith
192
Polnessan
Patna
Burnfoot
429
KILMEIN HILL
196
Burnside
Dalleagles
Afton Water
Aitkenhead
Loch Spallander Reservoir
Waterside
SCOTTISH INDUSTRIAL RAILWAY CENTRE
BENBEOCH
464
Doon
Burnton
Dalmellington
569
ENOCH HILL
BLAIRQUHAN
Straiton
181
Bogton Loch
Bellsbank
Afton Reserv
361
CAMPBELLS HILL
453
425
BIG HILL OF GLENMOUNT
382
Carsphairn Forest
Linfern Loch
Tairlaw Forest
Loch Finlas
LOCH DOON
Loch Bradan
797
CAIRNSMORE OF CARSPHAIRN
Lamloch
Brockloch
472
LOCH DOON CASTLE
Craigmalloch
Water of Ken
CARRICK FOREST
Loch Riecawr
Garryhorn
Carsphairn
CAIRN AVEL
Bardennoch
Loch Macaterick
MEAUL
695
768
Dundeugh Forest
Knowehead
EOCH
G A L L O W A Y
THE GLENKENS
Kendoon Loch
Gala Lane
Castlemaddy
Dundeugh
KENDOON
CORSERINE
814
Loch Harrow
Kendoon
Glenhoul
Forrest Lodge
Carsfad Loch
F O R E S T
692
MULLWHARCHAR
843
MERRICK
Loch Moan
Loch Enoch
Loch Dungeon
RHINNS OF KELLS
Water of Minnoch
Palgowan
Millquarter
P A R K
Loch Neldricken
SILVER FLOWE
746
Earlstoun Loch
Loch Valley
St John's Town of Dalry
Drumbuie
Bogue
Forest
BRUCE'S STONE
1307
Glen Trool Lodge
Trool
Garroch
Clatteringshaws Forest
Glenlee
172
Loch Trool
Loch Dee
Clatteringshaws Loch
381
New Galloway
0 1 2 3 miles
0 1 2 3 4 5 km

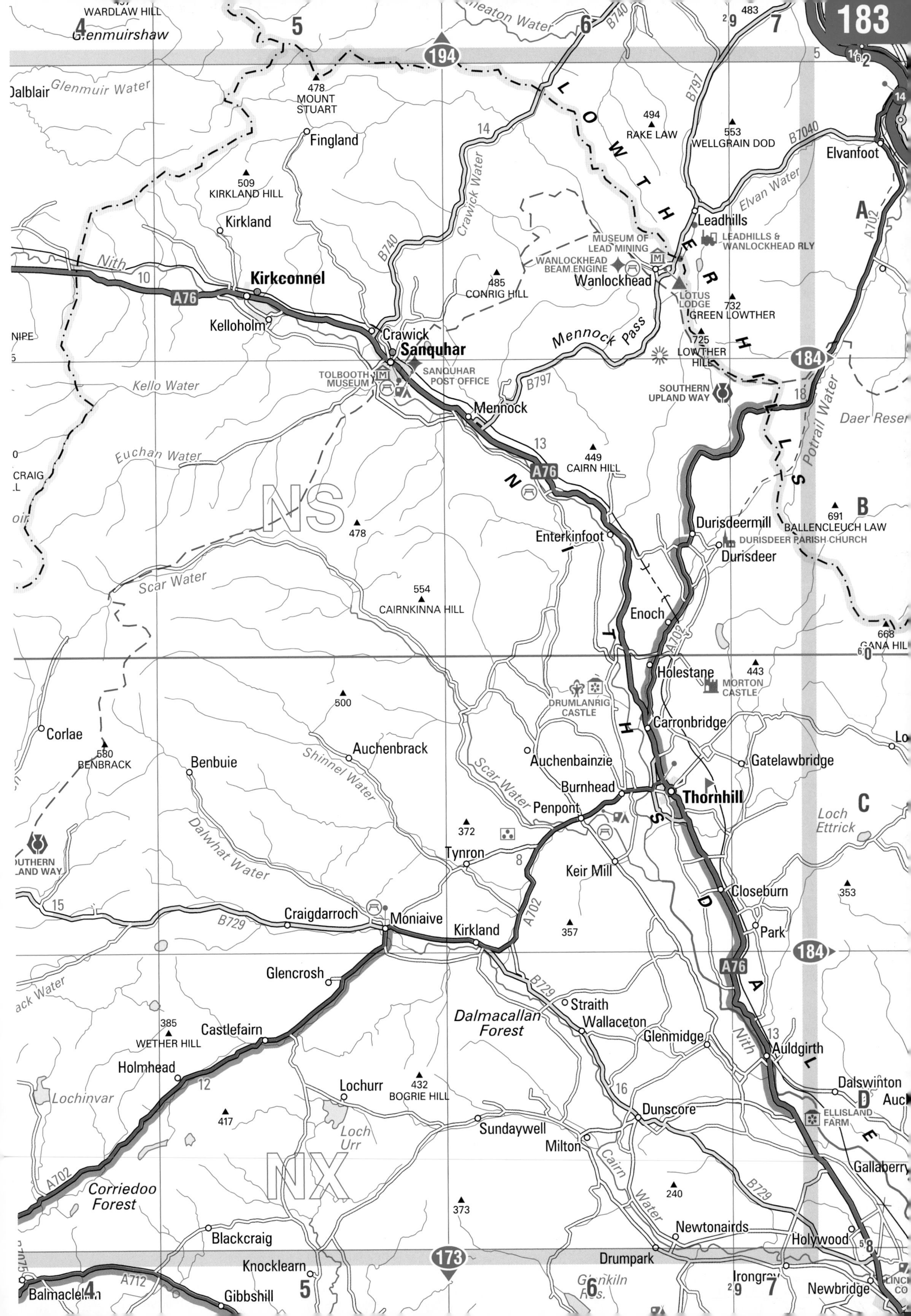

WARDLAW HILL
Glenmuirshaw
Dalblair
Glenmuir Water
478
MOUNT
STUART
Fingland
194
Wanlockhead
LOWTHER HILLS
494
RAKE LAW
553
WELLGRAIN DOD
B797
B7040
Elvanfoot
Elvan Water
509
KIRKLAND HILL
Kirkland
Crawick Water
B740
Leadhills
LEADHILLS &
WANLOCKHEAD RLY
MUSEUM OF
LEAD MINING
WANLOCKHEAD
BEAM ENGINE
Nith
A76
Kirkconnel
Kelloholm
485
CONRIG HILL
LOTUS
LODGE
732
GREEN LOWTHER
725
LOWTHER
HILL
Mennock Pass
Crawick
Sanquhar
TOLBOOTH
MUSEUM
SANQUHAR
POST OFFICE
B797
184
SOUTHERN
UPLAND WAY
A702
Kello Water
Mennock
Potrail Water
Daer Reser
Euchan Water
449
CAIRN HILL
CRAIG
NS
NITHSDALE
478
Durisdeermill
691
BALLENCLEUCH LAW
DURISDEER PARISH CHURCH
Enterkinfoot
Durisdeer
Scar Water
554
CAIRNKINNA HILL
Enoch
668
GANA HIL
Holestane
443
MORTON
CASTLE
500
DRUMLANRIG
CASTLE
Carronbridge
Corlae
580
BENBRACK
Auchenbrack
Benbuie
Shinnel Water
Auchenbainzie
Gatelawbridge
Scar Water
Burnhead
Thornhill
Penpont
Loch
Ettrick
372
Dalwhat Water
Tynron
Keir Mill
SOUTHERN
UPLAND WAY
Closeburn
353
B729
Craigdarroch
Moniaive
Kirkland
357
Park
A702
A76
Glencrosh
B729
Straith
Dalmacallan
Forest
Wallaceton
385
WETHER HILL
Castlefairn
Glenmidge
Auldgirth
Holmhead
Dalswinton
Lochinvar
Lochurr
432
BOGRIE HILL
417
ELLISLAND
FARM
Dunscore
Sundaywell
Loch
Urr
Milton
Cairn Water
A702
NX
240
Gallaberry
Corriedoo
Forest
373
B729
Newtonairds
Blackcraig
Holywood
173
Drumpark
Knocklearn
Irongray
A712
Balmaclellan
Gibbshill
Glenkiln
Newbridge

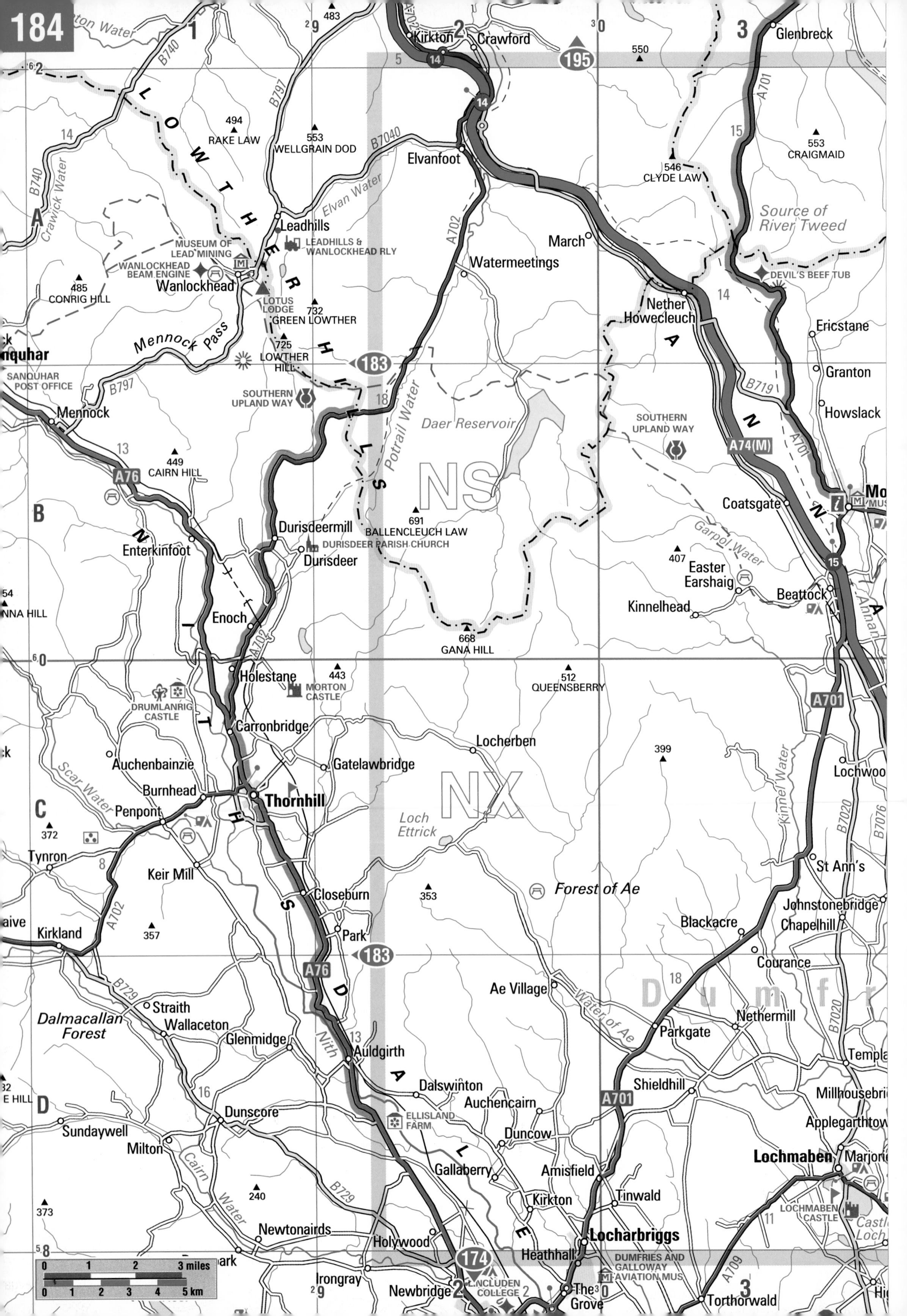
LOWTHER HILLS
NITHSDALE
NS
NX
Dumfr
Kirkton
Crawford
Glenbreck
RAKE LAW
WELLGRAIN DOD
Elvanfoot
CLYDE LAW
CRAIGMAID
Source of River Tweed
Leadhills
LEADHILLS & WANLOCKHEAD RLY
MUSEUM OF LEAD MINING
WANLOCKHEAD BEAM ENGINE
Wanlockhead
March
Watermeetings
DEVIL'S BEEF TUB
CONRIG HILL
LOTUS LODGE
GREEN LOWTHER
Nether Howecleuch
Ericstane
Mennock Pass
LOWTHER HILL
Granton
SANQUHAR POST OFFICE
SOUTHERN UPLAND WAY
Mennock
Howslack
Daer Reservoir
Potrail Water
CAIRN HILL
Coatsgate
BALLENCLEUCH LAW
Durisdeermill
DURISDEER PARISH CHURCH
Durisdeer
Enterkinfoot
Easter Earshaig
Beattock
Kinnelhead
Enoch
GANA HILL
Holestane
MORTON CASTLE
QUEENSBERRY
DRUMLANRIG CASTLE
Carronbridge
Locherben
Auchenbainzie
Gatelawbridge
Burnhead
Thornhill
Penpont
Loch Ettrick
Tynron
Keir Mill
St Ann's
Closeburn
Forest of Ae
Johnstonebridge
Chapelhill
Blackacre
Kirkland
Park
Courance
Ae Village
Water of Ae
Straith
Nethermill
Dalmacallan Forest
Wallaceton
Glenmidge
Parkgate
Auldgirth
Shieldhill
Dalswinton
Auchencairn
ELLISLAND FARM
Dunscore
Sundaywell
Duncow
Milton
Cairn Water
Gallaberry
Amisfield
Lochmaben
LOCHMABEN CASTLE
Tinwald
Newtonairds
Holywood
Locharbriggs
Heathhall
DUMFRIES AND GALLOWAY AVIATION MUS
Irongray
Newbridge
LINCLUDEN COLLEGE
The Grove
Torthorwald
Scar Water
Crawick Water
Elvan Water
Garpol Water
Kinnel Water
Nith
0 1 2 3 miles
0 1 2 3 4 5 km

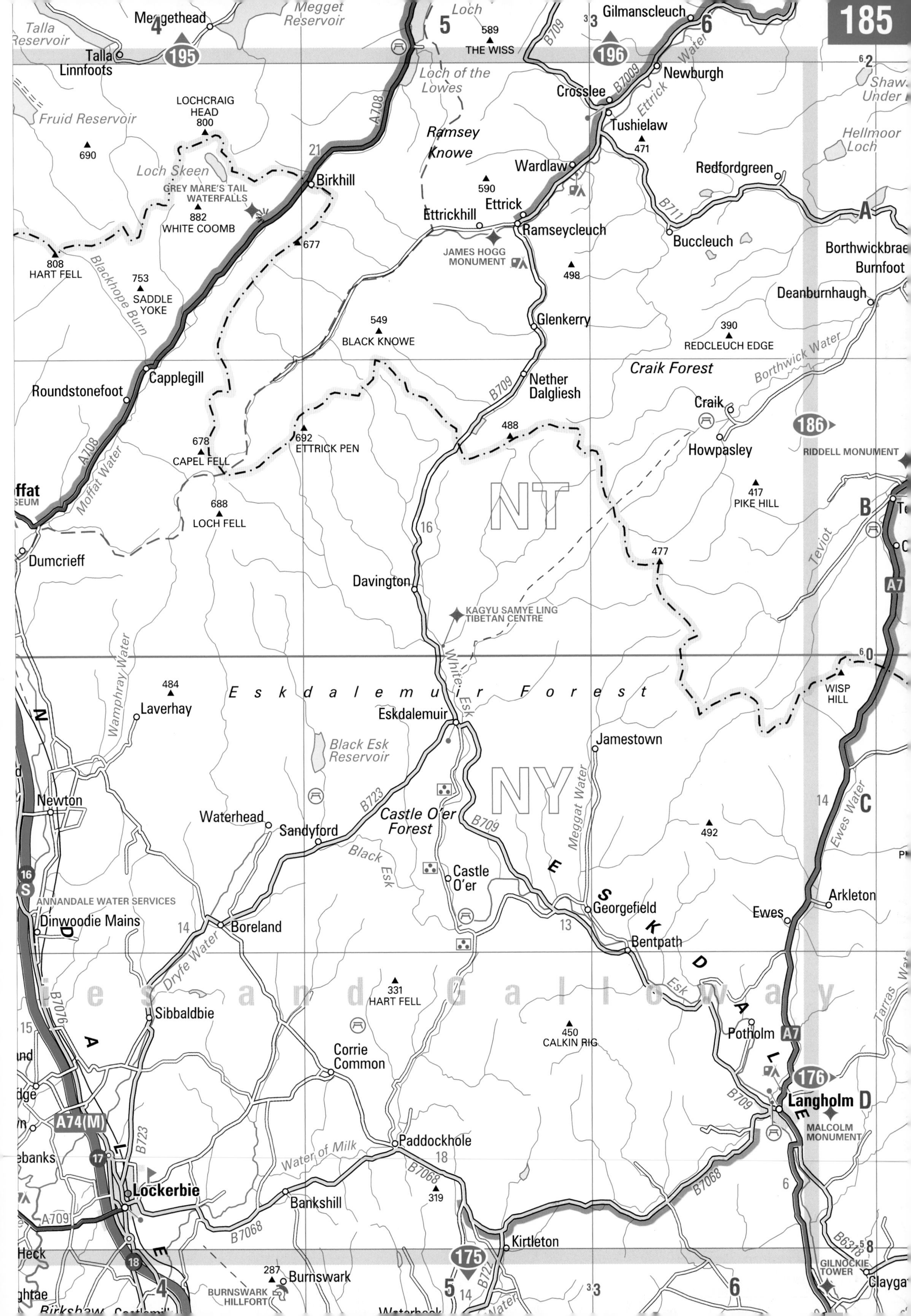
Megget Reservoir
Meggethead
Talla Reservoir
Talla
Linnfoots
195
Loch
589
THE WISS
Gilmanscleuch
196
Newburgh
Loch of the Lowes
Crosslee
Ettrick Water
Tushielaw
471
Shaw Under
Hellmoor Loch
LOCHCRAIG HEAD 800
Fruid Reservoir
690
Loch Skeen
GREY MARE'S TAIL WATERFALLS
882
WHITE COOMB
Birkhill
A708
Ramsey Knowe
590
Wardlaw
Ettrick
Ettrickhill
Ramseycleuch
Redfordgreen
B711
Buccleuch
JAMES HOGG MONUMENT
498
Borthwickbrae
Burnfoot
Deanburnhaugh
677
808
HART FELL
753
SADDLE YOKE
Blackhope Burn
549
BLACK KNOWE
Glenkerry
390
REDCLEUCH EDGE
Borthwick Water
Craik Forest
Capplegill
Roundstonefoot
Nether Dalgliesh
B709
Craik
Howpasley
186
RIDDELL MONUMENT
692
ETTRICK PEN
678
CAPEL FELL
488
Moffat Water
688
LOCH FELL
NT
417
PIKE HILL
Teviot
Dumcrieff
477
Davington
KAGYU SAMYE LING TIBETAN CENTRE
A7
484
Laverhay
Wamphray Water
White Esk
Eskdalemuir Forest
Eskdalemuir
WISP HILL
Jamestown
Black Esk Reservoir
NY
Meggat Water
Newton
Waterhead
Sandyford
B723
Castle O'er Forest
Ewes Water
492
Black Esk
Castle O'er
ANNANDALE WATER SERVICES
Dinwoodie Mains
Boreland
Dryfe Water
Georgefield
Arkleton
Ewes
Bentpath
ESKDALE
Dumfries and Galloway
331
HART FELL
Esk
Sibbaldbie
B7076
450
CALKIN RIG
Potholm
Corrie Common
Tarras Water
176
Langholm
MALCOLM MONUMENT
A74(M)
Paddockhole
Water of Milk
B7068
319
Lockerbie
A709
Bankshill
Kirtleton
175
B6318
GILNOCKIE TOWER
Claygate
Heck
287
Burnswark
BURNSWARK HILLFORT
B722
Birkshaw
Waterbeck

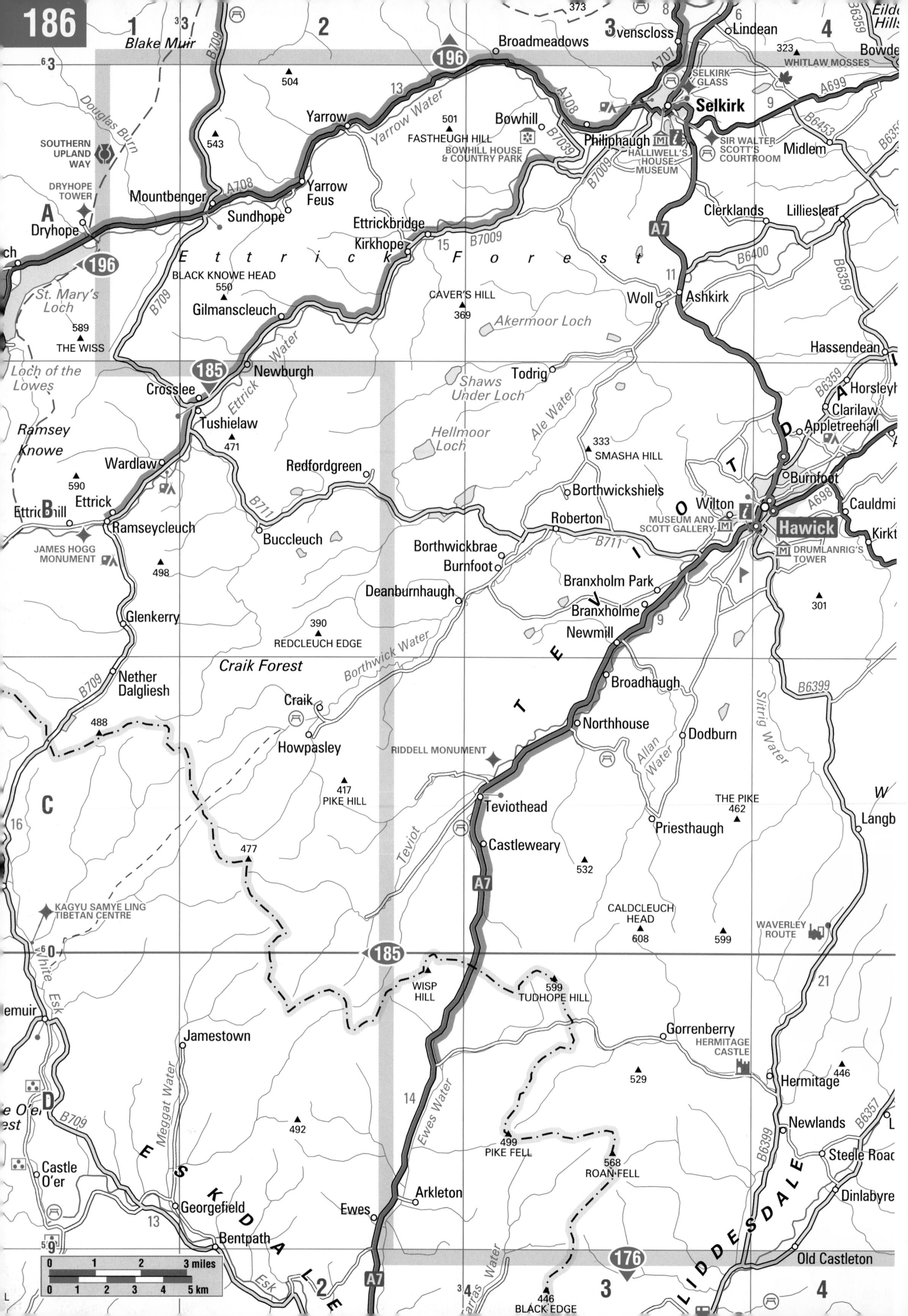

186
Blake Muir
Broadmeadows
Lindean
Selkirk
SELKIRK GLASS
WHITLAW MOSSES
Yarrow
Yarrow Water
FASTHEUGH HILL
Bowhill
BOWHILL HOUSE & COUNTRY PARK
Philiphaugh
HALLIWELL'S HOUSE MUSEUM
SIR WALTER SCOTT'S COURTROOM
Midlem
Douglas Burn
SOUTHERN UPLAND WAY
DRYHOPE TOWER
Mountbenger
Yarrow Feus
Sundhope
Dryhope
Ettrickbridge
Kirkhope
Clerklands
Lilliesleaf
Ettrick Forest
BLACK KNOWE HEAD
St. Mary's Loch
THE WISS
Gilmanscleuch
CAVER'S HILL
Akermoor Loch
Woll
Ashkirk
Hassendean
Loch of the Lowes
Newburgh
Crosslee
Ettrick Water
Todrig
Shaws Under Loch
Horsleyhill
Clarilaw
Appletreehall
Tushielaw
Ramsey Knowe
Hellmoor Loch
Ale Water
SMASHA HILL
Wardlaw
Redfordgreen
Burnfoot
Borthwickshiels
Wilton
Cauldmill
Ettrick
Ettrickhill
Ramseycleuch
Buccleuch
Roberton
MUSEUM AND SCOTT GALLERY
Hawick
Kirkton
JAMES HOGG MONUMENT
Borthwickbrae
Burnfoot
DRUMLANRIG'S TOWER
Deanburnhaugh
Branxholm Park
Branxholme
Glenkerry
REDCLEUCH EDGE
Newmill
Craik Forest
Borthwick Water
Nether Dalgliesh
Craik
Broadhaugh
TEVIOTDALE
Northhouse
Howpasley
Dodburn
RIDDELL MONUMENT
Allan Water
Slitrig Water
PIKE HILL
Teviothead
THE PIKE
Langburnshiels
Castleweary
Priesthaugh
Teviot
KAGYU SAMYE LING TIBETAN CENTRE
CALDCLEUCH HEAD
WAVERLEY ROUTE
White Esk
WISP HILL
TUDHOPE HILL
Eskdalemuir
Jamestown
Gorrenberry
HERMITAGE CASTLE
Hermitage
Meggat Water
Ewes Water
Newlands
Castle O'er Forest
Castle O'er
PIKE FELL
ROAN FELL
Steele Road
ESKDALE
Georgefield
Arkleton
Ewes
Dinlabyre
Bentpath
LIDDESDALE
Old Castleton
Tarras Water
BLACK EDGE
Esk
0 1 2 3 miles
0 1 2 3 4 5 km

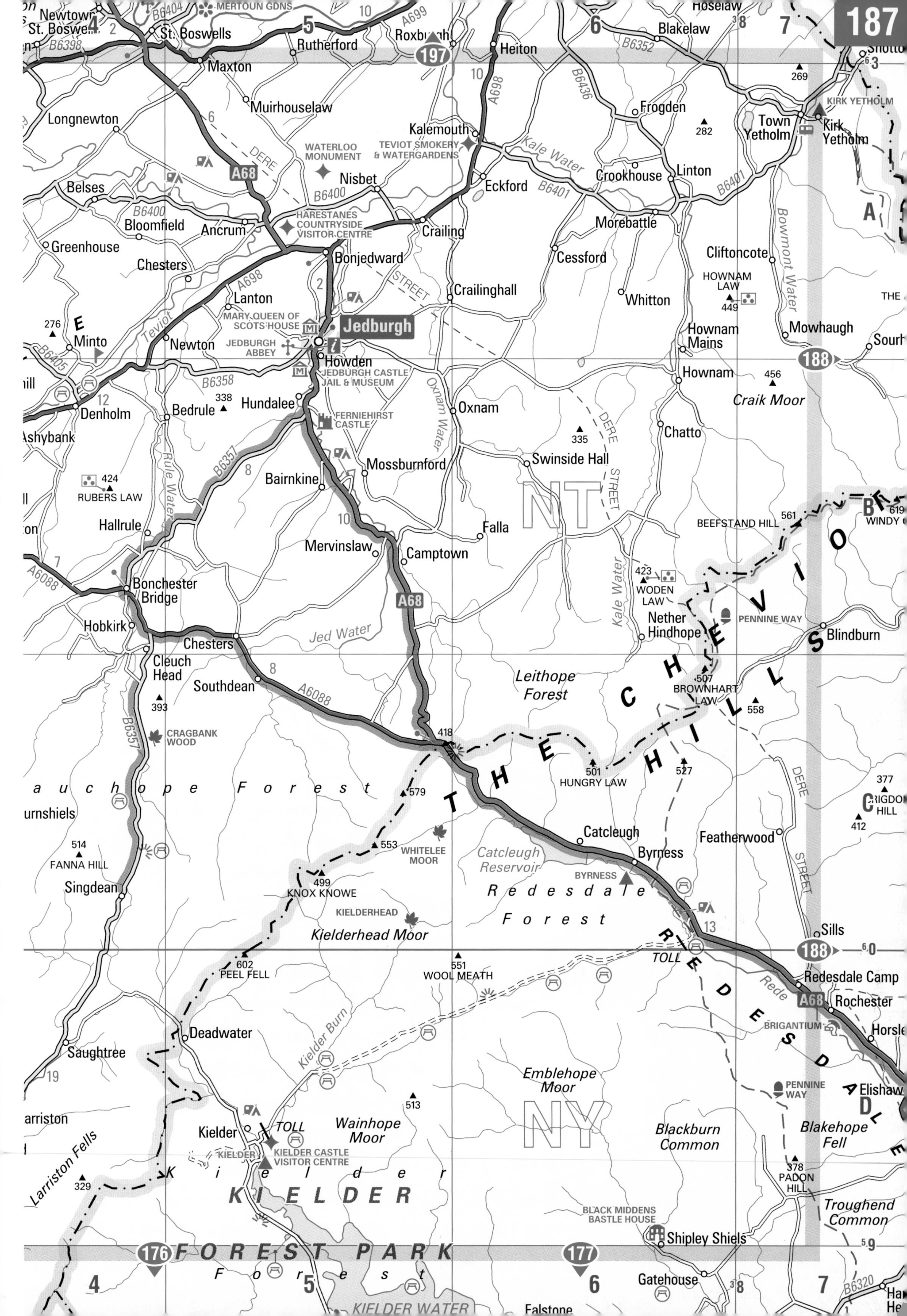
Jedburgh
St. Boswells
Newtown St. Boswells
Mertoun Gdns
Rutherford
Roxburgh
Heiton
Blakelaw
Maxton
Muirhouselaw
Longnewton
Kalemouth
Teviot Smokery & Watergardens
Waterloo Monument
Nisbet
Eckford
Kale Water
Frogden
Crookhouse
Linton
Town Yetholm
Kirk Yetholm
Belses
Bloomfield
Ancrum
Harestanes Countryside Visitor Centre
Crailing
Morebattle
Cessford
Greenhouse
Chesters
Bonjedward
Crailinghall
Whitton
Cliftoncote
Hownam Law
Bowmont Water
Lanton
Mary Queen of Scots House
Jedburgh Abbey
Newton
Minto
Howden
Jedburgh Castle Jail & Museum
Hownam Mains
Mowhaugh
Hownam
Craik Moor
Denholm
Bedrule
Hundalee
Oxnam
Oxnam Water
Ferniehirst Castle
Chatto
Ashybank
Swinside Hall
Rubers Law
Bairnkine
Mossburnford
Hallrule
Rule Water
Mervinslaw
Camptown
Falla
Beefstand Hill
Windy
Woden Law
Kale Water
Nether Hindhope
Pennine Way
Blindburn
Bonchester Bridge
Hobkirk
Chesters
Jed Water
Cleuch Head
Southdean
Leithope Forest
Brownhart Law
The Cheviot Hills
Cragbank Wood
Hungry Law
Wauchope Forest
Burnshiels
Catcleugh
Catcleugh Reservoir
Byrness
Featherwood
Rigdon Hill
Fanna Hill
Whitelee Moor
Singdean
Knox Knowe
Kielderhead
Kielderhead Moor
Redesdale Forest
Sills
Toll
Peel Fell
Wool Meath
Redesdale Camp
Rochester
Rede
Brigantium
Horsley
Deadwater
Saughtree
Kielder Burn
Emblehope Moor
Elishaw
Pennine Way
Redesdale
Wainhope Moor
Kielder
Kielder Castle Visitor Centre
Blackburn Common
Blakehope Fell
Larriston Fells
Kielder Forest Park
Padon Hill
Troughend Common
Black Middens Bastle House
Shipley Shiels
Gatehouse
Kielder Water
Falstone
A68
A698
A699
A6088
B6400
B6401
B6352
B6436
B6357
B6358
B6398
B6405
B6404
B6320
Dere Street
NT
NY
176
177
188
197

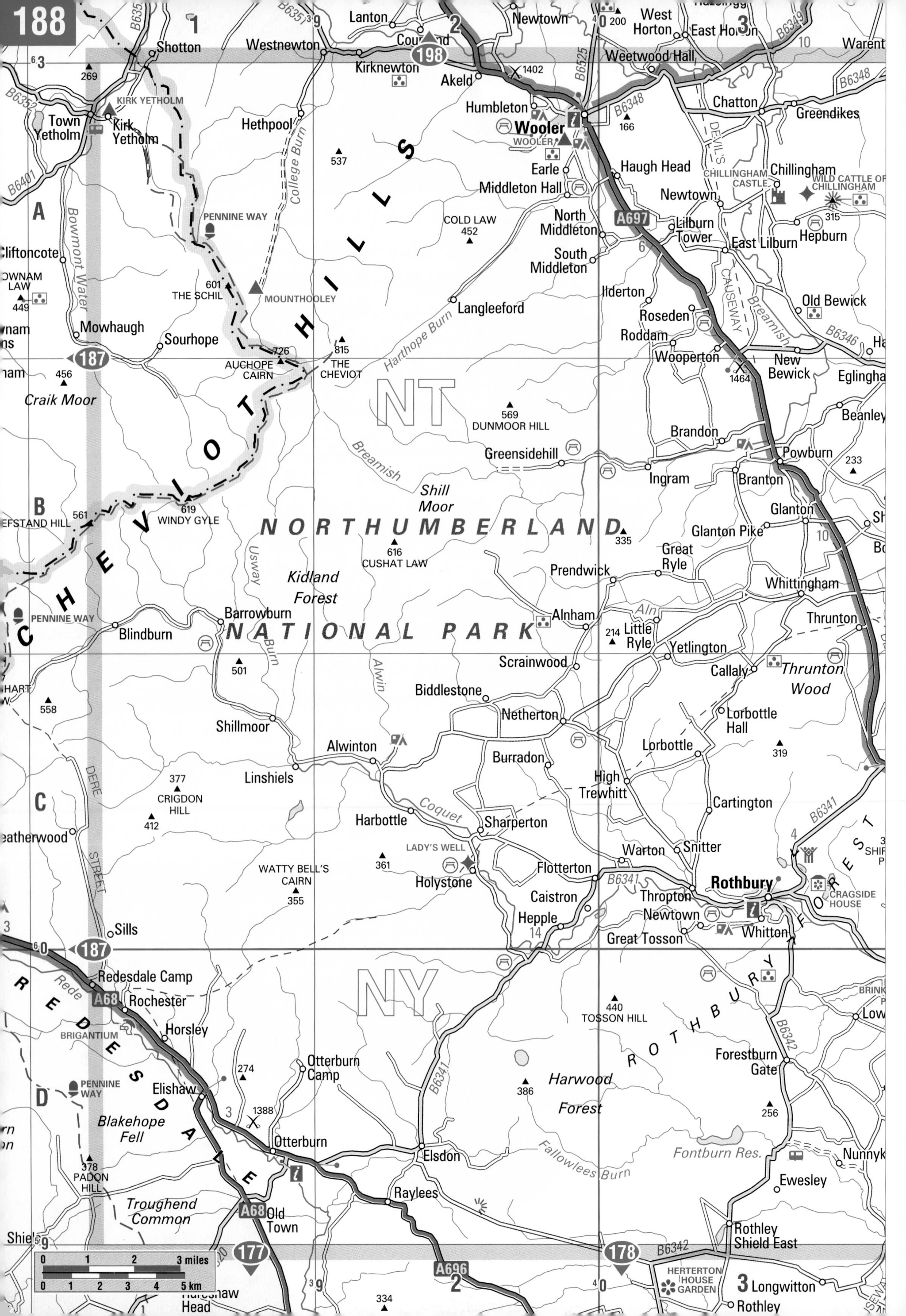
Shotton
Westnewton
Lanton
Kirknewton
Akeld
Newtown
West Horton
East Horton
Weetwood Hall
Warenton
198
Kirk Yetholm
Town Yetholm
Hethpool
College Burn
537
Humbleton
Wooler
Wooler
166
Chatton
Greendikes
Chillingham
Chillingham Castle
Wild Cattle of Chillingham
Devil's Causeway
Earle
Middleton Hall
Haugh Head
Newtown
Lilburn Tower
East Lilburn
Hepburn
315
A697
North Middleton
South Middleton
Cold Law
452
Pennine Way
Bowmont Water
Cliftoncote
601
The Schil
Mountholley
Langleeford
Ilderton
Roseden
Roddam
Wooperton
1464
New Bewick
Old Bewick
Breamish
B6346
Eglingham
Mowhaugh
Sourhope
726
Auchope Cairn
815
The Cheviot
Harthope Burn
187
456
Craik Moor
NT
569
Dunmoor Hill
Brandon
Beanley
Powburn
233
Greensidehill
Ingram
Branton
Shill Moor
Cheviot Hills
619
Windy Gyle
561
Northumberland National Park
335
Glanton
Glanton Pike
Great Ryle
616
Cushat Law
Usway Burn
Kidland Forest
Prendwick
Whittingham
Pennine Way
Blindburn
Barrowburn
Alnham
Aln
214
Little Ryle
Yetlington
Thrunton
Callaly
Thrunton Wood
501
Scrainwood
Biddlestone
Alwin
558
Netherton
Lorbottle Hall
Shillmoor
Alwinton
Linshiels
Burradon
Lorbottle
319
377
Crigdon Hill
412
High Trewhitt
Cartington
Dere Street
Harbottle
Coquet
Sharperton
B6341
Lady's Well
Holystone
361
Watty Bell's Cairn
355
Warton
Snitter
Flotterton
Rothbury
Caistron
Thropton
Cragside House
Hepple
Newtown
Whitton
Great Tosson
Sills
Rothbury Forest
187
Redesdale Camp
Rede
A68
Rochester
NY
Horsley
Brigantium
440
Tosson Hill
Redesdale
Pennine Way
Elishaw
274
Otterburn Camp
Harwood Forest
386
Forestburn Gate
B6342
256
Blakehope Fell
1388
Otterburn
Elsdon
Fallowlees Burn
Fontburn Res.
Nunnykirk
378
Padon Hill
Ewesley
Troughend Common
Raylees
A68
Old Town
Rothley Shield East
177
178
B6342
A696
Herterton House Garden
Longwitton
Rothley
334
Hareshaw Head
0 1 2 3 miles
0 1 2 3 4 5 km

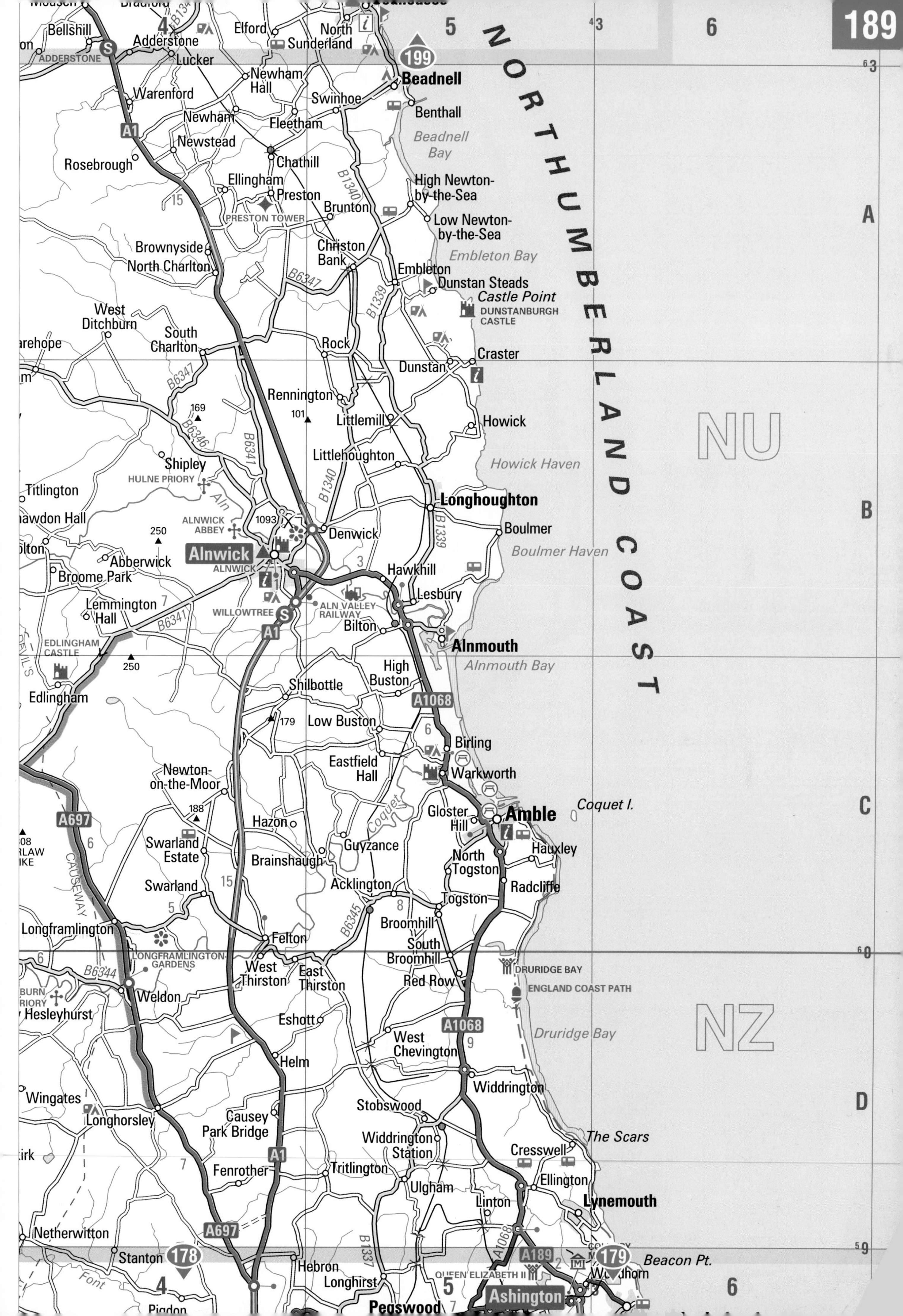
NORTHUMBERLAND COAST
NU
NZ
Bellshill
Adderstone
ADDERSTONE
Lucker
Elford
North Sunderland
Beadnell
Benthall
Beadnell Bay
Newham Hall
Warenford
Swinhoe
Newham
Fleetham
Newstead
Rosebrough
Chathill
Ellingham
Preston
PRESTON TOWER
Brunton
High Newton-by-the-Sea
Low Newton-by-the-Sea
Embleton Bay
Brownyside
North Charlton
Christon Bank
Embleton
Dunstan Steads
Castle Point
DUNSTANBURGH CASTLE
West Ditchburn
South Charlton
Rock
Craster
Dunstan
Rennington
Littlemill
Howick
Littlehoughton
Howick Haven
Shipley
HULNE PRIORY
Titlington
Longhoughton
Boulmer
Boulmer Haven
ALNWICK ABBEY
Denwick
Alnwick
ALNWICK
Abberwick
Broome Park
Hawkhill
Lesbury
Lemmington Hall
WILLOWTREE
ALN VALLEY RAILWAY
Bilton
Alnmouth
Alnmouth Bay
EDLINGHAM CASTLE
Edlingham
High Buston
Shilbottle
Low Buston
Birling
Eastfield Hall
Warkworth
Newton-on-the-Moor
Coquet I.
Gloster Hill
Amble
Hazon
Guyzance
Hauxley
Swarland Estate
Brainshaugh
North Togston
Radcliffe
Acklington
Swarland
Togston
Broomhill
South Broomhill
Longframlington
Felton
LONGFRAMLINGTON GARDENS
West Thirston
East Thirston
Red Row
DRURIDGE BAY
ENGLAND COAST PATH
Weldon
Hesleyhurst
Eshott
Druridge Bay
West Chevington
Helm
Widdrington
Wingates
Longhorsley
Stobswood
Causey Park Bridge
Widdrington Station
The Scars
Cresswell
Fenrother
Tritlington
Ulgham
Ellington
Linton
Lynemouth
Netherwitton
Stanton
Hebron
Longhirst
QUEEN ELIZABETH II
Beacon Pt.
Woodhorn
Ashington
Pegswood
Pigdon
Font
Coquet
Aln
CAUSEWAY
A1
A697
A1068
A189
B6347
B6346
B6341
B1340
B1339
B6345
B6344
B1337
178
179
199

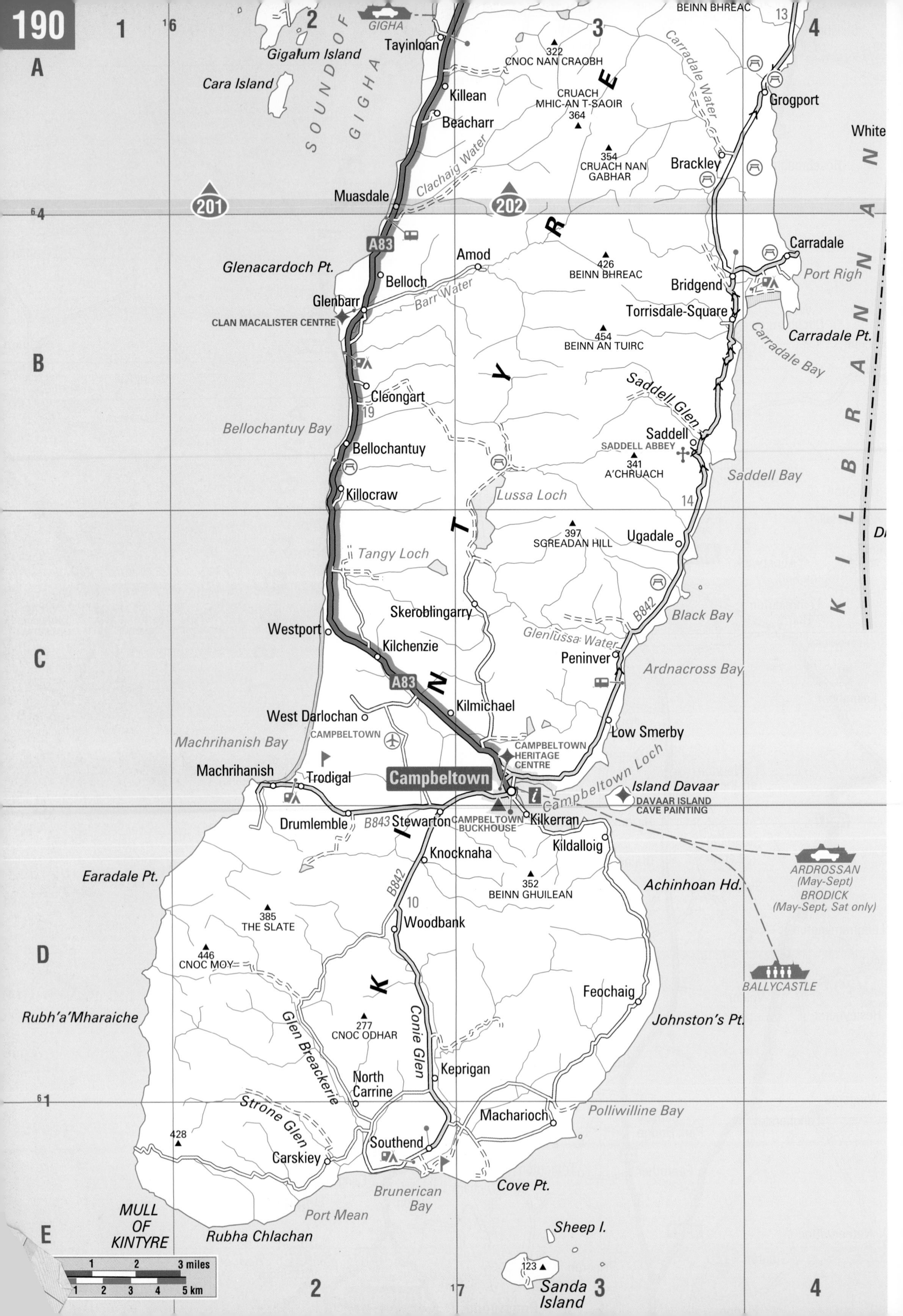

Gigalum Island
Cara Island
SOUND OF GIGHA
GIGHA
Tayinloan
Killean
Beacharr
Muasdale
Clachaig Water
201
202
A83
Glenacardoch Pt.
Belloch
Amod
Barr Water
Glenbarr
CLAN MACALISTER CENTRE
Cleongart
Bellochantuy Bay
Bellochantuy
Killocraw
Tangy Loch
Lussa Loch
Westport
Skeroblingarry
Kilchenzie
Kilmichael
West Darlochan
CAMPBELTOWN
Machrihanish Bay
Machrihanish
Trodigal
Campbeltown
CAMPBELTOWN HERITAGE CENTRE
Drumlemble
B843
Stewarton
CAMPBELTOWN BUCKHOUSE
Kilkerran
Knocknaha
B842
Woodbank
Earadale Pt.
385 THE SLATE
446 CNOC MOY
Rubh'a'Mharaiche
Glen Breackerie
Conie Glen
277 CNOC ODHAR
North Carrine
Keprigan
Strone Glen
428
Carskiey
Southend
Brunerican Bay
Port Mean
Rubha Chlachan
MULL OF KINTYRE
Cove Pt.
Sheep I.
123
Sanda Island
Macharioch
Polliwilline Bay
Feochaig
Johnston's Pt.
352 BEINN GHUILEAN
Kildalloig
Achinhoan Hd.
Island Davaar
DAVAAR ISLAND CAVE PAINTING
Campbeltown Loch
Low Smerby
Ardnacross Bay
Peninver
Glenlussa Water
Black Bay
Ugadale
397 SGREADAN HILL
341 A'CHRUACH
SADDELL ABBEY
Saddell
Saddell Glen
Saddell Bay
Carradale Bay
Carradale Pt.
Torrisdale-Square
Bridgend
Port Righ
Carradale
454 BEINN AN TUIRC
426 BEINN BHREAC
Brackley
354 CRUACH NAN GABHAR
364 CRUACH MHIC-AN T-SAOIR
322 CNOC NAN CRAOBH
BEINN BHREAC
Carradale Water
Grogport
White
KILBRANNAN
KINTYRE
ARDROSSAN (May-Sept)
BRODICK (May-Sept, Sat only)
BALLYCASTLE
1 2 3 miles
1 2 3 4 5 km

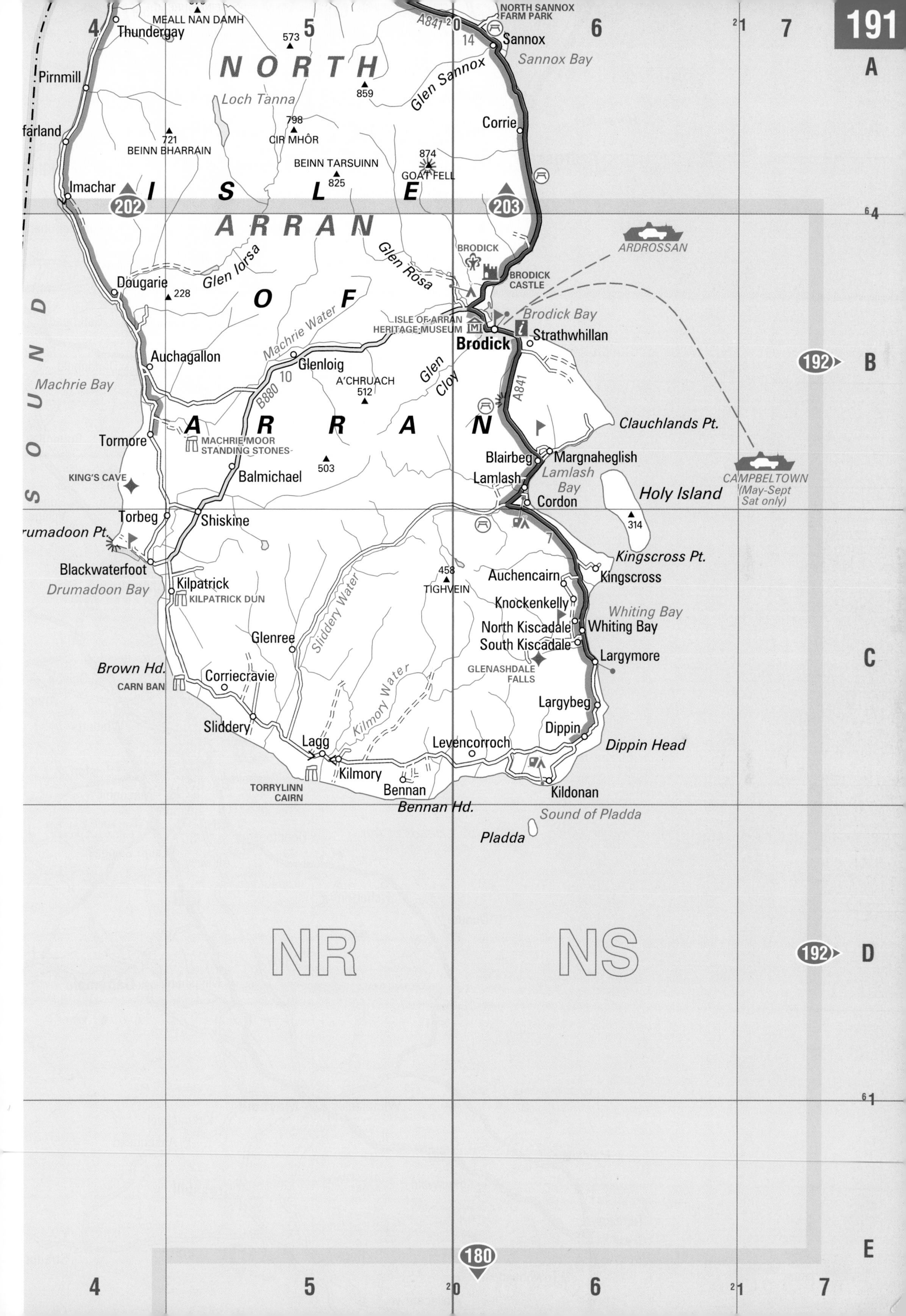

A
B
C
D
E

4 5 6 7

NORTH

MEALL NAN DAMH
Thundergay
573
859
Loch Tanna
798
CIR MHÔR
721
BEINN BHARRAIN
825
BEINN TARSUINN
874
GOAT FELL
Pirnmill
farland

ISLE

A R R A N

O F

Imachar
202

Dougarie
228
Glen Iorsa

Auchagallon

Glenloig
A'CHRUACH
512

Tormore
MACHRIE MOOR
STANDING STONES
503

KING'S CAVE
Balmichael

Torbeg
Shiskine

Drumadoon Pt.

Blackwaterfoot
Drumadoon Bay
Kilpatrick
KILPATRICK DUN

Glenree

Brown Hd.
CARN BAN
Corriecravie

Sliddery
Lagg

TORRYLINN
CAIRN
Kilmory
Bennan

Bennan Hd.

Machrie Bay

Machrie Water

NORTH SANNOX
FARM PARK
Sannox
14
Sannox Bay
A841

Glen Sannox

Corrie

203

BRODICK
BRODICK
CASTLE

ISLE OF ARRAN
HERITAGE MUSEUM
Brodick

Brodick Bay

Strathwhillan

Glen Rosa

Glen
Cloy

B880
10

A841

Clauchlands Pt.

Blairbeg
Lamlash
Margnaheglish

Lamlash
Bay

Cordon

Holy Island

314

Sliddery Water

Kilmory Water

458
TIGHVEIN

Auchencairn

Knockenkelly

North Kiscadale
South Kiscadale
GLENASHDALE
FALLS

Kingscross Pt.
Kingscross

Whiting Bay
Whiting Bay

Largymore

Largybeg
Dippin

Dippin Head

Levencorroch

Kildonan

Sound of Pladda
Pladda

S O U N D

ARDROSSAN

CAMPBELTOWN
(May-Sept
Sat only)

192

192

NR

NS

180

4 5 6 7

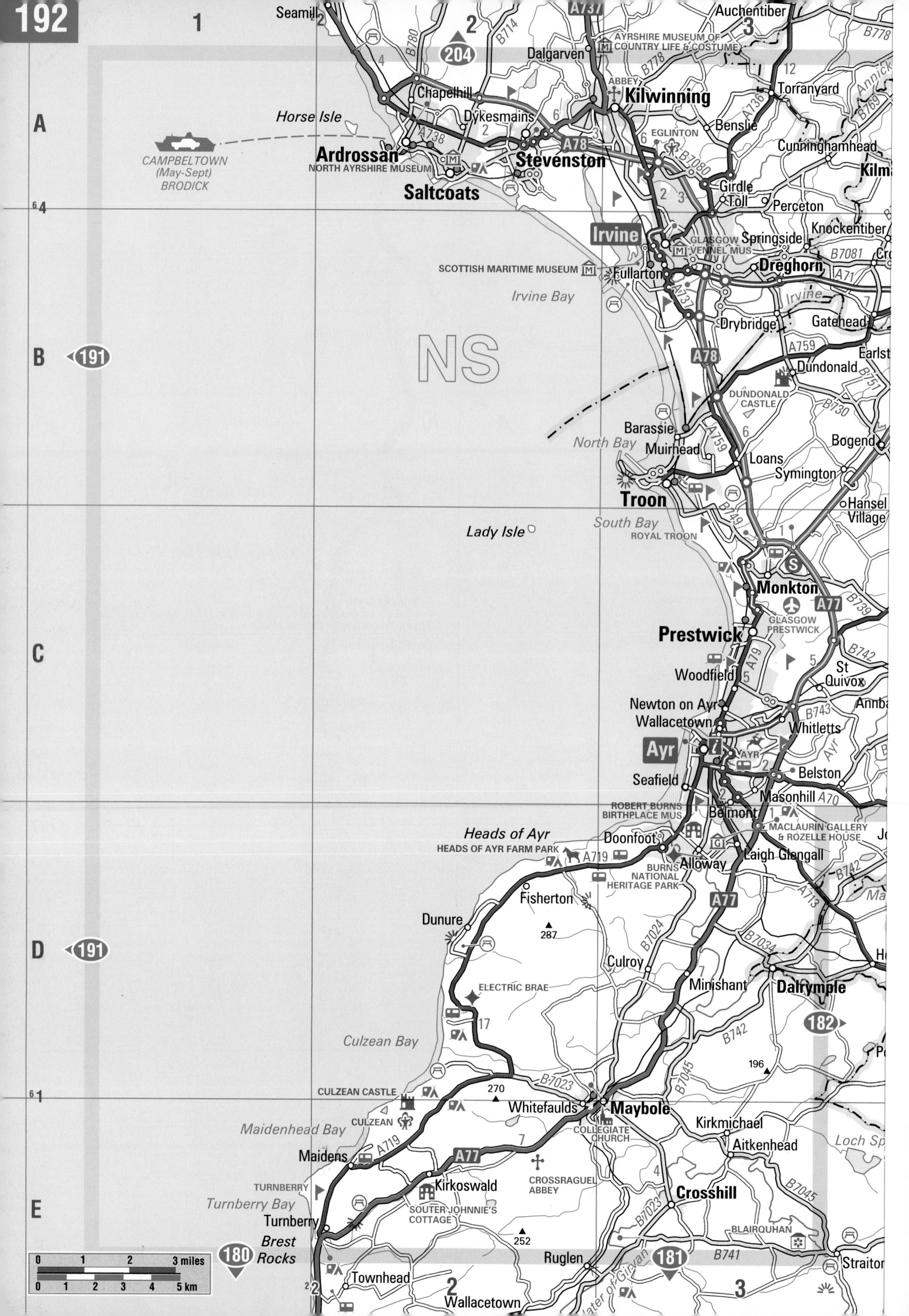

1   2   3

A

B

C

D

E

Seamill
A737
Auchentiber
B714
B780
B778
204
Dalgarven
AYRSHIRE MUSEUM OF
COUNTRY LIFE & COSTUME
B778
Torranyard
Annick
12
Chapelhill
ABBEY
Kilwinning
A736
B769
Dykesmains
A738
6
EGLINTON
Benslie
Cunninghamhead
Horse Isle
A78
B7080
6
Kilm
CAMPBELTOWN
(May-Sept)
BRODICK
Ardrossan
NORTH AYRSHIRE MUSEUM
Stevenston
Girdle
Toll
Perceton
Saltcoats
2 3
Springside
Knockentiber
Cro
Irvine
GLASGOW
VENNEL MUS
B7081
Dreghorn
A71
SCOTTISH MARITIME MUSEUM
Fullarton
Irvine
7
Irvine Bay
A737
Drybridge
Gatehead
NS
A759
Earls
A78
Dundonald
B751
DUNDONALD
CASTLE
B730
Barassie
Muirhead
A759
6
Bogend
North Bay
Loans
Symington
Troon
B749
Hansel
Village
South Bay
Lady Isle
ROYAL TROON
1
S
Monkton
A77
B739
GLASGOW
PRESTWICK
Prestwick
B742
Woodfield
A79
5
St
Quivox
Annb
Newton on Ayr
Wallacetown
B743
Whitletts
Ayr
Ayr
2
Belston
Seafield
Masonhill
A70
ROBERT BURNS
BIRTHPLACE MUS
Belmont
1
MACLAURIN GALLERY
& ROZELLE HOUSE
Jo
Heads of Ayr
Doonfoot
Laigh Glengall
HEADS OF AYR FARM PARK
A719
BURNS
NATIONAL
HERITAGE PARK
Alloway
A77
Fisherton
287
B7024
Culroy
Ma
Dunure
Minishant
Dalrymple
ELECTRIC BRAE
A713
182
17
B742
Culzean Bay
196
Po
CULZEAN CASTLE
270
B7023
CULZEAN
Whitefaulds
Maybole
Kirkmichael
Maidenhead Bay
A719
COLLEGIATE
CHURCH
Aitkenhead
Loch Sp
Maidens
A77
7
CROSSRAGUEL
ABBEY
Crosshill
B7045
TURNBERRY
Kirkoswald
SOUTER JOHNNIE'S
COTTAGE
B7023
Turnberry Bay
BLAIRQUHAN
Turnberry
252
180
Brest
Rocks
181
Ruglen
B741
Straitor
Townhead
Wallacetown

191 (B)

191 (D)

0   1   2   3 miles
0   1   2   3   4   5 km

2   3

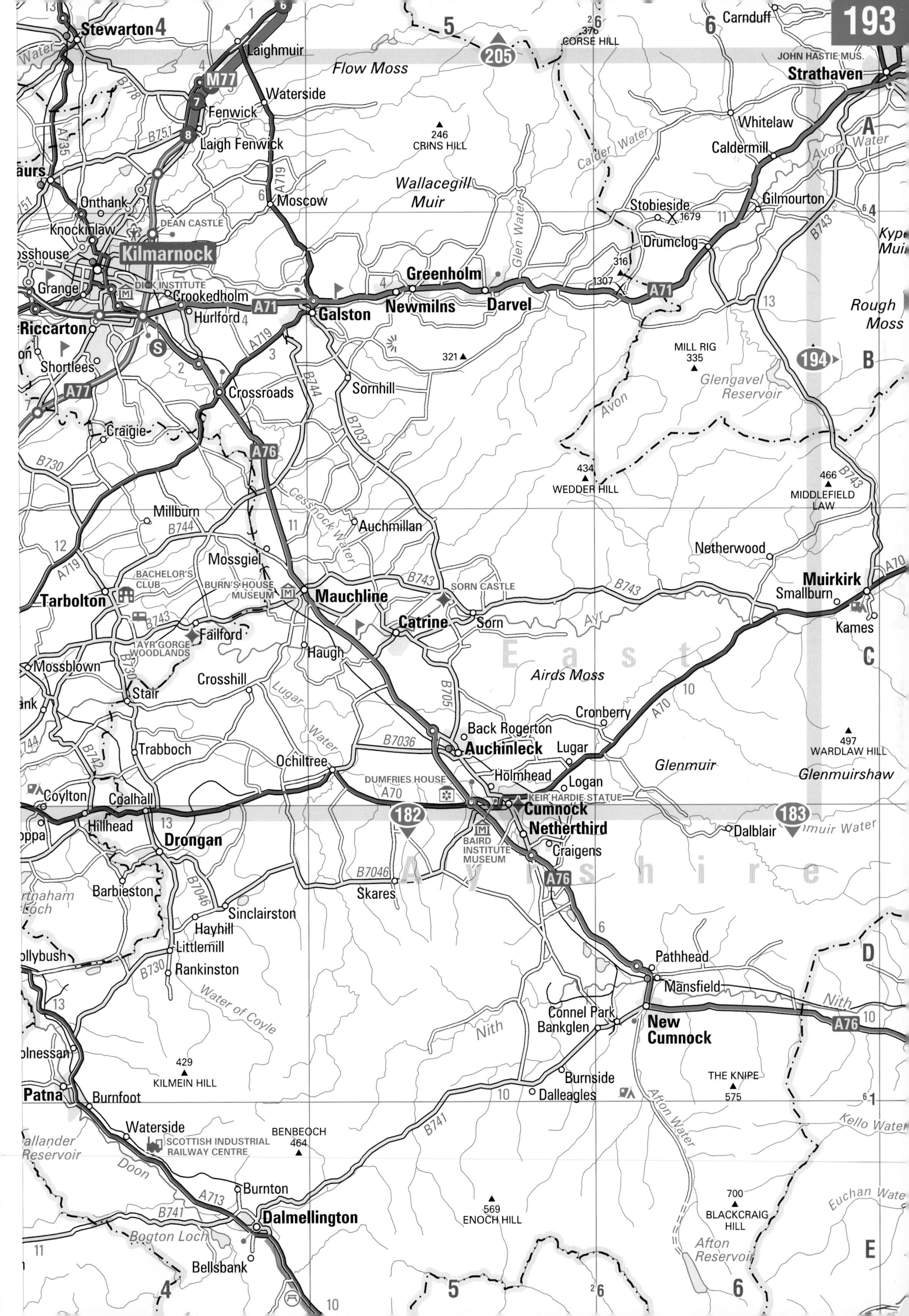
Stewarton
Laighmuir
Flow Moss
CORSE HILL
Carnduff
JOHN HASTIE MUS.
Strathaven
Waterside
Fenwick
Laigh Fenwick
CRINS HILL
Whitelaw
Caldermill
Wallacegill Muir
Moscow
Onthank
Knockinlaw
DEAN CASTLE
Kilmarnock
Stobieside
Gilmourton
Drumclog
Greenholm
Darvel
Newmilns
Galston
DICK INSTITUTE
Grange
Crookedholm
Hurlford
Riccarton
Shortlees
MILL RIG
Glengavel Reservoir
Rough Moss
Sornhill
Crossroads
Craigie
WEDDER HILL
MIDDLEFIELD LAW
Millburn
Auchmillan
Cessnock Water
Netherwood
Mossgiel
BACHELOR'S CLUB
BURN'S HOUSE MUSEUM
Tarbolton
Mauchline
SORN CASTLE
Muirkirk
Smallburn
Kames
Catrine
Sorn
Failford
AYR GORGE WOODLANDS
Mossblown
Haugh
East Ayrshire
Airds Moss
Crosshill
Stair
Cronberry
Back Rogerton
Auchinleck
Lugar
WARDLAW HILL
Trabboch
Ochiltree
Glenmuir
Glenmuirshaw
DUMFRIES HOUSE
Holmhead
Logan
KEIR HARDIE STATUE
Coylton
Coalhall
Cumnock
Hillhead
Drongan
Netherthird
BAIRD INSTITUTE MUSEUM
Craigens
Dalblair
Barbieston
Skares
Sinclairston
Hayhill
Littlemill
Rankinston
Water of Coyle
Pathhead
Mansfield
Connel Park
Bankglen
New Cumnock
Nith
KILMEIN HILL
Patna
Burnfoot
Burnside
Dalleagles
THE KNIPE
Afton Water
Waterside
SCOTTISH INDUSTRIAL RAILWAY CENTRE
BENBEOCH
Doon
Burnton
Dalmellington
Bogton Loch
Bellsbank
ENOCH HILL
BLACKCRAIG HILL
Afton Reservoir
Euchan Water
Kello Water

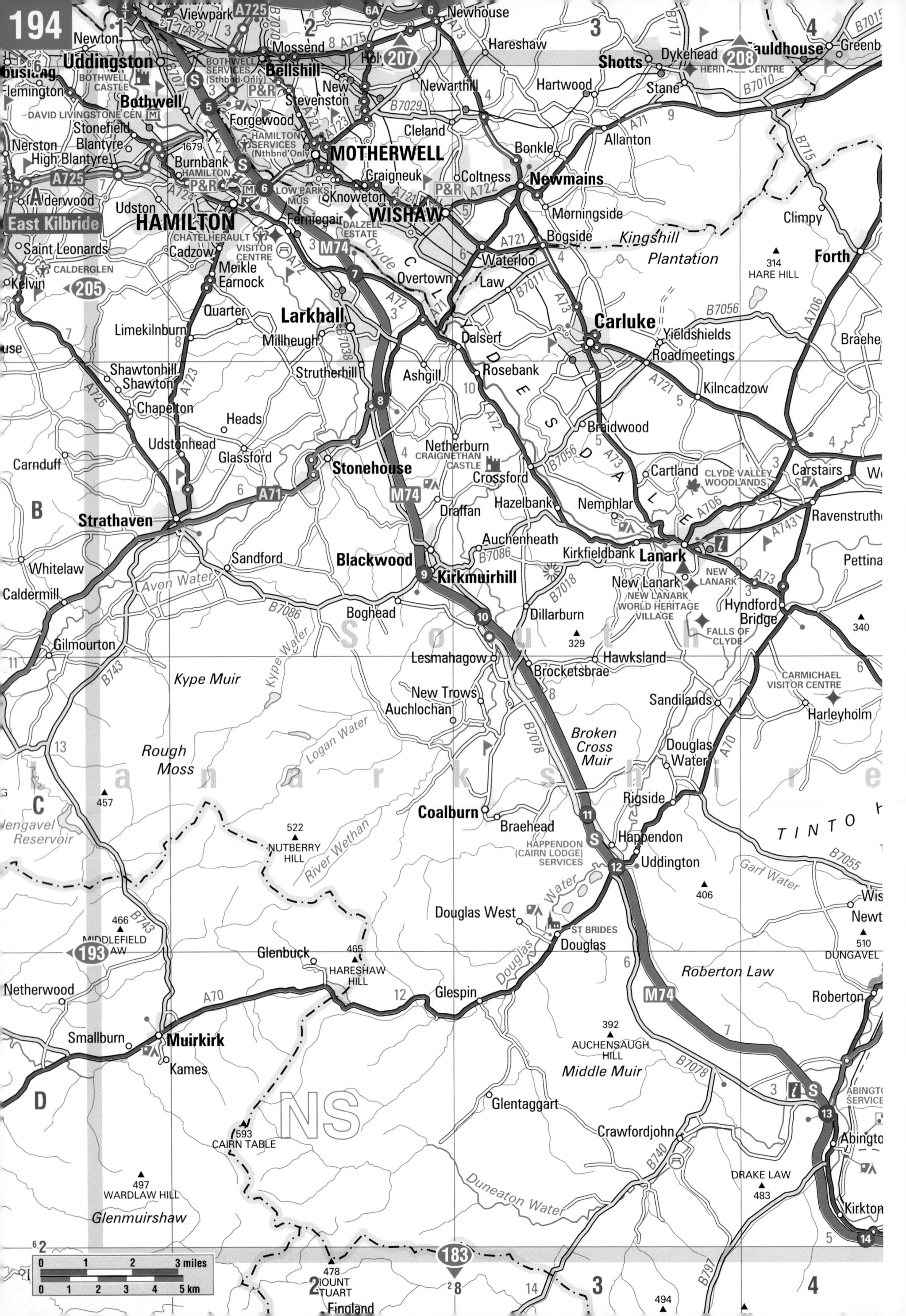
194
Uddingston
Bothwell
Bellshill
Mossend
Newhouse
Hareshaw
Shotts
Dykehead
Fauldhouse
Stane
Hartwood
Newarthill
Stevenston
Forgewood
Cleland
Allanton
Bonkle
MOTHERWELL
Craigneuk
Coltness
Newmains
Stonefield
Blantyre
High Blantyre
Burnbank
Nerston
Flemington
Newton
Viewpark
BOTHWELL CASTLE
DAVID LIVINGSTONE CEN
BOTHWELL SERVICES (Sthbnd Only)
HAMILTON SERVICES (Nthbnd Only)
Alderwood
Udston
HAMILTON
East Kilbride
Knoweton
WISHAW
Ferniegair
LOW PARKS MUS
DALZELL ESTATE
CHATELHERAULT
VISITOR CENTRE
Cadzow
Saint Leonards
CALDERGLEN
Kelvin
Meikle Earnock
Morningside
Bogside
Kingshill Plantation
Waterloo
Overtown
Law
Climpy
Forth
314 HARE HILL
Quarter
Larkhall
Millheugh
Limekilnburn
Dalserf
Carluke
Yieldshields
Roadmeetings
Braehead
Shawtonhill
Shawton
Struthernill
Ashgill
Rosebank
Kilncadzow
Chapelton
Heads
Braidwood
Udstonhead
Glassford
Netherburn
CRAIGNETHAN CASTLE
Crossford
Stonehouse
Carnduff
Cartland
CLYDE VALLEY WOODLANDS
Carstairs
Strathaven
Hazelbank
Nemphlar
Draffan
Ravenstruther
Auchenheath
Kirkfieldbank
Lanark
Sandford
Blackwood
Kirkmuirhill
Whitelaw
Pettinain
New Lanark
NEW LANARK WORLD HERITAGE VILLAGE
Caldermill
Avon Water
Boghead
Dillarburn
Hyndford Bridge
FALLS OF CLYDE
Gilmourton
Lesmahagow
Hawksland
Brocketsbrae
Kype Muir
Kype Water
CARMICHAEL VISITOR CENTRE
New Trows
Auchlochan
Sandilands
Harleyholm
Rough Moss
Logan Water
Broken Cross Muir
Douglas Water
South Lanarkshire
Glengavel Reservoir
457
522 NUTBERRY HILL
River Wethan
Coalburn
Braehead
Rigside
TINTO
Happendon
HAPPENDON (CAIRN LODGE) SERVICES
Uddington
Garf Water
406
Douglas West
ST BRIDES
Douglas
466 MIDDLEFIELD LAW
Glenbuck
465 HARESHAW HILL
510 DUNGAVEL
Roberton Law
Netherwood
Glespin
Roberton
Smallburn
Muirkirk
Kames
392 AUCHENSAUGH HILL
Middle Muir
ABINGTON SERVICES
Glentaggart
NS
593 CAIRN TABLE
Crawfordjohn
Abington
Duneaton Water
497 WARDLAW HILL
DRAKE LAW 483
Glenmuirshaw
Kirkton
478
Fingland
494
0 1 2 3 miles
0 1 2 3 4 5 km

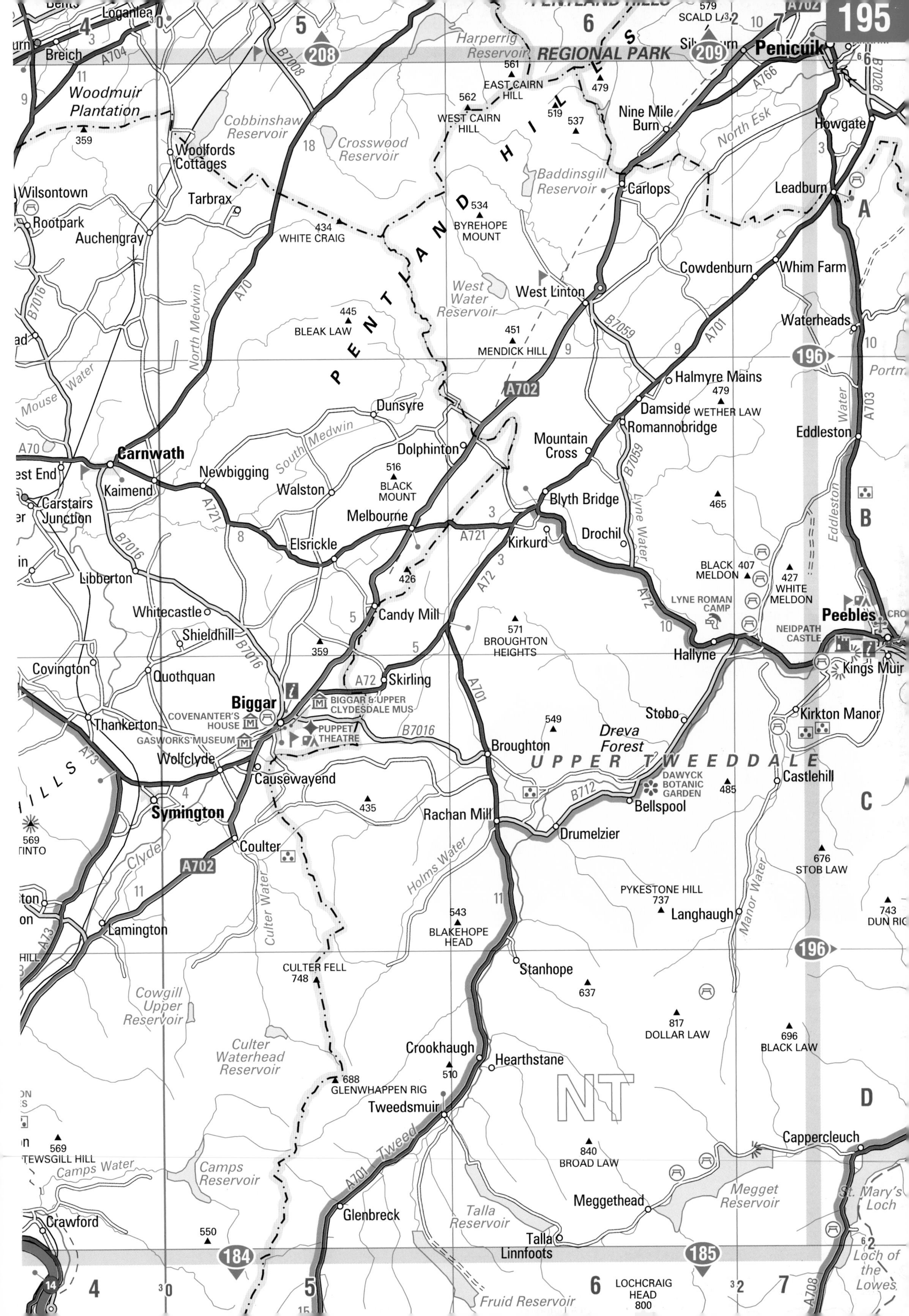

PENTLAND HILLS REGIONAL PARK
Penicuik
Loganlea
Breich
Woodmuir Plantation
Cobbinshaw Reservoir
Crosswood Reservoir
Harperrig Reservoir
EAST CAIRN HILL
WEST CAIRN HILL
SCALD LAW
Nine Mile Burn
Howgate
North Esk
Woolfords Cottages
Wilsontown
Tarbrax
Rootpark
Auchengray
WHITE CRAIG
BYREHOPE MOUNT
Baddinsgill Reservoir
Carlops
Leadburn
Cowdenburn
Whim Farm
West Water Reservoir
West Linton
BLEAK LAW
MENDICK HILL
Waterheads
North Medwin
Mouse Water
Halmyre Mains
WETHER LAW
Damside
Romannobridge
Dunsyre
South Medwin
Dolphinton
Mountain Cross
Eddleston
Carnwath
Kaimend
Newbigging
Walston
BLACK MOUNT
Blyth Bridge
Carstairs Junction
Melbourne
Elsrickle
Kirkurd
Drochil
Lyne Water
Libberton
BLACK MELDON
WHITE MELDON
LYNE ROMAN CAMP
Whitecastle
Candy Mill
BROUGHTON HEIGHTS
Peebles
NEIDPATH CASTLE
Shieldhill
Hallyne
Kings Muir
Covington
Quothquan
Skirling
Biggar
BIGGAR & UPPER CLYDESDALE MUS
COVENANTER'S HOUSE
Thankerton
GASWORKS MUSEUM
PUPPET THEATRE
Stobo
Kirkton Manor
Broughton
Dreva Forest
UPPER TWEEDDALE
Wolfclyde
Causewayend
DAWYCK BOTANIC GARDEN
Castlehill
Symington
Bellspool
Rachan Mill
Drumelzier
TINTO
Coulter
Clyde
Holms Water
STOB LAW
PYKESTONE HILL
Langhaugh
Manor Water
Lamington
Culter Water
BLAKEHOPE HEAD
DUN RIG
CULTER FELL
Stanhope
Cowgill Upper Reservoir
DOLLAR LAW
BLACK LAW
Crookhaugh
Hearthstane
Culter Waterhead Reservoir
GLENWHAPPEN RIG
Tweedsmuir
NT
Cappercleuch
TEWSGILL HILL
Camps Water
Camps Reservoir
BROAD LAW
Tweed
Meggethead
Megget Reservoir
St. Mary's Loch
Crawford
Glenbreck
Talla Reservoir
Talla Linnfoots
Loch of the Lowes
LOCHCRAIG HEAD
Fruid Reservoir
A70 A702 A721 A72 A701 A703 A766 A704 A73 A708 B7008 B7026 B7016 B7059 B712
208 209 196 184 185

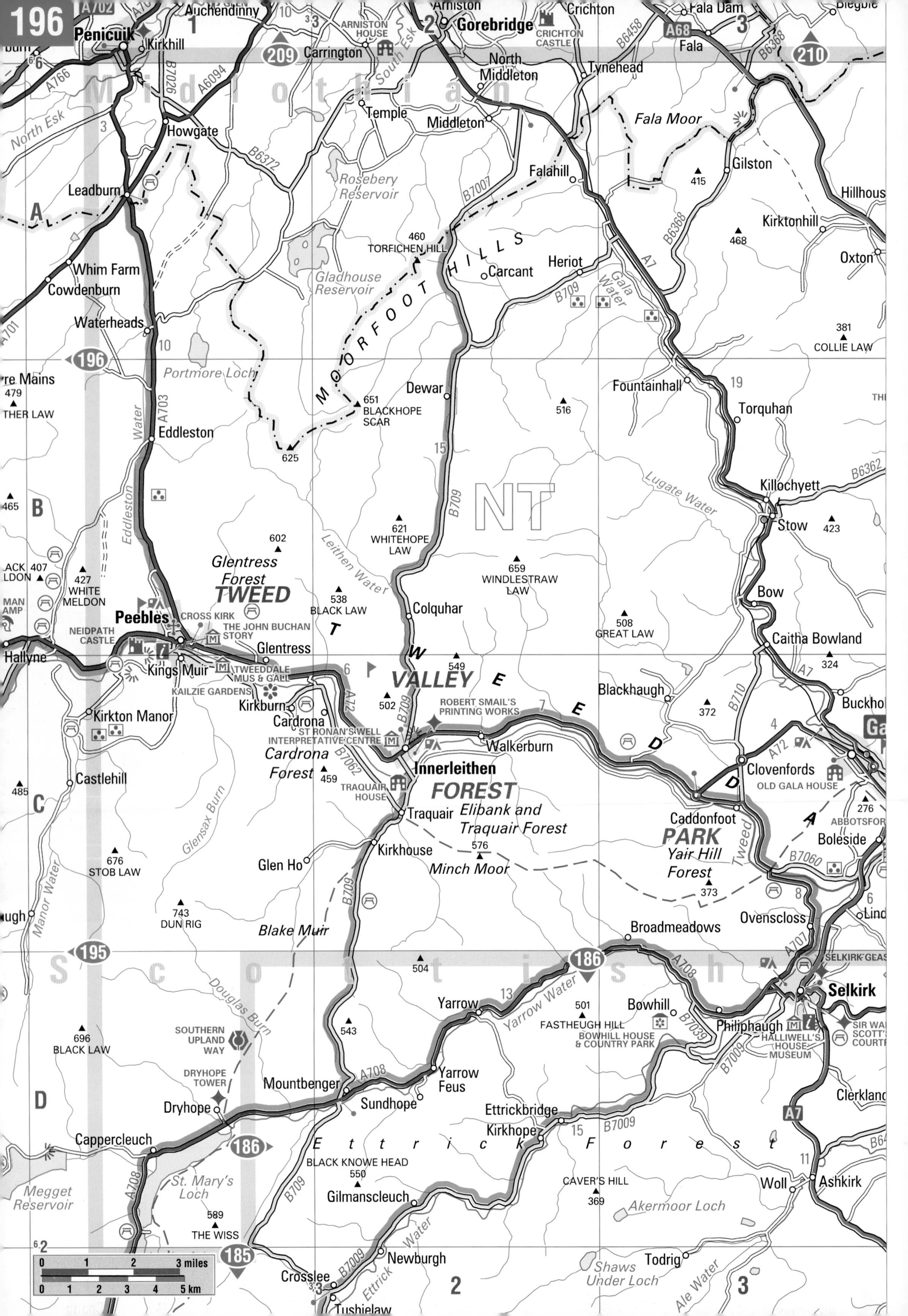
Penicuik
Auchendinny
Kirkhill
Arniston
Gorebridge
Crichton
Fala Dam
Fala
ARNISTON HOUSE
CRICHTON CASTLE
Carrington
North Middleton
Tynehead
Midlothian
Temple
Middleton
Howgate
Fala Moor
North Esk
South Esk
Gilston
Falahill
Leadburn
Rosebery Reservoir
Hillhouse
Kirktonhill
TORFICHEN HILL
MOORFOOT HILLS
Carcant
Heriot
Oxton
Whim Farm
Cowdenburn
Gladhouse Reservoir
Gala Water
Waterheads
COLLIE LAW
Portmore Loch
Dewar
Fountainhall
Torquhan
BLACKHOPE SCAR
Eddleston
Eddleston Water
Killochyett
Lugate Water
NT
Stow
WHITEHOPE LAW
Glentress Forest
TWEED
Leithen Water
WINDLESTRAW LAW
WHITE MELDON
Bow
Colquhar
Peebles
CROSS KIRK
THE JOHN BUCHAN STORY
BLACK LAW
GREAT LAW
NEIDPATH CASTLE
Glentress
Caitha Bowland
Hallyne
Kings Muir
TWEEDDALE MUS & GALL
VALLEY
KAILZIE GARDENS
Blackhaugh
Kirkburn
Cardrona
ROBERT SMAIL'S PRINTING WORKS
Kirkton Manor
ST RONAN'S WELL INTERPRETATIVE CENTRE
Walkerburn
Clovenfords
OLD GALA HOUSE
Cardrona Forest
Innerleithen
Castlehill
TRAQUAIR HOUSE
FOREST
Traquair
Elibank and Traquair Forest
Caddonfoot
PARK
Boleside
Glensax Burn
Kirkhouse
STOB LAW
Glen Ho
Minch Moor
Yair Hill Forest
Manor Water
DUN RIG
Blake Muir
Broadmeadows
Ovenscloss
SELKIRK GLASS
Scottish
Douglas Burn
Yarrow
Yarrow Water
FASTHEUGH HILL
Bowhill
Selkirk
BOWHILL HOUSE & COUNTRY PARK
Philiphaugh
HALLIWELL'S HOUSE MUSEUM
SIR WALTER SCOTT'S COURTROOM
SOUTHERN UPLAND WAY
BLACK LAW
DRYHOPE TOWER
Mountbenger
Yarrow Feus
Sundhope
Dryhope
Ettrickbridge
Kirkhope
Clerklands
Cappercleuch
Ettrick Forest
BLACK KNOWE HEAD
Ashkirk
Woll
CAVER'S HILL
Megget Reservoir
St. Mary's Loch
Gilmanscleuch
Akermoor Loch
THE WISS
Newburgh
Todrig
Crosslee
Shaws Under Loch
Ale Water
Ettrick Water
Tushielaw
miles
km

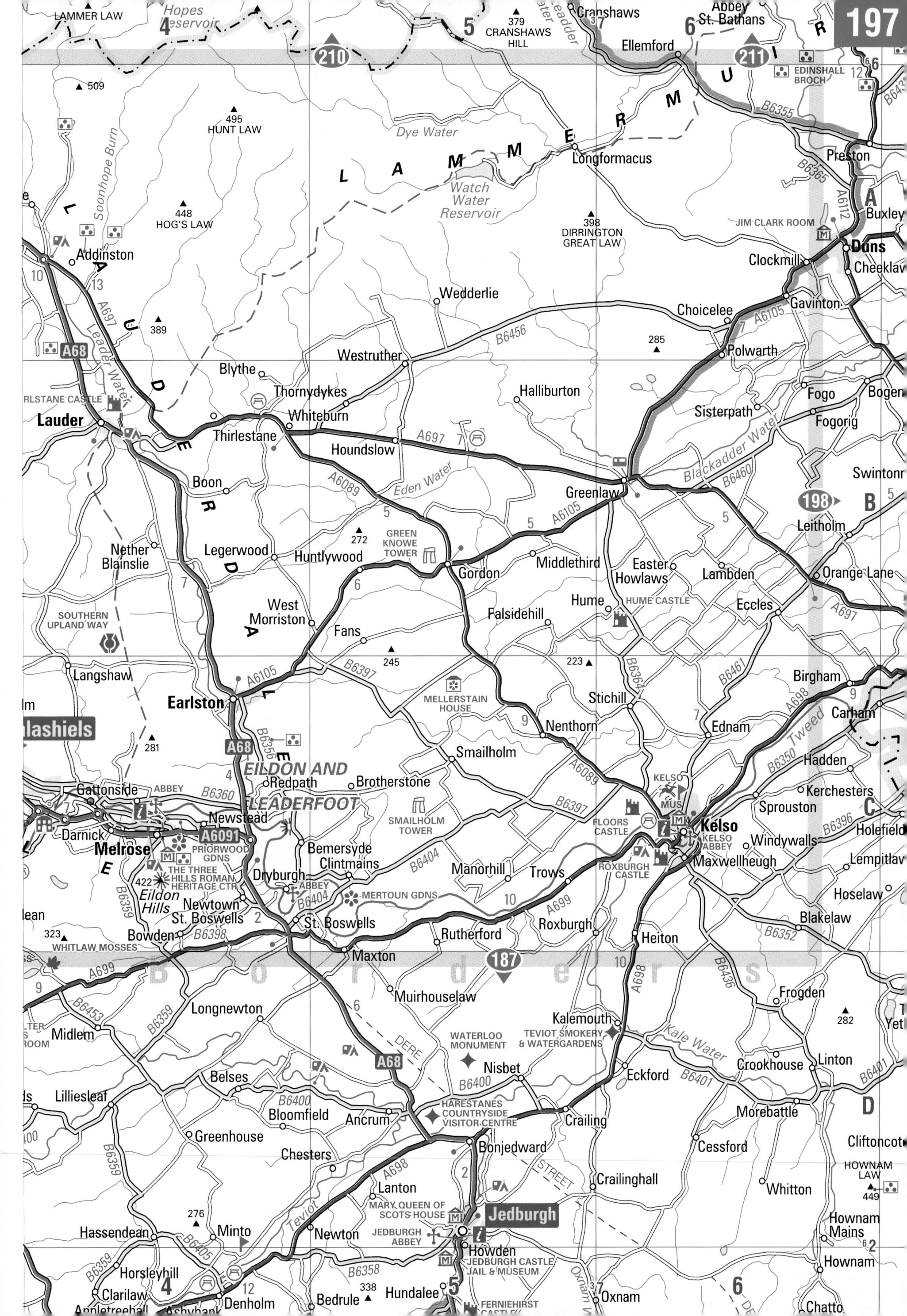
LAMMER LAW
Hopes Reservoir
CRANSHAWS HILL
Cranshaws
Abbey St. Bathans
Ellemford
EDINSHALL BROCH
LAMMERMUIR
HUNT LAW
Dye Water
Longformacus
Preston
Watch Water Reservoir
HOG'S LAW
DIRRINGTON GREAT LAW
JIM CLARK ROOM
Buxley
Duns
Addinston
Clockmill
Cheeklaw
Wedderlie
Choicelee
Gavinton
Westruther
Polwarth
Blythe
Thornydykes
Halliburton
Fogo
Bogend
THIRLESTANE CASTLE
Lauder
Whiteburn
Sisterpath
Fogorig
Thirlestane
Houndslow
Eden Water
Blackadder Water
Swinton
Boon
Greenlaw
LAUDERDALE
Leithholm
Nether Blainslie
Legerwood
Huntlywood
GREEN KNOWE TOWER
Gordon
Middlethird
Easter Howlaws
Lambden
Orange Lane
West Morriston
Hume
HUME CASTLE
Eccles
SOUTHERN UPLAND WAY
Fans
Falsidehill
Langshaw
Birgham
Earlston
MELLERSTAIN HOUSE
Stichill
Carham
Galashiels
Nenthorn
Ednam
Tweed
Smailholm
Hadden
EILDON AND LEADERFOOT
Redpath
Brotherstone
KELSO
Kerchesters
Gattonside
ABBEY
Sprouston
Newstead
SMAILHOLM TOWER
FLOORS CASTLE
Kelso
Holefield
Darnick
Melrose
PRIORWOOD GDNS
Bemersyde
KELSO ABBEY
Windywalls
Lempitlaw
Clintmains
Maxwellheugh
THE THREE HILLS ROMAN HERITAGE CTR
Dryburgh
Manorhill
Trows
ROXBURGH CASTLE
Eildon Hills
ABBEY
MERTOUN GDNS
Hoselaw
Newtown St. Boswells
St. Boswells
Roxburgh
Blakelaw
Bowden
Rutherford
Heiton
WHITLAW MOSSES
Maxton
Borders
Frogden
Muirhouselaw
Longnewton
Kalemouth
Midlem
WATERLOO MONUMENT
TEVIOT SMOKERY & WATERGARDENS
Kale Water
Nisbet
Crookhouse
Linton
Eckford
DERE STREET
Belses
Lilliesleaf
Bloomfield
Ancrum
HARESTANES COUNTRYSIDE VISITOR CENTRE
Crailing
Morebattle
Greenhouse
Bonjedward
Cessford
Cliftoncote
Chesters
Crailinghall
HOWNAM LAW
Lanton
Whitton
MARY QUEEN OF SCOTS HOUSE
Jedburgh
Hassendean
Minto
Newton
JEDBURGH ABBEY
Hownam Mains
Teviot
Howden
Horsleyhill
JEDBURGH CASTLE JAIL & MUSEUM
Hownam
Oxnam Water
Clarilaw
Denholm
Bedrule
Hundalee
FERNIEHIRST CASTLE
Oxnam
Chatto
A68
A697
A6105
A6089
A6091
A699
A698
A6112
B6456
B6355
B6365
B6460
B6364
B6461
B6397
B6356
B6360
B6404
B6359
B6398
B6453
B6400
B6401
B6436
B6352
B6396
B6350
B6405
B6358
210
211
198
187

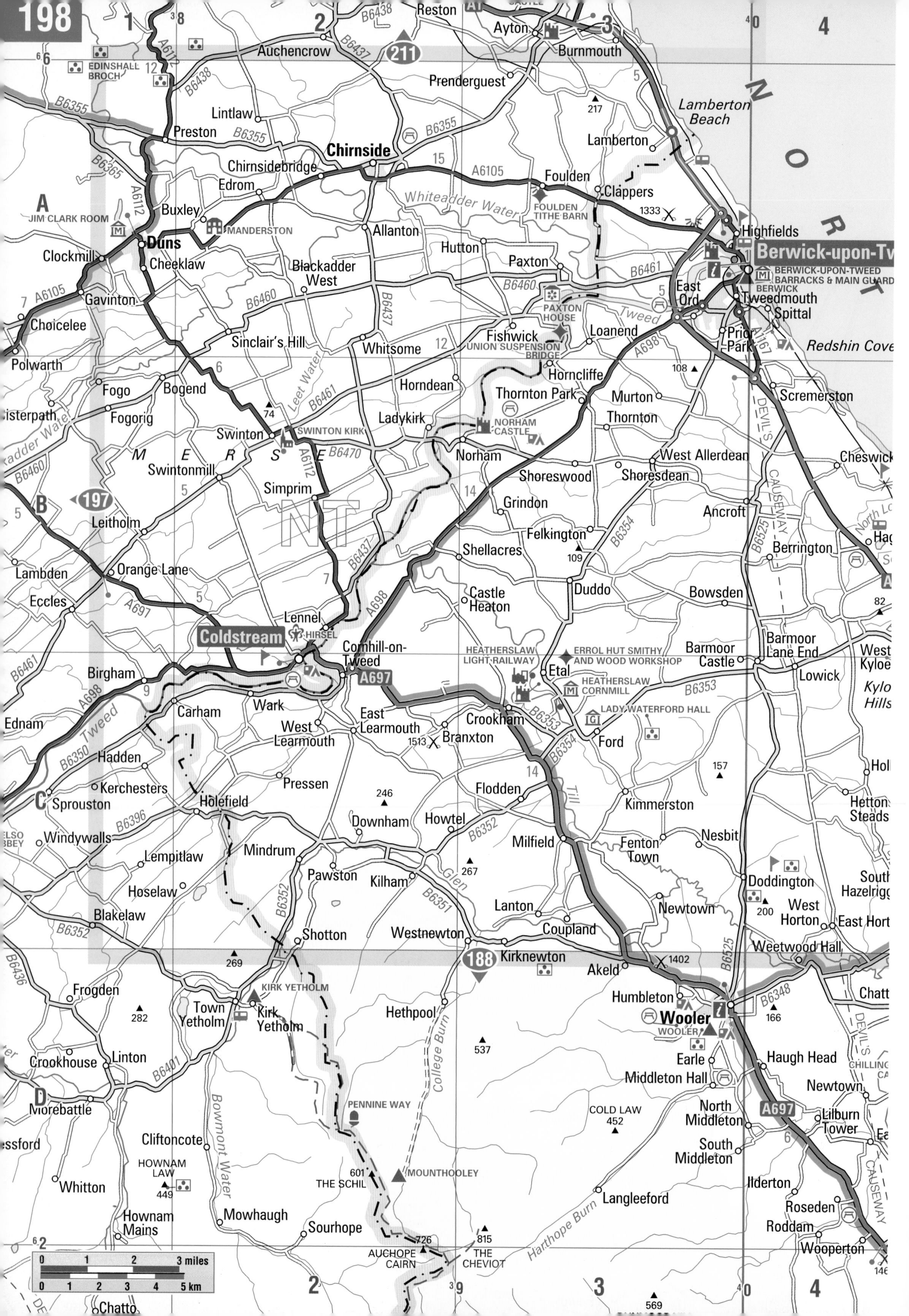

1
2
3
4
A
B
C
D
211
197
188
Reston
Ayton
Burnmouth
Auchencrow
EDINSHALL BROCH
Prenderguest
Lamberton Beach
Lintlaw
Preston
Chirnside
Lamberton
Chirnsidebridge
Edrom
Foulden
Clappers
Whiteadder Water
FOULDEN TITHE BARN
JIM CLARK ROOM
Buxley
MANDERSTON
Allanton
Highfields
Berwick-upon-Tw
Clockmill
Duns
Cheeklaw
Hutton
Paxton
Blackadder West
BERWICK-UPON-TWEED BARRACKS & MAIN GUARD
BERWICK
East Ord
Tweedmouth
Gavinton
PAXTON HOUSE
Tweed
Spittal
Choicelee
Sinclair's Hill
Fishwick
Loanend
Prior Park
Polwarth
Whitsome
UNION SUSPENSION BRIDGE
Redshin Cove
Horncliffe
Fogo
Bogend
Leet Water
Horndean
Thornton Park
Murton
Scremerston
Fogorig
Ladykirk
NORHAM CASTLE
Thornton
Swinton
SWINTON KIRK
MERSE
Norham
West Allerdean
Cheswick
Swintonmill
Shoreswood
Shoresdean
Simprim
NT
Grindon
Ancroft
Leitholm
Felkington
Shellacres
Berrington
Lambden
Orange Lane
Duddo
Eccles
Castle Heaton
Bowsden
Lennel
Coldstream
HIRSEL
Cornhill-on-Tweed
HEATHERSLAW LIGHT RAILWAY
ERROL HUT SMITHY AND WOOD WORKSHOP
Barmoor Castle
Barmoor Lane End
West Kyloe
Lowick
Kyloe Hills
Birgham
Etal
HEATHERSLAW CORNMILL
Carham
Wark
Crookham
LADY WATERFORD HALL
Ednam
East Learmouth
West Learmouth
Branxton
Ford
Hadden
Kerchesters
Pressen
Flodden
Sprouston
Holefield
Kimmerston
Hetton Steads
Windywalls
Downham
Howtel
Milfield
Fenton Town
Nesbit
Mindrum
Lempitlaw
Pawston
Kilham
Glen
Doddington
South Hazelrigg
Hoselaw
Lanton
Newtown
West Horton
East Hort
Blakelaw
Shotton
Westnewton
Coupland
Weetwood Hall
Kirknewton
Akeld
Frogden
KIRK YETHOLM
Humbleton
Chatt
Town Yetholm
Kirk Yetholm
Hethpool
Wooler
WOOLER
College Burn
Linton
Crookhouse
Earle
Haugh Head
CHILLING
Middleton Hall
Newtown
Bowmont Water
PENNINE WAY
North Middleton
Morebattle
COLD LAW
Lilburn Tower
Cliftoncote
South Middleton
essford
HOWNAM LAW
THE SCHIL
MOUNTHOOLEY
Langleeford
Ilderton
Whitton
Mowhaugh
Harthope Burn
Roseden
Hownam Mains
Sourhope
Roddam
AUCHOPE CAIRN
THE CHEVIOT
Wooperton
Chatto
DEVIL'S CAUSEWAY
NORTH
Till
A1
A6112
A6105
A698
A697
A6112
A1167
B6438
B6437
B6355
B6365
B6460
B6461
B6437
B6470
B6354
B6525
B6353
B6350
B6396
B6352
B6351
B6401
B6436
B6348
0 1 2 3 miles
0 1 2 3 4 5 km

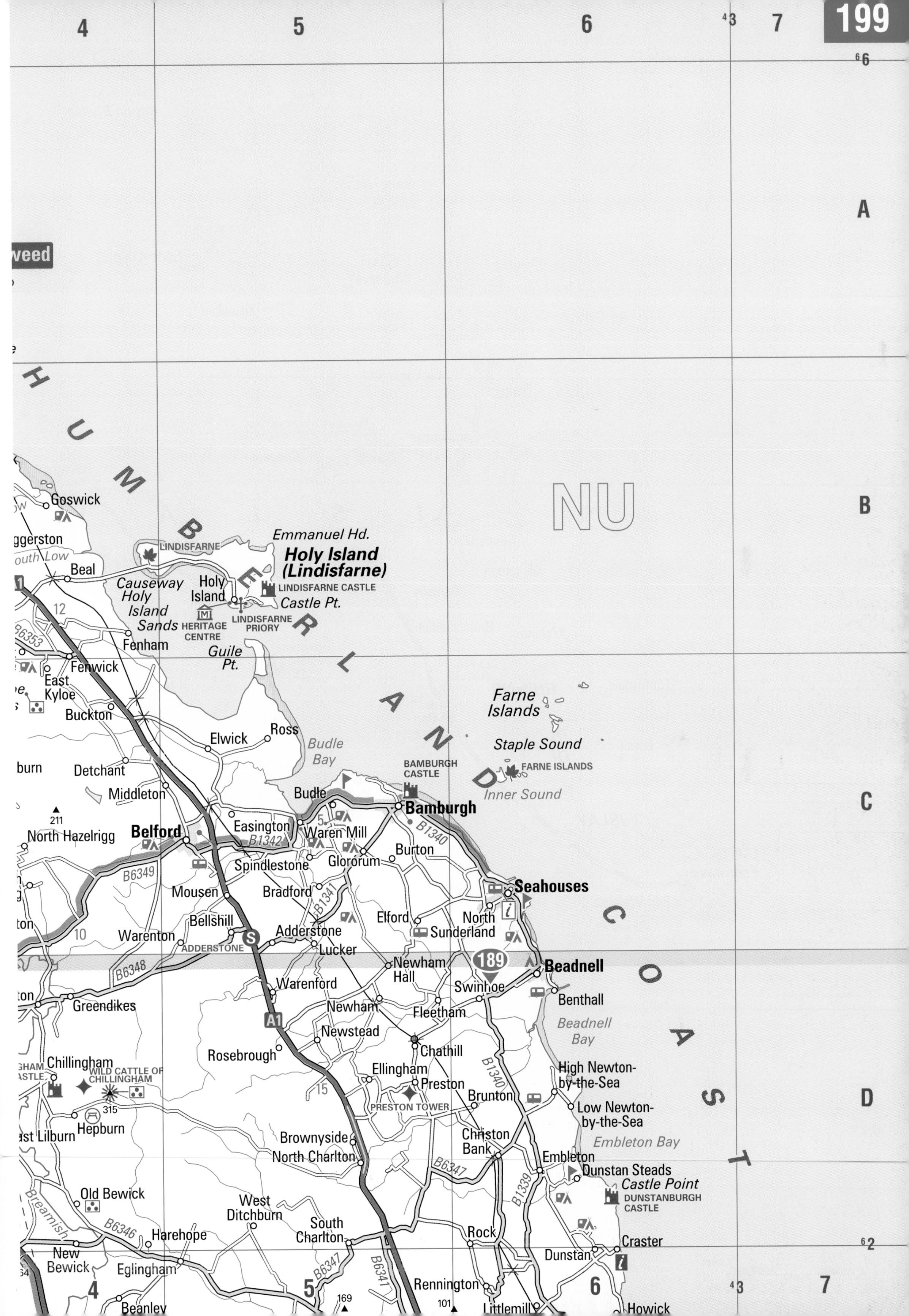

4
5
6
7
A
B
C
D
NU
NORTHUMBERLAND COAST
Goswick
Beal
Holy Island (Lindisfarne)
Emmanuel Hd.
LINDISFARNE CASTLE
Castle Pt.
LINDISFARNE PRIORY
HERITAGE CENTRE
Causeway
Holy Island Sands
Guile Pt.
Fenham
Fenwick
East Kyloe
Buckton
Elwick
Ross
Budle Bay
Detchant
Middleton
Belford
North Hazelrigg
Easington
Budle
BAMBURGH CASTLE
Bamburgh
Waren Mill
Spindlestone
Glororum
Burton
Mousen
Bradford
Bellshill
Warenton
ADDERSTONE
Adderstone
Lucker
Elford
North Sunderland
Seahouses
Farne Islands
Staple Sound
FARNE ISLANDS
Inner Sound
Beadnell
Benthall
Beadnell Bay
Newham Hall
Swinhoe
Warenford
Newham
Fleetham
Newstead
Chathill
Rosebrough
Greendikes
Chillingham
WILD CATTLE OF CHILLINGHAM
Hepburn
Ellingham
Preston
PRESTON TOWER
Brunton
High Newton-by-the-Sea
Low Newton-by-the-Sea
Embleton Bay
Christon Bank
Brownyside
North Charlton
Embleton
Dunstan Steads
Castle Point
DUNSTANBURGH CASTLE
Old Bewick
West Ditchburn
South Charlton
Harehope
New Bewick
Eglingham
Rock
Craster
Dunstan
Rennington
Littlemill
Howick
Beanley
A1
B1340
B1342
B1341
B6349
B6348
B6353
B1339
B6347
B6346
B6341
189
211
315
169
101

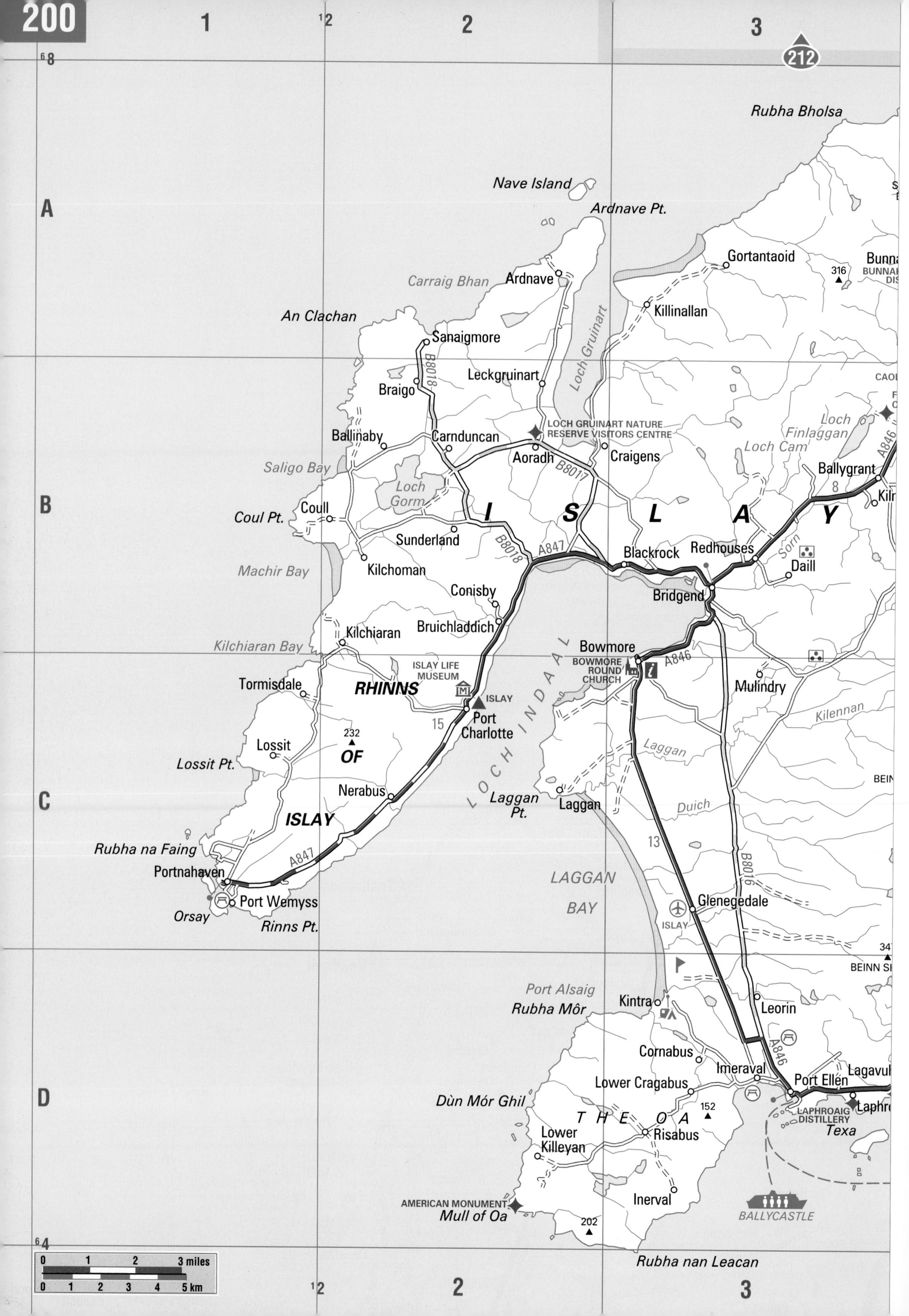

Rubha Bholsa

Nave Island

Ardnave Pt.

Carraig Bhan

Gortantaoid

Bunn

316

BUNNA
DIS

An Clachan

Ardnave

Killinallan

Sanaigmore

B8018

Loch Gruinart

CAO

Leckgruinart

Braigo

LOCH GRUINART NATURE
RESERVE VISITORS CENTRE

Loch
Finlaggan

Loch Cam

Carnduncan

Ballinaby

Aoradh

B8017

Craigens

Ballygrant

Saligo Bay

I   S   L   A   Y

Loch
Gorm

Coul Pt.

Coull

B8018

A847

Blackrock

Redhouses

Sorn

8

Kilr

Sunderland

Daill

Machir Bay

Kilchoman

Bridgend

Conisby

Kilchiaran

Kilchiaran Bay

Bruichladdich

Bowmore

BOWMORE
ROUND
CHURCH

A846

ISLAY LIFE
MUSEUM

ISLAY

Mulindry

Tormisdale

RHINNS

Port
Charlotte

Kilennan

232

OF

15

Lossit

Laggan
Pt.

Laggan

Duich

LOCH INDAAL

Lossit Pt.

Nerabus

13

B8016

Rubha na Faing

ISLAY

BEIN

Portnahaven

A847

LAGGAN

Glenegedale

Port Wemyss

BAY

ISLAY

Orsay

Rinns Pt.

341

BEINN SI

Port Alsaig
Rubha Môr

Kintra

Leorin

A846

Dùn Mór Ghil

Cornabus

Imeraval

Lagavul

Lower Cragabus

Port Ellen

Lower
Killeyan

152

Risabus

T H E   O A

LAPHROAIG
DISTILLERY

Laphro

Texa

AMERICAN MONUMENT
Mull of Oa

Inerval

BALLYCASTLE

202

Rubha nan Leacan

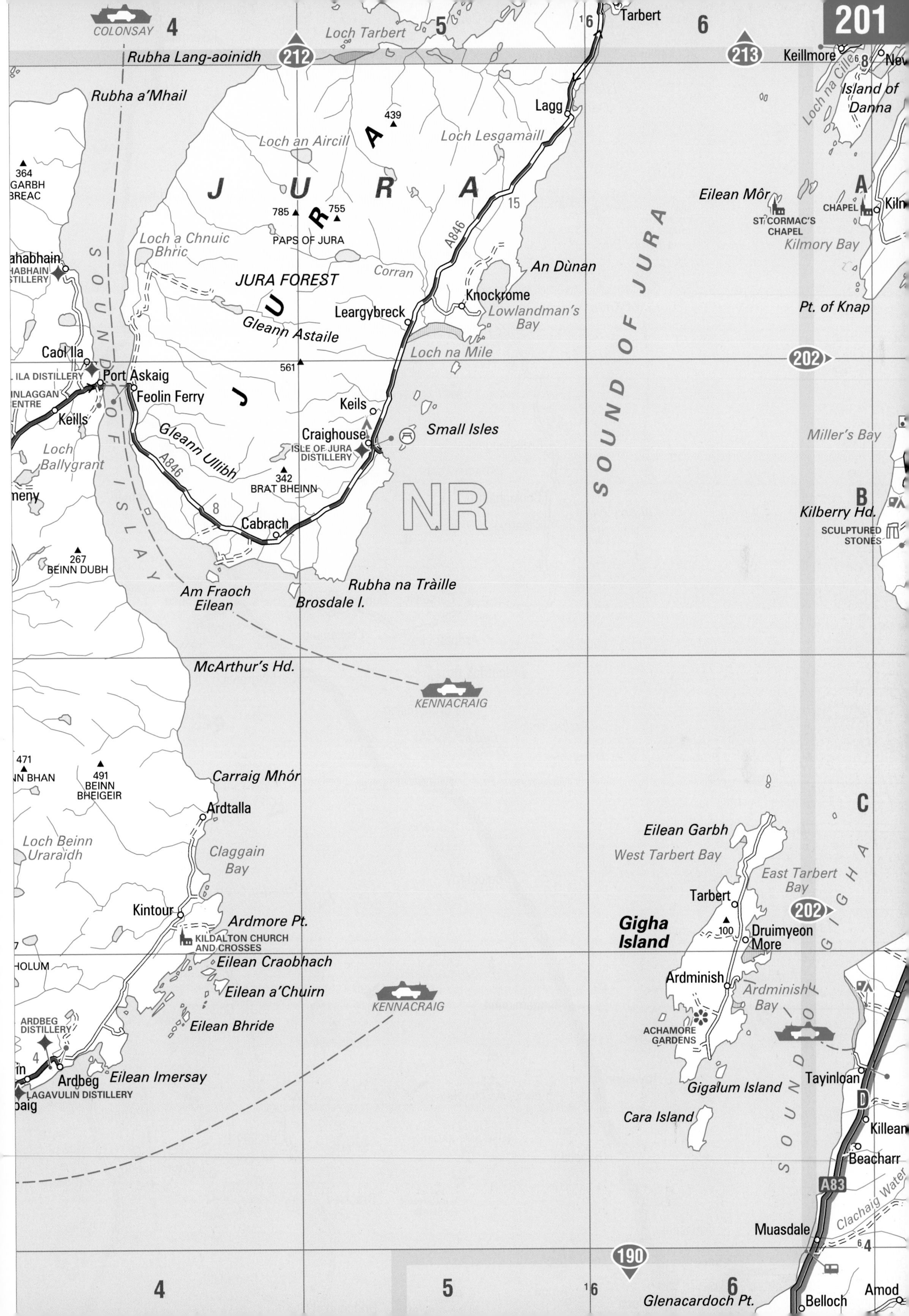
COLONSAY
4
5
6
Loch Tarbert
Tarbert
212
213
Rubha Lang-aoinidh
Keillmore
Rubha a'Mhail
Island of Danna
Loch na Cille
Lagg
439
Loch an Aircill
Loch Lesgamaill
364
GARBH
BREAC
JURA
785
755
PAPS OF JURA
Eilean Môr
CHAPEL
ST CORMAC'S CHAPEL
Kilmory Bay
A
Loch a Chnuic Bhric
A846
15
An Dùnan
JURA FOREST
Corran
Knockrome
Lowlandman's Bay
Leargybreck
Gleann Astaile
Pt. of Knap
SOUND OF JURA
Caol Ila
Loch na Mile
561
202
ILA DISTILLERY
Port Askaig
Feolin Ferry
Keils
Keills
Small Isles
Craighouse
ISLE OF JURA DISTILLERY
Loch Ballygrant
Gleann Ullibh
Miller's Bay
342
BRAT BHEINN
NR
SOUND OF ISLAY
8
Cabrach
B
Kilberry Hd.
SCULPTURED STONES
267
BEINN DUBH
Am Fraoch Eilean
Rubha na Tràille
Brosdale I.
McArthur's Hd.
KENNACRAIG
471
491
BEINN BHEIGEIR
Carraig Mhór
Ardtalla
C
Eilean Garbh
West Tarbert Bay
East Tarbert Bay
Loch Beinn Uraraidh
Claggain Bay
Tarbert
Kintour
Ardmore Pt.
Gigha Island
100
Druimyeon More
KILDALTON CHURCH AND CROSSES
Eilean Craobhach
Ardminish
Ardminish Bay
Eilean a'Chuirn
KENNACRAIG
ARDBEG DISTILLERY
Eilean Bhride
ACHAMORE GARDENS
SOUND OF GIGHA
Ardbeg
Eilean Imersay
Tayinloan
LAGAVULIN DISTILLERY
Gigalum Island
D
Killean
Cara Island
Beacharr
A83
Clachaig Water
Muasdale
190
4
5
6
Glenacardoch Pt.
Belloch
Amod

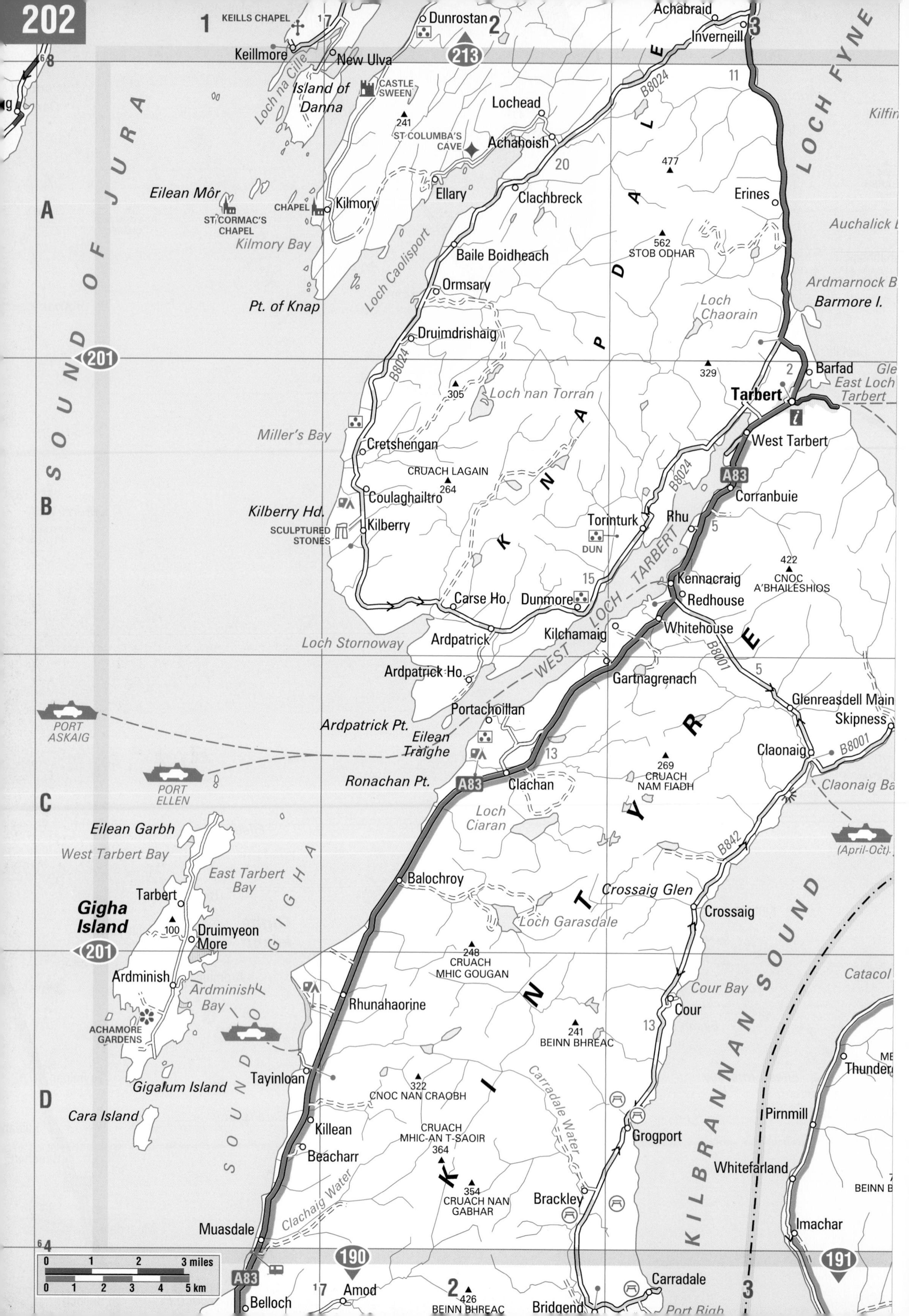

KEILLS CHAPEL
Keillmore
New Ulva
Dunrostan
213
Achabraid
Inverneill
LOCH FYNE

Loch na Cille
Island of Danna
CASTLE SWEEN
Lochead
11
Kilfin

241
ST COLUMBA'S CAVE
Achahoish
477
Erines

Ellary
Clachbreck
20

K
N
A
P
D
A
L
E

St CORMAC'S CHAPEL
CHAPEL
Kilmory
Baile Boidheach
562
STOB ODHAR
Ardmarnock B.
Auchalick

Eilean Môr
Ormsary
Loch Chaorain
Barmore I.

SOUND OF JURA
Kilmory Bay
Pt. of Knap
Loch Caolisport
Druimdrishaig
329
2
Barfad
East Loch Tarbert
Gle

201
305
Loch nan Torran
Tarbert
i
West Tarbert
A83

Miller's Bay
Cretshengan
264
CRUACH LAGAIN
Torinturk
DUN
Rhu
B8024
5
Corranbuie

B
Kilberry Hd.
SCULPTURED STONES
Coulaghailtro
Kilberry
15
Dunmore
LOCH TARBERT
Kennacraig
Redhouse
422
CNOC A'BHAILESHIOS

Carse Ho.
WEST
Whitehouse

Loch Stornoway
Ardpatrick
Kilchamaig
B8001
5

PORT ASKAIG
Ardpatrick Ho.
Gartnagrenach
Glenreasdell Main
Skipness

PORT ELLEN
Ardpatrick Pt.
Eilean Tràighe
Portachoillan
K
I
N
T
Y
R
E
B8001
Claonaig
Claonaig Ba

C
Eilean Garbh
West Tarbert Bay
Ronachan Pt.
A83
Clachan
13
269
CRUACH NAM FIADH
B842
(April-Oct).

East Tarbert Bay
Loch Ciaran

Gigha Island
Tarbert
100
Druimyeon More
201
Balochroy
Loch Garasdale
Crossaig Glen
Crossaig

Ardminish
Ardminish Bay
248
CRUACH MHIC GOUGAN
Cour Bay
Cour
Catacol

ACHAMORE GARDENS
Rhunahaorine
241
BEINN BHREAC
13

D
Cara Island
Gigalum Island
Tayinloan
322
CNOC NAN CRAOBH
Carradale Water
Grogport
Pirnmill
Thunder

SOUND OF GIGHA
Killean
CRUACH MHIC-AN T-SAOIR
364
Whitefarland
BEINN B

Beacharr
354
CRUACH NAN GABHAR
Brackley
Imachar

Muasdale
Clachaig Water
190
191

0 1 2 3 miles
0 1 2 3 4 5 km
A83
Belloch
Amod
BEINN BHREAC
426
Bridgend
Carradale
Port Righ

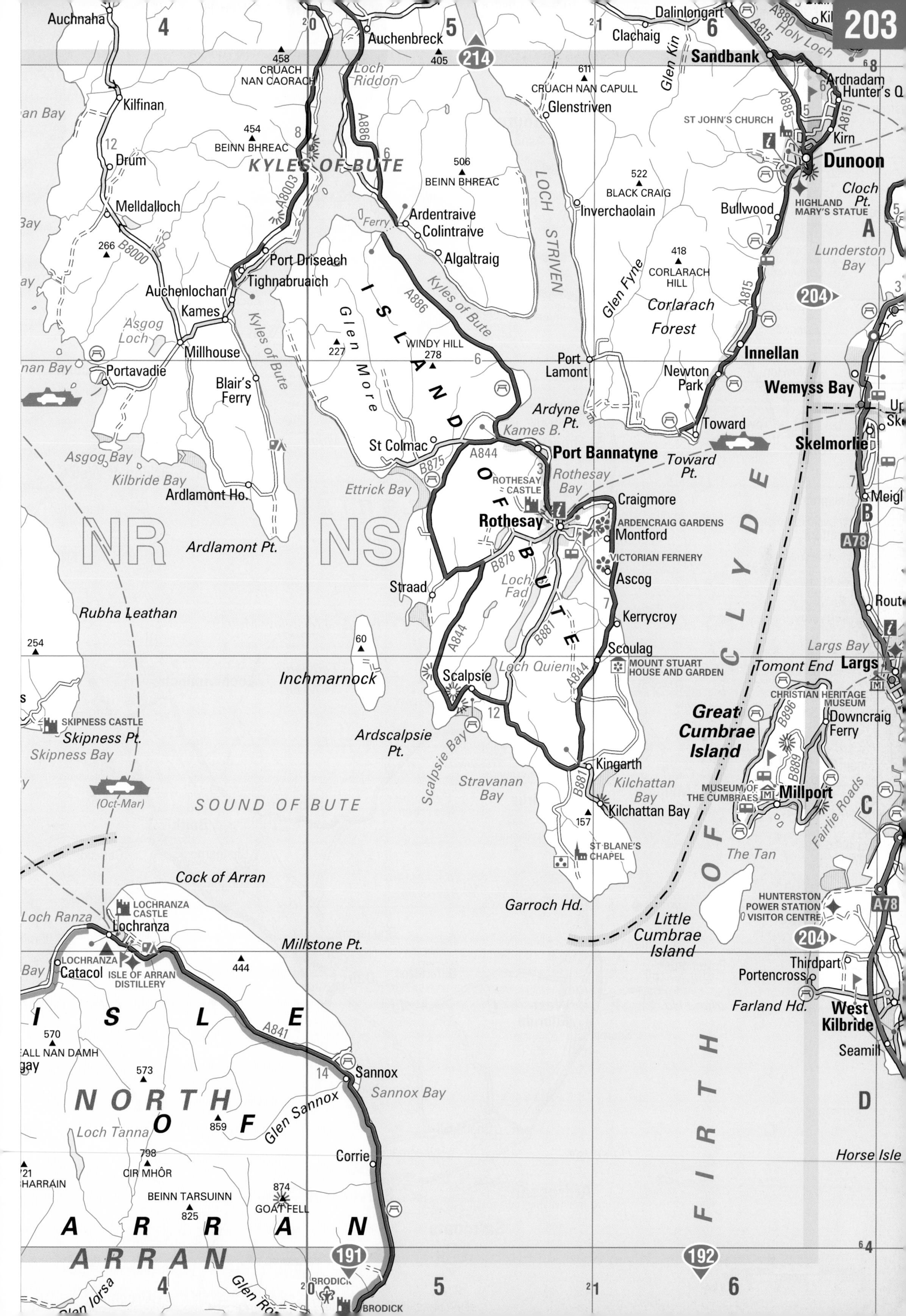

Auchnaha 4 Auchenbreck 5 Dalinlongart 6 Clachaig A880 Holy Loch

458 CRUACH NAN CAORACH
405 214 Sandbank A815

Kilfinan
Loch Riddon
Glen Kin
Ardnadam Hunter's Q.

Drum 12
454 BEINN BHREAC
CRUACH NAN CAPULL
611
A885
Kirn
A815
Dunoon

Melldalloch
KYLES OF BUTE
Glenstriven
ST JOHN'S CHURCH
Cloch Pt.
A

266 B8000
BEINN BHREAC
506
BLACK CRAIG 522
HIGHLAND MARY'S STATUE
Lunderston Bay

Ardentraive
Colintraive
A886
Inverchaolain
Bullwood 7
204

Port Driseach
Algaltraig
418 CORLARACH HILL
Corlarach Forest

Tighnabruaich
Auchenlochan
Kames
Ferry
LOCH STRIVEN
Glen Fyne
Innellan

Millhouse
Asgog Loch
WINDY HILL 278
A886
Port Lamont
Newton Park
A815
Wemyss Bay

Portavadie
Blair's Ferry
227
Glen More
6
Ardyne Pt.
Toward
Up Sk.

Asgog Bay
ISLAND OF BUTE
Kames B.
Toward Pt.
Skelmorlie
A78

Kilbride Bay
St Colmac
A844
Port Bannatyne
Rothesay Bay
B

Ardlamont Ho.
Ettrick Bay
ROTHESAY CASTLE
Rothesay
Craigmore
Meigl

NR NS
Rubha Leathan
Straad
B878
Loch Fad
B875
ARDENCRAIG GARDENS
Montford
VICTORIAN FERNERY
Ascog
A78

254
60
Scalpsie
B881
Kerrycroy
7
Route

Inchmarnock
Ardscalpsie Pt.
Scalpsie Bay
A844
Loch Quien
Scoulag
MOUNT STUART HOUSE AND GARDEN
Largs Bay
Tomont End
Largs

SKIPNESS CASTLE
Skipness Pt.
Skipness Bay
12
Kingarth
CHRISTIAN HERITAGE MUSEUM
Great Cumbrae Island
Downcraig Ferry
B896

SOUND OF BUTE
Stravanan Bay
Kilchattan Bay
Kilchattan Bay
157
MUSEUM OF THE CUMBRAES
Millport
B889

Cock of Arran
ST BLANE'S CHAPEL
Garroch Hd.
The Tan
C

LOCHRANZA CASTLE
Loch Ranza
Lochranza
Millstone Pt.
Little Cumbrae Island
HUNTERSTON POWER STATION VISITOR CENTRE
204
A78

Catacol
LOCHRANZA
ISLE OF ARRAN DISTILLERY
444
Thirdpart
Portencross
Farland Hd.
West Kilbride

ISLE
570 BEALL NAN DAMH
gay
A841
Seamill

NORTH OF
573
798 CIR MHÔR
859
Glen Sannox
14
Sannox
Sannox Bay
D

Loch Tanna
874
BEINN TARSUINN 825
GOAT FELL
Corrie
Horse Isle

'21 HARRAIN
ARRAN
191 BRODICK
192

Glen Iorsa
BRODICK
FIRTH OF CLYDE

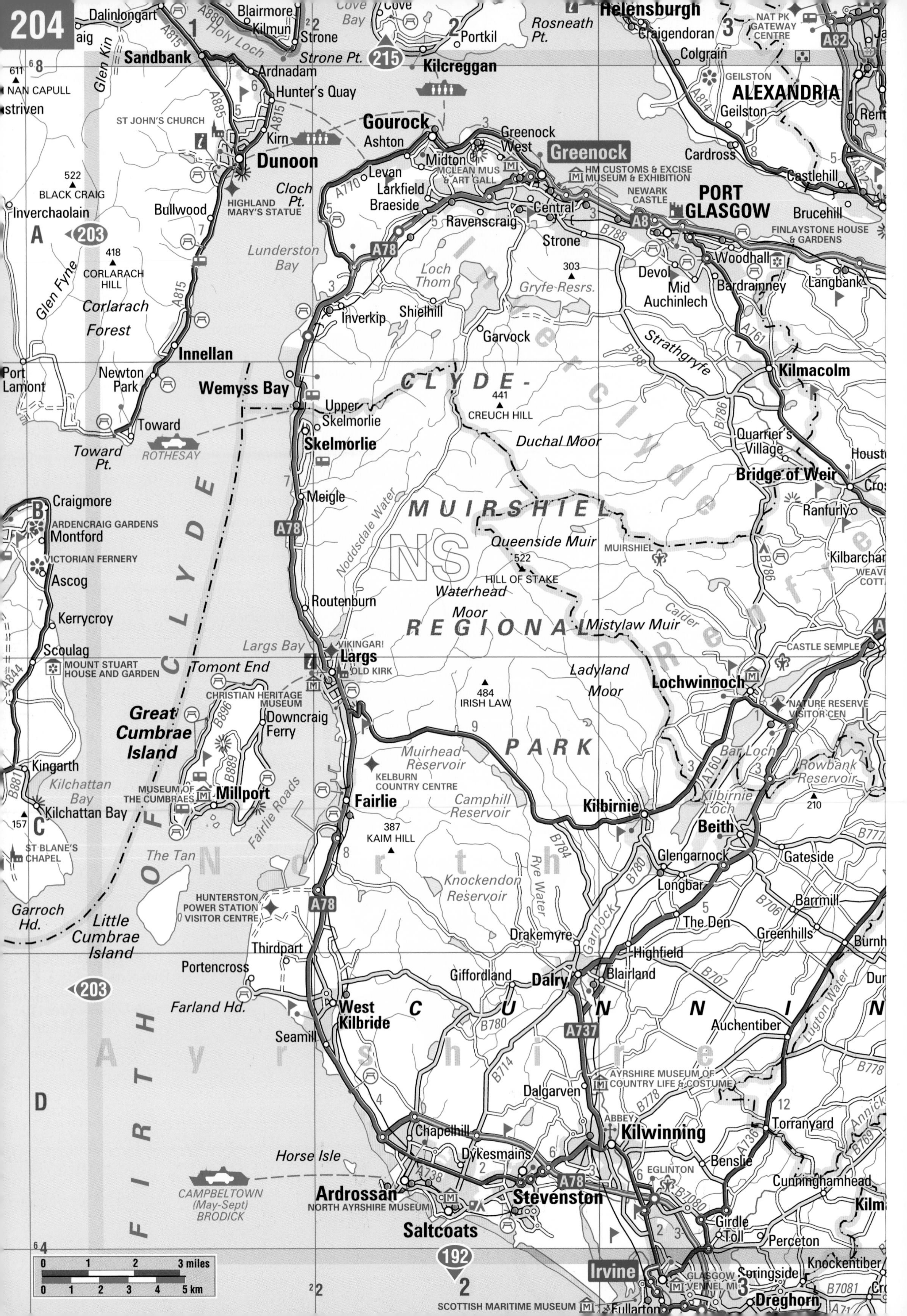

Dalinlongart
Blairmore
Kilmun
Holy Loch
Strone
Cove
Cove Bay
Portkil
Rosneath Pt.
Helensburgh
Craigendoran
NAT PK GATEWAY CENTRE
Sandbank
Glen Kin
Strone Pt.
215
Kilcreggan
Colgrain
NAN CAPULL
Ardnadam
Hunter's Quay
GEILSTON
ALEXANDRIA
Geilston
ST JOHN'S CHURCH
Gourock
Ashton
Greenock West
Greenock
Kirn
Dunoon
Cardross
Midton
MCLEAN MUS & ART GALL
HM CUSTOMS & EXCISE MUSEUM & EXHIBITION
Castlehill
522
BLACK CRAIG
Levan
Larkfield
Braeside
Cloch Pt.
NEWARK CASTLE
PORT GLASGOW
Inverchaolain
Bullwood
HIGHLAND MARY'S STATUE
Central
Ravenscraig
Brucehill
A
203
Strone
FINLAYSTONE HOUSE & GARDENS
Lunderston Bay
418
CORLARACH HILL
Glen Fyne
Loch Thom
303
Gryfe Resrs.
Devol
Mid Auchinlech
Woodhall
Bardrainney
Langbank
Corlarach Forest
Inverkip
Shielhill
Garvock
Strathgryfe
Innellan
Port Lamont
Newton Park
Wemyss Bay
CLYDE-
441
CREUCH HILL
Kilmacolm
Upper Skelmorlie
Toward
Toward Pt.
ROTHESAY
Skelmorlie
Duchal Moor
Quarrier's Village
Houst
Bridge of Weir
Meigle
Craigmore
B
MUIRSHIEL
Ranfurly
ARDENCRAIG GARDENS
Montford
Noddsdale Water
A78
Queenside Muir
MUIRSHIEL
NS
522
HILL OF STAKE
Kilbarchan
VICTORIAN FERNERY
Ascog
Waterhead Moor
Routenburn
REGIONAL
Mistylaw Muir
Calder
Kerrycroy
Scoulag
Largs Bay
VIKINGAR!
Largs
OLD KIRK
CASTLE SEMPLE
MOUNT STUART HOUSE AND GARDEN
Tomont End
Ladyland Moor
Lochwinnoch
484
IRISH LAW
CHRISTIAN HERITAGE MUSEUM
Great Cumbrae Island
Downcraig Ferry
NATURE RESERVE VISITOR CEN
PARK
Muirhead Reservoir
Barr Loch
Rowbank Reservoir
Kingarth
Kilchattan Bay
KELBURN COUNTRY CENTRE
MUSEUM OF THE CUMBRAES
Millport
Fairlie
Camphill Reservoir
Kilbirnie
Kilbirnie Loch
210
Beith
157
C
Kilchattan Bay
Fairlie Roads
387
KAIM HILL
ST BLANE'S CHAPEL
The Tan
Glengarnock
Gateside
Longbar
Knockendon Reservoir
Rye Water
Barrmill
HUNTERSTON POWER STATION VISITOR CENTRE
Garroch Hd.
Little Cumbrae Island
The Den
Drakemyre
Greenhills
Garnock
Burnh
Highfield
Thirdpart
Blairland
Portencross
Giffordland
Dalry
203
Farland Hd.
West Kilbride
Auchentiber
Lugton Water
Seamill
A737
AYRSHIRE MUSEUM OF COUNTRY LIFE & COSTUME
D
Dalgarven
ABBEY
Kilwinning
Torranyard
Chapelhill
Horse Isle
Dykesmains
Benslie
EGLINTON
Cunninghamhead
CAMPBELTOWN (May-Sept) BRODICK
Ardrossan
NORTH AYRSHIRE MUSEUM
Stevenston
A78
Saltcoats
Girdle Toll
Perceton
192
Irvine
GLASGOW VENNEL MU
Springside
Knockentiber
Dreghorn
SCOTTISH MARITIME MUSEUM
Fullarton
FIRTH OF CLYDE
Ayrshire
North
CUNNINGHAME
Inverclyde
Renfrewshire
0 1 2 3 miles
0 1 2 3 4 5 km

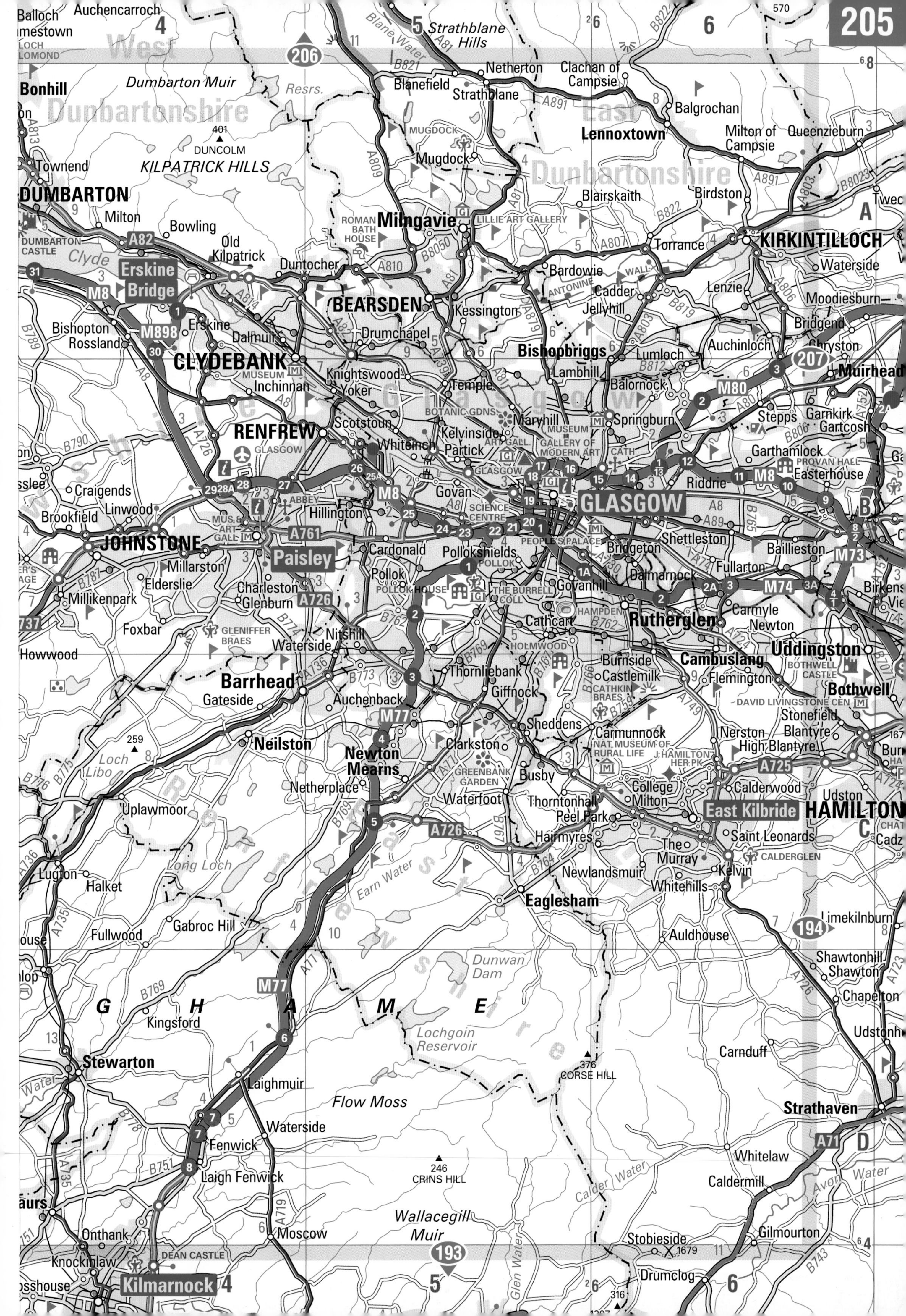

Balloch
Auchencarroch
Jamestown
LOCH LOMOND
West Dunbartonshire
Strathblane Hills
Blane Water
206
Netherton
Clachan of Campsie
570
Blanefield
Strathblane
Bonhill
Dumbarton Muir
Resrs.
A891
East Dunbartonshire
Balgrochan
Lennoxtown
Milton of Campsie
Queenzieburn
401
DUNCOLM
KILPATRICK HILLS
MUGDOCK
Mugdock
Townend
DUMBARTON
Milton
Bowling
Old Kilpatrick
ROMAN BATH HOUSE
Milngavie
LILLIE ART GALLERY
Blairskaith
Birdston
Twechar
DUMBARTON CASTLE
Clyde
Erskine Bridge
Duntocher
Bardowie
Torrance
KIRKINTILLOCH
Waterside
ANTONINE WALL
Cadder
Lenzie
Moodiesburn
M8
BEARSDEN
Kessington
Jellyhill
Bishopton
Rossland
M898
Erskine
Dalmuir
Drumchapel
Bridgend
Auchinloch
Chryston
CLYDEBANK
Bishopbriggs
Lumloch
207
Muirhead
MUSEUM
Inchinnan
Knightswood
Yoker
Temple
Lambhill
Balornock
M80
Glasgow
BOTANIC GDNS
Maryhill
MUSEUM
Springburn
Stepps
Garnkirk
Gartcosh
RENFREW
Scotstoun
Kelvinside
ART GALL.
GALLERY OF MODERN ART
GLASGOW
Whiteinch
Partick
CATH
Garthamlock
PROVAN HALL
Easterhouse
Craigends
Linwood
Brookfield
ABBEY
Hillington
Govan
SCIENCE CENTRE
GLASGOW
Riddrie
JOHNSTONE
MUS. & ART GALL.
A761
Paisley
Cardonald
Pollokshields
PEOPLE'S PALACE
Bridgeton
Shettleston
Baillieston
M73
Millarston
Elderslie
Pollok
POLLOK
POLLOK HOUSE
THE BURRELL COLL.
Govanhill
Dalmarnock
Fullarton
M74
Birkenshaw
Millikenpark
Charleston
Glenburn
A726
HAMPDEN
Cathcart
Rutherglen
Carmyle
Newton
Foxbar
GLENIFFER BRAES
Nitshill
Waterside
HOLMWOOD
Uddingston
Howwood
Barrhead
Gateside
Auchenback
Thornliebank
Burnside
Castlemilk
Cambuslang
Flemington
BOTHWELL CASTLE
Bothwell
Giffnock
CATHKIN BRAES
DAVID LIVINGSTONE CEN
Stonefield
M77
Sheddens
Carmunnock
Nerston
Blantyre
259
Neilston
Clarkston
NAT. MUSEUM OF RURAL LIFE
J. HAMILTON HER. PK
High Blantyre
A725
Loch Libo
Newton Mearns
GREENBANK GARDEN
Busby
College Milton
Calderwood
Netherplace
Waterfoot
Thorntonhall
Peel Park
East Kilbride
Udston
HAMILTON
Uplawmoor
A726
Hairmyres
The Murray
Saint Leonards
CALDERGLEN
Long Loch
Newlandsmuir
Kelvin
Lugton
Halket
Earn Water
Whitehills
Eaglesham
Renfrewshire
East Renfrewshire
Limekilnburn
194
Gabroc Hill
Fullwood
Auldhouse
Dunwan Dam
Shawtonhill
Shawton
Chapelton
B769
G
H
A
M
E
Kingsford
Lochgoin Reservoir
Udstonhead
376
CORSE HILL
Carnduff
Stewarton
Laighmuir
Flow Moss
Strathaven
Waterside
Fenwick
A71
D
Whitelaw
246
CRINS HILL
Laigh Fenwick
Calder Water
Avon Water
Caldermill
Wallacegill Muir
Onthank
Moscow
Glen Water
Stobieside
1679
Gilmourton
Knockinlaw
DEAN CASTLE
193
Kilmarnock
Drumclog
316

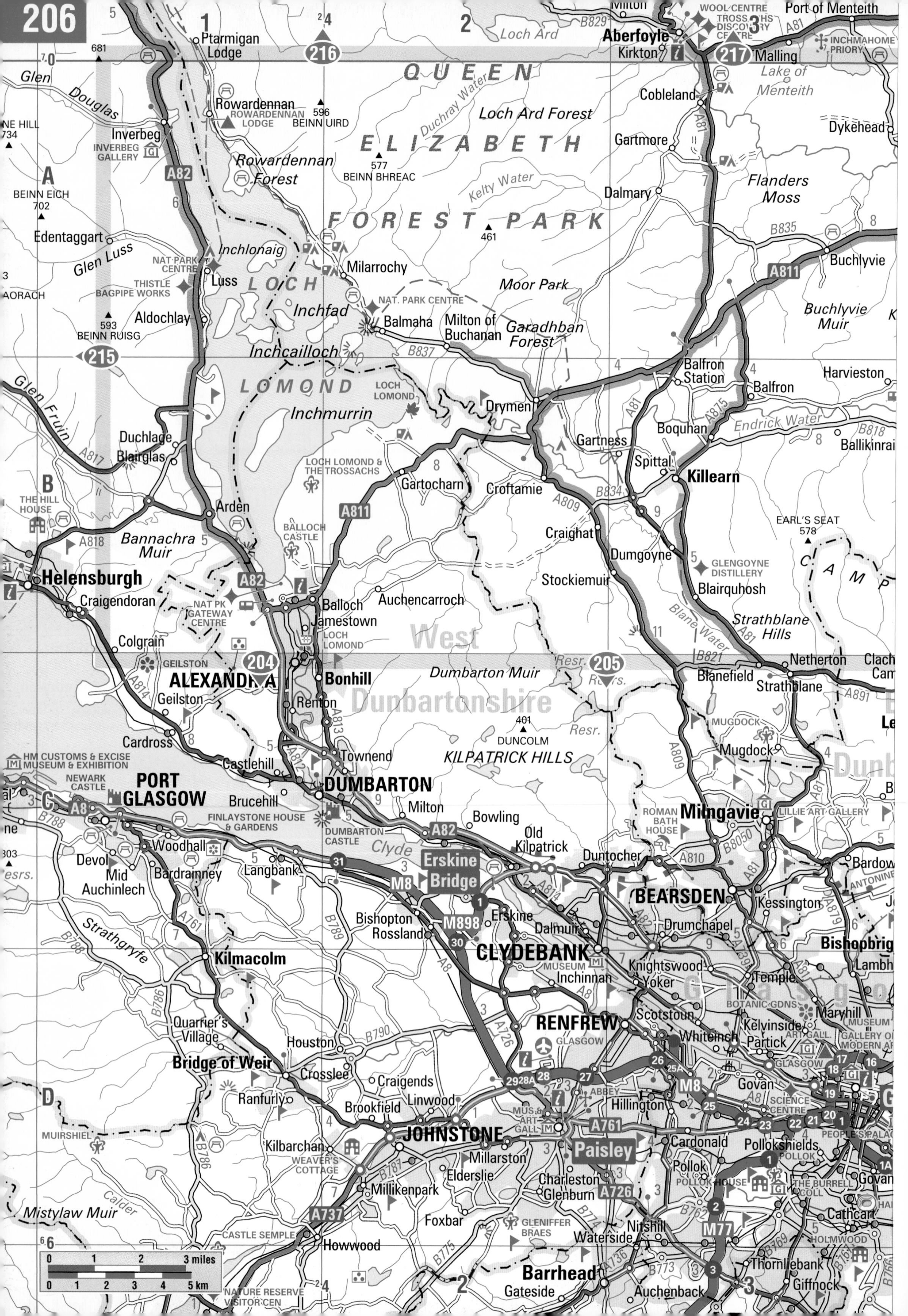

216
217
215
204
205
QUEEN ELIZABETH FOREST PARK
LOCH LOMOND
Aberfoyle
Kirkton
Port of Menteith
Malling
Lake of Menteith
INCHMAHOME PRIORY
Loch Ard
Loch Ard Forest
Cobleland
Gartmore
Dalmary
Flanders Moss
Dykehead
Buchlyvie
Buchlyvie Muir
Ptarmigan Lodge
Rowardennan
ROWARDENNAN LODGE
BEINN UIRD
BEINN BHREAC
Rowardennan Forest
Inverbeg
INVERBEG GALLERY
Glen Douglas
BEINN EICH
Edentaggart
Glen Luss
Inchlonaig
NAT PARK CENTRE
Luss
THISTLE BAGPIPE WORKS
Aldochlay
BEINN RUISG
Milarrochy
NAT. PARK CENTRE
Inchfad
Balmaha
Milton of Buchanan
Garadhban Forest
Moor Park
Inchcailloch
Inchmurrin
Glen Fruin
Duchlage
Blairglas
Drymen
Balfron Station
Balfron
Harvieston
Boquhan
Endrick Water
Ballikinrain
Gartness
Spittal
Killearn
LOCH LOMOND & THE TROSSACHS
Gartocharn
Croftamie
Arden
THE HILL HOUSE
Bannachra Muir
Helensburgh
Craigendoran
BALLOCH CASTLE
Craighat
Dumgoyne
EARL'S SEAT
GLENGOYNE DISTILLERY
Blairquhosh
Stockiemuir
NAT PK GATEWAY CENTRE
Balloch
Jamestown
Auchencarroch
Strathblane Hills
Colgrain
GEILSTON
ALEXANDRIA
Bonhill
West Dunbartonshire
Dumbarton Muir
Netherton
Blanefield
Strathblane
Geilston
Renton
DUNCOLM
KILPATRICK HILLS
MUGDOCK
Mugdock
Cardross
Castlehill
Townend
HM CUSTOMS & EXCISE MUSEUM & EXHIBITION
NEWARK CASTLE
PORT GLASGOW
Brucehill
DUMBARTON
Milton
Bowling
Old Kilpatrick
FINLAYSTONE HOUSE & GARDENS
DUMBARTON CASTLE
Clyde
ROMAN BATH HOUSE
Milngavie
LILLIE ART GALLERY
Woodhall
Devol
Mid Auchinlech
Bardrainney
Langbank
Erskine Bridge
Duntocher
BEARSDEN
Kessington
Bardowie
Strathgryfe
Bishopton
Rossland
Erskine
Dalmuir
Drumchapel
Bishopbriggs
Kilmacolm
CLYDEBANK
MUSEUM
Knightswood
Yoker
Inchinnan
Temple
Lambhill
BOTANIC GDNS
Maryhill
Quarrier's Village
RENFREW
Scotstoun
Whiteinch
Kelvinside
Partick
Houston
GLASGOW
Bridge of Weir
Crosslee
Craigends
Ranfurly
Linwood
Brookfield
ABBEY
Hillington
Govan
SCIENCE CENTRE
MUIRSHIEL
JOHNSTONE
MUS & ART GALL
Paisley
Cardonald
Pollokshields
Kilbarchan
WEAVER'S COTTAGE
Millarston
Elderslie
Charleston
Glenburn
Pollok
POLLOK HOUSE
THE BURRELL COLL
Millikenpark
Cathcart
Mistylaw Muir
Calder
Foxbar
GLENIFFER BRAES
Nitshill
Waterside
CASTLE SEMPLE
Howwood
Thornliebank
Giffnock
Barrhead
Gateside
Auchenback
NATURE RESERVE VISITOR CEN
0 1 2 3 miles
0 1 2 3 4 5 km

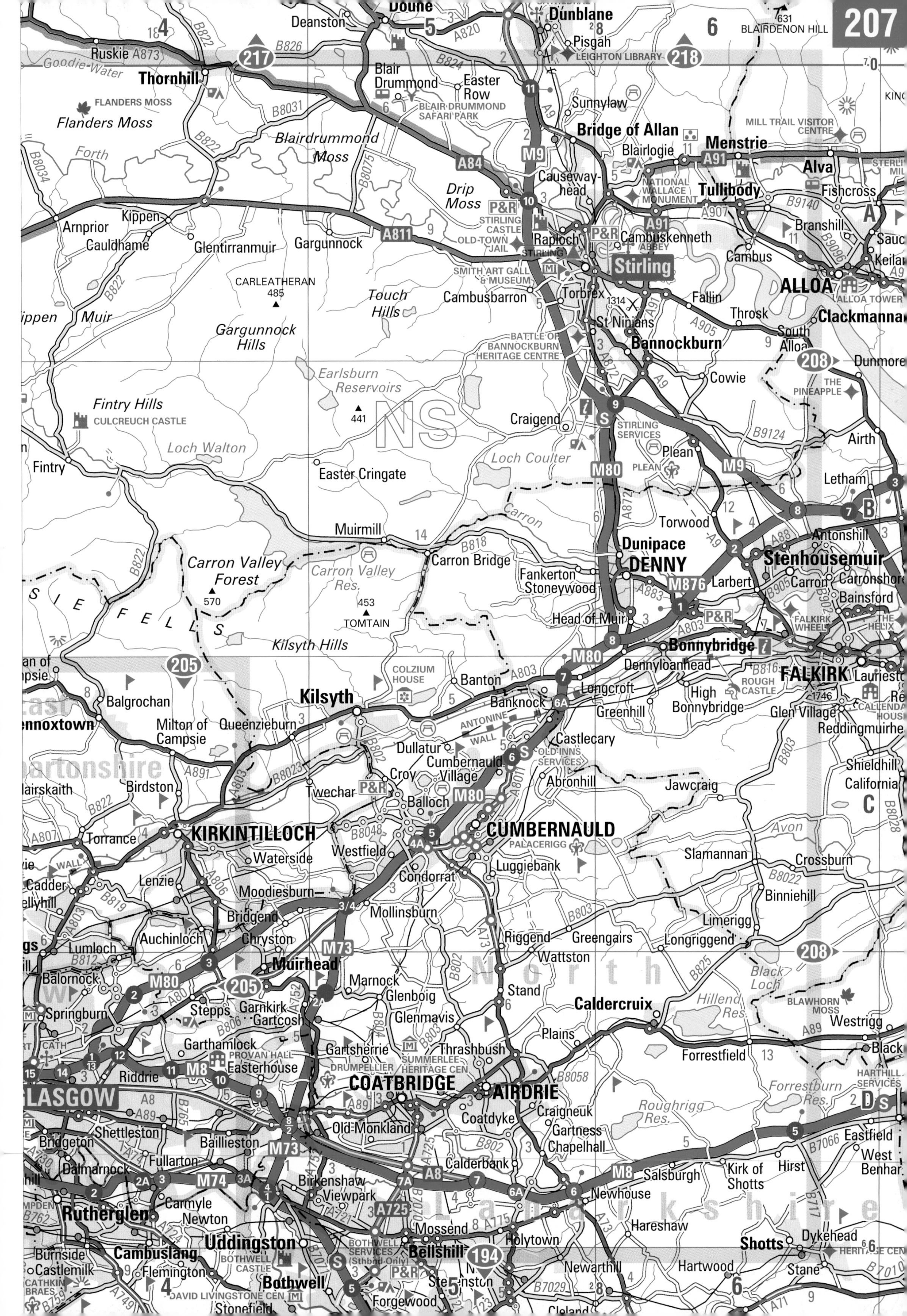

Doune
Deanston
Dunblane
Pisgah
631
BLAIRDENON HILL
LEIGHTON LIBRARY
217
218
Ruskie
Goodie Water
Thornhill
Blair Drummond
Easter Row
BLAIR DRUMMOND SAFARI PARK
FLANDERS MOSS
Flanders Moss
Sunnylaw
Bridge of Allan
MILL TRAIL VISITOR CENTRE
Menstrie
Blairdrummond Moss
Forth
Blairlogie
Alva
Causewayhead
NATIONAL WALLACE MONUMENT
Tullibody
Fishcross
Drip Moss
P&R
STIRLING CASTLE
Branshill
Arnprior
Kippen
Raploch
Cambuskenneth
ABBEY
Cauldhame
Glentirranmuir
Gargunnock
OLD TOWN JAIL
Cambus
Stirling
SMITH ART GALL & MUSEUM
ALLOA
ALLOA TOWER
CARLEATHERAN
485
Touch Hills
Cambusbarron
Torbrex
Fallin
Throsk
Clackmannan
Muir
St Ninians
Gargunnock Hills
BATTLE OF BANNOCKBURN HERITAGE CENTRE
Bannockburn
South Alloa
208
Dunmore
Earlsburn Reservoirs
Cowie
THE PINEAPPLE
Fintry Hills
CULCREUCH CASTLE
441
NS
Craigend
STIRLING SERVICES
Airth
Loch Walton
Plean
PLEAN
Loch Coulter
Fintry
Easter Cringate
Letham
Carron
Torwood
Muirmill
Dunipace
Antonshill
DENNY
Stenhousemuir
Carron Valley Forest
Carron Bridge
Carron Valley Res.
Fankerton
Stoneywood
Larbert
Carronshore
Bainsford
570
453
TOMTAIN
Head of Muir
FALKIRK WHEEL
THE HELIX
Kilsyth Hills
Bonnybridge
205
COLZIUM HOUSE
Banton
Dennyloanhead
ROUGH CASTLE
FALKIRK
Laurieston
Balgrochan
Kilsyth
Banknock
Longcroft
High Bonnybridge
1746
Greenhill
Glen Village
Lennoxtown
Milton of Campsie
Queenzieburn
ANTONINE WALL
Reddingmuirhead
Dullatur
Castlecary
OLD INNS SERVICES
Cumbernauld Village
Shieldhill
Croy
California
Birdston
Twechar
Abronhill
Jawcraig
Balloch
KIRKINTILLOCH
CUMBERNAULD
Torrance
PALACERIGG
Avon
Waterside
Westfield
Slamannan
Crossburn
Luggiebank
Lenzie
Condorrat
Moodiesburn
Binniehill
Mollinsburn
Bridgend
Limerigg
Auchinloch
Chryston
Riggend
Greengairs
Longriggend
Lumloch
Wattston
North
Muirhead
Balornock
Marnock
Black Loch
Stand
Glenboig
Hillend Res.
BLAWHORN MOSS
Springburn
Stepps
Garnkirk
Caldercruix
Gartcosh
Glenmavis
Westrigg
Plains
Garthamlock
Gartsherrie
Thrashbush
Forrestfield
PROVAN HALL
SUMMERLEE HERITAGE CEN
DRUMPELLIER
Riddrie
Easterhouse
HARTHILL SERVICES
COATBRIDGE
AIRDRIE
Forrestburn Res.
GLASGOW
Craigneuk
Roughrigg Res.
Coatdyke
Shettleston
Old Monkland
Gartness
Eastfield
Bridgeton
Baillieston
Chapelhall
Fullarton
West Benhar
Dalmarnock
Calderbank
Salsburgh
Kirk of Shotts
Hirst
Birkenshaw
Viewpark
Newhouse
Rutherglen
Carmyle
Newton
Lanarkshire
Mossend
Hareshaw
Uddingston
Holytown
Dykehead
Cambuslang
BOTHWELL SERVICES (Sthbnd Only)
Bellshill
194
Shotts
HERITAGE CEN
Burnside
BOTHWELL CASTLE
Castlemilk
Flemington
Newarthill
Hartwood
Stane
CATHKIN BRAES
Bothwell
DAVID LIVINGSTONE CEN
Forgewood
Cleland
Stonefield
Wall
M9
M80
M876
M73
M8
M74
A84
A811
A91
A9
A905
A88
A803
A80
A8
A725
A89
A73
A71

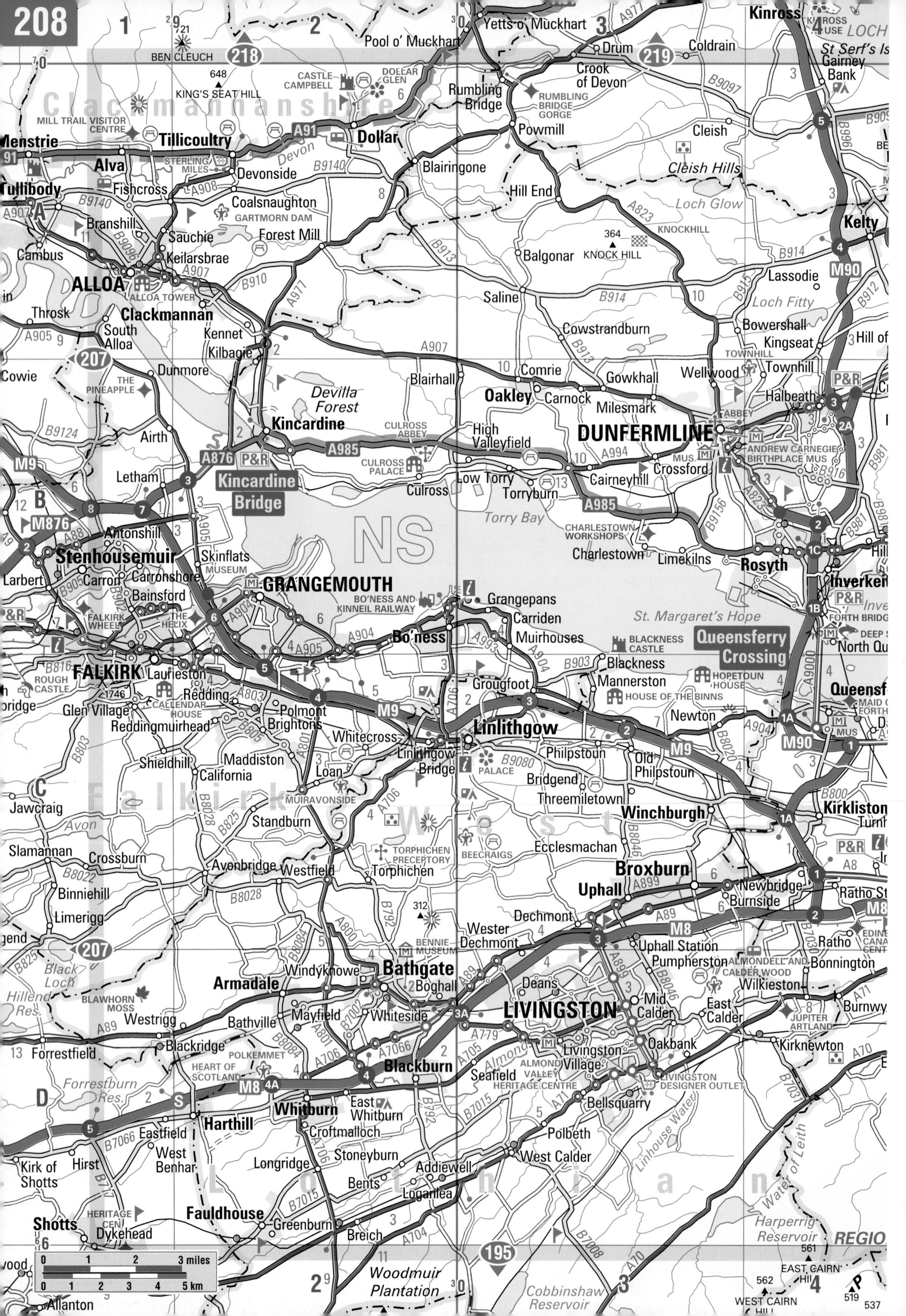
Clackmannanshire
Falkirk
West Lothian
BEN CLEUCH
KING'S SEAT HILL
648
218
219
207
195
Yetts o' Muckhart
Pool o' Muckhart
Drum
Coldrain
Kinross
KINROSS HOUSE
LOCH
St Serf's Is
Gairney Bank
Crook of Devon
Rumbling Bridge
RUMBLING BRIDGE GORGE
CASTLE CAMPBELL
DOLLAR GLEN
MILL TRAIL VISITOR CENTRE
Menstrie
Tillicoultry
Dollar
Powmill
Cleish
Cleish Hills
Alva
STERLING MILLS
Devonside
Blairingone
Tullibody
Fishcross
Coalsnaughton
GARTMORN DAM
Hill End
Loch Glow
Branshill
Sauchie
Forest Mill
Cambus
Keilarsbrae
KNOCKHILL
364
KNOCK HILL
Balgonar
Kelty
ALLOA
ALLOA TOWER
Saline
Lassodie
Loch Fitty
Throsk
Clackmannan
Kennet
Kilbagie
South Alloa
Cowstrandburn
Bowershall
Kingseat
Hill of
Cowie
THE PINEAPPLE
Dunmore
Comrie
Blairhall
Devilla Forest
Gowkhall
Wellwood
TOWNHILL
Townhill
Halbeath
Oakley
Carnock
Milesmark
ABBEY
Kincardine
CULROSS ABBEY
High Valleyfield
DUNFERMLINE
ANDREW CARNEGIE BIRTHPLACE MUS
Airth
Letham
CULROSS PALACE
Low Torry
Culross
Torryburn
Cairneyhill
Crossford
MUS.
Kincardine Bridge
Torry Bay
NS
CHARLESTOWN WORKSHOPS
Charlestown
Limekilns
Rosyth
Inverkeit
Antonshill
Stenhousemuir
Skinflats
MUSEUM
Larbert
Carron
Carronshore
GRANGEMOUTH
BO'NESS AND KINNEIL RAILWAY
Grangepans
Bainsford
Carriden
FALKIRK WHEEL
THE HELIX
St. Margaret's Hope
FORTH BRIDG
DEEP S
North Qu
Queensferry Crossing
Bo'ness
Muirhouses
BLACKNESS CASTLE
Blackness
ROUGH CASTLE
FALKIRK
Laurieston
1746
Redding
CALLENDAR HOUSE
Mannerston
HOPETOUN HOUSE
HOUSE OF THE BINNS
Grougfoot
Queensf
MAID O FORTH
Glen Village
Reddingmuirhead
Polmont
Brightons
Linlithgow
Newton
Whitecross
Linlithgow Bridge
PALACE
Philpstoun
Old Philpstoun
Shieldhill
Maddiston
California
Loan
Bridgend
Threemiletown
Jawcraig
MUIRAVONSIDE
Winchburgh
Kirkliston
Turnh
Avon
Standburn
Slamannan
Crossburn
TORPHICHEN PRECEPTORY
BEECRAIGS
Ecclesmachan
Avonbridge
Westfield
Torphichen
Broxburn
Binniehill
Uphall
Newbridge
Burnside
Ratho St
Limerigg
312
Dechmont
Wester Dechmont
BENNIE MUSEUM
Uphall Station
Ratho
EDIN CANA CENT
Black Loch
Pumpherston
ALMONDELL AND CALDER WOOD
Bonnington
Windyknowe
Bathgate
Armadale
Boghall
Deans
Wilkieston
Hillend Res.
BLAWHORN MOSS
Mayfield
Whiteside
LIVINGSTON
Mid Calder
East Calder
Burnwy
Westrigg
Bathville
JUPITER ARTLAND
Forrestfield
Blackridge
POLKEMMET
Livingston Village
Oakbank
Kirknewton
HEART OF SCOTLAND
Blackburn
Seafield
ALMOND VALLEY HERITAGE CENTRE
LIVINGSTON DESIGNER OUTLET
Forrestburn Res.
Whitburn
East Whitburn
Bellsquarry
Harthill
Eastfield
Croftmalloch
Polbeth
West Benhar
Stoneyburn
West Calder
Kirk of Shotts
Hirst
Longridge
Addiewell
Linhouse Water
Bents
Loganlea
Water of Leith
HERITAGE CEN
Shotts
Fauldhouse
Greenburn
Dykehead
Breich
Harperrig Reservoir
REGIO
Woodmuir Plantation
561
EAST CAIRN HILL
562
WEST CAIRN HILL
Cobbinshaw Reservoir
Allanton
P&R
M9
M876
M90
M8
A91
A908
A907
A905
A977
A876
A985
A994
A823
B914
B9097
B996
A904
A905
A803
B805
B803
B816
A801
A706
B9080
A993
B903
B8020
A9000
B800
B8046
A899
A89
A8
B7030
A71
A70
A779
A705
A7066
B8084
B7002
B7015
B792
B7066
A704
B7008
B7031
B825
B8022
B8028
B8028
B9124
B9140
B9096
B910
B913
B915
B912
B981
B916
B9156
0 1 2 3 miles
0 1 2 3 4 5 km
537
519

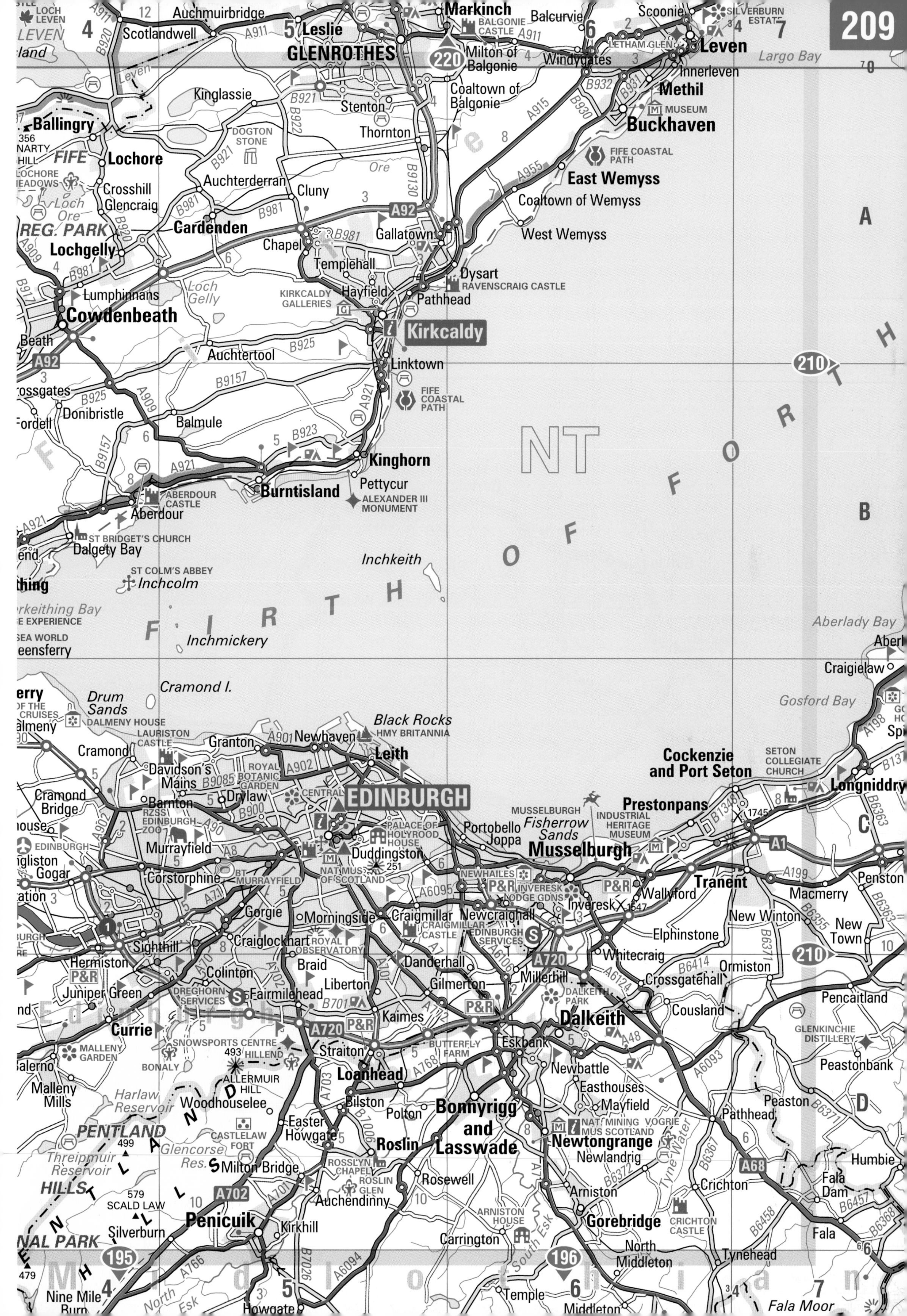

209
Scotlandwell
Auchmuirbridge
Leslie
GLENROTHES
Markinch
Balgonie Castle
Milton of Balgonie
Balcurvie
Windygates
Scoonie
Silverburn Estate
Letham Glen
Leven
Largo Bay
Innerleven
Methil
Museum
Buckhaven
Coaltown of Balgonie
Stenton
Thornton
Kinglassie
Ballingry
Dogton Stone
Lochore
FIFE
Lochore Meadows
Crosshill
Glencraig
Loch Ore
Auchterderran
Cluny
Cardenden
Reg. Park
Lochgelly
Chapel
Gallatown
Templehall
Fife Coastal Path
East Wemyss
Coaltown of Wemyss
West Wemyss
Dysart
Ravenscraig Castle
Lumphinnans
Loch Gelly
Kirkcaldy Galleries
Hayfield
Pathhead
Cowdenbeath
Kirkcaldy
Auchtertool
Linktown
Donibristle
Balmule
Kinghorn
Burntisland
Pettycur
Alexander III Monument
Aberdour Castle
Aberdour
St Bridget's Church
Dalgety Bay
NT
FIRTH OF FORTH
Inchkeith
St Colm's Abbey
Inchcolm
Inchmickery
Cramond I.
Drum Sands
Dalmeny House
Black Rocks
HMY Britannia
Newhaven
Granton
Leith
Lauriston Castle
Cramond
Davidson's Mains
Royal Botanic Garden
Drylaw
Cramond Bridge
Barnton
EDINBURGH
RZSS Edinburgh Zoo
Murrayfield
Palace of Holyroodhouse
Duddingston
Nat. Mus. of Scotland
BT Murrayfield
Corstorphine
Gogar
Gorgie
Morningside
Craigmillar
Craigmillar Castle
Newcraighall
Sighthill
Craiglockhart
Royal Observatory
Hermiston
Colinton
Braid
Danderhall
Juniper Green
Dreghorn Services
Fairmilehead
Liberton
Gilmerton
Kaimes
Currie
Malleny Garden
Snowsports Centre
Hillend
Straiton
Butterfly Farm
Eskbank
Loanhead
Allermuir Hill
Bonaly
Malleny Mills
Harlaw Reservoir
Woodhouselee
Bilston
Polton
Bonnyrigg and Lasswade
PENTLAND HILLS
Easter Howgate
Castlelaw Fort
Roslin
Glencorse Res.
Milton Bridge
Rosslyn Chapel
Roslin Glen
Threipmuir Reservoir
Auchendinny
Rosewell
Scald Law
Penicuik
Kirkhill
Silverburn
Carrington
Arniston House
Nine Mile Burn
Howgate
Temple
Midlothian
Portobello
Joppa
Musselburgh
Fisherrow Sands
Industrial Heritage Museum
Prestonpans
Cockenzie and Port Seton
Seton Collegiate Church
Longniddry
Newhailes
Inveresk Lodge Gdns
Inveresk
Wallyford
Tranent
Edinburgh Services
Elphinstone
Whitecraig
Millerhill
Dalkeith Park
Dalkeith
Crossgatehall
Ormiston
Cousland
Newbattle
Easthouses
Mayfield
Nat. Mining Mus Scotland
Newtongrange
Newlandrig
Vogrie
Arniston
Gorebridge
Crichton
Crichton Castle
North Middleton
Middleton
Pathhead
Tynehead
Macmerry
New Winton
Penston
New Town
Pencaitland
Glenkinchie Distillery
Peastonbank
Peaston
Humbie
Fala Dam
Fala
Fala Moor
Aberlady Bay
Craigielaw
Gosford Bay
Tyne Water
South Esk

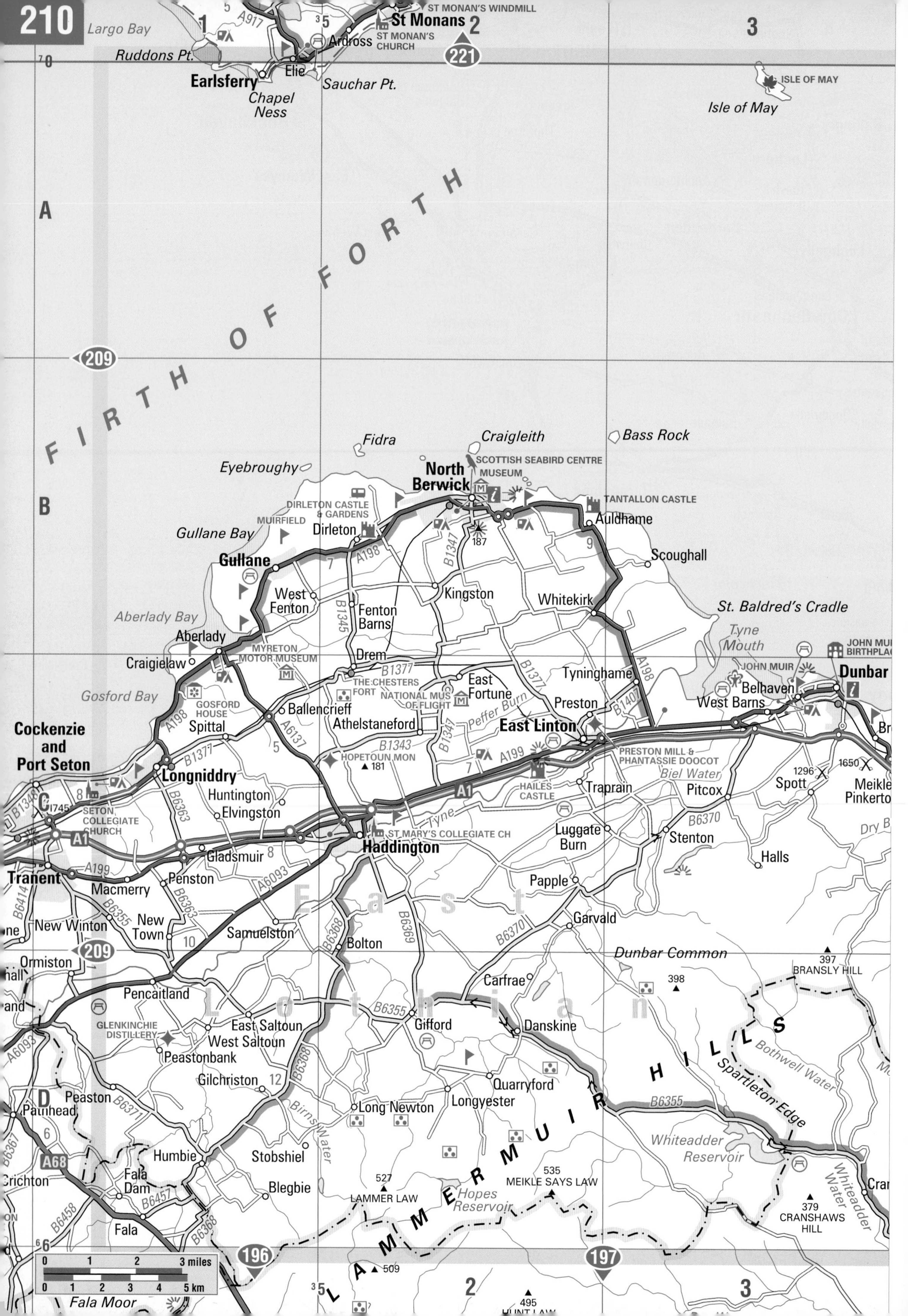
Largo Bay
Ruddons Pt.
Earlsferry
Elie
Chapel Ness
Sauchar Pt.
Ardross
St Monans
ST MONAN'S WINDMILL
ST MONAN'S CHURCH
221
Isle of May
ISLE OF MAY
FIRTH OF FORTH
209
Fidra
Craigleith
Bass Rock
Eyebroughy
North Berwick
SCOTTISH SEABIRD CENTRE
MUSEUM
TANTALLON CASTLE
Auldhame
DIRLETON CASTLE & GARDENS
MUIRFIELD
Dirleton
Gullane Bay
Gullane
Scoughall
West Fenton
Fenton Barns
Kingston
Whitekirk
St. Baldred's Cradle
Aberlady Bay
Aberlady
Tyne Mouth
JOHN MUIR
Dunbar
Craigielaw
MYRETON MOTOR MUSEUM
Drem
Gosford Bay
GOSFORD HOUSE
THE CHESTERS FORT
NATIONAL MUS OF FLIGHT
East Fortune
Tyninghame
Belhaven
West Barns
Ballencrieff
Preston
Cockenzie and Port Seton
Spittal
Athelstaneford
Peffer Burn
East Linton
HOPETOUN MON
PRESTON MILL & PHANTASSIE DOOCOT
Longniddry
Biel Water
HAILES CASTLE
Traprain
Pitcox
Spott
Meikle Pinkerton
SETON COLLEGIATE CHURCH
Huntington
Elvingston
Tyne
ST MARY'S COLLEGIATE CH
Luggate Burn
Stenton
Haddington
Gladsmuir
Halls
Tranent
Macmerry
Penston
Papple
East Lothian
New Winton
New Town
Samuelston
Bolton
Garvald
Ormiston
Dunbar Common
BRANSLY HILL
Carfrae
Pencaitland
GLENKINCHIE DISTILLERY
East Saltoun
West Saltoun
Gifford
Danskine
Peastonbank
Bothwell Water
Gilchriston
Quarryford
Longyester
Spartleton Edge
LAMMERMUIR HILLS
Peaston
Pathhead
Long Newton
Whiteadder Reservoir
Humbie
Stobshiel
Birns Water
Crichton
Fala Dam
Blegbie
LAMMER LAW
MEIKLE SAYS LAW
Hopes Reservoir
CRANSHAWS HILL
Whiteadder Water
Fala
196
197
Fala Moor
HUNT LAW
0 1 2 3 miles
0 1 2 3 4 5 km

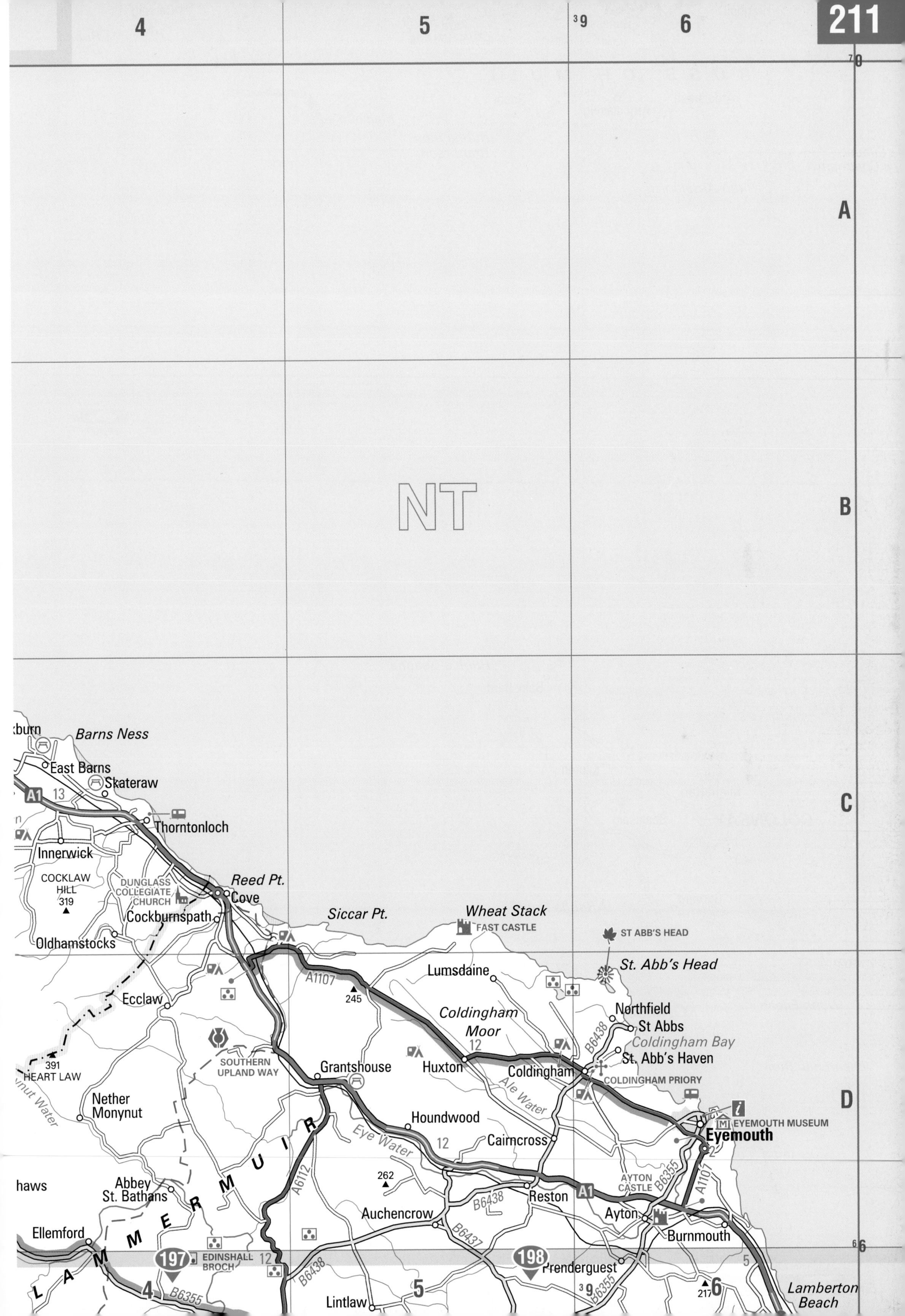

4   **5**   ³**9**   **6**

A

B

NT

C

:burn   *Barns Ness*

East Barns

Skateraw

A1 13

Thorntonloch

Innerwick

COCKLAW HILL 319

DUNGLASS COLLEGIATE CHURCH

Reed Pt.

Cove

Cockburnspath

Oldhamstocks

Siccar Pt.

Wheat Stack

FAST CASTLE

ST ABB'S HEAD

St. Abb's Head

Ecclaw

A1107

245

Lumsdaine

Northfield

St Abbs

Coldingham Bay

391 HEART LAW

:nut Water

Nether Monynut

Coldingham Moor

12

SOUTHERN UPLAND WAY

Grantshouse

Huxton

St. Abb's Haven

COLDINGHAM PRIORY

B6438

Coldingham

Ale Water

EYEMOUTH MUSEUM

Eyemouth

D

Houndwood

Eye Water

12

Cairncross

:haws

Abbey St. Bathans

A6112

262

A1

Reston

AYTON CASTLE

B6355

A1107

Ellemford

197

EDINSHALL BROCH

12

B6438

Auchencrow

B6437

B6438

198

Prenderguest

Ayton

Burnmouth

6

6

5

LAMMERMUIR

B6355

4

B6355

Lintlaw

5

³**9**

B6355

217

6

Lamberton Beach

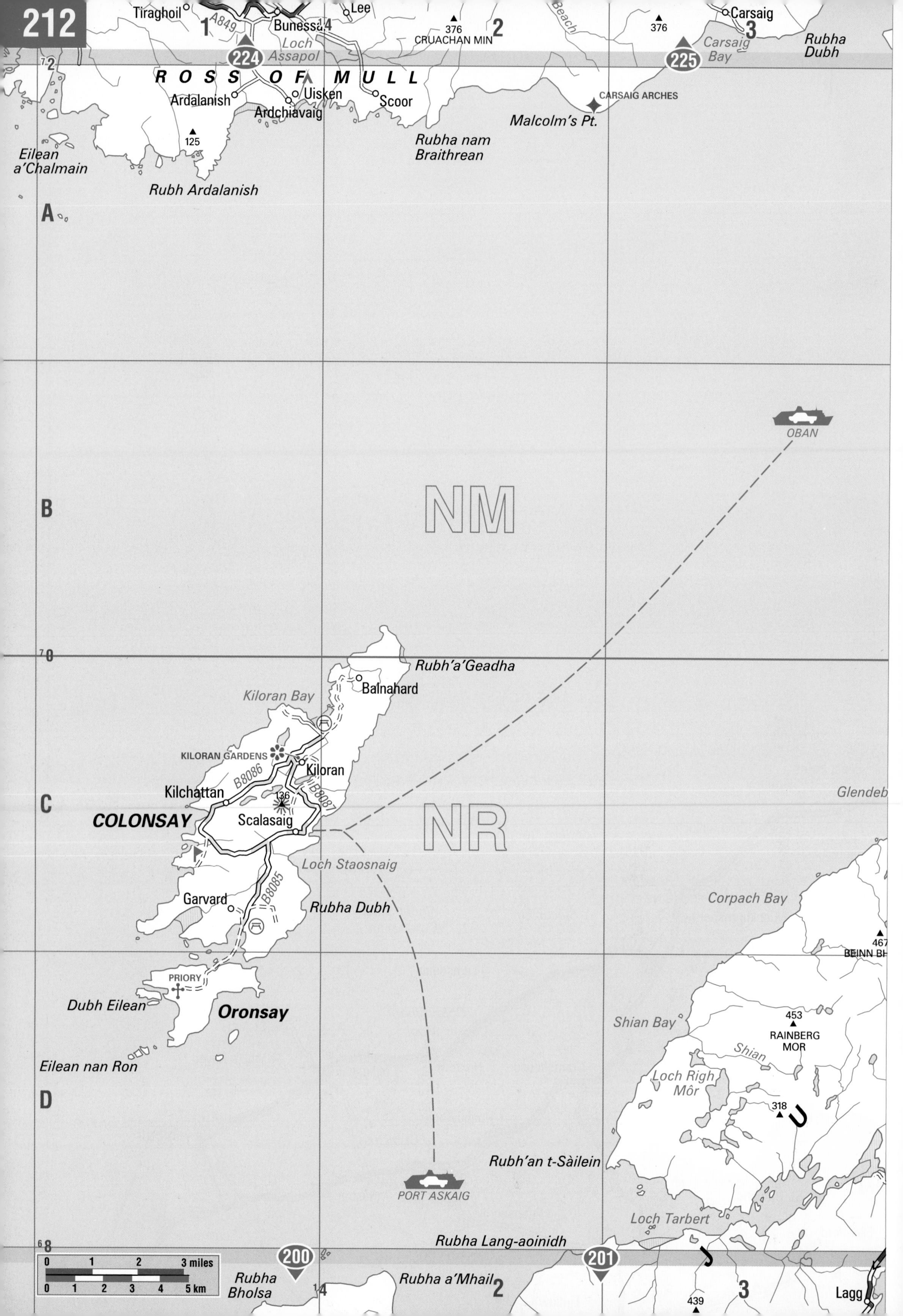

1   2   3

Tiraghoil
Lee
Carsaig
A849
Bunessan
376
376
Rubha
Dubh
224
Loch
Assapol
CRUACHAN MIN
225
Carsaig
Bay

R O S S   O F   M U L L

Ardalanish
Uisken
Scoor
CARSAIG ARCHES
Ardchiavaig
Malcolm's Pt.

125
Rubha nam
Braithrean

Eilean
a'Chalmain

Rubh Ardalanish

A

NM

OBAN

B

7 0

Rubh'a'Geadha

Kiloran Bay
Balnahard

KILORAN GARDENS
Glendeb

B8086
Kiloran

Kilchattan
136
B8087

NR

C

COLONSAY
Scalasaig

Corpach Bay

Loch Staosnaig

467
BEINN BH

Garvard
B8085
Rubha Dubh

PRIORY

Shian Bay
453
RAINBERG
MOR

Dubh Eilean
Oronsay

Shian

Eilean nan Ron

Loch Righ
Môr

318

D

Rubh'an t-Sàilein

PORT ASKAIG

6 8

Rubha Lang-aoinidh

Loch Tarbert

0   1   2   3 miles
0   1   2   3   4   5 km

200
Rubha
Bholsa
Rubha a'Mhail
201
Lagg

1   4   2   3

439

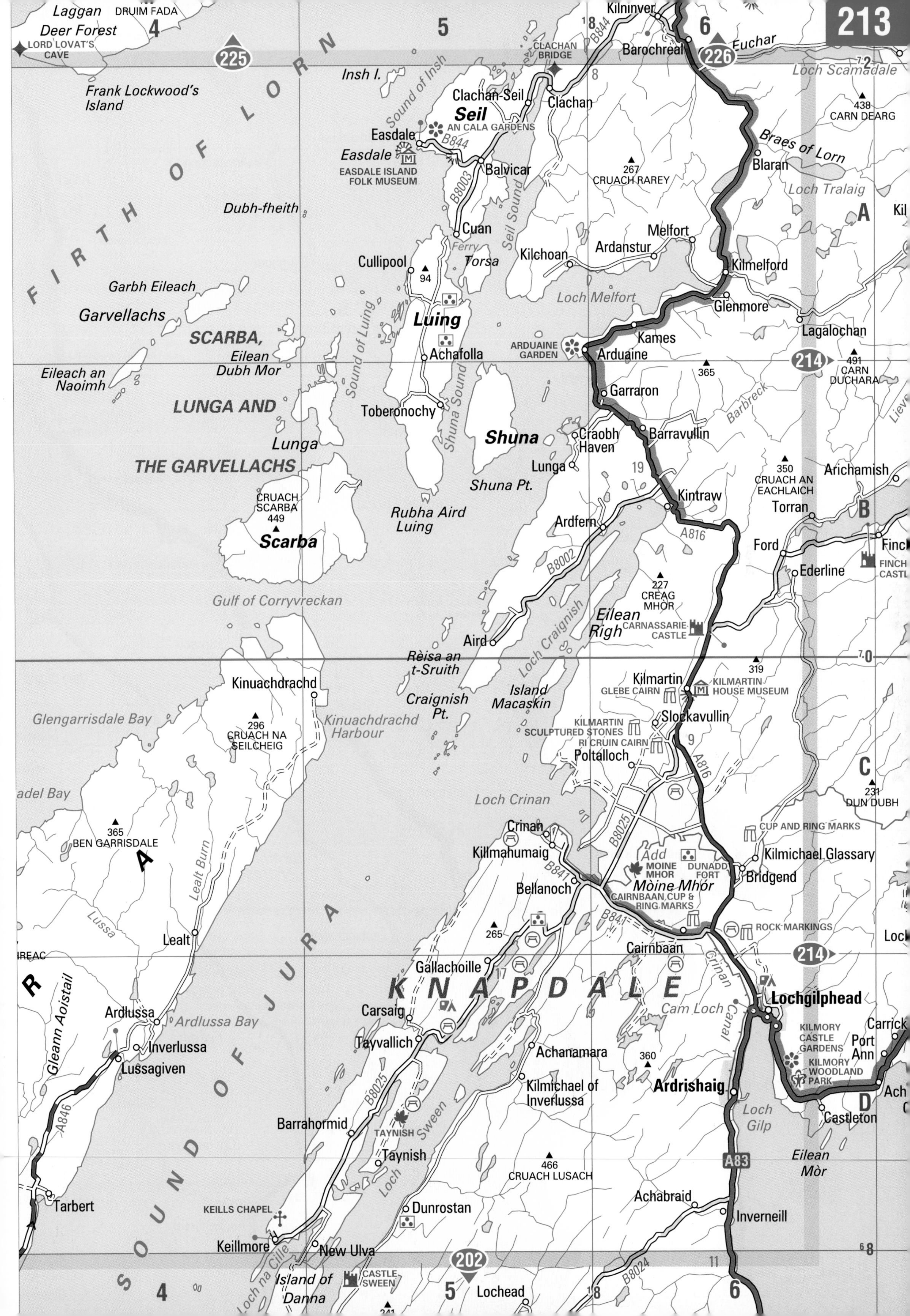
Laggan Deer Forest
DRUIM FADA
LORD LOVAT'S CAVE
225
226
202
214
Kilninver
Barochreal
Euchar
Loch Scamadale
CLACHAN BRIDGE
Clachan-Seil
Clachan
Insh I.
Sound of Insh
Frank Lockwood's Island
FIRTH OF LORN
Seil
AN CALA GARDENS
Easdale
EASDALE ISLAND FOLK MUSEUM
Balvicar
Cuan
Seil Sound
Dubh-fheith
267 CRUACH RAREY
438 CARN DEARG
Braes of Lorn
Blaran
Loch Tralaig
Melfort
Ardanstur
Kilchoan
Kilmelford
Glenmore
Loch Melfort
Cullipool
Torsa
Luing
Garbh Eileach
Garvellachs
SCARBA, LUNGA AND THE GARVELLACHS
Eilean Dubh Mor
Eileach an Naoimh
Sound of Luing
Achafolla
ARDUAINE GARDEN
Arduaine
Kames
Lagalochan
491 CARN DUCHARA
365
Garraron
Toberonochy
Shuna Sound
Shuna
Craobh Haven
Barravullin
Barbreck
Lunga
Shuna Pt.
350 CRUACH AN EACHLAICH
Arichamish
Kintraw
Torran
CRUACH SCARBA 449
Scarba
Rubha Aird Luing
Ardfern
A816
Ford
Ederline
FINCH CASTLE
B8002
227 CREAG MHOR
Eilean Righ
CARNASSARIE CASTLE
Gulf of Corryvreckan
Aird
Loch Craignish
Rèisa an t-Sruith
319
Kinuachdrachd
Kilmartin
KILMARTIN HOUSE MUSEUM
GLEBE CAIRN
Craignish Pt.
Island Macaskin
Slockavullin
Glengarrisdale Bay
Kinuachdrachd Harbour
296 CRUACH NA SEILCHEIG
KILMARTIN SCULPTURED STONES
RI CRUIN CAIRN
Poltalloch
231 DUN DUBH
Loch Crinan
B8025
CUP AND RING MARKS
365 BEN GARRISDALE
Crinan
Kilmahumaig
Add
MOINE MHOR
DUNADD FORT
Kilmichael Glassary
Bridgend
Bellanoch
Mòine Mhór
CAIRNBAAN CUP & RING MARKS
B841
Lealt Burn
Lussa
265
ROCK MARKINGS
Lealt
Cairnbaan
Gallachoille
KNAPDALE
Crinan Canal
Lochgilphead
Carsaig
Cam Loch
Ardlussa
Ardlussa Bay
KILMORY CASTLE GARDENS
Carrick
Port Ann
Tayvallich
Inverlussa
Achanamara
Lussagiven
360
KILMORY WOODLAND PARK
Gleann Aoistail
SOUND OF JURA
Kilmichael of Inverlussa
Ardrishaig
Loch Gilp
Castleton
A846
Barrahormid
TAYNISH
Loch Sween
Taynish
A83
Eilean Mòr
466 CRUACH LUSACH
Tarbert
KEILLS CHAPEL
Dunrostan
Achabraid
Inverneill
Keillmore
New Ulva
Loch na Cille
Island of Danna
CASTLE SWEEN
B8024
Lochead
A
B
C
D
4
5
6

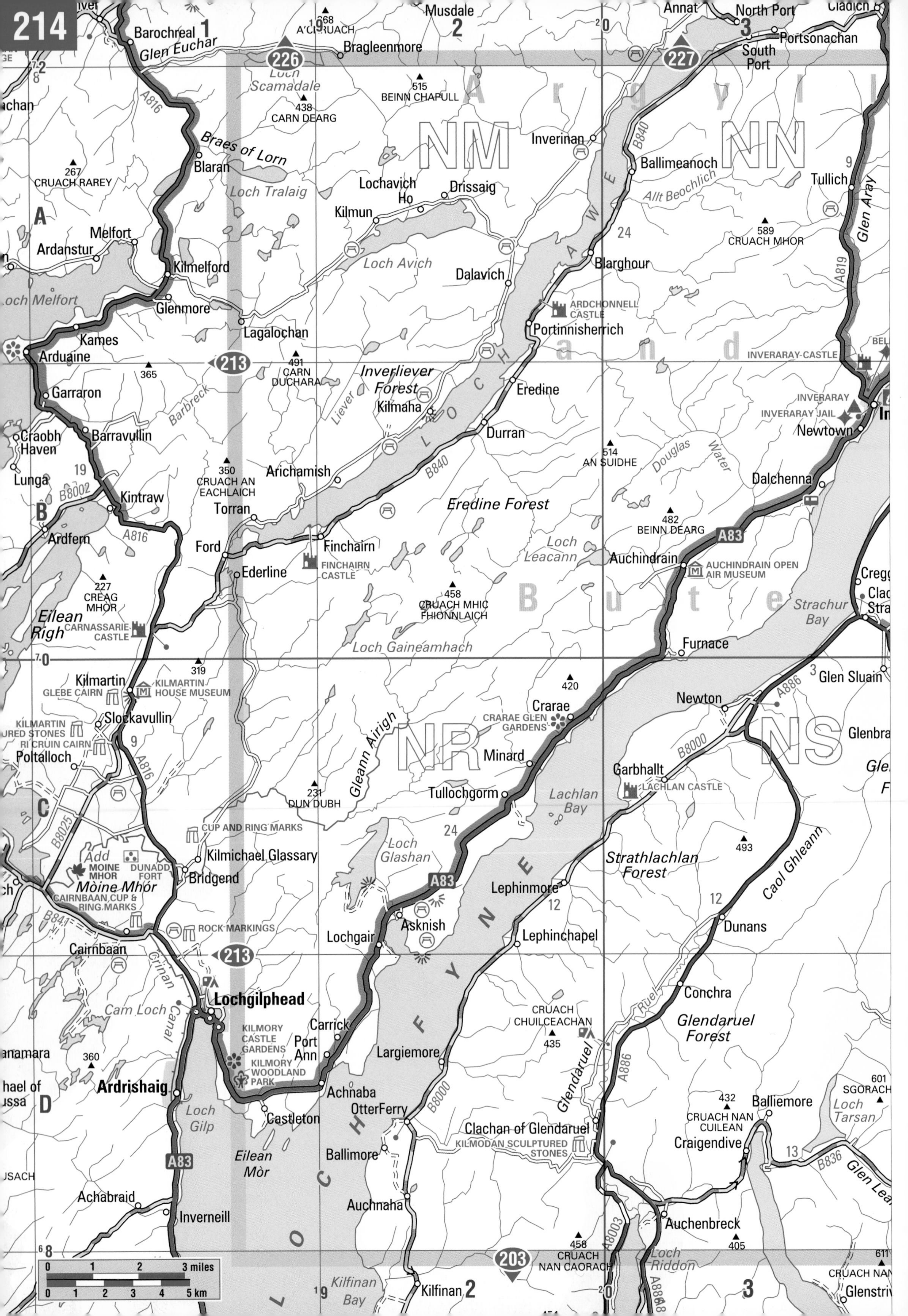

Barochreal
Glen Euchar
A'CHRUACH
668
Musdale
Bragleenmore
Annat
North Port
Cladich
Portsonachan
South Port
226
227
Loch Scamadale
515 BEINN CHAPULL
438 CARN DEARG
Braes of Lorn
Argyll and Bute
NM
NN
Inverinan
B840
Ballimeanoch
Allt Beochlich
Tullich
Glen Aray
267 CRUACH RAREY
Blaran
Loch Tralaig
Lochavich Ho
Drissaig
Kilmun
A
Melfort
Ardanstur
Kilmelford
Loch Avich
589 CRUACH MHOR
Blarghour
Dalavich
A819
Loch Melfort
Glenmore
ARDCHONNELL CASTLE
Portinnisherrich
Lagalochan
Kames
Arduaine
491 CARN DUCHARA
213
365
Inverliever Forest
Kilmaha
INVERARAY CASTLE
Eredine
INVERARAY
INVERARAY JAIL
Newtown
Garraron
Barbreck
Liever
LOCH AWE
Craobh Haven
Barravullin
Durran
514 AN SUIDHE
Douglas Water
Lunga
19
350 CRUACH AN EACHLAICH
Arichamish
Dalchenna
B8002
Kintraw
B
Torran
Eredine Forest
482 BEINN DEARG
A83
Ardfern
A816
Ford
Finchairn
Loch Leacann
Auchindrain
AUCHINDRAIN OPEN AIR MUSEUM
Ederline
FINCHAIRN CASTLE
227 CREAG MHOR
458 CRUACH MHIC FHIONNLAICH
Creggans
Strachur Bay
Eilean Righ
CARNASSARIE CASTLE
Loch Gaineamhach
Furnace
319
Glen Sluain
Kilmartin
KILMARTIN HOUSE MUSEUM
GLEBE CAIRN
420
Newton
Crarae
A886
KILMARTIN
Slockavullin
CRARAE GLEN GARDENS
STANDING STONES
RI CRUIN CAIRN
9
Gleann Airigh
NR
NS
Poltalloch
Minard
B8000
Garbhallt
LACHLAN CASTLE
C
231 DUN DUBH
Tullochgorm
Lachlan Bay
B8025
CUP AND RING MARKS
Loch Glashan
24
493
Kilmichael Glassary
Add
MOINE MHOR
DUNADD FORT
Bridgend
Strathlachlan Forest
Caol Ghleann
Moine Mhor
CAIRNBAAN CUP & RING MARKS
Lephinmore
12
Dunans
B841
ROCK MARKINGS
Asknish
Lochgair
Lephinchapel
Cairnbaan
Crinan Canal
Conchra
Lochgilphead
Cam Loch
CRUACH CHUILCEACHAN
435
Glendaruel Forest
Ruel
KILMORY CASTLE GARDENS
Carrick
Port Ann
360
KILMORY WOODLAND PARK
Largiemore
Ardrishaig
Achnaba
601 SGORACH
D
432 CRUACH NAN CUILEAN
Balliemore
Loch Tarsan
Loch Gilp
Castleton
Otter Ferry
Glendaruel
Clachan of Glendaruel
KILMODAN SCULPTURED STONES
Craigendive
Eilean Mòr
Ballimore
B836
Glen Lean
A83
LOCH FYNE
Achabraid
Auchnaha
Inverneill
Auchenbreck
458 CRUACH NAN CAORACH
405
A8003
Loch Riddon
203
611 CRUACH NAN
Kilfinan Bay
Kilfinan
Glenstriven
0 1 2 3 miles
0 1 2 3 4 5 km

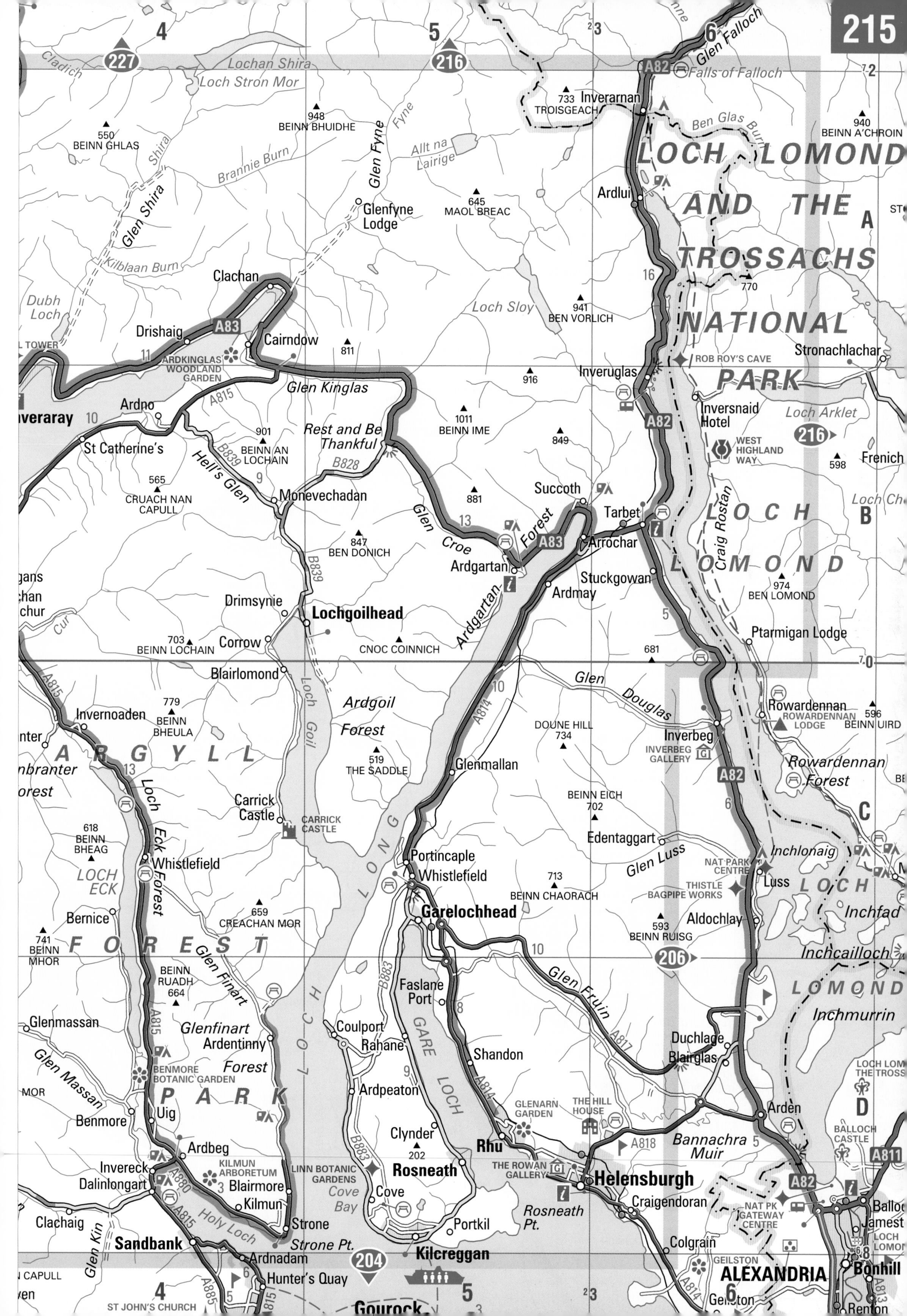

Lochan Shira
Loch Stron Mor
Glen Fyne
Glen Falloch
Falls of Falloch
Inverarnan
TROISGEACH
BEINN BHUIDHE
BEINN GHLAS
BEINN A'CHROIN
Allt na Lairige
Brannie Burn
Glen Shira
Glenfyne Lodge
MAOL BREAC
Ardlui
LOCH LOMOND AND THE TROSSACHS NATIONAL PARK
Kilblaan Burn
Clachan
Dubh Loch
Drishaig
Cairndow
Loch Sloy
BEN VORLICH
ARDKINGLAS WOODLAND GARDEN
Inveruglas
ROB ROY'S CAVE
Stronachlachar
Glen Kinglas
Inversnaid Hotel
Loch Arklet
Ardno
Inveraray
St Catherine's
Rest and Be Thankful
BEINN IME
BEINN AN LOCHAIN
Hell's Glen
WEST HIGHLAND WAY
Frenich
CRUACH NAN CAPULL
Monevechadan
Succoth
Tarbet
Glen Croe
Forest
Arrochar
LOCH LOMOND
Craig Rostan
BEN DONICH
Ardgartan
Stuckgowan
Ardmay
BEN LOMOND
Drimsynie
Lochgoilhead
Ardgartan
Ptarmigan Lodge
BEINN LOCHAIN
Corrow
CNOC COINNICH
Blairlomond
Loch Goil
Glen Douglas
Rowardennan
ROWARDENNAN LODGE
BEINN UIRD
Ardgoil Forest
Invernoaden
BEINN BHEULA
DOUNE HILL
Inverbeg
INVERBEG GALLERY
ARGYLL FOREST PARK
THE SADDLE
Glenmallan
Rowardennan Forest
Carrick Castle
CARRICK CASTLE
BEINN EICH
Loch Eck
Forest
BEINN BHEAG
Edentaggart
Glen Luss
Inchlonaig
Whistlefield
LOCH ECK
Portincaple
Whistlefield
NAT PARK CENTRE
Luss
LOCH LONG
THISTLE BAGPIPE WORKS
BEINN CHAORACH
Bernice
CREACHAN MOR
Garelochhead
Aldochlay
Inchfad
BEINN RUISG
BEINN MHOR
Glen Finart
Inchcailloch
BEINN RUADH
Glen Fruin
Faslane Port
GARE LOCH
LOMOND
Glenmassan
Inchmurrin
Glenfinart
Ardentinny
Coulport
Rahane
Shandon
Duchlage
Blairglas
Glen Massan
Forest
BENMORE BOTANIC GARDEN
Ardpeaton
LOCH LOMOND & THE TROSSACHS
Benmore
Uig
Clynder
GLENARN GARDEN
THE HILL HOUSE
Arden
Ardbeg
Bannachra Muir
BALLOCH CASTLE
Rhu
Invereck
KILMUN ARBORETUM
LINN BOTANIC GARDENS
Rosneath
THE ROWAN GALLERY
Helensburgh
Dalinlongart
Blairmore
Cove Bay
Cove
Craigendoran
Kilmun
Rosneath Pt.
NAT PK GATEWAY CENTRE
Balloch
Jamestown
Clachaig
Strone
Portkil
Holy Loch
LOCH LOMOND
Glen Kin
Sandbank
Strone Pt.
Colgrain
Ardnadam
Kilcreggan
GEILSTON
ALEXANDRIA
Bonhill
Hunter's Quay
ST JOHN'S CHURCH
Gourock
Geilston
Renton

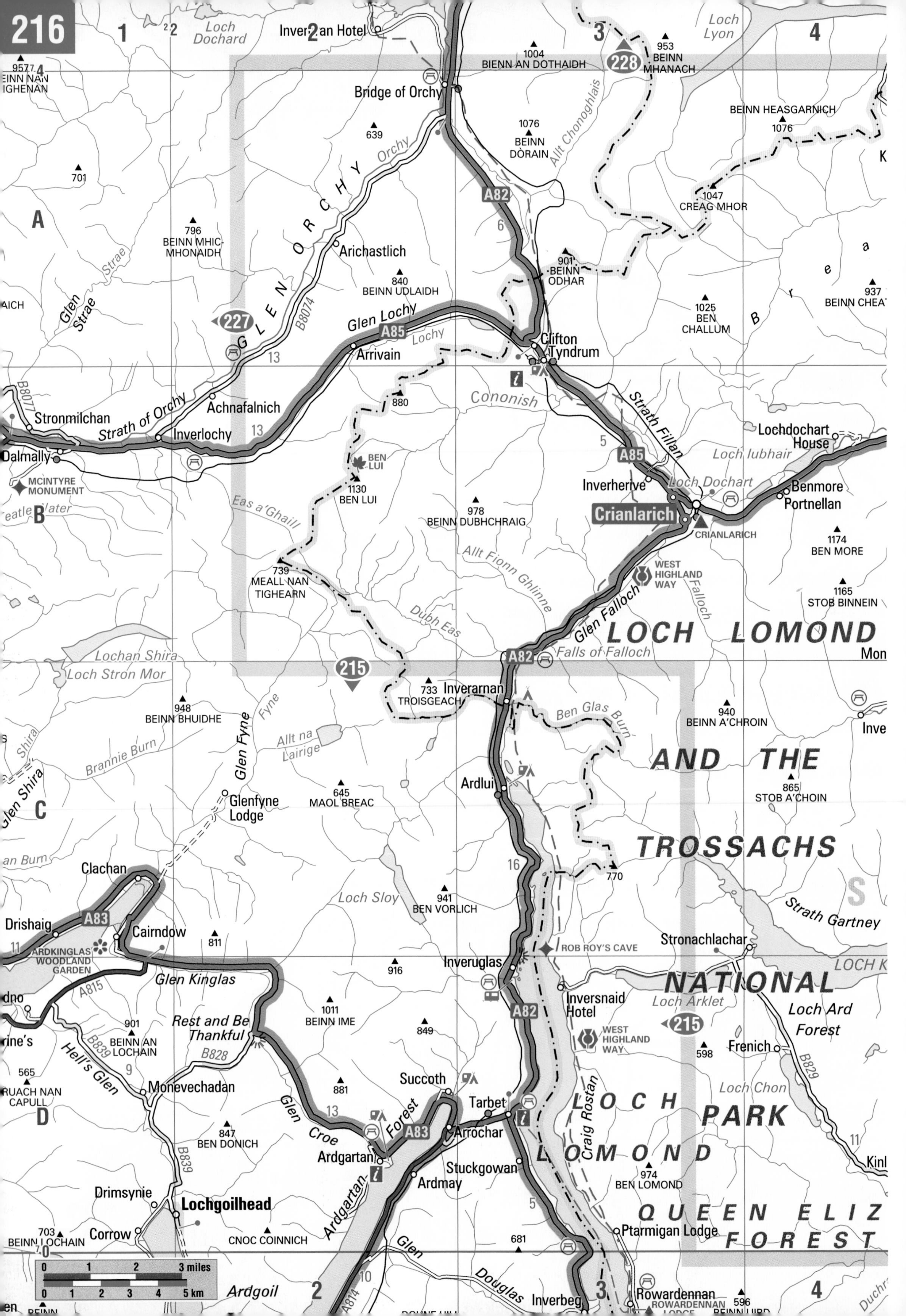

Inveroran Hotel
Loch Dochard
Bridge of Orchy
1004 BIENN AN DOTHAIDH
953 BEINN MHANACH
228
Loch Lyon
GLEN ORCHY
Arichastlich
1076 BEINN DÒRAIN
Allt Chonoghlais
BEINN HEASGARNICH 1076
1047 CREAG MHOR
796 BEINN MHIC-MHONAIDH
840 BEINN UDLAIDH
901 BEINN ODHAR
Glen Strae
227
B8074
Glen Lochy
A85
A82
Arrivain
Clifton
Tyndrum
1025 BEN CHALLUM
937 BEINN CHEAT
Stronmilchan
Strath of Orchy
Achnafalnich
Inverlochy
Dalmally
B8077
880
Cononish
Strath Fillan
Lochdochart House
Loch Iubhair
MCINTYRE MONUMENT
BEN LUI
1130 BEN LUI
978 BEINN DUBHCHRAIG
Inverherive
Loch Dochart
Benmore
Portnellan
Crianlarich
CRIANLARICH
1174 BEN MORE
Eas a'Ghaill
Allt Fionn Ghlinne
WEST HIGHLAND WAY
Falloch
739 MEALL NAN TIGHEARN
1165 STOB BINNEIN
Dubh Eas
Glen Falloch
LOCH LOMOND
Lochan Shira
Loch Stron Mor
215
Falls of Falloch
733 TROISGEACH
Inverarnan
948 BEINN BHUIDHE
Glen Fyne
Fyne
Allt na Lairige
Ben Glas Burn
940 BEINN A'CHROIN
AND THE
Brannie Burn
Glen Shira
Ardlui
645 MAOL BREAC
865 STOB A'CHOIN
Glenfyne Lodge
TROSSACHS
Clachan
Loch Sloy
770
941 BEN VORLICH
Drishaig
A83
Cairndow
ARDKINGLAS WOODLAND GARDEN
811
916
Inveruglas
ROB ROY'S CAVE
Stronachlachar
Strath Gartney
Glen Kinglas
A815
1011 BEINN IME
Inversnaid Hotel
NATIONAL
Loch Arklet
Loch Ard Forest
901 BEINN AN LOCHAIN
Rest and Be Thankful
849
WEST HIGHLAND WAY
215
598
Frenich
Hell's Glen
B839
B828
565 RUACH NAN CAPULL
Monevechadan
881
Succoth
Glen Croe
Tarbet
LOCH LOMOND
Craig Rostan
Loch Chon
PARK
B829
847 BEN DONICH
Ardgartan Forest
Arrochar
Ardgartan
Stuckgowan
Ardmay
974 BEN LOMOND
Drimsynie
Lochgoilhead
QUEEN ELIZ FOREST
703 BEINN LOCHAIN
Corrow
CNOC COINNICH
Ardgartan
681
Ptarmigan Lodge
Glen Douglas
Ardgoil
A814
Inverbeg
Rowardennan
596
0 1 2 3 miles
0 1 2 3 4 5 km

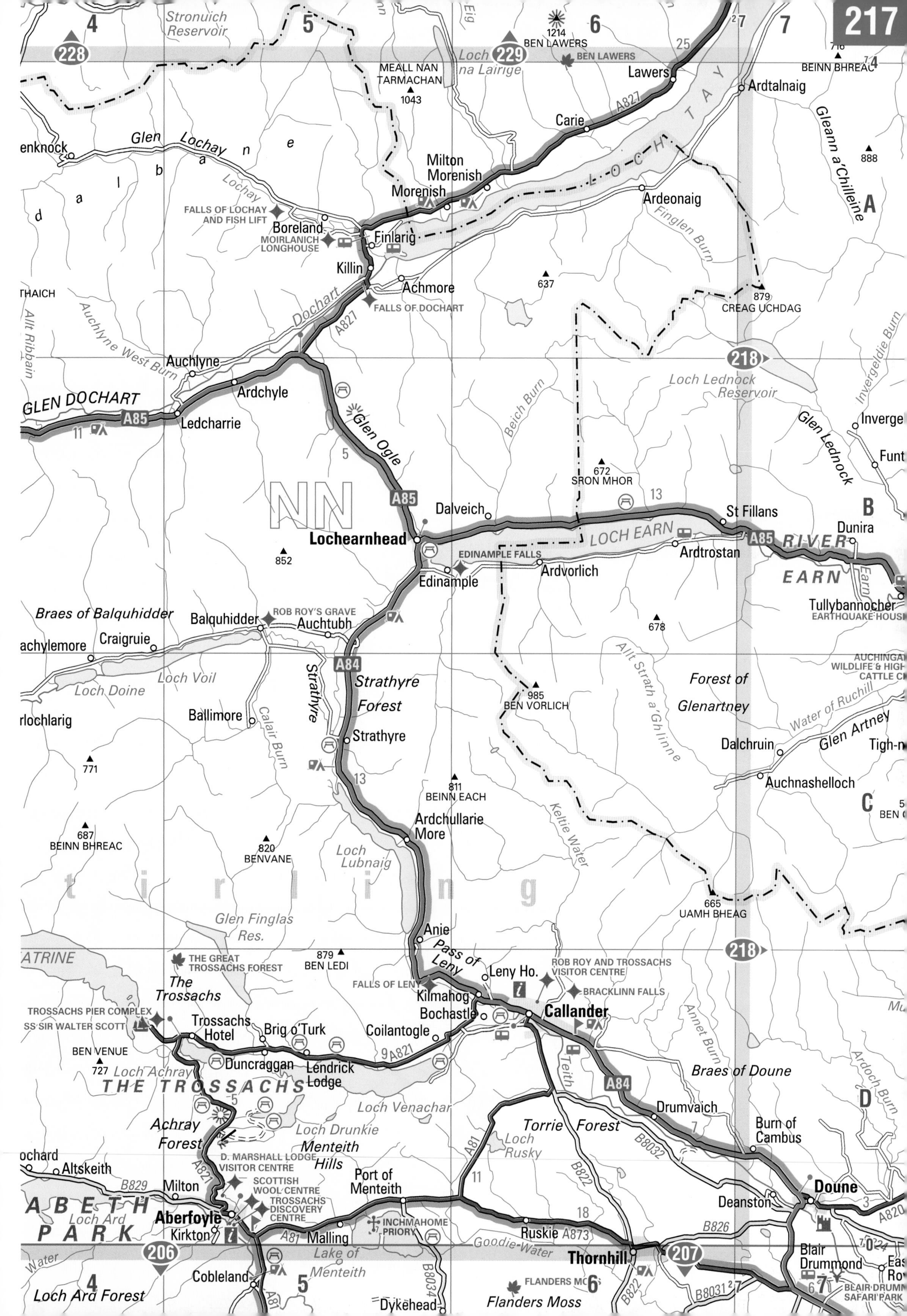
228
229
Stronuich Reservoir
1214 BEN LAWERS
BEN LAWERS
Loch na Lairige
MEALL NAN TARMACHAN
1043
Lawers
Ardtalnaig
BEINN BHREAC
A827
Carie
LOCH TAY
Gleann a'Chilleine
888
Glen Lochay
Breadalbane
Milton Morenish
Morenish
Ardeonaig
FALLS OF LOCHAY AND FISH LIFT
Boreland
MOIRLANICH LONGHOUSE
Finlarig
Finglen Burn
Killin
Achmore
637
FALLS OF DOCHART
879 CREAG UCHDAG
Dochart
Allt Ribbain
Auchlyne West Burn
Auchlyne
218
Loch Lednock Reservoir
Invergeldie Burn
Ardchyle
GLEN DOCHART
A85
Ledcharrie
Glen Ogle
Beich Burn
Glen Lednock
NN
672 SRON MHOR
Dalveich
St Fillans
Dunira
Lochearnhead
LOCH EARN
852
EDINAMPLE FALLS
Ardvorlich
Ardtrostan
RIVER EARN
Edinample
Tullybannocher
Braes of Balquhidder
Balquhidder
ROB ROY'S GRAVE
Auchtubh
678
Craigruie
A84
Allt Strath a'Ghlinne
Loch Voil
Strathyre Forest
Forest of Glenartney
Loch Doine
985 BEN VORLICH
Water of Ruchill
Ballimore
Calair Burn
Strathyre
Dalchruin
Glen Artney
771
811 BEINN EACH
Auchnashelloch
Ardchullarie More
Keltie Water
687 BEINN BHREAC
820 BENVANE
Loch Lubnaig
Stirling
665 UAMH BHEAG
Glen Finglas Res.
Anie
Pass of Leny
THE GREAT TROSSACHS FOREST
879 BEN LEDI
Leny Ho.
ROB ROY AND TROSSACHS VISITOR CENTRE
The Trossachs
FALLS OF LENY
Kilmahog
BRACKLINN FALLS
TROSSACHS PIER COMPLEX
SS SIR WALTER SCOTT
Trossachs Hotel
Brig o'Turk
Bochastle
Callander
Coilantogle
Annet Burn
BEN VENUE
727
Loch Achray
Duncraggan
A821
Lendrick Lodge
Braes of Doune
THE TROSSACHS
Loch Venachar
Teith
Ardoch Burn
Achray Forest
Loch Drunkie
Torrie Forest
Drumvaich
Loch Rusky
Burn of Cambus
Menteith Hills
D. MARSHALL LODGE VISITOR CENTRE
B8032
Altskeith
A81
B822
Milton
SCOTTISH WOOL CENTRE
Port of Menteith
Doune
TROSSACHS DISCOVERY CENTRE
Deanston
Loch Ard
Aberfoyle
INCHMAHOME PRIORY
Ruskie
A873
B826
Kirkton
Malling
Goodie Water
Lake of Menteith
Thornhill
207
206
B8034
FLANDERS MOSS
Blair Drummond
Cobleland
Loch Ard Forest
Flanders Moss
B8031
BLAIR DRUMMOND SAFARI PARK
Dykehead

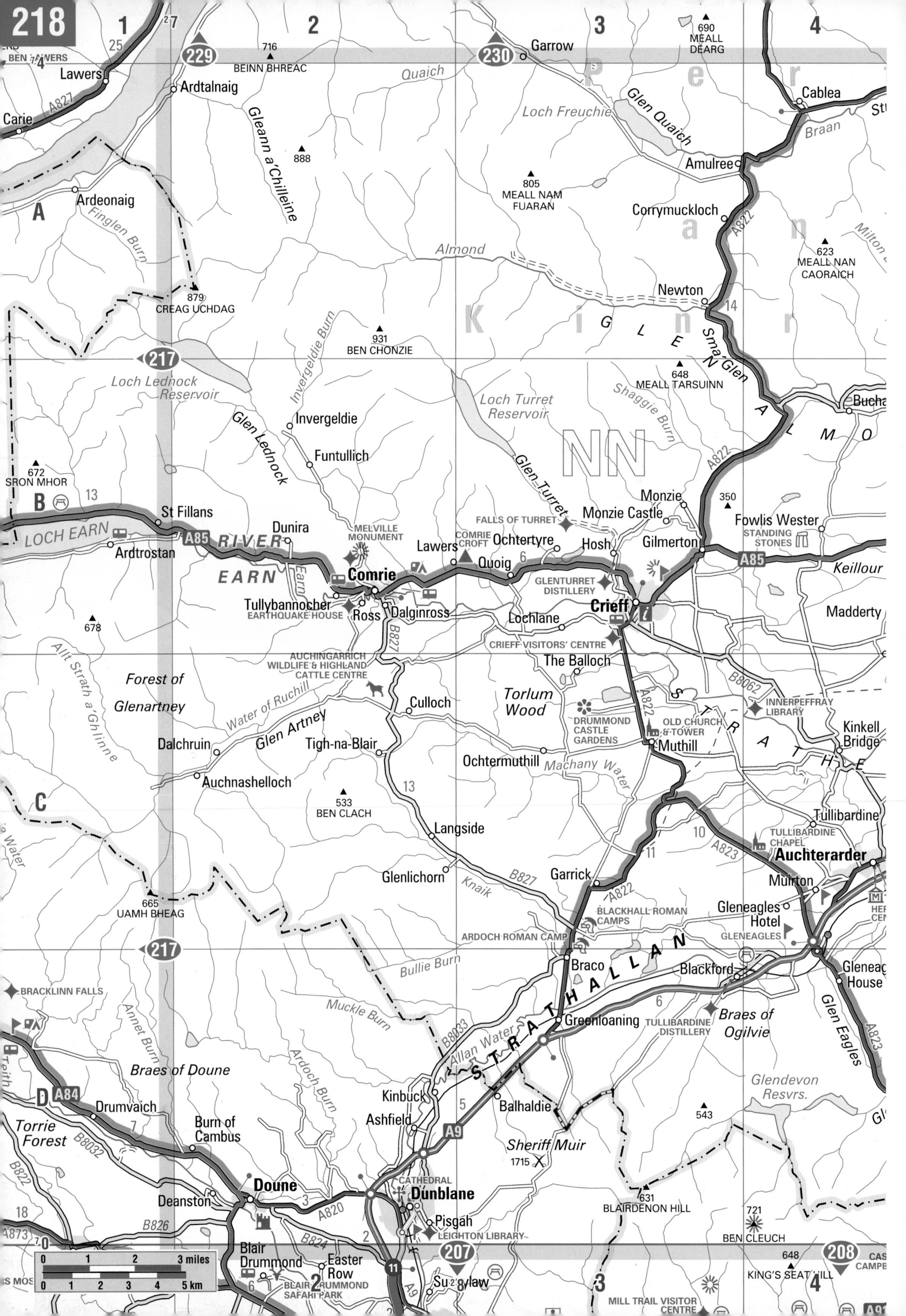
1
2
3
4
A
B
C
D
229
230
217
207
208
Lawers
Carie
Ardtalnaig
Ardeonaig
Finglen Burn
716
BEINN BHREAC
Quaich
Garrow
690
MEALL DEARG
Cablea
Braan
Loch Freuchie
Glen Quaich
Amulree
Gleann a'Chilleine
888
805
MEALL NAM FUARAN
Corrymuckloch
A822
623
MEALL NAN CAORAICH
Almond
Newton
879
CREAG UCHDAG
931
BEN CHONZIE
Invergeldie Burn
GLEN ALMOND
Sma' Glen
648
MEALL TARSUINN
Loch Lednock Reservoir
Loch Turret Reservoir
Shaggie Burn
Invergeldie
Glen Lednock
Funtullich
Glen Turret
NN
672
SRON MHOR
Monzie
350
St Fillans
Monzie Castle
Fowlis Wester
LOCH EARN
Dunira
MELVILLE MONUMENT
FALLS OF TURRET
STANDING STONES
Ardtrostan
A85
RIVER EARN
COMRIE CROFT
Lawers
Ochtertyre
Hosh
Gilmerton
Quoig
Keillour
Comrie
GLENTURRET DISTILLERY
Crieff
Madderty
Tullybannocher
EARTHQUAKE HOUSE
Ross
Dalginross
Lochlane
678
B827
CRIEFF VISITORS' CENTRE
AUCHINGARRICH WILDLIFE & HIGHLAND CATTLE CENTRE
The Balloch
Allt Strath a'Ghlinne
Forest of Glenartney
Water of Ruchill
Torlum Wood
B8062
INNERPEFFRAY LIBRARY
Culloch
DRUMMOND CASTLE GARDENS
OLD CHURCH & TOWER
Kinkell Bridge
Glen Artney
STRATHEARN
Dalchruin
Tigh-na-Blair
Muthill
Ochtermuthill
Machany Water
Auchnashelloch
533
BEN CLACH
Tullibardine
Langside
TULLIBARDINE CHAPEL
A823
Auchterarder
Glenlichorn
Knaik
Garrick
Muirton
665
UAMH BHEAG
BLACKHALL ROMAN CAMPS
Gleneagles Hotel
GLENEAGLES
ARDOCH ROMAN CAMP
Braco
Bullie Burn
Blackford
Gleneagles House
BRACKLINN FALLS
STRATHALLAN
Muckle Burn
Annet Burn
B8033
Allan Water
Greenloaning
TULLIBARDINE DISTILLERY
Braes of Ogilvie
Glen Eagles
Ardoch Burn
Braes of Doune
Glendevon Resvrs.
Kinbuck
A84
Drumvaich
Balhaldie
543
Torrie Forest
Burn of Cambus
Ashfield
A9
B8032
Sheriff Muir
1715
B822
Doune
CATHEDRAL
Dunblane
631
BLAIRDENON HILL
Deanston
A820
721
Pisgah
B826
B824
LEIGHTON LIBRARY
BEN CLEUCH
A873
Blair Drummond
Easter Row
648
KING'S SEAT HILL
3 miles
5 km
BLAIR DRUMMOND SAFARI PARK
Sunnylaw
MILL TRAIL VISITOR CENTRE

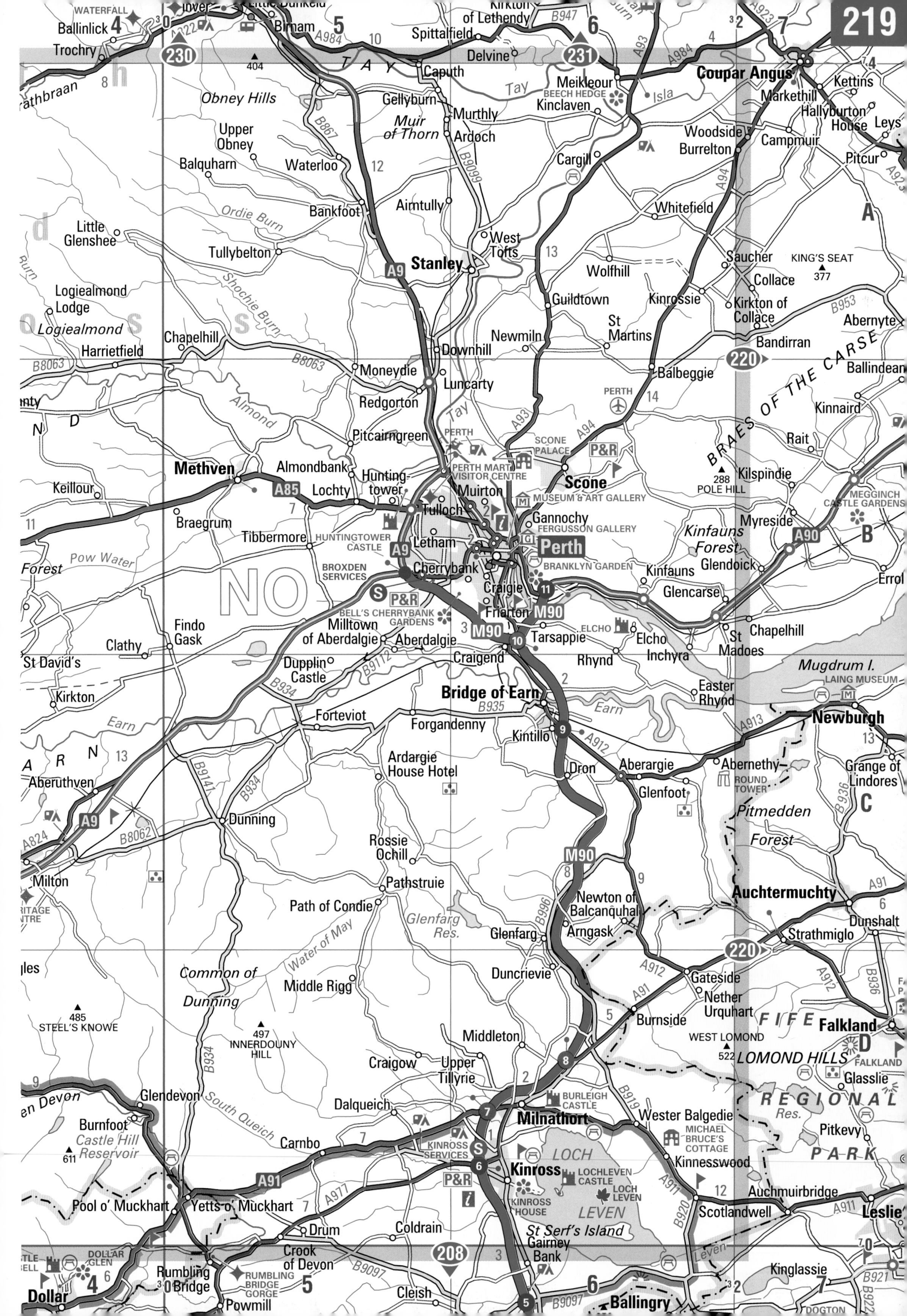
WATERFALL
Ballinlick
Trochry
Birnam
of Lethendy
Spittalfield
Delvine
Caputh
Coupar Angus
Meikleour
BEECH HEDGE
Kinclaven
Markethill
Kettins
Hallyburton House
Leys
Woodside
Burrelton
Campmuir
Pitcur
Obney Hills
Upper Obney
Gellyburn
Murthly
Muir of Thorn
Ardoch
Balquharn
Waterloo
Cargill
Bankfoot
Airntully
Whitefield
Ordie Burn
Little Glenshee
Tullybelton
West Tofts
Stanley
Wolfhill
Saucher
KING'S SEAT
377
Collace
Kirkton of Collace
Logiealmond Lodge
Logiealmond
Shochie Burn
Guildtown
Kinrossie
St Martins
Abernyte
Chapelhill
Harrietfield
Newmiln
Downhill
Bandirran
BRAES OF THE CARSE
Ballindean
Moneydie
Luncarty
Balbeggie
Redgorton
PERTH
Kinnaird
Almond
Tay
Pitcairngreen
SCONE PALACE
P&R
Rait
Methven
Almondbank
PERTH MART VISITOR CENTRE
Scone
288
POLE HILL
Kilspindie
Keillour
Lochty
Huntingtower
Muirton
MUSEUM & ART GALLERY
MEGGINCH CASTLE GARDENS
Braegrum
Tulloch
Gannochy
FERGUSSON GALLERY
Myreside
Tibbermore
HUNTINGTOWER CASTLE
Letham
Perth
Kinfauns Forest
Pow Water
Forest
BROXDEN SERVICES
Cherrybank
BRANKLYN GARDEN
Kinfauns
Glendoick
Errol
NO
Craigie
Glencarse
BELL'S CHERRYBANK GARDENS
Friarton
Findo Gask
Milltown of Aberdalgie
Aberdalgie
Tarsappie
ELCHO
Elcho
Chapelhill
St Madoes
Clathy
Inchyra
St David's
Dupplin Castle
Craigend
Rhynd
Mugdrum I.
LAING MUSEUM
Kirkton
Bridge of Earn
Easter Rhynd
Earn
Forteviot
Forgandenny
Kintillo
Newburgh
Aberuthven
Ardargie House Hotel
Dron
Aberargie
Abernethy
ROUND TOWER
Grange of Lindores
Glenfoot
Pitmedden Forest
Dunning
Rossie Ochill
Milton
Pathstruie
Path of Condie
Glenfarg Res.
Newton of Balcanquhal
Auchtermuchty
Dunshalt
Glenfarg
Arngask
Strathmiglo
Water of May
Common of Dunning
Middle Rigg
Duncrievie
Gateside
Nether Urquhart
Burnside
FIFE
Falkland
485
STEEL'S KNOWE
497
INNERDOUNY HILL
Middleton
WEST LOMOND
522
LOMOND HILLS
FALKLAND
Craigow
Upper Tillyrie
Glasslie
Glendevon
South Queich
BURLEIGH CASTLE
REGIONAL PARK
Dalqueich
Milnathort
Wester Balgedie
Burnfoot
Castle Hill Reservoir
611
Carnbo
KINROSS SERVICES
LOCH
MICHAEL BRUCE'S COTTAGE
Pitkevy
Kinnesswood
Kinross
LOCHLEVEN CASTLE
LOCH LEVEN
KINROSS HOUSE
LEVEN
Auchmuirbridge
Pool o' Muckhart
Yetts o' Muckhart
Coldrain
Scotlandwell
Leslie
Drum
St Serf's Island
Gairney Bank
Crook of Devon
DOLLAR GLEN
Rumbling Bridge
RUMBLING BRIDGE GORGE
Kinglassie
Dollar
Cleish
Powmill
Ballingry
DOGTON
A9
A85
M90
A91
A93
A94
A90
A912
A913
A977
A911
A984
A923
A824
A921
B867
B9099
B8063
B9112
B934
B935
B9141
B8062
B996
B919
B920
B9097
B953
B936
B947
B921
B922
230
231
220
208

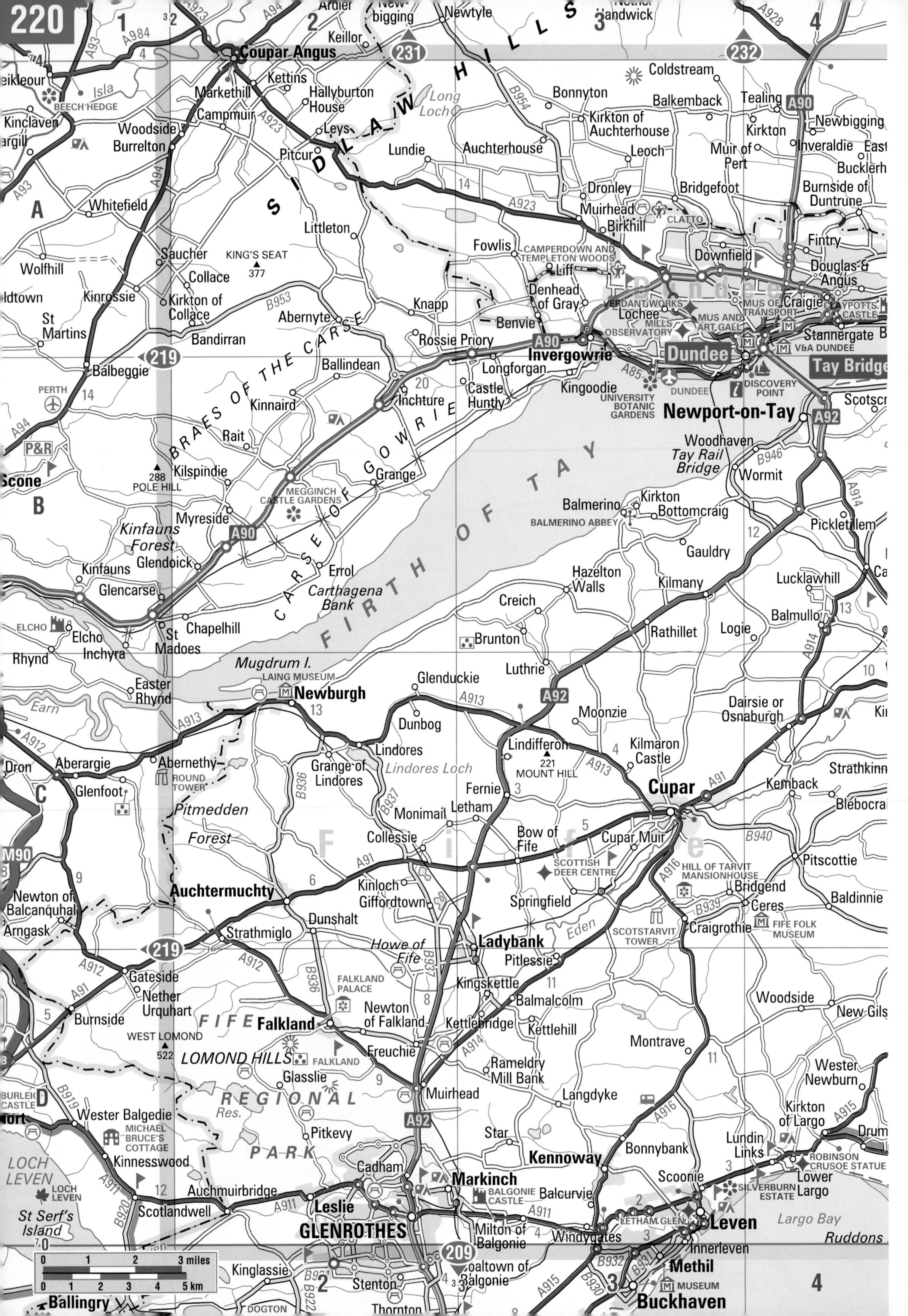

Coupar Angus
Keillor
Newtyle
SIDLAW HILLS
Kettins
Markethill
Hallyburton House
Long Loch
Campmuir
Woodside
Burrelton
Leys
Pitcur
Lundie
Auchterhouse
Bonnyton
Coldstream
Balkemback
Tealing
Kirkton of Auchterhouse
Leoch
Kirkton
Newbigging
Muir of Pert
Inveraldie
Bucklerh
Dronley
Bridgefoot
Burnside of Duntrune
Muirhead
Birkhill
CLATTO
Fintry
Downfield
Douglas & Angus
Craigie
CLAYPOTTS CASTLE
Stannergate
Meikleour
Isla
BEECH HEDGE
Kinclaven
Whitefield
Littleton
Fowlis
CAMPERDOWN AND TEMPLETON WOODS
Liff
Denhead of Gray
Lochee
VERDANT WORKS
MUS OF TRANSPORT
MUS AND ART GALL
MILLS OBSERVATORY
V&A DUNDEE
Dundee
Tay Bridge
Saucher
KING'S SEAT 377
Wolfhill
Collace
Kinrossie
Kirkton of Collace
St Martins
B953
Abernyte
Knapp
Benvie
Bandirran
Rossie Priory
Invergowrie
Longforgan
Kingoodie
UNIVERSITY BOTANIC GARDENS
DUNDEE
DISCOVERY POINT
Newport-on-Tay
Scotscr
Balbeggie
219
PERTH
BRAES OF THE CARSE
Ballindean
Kinnaird
Inchture
Castle Huntly
CARSE OF GOWRIE
Rait
P&R
Scone
288 POLE HILL
Kilspindie
Grange
MEGGINCH CASTLE GARDENS
FIRTH OF TAY
Woodhaven
Tay Rail Bridge
Wormit
Kirkton
Balmerino
Bottomcraig
BALMERINO ABBEY
Pickletillem
Myreside
Kinfauns Forest
Gauldry
Kinfauns
Glendoick
Errol
Carthagena Bank
Hazelton Walls
Kilmany
Lucklawhill
Glencarse
Creich
Balmullo
ELCHO
Elcho
Inchyra
Chapelhill
St Madoes
Rathillet
Logie
Brunton
Rhynd
Mugdrum I.
LAING MUSEUM
Newburgh
Luthrie
Glenduckie
Easter Rhynd
Earn
A913
Dunbog
Moonzie
Dairsie or Osnaburgh
Lindores
Lindifferon
221 MOUNT HILL
Kilmaron Castle
Dron
Aberargie
Abernethy
ROUND TOWER
Grange of Lindores
Lindores Loch
Strathkinn
Glenfoot
Fernie
Cupar
Kemback
Pitmedden Forest
Monimail
Letham
Blebocrai
Collessie
Bow of Fife
Cupar Muir
Fife
SCOTTISH DEER CENTRE
HILL OF TARVIT MANSIONHOUSE
Pitscottie
Newton of Balcanquhal
Auchtermuchty
Kinloch
Giffordtown
Springfield
Bridgend
Ceres
Baldinnie
Arngask
Strathmiglo
Dunshalt
Ladybank
Eden
SCOTSTARVIT TOWER
Craigrothie
FIFE FOLK MUSEUM
Howe of Fife
Pitlessie
Gateside
Nether Urquhart
FALKLAND PALACE
Kingskettle
Balmalcolm
Woodside
New Gils
Burnside
FIFE
Falkland
Newton of Falkland
Kettlebridge
Kettlehill
WEST LOMOND 522
LOMOND HILLS
FALKLAND
Freuchie
Montrave
Rameldry Mill Bank
Wester Newburn
Glasslie
REGIONAL PARK
Muirhead
Langdyke
Kirkton of Largo
Wester Balgedie
Res.
MICHAEL BRUCE'S COTTAGE
Pitkevy
Star
Lundin Links
Bonnybank
Kennoway
Kinnesswood
ROBINSON CRUSOE STATUE
LOCH LEVEN
Cadham
Markinch
Scoonie
Lower Largo
SILVERBURN ESTATE
BALGONIE CASTLE
Balcurvie
Auchmuirbridge
Leslie
Scotlandwell
LETHAM GLEN
Leven
Largo Bay
St Serf's Island
GLENROTHES
Milton of Balgonie
Windygates
Ruddons
Innerleven
209
Methil
Kinglassie
Coaltown of Balgonie
MUSEUM
Buckhaven
Stenton
Ballingry
DOGTON
Thornton
0 1 2 3 miles
0 1 2 3 4 5 km
A90
A92
A91
A912
A914
A916
A915
A911
A923
A94
A93
A984
A85
A928
B954
B946
B936
B937
B939
B940
B932
B930
B931
B919
B920
B922
M90
231
232

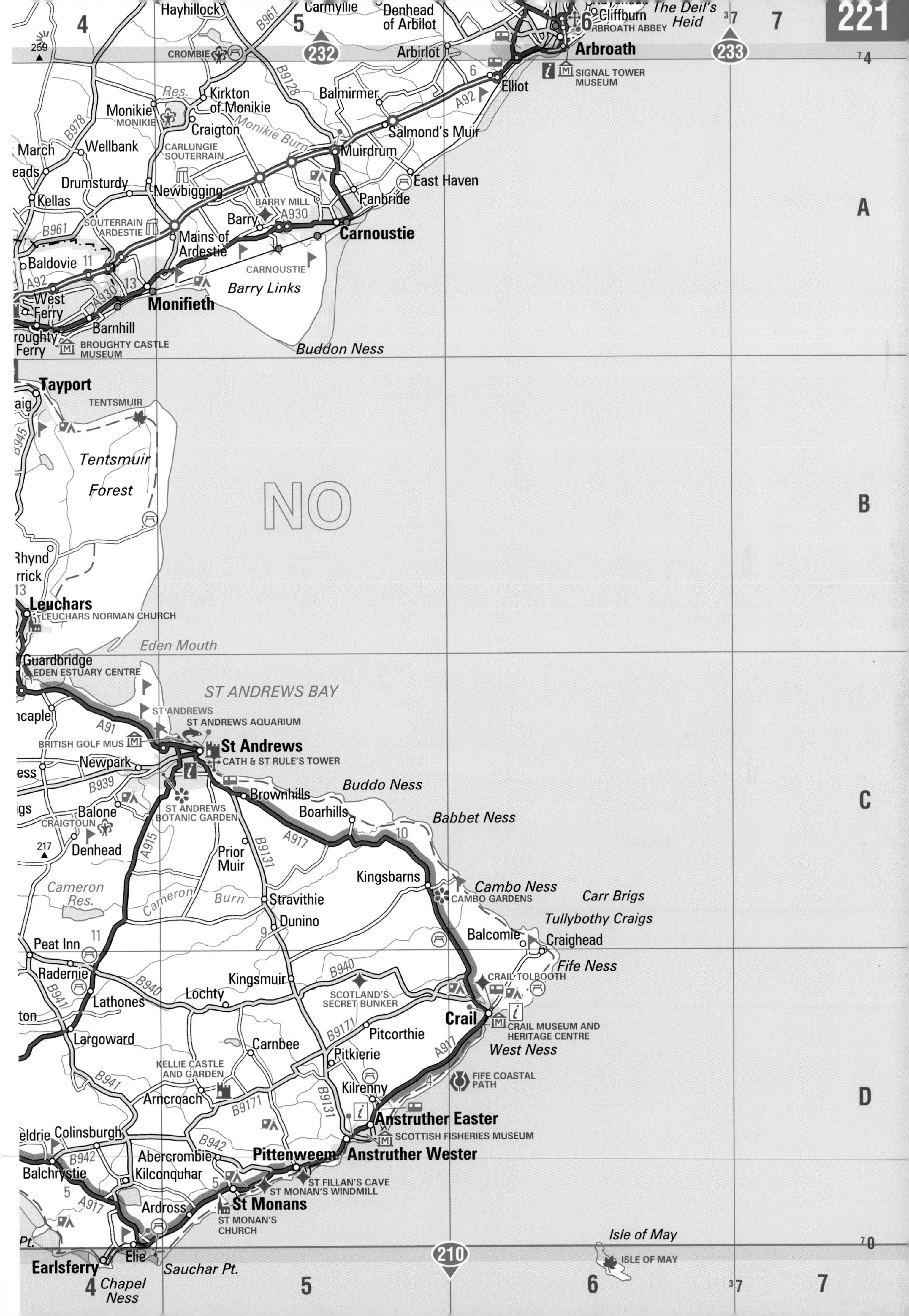

4   5   7   7

Hayhillock   Carmyllie   Denhead   Cliffburn
of Arbilot   The Deil's   Heid

259

CROMBIE   232   Arbilot   Arbroath   233   7 4
ARBROATH ABBEY

B961   B9128   Balmirmer   A92   Elliot   SIGNAL TOWER MUSEUM

Kirkton   of Monikie   Craigton   Salmond's Muir

Monikie   MONIKIE   Muirdrum

March   Wellbank   CARLUNGIE SOUTERRAIN   Monikie Burn

eads   Drumsturdy   Newbigging   BARRY MILL   Panbride   East Haven

Kellas   SOUTERRAIN ARDESTIE   Barry   A930

Baldovie   11   Mains of Ardestie   Carnoustie

B961   A930   13

West Ferry   CARNOUSTIE   **A**

Monifieth   Barry Links

Barnhill   Buddon Ness

roughty Ferry   BROUGHTY CASTLE MUSEUM

Tayport   TENTSMUIR

raig   Tentsmuir Forest

B945   **NO**   **B**

Rhynd   rrick

13

Leuchars   LEUCHARS NORMAN CHURCH

Guardbridge   Eden Mouth
EDEN ESTUARY CENTRE

ncaple   ST ANDREWS BAY

A91   St Andrews   ST ANDREWS AQUARIUM

BRITISH GOLF MUS   **St Andrews**   **C**
Newpark   CATH & ST RULE'S TOWER

B939   ST ANDREWS BOTANIC GARDEN   Brownhills   Buddo Ness

ess   Balone   Boarhills   Babbet Ness

igs   CRAIGTOUN   Prior Muir   10

217   Denhead   A915   B9131   A917   Kingsbarns   Cambo Ness   Carr Brigs
CAMBO GARDENS

Cameron Res.   Cameron Burn   Stravithie   Tullybothy Craigs

Peat Inn   11   Dunino   9   Balcomie   Craighead

Radernie   Kingsmuir   B940   Fife Ness

B941   Lochty   SCOTLAND'S SECRET BUNKER   CRAIL TOLBOOTH

Lathones   B940   B9171   Pitcorthie   **Crail**   CRAIL MUSEUM AND HERITAGE CENTRE

Largoward   Carnbee   Pitkierie   A917   West Ness

ton   B941   KELLIE CASTLE AND GARDEN   B9131   Kilrenny   FIFE COASTAL PATH   **D**

eldrie   Colinsburgh   Arncroach   B9171   **Anstruther Easter**
SCOTTISH FISHERIES MUSEUM

B942   Abercrombie   B942   **Pittenweem**   **Anstruther Wester**

Balchrystie   Kilconquhar   ST FILLAN'S CAVE   ST MONAN'S WINDMILL

A917   5   Ardross   **St Monans**   ST MONAN'S CHURCH

Pt.   Elie   Isle of May   210   ISLE OF MAY   7 0

Earlsferry   Chapel Ness   Sauchar Pt.

4   5   6   7

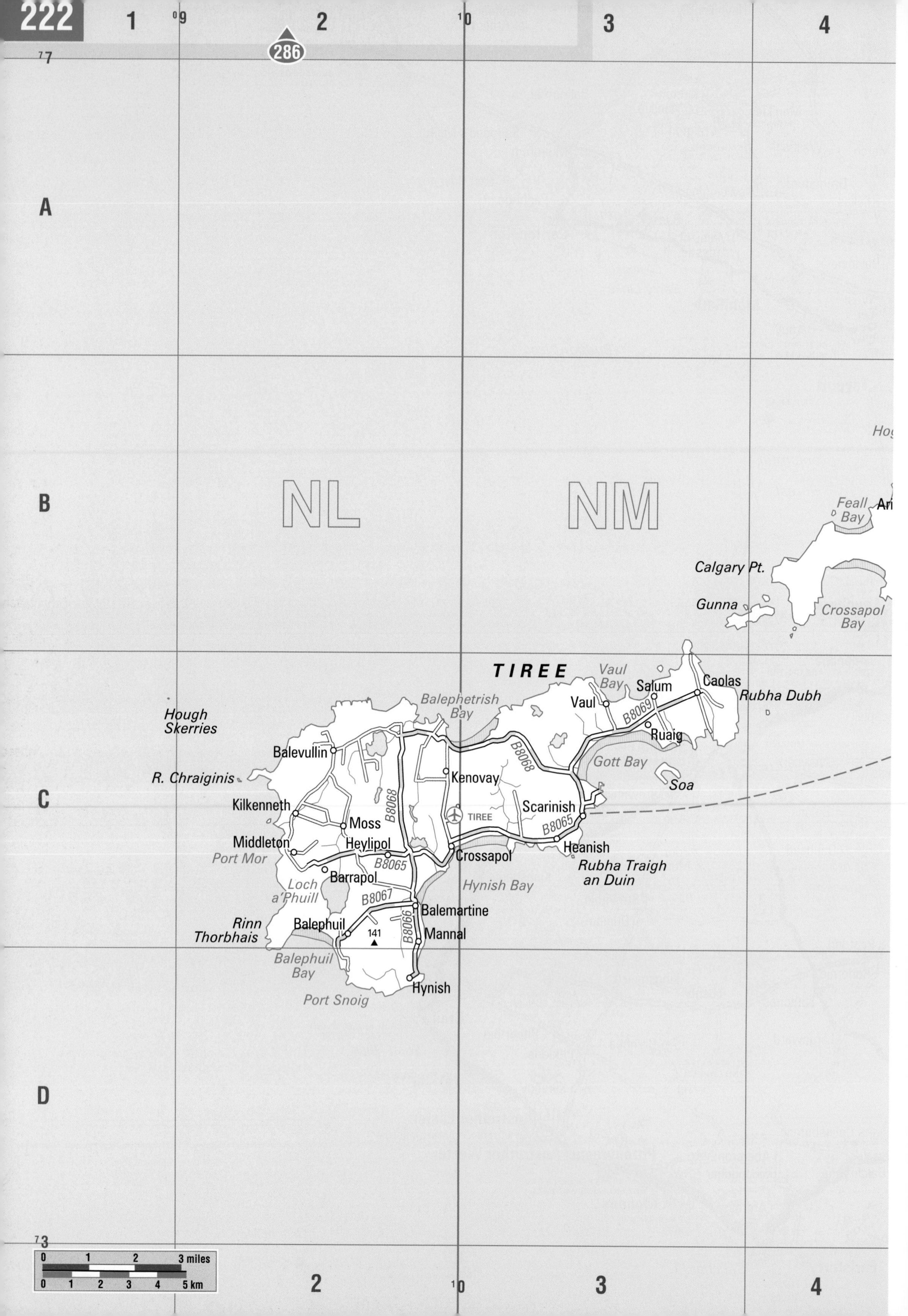

1 09 2 10 3 4

A

NL NM

B

Hog

Feall Bay Ari

Calgary Pt.

Gunna Crossapol Bay

TIREE

Vaul Bay

Salum Caolas

Vaul B8069 Rubha Dubh

Ruaig

Hough Skerries

Balephetrish Bay

Gott Bay

Balevullin

Soa

R. Chraiginis

Kenovay

C

Kilkenneth

B8068

Scarinish

Moss

B8065

Middleton Heylipol TIREE Heanish

Port Mor Crossapol Rubha Traigh
an Duin

B8065

Barrapol

Loch a'Phuill Hynish Bay

B8067

Rinn
Thorbhais Balephuil Balemartine

141 B8066 Mannal

Balephuil Bay

Port Snoig Hynish

D

73

0 1 2 3 miles
0 1 2 3 4 5 km

2 10 3 4

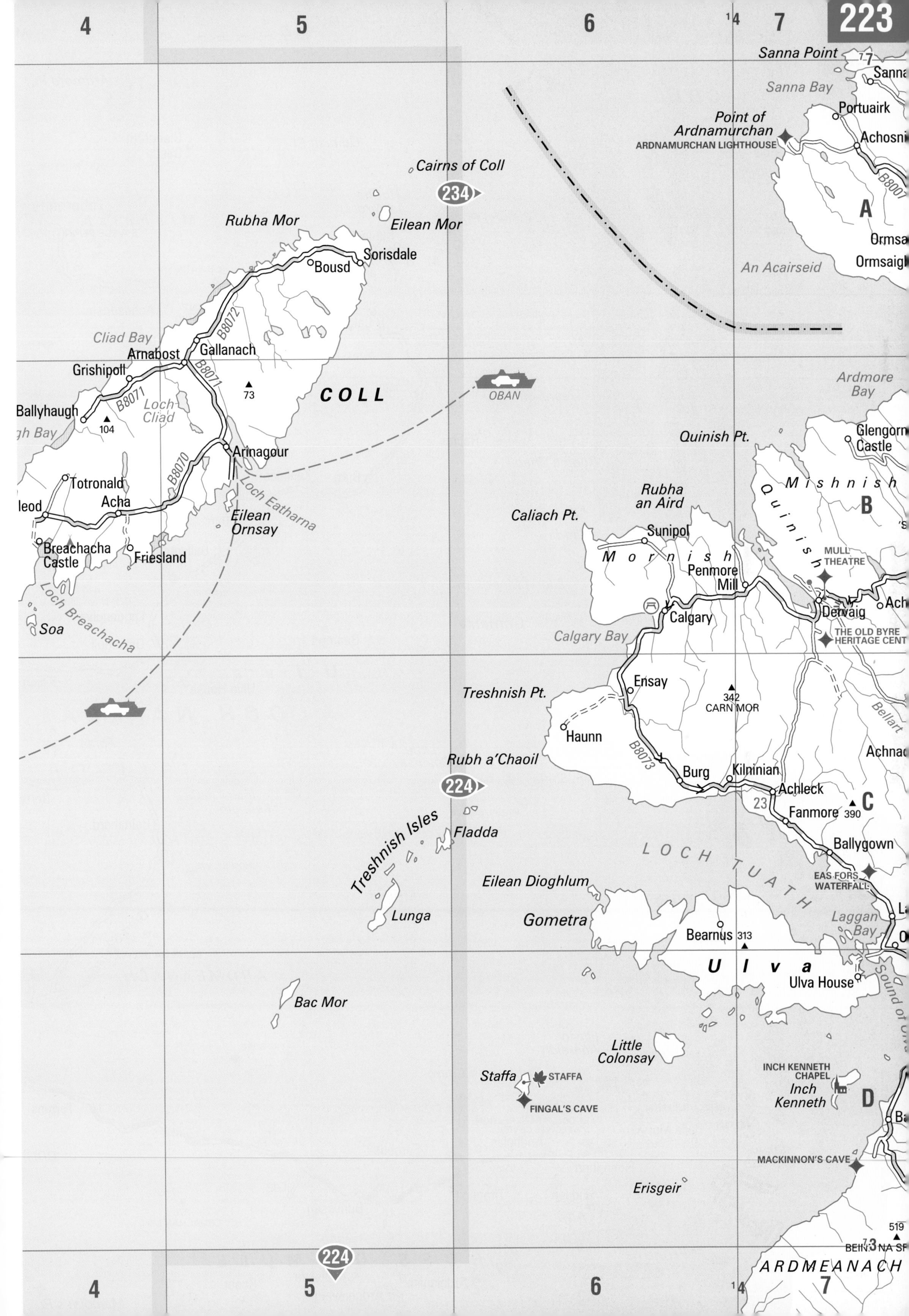

4 **5** **6** **7**

Sanna Point

Sanna Bay

Sanna

Point of
Ardnamurchan
ARDNAMURCHAN LIGHTHOUSE

Portuairk

Achosni

A

Cairns of Coll

234 ▷

Eilean Mor

An Acairseid

Ormsa

Ormsaig

Rubha Mor

Bousd

Sorisdale

Ardmore
Bay

Cliad Bay

Arnabost   Gallanach

Grishipoll

B8072

B8071

▲ 73

C O L L

OBAN 🚢

Quinish Pt.

Glengorn
Castle

M i s h n i s h

Ballyhaugh

B8071

Loch
Cliad

▲
104

gh Bay

Rubha
an Aird

Caliach Pt.

Sunipol

M o r n i s h

Q u i n i s h

MULL
THEATRE

B

Totronald

Acha

Arinagour

Penmore
Mill

Derviag

Ach

leod

B8070

Loch Eatharna

Eilean
Ornsay

🅿

Calgary

THE OLD BYRE
HERITAGE CENT

Breachacha
Castle

Friesland

Calgary Bay

Loch Breachacha

Soa

🚢

Treshnish Pt.

Ensay

▲ 342
CARN MOR

Bellart

Achna

Haunn

B8073

Rubh a'Chaoil

224 ▷

Burg   Kilninian

Achleck

Fanmore ▲ 390

C

Treshnish Isles

Fladda

Eilean Dioghlum

L   O   C   H   T   U   A   T   H

Ballygown

EAS FORS
WATERFALL

La

Lunga

Gometra

Bearnus ▲ 313

Laggan
Bay

O

U l v a

Ulva House

Bac Mor

INCH KENNETH
CHAPEL

*Inch
Kenneth*

D

Little
Colonsay

Ba

Staffa 🍁 STAFFA

MACKINNON'S CAVE

🔹 FINGAL'S CAVE

Erisgeir

▲ 519

BEINN NA SF

A R D M E A N A C H

224
▽

4 **5** **6** **7**

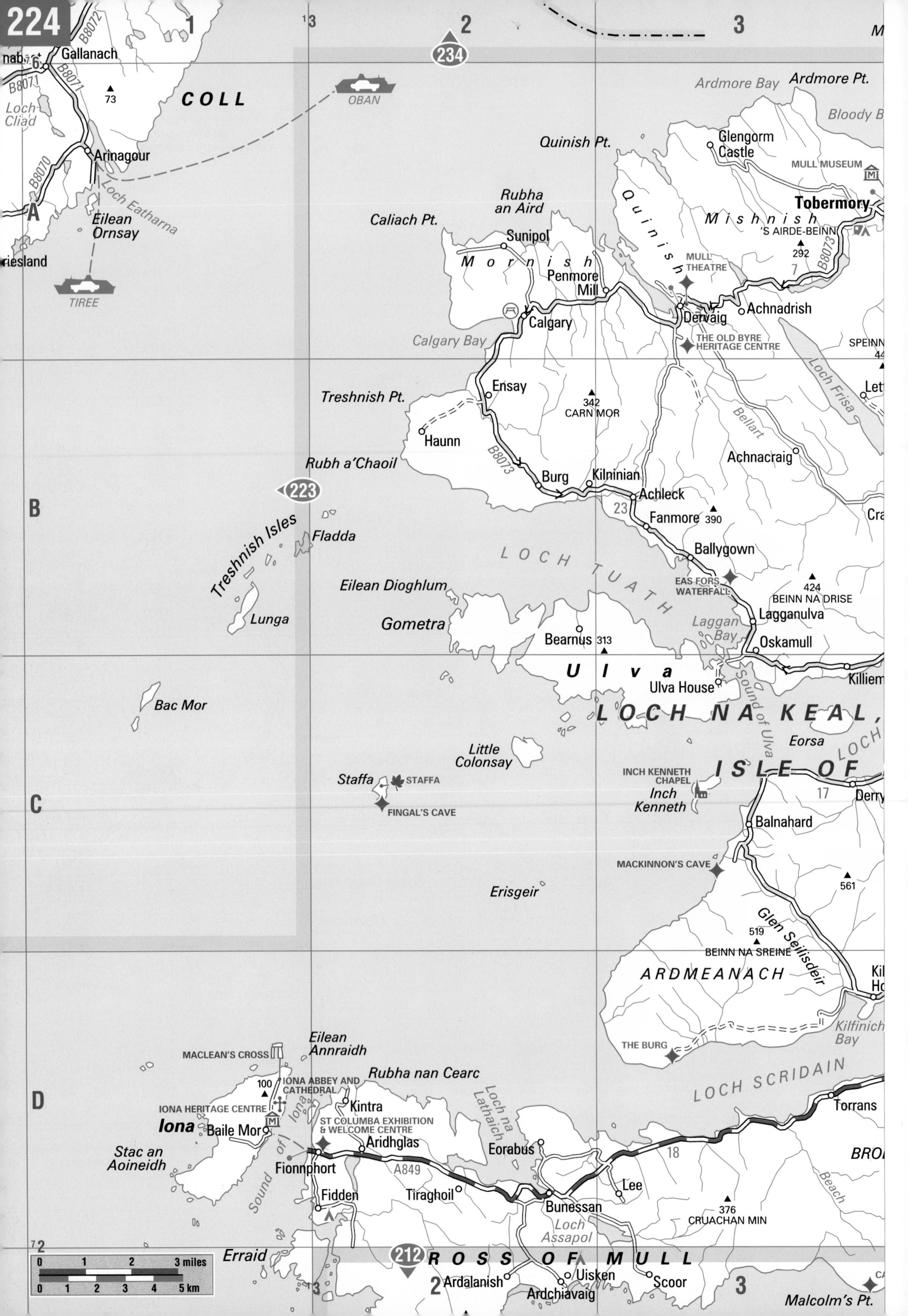

COLL

Gallanach

nab

B8072

B8071

Loch Cliad

Eilean Ornsay

B8070

Arinagour

Loch Eatharna

73

iesland

TIREE

OBAN

234

1 ³3 **2** **3** M

Ardmore Bay Ardmore Pt.

Bloody B

Quinish Pt.

Glengorm Castle

MULL MUSEUM

Tobermory

Quinish

Mishnish

'S AIRDE-BEINN

292

7

B8073

Let

Loch Frisa

Caliach Pt.

Rubha an Aird

Sunipol

Mornish

Penmore Mill

Calgary

MULL THEATRE

Dervaig

Achnadrish

Calgary Bay

THE OLD BYRE HERITAGE CENTRE

SPEINN 44

Treshnish Pt.

Ensay

342 CARN MOR

Bellart

Achnacraig

Haunn

Rubh a'Chaoil

B8073

Burg

Kilninian

Achleck

23

Fanmore

390

Cra

223

Treshnish Isles

Fladda

Ballygown

EAS FORS WATERFALL

424 BEINN NA DRISE

Eilean Dioghlum

LOCH TUATH

Lagganulva

Lunga

Gometra

Bearnus 313

Laggan Bay

Oskamull

U l v a

Killiem

Bac Mor

Ulva House

LOCH NA KEAL,

Eorsa

Loch

ISLE OF

Little Colonsay

17

Derry

INCH KENNETH CHAPEL

Inch Kenneth

Staffa ★ STAFFA

Balnahard

★ FINGAL'S CAVE

Erisgeir

MACKINNON'S CAVE

561

Glen Seilisdeir

519 BEINN NA SREINE

ARDMEANACH

Kil Ho

Kilfinich Bay

THE BURG

LOCH SCRIDAIN

Eilean Annraidh

MACLEAN'S CROSS

Rubha nan Cearc

Loch na Lathaich

Torrans

100

IONA ABBEY AND CATHEDRAL

18

BRO

IONA HERITAGE CENTRE

Kintra

Iona

Baile Mor

ST COLUMBA EXHIBITION & WELCOME CENTRE

Stac an Aoineidh

Sound of Iona

Aridhglas

Eorabus

Lee

Fionnphort

A849

Fidden

Tiraghoil

Bunessan

376 CRUACHAN MIN

Erraid

212

R O S S O F M U L L

Loch Assapol

Ardalanish

Ardchiavaig

Uisken

Scoor

Malcolm's Pt.

CA

3

0   1   2   3 miles
0 1 2 3 4 5 km

7 2
³3
2
2

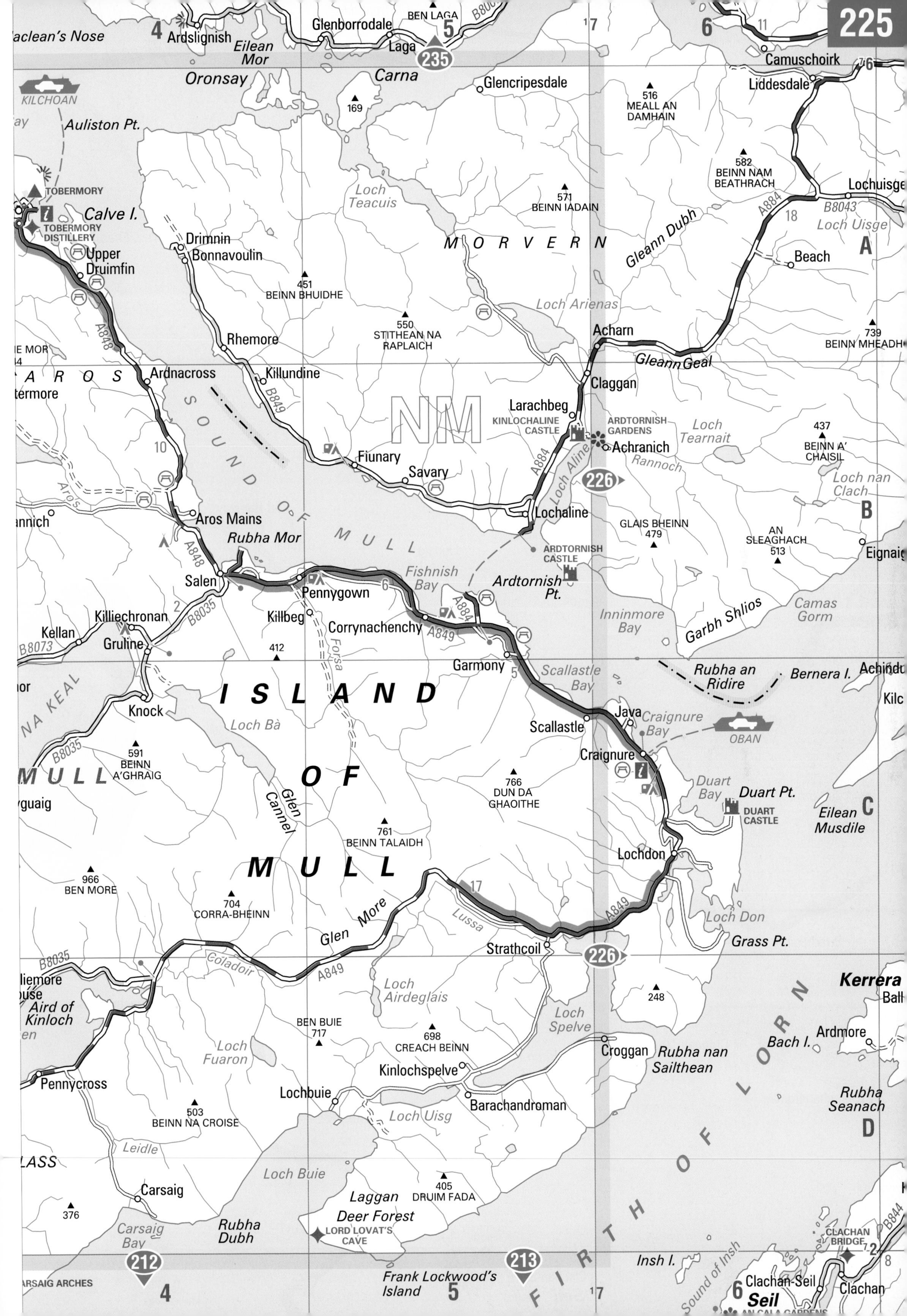

Maclean's Nose
Ardslignish
Eilean Mor
Glenborrodale
Laga
BEN LAGA
235
Oronsay
Carna
KILCHOAN
Auliston Pt.
Glencripesdale
516 MEALL AN DAMHAIN
Camuschoirk
Liddesdale
TOBERMORY
Calve I.
TOBERMORY DISTILLERY
Loch Teacuis
571 BEINN IADAIN
582 BEINN NAM BEATHRACH
Lochuisge
B8043
Loch Uisge
Drimnin
Bonnavoulin
Upper Druimfin
MORVERN
Gleann Dubh
Beach
451 BEINN BHUIDHE
550 STITHEAN NA RAPLAICH
Loch Arienas
Acharn
739 BEINN MHEADH
A848
Rhemore
Ardnacross
Killundine
Gleann Geal
Claggan
ARO S
B849
SOUND OF MULL
NM
Larachbeg
KINLOCHALINE CASTLE
ARDTORNISH GARDENS
Achranich
Loch Tearnait
Rannoch
437 BEINN A' CHAISIL
Loch nan Clach
Fiunary
Savary
A884
Loch Aline
226
Aros Mains
Lochaline
GLAIS BHEINN 479
AN SLEAGHACH 513
Eignaig
Rubha Mor
ARDTORNISH CASTLE
Fishnish Bay
Ardtornish Pt.
Salen
Pennygown
B8035
Killiechronan
Kellan
Gruline
B8073
Killbeg
Corrynachenchy
A849
Inninmore Bay
Garbh Shlios
Camas Gorm
412
Forsa
Garmony
Scallastle Bay
Rubha an Ridire
Bernera I.
ISLAND OF MULL
Knock
Loch Bà
Java
Scallastle
Craignure Bay
OBAN
591 BEINN A'GHRAIG
Craignure
766 DUN DA GHAOITHE
Glen Cannel
Duart Bay
Duart Pt.
DUART CASTLE
Eilean Musdile
761 BEINN TALAIDH
Lochdon
966 BEN MORE
704 CORRA-BHEINN
Glen More
Lussa
Loch Don
Grass Pt.
Strathcoil
Coladoir
Aird of Kinloch
Loch Airdeglais
248
Kerrera
FIRTH OF LORN
BEN BUIE 717
698 CREACH BEINN
Loch Spelve
Croggan
Rubha nan Sailthean
Bach I.
Ardmore
Loch Fuaron
Kinlochspelve
Pennycross
Lochbuie
Barachandroman
503 BEINN NA CROISE
Loch Uisg
Rubha Seanach
Leidle
Loch Buie
405 DRUIM FADA
Carsaig
376
Laggan Deer Forest
Rubha Dubh
Carsaig Bay
LORD LOVAT'S CAVE
CLACHAN BRIDGE
212
213
Insh I.
Sound of Insh
CARSAIG ARCHES
Frank Lockwood's Island
Clachan-Seil
Seil
Clachan
B844

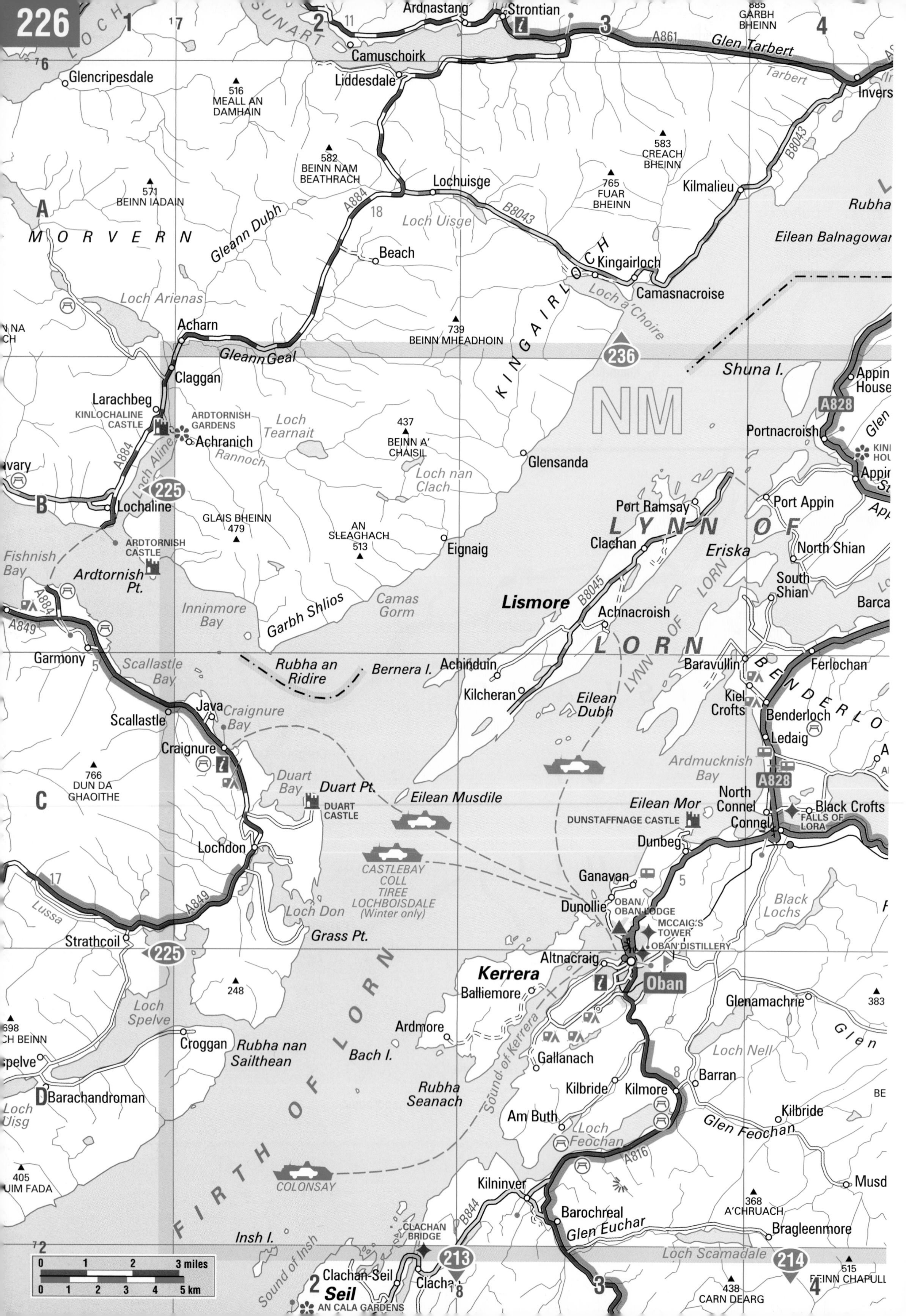
Ardnastang
Strontian
Loch Sunart
Camuschoirk
Glencripesdale
Liddesdale
516 MEALL AN DAMHAIN
885 GARBH BHEINN
A861
Glen Tarbert
Tarbert
Inversanda
582 BEINN NAM BEATHRACH
583 CREACH BHEINN
571 BEINN IADAIN
Lochuisge
765 FUAR BHEINN
Kilmalieu
B8043
A884
Loch Uisge
MORVERN
Gleann Dubh
Beach
Kingairloch
Camasnacroise
Rubha
Eilean Balnagowan
Loch Arienas
Loch a'Choire
Acharn
739 BEINN MHEADHOIN
Gleann Geal
236
Shuna I.
Claggan
KINGAIRLOCH
Appin House
Larachbeg
KINLOCHALINE CASTLE
ARDTORNISH GARDENS
Loch Tearnait
437 BEINN A' CHAISIL
NM
A828
Portnacroish
Achranich
Rannoch
Glensanda
Loch nan Clach
Loch Aline
225
Lochaline
GLAIS BHEINN 479
AN SLEAGHACH 513
Eignaig
Port Ramsay
Port Appin
LYNN OF
ARDTORNISH CASTLE
Clachan
Eriska
North Shian
Fishnish Bay
Ardtornish Pt.
South Shian
Lismore
B8045
Inninmore Bay
Garbh Shlios
Camas Gorm
Achnacroish
A849
Garmony
LORN
Baravullin
Ferlochan
Scallastle Bay
Rubha an Ridire
Bernera I.
Achinduin
BENDERLOCH
Kilcheran
LYNN OF LORN
Eilean Dubh
Kiel Crofts
Benderloch
Scallastle
Java
Craignure Bay
Ledaig
Craignure
766 DUN DA GHAOITHE
Duart Bay
Duart Pt.
Ardmucknish Bay
A828
Eilean Musdile
DUART CASTLE
Eilean Mor
DUNSTAFFNAGE CASTLE
North Connel
Connel
Black Crofts
FALLS OF LORA
Lochdon
Dunbeg
CASTLEBAY COLL TIREE LOCHBOISDALE (Winter only)
Ganavan
Lussa
Loch Don
Dunollie
OBAN/OBAN LODGE
MCCAIG'S TOWER
OBAN DISTILLERY
Black Lochs
Strathcoil
225
Grass Pt.
Altnacraig
Kerrera
Oban
248
Balliemore
Glenamachrie
383
Loch Spelve
698
Croggan
Rubha nan Sailthean
Ardmore
Sound of Kerrera
Glen
Bach I.
Gallanach
Loch Nell
Barachandroman
Rubha Seanach
Kilbride
Kilmore
Barran
Loch Uisg
Am Buth
Loch Feochan
Kilbride
Glen Feochan
A816
FIRTH OF LORN
405
COLONSAY
Kilninver
Musd
368 A'CHRUACH
B844
Barochreal
Glen Euchar
Insh I.
CLACHAN BRIDGE
Bragleenmore
Loch Scamadale
213
214
515
Sound of Insh
Clachan-Seil
Clachan
Seil
438 CARN DEARG
AN CALA GARDENS
0 1 2 3 miles
0 1 2 3 4 5 km

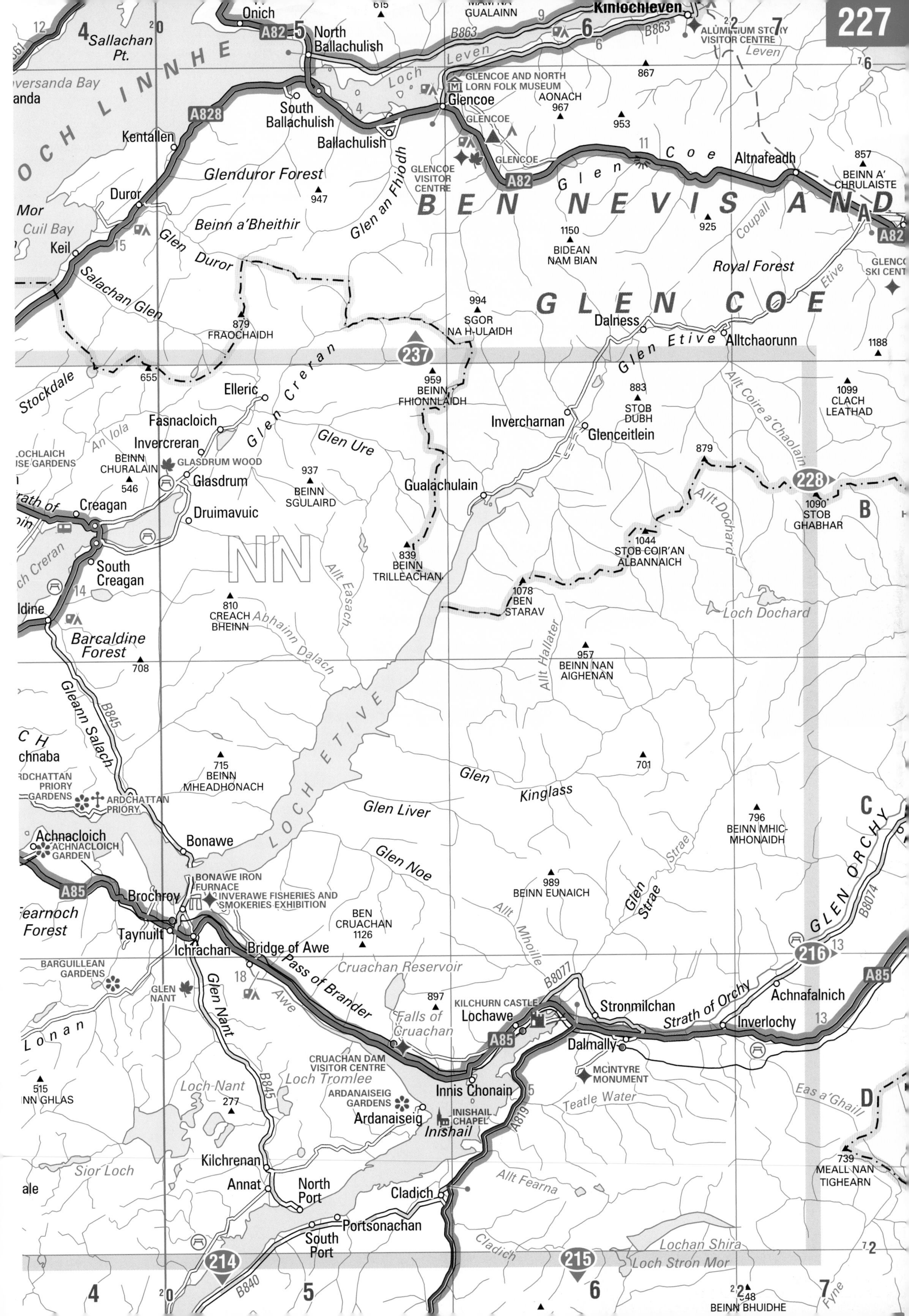

Onich
North Ballachulish
Kinlochleven
ALUMINIUM STORY VISITOR CENTRE
Sallachan Pt.
LOCH LINNHE
A82
A828
B863
Loch Leven
GLENCOE AND NORTH LORN FOLK MUSEUM
Glencoe
AONACH 967
867
953
South Ballachulish
Ballachulish
Kentallen
GLENCOE
Glen an Fhiodh
Glen Coe
Altnafeadh
857
BEINN A' CHRULAISTE
Glenduror Forest
947
GLENCOE VISITOR CENTRE
BEN NEVIS AND
Mor
Cuil Bay
Duror
Beinn a'Bheithir
1150
BIDEAN NAM BIAN
925
Coupall
Keil
Glen Duror
Royal Forest
Etive
GLENCOE SKI CENT
Salachan Glen
879
FRAOCHAIDH
994
SGOR NA H-ULAIDH
GLEN COE
Dalness
Glen Etive
Alltchaorunn
1188
237
Stockdale
655
Glen Creran
959
BEINN FHIONNLAIDH
883
STOB DUBH
Allt Coire a'Chaolain
1099
CLACH LEATHAD
Elleric
Fasnacloich
Inverchanan
Glenceitlein
An Iola
Invercreran
Glen Ure
879
LOCHLAICH HOUSE GARDENS
BEINN CHURALAIN 546
GLASDRUM WOOD
Glasdrum
937
BEINN SGULAIRD
Gualachulain
228
1090
STOB GHABHAR
Allt Dochard
Creagan
Druimavuic
NN
1044
STOB COIR'AN ALBANNAICH
South Creagan
Loch Creran
839
BEINN TRILLEACHAN
Allt Easach
810
CREACH BHEINN
1078
BEN STARAV
Loch Dochard
Barcaldine Forest
708
Abhainn Dalach
Allt Hallater
957
BEINN NAN AIGHENAN
Gleann Salach
B845
LOCH ETIVE
715
BEINN MHEADHONACH
701
Glen Kinglass
ARDCHATTAN PRIORY GARDENS
ARDCHATTAN PRIORY
Glen Liver
796
BEINN MHIC-MHONAIDH
GLEN ORCHY
Achnacloich
ACHNACLOICH GARDEN
Bonawe
Glen Noe
Strae
B8074
BONAWE IRON FURNACE
INVERAWE FISHERIES AND SMOKERIES EXHIBITION
989
BEINN EUNAICH
Glen Strae
A85
Brochroy
Fearnoch Forest
BEN CRUACHAN 1126
Allt Mhoille
Taynuilt
Ichrachan
Bridge of Awe
216
BARGUILLEAN GARDENS
Pass of Brander
Cruachan Reservoir
B8077
GLEN NANT
Glen Nant
Awe
897
KILCHURN CASTLE
Lochawe
Stronmilchan
Strath of Orchy
Achnafalnich
Inverlochy
Lonan
Falls of Cruachan
Dalmally
CRUACHAN DAM VISITOR CENTRE
Loch Tromlee
MCINTYRE MONUMENT
515
Loch Nant
277
ARDANAISEIG GARDENS
Innis Chonain
Teatle Water
Eas a'Ghaill
Ardanaiseig
INISHAIL CHAPEL
Inishail
A819
Kilchrenan
Sior Loch
739
MEALL NAN TIGHEARN
Annat
North Port
Cladich
Allt Fearna
Portsonachan
South Port
Cladich
Lochan Shira
214
215
Loch Stron Mor
B840
BEINN BHUIDHE
Fyne

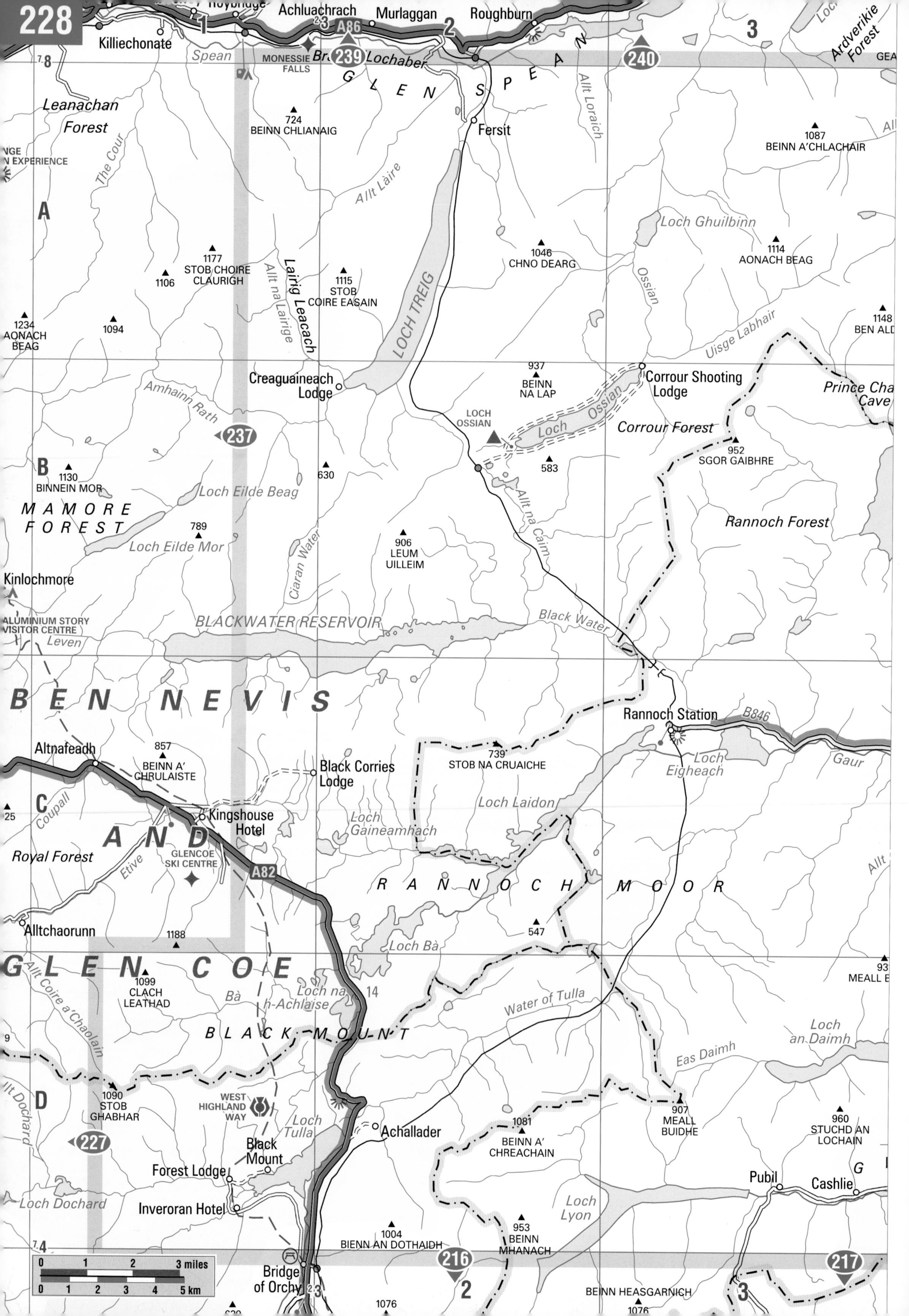

Roybridge
Achluachrach
Murlaggan
Roughburn
Killiechonate
A86
Spean
MONESSIE FALLS
Lochaber
239
240
Ardverikie Forest
GLEN SPEAN
Leanachan Forest
The Cour
724
BEINN CHLIANAIG
Fersit
Allt Loraich
1087
BEINN A'CHLACHAIR
Allt Làire
Loch Ghuilbinn
1177
STOB CHOIRE CLAURIGH
1106
Allt na Lairige
Lairig Leacach
1115
STOB COIRE EASAIN
LOCH TREIG
1046
CHNO DEARG
Ossian
1114
AONACH BEAG
1234
AONACH BEAG
1094
Uisge Labhair
1148
937
BEINN NA LAP
Corrour Shooting Lodge
Creaguaineach Lodge
Amhainn Rath
237
LOCH OSSIAN
Loch Ossian
Corrour Forest
952
SGOR GAIBHRE
583
630
B
1130
BINNEIN MOR
Loch Eilde Beag
MAMORE FOREST
789
Loch Eilde Mor
Allt na Cam
906
LEUM UILLEIM
Rannoch Forest
Ciaran Water
Kinlochmore
ALUMINIUM STORY VISITOR CENTRE
Leven
BLACKWATER RESERVOIR
Black Water
BEN NEVIS
AND
GLEN COE
Rannoch Station
B846
Altnafeadh
857
BEINN A' CHRULAISTE
739
STOB NA CRUAICHE
Black Corries Lodge
Loch Eigheach
Gaur
C
Coupall
Kingshouse Hotel
Loch Laidon
Loch Gaineamhach
Royal Forest
Etive
GLENCOE SKI CENTRE
A82
RANNOCH MOOR
Alltchaorunn
1188
547
Loch Bà
1099
CLACH LEATHAD
Allt Coire a' Chaolain
Bà
Loch na h-Achlaise
14
Water of Tulla
BLACK MOUNT
Loch an Daimh
Eas Daimh
D
1090
STOB GHABHAR
WEST HIGHLAND WAY
907
MEALL BUIDHE
960
STUCHD AN LOCHAIN
227
Loch Tulla
Achallader
1081
BEINN A' CHREACHAIN
Black Mount
Forest Lodge
Pubil
Cashlie
Loch Dochard
Inveroran Hotel
Loch Lyon
1004
BIENN AN DOTHAIDH
953
BEINN MHANACH
216
217
Bridge of Orchy
BEINN HEASGARNICH
1076
0 1 2 3 miles
0 1 2 3 4 5 km

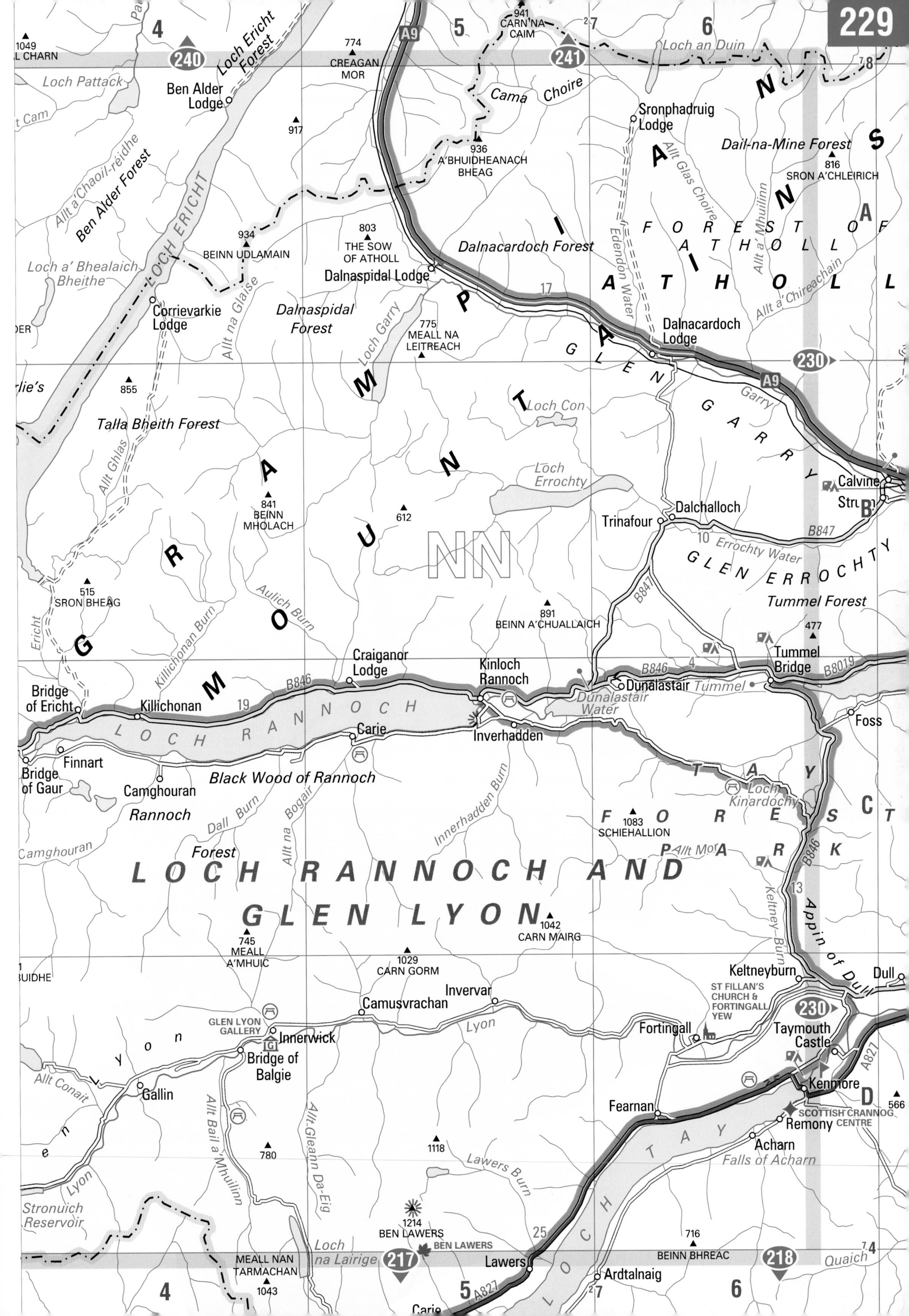

Loch Ericht Forest
Ben Alder Lodge
Loch Pattack
Ben Alder Forest
LOCH ERICHT
940
241
A9
774 CREAGAN MOR
917
941 CARN NA CAIM
Cama Choire
936 A'BHUIDHEANACH BHEAG
Loch an Duin
Sronphadruig Lodge
Dail-na-Mine Forest
816 SRON A'CHLEIRICH
FOREST OF ATHOLL
934 BEINN UDLAMAIN
803 THE SOW OF ATHOLL
Dalnaspidal Lodge
Dalnacardoch Forest
Edendon Water
Loch a' Bhealaich Bheithe
Corrievarkie Lodge
Allt na Glaise
Dalnaspidal Forest
Loch Garry
775 MEALL NA LEITREACH
Dalnacardoch Lodge
GLEN GARRY
230
855
Talla Bheith Forest
Loch Con
Loch Errochty
GRAMPIAN MOUNTAINS
841 BEINN MHOLACH
612
NN
Calvine
Dalchalloch
Trinafour
B847
Errochty Water
GLEN ERROCHTY
Tummel Forest
515 SRON BHEAG
Aulich Burn
891 BEINN A'CHUALLAICH
477
Killichonan Burn
Craiganor Lodge
Kinloch Rannoch
Tummel Bridge
B846
B8019
Bridge of Ericht
Killichonan
LOCH RANNOCH
Dunalastair
Dunalastair Water
Tummel
Carie
Inverhadden
Foss
Finnart
Bridge of Gaur
Camghouran
Black Wood of Rannoch
Rannoch Forest
Dall Burn
Allt na Bogair
Innerhadden Burn
TAY FOREST PARK
Loch Kinardochy
1083 SCHIEHALLION
Allt Mor
LOCH RANNOCH AND GLEN LYON
Keltney Burn
Appin of Dull
745 MEALL A'MHUIC
1042 CARN MAIRG
1029 CARN GORM
Keltneyburn
Dull
ST FILLAN'S CHURCH & FORTINGALL YEW
Inervar
Camusvrachan
GLEN LYON GALLERY
Innerwick
Bridge of Balgie
Lyon
Fortingall
Taymouth Castle
A827
Kenmore
Allt Conait
Gallin
Fearnan
SCOTTISH CRANNOG CENTRE
Remony
566
Allt Bail a' Mhuilinn
Allt Gleann Da-Eig
780
1118
Acharn
Falls of Acharn
LOCH TAY
Lawers Burn
Stronuich Reservoir
1214 BEN LAWERS
BEN LAWERS
716
Loch na Lairige
MEALL NAN TARMACHAN
1043
217
Lawers
BEINN BHREAC
Ardtalnaig
218
Quaich
Carie
4
5
6

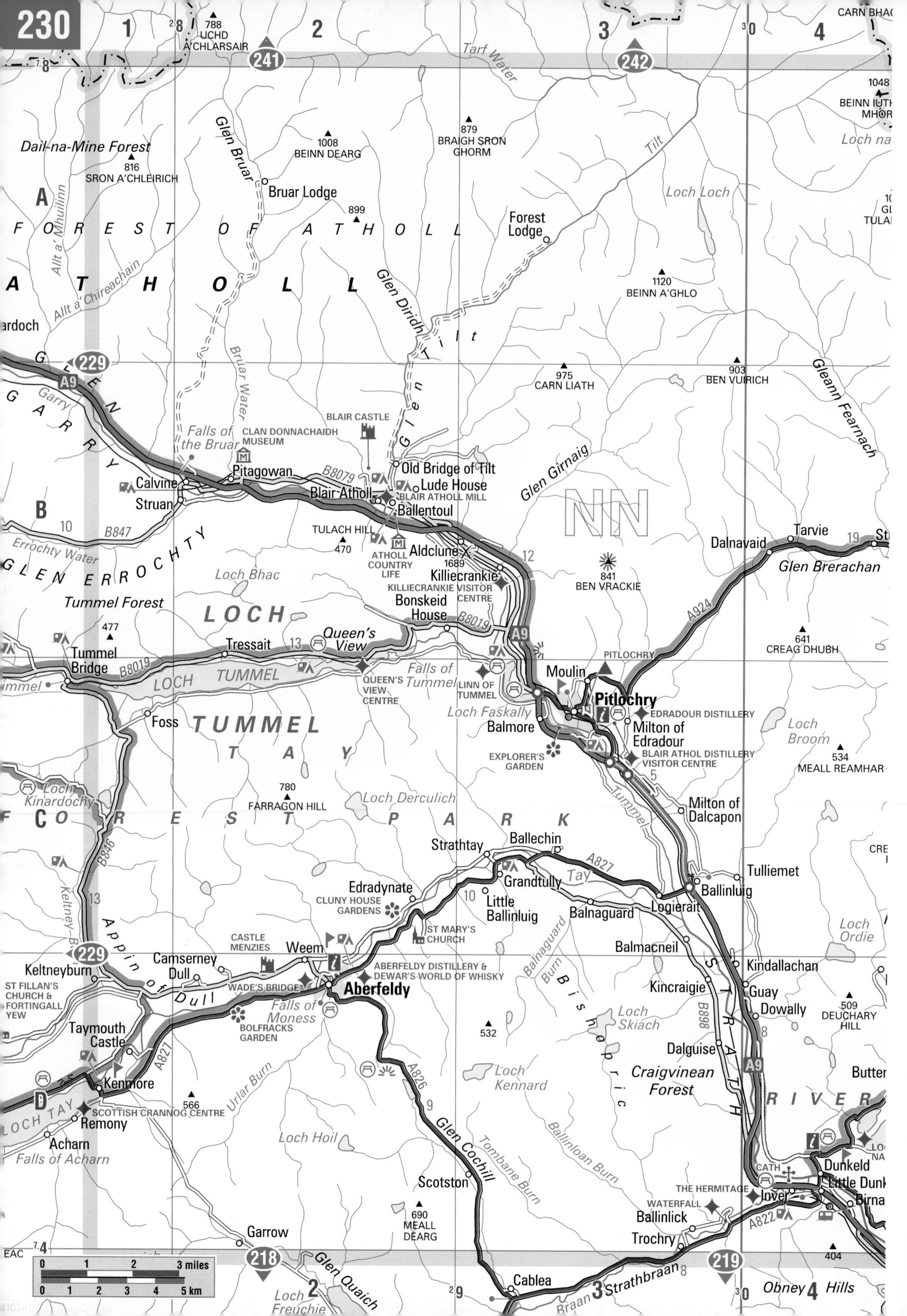

788 UCHD A'CHLARSAIR
241
242
Tarf Water
1048 BEINN IUTH MHOR
Dail-na-Mine Forest
816 SRON A'CHLEIRICH
Glen Bruar
1008 BEINN DEARG
879 BRAIGH SRON GHORM
Tilt
Loch na
Bruar Lodge
899
Loch Loch
Forest Lodge
FOREST OF ATHOLL
ATHOLL
Allt a' Mhuilinn
Allt a' Chireachain
Glen Diridh
1120 BEINN A'GHLO
Glen Tilt
229
A9
GLEN GARRY
Bruar Water
975 CARN LIATH
903 BEN VUIRICH
Gleann Fearnach
BLAIR CASTLE
Falls of the Bruar
CLAN DONNACHAIDH MUSEUM
Old Bridge of Tilt
Pitagowan
B8079
Lude House
Glen Girnaig
Calvine
Blair Atholl
BLAIR ATHOLL MILL
Struan
Ballentoul
NN
B847
TULACH HILL 470
ATHOLL COUNTRY LIFE
Aldclune
1689
Tarvie
Dalnavaid
Errochty Water
GLEN ERROCHTY
Killiecrankie
841 BEN VRACKIE
Glen Brerachan
Loch Bhac
KILLIECRANKIE VISITOR CENTRE
Tummel Forest
Bonskeid House
B8019
A924
LOCH
477
641 CREAG DHUBH
Queen's View
Tressait
Tummel Bridge
PITLOCHRY
LOCH TUMMEL
QUEEN'S VIEW CENTRE
Falls of Tummel
LINN OF TUMMEL
Moulin
Pitlochry
EDRADOUR DISTILLERY
Loch Faskally
Balmore
Milton of Edradour
Foss
TUMMEL
TAY
Loch Broom
BLAIR ATHOL DISTILLERY VISITOR CENTRE
EXPLORER'S GARDEN
534 MEALL REAMHAR
Loch Kinardochy
780 FARRAGON HILL
Loch Derculich
Milton of Dalcapon
FOREST PARK
Tummel
Strathtay
Ballechin
A827
B846
Tay
Tulliemet
Grandtully
Ballinluig
Edradynate
CLUNY HOUSE GARDENS
Little Ballinluig
Logierait
Balnaguard
Loch Ordie
Keltney Burn
Appin of Dull
ST MARY'S CHURCH
CASTLE MENZIES
Weem
Balnaguard Burn
Balmacneil
Camserney
Keltneyburn
Dull
ABERFELDY DISTILLERY & DEWAR'S WORLD OF WHISKY
Kindallachan
ST FILLAN'S CHURCH & FORTINGALL YEW
WADE'S BRIDGE
Aberfeldy
Kincraigie
Guay
Bishopric
Falls of Moness
Loch Skiach
B898
Dowally
509 DEUCHARY HILL
Taymouth Castle
BOLFRACKS GARDEN
532
Dalguise
STRATH
A827
Urlar Burn
A826
Loch Kennard
Craigvinean Forest
Butter
Kenmore
LOCH TAY
566
RIVER
SCOTTISH CRANNOG CENTRE
Remony
Glen Cochill
Acharn
Falls of Acharn
Loch Hoil
Tombane Burn
Ballinloan Burn
Dunkeld
Little Dunk
CATH
Scotston
THE HERMITAGE
Inver
Birna
690 MEALL DEARG
WATERFALL
Ballinlick
A822
Garrow
Trochry
218
Glen Quaich
404
219
Cablea
Strathbraan
Braan
Obney Hills
Loch Freuchie
0 1 2 3 miles
0 1 2 3 4 5 km

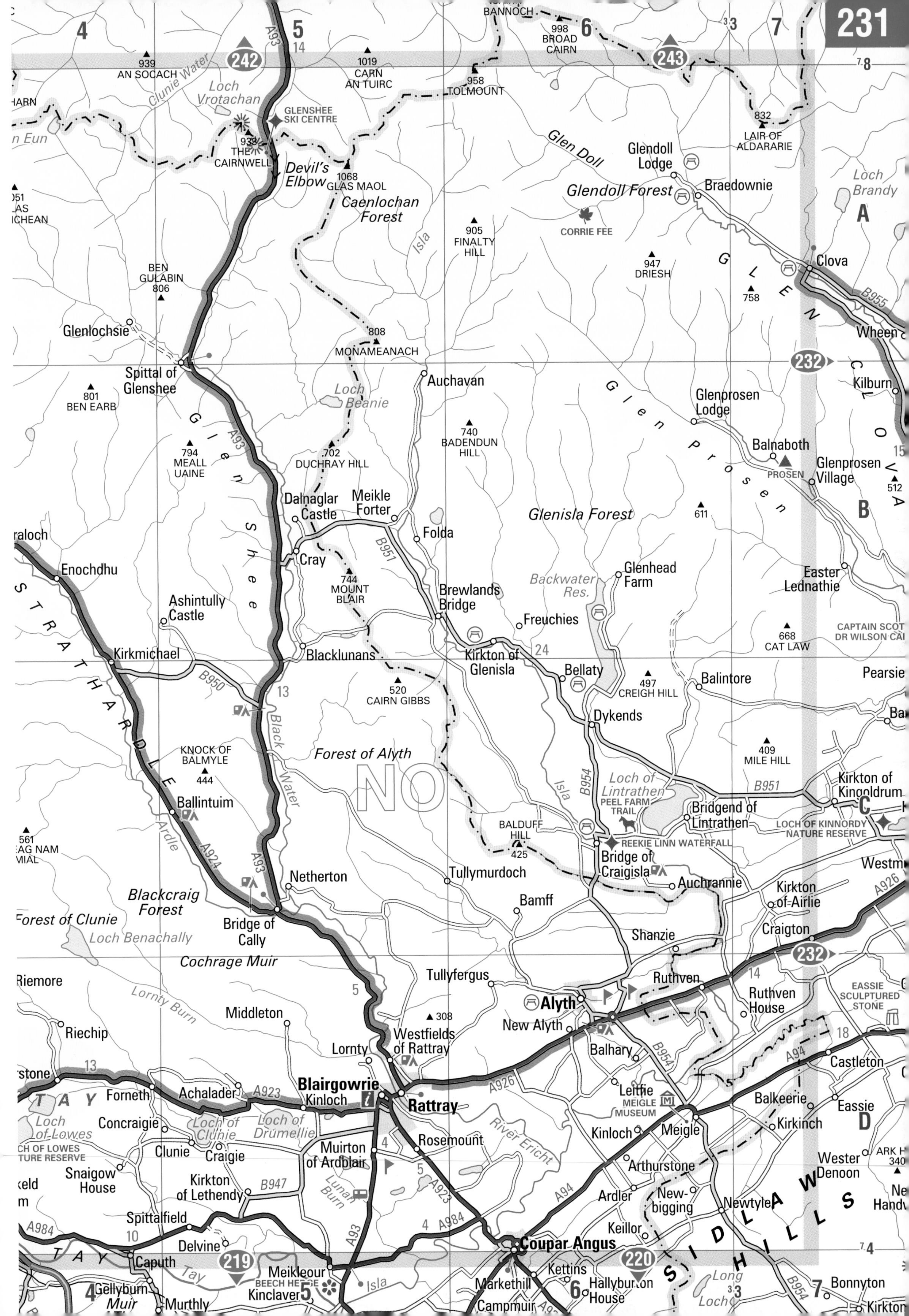

4 **5** **6** **7**

BANNOCH
998
BROAD
CAIRN
242
14
939
AN SOCACH
1019
CARN
AN TUIRC
243
3 3
7 8
Cluinie Water
Loch
Vrotachan
958
T.OLMOUNT
832
LAIR OF
ALDARARIE
HARN
GLENSHEE
SKI CENTRE
Glen Doll
Glendoll
Lodge
Braedownie
Loch
Brandy
A
n Eun
939
THE
CAIRNWELL
Devil's
Elbow
Glendoll Forest
1068
GLAS MAOL
Caenlochan
Forest
CORRIE FEE
Clova
051
LAS
CHEAN
905
FINALTY
HILL
947
DRIESH
758
B955
BEN
GULABIN
806
808
MONAMEANACH
Auchavan
Glenprosen
Lodge
232
Kilburn
Glenlochsie
Loch
Beanie
Balnaboth
PROSEN
Glenprosen
Village
15
512
Spittal of
Glenshee
740
BADENDUN
HILL
B
801
BEN EARB
794
MEALL
UAINE
702
DUCHRAY HILL
Glenisla Forest
611
raloch
Dalnaglar
Castle
Meikle
Forter
Folda
Easter
Lednathie
Enochdhu
Cray
744
MOUNT
BLAIR
Brewlands
Bridge
Glenhead
Farm
STRATHARDLE
Ashintully
Castle
Blacklunans
Backwater
Res.
Freuchies
Kirkton of
Glenisla
24
668
CAT LAW
CAPTAIN SCOT
DR WILSON CAI
Kirkmichael
B950
520
CAIRN GIBBS
Bellaty
497
CREIGH HILL
Balintore
Pearsie
13
Forest of Alyth
NO
Dykends
409
MILE HILL
Ba
KNOCK OF
BALMYLE
444
Black Water
Loch of
Lintrathen
Kirkton of
Kingoldrum
561
AG NAM
MIAL
Ballintuim
PEEL FARM
TRAIL
Bridgend of
Lintrathen
C
B951
BALDUFF
HILL
425
REEKIE LINN WATERFALL
LOCH OF KINNORDY
NATURE RESERVE
Blackcraig
Forest
Netherton
Tullymurdoch
Bridge of
Craigisla
Auchrannie
Kirkton
of-Airlie
Westm
Forest of Clunie
Bridge of
Cally
Bamff
Shanzie
Craigton
Loch Benachally
Cochrage Muir
Tullyfergus
Ruthven
232
14
EASSIE
SCULPTURED
STONE
Riemore
Lornty Burn
5
Alyth
Ruthven
House
Riechip
Middleton
308
New Alyth
Balhary
Castleton
18
stone
13
Forneth
Achalader
A923
Blairgowrie
Kinloch
Westfields
of Rattray
Lornty
B954
Leitfie
MEIGLE
MUSEUM
Balkeerie
Eassie
D
TAY
Concraigie
Clunie
Craigie
Loch
of-Lowes
Loch of
Clunie
Loch of
Drumellie
Rattray
Kinloch
Meigle
Kirkinch
CH OF LOWES
URE RESERVE
Snaigow
House
Kirkton
of Lethendy
Muirton
of Ardblair
Rosemount
4
Arthurstone
Wester
Denoon
Ne
Handw
keld
m
Spittalfield
B947
Lunan Burn
New-
bigging
Ardler
ARK H
340
A984
Delvine
A923
Kinclaven
Meikleour
BEECH HEDGE
Caputh
219
5
River Ericht
Coupar Angus
Kettins
Hallyburton
House
220
Long
Loch
Bonnyton
Kirkton
Gellyburn
Murthly
Muir
Kinclaven
Isla
Markethill
Campmuir
SIDLAW HILLS
B954

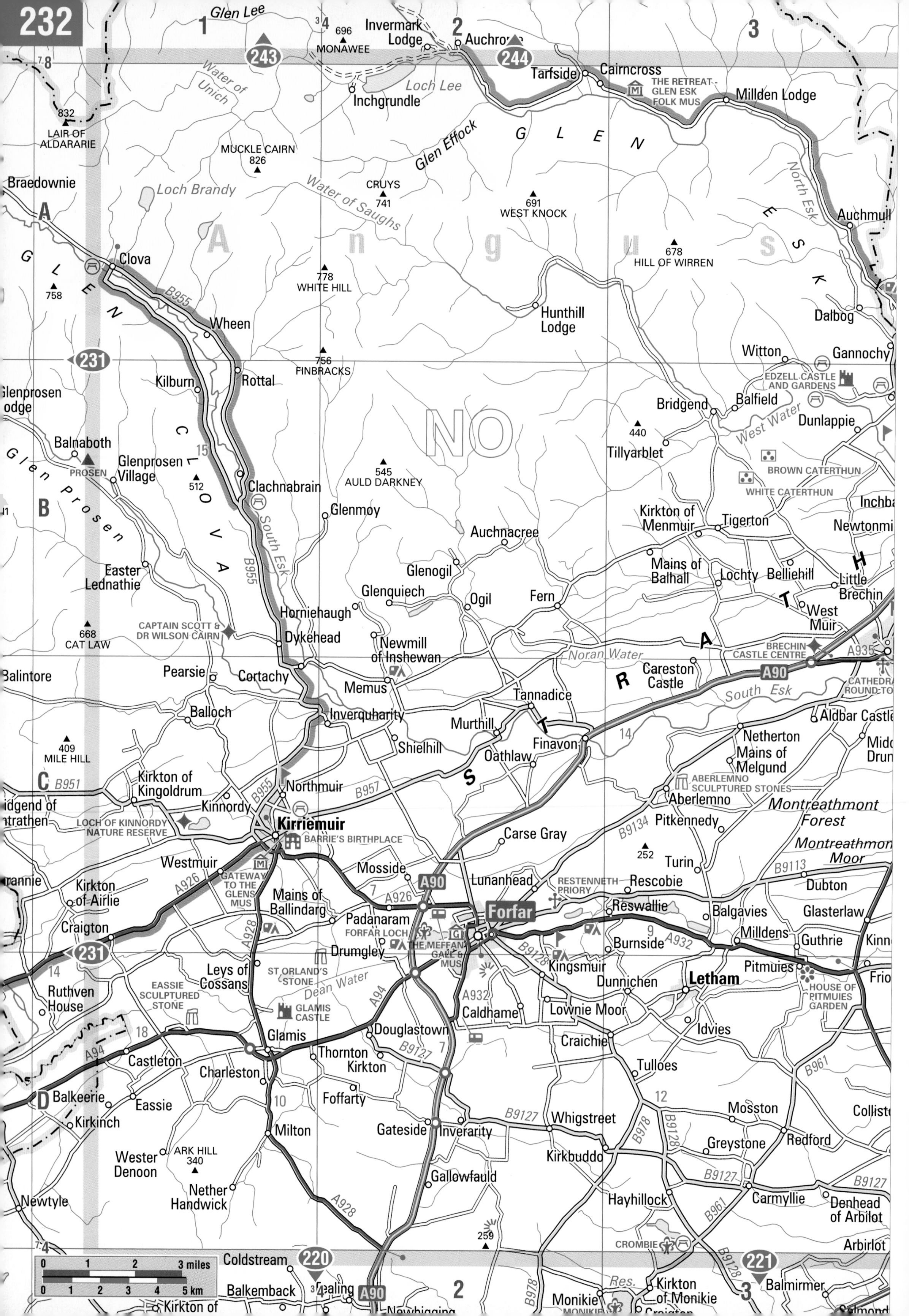

Glen Lee
Invermark Lodge
Auchronie
696 MONAWEE
243
244
Tarfside
Cairncross
THE RETREAT GLEN ESK FOLK MUS
Millden Lodge
Loch Lee
Inchgrundle
Water of Unich
832 LAIR OF ALDARARIE
MUCKLE CAIRN 826
Glen Effock
G L E N E S K
Braedownie
Loch Brandy
Water of Saughs
CRUYS 741
691 WEST KNOCK
North Esk
Auchmull
A n g u s
678 HILL OF WIRREN
Clova
778 WHITE HILL
758
GLEN CLOVA
B955
Wheen
Hunthill Lodge
Dalbog
231
756 FINBRACKS
Witton
Gannochy
Kilburn
Rottal
Glenprosen Lodge
EDZELL CASTLE AND GARDENS
Bridgend
Balfield
NO
West Water
Dunlappie
440
Tillyarblet
Balnaboth
PROSEN
Glenprosen Village
Glen Prosen
512
545 AULD DARKNEY
Clachnabrain
BROWN CATERTHUN
WHITE CATERTHUN
Glenmoy
South Esk
Kirkton of Menmuir
Tigerton
Inchbare
Newtonmill
Auchnacree
Easter Lednathie
Mains of Balhall
Lochty
Belliehill
Little Brechin
Glenogil
Glenquiech
Ogil
Fern
West Muir
Horniehaugh
668 CAT LAW
CAPTAIN SCOTT & DR WILSON CAIRN
Dykehead
Newmill of Inshewan
Noran Water
BRECHIN CASTLE CENTRE
A935
Balintore
Pearsie
Cortachy
Memus
Careston Castle
A90
STRATHMORE
CATHEDRAL ROUND TOWER
South Esk
Tannadice
Balloch
Inverquharity
Murthill
Aldbar Castle
409 MILE HILL
Shielhill
Finavon
Netherton
Mains of Melgund
Oathlaw
B951
Kirkton of Kingoldrum
B957
Northmuir
ABERLEMNO SCULPTURED STONES
Aberlemno
Montreathmont Forest
Kinnordy
Pitkennedy
LOCH OF KINNORDY NATURE RESERVE
Kirriemuir
B9134
BARRIE'S BIRTHPLACE
Carse Gray
Montreathmont Moor
252
Westmuir
Turin
Mosside
Lunanhead
RESTENNETH PRIORY
Rescobie
B9113
GATEWAY TO THE GLENS MUS
Dubton
Kirkton of Airlie
A926
Mains of Ballindarg
Forfar
Reswallie
Balgavies
Glasterlaw
Craigton
Padanaram
FORFAR LOCH
THE MEFFAN GALL & MUS
Burnside
A932
Milldens
Guthrie
Drumgley
B9128
Kingsmuir
Pitmuies
Letham
Leys of Cossans
ST ORLAND'S STONE
Dunnichen
HOUSE OF PITMUIES GARDEN
EASSIE SCULPTURED STONE
Dean Water
Ruthven House
GLAMIS CASTLE
A94
Caldhame
Lownie Moor
Idvies
Glamis
Douglastown
Craichie
Castleton
Thornton Kirkton
B9127
Tulloes
Charleston
B961
Balkeerie
Eassie
Foffarty
Mosston
Colliston
Kirkinch
Milton
Gateside
Inverarity
Whigstreet
B978
Greystone
Redford
Wester Denoon
ARK HILL 340
Kirkbuddo
Gallowfauld
Nether Handwick
B9127
Newtyle
Hayhillock
Carmyllie
Denhead of Arbilot
A928
259
CROMBIE
Arbirlot
Coldstream
220
221
Balkemback
Tealing
Res.
Kirkton of Monikie
Monikie
Balmirmer
Newbigging
0 1 2 3 miles
0 1 2 3 4 5 km

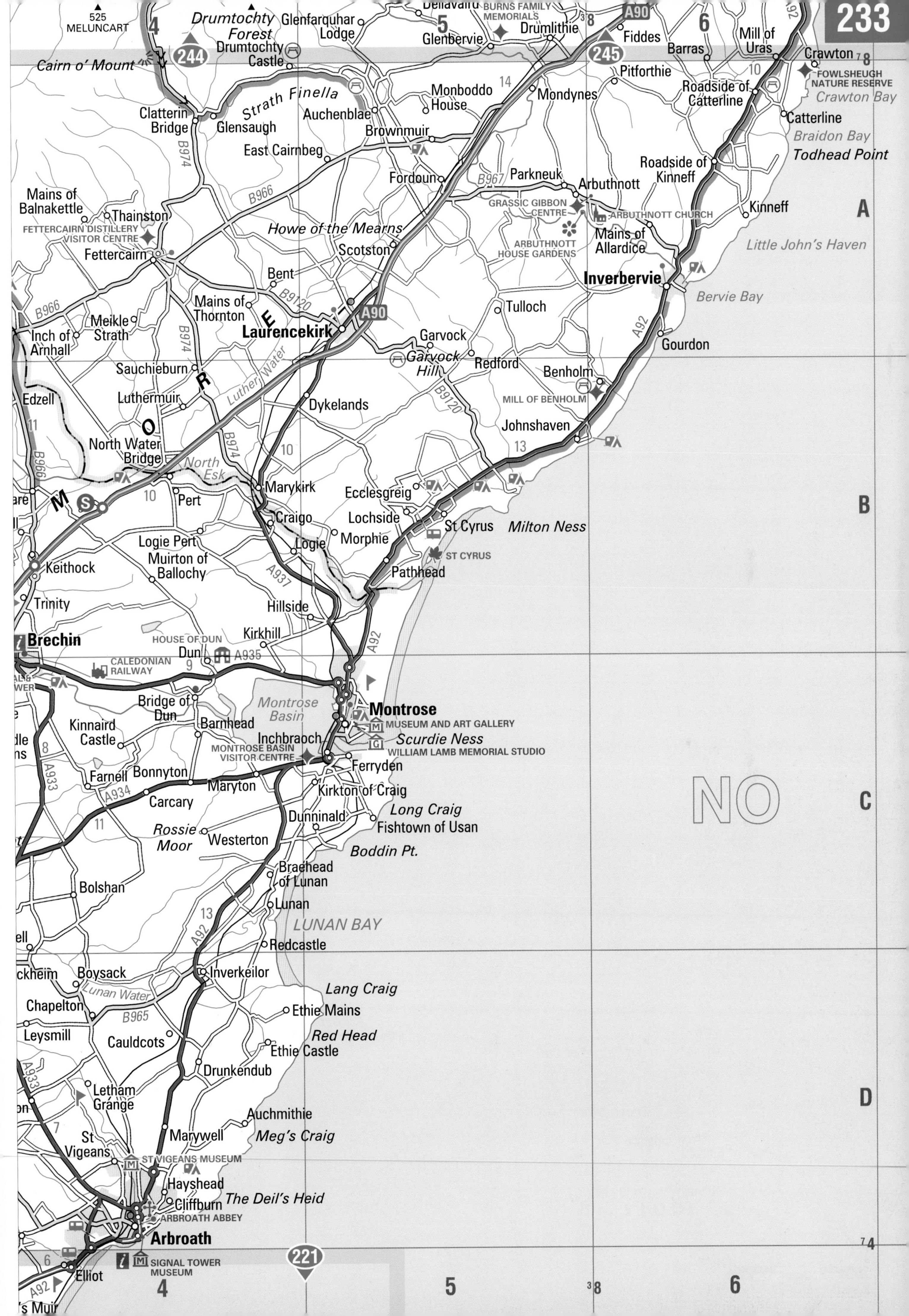

Drumtochty Forest
Glenfarquhar Lodge
Drumtochty Castle
Cairn o' Mount
Glenbervie
BURNS FAMILY MEMORIALS
Drumlithie
Fiddes
Barras
Mill of Uras
Crawton
FOWLSHEUGH NATURE RESERVE
Crawton Bay
Pitforthie
Monboddo House
Mondynes
Roadside of Catterline
Catterline
Braidon Bay
Todhead Point
Strath Finella
Clatterin Bridge
Glensaugh
Auchenblae
Brownmuir
East Cairnbeg
Fordoun
Parkneuk
Arbuthnott
Roadside of Kinneff
Kinneff
GRASSIC GIBBON CENTRE
ARBUTHNOTT CHURCH
ARBUTHNOTT HOUSE GARDENS
Mains of Allardice
Little John's Haven
Mains of Balnakettle
Thainston
FETTERCAIRN DISTILLERY VISITOR CENTRE
Fettercairn
Howe of the Mearns
Scotston
Bent
Inverbervie
Bervie Bay
Tulloch
Mains of Thornton
Laurencekirk
Meikle Strath
Inch of Arnhall
Garvock
Garvock Hill
Redford
Gourdon
Sauchieburn
Luther Water
Benholm
MILL OF BENHOLM
Luthermuir
Dykelands
Edzell
Johnshaven
North Water Bridge
North Esk
Marykirk
Pert
Ecclesgreig
Lochside
St Cyrus
Milton Ness
Craigo
Logie Pert
Logie
Morphie
ST CYRUS
Muirton of Ballochy
Keithock
Pathhead
Trinity
Hillside
Brechin
HOUSE OF DUN
Kirkhill
Dun
CALEDONIAN RAILWAY
Bridge of Dun
Montrose Basin
Montrose
MUSEUM AND ART GALLERY
Kinnaird Castle
Barnhead
Inchbraoch
Scurdie Ness
MONTROSE BASIN VISITOR CENTRE
WILLIAM LAMB MEMORIAL STUDIO
Ferryden
Farnell
Bonnyton
Maryton
Kirkton of Craig
Carcary
Long Craig
Dunninald
Fishtown of Usan
Rossie Moor
Westerton
Boddin Pt.
Braehead of Lunan
Bolshan
Lunan
LUNAN BAY
Redcastle
Boysack
Inverkeilor
Lang Craig
Lunan Water
Chapelton
Ethie Mains
Leysmill
Cauldcots
Red Head
Ethie Castle
Drunkendub
Letham Grange
Auchmithie
Meg's Craig
St Vigeans
Marywell
ST VIGEANS MUSEUM
Hayshead
Cliffburn
The Deil's Heid
ARBROATH ABBEY
Arbroath
SIGNAL TOWER MUSEUM
Elliot
NO
MELUNCART

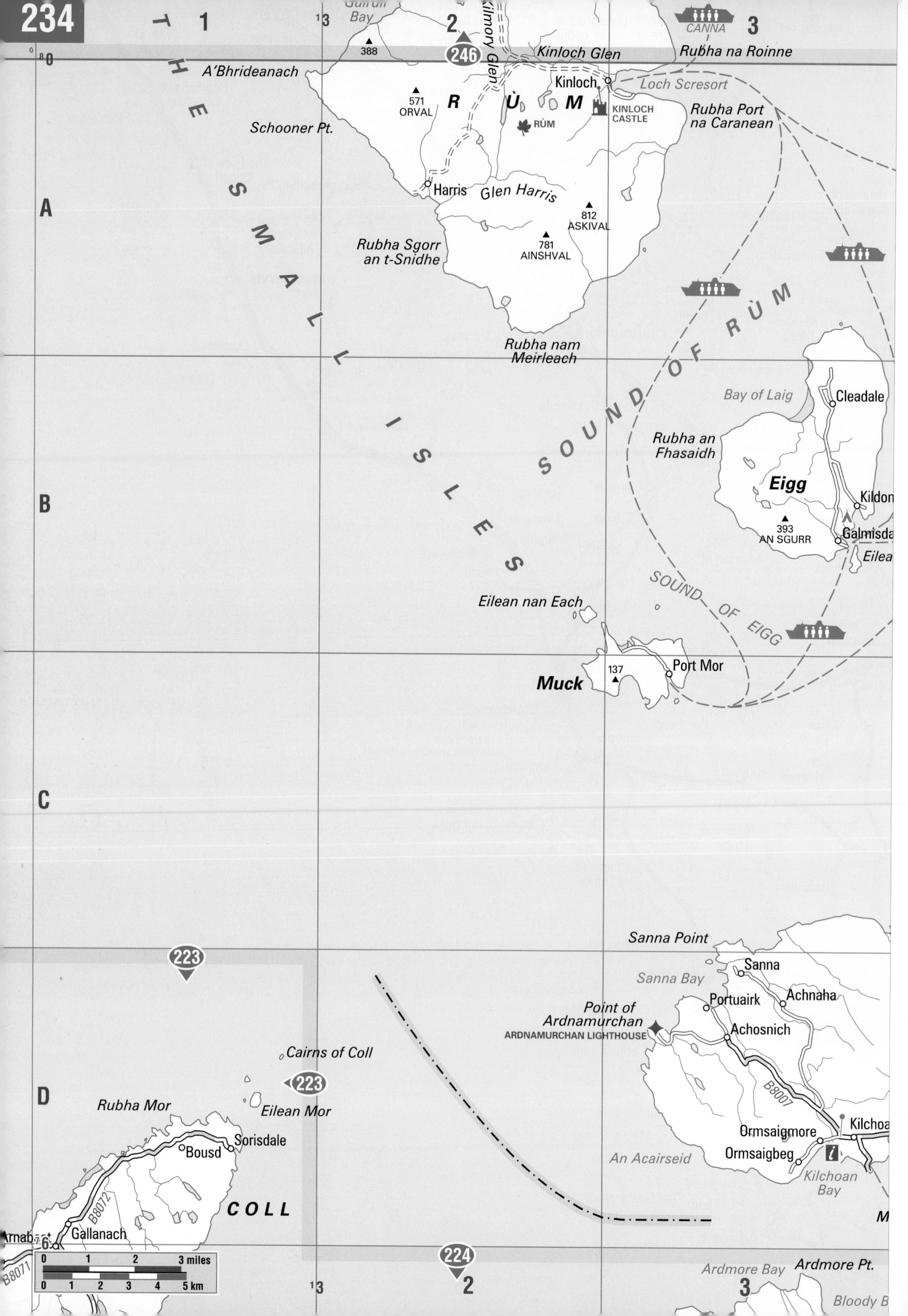

1
3
2
246
3

Gurdil
Bay
388
Kilmory Glen
Kinloch Glen
CANNA
Rubha na Roinne

A'Bhrideanach
R Ù M
Kinloch
Loch Scresort

Schooner Pt.
571
ORVAL
RÙM
KINLOCH
CASTLE
Rubha Port
na Caranean

A

Harris
Glen Harris

812
ASKIVAL

Rubha Sgorr
an t-Snidhe
781
AINSHVAL

Rubha nam
Meirleach

SOUND OF RÙM

Bay of Laig
Cleadale

Rubha an
Fhasaidh

Eigg
Kildon

B

Galmisda

An Sgurr
393
AN SGURR
Eilea

SOUND OF EIGG

Eilean nan Each

Muck
137
Port Mor

C

Sanna Point

Sanna

223
Sanna Bay
Portuairk
Achnaha

Point of
Ardnamurchan
ARDNAMURCHAN LIGHTHOUSE
Achosnich

Cairns of Coll
223

D
Rubha Mor
Eilean Mor
B8007

Sorisdale
Ormsaigmore
Kilchoa

Bousd
Ormsaigbeg
i

B8072
COLL
An Acairseid
Kilchoan
Bay

Arnaba t
Gallanach
B8071

224
M

0   1   2   3 miles
0 1 2 3 4 5 km

3
2
3
Ardmore Bay
Ardmore Pt.
Bloody B

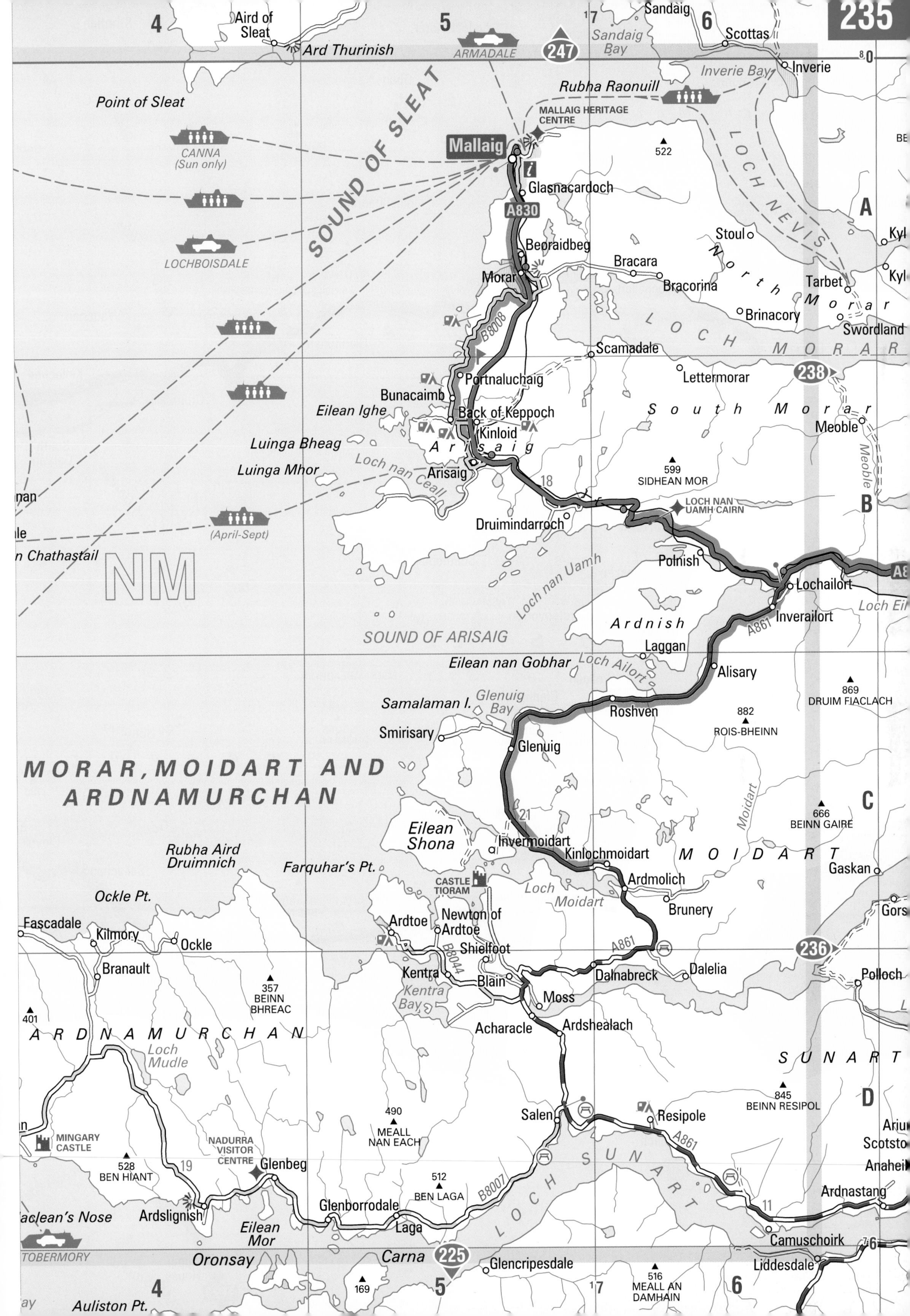
4
Aird of Sleat
Ard Thurinish
5
ARMADALE
247
Sandaig
Sandaig Bay
6
Scottas
Inverie
Inverie Bay
Point of Sleat
SOUND OF SLEAT
Rubha Raonuill
MALLAIG HERITAGE CENTRE
Mallaig
CANNA
(Sun only)
522
LOCH NEVIS
Glasnacardoch
A830
A
LOCHBOISDALE
Beoraidbeg
Stoul
Bracara
Bracorina
North Morar
Morar
Tarbet
Brinacory
LOCH MORAR
Swordland
B8008
Scamadale
Lettermorar
238
Portnaluchaig
Bunacaimb
Eilean Ighe
Back of Keppoch
South Morar
Kinloid
Meoble
Arisaig
Luinga Bheag
Luinga Mhor
Loch nan Ceall
599
SIDHEAN MOR
18
Meoble
LOCH NAN UAMH CAIRN
B
Druimindarroch
(April-Sept)
Chathastail
NM
Loch nan Uamh
Polnish
Lochailort
Loch Eil
Ardnish
Inverailort
A861
SOUND OF ARISAIG
Laggan
Eilean nan Gobhar
Loch Ailort
Alisary
869
DRUIM FIACLACH
Samalaman I.
Glenuig Bay
Roshven
882
ROIS-BHEINN
Smirisary
Glenuig
MORAR, MOIDART AND ARDNAMURCHAN
Moidart
666
BEINN GAIRE
C
21
Eilean Shona
Invermoidart
Kinlochmoidart
MOIDART
Rubha Aird Druimnich
Farquhar's Pt.
Gaskan
CASTLE TIORAM
Ardmolich
Loch Moidart
Ockle Pt.
Brunery
Fascadale
Ardtoe
Newton of Ardtoe
Gorsten
Kilmory
Ockle
Shielfoot
A861
236
B8044
Branault
Kentra
Blain
Dalnabreck
Dalelia
Polloch
357
BEINN BHREAC
Kentra Bay
Moss
401
Acharacle
Ardshealach
ARDNAMURCHAN
Loch Mudle
SUNART
845
BEINN RESIPOL
D
490
MEALL NAN EACH
Salen
Resipole
MINGARY CASTLE
NADURRA VISITOR CENTRE
Glenbeg
A861
528
BEN HIANT
19
512
BEN LAGA
LOCH SUNART
B8007
Ardnastang
Ardslignish
Glenborrodale
11
aclean's Nose
Eilean Mor
Laga
Camuschoirk
TOBERMORY
Oronsay
Carna
225
Glencripesdale
Liddesdale
4
169
5
17
516
MEALL AN DAMHAIN
6
Auliston Pt.

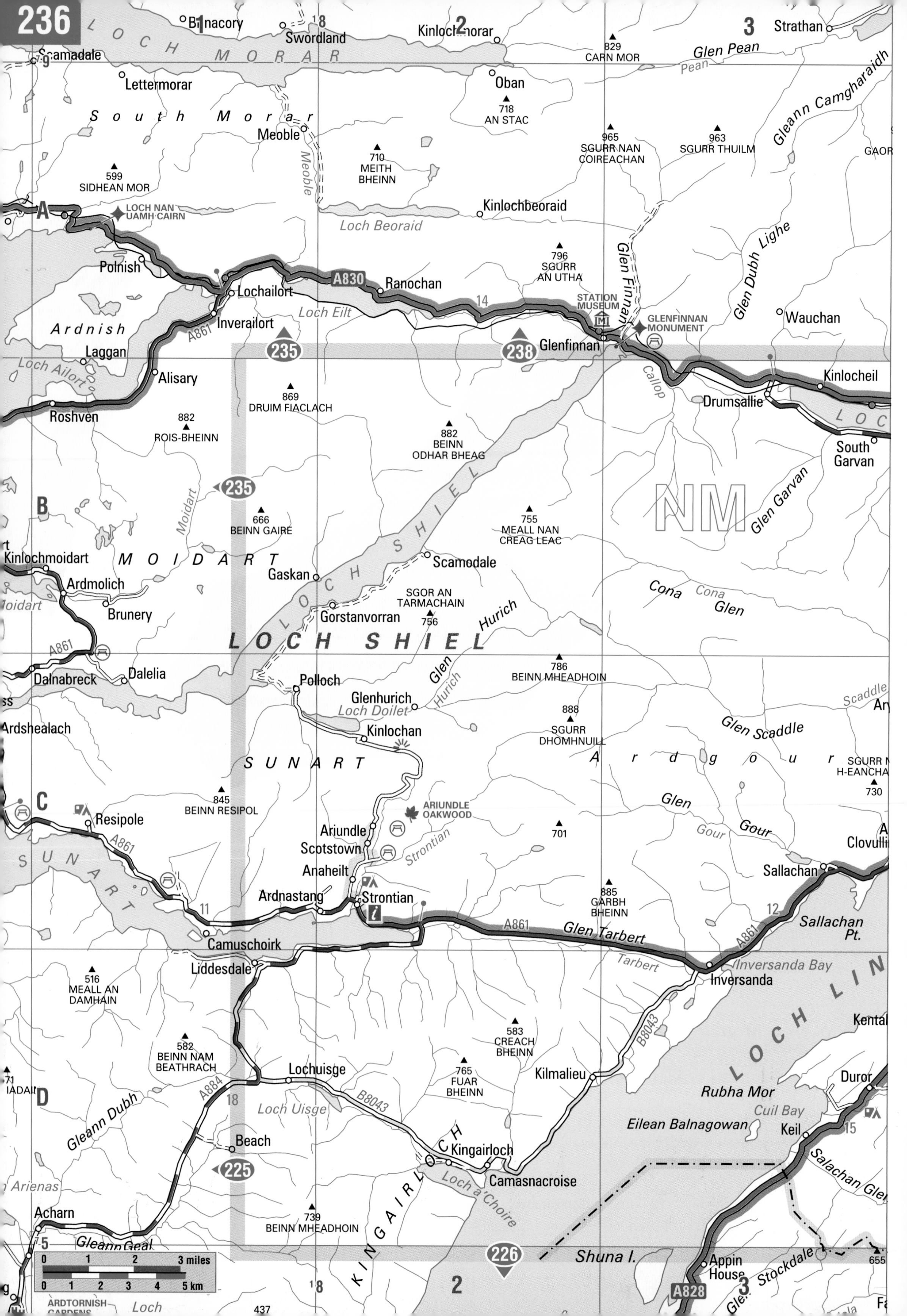
236
1
2
3
A
B
C
D
18
Bunacory
Swordland
Kinlochmorar
Strathan
LOCH MORAR
Scamadale
829
CARN MOR
Glen Pean
Pean
Lettermorar
Oban
Gleann Camgharaidh
South Morar
718
AN STAC
Meoble
965
SGURR NAN COIREACHAN
963
SGURR THUILM
GAOR
710
MEITH BHEINN
599
SIDHEAN MOR
Meoble
Kinlochbeoraid
LOCH NAN UAMH CAIRN
Loch Beoraid
796
SGURR AN UTHA
Glen Finnan
Glen Dubh Lighe
Polnish
A830
Ranochan
Lochailort
14
STATION MUSEUM
Inverailort
Loch Eilt
GLENFINNAN MONUMENT
Wauchan
Ardnish
A861
235
238
Glenfinnan
Laggan
Loch Ailort
Alisary
869
DRUIM FIACLACH
Callop
Kinlocheil
Drumsallie
Roshven
882
ROIS-BHEINN
882
BEINN ODHAR BHEAG
LOCH
South Garvan
Moidart
235
NM
Glen Garvan
666
BEINN GAIRE
755
MEALL NAN CREAG LEAC
LOCH SHIEL
Kinlochmoidart
MOIDART
Scamodale
Gaskan
Ardmolich
Moidart
Brunery
SGOR AN TARMACHAIN
Gorstanvorran
756
Cona
Cona Glen
A861
LOCH SHIEL
Glen Hurich
Hurich
786
BEINN MHEADHOIN
Dalnabreck
Dalelia
Polloch
Glenhurich
Loch Doilet
Scaddle
Ardshealach
Kinlochan
888
SGURR DHOMHNUILL
Glen Scaddle
SUNART
Ardgour
SGURR NA H-EANCHA
730
845
BEINN RESIPOL
Resipole
ARIUNDLE OAKWOOD
Glen Gour
Gour
A861
Ariundle
701
Clovullin
SUNART
Scotstown
Strontian
Anaheilt
Sallachan
Ardnastang
Strontian
885
GARBH BHEINN
12
Sallachan Pt.
11
A861
Glen Tarbert
Camuschoirk
Liddesdale
Tarbert
Inversanda Bay
Inversanda
516
MEALL AN DAMHAIN
LOCH LINNHE
B8043
583
CREACH BHEINN
Kentallen
582
BEINN NAM BEATHRACH
765
FUAR BHEINN
Lochuisge
Kilmalieu
Duror
A884
18
Loch Uisge
B8043
Rubha Mor
Cuil Bay
Gleann Dubh
Eilean Balnagowan
Keil
15
Beach
Kingairloch
225
Salachan Glen
Camasnacroise
Loch a'Choire
Arienas
Acharn
739
BEINN MHEADHOIN
KINGAIRLOCH
Gleann Geal
226
Shuna I.
655
0 1 2 3 miles
0 1 2 3 4 5 km
Appin House
Glen Stockdale
ARDTORNISH GARDENS
Loch
437
A828

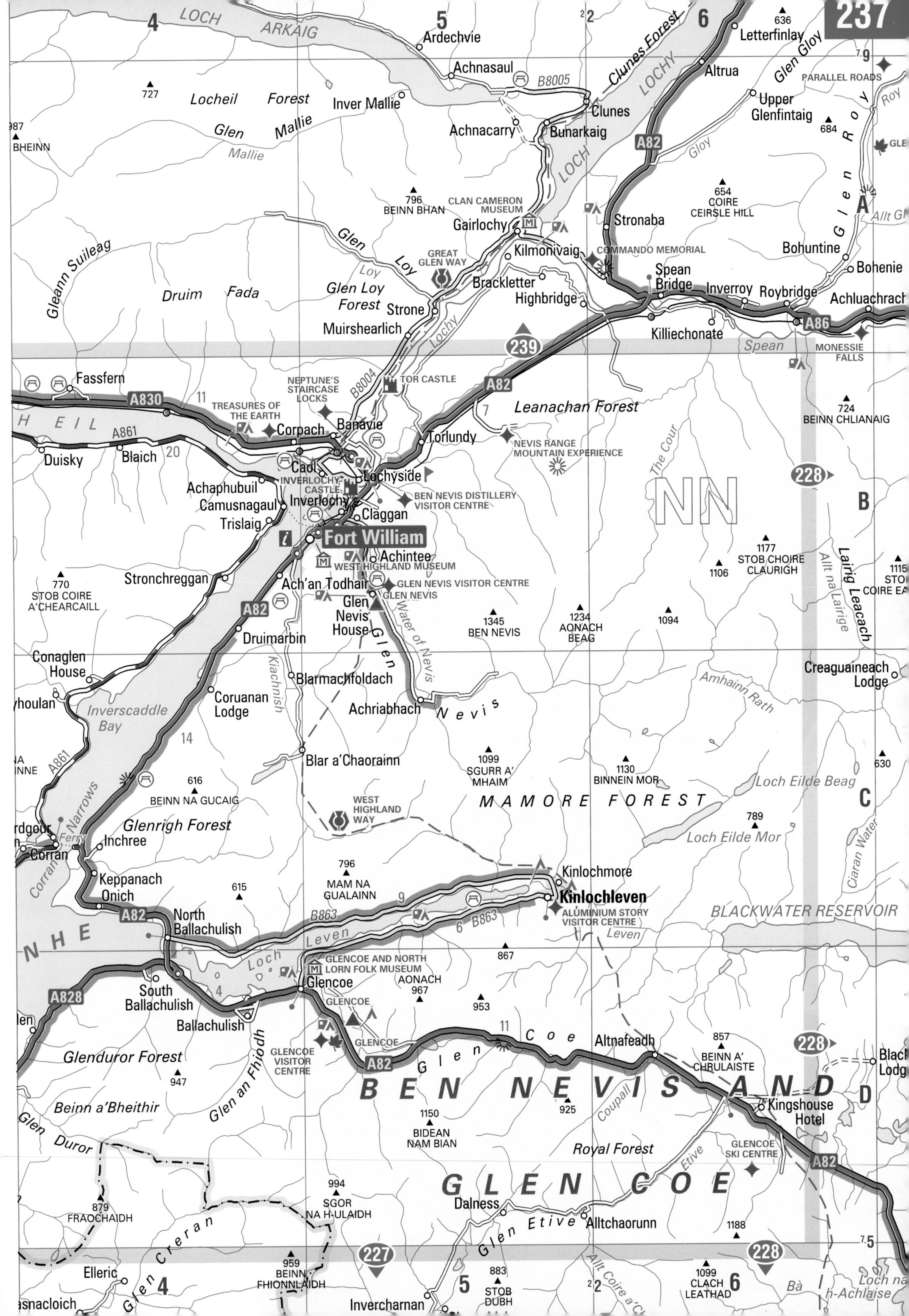

LOCH ARKAIG
Ardechvie
Achnasaul
B8005
Clunes Forest
Letterfinlay
Altrua
Glen Gloy
PARALLEL ROADS
Locheil Forest
Inver Mallie
Glen Mallie
Achnacarry
Clunes
Bunarkaig
LOCH LOCHY
A82
Upper Glenfintaig
Glen Roy
BEINN BHAN
CLAN CAMERON MUSEUM
Gairlochy
Stronaba
COIRE CEIRSLE HILL
Glen Loy
GREAT GLEN WAY
Kilmonivaig
COMMANDO MEMORIAL
Bohuntine
Bohenie
Spean Bridge
Inverroy
Roybridge
Achluachrach
Gleann Suileag
Druim Fada
Glen Loy Forest
Strone
Brackletter
Highbridge
Muirshearlich
Killiechonate
A86
Spean
MONESSIE FALLS
Fassfern
NEPTUNE'S STAIRCASE LOCKS
B8004
TOR CASTLE
A830
TREASURES OF THE EARTH
Corpach
Banavie
Leanachan Forest
BEINN CHLIANAIG
A861
Duisky
Blaich
Torlundy
NEVIS RANGE MOUNTAIN EXPERIENCE
The Cour
Caol
Lochyside
INVERLOCHY CASTLE
Achaphubuil
Camusnagaul
Inverlochy
BEN NEVIS DISTILLERY VISITOR CENTRE
NN
Claggan
Trislaig
Fort William
Achintee
WEST HIGHLAND MUSEUM
STOB CHOIRE CLAURIGH
STOB COIRE A'CHEARCAILL
Stronchreggan
Ach'an Todhair
GLEN NEVIS VISITOR CENTRE
GLEN NEVIS
Glen Nevis House
Water of Nevis
BEN NEVIS
AONACH BEAG
Allt na Lairige
Lairig Leacach
Druimarbin
Conaglen House
Kiachnish
Blarmachfoldach
Creaguaineach Lodge
Amhainn Rath
Coruanan Lodge
Inverscaddle Bay
Achriabhach
Glen Nevis
Blar a'Chaorainn
SGURR A' MHAIM
BINNEIN MOR
Loch Eilde Beag
BEINN NA GUCAIG
MAMORE FOREST
WEST HIGHLAND WAY
Loch Eilde Mor
Glenrigh Forest
Corran Narrows
Ferry
Inchree
Corran
Ciaran Water
Kinlochmore
Keppanach
MAM NA GUALAINN
Onich
Kinlochleven
ALUMINIUM STORY VISITOR CENTRE
BLACKWATER RESERVOIR
North Ballachulish
B863
Loch Leven
Leven
GLENCOE AND NORTH LORN FOLK MUSEUM
Glencoe
AONACH
A828
South Ballachulish
GLENCOE
Ballachulish
Glen an Fhiodh
Coe
Altnafeadh
BEINN A' CHRULAISTE
Glendurор Forest
GLENCOE VISITOR CENTRE
Glen Coe
BEN NEVIS AND
Kingshouse Hotel
Beinn a'Bheithir
Coupall
BIDEAN NAM BIAN
Glen Duror
Royal Forest
Etive
GLENCOE SKI CENTRE
FRAOCHAIDH
SGOR NA H-ULAIDH
GLEN COE
Dalness
Glen Etive
Alltchaorunn
Glen Creran
227
228
239
BEINN FHIONNLAIDH
Elleric
STOB DUBH
CLACH LEATHAD
Allt Coire a'Ch
Inverchanan
Loch na h-Achlaise

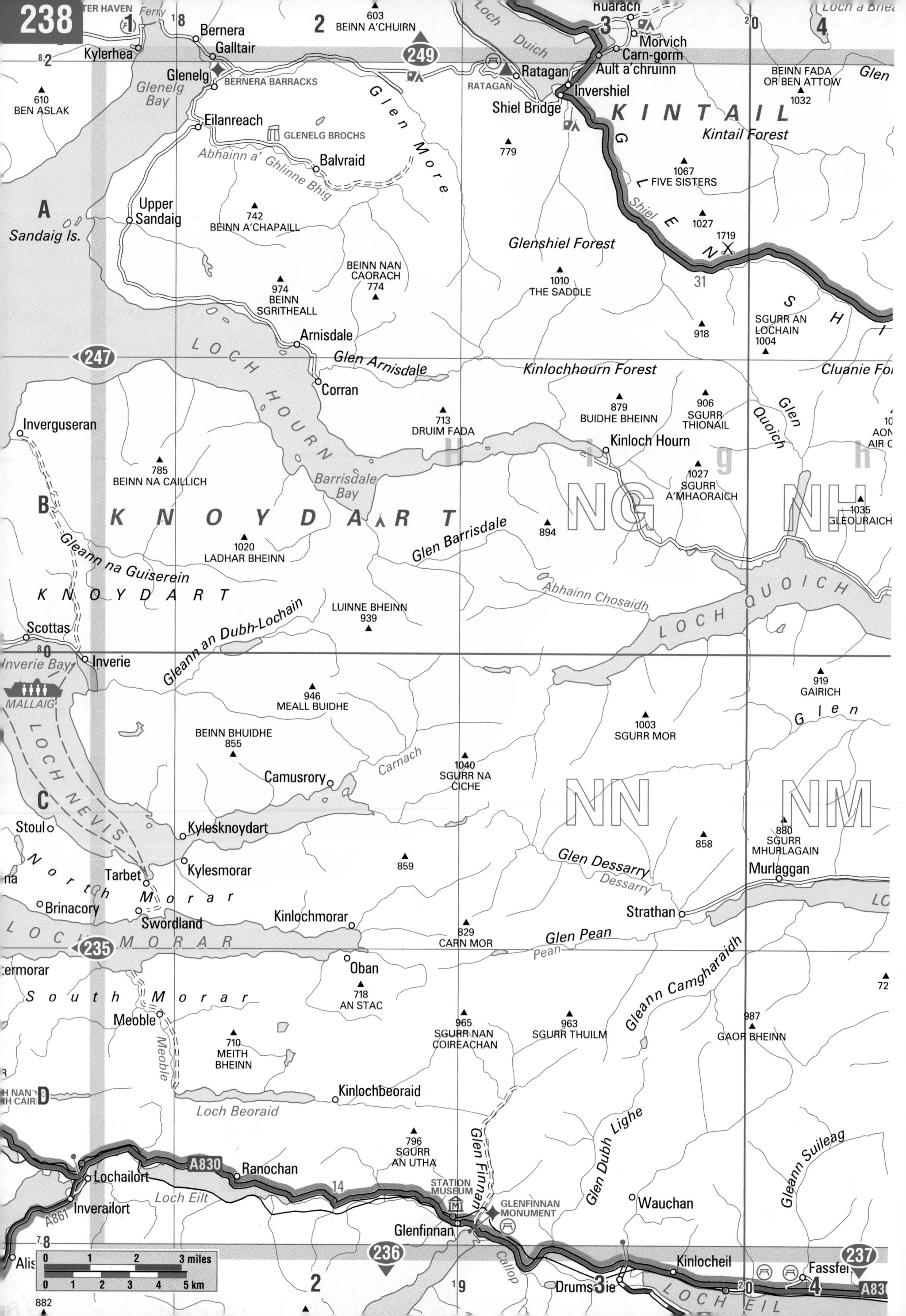
Bernera
Galltair
Kylerhea
Glenelg
Glenelg Bay
BERNERA BARRACKS
610
BEN ASLAK
603
BEINN A'CHUIRN
249
Loch Duich
Ratagan
RATAGAN
Ruarach
Morvich
Carn-gorm
Ault a'chruinn
Inverhsiel
Shiel Bridge
BEINN FADA OR BEN ATTOW
1032
K I N T A I L
Kintail Forest
Eilanreach
GLENELG BROCHS
Abhainn a' Ghlinne Bhig
Balvraid
Glen More
779
1067
FIVE SISTERS
Upper Sandaig
Sandaig Is.
742
BEINN A'CHAPAILL
Shiel
G L E N
1027
1719
Glenshiel Forest
31
974
BEINN SGRITHEALL
BEINN NAN CAORACH
774
1010
THE SADDLE
918
SGURR AN LOCHAIN
1004
S H I
Arnisdale
247
LOCH HOURN
Glen Arnisdale
Corran
Kinlochhourn Forest
Cluanie Fo
879
BUIDHE BHEINN
906
SGURR THIONAIL
Glen Quoich
713
DRUIM FADA
Kinloch Hourn
Inverguseran
785
BEINN NA CAILLICH
Barrisdale Bay
1027
SGURR A'MHAORAICH
NG
NH
1035
GLEOURAICH
K N O Y D A R T
1020
LADHAR BHEINN
Glen Barrisdale
894
Gleann na Guiserein
K N O Y D A R T
Abhainn Chosaidh
LOCH QUOICH
LUINNE BHEINN
939
Gleann an Dubh-Lochain
Scottas
Inverie
Inverie Bay
MALLAIG
946
MEALL BUIDHE
919
GAIRICH
Glen
1003
SGURR MOR
BEINN BHUIDHE
855
Carnach
1040
SGURR NA CICHE
Camusrory
LOCH NEVIS
NN
NM
Stoul
Kyleknoydart
858
880
SGURR MHURLAGAIN
North Morar
Tarbet
Kylesmorar
859
Glen Dessarry
Dessarry
Murlaggan
Brinacory
Swordland
Kinlochmorar
Strathan
LOCH MORAR
235
829
CARN MOR
Glen Pean
Pean
Oban
718
AN STAC
Gleann Camgharaidh
South Morar
Meoble
965
SGURR NAN COIREACHAN
963
SGURR THUILM
987
GAOR BHEINN
710
MEITH BHEINN
Kinlochbeoraid
Loch Beoraid
Glen Finnan
Glen Dubh Lighe
796
SGURR AN UTHA
Gleann Suileag
A830
Ranochan
Lochailort
Inverailort
Loch Eilt
A861
14
STATION MUSEUM
GLENFINNAN MONUMENT
Wauchan
Glenfinnan
236
Callop
Kinlocheil
237
Fassfe
Drumsallie
LOCH EIL
3 miles
5 km
882

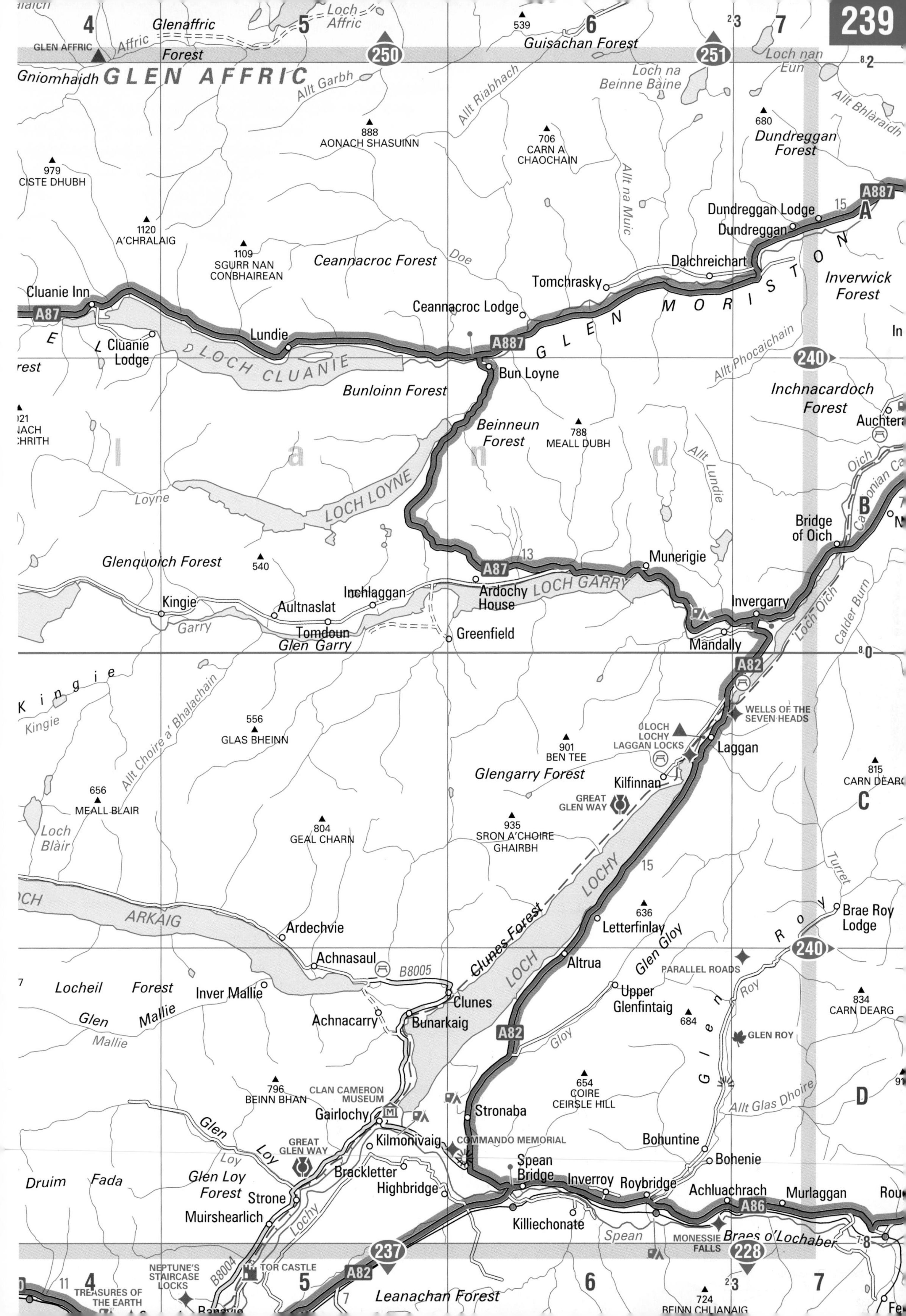

GLEN AFFRIC
Glenaffric
Forest
Loch Affric
Guisachan Forest
Loch nan Eun
Loch na Beinne Bàine
Allt Garbh
Allt Riabhach
Allt Bhlàraidh
888 AONACH SHASUINN
706 CARN A CHAOCHAIN
680
Dundreggan Forest
979 CISTE DHUBH
1120 A'CHRALAIG
1109 SGURR NAN CONBHAIREAN
Ceannacroc Forest
Allt na Muic
Dundreggan Lodge
Dundreggan
Dalchreichart
Tomchrasky
Inverwick Forest
Cluanie Inn
Ceannacroc Lodge
GLEN MORISTON
Lundie
Cluanie Lodge
LOCH CLUANIE
Bun Loyne
Bunloinn Forest
Allt Phocaichain
Inchnacardoch Forest
Beinneun Forest
788 MEALL DUBH
Allt Lundie
LOCH LOYNE
Loyne
Bridge of Oich
Glenquoich Forest
540
Munerigie
Kingie
Aultnaslat
Inchlaggan
Ardochy House
LOCH GARRY
Invergarry
Garry
Tomdoun
Glen Garry
Greenfield
Mandally
Loch Oich
Calder Burn
Kingie
Allt Choire a' Bhalachain
556 GLAS BHEINN
WELLS OF THE SEVEN HEADS
LOCH LOCHY LAGGAN LOCKS
Laggan
901 BEN TEE
Glengarry Forest
Kilfinnan
815 CARN DEARG
656 MEALL BLAIR
GREAT GLEN WAY
Loch Blàir
804 GEAL CHARN
935 SRON A'CHOIRE GHAIRBH
LOCH LOCHY
Turret
ARKAIG
636
Letterfinlay
Brae Roy Lodge
Clunes Forest
Ardechvie
Glen Gloy
Achnasaul
Altrua
Glen Roy
PARALLEL ROADS
Locheil Forest
Inver Mallie
Clunes
Upper Glenfintaig
834 CARN DEARG
Glen Mallie
Achnacarry
Bunarkaig
684
Mallie
Gloy
GLEN ROY
796 BEINN BHAN
CLAN CAMERON MUSEUM
654 COIRE CEIRSLE HILL
Allt Glas Dhoire
Gairlochy
Stronaba
Glen Loy
GREAT GLEN WAY
Kilmonivaig
COMMANDO MEMORIAL
Bohuntine
Bohenie
Druim Fada
Glen Loy Forest
Strone
Brackletter
Highbridge
Spean Bridge
Inverroy
Roybridge
Achluachrach
Murlaggan
Muirshearlich
Killiechonate
Spean
MONESSIE FALLS
Braes o'Lochaber
NEPTUNE'S STAIRCASE LOCKS
TOR CASTLE
TREASURES OF THE EARTH
Leanachan Forest
724 BEINN CHLIANAIG
A87 A887 A82 A86 B8005 B8004
250 251 240 237 228

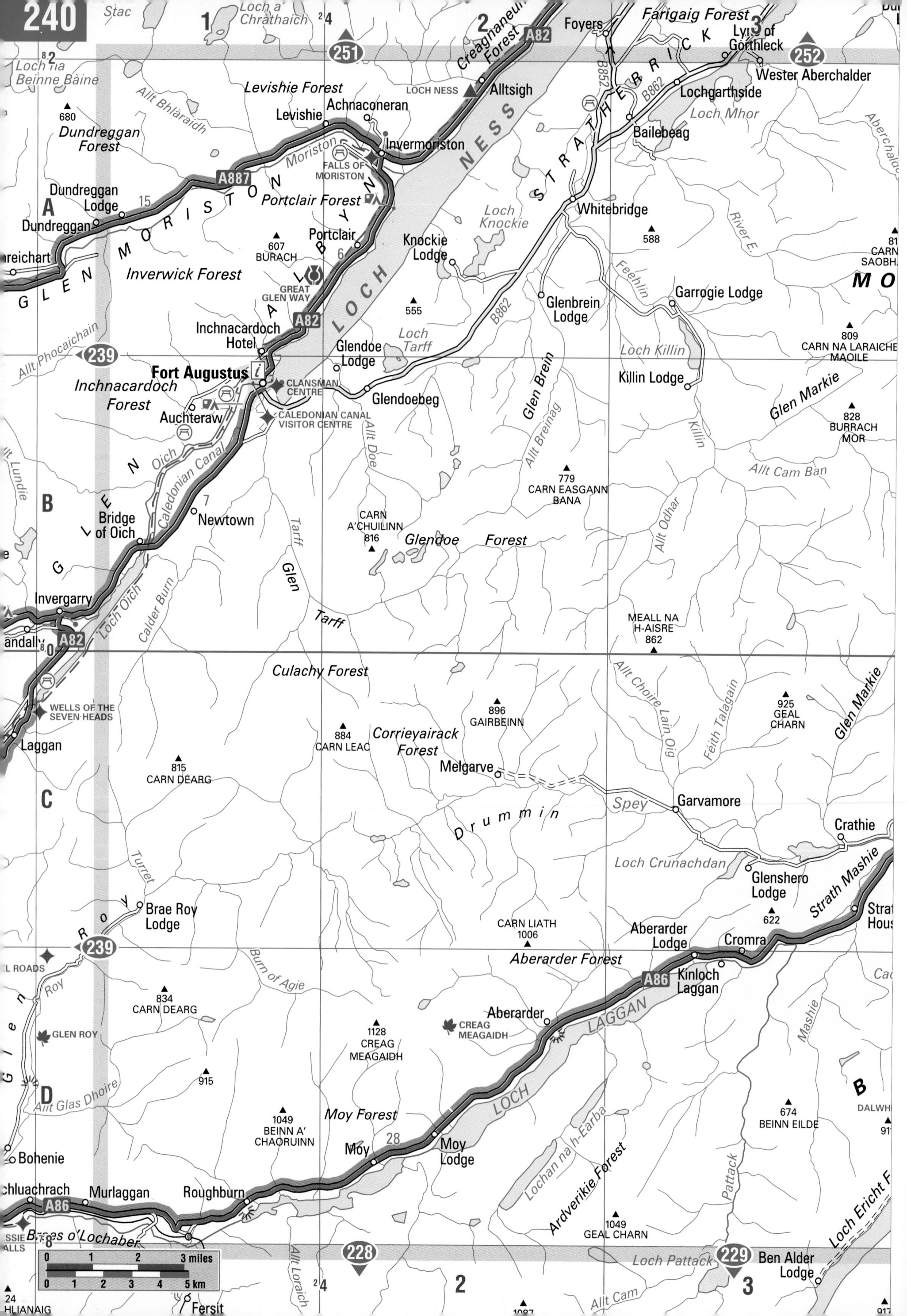

1   **2**   **3**

Stac
Loch a'
Chrathaich
251
Creagnaneun Forest
A82
Foyers
Farigaig Forest
Lyn of Gorthleck
252
Loch na
Beinne Bàine
680
Dundreggan Forest
Levishie Forest
Achnaconeran
LOCH NESS
Alltsigh
Wester Aberchalder
Levishie
Lochgarthside
Baile beag
Loch Mhor
Dundreggan Lodge
A887
Moriston
Invermoriston
FALLS OF MORISTON
Portclair Forest
607 BURACH
Portclair
Whitebridge
588
81 CARN SAOBHA
A
Dundreggan
15
MORISTON
GLEN
Inverwick Forest
GREAT GLEN WAY
A82
Loch Knockie
Knockie Lodge
River E.
MO
reichart
GLEN
Loch Knockie
555
B862
Glenbrein Lodge
Feehlin
Garrogie Lodge
809 CARN NA LARAICHE MAOILE
Inchnacardoch Hotel
Glendoe Lodge
Loch Tarff
Loch Killin
Killin Lodge
239
Fort Augustus
Glendoebeg
828 BURRACH MOR
Inchnacardoch Forest
CLANSMAN CENTRE
Glen Brein
Allt Breinag
Glen Markie
Auchteraw
CALEDONIAN CANAL VISITOR CENTRE
Allt Doe
779 CARN EASGANN BANA
Allt Cam Ban
B
Bridge of Oich
Newtown
7
CARN A'CHUILINN 816
Glendoe Forest
Allt Odhar
Allt Choire Iain Oig
MEALL NA H-AISRE 862
Feith Talagain
925 GEAL CHARN
Glen Markie
Invergarry
A82
andally
Loch Oich
Calder Burn
Glen
Tarff
Culachy Forest
896 GAIRBEINN
Drummin
Spey
Garvamore
Crathie
C
WELLS OF THE SEVEN HEADS
884 CARN LEAC
Corrieyairack Forest
Melgarve
Loch Crunachdan
Glenshero Lodge
Strath Mashie
Laggan
815 CARN DEARG
Strat Hous
Turret
Brae Roy Lodge
Burn of Agie
CARN LIATH 1006
Aberarder Lodge
Cromra
622
239
834 CARN DEARG
Aberarder Forest
A86
Kinloch Laggan
GLEN ROY
915
1128 CREAG MEAGAIDH
CREAG MEAGAIDH
Aberarder
LAGGAN
LOCH
B
D
L ROADS
GLEN ROY
Allt Glas Dhoire
Moy Forest
674 BEINN EILDE
DALWHI
91
Bohenie
1049 BEINN A' CHAORUINN
Moy
28
Moy Lodge
Ardverikie Forest
Loch Ericht F
chluachrach
Murlaggan
Roughburn
Pattack
A86
Brees o' Lochaber
SSIE
ALLS
228
1049 GEAL CHARN
Loch Pattack
229
Ben Alder Lodge
24
HLIANAIG
Fersit
Allt Loraich
2
Allt Cam
3

0	1	2	3 miles
0	1 2 3 4		5 km

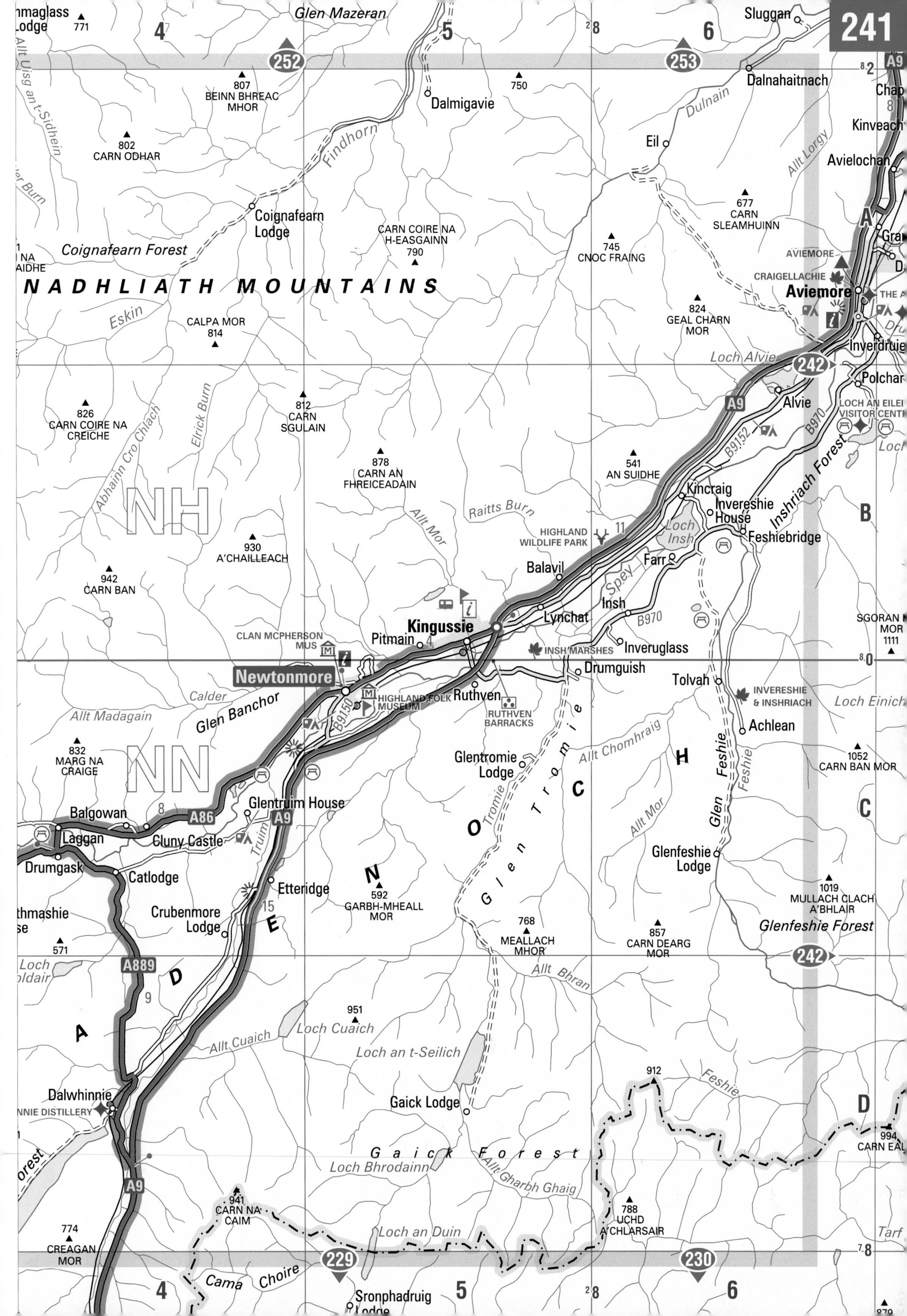
Glen Mazeran
Dalmigavie
Dalnahaitnach
Sluggan
BEINN BHREAC MHOR
CARN ODHAR
Coignafearn Lodge
Coignafearn Forest
CARN COIRE NA H-EASGAINN
MONADHLIATH MOUNTAINS
CALPA MOR
CNOC FRAING
GEAL CHARN MOR
CARN SLEAMHUINN
Eil
Aviemore
Avielochan
Kinveach
Loch Alvie
Alvie
Polchar
Inverdruie
LOCH AN EILEIN VISITOR CENTRE
CARN COIRE NA CREICHE
CARN SGULAIN
CARN AN FHREICEADAIN
AN SUIDHE
Kincraig
Invereshie House
Feshiebridge
Inshriach Forest
HIGHLAND WILDLIFE PARK
Loch Insh
A'CHAILLEACH
CARN BAN
Balavil
Farr
Insh
Lynchat
Kingussie
Pitmain
CLAN MCPHERSON MUS
INSH MARSHES
Inveruglass
Drumguish
Tolvah
Newtonmore
HIGHLAND FOLK MUSEUM
Ruthven
RUTHVEN BARRACKS
INVERESHIE & INSHRIACH
Achlean
Glen Banchor
MARG NA CRAIGE
Glentromie Lodge
Glen Tromie
Glen Feshie
CARN BAN MOR
Balgowan
Laggan
Cluny Castle
Glentruim House
Drumgask
Catlodge
Etteridge
Crubenmore Lodge
GARBH-MHEALL MOR
MEALLACH MHOR
CARN DEARG MOR
Glenfeshie Lodge
MULLACH CLACH A'BHLAIR
Glenfeshie Forest
Loch Cuaich
Loch an t-Seilich
Dalwhinnie
Gaick Lodge
Gaick Forest
Loch Bhrodainn
CARN NA CAIM
UCHD A'CHLARSAIR
Loch an Duin
CREAGAN MOR
Cama Choire
Sronphadruig Lodge
CARN EALAR
SGORAN MOR
Loch Einich

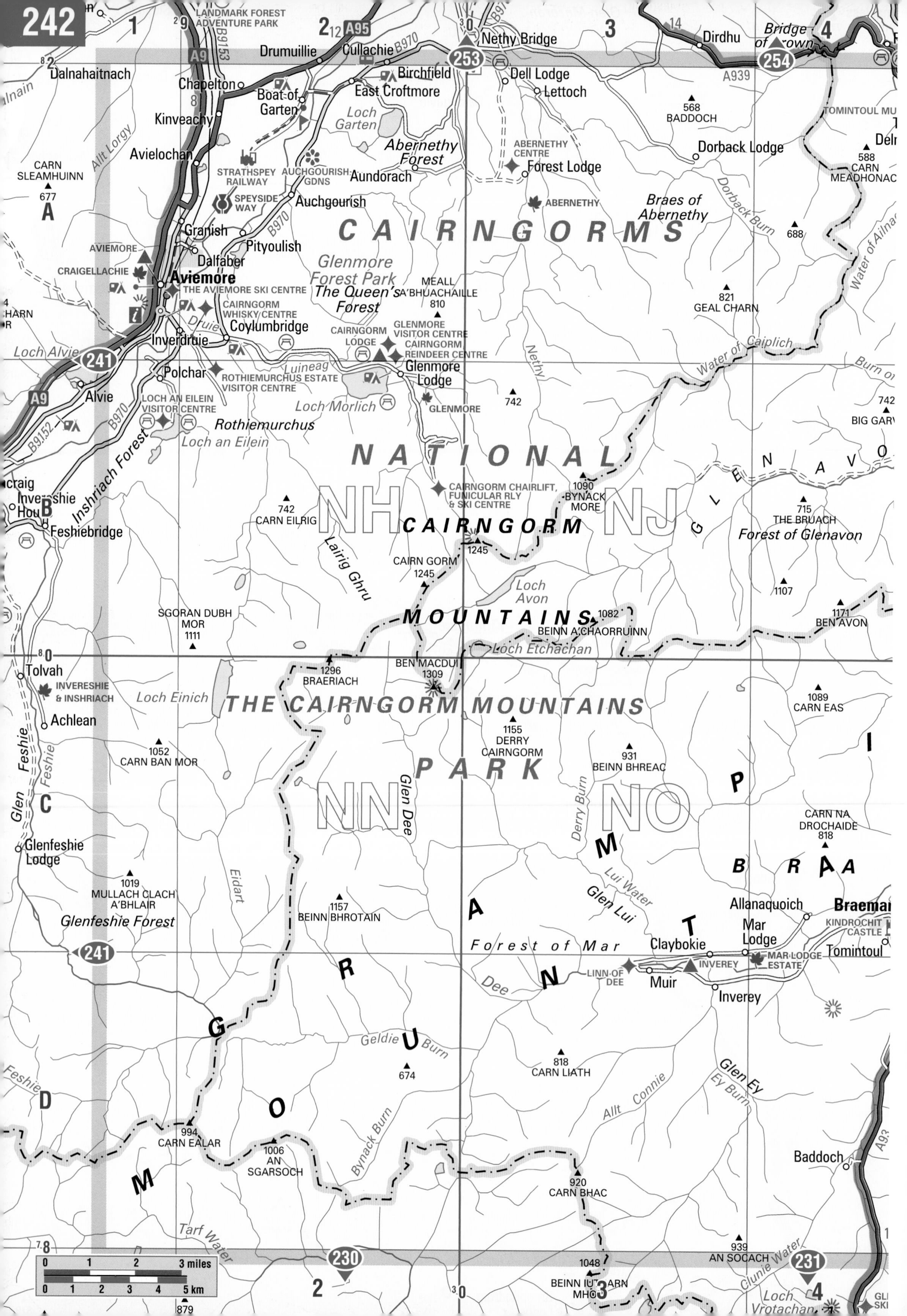
LANDMARK FOREST ADVENTURE PARK
Drumuillie
Cullachie
Nethy Bridge
Dirdhu
Bridge of Brown
Dalnahaitnach
Chapelton
Boat of Garten
Birchfield
East Croftmore
Dell Lodge
Lettoch
Kinveachy
Loch Garten
568 BADDOCH
Avielochan
Abernethy Forest
Aundorach
ABERNETHY CENTRE
Forest Lodge
Dorback Lodge
588 CARN MEADHONACH
CARN SLEAMHUINN 677
STRATHSPEY RAILWAY
AUCHGOURISH GDNS
SPEYSIDE WAY
Auchgourish
ABERNETHY
Braes of Abernethy
Dorback Burn
688
Granish
Pityoulish
CAIRNGORMS
AVIEMORE
Dalfaber
CRAIGELLACHIE
Aviemore
THE AVIEMORE SKI CENTRE
Glenmore Forest Park
The Queen's Forest
MEALL A'BHUACHAILLE 810
821 GEAL CHARN
CAIRNGORM WHISKY CENTRE
Coylumbridge
CAIRNGORM LODGE
GLENMORE VISITOR CENTRE
CAIRNGORM REINDEER CENTRE
Inverdruie
Druie
Loch Alvie
Luineag
Glenmore Lodge
Water of Caiplich
Nethy
Polchar
ROTHIEMURCHUS ESTATE VISITOR CENTRE
Alvie
LOCH AN EILEIN VISITOR CENTRE
Loch Morlich
GLENMORE
742
742 BIG GARVOUN
Rothiemurchus
Loch an Eilein
Inshriach Forest
NATIONAL
GLEN AVON
CAIRNGORM CHAIRLIFT, FUNICULAR RLY & SKI CENTRE
1090 BYNACK MORE
715 THE BRUACH
Invereshie House
Feshiebridge
742 CARN EILRIG
NH
CAIRNGORM
NJ
Forest of Glenavon
1245
Lairig Ghru
CAIRN GORM 1245
Loch Avon
1107
SGORAN DUBH MOR 1111
MOUNTAINS
1082
1171 BEN AVON
BEINN A'CHAORRUINN
Loch Etchachan
Tolvah
1296 BRAERIACH
BEN MACDUI 1309
1089 CARN EAS
INVERESHIE & INSHRIACH
Loch Einich
THE CAIRNGORM MOUNTAINS
Achlean
1155 DERRY CAIRNGORM
1052 CARN BAN MOR
931 BEINN BHREAC
PARK
Glen Feshie
NN
Glen Dee
Derry Burn
NO
CARN NA DROCHAIDE 818
Glenfeshie Lodge
1019 MULLACH CLACH A'BHLAIR
Eidart
Lui Water
Glen Lui
Allanaquoich
Braemar
1157 BEINN BHROTAIN
Glenfeshie Forest
Mar Lodge
Claybokie
KINDROCHIT CASTLE
Forest of Mar
MAR LODGE ESTATE
Tomintoul
INVEREY
LINN OF DEE
Muir
Inverey
Dee
Geldie Burn
674
818 CARN LIATH
Glen Ey
Ey Burn
Allt Connie
994 CARN EALAR
1006 AN SGARSOCH
Bynack Burn
Baddoch
920 CARN BHAC
Tarf Water
939 AN SOCACH
Clunie Water
1048
BEINN IUTHARN MHOR
Loch Vrotachan
0 1 2 3 miles
0 1 2 3 4 5 km
879

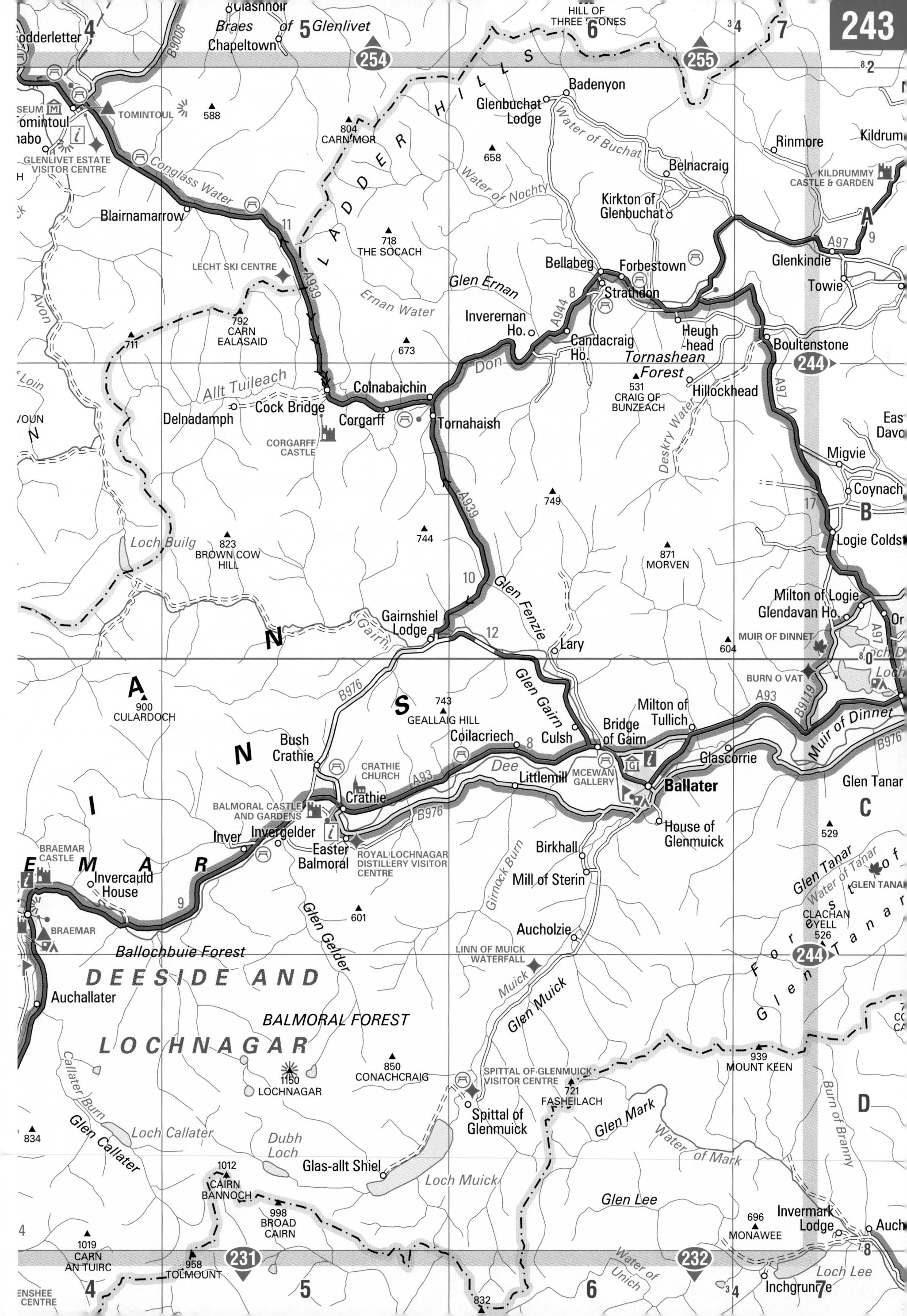
Braes of Glenlivet
Chapeltown
HILL OF THREE STONES
LADDER HILLS
Badenyon
Glenbuchat Lodge
Water of Buchat
Rinmore
Kildrummy
KILDRUMMY CASTLE & GARDEN
Belnacraig
Kirkton of Glenbuchat
Water of Nochty
TOMINTOUL
Tomintoul
GLENLIVET ESTATE VISITOR CENTRE
Conglass Water
804 CARN MOR
658
588
Blairnamarrow
718 THE SOCACH
LECHT SKI CENTRE
A939
Glen Ernan
Ernan Water
Bellabeg
Forbestown
Strathdon
Glenkindie
Towie
A97
Inverernan Ho.
Candacraig Ho.
Heugh-head
Boultenstone
Tornashean Forest
531 CRAIG OF BUNZEACH
Hillockhead
792 CARN EALASAID
711
673
Don
Allt Tuileach
Colnabaichin
Cock Bridge
Delnadamph
Corgarff
CORGARFF CASTLE
Tornahaish
Deskry Water
Migvie
Coynach
Logie Coldstone
749
744
823 BROWN COW HILL
Loch Builg
871 MORVEN
Avon
Glen Fenzie
Milton of Logie
Glendavan Ho.
Gairnshiel Lodge
Gairn
Lary
MUIR OF DINNET
604
BURN O VAT
900 CULARDOCH
743 GEALLAIG HILL
Glen Gairn
B976
Milton of Tullich
Bridge of Gairn
Culsh
Coilacriech
Bush Crathie
CRATHIE CHURCH
Crathie
Dee
Littlemill
MCEWAN GALLERY
Ballater
Glascorrie
Muir of Dinnet
Glen Tanar
BALMORAL CASTLE AND GARDENS
House of Glenmuick
529
BRAEMAR CASTLE
Inver
Invergelder
Easter Balmoral
ROYAL LOCHNAGAR DISTILLERY VISITOR CENTRE
Birkhall
Mill of Sterin
Girnock Burn
Invercauld House
BRAEMAR
Glen Gelder
601
Aucholzie
CLACHAN YELL 526
Water of Tanar
GLEN TANAR
Forest of Glen Tanar
Ballochbuie Forest
LINN OF MUICK WATERFALL
Muick
Glen Muick
CAIRNGORMS NATIONAL PARK
DEESIDE AND LOCHNAGAR
Auchallater
BALMORAL FOREST
939 MOUNT KEEN
850 CONACHCRAIG
1150 LOCHNAGAR
SPITTAL OF GLENMUICK VISITOR CENTRE
721 FASHEILACH
Spittal of Glenmuick
Glen Mark
Burn of Branny
Callater Burn
Glen Callater
834
Loch Callater
Dubh Loch
Glas-allt Shiel
Water of Mark
Loch Muick
Glen Lee
1012 CAIRN BANNOCH
998 BROAD CAIRN
696 MONAWEE
Invermark Lodge
1019 CARN AN TUIRC
958 TOLMOUNT
Water of Unich
Loch Lee
Inchgrundle
832
254
255
244
231
232
A93
A944
B9119

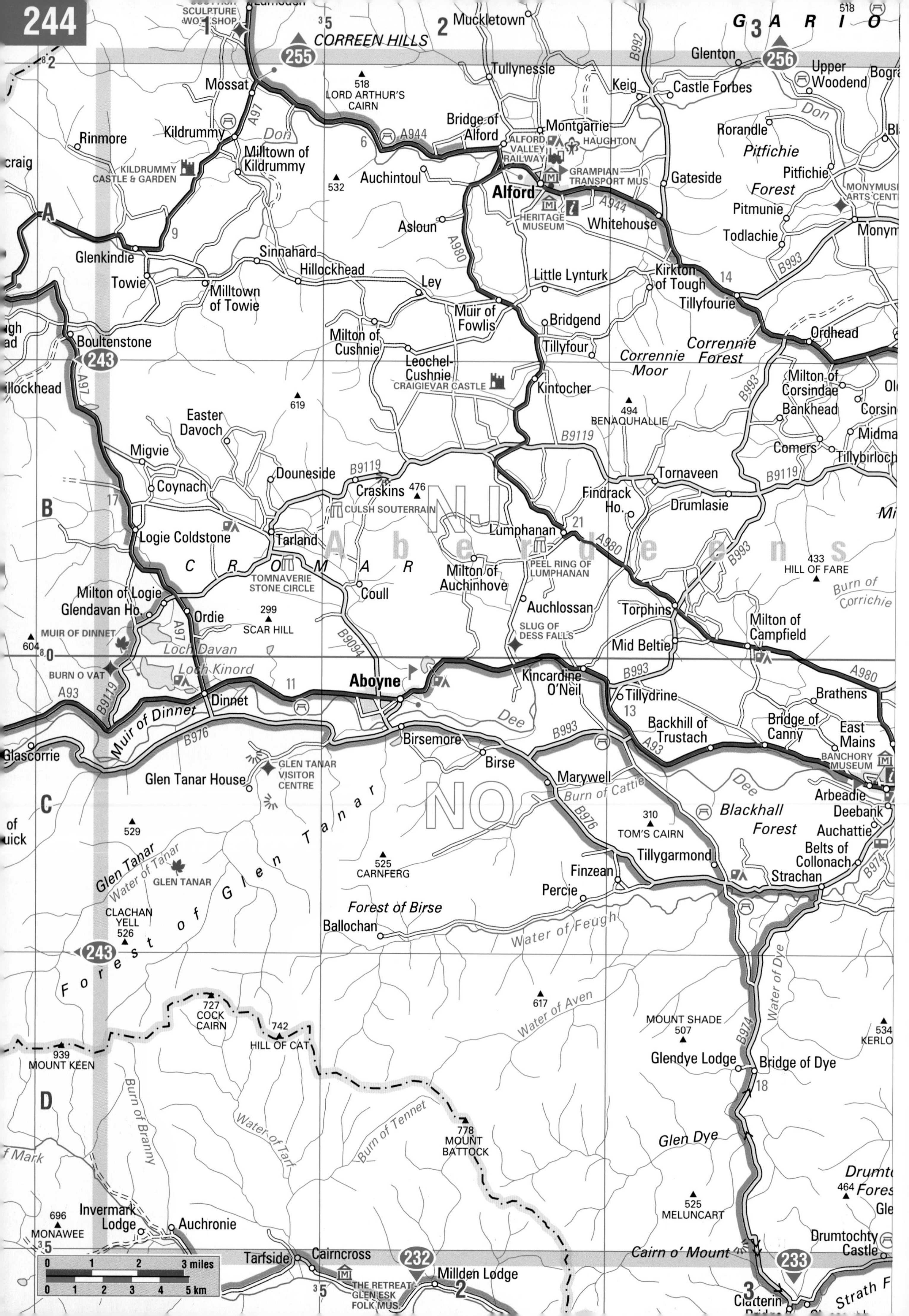
CORREEN HILLS
Muckletown
Mossat
Tullynessle
LORD ARTHUR'S CAIRN
Glenton
Upper Woodend
Keig
Castle Forbes
Kildrummy
Rinmore
Milltown of Kildrummy
KILDRUMMY CASTLE & GARDEN
Bridge of Alford
Montgarrie
ALFORD VALLEY RAILWAY
HAUGHTON
GRAMPIAN TRANSPORT MUS
Auchintoul
Alford
HERITAGE MUSEUM
Gateside
Rorandle
Pitfichie
Pitfichie Forest
Pitmunie
Todlachie
Asloun
Whitehouse
Glenkindie
Towie
Sinnahard
Hillockhead
Milltown of Towie
Ley
Little Lynturk
Kirkton of Tough
Tillyfourie
Muir of Fowlis
Bridgend
Boultenstone
Milton of Cushnie
Leochel-Cushnie
CRAIGIEVAR CASTLE
Tillyfour
Corrennie Moor
Corrennie Forest
Ordhead
Kintocher
Milton of Corsindae
Bankhead
BENAQUHALLIE
Comers
Tillybirloch
Easter Davoch
Migvie
Coynach
Douneside
Craskins
CULSH SOUTERRAIN
Tornaveen
Findrack Ho.
Drumlasie
Logie Coldstone
Tarland
Lumphanan
CROMAR
Aberdeens
TOMNAVERIE STONE CIRCLE
Milton of Auchinhove
PEEL RING OF LUMPHANAN
Coull
Auchlossan
Torphins
HILL OF FARE
Burn of Corrichie
Milton of Logie
Glendavan Ho.
Ordie
SCAR HILL
MUIR OF DINNET
SLUG OF DESS FALLS
Milton of Campfield
Mid Beltie
Loch Davan
Loch Kinord
BURN O VAT
Aboyne
Kincardine O'Neil
Tillydrine
Brathens
Dinnet
Muir of Dinnet
Dee
Backhill of Trustach
Bridge of Canny
East Mains
Glascorrie
Birsemore
Birse
BANCHORY MUSEUM
Glen Tanar House
GLEN TANAR VISITOR CENTRE
Marywell
Burn of Cattie
Arbeadie
Deebank
Blackhall Forest
TOM'S CAIRN
Auchattie
Belts of Collonach
Glen Tanar
Water of Tanar
GLEN TANAR
CARNFERG
Tillygarmond
Finzean
Strachan
Percie
Forest of Birse
Forest of Glen Tanar
CLACHAN YELL
Ballochan
Water of Feugh
COCK CAIRN
HILL OF CAT
MOUNT KEEN
Water of Aven
MOUNT SHADE
Water of Dye
KERLOCH
Glendye Lodge
Bridge of Dye
Burn of Branny
Water of Tarf
Burn of Tennet
MOUNT BATTOCK
Glen Dye
Invermark Lodge
Auchronie
MONAWEE
MELUNCART
Drumtochty Castle
Cairn o' Mount
Tarfside
Cairncross
Millden Lodge
THE RETREAT GLEN ESK FOLK MUS
Clatterin Bridge
Strath F
0 1 2 3 miles
0 1 2 3 4 5 km

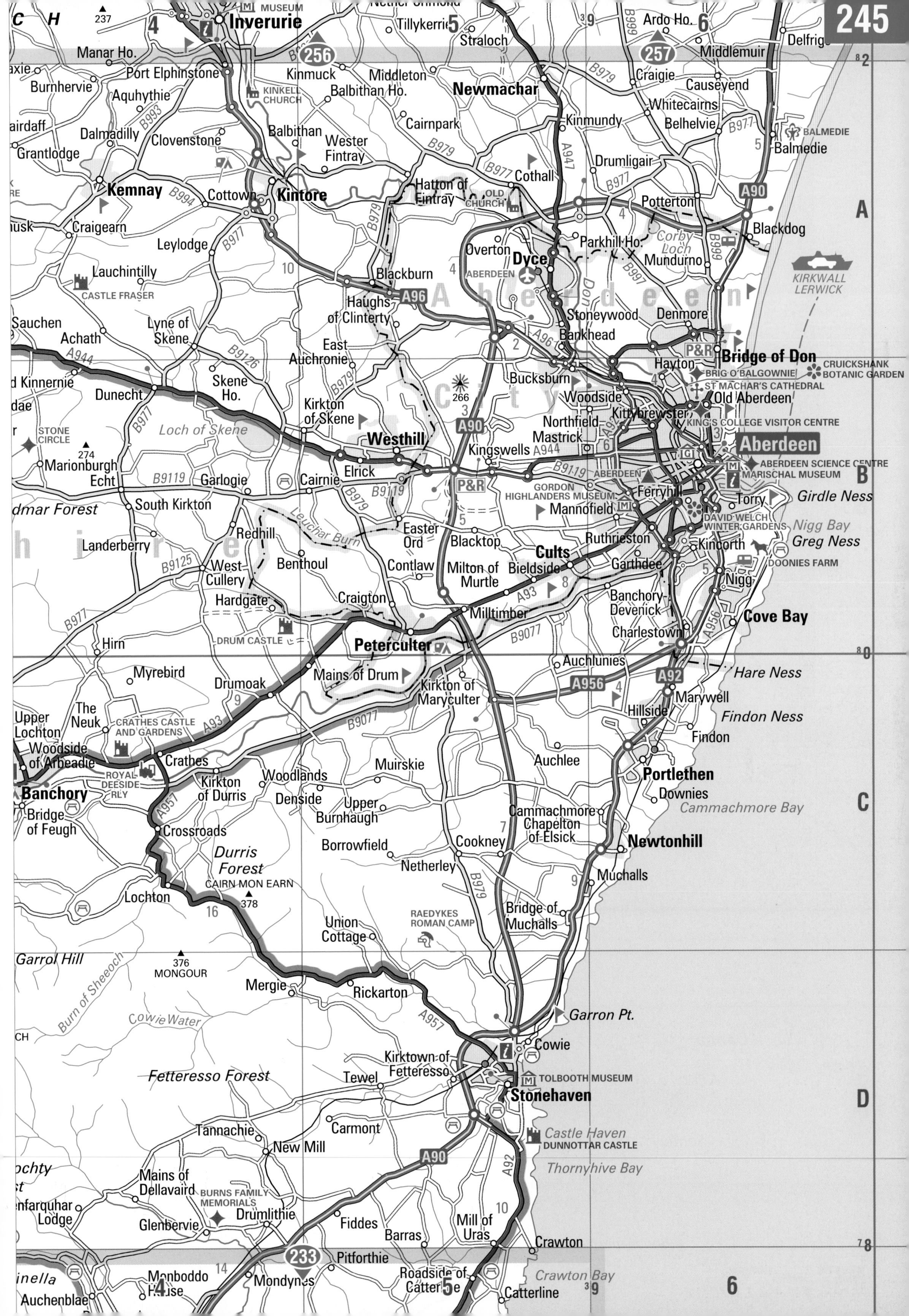
Inverurie
MUSEUM
Tillykerrie
Straloch
Ardo Ho.
Delfrig
Manar Ho.
256
257
Middlemuir
Port Elphinstone
Kinmuck
Middleton
Craigie
Burnhervie
Aquhythie
KINKELL CHURCH
Balbithan Ho.
Newmachar
Causeyend
Whitecairns
Dalmadilly
Clovenstone
Cairnpark
Kinmundy
Belhelvie
BALMEDIE
Grantlodge
Balbithan
Wester Fintray
Balmedie
Drumligair
Kemnay
Cottown
Kintore
Hatton of Fintray
Cothall
OLD CHURCH
Potterton
A90
Craigearn
Leylodge
Overton
Dyce
Parkhill Ho.
Corby Loch
Blackdog
Mundurno
Lauchintilly
CASTLE FRASER
Blackburn
ABERDEEN
KIRKWALL LERWICK
Haughs of Clinterty
A96
Stoneywood
Denmore
Sauchen
Achath
Lyne of Skene
Bankhead
Bridge of Don
East Auchronie
Hayton
CRUICKSHANK BOTANIC GARDEN
BRIG O' BALGOWNIE
Kinnernie
Dunecht
Skene Ho.
Bucksburn
ST MACHAR'S CATHEDRAL
Old Aberdeen
266
Woodside
Kirkton of Skene
Kittybrewster
KING'S COLLEGE VISITOR CENTRE
STONE CIRCLE
Loch of Skene
Westhill
Northfield
Mastrick
Aberdeen
274
Marionburgh
Kingswells
A944
ABERDEEN SCIENCE CENTRE
MARISCHAL MUSEUM
Echt
Garlogie
Cairnie
Elrick
P&R
GORDON HIGHLANDERS MUSEUM
Ferryhill
Torry
Girdle Ness
South Kirkton
Mannofield
DAVID WELCH WINTER GARDENS
Nigg Bay
Leuchar Burn
Easter Ord
Redhill
Blacktop
Ruthrieston
Greg Ness
Landerberry
Cults
Kincorth
DOONIES FARM
Benthoul
Contlaw
Milton of Murtle
Bieldside
Garthdee
West Cullery
Nigg
Hardgate
Craigton
Banchory-Devenick
Cove Bay
Milltimber
A93
Hirn
DRUM CASTLE
Peterculter
Charlestown
Myrebird
Auchlunies
Hare Ness
Drumoak
Mains of Drum
A92
Kirkton of Maryculter
A956
Marywell
The Neuk
Hillside
Findon Ness
Upper Lochton
CRATHES CASTLE AND GARDENS
Findon
Woodside of Arbeadie
Crathes
Muirskie
Auchlee
ROYAL DEESIDE RLY
Kirkton of Durris
Woodlands
Portlethen
Banchory
Denside
Downies
Bridge of Feugh
Upper Burnhaugh
Cammachmore
Cammachmore Bay
Chapelton of Elsick
Crossroads
Borrowfield
Cookney
Newtonhill
Durris Forest
Netherley
Muchalls
Lochton
CAIRN MON EARN
378
Union Cottage
RAEDYKES ROMAN CAMP
Bridge of Muchalls
Garrol Hill
376 MONGOUR
Burn of Sheeoch
Mergie
Rickarton
Garron Pt.
Cowie Water
A957
Cowie
Kirktown of Fetteresso
Fetteresso Forest
Tewel
TOLBOOTH MUSEUM
Stonehaven
Tannachie
Carmont
Castle Haven
DUNNOTTAR CASTLE
New Mill
Thornyhive Bay
Mains of Dellavaird
BURNS FAMILY MEMORIALS
Drumlithie
Fiddes
Glenbervie
Mill of Uras
Barras
Crawton
233
Pitforthie
Crawton Bay
Monboddo House
Mondynes
Roadside of Catterline
Catterline
Auchenblae
A
B
C
D

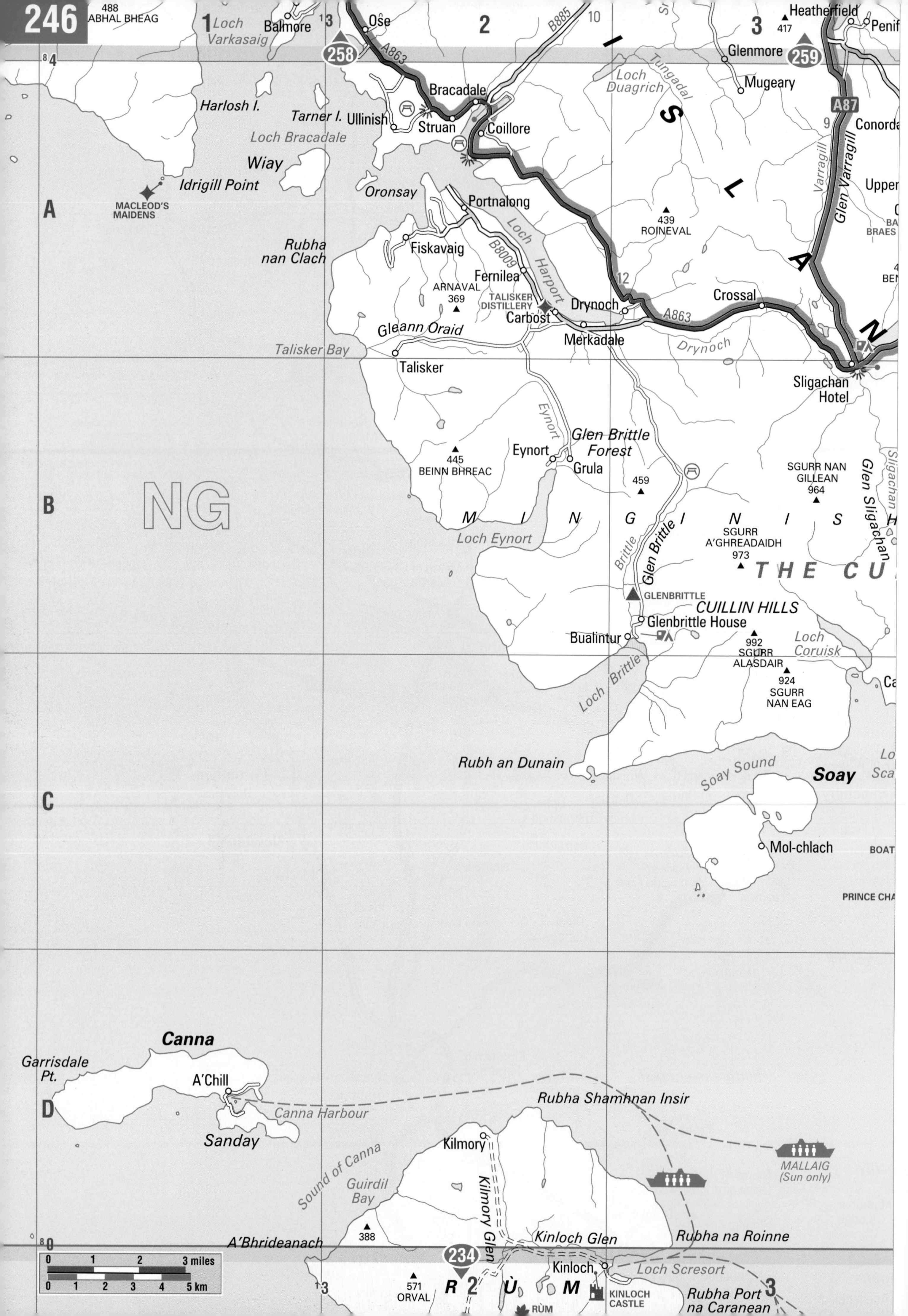

488
ABHAL BHEAG

1 Loch
Varkasaig
Balmore
Ose
3
2
B885
10
3
Heatherfield
417
Glenmore
Penif

258

A863

ISLAN

A87

259

Loch
Duagrich
Tungadal
Mugeary
Conorda

9

Glen Varragill

Upper
BA
BRAES

Harlosh I.

Tarner I.
Ullinish
Bracadale
Coillore

Struan

Loch Bracadale

Wiay

Oronsay

Portnalong

439
ROINEVAL

A

Idrigill Point

MACLEOD'S
MAIDENS

Rubha
nan Clach

Fiskavaig

Fernilea

ARNAVAL
369

TALISKER
DISTILLERY

B8009

Loch Harport

Drynoch

Crossal

Varragill

Carbost

A863

Gleann Oraid

Merkadale

Drynoch

Talisker Bay

Talisker

Sligachan
Hotel

NG

Eynort
Eynort

Glen Brittle
Forest

445
BEINN BHREAC

Grula

459

SGURR NAN
GILLEAN
964

Glen Sligachan

B

M
I
N
G
I
N
I
S
THE CU

Loch Eynort

Brittle

Glen Brittle

SGURR
A'GHREADAIDH
973

GLENBRITTLE

CUILLIN HILLS

Glenbrittle House

Bualintur

Loch
Coruisk

992
SGURR
ALASDAIR

924
SGURR
NAN EAG

Ca

Loch Brittle

C

Rubh an Dunain

Soay Sound

Soay

Lo
Sca

Mol-chlach

BOAT

PRINCE CHA

Canna

Garrisdale
Pt.

A'Chill

Canna Harbour

Rubha Shamhnan Insir

D

Sanday

Kilmory

Sound of Canna

Guirdil
Bay

Kilmory Glen

MALLAIG
(Sun only)

0

A'Bhrideanach

388

Kinloch Glen

Rubha na Roinne

Loch Scresort

234

Kinloch

R 2 Ù M

571
ORVAL

RÙM

KINLOCH
CASTLE

Rubha Port
na Caranean

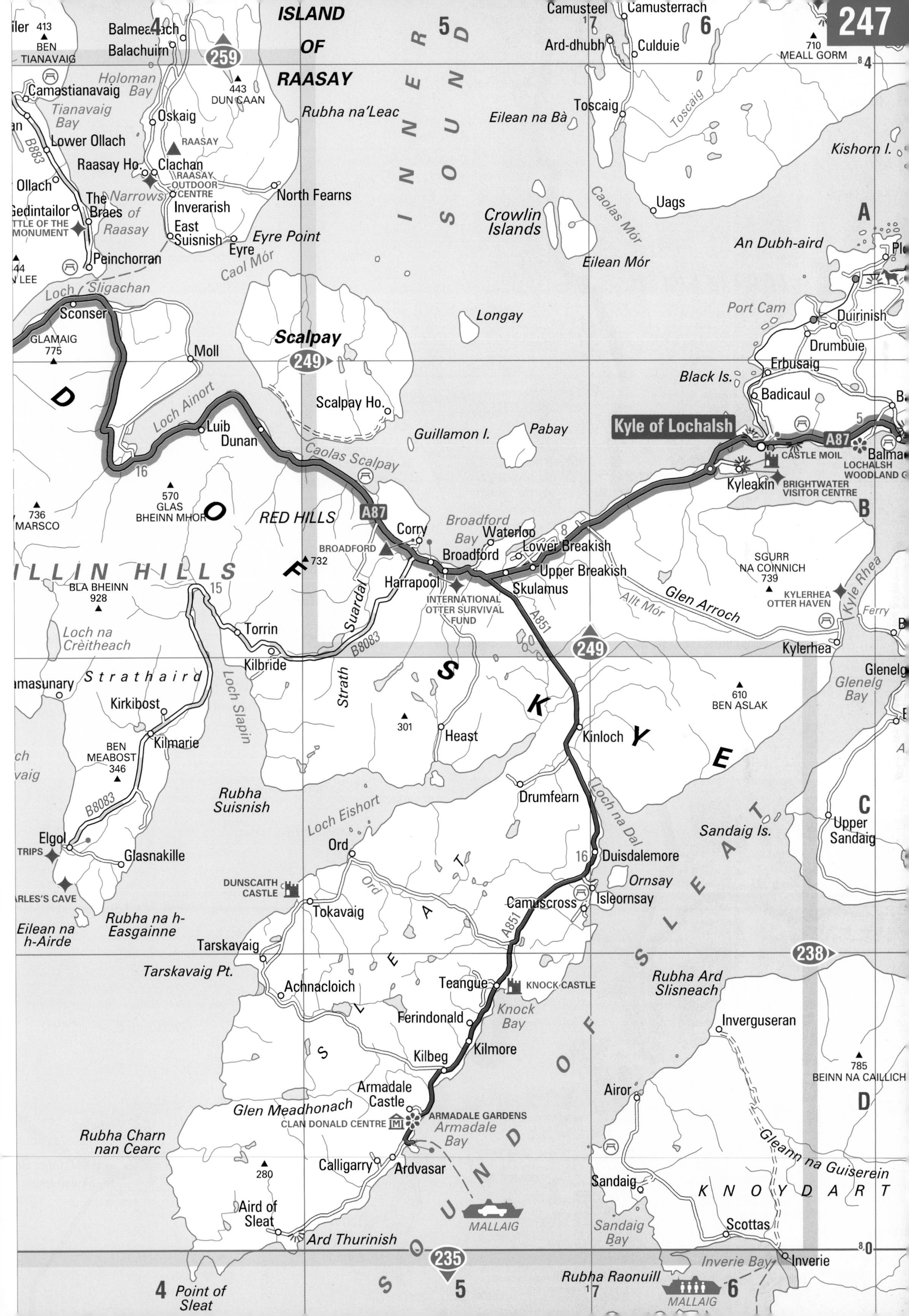
ISLAND OF RAASAY
INNER SOUND
Scalpay
Crowlin Islands
Kyle of Lochalsh
SKYE
SLEAT
SOUND OF SLEAT
KNOYDART
RED HILLS
CUILLIN HILLS
Camasunary
Strathaird
Kirkibost
Kilmarie
Elgol
Glasnakille
Torrin
Kilbride
Broadford
Harrapool
Corry
Waterloo
Lower Breakish
Upper Breakish
Skulamus
Kylerhea
Kyleakin
Heast
Kinloch
Drumfearn
Duisdalemore
Isleornsay
Camuscross
Ord
Tokavaig
Tarskavaig
Achnacloich
Teangue
Ferindonald
Kilmore
Kilbeg
Armadale Castle
Calligarry
Ardvasar
Aird of Sleat
Sconser
Moll
Luib
Dunan
Erbusaig
Badicaul
Drumbuie
Duirinish
Toscaig
Uags
Culduie
Camusterrach
Camusteel
Ard-dhubh
Inverguseran
Airor
Sandaig
Scottas
Inverie
Upper Sandaig
Glenelg
Oskaig
Clachan
Inverarish
East Suisnish
Eyre
North Fearns
Raasay Ho.
Lower Ollach
Camastianavaig
Balmeanach
Balachuirn
Peinchorran
The Braes
Gedintailor
Ollach
Pabay
Longay
Guillamon I.
Black Is.
Kishorn I.
Eilean na Bà
Eilean Mór
Ornsay
Sandaig Is.
Point of Sleat
Rubha Raonuill
Ard Thurinish
Rubha Ard Slisneach
Tarskavaig Pt.
Rubha na h-Easgainne
Eilean na h-Airde
Rubha Suisnish
Rubha Charn nan Cearc
Rubha na'Leac
Eyre Point
An Dubh-aird
Loch Sligachan
Loch Ainort
Loch Slapin
Loch Eishort
Loch na Dal
Loch na Crèitheach
Caolas Scalpay
Caolas Mór
Caol Mór
Broadford Bay
Knock Bay
Armadale Bay
Sandaig Bay
Inverie Bay
Glenelg Bay
Port Cam
Kyle Rhea
Glen Arroch
Allt Mór
Glen Meadhonach
Gleann na Guiserein
Strath
Suardal
Holoman Bay
Tianavaig Bay
Narrows of Raasay
GLAMAIG 775
570 GLAS BHEINN MHOR
736 MARSCO
BLA BHEINN 928
BEN MEABOST 346
732
301
280
610 BEN ASLAK
SGURR NA COINNICH 739
785 BEINN NA CAILLICH
710 MEALL GORM
443 DUN CAAN
413 BEN TIANAVAIG
RAASAY
BROADFORD
RAASAY OUTDOOR CENTRE
INTERNATIONAL OTTER SURVIVAL FUND
CASTLE MOIL
BRIGHTWATER VISITOR CENTRE
LOCHALSH WOODLAND
KYLERHEA OTTER HAVEN
DUNSCAITH CASTLE
KNOCK CASTLE
ARMADALE GARDENS
CLAN DONALD CENTRE
TRIPS
MALLAIG
A87
A851
B8083
B883
259
249
238
235

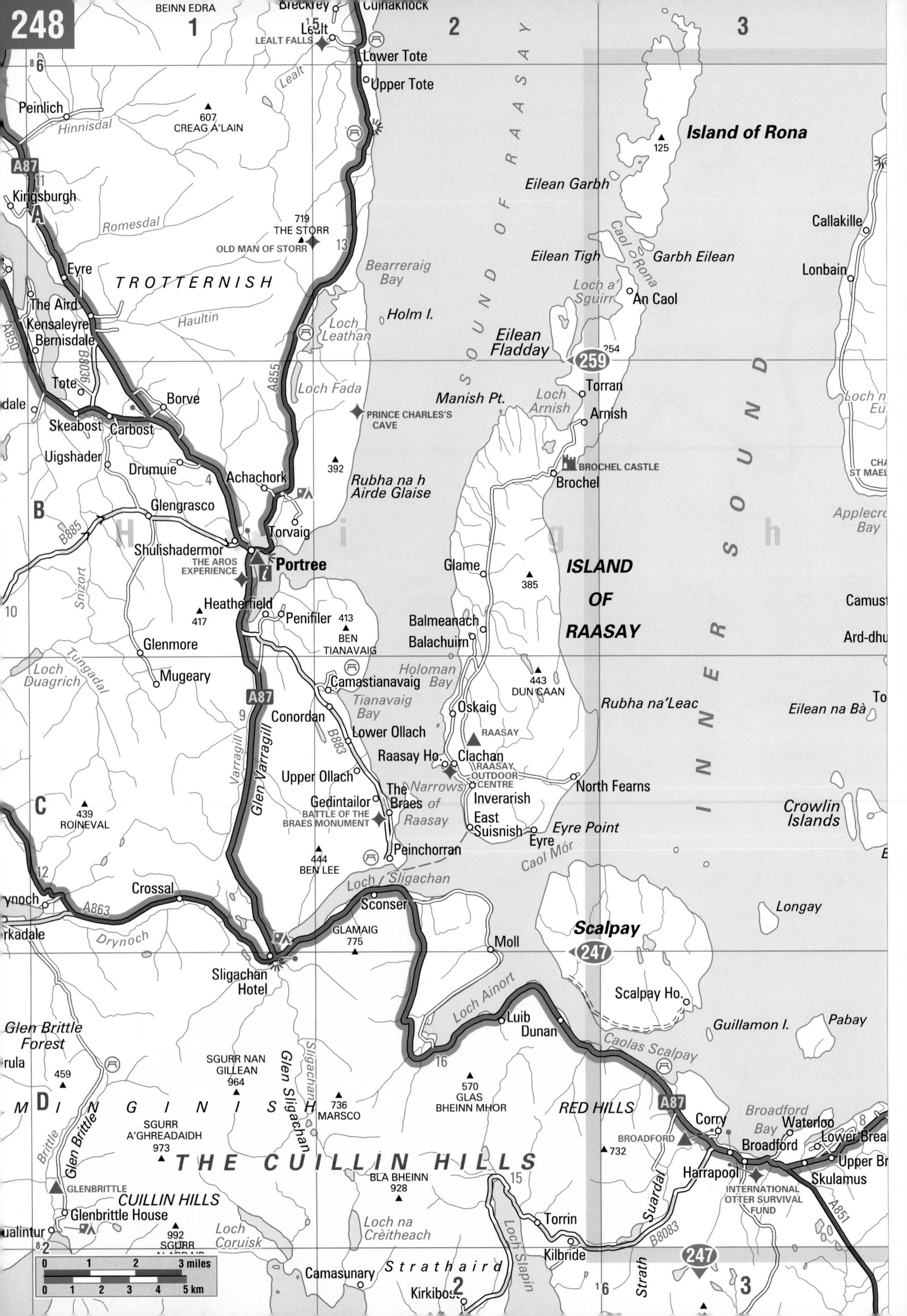

Island of Rona
Eilean Garbh
Eilean Tigh
Garbh Eilean
Caol Rona
Loch a' Sguirr
An Caol
Eilean Fladday
259
254
Torran
Arnish
Loch Arnish
Manish Pt.
Brochel Castle
Brochel
Sound of Raasay
Inner Sound
Island of Raasay
Glame
385
Balmeanach
Balachuirn
443
Dun Caan
Oskaig
Raasay
Clachan
Raasay Ho.
Raasay Outdoor Centre
North Fearns
Inverarish
East Suisnish
Eyre
Eyre Point
Rubha na'Leac
Narrows of Raasay
Caol Mòr
Holoman Bay
Callakille
Lonbain
Applecross Bay
Camust
Ard-dhu
Eilean na Bà
Crowlin Islands
Longay
Scalpay
247
Scalpay Ho.
Guillamon I.
Pabay
Caolas Scalpay
Beinn Edra
Breckrey
Culnaknock
Lealt
Lealt Falls
Lower Tote
Upper Tote
Lealt
Peinlich
Hinnisdal
607
Creag a'Lain
A87
Kingsburgh
Romesdal
719
The Storr
Old Man of Storr
Bearreraig Bay
Holm I.
Trotternish
Eyre
The Aird
Kensaleyre
Bernisdale
A850
B8036
Haultin
Loch Leathan
Loch Fada
A855
Tote
Borve
Skeabost
Carbost
Prince Charles's Cave
Uigshader
Drumuie
Achachork
392
Rubha na h Airde Glaise
Glengrasco
Torvaig
B885
Shulishadermor
The Aros Experience
Portree
Snizort
Heatherfield
417
Penifiler
413
Ben Tianavaig
Glenmore
Loch Duagrich
Tungadal
Mugeary
Camastianavaig
Tianavaig Bay
A87
Conordan
Varragill
Glen Varragill
B883
Lower Ollach
Upper Ollach
The Braes
Gedintailor
Battle of the Braes Monument
439
Roineval
444
Ben Lee
Peinchorran
Loch Sligachan
Crossal
Drynoch
A863
Carkadale
Sconser
Glamaig
775
Moll
Sligachan Hotel
Loch Ainort
Luib
Dunan
Glen Brittle Forest
459
Sgurr nan Gillean
964
Glen Sligachan
Sligachan
736
Marsco
570
Glas Bheinn Mhor
Red Hills
Minginish
Sgurr a'Ghreadaidh
973
The Cuillin Hills
Glen Brittle
Brittle
Glenbrittle
Cuillin Hills
Bla Bheinn
928
Glenbrittle House
992
Loch Coruisk
Loch na Crèitheach
Strathaird
Camasunary
Kirkibost
Loch Slapin
Torrin
Kilbride
B8083
Suardal
Strath
Broadford
732
Corry
Broadford Bay
Waterloo
Lower Breakish
Upper Breakish
Harrapool
International Otter Survival Fund
Skulamus
A851
3 miles
5 km

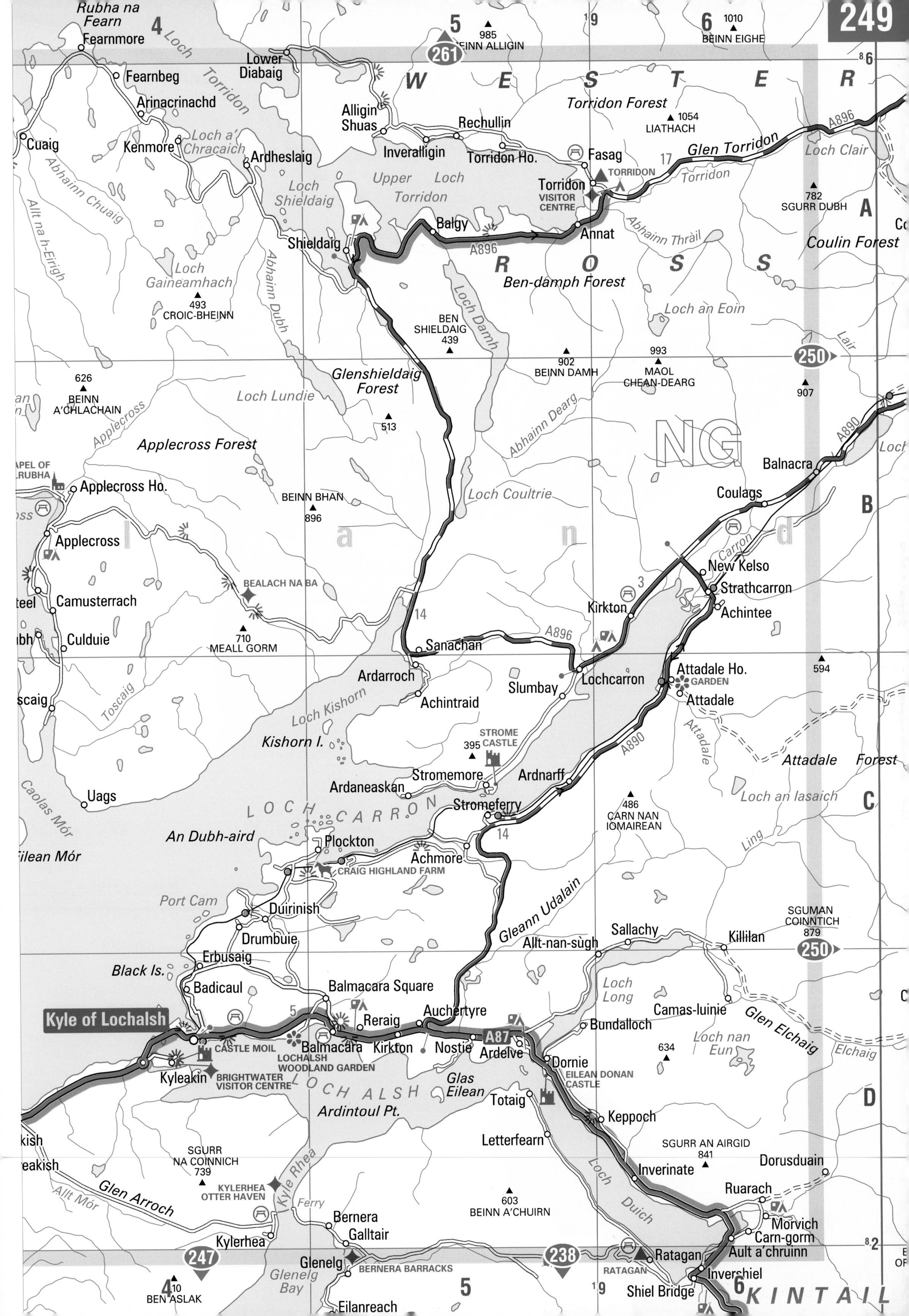
Rubha na Fearn
Fearnmore
Fearnbeg
Arinacrinachd
Cuaig
Kenmore
Loch Torridon
Loch a' Chracaich
Ardheslaig
Lower Diabaig
Alligin Shuas
Inveralligin
Rechullin
Torridon Ho.
Fasag
Torridon
TORRIDON
VISITOR CENTRE
Upper Loch Torridon
Loch Shieldaig
Shieldaig
Balgy
Annat
A896
WESTER ROSS
Torridon Forest
1054 LIATHACH
985 BEINN ALLIGIN
1010 BEINN EIGHE
261
Glen Torridon
Loch Clair
A896
782 SGURR DUBH
Coulin Forest
Abhainn Thràil
Ben-damph Forest
Loch an Eoin
Loch Damh
BEN SHIELDAIG 439
902 BEINN DAMH
993 MAOL CHEAN-DEARG
907
250
Abhainn Chuaig
Allt na h-Eirigh
Loch Gaineamhach
493 CROIC-BHEINN
Abhainn Dubh
Glenshieldaig Forest
Loch Lundie
513
626 BEINN A'CHLACHAIN
Applecross
Applecross Forest
Abhainn Dearg
NG
Highland
A890
Balnacra
Coulags
Loch Coultrie
BEINN BHAN 896
Applecross Ho.
Applecross
Camusterrach
Culduie
BEALACH NA BA
710 MEALL GORM
Carron
New Kelso
Strathcarron
Achintee
Kirkton
Sanachan
A896
Ardarroch
Achintraid
Toscaig
Loch Kishorn
Kishorn I.
Slumbay
Lochcarron
Attadale Ho.
GARDEN
Attadale
594
STROME CASTLE
395
Stromemore
Ardaneaskan
Ardnarff
A890
Attadale Forest
Loch an Iasaich
Uags
Caolas Mór
LOCH CARRON
Stromeferry
486 CARN NAN IOMAIREAN
An Dubh-aird
Plockton
Achmore
CRAIG HIGHLAND FARM
Port Cam
Duirinish
Drumbuie
Erbusaig
Black Is.
Badicaul
Gleann Udalain
Allt-nan-sùgh
Sallachy
Killilan
SGUMAN COINNTICH 879
250
Loch Long
Camas-luinie
Glen Elchaig
Kyle of Lochalsh
Balmacara Square
Reraig
Auchertyre
A87
Bundalloch
CASTLE MOIL
Balmacara
Kirkton
Nostie
Ardelve
Dornie
EILEAN DONAN CASTLE
Loch nan Eun
634
LOCHALSH WOODLAND GARDEN
Kyleakin
BRIGHTWATER VISITOR CENTRE
LOCH ALSH
Glas Eilean
Totaig
Ardintoul Pt.
Keppoch
Letterfearn
SGURR NA COINNICH 739
Glen Arroch
Allt Mór
KYLERHEA OTTER HAVEN
Kyle Rhea
Ferry
SGURR AN AIRGID 841
Inverinate
Dorusduain
Ruarach
Morvich
Carn-gorm
Ault a'chruinn
603 BEINN A'CHUIRN
Loch Duich
Bernera
Galltair
Kylerhea
247
238
Glenelg
BERNERA BARRACKS
Glenelg Bay
Ratagan
RATAGAN
Inverchiel
Shiel Bridge
Eilanreach
610 BEN ASLAK
KINTAIL
Elchaig
4
5
6

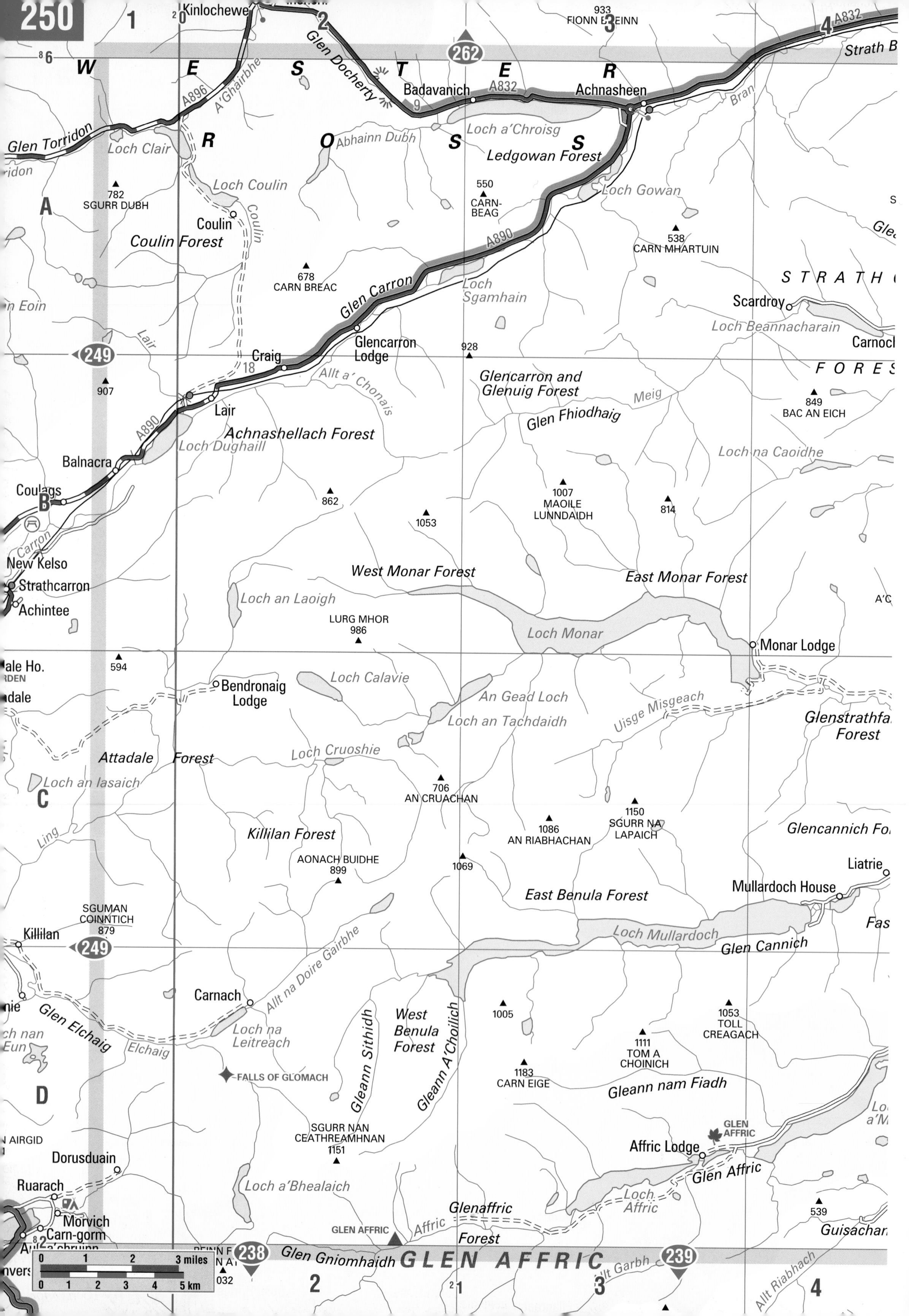

W E S T E R

O S S

Kinlochewe

FIONN BEINN
933

A832

Strath B

262

Glen Docherty

Badavanich

A832

Achnasheen

Bran

Glen Torridon

A896

A'Ghairbhe

Loch a'Chroisg

Ledgowan Forest

Loch Gowan

Loch Clair

Abhainn Dubh

Loch Coulin

CARN-BEAG
550

A890

CARN MHARTUIN
538

STRATH

SGURR DUBH
782

Coulin

Coulin Forest

Coulin

CARN BREAC
678

Glen Carron

Loch Sgamhain

Scardroy

Loch Beannacharain

Carnoch

Glen Carron

F O R E S

249

907

Craig

Glencarron Lodge

928

Glencarron and Glenuig Forest

Meig

BAC AN EICH
849

18

Allt a'Chonais

Glen Fhiodhaig

Loch na Caoidhe

Lair

Achnashellach Forest

Balnacra

Loch Dughaill

862

1053

MAOILE LUNNDAIDH
1007

814

Coulags

Carron

West Monar Forest

East Monar Forest

A'C

New Kelso

Strathcarron

Loch an Laoigh

Achintee

LURG MHOR
986

Loch Monar

Monar Lodge

ale Ho.
RDEN

594

Loch Calavie

Bendronaig Lodge

An Gead Loch

Loch an Tachdaidh

Uisge Misgeach

Glenstrathfa
Forest

dale

Ling

Loch an Iasaich

Attadale   Forest

Loch Cruoshie

AN CRUACHAN
706

SGURR NA LAPAICH
1150

Glencannich Fo

C

Killilan Forest

AN RIABHACHAN
1086

1069

Liatrie

AONACH BUIDHE
899

East Benula Forest

Mullardoch House

Fas

SGUMAN COINNTICH
879

Killilan

249

Loch Mullardoch

Glen Cannich

Carnach

Allt na Doire Gairbhe

Gleann Sithidh

West Benula Forest

Gleann A'Choilich

1005

TOLL CREAGACH
1053

nie

ch nan
Eun

Glen Elchaig

Elchaig

Loch na Leitreach

FALLS OF GLOMACH

Gleann nam Fiadh

TOM A CHOINICH
1111

GLEN AFFRIC

AIRGID

Dorusduain

SGURR NAN CEATHREAMHNAN
1151

CARN EIGE
1183

Affric Lodge

Glen Affric

Ruarach

Loch a'Bhealaich

Loch Affric

539

Morvich

Carn-gorm

Loch a'M

Guisacha

An t-sa'chruinn

BEINN NA
032

GLEN AFFRIC

238

Glen Gniomhaidh

G L E N   A F F R I C

Affric

Glenaffric Forest

Allt Garbh

239

Allt Riabhach

0   1   2   3 miles

0 1 2 3 4 5 km

2

3

4

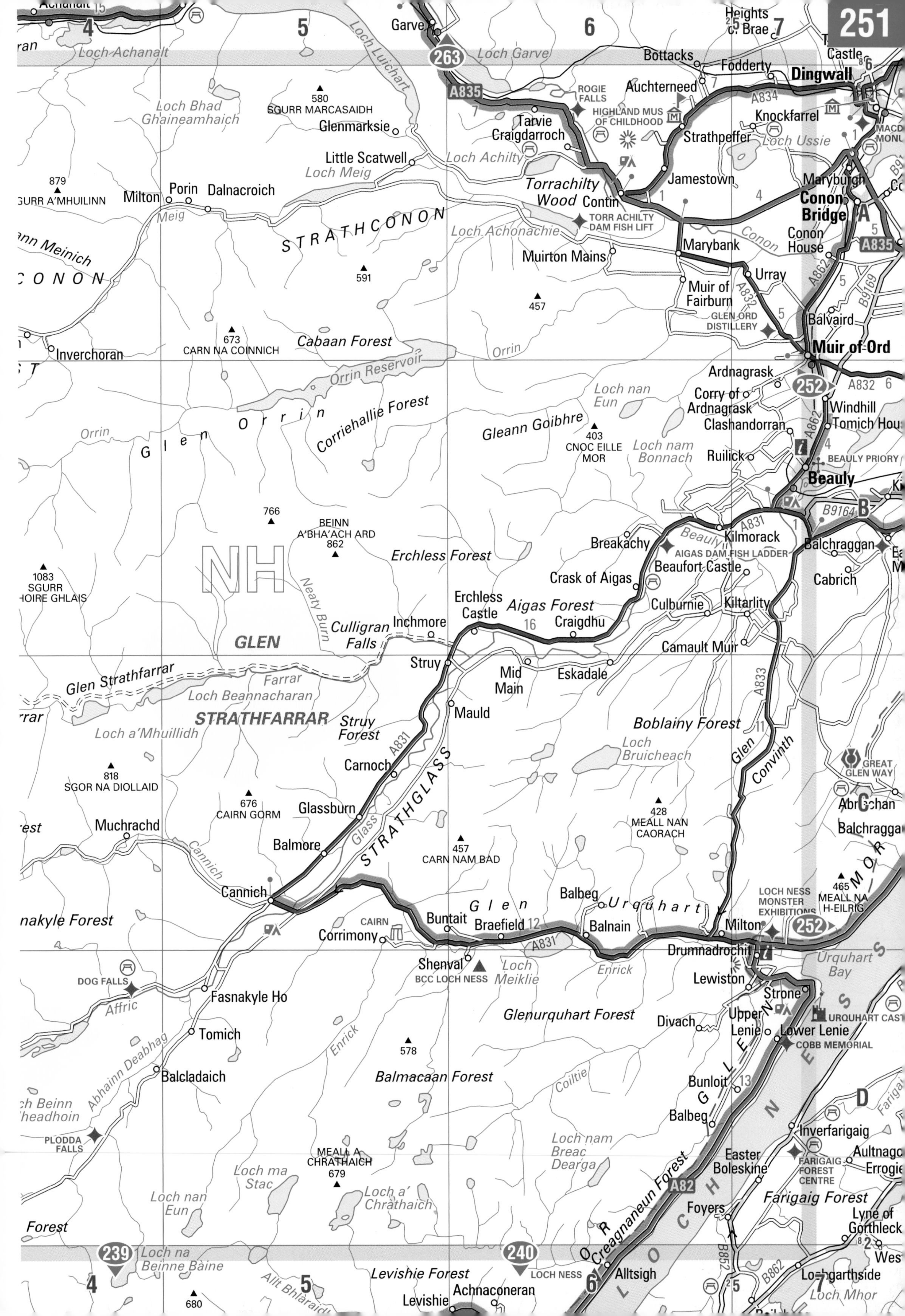

Garve
Loch Luichart
263
Loch Garve
Loch Achanalt
Heights of Brae
Bottacks
Fodderty
Castle
Dingwall
A835
ROGIE FALLS
Auchterneed
HIGHLAND MUS OF CHILDHOOD
A834
Knockfarrel
580
SGURR MARCASAIDH
Loch Bhad Ghaineamhaich
Glenmarksie
Tarvie
Craigdarroch
Strathpeffer
Loch Ussie
Little Scatwell
Loch Achilty
Loch Meig
Jamestown
879
SGURR A'MHUILINN
Milton
Porin
Dalnacroich
Torrachilty Wood
Contin
Maryburgh
Conon Bridge
Meig
STRATHCONON
TORR ACHILTY DAM FISH LIFT
Loch Achonachie
Conon
Conon House
Marybank
A835
Muirton Mains
Urray
A862
B9169
591
Muir of Fairburn
A832
457
GLEN ORD DISTILLERY
Balvaird
673
CARN NA COINNICH
Cabaan Forest
Muir of Ord
Inverchoran
Orrin
Orrin Reservoir
Ardnagrask
252
A832
Loch nan Eun
Corry of Ardnagrask
Windhill
Corriehallie Forest
Clashandorran
Tomich House
Glen Orrin
Gleann Goibhre
403
CNOC EILLE MOR
Loch nam Bonnach
Ruilick
BEAULY PRIORY
Beauly
766
BEINN A'BHA'ACH ARD
862
B9164
A831
Breakachy
Kilmorack
Beauly
NH
Erchless Forest
AIGAS DAM FISH LADDER
Balchraggan
1083
SGURR
HOIRE GHLAIS
Beaufort Castle
Crask of Aigas
Cabrich
Neaty Burn
Erchless Castle
Aigas Forest
Culburnie
Kiltarlity
Inchmore
Craigdhu
Culligran Falls
GLEN
Camault Muir
Struy
Mid Main
Eskadale
A833
Glen Strathfarrar
Farrar
Loch Beannacharan
Mauld
STRATHFARRAR
Struy Forest
Boblainy Forest
Loch a'Mhuillidh
Loch Bruicheach
A831
Glen Convinth
GREAT GLEN WAY
818
SGOR NA DIOLLAID
Carnoch
STRATHGLASS
676
CAIRN GORM
Glassburn
428
MEALL NAN CAORACH
Abriachan
Muchrachd
Balchraggan
Balmore
Glass
457
CARN NAM BAD
Cannich
LOCH NESS MONSTER EXHIBITIONS
465
MEALL NA H-EILRIG
Glen Urquhart
Balbeg
Buntait
Braefield
Balnain
Milton
Corrimony
CAIRN
A831
Drumnadrochit
Urquhart Bay
DOG FALLS
Shenval
BCC LOCH NESS
Loch Meiklie
Enrick
Lewiston
Strone
Affric
Fasnakyle Ho
Glenurquhart Forest
URQUHART CASTLE
Tomich
Divach
Upper Lenie
Lower Lenie
COBB MEMORIAL
Abhainn Deabhag
Enrick
578
Balcladaich
Balmacaan Forest
Coiltie
Bunloit
D
PLODDA FALLS
Balbeg
Inverfarigaig
Loch nam Breac Dearga
MEALL A CHRATHAICH
679
Loch ma Stac
Easter Boleskine
FARIGAIG FOREST CENTRE
Aultnagoire
Errogie
Loch nan Eun
Loch a' Chrathaich
Creagnaneun Forest
A82
Foyers
Farigaig Forest
Forest
Lyne of Gorthleck
239
Loch na Beinne Bàine
240
LOCH NESS
Levishie Forest
Alltsigh
B862
Wester
Achnaconeran
Levishie
Allt Bhlàraidh
680
Loch Mhor
Loch Ness

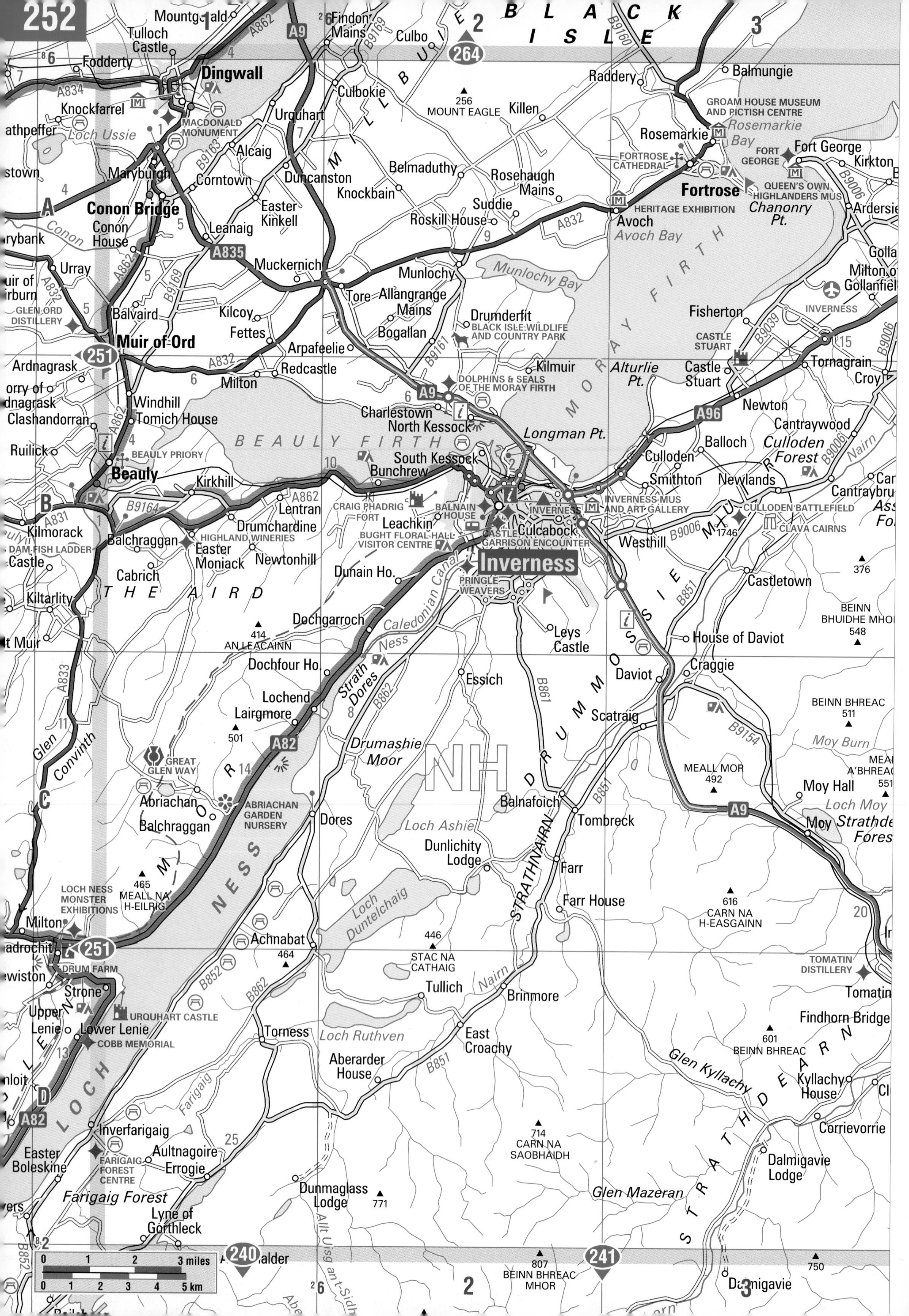
BLACK ISLE
MILLBUIE
Dingwall
Conon Bridge
Muir of Ord
Beauly
Fortrose
Rosemarkie
Avoch
Fort George
Inverness
BEAULY FIRTH
MORAY FIRTH
THE AIRD
LOCH NESS
DRUMMOSSIE MUIR
STRATHNAIRN
STRATHDEARN
GROAM HOUSE MUSEUM AND PICTISH CENTRE
FORTROSE CATHEDRAL
QUEEN'S OWN HIGHLANDERS MUS
HERITAGE EXHIBITION
BLACK ISLE WILDLIFE AND COUNTRY PARK
DOLPHINS & SEALS OF THE MORAY FIRTH
INVERNESS MUS AND ART GALLERY
CULLODEN BATTLEFIELD
CLAVA CAIRNS
CRAIG PHADRIG FORT
BALNAIN HOUSE
BUGHT FLORAL HALL VISITOR CENTRE
CASTLE GARRISON ENCOUNTER
PRINGLE WEAVERS
HIGHLAND WINERIES
DAM FISH LADDER
BEAULY PRIORY
MACDONALD MONUMENT
GLEN ORD DISTILLERY
GREAT GLEN WAY
ABRIACHAN GARDEN NURSERY
LOCH NESS MONSTER EXHIBITIONS
URQUHART CASTLE
COBB MEMORIAL
FARIGAIG FOREST CENTRE
TOMATIN DISTILLERY
Loch Ashie
Loch Duntelchaig
Loch Ruthven
Loch Moy
Culloden Forest
Farigaig Forest
Glen Kyllachy
Glen Mazeran
Drumashie Moor
NH
A9
A82
A96
A835
A862
A832
A831
A833
B851
B861
B862
B9006
B9154
0 1 2 3 miles
0 1 2 3 4 5 km

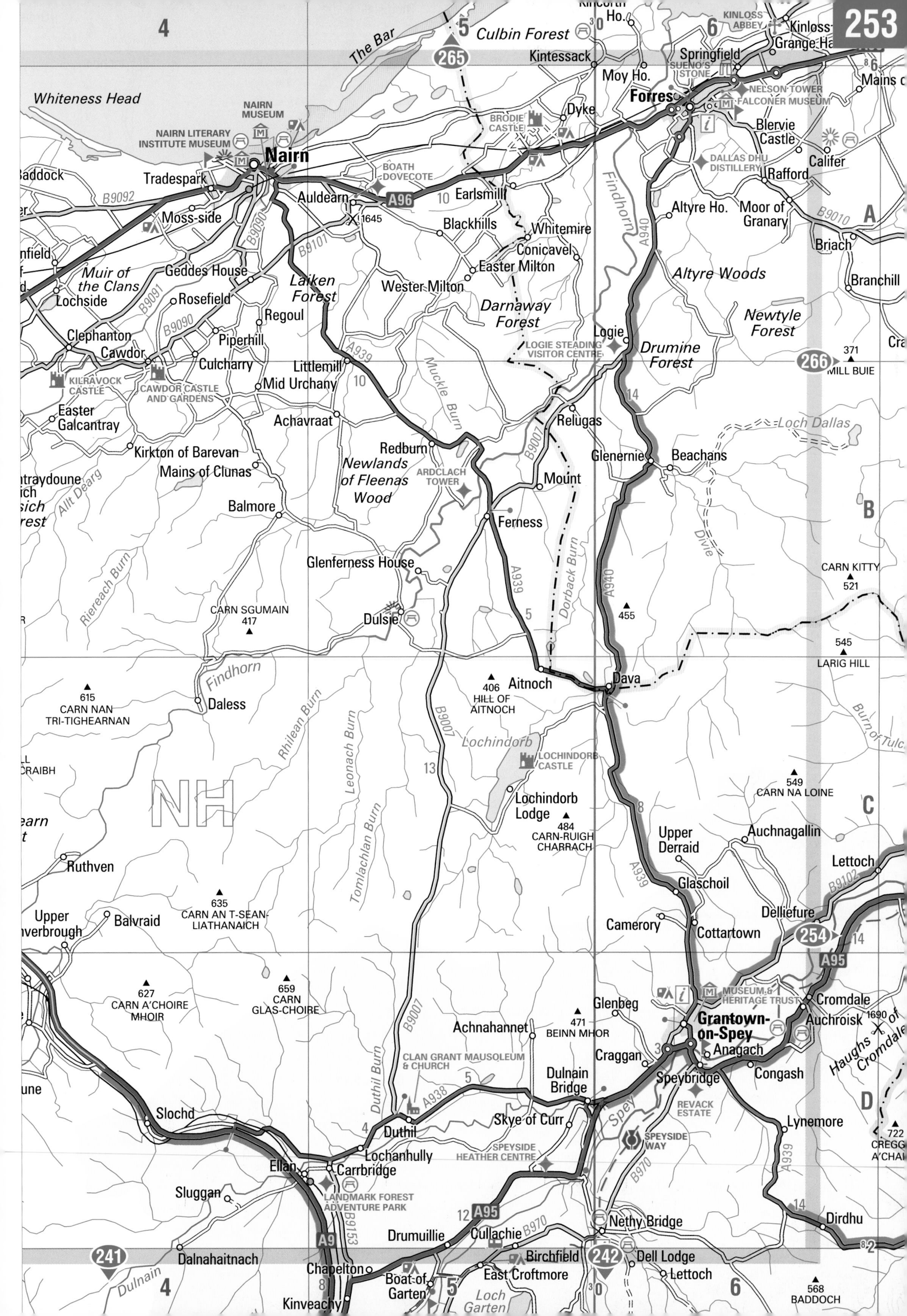

Culbin Forest
The Bar
Whiteness Head
Kintessack
Moy Ho.
Springfield
Kinloss
Grange Ha
Forres
Dyke
NAIRN MUSEUM
NAIRN LITERARY INSTITUTE MUSEUM
Nairn
BRODIE CASTLE
Tradespark
BOATH DOVECOTE
Auldearn
A96
Earlsmill
NELSON TOWER
FALCONER MUSEUM
Blervie Castle
Califer
DALLAS DHU DISTILLERY
Rafford
Altyre Ho.
Moor of Granary
Briach
Branchill
Moss-side
Blackhills
Whitemire
Conicavel
Easter Milton
Wester Milton
Muir of the Clans
Geddes House
Lochside
Laiken Forest
Rosefield
Regoul
Darnaway Forest
Altyre Woods
Newtyle Forest
Clephanton
Cawdor
Piperhill
Culcharry
Logie
LOGIE STEADING VISITOR CENTRE
Drumine Forest
MILL BUIE
KILRAVOCK CASTLE
CAWDOR CASTLE AND GARDENS
Littlemill
Mid Urchany
Easter Galcantray
Achavraat
Muckle Burn
Relugas
Loch Dallas
Kirkton of Barevan
Mains of Clunas
Redburn
Newlands of Fleenas Wood
ARDCLACH TOWER
Glenernie
Beachans
Mount
Balmore
Ferness
Allt Dearg
Glenferness House
CARN KITTY
Riereach Burn
CARN SGUMAIN
Dulsie
Dorback Burn
Divie
LARIG HILL
Findhorn
Daless
Aitnoch
HILL OF AITNOCH
Dava
CARN NAN TRI-TIGHEARNAN
Rhilean Burn
Leonach Burn
Lochindorb
LOCHINDORB CASTLE
Lochindorb Lodge
CARN-RUIGH CHARRACH
CARN NA LOINE
NH
Upper Derraid
Auchnagallin
Ruthven
Tomlachlan Burn
Glaschoil
Lettoch
Upper Inverbrough
Balvraid
CARN AN T-SEAN-LIATHANAICH
Camerory
Cottartown
Delliefure
CARN A'CHOIRE MHOIR
CARN GLAS-CHOIRE
MUSEUM & HERITAGE TRUST
Cromdale
Glenbeg
BEINN MHOR
Grantown-on-Spey
Auchroisk
Achnahannet
Haughs of Cromdale
Craggan
Anagach
CLAN GRANT MAUSOLEUM & CHURCH
Dulnain Bridge
Speybridge
Congash
REVACK ESTATE
Slochd
Duthil
Skye of Curr
Lynemore
Duthil Burn
SPEYSIDE WAY
Lochanhully
SPEYSIDE HEATHER CENTRE
CREGG A'CHAI
Ellan
Carrbridge
Spey
Sluggan
LANDMARK FOREST ADVENTURE PARK
Dirdhu
Drumuillie
Cullachie
Nethy Bridge
Dalnahaitnach
Birchfield
Dell Lodge
Chapelton
Boat-of-Garten
East Croftmore
Lettoch
Dulnain
Loch Garten
Kinveachy
BADDOCH

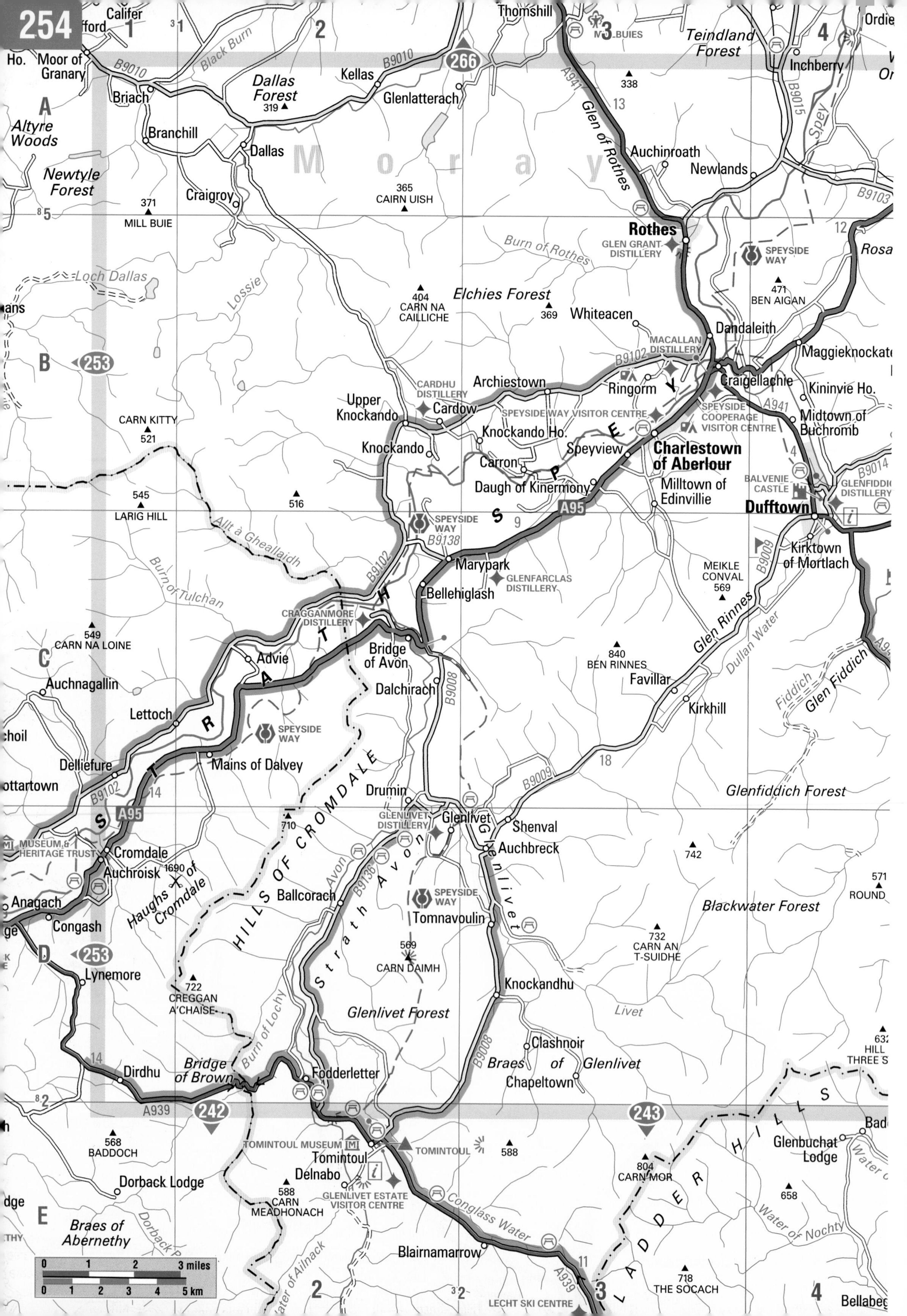

Moray
Rothes
Charlestown of Aberlour
Dufftown
Tomintoul
Cromdale
Dallas
Dallas Forest
Kellas
Glenlatterach
Briach
Branchill
Craigroy
Moor of Granary
Altyre Woods
Newtyle Forest
Loch Dallas
Lossie
Elchies Forest
Whiteacen
Dandaleith
Craigellachie
Archiestown
Cardow
Upper Knockando
Knockando
Knockando Ho.
Carron
Speyview
Daugh of Kinermony
Marypark
Bellehiglash
Bridge of Avon
Dalchirach
Advie
Lettoch
Auchnagallin
Dellefure
Mains of Dalvey
Drumin
Glenlivet
Shenval
Auchbreck
Ballcorach
Tomnavoulin
Knockandhu
Clashnoir
Braes of Glenlivet
Chapeltown
Fodderletter
Bridge of Brown
Dirdhu
Lynemore
Congash
Anagach
Auchroisk
Haughs of Cromdale
HILLS OF CROMDALE
STRATH SPEY
Strath Avon
Glenlivet Forest
Glenfiddich Forest
Blackwater Forest
Glen Rinnes
Glen Fiddich
Glen of Rothes
Kirktown of Mortlach
Milltown of Edinvillie
Favillar
Kirkhill
Maggieknockater
Kininvie Ho.
Midtown of Buchromb
Auchinroath
Newlands
Inchberry
Teindland Forest
Thornshill
Delnabo
Dorback Lodge
Braes of Abernethy
Blairnamarrow
Glenbuchat Lodge
LADDER HILLS
Conglass Water
Water of Nochty
LECHT SKI CENTRE
GLEN GRANT DISTILLERY
MACALLAN DISTILLERY
CARDHU DISTILLERY
CRAGGANMORE DISTILLERY
GLENFARCLAS DISTILLERY
GLENLIVET DISTILLERY
GLENFIDDICH DISTILLERY
BALVENIE CASTLE
SPEYSIDE COOPERAGE VISITOR CENTRE
SPEYSIDE WAY VISITOR CENTRE
SPEYSIDE WAY
MUSEUM & HERITAGE TRUST
TOMINTOUL MUSEUM
GLENLIVET ESTATE VISITOR CENTRE
840 BEN RINNES
471 BEN AIGAN
569 MEIKLE CONVAL
404 CARN NA CAILLICHE
365 CAIRN UISH
371 MILL BUIE
521 CARN KITTY
545 LARIG HILL
549 CARN NA LOINE
722 CREGGAN A'CHAISE
569 CARN DAIMH
732 CARN AN T-SUIDHE
804 CARN MOR
718 THE SOCACH
568 BADDOCH
588 CARN MEADHONACH
A95
A941
A939
B9010
B9102
B9008
B9009
B9136
B9138
B9015
B9103
B9014
253
266
242
243
0 1 2 3 miles
0 1 2 3 4 5 km

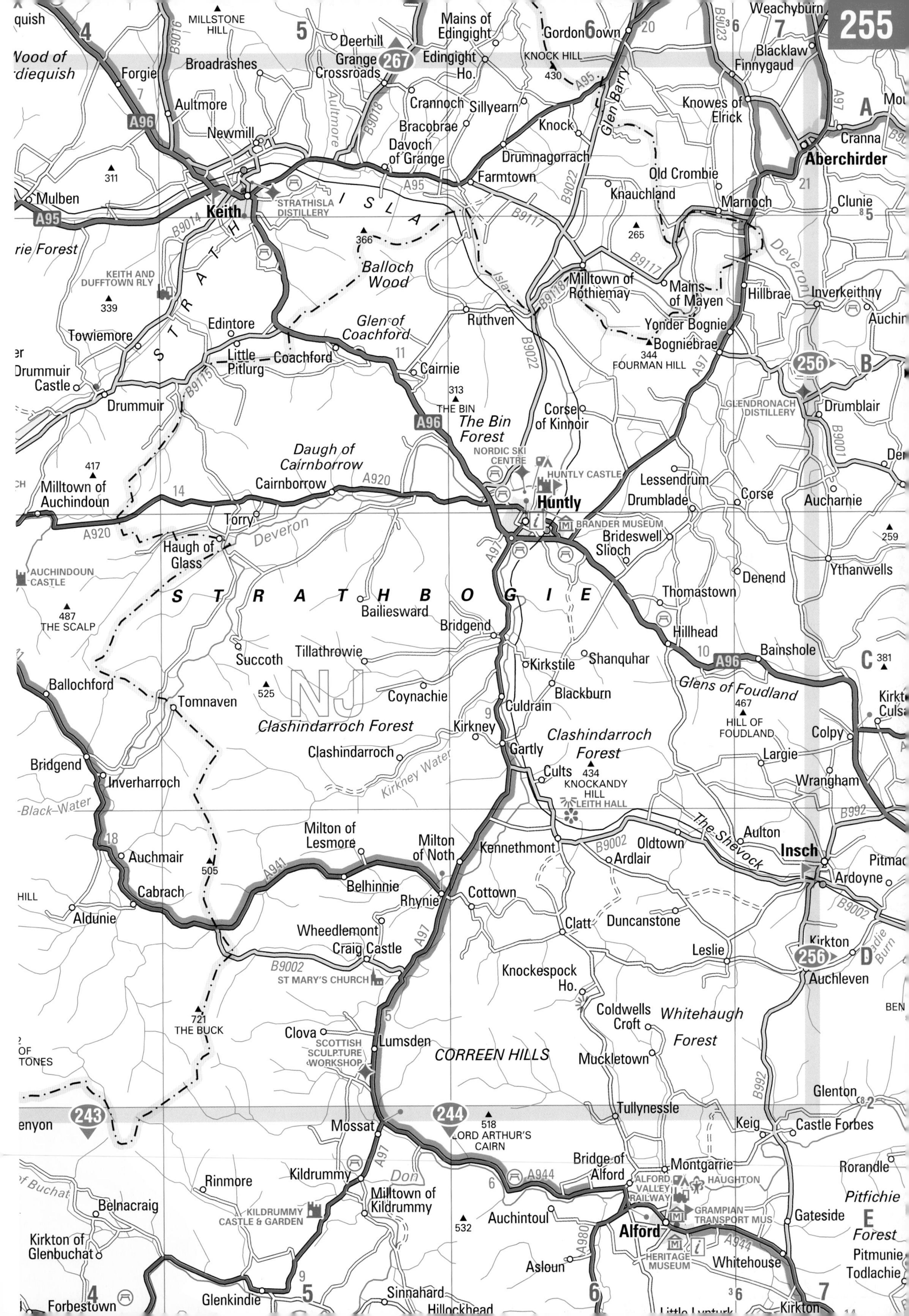
quish
4
5
6
7
MILLSTONE HILL
B9016
Deerhill
Mains of Edingight
Gordontown
20
B9023
Weachyburn
Wood of
rdiequish
Broadrashes
Grange
267
Crossroads
Edingight Ho.
KNOCK HILL
430
A95
Blacklaw
Finnygaud
Forgie
Aultmore
Crannoch
Sillyearn
Glen Barry
Knowes of Elrick
A97
A
Aultmore
A96
B9018
Bracobrae
Knock
Newmill
Davoch of Grange
Drumnagorrach
Old Crombie
Cranna
Aberchirder
311
Farmtown
A95
B9022
Knauchland
21
Mulben
Keith
STRATHISLA DISTILLERY
I S L A
Marnoch
Clunie
5
A95
B9014
B9117
265
rie Forest
366
Deveron
Balloch Wood
KEITH AND DUFFTOWN RLY
B9117
Isla
Milltown of Rothiemay
Mains of Mayen
Hillbrae
Inverkeithny
339
B9118
Auchin
Glen of Coachford
Ruthven
Edintore
Yonder Bognie
Towiemore
S T R A T H
Bogniebrae
11
B9022
344
FOURMAN HILL
er
Little Pitlurg
Coachford
Cairnie
256
B
Drummuir Castle
B9115
313
THE BIN
A97
Drummuir
GLENDRONACH DISTILLERY
Drumblair
A96
The Bin Forest
Corse of Kinnoir
B9001
Daugh of Cairnborrow
NORDIC SKI CENTRE
De
417
HUNTLY CASTLE
Lessendrum
CH
Milltown of Auchindoun
14
Cairnborrow
A920
Huntly
Corse
Aucharnie
Drumblade
A920
Torry
BRANDER MUSEUM
Deveron
259
Brideswell
Haugh of Glass
A97
Slioch
AUCHINDOUN CASTLE
Ythanwells
Denend
S T R A T H B O G I E
Thomastown
487
THE SCALP
Bailiesward
Bridgend
Hillhead
Succoth
Tillathrowie
10
Bainshole
Shanquhar
C
381
A96
Kirkstile
Glens of Foudland
Ballochford
525
Blackburn
Kirkt
Tomnaven
NJ
Coynachie
Culsa
Culdrain
467
HILL OF FOUDLAND
9
Clashindarroch Forest
Kirkney
Colpy
Clashindarroch Forest
Gartly
Bridgend
Clashindarroch
Largie
Kirkney Water
Cults
434
KNOCKANDY HILL
Inverharroch
Wrangham
LEITH HALL
Black Water
B992
The Shevock
18
Milton of Lesmore
Milton of Noth
Aulton
Kennethmont
B9002
Oldtown
Insch
Auchmair
Pitmac
505
Ardlair
A941
Ardoyne
HILL
Cabrach
Belhinnie
Cottown
Rhynie
B9002
Aldunie
Duncanstone
Clatt
Wheedlemont
Kirkton
Craig Castle
A97
Leslie
Badie Burn
B9002
256
D
Knockespock Ho.
ST MARY'S CHURCH
Auchleven
BEN
721
Coldwells Croft
Whitehaugh Forest
THE BUCK
5
Clova
SCOTTISH SCULPTURE WORKSHOP
Lumsden
OF
CORREEN HILLS
Muckletown
TONES
B992
Glenton
8 2
Tullynessle
243
244
518
LORD ARTHUR'S CAIRN
enyon
Mossat
Keig
Castle Forbes
A97
Bridge of Alford
Montgarrie
Rorandle
Kildrummy
Don
A944
Rinmore
6
ALFORD VALLEY RAILWAY
HAUGHTON
of Buchat
Milltown of Kildrummy
Pitfichie
Belnacraig
KILDRUMMY CASTLE & GARDEN
GRAMPIAN TRANSPORT MUS
532
Auchintoul
Gateside
E
Kirkton of Glenbuchat
Alford
A980
A944
Forest
HERITAGE MUSEUM
Pitmunie
Asloun
Whitehouse
Todlachie
9
4
5
6
3 6
7
Forbestown
Glenkindie
Sinnahard
Hillockhead
Little Lynturk
Kirkton

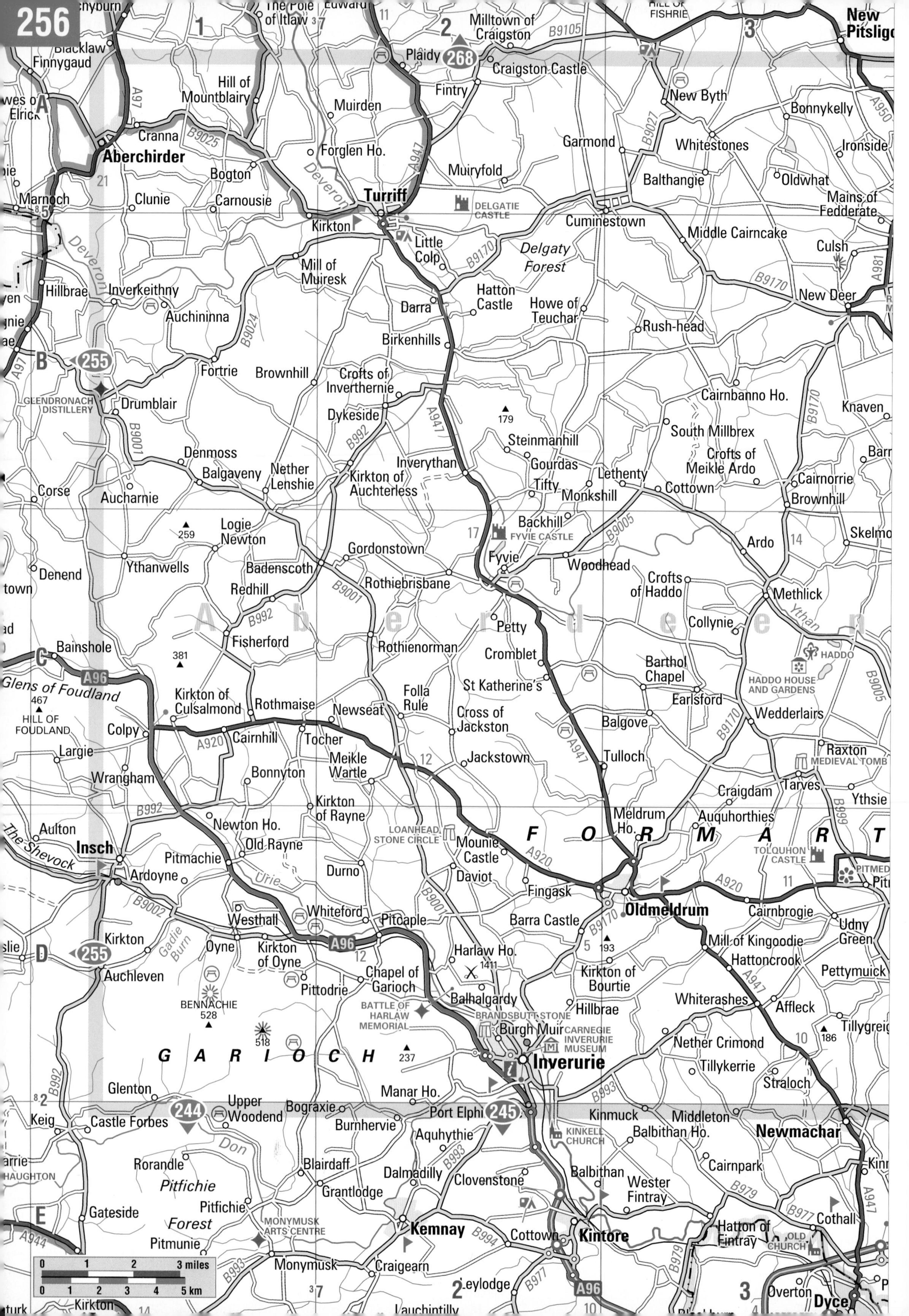

Aberchirder
Turriff
Cuminestown
New Pitsligo
New Byth
New Deer
Fyvie
FYVIE CASTLE
DELGATIE CASTLE
Methlick
HADDO HOUSE AND GARDENS
Insch
Oldmeldrum
Inverurie
CARNEGIE INVERURIE MUSEUM
Kintore
Kemnay
Newmachar
Dyce
Monymusk
MONYMUSK ARTS CENTRE
Glens of Foudland
HILL OF FOUDLAND
BENNACHIE
GARIOCH
FORMARTINE
Aberdeen
Pitfichie Forest
Delgaty Forest
GLENDRONACH DISTILLERY
LOANHEAD STONE CIRCLE
BATTLE OF HARLAW MEMORIAL
BRANDSBUTT STONE
KINKELL CHURCH
TOLQUHON CASTLE
MEDIEVAL TOMB
Deveron
Ythan
Don
Urie
The Shevock
Gadie Burn
A96
A97
A920
A947
A981
A950
A944
B9001
B9005
B9170
B992
B993
B994
B977
B979
B9002
B9024
B9025
B9027
B9105
B999
255
268
244
245
0 1 2 3 miles
0 1 2 3 4 5 km

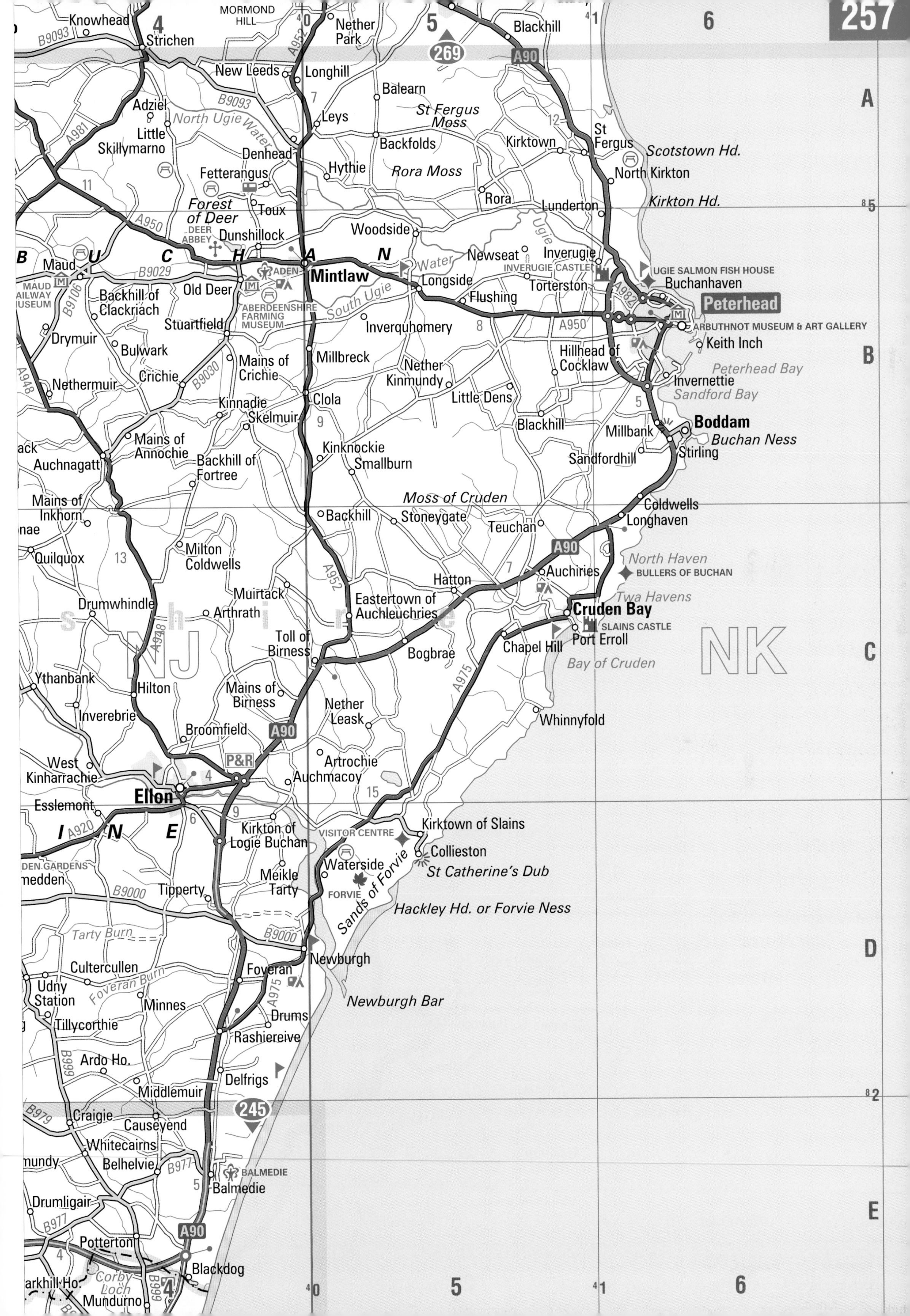
4
5
6
40
41
A
B
C
D
E
NJ
NK
Knowhead
Strichen
MORMOND HILL
Nether Park
Blackhill
269
A90
B9093
A952
New Leeds
Longhill
Balearn
Adziel
B9093
North Ugie Water
Leys
St Fergus Moss
Little Skillymarno
A981
Backfolds
Kirktown
St Fergus
Scotstown Hd.
Denhead
Hythie
Rora Moss
North Kirkton
Fetterangus
Forest of Deer
Toux
Rora
Lunderton
Kirkton Hd.
A950
DEER ABBEY
Dunshillock
Woodside
BUCHAN
Maud
Mintlaw
ADEN
Water
Newseat
Inverugie
INVERUGIE CASTLE
UGIE SALMON FISH HOUSE
Buchanhaven
MAUD RAILWAY MUSEUM
B9029
Old Deer
Longside
Torterston
Backhill of Clackriach
B9106
Flushing
South Ugie
A982
Peterhead
ABERDEENSHIRE FARMING MUSEUM
Stuartfield
Drymuir
Inverquhomery
A950
ARBUTHNOT MUSEUM & ART GALLERY
Keith Inch
Bulwark
Millbreck
Hillhead of Cocklaw
Peterhead Bay
Mains of Crichie
Nether Kinmundy
A948
Nethermuir
Crichie
B9030
Invernettie
Sandford Bay
Clola
Little Dens
Kinnadie
Skelmuir
Boddam
Blackhill
Millbank
Buchan Ness
Mains of Annochie
Kinknockie
Stirling
Auchnagatt
Backhill of Fortree
Smallburn
Sandfordhill
Mains of Inkhorn
Moss of Cruden
Coldwells
Backhill
Stoneygate
Longhaven
Teuchan
Milton Coldwells
A90
North Haven
Quilquox
Auchiries
BULLERS OF BUCHAN
A952
Hatton
Muirtack
Drumwhindle
Eastertown of Auchleuchries
Twa Havens
Arthrath
Cruden Bay
SLAINS CASTLE
Toll of Birness
Port Erroll
A948
Bogbrae
Chapel Hill
Bay of Cruden
Ythanbank
A975
Hilton
Mains of Birness
Nether Leask
Inverebrie
Whinnyfold
Broomfield
A90
West Kinharrachie
P&R
Artrochie
Auchmacoy
Ellon
Esslemont
Kirkton of Logie Buchan
Kirktown of Slains
A920
VISITOR CENTRE
Collieston
Waterside
St Catherine's Dub
GARDENS
Meikle Tarty
Sands of Forvie
FORVIE
Hackley Hd. or Forvie Ness
B9000
Tipperty
Tarty Burn
B9000
Newburgh
Cultercullen
Foveran
Udny Station
Foveran Burn
A975
Minnes
Newburgh Bar
Drums
Tillycorthie
Rashiereive
B999
Ardo Ho.
Delfrigs
Middlemuir
B979
245
Craigie
Causeyend
Whitecairns
Belhelvie
B977
BALMEDIE
Balmedie
Drumligair
B977
A90
Potterton
Corby Loch
Blackdog
B999
Mundurno

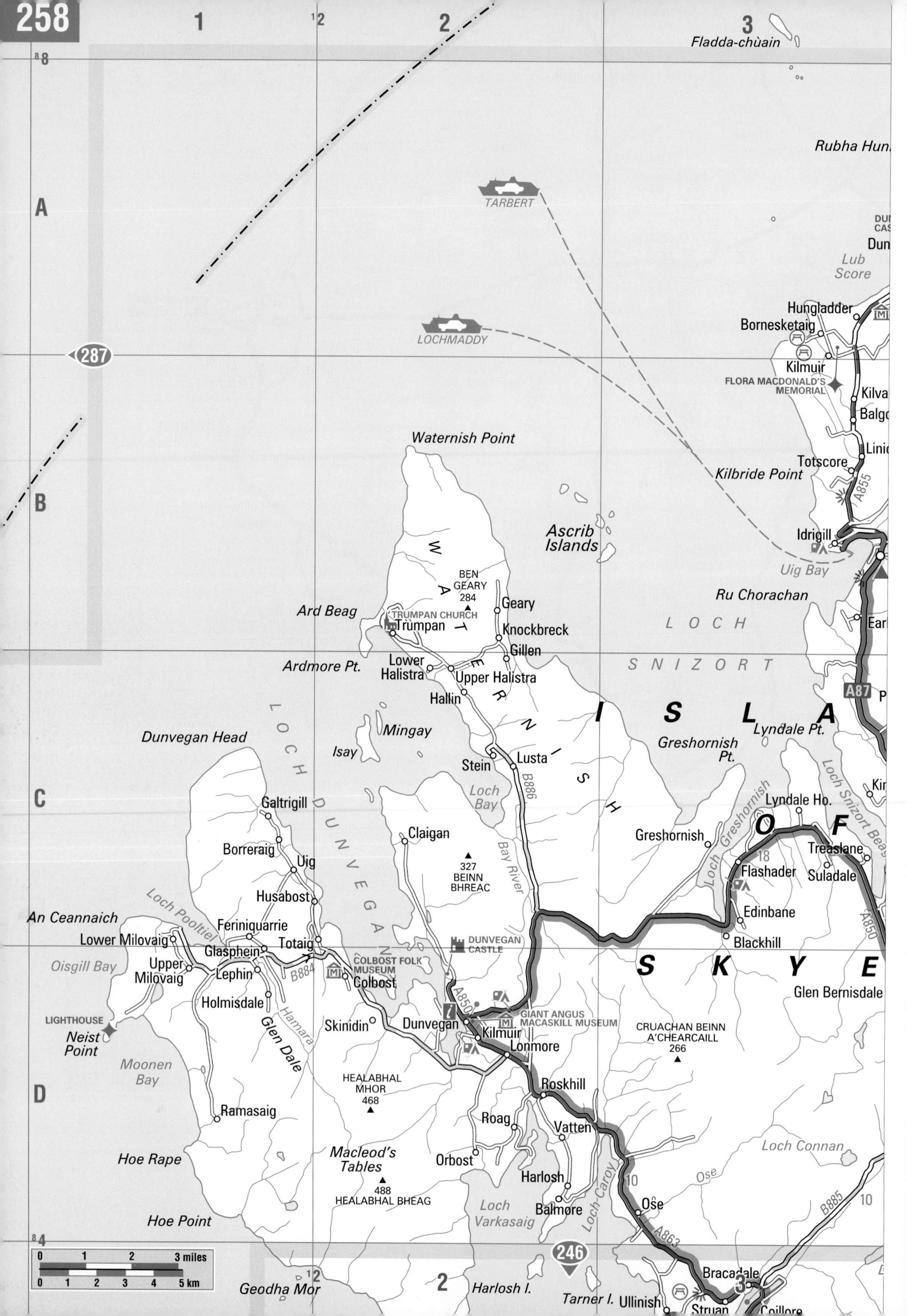

1 2 2 3

Fladda-chùain

A

Rubha Hun...

TARBERT

LOCHMADDY

⟨287⟩

DUN
CAS
Dun

Lub
Score

Hungladder
Bornesketaig

Kilmuir
FLORA MACDONALD'S
MEMORIAL
Kilva
Balgo

Linic

Totscore
Kilbride Point

Idrigill

B

Waternish Point

Ascrib
Islands

Uig Bay

Ru Chorachan

LOCH

A87 P

Ard Beag

BEN
GEARY
284
TRUMPAN CHURCH
Trùmpan

Geary
Knockbreck
Gillen

SNIZORT

ISLA

Ardmore Pt.

Lower
Halistra
Upper Halistra

Hallin

W
A
T
E
R
N
I
S
H

Lyndale Pt.

Greshornish
Pt.

Earl

Dunvegan Head

Isay
Mingay

Stein

Loch
Bay

Lusta

B886

Bay River

Greshornish

Lyndale Ho.

Kir

C

Galtrigill

Claigan

327
BEINN
BHREAC

Loch Greshornish

18

Treaslane
Suladale

Borreraig
Uig

OF

Flashader

Husabost

LOCH
DUNVEGAN

Edinbane

An Ceannaich
Lower Milovaig

Feriniquarrie
Totaig

Blackhill

Loch Pooltiel

Glasphein

SKYE

Oisgill Bay
Upper
Milovaig
Lephin

B884

COLBOST FOLK
MUSEUM
Colbost

DUNVEGAN
CASTLE

A850

Glen Bernisdale

LIGHTHOUSE

Holmisdale

Skinidin

Dunvegan

GIANT ANGUS
MACASKILL MUSEUM

CRUACHAN BEINN
A'CHEARCAILL
266

Neist
Point

Glen Dale

Hamara

Kilmuir
Lonmore

Moonen
Bay

HEALABHAL
MHOR
468

D

Ramasaig

Roskhill

Roag

Vatten

Loch Connan

Hoe Rape

Macleod's
Tables

Orbost

Harlosh

Loch Caroy

10
Ose

Ose

B885

10

Hoe Point

488
HEALABHAL BHEAG

Loch
Varkasaig

Balmore

A863

Bracadale

⟨246⟩

3

Geodha Mor
Harlosh I.
Tarner I. Ullinish

Struan
Coillore

0   1   2   3 miles
0 1 2 3 4 5 km

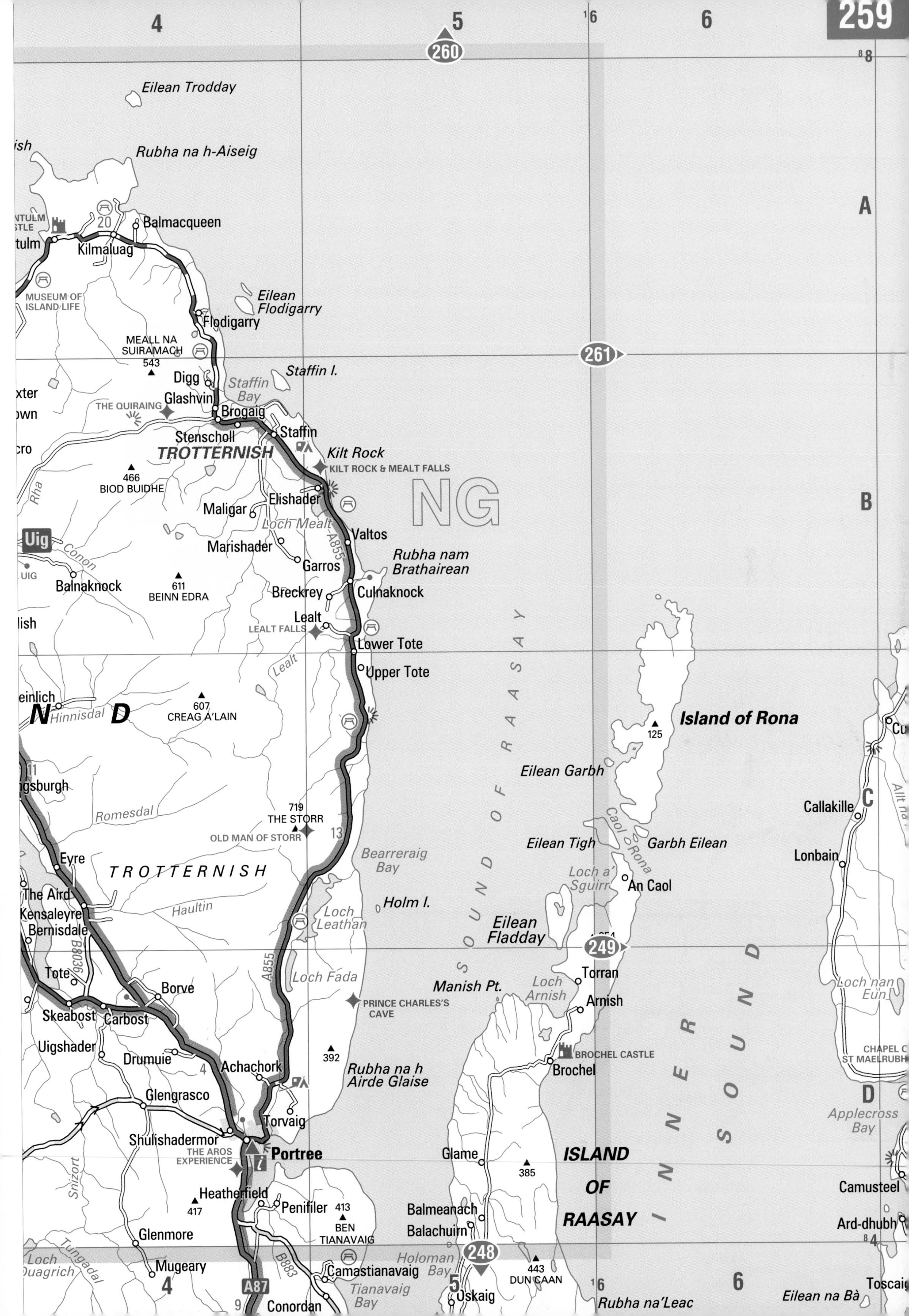

4
5
6
260
261
249
248
A
B
C
D
Eilean Trodday
Rubha na h-Aiseig
Balmacqueen
Kilmaluag
MUSEUM OF ISLAND LIFE
Eilean Flodigarry
Flodigarry
MEALL NA SUIRAMACH
543
Digg
Staffin I.
Staffin Bay
Glashvin
THE QUIRAING
Brogaig
Staffin
Stenscholl
TROTTERNISH
Kilt Rock
KILT ROCK & MEALT FALLS
466
BIOD BUIDHE
Elishader
Maligar
Loch Mealt
NG
Valtos
Uig
Conon
Marishader
Garros
Rubha nam Brathairean
Balnaknock
611
BEINN EDRA
Breckrey
Culnaknock
Lealt
LEALT FALLS
Lower Tote
Upper Tote
Lealt
607
CREAG A'LAIN
Hinnisdal
Island of Rona
125
Eilean Garbh
SOUND OF RAASAY
719
THE STORR
OLD MAN OF STORR
Romesdal
Callakille
Caol Rona
Eilean Tigh
Garbh Eilean
Bearreraig Bay
Lonbain
Eyre
TROTTERNISH
Loch a' Sguirr
An Caol
The Aird
Holm I.
Haultin
Kensaleyre
Loch Leathan
Eilean Fladday
Bernisdale
B8036
A855
Torran
Tote
Loch Fada
Manish Pt.
Loch Arnish
Arnish
Loch nan Eun
Borve
PRINCE CHARLES'S CAVE
Skeabost
Carbost
Uigshader
392
BROCHEL CASTLE
CHAPEL OF ST MAELRUBHA
Drumuie
Achachork
Rubha na h Airde Glaise
Brochel
INNER SOUND
Glengrasco
Torvaig
Applecross Bay
Shulishadermor
Portree
THE AROS EXPERIENCE
Glame
385
ISLAND OF RAASAY
Snizort
Camusteel
Heatherfield
417
Penifiler
413
BEN TIANAVAIG
Balmeanach
Balachuirn
Ard-dhubh
Glenmore
Holoman Bay
443
DUN CAAN
Loch Duagrich
Tungadal
Mugeary
B883
Camastianavaig
A87
Tianavaig Bay
Oskaig
Rubha na'Leac
Eilean na Bà
Toscaig
Conordan

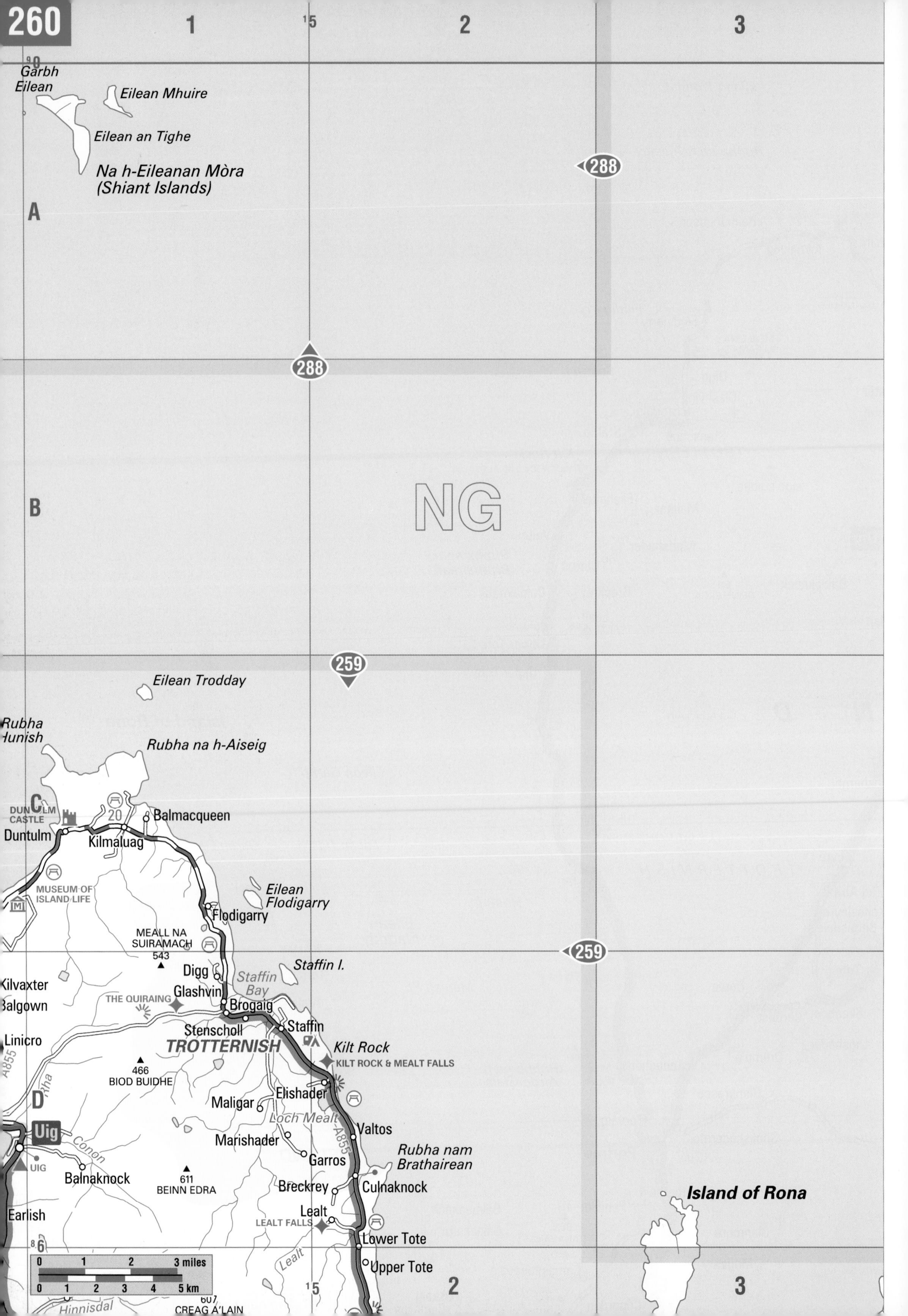

1 ¹5 2 3

Garbh Eilean

Eilean Mhuire

Eilean an Tighe

Na h-Eileanan Mòra (Shiant Islands)

A

◄288

B

NG

▲288

C

259

Eilean Trodday

Rubha Hunish

Rubha na h-Aiseig

DUN
CASTLE LM 🏰
Duntulm 20 🚻
Kilmaluag Balmacqueen

🚻 MUSEUM OF
ISLAND LIFE
M 🏛

Eilean Flodigarry

Flodigarry

MEALL NA
SUIRAMACH 🚻

543 ▲

Digg *Staffin Bay* *Staffin I.*

Kilvaxter THE QUIRAING ☀ Glashvin

Balgown ◆ Brogaig ►259

Linicro Stenscholl Staffin

TROTTERNISH 🚻 *Kilt Rock*
KILT ROCK & MEALT FALLS

466 ▲
BIOD BUIDHE

A855 Maligar Elishader 🚻

D *Loch Mealt*

Uig Marishader Valtos A855

UIG ▲ Garros *Rubha nam Brathairean*

Balnaknock 611 ▲ Breckrey Culnaknock

BEINN EDRA

Earlish Lealt **Island of Rona**

LEALT FALLS ◆

⁸6 Lower Tote 🚻

0 1 2 3 miles

0 1 2 3 4 5 km

Upper Tote

Hinnisdal 607 ▲
CREAG A'LAIN

¹5 2 3

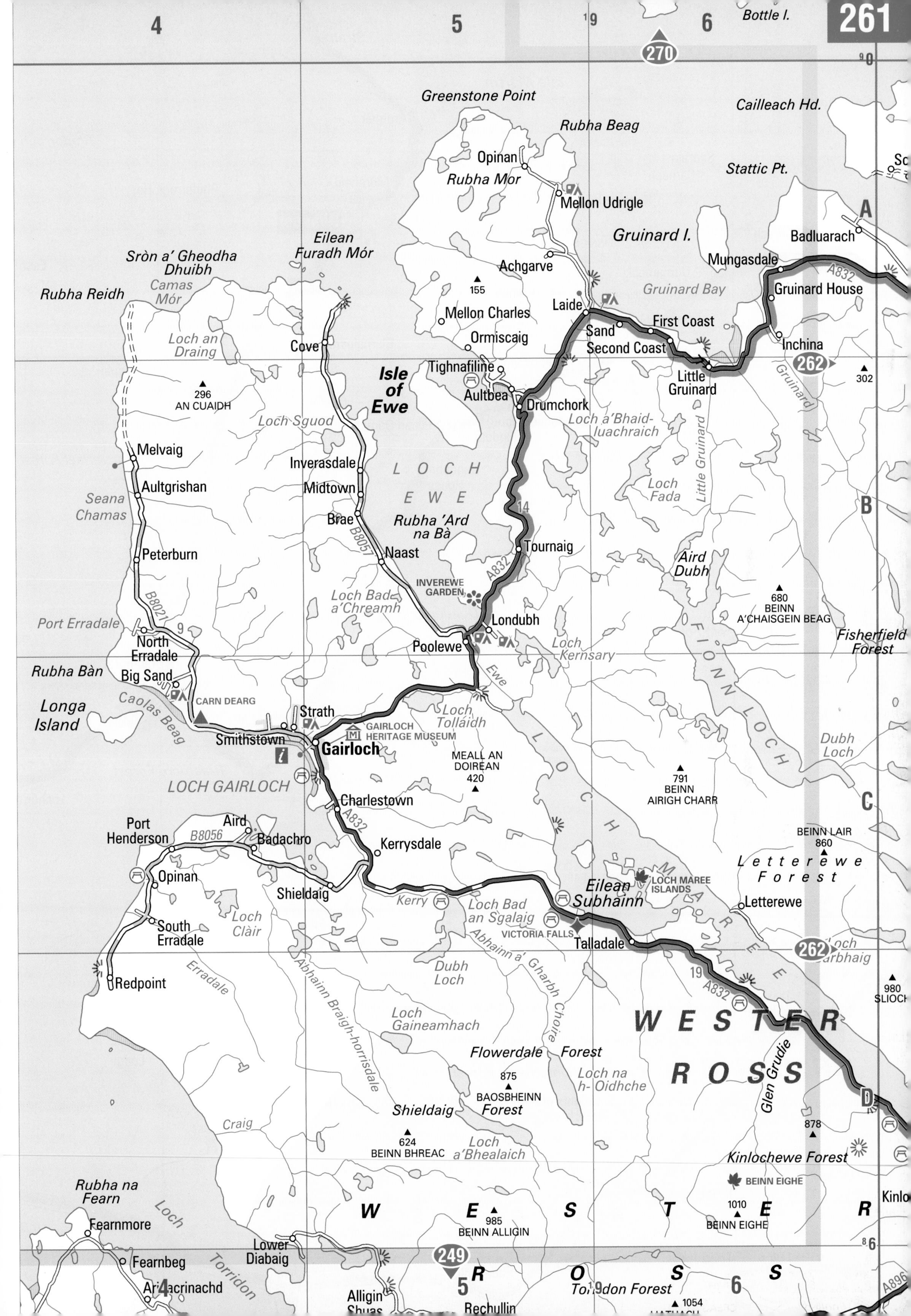

Greenstone Point
Cailleach Hd.
Rubha Beag
Opinan
Rubha Mor
Static Pt.
Mellon Udrigle
Gruinard I.
Badluarach
Mungasdale
Achgarve
Gruinard Bay
Gruinard House
Laide
Mellon Charles
First Coast
Sand
Second Coast
Inchina
Ormiscaig
Tighnafiline
Little Gruinard
Aultbea
Drumchork
Isle of Ewe
Eilean Furadh Mór
Sròn a' Gheodha Dhuibh
Camas Mór
Rubha Reidh
Loch an Draing
Cove
296 AN CUAIDH
Loch Sguod
Loch a'Bhaid-luachraich
Melvaig
Aultgrishan
Inverasdale
Midtown
LOCH EWE
Loch Fada
Little Gruinard
Seana Chamas
Brae
Rubha 'Ard na Bà
Peterburn
Naast
Tournaig
Aird Dubh
INVEREWE GARDEN
Loch Bad a'Chreamh
680 BEINN A'CHAISGEIN BEAG
Londubh
Port Erradale
North Erradale
Poolewe
Loch Kernsary
Fisherfield Forest
Rubha Bàn
Big Sand
FIONN LOCH
Longa Island
Caolas Beag
CARN DEARG
Strath
Loch Tolláidh
GAIRLOCH HERITAGE MUSEUM
Smithstown
Gairloch
Dubh Loch
MEALL AN DOIREAN 420
791 BEINN AIRIGH CHARR
LOCH GAIRLOCH
Charlestown
LOCH MAREE
Port Henderson
Aird
Badachro
BEINN LAIR 860
Letterewe Forest
Kerrysdale
Opinan
Shieldaig
Kerry
Eilean Subhainn
LOCH MAREE ISLANDS
Letterewe
Loch Bad an Sgalaig
Loch Clàir
South Erradale
VICTORIA FALLS
Talladale
Dubh Loch
Redpoint
Erradale
Abhainn a' Gharbh Choire
980 SLIOCH
Abhainn Braigh-horrisdale
Loch Gaineamhach
WESTER ROSS
Flowerdale Forest
Glen Grudie
Loch na h-Oidhche
875 BAOSBHEINN Forest
Shieldaig
878
624 BEINN BHREAC
Loch a'Bhealaich
Craig
Kinlochewe Forest
BEINN EIGHE
Rubha na Fearn
Loch Torridon
Fearnmore
985 BEINN ALLIGIN
1010 BEINN EIGHE
WESTER ROSS
Lower Diabaig
Fearnbeg
Arinacrinachd
Alligin Shuas
Rechullin
Torridon Forest
1054
Bottle I.
A832
B8057
B8021
B8056
A896
270
262
249

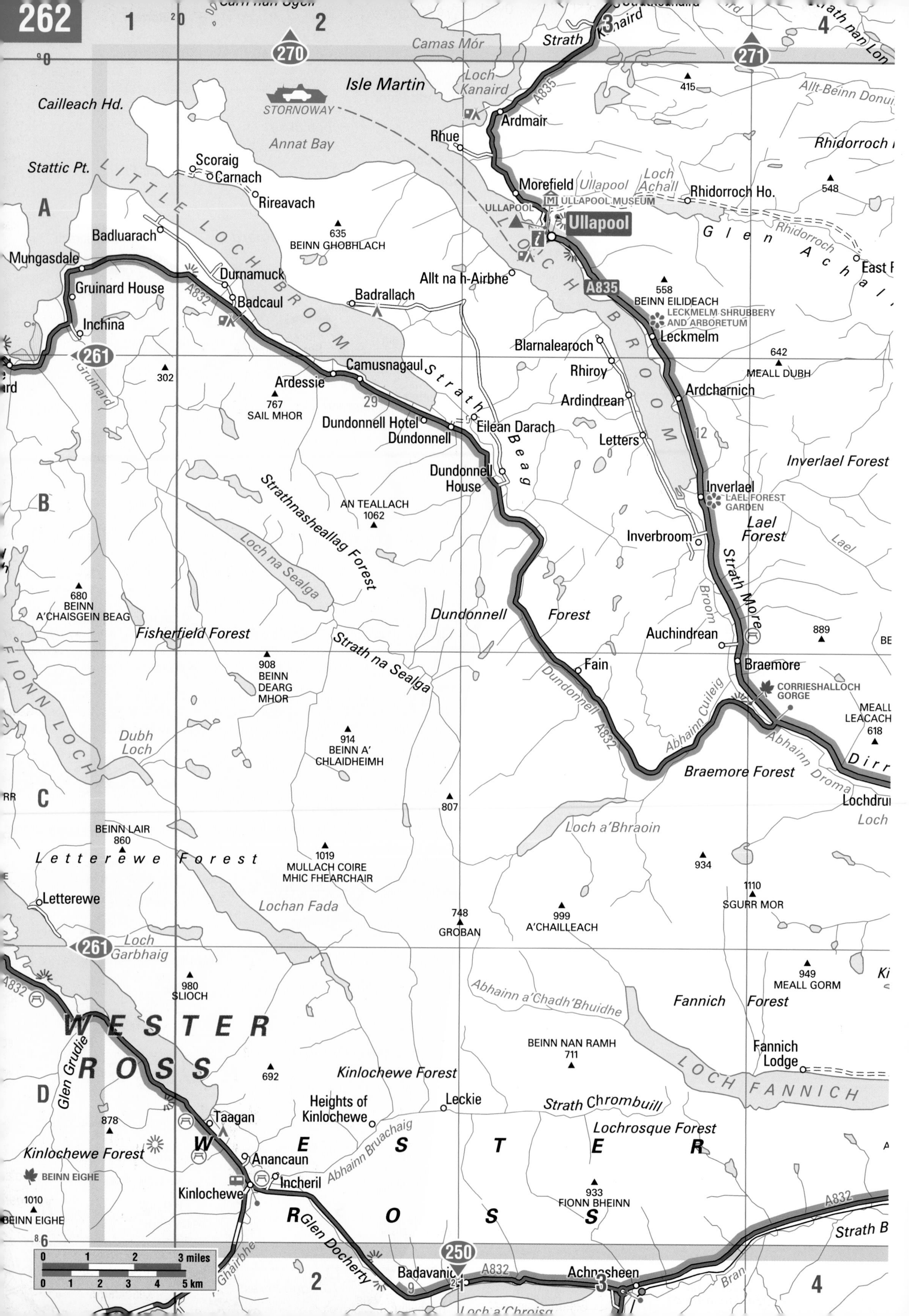
Isle Martin
Cailleach Hd.
STORNOWAY
Annat Bay
Camas Mór
Loch Kanaird
Strath Kanaird
Ardmair
Rhue
Stattic Pt.
Scoraig
Carnach
Rireavach
LITTLE LOCH BROOM
Morefield
Ullapool
Loch Achall
ULLAPOOL MUSEUM
Rhidorroch Ho.
Rhidorroch
Glen Achall
East
Alt-Beinn Donuil
548
415
Badluarach
635
BEINN GHOBHLACH
Mungasdale
Gruinard House
Inchina
Durnamuck
Badcaul
Badrallach
Allt na h-Airbhe
LOCH BROOM
A835
558
BEINN EILIDEACH
LECKMELM SHRUBBERY AND ARBORETUM
Leckmelm
Blarnalearoch
642
MEALL DUBH
Rhiroy
Ardindrean
Ardcharnich
Letters
261
302
Camusnagaul
Strath Beag
Ardessie
767
SAIL MHOR
Dundonnell Hotel
Dundonnell
Eilean Darach
Dundonnell House
Inverlael Forest
Inverlael
LAEL FOREST GARDEN
Lael Forest
Inverbroom
Strathnasheallag Forest
AN TEALLACH
1062
Loch na Sealga
680
BEINN A'CHAISGEIN BEAG
Fisherfield Forest
Dundonnell Forest
Strath More
Broom
Auchindrean
889
Braemore
CORRIESHALLOCH GORGE
Strath na Sealga
908
BEINN DEARG MHOR
Fain
Dundonnell
A832
FIONN LOCH
Dubh Loch
914
BEINN A' CHLAIDHEIMH
Abhainn Cuileig
MEALL LEACACH
618
Abhainn Droma
Braemore Forest
807
Lochdrum
Loch a'Bhraoin
BEINN LAIR
860
Letterewe Forest
1019
MULLACH COIRE MHIC FHEARCHAIR
934
1110
SGURR MOR
Letterewe
Lochan Fada
748
GROBAN
999
A'CHAILLEACH
Loch Garbhaig
949
MEALL GORM
980
SLIOCH
Abhainn a'Chadh'Bhuidhe
Fannich Forest
WESTER ROSS
BEINN NAN RAMH
711
Fannich Lodge
LOCH FANNICH
Glen Grudie
692
Kinlochewe Forest
Heights of Kinlochewe
Leckie
Strath Chrombuill
Lochrosque Forest
Taagan
878
Kinlochewe Forest
Anancaun
Abhainn Bruachaig
BEINN EIGHE
Incheril
Kinlochewe
933
FIONN BHEINN
1010
BEINN EIGHE
Glen Docherty
A832
Strath Bran
250
270
271
Badavanich
Achnasheen
Gharbhe
Loch a'Chroisg
0 1 2 3 miles
0 1 2 3 4 5 km
1 2 3 4
A B C D

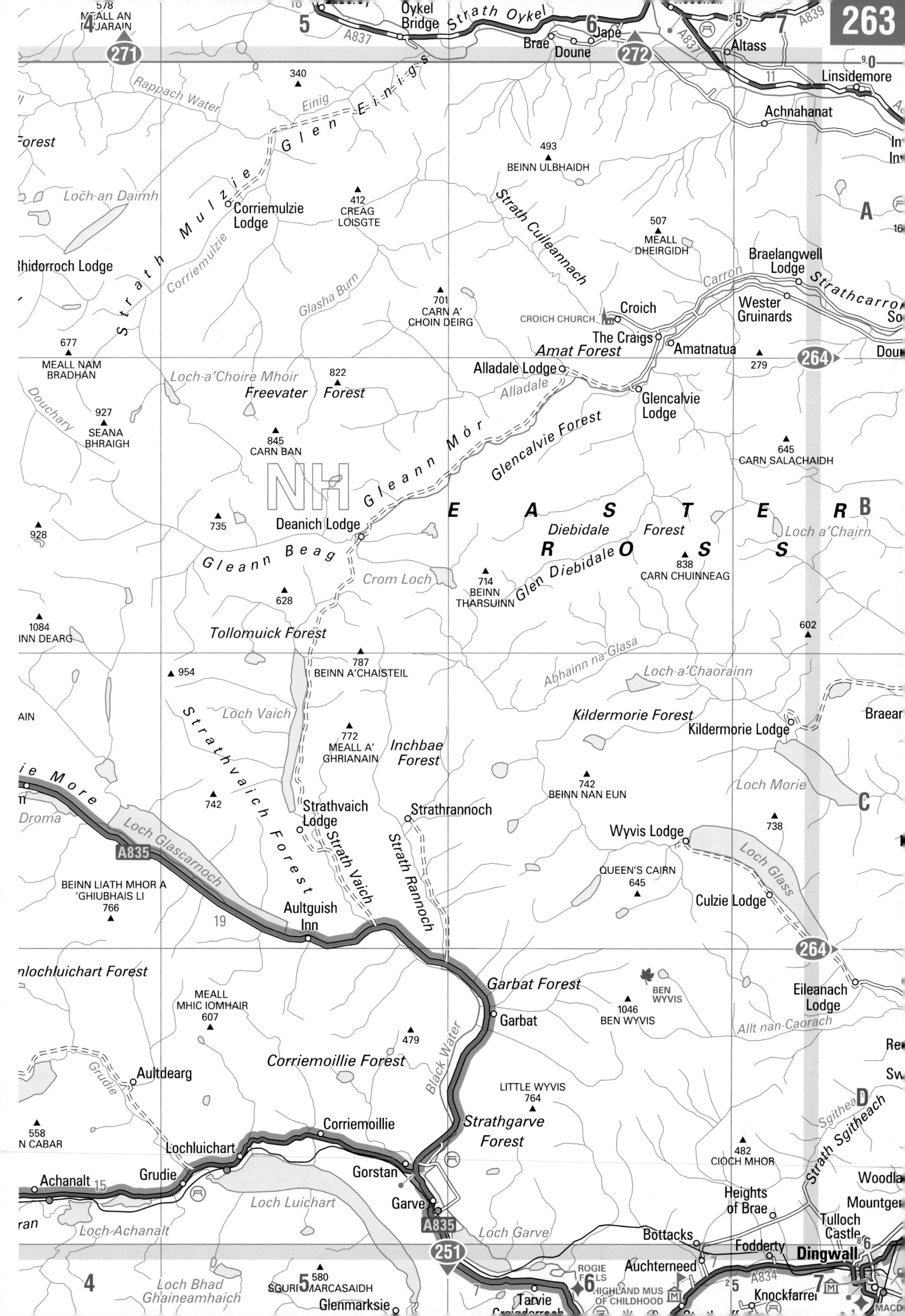
271
272
Oykel Bridge
Strath Oykel
A837
Brae
Doune
Altass
A839
Linsidemore
Achnahanat
Rappach Water
Einig
Glen Einig
340
Forest
Loch an Daimh
Strath Mulzie
Corriemulzie Lodge
412
CREAG LOISGTE
493
BEINN ULBHAIDH
Strath Cuileannach
507
MEALL DHEIRGIDH
Braelangwell Lodge
Strathcarron
Carron
Rhidorroch Lodge
Corriemulzie
Glasha Burn
701
CARN A' CHOIN DEIRG
CROICH CHURCH
Croich
Wester Gruinards
The Craigs
Amatnatua
Amat Forest
677
MEALL NAM BRADHAN
279
264
Loch-a'Choire Mhoir
822
Freevater
Forest
Alladale Lodge
Alladale
Glencalvie Lodge
Douchary
927
SEANA BHRAIGH
845
CARN BAN
Glencalvie Forest
Gleann Mór
645
CARN SALACHAIDH
NH
EASTER ROSS
Diebidale
Forest
Loch a'Chairn
928
735
Deanich Lodge
Gleann Beag
Crom Loch
714
BEINN THARSUINN
Glen Diebidale
838
CARN CHUINNEAG
628
1084
INN DEARG
Tollomuick Forest
602
787
BEINN A'CHAISTEIL
954
Abhainn na Glasa
Loch-a'Chaorainn
Loch Vaich
Strathvaich Forest
Kildermorie Forest
Kildermorie Lodge
Braear
772
MEALL A' GHRIANAIN
Inchbae Forest
742
BEINN NAN EUN
Loch Morie
742
Strathvaich Lodge
Strathrannoch
Droma
Loch Glascarnoch
A835
Strath Vaich
Strath Rannoch
Wyvis Lodge
738
Loch Glass
QUEEN'S CAIRN 645
Culzie Lodge
BEINN LIATH MHOR A 'GHIUBHAIS LI
766
19
Aultguish Inn
264
nlochluichart Forest
Garbat Forest
BEN WYVIS
1046
BEN WYVIS
Eileanach Lodge
MEALL MHIC IOMHAIR
607
Garbat
Allt nan Caorach
479
Black Water
Corriemoillie Forest
Aultdearg
Grudie
LITTLE WYVIS
764
Strathgarve Forest
Sgithea
Strath Sgitheach
558
N CABAR
Corriemoillie
482
CIOCH MHOR
Lochluichart
Gorstan
Achanalt
15
Grudie
Garve
Heights of Brae
Woodla
Mountger
Tulloch Castle
Loch Luichart
A835
Loch Garve
Loch Achanalt
Bottacks
Fodderty
Dingwall
251
Auchterneed
ROGIE FALLS
HIGHLAND MUS OF CHILDHOOD
A834
580
SGURR MARCASAIDH
Loch Bhad Ghaineamhaich
Glenmarksie
Tarvie
Knockfarrel
A
B
C
D
4
5
6
7

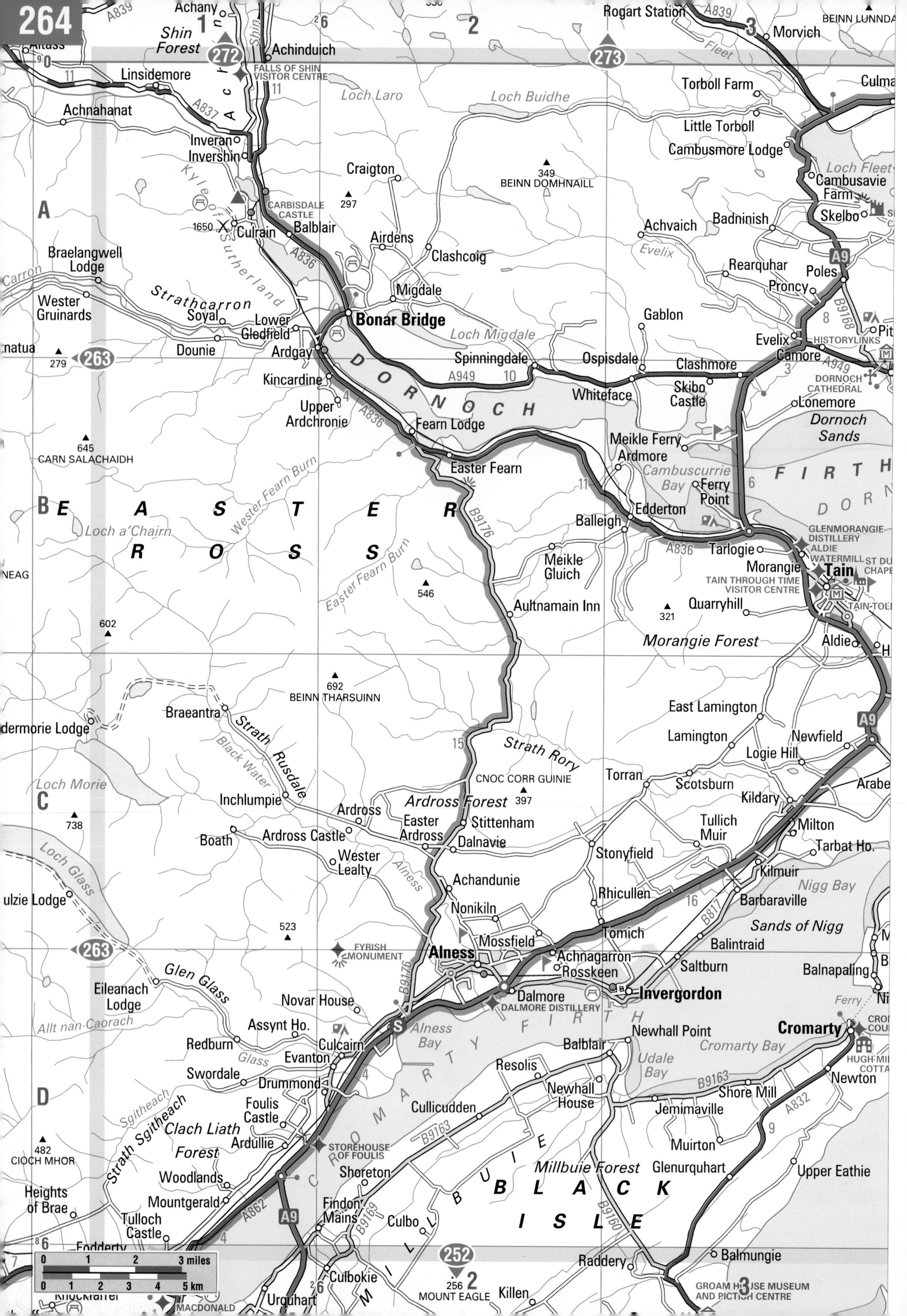

Achany
Shin Forest
272
Achinduich
Rogart Station
A839
273
Morvich
BEINN LUNNDA
Fleet
Linsidemore
FALLS OF SHIN VISITOR CENTRE
Loch Laro
Loch Buidhe
Torboll Farm
Culma
Achnahanat
A837
Little Torboll
Cambusmore Lodge
Inveran
Invershin
Craigton
349
BEINN DOMHNAILL
Loch Fleet
Cambusavie Farm
Kyle of Sutherland
CARBISDALE CASTLE
297
A
1650
Culrain
Balblair
Achvaich
Badninish
Skelbo
Braelangwell Lodge
Carron
A836
Airdens
Clashcoig
Evelix
A9
Rearquhar
Poles
Proncy
Wester Gruinards
Strathcarron
Migdale
Soyal
Lower Gledfield
Bonar Bridge
Gablon
B9168
Loch Migdale
Evelix
HISTORYLINKS
Dounie
Ardgay
279
263
Spinningdale
Ospisdale
Clashmore
Camore
A949
DORNOCH CATHEDRAL
Kincardine
DORNOCH
A949
Whiteface
Skibo Castle
Lonemore
Upper Ardchronie
A836
Fearn Lodge
Dornoch Sands
645
CARN SALACHAIDH
Meikle Ferry
Ardmore
Easter Fearn
Cambuscurrie Bay
Ferry Point
FIRTH
DORN
Wester Fearn Burn
B
EASTER ROSS
B9176
Edderton
Balleigh
GLENMORANGIE DISTILLERY
ALDIE WATERMILL
Loch a'Chairn
A836
Tarlogie
Meikle Gluich
Morangie
Tain
TAIN THROUGH TIME VISITOR CENTRE
NEAG
Easter Fearn Burn
546
Aultnamain Inn
321
Quarryhill
602
Morangie Forest
Aldie
692
BEINN THARSUINN
East Lamington
Braeantra
Strath Rusdale
dermorie Lodge
Black Water
15
Strath Rory
Lamington
Newfield
Logie Hill
A9
Loch Morie
CNOC CORR GUINIE
397
Torran
Scotsburn
Kildary
Arabe
C
Inchlumpie
Ardross
Ardross Forest
Easter Ardross
Stittenham
Tullich Muir
Milton
738
Boath
Ardross Castle
Dalnavie
Tarbat Ho.
Wester Lealty
Alness
Stonyfield
Kilmuir
Loch Glass
Achandunie
Nigg Bay
ulzie Lodge
Rhicullen
16
Barbaraville
Nonikiln
B817
Sands of Nigg
523
Tomich
Mossfield
Balintraid
263
FYRISH MONUMENT
Alness
Achnagarron
B9176
Rosskeen
Saltburn
Balnapaling
Eileanach Lodge
Glen Glass
Dalmore
Invergordon
Ferry
Novar House
DALMORE DISTILLERY
Allt nan Caorach
Assynt Ho.
Alness Bay
CROMARTY FIRTH
Cromarty
Culcairn
Newhall Point
Redburn
Balblair
Cromarty Bay
Glass
Evanton
Udale Bay
Resolis
HUGH MI COTTA
Swordale
Drummond
Newhall House
B9163
Newton
D
Foulis Castle
Shore Mill
Cullicudden
Jemimaville
A832
Sgitheach
Strath Sgitheach
Clach Liath
Ardullie
B9163
482
CIOCH MHOR
Forest
STOREHOUSE OF FOULIS
Muirton
Millbuie Forest
Glenurquhart
Woodlands
Shoreton
Upper Eathie
BLACK ISLE
Heights of Brae
Mountgerald
A862
Findon Mains
B9169
Culbo
B9160
Tulloch Castle
A9
Fodderty
252
Balmungie
Raddery
Culbokie
256
MOUNT EAGLE
Killen
GROAM HOUSE MUSEUM AND PICTISH CENTRE
Knockfarrel
MACDONALD
Urquhart
0 1 2 3 miles
0 1 2 3 4 5 km

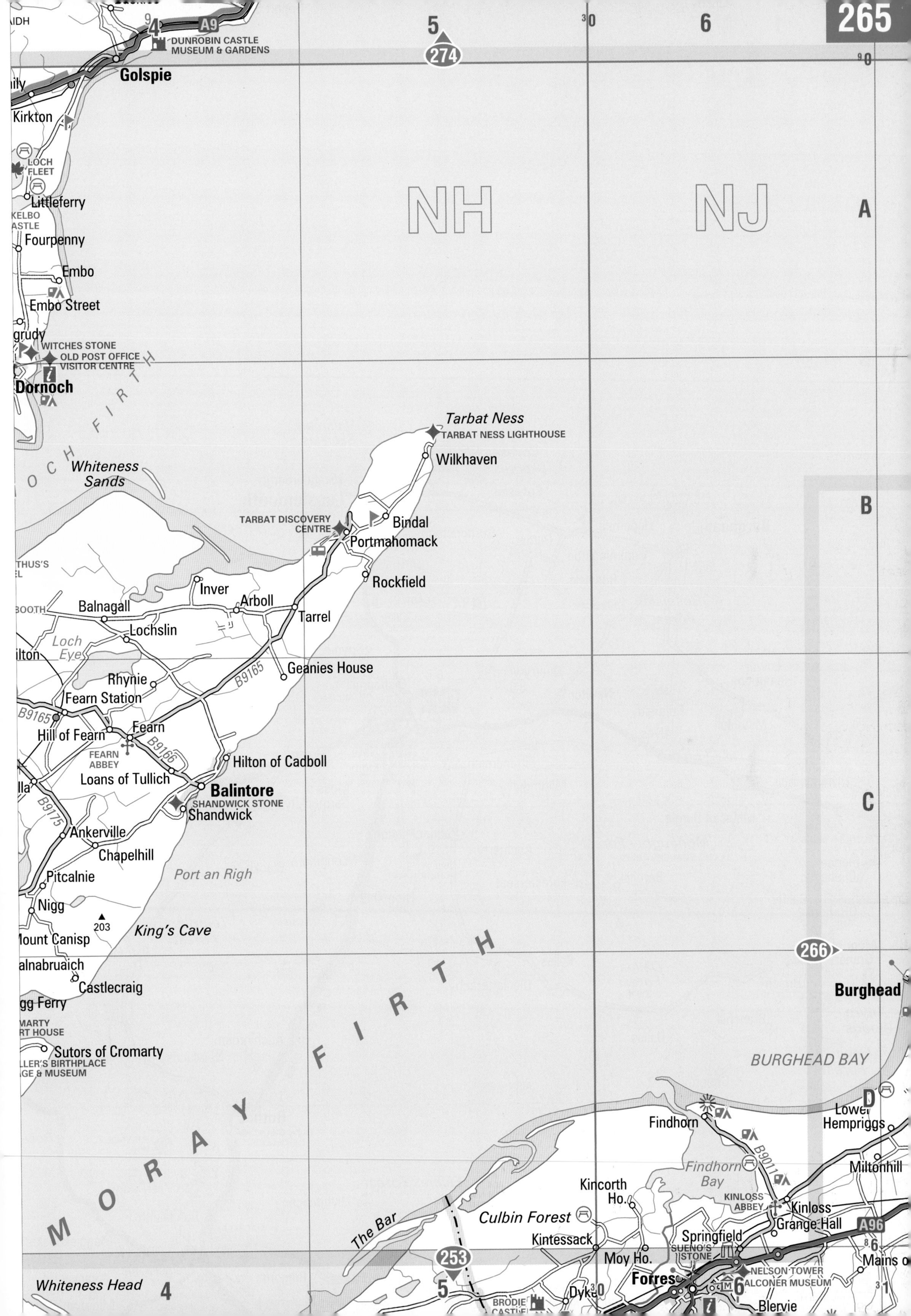

NH

NJ

A

B

C

D

Golspie

Kirkton

LOCH FLEET

Littleferry

KELBO CASTLE

Fourpenny

Embo

Embo Street

grudy

WITCHES STONE
OLD POST OFFICE
VISITOR CENTRE

Dornoch

Whiteness Sands

THUS'S

BOOTH

Inver

Balnagall

Lochslin

Loch Eye

ilton

Rhynie

Fearn Station

Hill of Fearn

Fearn

FEARN ABBEY

Loans of Tullich

lla

Ankerville

Chapelhill

Pitcalnie

Nigg

203

Mount Canisp

lnabruaich

Castlecraig

gg Ferry

MARTY
RT HOUSE

Sutors of Cromarty

LLER'S BIRTHPLACE
GE & MUSEUM

Tarbat Ness
TARBAT NESS LIGHTHOUSE

Wilkhaven

TARBAT DISCOVERY CENTRE

Bindal

Portmahomack

Rockfield

Arboll

Tarrel

B9165

Geanies House

B9165

B9166

Hilton of Cadboll

Balintore

SHANDWICK STONE

Shandwick

B9175

Port an Righ

King's Cave

M O R A Y

F I R T H

266

Burghead

BURGHEAD BAY

Lower Hempriggs

Miltonhill

Findhorn

B9011

Findhorn Bay

KINLOSS ABBEY

Kinloss

Grange Hall

A96

Kincorth Ho.

The Bar

Culbin Forest

Kintessack

Springfield

SUENO'S STONE

Moy Ho.

NELSON TOWER
ALCONER MUSEUM

Forres

Dyke

253

BRODIE CASTLE

Blervie

Mains o

Whiteness Head

A9

DUNROBIN CASTLE
MUSEUM & GARDENS

274

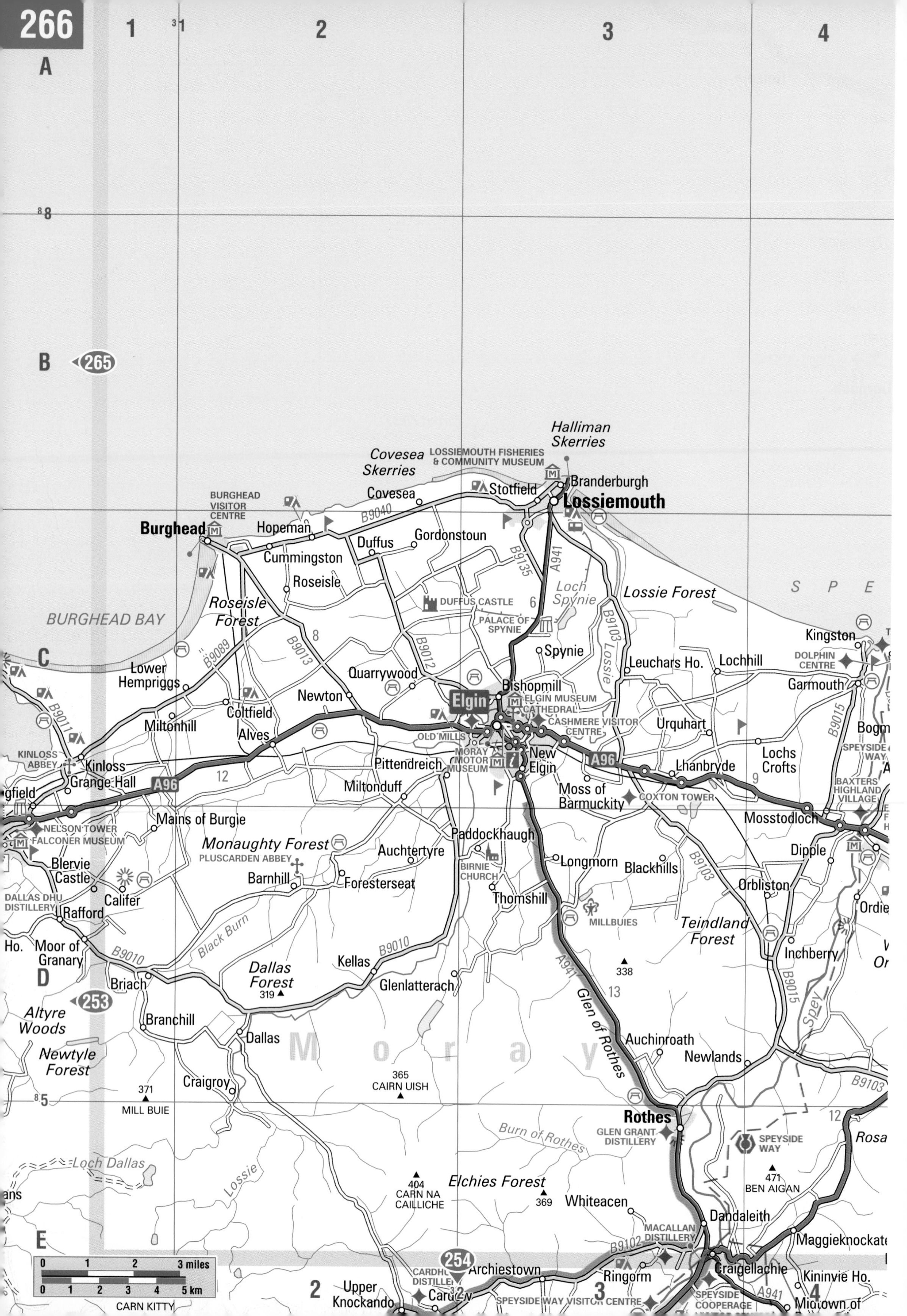
Halliman Skerries
Covesea Skerries
LOSSIEMOUTH FISHERIES & COMMUNITY MUSEUM
Branderburgh
Stotfield
Lossiemouth
Covesea
BURGHEAD VISITOR CENTRE
Burghead
Hopeman
Duffus
Gordonstoun
Cummingston
Roseisle
Roseisle Forest
BURGHEAD BAY
DUFFUS CASTLE
Loch Spynie
Lossie Forest
PALACE OF SPYNIE
Spynie
Kingston
DOLPHIN CENTRE
Garmouth
Leuchars Ho.
Lochhill
Lower Hempriggs
Quarrywood
Newton
Bishopmill
Elgin
ELGIN MUSEUM
CATHEDRAL
CASHMERE VISITOR CENTRE
Coltfield
Miltonhill
Alves
OLD MILLS
MORAY MOTOR MUSEUM
New Elgin
Urquhart
Lochs Crofts
Lhanbryde
KINLOSS ABBEY
Kinloss
Grange Hall
Pittendreich
Miltonduff
Moss of Barmuckity
COXTON TOWER
BAXTERS HIGHLAND VILLAGE
SPEYSIDE WAY
Mosstodloch
NELSON TOWER
FALCONER MUSEUM
Mains of Burgie
Monaughty Forest
PLUSCARDEN ABBEY
Auchtertyre
Paddockhaugh
Longmorn
Blackhills
Dipple
Blervie Castle
Barnhill
Foresterseat
BIRNIE CHURCH
Thomshill
Orbliston
DALLAS DHU DISTILLERY
Califer
Rafford
MILLBUIES
Teindland Forest
Moor of Granary
Black Burn
Dallas Forest
Kellas
Inchberry
Briach
Glenlatterach
Glen of Rothes
Altyre Woods
Branchill
Dallas
Moray
Auchinroath
Newlands
Newtyle Forest
Craigroy
MILL BUIE
CAIRN UISH
Rothes
GLEN GRANT DISTILLERY
SPEYSIDE WAY
Burn of Rothes
BEN AIGAN
Loch Dallas
Lossie
CARN NA CAILLICHE
Elchies Forest
Whiteacen
Dandaleith
MACALLAN DISTILLERY
Maggieknockater
Archiestown
Ringorm
Craigellachie
Kininvie Ho.
Upper Knockando
SPEYSIDE WAY VISITOR CENTRE
SPEYSIDE COOPERAGE
Midtown of
CARN KITTY
0 1 2 3 miles
0 1 2 3 4 5 km
265
253
254

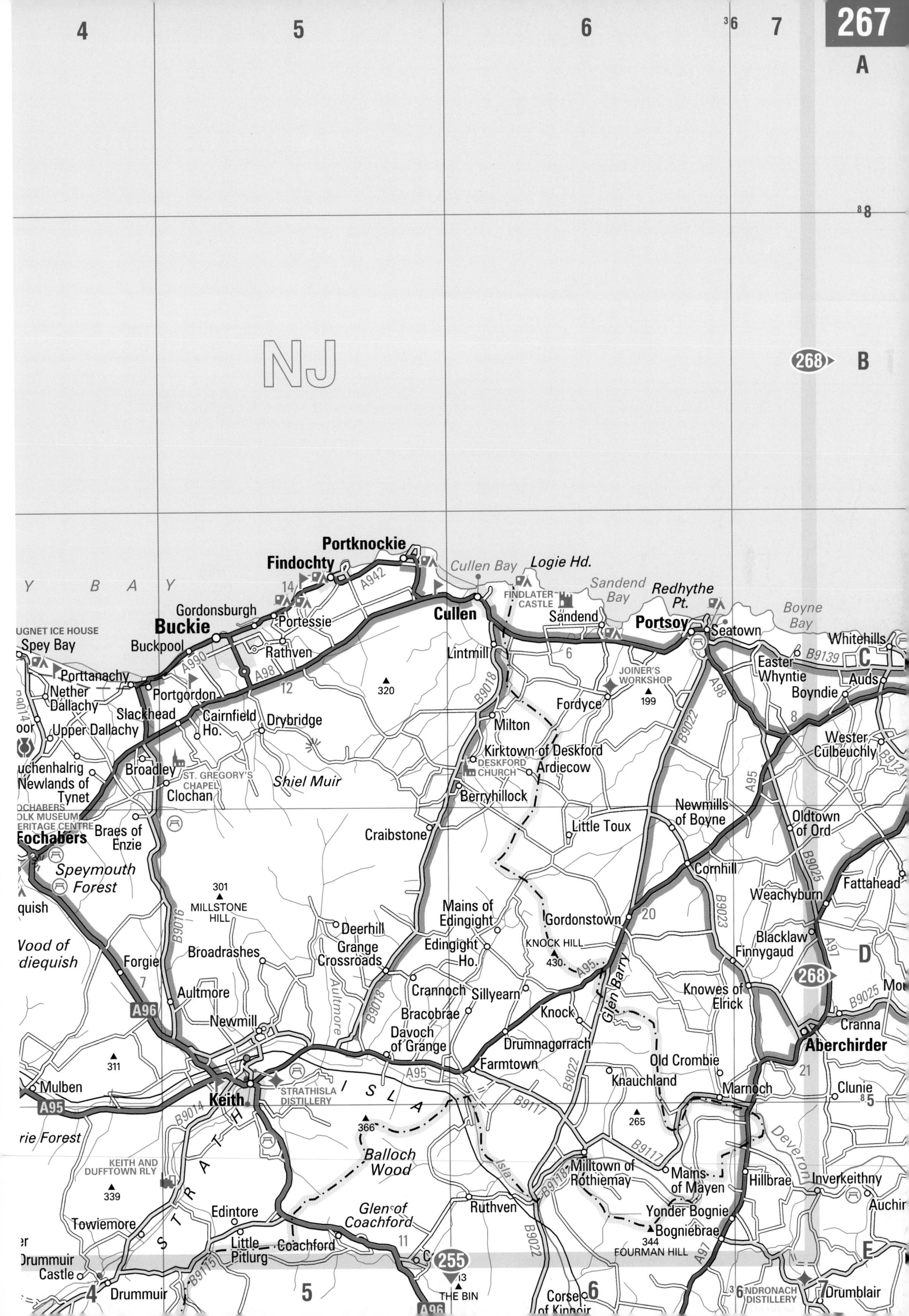
NJ
Portknockie
Findochty
Cullen Bay
Logie Hd.
Sandend Bay
Redhythe Pt.
Boyne Bay
Buckie
Gordonsburgh
Portessie
Rathven
Cullen
Findlater Castle
Sandend
Portsoy
Seatown
Whitehills
Spey Bay
Buckpool
Portgordon
Porttanachy
Nether Dallachy
Upper Dallachy
Slackhead
Cairnfield Ho.
Drybridge
Lintmill
Joiner's Workshop
Easter Whyntie
Auds
Boyndie
Fordyce
Milton
Kirktown of Deskford
Deskford Church
Ardiecow
Wester Culbeuchly
Broadley
St. Gregory's Chapel
Clochan
Shiel Muir
Berryhillock
Newlands of Tynet
Fochabers Folk Museum Heritage Centre
Fochabers
Braes of Enzie
Craibstone
Little Toux
Newmills of Boyne
Oldtown of Ord
Speymouth Forest
Cornhill
Fattahead
Weachyburn
Millstone Hill
Mains of Edingight
Gordonstown
Deerhill
Grange Crossroads
Edingight Ho.
Knock Hill
Blacklaw
Finnygaud
Broadrashes
Forgie
Aultmore
Crannoch
Sillyearn
Knowes of Elrick
Glen Barry
Knock
Cranna
Bracobrae
Newmill
Davoch of Grange
Drumnagorrach
Aberchirder
Farmtown
Old Crombie
Knauchland
Mulben
Keith
Strathisla Distillery
Strath Isla
Marnoch
Clunie
Balloch Wood
Milltown of Rothiemay
Mains of Mayen
Hillbrae
Inverkeithny
Keith and Dufftown Rly
Edintore
Glen of Coachford
Ruthven
Yonder Bognie
Bogniebrae
Fourman Hill
Towiemore
Little Pitlurg
Coachford
Drummuir Castle
Drummuir
The Bin
Corse of Kinnoir
Glendronach Distillery
Drumblair
Deveron
Isla
A95
A96
A98
A942
A990
A97
B9018
B9022
B9023
B9025
B9016
B9014
B9117
B9118
B9115
B9139
268
255

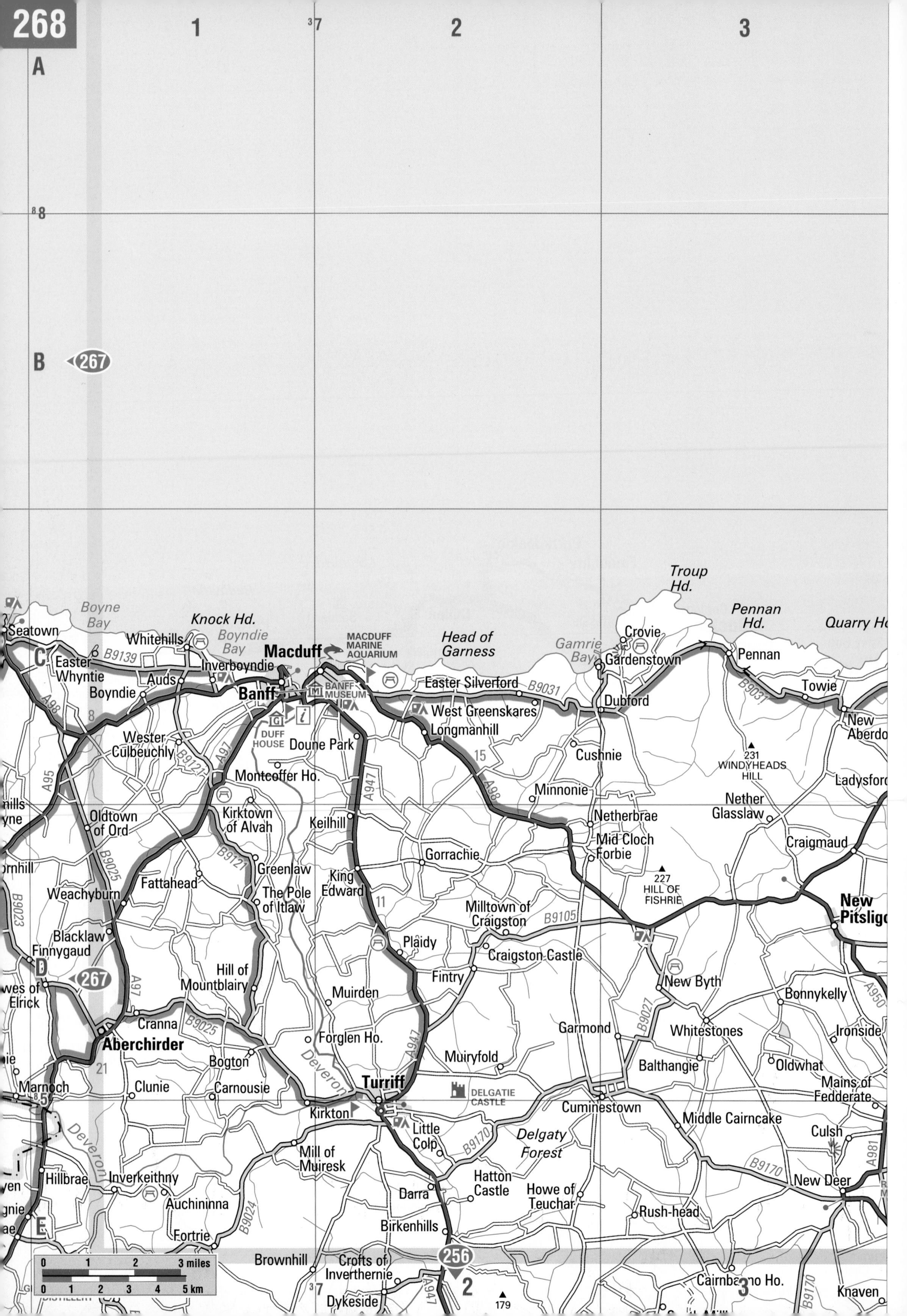

A

1   ³7   2   3

B   ◄ 267

Troup
Hd.

Pennan
Hd.

Quarry Ho

Boyne
Bay

Seatown

Knock Hd.

Boyndie
Bay

Whitehills

MACDUFF
MARINE
AQUARIUM

Head of
Garness

Gamrie
Bay

Crovie

Gardenstown

Pennan

C   Easter
Whyntie

B9139

Inverboyndie

Macduff

Easter Silverford

Dubford

Towie

Boyndie

Auds

Banff

BANFF
MUSEUM

West Greenskares

B9031

New
Aberdo

A98

Wester
Culbeuchly

A97

DUFF
HOUSE

Doune Park

Longmanhill

Cushnie

B9121

Montcoffer Ho.

A947

15

Minnonie

231
WINDYHEADS
HILL

Ladysford

hills
yne

A95

Oldtown
of Ord

Kirktown
of Alvah

Keilhill

A98

Netherbrae

Nether
Glasslaw

B9121

Greenlaw

Gorrachie

Mid Cloch
Forbie

Craigmaud

rnhill

B9025

Fattahead

King
Edward

Milltown of
Craigston

227
HILL OF
FISHRIE

New
Pitsligo

Weachyburn

The Pole
of Itlaw

11

B9105

B9023

Blacklaw
Finnygaud

Hill of
Mountblairy

Plaidy

Craigston Castle

New Byth

Bonnykelly

A950

D   ◄ 267

A97

Muirden

Fintry

B9027

wes of
Elrick

Cranna

B9025

Forglen Ho.

Garmond

Whitestones

Ironside

Aberchirder

Bogton

Muiryfold

Balthangie

Oldwhat

Mains of
Fedderate

21

Deveron

Clunie

Carnousie

Turriff

DELGATIE
CASTLE

Cuminestown

Middle Cairncake

Culsh

Marnoch

Kirkton

B9170

Delgaty
Forest

B9981

A95

Deveron

Mill of
Muiresk

Little
Colp

Hatton
Castle

Howe of
Teuchar

Rush-head

New Deer

Hillbrae

Inverkeithny

Darra

B9024

B9170

ven
gnie
ae

Auchininna

Fortrie

Birkenhills

256

Brownhill

Crofts of
Inverthernie

³7   2

Cairnbano Ho.

3

Dykeside

A947

179

Knaven

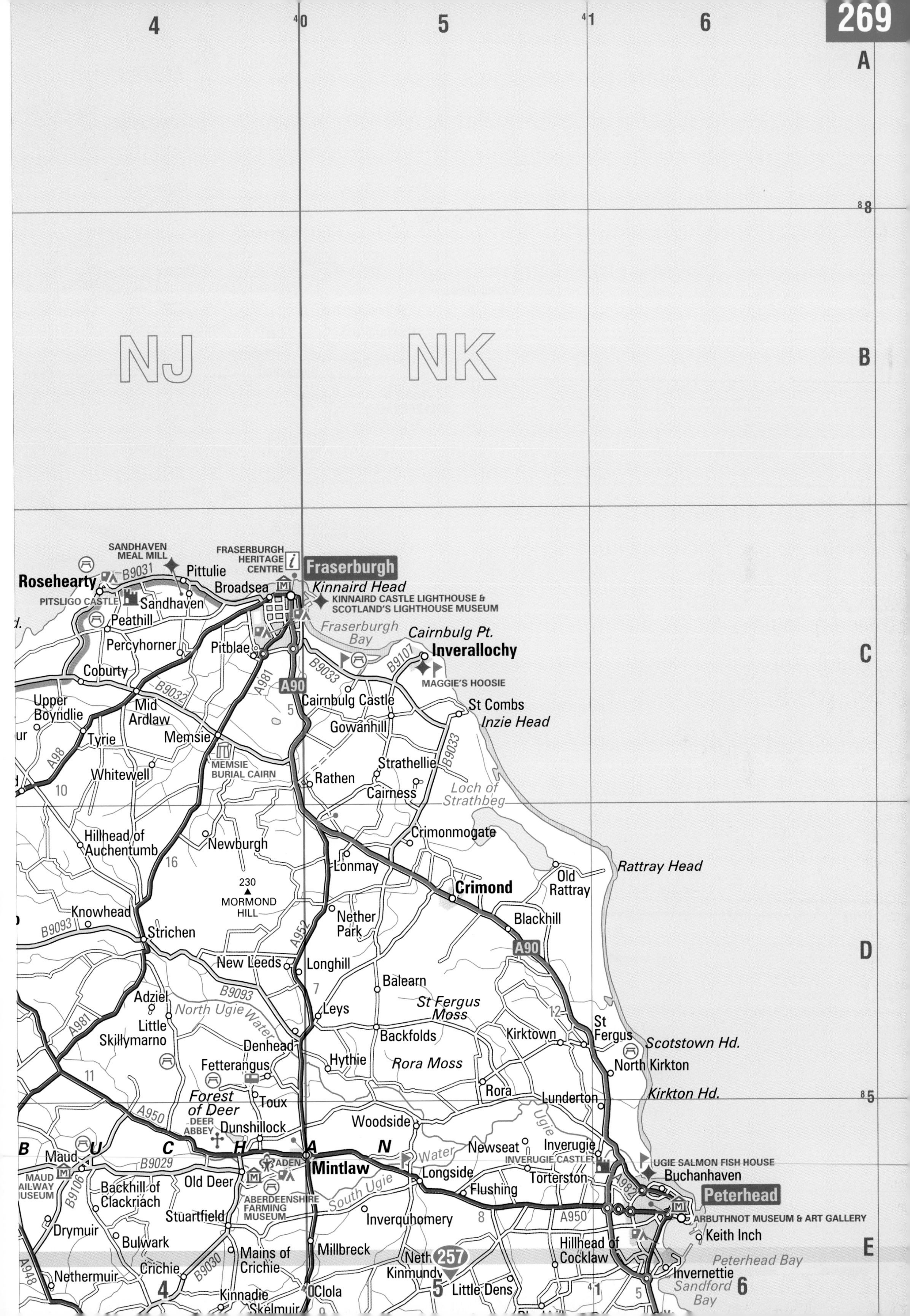

A

8

B

NJ   NK

C

SANDHAVEN
MEAL MILL
Rosehearty
Pittulie
PITSLIGO CASTLE
Sandhaven
Broadsea
Peathill
Percyhorner
Pitblae
Coburty
B9032
B9031
B9033
FRASERBURGH
HERITAGE
CENTRE
Fraserburgh
Kinnaird Head
KINNAIRD CASTLE LIGHTHOUSE &
SCOTLAND'S LIGHTHOUSE MUSEUM
Fraserburgh
Bay
Cairnbulg Pt.
Inverallochy
MAGGIE'S HOOSIE
Upper
Boyndlie
Mid
Ardlaw
Memsie
A981
A90
5
Cairnbulg Castle
Gowanhill
St Combs
Inzie Head
A98
Tyrie
Whitewell
10
MEMSIE
BURIAL CAIRN
Rathen
Strathellie
Cairness
B9107
B9033
Loch of
Strathbeg
Hillhead of
Auchentumb
Newburgh
16
230
MORMOND
HILL
Lonmay
Crimonmogate
Old
Rattray
Crimond
Rattray Head
Knowhead
B9093
Strichen
A952
Nether
Park
Blackhill
A90
D

New Leeds
Longhill
7
Balearn
St Fergus
Moss
Kirktown
St
Fergus
Scotstown Hd.
Adziel
North Ugie Water
B9093
Little
Skillymarno
Leys
Backfolds
Rora Moss
North Kirkton
Denhead
Hythie
Kirkton Hd.
8
Fetterangus
11
Toux
Forest
of Deer
DEER
ABBEY
Dunshillock
Woodside
Rora
Lunderton
Ugie
Water
Newseat
Inverugie
INVERUGIE CASTLE
UGIE SALMON FISH HOUSE
A950
B   **U**   **C**   **H**   **A**   **N**
Maud
MAUD
RAILWAY
MUSEUM
B9029
B9106
Backhill of
Clackriach
Old Deer
ABERDEENSHIRE
FARMING
MUSEUM
Mintlaw
South Ugie
Longside
Torterston
A982
Buchanhaven
Peterhead
ARBUTHNOT MUSEUM & ART GALLERY
Keith Inch
Drymuir
Stuartfield
Flushing
Inverquhomery
8
Bulwark
Mains of
Crichie
Millbreck
257
Hillhead of
Cocklaw
Peterhead Bay
E
Nethermuir
A948
Crichie
B9030
Neth
Kinmundy
A950
Invernettie
Sandford
Bay
Kinnadie
Clola
Little Dens
Skelmuir

4   0   5   1   6

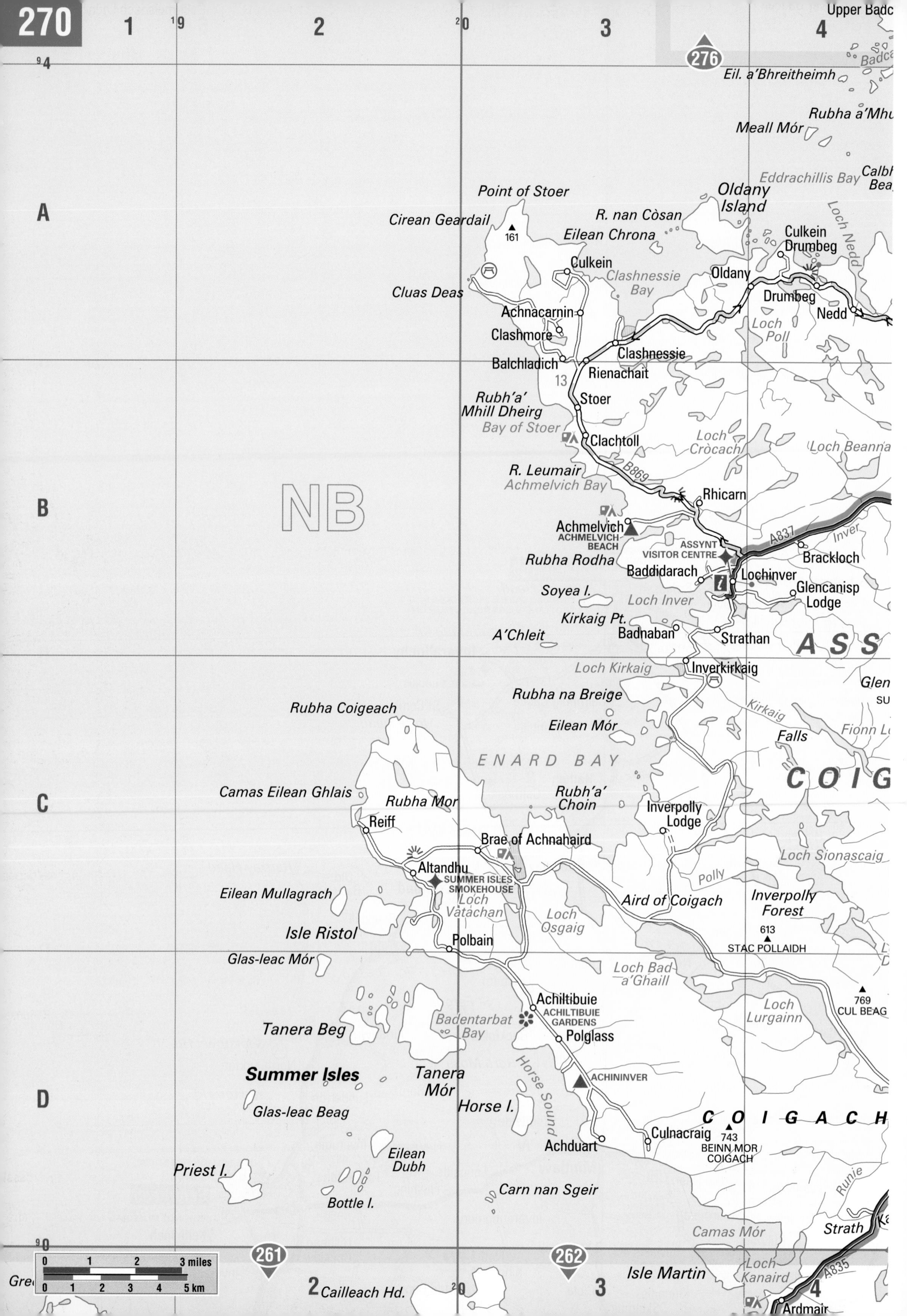
Upper Badc
Eil. a'Bhreitheimh
Rubha a'Mhu
Meall Mór
Eddrachillis Bay
Oldany Island
Point of Stoer
Cirean Geardail
R. nan Còsan
Eilean Chrona
161
Culkein
Drumbeg
Loch Nedd
Culkein
Clashnessie Bay
Oldany
Cluas Deas
Drumbeg
Nedd
Achnacarnin
Clashmore
Loch Poll
Balchladich
Clashnessie
Rienachait
13
Rubh'a' Mhill Dheirg
Stoer
Bay of Stoer
Clachtoll
Loch Cròcach
Loch Beanna
R. Leumair
B869
Achmelvich Bay
Rhicarn
NB
Achmelvich
ACHMELVICH BEACH
ASSYNT VISITOR CENTRE
A837
Inver
Brackloch
Rubha Rodha
Baddidarach
Lochinver
Glencanisp Lodge
Soyea I.
Loch Inver
Kirkaig Pt.
Badnaban
Strathan
A'Chleit
ASS
Loch Kirkaig
Inverkirkaig
Glen
Rubha na Breige
Rubha Coigeach
Kirkaig
Eilean Mór
Falls
Fionn L
ENARD BAY
COIG
Camas Eilean Ghlais
Rubha Mor
Rubh'a' Choin
Inverpolly Lodge
Reiff
Brae of Achnahaird
Loch Sionascaig
Altandhu
SUMMER ISLES SMOKEHOUSE
Polly
Eilean Mullagrach
Loch Vatachan
Aird of Coigach
Inverpolly Forest
Loch Osgaig
Isle Ristol
613
Polbain
STAC POLLAIDH
Glas-leac Mór
Loch Bad a'Ghaill
769
CUL BEAG
Achiltibuie
ACHILTIBUIE GARDENS
Loch Lurgainn
Tanera Beg
Badentarbat Bay
Polglass
Horse Sound
Summer Isles
Tanera Mór
ACHININVER
Glas-leac Beag
Horse I.
COIGACH
Culnacraig
743
BEINN MOR COIGACH
Achduart
Eilean Dubh
Priest I.
Runie
Carn nan Sgeir
Bottle I.
Camas Mór
Strath
Loch Kanaird
A835
Isle Martin
Cailleach Hd.
Ardmair
0 1 2 3 miles
0 1 2 3 4 5 km
276
261
262
1 2 3 4
A B C D

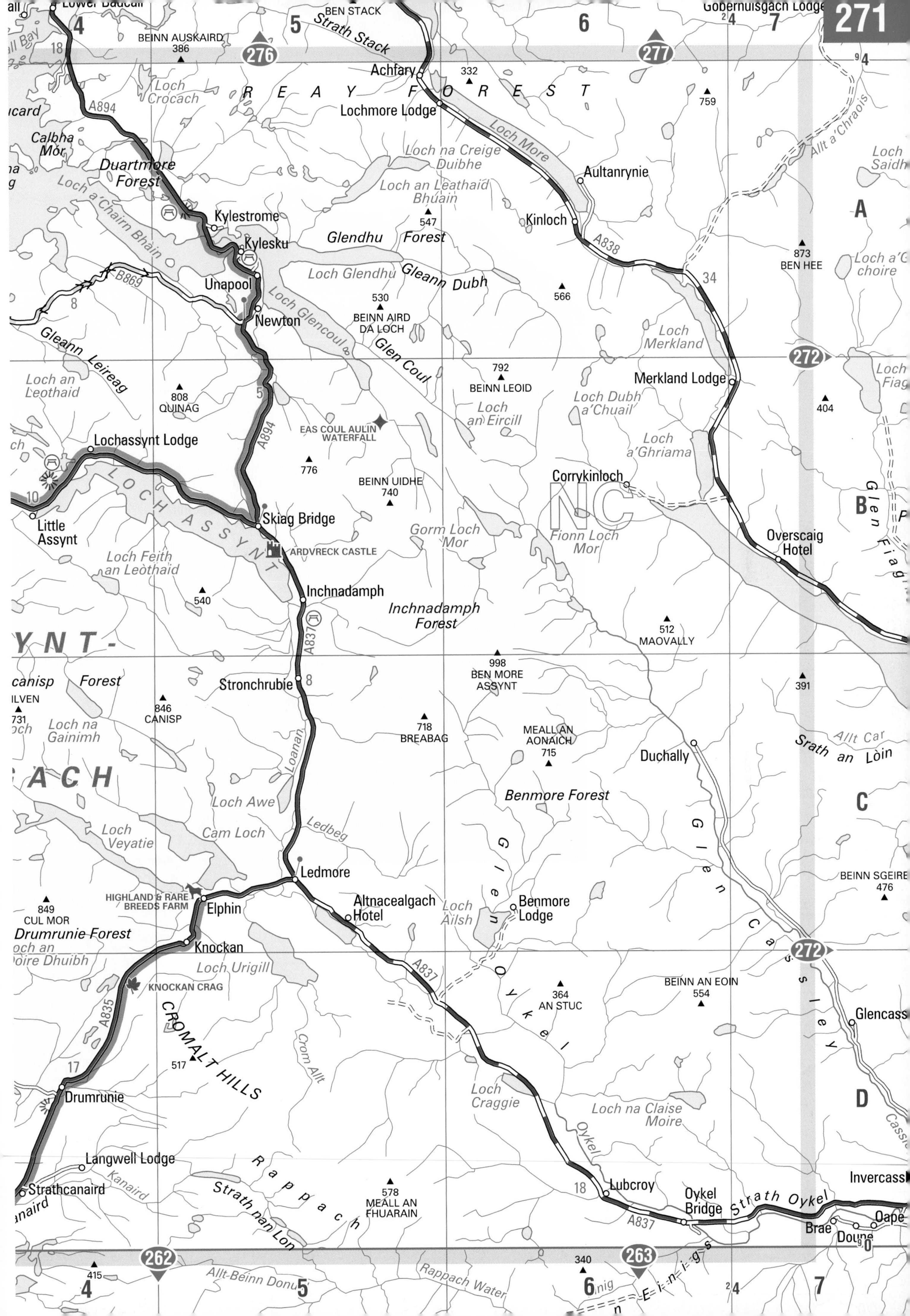

REAY FOREST
Achfary
Lochmore Lodge
Loch More
Aultanrynie
Kinloch
A838
Loch Merkland
Merkland Lodge
BEN HEE
Kylestrome
Kylesku
Unapool
Newton
Loch Glendhu
Glendhu Forest
Loch Glencoul
Glen Coul
EAS COUL AULIN WATERFALL
BEINN LEOID
QUINAG
Lochassynt Lodge
LOCH ASSYNT
Skiag Bridge
ARDVRECK CASTLE
Little Assynt
Inchnadamph
Inchnadamph Forest
Corrykinloch
Overscaig Hotel
Fionn Loch Mor
Gorm Loch Mor
BEN MORE ASSYNT
MAOVALLY
Stronchrubie
CANISP
BREABAG
Duchally
Benmore Forest
Loch Awe
Cam Loch
Loch Veyatie
Ledmore
Elphin
HIGHLAND & RARE BREEDS FARM
Knockan
KNOCKAN CRAG
Altnacealgach Hotel
Benmore Lodge
Glen Oykel
Glen Cassley
CUL MOR
Drumrunie Forest
CROMALT HILLS
Drumrunie
Langwell Lodge
Strathcanaird
Strath nan Lon
Rappach
MEALL AN FHUARAIN
Loch Craggie
Lubcroy
Oykel Bridge
Strath Oykel
A837
A835
A894
B869
Glencassley
Invercassley

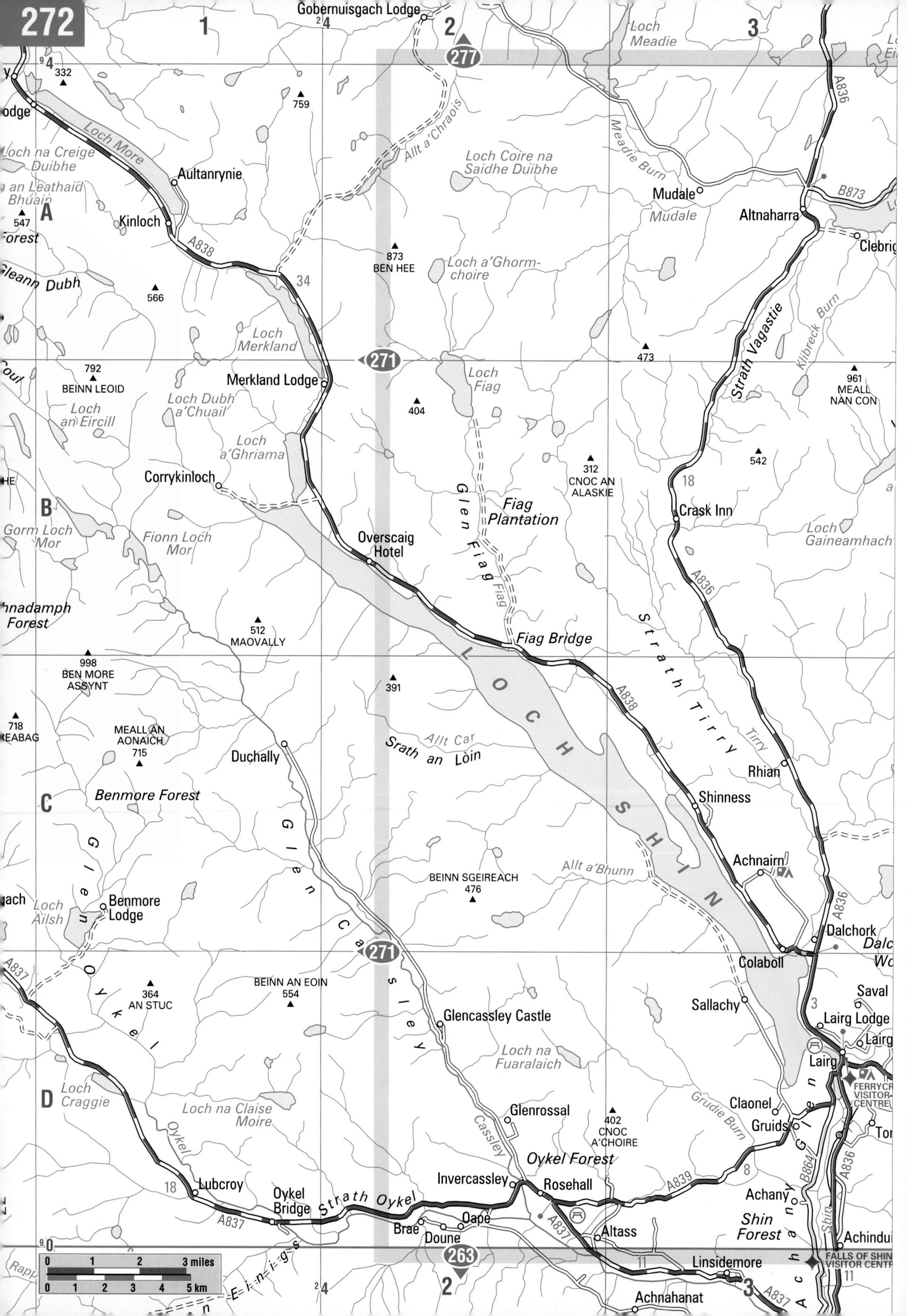
Gobernuisgach Lodge
277
Loch Meadie
Loch More
Aultanrynie
Kinloch
A838
Loch na Creige Duibhe
Allt a'Chraois
Loch Coire na Saidhe Duibhe
Meadie Burn
Mudale
Altnaharra
B873
Clebrig
873
BEN HEE
Loch a'Ghorm-choire
Loch Merkland
Merkland Lodge
271
Loch Fiag
Strath Vagastie
Kilbreck Burn
961
MEALL NAN CON
792
BEINN LEOID
Loch an Eircill
Loch Dubh a'Chuail
Loch a'Ghriama
Corrykinloch
Glen Fiag
Fiag Plantation
312
CNOC AN ALASKIE
Crask Inn
Loch Gaineamhach
Gorm Loch Mor
Fionn Loch Mor
Overscaig Hotel
A836
Forest
512
MAOVALLY
Fiag Bridge
Strath Tirry
998
BEN MORE ASSYNT
LOCH SHIN
391
718
MEALL AN AONAICH
715
Allt Car
Srath an Lòin
Duchally
Rhian
Benmore Forest
Shinness
Glen Cassley
Achnairn
Allt a'Bhunn
BEINN SGEIREACH
476
Loch Ailsh
Benmore Lodge
Glen Oykel
Dalchork
Colaboll
A837
364
AN STUC
BEINN AN EOIN
554
Glencassley Castle
Sallachy
Saval
Lairg Lodge
Lairg
Loch na Fuaralaich
Grudie Burn
FERRYCROFT VISITOR CENTRE
Loch Craggie
Loch na Claise Moire
Glenrossal
402
CNOC A'CHOIRE
Claonel
Gruids
Oykel
Cassley
Oykel Forest
A839
B864
Lubcroy
Oykel Bridge
Strath Oykel
Invercassley
Rosehall
Achany
Shin Forest
Brae
Doune
Oape
Altass
Achinduich
263
Linsidemore
FALLS OF SHIN VISITOR CENTRE
Achnahanat
0 1 2 3 miles
0 1 2 3 4 5 km

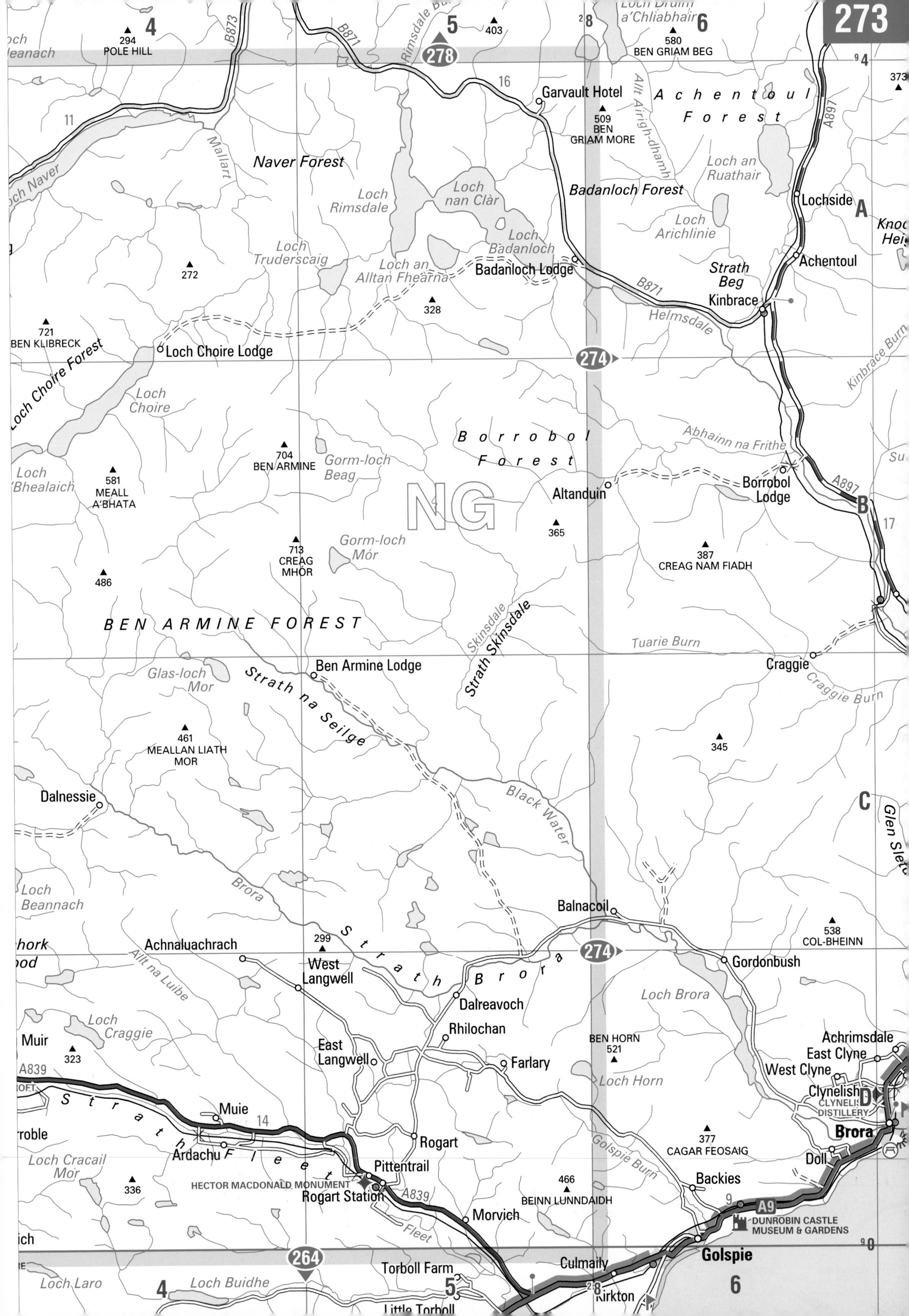
POLE HILL
294
B873
B871
Rimsdale Burn
278
403
Loch Druim a'Chliabhair
580
BEN GRIAM BEG
A897
Garvault Hotel
Achentoul Forest
509
BEN GRIAM MORE
Allt Airigh-dhamh
Loch an Ruathair
Naver Forest
Mallart
Loch Naver
Loch Rimsdale
Loch nan Clàr
Badanloch Forest
Lochside
Loch Arichlinie
Loch Badanloch
Loch Truderscaig
272
Loch an Alltan Fhearna
Badanloch Lodge
Achentoul
Strath Beg
Kinbrace
328
721
BEN KLIBRECK
Loch Choire Forest
Loch Choire Lodge
Helmsdale
274
Kinbrace Burn
Loch Choire
Borrobol Forest
Abhainn na Frithe
Loch Bhealaich
581
MEALL A'BHATA
704
BEN ARMINE
Gorm-loch Beag
NG
Altanduin
Borrobol Lodge
365
17
713
CREAG MHÒR
Gorm-loch Mór
387
CREAG NAM FIADH
486
BEN ARMINE FOREST
Skinsdale
Strath Skinsdale
Tuarie Burn
Glas-loch Mor
Ben Armine Lodge
Strath na Seilge
Craggie
Craggie Burn
461
MEALLAN LIATH MOR
345
Dalnessie
Black Water
Glen Sletdale
Loch Beannach
Brora
Balnacoil
538
COL-BHEINN
299
Achnaluachrach
West Langwell
Strath Brora
Allt na Luibe
Gordonbush
Dalreavoch
Loch Brora
Loch Craggie
Muir
323
Rhilochan
BEN HORN
521
Achrimsdale
East Clyne
East Langwell
Farlary
West Clyne
A839
Loch Horn
Clynelish
CLYNELISH DISTILLERY
Muie
14
Strath Fleet
Brora
Rogart
377
CAGAR FEOSAIG
Ardachu
Golspie Burn
Loch Cracail Mor
Pittentrail
Doll
466
Backies
336
HECTOR MACDONALD MONUMENT
Rogart Station
BEINN LUNNDAIDH
A9
DUNROBIN CASTLE MUSEUM & GARDENS
Morvich
Fleet
264
Torboll Farm
Culmaily
Golspie
Loch Laro
Loch Buidhe
Kirkton
Little Torboll

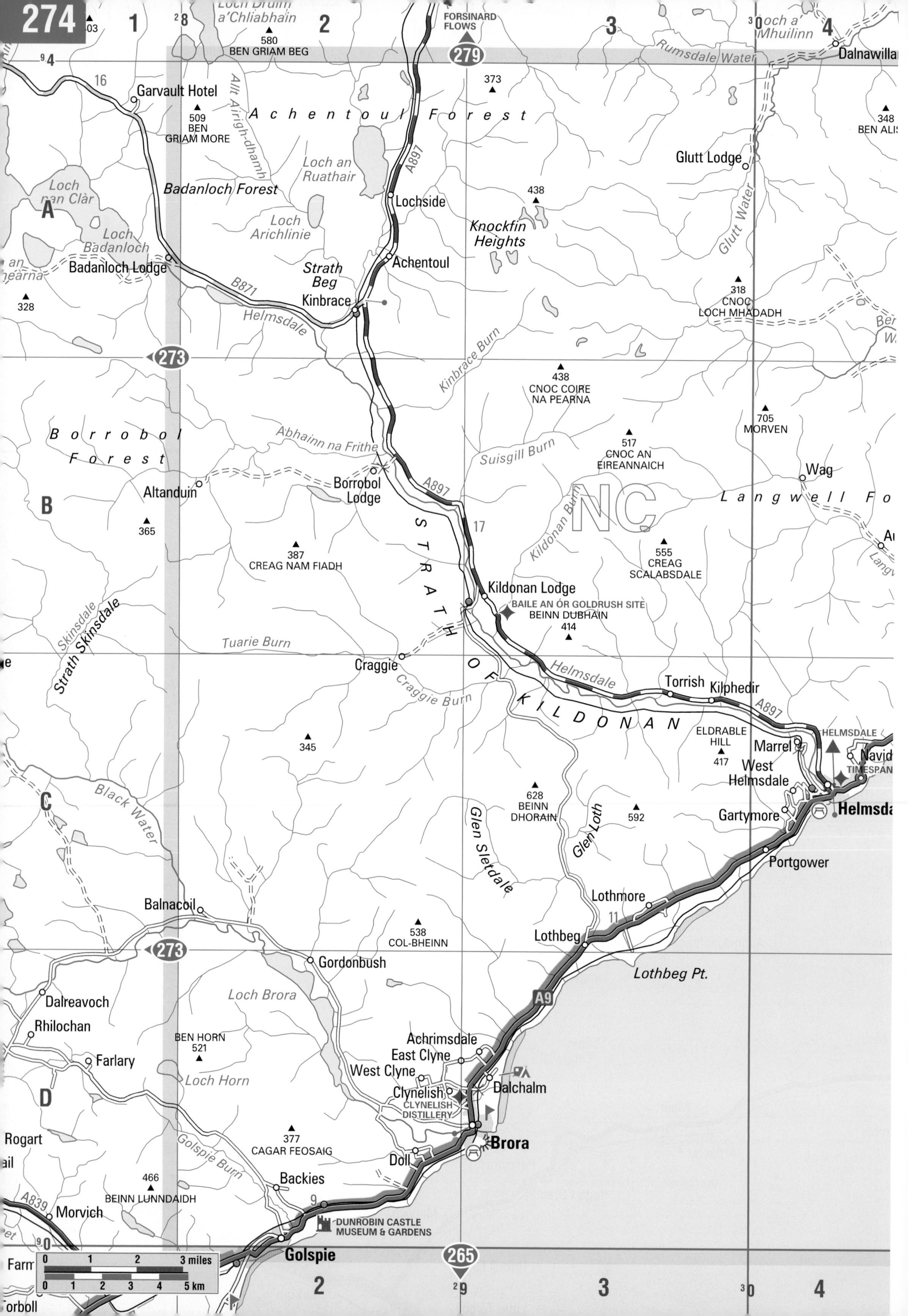
Garvault Hotel
Achentoul Forest
Badanloch Forest
Loch an Ruathair
Loch Arichlinie
Lochside
Achentoul
Kinbrace
Strath Beg
Badanloch Lodge
Loch Badanloch
Loch nan Clàr
B871
Helmsdale
Knockfin Heights
Glutt Lodge
Glutt Water
Rumsdale Water
Dalnawillan
BEN GRIAM BEG
580
509 BEN GRIAM MORE
Allt Airigh-dhamh
A897
FORSINARD FLOWS
279
273
Borrobol Forest
Altanduin
Borrobol Lodge
Abhainn na Frithe
Suisgill Burn
Kinbrace Burn
CNOC COIRE NA PEARNA
517 CNOC AN EIREANNAICH
705 MORVEN
Wag
Langwell Fo
NC
STRATH OF KILDONAN
Kildonan Burn
387 CREAG NAM FIADH
555 CREAG SCALABSDALE
Kildonan Lodge
BAILE AN ÒR GOLDRUSH SITE
BEINN DUBHAIN 414
Strath Skinsdale
Skinsdale
Tuarie Burn
Craggie
Craggie Burn
Torrish
Kilphedir
ELDRABLE HILL 417
Marrel
West Helmsdale
HELMSDALE
TIMESPAN
Navid
Helmsda
Gartymore
Portgower
628 BEINN DHORAIN
Glen Loth
Glen Sletdale
Black Water
Lothmore
Lothbeg
Lothbeg Pt.
Balnacoil
538 COL-BHEINN
Gordonbush
Loch Brora
A9
Dalreavoch
Rhilochan
Farlary
BEN HORN 521
Loch Horn
Achrimsdale
East Clyne
West Clyne
Clynelish
CLYNELISH DISTILLERY
Dalchalm
Brora
377 CAGAR FEOSAIG
Doll
Golspie Burn
Backies
466 BEINN LUNNDAIDH
A839
Morvich
Rogart
DUNROBIN CASTLE MUSEUM & GARDENS
Golspie
265
3 miles
5 km

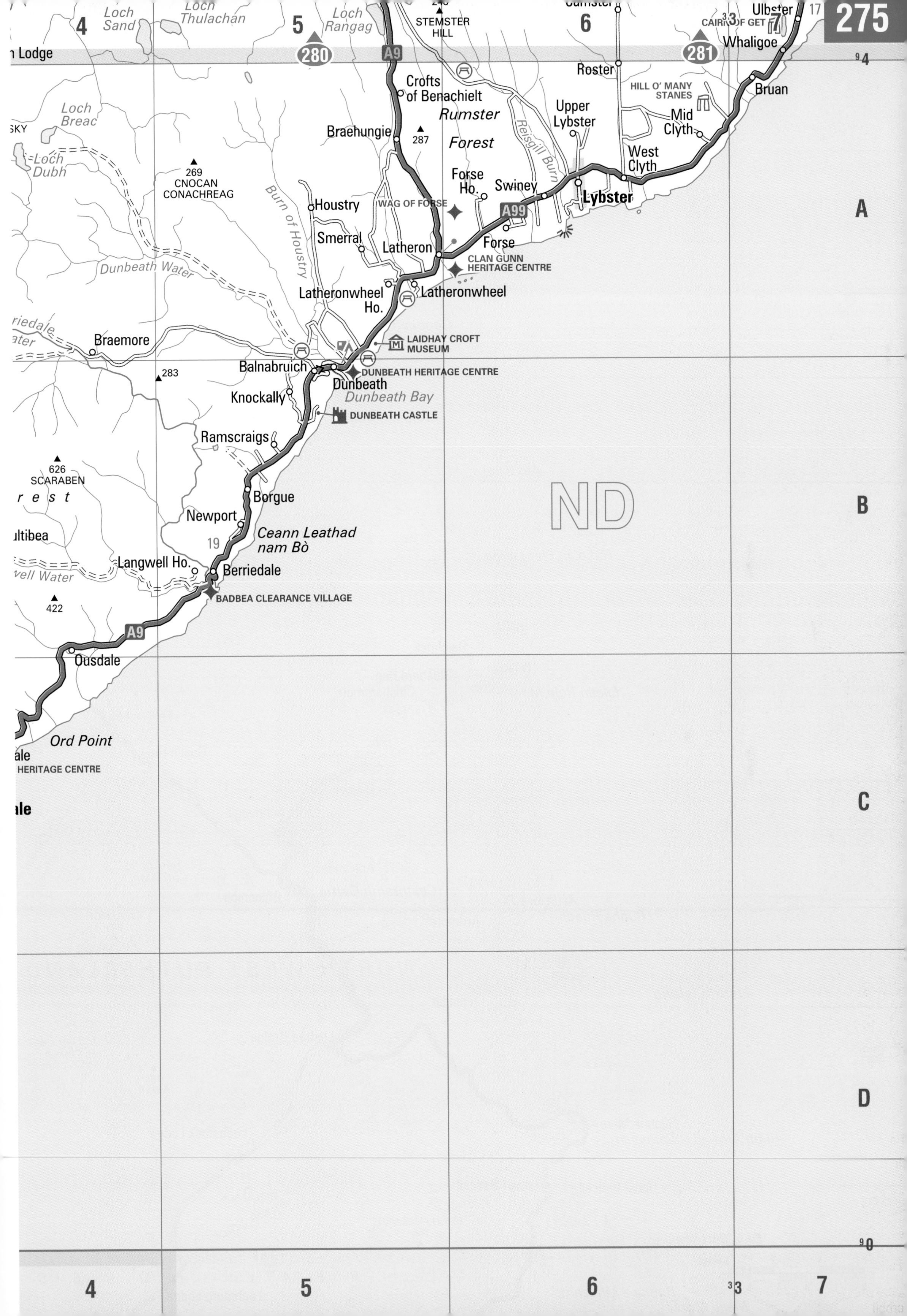

4 **5** **6** **7**

Lodge

Loch Sand
Loch Thulachan
Loch Rangag

STEMSTER HILL

Cairn of Get
Ulbster

CAIRN OF GET

Whaligoe

Roster

Crofts of Benachielt

Loch Breac

Rumster Forest

Upper Lybster

Hill O' Many Stanes

Bruan

Braehungie

▲ 287

Mid Clyth

SKY

269 ▲ CNOCAN CONACHREAG

West Clyth

Loch Dubh

Houstry

WAG OF FORSE

Forse Ho.

Swiney

Lybster

Smerral

Latheron

Forse

A99

A

Dunbeath Water

CLAN GUNN HERITAGE CENTRE

Latheronwheel Ho.

Latheronwheel

iedale ater

LAIDHAY CROFT MUSEUM

Braemore

▲ 283

Balnabruich

DUNBEATH HERITAGE CENTRE

Dunbeath

Knockally

Dunbeath Bay

DUNBEATH CASTLE

Ramscraigs

626 ▲ SCARABEN

B

rest

Borgue

ND

Newport

Ceann Leathad nam Bò

ultibea

19

Langwell Ho.

Berriedale

▲ 422

BADBEA CLEARANCE VILLAGE

ell Water

A9

Ousdale

C

Ord Point

HERITAGE CENTRE

ale

D

4 **5** **6** **7**

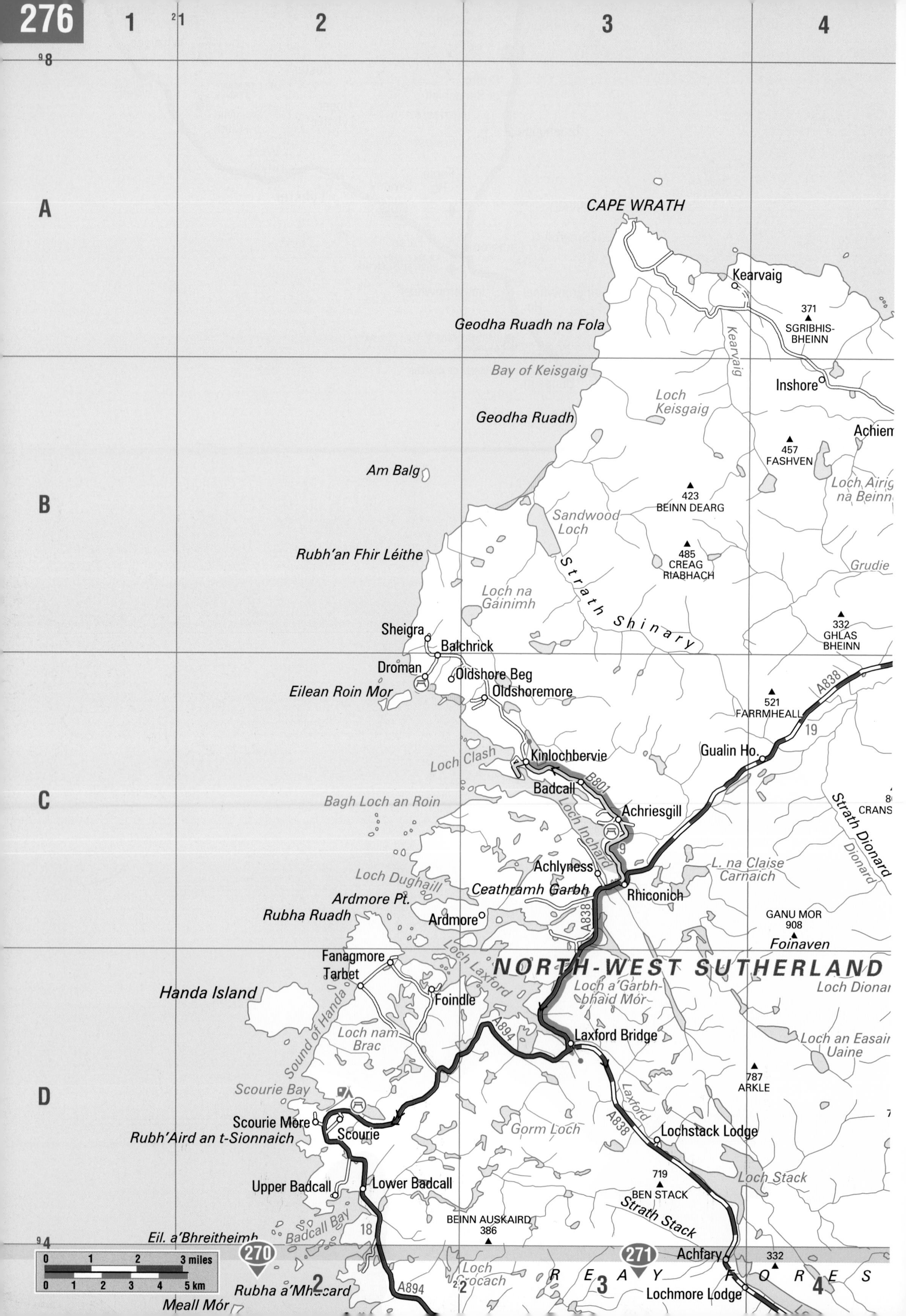
CAPE WRATH
Kearvaig
371
SGRIBHIS-BHEINN
Geodha Ruadh na Fola
Kearvaig
Bay of Keisgaig
Inshore
Loch Keisgaig
Geodha Ruadh
457
FASHVEN
Am Balg
Loch Airig na Beinn
423
BEINN DEARG
Sandwood Loch
485
CREAG RIABHACH
Rubh'an Fhir Léithe
Grudie
Strath Shinary
Loch na Gainimh
332
GHLAS BHEINN
Sheigra
Balchrick
Droman
Oldshore Beg
Oldshoremore
Eilean Roin Mor
521
FARRMHEALL
A838
19
Gualin Ho.
Kinlochbervie
Loch Clash
Badcall
B801
Bagh Loch an Roin
Achriesgill
Loch Inchard
Strath Dionard
Dionard
CRANS
Achlyness
L. na Claise Carnaich
Loch Dughaill
Ceathramh Garbh
Rhiconich
Ardmore Pt.
Rubha Ruadh
Ardmore
GANU MOR
908
Foinaven
Fanagmore
Tarbet
NORTH-WEST SUTHERLAND
Loch Laxford
Handa Island
Loch a'Garbh-bhaid Mór
Loch Dionar
Foindle
Sound of Handa
A894
Loch nam Brac
Laxford Bridge
Loch an Easain Uaine
787
ARKLE
Scourie Bay
Laxford
Scourie More
Scourie
Gorm Loch
A838
Rubh'Aird an t-Sionnaich
Lochstack Lodge
Loch Stack
Upper Badcall
Lower Badcall
719
BEN STACK
Strath Stack
BEINN AUSKAIRD
386
Badcall Bay
18
Eil. a'Bhreitheimh
0 1 2 3 miles
0 1 2 3 4 5 km
270
271
Achfary
332
Loch Crocach
REAY FOREST
Rubha a'Mhucard
Lochmore Lodge
A894
Meall Mór
1
2
3
4
A
B
C
D

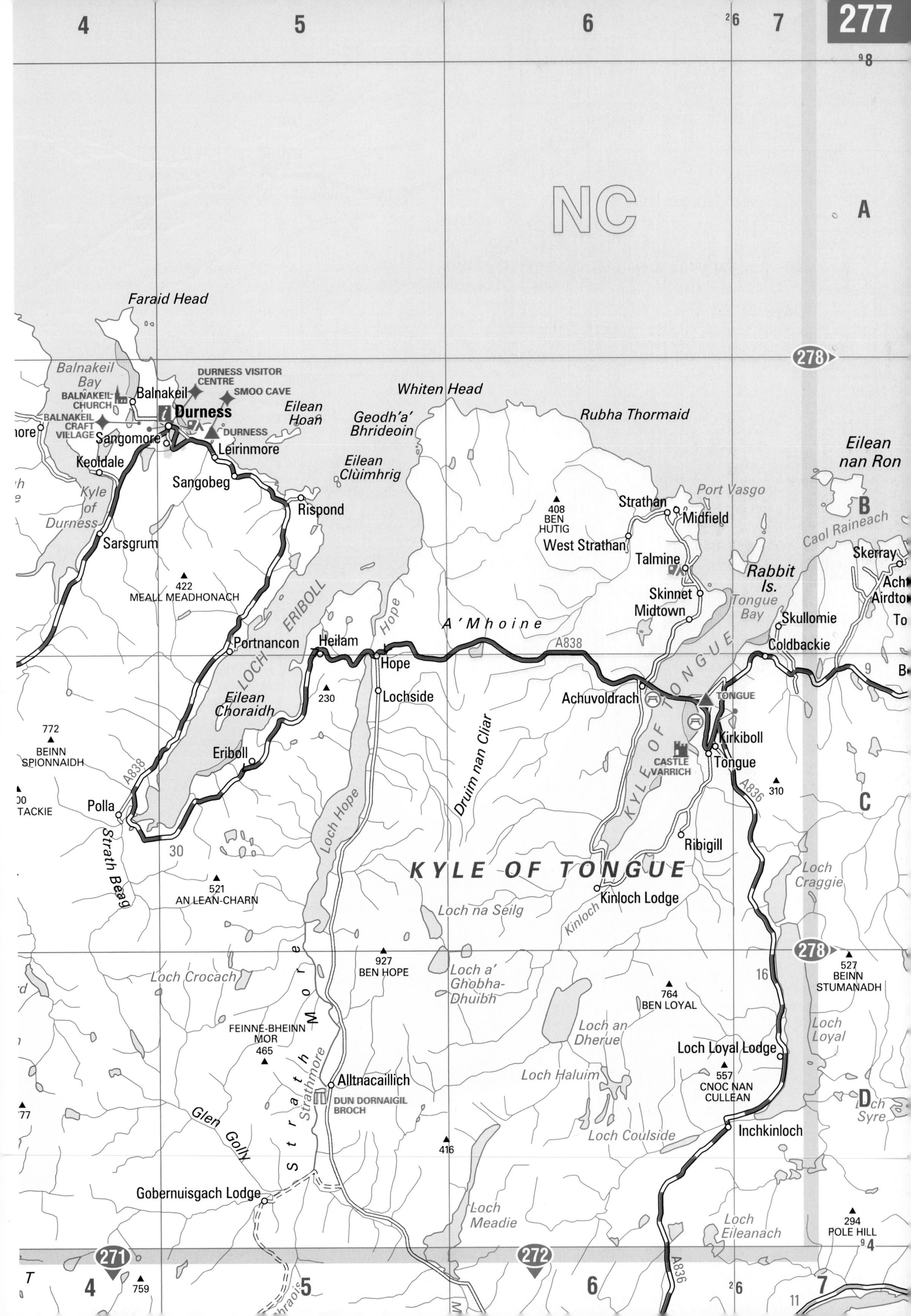
4
5
6
7
NC
A
B
C
D
Faraid Head
Balnakeil Bay
BALNAKEIL CHURCH
Balnakeil
DURNESS VISITOR CENTRE
SMOO CAVE
Durness
DURNESS
BALNAKEIL CRAFT VILLAGE
Sangomore
Leirinmore
Keoldale
Sangobeg
Kyle of Durness
Rispond
Sarsgrum
Eilean Hoan
Whiten Head
Geodh'a' Bhrideoin
Eilean Clùimhrig
Rubha Thormaid
Eilean nan Ron
Port Vasgo
Strathan
Midfield
408 BEN HUTIG
West Strathan
Talmine
Caol Raineach
Skerray
Rabbit Is.
Skinnet
Midtown
Tongue Bay
Skullomie
Coldbackie
422 MEALL MEADHONACH
LOCH ERIBOLL
Portnancon
Heilam
Hope
A'Mhoine
A838
Hope
Lochside
230
Eilean Choraidh
Achuvoldrach
TONGUE
KYLE OF TONGUE
Kirkiboll
Tongue
CASTLE VARRICH
772 BEINN SPIONNAIDH
Eriboll
A838
Polla
TACKIE
Strath Beag
Loch Hope
Druim nan Cliar
A836
310
Ribigill
30
521 AN LEAN-CHARN
KYLE OF TONGUE
Loch Craggie
Kinloch Lodge
Kinloch
Loch na Seilg
927 BEN HOPE
Loch a' Ghobha-Dhuibh
Loch Crocach
527 BEINN STUMANADH
764 BEN LOYAL
16
FEINNE-BHEINN MOR 465
Strath More
Loch an Dherue
Loch Loyal Lodge
Loch Loyal
557 CNOC NAN CULLEAN
Alltnacaillich
Strathmore
DUN DORNAIGIL BROCH
Loch Haluim
Loch Syre
Glen Golly
Loch Coulside
Inchkinloch
416
Gobernuisgach Lodge
Loch Meadie
Loch Eileanach
294 POLE HILL
A836
759
11
9

278
278
271
272

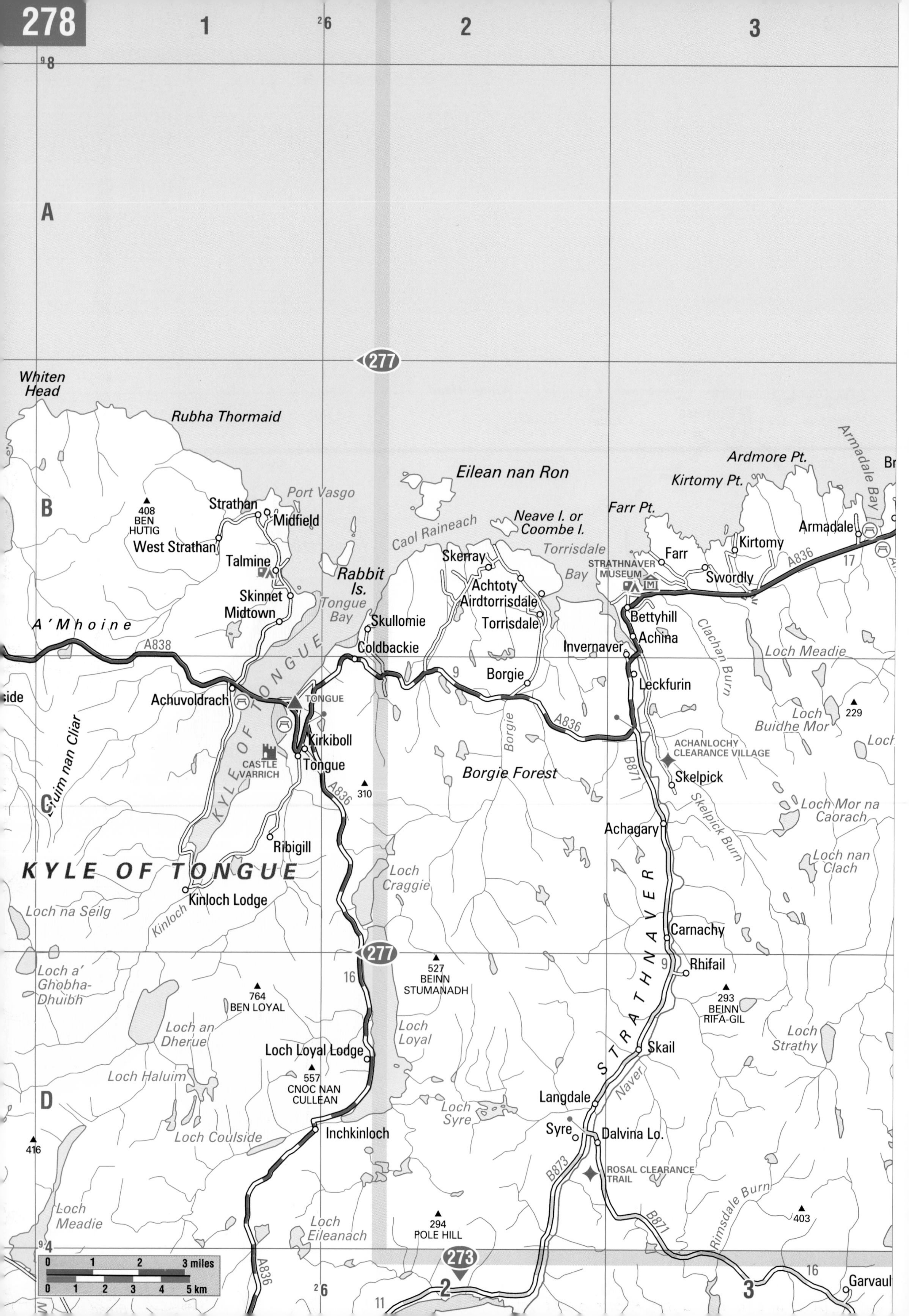
A
B
C
D
1
2
3
277
273
Whiten Head
Rubha Thormaid
Eilean nan Ron
Ardmore Pt.
Kirtomy Pt.
Armadale Bay
Port Vasgo
Strathan
Midfield
408 BEN HUTIG
West Strathan
Talmine
Skinnet
Midtown
Rabbit Is.
Tongue Bay
Caol Raineach
Neave I. or Coombe I.
Farr Pt.
Torrisdale Bay
Skerray
Achtoty
Airdtorrisdale
Torrisdale
Farr
Kirtomy
Armadale
Swordly
STRATHNAVER MUSEUM
A836
17
Bettyhill
Achina
Invernaver
Clachan Burn
Loch Meadie
A'Mhoine
A838
Skullomie
Coldbackie
Borgie
Leckfurin
Achuvoldrach
TONGUE
Kirkiboll
Tongue
CASTLE VARRICH
KYLE OF TONGUE
Borgie Forest
Borgie
B871
ACHANLOCHY CLEARANCE VILLAGE
Skelpick
Skelpick Burn
Loch Buidhe Mor
229
Loch Mor na Caorach
Loch nan Clach
310
Ribigill
Achagary
Loch Craggie
STRATHNAVER
Kinloch Lodge
Kinloch
Loch na Seilg
Carnachy
Rhifail
527 BEINN STUMANADH
293 BEINN RIFA-GIL
Loch a' Ghobha-Dhuibh
764 BEN LOYAL
16
Loch an Dherue
Loch Loyal Lodge
Loch Loyal
Loch Strathy
Skail
Loch Haluim
557 CNOC NAN CULLEAN
Naver
Langdale
Loch Syre
Syre
Dalvina Lo.
Inchkinloch
Loch Coulside
416
ROSAL CLEARANCE TRAIL
B873
Rimsdale Burn
403
Loch Meadie
Loch Eileanach
294 POLE HILL
Garvault
0 1 2 3 miles
0 1 2 3 4 5 km

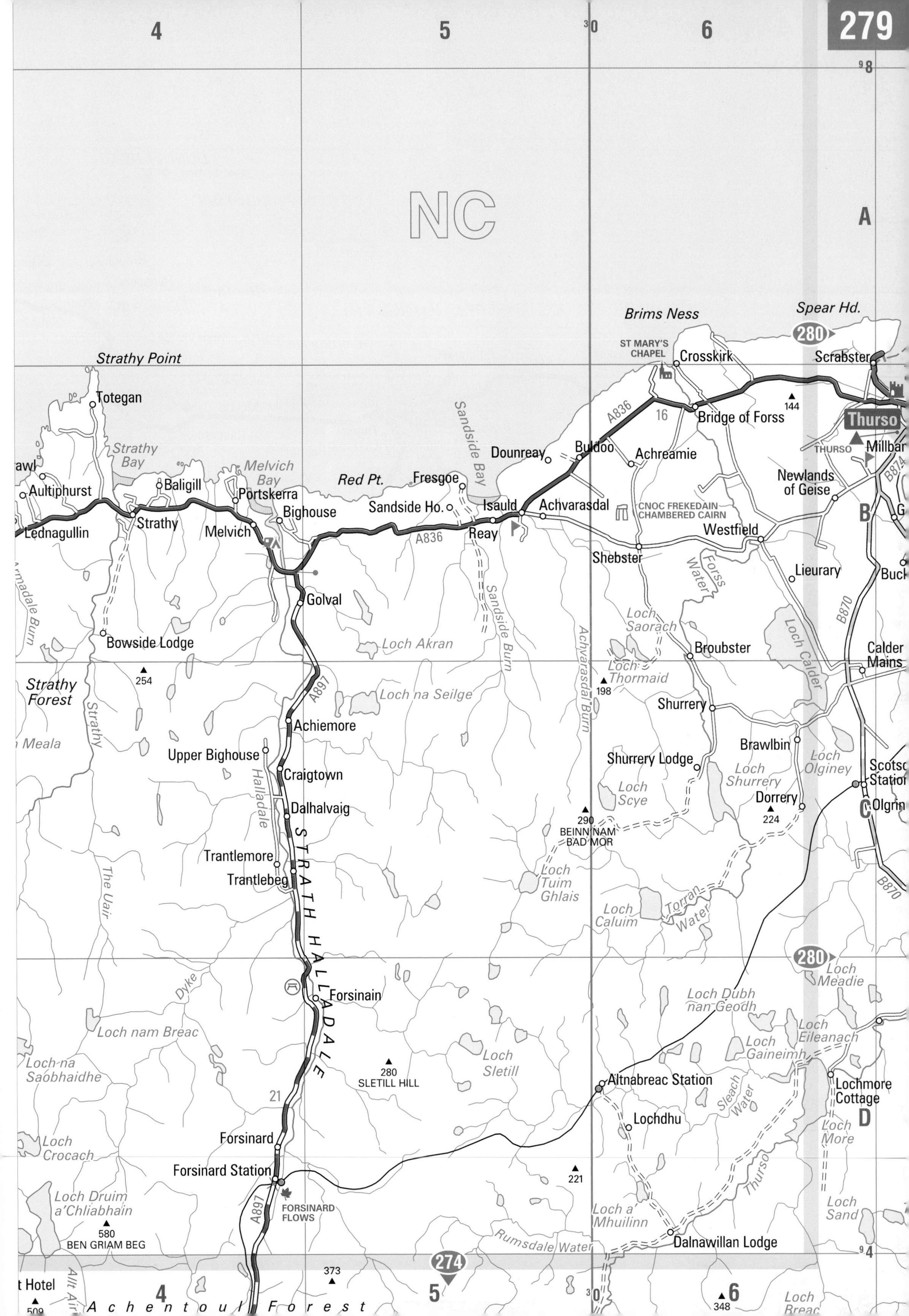

4   5   30   6

98

NC

A

Brims Ness   Spear Hd.

280

ST MARY'S CHAPEL   Crosskirk   Scrabster

Strathy Point

A836   16   Bridge of Forss ▲144

Thurso

Totegan   Dounreay   Buldoo   Achreamie   THURSO ▲   Millbar

Strathy Bay   Melvich Bay   Red Pt.   Fresgoe   Sandside Bay   Newlands of Geise   B874

awl   Aultiphurst   Baligill   Portskerra   Bighouse   Sandside Ho.   Isauld   Achvarasdal   Westfield   B

Lednagullin   Strathy   Melvich   A836   Reay   CNOC FREKEDAIN CHAMBERED CAIRN   Buck

G

Shebster   Lieurary

Golval   Forss Water   Loch Calder

Loch Akran   Sandside Burn   Loch Saorach   Calder Mains

Bowside Lodge   Broubster

Strathy Forest   ▲254   Loch Thormaid   ▲198   Shurrery

Meala   A897   Loch na Seilge   Achvarasdal Burn   Brawlbin   Loch Olginey   Scotsc Station

Achiemore   Shurrery Lodge   Loch Shurrery   Dorrery   C

Upper Bighouse   Halladale   Loch Scye   ▲224   Olgrin

Craigtown   STRATH HALLADALE

Dalhalvaig   ▲290 BEINN NAM BAD MOR

The Uair   Trantlemore   Loch Tuim Ghlais   B870

Trantlebeg   Loch Caluim   Torran Water

Dyke   280   Loch Meadie

Loch nam Breac   Forsinain   Loch Dubh nan Geodh   Loch Eileanach

Loch na Saobhaidhe   ▲280 SLETILL HILL   Loch Sletill   Loch Gaineimh

Altnabreac Station   Sleach Water   Lochmore Cottage   D

21   Lochdhu   Loch More

Loch Crocach   Forsinard   Thurso

Forsinard Station   ▲221   Loch Sand

Loch Druim a'Chliabhain   A897   FORSINARD FLOWS   Dalnawillan Lodge

▲580 BEN GRIAM BEG   Rumsdale Water   94

t Hotel   4   373   274   5   30   ▲348   6   Loch Breac

509   A c h e n t o u l   F o r e s t

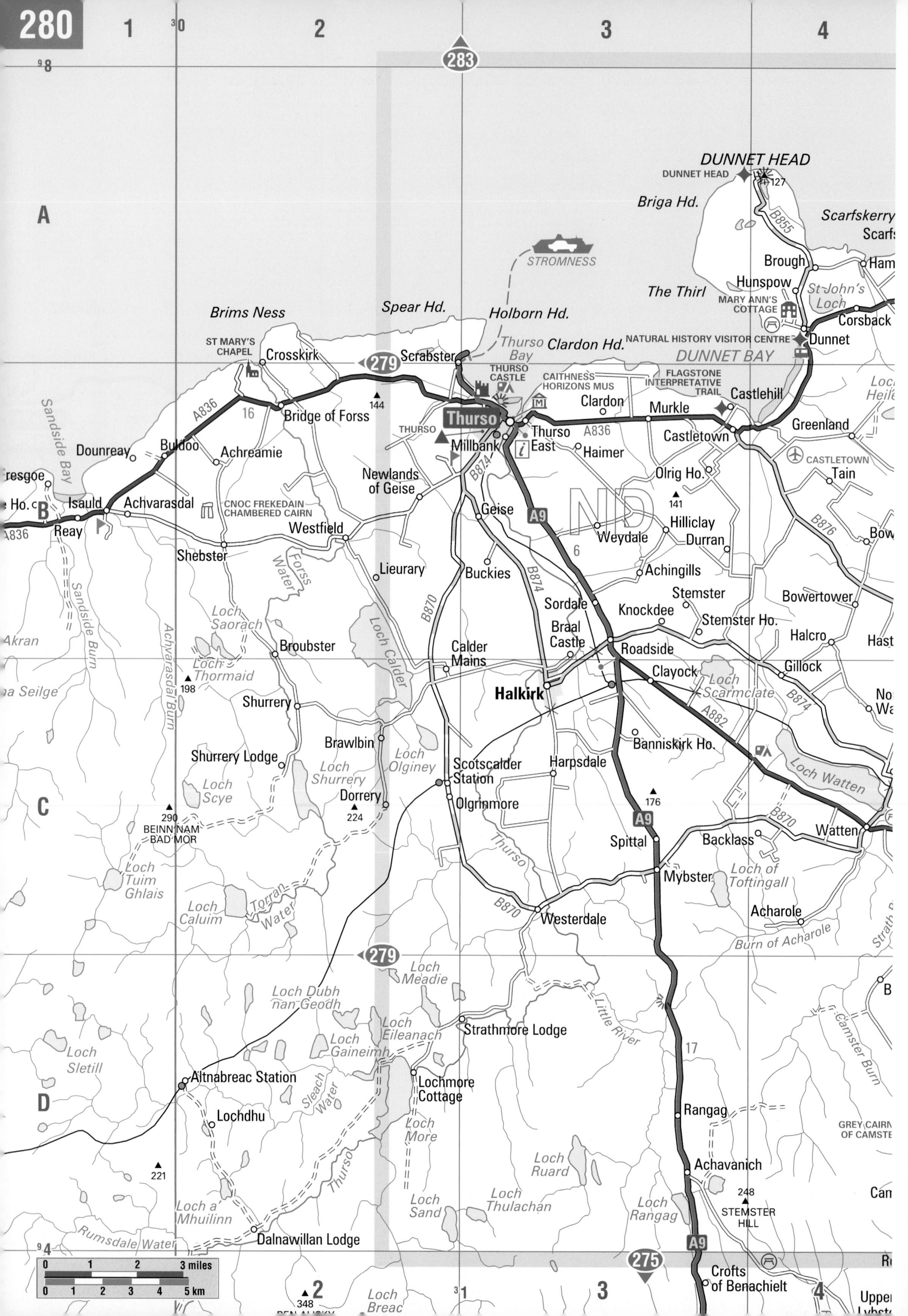
1
2
3
4
283
A
DUNNET HEAD
DUNNET HEAD
127
Briga Hd.
B855
Scarfskerry
STROMNESS
Brough
Ham
Hunspow
St John's Loch
The Thirl
MARY ANN'S COTTAGE
Corsback
Dunnet
Brims Ness
Spear Hd.
Holborn Hd.
Thurso Bay
Clardon Hd.
NATURAL HISTORY VISITOR CENTRE
DUNNET BAY
ST MARY'S CHAPEL
Crosskirk
279
Scrabster
THURSO CASTLE
CAITHNESS HORIZONS MUS
FLAGSTONE INTERPRETATIVE TRAIL
Castlehill
Clardon
Murkle
144
A836
16
Bridge of Forss
Thurso
THURSO
Millbank
Thurso East
A836
Haimer
Castletown
Greenland
Sandside Bay
Dounreay
Buldoo
Achreamie
CASTLETOWN
Olrig Ho.
Tain
Newlands of Geise
B874
Fresgoe
141
Isauld
Achvarasdal
CNOC FREKEDAIN CHAMBERED CAIRN
Geise
ND
Hilliclay
B876
B
Reay
A836
Westfield
A9
Weydale
Durran
Shebster
6
Forss Water
Lieurary
Buckies
B874
Achingills
Sandside Burn
B870
Stemster
Bowertower
Loch Saorach
Sordale
Knockdee
Stemster Ho.
Akran
Achvarasdal Burn
Loch Calder
Braal Castle
Broubster
Calder Mains
Roadside
Halcro
Loch Thormaid
198
Clayock
Loch Scarmclate
Gillock
Halkirk
B874
Shurrery
A882
Brawlbin
Banniskirk Ho.
Shurrery Lodge
Loch Olginey
Loch Shurrery
Scotscalder Station
Harpsdale
Loch Watten
Loch Scye
Dorrery
224
176
C
290
BEINN NAM BAD MOR
Olgrinmore
A9
B870
Watten
Thurso
Spittal
Backlass
Loch Tuim Ghlais
Mybster
Loch of Toftingall
Loch Caluim
Torran Water
B870
Westerdale
Acharole
Burn of Acharole
279
Loch Meadie
Loch Dubh nan Geodh
Little River
Loch Eileanach
Strathmore Lodge
Camster Burn
Loch Sletill
Loch Gaineimh
17
Altnabreac Station
Sleach Water
Lochmore Cottage
D
Lochdhu
Rangag
Loch More
GREY CAIRN OF CAMSTER
Loch Ruard
221
Achavanich
Thurso
248
Loch Thulachan
Loch a' Mhuilinn
Loch Sand
Loch Rangag
STEMSTER HILL
Rumsdale Water
Dalnawillan Lodge
A9
275
0 1 2 3 miles
0 1 2 3 4 5 km
348
Loch Breac
Crofts of Benachielt
Upper Lybster

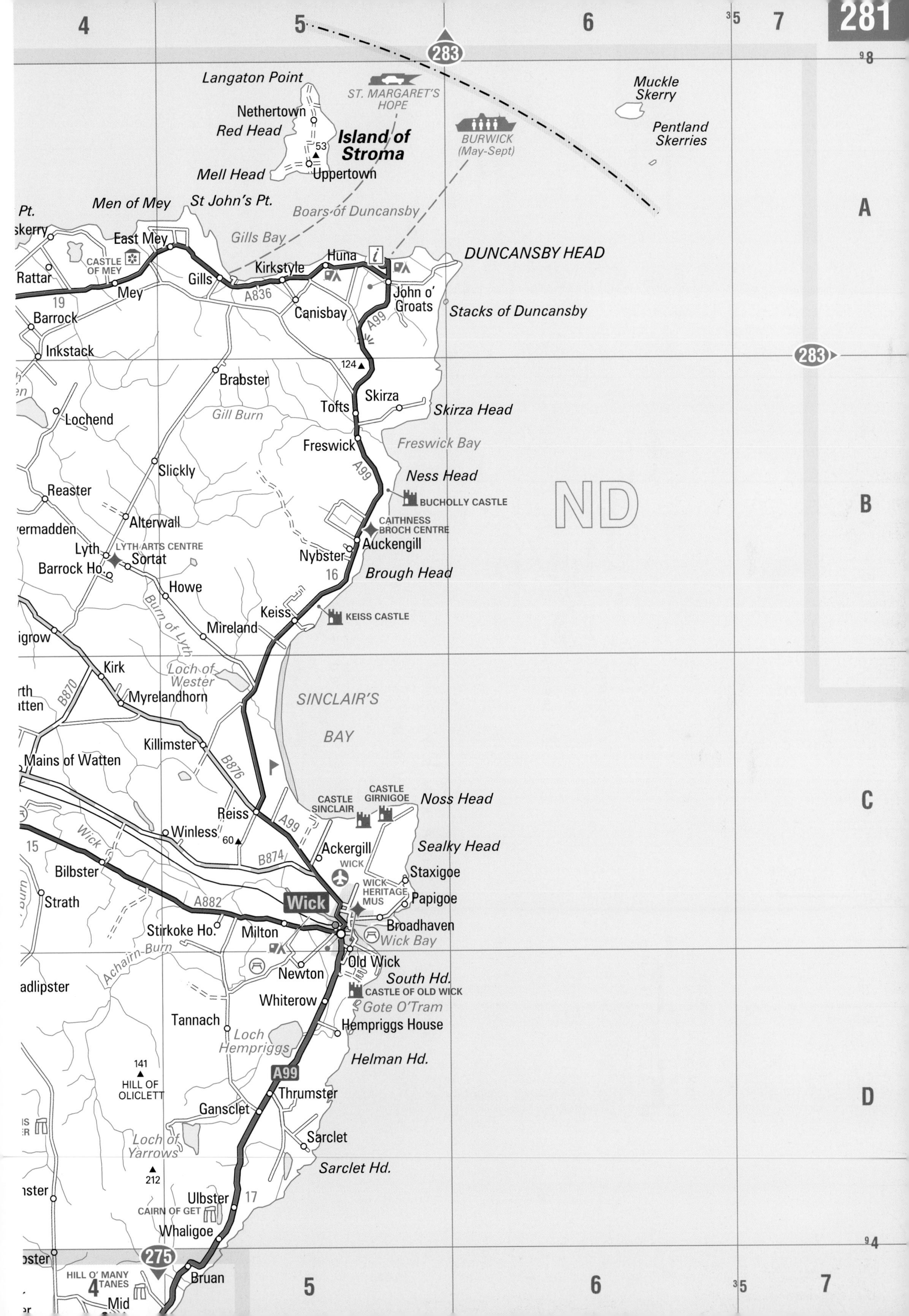

Langaton Point
Nethertown
Red Head
53
Island of Stroma
Mell Head
Uppertown

ST. MARGARET'S HOPE
283

Muckle Skerry
Pentland Skerries

BURWICK (May-Sept)

Men of Mey
St John's Pt.
Boars of Duncansby

DUNCANSBY HEAD

A
Pt.
skerry
Rattar
East Mey
CASTLE OF MEY
Gills
Mey
A836
Kirkstyle
Huna
Canisbay
A99
John o' Groats
Stacks of Duncansby
Barrock
Inkstack

124
Brabster
Gill Burn
Tofts
Skirza
Skirza Head
Freswick
Freswick Bay
A99

ND

B
Lochend
Slickly
Ness Head
Reaster
Alterwall
BUCHOLLY CASTLE
ermadden
Lyth
LYTH ARTS CENTRE
Sortat
CAITHNESS BROCH CENTRE
Barrock Ho.
Howe
Nybster
Auckengill
16
Brough Head
Keiss
KEISS CASTLE
Mireland

igrow
Kirk
Loch of Wester
B870
Myrelandhorn
SINCLAIR'S BAY

C
rth
atten
Killimster
B876

Mains of Watten
Reiss
CASTLE SINCLAIR
CASTLE GIRNIGOE
Noss Head
15
Winless
60
A99
Ackergill
Sealky Head
Bilbster
B874
WICK
Staxigoe
Strath
A882
WICK HERITAGE MUS
Papigoe
Wick
Stirkoke Ho.
Milton
Broadhaven
Wick Bay
Newton
Old Wick
South Hd.
adlipster
Whiterow
CASTLE OF OLD WICK
Gote O'Tram
Tannach
Hempriggs House
Loch Hempriggs
Helman Hd.
141
HILL OF OLICLETT
A99
Gansclet
Thrumster

D

Loch of Yarrows
Sarclet
Sarclet Hd.
212
Ulbster
17
CAIRN OF GET
Whaligoe
275
ster
HILL O' MANY TANES
Bruan
Mid

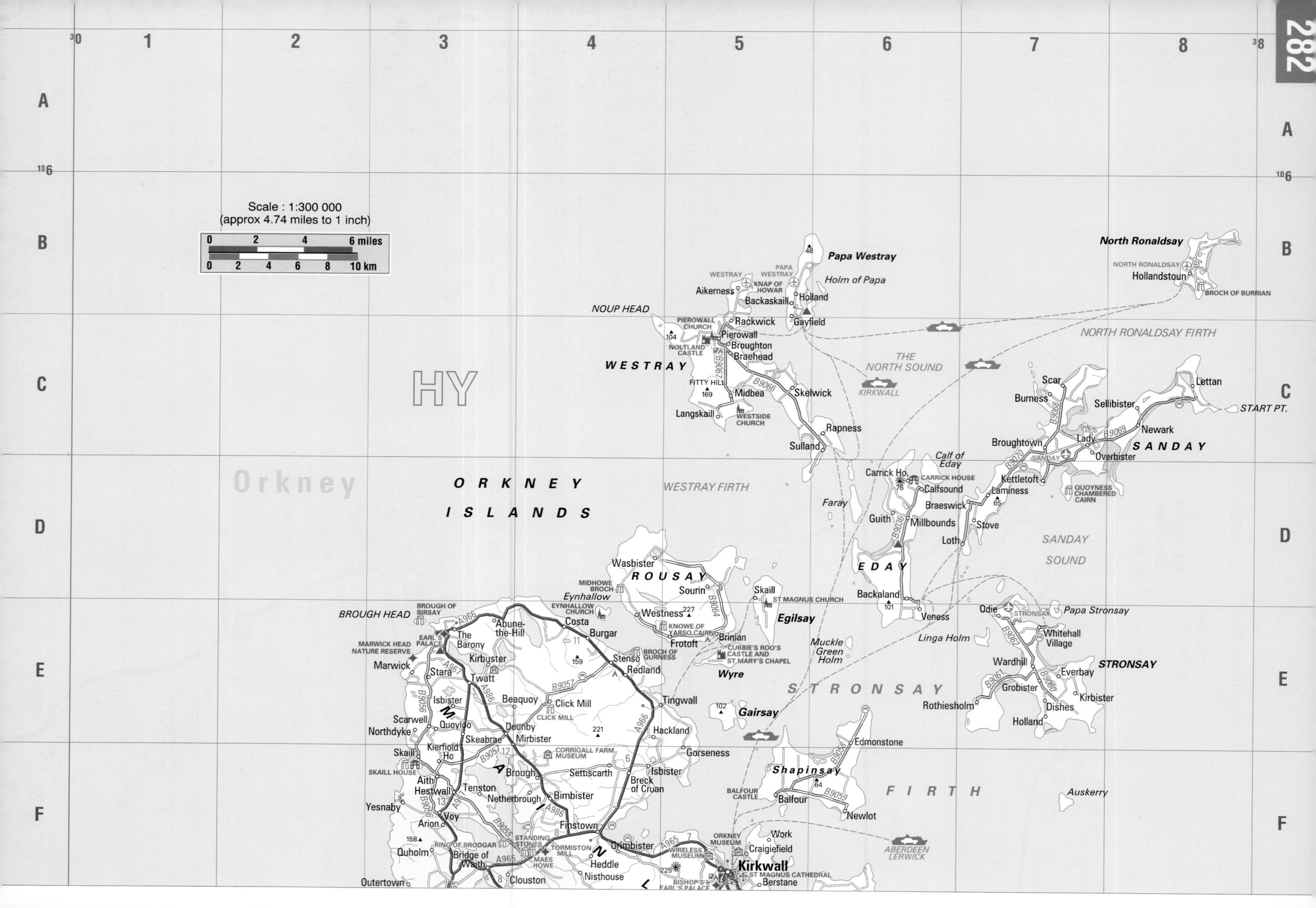

HY

Orkney

ORKNEY ISLANDS

Scale : 1:300 000
(approx 4.74 miles to 1 inch)

0   2   4   6 miles
0   2   4   6   8   10 km

North Ronaldsay

Hollandstoun
NORTH RONALDSAY
BROCH OF BURRIAN

NORTH RONALDSAY FIRTH

SANDAY

START PT.
Lettan
Newark
Sellibister
Overbister
Lady
B9069
QUOYNESS CHAMBERED CAIRN
SANDAY
Scar
Burness
Broughtown
B9068
Kettletoft
Lamiress
Stove
Overbister

Calf of Eday
CARRICK HOUSE
Carrick Ho.
Calfsound
Braeswick
Millbounds
Loth
B9063
Guith
Backaland
Veness
EDAY

Papa Westray
Holm of Papa
Gayfield
Holland
PAPA WESTRAY
KNAP OF HOWAR
48

THE NORTH SOUND

KIRKWALL

Papa Stronsay
Odie
Whitehall Village
Everbay
Kirbister
Dishes
Holland
Wardhill
Grobister
Rothiesholm
STRONSAY
B9062
B9060

SANDAY SOUND

Auskerry

ABERDEEN LERWICK

STRONSAY FIRTH

Linga Holm

Rapness
Skelwick
Midbea
WESTSIDE CHURCH
B9066
Sulland
Langskaill
Brough
Brachead
Rackwick
Backaskaill
Aikerness
PIEROWALL CHURCH
NOLTLAND CASTLE
104
B9067
FITTY HILL
169
Pierowall

WESTRAY

NOUP HEAD

WESTRAY FIRTH

Faray

St Magnus Church
Muckle Green Holm

Egilsay
ST MAGNUS CHURCH
CUBBIE ROO'S CASTLE AND ST MARY'S CHAPEL
Brinian
Wyre
Gairsay
102

Edmonstone
B9068
Balfour
Shapinsay
B9059
54
Newlot
Work

Craigiefield
Berstane
Kirkwall
ST MAGNUS CATHEDRAL
ORKNEY MUSEUM
WIRELESS MUSEUM
BISHOP'S & EARL'S PALACE
A960

Skaill
Westness
KNOWE OF YARSO
Frotoft
BROCH OF GURNESS
227
159
ROUSAY
Sourin
B9064
Washbister
MIDHOWE BROCH
EYNHALLOW CHURCH
Eynhallow
Costa
Burgar
11
Redland
Stenso
Tingwall
Hackland
Gorseness
Isbister
Breck of Cruan
Grimbister
A966
996
BALFOUR CASTLE
Finstown
8
TORMISTON
STANDING STONES
MAES HOWE
Clouston
Quanterness
Heddle
Nisthouse
N
Settiscarth
Bimbister
CORRIGALL FARM MUSEUM
221
A986
Mirbister
Beaquoy
Dounby
CLICK MILL
Click Mill
B9057
M
Broughs
Nethertown
Tenston
A986
B9055
A965
Bridge of Waith
8
RING OF BRODGAR
168
Quoyloo
Kierfold Ho.
Skeabrae
Twatt
A986
Abune-the-Hill
Kirbuster
The Barony
EARL'S PALACE
BROUGH OF BIRSAY
MARWICK HEAD NATURE RESERVE
Marwick
A967
Stara
Isbister
B9056
Scarwell
Northdyke
Skaill
SKAILL HOUSE
Yesnaby
Hestwall
Aith
Arion
A967
Quoyloo
Stromness
Outertown
BROUGH HEAD

Abune-the-Hill

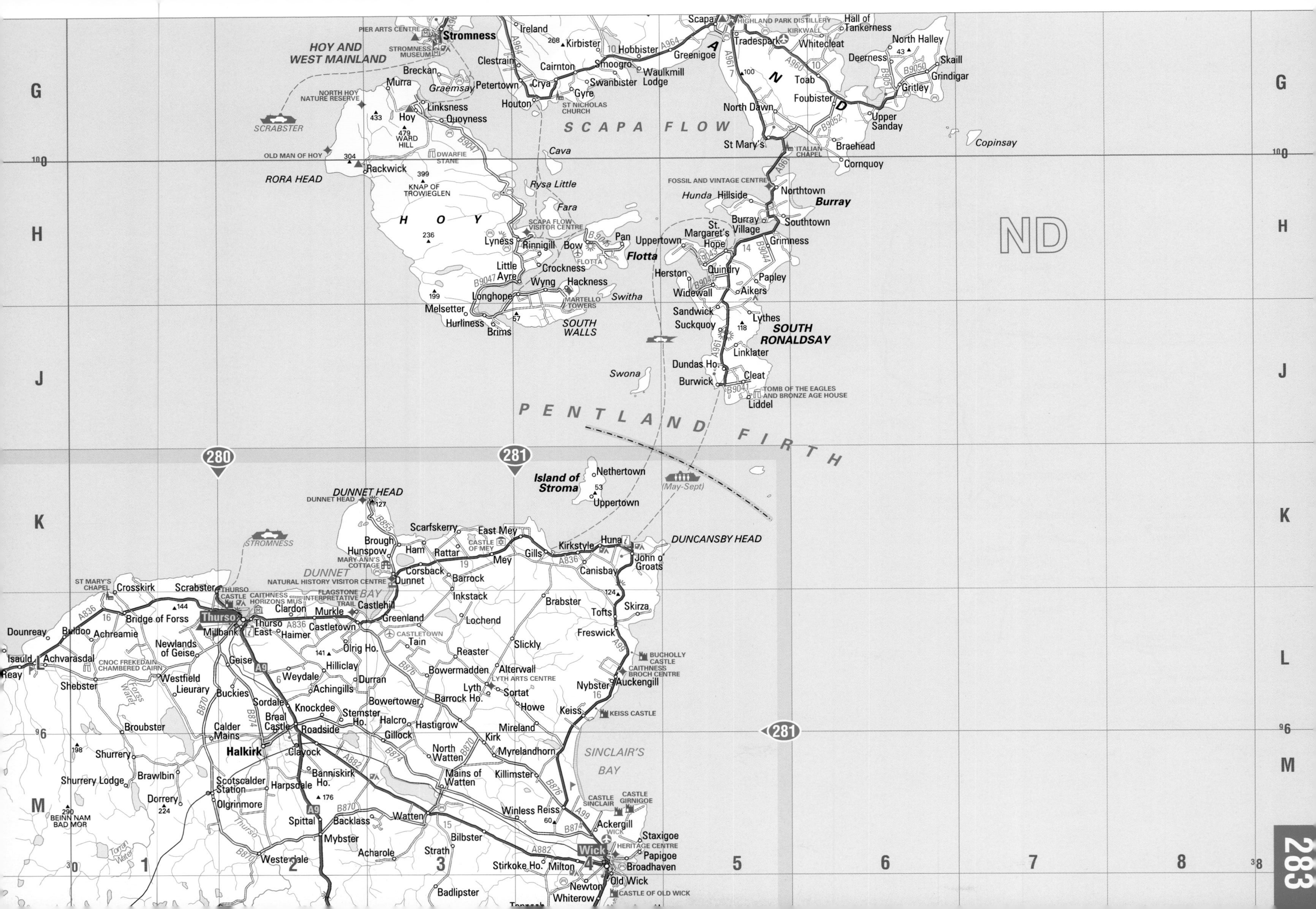
ND
HOY AND WEST MAINLAND
PIER ARTS CENTRE
Stromness
STROMNESS MUSEUM
Ireland
Kirbister
Hobbister
Greenigoe
Scapa
HIGHLAND PARK DISTILLERY
KIRKWALL
Hall of Tankerness
Tradespark
Whitecleat
North Halley
Deerness
Skaill
Grindigar
Gritley
Toab
Foubister
Upper Sanday
North Dawn
St Mary's
ITALIAN CHAPEL
Braehead
Cornquoy
Copinsay
Clestrain
Cairnton
Smoogro
Waulkmill
Lodge
Swanbister
Gyre
Crya
Petertown
Houton
ST NICHOLAS CHURCH
Breckan
Murra
Graemsay
Linksness
Quoyness
Hoy
WARD HILL
NORTH HOY NATURE RESERVE
SCRABSTER
OLD MAN OF HOY
RORA HEAD
Rackwick
DWARFIE STANE
KNAP OF TROWIEGLEN
SCAPA FLOW
Cava
Rysa Little
Fara
HOY
SCAPA FLOW VISITOR CENTRE
Lyness
Rinnigill
Bow
FLOTTA
Pan
Uppertown
Flotta
Little Ayre
Crockness
Wyng
Hackness
Longhope
MARTELLO TOWERS
Switha
Melsetter
Hurliness
Brims
SOUTH WALLS
FOSSIL AND VINTAGE CENTRE
Northtown
Hunda
Hillside
Burray
Burray Village
Southtown
St. Margaret's Hope
Grimness
Herston
Quindry
Papley
Widewall
Aikers
Sandwick
Lythes
Suckquoy
SOUTH RONALDSAY
Linklater
Dundas Ho.
Cleat
Burwick
TOMB OF THE EAGLES AND BRONZE AGE HOUSE
Liddel
Swona
PENTLAND FIRTH
Island of Stroma
Nethertown
Uppertown
(May-Sept)
DUNNET HEAD
DUNCANSBY HEAD
STROMNESS
Scarfskerry
East Mey
CASTLE OF MEY
Brough
Hunspow
Ham
Rattar
Mey
Gills
Kirkstyle
Huna
John o' Groats
Canisbay
MARY-ANN'S COTTAGE
DUNNET BAY
Corsback
Dunnet
Barrock
NATURAL HISTORY VISITOR CENTRE
ST MARY'S CHAPEL
Crosskirk
Scrabster
THURSO CASTLE
CAITHNESS HORIZONS MUS
FLAGSTONE INTERPRETATIVE TRAIL
Castlehill
Inkstack
Brabster
Skirza
Tofts
Clardon
Murkle
Greenland
Lochend
Freswick
Bridge of Forss
Thurso
Millbank
East
Haimer
Castletown
CASTLETOWN
Tain
Dounreay
Buldoo
Achreamie
Newlands of Geise
Olrig Ho.
Reaster
Slickly
BUCHOLLY CASTLE
CAITHNESS BROCH CENTRE
Isauld
Reay
Achvarasdal
CNOC FREKEDAL CHAMBERED CAIRN
Geise
Hilliclay
Bowermadden
Alterwall
LYTH ARTS CENTRE
Nybster
Auckengill
Shebster
Westfield
Lieurary
Weydale
Durran
Lyth
Sortat
Forss Water
Buckies
Achingills
Bowertower
Barrock Ho.
Howe
Keiss
KEISS CASTLE
Sordale
Knockdee
Stemster Ho.
Halcro
Hastigrow
Mireland
Broubster
Calder Mains
Braal Castle
Roadside
Gillock
Kirk
Halkirk
Clayock
North Watten
Myrelandhorn
SINCLAIR'S BAY
Shurrery
Shurrery Lodge
Brawlbin
Banniskirk Ho.
Mains of Watten
Killimster
Scotscalder Station
Harpsdale
Dorrery
Olgrinmore
CASTLE SINCLAIR
CASTLE GIRNIGOE
BEINN NAM BAD MOR
Spittal
Backlass
Watten
Winless
Reiss
Ackergill
Mybster
Bilbster
WICK
Staxigoe
HERITAGE CENTRE
Acharole
Strath
Wick
Papigoe
Westerdale
Stirkoke Ho.
Milton
Broadhaven
Newton
Old Wick
CASTLE OF OLD WICK
Whiterow
Badlipster
Thurso
Torran Water
A9
A99
A836
A882
A960
A961
A964
A965
B855
B870
B874
B876
B9041
B9043
B9044
B9045
B9047
B9050
B9052
280
281
G
H
J
K
L
M
1
2
3
4
5
6
7
8

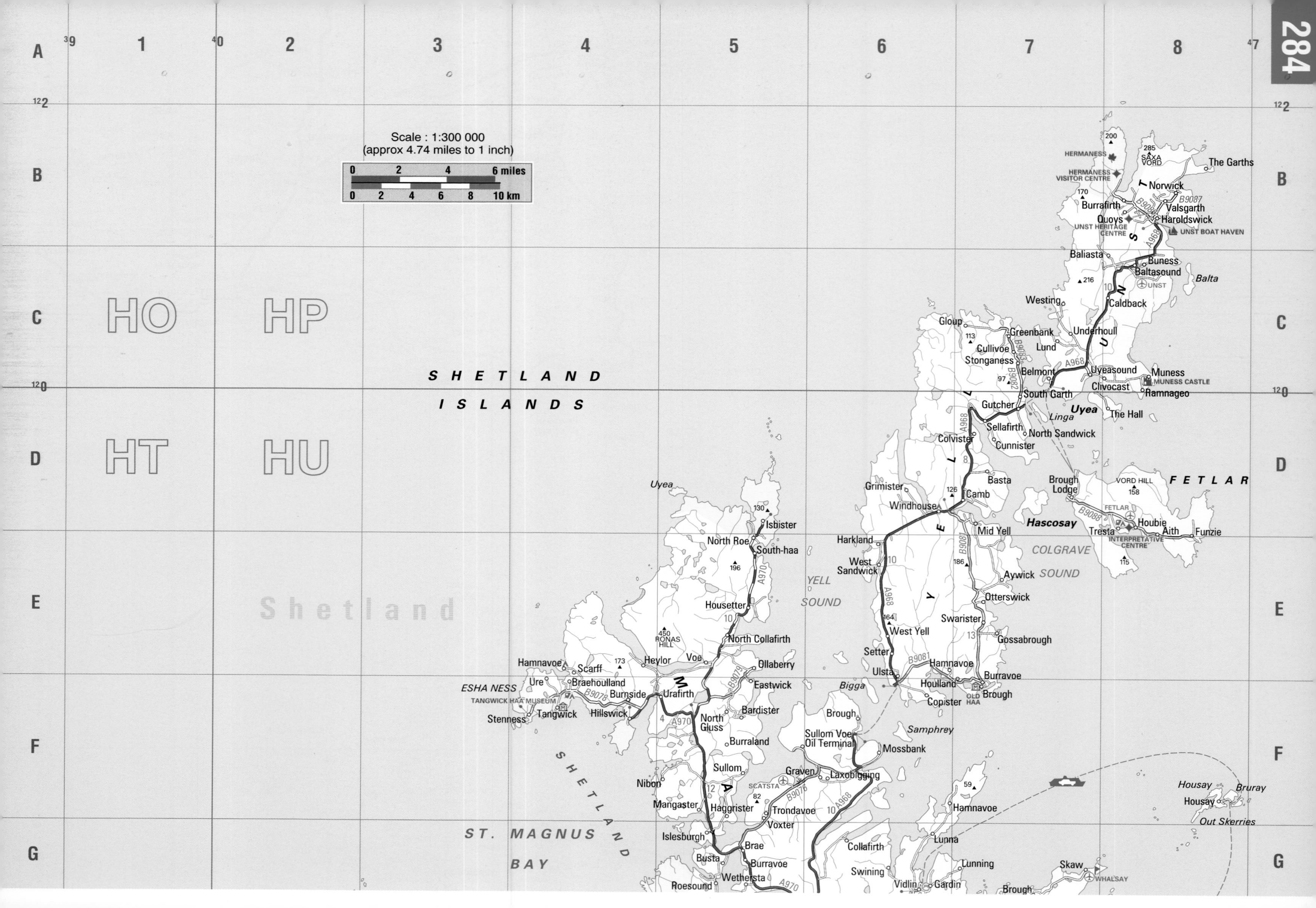
Scale : 1:300 000
(approx 4.74 miles to 1 inch)
0 2 4 6 miles
0 2 4 6 8 10 km
HO
HP
HT
HU
SHETLAND
ISLANDS
Shetland
Hermaness
Hermaness Visitor Centre
Saxa Vord
The Garths
Norwick
Valsgarth
Haroldswick
Unst Boat Haven
Burrafirth
Quoys
Unst Heritage Centre
Baliasta
Buness
Baltasound
Unst
Balta
Westing
Caldback
Gloup
Greenbank
Underhoull
Cullivoe
Lund
Stonganess
Belmont
Uyeasound
Muness
Muness Castle
Clivocast
Ramnageo
South Garth
Gutcher
Uyea
Linga
The Hall
Sellafirth
North Sandwick
Colvister
Cunnister
Basta
Grimister
Camb
Windhouse
Brough Lodge
Vord Hill
FETLAR
Fetlar
Houbie
Hascosay
Tresta
Aith
Funzie
Interpretative Centre
Mid Yell
Harkland
West Sandwick
Colgrave Sound
Aywick
Otterswick
Swarister
West Yell
Gossabrough
Setter
Hamnavoe
Ulsta
Burravoe
Houlland
Brough
Old Haa
Copister
Bigga
Samphrey
Yell Sound
Uyea
Isbister
North Roe
South-haa
Housetter
North Collafirth
Ronas Hill
Heylor
Voe
Ollaberry
Hamnavoe
Scarff
Ure
Braehoulland
Esha Ness
Tangwick Haa Museum
Burnside
Urafirth
Eastwick
Stenness
Tangwick
Hillswick
Bardister
North Gluss
Burraland
Brough
Sullom Voe Oil Terminal
Mossbank
Sullom
Graven
Laxobigging
Scatsta
Nibon
Mangaster
Haggrister
Trondavoe
Voxter
Hamnavoe
Lunna
Islesburgh
Brae
Collafirth
Busta
Burravoe
Swining
Lunning
Wethersta
Roesound
Vidlin
Gardin
Brough
Skaw
Whalsay
Housay
Bruray
Out Skerries
SHETLAND
ST. MAGNUS BAY
A968
A970
B9081
B9082
B9083
B9086
B9087
B9088
B9076
B9078
B9079

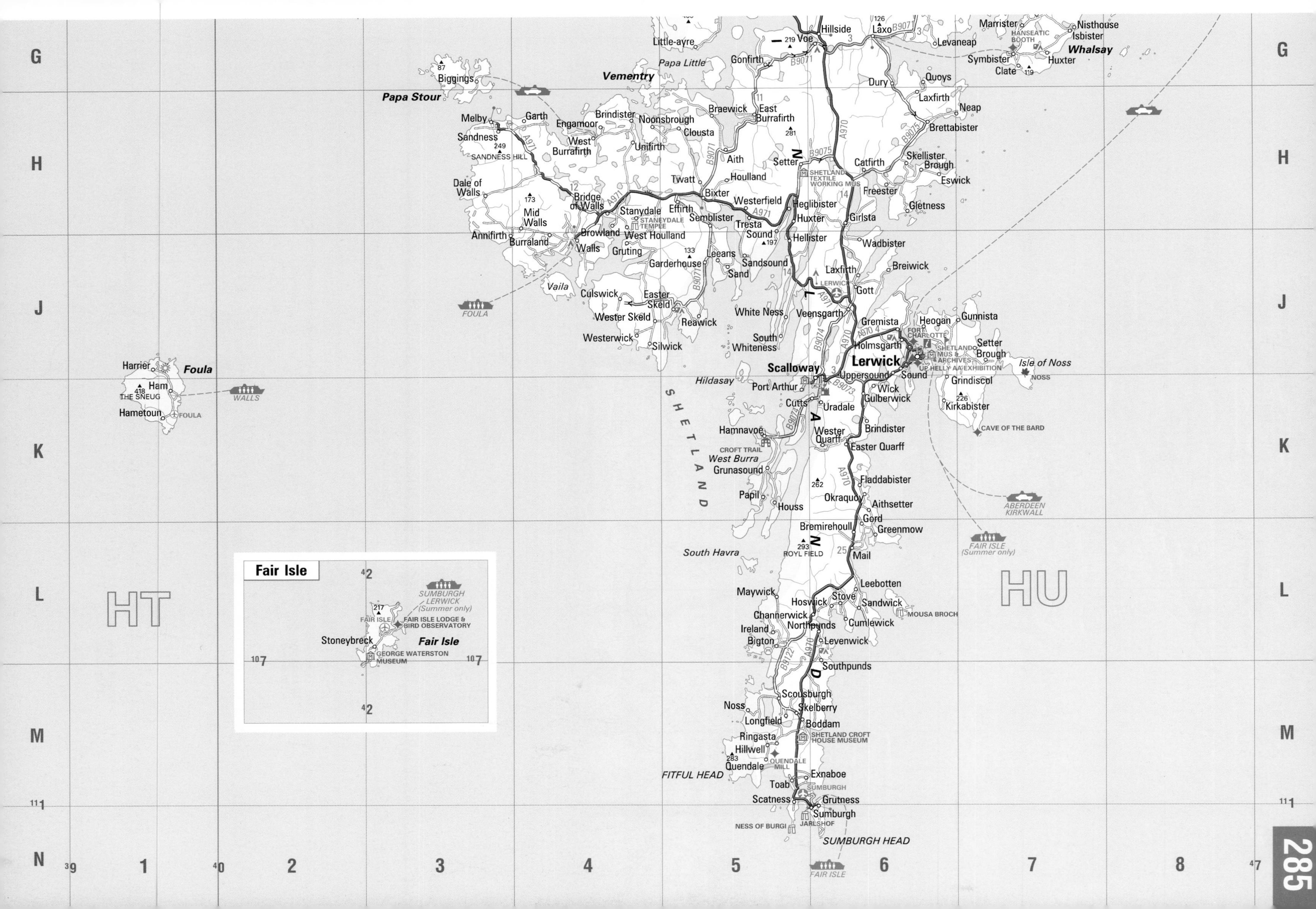
Hillside
Voe
Laxo
Levaneap
Marrister
Nisthouse
Isbister
Whalsay
Symbister
Huxter
Clate
HANSEATIC BOOTH
Little-ayre
Papa Little
Gonfirth
Vementry
Biggings
Papa Stour
Dury
Quoys
Laxfirth
Neap
Brettabister
Melby
Garth
Sandness
SANDNESS HILL
Engamoor
Brindister
Noonsbrough
Clousta
West Burrafirth
Unifirth
Braewick
East Burrafirth
Aith
Setter
Catfirth
Skellister
Brough
Eswick
SHETLAND TEXTILE WORKING MUS
Dale of Walls
Mid Walls
Bridge of Walls
Twatt
Houlland
Bixter
Westerfield
Heglibister
Freester
Gletness
Stanydale
Effirth
STANEYDALE TEMPLE
Semblister
Tresta
Sound
Huxter
Girlsta
Annifirth
Burraland
Browland
West Houlland
Walls
Gruting
Hellister
Wadbister
Garderhouse
Leeans
Sandsound
Sand
Laxfirth
Breiwick
Vaila
LERWICK
FOULA
Culswick
Easter Skeld
Gott
Wester Skeld
Reawick
White Ness
Veensgarth
Gremista
Heogan
Gunnista
Westerwick
Silwick
South Whiteness
FORT CHARLOTTE
Holmsgarth
SHETLAND MUS & ARCHIVES
Setter
Brough
Harrier
Foula
Lerwick
Isle of Noss
Ham
THE SNEUG
Hametoun
WALLS
Scalloway
Hildasay
Uppersound
Sound
UP HELLY AA EXHIBITION
Grindiscol
NOSS
Port Arthur
Wick
Gulberwick
Cutts
Uradale
Kirkabister
SHETLAND
Hamnavoe
Wester Quarff
Brindister
CAVE OF THE BARD
CROFT TRAIL
West Burra
Easter Quarff
Grunasound
Fladdabister
Papil
Houss
Okraquoy
Aithsetter
ABERDEEN KIRKWALL
Gord
Bremirehoull
Greenmow
ROYL FIELD
Mail
FAIR ISLE (Summer only)
South Havra
Fair Isle
SUMBURGH LERWICK (Summer only)
FAIR ISLE LODGE & BIRD OBSERVATORY
Stoneybreck
GEORGE WATERSTON MUSEUM
HT
HU
Leebotten
Maywick
Hoswick
Stove
Sandwick
MOUSA BROCH
Channerwick
Northpunds
Cumlewick
Ireland
Bigton
Levenwick
Southpunds
Scousburgh
Noss
Skelberry
Longfield
Boddam
Ringasta
SHETLAND CROFT HOUSE MUSEUM
Hillwell
QUENDALE MILL
Quendale
FITFUL HEAD
Exnaboe
Toab
SUMBURGH
Scatness
Grutness
Sumburgh
NESS OF BURGI
JARLSHOF
SUMBURGH HEAD
A970
A971
B9071
B9075
B9074
B9073
B9122
G
H
J
K
L
M
N
1
2
3
4
5
6
7
8

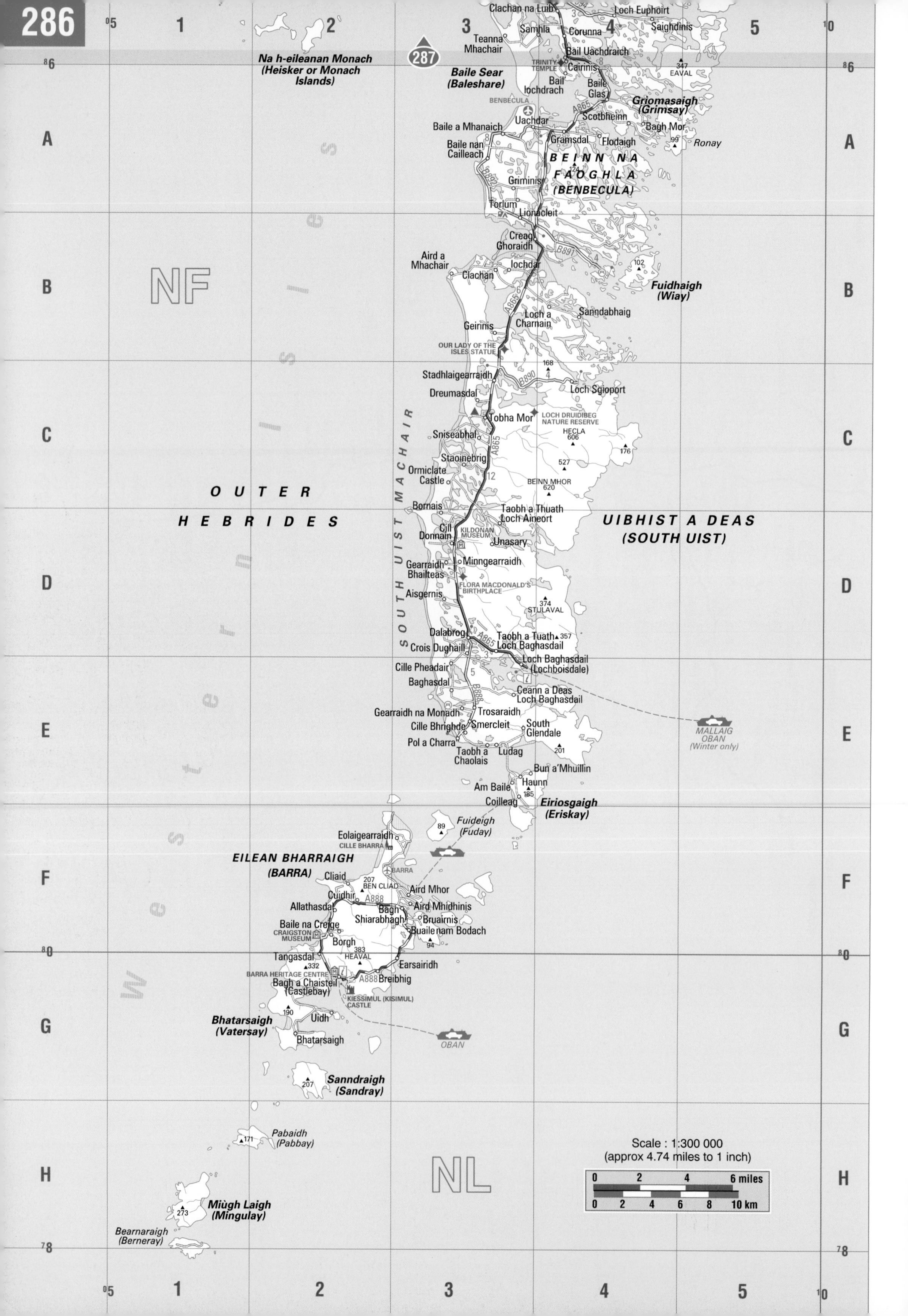

Na h-eileanan Monach (Heisker or Monach Islands)
Baile Sear (Baleshare)
Clachan na Luib
Loch Euphoirt
Saighdinis
Samhla
Corunna
Teanna Mhachair
Bail Uachdraich
Cairinis
Bail Iochdrach
Baile Glas
Griomasaigh (Grimsay)
Uachdar
Scotbheinn
Baile a Mhanaich
Bagh Mor
Gramsdal
Flodaigh
Ronay
Baile nan Cailleach
BEINN NA FAOGHLA (BENBECULA)
Griminis
Torlum
Lionacleit
Creag Ghoraidh
Aird a Mhachair
Iochdar
Clachan
Fuidhaigh (Wiay)
Loch a Charnain
Sanndabhaig
Geirinis
OUR LADY OF THE ISLES STATUE
Stadhlaigearraidh
Loch Sgioport
Dreumasdal
Tobha Mor
LOCH DRUIDIBEG NATURE RESERVE
Sniseabhal
HECLA 606
Staoinebrig
Ormiclate Castle
BEINN MHOR 620
OUTER HEBRIDES
Bornais
Taobh a Thuath Loch Aineort
UIBHIST A DEAS (SOUTH UIST)
Cill Donnain
KILDONAN MUSEUM
Unasary
SOUTH UIST MACHAIR
Gearraidh Bhailteas
Minngearraidh
FLORA MACDONALD'S BIRTHPLACE
Aisgernis
STULAVAL
Dalabrog
Taobh a Tuath Loch Baghasdail
Crois Dughaill
Loch Baghasdail (Lochboisdale)
Cille Pheadair
Baghasdal
Ceann a Deas Loch Baghasdail
Gearraidh na Monadh
Trosaraidh
MALLAIG OBAN (Winter only)
Cille Bhrighde
Smercleit
South Glendale
Pol a Charra
Taobh a Chaolais
Ludag
Bun a'Mhuillin
Am Baile
Haunn
Coilleag
Eiriosgaigh (Eriskay)
Fuideigh (Fuday)
Eolaigearraidh
CILLE BHARRA
EILEAN BHARRAIGH (BARRA)
BARRA
Cliaid
BEN CLIAD
Aird Mhor
Cuidhir
Allathasdal
Aird Mhidhinis
Bagh Shiarabhagh
Bruairnis
Baile na Creige
CRAIGSTON MUSEUM
Buaile nam Bodach
Borgh
HEAVAL
Tangasdal
Earsairidh
BARRA HERITAGE CENTRE
Breibhig
Bagh a Chaisteil (Castlebay)
KIESSIMUL (KISIMUL) CASTLE
Bhatarsaigh (Vatersay)
Uidh
Bhatarsaigh
OBAN
Sanndraigh (Sandray)
Pabaidh (Pabbay)
Miùgh Laigh (Mingulay)
Bearnaraigh (Berneray)
NF
NL
Scale : 1:300 000
(approx 4.74 miles to 1 inch)
0 2 4 6 miles
0 2 4 6 8 10 km

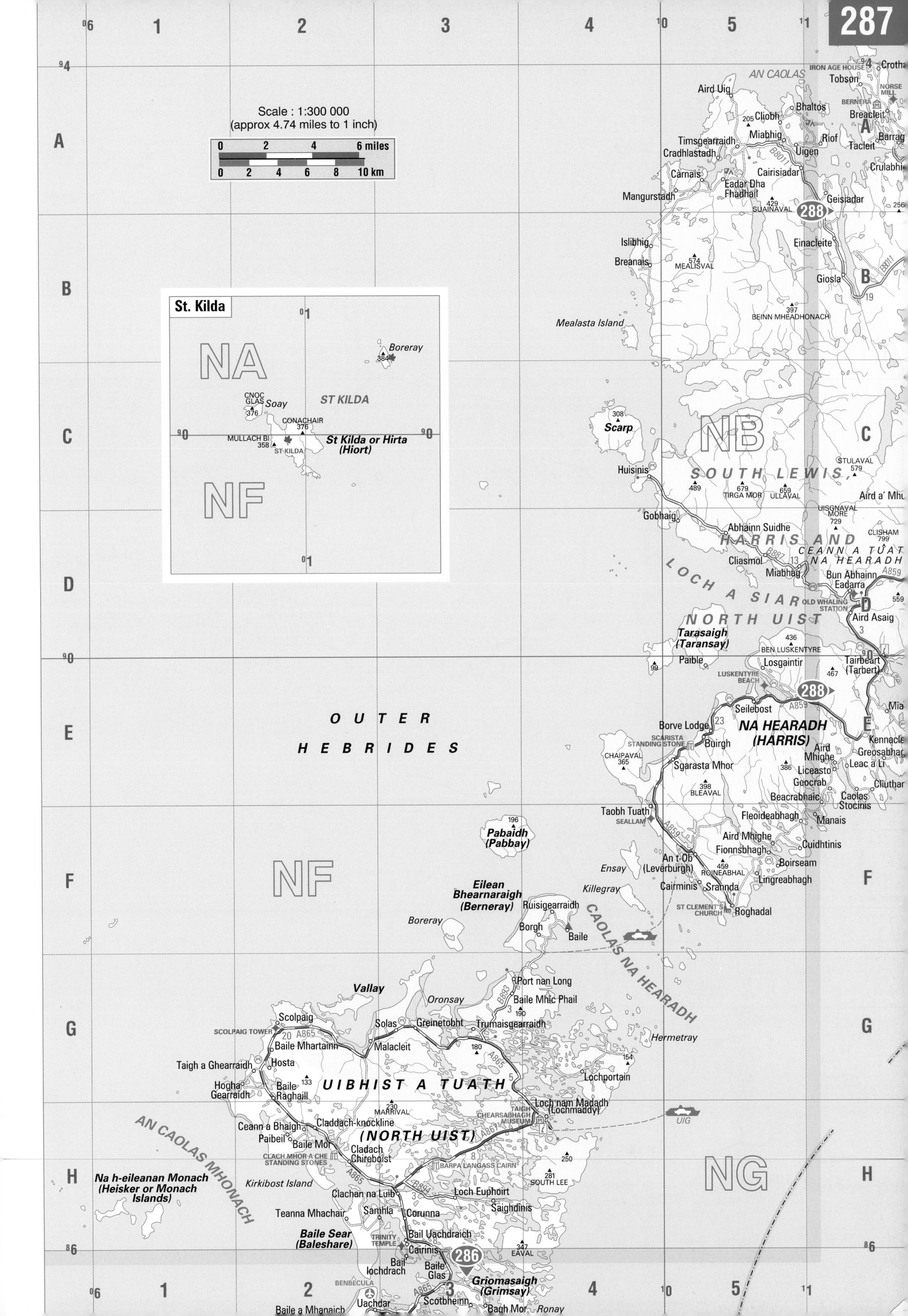

St. Kilda

NA

NF

ST KILDA

Boreray
384

CNOC GLAS 376 *Soay*
CONACHAIR 376

MULLACH BI 358 ST-KILDA **St Kilda or Hirta (Hiort)**

Scale : 1:300 000
(approx 4.74 miles to 1 inch)

0 2 4 6 miles
0 2 4 6 8 10 km

AN CAOLAS
IRON AGE HOUSE
Tobson Crotha
NORSE MILL
Aird Uig
BERNERA
Cliobh Bhaltos Breaclait
205 Miabhig Riof Barrag
Timsgearraidh Uigen Tacleit
Cradhlastadh Cairisiadar Geisiadar Crulabhi
Carnais Eadar Dha Fhadhail 256
Mangurstadh 429 SUAINAVAL **288**

Islibhig Einacleite
Breanais 574 MEALISVAL Giosla
19

Mealasta Island 397 BEINN MHEADHONACH

NB

Scarp 308 STULAVAL 579
SOUTH LEWIS
Huisinis 489 TIRGA MOR ULLAVAL Aird a' Mhu
679 659
Gobhaig UISGNAVAL MORE 729 CLISHAM 799
Abhainn Suidhe 13 HARRIS AND CEANN A TUAT NA HEARADH
Cliasmol Bun Abhainn Eadarra
Miabhag OLD WHALING STATION 559
NORTH UIST 3 Aird Asaig
Tarasaigh (Taransay) 436 BEN LUSKENTYRE
Paible 99 Losgaintir Tairbeart (Tarbert)
LUSKENTYRE BEACH 467 **288**
Seilebost Mia
Borve Lodge 23 A859
SCARISTA STANDING STONE Buirgh **NA HEARADH (HARRIS)**
CHAIPAVAL 365 Sgarasta Mhor Aird Mhighe Kennacle
386 Liceasto Greosabhac Leac a Li
398 Geocrab Cliuthar
BLEAVAL Beacrabhaic Caolas Stocinis
Taobh Tuath Fleoideabhagh Manais
SEALLAM A859 Aird Mhighe Cuidhtinis
Pabaidh (Pabbay) 196 Fionnsbhagh Boirseam
An t-Ob 459 Lingreabhagh
Ensay (Leverburgh) ROINEABHAL
Killegray Cairinis Srannda
Eilean Bhearnaraigh (Berneray) ST CLEMENT'S CHURCH Roghadal
Ruisigearraidh
Boreray Borgh Baile

O U T E R
H E B R I D E S

N F

CAOLAS NA HEARADH

Port nan Long
Valley *Oronsay* Baile Mhic Phail
Scolpaig Solas Greinetobht 3 Trumaisgearraidh
SCOLPAIG TOWER 20 A865 Malacleit 190 *Hermetray*
Baile Mhartainn 180 A865
Taigh a Ghearraidh Hosta 5
Hogha Gearraidh Baile 133 Lochportain
Raghaill **UIBHIST A TUATH** Loch nam Madadh (Lochmaddy)
Ceann a Bhaigh Claddach-knockline TAIGH CHEARSABHAGH MUSEUM UIG
Paibeil Baile Mor Cladach 230 A867
CLACH MHOR A CHE STANDING STONES Chireboist **(NORTH UIST)** 8
Na h-eileanan Monach (Heisker or Monach Islands) *Kirkibost Island* BARPA LANGASS CAIRN 250
Clachan na Luib A865 Loch Euphoirt 281 SOUTH LEE
Teanna Mhachair Samhla Corunna Saighdinis
Ronay
Baile Sear (Baleshare) TRINITY TEMPLE Bail Uachdraich 347 EAVAL
Cairinis Baile Glas **286**
Bail Iochdrach BENBECULA A865 **Griomasaigh (Grimsay)**
Baile a Mhanaich Uachdar Scotbheinn Bagh Mor *Ronay*

AN CAOLAS MHONACH

NG

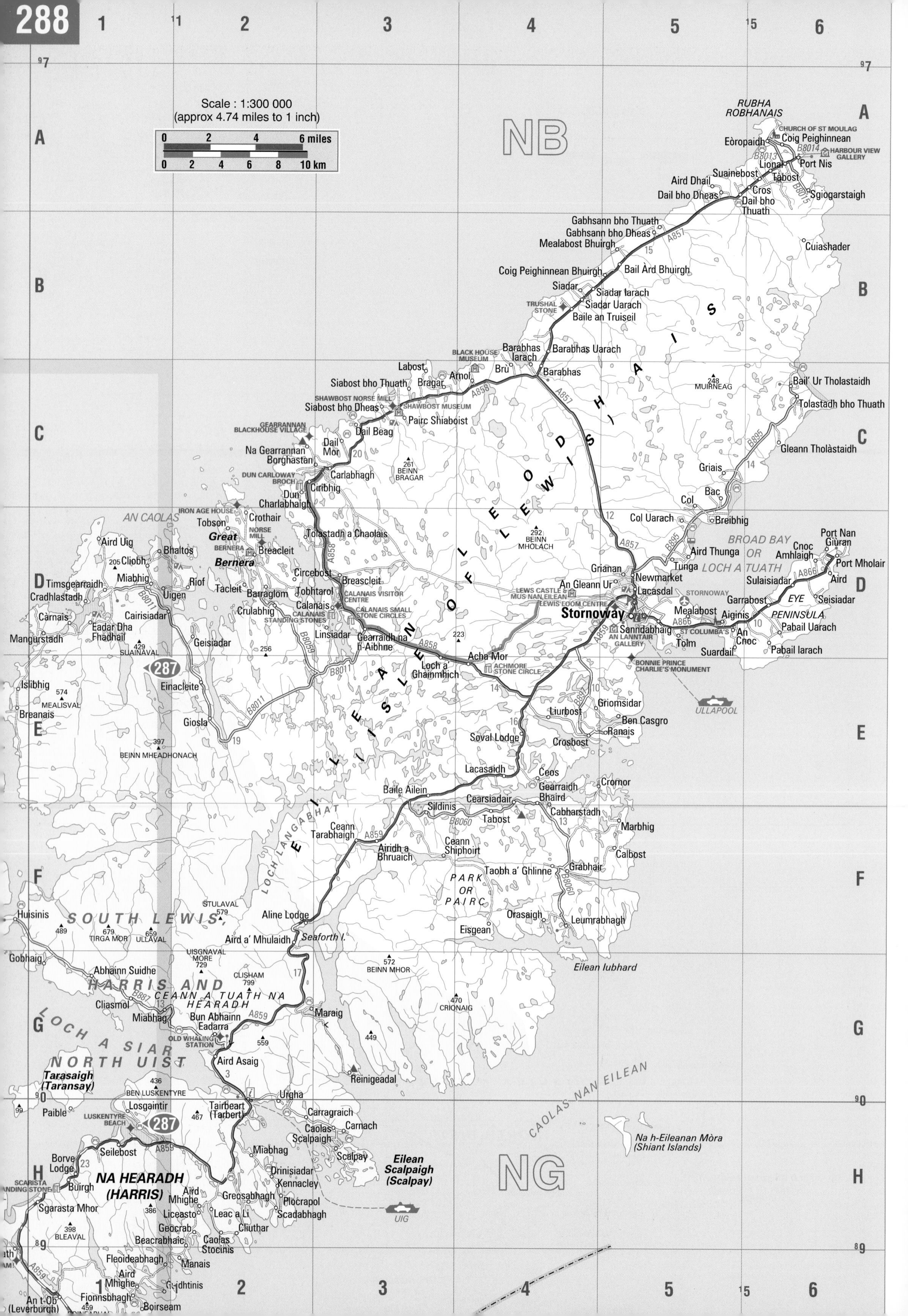
Scale : 1:300 000
(approx 4.74 miles to 1 inch)
0 2 4 6 miles
0 2 4 6 8 10 km
NB
NG
RUBHA ROBHANAIS
CHURCH OF ST MOULAG
Eòropaidh
Coig Peighinnean
HARBOUR VIEW GALLERY
Lional
Port Nis
Suainebost
Tabost
Aird Dhail
Cros
Dail bho Dheas
Dail bho Thuath
Sgiogarstaigh
Gabhsann bho Thuath
Gabhsann bho Dheas
Mealabost Bhuirgh
Cuiashader
Coig Peighinnean Bhuirgh
Bail Àrd Bhuirgh
Siadar
Siadar Iarach
Siadar Uarach
TRUSHAL STONE
Baile an Truiseil
BLACK HOUSE MUSEUM
Barabhas Iarach
Barabhas Uarach
Labost
Arnol
Brù
Barabhas
Siabost bho Thuath
Bragar
SHAWBOST NORSE MILL
Siabost bho Dheas
SHAWBOST MUSEUM
Pairc Shiaboist
248 MUIRNEAG
Bail' Ur Tholastaidh
Tolastadh bho Thuath
GEARRANNAN BLACKHOUSE VILLAGE
Dail Beag
Dail Mor
Na Gearrannan
Borghastan
261 BEINN BRAGAR
Gleann Tholàstaidh
DUN CARLOWAY BROCH
Carlabhagh
Griais
Dun Charlabhaigh
Ciribhig
Bac
Col
IRON AGE HOUSE
AN CAOLAS
Crothair
Tobson
NORSE MILL
Col Uarach
Breibhig
Great Bernera
Tolastadh a Chaolais
292 BEINN MHOLACH
BROAD BAY OR LOCH A TUATH
Port Nan Giùran
Cnoc
Amhlaigh
Aird Uig
Bhaltos
Breacleit
Aird Thunga
Tunga
205
Cliobh
Circebost
Grianan
Newmarket
Port Mholair
Timsgearraidh
Miabhig
Riof
Breascleit
An Gleann Ur
Sulaisiadar
Aird
Cradhlastadh
Uigen
Tacleit
Barraglom
Tobhtarol
CALANAIS VISITOR CENTRE
LEWS CASTLE & MUS NAN EILEAN
Lacasdal
STORNOWAY
Garrabost
EYE PENINSULA
Seisiadar
Càrnais
Cairisiadar
Crulabhig
Calanais
CALANAIS STANDING STONES
CALANAIS SMALL STONE CIRCLES
LEWIS LOOM CENTRE
Stornoway
Mealabost
Aiginis
Eadar Dha Fhadhail
Linsiadar
Sanndabhaig
ST COLUMBA'S
Pabail Uarach
Mangurstadh
429 SUAINAVAL
Geisiadar
256
Gearraidh na h-Aibhne
223
AN LANNTAIR GALLERY
Tolm
An Cnoc
Suardail
Pabail Iarach
287
Acha Mor
ACHMORE STONE CIRCLE
Loch a' Ghainmhich
BONNIE PRINCE CHARLIE'S MONUMENT
Islibhig
Einacleite
574 MEALISVAL
ULLAPOOL
Breanais
Griomsidar
Liurbost
Ben Casgro
Giosla
Ranais
397 BEINN MHEADHONACH
Soval Lodge
Crosbost
Lacasaidh
Ceos
Baile Ailein
Gearraidh Bhaird
Cromor
Sildinis
Cearsiadair
Tabost
Cabharstadh
EILEAN LANGABHAT
ISLE OF LEWIS
EILEAN LEODHAIS
Ceann Tarabhaigh
Airidh a Bhruaich
Ceann Shiphoirt
Marbhig
Calbost
LOCH LANGABHAT
PARK OR PAIRC
Taobh a' Ghlinne
Grabhair
STULAVAL 579
Huisinis
SOUTH LEWIS
Aline Lodge
Orasaigh
Leumrabhagh
489
679 TIRGA MOR
659 ULLAVAL
Eisgean
Aird a' Mhulaidh
Seaforth I.
Gobhaig
UISGNAVAL MORE 729
572 BEINN MHOR
Eilean Iubhard
Abhainn Suidhe
CLISHAM 799
HARRIS AND CEANN A TUATH NA HEARADH
470 CRIONAIG
Cliasmol
Miabhag
Bun Abhainn Eadarra
Maraig
LOCH A SIAR
OLD WHALING STATION
559
449
NORTH UIST
Aird Asaig
Reinigeadal
Tarasaigh (Taransay)
436 BEN LUSKENTYRE
CAOLAS NAN EILEAN
Urgha
Losgaintir
Tairbeart (Tarbert)
467
Carragraich
Paible
LUSKENTYRE BEACH
Caolas
Carnach
Na h-Eileanan Mòra (Shiant Islands)
Seilebost
Scalpaigh
Borve Lodge
Miabhag
Scalpay
Eilean Scalpaigh (Scalpay)
SCARISTA STANDING STONE
Drinisiadar
Kennacley
NA HEARADH (HARRIS)
Buirgh
Aird Mhighe
Greosabhagh
Plocrapol
Sgarasta Mhor
386
Liceasto
Leac a Li
Scadabhagh
UIG
398 BLEAVAL
Geocrab
Cluithar
Beacrabhaic
Caolas Stocinis
Fleoideabhagh
Manais
Aird Mhighe
Gèidhtinis
An t-Ób (Leverburgh)
Fionnsbhagh
459
Boirseam
A857
A858
A859
A866
B8011
B8013
B8014
B8015
B895
B8059
B8060
B887
B897
1 2 3 4 5 6
A B C D E F G H

Index to road maps of Britain

Abbreviations used in the index

Abbreviation	County or unitary authority	Abbreviation	County or unitary authority
Aberdeen	Aberdeen City	M Keynes	Milton Keynes
Aberds	Aberdeenshire	M Tydf	Merthyr Tydfil
Ald	Alderney	Mbro	Middlesbrough
Anglesey	Isle of Anglesey	Medway	Medway
Angus	Angus	Mers	Merseyside
Argyll	Argyll and Bute	Midloth	Midlothian
Bath	Bath and North East Somerset	Mon	Monmouthshire
Bedford	Bedford	Moray	Moray
Bl Gwent	Blaenau Gwent	N Ayrs	North Ayrshire
Blackburn	Blackburn with Darwen	N Lincs	North Lincolnshire
Blackpool	Blackpool	N Lanark	North Lanarkshire
BCP	Bournemouth, Christchurch and Poole	N Som	North Somerset
		N Yorks	North Yorkshire
Borders	Scottish Borders	NE Lincs	North East Lincolnshire
Brack	Bracknell	Neath	Neath Port Talbot
Bridgend	Bridgend	Newport	City and County of Newport
Brighton	City of Brighton and Hove	Norf	Norfolk
Bristol	City and County of Bristol	Northants	Northamptonshire
Bucks	Buckinghamshire	Northumb	Northumberland
C Beds	Central Bedfordshire	Nottingham	City of Nottingham
Caerph	Caerphilly	Notts	Nottinghamshire
Cambs	Cambridgeshire	Orkney	Orkney
Cardiff	Cardiff	Oxon	Oxfordshire
Carms	Carmarthenshire	Pboro	Peterborough
Ceredig	Ceredigion	Pembs	Pembrokeshire
Ches E	Cheshire East	Perth	Perth and Kinross
Ches W	Cheshire West and Chester	Plym	Plymouth
Clack	Clackmannanshire	Powys	Powys
Conwy	Conwy	Ptsmth	Portsmouth
Corn	Cornwall	Reading	Reading
Cumb	Cumbria	Redcar	Redcar and Cleveland
Darl	Darlington	Renfs	Renfrewshire
Denb	Denbighshire	Rhondda	Rhondda Cynon Taff
Derby	City of Derby	Rutland	Rutland
Derbys	Derbyshire	S Ayrs	South Ayrshire
Devon	Devon	S Glos	South Gloucestershire
Dorset	Dorset	S Lanark	South Lanarkshire
Dumfries	Dumfries and Galloway	S Yorks	South Yorkshire
Dundee	Dundee City	Scilly	Scilly
Durham	Durham	Shetland	Shetland
E Ayrs	East Ayrshire	Shrops	Shropshire
E Dunb	East Dunbartonshire	Slough	Slough
E Loth	East Lothian	Som	Somerset
E Renf	East Renfrewshire	Soton	Southampton
E Sus	East Sussex	Staffs	Staffordshire
E Yorks	East Riding of Yorkshire	Southend	Southend-on-Sea
Edin	City of Edinburgh	Stirling	Stirling
Essex	Essex	Stockton	Stockton-on-Tees
Falk	Falkirk	Stoke	Stoke-on-Trent
Fife	Fife	Suff	Suffolk
Flint	Flintshire	Sur	Surrey
Glasgow	City of Glasgow	Swansea	Swansea
Glos	Gloucestershire	Swindon	Swindon
Gtr Man	Greater Manchester	T&W	Tyne and Wear
Guern	Guernsey	Telford	Telford and Wrekin
Gwyn	Gwynedd	Thurrock	Thurrock
Halton	Halton	Torbay	Torbay
Hants	Hampshire	Torf	Torfaen
Hereford	Herefordshire	V Glam	The Vale of Glamorgan
Herts	Hertfordshire	W Berks	West Berkshire
Highld	Highland	W Dunb	West Dunbartonshire
Hrtlpl	Hartlepool	W Isles	Western Isles
Hull	Hull	W Loth	West Lothian
IoM	Isle of Man	W Mid	West Midlands
IoW	Isle of Wight	W Sus	West Sussex
Invclyd	Inverclyde	W Yorks	West Yorkshire
Jersey	Jersey	Warks	Warwickshire
Kent	Kent	Warr	Warrington
Lancs	Lancashire	Wilts	Wiltshire
Leicester	City of Leicester	Windsor	Windsor and Maidenhead
Leics	Leicestershire	Wokingham	Wokingham
Lincs	Lincolnshire	Worcs	Worcestershire
London	Greater London	Wrex	Wrexham
Luton	Luton	York	City of York

How to use the index

A

Abbas Combe 29 C7
Abberley 79 A5
Abberton
Essex 71 B4
Worcs 80 B2
Abberwick 189 B4
Abbess Roding 69 B5
Abbey 27 D6
Abbey-cwm-hir 93 D4
Abbeydale 130 A3
Abbey Dore 78 D1
Abbey Field 70 A3
Abbey Hulton 112 A3
Abbey St Bathans . . 211 D4
Abbeystead 145 B5
Abbey Town 175 C4
Abbey Village 137 A5
Abbey Wood 50 B1
Abbots Bickington . . 25 D4
Abbots Bromley 113 C4
Abbotsbury 15 C5
Abbotsham 25 C5
Abbotskerswell 8 A2
Abbots Langley 67 C5
Abbots Leigh 43 B4
Abbotsley 84 B4
Abbots Morton 80 B3
Abbots Ripton 100 D4
Abbots Salford 80 B3
Abbotswood 32 C2
Abbotts Ann 32 A2
Abcott 94 D1
Abdon 94 C3
Aber 74 D3
Aberaeron 74 B3
Aberaman 41 A5
Aberangell 91 A6
Aber-Arad 73 C6
Aberarder 240 D2
Aberarder House . . . 252 D2
Aberarder Lodge . . . 240 D3
Aberargie 219 C6
Aberarth 74 B3
Aberavon 40 B2
Aber-banc 73 B6
Aberbeeg 41 A7
Abercanaid 41 A5
Abercarn 41 B7
Abercastle 55 A4
Abercegir 91 B6
Aberchirder 268 D1
Aber Cowarch 91 A6
Abercraf 59 D5
Abercrombie 221 D5
Abercych 73 B5
Abercynafon 60 B2
Abercynon 41 B5
Aberdalgie 219 B5
Aberdâr = *Aberdare* . . 41 A4
Aberdare = *Aberdâr* . . 41 A4
Aberdaron 106 D1
Aberdaugleddau
= *Milford Haven* 55 D5
Aberdeen 245 B6
Aberdesach 107 A4
Aberdour 209 B4
Aberdovey 90 C4
Aberdulais 40 A2
Aberedw 77 C4
Abereiddy 54 A3
Abererch 106 C3
Aberfan 41 A5
Aberfeldy 230 D2
Aberffraw 122 D3
Aberffrwd 75 A5
Aberford 148 D3
Aberfoyle 217 D5
Abergavenny =
Y Fenni 61 B4
Abergele 125 B4
Aber-Giâr 58 A2
Abergorlech 58 B2
Abergwaun
= *Fishguard* 72 C2
Abergwesyn 76 B2
Abergwili 58 C1
Abergwynant 91 A4
Aber-gwynfi 40 B3
Abergwyngregyn . . . 123 C6
Abergynolwyn 91 B4
Aber-Hirnant 109 B4
Aberhonddu
= *Brecon* 60 A2
Aberhosan 91 C6
Aberkenfig 40 C3
Aberlady 210 B1
Aberlemno 232 C3
Aberllefenni 91 B5
Abermagwr 75 A5
Abermaw
= *Barmouth* 90 A4
Abermeurig 75 C4
Abermule 93 B5

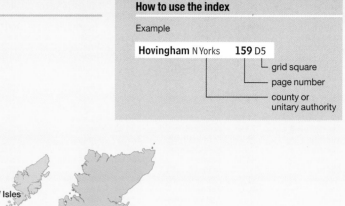

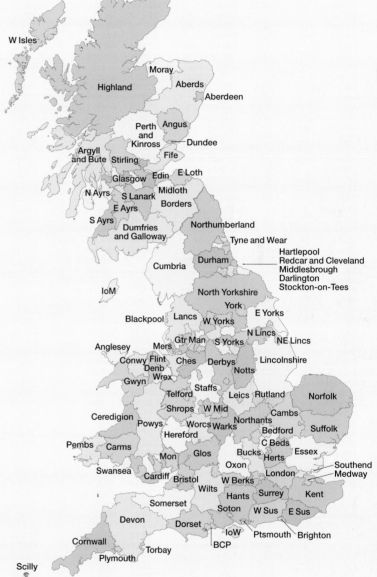

Abernaint 109 C6
Abernant 73 D6
Aber-nant 41 A5
Abernethy 219 C6
Abernyte 220 A2
Aberpennar
=Mountain Ash 41 B5
Aberporth 73 A5
Aber-Rhiwlech 108 C4
Abersoch 106 D3
Abersychan 61 C4
Abertawe
=Swansea 57 C6
Aberteifi =Cardigan 73 B4
Aberthin 41 D5
Abertillery
=Abertyleri 41 A7
Abertridwr
Caerph 41 C6
Powys 109 D5
Abertyleri
=Abertillery 41 A7
Abertysswg 60 C3
Aberuthven 219 C4
Aber-Village 60 A3
Aberyscir 60 A1
Aberystwyth 90 D3
Abhainn Suidhe 287 D5
Abingdon-on-Thames 65 D5
Abinger Common 35 B4
Abinger Hammer 34 B3
Abington 194 D4
Abington Pigotts 85 C5
Ab Kettleby 115 C5
Ab Lench 80 B3
Ablington
Glos 64 C2
Wilts 31 A5
Abney 130 B1
Aboyne 244 C2
Abram 137 C5
Abriachan 252 C1
Abridge 69 D4
Abronhill 207 C5
Abson 43 B6
Abthorpe 82 C3
Abune-the-Hill 282 E3
Aby 135 B4
Acaster Malbis 149 C4
Acaster Selby 149 C4
Accrington 137 A6
Acha 223 B4
Achabraid 213 D6
Achachork 259 D4
Achafolla 213 A5
Achagary 278 C3
Achahoish 202 A2
Achalader 231 D5
Achallader 228 D2
Acha Mor 288 E4
Achanalt 263 D4
Achanamara 213 D5
Achandunie 264 C2
Ach'an Todhair 237 B4
Achany 272 D3
Achaphubuil 237 B4
Acharacle 235 D5
Acharn
Highld 236 D1
Perth 229 D6
Acharole 280 C4
Achath 245 A4
Achavanich 280 D3
Achavraat 253 B5
Achddu 57 B4
Achduart 270 D3
Achentoul 274 A2
Achfary 271 A5
Achgarve 261 A5
Achiemore
Highld 277 B4
Highld 279 C4
A'Chill 246 D1
Achiltibuie 270 D3
Achina 278 B3
Achinduich 272 D3
Achinduin 226 C3
Achingills 280 B3
Achintee
Highld 237 B5
Highld 249 B6
Achintraid 249 C5
Achlean 241 C6
Achleck 224 B3
Achluachrach 239 D6
Achlyness 276 C3
Achmelvich 270 B3
Achmore
Highld 249 C5
Stirling 217 A5
Achnaba
Argyll 214 D2
Argyll 226 C4
Achnabat 252 C1
Achnacarnin 270 A3
Achnacarry 239 D5
Achnacloich
Argyll 227 C4
Highld 247 D4
Achnaconeran 240 A2
Achnacraig 224 B3
Achnacroish 226 B3
Achnadrish 224 A3
Achnafalnich 227 D7
Achnagarron 264 D2
Achnaha 234 D3
Achnahanat 263 A7
Achnahannet 253 D5
Achnairn 272 C3
Achnaluachrach 273 D4
Achnasaul 239 D5
Achnasheen 250 A3
Achosnich 234 D3
Achranich 226 B2
Achreamie 279 B6
Achriabhach 237 C5
Achriesgill 276 C3
Achrimsdale 274 D3
Achtoty 278 B2
Achurch 100 C2
Achuvoldrach 277 C6
Achvaich 264 A3
Achvarasdal 279 B5
Ackergill 281 C5
Acklam
Mbro 168 D2
N Yorks 149 A6
Ackleton 95 B5
Acklington 189 C5
Ackton 140 A2
Ackworth Moor Top 140 B2
Acle 121 D6
Acock's Green 96 C4
Acol 53 C5
Acomb
Northumb 178 C1
York 149 B4
Aconbury 78 D3
Acre 137 A6
Acrefair 110 A1
Acre Street 19 B6
Acton
Ches E 127 D6
Dorset 16 D3
London 49 A5
Shrops 93 C7
Suff 87 C4
Wrex 126 D3
Acton Beauchamp 79 B4
Acton Bridge 127 B5
Acton Burnell 94 A3
Acton Green 79 B4
Acton Pigott 94 A3
Acton Round 95 B4
Acton Scott 94 C2
Acton Trussell 112 D3
Acton Turville 44 A2
Adbaston 111 C6
Adber 29 C5
Adderley 111 A5
Adderstone 199 C5
Addiewell 208 D2
Addingham 147 C4
Addington
Bucks 66 A2
Kent 37 A4
London 49 C6
Addinston 197 A4
Addiscombe 49 C6
Addlestone 48 C3
Addlethorpe 135 C5
Adel 148 D1
Adeney 111 D6
Adfa 93 A4
Adforton 94 D2
Adisham 53 D4
Adlestrop 64 A3
Adlingfleet 141 A6
Adlington 137 B5
Admaston
Staffs 112 C4
Telford 111 D5
Admington 81 C5
Adstock 83 D4
Adstone 82 B2
Adversane 34 D3
Advie 254 C2
Adwalton 139 A5
Adwell 66 D1
Adwick le Street 140 C3
Adwick upon Dearne 140 C2
Adziel 269 D4
Ae Village 184 D2
Affleck 256 D3
Affpuddle 16 B2
Affric Lodge 250 D3
Afon-wen 125 B6
Afton 18 C2
Agglethorpe 157 C4
Agneash 152 C4
Aigburth 126 A3
Aiginis 288 D5
Aike 150 C3
Aikerness 282 B5
Aikers 283 H5
Aiketgate 164 A2
Aikton 175 C5
Ailey 78 C1
Ailstone 81 B5
Ailsworth 100 B3
Ainderby Quernhow 158 C2
Ainderby Steeple 158 B2
Aingers Green 71 A5
Ainsdale 136 B2
Ainsdale-on-Sea 136 B2
Ainstable 164 A3
Ainsworth 137 B6
Ainthorpe 159 A6
Aintree 136 D2
Aird
Argyll 213 B5
Dumfries 170 A2
Highld 261 C4
W Isles 288 D6
Aird a Mhachair 286 B3
Aird a' Mhulaidh 288 F2
Aird Asaig 288 G2
Aird Dhail 288 A5
Airdens 264 A2
Aird Mhidhinis 286 F3
Aird Mhighe
W Isles 287 F5
W Isles 288 H2
Aird Mhor 286 F3
Aird of Sleat 247 D4
Airdrie 207 D5
Aird Thunga 288 D5
Airdtorrisdale 278 B2
Aird Uig 287 A5
Airidh a Bhruaich 288 F3
Airieland 173 C5
Airmyn 141 A5
Airntully 219 A5
Airor 247 D6
Airth 208 B1
Airton 146 B3
Airyhassen 171 C5
Aisby
Lincs 116 B3
Lincs 141 D6
Aisgernis 286 D3
Aiskew 157 C6
Aislaby
N Yorks 159 C6
N Yorks 160 A2
Stockton 168 D2
Aisthorpe 133 A4
Aith
Orkney 282 F3
Shetland 284 D8
Shetland 285 H5
Aithsetter 285 K6
Aitkenhead 192 E3
Aitnoch 253 C5
Akeld 188 A2
Akeley 83 D4
Akenham 88 C2
Albaston 11 D5
Alberbury 110 D2
Albourne 21 A5
Albrighton
Shrops 95 A6
Shrops 110 D3
Alburgh 104 C3
Albury
Herts 68 A4
Sur 34 B3
Albury End 68 A4
Alby Hill 120 B3
Alcaig 252 A1
Alcaston 94 C2
Alcester 80 B3
Alciston 22 B3
Alcombe
Som 27 A4
Wilts 44 C2
Alconbury 100 D3
Alconbury Weston 100 D3
Aldbar Castle 232 C3
Aldborough
Norf 120 B3
N Yorks 148 A3
Aldbourne 45 B6
Aldbrough 151 D5
Aldbrough St John 167 D5
Aldbury 67 B4
Aldcliffe 145 A4
Aldclune 230 B3
Aldeburgh 89 B5
Aldeby 105 B5
Aldenham 67 D6
Alderbury 31 C5
Aldercar 114 A2
Alderford 120 D3
Alderholt 31 D5
Alderley 62 D3
Alderley Edge 128 B3
Aldermaston 46 C3
Aldermaston Wharf 47 C4
Alderminster 81 C5
Alder's End 79 C4
Aldersey Green 127 D4
Aldershot 34 A1
Alderton
Glos 80 D3
Northants 83 C4
Shrops 110 C3
Suff 88 C4
Wilts 44 A2
Alderwasley 130 D3
Aldfield 147 A6
Aldford 127 D4
Aldham
Essex 70 A3
Suff 87 C6
Aldie 264 B3
Aldingbourne 20 B2
Aldingham 154 D1
Aldington
Kent 38 B2
Worcs 80 C3
Aldington Frith 38 B2
Aldochlay 206 A1
Aldreth 101 D6
Aldridge 96 A3
Aldringham 89 A5
Aldsworth 64 B2
Aldunie 255 D4
Aldwark
Derbys 130 D2
N Yorks 148 A3
Aldwick 20 C2
Aldwincle 100 C2
Aldworth 46 B3
Alexandria 206 C1
Alfardisworthy 24 D3
Alfington 13 B6
Alfold 34 C3
Alfold Bars 34 C3
Alfold Crossways 34 C3
Alford
Aberds 244 A2
Lincs 135 B4
Som 29 B6
Alfreton 131 D4
Alfrick 79 B5
Alfrick Pound 79 B5
Alfriston 22 B3
Algaltraig 203 A5
Algarkirk 117 B5
Alhampton 29 B6
Aline Lodge 288 F2
Alisary 235 C6
Alkborough 141 A6
Alkerton 81 C6
Alkham 39 A4
Alkington 111 B4
Alkmonton 113 B5
Alladale Lodge 263 B6
Allaleigh 8 B2
Allanaquoich 242 C4
Allangrange Mains 252 A2
Allanton
Borders 198 A2
N Lanark 194 A3
Allathasdal 286 F2
All Cannings 45 C4
Allendale Town 177 D6
Allenheads 165 A6
Allensford 178 D2
Allens Green 69 B4
Allensmore 78 D2
Allenton 114 B1
Aller 28 C4
Allerby 162 A3
Allerford 27 A4
Allerston 160 C2
Allerthorpe 149 C6
Allerton
Mers 127 A4
W Yorks 147 D5
Allerton Bywater 140 A2
Allerton Mauleverer 148 B3
Allesley 97 C6
Allestree 114 B1
Allet 4 C2
Allexton 99 A5
Allgreave 129 C4
Allhallows 51 B5
Allhallows-on-Sea 51 B5
Alligin Shuas 249 A5
Allimore Green 112 D2
Allington
Lincs 115 A6
Wilts 31 B6
Wilts 45 C4
Allithwaite 154 D2
Alloa 208 A1
Allonby 174 D3
Alloway 192 D3
All Saints South Elmham 104 C4
All Stretton 94 B2
Allt 57 B5
Alltchaorunn 237 D5
Alltforgan 109 C4
Alltmawr 77 C4
Alltnacaillich 277 D5
Allt na h-Airbhe 262 A3
Allt-nan-sùgh 249 D6
Alltsigh 240 A2
Alltwalis 58 B1
Alltwen 40 A2
Alltyblaca 75 D4
Allwood Green 103 D6
Almeley 78 B1
Almer 16 B3
Almholme 140 C3
Almington 111 B6
Alminstone Cross 24 C4
Almondbank 219 B5
Almondbury 139 B4
Almondsbury 43 A5
Alne 148 A3
Alness 264 D2
Alnham 188 B2
Alnmouth 189 B5
Alnwick 189 B4
Alperton 49 A4
Alphamstone 87 D4
Alpheton 87 B4
Alphington 13 B4
Alport 130 C2
Alpraham 127 D5
Alresford 71 A4
Alrewas 113 D5
Alsager 128 D2
Alsagers Bank 112 A2
Alsop en le Dale 129 D6
Alston
Cumb 165 A5
Devon 14 A3
Alstone 80 D2
Alstonefield 129 D6
Alswear 26 C2
Altandhu 270 C2
Altanduin 274 B2
Altarnun 10 C3
Altass 272 D2
Alterwall 281 B4
Altham 146 D1
Althorne 70 D3
Althorpe 141 C6
Alticry 171 B4
Altnabreac Station 279 D6
Altnacealgach Hotel 271 C5
Altnacraig 226 D3
Altnafeadh 237 D6
Altnaharra 272 A3
Altofts 139 A6
Alton
Derbys 130 C3
Hants 33 B6
Staffs 113 A4
Alton Pancras 15 A7
Alton Priors 45 C5
Altrincham 128 A2
Altrua 239 D6
Altskeith 217 D4
Altyre House 253 A6
Alva 208 A1
Alvanley 127 B4
Alvaston 114 B1
Alvechurch 96 D3
Alvecote 97 A5
Alvediston 30 C3
Alveley 95 C5
Alverdiscott 25 C6
Alverstoke 19 B5
Alverstone 19 C4
Alverton 115 A5
Alves 266 C2
Alvescot 64 C3
Alveston
S Glos 43 A5
Warks 81 B5
Alvie 241 B6
Alvingham 143 D5
Alvington 62 C2
Alwalton 100 B3
Alweston 29 D6
Alwinton 188 C2
Alwoodley 148 C1
Alyth 231 D6
Amatnatua 263 A6
Am Baile 286 E3
Ambergate 130 D3
Amber Hill 117 A5
Amberley
Glos 63 C4
W Sus 20 A3
Amble 189 C5
Amblecote 96 C1
Ambler Thorn 138 A3
Ambleside 154 A2
Ambleston 55 B6
Ambrosden 65 B7
Am Buth 226 D3
Amcotts 141 B6
Amersham 67 D4
Amesbury 31 A5
Amington 97 A5
Amisfield 184 D2
Amlwch 123 A4
Amlwch Port 123 A4
Ammanford
=Rhydaman 57 A6
Amod 190 B3
Amotherby 159 D6
Ampfield 32 C3
Ampleforth 159 D4
Ampney Crucis 63 C6
Ampney St Mary 64 C1
Ampney St Peter 64 C1
Amport 32 A1
Ampthill 84 D2
Ampton 103 D4
Amroth 56 B1
Amulree 218 A3
Anagach 253 D6
Anaheilt 236 C2
Anancaun 262 D2
An Caol 248 A3
Ancaster 116 A2
Anchor 93 C5
Anchorsholme 144 C3
An Cnoc 288 D5
Ancroft 198 B3
Ancrum 187 A5
Anderby 135 B5
Anderson 16 B2
Anderton 127 B6
Andover 32 A2
Andover Down 32 A2
Andoversford 63 B6
Andreas 152 B4
Anfield 136 D2
Angersleigh 28 D1
Angle 55 D4
An Gleann Ur 288 D5
Angmering 20 B3
Angram
N Yorks 148 C4
N Yorks 156 B2
Anie 217 C5
Ankerville 265 C4
Anlaby 142 A2
Anmer 119 C4
Annan 175 B4
Annat
Argyll 227 D5
Highld 249 A5
Anna Valley 32 A2
Annbank 193 C4
Annesley 131 D5
Annesley Woodhouse 131 D4
Annfield Plain 178 D3
Annifirth 285 J3
Annitsford 179 B4
Annscroft 94 A2

Ansdell 136 A2
Ansford 29 B6
Ansley 97 B5
Anslow 113 C6
Anslow Gate 113 C5
Anstey
  Herts 85 D6
  Leics 98 A3
Anstruther Easter . . 221 D5
Anstruther Wester . 221 D5
Ansty
  Hants 33 A6
  Warks 97 C6
  Wilts 30 C3
  W Sus 35 A3
Anthill Common 33 D5
Anthorn 175 C4
Antingham 121 B4
An t-Ob
  = Leverburgh 287 F5
Anton's Gowt 117 A5
Antonshill 208 B1
Antony 6 B3
Anwick 133 D6
Anwoth 172 C3
Aoradh 200 B2
Apes Hall 102 B1
Apethorpe 100 B2
Apeton 112 D2
Apley 133 B6
Apperknowle 130 B3
Apperley 63 A4
Apperley Bridge . . . 147 D5
Appersett 156 B2
Appin 226 B4
Appin House 226 B4
Appleby 142 B1
Appleby-in-
  Westmorland 165 C4
Appleby Magna . . 97 A6
Appleby Parva . . 97 A6
Applecross 249 B4
Applecross House . . 249 B4
Appledore
  Devon 25 B5
  Devon 27 D5
  Kent 38 C1
Appledore Heath . . . 38 B1
Appleford 65 D6
Applegarthtown . . . 185 D4
Appleshaw 32 A2
Applethwaite 163 B5
Appleton
  Halton 127 A5
  Oxon 65 C5
Appleton-le-
  Moors 159 C6
Appleton-le-Street 159 D6
Appleton Roebuck . 149 C4
Appleton Thorn . . . 127 A6
Appleton Wiske . . . 158 A2
Appletreehall 186 B4
Appletreewick . . . 147 A4
Appley 27 C5
Appley Bridge . . . 136 C4
Apse Heath 19 C4
Apsley End 84 D3
Apuldram 20 B1
Aquhythie 245 A4
Arabella 265 C4
Arbeadie 244 C3
Arberth = Narberth . . 55 C7
Arbirlot 233 D4
Arboll 265 B4
Arborfield 47 C5
Arborfield Cross . . . 47 C5
Arborfield Garrison . 47 C5
Arbourthorne 130 A3
Arbroath 233 D4
Arbuthnott 233 A5
Archiestown 254 B3
Arclid 128 C2
Ardachu 273 D4
Ardalanish 224 E2
Ardanaiseig 227 D5
Ardaneaskan 249 C5
Ardanstur 213 A6
Ardargie House
  Hotel 219 C5
Ardarroch 249 C5
Ardbeg
  Argyll 201 D4
  Argyll 215 D4
Ardcharnich 262 B3
Ardchiavaig 224 E2
Ardchullarie More . 217 C5
Ardchyle 217 B5
Ard-dhubh 249 B4
Arddleen 110 D1
Ardechive 239 C5

Ardeley 68 A3
Ardelve 249 D5
Arden 206 B1
Ardens Grafton 80 B4
Ardentinny 215 D4
Ardentraive 203 A5
Ardeonaig 217 A6
Ardersier 252 A3
Ardessie 262 B2
Ardfern 213 B6
Ardgartan 215 B5
Ardgay 264 A1
Ardgour 237 C4
Ardheslaig 249 A4
Ardiecow 267 C6
Ardindrean 262 B3
Ardingly 35 D6
Ardington 46 A2
Ardlair 255 D6
Ardlamont House . . 203 B4
Ardleigh 71 A4
Ardler 231 D6
Ardley 65 A6
Ardlui 215 B5
Ardlussa 213 D4
Ardmair 262 A3
Ardmay 215 B5
Ardminish 202 D1
Ardmolich 235 C6
Ardmore
  Argyll 226 D2
  Highld 264 B3
  Highld 276 C3
Ardnacross 225 B4
Ardnadam 203 A6
Ardnagrask 251 B7
Ardnarff 249 C5
Ardnastang 236 C2
Ardnave 200 A2
Ardno 215 B4
Ardo 256 C3
Ardoch 219 A5
Ardochy House . . . 239 B6
Ardo House 257 D4
Ardoyne 256 D1
Ardpatrick 202 B2
Ardpatrick House . . 202 C2
Ardpeaton 215 D5
Ardrishaig 213 D6
Ardross
  Fife 221 D5
  Highld 264 C2
Ardrossan 204 D2
Ardross Castle 264 C2
Ardshealach 235 D5
Ardsley 140 C1
Ardslignish 235 D4
Ardtalla 201 C4
Ardtalnaig 218 A2
Ardtoe 235 C5
Ardtrostan 217 B6
Arduaine 213 A5
Ardullie 264 D1
Ardvasar 247 D5
Ardvorlich 217 B6
Ardwell 170 C3
Ardwell Mains 170 C3
Ardwick 138 D1
Areley Kings 95 D6
Arford 34 C1
Argoed
  Caerph 41 B6
  Powys 76 A3
Arichamish 214 B2
Arichastlich 216 A2
Aridhglas 224 D2
Arileod 223 B4
Arinacrinachd 249 A4
Arinagour 223 B5
Arion 282 F3
Arisaig 235 B5
Ariundle 236 C2
Arkendale 148 A2
Arkesden 85 D6
Arkholme 155 D4
Arkleton 186 D2
Arkle Town 156 A4
Arkley 68 D2
Arksey 140 C3
Arkwright Town . . . 131 B4
Arle 63 A5
Arlecdon 162 C3
Arlesey 84 D3
Arleston 111 D5
Arley 128 A1
Arlingham 62 B3
Arlington
  Devon 25 A7
  E Sus 22 B3
  Glos 64 C2

Armadale
  Highld 278 B3
  W Loth 208 D2
Armadale Castle . . . 247 D5
Armathwaite 164 A3
Arminghall 104 A3
Armitage 113 D4
Armley 148 D1
Armscote 81 C5
Armthorpe 140 C4
Arnabost 223 B5
Arncliffe 156 D3
Arncroach 221 D5
Arne 16 C3
Arnesby 98 B3
Arngask 219 C6
Arnisdale 238 A2
Arnish 248 B2
Arniston Engine . . . 209 D6
Arnol 288 C4
Arnold
  E Yorks 151 C4
  Notts 114 A3
Arnprior 207 A4
Arnside 154 D3
Aros Mains 225 B4
Arowry 110 B3
Arpafeelie 252 A2
Arrad Foot 154 C2
Arram 150 C3
Arrathorne 157 B6
Arreton 18 C4
Arrington 85 B5
Arrivain 216 A2
Arrochar 215 B5
Arrow 80 B3
Arthington 147 C6
Arthingworth 99 C4
Arthog 90 A4
Arthrath 257 C4
Arthurstone 231 D6
Artrochie 257 C5
Arundel 20 B3
Aryhoulan 237 C4
Asby 162 B3
Ascog 203 B6
Ascot 48 C2
Ascott 81 D6
Ascott-under-
  Wychwood 64 B4
Asenby 158 D2
Asfordby 115 D5
Asfordby Hill 115 D5
Asgarby
  Lincs 116 A4
  Lincs 134 C3
Ash
  Kent 50 C2
  Kent 53 D4
  Som 29 C4
  Sur 34 A1
Ashampstead 46 B3
Ashbocking 88 B2
Ashbourne 113 A5
Ashbrittle 27 C5
Ash Bullayne 12 A2
Ashburton 7 A6
Ashbury
  Devon 11 B6
  Oxon 45 A6
Ashby 141 C7
Ashby by Partney . . 135 C4
Ashby cum Fenby . . 143 C4
Ashby de la
  Launde 133 D5
Ashby-de-la-
  Zouch 114 D1
Ashby Folville 115 D5
Ashby Magna 98 B2
Ashby Parva 98 C2
Ashby Puerorum . . 134 B3
Ashby St Ledgers . . 82 A2
Ashby St Mary 104 A4
Ashchurch 80 D2
Ashcombe 13 D4
Ashcott 28 B4
Ashdon 86 C1
Ashe 32 A4
Asheldham 70 C3
Ashen 86 C3
Ashendon 66 B2
Ashfield
  Carms 58 C3
  Stirling 218 D2
  Suff 88 A3
Ashfield Green . . . 104 D3
Ashfold Crossways . 35 D5
Ashford
  Devon 25 B6
  Hants 31 D5

Ashford continued
  Kent 38 A2
  Sur 48 B3
Ashford Bowdler . . . 94 D3
Ashford Carbonell . . 94 D3
Ashford Hill 46 C3
Ashford in the
  Water 130 C1
Ashgill 194 B2
Ash Green 97 C6
Ashill
  Devon 27 D5
  Norf 103 A4
  Som 28 D3
Ashingdon 70 D2
Ashington
  Northumb 179 A4
  Som 29 C5
  W Sus 21 A4
Ashintully Castle . . 231 B5
Ashkirk 186 A3
Ashlett 18 A3
Ashleworth 63 A4
Ashley
  Cambs 86 A2
  Ches E 128 A2
  Devon 26 D1
  Dorset 17 A5
  Glos 63 D5
  Hants 17 B6
  Hants 32 B2
  Northants 99 B4
  Staffs 111 B6
Ashley Green 67 C4
Ashley Heath
  Dorset 17 A5
  Staffs 111 B6
Ash Magna 111 B4
Ashmanhaugh 121 C5
Ashmansworth 46 D2
Ashmansworthy . . . 24 D4
Ash Mill 26 C2
Ashmore 30 D3
Ashorne 81 B6
Ashover 130 C3
Ashow 97 D6
Ashprington 8 B2
Ash Priors 27 C6
Ashreigney 26 D1
Ash Street 87 C6
Ashtead 35 A4
Ash Thomas 27 D5
Ashton
  Ches W 127 C5
  Corn 3 C4
  Hants 33 D4
  Hereford 78 A3
  Invclyd 204 A2
  Northants 83 C4
  Northants 100 C2
Ashton Common . . . 44 D2
Ashton-In-
  Makerfield 137 D4
Ashton Keynes 63 D6
Ashton under Hill . . 80 D2
Ashton-under-
  Lyne 138 D2
Ashton upon
  Mersey 137 D6
Ashurst
  Hants 32 D2
  Kent 36 C3
  W Sus 21 A4
Ashurstwood 36 C2
Ash Vale 34 A1
Ashwater 11 B4
Ashwell
  Herts 85 D4
  Rutland 115 D6
  Som 28 D3
Ashwellthorpe . . . 104 B2
Ashwick 29 A6
Ashwicken 119 D4
Ashybank 186 B4
Askam in Furness . 153 C2
Askern 140 B3
Askerswell 15 B5
Askett 66 C2
Askham
  Cumb 164 C3
  Notts 132 B2
Askham Bryan . . . 149 C4
Askham Richard . . 148 C4
Asknish 214 C2
Askrigg 156 B3
Askwith 147 C5
Aslackby 116 B3
Aslacton 104 B2
Aslockton 115 B5
Asloun 244 A2

Aspatria 174 D4
Aspenden 68 A3
Asperton 117 B5
Aspley Guise 83 D6
Aspley Heath 83 D6
Aspull 137 C5
Asselby 141 A5
Asserby 135 B4
Assington 87 D5
Assynt House 264 D1
Astbury 128 C3
Astcote 82 B3
Asterley 94 A1
Asterton 94 B1
Asthall 64 B3
Asthall Leigh 64 B3
Astley
  Shrops 111 D4
  Warks 97 C6
  Worcs 79 A5
Astley Abbotts . . . 95 B5
Astley Bridge 137 B6
Astley Cross 79 A6
Astley Green 137 D6
Aston
  Ches E 111 A5
  Ches W 127 B5
  Derbys 130 A1
  Hereford 94 D2
  Herts 68 A2
  Oxon 64 C4
  Shrops 111 C4
  Staffs 111 A6
  S Yorks 131 A4
  Telford 95 A4
  W Mid 96 C3
  Wokingham 47 A5
Aston Abbotts 66 A3
Aston Botterell . . . 95 C4
Aston-By-Stone . . . 112 B3
Aston Cantlow 80 B4
Aston Clinton 66 B3
Aston Crews 62 A2
Aston Cross 80 D2
Aston End 68 A2
Aston Eyre 95 B4
Aston Fields 80 A2
Aston Flamville . . . 98 B1
Aston Ingham 62 A2
Aston juxta
  Mondrum 127 D6
Aston le Walls . . . 82 B1
Aston Magna 81 D4
Aston Munslow . . . 94 C3
Aston on Clun 94 C1
Aston-on-Trent . . . 114 C2
Aston Rogers 94 A1
Aston Rowant 66 D2
Aston Sandford . . . 66 C2
Aston Somerville . . 80 D3
Aston Subedge . . . 80 C4
Aston Tirrold 46 A3
Aston Upthorpe . . . 46 A3
Astrop 82 D2
Astwick 84 D4
Astwood
  M Keynes 83 C6
  Worcs 79 B6
Astwood Bank 80 A3
Aswarby 116 B3
Aswardby 134 B3
Atcham 94 A3
Atch Lench 80 B3
Athelhampton 16 B1
Athelington 104 D3
Athelney 28 C3
Athelstaneford . . . 210 C2
Atherington 25 C6
Atherstone 97 B6
Atherstone on Stour 81 B5
Atherton 137 C5
Atley Hill 157 A6
Atlow 113 A6
Attadale 249 C6
Attadale House . . 249 C6
Attenborough . . . 114 B3
Atterby 142 D1
Attercliffe 130 A3
Attleborough
  Norf 103 B6
  Warks 97 B6
Attlebridge 120 D3
Atwick 151 B4
Atworth 44 C2
Auberrow 78 C2
Aubourn 133 C4
Auchagallon 191 B4
Auchallater 243 D4
Aucharnie 256 B1
Auchattie 244 C3
Auchavan 231 B5

Auchbreck 254 D3
Auchenback 205 C5
Auchenbainzie . . . 183 C6
Auchenblae 233 A5
Auchenbrack 183 C5
Auchenbreck 214 D3
Auchencairn
  Dumfries 173 C5
  Dumfries 184 D2
  N Ayrs 191 C6
Auchencrosh 180 D3
Auchencrow 211 D5
Auchendinny 209 D5
Auchengray 195 A4
Auchenhalrig 267 C4
Auchenheath 194 B3
Auchenlochan . . . 203 A4
Auchenmalg 171 B4
Auchensoul 181 B4
Auchentiber 204 D3
Auchertyre 249 D5
Auchgourish 242 A2
Auchincarroch . . . 206 B2
Auchindrain 214 B3
Auchindrean 262 B3
Auchininna 256 B1
Auchinleck 193 C5
Auchinloch 205 A6
Auchinroath 266 D3
Auchintoul 244 A2
Auchiries 257 C5
Auchlee 245 C5
Auchleven 256 D1
Auchlochan 194 C3
Auchlossan 244 B2
Auchlunies 245 C5
Auchlyne 217 B5
Auchmacoy 257 C5
Auchmair 255 D4
Auchmantle 170 A3
Auchmillan 193 C5
Auchmithie 233 D4
Auchmuirbridge . . 220 D2
Auchmull 232 A3
Auchnacree 232 B2
Auchnagallin . . . 253 C6
Auchnagatt 257 B4
Auchnaha 214 D2
Auchnashelloch . . 218 C2
Aucholzie 243 C6
Auchrannie 231 C6
Auchroisk 253 D6
Auchronie 244 D1
Auchterarder 218 C4
Auchteraw 240 B1
Auchterderran . . . 209 A5
Auchterhouse . . . 220 A3
Auchtermuchty . . 220 C2
Auchterneed 251 A6
Auchtertool 209 A5
Auchtertyre 266 D2
Auchtubh 217 B5
Auckengill 281 B5
Auckley 140 C4
Audenshaw 138 D2
Audlem 111 A5
Audley 128 D2
Audley End 87 D4
Auds 268 C1
Aughton
  E Yorks 149 D6
  Lancs 136 C2
  Lancs 145 A5
  S Yorks 131 A4
  Wilts 45 D6
Aughton Park . . . 136 C3
Auldearn 253 A5
Aulden 78 B2
Auldgirth 183 D7
Auldhame 210 B2
Auldhouse 205 C6
Ault a'chruinn . . . 249 D6
Aultanrynie 271 A6
Aultbea 261 B5
Aultdearg 263 D4
Aultgrishan 261 B4
Aultguish Inn . . . 263 C5
Aultibea 274 B4
Aultiphurst 279 B4
Aultmore 267 C5
Aultnagoire 252 D1
Aultnamain Inn . . 264 B2
Aultnaslat 239 B5
Aulton 255 D7
Aundorach 242 A2
Aunsby 116 B3
Auquhorthies . . . 256 D3
Aust 43 A4

Austendike 117 C5
Austerfield 141 D4
Austrey 97 A5
Austwick 146 A1
Authorpe 135 A4
Authorpe Row . . .135 B5
Avebury 45 C5
Aveley 50 A2
Avening 63 D4
Averham 132 D2
Aveton Gifford 7 C5
Avielochan 242 A2
Aviemore 242 A1
Avington
  Hants 32 B4
  W Berks 46 C1
Avoch 252 A3
Avon 17 B5
Avonbridge 208 C2
Avon Dassett 81 C7
Avonmouth 43 B4
Avonwick 7 B6
Awbridge 32 C2
Awhirk 170 B2
Awkley 43 A4
Awliscombe 13 A6
Awre 62 C3
Awsworth 114 A2
Axbridge 42 D3
Axford
  Hants 33 A5
  Wilts 45 C6
Axminster 14 B2
Axmouth 14 B2
Axton 125 A6
Aycliff 39 A5
Aycliffe 167 C5
Aydon 178 C2
Aylburton 62 C2
Ayle 165 A5
Aylesbeare 13 B5
Aylesbury 66 B3
Aylesby 143 C4
Aylesford 37 A5
Aylesham 53 D4
Aylestone 98 A2
Aylmerton 120 B3
Aylsham 120 C3
Aylton 79 D4
Aymestrey 78 A2
Aynho 82 D2
Ayot St Lawrence . . 68 B1
Ayot St Peter 68 B2
Ayr 192 C3
Aysgarth 156 C4
Ayside 154 C2
Ayston 99 A5
Aythorpe Roding . . . 69 B5
Ayton 211 D6
Aywick 284 E7
Azerley 157 D6

B

Babbacombe 8 A3
Babbinswood 110 B2
Babcary 29 C5
Babel 59 B5
Babell 125 B6
Babraham 85 B7
Babworth 132 A1
Bac 288 C5
Bachau 123 B4
Backaland 282 D6
Backaskaill 282 B5
Backbarrow 154 C2
Backe 56 A2
Backfolds 269 D5
Backford 127 B4
Backford Cross . .126 B3
Backhill
  Aberds 256 C2
  Aberds 257 C5
Backhill of
  Clackriach 257 B4
Backhill of
  Fortree 257 B4
Backhill of
  Trustach 244 C3
Backies 274 D2
Backlass 280 C4
Back of Keppoch .235 B5
Back Rogerton . . .193 C5
Backwell 42 C3
Backworth 179 B5
Bacon End 69 B6
Baconsthorpe 120 B3

Bacton
  Hereford 78 D1
  Norf 121 B5
  Suff 87 A6
Bacton Green 87 A6
Bacup 138 A1
Badachro 261 C4
Badanloch Lodge . .273 A5
Badavanich 250 A3
Badbury 45 A5
Badby 82 B2
Badcall 276 C3
Badcaul 262 A2
Baddeley Green . . .129 D4
Baddesley Clinton . .97 D5
Baddesley Ensor . . .97 B5
Baddidarach 270 B3
Baddoch 242 D4
Baddock 252 A3
Badenscoth 256 C2
Badenyon 243 A6
Badger 95 B5
Badger's Mount 50 C1
Badgeworth 63 B5
Badgworth 42 D2
Badicaul 249 D4
Badingham 88 A4
Badlesmere 52 D2
Badlipster 280 D4
Badluarach 262 A1
Badminton 44 A2
Badnaban 270 B3
Badninish 264 A3
Badrallach 262 A2
Badsey 80 C3
Badshot Lea 34 B1
Badsworth 140 B2
Badwell Ash 87 A5
Bae Colwyn
  = Colwyn Bay 124 B3
Bagby 158 C3
Bag Enderby 134 B3
Bagendon 63 C6
Bagh a Chaisteil
  = Castlebay 286 G2
Baghasdal 286 E3
Bagh Mor 286 A4
Bagh Shiarabhagh .286 F3
Bagillt 126 B2
Baginton 97 D6
Baglan 40 B2
Bagley 110 C3
Bagnall 129 D4
Bagnor 46 C2
Bagshot
  Sur 48 C2
  Wilts 45 C7
Bagthorpe
  Norf 119 B4
  Notts 131 D4
Bagworth 98 A1
Bagwy Llydiart . . .61 A6
Bail Àrd Bhuirgh . .288 B5
Baildon 147 D5
Baile 287 F4
Baile Ailein 288 E3
Baile a Mhanaich .286 A3
Baile an Truiseil . .288 B4
Bailebeag 240 A3
Baile Boidheach . .202 A2
Baile Glas 286 A4
Baile Mhartainn . . .287 G2
Baile Mhic Phail . .287 G3
Baile Mor
  Argyll 224 D1
  W Isles 287 H2
Baile na Creige . . .286 F2
Baile nan
  Cailleach 286 A3
Baile Raghaill 287 G2
Baileyhead 176 B3
Bailiesward 255 C5
Baillieston 205 B6
Bail' Iochdrach . . .286 A4
Bail Uachdraich . . .287 H3
Bail' Ur
  Tholastaidh 288 C6
Bainbridge 156 B3
Bainsford 208 B1
Bainshole 255 C7
Bainton
  E Yorks 150 B2
  Pboro 100 A2
Bairnkine 187 B5
Baker's End 68 B3
Baker Street 50 A3
Bakewell 130 C2
Bala = Y Bala 108 B4
Balachuirn 248 B2
Balavil 241 B5

Balbeg
  Highld 251 C6
  Highld 251 D6
Balbeggie 219 B6
Balbithan 245 A4
Balbithan House . .245 A5
Balblair
  Highld 264 A1
  Highld 264 D3
Balby 140 C3
Balchladich 270 A3
Balchraggan
  Highld 252 B1
  Highld 252 C1
Balchrick 276 C2
Balchrystie 221 D4
Balcladaich 251 D4
Balcombe 35 C6
Balcombe Lane . . .35 C6
Balcomie 221 C6
Balcurvie 220 D3
Baldersby 158 D2
Baldersby
  St James 158 D2
Balderstone 145 D6
Balderton
  Ches W 126 C3
  Notts 132 D3
Baldhu 4 C2
Baldinnie 220 C4
Baldock 84 D4
Baldovie 221 A4
Baldrine 152 C4
Baldslow 23 A5
Baldwin 152 C3
Baldwinholme . . .175 C6
Baldwin's Gate . . .112 A1
Bale 120 B2
Balearn 269 D5
Balemartine 222 C2
Balephuil 222 C2
Balerno 209 D4
Balevullin 222 C2
Balfield 232 B3
Balfour 282 F5
Balfron 206 B3
Balfron Station . . .206 B3
Balgaveny 256 B1
Balgavies 232 C3
Balgonar 208 A3
Balgove 256 C3
Balgowan 241 C4
Balgown 258 B3
Balgrochan 205 A6
Balgy 249 A5
Balhaldie 218 D3
Balhalgardy 256 D2
Balham 49 B5
Balhary 231 D6
Baliasta 284 C8
Baligill 279 B4
Balintore
  Angus 231 C6
  Highld 265 C4
Balintraid 264 C3
Balk 158 C3
Balkeerie 232 D1
Balkemback 220 A3
Balkholme 141 A5
Balkissock 180 C3
Ball 110 C2
Ballabeg 152 D2
Ballacannel 152 C4
Ballachulish 237 D4
Ballajora 152 B4
Ballaleigh 152 C3
Ballamodha 152 D2
Ballantrae 180 C2
Ballaquine 152 C4
Ballards Gore 70 D3
Ballasalla
  IoM 152 B3
  IoM 152 D2
Ballater 243 C6
Ballaugh 152 B3
Ballaveare 152 D2
Ballcorach 254 D2
Ballechin 230 C3
Balleigh 264 B3
Ballencrieff 210 C1
Ballentoul 230 B2
Ball Haye
  Green 129 D4
Ball Hill 46 C2
Ballidon 130 D2
Balliemore
  Argyll 214 D3
  Argyll 226 D3
Ballikinrain 206 B3
Ballimeanoch 214 A3

Ballimore
  Argyll 214 D2
  Stirling 217 C5
Ballinaby 200 B2
Ballindean 220 B2
Ballingdon 87 C4
Ballinger Common . . 67 C4
Ballingham 78 D3
Ballingry 209 A4
Ballinlick 230 D3
Ballinluig 230 C3
Ballintuim 231 C5
Balloch
  Angus 232 C1
  Highld 252 B3
  N Lanark 207 C5
  W Dunb 206 B1
Ballochan 244 C2
Ballochford 255 C4
Ballochmorrie 181 C4
Balls Cross 34 D2
Balls Green 71 A4
Ballygown 224 B3
Ballygrant 200 B3
Ballyhaugh 223 B4
Balmacara 249 D5
Balmacara Square . .249 D5
Balmaclellan 173 A4
Balmacneil 230 C3
Balmacqueen 259 A4
Balmae 173 D4
Balmaha 206 A2
Balmalcolm 220 D3
Balmeanach 248 B2
Balmedie 245 A6
Balmer Heath 110 B3
Balmerino 220 B3
Balmerlawn 18 A2
Balmichael 191 B5
Balmirmer 221 A5
Balmore
  Highld 251 C5
  Highld 253 B4
  Highld 258 D2
  Perth 230 C3
Balmule 209 B5
Balmullo 220 B4
Balmungie 252 A3
Balnaboth 231 B7
Balnabruaich 264 D3
Balnabruich 275 B5
Balnacoil 274 C2
Balnacra 250 B1
Balnafoich 252 C2
Balnagall 265 B4
Balnaguard 230 C3
Balnahard
  Argyll 212 C2
  Argyll 224 C3
Balnain 251 C6
Balnakeil 277 B4
Balnaknock 259 B4
Balnapaling 264 D3
Balne 140 B3
Balochroy 202 C2
Balone 221 C4
Balornock 205 B6
Balquharn 219 A5
Balquhidder 217 B5
Balsall 97 D5
Balsall Common . . .97 D5
Balsall Heath 96 C3
Balscott 81 C6
Balsham 86 B1
Baltasound 284 C8
Balterley 128 D2
Baltersan 171 A6
Balthangie 268 D3
Baltonsborough . . .29 B5
Balvaird 252 A1
Balvicar 213 A5
Balvraid
  Highld 238 A2
  Highld 253 C4
Bamber Bridge . . .137 A4
Bambers Green . . .69 A5
Bamburgh 199 C5
Bamff 231 C6
Bamford
  Derbys 130 A2
  Gtr Man 138 B1
Bampton
  Cumb 164 D3
  Devon 27 C4
  Oxon 64 C4
Bampton Grange . .164 D3
Banavie 237 B5
Banbury 82 C1
Bancffosfelen 57 A4
Banchory 244 C3

Banchory-
  Devenick 245 B6
Bancycapel 57 A4
Bancyfelin 56 A3
Bancyffordd 73 C7
Bandirran 220 A2
Banff 268 C1
Bangor-is-y-coed
  = Bangor-on-Dee . .110 A2
Bangor-on-Dee
  = Bangor-is-y-coed . .110 A2
Banham 103 C6
Bank 18 A1
Bankend 174 B3
Bankfoot 219 A5
Bankglen 182 A4
Bankhead
  Aberdeen 245 A5
  Aberds 244 B3
Bank Newton 146 B3
Banknock 207 C5
Banks
  Cumb 176 C3
  Lancs 136 A2
Bankshill 185 D4
Bank Street 79 A4
Banningham 120 C4
Banniskirk House . .280 C3
Bannister Green . . .69 A6
Bannockburn 207 A6
Banstead 35 A5
Bantham 7 C5
Banton 207 C5
Banwell 42 D2
Banyard's Green . .104 D3
Bapchild 51 C6
Barabhas 288 C4
Barabhas Iarach . .288 C4
Barabhas Uarach . .288 B4
Barachandroman . .225 D5
Barassie 192 B3
Barbaraville 264 C3
Barber Booth 129 A6
Barbieston 182 A2
Barbon 155 C5
Barbridge 127 D6
Barbrook 26 A2
Barby 98 D2
Barcaldine 227 B4
Barcheston 81 D5
Barcombe 22 A2
Barcombe Cross . .22 A2
Barden 157 B5
Bardennoch 182 C3
Barden Scale 147 B4
Bardfield Saling . . .69 A6
Bardister 284 F5
Bardney 133 C6
Bardon 114 D2
Bardon Mill 177 C5
Bardowie 205 A5
Bardrainney 204 A3
Bardsea 154 D2
Bardsey 148 C2
Bardwell 103 D5
Bare 145 A4
Barfad 202 B3
Barford
  Norf 104 A2
  Warks 81 A5
Barford St John 82 D1
Barford St Martin . . 31 B4
Barford
  St Michael 82 D1
Barfrestone 53 D4
Bargod = Bargoed . .41 B6
Bargoed = Bargod . .41 B6
Bargrennan 181 D5
Barham
  Cambs 100 D3
  Kent 53 D4
  Suff 88 B2
Barharrow 172 C4
Barhill 173 B6
Bar Hill 85 A5
Barholm 116 D3
Barkby 98 A3
Barkestone-
  le-Vale 115 B5
Barkham 47 C5
Barking
  London 50 A1
  Suff 87 B6
Barkingside 50 A1
Barking Tye 87 B6
Barkisland 138 B3
Barkston
  Lincs 116 A2

Barkston continued
  N Yorks 148 D3
Barkway 85 D5
Barlaston 112 B2
Barlavington 20 A2
Barlborough 131 B4
Barlby 149 D5
Barlestone 98 A1
Barley
  Herts 85 D5
  Lancs 146 C2
Barley Mow 179 D4
Barleythorpe 99 A5
Barling 51 A6
Barlow
  Derbys 130 B3
  N Yorks 140 A4
  T&W 178 C3
Barmby Moor 149 C6
Barmby on the
  Marsh 141 A4
Barmer 119 B5
Barmoor Castle . . .198 C3
Barmoor Lane End .198 C4
Barmouth
  = Abermaw 90 A4
Barmpton 167 D6
Barmston 151 B4
Barnack 100 A2
Barnacle 97 C6
Barnard Castle . . .166 D3
Barnard Gate 65 B5
Barnardiston 86 C3
Barnbarroch 173 C6
Barnburgh 140 C2
Barnby 105 C5
Barnby Dun 140 C4
Barnby in the
  Willows 132 D3
Barnby Moor 131 A6
Barnes Street 36 B4
Barnet 68 D2
Barnetby le Wold . .142 C2
Barney 120 B1
Barnham
  Suff 103 D4
  W Sus 20 B2
Barnham Broom . .104 A1
Barnhead 233 C4
Barnhill
  Ches W 127 D4
  Dundee 221 A4
  Moray 266 D2
Barnhills 180 D1
Barningham
  Durham 166 D3
  Suff 103 D5
Barnoldby le Beck . .143 C4
Barnoldswick 146 C2
Barns Green 35 D4
Barnsley
  Glos 64 C1
  S Yorks 139 C6
Barnstaple 25 C6
Barnston
  Essex 69 B6
  Mers 126 A2
Barnstone 115 B5
Barnt Green 96 D3
Barnton
  Ches W 127 B6
  Edin 209 C4
Barnwell All Saints .100 C2
Barnwell
  St Andrew 100 C2
Barnwood 63 B4
Barochreal 226 D3
Barons Cross 78 B2
Barr 181 B4
Barra Castle 256 D2
Barrachan 171 C5
Barrack 256 B3
Barraglom 288 D2
Barrahormid 213 D5
Barran 226 D3
Barrapol 222 C2
Barras
  Aberds 245 D5
  Cumb 165 D6
Barrasford 177 B7
Barravullin 213 B6
Barregarrow 152 C3
Barrhead 205 C4
Barrhill 181 C4
Barrington
  Cambs 85 C5
  Som 28 D3
Barripper 3 C4
Barrmill 204 C3
Barrock 281 A4

Barrock House 281 B4
Barrow
Lancs 146 D1
Rutland 116 D1
Suff 86 A3
Barroway Drove 102 A1
Barrowburn 188 B1
Barrowby 116 B1
Barrowcliff 160 C4
Barrowden 99 A6
Barrowford 146 D2
Barrow Green 51 C6
Barrow Gurney 43 C4
Barrow Haven 142 A2
Barrow-in-Furness 153 D3
Barrow Island 153 D2
Barrow Nook 136 C3
Barrows Green
Ches E 128 D1
Cumb 154 C4
Barrow's Green 127 A5
Barrow Street 30 B2
Barrow upon Humber 142 A2
Barrow upon Soar 114 D3
Barrow upon Trent 114 C1
Barry 221 A5
Barry = Y Barri 41 E6
Barry Island 41 E6
Barsby 115 D4
Barsham 105 C4
Barston 97 D5
Bartestree 78 C3
Barthol Chapel 256 C3
Barthomley 128 D2
Bartley 32 D2
Bartley Green 96 C3
Bartlow 86 C1
Barton
Cambs 85 B6
Ches W 127 D4
Glos 64 A2
Lancs 136 C2
Lancs 145 D5
N Yorks 157 A6
Oxon 65 C6
Torbay 8 A3
Warks 80 B4
Barton Bendish 102 A3
Barton Hartshorn 82 D3
Barton in Fabis 114 B3
Barton in the Beans 97 A6
Barton-le-Clay 84 D2
Barton-le-Street 159 D6
Barton-le-Willows 149 A6
Barton Mills 102 D3
Barton on Sea 17 B6
Barton on the Heath 81 D5
Barton St David 29 B5
Barton Seagrave 99 D5
Barton Stacey 32 A3
Barton Turf 121 C5
Barton-under-Needwood 113 D5
Barton-upon-Humber 142 A2
Barton Waterside 142 A2
Barugh 139 C6
Barway 102 D1
Barwell 98 B1
Barwick
Herts 68 B3
Som 29 D5
Barwick in Elmet 148 D2
Baschurch 110 C3
Bascote 81 A7
Basford Green 129 D4
Bashall Eaves 145 C6
Bashley 17 B6
Basildon 51 A4
Basingstoke 47 D4
Baslow 130 B2
Bason Bridge 28 A3
Bassaleg 42 A1
Bassenthwaite 163 A5
Bassett 32 D3
Bassingbourn 85 C5
Bassingfield 115 B4
Bassingham 133 C4
Bassingthorpe 116 C2
Basta 284 D7
Baston 116 D4
Bastwick 121 D6
Baswick Steer 150 C3
Batchworth Heath 67 D5
Batcombe
Dorset 15 A6
Som 29 B6
Bate Heath 128 B1
Batford 67 B6
Bath 43 C6
Bathampton 44 C1
Bathealton 27 C5
Batheaston 44 C1
Bathford 44 C1
Bathgate 208 D2
Bathley 132 D2
Bathpool
Corn 10 D3
Som 28 C2
Bathville 208 D2
Batley 139 A5
Batsford 81 D4
Battersby 159 A4
Battersea 49 B5
Battisborough Cross 7 C4
Battisford 87 B6
Battisford Tye 87 B6
Battle
E Sus 23 A5
Powys 76 D4
Battledown 63 A5
Battlefield 111 D4
Battlesbridge 70 D1
Battlesden 67 A4
Battlesea Green 104 D3
Battleton 27 C4
Battram 98 A1
Battramsley 18 B2
Baughton 80 C1
Baughurst 46 D3
Baulking 64 D4
Baumber 134 B2
Baunton 63 C6
Baverstock 31 B4
Bawburgh 104 A2
Bawdeswell 120 C2
Bawdrip 28 B3
Bawdsey 88 C4
Bawtry 141 D4
Baxenden 137 A6
Baxterley 97 B5
Baybridge 32 C4
Baycliff 154 D1
Baydon 45 B6
Bayford
Herts 68 C3
Som 30 C1
Bayles 165 A5
Baylham 88 B2
Baynard's Green 65 A6
Bayston Hill 94 A2
Baythorn End 86 C3
Bayton 95 D4
Beach 236 D1
Beachampton 83 D4
Beachamwell 102 A3
Beachans 253 B6
Beacharr 202 D1
Beachborough 38 B3
Beachley 62 D1
Beacon 14 A1
Beacon End 70 A3
Beacon Hill 34 C1
Beacon's Bottom 66 D2
Beaconsfield 67 E4
Beacrabhaic 288 H2
Beadlam 159 C5
Beadlow 84 D3
Beadnell 189 A5
Beaford 25 D6
Beal
Northumb 199 B4
N Yorks 140 A3
Beamhurst 113 B4
Beaminster 15 A4
Beamish 179 D4
Beamsley 147 B4
Bean 50 B2
Beanacre 44 C3
Beanley 188 B3
Beaquoy 282 E4
Bear Cross 17 B4
Beardwood 137 A5
Beare Green 35 B4
Bearley 81 A4
Bearnus 224 B2
Bearpark 167 A5
Bearsbridge 177 D5
Bearsden 205 A5
Bearsted 37 A5
Bearstone 111 B6
Bearwood
BCP 17 B4
Hereford 78 B1
W Mid 96 C3
Beattock 184 B3
Beauchamp Roding 69 B5
Beauchief 130 A3
Beaufort 60 B3
Beaufort Castle 251 B7
Beaulieu 18 A2
Beauly 252 B1
Beaumaris 123 C6
Beaumont
Cumb 175 C6
Essex 71 A5
Beaumont Hill 167 D5
Beausale 97 D5
Beauworth 33 C4
Beaworthy 11 B5
Beazley End 70 A1
Bebington 126 A3
Bebside 179 A4
Beccles 105 B5
Becconsall 136 A3
Beckbury 95 A5
Beckenham 49 C6
Beckermet 162 D3
Beckfoot
Cumb 163 D4
Cumb 174 D3
Beck Foot 155 B5
Beckford 80 D2
Beckhampton 45 C4
Beck Hole 159 A7
Beckingham
Lincs 132 D3
Notts 141 E5
Beckington 44 D2
Beckley
E Sus 37 D6
Hants 17 B6
Oxon 65 B6
Beck Row 102 D2
Beck Side 153 B3
Beckton 50 A1
Beckwithshaw 147 B6
Becontree 50 A1
Bedale 157 C6
Bedburn 166 B4
Bedchester 30 D2
Beddau 41 C5
Beddgelert 107 B5
Beddingham 22 B2
Beddington 49 C6
Bedfield 88 A3
Bedford 84 B2
Bedham 34 D3
Bedhampton 19 A6
Bedingfield 88 A2
Bedlam 147 A6
Bedlington 179 A4
Bedlington Station 179 A4
Bedlinog 41 A5
Bedminster 43 B4
Bedmond 67 C5
Bednall 112 D3
Bedrule 187 B5
Bedstone 94 D1
Bedwas 41 C6
Bedworth 97 C6
Bedworth Heath 97 C6
Bed-y-coedwr 108 C2
Beeby 98 A3
Beech
Hants 33 B5
Staffs 112 B2
Beech Hill
Gtr Man 137 C4
W Berks 47 C4
Beechingstoke 45 D4
Beedon 46 B2
Beeford 151 B4
Beeley 130 C2
Beelsby 143 C4
Beenham 46 C3
Beeny 10 B2
Beer 14 C2
Beercrocombe 28 C3
Beer Hackett 29 D6
Beesands 8 C2
Beesby 135 A4
Beeson 8 C2
Beeston
C Beds 84 C3
Ches W 127 D5
Norf 119 D6
Notts 114 B3
W Yorks 148 D1
Beeston Regis 120 A3
Beeswing 173 B6
Beetham 154 D3
Beetley 119 D6
Begbroke 65 B5
Begelly 55 D7
Beggar's Bush 77 A6
Beguildy 93 D5
Beighton
Norf 105 A4
Beighton *continued*
S Yorks 131 A4
Beighton Hill 130 D2
Beith 204 C3
Bekesbourne 52 D3
Belaugh 121 D4
Belbroughton 96 D2
Belchamp Otten 87 C4
Belchamp St Paul 86 C3
Belchamp Walter 87 C4
Belchford 134 B2
Belford 199 C5
Belhaven 210 C3
Belhelvie 245 A6
Belhinnie 255 D5
Bellabeg 243 A6
Bellamore 181 C4
Bellanoch 213 C5
Bellaty 231 C6
Bell Bar 68 C2
Bell Busk 146 B3
Belleau 135 B4
Bellehiglash 254 C2
Bell End 96 D2
Bellerby 157 B5
Bellever 12 D1
Belliehill 232 B3
Bellingdon 67 C4
Bellingham 177 A6
Belloch 190 B2
Bellochantuy 190 B2
Bell o' th' Hill 111 A4
Bellsbank 182 B2
Bellshill
N Lanark 207 D5
Northumb 199 C5
Bellspool 195 C6
Bellsquarry 208 D3
Bells Yew Green 36 C4
Belmaduthy 252 A2
Belmesthorpe 116 D3
Belmont
Blackburn 137 B5
London 49 C5
S Ayrs 192 C3
Shetland 284 C7
Belnacraig 243 A6
Belowda 5 A4
Belper 114 A1
Belper Lane End 114 A1
Belsay 178 B3
Belses 187 A4
Belsford 7 B6
Belstead 88 C2
Belston 192 C3
Belstone 11 B7
Belthorn 137 A6
Beltinge 52 C3
Beltoft 141 C6
Belton
Leics 114 C2
Lincs 116 B2
N Lincs 141 C5
Norf 105 A5
Belton in Rutland 99 A5
Beltring 37 B4
Belts of Collonach 244 C3
Belvedere 50 B1
Belvoir 115 B6
Bembridge 19 C5
Bemersyde 197 C4
Bemerton 31 B5
Bempton 161 D5
Benacre 105 C6
Ben Alder Lodge 229 A4
Ben Armine Lodge 273 C5
Benbuie 183 C5
Ben Casgro 288 E5
Benderloch 226 C4
Bendronaig Lodge 250 C2
Benenden 37 C6
Benfield 171 A5
Bengate 121 C5
Bengeworth 80 C3
Benhall Green 89 A4
Benhall Street 89 A4
Benholm 233 B6
Beningbrough 148 B4
Benington
Herts 68 A2
Lincs 117 A6
Benllech 123 B5
Benmore
Argyll 215 D4
Stirling 216 B4
Benmore Lodge 271 C6
Bennacott 10 B3
Bennan 191 C5
Benniworth 134 A2
Benover 37 B5
Bensham 179 C4
Benslie 204 D3
Benson 65 D7
Bent 233 A4
Bent Gate 137 A6
Benthall
Northumb 189 A5
Shrops 95 A4
Bentham 63 B5
Benthoul 245 B5
Bentlawnt 94 A1
Bentley
E Yorks 150 D3
Hants 33 A6
Suff 88 D2
S Yorks 140 C3
Warks 97 B5
Worcs 80 A2
Bentley Heath 97 D4
Benton 26 B1
Bentpath 185 C6
Bents 208 D2
Bentworth 33 A5
Benvie 220 A3
Benwick 101 B5
Beoley 80 A3
Beoraidbeg 235 A5
Bepton 20 A1
Berden 69 A4
Bere Alston 6 A3
Bere Ferrers 6 A3
Berepper 3 C4
Bere Regis 16 B2
Bergh Apton 104 A4
Berinsfield 65 D6
Berkeley 62 D2
Berkhamsted 67 C4
Berkley 30 A2
Berkswell 97 D5
Bermondsey 49 B6
Bernera 249 D5
Bernice 215 C4
Bernisdale 259 C4
Berrick Salome 65 D7
Berriedale 275 B5
Berrier 164 C1
Berriew 93 A5
Berrington
Northumb 198 B4
Shrops 94 A3
Berrow 42 D2
Berrow Green 79 B5
Berry Down Cross 25 A6
Berry Hill
Glos 62 B1
Pembs 72 B3
Berryhillock 267 C6
Berrynarbor 25 A6
Berry Pomeroy 8 A2
Bersham 110 A2
Berstane 282 F5
Berwick 22 B3
Berwick Bassett 45 B4
Berwick Hill 178 B3
Berwick St James 31 B4
Berwick St John 30 C3
Berwick St Leonard 30 B3
Berwick-upon-Tweed 198 A3
Bescar 136 B2
Besford 80 C2
Bessacarr 140 C4
Bessels Leigh 65 C5
Bessingby 151 A4
Bessingham 120 B3
Bestbeech Hill 36 C4
Besthorpe
Norf 103 B6
Notts 132 C3
Bestwood 114 A3
Bestwood Village 114 A3
Beswick 150 C3
Betchworth 35 B5
Bethania
Ceredig 75 B4
Gwyn 107 A6
Gwyn 108 A2
Bethel
Anglesey 122 C3
Gwyn 109 B4
Gwyn 123 D5
Bethersden 38 A1
Bethesda
Gwyn 123 D6
Pembs 55 C6
Bethlehem 58 C3
Bethnal Green 49 A6
Betley 111 A6
Betsham 50 B3
Betteshanger 53 D5
Bettiscombe 14 B3
Bettisfield 110 B3
Betton
Shrops 93 A7
Shrops 111 B5
Bettws
Bridgend 40 C4
Mon 61 B4
Newport 61 D4
Bettws Cedewain 93 B5
Bettws Gwerfil Goch 109 A5
Bettws Ifan 73 B6
Bettws Newydd 61 C5
Bettws-y-crwyn 93 C6
Bettyhill 278 B3
Betws 57 A6
Betws Bledrws 75 C4
Betws-Garmon 107 A5
Betws-y-Coed 124 D2
Betws-yn-Rhos 125 B4
Beulah
Ceredig 73 B5
Powys 76 B3
Bevendean 21 B6
Bevercotes 132 B1
Beverley 150 D3
Beverston 63 D4
Bevington 62 D2
Bewaldeth 163 A5
Bewcastle 176 B3
Bewdley 95 D5
Bewerley 147 A5
Bewholme 151 B4
Bexhill 23 B5
Bexley 50 B1
Bexleyheath 50 B1
Bexwell 102 A2
Beyton 87 A5
Bhaltos 287 A5
Bhatarsaigh 286 G2
Bibury 64 C2
Bicester 65 A6
Bickenhall 28 D2
Bickenhill 97 C4
Bicker 117 B5
Bickershaw 137 C5
Bickerstaffe 136 C3
Bickerton
Ches E 127 D5
N Yorks 148 B3
Bickington
Devon 12 D2
Devon 25 B6
Bickleigh
Devon 7 A4
Devon 13 A4
Bickleton 25 B6
Bickley 49 C7
Bickley Moss 111 A4
Bicknacre 70 C1
Bicknoller 27 B6
Bicknor 37 A6
Bickton 31 D5
Bicton
Shrops 93 C6
Shrops 110 D3
Bidborough 36 B3
Biddenden 37 C6
Biddenham 84 C2
Biddestone 44 B2
Biddisham 42 D2
Biddlesden 82 C3
Biddlestone 188 C2
Biddulph 128 D3
Biddulph Moor 129 D4
Bideford 25 C5
Bidford-on-Avon 80 B4
Bidston 136 D1
Bielby 149 C6
Bieldside 245 B5
Bierley
IoW 18 D4
W Yorks 147 D5
Bierton 66 B3
Bigbury 7 C5
Bigbury on Sea 7 C5
Bigby 142 C2
Biggar
Cumb 153 D2
S Lanark 195 C5
Biggin
Derbys 113 A6
Derbys 129 D6
N Yorks 148 D4
Biggings 285 G3
Biggin Hill 36 A2
Biggleswade 84 C3

Bighouse 279 B4
Bighton 33 B5
Bignor 20 A2
Big Sand 261 C4
Bigton 285 L5
Bilberry 5 A5
Bilborough 114 A3
Bilbrook 27 A5
Bilbrough 148 C4
Bilbster 281 C4
Bildershaw 167 C5
Bildeston 87 C5
Billericay 69 D6
Billesdon 99 A4
Billesley 80 B4
Billingborough 116 B4
Billinge 136 C4
Billingford 120 C2
Billingham 168 C2
Billinghay 133 D6
Billingley 140 C2
Billingshurst 34 D3
Billingsley 95 C5
Billington
C Beds 67 A4
Lancs 145 D7
Billockby 121 D6
Billy Row 167 B4
Bilsborrow 145 D5
Bilsby 135 B4
Bilsham 20 B2
Bilsington 38 B2
Bilson Green 62 B2
Bilsthorpe 131 C6
Bilsthorpe Moor 131 D6
Bilston
Midloth 209 D5
W Mid 96 B2
Bilstone 97 A6
Bilting 38 A2
Bilton
E Yorks 151 D4
Northumb 189 B5
Warks 98 D1
Bilton in Ainsty 148 C3
Bimbister 282 F4
Binbrook 143 D4
Binchester Blocks 167 B5
Bincombe 15 C6
Bindal 265 B5
Binegar 29 A6
Binfield 47 B6
Binfield Heath 47 B5
Bingfield 178 B1
Bingham 115 B5
Bingley 147 D5
Bings Heath 111 D4
Binham 120 B1
Binley
Hants 46 D2
W Mid 97 D6
Binley Woods 97 D6
Binniehill 207 C6
Binsoe 157 D6
Binstead 19 B4
Binsted 33 A6
Binton 80 B4
Bintree 120 C2
Binweston 93 A7
Birch
Essex 70 B3
Gtr Man 138 C1
Bircham Newton 119 B4
Bircham Tofts 119 B4
Birchanger 69 A5
Birchencliffe 139 B4
Bircher 78 A2
Birch Green 70 B3
Birchgrove
Cardiff 41 D6
Swansea 40 B2
Birch Heath 127 C5
Birch Hill 127 B5
Birchington 53 C4
Birchmoor 97 A5
Birchover 130 C2
Birch Vale 129 A5
Birchwood
Lincs 133 C4
Warr 137 D5
Bircotes 140 D4
Birdbrook 86 C3
Birdforth 158 D3
Birdham 20 C1
Birdholme 130 C3
Birdingbury 82 A1
Birdlip 63 B5
Birdsall 149 A7
Birds Edge 139 C5
Birdsgreen 95 C5
Birdsmoor Gate 14 A3
Birdston 205 A6
Birdwell 139 C6
Birdwood 62 B3
Birgham 198 C1
Birkby 158 A2
Birkdale 136 B2
Birkenhead 126 A3
Birkenhills 256 B2
Birkenshaw
N Lanark 207 D4
W Yorks 139 A5
Birkhall 243 C6
Birkhill
Angus 220 A3
Borders 185 A5
Birkholme 116 C2
Birkin 140 A3
Birley 78 B2
Birling
Kent 50 C3
Northumb 189 C5
Birling Gap 22 C3
Birlingham 80 C2
Birmingham 96 C3
Birnam 230 D4
Birse 244 C2
Birsemore 244 C2
Birstall
Leics 98 A2
W Yorks 139 A5
Birstwith 147 B6
Birthorpe 116 B4
Birtley
Hereford 78 A1
Northumb 177 B6
T&W 179 D4
Birts Street 79 D5
Bisbrooke 99 B5
Biscathorpe 134 A2
Biscot 67 A5
Bisham 47 A6
Bishampton 80 B2
Bish Mill 26 C2
Bishop Auckland 167 C5
Bishopbridge 142 D2
Bishopbriggs 205 B6
Bishop Burton 150 D2
Bishop Middleham 167 B6
Bishopmill 266 C3
Bishop Monkton 148 A2
Bishop Norton 142 D1
Bishopsbourne 52 D3
Bishops Cannings 44 C4
Bishop's Castle 93 C7
Bishop's Caundle 29 D6
Bishop's Cleeve 63 A5
Bishops Frome 79 C4
Bishop's Green 69 B6
Bishop's Hull 28 C2
Bishop's Itchington 81 B6
Bishops Lydeard 27 C6
Bishops Nympton 26 C2
Bishop's Offley 112 C1
Bishop'S Stortford 69 A4
Bishop's Sutton 33 B5
Bishop's Tachbrook 81 A6
Bishops Tawton 25 B6
Bishopsteignton 13 D4
Bishopstoke 32 D3
Bishopston 57 D5
Bishopstone
Bucks 66 B3
E Sus 22 B2
Hereford 78 C2
Swindon 45 A6
Wilts 31 C4
Bishopstrow 30 A2
Bishop Sutton 43 D4
Bishop's Waltham 33 D4
Bishopswood 28 D2
Bishop's Wood 95 A6
Bishopsworth 43 C4
Bishop Thornton 147 A6
Bishopthorpe 149 C4
Bishopton
Darl 167 C6
Dumfries 171 C6
N Yorks 157 D7
Renfs 205 A4
Warks 81 B4
Bishop Wilton 149 B6
Bishton 42 A2
Bisley
Glos 63 C5
Sur 34 A2
Bispham 144 C3
Bispham Green 136 B3
Bissoe 4 C2
Bisterne Close 17 A6
Bitchfield 116 C2
Bittadon 25 A6
Bittaford 7 B5
Bittering 119 D6
Bitterley 94 D3
Bitterne 32 D3
Bitteswell 98 C2
Bitton 43 C5
Bix 47 A5
Bixter 285 H5
Blaby 98 B2
Blackacre 184 C3
Blackadder West 198 A2
Blackawton 8 B2
Blackborough 13 A5
Blackborough End 118 D3
Black Bourton 64 C3
Blackboys 36 D3
Blackbrook
Derbys 114 A1
Mers 136 D4
Staffs 111 B6
Blackburn
Aberds 245 A5
Aberds 255 C6
Blackburn 137 A5
W Loth 208 D2
Black Callerton 178 C3
Black Clauchrie 181 C4
Black Corries
Lodge 228 C1
Blackcraig 183 D5
Black Crofts 226 C4
Blackden Heath 128 B2
Blackdog 245 A6
Black Dog 12 A3
Blackfell 179 D4
Blackfield 18 A3
Blackford
Cumb 175 B6
Perth 218 D3
Som 28 A4
Som 29 C6
Blackfordby 114 D1
Blackgang 18 D3
Blackhall Colliery 168 B2
Blackhall Mill 178 D3
Blackhall Rocks 168 B2
Blackham 36 C2
Blackhaugh 196 C3
Blackheath
Essex 71 A4
Suff 105 D5
Sur 34 B3
W Mid 96 C2
Black Heddon 178 B2
Blackhill
Aberds 257 B5
Aberds 269 D5
Highld 258 C3
Blackhills
Highld 253 A5
Moray 266 D3
Blackhorse 43 B5
Blackland 44 C4
Black Lane 137 C6
Blacklaw 268 D1
Blackley 138 C1
Blacklunans 231 B5
Black Marsh 94 B1
Blackmill 40 C4
Blackmoor 33 B6
Blackmoor Gate 26 A1
Blackmore 69 C6
Blackmore End
Essex 86 D3
Herts 67 B6
Black Mount 228 D1
Blackness 208 C3
Blacknest 33 A6
Black Notley 70 A1
Blacko 146 C2
Black Pill 57 C6
Blackpool
Blackpool 144 D3
Devon 8 C2
Pembs 55 C6
Blackpool Gate 176 B3
Blackridge 208 D1
Blackrock
Argyll 200 B3
Mon 60 B4
Blackrod 137 B5
Blackshaw 174 B3
Blackshaw Head 138 A2
Blacksmith's Green 88 A2
Blackstone 21 A5
Black Tar 55 D5
Blackthorn 65 B7
Blackthorpe 87 A5
Blacktoft 141 A6
Blacktop 245 B5
Black Torrington 11 A5
Blacktown 42 A1
Blackwall Tunnel 49 A6
Blackwater
Corn 4 C2
Hants 34 A1
IoW 18 C4
Blackwaterfoot 191 C4
Blackwell
Darl 167 D5
Derbys 129 B6
Derbys 131 D4
Warks 81 C5
Worcs 96 D2
W Sus 36 C1
Blackwood 194 B2
Blackwood
=Coed Duon 41 B6
Blackwood Hill 129 D4
Blacon 126 C3
Bladnoch 171 B6
Bladon 65 B5
Blaenannerch 73 B5
Blaenau Ffestiniog 108 A2
Blaenavon 61 C4
Blaencelyn 73 A6
Blaendyryn 59 B6
Blaenffos 73 C4
Blaengarw 40 B4
Blaengwrach 59 E5
Blaen-gwynfi 40 B3
Blaenpennal 75 B5
Blaenplwyf 75 A4
Blaenporth 73 B5
Blaenrhondda 40 A4
Blaen-waun 73 D5
Blaen-y-coed 73 D6
Blaenycwm 92 D2
Blaen-y-Cwm
Denb 109 B5
Gwyn 108 C2
Powys 109 C5
Blagdon
N Som 43 D4
Torbay 8 A2
Blagdon Hill 28 D2
Blagill 165 A5
Blaguegate 136 C3
Blaich 237 B4
Blain 235 D5
Blaina 60 C4
Blair Atholl 230 B2
Blairbeg 191 B6
Blairdaff 244 A3
Blair Drummond 207 A5
Blairglas 206 B1
Blairgowrie 231 D5
Blairhall 208 B3
Blairingone 208 A2
Blairland 204 D3
Blairlogie 207 A6
Blairlomond 215 C4
Blairmore 215 D4
Blairnamarrow 243 A5
Blairquhosh 206 B3
Blair's Ferry 203 B4
Blairskaith 205 A5
Blaisdon 62 B3
Blakebrook 95 D6
Blakedown 96 D1
Blakelaw 197 C6
Blakeley 95 B6
Blakeley Lane 112 A3
Blakemere 78 C1
Blakeney
Glos 62 C2
Norf 120 A2
Blakenhall
Ches E 111 A6
W Mid 96 B2
Blakeshall 95 C6
Blakesley 82 B3
Blanchland 178 D1
Blandford Forum 16 A2
Blandford St Mary 16 A2
Bland Hill 147 B6
Blanefield 205 A5
Blankney 133 C5
Blantyre 194 A1
Blar a'Chaorainn 237 C5
Blaran 214 A1
Blarghour 214 A2
Blarmachfoldach 237 C4
Blarnalearoch 262 A3
Blashford 17 A5
Blaston 99 B5
Blatherwycke 99 B6
Blawith 154 C1
Blaxhall 89 B4
Blaxton 141 C4
Blaydon 178 C3
Bleadon 42 D2
Bleak Hey Nook 138 C3
Blean 52 C3
Bleasby
Lincs 133 A6
Notts 115 A5
Bleasdale 145 C5
Bleatarn 165 D5
Blebocraigs 220 C4
Bleddfa 77 A6
Bledington 64 A3
Bledlow 66 C2
Bledlow Ridge 66 D2
Blegbie 210 D1
Blencarn 165 B4
Blencogo 175 D4
Blendworth 33 D6
Blenheim Park 119 B5
Blennerhasset 175 D4
Blervie Castle 253 A6
Bletchingdon 65 B6
Bletchingley 35 A6
Bletchley
M Keynes 83 D5
Shrops 111 B5
Bletherston 55 B6
Bletsoe 84 B2
Blewbury 46 A3
Blickling 120 C3
Blidworth 131 D5
Blindburn 188 B1
Blindcrake 163 A4
Blindley Heath 35 B6
Blisland 10 D2
Blissford 31 D5
Bliss Gate 95 D5
Blisworth 83 B4
Blithbury 113 C4
Blitterlees 174 C4
Blockley 81 D4
Blofield 104 A4
Blofield Heath 121 D5
Blo' Norton 103 D6
Bloomfield 187 A4
Blore 113 A5
Blount's Green 113 B4
Blowick 136 B2
Bloxham 82 D1
Bloxholm 133 D5
Bloxwich 96 A2
Bloxworth 16 B2
Blubberhouses 147 B5
Blue Anchor
Som 27 A5
Swansea 57 C5
Blue Row 71 B4
Blundeston 105 B6
Blunham 84 B3
Blunsdon St Andrew 45 A5
Bluntington 96 D1
Bluntisham 101 D5
Blunts 6 A2
Blyborough 142 D1
Blyford 105 D5
Blymhill 112 D2
Blyth
Northumb 179 A5
Notts 131 A6
Blyth Bridge 195 B6
Blythburgh 105 D5
Blythe 197 B4
Blythe Bridge 112 A3
Blyton 141 D6
Boarhills 221 C5
Boarhunt 19 A5
Boarshead 36 C3
Boars Head 137 C4
Boars Hill 65 C5
Boarstall 66 B1
Boasley Cross 11 B5
Boath 264 C1
Boat of Garten 242 A2
Bobbing 51 C5
Bobbington 95 B6
Bobbingworth 69 C5
Bocaddon 5 B6
Bochastle 217 D6
Bocking 70 A1
Bocking
Churchstreet 70 A1
Boddam
Aberds 257 B6
Shetland 285 M5
Boddington 63 A4
Bodedern 122 B3
Bodelwyddan 125 B5
Bodenham
Hereford 78 B3
Wilts 31 C5
Bodenham Moor 78 B3
Bodermid 106 D1
Bodewryd 122 A3
Bodfari 125 B5
Bodffordd 123 C4
Bodham 120 A3
Bodiam 37 D5
Bodicote 82 D1
Bodieve 9 D5
Bodinnick 5 B6
Bodle Street Green 23 A4
Bodmin 5 A5
Bodney 103 B4
Bodorgan 122 D3
Bodsham 38 A3
Boduan 106 C3
Bodymoor Heath 97 B4
Bogallan 252 A2
Bogbrae 257 C5
Bogend
Borders 198 B1
S Ayrs 192 B3
Boghall 208 D2
Boghead 194 B2
Bogmoor 267 C4
Bogniebrae 255 B6
Bognor Regis 20 C2
Bograxie 256 E2
Bogside 194 A3
Bogton 268 D1
Bogue 182 D4
Bohenie 239 D6
Bohortha 4 D3
Bohuntine 239 D6
Boirseam 287 F5
Bojewyan 2 B1
Bolam
Durham 167 C4
Northumb 178 A2
Bolberry 7 D5
Bold Heath 127 A5
Boldon 179 C5
Boldon Colliery 179 C5
Boldre 18 B2
Boldron 166 D3
Bole 132 A2
Bolehill 130 D2
Boleside 196 C3
Bolham 27 D4
Bolham Water 27 D6
Bolingey 4 B2
Bollington 129 B4
Bollington Cross 129 B4
Bolney 35 D5
Bolnhurst 84 B2
Bolshan 233 C4
Bolsover 131 B4
Bolsterstone 139 D5
Bolstone 78 D3
Boltby 158 C3
Bolter End 66 D2
Bolton
Cumb 165 C4
E Loth 210 C2
E Yorks 149 B6
Gtr Man 137 C6
Northumb 189 B4
Bolton Abbey 147 B4
Bolton Bridge 147 B4
Bolton-by-
Bowland 146 C1
Boltonfellend 176 C2
Boltongate 175 D5
Bolton-le-Sands 145 A4
Bolton Low Houses 175 D5
Bolton-on-Swale 157 B6
Bolton Percy 148 C4
Bolton Town End 145 A4
Bolton upon
Dearne 140 C2
Bolventor 10 D2
Bomere Heath 110 D3
Bonar Bridge 264 A2
Bonawe 227 C5
Bonby 142 B2
Boncath 73 C5
Bonchester Bridge 187 B4
Bonchurch 19 D4
Bondleigh 12 A1
Bonehill
Devon 12 D2
Staffs 97 A4
Bo'ness 208 B2
Bonhill 206 C1
Boningale 95 A6
Bonjedward 187 A5

Bonkle 194 A3
Bonnavoulin 225 A4
Bonnington
- Edin 208 D4
- Kent 38 B2

Bonnybank 220 D3
Bonnybridge 207 B6
Bonnykelly 268 D3
Bonnyrigg and Lasswade 209 D6
Bonnyton
- Aberds 256 C1
- Angus 220 A3
- Angus 233 C4

Bonsall 130 D2
Bonskeid House 230 B2
Bont 61 B5
Bontddu 91 A4
Bont-Dolgadfan 91 B6
Bont-goch 91 D4
Bonthorpe 135 B4
Bontnewydd
- Ceredig 75 B5
- Gwyn 107 A4

Bont-newydd 125 B5
Bont Newydd
- Gwyn 108 A2
- Gwyn 108 C2

Bontuchel 125 D5
Bonvilston 41 D5
Bon-y-maen 57 C6
Booker 66 D3
Boon 197 B4
Boosbeck 169 D4
Boot 163 D4
Booth 138 A3
Boothby Graffoe 133 D4
Boothby Pagnell 116 B2
Boothen 112 A2
Boothferry 141 A5
Boothville 83 A4
Booth Wood 138 B3
Bootle
- Cumb 153 B2
- Mers 136 D2

Booton 120 C3
Boot Street 88 C3
Boquhan 206 B3
Boraston 95 D4
Borden
- Kent 51 C5
- W Sus 34 D1

Bordley 146 A3
Bordon 33 B7
Bordon Camp 33 B6
Boreham
- Essex 70 C1
- Wilts 30 A2

Boreham Street 23 A4
Borehamwood 68 D1
Boreland
- Dumfries 185 C4
- Stirling 217 A5

Borgh
- W Isles 286 F2
- W Isles 287 F4

Borghastan 288 C3
Borgie 278 C2
Borgue
- Dumfries 172 D4
- Highld 275 B5

Borley 87 C4
Bornais 286 D3
Bornesketaig 258 A3
Borness 172 D4
Boroughbridge 148 A2
Borough Green 36 A4
Borras Head 126 D3
Borreraig 258 C1
Borrobol Lodge 274 B2
Borrowash 114 B2
Borrowby 158 C3
Borrowdale 163 C5
Borrowfield 245 C5
Borth 90 C4
Borthwickbrae 186 B3
Borthwickshiels 186 B3
Borth-y-Gest 107 C5
Borve 259 D4
Borve Lodge 287 E5
Borwick 154 D4
Bosavern 2 B1
Bosbury 79 C4
Boscastle 10 B2
Boscombe
- BCP 17 B5
- Wilts 31 B6

Boscoppa 5 B5
Bosham 19 A7
Bosherston 55 E5
Boskenna 2 C2
Bosley 129 C4
Bossall 149 A6
Bossiney 9 C6
Bossingham 38 A3
Bossington 26 A3
Bostock Green 127 C6
Boston 117 A6
Boston Long Hedges 117 A6
Boston Spa 148 C3
Boston West 117 A5
Boswinger 5 C4
Botallack 2 B1
Botany Bay 68 D2
Botcherby 175 C7
Botcheston 98 A1
Botesdale 103 D6
Bothal 179 A4
Bothamsall 131 B6
Bothel 163 A4
Bothenhampton 15 B4
Bothwell 194 A2
Botley
- Bucks 67 C4
- Hants 32 D4
- Oxon 65 C5

Botolph Claydon 66 A2
Botolphs 21 B4
Bottacks 263 D6
Bottesford
- Leics 115 B6
- N Lincs 141 C6

Bottisham 86 A1
Bottlesford 45 D5
Bottom Boat 139 A6
Bottomcraig 220 B3
Bottom House 129 D5
Bottom of Hutton 136 A3
Bottom o' th' Moor 137 B5
Botusfleming 6 A3
Botwnnog 106 C2
Bough Beech 36 B2
Boughrood 77 D5
Boughspring 62 D1
Boughton
- Norf 102 A2
- Northants 83 A4
- Notts 131 C6

Boughton Aluph 38 A2
Boughton Lees 38 A2
Boughton Malherbe 37 B6
Boughton Monchelsea 37 A5
Boughton Street 52 D2
Boulby 169 D5
Boulden 94 C3
Boulmer 189 B5
Boulston 55 C5
Boultenstone 243 A7
Boultham 133 C4
Bourn 85 B5
Bourne 116 C3
Bourne End
- Bucks 48 A1
- C Beds 83 C6
- Herts 67 C5

Bournemouth 17 B4
Bournes Green
- Glos 63 C5
- Southend 51 A6

Bournheath 96 D2
Bournmoor 179 D5
Bournville 96 C3
Bourton
- Dorset 30 B1
- N Som 42 C2
- Oxon 45 A6
- Shrops 94 B3

Bourton on Dunsmore 98 D1
Bourton on the Hill 81 D4
Bourton-on-the-Water 64 A2
Bousd 223 A5
Boustead Hill 175 C5
Bouth 154 C2
Bouthwaite 157 D5
Boveney 48 B2
Boverton 41 E4
Bovey Tracey 12 D3
Bovingdon 67 C5
Bovingdon Green
- Bucks 47 A6
- Herts 67 C5

Bovinger 69 C5
Bovington Camp 16 C2
Bow
- Borders 196 B3
- Devon 12 A2

Bow *continued*
- Orkney 283 H4

Bowbank 166 C2
Bow Brickhill 83 D6
Bowburn 167 B6
Bowcombe 18 C3
Bowd 13 B6
Bowden
- Borders 197 C4
- Devon 8 C2

Bowden Hill 44 C3
Bowderdale 155 A5
Bowdon 128 A2
Bower 177 A5
Bowerchalke 31 C4
Bowerhill 44 C3
Bower Hinton 29 D4
Bowermadden 280 B4
Bowers Gifford 51 A4
Bowershall 208 A3
Bowertower 280 B4
Bowes 166 D2
Bowgreave 145 C4
Bowgreen 128 A2
Bowhill 186 A3
Bowhouse 174 B3
Bowland Bridge 154 C3
Bowley 78 B3
Bowlhead Green 34 C2
Bowling
- W Dunb 205 A4
- W Yorks 147 D5

Bowling Bank 110 A2
Bowling Green 79 B6
Bowmanstead 154 B2
Bowmore 200 C3
Bowness-on-Solway 175 B5
Bowness-on-Windermere 154 B3
Bow of Fife 220 C3
Bowsden 198 B3
Bowside Lodge 279 B4
Bowston 154 B3
Bow Street 90 D4
Bowthorpe 104 A2
Box
- Glos 63 C4
- Wilts 44 C2

Boxbush 62 B3
Box End 84 C2
Boxford
- Suff 87 C5
- W Berks 46 B2

Boxgrove 20 B2
Boxley 37 A5
Boxmoor 67 C5
Boxted
- Essex 87 D6
- Suff 87 B4

Boxted Cross 87 D6
Boxted Heath 87 D6
Boxworth 85 A5
Boxworth End 85 A5
Boyden Gate 53 C4
Boylestone 113 B5
Boyndie 268 C1
Boynton 151 A4
Boysack 233 D4
Boyton
- Corn 10 B4
- Suff 89 C4
- Wilts 30 B3

Boyton Cross 69 C6
Boyton End 86 C3
Bozeat 83 B6
Braaid 152 D3
Braal Castle 280 B3
Brabling Green 88 A3
Brabourne 38 A2
Brabourne Lees 38 A2
Brabster 281 B5
Bracadale 246 A2
Bracara 235 A6
Braceborough 116 D3
Bracebridge 133 C4
Bracebridge Heath 133 C4
Bracebridge Low Fields 133 C4
Braceby 116 B3
Bracewell 146 C2
Brackenfield 130 D3
Brackenthwaite
- Cumb 175 D5
- N Yorks 148 B1

Bracklesham 19 B7
Brackletter 239 D5
Brackley
- Argyll 202 D2
- Northants 82 D2

Brackloch 270 B4
Bracknell 47 C6
Braco 218 D3
Bracobrae 267 D6
Bracon Ash 104 B2
Bracorina 235 A6
Bradbourne 130 D2
Bradbury 167 C6
Bradda 152 E1
Bradden 82 C3
Braddock 5 A6
Bradeley 128 D3
Bradenham
- Bucks 66 D3
- Norf 103 A5

Bradenstoke 44 B4
Bradfield
- Essex 88 D2
- Norf 121 B4
- W Berks 47 B4

Bradfield Combust 87 B4
Bradfield Green 128 D1
Bradfield Heath 71 A5
Bradfield St Clare 87 B5
Bradfield St George 87 A5
Bradford
- Corn 10 D2
- Derbys 130 C2
- Devon 11 A5
- Northumb 199 C5
- W Yorks 147 D5

Bradford Abbas 29 D5
Bradford Leigh 44 C2
Bradford-on-Avon 44 C2
Bradford-on-Tone 28 C1
Bradford Peverell 15 B6
Brading 19 C5
Bradley
- Derbys 113 A6
- Hants 33 A5
- NE Lincs 143 C4
- Staffs 112 D2
- W Mid 96 B2
- W Yorks 139 A4

Bradley Green 80 A2
Bradley in the Moors 113 A4
Bradley Stoke 43 A5
Bradlow 79 D5
Bradmore
- Notts 114 B3
- W Mid 96 B1

Bradninch 13 A5
Bradnop 129 D5
Bradpole 15 B4
Bradshaw
- Gtr Man 137 B6
- W Yorks 138 B3

Bradstone 11 C4
Bradwall Green 128 C2
Bradway 130 A3
Bradwell
- Derbys 129 A6
- Essex 70 A2
- M Keynes 83 D5
- Norf 105 A6
- Staffs 112 A2

Bradwell Grove 64 C3
Bradwell on Sea 71 C4
Bradwell Waterside 70 C3
Bradworthy 24 D4
Bradworthy Cross 24 D4
Brae
- Dumfries 173 A6
- Highld 261 B5
- Highld 272 D2
- Shetland 284 G5

Braeantra 264 C1
Braedownie 231 A6
Braefield 251 C6
Braegrum 219 B5
Braehead
- Dumfries 171 B6
- Orkney 282 C5
- Orkney 283 G6
- S Lanark 194 C3
- S Lanark 195 A4

Braehead of Lunan 233 C4
Braehoulland 284 F4
Braehungie 275 A5
Braelangwell Lodge 263 A7
Braemar 243 C4
Braemore
- Highld 262 C3
- Highld 275 A4

Brae of Achnahaird 270 C3
Brae Roy Lodge 240 C1
Braeside 204 A2
Braes of Enzie 267 D4
Braeswick 282 D7
Braewick 285 H5
Brafferton
- Darl 167 C5
- N Yorks 158 D3

Brafield-on-the-Green 83 B5
Bragar 288 C3
Bragbury End 68 A2
Bragleenmore 226 D4
Braichmelyn 123 D6
Braid 209 D5
Braides 144 B4
Braidley 156 C4
Braidwood 194 B3
Braigo 200 B2
Brailsford 113 A6
Brainshaugh 189 C5
Braintree 70 A1
Braiseworth 104 D2
Braishfield 32 C2
Braithwaite
- Cumb 163 B5
- S Yorks 140 B4
- W Yorks 147 C4

Braithwell 140 D3
Bramber 21 A4
Bramcote
- Notts 114 B3
- Warks 97 C7

Bramdean 33 C5
Bramerton 104 A3
Bramfield
- Herts 68 B2
- Suff 105 D4

Bramford 88 C2
Bramhall 128 A3
Bramham 148 C3
Bramhope 147 C6
Bramley
- Hants 47 D4
- Sur 34 B3
- S Yorks 140 D2
- W Yorks 147 D6

Bramling 53 D4
Brampford Speke 13 B4
Brampton
- Cambs 100 D4
- Cumb 165 C4
- Cumb 176 C3
- Derbys 130 B3
- Hereford 78 D2
- Lincs 132 B3
- Norf 120 C4
- Suff 105 C5
- S Yorks 140 C2

Brampton Abbotts 62 A2
Brampton Ash 99 C4
Brampton Bryan 94 D1
Brampton en le Morthen 131 A4
Bramshall 113 B4
Bramshaw 31 D6
Bramshill 47 C5
Bramshott 34 C1
Branault 235 D4
Brancaster 119 A4
Brancaster Staithe 119 A4
Brancepeth 167 B5
Branch End 178 C2
Branchill 266 D1
Branderburgh 266 B3
Brandesburton 151 C4
Brandeston 88 A3
Brand Green 62 A3
Brandhill 94 D2
Brandis Corner 11 A5
Brandiston 120 C3
Brandon
- Durham 167 B5
- Lincs 116 A2
- Northumb 188 B3
- Suff 102 C3
- Warks 97 D7

Brandon Bank 102 C2
Brandon Creek 102 B2
Brandon Parva 104 A1
Brandsby 159 D4
Brandy Wharf 142 D2
Brane 2 C2
Bran End 69 A6
Branksome 17 B4
Branksome Park 17 B4
Bransby 132 B3
Branscombe 14 C1
Bransford 79 B5
Bransgore 17 B5
Branshill 208 A1
Bransholme 151 D4
Branson's Cross 96 D3
Branston
- Leics 115 C6
- Lincs 133 C5
- Staffs 113 C6

Branston Booths 133 C5
Branstone 19 C4
Bransty 162 C2
Brant Broughton 133 D4
Brantham 88 D2
Branthwaite
- Cumb 162 B3
- Cumb 163 A5

Brantingham 142 A1
Branton
- Northumb 188 B3
- S Yorks 140 C4

Branxholme 186 B3
Branxholm Park 186 B3
Branxton 198 C2
Brassey Green 127 C5
Brassington 130 D2
Brasted 36 A2
Brasted Chart 36 A2
Brathens 244 C3
Bratoft 135 C4
Brattleby 133 A4
Bratton
- Telford 111 D5
- Wilts 44 D3

Bratton Clovelly 11 B5
Bratton Fleming 26 B1
Bratton Seymour 29 C6
Braughing 68 A3
Braunston 82 A2
Braunstone Town 98 A2
Braunston-in-Rutland 99 A5
Braunton 25 B5
Brawby 159 D6
Brawl 279 B4
Brawlbin 279 C6
Bray 48 B2
Braybrooke 99 C4
Braye 7
Brayford 26 B1
Bray Shop 10 D4
Braystones 162 D3
Braythorn 147 C6
Brayton 149 D5
Bray Wick 48 B1
Brazacott 10 B3
Breach 51 C5
Breachacha Castle 223 B4
Breachwood Green 67 A6
Breacleit 288 D2
Breaden Heath 110 B3
Breadsall 114 B1
Breadstone 62 C3
Breage 3 C4
Breakachy 251 B6
Bream 62 C2
Breamore 31 D5
Brean 42 D1
Breanais 287 B4
Brearton 148 A2
Breascleit 288 D3
Breaston 114 B2
Brechfa 58 B2
Brechin 232 B3
Breckan 283 G3
Breck of Cruan 282 F4
Breckrey 259 B5
Brecon
- *=Aberhonddu* 60 A2

Bredbury 138 D2
Brede 23 A6
Bredenbury 79 B4
Bredfield 88 B3
Bredgar 51 C5
Bredhurst 51 C4
Bredicot 80 B2
Bredon 80 D2
Bredon's Norton 80 D2
Bredwardine 78 C1
Breedon on the Hill 114 C2
Breibhig
- W Isles 286 G2
- W Isles 288 D5

Breich 208 D2
Breightmet 137 C6
Breighton 149 D6
Breinton 78 D2
Breinton Common 78 C2
Breiwick 285 J6
Bremhill 44 B3
Bremirehoull 285 L6
Brenchley 37 B4

Brendon 26 A2
Brenkley 179 B4
Brent Eleigh 87 C5
Brentford 49 B4
Brentingby 115 D5
Brent Knoll 42 D2
Brent Pelham......85 D6
Brentwood 69 D5
Brenzett..........38 C2
Brereton 113 D4
Brereton Green ...128 C2
Brereton Heath ...128 C3
Bressingham 104 C1
Bretby 113 C6
Bretford 98 D1
Bretforton 80 C3
Bretherdale Head ..155 A4
Bretherton 136 A3
Brettabister 285 H6
Brettenham
  Norf 103 C5
  Suff 87 B5
Bretton
  Derbys 130 B2
  Flint 126 C3
Brewer Street......35 A6
Brewlands Bridge .. 231 B5
Brewood 96 A1
Briach 266 D1
Briants Puddle 16 B2
Brick End 69 A5
Brickendon 68 C3
Bricket Wood 67 C6
Bricklehampton ...80 C2
Bride 152 A4
Bridekirk 163 A4
Bridell 73 B4
Bridestowe 11 C6
Brideswell 255 C6
Bridford 12 C3
Bridfordmills 12 C3
Bridge 52 D3
Bridge End 116 B4
Bridgefoot
  Angus 220 A3
  Cumb 162 B3
Bridge Green 85 D6
Bridgehampton ...29 C5
Bridge Hewick....158 D2
Bridgehill 178 D2
Bridgemary 19 A4
Bridgemont 129 A5
Bridgend
  Aberds 244 A2
  Aberds 255 C6
  Angus 232 B3
  Argyll 190 B3
  Argyll 200 B3
  Argyll 214 C1
  Cumb 164 D1
  Fife 220 C3
  Moray 255 C4
  N Lanark 207 C4
  Pembs 73 B4
  W Loth 208 C3
Bridgend = Pen-y-bont
  ar Ogwr 40 D4
Bridgend of
  Lintrathen ...231 C6
Bridge of Alford...244 A2
Bridge of Allan ...207 A5
Bridge of Avon ...254 C2
Bridge of Awe ...227 D5
Bridge of Balgie ..229 D4
Bridge of Cally 231 C5
Bridge of Canny ...244 C3
Bridge of Craigisla .231 C6
Bridge of Dee 173 C5
Bridge of Don 245 A6
Bridge of Dun 233 C4
Bridge of Dye 244 D3
Bridge of Earn 219 C6
Bridge of Ericht ...229 C4
Bridge of Feugh...245 C4
Bridge of Forss ...279 B6
Bridge of Gairn ...243 C6
Bridge of Gaur ...229 C4
Bridge of Muchalls .245 C5
Bridge of Oich ...240 B1
Bridge of Orchy ..216 A2
Bridge of Waith ...282 F3
Bridge of Walls ...285 H4
Bridge of Weir ...204 B3
Bridgerule 10 A3
Bridges 94 B1
Bridge Sollers 78 C2
Bridge Street 87 C4
Bridgeton 205 B6

Bridgetown
  Corn 10 C4
  Som. 27 B4
Bridge Trafford....127 B4
Bridge Yate 43 B5
Bridgham 103 C5
Bridgnorth 95 B5
Bridgtown 96 A2
Bridgwater 28 B3
Bridlington 151 A4
Bridport 15 B4
Bridstow 62 A1
Brierfield 146 D2
Brierley
  Glos 62 B2
  Hereford 78 B2
  S Yorks 140 B2
Brierley Hill 96 C2
Briery Hill 60 C3
Brigg 142 C2
Briggswath 160 A2
Brigham
  Cumb 162 A3
  E Yorks 150 B3
Brighouse 139 A4
Brighstone 18 C3
Brightgate 130 D2
Brighthampton ...65 C4
Brightling 37 D4
Brightlingsea 71 B4
Brighton
  Brighton 21 B6
  Corn 4 B4
Brighton Hill 33 A5
Brightons 208 C2
Brightwalton 46 B2
Brightwell 88 C3
Brightwell Baldwin .66 D1
Brightwell cum
  Sotwell 65 D6
Brignall 166 D3
Brig o'Turk 217 D5
Brigsley 143 C4
Brigsteer 154 C3
Brigstock 99 C6
Brill 66 B1
Brilley 77 C6
Brimaston 55 B5
Brimfield 78 A3
Brimington 131 B4
Brimley 12 D2
Brimpsfield 63 B5
Brimpton 46 C3
Brims 283 J3
Brimscombe 63 C4
Brimstage 126 A3
Brinacory 235 A6
Brind 149 D6
Brindister
  Shetland 285 H4
  Shetland 285 K6
Brindle 137 A5
Brindley Ford 128 D3
Brineton 112 D2
Bringhurst 99 B5
Brington 100 D2
Brinian 282 E5
Briningham 120 B2
Brinkhill 134 B3
Brinkley 86 B2
Brinklow 98 D1
Brinkworth 44 A4
Brinmore 252 D2
Brinscall 137 A5
Brinsea 42 C3
Brinsley 114 A2
Brinsop 78 C2
Brinsworth 131 A4
Brinton 120 B2
Brisco 175 C7
Brisley 119 C6
Brislington 43 B5
Bristol 43 B4
Briston 120 B2
Britannia 138 A1
Britford 31 C5
Brithdir 91 A5
British Legion
  Village 37 A5
Briton Ferry 40 B2
Britwell Salome....66 D1
Brixham 8 B3
Brixton
  Devon 7 B4
  London 49 B6
Brixton Deverill ...30 B2
Brixworth 99 D4
Brize Norton 64 C4
Broad Blunsdon ...64 D2
Broadbottom 138 D2

Broadbridge 19 A7
Broadbridge Heath .35 C4
Broad Campden...81 D4
Broad Chalke 31 C4
Broadclyst 13 B4
Broadfield
  Gtr Man 138 B1
  Lancs 136 A4
  Pembs 56 B1
  W Sus 35 C5
Broadford 247 B5
Broadford Bridge ..34 D3
Broad Green
  C Beds 83 C6
  Essex 70 A2
  Worcs 79 B5
Broadhaugh 186 C3
Broadhaven 281 C5
Broad Haven 55 C4
Broadheath 128 A2
Broad Heath 79 A4
Broadhembury ...13 A6
Broadhempston 8 A2
Broad Hill 102 D1
Broad Hinton 45 B5
Broadholme
  Derbys 114 A1
  Lincs 132 B3
Broadland Row ...23 A6
Broadlay 56 B3
Broad Laying 46 C2
Broadley
  Lancs 138 B1
  Moray 267 C4
Broadley Common ..68 C4
Broad Marston ...80 C4
Broadmayne 16 C1
Broadmeadows ...196 C3
Broadmere 33 A5
Broadmoor 55 D6
Broadoak 52 C3
Broad Oak
  Carms 58 C2
  Cumb 153 A2
  Dorset 14 B4
  Dorset 30 D1
  E Sus 23 A6
  E Sus 36 D4
  Hereford 61 A6
  Mers 136 D4
Broadrashes 267 D5
Broadsea 269 C4
Broadstairs 53 C5
Broadstone
  BCP 17 B4
  Shrops 94 C3
Broad Street 37 A6
Broad Street Green. .70 C2
Broad Town 45 B4
Broadtown Lane ...45 B4
Broadwas 79 B5
Broadwater
  Herts 68 A2
  W Sus 21 B4
Broadway
  Carms 56 B2
  Pembs 55 C4
  Som. 28 D3
  Suff 105 D4
  Worcs 80 D3
Broadwell
  Glos 62 B1
  Glos 64 A3
  Oxon 64 C3
  Warks 82 A1
Broadwell House ...177 D7
Broadwey 15 C6
Broadwindsor 14 A4
Broadwood Kelly ..11 A7
Broadwoodwidger ..11 C5
Brobury 78 C1
Brochel 248 B2
Brochloch 182 C3
Brochroy 227 C5
Brockamin 79 B5
Brockbridge 33 D5
Brockdam 189 A4
Brockdish 104 D3
Brockenhurst 18 A2
Brocketsbrae 194 C3
Brockford Street ...88 A2
Brockhall 82 A3
Brockham 35 B4
Brockhampton
  Glos 63 A6
  Hereford 78 D3
Brockholes 139 B4
Brockhurst
  Derbys 130 C3
  Hants 19 A5

Brocklebank 175 D6
Brocklesby 142 B3
Brockley 42 C3
Brockley Green ...87 B4
Brockleymoor 164 B2
Brockton
  Shrops 93 A7
  Shrops 94 B3
  Shrops 94 C1
  Shrops 95 A5
  Telford 111 D6
Brockweir 62 C1
Brockwood 33 C5
Brockworth 63 B4
Brocton 112 D3
Brodick 191 B6
Brodsworth 140 C1
Brogaig 259 B4
Brogborough 83 D6
Brokenborough ...44 A3
Broken Cross
  Ches E. 128 B3
  Ches W 128 B1
Bromborough 126 A3
Brome 104 D2
Brome Street 104 D2
Bromeswell 88 B4
Bromfield
  Cumb 175 D4
  Shrops 94 D2
Bromham
  Bedford 84 B2
  Wilts 44 C3
Bromley
  London 49 C7
  W Mid 96 C2
Bromley Common ..49 C7
Bromley Green ...38 B1
Brompton
  Medway 51 C4
  N Yorks 158 B2
  N Yorks 160 C3
Brompton-on-
  Swale 157 B6
Brompton Ralph ...27 B5
Brompton Regis ...27 B4
Bromsash 62 A2
Bromsberrow Heath .79 D5
Bromsgrove 96 D2
Bromyard 79 B4
Bromyard Downs ...79 B4
Bronaber 108 B2
Brongest 73 B6
Bronington 110 B3
Bronllys 77 D5
Bronnant 75 B5
Bronwydd Arms...73 D7
Bronydd 77 C6
Bronygarth 110 B1
Brook
  Carms 56 B2
  Hants 32 C2
  Hants 32 D1
  IoW. 18 C2
  Kent 38 A2
  Sur 34 B3
  Sur 34 C2
Brooke
  Norf 104 B3
  Rutland 99 A5
Brookenby 143 D4
Brookend 62 D1
Brook End 84 A2
Brookfield 205 B4
Brook Hill 31 D6
Brookhouse 145 A5
Brookhouse Green .128 C3
Brookland 38 C1
Brooklands
  Dumfries 173 A6
  Gtr Man 137 D6
  Shrops 111 A4
Brookmans Park ...68 C2
Brooks 93 B5
Brooks Green 35 D4
Brook Street
  Kent 36 B2
  Kent 38 B1
  W Sus 35 D6
Brookthorpe 63 B4
Brookville 102 B3
Brookwood 34 A2
Broom
  C Beds 84 C3
  S Yorks 140 D2
  Warks 80 B3
  Worcs 96 D2
Broome
  Norf 105 B4
  Shrops 94 C2

Broomedge 128 A2
Broome Park 189 B4
Broomer's Corner...35 D4
Broomfield
  Aberds 257 C4
  Essex 69 B7
  Kent 37 A6
  Kent 52 C3
  Som. 28 B2
Broomfleet 141 A6
Broom Green 120 C1
Broomhall
  Ches E. 111 A5
  Windsor 48 C3
Broomhaugh 178 C2
Broomhill
  Norf 102 A2
  Northumb 189 C5
  S Yorks 140 C2
Broom Hill 17 A4
Broomholm 121 B5
Broomley 178 C2
Broompark 167 A5
Broom's Green 79 D5
Broomy Lodge 31 D6
Brora 274 D3
Broseley 95 A4
Brotherhouse Bar ..117 D5
Brotherstone 197 C5
Brothertoft 117 A5
Brotherton 140 A2
Brotton 169 D4
Broubster 279 B6
Brough
  Cumb 165 D5
  Derbys 130 A1
  E Yorks 142 A1
  Highld 280 A4
  Notts 132 D3
  Orkney 282 F4
  Shetland 284 F6
  Shetland 284 F7
  Shetland 284 G7
  Shetland 285 H6
  Shetland 285 J7
Broughall 111 A4
Brough Lodge 284 D7
Brough Sowerby ..165 D5
Broughton
  Borders 195 C6
  Cambs 101 D4
  Flint 126 C3
  Hants 32 B2
  Lancs 145 D5
  M Keynes 83 C5
  N Lincs 142 C1
  Northants 99 D5
  N Yorks 146 B3
  N Yorks 159 D6
  Orkney 282 C5
  Oxon 81 D2
  V Glam 40 D4
Broughton Astley ..98 B2
Broughton Beck ...154 C1
Broughton
  Common 44 C2
Broughton Gifford ..44 C2
Broughton Hackett .80 B2
Broughton in
  Furness 153 B3
Broughton Mills ...153 A3
Broughton Moor ...162 A3
Broughton Park ...138 C1
Broughton Poggs ..64 C3
Broughtown 282 C7
Broughty Ferry ...221 A4
Browhouses 175 B5
Browland 285 H4
Brown Candover ...33 B4
Brown Edge
  Lancs 136 B2
  Staffs 129 D4
Brown Heath 127 C4
Brownhill
  Aberds 256 B1
  Aberds 256 B3
  Blackburn 145 D6
  Shrops 110 C3
Brownhills
  Fife 221 C5
  W Mid 96 A3
Brownlow 128 C3
Brownlow Heath ...128 C3
Brownmuir 233 A5
Brown's End 79 D5
Brownshill 63 C4
Brownston 7 B6
Brownyside 189 A4
Broxa 160 B3
Broxbourne 68 C3

Broxburn
  E Loth 210 C3
  W Loth 208 C3
Broxholme 133 B4
Broxted 69 A5
Broxton 127 D4
Broxwood 78 B1
Broyle Side 22 A2
Brù 288 C4
Bruairnis 286 F3
Bruan 275 A7
Bruar Lodge 230 A2
Brucehill 206 C1
Bruera 127 C4
Bruern Abbey 64 A3
Bruichladdich 200 B2
Bruisyard 88 A4
Brumby 141 C6
Brund 129 C6
Brundall 104 A4
Brundish 88 A3
Brundish Street ...104 D3
Brunery 235 C6
Brunshaw 146 D2
Brunswick Village ..179 B4
Bruntcliffe 139 A5
Bruntingthorpe ...98 B3
Brunton
  Fife 220 B3
  Northumb 189 A5
  Wilts 45 D6
Brushford
  Devon 12 A1
  Som. 27 C4
Bruton 29 B6
Bryanston 16 A2
Brydekirk 175 A4
Bryher Scilly 2 E3
Brymbo 126 D2
Brympton 29 D5
Bryn
  Carms 57 B5
  Gtr Man 137 C4
  Neath 40 B3
  Shrops 93 C6
Brynamman 59 D4
Brynberian 72 C4
Brynbryddan 40 B2
Brynbuga = Usk ...61 C5
Bryncae 41 C4
Bryncethin 40 C4
Bryncir 107 B4
Bryn-coch 40 B2
Bryncroes 106 C2
Bryncrug 90 B4
Bryn Du 122 C3
Bryneglwys 109 A6
Brynford 126 B1
Bryn Gates 137 C4
Bryn-glas 124 C3
Bryn Golau 41 C4
Bryngwran 122 C3
Bryngwyn
  Ceredig. 73 B5
  Mon. 61 C5
  Powys 77 C5
Brynhenllan 72 C3
Brynhoffnant 73 A6
Brynithel 41 A7
Bryn-Iwan 73 C6
Brynmawr 60 B3
Bryn-mawr 106 C2
Brynmenyn 40 C4
Brynmill 57 C6
Brynna 41 C4
Bryn-nantllech ...125 C4
Bryn-penarth 93 A5
Brynrefail
  Anglesey 123 B4
  Gwyn. 123 D5
Bryn Rhyd-yr-
  Arian. 125 C4
Brynsadler 41 C5
Bryn Saith
  Marchog 125 D5
Brynsiencyn 123 D4
Bryn Sion 91 A6
Brynteg
  Anglesey 123 B4
  Ceredig. 58 A1
Bryn-y-gwenin ...61 B5
Bryn-y-maen 124 B3
Bryn-yr-eryr 106 B3
Buaile nam Bodach 286 F3
Bualintur 246 B3
Buarthmeini 108 B3
Bubbenhall 97 D6
Bubwith 149 D6
Buccleuch 185 A6
Buchanhaven 257 B6

Buchanty....218 B4
Buchlyvie....206 A3
Buckabank....164 A1
Buckden
  Cambs....84 A3
  N Yorks....156 D3
Buckenham....105 A4
Buckerell....13 A6
Buckfast....7 A6
Buckfastleigh....7 A6
Buckhaven....209 A6
Buckholm....196 C3
Buckholt....61 B7
Buckhorn Weston..30 C1
Buckhurst Hill....68 D4
Buckie....267 C5
Buckies....280 B3
Buckingham....82 D3
Buckland
  Bucks....66 B3
  Devon....7 C5
  Glos....80 D3
  Hants....18 B2
  Herts....85 D5
  Kent....39 A5
  Oxon....64 D4
  Sur....35 A5
Buckland Brewer...25 C5
Buckland Common..67 C4
Buckland Dinham...43 D6
Buckland Filleigh..11 A5
Buckland in the
  Moor....12 D2
Buckland
  Monachorum...6 A3
Buckland Newton..15 A6
Buckland St Mary..28 D2
Bucklebury....46 B3
Bucklegate....117 B6
Bucklerheads....221 A4
Bucklers Hard....18 B3
Bucklesham....88 C3
Buckley =Bwcle....126 C2
Bucklow Hill....128 A2
Buckminster....116 C1
Bucknall
  Lincs....133 C6
  Stoke....112 A3
Bucknell
  Oxon....65 A6
  Shrops....94 D1
Buckpool....267 C5
Bucksburn....245 B5
Buck's Cross....24 C4
Bucks Green....34 C3
Buckshaw Village..137 A4
Bucks Horn Oak...33 A7
Buckskin....47 D4
Buck's Mills....25 C4
Buckton
  E Yorks....161 D5
  Hereford....94 D1
  Northumb....199 C4
Buckworth....100 D3
Budbrooke....81 A5
Budby....131 C6
Budd's Titson....10 A3
Bude....10 A3
Budlake....13 B4
Budle....199 C5
Budleigh Salterton..13 C5
Budock Water....4 D2
Buerton....111 A5
Buffler's Holt....82 D3
Bugbrooke....82 B3
Buglawton....128 C3
Bugle....5 B5
Bugley....30 A2
Bugthorpe....149 B6
Buildwas....95 A4
Builth Road....76 B4
Builth Wells
  =Llanfair-ym-Muallt.76 B4
Buirgh....287 E5
Bulby....116 C3
Bulcote....115 A4
Buldoo....279 B5
Bulford....31 A5
Bulford Camp....31 A5
Bulkeley....127 D5
Bulkington
  Warks....97 C6
  Wilts....44 B3
Bulkworthy....25 D4
Bullamoor....158 B2
Bullbridge....130 D3
Bullbrook....48 C1
Bulley....62 B3
Bullgill....162 A3
Bull Hill....18 B2

Bullington
  Hants....32 A3
  Lincs....133 B5
Bull's Green....68 B2
Bullwood....203 A6
Bulmer
  Essex....87 C4
  N Yorks....149 A5
Bulmer Tye....87 D4
Bulphan....50 A3
Bulverhythe....23 B5
Bulwark....257 B4
Bulwell....114 A3
Bulwick....99 B6
Bumble's Green....68 C4
Bun Abhainn
  Eadarra....288 G2
Bunacaimb....235 B5
Bun a'Mhuillin....286 E3
Bunarkaig....239 D5
Bunbury....127 D5
Bunbury Heath...127 D5
Bunchrew....252 B2
Bundalloch....249 D5
Buness....284 C8
Bunessan....224 D2
Bungay....104 C4
Bunkers Hill....65 B5
Bunker's Hill
  Lincs....133 B4
  Lincs....134 D2
Bunloit....251 D7
Bun Loyne....239 B6
Bunnahabhain....201 A4
Bunny....114 C3
Buntait....251 C5
Buntingford....68 A3
Bunwell....104 B2
Burbage
  Derbys....129 B5
  Leics....98 B1
  Wilts....45 C6
Burchett's Green...47 A6
Burcombe....31 B4
Burcot....65 D6
Burcott....66 A3
Burdon....179 D5
Bures....87 D5
Bures Green....87 D5
Burford
  Ches E....127 D6
  Oxon....64 B3
  Shrops....78 A3
Burg....224 B2
Burgar....282 E4
Burgate
  Hants....31 D5
  Suff....104 D1
Burgess Hill....21 A6
Burgh....88 B3
Burgh by Sands...175 C6
Burgh Castle....105 A5
Burghclere....46 C2
Burghead....266 C2
Burghfield....47 C4
Burghfield Common.47 C4
Burghfield Hill....47 C4
Burgh Heath....35 A5
Burghill....78 C2
Burgh le Marsh....135 C5
Burgh Muir....256 D2
Burgh next
  Aylsham....120 C4
Burgh on Bain....134 A2
Burgh St Margaret.121 D6
Burgh St Peter....105 B5
Burghwallis....140 B3
Burham....51 C4
Buriton....33 C6
Burland....127 D6
Burlawn....9 D5
Burleigh....48 C1
Burlescombe....27 D5
Burleston....16 B1
Burley
  Hants....17 A6
  Rutland....116 D1
  W Yorks....148 D1
Burleydam....111 A5
Burley Gate....78 C3
Burley in
  Wharfedale....147 C5
Burley Lodge....17 A6
Burley Street....17 A6
Burlingjobb....77 B6
Burlow....22 A3
Burlton....110 C3
Burmarsh....38 B2
Burmington....81 D5
Burn....140 A3

Burnaston....113 B6
Burnbank....194 A2
Burnby....150 C1
Burncross....139 D6
Burneside....154 B4
Burness....282 C7
Burneston....157 C7
Burnett....43 C5
Burnfoot
  Borders....186 B3
  Borders....186 B4
  E Ayrs....182 B2
  Perth....219 D4
Burnham
  Bucks....48 A2
  N Lincs....142 B2
Burnham Deepdale.119 A5
Burnham Green....68 B2
Burnham Market...119 A5
Burnham Norton...119 A5
Burnham-on-
  Crouch....70 D3
Burnham-on-Sea...28 A3
Burnham Overy
  Staithe....119 A5
Burnham Overy
  Town....119 A5
Burnham Thorpe...119 A5
Burnhead
  Dumfries....183 C6
  S Ayrs....181 A4
Burnhervie....245 A4
Burnhill Green....95 A5
Burnhope....167 A4
Burnhouse....204 C3
Burniston....160 B4
Burnlee....139 C4
Burnley....146 D2
Burnley Lane....146 D2
Burnmouth....211 D6
Burn of Cambus...218 D2
Burnopfield....178 D3
Burnsall....147 A4
Burnside
  Angus....232 C3
  E Ayrs....182 A3
  Fife....219 D6
  Shetland....284 F4
  S Lanark....205 B6
  W Loth....208 C3
Burnside of
  Duntrune....220 A4
Burnswark....175 A4
Burntcommon....34 A3
Burnt Heath....130 B2
Burnthouse....4 D2
Burnt Houses....166 C4
Burntisland....209 B5
Burnton....182 B2
Burntwood....96 A3
Burnt Yates....147 A6
Burnwynd....208 D4
Burpham
  Sur....34 A3
  W Sus....20 B3
Burradon
  Northumb....188 C2
  T&W....179 B4
Burrafirth....284 B8
Burraland
  Shetland....284 F5
  Shetland....285 J4
Burras....3 B4
Burravoe
  Shetland....284 F7
  Shetland....284 G5
Burray Village....283 H5
Burrells....165 D4
Burrelton....220 A2
Burridge
  Devon....25 B6
  Hants....32 A4
Burrill....157 C6
Burringham....141 C6
Burrington
  Devon....26 D1
  Hereford....94 D2
  N Som....42 D3
Burrough Green....86 B2
Burrough on the
  Hill....115 D5
Burrow-bridge....28 C3
Burrowhill....48 C2
Burry....57 C4
Burry Green....57 C4
Burry Port
  =Porth Tywyn....57 B4
Burscough....136 B3
Burscough Bridge..136 B3
Bursea....149 D7

Burshill....150 C3
Bursledon....18 A3
Burslem....112 A2
Burstall....88 C1
Burstock....14 A4
Burston
  Norf....104 C2
  Staffs....112 B3
Burstow....35 B6
Burstwick....143 A4
Burtersett....156 C2
Burtle....28 A3
Burton
  BCP....17 B5
  Ches W....126 B3
  Ches W....127 C5
  Lincs....133 B4
  Northumb....199 C5
  Pembs....55 D5
  Som....28 A1
  Wilts....44 B2
Burton Agnes....151 A4
Burton Bradstock..15 C4
Burton Dassett....81 B6
Burton Fleming...161 D4
Burton Green
  W Mid....97 D5
  Wrex....126 D3
Burton Hastings...97 B7
Burton-in-Kendal..154 D4
Burton in Lonsdale.155 D5
Burton Joyce....115 A4
Burton Latimer....99 D6
Burton Lazars....115 D5
Burton-le-Coggles.116 C2
Burton Leonard...148 A2
Burton on the
  Wolds....114 C3
Burton Overy....98 B3
Burton Pedwardine 116 A4
Burton Pidsea....151 D5
Burton Salmon...140 A2
Burton Stather....141 B6
Burton upon
  Stather....141 B6
Burton upon Trent..113 C6
Burtonwood....137 D4
Burwardsley....127 D5
Burwarton....95 C4
Burwash....37 D4
Burwash Common..36 D4
Burwash Weald....36 D4
Burwell
  Cambs....86 A1
  Lincs....134 B3
Burwen....123 A4
Burwick....283 J5
Bury
  Cambs....101 C4
  Gtr Man....137 B7
  Som....27 C4
  W Sus....20 A3
Bury Green....68 A4
Bury St Edmunds...87 A4
Burythorpe....149 A6
Busby....205 C5
Buscot....64 D3
Bush Bank....78 B2
Bushbury....96 A2
Bushby....98 A3
Bush Crathie....243 C5
Bushey....67 D6
Bushey Heath....67 D6
Bush Green....104 C3
Bushley....80 D1
Bushton....45 B4
Buslingthorpe....133 A5
Busta....284 G5
Butcher's Cross....36 D3
Butcombe....43 C4
Butetown....41 D6
Butleigh....29 B5
Butleigh Wootton..29 B5
Butler's Cross....66 C3
Butler's End....97 C5
Butlers Marston....81 C6
Butley....89 B4
Butley High Corner.89 C4
Butterburn....177 B4
Buttercrambe....149 B6
Butterknowle....166 C4
Butterleigh....13 A4
Buttermere
  Cumb....163 C4
  Wilts....46 C1
Buttershaw....139 A4
Butterstone....231 D4
Butterton....129 D5
Butterwick
  Durham....167 C6

Butterwick *continued*
  Lincs....117 A6
  N Yorks....159 D6
  N Yorks....160 D3
Butt Green....127 D6
Buttington....93 A6
Buttonoak....95 D5
Buttsash....18 A3
Butt's Green....32 C2
Buxhall....87 B6
Buxhall Fen Street..87 B6
Buxley....198 A2
Buxted....36 D2
Buxton
  Derbys....129 B5
  Norf....120 C4
Buxworth....129 A5
Bwcle =Buckley....126 C2
Bwlch....60 A3
Bwlchgwyn....126 C2
Bwlch-Llan....75 C4
Bwlchnewydd....73 D6
Bwlchtocyn....106 D3
Bwlch-y-cibau....109 D6
Bwlchyddar....109 C6
Bwlch-y-fadfa....74 D3
Bwlch-y-ffridd....93 B4
Bwlchygroes....73 C5
Bwlch-y-sarnau....92 D4
Byermoor....178 D3
Byers Green....167 C4
Byfield....82 B2
Byfleet....48 C3
Byford....78 C1
Bygrave....85 D4
Byker....179 C4
Bylchau....125 C4
Byley....128 C2
Bynea....57 C5
Byness....187 C6
Bythorn....100 D2
Byton....78 A1
Byworth....34 D2

C

Cabharstadh....288 E4
Cablea....218 A4
Cabourne....142 C3
Cabrach
  Argyll....201 B4
  Moray....255 D4
Cabrich....252 B1
Cabus....145 C4
Cackle Street....36 D2
Cadbury....13 A4
Cadbury Barton....26 D1
Cadder....205 A6
Caddington....67 B5
Caddonfoot....196 C3
Cadeby
  Leics....97 A7
  S Yorks....140 C3
Cadeleigh....13 A4
Cade Street....36 D4
Cadgwith....3 D5
Cadham....220 D2
Cadishead....137 D6
Cadle....57 C6
Cadley
  Lancs....145 D5
  Wilts....45 C6
  Wilts....45 D6
Cadmore End....66 D2
Cadnam....32 D1
Cadney....142 C2
Cadole....126 C2
Cadoxton....41 E6
Cadoxton-Juxta-
  Neath....40 B2
Cadshaw....137 B6
Cadzow....194 A2
Caeathro....123 D4
Caehopkin....59 D5
Caenby....133 A5
Caenby Corner....133 A4
Caerau
  Bridgend....40 B2
  Cardiff....41 D6
Caér-bryn....57 A5
Caerdeon....90 A4
Caerdydd =Cardiff..41 D6
Caerfarchell....54 B3
Caerffili
  =Caerphilly....41 C6
Caerfyrddin
  =Carmarthen....73 D7
Caergeiliog....122 C3
Caergwrle....126 D3

Caergybi
  =Holyhead....122 B2
Caerleon
  =Caerllion....61 D5
Caer Llan....61 C6
Caerllion
  =Caerleon....61 D5
Caernarfon....123 D4
Caerphilly
  =Caerffili....41 C6
Caersws....92 B4
Caerwedros....73 A6
Caerwent....61 D6
Caerwych....107 C6
Caerwys....125 B6
Caethle....90 C4
Caim....123 B6
Caio....58 B3
Cairinis....287 H3
Cairisiadar....287 A5
Cairminis....287 F5
Cairnbaan....213 C6
Cairnborrow....255 B5
Cairnbrogie....256 D3
Cairnbulg Castle...269 C5
Cairncross
  Angus....232 A2
  Borders....211 D5
Cairndow....215 A4
Cairness....269 C5
Cairneyhill....208 B3
Cairnfield House...267 C5
Cairngaan....170 D3
Cairngarroch....170 C2
Cairnhill....256 C1
Cairnie
  Aberds....245 B5
  Aberds....255 B5
Cairnorrie....256 B3
Cairnpark....245 A5
Cairnryan....170 A2
Cairnton....283 G4
Caister-on-Sea....121 D7
Caistor....142 C3
Caistor St Edmund.104 A3
Caistron....188 C2
Caitha Bowland....196 B3
Calais Street....87 D5
Calanais....288 D3
Calbost....288 F5
Calbourne....18 C3
Calceby....134 B3
Calcot Row....47 B4
Calcott....52 C3
Caldback....284 C8
Caldbeck....163 A6
Caldbergh....157 C4
Caldecote
  Cambs....85 B5
  Cambs....100 C3
  Herts....84 D4
  Northants....82 B3
Caldecott
  Northants....84 A1
  Oxon....65 D5
  Rutland....99 B5
Calderbank....207 D5
Calder Bridge....162 D3
Calderbrook....138 B2
Caldercruix....207 D6
Calder Hall....162 D3
Calder Mains....280 C2
Caldermill....205 D6
Calder Vale....145 C5
Calderwood....205 C6
Caldhame....232 D2
Caldicot....42 A3
Caldwell
  Derbys....113 D6
  N Yorks....167 D4
Caldy....126 A2
Caledrhydiau....74 C3
Calfsound....282 D6
Calgary....224 A2
Califer....266 D1
California
  Falk....208 C2
  Norf....121 D7
Calke....114 C3
Callakille....248 A3
Callaly....188 C3
Callander....217 D6
Callaughton....95 B4
Callestick....4 B2
Calligarry....247 D5
Callington....6 A2
Callow....78 D2

Callow End 79 C6
Callow Hill
Wilts 44 A4
Worcs 95 D5
Callows Grave 78 A3
Calmore 32 D2
Calmsden 63 C6
Calne 44 B4
Calow 131 B4
Calshot 18 A3
Calstock 6 A3
Calstone Wellington 44 C4
Calthorpe 120 B3
Calthwaite 164 A2
Calton
N Yorks 146 B3
Staffs 129 D6
Calveley 127 D5
Calver 130 B2
Calverhall 111 B5
Calver Hill 78 C1
Calverleigh 27 D4
Calverley 147 D6
Calvert 66 A1
Calverton
M Keynes 83 D4
Notts 115 A4
Calvine 230 B2
Calvo 174 C4
Cam 62 D3
Camas-luinie 249 D6
Camasnacroise 236 D2
Camastianavaig 247 A4
Camasunary 247 C4
Camault Muir 251 B7
Camb 284 D7
Camber 38 D1
Camberley 47 C6
Camberwell 49 B6
Camblesforth 141 A4
Cambo 178 A2
Cambois 179 A5
Camborne 3 A4
Cambourne 85 B5
Cambridge
Cambs 85 B6
Glos 62 C3
Cambridge Town 51 A6
Cambus 207 A6
Cambusavie Farm 264 A3
Cambusbarron 207 A5
Cambuskenneth 207 A6
Cambuslang 205 B6
Cambusmore Lodge 264 A3
Camden 49 A5
Camelford 10 C2
Camelsdale 34 C1
Camerory 253 C6
Camer's Green 79 D5
Camerton
Bath 43 D5
Cumb 162 A3
E Yorks 143 A4
Camghouran 229 C4
Cammachmore 245 C6
Cammeringham 133 A4
Camore 264 A3
Campbeltown 190 C3
Camperdown 179 B4
Camp Hill 97 B6
Campmuir 220 A2
Campsall 140 B3
Campsey Ash 88 B4
Campton 84 D3
Camptown 187 B5
Camrose 55 B5
Camserney 230 D2
Camster 281 D4
Camuschoirk 235 D6
Camuscross 247 C5
Camusnagaul
Highld 237 B4
Highld 262 B2
Camusrory 238 C2
Camusteel 249 B4
Camusterrach 249 B4
Camusvrachan 229 D5
Canada 32 D1
Canadia 23 A5
Canal Side 141 B4
Candacraig House 243 A6
Candlesby 135 C4
Candy Mill 195 B5
Cane End 47 B4
Canewdon 70 D2
Canford Bottom 17 A4
Canford Cliffs 17 C4
Canford Magna 17 B4
Canham's Green 87 A6
Canholes 129 B5
Canisbay 281 A5
Cann 30 C2
Cannard's Grave 29 A6
Cann Common 30 C2
Cannich 251 C5
Cannington 28 B2
Cannock 96 A2
Cannock Wood 112 D4
Canonbie 175 A6
Canon Bridge 78 C2
Canon Frome 79 C4
Canon Pyon 78 C2
Canons Ashby 82 B2
Canonstown 2 B3
Canterbury 52 D3
Cantley
Norf 105 A4
S Yorks 140 C4
Cantlop 94 A3
Canton 41 D6
Cantraybruich 252 B3
Cantraydoune 252 B3
Cantraywood 252 B3
Cantsfield 155 D5
Canvey Island 51 A4
Canwick 133 C4
Canworthy Water 10 B3
Caol 237 B5
Caolas 222 C3
Caolas Scalpaigh 288 H3
Caolas Stocinis 288 H2
Caol Ila 201 A4
Capel 35 B4
Capel Bangor 91 D4
Capel Betws Lleucu 75 C5
Capel Carmel 106 D1
Capel Coch 123 B4
Capel Curig 124 D2
Capel Cynon 73 B6
Capel Dewi
Carms 58 C1
Ceredig 58 A1
Ceredig 90 D4
Capel Garmon 124 D3
Capel-gwyn 122 C3
Capel Gwyn 58 C1
Capel Gwynfe 59 C4
Capel Hendre 57 A5
Capel Hermon 108 C2
Capel Isaac 58 C2
Capel Iwan 73 C5
Capel le Ferne 39 B4
Capel Llanilltern 41 C5
Capel Mawr 123 C4
Capel St Andrew 89 C4
Capel St Mary 88 D1
Capel Seion 75 A5
Capel Tygwydd 73 B5
Capel Uchaf 107 B4
Capelulo 124 B2
Capel-y-graig 123 D5
Capenhurst 126 B3
Capernwray 154 D4
Capheaton 178 A2
Cappercleuch 196 D1
Capplegill 185 B4
Capton 8 B2
Caputh 219 A5
Carbis Bay 2 B3
Carbost
Highld 246 A2
Highld 259 D4
Carbrook 130 A3
Carbrooke 103 A5
Carburton 131 B6
Carcant 196 A2
Carcary 233 C4
Carclaze 5 B5
Car Colston 115 A5
Carcroft 140 B3
Cardenden 209 A5
Cardeston 110 D2
Cardiff = *Caerdydd* 41 D6
Cardigan = *Aberteifi* 73 B4
Cardington
Bedford 84 C2
Shrops 94 B3
Cardinham 5 A6
Cardonald 205 B5
Cardow 254 B2
Cardrona 196 C2
Cardross 206 C1
Cardurnock 175 C4
Careby 116 D3
Careston Castle 232 C3
Carew 55 D6
Carew Cheriton 55 D6
Carew Newton 55 D6
Carey 78 D3
Carfrae 210 D2
Cargenbridge 174 A2
Cargill 219 A6
Cargo 175 C6
Cargreen 6 A3
Carham 198 C2
Carhampton 27 A5
Carharrack 4 C2
Carie
Perth 217 A6
Perth 229 C5
Carines 4 B2
Carisbrooke 18 C3
Cark 154 D2
Carlabhagh 288 C3
Carland Cross 4 B3
Carlby 116 D3
Carlecotes 139 C4
Carlesmoor 157 D5
Carleton
Cumb 164 C3
Cumb 176 D2
Lancs 144 D3
N Yorks 146 C3
Carleton Forehoe 104 A1
Carleton Rode 104 B2
Carlingcott 43 D5
Carlin How 169 D5
Carlisle 175 C7
Carlops 195 A6
Carlton
Bedford 83 B6
Cambs 86 B2
Leics 97 A6
Notts 115 A4
N Yorks 140 A4
N Yorks 157 C4
N Yorks 159 C5
N Yorks 167 D4
Stockton 167 C6
Suff 89 A4
S Yorks 139 B6
W Yorks 139 A6
Carlton Colville 105 C6
Carlton Curlieu 98 B3
Carlton Husthwaite 158 D3
Carlton in Cleveland 158 A4
Carlton in Lindrick 131 A5
Carlton le Moorland 133 D4
Carlton Miniott 158 C2
Carlton on Trent 132 C2
Carlton Scroop 116 A2
Carluke 194 A3
Carmarthen = *Caerfyrddin* 73 D7
Carmel
Anglesey 122 B3
Carms 57 A5
Flint 125 B6
Guern 6
Gwyn 107 A4
Carmont 245 D5
Carmunnock 205 C6
Carmyle 205 B6
Carmyllie 232 D3
Carnaby 151 A4
Carnach
Highld 250 D2
Highld 262 A2
W Isles 288 H3
Carnachy 278 C3
Càrnais 287 A5
Carnbee 221 D5
Carnbo 219 D5
Carnbrea 3 A4
Carnduff 205 D6
Carnduncan 200 B2
Carne 4 D4
Carnforth 154 D3
Carn-gorm 249 D6
Carnhedryn 54 B4
Carnhell Green 3 B4
Carnkie
Corn 3 B4
Corn 4 D2
Carno 92 B3
Carnoch
Highld 251 A4
Highld 251 C5
Carnock 208 B3
Carnon Downs 4 C2
Carnousie 268 D1
Carnoustie 221 A5
Carnwath 195 B4
Carnyorth 2 B1
Carperby 156 C4
Carpley Green 156 C3
Carr 140 D3
Carradale 190 B4
Carragraich 288 H2
Carrbridge 253 D5
Carrefour Selous 6
Carreglefn 122 B3
Carreg-wen 73 B5
Carr Hill 179 C4
Carrick
Argyll 214 D2
Fife 220 B4
Carrick Castle 215 C4
Carrick House 282 D6
Carriden 208 B3
Carrington
Gtr Man 137 D6
Lincs 134 D3
Midloth 209 D6
Carrog
Conwy 108 A2
Denb 109 A6
Carron
Falk 208 B1
Moray 254 B3
Carronbridge 183 C6
Carron Bridge 207 B5
Carronshore 208 B1
Carrshield 165 A6
Carrutherstown 174 A4
Carrville 167 A6
Carsaig
Argyll 213 D5
Argyll 225 D4
Carscreugh 171 B4
Carsegowan 171 B6
Carse Gray 232 C2
Carse House 202 B2
Carseriggan 171 A5
Carsethorn 174 C2
Carshalton 49 C5
Carsington 130 D2
Carskiey 190 E2
Carsluith 171 B6
Carsphairn 182 C3
Carstairs 194 B4
Carstairs Junction 195 B4
Carswell Marsh 64 D4
Carter's Clay 32 C2
Carterton 64 C3
Carterway Heads 178 D2
Carthew 5 B5
Carthorpe 157 C7
Cartington 188 C3
Cartland 194 B3
Cartmel 154 D2
Cartmel Fell 154 C3
Carway 57 B4
Cary Fitzpaine 29 C5
Cascob 77 A6
Cas-gwent = *Chepstow* 62 D1
Cashlie 228 D3
Cashmoor 30 D3
Casnewydd = *Newport* 42 A2
Cassey Compton 63 B6
Cassington 65 B5
Cassop 167 B6
Castell 125 C6
Castellau 41 C5
Castell-Howell 74 D3
Castell-Nedd = *Neath* 40 B2
Castell Newydd Emlyn = *Newcastle Emlyn* 73 B6
Castell-y-bwch 61 D4
Casterton 155 D5
Castle Acre 119 D5
Castle Ashby 83 B5
Castlebay = *Bagh a Chaisteil* 286 G2
Castle Bolton 156 B4
Castle Bromwich 96 C4
Castle Bytham 116 D2
Castlebythe 55 B6
Castle Caereinion 93 A5
Castle Camps 86 C2
Castle Carrock 176 D3
Castlecary 207 C5
Castle Cary 29 B6
Castle Combe 44 B2
Castlecraig 265 D4
Castle Donington 114 C2
Castle Douglas 173 B5
Castle Eaton 64 D2
Castle Eden 168 B2
Castlefairn 183 D5
Castle Forbes 244 A3
Castleford 140 A2
Castle Frome 79 C4
Castle Green 48 C2
Castle Gresley 113 D6
Castle Heaton 198 B3
Castle Hedingham 86 D3
Castlehill
Borders 195 C7
Highld 280 B3
W Dunb 206 C1
Castle Hill 37 B4
Castle Huntly 220 B3
Castle Kennedy 170 B3
Castlemaddy 182 D3
Castlemartin 55 E5
Castlemilk
Dumfries 174 A4
Glasgow 205 C6
Castlemorris 55 A5
Castlemorton 79 D5
Castle O'er 185 C5
Castle Pulverbatch 94 A2
Castle Rising 118 C3
Castleside 166 A3
Castle Stuart 252 B3
Castlethorpe 83 C5
Castleton
Angus 232 D1
Argyll 214 D1
Derbys 129 A6
Gtr Man 138 B1
Newport 42 A1
N Yorks 159 A5
Castletown
Ches W 127 D4
Highld 252 B3
Highld 280 B3
IoM 152 E2
T&W 179 D5
Castleweary 186 C3
Castley 147 C6
Caston 103 B5
Castor 100 B3
Catacol 203 D4
Catbrain 43 A4
Catbrook 61 C7
Catchall 2 C2
Catchems Corner 97 D5
Catchgate 178 D3
Catcleugh 187 C6
Catcliffe 131 A4
Catcott 28 B3
Caterham 35 A6
Catfield 121 C5
Catfirth 285 H6
Catford 49 B6
Catforth 145 D4
Cathays 41 D6
Cathcart 205 B5
Cathedine 60 A3
Catherington 33 D5
Catherton 95 D4
Catlodge 241 C4
Catlowdy 176 B2
Catmore 46 A2
Caton 145 A5
Caton Green 145 A5
Catrine 193 C5
Cat's Ash 61 D5
Catsfield 23 A5
Catshill 96 D2
Cattal 148 B3
Cattawade 88 D2
Catterall 145 C4
Catterick 157 B6
Catterick Bridge 157 B6
Catterick Garrison 157 B5
Catterlen 164 B2
Catterline 233 A6
Catterton 148 C4
Catthorpe 98 D2
Cattistock 15 B5
Catton
Northumb 177 D6
N Yorks 158 D2
Catwick 151 C4
Catworth 100 D2
Caudlesprings 103 A5
Caulcott 65 A6
Cauldcots 233 D4
Cauldhame 207 A4
Cauldmill 186 B4
Cauldon 113 A4
Caulkerbush 174 C2
Caulside 176 A2
Caunsall 95 C6
Caunton 132 D2
Causewayend 195 C5
Causeway End 171 A6
Causeway Foot 147 D4
Causewayhead 174 C4
Causeway-head 207 A5
Causeyend 245 A6
Causey Park Bridge 189 D4
Cautley 155 B5
Cavendish 87 C4
Cavendish Bridge 114 C2
Cavenham 86 A3
Caversfield 65 A6
Caversham 47 B5
Caverswall 112 A3
Cavil 149 D6
Cawdor 253 B4
Cawkwell 134 B2
Cawood 149 D4
Cawsand 6 B3
Cawston 120 C3
Cawthorne 139 C5
Cawthorpe 116 C3
Cawton 159 D5
Caxton 85 B5
Caynham 94 D3
Caythorpe
Lincs 116 A2
Notts 115 A4
Cayton 161 C4
Ceann a Bhaigh 287 H2
Ceannacroc Lodge 239 A6
Ceann a Deas Loch Baghasdail 286 E3
Ceann Shiphoirt 288 F3
Ceann Tarabhaigh 288 F3
Cearsiadair 288 E4
Cefn Berain 125 C4
Cefn-brith 125 D4
Cefn Canol 110 B1
Cefn-coch 124 C3
Cefn Coch 109 C6
Cefn-coed-y-cymmer 60 C2
Cefn Cribbwr 40 C3
Cefn Cross 40 C3
Cefn-ddwysarn 109 B4
Cefn Einion 93 C6
Cefneithin 57 A5
Cefn-gorwydd 76 C3
Cefn-mawr 110 A1
Cefn-y-bedd 126 D3
Cefn-y-pant 73 D4
Cei-bach 73 A7
Ceinewydd = *New Quay* 73 A6
Ceint 123 C4
Cellan 75 D5
Cellarhead 112 A3
Cemaes 122 A3
Cemmaes 91 B6
Cemmaes Road 91 B6
Cenarth 73 B5
Cenin 107 B4
Central 204 A2
Ceos 288 E4
Ceres 220 C4
Cerne Abbas 15 A6
Cerney Wick 63 D6
Cerrigceinwen 123 C4
Cerrigydrudion 109 A4
Cessford 187 A6
Ceunant 123 D5
Chaceley 79 D6
Chacewater 4 C2
Chackmore 82 D3
Chacombe 82 C1
Chadderton 138 C2
Chadderton Fold 138 C1
Chaddesden 114 B1
Chaddesley Corbett 96 D1
Chaddleworth 46 B2
Chadlington 64 A4
Chadshunt 81 B6
Chad Valley 96 C3
Chadwell 115 C5
Chadwell St Mary 50 B3
Chadwick End 97 D5
Chadwick Green 136 D4
Chaffcombe 28 D3
Chagford 12 C2
Chailey 22 A1
Chainbridge 101 A6
Chain Bridge 117 A6
Chainhurst 37 B5
Chalbury 17 A4
Chalbury Common 17 A4
Chaldon 35 A6
Chaldon Herring or 16 C1
Chale 18 D3
Chale Green 18 D3
Chalfont Common 67 D5
Chalfont St Giles 67 D4
Chalfont St Peter 67 D5

Chalford 63 C4
Chalgrove 66 D1
Chalk 50 B3
Challacombe 26 A1
Challoch 171 A5
Challock 52 D2
Chalton
  C Beds 67 A5
  Hants 33 D6
Chalvington 22 B3
Chancery 75 A4
Chandler's Ford 32 C3
Channel Tunnel 38 B3
Channerwick 285 L6
Chantry
  Som 29 A7
  Suff 88 C2
Chapel 209 A5
Chapel Allerton
  Som 42 D3
  W Yorks 148 D2
Chapel Amble 9 D5
Chapel Brampton 83 A4
Chapel Chorlton 112 B2
Chapel End 97 B6
Chapel-en-le-Frith 129 A5
Chapelgate 117 C7
Chapel Green
  Warks 82 A1
  Warks 97 C5
Chapel Haddlesey 140 A3
Chapelhall 207 D5
Chapel Head 101 C5
Chapelhill
  Dumfries 184 C3
  Highld 265 C4
  N Ayrs 204 D2
  Perth 219 A5
  Perth 220 B2
Chapel Hill
  Aberds 257 C5
  Lincs 134 D2
  Mon 62 D1
  N Yorks 148 C2
Chapelknowe 175 A6
Chapel Lawn 93 D7
Chapel-le-Dale 155 D6
Chapel Milton 129 A5
Chapel of Garioch 256 D2
Chapel Row 46 C3
Chapel St Leonards 135 B5
Chapel Stile 154 A2
Chapelton
  Angus 233 D4
  Devon 25 C6
  Highld 242 A2
  S Lanark 194 B1
Chapeltown
  Blackburn 137 B6
  Moray 254 D3
  S Yorks 139 D6
Chapmanslade 30 A2
Chapmans Well 11 B4
Chapmore End 68 B3
Chappel 70 A2
Chard 14 A3
Chardstock 14 A3
Charfield 62 D3
Charford 80 A2
Charing 38 A1
Charing Cross 31 D5
Charing Heath 38 A1
Charingworth 81 D5
Charlbury 65 B4
Charlcombe 43 C6
Charlecote 81 B5
Charles 26 B1
Charlesfield 175 B4
Charleston
  Angus 232 D1
  Renfs 205 B4
Charlestown
  Aberdeen 245 B6
  Corn 5 B5
  Derbys 138 D3
  Dorset 15 D6
  Fife 208 B3
  Gtr Man 137 C7
  Highld 252 B2
  Highld 261 C5
  W Yorks 138 A2
Charlestown of
  Aberlour 254 B3
Charles Tye 87 B6
Charlesworth 138 D3
Charleton 7 C6
Charlton
  Hants 32 A2
  Herts 68 A1
  London 49 B7
Charlton *continued*
  Northants 82 D2
  Northumb 177 A6
  Som 43 D5
  Telford 111 D4
  Wilts 30 C3
  Wilts 44 A3
  Wilts 45 D5
  Worcs 80 C3
  W Sus 20 A1
Charlton Abbots 63 A6
Charlton Adam 29 C5
Charlton-All-Saints 31 C5
Charlton Down 15 B6
Charlton
  Horethorne 29 C6
Charlton Kings 63 A5
Charlton Mackerell 29 C5
Charlton Marshall 16 A2
Charlton Musgrove 29 C7
Charlton on Otmoor 65 B6
Charltons 168 D4
Charlwood 35 B5
Charlynch 28 B2
Charminster 15 B6
Charmouth 14 B3
Charndon 66 A1
Charney Bassett 65 D4
Charnock Richard 137 B4
Charsfield 88 B3
Chart Corner 37 A5
Charter Alley 46 D3
Charterhouse 42 D3
Charterville
  Allotments 64 B4
Chartham 52 D3
Chartham Hatch 52 D3
Chartridge 67 C4
Chart Sutton 37 B6
Charvil 47 B5
Charwelton 82 B2
Chasetown 96 A3
Chastleton 64 A3
Chasty 10 A4
Chatburn 146 C1
Chatcull 112 B1
Chatham 51 C4
Chathill 189 A4
Chattenden 51 B4
Chatteris 101 C5
Chattisham 88 C1
Chatto 187 B6
Chatton 188 A3
Chawleigh 26 D2
Chawley 65 C5
Chawston 84 B3
Chawton 33 B6
Cheadle
  Gtr Man 128 A3
  Staffs 112 A4
Cheadle Heath 128 A3
Cheadle Hulme 128 A3
Cheam 49 C5
Cheapside 34 A3
Chearsley 66 B2
Chebsey 112 C2
Checkendon 47 A4
Checkley
  Ches E 111 A6
  Hereford 78 D3
  Staffs 112 B4
Chedburgh 86 B3
Cheddar 42 D3
Cheddington 67 B4
Cheddleton 129 D4
Cheddon Fitzpaine 28 C2
Chedglow 63 D5
Chedgrave 105 B4
Chedington 15 A4
Chediston 105 D4
Chedworth 63 B6
Chedzoy 28 B3
Cheeklaw 198 A1
Cheeseman's Green 38 B2
Cheglinch 25 A6
Cheldon 26 D2
Chelford 128 B3
Chellaston 114 B1
Chell Heath 128 D3
Chellington 83 B6
Chelmarsh 95 C5
Chelmer Village 70 C1
Chelmondiston 88 D3
Chelmorton 129 C6
Chelmsford 69 C7
Chelsea 49 B5
Chelsfield 50 C1
Chelsworth 87 C5
Cheltenham 63 A5
Chelveston 84 A1
Chelvey 42 C3
Chelwood 43 C5
Chelwood Common 36 D2
Chelwood Gate 36 D2
Chelworth 63 D5
Chelworth Green 64 D1
Chemistry 111 A4
Chenies 67 D5
Cheny Longville 94 C2
Chepstow
  = Cas-gwent 62 D1
Chequerfield 140 A2
Cherhill 44 B4
Cherington
  Glos 63 D5
  Warks 81 D5
Cheriton
  Devon 26 A2
  Hants 33 C4
  Kent 38 B3
  Swansea 57 C4
Cheriton Bishop 12 B2
Cheriton Fitzpaine 12 A3
Cheriton or Stackpole
  Elidor 55 E5
Cherrington 111 C5
Cherrybank 219 B6
Cherry Burton 150 C2
Cherry Hinton 85 B6
Cherry Orchard 79 B6
Cherry Willingham 133 B5
Chertsey 48 C3
Cheselbourne 16 B1
Chesham 67 C4
Chesham Bois 67 D4
Cheshunt 68 C3
Cheslyn Hay 96 A2
Chessington 49 C4
Chester 127 C4
Chesterblade 29 A6
Chesterfield 130 B3
Chester-le-Street 179 D4
Chester Moor 167 A5
Chesters
  Borders 187 A5
  Borders 187 B5
Chesterton
  Cambs 85 A6
  Cambs 100 B3
  Glos 63 C6
  Oxon 65 A6
  Shrops 95 B5
  Staffs 112 A2
  Warks 81 B6
Chesterwood 177 C6
Chestfield 52 C3
Cheston 7 B5
Cheswardine 111 C6
Cheswick 198 B4
Chetnole 15 A6
Chettiscombe 27 D4
Chettisham 102 C1
Chettle 30 D3
Chetton 95 B4
Chetwode 66 A1
Chetwynd Aston 111 D6
Cheveley 86 A2
Chevening 36 A2
Chevington 86 B3
Chevithorne 27 D4
Chew Magna 43 C4
Chew Stoke 43 C4
Chewton Keynsham 43 C5
Chewton Mendip 43 D4
Chicheley 83 C6
Chichester 20 B1
Chickerell 15 C6
Chicklade 30 B3
Chicksgrove 30 B3
Chidden 33 D5
Chiddingfold 34 C2
Chiddingly 22 A3
Chiddingstone 36 B2
Chiddingstone
  Causeway 36 B3
Chiddingstone
  Hoath 36 B2
Chideock 14 B4
Chidham 19 A6
Chidswell 139 A5
Chieveley 46 B2
Chignall St James 69 C6
Chignall Smealy 69 B6
Chigwell 68 D4
Chigwell Row 69 D4
Chilbolton 32 B2
Chilcomb 32 C4
Chilcombe 15 B5
Chilcompton 43 D5
Chilcote 113 D6
Childer Thornton 126 B3
Child Okeford 30 D2
Childrey 46 A1
Child's Ercall 111 C5
Childswickham 80 D3
Childwall 127 A4
Childwick Green 67 B6
Chilfrome 15 B5
Chilgrove 20 A1
Chilham 52 D2
Chilhampton 31 B4
Chilla 11 A5
Chillaton 11 C5
Chillenden 53 D4
Chillerton 18 C3
Chillesford 89 B4
Chillingham 188 A3
Chillington
  Devon 8 C1
  Som 28 D3
Chilmark 30 B3
Chilson 64 B4
Chilsworthy
  Corn 11 D5
  Devon 10 A4
Chilthorne Domer 29 D5
Chiltington 22 A1
Chilton
  Bucks 66 B1
  Durham 167 C5
  Oxon 46 A2
Chilton Cantelo 29 C5
Chilton Foliat 45 B7
Chilton Lane 167 B6
Chilton Polden 28 B3
Chilton Street 86 C3
Chilton Trinity 28 B2
Chilvers Coton 97 B6
Chilwell 114 B3
Chilworth
  Hants 32 D3
  Sur 34 B3
Chimney 65 C4
Chineham 47 D4
Chingford 68 D3
Chinley 129 A5
Chinley Head 129 A5
Chinnor 66 C2
Chipnall 111 B6
Chippenhall Green 104 D3
Chippenham
  Cambs 86 A2
  Wilts 44 B3
Chipperfield 67 C5
Chipping
  Herts 85 D5
  Lancs 145 C6
Chipping Campden 81 D4
Chipping Hill 70 B2
Chipping Norton 64 A4
Chipping Ongar 69 C5
Chipping Sodbury 43 A6
Chipping Warden 82 C1
Chipstable 27 C5
Chipstead
  Kent 36 A2
  Sur 35 A5
Chirbury 93 B6
Chirk *= Y Waun* 110 B1
Chirk Bank 110 B1
Chirmorrie 181 D4
Chirnside 198 A2
Chirnsidebridge 198 A2
Chirton 45 D4
Chisbury 45 C6
Chiselborough 29 D4
Chiseldon 45 B5
Chiserley 138 A3
Chislehampton 65 D6
Chislehurst 50 B1
Chislet 53 C4
Chiswell Green 67 C6
Chiswick 49 B5
Chiswick End 85 C5
Chisworth 138 D2
Chithurst 34 D1
Chittering 101 D6
Chitterne 30 A3
Chittlehamholt 26 C1
Chittlehampton 26 C1
Chittoe 44 C3
Chivenor 25 B6
Chobham 48 C2
Choicelee 197 A6
Cholderton 31 A6
Cholesbury 67 C4
Chollerford 177 B7
Chollerton 178 B1
Cholmondeston 127 C6
Cholsey 46 A3
Cholstrey 78 B2
Chop Gate 159 B4
Choppington 179 A4
Chopwell 178 D3
Chorley
  Ches E 127 D5
  Lancs 137 B4
  Shrops 95 C4
  Staffs 113 D4
Chorleywood 67 D5
Chorlton cum
  Hardy 137 D7
Chorlton Lane 110 A3
Choulton 94 C1
Chowdene 179 D4
Chowley 127 D4
Chrishall 85 D6
Christchurch
  BCP 17 B5
  Cambs 101 B6
  Glos 62 B1
  Newport 42 A2
Christian Malford 44 B3
Christleton 127 C4
Christmas Common 66 D2
Christon 42 D2
Christon Bank 189 A5
Christow 12 C3
Chryston 207 C4
Chudleigh 12 D3
Chudleigh Knighton 12 D3
Chulmleigh 26 D1
Chunal 138 D3
Church 137 A6
Churcham 62 B3
Church Aston 111 D6
Churchbank 93 D7
Church Brampton 83 A4
Churchbridge 96 A2
Church Broughton 113 B6
Church Crookham 47 D6
Churchdown 63 B4
Church Eaton 112 D2
Churchend
  Essex 69 A6
  Essex 71 D4
  S Glos 62 D3
Church End
  Cambs 100 C4
  Cambs 101 A5
  C Beds 67 A4
  C Beds 84 D1
  C Beds 84 D3
  Essex 69 A7
  Essex 86 C1
  E Yorks 150 B3
  Hants 47 D4
  Lincs 117 B5
  Warks 97 B5
  Warks 97 B5
  Wilts 44 B4
Church Enstone 65 A4
Church Fenton 148 D4
Churchfield 96 B3
Churchgate Street 69 B4
Church Green
  Devon 14 B1
  Norf 103 B6
Church Gresley 113 D6
Church Hanborough 65 B5
Church Hill 127 C6
Church Houses 159 B5
Churchill
  Devon 14 A3
  Devon 25 A6
  N Som 42 D3
  Oxon 64 A3
  Worcs 80 B2
  Worcs 96 D1
Churchinford 28 D2
Church Knowle 16 C3
Church Laneham 132 B3
Church Langton 99 B4
Church Lawford 98 D1
Church Lawton 128 D3
Church Leigh 112 B4
Church Lench 80 B3
Church Mayfield 113 A5
Church Minshull 127 C6
Church Norton 20 C1
Churchover 98 C2
Church Preen 94 B3
Church
  Pulverbatch 94 A2
Churchstanton 28 D1
Church Stoke 93 B6
Churchstow 7 C6
Church Stowe 82 B3
Church Street 51 B4
Church Stretton 94 B2
Churchtown
  Derbys 130 C2
  IoM 152 B4
  Lancs 145 C4
  Mers 136 B2
Church Town
  N Lincs 141 C5
  Sur 35 A6
Church Village 41 C5
Church Warsop 131 C5
Churnsike Lodge 177 B4
Churston Ferrers 8 B3
Churt 34 C1
Churton 127 D4
Churwell 139 A5
Chute Standen 45 D7
Chwilog 107 C4
Chyandour 2 B2
Cilan Uchaf 106 D2
Cilcain 126 C1
Cilcennin 75 B4
Cilfor 107 C6
Cilfrew 40 A2
Cilfynydd 41 B5
Cilgerran 73 B4
Cilgwyn
  Carms 59 C4
  Gwyn 107 A4
  Pembs 72 C3
Ciliau Aeron 74 C3
Cill Donnain 286 D3
Cille Bhrighde 286 E3
Cille Pheadair 286 E3
Cilmery 76 B4
Cilsan 58 C2
Ciltalgarth 108 A3
Cilwendeg 73 C5
Cilybebyll 40 A2
Cilycwm 59 B4
Cimla 40 B2
Cinderford 62 B2
Cippyn 72 B4
Circebost 288 D2
Cirencester 63 C6
Ciribhig 288 C2
City
  London 49 A6
  Powys 93 C6
City Dulas 123 B4
Clachaig 215 D4
Clachan
  Argyll 202 C2
  Argyll 213 A5
  Argyll 215 A4
  Argyll 226 B3
  Highld 248 C2
  W Isles 286 B3
Clachaneasy 181 D5
Clachanmore 170 C2
Clachan na Luib 287 H3
Clachan of
  Campsie 205 A6
Clachan of
  Glendaruel 214 D2
Clachan-Seil 213 A5
Clachan Strachur 214 B3
Clachbreck 202 A2
Clachnabrain 232 B1
Clachtoll 270 B3
Clackmannan 208 A2
Clacton-on-Sea 71 B5
Cladach Chireboist 287 H2
Claddach-
  knockline 287 H2
Cladich 227 D5
Claggan
  Highld 225 B5
  Highld 237 B5
Claigan 258 C2
Claines 79 B6
Clandown 43 D5
Clanfield
  Hants 33 D5
  Oxon 64 C3
Clanville 32 A2
Claonaig 202 C3
Claonel 272 D3
Clapgate
  Dorset 17 A4
  Herts 68 A4
Clapham
  Bedford 84 B2
  London 49 B5
  N Yorks 146 A1
  W Sus 20 B3
Clap Hill 38 B2
Clappers 198 A3
Clappersgate 154 A2

Clapton 14 A4
Clapton-in-Gordano 42 B3
Clapton-on-the-Hill 64 B2
Clapworthy 26 C1
Clarach 90 D4
Clara Vale 178 C3
Clarbeston 55 B6
Clarbeston Road 55 B6
Clarborough 132 A2
Clardon 280 B3
Clare 86 C3
Clarebrand 173 B5
Clarencefield 174 B3
Clarilaw 186 B4
Clark's Green 35 C4
Clarkston 205 C5
Clashandorran 251 B7
Clashcoig 264 A2
Clashindarroch 255 C5
Clashmore
  Highld 264 B3
  Highld 270 A3
Clashnessie 270 A3
Clashnoir 254 D3
Clate 285 G7
Clathy 219 C4
Clatt 255 D6
Clatter 92 B3
Clatterford 18 C3
Clatterin Bridge . . . 233 A4
Clatworthy 27 B5
Claughton
  Lancs 145 A5
  Lancs 145 C5
  Mers 126 A3
Claverdon 81 A4
Claverham 42 C3
Clavering 85 D6
Claverley 95 B5
Claverton 44 C1
Clawdd-newydd . . . 125 D5
Clawthorpe 154 D4
Clawton 11 B4
Claxby
  Lincs 135 B4
  Lincs 142 D3
Claxton
  Norf 104 A4
  N Yorks 149 A5
Claybokie 242 D3
Claybrooke Magna . . 98 C1
Claybrooke Parva . . . 98 C1
Clay Common 105 C5
Clay Coton 98 D2
Clay Cross 130 C3
Claydon
  Oxon 82 B1
  Suff 88 B2
Claygate
  Dumfries 175 A6
  Kent 37 B5
  Sur 49 C4
Claygate Cross 36 A4
Clayhanger
  Devon 27 C5
  W Mid 96 A3
Clayhidon 27 D6
Clayhill
  E Sus 37 D6
  Hants 18 A2
Clay Hill 46 B3
Clay Lake 117 C5
Clayock 280 C3
Claypole 115 A6
Clayton
  Staffs 112 A2
  S Yorks 140 C2
  W Sus 21 A5
  W Yorks 147 D5
Clayton Green 137 A4
Clayton-le-Moors . . 146 D1
Clayton-le-Woods . . 137 A4
Clayton West 139 B5
Clayworth 132 A2
Cleadale 234 B3
Cleadon 179 C5
Clearbrook 7 A4
Clearwell 62 C1
Cleasby 167 D5
Cleat 283 J5
Cleatlam 166 D4
Cleator 162 C3
Cleator Moor 162 C3
Clebrig 272 A3
Cleckheaton 139 A4
Cleedownton 94 C3
Cleehill 94 D3
Clee St Margaret . . . 94 C3

Cleethorpes 143 C5
Cleeton St Mary 95 D4
Cleeve 42 C3
Cleeve Hill 63 A5
Cleeve Prior 80 C3
Clegyrnant 91 B7
Clehonger 78 D2
Cleish 208 A3
Cleland 194 A3
Clench Common 45 C5
Clenchwarton 118 C2
Clent 96 D2
Cleobury Mortimer . . 95 D4
Cleobury North 95 C4
Cleongart 190 B2
Clephanton 253 A4
Clerklands 186 A4
Clestrain 283 G5
Cleuch Head 187 B4
Cleughbrae 174 A3
Clevancy 45 B4
Clevedon 42 B3
Cleveley 65 A4
Cleveleys 144 C3
Cleverton 44 A3
Clevis 40 D3
Clewer 42 C3
Cley next the Sea . . 120 A2
Cliaid 286 F2
Cliasmol 287 D5
Cliburn 164 C3
Click Mill 282 E4
Cliddesden 33 A5
Cliffburn 233 D4
Cliffe
  Medway 51 B4
  N Yorks 149 D5
Cliff End 23 A6
Cliffe Woods 51 B4
Clifford
  Hereford 77 C6
  W Yorks 148 C3
Clifford Chambers . . 81 B4
Clifford's Mesne . . . 62 A3
Cliffsend 53 C5
Clifton
  Bristol 43 B4
  C Beds 84 D3
  Cumb 164 C3
  Derbys 113 A5
  Lancs 145 D4
  Northumb 179 A4
  Nottingham 114 B3
  N Yorks 147 C5
  Oxon 82 D1
  Stirling 216 A3
  S Yorks 140 D3
  Worcs 79 C6
  York 149 B4
Clifton Campville . . 113 D6
Cliftoncote 187 A7
Clifton Green 137 C6
Clifton Hampden . . . 65 D6
Clifton Reynes 83 B6
Clifton upon
  Dunsmore 98 D2
Clifton upon Teme . . 79 A5
Cliftonville 53 B5
Climaen gwyn 59 E4
Climping 20 B3
Climpy 194 A4
Clink 30 A1
Clint 147 B6
Clint Green 120 D2
Clintmains 197 C5
Cliobh 287 A5
Clippesby 121 D6
Clipsham 116 D2
Clipston 99 C4
Clipstone 131 C5
Clitheroe 146 C1
Cliuthar 288 H2
Clive 111 C4
Clivocast 284 C8
Clixby 142 C3
Clocaenog 125 D5
Clochan 267 C5
Clock Face 136 D4
Clockmill 197 A6
Cloddiau 93 A6
Clodock 61 A5
Clola 257 B5
Clophill 84 D2
Clopton
  Northants 100 C2
  Suff 88 B3
Clopton Corner 88 B3
Clopton Green 86 B3
Closeburn 183 C6
Close Clark 152 D2

Closworth 29 D5
Clothall 85 D4
Clotton 127 C5
Clough Foot 138 A2
Cloughton 160 B4
Cloughton
  Newlands 160 B4
Clousta 285 H5
Clouston 282 F3
Clova
  Aberds 255 D5
  Angus 232 A1
Clovelly 24 C4
Clove Lodge 166 D2
Clovenfords 196 C3
Clovenstone 245 A4
Clovullin 237 C4
Clow Bridge 137 A7
Clowne 131 B4
Clows Top 95 D5
Cloy 110 A2
Cluanie Inn 239 A4
Cluanie Lodge 239 A4
Clun 93 C7
Clunbury 94 C1
Clunderwen 55 C7
Clune 252 D3
Clunes 239 D6
Clungunford 94 D1
Clunie
  Aberds 268 D1
  Perth 231 D5
Clunton 94 C1
Cluny 209 A5
Cluny Castle 241 C4
Clutton
  Bath 43 D5
  Ches W 127 D4
Clwt-grugoer 125 C4
Clwt-y-bont 123 D5
Clydach
  Mon 60 B4
  Swansea 40 A1
Clydach Vale 41 B4
Clydebank 205 A4
Clydey 73 C5
Clyffe Pypard 45 B4
Clynder 215 D5
Clyne 40 A3
Clynelish 274 D2
Clynnog-fawr 107 A4
Clyro 77 C6
Clyst Honiton 13 B4
Clyst Hydon 13 A5
Clyst St George 13 C4
Clyst St Lawrence . . 13 A5
Clyst St Mary 13 B4
Cnoc Amhlaigh . . . 288 D6
Cnwch-coch 75 A5
Coachford 255 B5
Coad's Green 10 D3
Coal Aston 130 B3
Coalbrookdale 95 A4
Coalbrookvale 60 C3
Coalburn 194 C3
Coalburns 178 C3
Coalcleugh 165 A6
Coaley 62 C3
Coalhall 182 A2
Coalhill 70 D1
Coalpit Heath 43 B5
Coalport 95 A4
Coalsnaughton 208 A2
Coaltown of
  Balgonie 209 A5
Coaltown of
  Wemyss 209 A6
Coalville 114 D2
Coalway 62 B1
Coat 29 C4
Coatbridge 207 D5
Coatdyke 207 D5
Coate
  Swindon 45 A5
  Wilts 44 C4
Coates
  Cambs 101 B5
  Glos 63 C5
  Lancs 146 C2
  Notts 132 A3
  W Sus 20 A2
Coatham 168 C3
Coatham
  Mundeville 167 C5
Coatsgate 184 B3
Cobbaton 25 C7
Cobbler's Green . . . 104 B3
Coberley 63 B5
Cobham
  Kent 50 C3

Cobham continued
  Sur 48 C4
Cobholm Island . . . 105 A6
Cobleland 206 A3
Cobnash 78 A2
Coburty 269 C4
Cockayne 159 B5
Cockayne Hatley . . . 85 C4
Cock Bank 110 A2
Cock Bridge 243 B5
Cockburnspath 211 C4
Cock Clarks 70 C2
Cockenzie and Port
  Seton 209 C7
Cockerham 145 B4
Cockermouth 163 A4
Cockernhoe Green . . 67 A6
Cockfield
  Durham 166 C4
  Suff 87 B5
Cockfosters 68 D2
Cocking 20 A1
Cockington 8 A2
Cocklake 28 A4
Cockley Beck 163 D5
Cockley Cley 102 A3
Cockshutt 110 C3
Cockthorpe 120 A1
Cockwood 13 C4
Cockyard 78 D2
Codda 10 D2
Coddenham 88 B2
Coddington
  Ches W 127 D4
  Hereford 79 C5
  Notts 132 D3
Codford St Mary . . . 30 B3
Codford St Peter . . . 30 B3
Codicote 68 B2
Codmore Hill 34 D3
Codnor 114 A2
Codrington 43 B6
Codsall 95 A6
Codsall Wood 95 A6
Coed Duon
  =Blackwood 41 B6
Coedely 41 C5
Coedkernew 42 A1
Coed Mawr 123 C5
Coed Morgan 61 B5
Coedpoeth 126 D2
Coed-Talon 126 D2
Coedway 110 D2
Coed-y-bryn 73 B6
Coed-y-paen 61 D5
Coed-yr-ynys 60 A3
Coed Ystumgwern . . 107 D5
Coelbren 59 D5
Coffinswell 8 A2
Cofton Hackett 96 D3
Cogan 41 D6
Cogenhoe 83 A5
Cogges 65 C4
Coggeshall 70 A2
Coggeshall Hamlet . 70 A2
Coggins Mill 36 D3
Coignafearn Lodge . 241 A4
Coig Peighinnean . . 288 A6
Coig Peighinnean
  Bhuirgh 288 B5
Coilacriech 243 C6
Coilantogle 217 D5
Coilleag 286 E3
Coillore 246 A2
Coity 40 C4
Col 288 C5
Colaboll 272 C3
Colan 4 A3
Colaton Raleigh 13 C5
Colbost 258 D2
Colburn 157 B5
Colby
  Cumb 165 C4
  IoM 152 D2
  Norf 120 B4
Colchester 71 A4
Colcot 41 E6
Cold Ash 46 C3
Cold Ashby 98 D3
Cold Ashton 43 B6
Cold Aston 64 B2
Coldbackie 277 C7
Coldbeck 155 A6
Coldblow 50 B2
Cold Blow 55 C7
Cold Brayfield 83 B6
Coldean 21 B6
Coldeast 12 D3
Colden 138 A2
Colden Common . . . 32 C3

Coldfair Green 89 A5
Coldham 101 A6
Cold Hanworth 133 A5
Coldharbour
  Glos 62 C1
  Kent 36 A3
  Sur 35 B4
Cold Harbour 116 B2
Cold Hatton 111 C5
Cold Hesledon 168 A2
Cold Higham 82 B3
Coldingham 211 D6
Cold Kirby 158 C4
Cold Newton 99 A4
Cold Northcott 10 C3
Cold Norton 70 C2
Cold Overton 115 D6
Coldrain 219 D5
Coldred 39 A4
Coldridge 12 A1
Coldstream
  Angus 220 A3
  Borders 198 C2
Coldwaltham 20 A3
Coldwells 257 B6
Coldwells Croft . . . 255 D6
Coldyeld 94 B1
Cole 29 B6
Colebatch 93 C7
Colebrook 13 A5
Colebrooke 12 B2
Coleby
  Lincs 133 C4
  N Lincs 141 B6
Coleford
  Devon 12 A2
  Glos 62 B1
  Som 29 A6
Cole Green 68 B2
Cole Henley 46 D2
Colehill 17 A4
Coleman's Hatch . . . 36 C2
Colemere 110 B3
Colemore 33 B6
Coleorton 114 D2
Colerne 44 B2
Colesbourne 63 B5
Colesden 84 B3
Coles Green 88 C1
Cole's Green 88 A3
Coleshill
  Bucks 67 D4
  Oxon 64 D3
  Warks 97 C5
Colestocks 13 A5
Colgate 35 C5
Colgrain 206 B1
Colinsburgh 221 D4
Colinton 209 D5
Colintraive 203 A5
Colkirk 119 C6
Collace 220 A2
Collafirth 284 G6
Collaton St Mary . . . 8 B2
College Milton 205 C6
Collessie 220 C2
Collier Row 69 D5
Collier's End 68 A3
Collier's Green 37 C5
Collier Street 37 B5
Colliery Row 167 A6
Collieston 257 D5
Collin 174 A3
Collingbourne Ducis 45 D6
Collingbourne
  Kingston 45 D6
Collingham
  Notts 132 C3
  W Yorks 148 C2
Collington 79 A4
Collingtree 83 B4
Collins Green 137 D4
Colliston 233 D4
Collycroft 97 C6
Collynie 256 C3
Collyweston 100 A1
Colmonell 180 C3
Colmworth 84 B3
Colnabaichin 243 B5
Colnbrook 48 B3
Colne
  Cambs 101 D5
  Lancs 146 C2
Colne Edge 146 C2
Colne Engaine 87 D4
Colney 104 A2
Colney Heath 68 C2
Colney Street 67 C6
Coln Rogers 64 C1
Coln St Aldwyn's . . . 64 C2

Coln St Dennis 64 B1
Colpy 256 C1
Colquhar 196 B2
Colsterdale 157 C5
Colsterworth 116 C2
Colston Bassett . . . 115 B4
Coltfield 266 C2
Colthouse 154 B2
Coltishall 121 D4
Coltness 194 A3
Colton
  Cumb 154 C2
  Norf 104 A2
  N Yorks 148 C4
  Staffs 113 C4
  W Yorks 148 D2
Col Uarach 288 D5
Colva 77 B6
Colvend 173 C6
Colvister 284 D7
Colwall Green 79 C5
Colwall Stone 79 C5
Colwell 178 B1
Colwich 112 C4
Colwick 115 A4
Colwinston 40 D4
Colworth 20 B2
Colwyn Bay
  =Bae Colwyn . . . 124 B3
Colyford 14 B2
Colyton 14 B2
Combe
  Hereford 78 A1
  Oxon 65 B5
  W Berks 46 C1
Combe Common . . . 34 C2
Combe Down 43 C6
Combe Florey 27 B6
Combe Hay 43 D6
Combeinteignhead . 13 D4
Combe Martin 25 A6
Combe Moor 78 A1
Combe Raleigh 13 A6
Comberbach 127 B6
Comberton
  Cambs 85 B5
  Hereford 78 A2
Combe St Nicholas . 28 D3
Combpyne 14 B2
Combridge 113 B4
Combrook 81 B6
Combs
  Derbys 129 B5
  Suff 87 B6
Combs Ford 87 B6
Combwich 28 A2
Comers 244 B3
Comins Coch 90 D4
Commercial End . . . 86 A1
Commins Capel
  Betws 75 C5
Commins Coch 91 B5
Commondale 169 D4
Common Edge 144 D3
Commonmoor 6 A1
Commonside 127 B5
Common Side 130 B3
Compstall 138 D2
Compton
  Devon 8 A2
  Hants 32 C3
  Sur 34 B1
  Sur 34 B2
  W Berks 46 B3
  Wilts 45 D5
  W Sus 33 D6
Compton Abbas . . . 30 D2
Compton Abdale . . . 63 B6
Compton Bassett . . 44 B4
Compton
  Beauchamp 45 A6
Compton Bishop . . . 42 D2
Compton
  Chamberlayne . . 31 C4
Compton Dando . . . 43 C5
Compton Dundon . . 29 B4
Compton Martin . . . 43 D4
Compton
  Pauncefoot 29 C6
Compton Valence . . 15 B5
Comrie
  Fife 208 B3
  Perth 218 B2
Conaglen House . . . 237 C4
Conchra 214 D3
Concraigie 231 D5
Conder Green 145 B4
Conderton 80 D2
Condicote 64 A2
Condorrat 207 C5

Condover . . . 94 A2
Coneyhurst . . . 35 D4
Coneysthorpe . . . 159 D6
Coneythorpe . . . 148 B2
Coney Weston . . . 103 D5
Conford . . . 33 B7
Congash . . . 253 D6
Congdon's Shop . . . 10 D3
Congerstone . . . 97 A6
Congham . . . 119 C4
Congleton . . . 128 C3
Congl-y-wal . . . 108 A2
Congresbury . . . 42 C3
Congreve . . . 112 D3
Conicavel . . . 253 A5
Coningsby . . . 134 D2
Conington
  Cambs . . . 85 A5
  Cambs . . . 100 A5
Conisbrough . . . 140 D3
Conisby . . . 200 B2
Conisholme . . . 143 D6
Coniston
  Cumb . . . 154 B2
  E Yorks . . . 151 D4
Coniston Cold . . . 146 B3
Conistone . . . 146 A3
Connah's Quay . . . 126 C2
Connel . . . 226 C4
Connel Park . . . 182 A4
Connor Downs . . . 2 B3
Conon Bridge . . . 252 A1
Conon House . . . 252 A1
Cononley . . . 146 C3
Conordan . . . 247 A4
Consall . . . 112 A3
Consett . . . 178 D3
Constable Burton . . . 157 B5
Constantine . . . 3 C5
Constantine Bay . . . 9 D4
Contin . . . 251 A6
Contlaw . . . 245 B5
Conwy . . . 124 B2
Conyer . . . 51 C6
Conyers Green . . . 87 A4
Cooden . . . 23 B5
Cooil . . . 152 D3
Cookbury . . . 11 A5
Cookham . . . 48 A1
Cookham Dean . . . 47 A6
Cookham Rise . . . 48 A1
Cookhill . . . 80 B3
Cookley
  Suff . . . 104 D4
  Worcs . . . 95 C6
Cookley Green . . . 66 D1
Cookney . . . 245 C5
Cookridge . . . 147 C6
Cooksbridge . . . 22 A2
Cooksmill Green . . . 69 C6
Coolham . . . 35 D4
Cooling . . . 51 B4
Coombe
  Corn . . . 4 B4
  Corn . . . 24 D3
  Hants . . . 33 C5
  Wilts . . . 45 D5
Coombe Bissett . . . 31 C5
Coombe Hill . . . 63 A4
Coombe Keynes . . . 16 C2
Coombes . . . 21 B4
Coopersale
  Common . . . 69 C4
Cootham . . . 20 A3
Copdock . . . 88 C2
Copford Green . . . 70 A3
Copgrove . . . 148 A2
Copister . . . 284 F6
Cople . . . 84 C3
Copley . . . 166 C3
Coplow Dale . . . 129 B6
Copmanthorpe . . . 149 C4
Coppathorne . . . 10 A3
Coppenhall . . . 112 D3
Coppenhall Moss . . . 128 C2
Copperhouse . . . 2 B3
Coppingford . . . 100 C3
Copplestone . . . 12 A2
Coppull . . . 137 B4
Coppull Moor . . . 137 B4
Copsale . . . 35 D4
Copster Green . . . 145 D6
Copston Magna . . . 98 C1
Copt Heath . . . 97 D4
Copt Hewick . . . 158 D2
Copthorne
  Shrops . . . 110 D3
  Sur . . . 35 C6
Copt Oak . . . 114 D2
Copy's Green . . . 119 B6

Copythorne . . . 32 D2
Corbets Tey . . . 50 A2
Corbridge . . . 178 C1
Corby . . . 99 C5
Corby Glen . . . 116 C2
Cordon . . . 191 B6
Coreley . . . 95 D4
Cores End . . . 48 A2
Corfe . . . 28 C2
Corfe Castle . . . 16 C3
Corfe Mullen . . . 16 B3
Corfton . . . 94 C2
Corgarff . . . 243 B5
Corhampton . . . 33 C5
Corlae . . . 183 C4
Corley . . . 97 C6
Corley Ash . . . 97 C5
Corley Moor . . . 97 C5
Cornaa . . . 152 C4
Cornabus . . . 200 D3
Cornel . . . 124 C2
Corner Row . . . 144 D4
Corney . . . 153 A2
Cornforth . . . 167 B6
Cornhill . . . 267 D6
Cornhill-on-Tweed . . . 198 C2
Cornholme . . . 138 A2
Cornish Hall End . . . 86 D2
Cornquoy . . . 283 H6
Cornsay . . . 166 A4
Cornsay Colliery . . . 167 A4
Corntown
  Highld . . . 252 A1
  V Glam . . . 40 D4
Cornwell . . . 64 A3
Cornwood . . . 7 B5
Cornworthy . . . 8 B2
Corpach . . . 237 B4
Corpusty . . . 120 B3
Corran
  Highld . . . 237 C4
  Highld . . . 238 B2
Corranbuie . . . 202 B3
Corrany . . . 152 C4
Corrie . . . 203 D5
Corrie Common . . . 185 D5
Corriecravie . . . 191 C5
Corriemoillie . . . 263 D5
Corriemulzie
  Lodge . . . 263 A5
Corrievarkie Lodge . . . 229 A4
Corrievorrie . . . 252 C3
Corrimony . . . 251 C5
Corringham
  Lincs . . . 141 D6
  Thurrock . . . 51 A4
Corris . . . 91 B5
Corris Uchaf . . . 91 B5
Corrour Shooting
  Lodge . . . 228 B3
Corrow . . . 215 B4
Corry . . . 247 B5
Corrykinloch . . . 271 B6
Corrymuckloch . . . 218 A3
Corrynachenchy . . . 225 B5
Corry of
  Ardnagrask . . . 251 B7
Corsback . . . 280 A4
Corscombe . . . 15 A5
Corse
  Aberds . . . 255 B7
  Glos . . . 62 A3
Corse Lawn . . . 79 D6
Corse of Kinnoir . . . 255 B6
Corsewall . . . 170 A2
Corsham . . . 44 B2
Corsindae . . . 244 B3
Corsley . . . 30 A2
Corsley Heath . . . 30 A2
Corsock . . . 173 A5
Corston
  Bath . . . 43 C5
  Wilts . . . 44 A3
Corstorphine . . . 209 C4
Cors-y-Gedol . . . 107 D5
Cortachy . . . 232 C1
Corton
  Suff . . . 105 B6
  Wilts . . . 30 A3
Corton Denham . . . 29 C6
Coruanan Lodge . . . 237 C4
Corunna . . . 287 H3
Corwen . . . 109 A5
Coryton
  Devon . . . 11 C5
  Thurrock . . . 51 A4
Cosby . . . 98 B2
Coseley . . . 96 B2
Cosgrove . . . 83 C4
Cosham . . . 19 A5

Cosheston . . . 55 D6
Cossall . . . 114 A2
Cossington
  Leics . . . 115 D4
  Som . . . 28 A3
Costa . . . 282 E4
Costessey . . . 120 D3
Costock . . . 114 C3
Coston . . . 115 C6
Cote . . . 64 C4
Cotebrook . . . 127 C5
Cotehill . . . 176 D2
Cotes
  Cumb . . . 154 C3
  Leics . . . 114 C3
  Staffs . . . 112 B2
Cotesbach . . . 98 C2
Cotgrave . . . 115 B4
Cothall . . . 245 A5
Cotham . . . 115 A5
Cothelstone . . . 28 B1
Cotherstone . . . 166 D3
Cothill . . . 65 D5
Cotleigh . . . 14 A2
Cotmanhay . . . 114 A2
Cotmaton . . . 13 C6
Coton
  Cambs . . . 85 B6
  Northants . . . 98 D3
  Staffs . . . 112 B3
  Staffs . . . 112 C2
Coton Clanford . . . 112 C2
Coton Hill
  Shrops . . . 110 D3
  Staffs . . . 112 B3
Coton in the Elms . . . 113 D6
Cott . . . 8 A1
Cottam
  E Yorks . . . 150 A2
  Lancs . . . 145 D5
  Notts . . . 132 B3
Cottartown . . . 253 C6
Cottenham . . . 85 A6
Cotterdale . . . 156 B2
Cotterstock . . . 100 B2
Cottesbrooke . . . 99 D4
Cottesmore . . . 116 D2
Cotteylands . . . 27 D4
Cottingham
  E Yorks . . . 150 D3
  Northants . . . 99 B5
Cottingley . . . 147 D5
Cottisford . . . 82 D2
Cotton
  Staffs . . . 113 A4
  Suff . . . 87 A6
Cotton End . . . 84 C2
Cottown
  Aberds . . . 245 A4
  Aberds . . . 255 D6
  Aberds . . . 256 B3
Cotwalton . . . 112 B3
Couch's Mill . . . 5 B6
Coughton
  Hereford . . . 62 A1
  Warks . . . 80 A3
Coulaghailtro . . . 202 B2
Coulags . . . 249 B6
Coulby Newham . . . 168 D3
Coulderton . . . 162 D2
Coulin . . . 250 A2
Coull
  Aberds . . . 244 B2
  Argyll . . . 200 B2
Coulport . . . 215 D5
Coulsdon . . . 35 A5
Coulston . . . 44 D3
Coulter . . . 195 C5
Coulton . . . 159 D5
Cound . . . 94 A3
Coundon
  Durham . . . 167 C5
  W Mid . . . 97 C6
Coundon Grange . . . 167 C5
Countersett . . . 156 C3
Countess . . . 31 A5
Countess Wear . . . 13 C4
Countesthorpe . . . 98 B2
Countisbury . . . 26 A2
County Oak . . . 35 C5
Coupar Angus . . . 231 D6
Coup Green . . . 137 A4
Coupland . . . 198 C3
Cour . . . 202 D3
Courance . . . 184 C3
Court-at-Street . . . 38 B2
Courteenhall . . . 83 B4
Court Henry . . . 58 C2

Courtsend . . . 71 D4
Courtway . . . 28 B2
Cousland . . . 209 D6
Cousley Wood . . . 37 C4
Cove
  Argyll . . . 215 D5
  Borders . . . 211 C4
  Devon . . . 27 D4
  Hants . . . 34 A1
  Highld . . . 261 A5
Cove Bay . . . 245 B6
Cove Bottom . . . 105 D5
Covehithe . . . 105 C6
Coven . . . 96 A2
Coveney . . . 101 C6
Covenham
  St Bartholomew . . . 143 D5
Covenham
  St Mary . . . 143 D5
Coventry . . . 97 D6
Coverack . . . 3 D5
Coverham . . . 157 C5
Covesea . . . 266 B2
Covington
  Cambs . . . 100 D2
  S Lanark . . . 195 C4
Cowan Bridge . . . 155 D5
Cow Ark . . . 145 C6
Cowbeech . . . 22 A4
Cowbit . . . 117 D5
Cowbridge
  Lincs . . . 117 A6
  Som . . . 27 A4
Cowbridge
  = Y Bont-Faen . . . 41 D4
Cowdale . . . 129 B5
Cowden . . . 36 B2
Cowdenbeath . . . 209 A4
Cowdenburn . . . 195 A7
Cowers Lane . . . 113 A7
Cowes . . . 18 B3
Cowesby . . . 158 C3
Cowfold . . . 35 D5
Cowgill . . . 155 C6
Cowie
  Aberds . . . 245 D5
  Stirling . . . 207 B6
Cowley
  Devon . . . 13 B4
  Glos . . . 63 B5
  London . . . 48 A3
  Oxon . . . 65 C6
Cowleymoor . . . 27 D4
Cowling
  Lancs . . . 137 B4
  N Yorks . . . 146 C3
  N Yorks . . . 157 C6
Cowlinge . . . 86 B3
Cowpe . . . 138 A1
Cowpen . . . 179 A4
Cowpen Bewley . . . 168 C2
Cowplain . . . 33 D5
Cowshill . . . 165 A6
Cowslip Green . . . 42 C3
Cowstrandburn . . . 208 A3
Cowthorpe . . . 148 B3
Coxbank . . . 111 A5
Coxbench . . . 114 A1
Cox Common . . . 105 C4
Coxford
  Norf . . . 119 C5
  Soton . . . 32 D2
Cox Green . . . 48 B1
Coxheath . . . 37 A5
Coxhill . . . 39 A4
Coxhoe . . . 167 B6
Coxley . . . 29 A5
Cox Moor . . . 131 D5
Coxwold . . . 158 D4
Coychurch . . . 40 D4
Coylton . . . 193 C4
Coylumbridge . . . 242 A2
Coynach . . . 244 B1
Coynachie . . . 255 C5
Coytrahen . . . 40 C3
Crabadon . . . 7 B6
Crabbs Cross . . . 80 A3
Crabtree . . . 35 D5
Crackenthorpe . . . 165 C4
Crackington Haven . . . 10 B2
Crackley . . . 97 D5
Crackleybank . . . 111 D6
Crackpot . . . 156 B3
Cracoe . . . 146 A3
Craddock . . . 27 D5
Cradhlastadh . . . 287 A5
Cradley . . . 79 C5
Cradley Heath . . . 96 C2
Crafthole . . . 6 B2
Craggan . . . 253 D6

Craggie
  Highld . . . 252 C3
  Highld . . . 274 C2
Cragg Vale . . . 138 A3
Craghead . . . 179 D5
Crai . . . 59 C5
Craibstone . . . 267 D5
Craichie . . . 232 D3
Craig
  Dumfries . . . 173 A4
  Dumfries . . . 173 B4
  Highld . . . 250 B2
Craiganor Lodge . . . 229 C5
Craig Castle . . . 255 D5
Craig-cefn-parc . . . 40 A1
Craigdam . . . 256 C3
Craigdarroch
  Dumfries . . . 183 C5
  Highld . . . 251 A6
Craigdhu . . . 251 B6
Craigearn . . . 245 A4
Craigellachie . . . 254 B3
Craigencross . . . 170 A2
Craigend
  Perth . . . 219 B6
  Stirling . . . 207 B5
Craigendive . . . 214 C3
Craigendoran . . . 215 D6
Craigends . . . 205 B4
Craigens
  Argyll . . . 200 B2
  E Ayrs . . . 182 A3
Craighat . . . 206 B2
Craighead . . . 221 D6
Craighlaw Mains . . . 171 A5
Craighouse . . . 201 B5
Craigie
  Aberds . . . 245 A6
  Dundee . . . 220 A4
  Perth . . . 219 B6
  Perth . . . 231 D5
  S Ayrs . . . 193 B4
Craigiefield . . . 282 F5
Craigielaw . . . 210 C1
Craiglockhart . . . 209 C5
Craigmalloch . . . 182 C2
Craigmaud . . . 268 D3
Craigmillar . . . 209 C5
Craigmore . . . 203 B6
Craignant . . . 110 B1
Craigneuk
  N Lanark . . . 194 A2
  N Lanark . . . 207 D5
Craignure . . . 225 C6
Craigo . . . 233 B4
Craigow . . . 219 D5
Craig Penllyn . . . 41 D4
Craigrothie . . . 220 C3
Craigroy . . . 266 D2
Craigruie . . . 217 B4
Craigston Castle . . . 268 D2
Craigton
  Aberdeen . . . 245 B5
  Angus . . . 221 A5
  Angus . . . 232 C1
  Highld . . . 264 A2
Craigtown . . . 279 C4
Craig-y-don . . . 124 A2
Craig-y-nos . . . 59 D5
Craik . . . 185 B6
Crail . . . 221 D6
Crailing . . . 187 A5
Crailinghall . . . 187 A5
Craiselound . . . 141 D5
Crakehill . . . 158 D3
Crakemarsh . . . 113 B4
Crambe . . . 149 A6
Cramlington . . . 179 B4
Cramond . . . 209 C4
Cramond Bridge . . . 209 C4
Cranage . . . 128 C2
Cranberry . . . 112 B2
Cranborne . . . 31 D4
Cranbourne . . . 48 B2
Cranbrook
  Devon . . . 13 B5
  Kent . . . 37 C5
Cranbrook Common . . . 37 C5
Crane Moor . . . 139 C6
Crane's Corner . . . 119 D6
Cranfield . . . 83 C6
Cranford . . . 48 B4
Cranford St Andrew . . . 99 D6
Cranford St John . . . 99 D6
Cranham
  Glos . . . 63 B4
  London . . . 50 A2
Crank . . . 136 D4
Crank Wood . . . 137 C5
Cranleigh . . . 34 C3

Cranley . . . 104 D2
Cranmer Green . . . 103 D6
Cranmore . . . 18 C2
Cranna . . . 268 D1
Crannich . . . 225 B4
Crannoch . . . 267 D5
Cranoe . . . 99 B4
Cransford . . . 88 A4
Cranshaws . . . 210 D3
Cranstal . . . 152 A4
Crantock . . . 4 C2
Cranwell . . . 116 A3
Cranwich . . . 102 B3
Cranworth . . . 103 A5
Craobh Haven . . . 213 B5
Crapstone . . . 7 A4
Crarae . . . 214 C2
Crask Inn . . . 272 B3
Craskins . . . 244 B2
Crask of Aigas . . . 251 B6
Craster . . . 189 B5
Craswall . . . 77 D6
Cratfield . . . 104 D4
Crathes . . . 245 C4
Crathie
  Aberds . . . 243 C5
  Highld . . . 240 C3
Crathorne . . . 158 A3
Craven Arms . . . 94 C2
Crawcrook . . . 178 C3
Crawford
  Lancs . . . 136 C3
  S Lanark . . . 195 D4
Crawfordjohn . . . 194 D3
Crawick . . . 183 A5
Crawley
  Hants . . . 32 B3
  Oxon . . . 64 B4
  W Sus . . . 35 C5
Crawley Down . . . 35 C6
Crawleyside . . . 166 A2
Crawshawbooth . . . 137 A7
Crawton . . . 233 A6
Cray
  N Yorks . . . 156 D3
  Perth . . . 231 B5
Crayford . . . 50 B2
Crayke . . . 159 D4
Crays Hill . . . 69 D7
Cray's Pond . . . 47 A4
Creacombe . . . 26 D3
Creagan . . . 227 B4
Creag Ghoraidh . . . 286 B3
Creaguaineach
  Lodge . . . 228 B2
Creaksea . . . 70 D3
Creaton . . . 99 D4
Creca . . . 175 A5
Credenhill . . . 78 C2
Crediton . . . 12 A3
Creebridge . . . 171 A6
Creech Heathfield . . . 28 C2
Creech St Michael . . . 28 C2
Creed . . . 4 C4
Creekmouth . . . 50 A1
Creeting Bottoms . . . 88 B2
Creeting St Mary . . . 88 B1
Creeton . . . 116 C3
Creetown . . . 171 B6
Creggans . . . 214 B3
Cregneash . . . 152 E1
Creg-ny-Baa . . . 152 C3
Cregrina . . . 77 B5
Creich . . . 220 B3
Creigiau . . . 41 C5
Cremyll . . . 6 B3
Creslow . . . 66 A3
Cressage . . . 94 A3
Cressbrook . . . 129 B6
Cresselly . . . 55 D6
Cressing . . . 70 A1
Cresswell
  Northumb . . . 189 D5
  Staffs . . . 112 B3
Cresswell Quay . . . 55 D6
Creswell . . . 131 B5
Cretingham . . . 88 A3
Cretshengan . . . 202 B2
Crewe
  Ches E . . . 128 D2
  Ches W . . . 127 D4
Crewgreen . . . 110 D2
Crewkerne . . . 14 A4
Crianlarich . . . 216 B3
Cribyn . . . 75 C4
Criccieth . . . 107 C4
Crich . . . 130 D3
Crichie . . . 257 B4

Crichton ... 209 D6
Crick
  Mon. ... 61 D6
  Northants ... 98 D2
Crickadarn ... 77 C4
Cricket Malherbie ... 28 D3
Cricket St Thomas ... 14 A3
Crickheath ... 110 C1
Crickhowell ... 60 B4
Cricklade ... 64 D2
Cricklewood ... 49 A5
Cridling Stubbs ... 140 A3
Crieff ... 218 B3
Criggion ... 110 D1
Crigglestone ... 139 B6
Crimond ... 269 D5
Crimonmogate ... 269 D5
Crimplesham ... 102 A2
Crinan ... 213 C5
Cringleford ... 104 A2
Cringles ... 147 C4
Crinow ... 56 A1
Cripplesease ... 2 B3
Cripplestyle ... 31 D4
Cripp's Corner ... 37 D5
Croasdale ... 162 C3
Crockenhill ... 50 C2
Crockernwell ... 12 B2
Crockerton ... 30 A2
Crocketford or Ninemile
  Bar ... 173 A6
Crockey Hill ... 149 C5
Crockham Hill ... 36 A2
Crockleford Heath ... 71 A4
Crockness ... 283 H4
Crock Street ... 28 D3
Croeserw ... 40 B3
Croes-goch ... 54 A4
Croes-lan ... 73 B6
Croesor ... 107 B6
Croesyceiliog
  Carms ... 57 A4
  Torf ... 61 D5
Croes-y-mwyalch ... 61 D5
Croesywaun ... 107 A5
Croft
  Leics ... 98 B2
  Lincs ... 135 C5
  Pembs ... 73 B4
  Warr ... 137 D5
Croftamie ... 206 B2
Croftmalloch ... 208 D2
Crofton
  Wilts ... 45 C6
  W Yorks ... 140 B1
Croft-on-Tees ... 157 A6
Crofts of
  Benachielt ... 275 A5
Crofts of Haddo ... 256 C3
Crofts of
  Inverthernie ... 256 B2
Crofts of Meikle
  Ardo ... 256 B3
Crofty ... 57 C5
Croggan ... 225 D6
Croglin ... 164 A3
Croich ... 263 A6
Crois Dughaill ... 286 D3
Cromarty ... 264 D3
Cromblet ... 256 C2
Cromdale ... 253 D6
Cromer
  Herts ... 68 A2
  Norf ... 120 A4
Cromford ... 130 D2
Cromhall ... 62 D2
Cromhall Common ... 43 A5
Cromor ... 288 E5
Cromra ... 240 C3
Cromwell ... 132 C2
Cronberry ... 193 C6
Crondall ... 33 A6
Cronk-y-Voddy ... 152 C3
Cronton ... 127 A4
Crook
  Cumb ... 154 B3
  Durham ... 167 B4
Crookedholm ... 193 B4
Crookes ... 130 A3
Crookham
  Northumb ... 198 C3
  W Berks ... 46 C3
Crookham Village ... 47 D5
Crookhaugh ... 195 D6
Crookhouse ... 187 A6
Crooklands ... 154 C4
Crook of Devon ... 219 D5
Cropredy ... 82 C1

Cropston ... 114 D3
Cropthorne ... 80 C2
Cropton ... 159 C6
Cropwell Bishop ... 115 B4
Cropwell Butler ... 115 B4
Cros ... 288 A6
Crosbost ... 288 E4
Crosby
  Cumb ... 162 A3
  IoM ... 152 D3
  N Lincs ... 141 B6
Crosby Garrett ... 155 A6
Crosby
  Ravensworth ... 165 D4
Crosby Villa ... 162 A3
Croscombe ... 29 A5
Cross ... 42 D3
Crossaig ... 202 C3
Crossal ... 246 A3
Crossapol ... 222 B1
Cross Ash ... 61 B6
Cross-at-Hand ... 37 B5
Crossburn ... 207 C6
Crossbush ... 20 B3
Crosscanonby ... 162 A3
Crossdale Street ... 120 B4
Crossens ... 136 B2
Crossflatts ... 147 C5
Crossford
  Fife ... 208 B3
  S Lanark ... 194 B3
Crossgate ... 117 C5
Crossgatehall ... 209 D6
Crossgates
  Fife ... 208 B4
  Powys ... 77 A4
Crossgill ... 145 A5
Cross Green
  Devon ... 11 C4
  Suff ... 87 B4
  Suff ... 87 B5
  Warks ... 81 B6
Cross Hands ... 57 A5
Cross-hands ... 73 D4
Cross Hands ... 55 C6
Crosshill
  E Ayrs ... 193 C4
  Fife ... 209 A4
  S Ayrs ... 192 E3
Cross Hill ... 114 A2
Crosshouse ... 192 B3
Cross Houses ... 94 A3
Crossings ... 176 B3
Cross in Hand
  E Sus. ... 36 D3
  Leics ... 98 C2
Cross Inn
  Ceredig. ... 73 A6
  Ceredig. ... 75 B4
  Rhondda ... 41 C5
Crosskeys ... 41 B7
Cross Keys ... 36 A3
Crosskirk ... 279 A6
Cross Lane Head ... 95 B5
Crosslanes ... 110 D2
Cross Lanes
  Corn ... 3 C4
  N Yorks ... 148 A4
  Wrex ... 110 A2
Crosslee
  Borders ... 185 A6
  Renfs ... 205 B4
Crossmichael ... 173 B5
Crossmoor ... 144 D4
Cross Oak ... 60 A3
Cross of Jackston ... 256 C2
Cross o' th' hands ... 113 A6
Crossroads
  Aberds ... 245 C4
  E Ayrs ... 193 B4
Cross Street ... 104 C2
Cross Trickett's ... 17 A4
Crossway
  Hereford ... 79 D4
  Mon. ... 61 B6
  Powys ... 77 B4
Crossway Green ... 79 A6
Crossways ... 16 C1
Crosswell ... 72 C4
Crosswood ... 75 A5
Crosthwaite ... 154 B3
Croston ... 136 B3
Crostwick ... 121 D4
Crostwight ... 121 C5
Crothair ... 288 D2
Crouch ... 36 A4
Croucheston ... 31 C4
Crouch Hill ... 29 D7
Crouch House Green 36 B2
Croughton ... 82 D2

Crovie ... 268 C3
Crowan ... 3 B4
Crowborough ... 36 C3
Crowcombe ... 27 B6
Crowdecote ... 129 C6
Crowden ... 138 D3
Crow Edge ... 139 C4
Crowell ... 66 D2
Crowfield
  Northants ... 82 C3
  Suff. ... 88 B2
Crow Hill ... 62 A2
Crowhurst
  E Sus. ... 23 A5
  Sur ... 36 B1
Crowhurst Lane End. 36 B1
Crowland ... 117 D5
Crowlas ... 2 B3
Crowle
  N Lincs ... 141 B5
  Worcs ... 80 B2
Crowmarsh Gifford.. 47 A4
Crown Corner ... 104 D3
Crownhill ... 6 B3
Crownland ... 103 E6
Crownthorpe ... 104 A1
Crowntown ... 3 B4
Crows-an-wra ... 2 C1
Crowshill ... 103 A5
Crowsnest ... 94 A1
Crowthorne ... 47 C6
Crowton ... 127 B5
Croxall ... 113 D5
Croxby ... 142 D3
Croxdale ... 167 B5
Croxden ... 113 B4
Croxley Green ... 67 D5
Croxton
  Cambs. ... 84 A4
  N Lincs ... 142 B2
  Norf ... 103 C4
  Staffs ... 112 B1
Croxtonbank ... 112 B1
Croxton Kerrial ... 115 C6
Croy
  Highld ... 252 B3
  N Lanark ... 207 C5
Croyde ... 25 B5
Croydon
  Cambs. ... 85 C5
  London ... 49 C6
Crubenmore Lodge 241 C4
Cruckmeole ... 94 A2
Cruckton ... 110 D3
Cruden Bay ... 257 C5
Crudgington ... 111 D5
Crudwell ... 63 D5
Crug ... 93 D5
Crugmeer ... 9 D5
Crugybar ... 58 B3
Crulabhig ... 288 D2
Crumlin = Crymlyn... 41 B7
Crumpsall ... 138 C1
Crundale
  Kent ... 38 A2
  Pembs. ... 55 C5
Cruwys Morchard ... 26 D3
Crux Easton ... 46 D2
Crwbin ... 57 A4
Crya ... 283 G4
Cryers Hill ... 66 D1
Crymlyn ... 123 C6
Crymlyn = Crumlin. 41 B7
Crymych ... 73 C4
Crynant ... 40 A2
Crynfryn ... 75 B4
Cuaig ... 249 A4
Cuan ... 213 A5
Cubbington ... 81 A6
Cubeck ... 156 C3
Cubert ... 4 B2
Cubley ... 139 C5
Cubley Common ... 113 B5
Cublington
  Bucks ... 66 A3
  Hereford ... 78 D2
Cuckfield ... 35 D6
Cucklington ... 30 C1
Cuckney ... 131 B5
Cuckoo Hill ... 141 D5
Cuddesdon ... 65 C7
Cuddington
  Bucks ... 66 B2
  Ches W ... 127 B6
Cuddington Heath . 110 A3
Cuddy Hill ... 145 D4
Cudham ... 36 A2
Cudliptown ... 11 D6
Cudworth
  Som. ... 28 D3

Cudworth *continued*
  S Yorks ... 140 C1
Cuffley ... 68 C3
Cuiashader ... 288 B6
Cuidhir ... 286 F2
Cuidhtinis ... 287 F5
Culbo ... 264 D2
Culbokie ... 252 A2
Culburnie ... 251 B6
Culcabock ... 252 B2
Culcairn ... 264 D2
Culcharry ... 253 A4
Culcheth ... 137 D5
Culdrain ... 255 C6
Culduie ... 249 B4
Culford ... 103 D4
Culgaith ... 165 C4
Culham ... 65 D6
Culkein ... 270 A3
Culkein Drumbeg ... 270 A4
Culkerton ... 63 D5
Cullachie ... 253 D5
Cullen ... 267 C6
Cullercoats ... 179 B5
Cullicudden ... 264 D2
Cullingworth ... 147 D4
Cullipool ... 213 A5
Cullivoe ... 284 C7
Culloch ... 218 C2
Culloden ... 252 B3
Cullompton ... 13 A5
Culmaily ... 265 A4
Culmazie ... 171 B5
Culmington ... 94 C2
Culmstock ... 27 D6
Culnacraig ... 270 D3
Culnaknock ... 259 B5
Culpho ... 88 C3
Culrain ... 264 A1
Culross ... 208 B2
Culroy ... 192 D3
Culsh
  Aberds ... 243 C6
  Aberds ... 256 B3
Culshabbin ... 171 B5
Culswick ... 285 J4
Cultercullen ... 257 D4
Cults
  Aberdeen ... 245 B5
  Aberds ... 255 C6
  Dumfries ... 171 C6
Culverstone Green ... 50 C3
Culverthorpe ... 116 A3
Culworth ... 82 C2
Culzie Lodge ... 263 C7
Cumberhead ... 194 C3
Cumbernauld ... 207 C5
Cumbernauld
  Village ... 207 C5
Cumberworth ... 135 B5
Cuminestown ... 268 D3
Cumlewick ... 285 L6
Cummersdale ... 175 C6
Cummertrees ... 174 B4
Cummingston ... 266 C2
Cumnock ... 193 C5
Cumnor ... 65 C5
Cumrew ... 176 D3
Cumwhinton ... 176 D2
Cumwhitton ... 176 D3
Cundall ... 158 D3
Cunninghamhead . 204 D3
Cunnister ... 284 D7
Cupar ... 220 C3
Cupar Muir ... 220 C3
Cupernham ... 32 C2
Curbar ... 130 B2
Curbridge
  Hants ... 32 D4
  Oxon ... 64 C4
Curdridge ... 32 D4
Curdworth ... 97 B4
Curland ... 28 D2
Curlew Green ... 89 A4
Currarie ... 180 B3
Curridge ... 46 B2
Currie ... 209 D4
Curry Mallet ... 28 C3
Curry Rivel ... 28 C3
Curtisden Green ... 37 B5
Curtisknowle ... 7 B6
Cury ... 3 C4
Cushnie ... 268 C2
Cushuish ... 28 B1
Cusop ... 77 C6
Cutcloy ... 171 D6
Cutcombe ... 27 B4
Cutgate ... 138 B1
Cutiau ... 90 A4
Cutlers Green ... 86 D1
Cutnall Green ... 80 A1

Cutsdean ... 80 D3
Cutthorpe ... 130 B3
Cutts ... 285 K6
Cuxham ... 66 D1
Cuxton ... 51 C4
Cuxwold ... 142 C3
Cwm
  Bl Gwent ... 60 C1
  Denb ... 125 B5
  Swansea ... 40 B1
Cwmafan ... 40 B2
Cwmaman ... 41 B5
Cwmann ... 75 D5
Cwmavon ... 61 C4
Cwmbach
  Carms ... 57 B4
  Carms ... 73 D5
  Powys ... 76 B4
  Powys ... 77 D5
Cwmbâch ... 41 A5
Cwmbelan ... 92 C3
Cwmbran
  =Cwmbrân ... 61 D4
Cwmbrân
  =Cwmbran ... 61 D4
Cwmbrwyno ... 91 D5
Cwm-byr ... 58 B3
Cwmcarn ... 41 B7
Cwmcarvan ... 61 C6
Cwm-Cewydd ... 91 A6
Cwm-cou ... 73 B5
Cwmcych ... 73 C5
Cwmdare ... 41 A4
Cwmderwen ... 92 A3
Cwmdu
  Carms ... 58 B3
  Powys ... 60 A3
  Swansea ... 57 C6
Cwmduad ... 73 C6
Cwm-Dulais ... 57 B6
Cwmdwr ... 59 B4
Cwmfelin
  Bridgend ... 40 C3
  M Tydf ... 41 A5
Cwmfelin Boeth ... 56 A1
Cwm-felin-fach ... 41 B6
Cwmfelin Mynach ... 73 D5
Cwmffrwd ... 57 A4
Cwm Ffrwd-oer ... 61 C4
Cwmgiedd ... 59 D4
Cwmgors ... 59 D4
Cwmgwili ... 57 A5
Cwmgwrach ... 40 A3
Cwm-hesgen ... 108 C2
Cwmhiraeth ... 73 C6
Cwm-hwnt ... 59 E6
Cwmifor ... 58 C3
Cwm Irfon ... 76 C2
Cwmisfael ... 57 A4
Cwm-Llinau ... 91 B6
Cwmllynfell ... 59 D4
Cwm-mawr ... 57 A5
Cwmorgan ... 73 C5
Cwm-parc ... 40 B4
Cwmpengraig ... 73 C6
Cwm Penmachno . 108 A2
Cwmrhos ... 60 A3
Cwmsychpant ... 74 D3
Cwmtillery ... 60 C4
Cwm-twrch Isaf ... 59 D4
Cwm-twrch Uchaf ... 59 D4
Cwmwysg ... 59 C5
Cwm-y-glo
  Carms ... 57 A5
  Gwyn. ... 123 D5
Cwmyoy ... 61 A4
Cwmystwyth ... 92 D1
Cwrt ... 91 B4
Cwrt-newydd ... 74 D3
Cwrt-y-cadno ... 58 A3
Cwrt-y-gollen ... 60 B4
Cydweli = Kidwelly. 57 B4
Cyffordd Llandudno
  =Llandudno
  Junction ... 124 B2
Cyffylliog ... 125 D5
Cyfronydd ... 93 A5
Cymer ... 40 B3
Cyncoed ... 41 C6
Cynghordy ... 59 A5
Cynheidre ... 57 B4
Cynwyd ... 109 A5
Cynwyl Elfed ... 73 D6
Cywarch ... 91 A6

D

Dacre
  Cumb ... 164 C2
  N Yorks ... 147 A5
Dacre Banks ... 147 A5
Daddry Shield ... 166 B3
Dadford ... 82 D3
Dadlington ... 97 B7
Dafarn Faig ... 107 B4
Dafen ... 57 B5
Daffy Green ... 103 A5
Dagenham ... 50 A1
Daglingworth ... 63 C5
Dagnall ... 67 B4
Dail Beag ... 288 C3
Dail bho Dheas ... 288 A5
Dail bho Thuath ... 288 A5
Daill ... 200 B3
Dailly ... 181 A4
Dail Mor. ... 288 C3
Dairsie or
  Osnaburgh ... 220 C4
Daisy Hill ... 137 C5
Dalabrog ... 286 D3
Dalavich ... 214 A2
Dalbeattie ... 173 B6
Dalblair ... 182 A4
Dalbog ... 232 A3
Dalbury ... 113 B6
Dalby
  IoM ... 152 D2
  N Yorks ... 159 D5
Dalchalloch ... 229 B6
Dalchalm ... 274 D3
Dalchenna ... 214 B3
Dalchirach ... 254 C2
Dalchork ... 272 C3
Dalchreichart ... 239 A6
Dalchruin ... 218 C2
Dalderby ... 134 C2
Dale ... 54 D4
Dale Abbey ... 114 B2
Dale Head ... 164 D2
Dalelia ... 235 D6
Dale of Walls ... 285 H3
Daless ... 253 C4
Dalfaber ... 242 A2
Dalgarven ... 204 D2
Dalgety Bay ... 209 B4
Dalginross ... 218 B2
Dalguise ... 230 D3
Dalhalvaig ... 279 C4
Dalham ... 86 A3
Dalinlongart ... 215 D4
Dalkeith ... 209 D6
Dallam ... 137 D4
Dallas ... 266 D2
Dalleagles ... 182 A3
Dallinghoo ... 88 B3
Dallington
  E Sus. ... 23 A4
  Northants ... 83 A4
Dallow ... 157 D5
Dalmadilly ... 245 A4
Dalmally ... 227 D6
Dalmarnock ... 205 B6
Dalmary ... 206 A3
Dalmellington ... 182 B2
Dalmeny ... 208 C4
Dalmigavie ... 241 A5
Dalmigavie Lodge. 252 D3
Dalmore ... 264 D2
Dalmuir ... 205 A4
Dalnabreck ... 235 D5
Dalnacardoch
  Lodge ... 229 B6
Dalnacroich ... 251 A5
Dalnaglar Castle . 231 B5
Dalnahaitnach ... 253 D4
Dalnaspidal Lodge 229 A5
Dalnavaid ... 230 B4
Dalnavie ... 264 C2
Dalnawillan Lodge 279 D6
Dalness ... 237 D5
Dalnessie ... 273 C4
Dalqueich ... 219 D5
Dalreavoch ... 273 D5
Dalry ... 204 D2
Dalrymple ... 192 D3
Dalserf ... 194 A3
Dalston ... 175 C6
Dalswinton ... 184 D2
Dalton
  Dumfries ... 174 A4
  Lancs ... 136 C3
  Northumb ... 177 D7
  Northumb ... 178 B3
  N Yorks ... 157 A5

Dalton continued
N Yorks 158 D3
S Yorks 140 D2
Dalton-in-Furness . 153 C3
Dalton-le-Dale . . . 168 A2
Dalton-on-Tees . . . 157 A6
Dalton Piercy 168 B2
Dalveich 217 B6
Dalwood 14 A2
Dalwyne 181 B5
Damerham 31 D5
Damgate 105 A5
Dam Green 103 C6
Damnaglaur 170 D3
Damside 195 B6
Dam Side 144 C4
Danbury 70 C1
Danby 159 A6
Danby Wiske 158 B2
Dandaleith 254 D1
Danderhall 209 D6
Danebridge 129 C4
Dane End 68 A3
Danehill 36 D2
Danemoor Green . . 103 A6
Danesford 95 B5
Daneshill 47 D4
Dangerous Corner . 136 B4
Danskine 210 D2
Darcy Lever 137 C6
Darenth 50 B2
Daresbury 127 A5
Darfield 140 C2
Darfoulds 131 B5
Dargate 52 C2
Darite 6 A1
Darlaston 96 B2
Darley 147 B6
Darley Bridge 130 C2
Darley Head 147 B5
Darlingscott 81 C5
Darlington 167 D5
Darliston 111 B4
Darlton 132 B2
Darnall 130 A3
Darnick 197 C4
Darowen 91 B6
Darra 256 B2
Darracott 25 B5
Darras Hall 178 B3
Darrington 140 A2
Darsham 89 A5
Dartford 50 B2
Dartford Crossing . . 50 B2
Dartington 8 A1
Dartmeet 12 D1
Dartmouth 8 B2
Darton 139 C6
Darvel 193 B5
Darwell Hole 23 A4
Darwen 137 A5
Datchet 48 B2
Datchworth 68 B2
Datchworth Green . . 68 B2
Daubhill 137 C6
Daugh of
Kinermony 254 B3
Dauntsey 44 A3
Dava 253 C6
Davenham 127 B6
Davenport Green . . 128 B3
Daventry 82 A2
Davidson's Mains . 209 C5
Davidstow 10 C2
David's Well 93 D4
Davington 185 B5
Daviot
Aberds 256 D2
Highld 252 C3
Davoch of Grange . 267 D5
Davyhulme 137 D6
Dawley 95 A4
Dawlish 13 D4
Dawlish Warren 13 D4
Dawn 124 B3
Daws Heath 51 A5
Daw's House 10 C4
Dawsmere 118 B1
Dayhills 112 B3
Daylesford 64 A3
Ddôl-Cownwy 109 D5
Ddrydwy 122 C3
Deadwater 187 D5
Deaf Hill 167 B6
Deal 53 D5
Deal Hall 71 D4
Dean
Cumb 162 B3

Dean continued
Devon 7 A6
Devon 25 A6
Dorset 30 D3
Hants 33 D4
Som 29 A6
Deanburnhaugh . . . 186 B2
Deane
Gtr Man 137 C5
Hants 46 D3
Deanich Lodge 263 B5
Deanland 30 D3
Dean Prior 7 A6
Dean Row 128 A3
Deans 208 D3
Deanscales 162 B3
Deanshanger 83 D4
Deanston 218 D2
Dearham 162 A3
Debach 88 B3
Debden
Essex 68 D4
Essex 86 D1
Debden Cross 86 D1
Debenham 88 A2
Dechmont 208 C3
Deddington 82 D1
Dedham 87 D6
Dedham Heath 87 D6
Deebank 244 C3
Deene 99 B6
Deenethorpe 99 B6
Deepcar 139 D5
Deepcut 34 A2
Deepdale 155 C6
Deeping Gate 100 A3
Deeping St James . 100 A3
Deeping
St Nicholas 117 D5
Deerhill 267 D5
Deerhurst 63 A4
Deerness 283 G6
Defford 80 C2
Defynnog 59 C6
Deganwy 124 B3
Deighton
N Yorks 158 A2
W Yorks 139 B4
York 149 C5
Deiniolen 123 D5
Delabole 9 C6
Delamere 127 C5
Delfrigs 257 D4
Delliefure 254 C1
Dell Lodge 242 A3
Delnabo 243 A4
Delnadamph 243 B5
Delph 138 C2
Delves 166 A4
Delvine 231 D5
Dembleby 116 B3
Denaby Main 140 D2
Denbigh =Dinbych . 125 C5
Denbury 8 A2
Denby 114 A1
Denby Dale 139 C5
Denchworth 65 D4
Dendron 153 C3
Denel End 84 D2
Denend 255 C2
Denford 100 D1
Dengie 70 C3
Denham
Bucks 48 A3
Suff 86 A3
Suff 104 D2
Denham Street 104 D2
Denhead
Aberds 269 D4
Fife 221 C4
Denhead of
Arbilot 232 D3
Denhead of Gray . . 220 A3
Denholm 187 B4
Denholme 147 D4
Denholme Clough . . 147 D4
Denio 106 C3
Denmead 33 D5
Denmore 245 A6
Denmoss 256 B1
Dennington 88 A3
Denny 207 B6
Dennyloanhead . . . 207 B6
Denny Lodge 18 A2
Denshaw 138 B2
Denside 245 C5
Densole 39 A4
Denston 86 B3
Denstone 113 A5
Dent 155 C6

Denton
Cambs 100 C3
Darl 167 D5
E Sus 22 B2
Gtr Man 138 D2
Kent 39 A4
Lincs 115 B6
Norf 104 C3
Northants 83 B5
N Yorks 147 C5
Oxon 65 C6
Denton's Green . . . 136 D3
Denver 102 A2
Denwick 189 B5
Deopham 103 A6
Deopham Green . . . 103 B6
Depden 86 B3
Depden Green 86 B3
Deptford
London 49 B6
Wilts 31 B4
Derby 114 B1
Derbyhaven 152 E2
Dereham 120 D1
Deri 41 A6
Derril 10 A4
Derringstone 39 A4
Derrington 112 C2
Derriton 10 A4
Derryguaig 224 C3
Derry Hill 44 B3
Derrythorpe 141 C6
Dersingham 118 B3
Dervaig 224 A3
Derwen 125 D5
Derwenlas 91 C5
Desborough 99 C5
Desford 98 A1
Detchant 199 C4
Detling 37 A5
Deuddwr 110 D1
Devauden 61 D6
Devil's Bridge 75 A6
Devizes 44 C4
Devol 204 A3
Devonport 6 B3
Devonside 208 A2
Devoran 4 D2
Dewar 196 B2
Dewlish 16 B1
Dewsbury 139 A5
Dewsbury Moor . . . 139 A5
Dewshall Court 78 D2
Dhoon 152 C4
Dhoor 152 B4
Dhowin 152 A4
Dial Post 21 A4
Dibden 18 A3
Dibden Purlieu 18 A3
Dickleburgh 104 C2
Didbrook 80 D3
Didcot 46 A3
Diddington 84 A3
Diddlebury 94 C3
Didley 78 D2
Didling 20 A1
Didmarton 44 A2
Didsbury 138 D1
Didworthy 7 A5
Digby 133 D5
Digg 259 B4
Diggle 138 C3
Digmoor 136 C3
Digswell Park 68 B2
Dihewyd 74 C3
Dilham 121 C5
Dilhorne 112 A3
Dillarburn 194 B3
Dillington 84 A3
Dilston 178 C1
Dilton Marsh 30 A2
Dilwyn 78 B2
Dinas
Carms 73 C5
Gwyn 106 C2
Dinas Cross 72 C3
Dinas Dinlle 107 A4
Dinas-Mawddwy . . 91 A6
Dinas Powys 41 D6
Dinbych =Denbigh . 125 C5
Dinbych-y-Pysgod
=Tenby 56 B1
Dinder 29 A5
Dinedor 78 D3
Dingestow 61 B6
Dingle 126 A3
Dingleden 37 C6
Dingley 99 C4
Dingwall 252 A1
Dinlabyre 186 D4

Dinmael 109 A5
Dinnet 244 C1
Dinnington
Som 28 D4
S Yorks 131 A5
T&W 179 B4
Dinorwic 123 D5
Dinton
Bucks 66 B2
Wilts 31 B4
Dinwoodie Mains . . 185 C4
Dinworthy 24 D4
Dippen 191 C6
Dippenhall 33 A7
Dipple
Moray 266 D4
S Ayrs 181 A4
Diptford 7 B6
Dipton 178 D3
Dirdhu 254 D1
Dirleton 210 B2
Dirt Pot 165 A6
Discoed 77 A6
Diseworth 114 C2
Dishes 282 E7
Dishforth 158 D2
Disley 129 A4
Diss 104 D2
Disserth 76 B4
Distington 162 B3
Ditchampton 31 B4
Ditcheat 29 B6
Ditchingham 104 B4
Ditchling 21 A6
Ditherington 111 D4
Dittisham 8 B2
Ditton
Halton 127 A4
Kent 37 A5
Ditton Green 86 B2
Ditton Priors 95 C4
Divach 251 D6
Divlyn 59 B4
Dixton
Glos 80 D2
Mon 61 B7
Dobcross 138 C2
Dobwalls 5 A7
Doccombe 12 C2
Dochfour House . . . 252 C2
Dochgarroch 252 B2
Docking 119 B4
Docklow 78 B3
Dockray 164 C1
Dockroyd 147 D4
Doc Penfro
=Pembroke Dock . . 55 D5
Dodburn 186 C3
Doddinghurst 69 D5
Doddington
Cambs 101 B5
Kent 51 D6
Lincs 133 B4
Northumb 198 C3
Shrops 95 D4
Doddiscombsleigh . 12 C3
Dodford
Northants 82 A3
Worcs 96 D2
Dodington 43 A6
Dodleston 126 C3
Dodworth 139 C6
Dods Leigh 112 B4
Doe Green 127 A5
Doe Lea 131 C4
Dogdyke 134 D2
Dogmersfield 47 D5
Dogridge 45 A4
Dogsthorpe 100 A3
Dog Village 13 B4
Dolanog 109 D5
Dolau
Powys 77 A5
Rhondda 41 C4
Dolbenmaen 107 B5
Dolfach 91 B7
Dolfor 93 C5
Dol-fôr 91 B6
Dolgarrog 124 C2
Dolgellau 91 A5
Dolgran 58 B1
Dolhendre 108 B3
Doll 274 D2
Dollar 208 A2
Dolley Green 77 A6
Dollwen 91 D4
Dolphin 126 B1
Dolphinholme 145 B5
Dolphinton 195 B6
Dolton 25 D6

Dolwen
Conwy 124 B3
Powys 92 A3
Dolwyd 124 B3
Dolwyddelan 124 D2
Dôl-y-Bont 90 D4
Dol-y-cannau 77 C6
Dolyhir 77 B6
Doncaster 140 C3
Dones Green 127 B6
Donhead St Andrew . 30 C3
Donhead St Mary . . 30 C3
Donibristle 209 B4
Donington 117 B5
Donington on Bain . 134 A2
Donington South
Ing 117 B5
Donisthorpe 113 D7
Donkey Town 48 C2
Donnington
Glos 64 A2
Hereford 79 D5
Shrops 94 A3
Telford 111 D6
W Berks 46 C2
W Sus 20 B1
Donnington Wood . . 111 D6
Donyatt 28 D3
Doonfoot 192 D3
Dorback Lodge 242 A3
Dorchester
Dorset 15 B6
Oxon 65 D6
Dordon 97 A5
Dore 130 A3
Dores 252 C1
Dorking 35 B4
Dormansland 36 B2
Dormanstown 168 C3
Dormington 78 C3
Dormston 80 B2
Dornal 181 D4
Dorney 48 B2
Dornie 249 D5
Dornoch 264 B3
Dornock 175 B5
Dorrery 279 C6
Dorridge 97 D4
Dorrington
Lincs 133 D5
Shrops 94 A2
Dorsington 80 C4
Dorstone 77 C7
Dorton 66 B1
Dorusduain 250 D1
Dosthill 97 B5
Dottery 15 B4
Doublebois 5 A6
Dougarie 191 B4
Doughton 63 D4
Douglas
IoM 152 D3
S Lanark 194 C3
Douglas & Angus . . 220 A4
Douglastown 232 D2
Douglas Water 194 C3
Douglas West 194 C3
Doulting 29 A6
Dounby 282 E3
Doune
Highld 272 D2
Stirling 218 D2
Doune Park 268 C2
Douneside 244 B1
Dounie 264 A1
Dounreay 279 B5
Dousland 7 A4
Dovaston 110 C2
Dove Holes 129 B5
Dovenby 162 A3
Dover 39 A6
Dovercourt 88 D3
Doverdale 79 A6
Doveridge 113 B5
Doversgreen 35 B5
Dowally 230 D4
Dowbridge 144 D4
Dowdeswell 63 B5
Dowlais 60 C2
Dowland 25 D6
Dowlish Wake 28 D3
Down Ampney 64 D2
Downcraig Ferry . . 204 C1
Downderry 6 B2
Downe 50 C1
Downend
IoW 18 C4
S Glos 43 B5
W Berks 46 B2
Downfield 220 A3

Downgate 11 D4
Downham
Essex 70 D1
Lancs 146 C1
Northumb 198 C3
Downham Market . . 102 A2
Down Hatherley . . . 63 A4
Downhead 29 A6
Downhill
Perth 219 A5
T&W 179 D5
Downholland Cross 136 C2
Downholme 157 B5
Downies 245 C6
Downley 66 D3
Down St Mary 12 A2
Downside
Som 29 A6
Sur 35 A4
Down Thomas 7 B4
Downton
Hants 17 B6
Wilts 31 C5
Downton on the
Rock 94 D2
Dowsby 116 C4
Dowsdale 117 D5
Dowthwaitehead . . 163 B6
Doxey 112 C3
Doxford 189 A4
Doxford Park 179 D5
Doynton 43 B6
Draffan 194 B2
Dragonby 141 B7
Drakeland Corner . . . 7 B4
Drakemyre 204 C2
Drake's Broughton . 80 C2
Drakes Cross 96 D3
Drakewalls 11 D5
Draughton
Northants 99 D4
N Yorks 147 B4
Drax 141 A4
Draycote 98 D1
Draycott
Derbys 114 B2
Glos 81 D4
Som 42 D3
Draycott in the
Clay 113 C5
Draycott in the
Moors 112 A3
Drayford 26 D2
Drayton
Leics 99 B5
Lincs 117 B5
Norf 120 D3
Oxon 65 D5
Oxon 82 C1
Ptsmth 19 A5
Som 28 C4
Worcs 96 D2
Drayton Bassett . . . 97 A4
Drayton Beauchamp 67 B4
Drayton Parslow . . . 66 A3
Drayton St Leonard . 65 D6
Drebley 147 B4
Dreemskerry 152 B4
Dreenhill 55 C5
Drefach
Carms 57 A5
Carms 73 C6
Dre-fach
Carms 57 A6
Ceredig 75 D4
Drefelin 73 C6
Dreghorn 192 B3
Drellingore 39 A4
Drem 210 C2
Dresden 112 A3
Dreumasdal 286 C3
Drewsteignton 12 B2
Driby 134 B3
Driffield
E Yorks 150 B3
Glos 63 D6
Drigg 153 A1
Drighlington 139 A5
Drimnin 225 A4
Drimpton 14 A4
Drimsynie 215 B4
Drinisiadar 288 H2
Drinkstone 87 A5
Drinkstone Green . . 87 A5
Drishaig 215 A4
Drissaig 214 A2
Drochil 195 B6
Drointon 112 C4

Droitwich Spa 80 A1
Droman 276 C2
Dron 219 C6
Dronfield 130 B3
Dronfield
  Woodhouse 130 B3
Drongan 182 A2
Dronley 220 A3
Droxford 33 D5
Droylsden 138 D2
Druid 109 A5
Druidston 55 C4
Druimarbin 237 B4
Druimavuic 227 B5
Druimdrishaig 202 A2
Druimindarroch 235 B5
Druimyeon More . . .202 C1
Drum
  Argyll 203 A4
  Perth 219 D5
Drumbeg 270 A4
Drumblade 255 B6
Drumblair 256 B1
Drumbuie
  Dumfries 182 D3
  Highld 249 C4
Drumburgh 175 C5
Drumburn 174 B2
Drumchapel 205 A5
Drumchardine 252 B1
Drumchork 261 B5
Drumclog 193 B6
Drumderfit 252 A2
Drumeldrie 220 D4
Drumelzier 195 C6
Drumfearn 247 C5
Drumgask 241 C4
Drumgley 232 C2
Drumguish 241 C5
Drumin 254 C2
Drumlasie 244 B3
Drumlemble 190 D2
Drumligair 245 A6
Drumlithie 245 D4
Drummoddie 171 C5
Drummond 264 D2
Drummore 170 D3
Drummuir 255 B4
Drummuir Castle . . .255 B4
Drumnadrochit 251 D7
Drumnagorrach 267 D6
Drumoak 245 C4
Drumpark 183 D6
Drumphail 171 A4
Drumrash 173 A4
Drumrunie 271 D4
Drums 257 D4
Drumsallie 236 B3
Drumstinchall 173 C6
Drumsturdy 221 A4
Drumtochty Castle . .244 E3
Drumtroddan 171 C5
Drumuie 259 D4
Drumuillie 253 D5
Drumvaich 217 D6
Drumwhindle 257 C4
Drunkendub 233 D4
Drury 126 C2
Drury Square 119 D6
Drybeck 165 D4
Drybridge
  Moray 267 C5
  N Ayrs 192 B3
Drybrook 62 B2
Dryburgh 197 C4
Dry Doddington 115 A6
Dry Drayton 85 A5
Dryhope 196 D1
Drylaw 209 C5
Drym 3 B4
Drymen 206 B2
Drymuir 257 B4
Drynoch 246 A3
Dryslwyn 58 C2
Dryton 94 A3
Dubford 268 C3
Dubton 232 C3
Duchally 271 C6
Duck Corner 89 C4
Duckington 127 C4
Ducklington 65 C4
Duckmanton 131 B4
Duck's Cross 84 B3
Duddenhoe End 85 D6
Duddingston 209 C5
Duddington 100 A1
Duddleswell 36 D2

Duddo 198 B3
Duddon 127 C5
Duddon Bridge 153 B3
Dudleston 110 B2
Dudleston Heath 110 B2
Dudley
  T&W 179 B4
  W Mid 96 B2
Dudley Port 96 B2
Duffield 114 A1
Duffryn
  Neath 40 B3
  Newport 42 A1
Dufftown 254 C4
Duffus 266 C2
Dufton 165 C4
Duggleby 150 A1
Duirinish 249 C4
Duisdalemore 247 C6
Duisky 237 B4
Dukestown 60 B3
Dukinfield 138 D2
Dulas 123 B4
Dulcote 29 A5
Dulford 13 A5
Dull 230 D2
Dullatur 207 C5
Dullingham 86 B2
Dulnain Bridge 253 D5
Duloe
  Bedford 84 A3
  Corn 6 B1
Dulsie 253 B5
Dulverton 27 C4
Dulwich 49 B6
Dumbarton 205 A3
Dumbleton 80 D3
Dumcrieff 185 B4
Dumfries 174 A2
Dumgoyne 206 B3
Dummer 33 A4
Dumpford 34 D1
Dumpton 53 C5
Dun 233 C4
Dunain House 252 B2
Dunalastair 229 C6
Dunan 247 B4
Dunans 214 C3
Dunball 28 A3
Dunbar 210 C3
Dunbeath 275 B5
Dunbeg 226 C3
Dunblane 218 D2
Dunbog 220 C2
Duncanston 252 A1
Duncanstone 255 D6
Dun Charlabhaigh . .288 C2
Dunchurch 98 D1
Duncote 82 B3
Duncow 184 D2
Duncraggan 217 D5
Duncrievie 219 D6
Duncton 20 A2
Dundas House 283 J5
Dundee 220 A4
Dundeugh 182 D3
Dundon 29 B4
Dundonald 192 B3
Dundonnell 262 B2
Dundonnell Hotel . .262 B2
Dundonnell House . .262 B3
Dundraw 175 D5
Dundreggan 239 A7
Dundreggan
  Lodge 240 A1
Dundrennan 173 D5
Dundry 43 C4
Dunecht 245 B4
Dunfermline 208 B3
Dunfield 64 D2
Dunford Bridge 139 C4
Dungworth 130 A2
Dunham 132 B3
Dunham-on-
  the-Hill 127 B4
Dunhampton 79 A6
Dunham Town 128 A2
Dunholme 133 B5
Dunino 221 C5
Dunipace 207 B6
Dunira 218 B2
Dunkeld 230 D4
Dunkerton 43 D6
Dunkeswell 13 A6
Dunkeswick 148 C2
Dunkirk
  Kent 52 D2
  Norf 120 C4
Dunk's Green 36 A4
Dunlappie 232 B3

Dunley
  Hants 46 D2
  Worcs 79 A5
Dunlichity Lodge . . .252 C2
Dunlop 205 D4
Dunmaglass Lodge . .252 D1
Dunmore
  Argyll 202 B2
  Falk 208 B1
Dunnet 280 A4
Dunnichen 232 D3
Dunninald 233 C5
Dunning 219 C5
Dunnington
  E Yorks 151 B4
  Warks 80 B3
  York 149 B5
Dunnockshaw 137 A7
Dunollie 226 C3
Dunoon 203 A6
Dunragit 170 B3
Dunrostan 213 D5
Duns 198 A1
Dunsby 116 C4
Dunscore 183 D6
Dunscroft 141 C4
Dunsdale 168 D4
Dunsden Green 47 B5
Dunsfold 34 C3
Dunsford 12 C3
Dunshalt 220 C2
Dunshillock 257 B4
Dunskey House 170 B2
Dunsley 169 D6
Dunsmore 66 C3
Dunsop Bridge 145 B6
Dunstable 67 A5
Dunstall 113 C5
Dunstall Common . . .80 C1
Dunstall Green 86 A3
Dunstan 189 B5
Dunstan Steads 189 A5
Dunster 27 A4
Duns Tew 65 A5
Dunston
  Lincs 133 C5
  Norf 104 A3
  Staffs 112 D3
  T&W 179 C4
Dunsville 140 C4
Dunswell 150 D3
Dunsyre 195 B5
Dunterton 11 D4
Duntisbourne
  Abbots 63 C5
Duntisbourne Leer . .63 C5
Duntisbourne Rouse .63 C5
Duntish 15 A6
Duntocher 205 A4
Dunton
  Bucks 66 A3
  C Beds 84 C4
  Norf 119 B5
Dunton Bassett 98 B2
Dunton Green 36 A3
Dunton Wayletts 69 D6
Duntulm 259 A4
Dunure 192 D2
Dunvant 57 C5
Dunvegan 258 D2
Dunwich 105 D5
Dunwood 129 D4
Dupplin Castle 219 C5
Durdar 175 C7
Durgates 36 C4
Durham 167 A5
Durisdeer 183 B6
Durisdeermill 183 B6
Durkar 139 B6
Durleigh 28 B2
Durley
  Hants 32 D4
  Wilts 45 C6
Durnamuck 262 A2
Durness 277 B5
Durno 256 D2
Duror 236 D3
Durran
  Argyll 214 B2
  Highld 280 B3
Durrington
  Wilts 31 A5
  W Sus 21 B4
Dursley 62 D3
Durston 28 C2
Durweston 16 A2
Dury 285 G6
Duston 83 A4
Duthil 253 D5
Dutlas 93 D6

Duton Hill 69 A6
Dutson 10 C4
Dutton 127 B5
Duxford
  Cambs 85 C6
  Oxon 65 D4
Dwygyfylchi 124 B2
Dwyran 123 D4
Dyce 245 A5
Dye House 178 D1
Dyffryn
  Bridgend 40 B3
  Carms 73 D6
  Pembs 72 C2
Dyffryn Ardudwy . . .107 D5
Dyffryn Castell 91 D5
Dyffryn Ceidrych . . .59 C4
Dyffryn Cellwen 59 E5
Dyke
  Lincs 116 C4
  Moray 253 A5
Dykehead
  Angus 232 B1
  N Lanark 207 E6
  Stirling 206 A3
Dykelands 233 B5
Dykends 231 C6
Dykeside 256 B2
Dykesmains 204 D2
Dylife 91 C6
Dymchurch 38 C2
Dymock 79 D5
Dyrham 43 B6
Dysart 209 A6
Dyserth 125 B5

E

Eachwick 178 B3
Eadar Dha
  Fhadhail 287 A5
Eagland Hill 144 C4
Eagle 132 C3
Eagle
  Barnsdale 132 C3
Eagle Moor 132 C3
Eaglescliffe 168 D2
Eaglesfield
  Cumb 162 B3
  Dumfries 175 A5
Eaglesham 205 C5
Eaglethorpe 100 B2
Eairy 152 D2
Eakley Lanes 83 B5
Eakring 132 C1
Ealand 141 B5
Ealing 49 A4
Eals 177 D4
Eamont Bridge 164 C3
Earby 146 C3
Earcroft 137 A5
Eardington 95 B5
Eardisland 78 B2
Eardisley 77 C7
Eardiston
  Shrops 110 C2
  Worcs 79 A4
Earith 101 D5
Earle 188 A2
Earley 47 B5
Earlham 104 A3
Earlish 258 B3
Earls Barton 83 A5
Earls Colne 70 A2
Earl's Croome 79 C6
Earlsdon 97 D6
Earlsferry 221 E4
Earlsfield 116 B2
Earlsford 256 C3
Earl's Green 87 A6
Earlsheaton 139 A5
Earl Shilton 98 B1
Earlsmill 253 A5
Earl Soham 88 A3
Earl Sterndale 129 C5
Earlston
  Borders 197 C4
  E Ayrs 193 B4
Earl Stonham 88 B2
Earlswood
  Mon 61 D6
  Sur 35 B5
  Warks 96 D4
Earnley 19 B7
Earsairidh 286 G3
Earsdon 179 B5
Earsham 104 C4
Earswick 149 B5
Eartham 20 B2

Easby
  N Yorks 157 A5
  N Yorks 159 A4
Easdale 213 A5
Easebourne 34 D1
Easenhall 98 D1
Eashing 34 B2
Easington
  Bucks 66 B1
  Durham 168 A2
  E Yorks 143 B5
  Northumb 199 C5
  Oxon 66 D1
  Oxon 82 D1
  Redcar 169 D5
Easington Colliery . .168 A2
Easington Lane 167 A6
Easingwold 148 A4
Easole Street 53 D4
Eassie 232 D1
East Aberthaw 41 E5
East Adderbury 82 D1
East Allington 7 C6
East Anstey 26 C3
East Appleton 157 B6
East Ardsley 139 A6
East Ashling 19 A7
East Auchronie 245 B5
East Ayton 160 C3
East Bank 60 C4
East Barkwith 133 A6
East Barming 37 A5
East Barnby 169 D6
East Barnet 68 D2
East Barns 211 C4
East Barsham 119 B6
East Beckham 120 B3
East Bedfont 48 B3
East Bergholt 87 D6
East Bilney 119 D6
East Blatchington 22 B2
East Boldre 18 A2
Eastbourne 22 C4
East Brent 42 D2
Eastbridge 89 A5
East Bridgford 115 A4
East Buckland 26 B1
East Budleigh 13 C5
Eastburn 147 C4
East Burrafirth 285 H5
East Burton 16 C2
Eastbury
  London 67 D5
  W Berks 46 B1
East Butsfield 166 A4
East Butterwick 141 C6
Eastby 147 B4
East Cairnbeg 233 A5
East Calder 208 D3
East Carleton 104 A2
East Carlton
  Northants 99 C5
  W Yorks 147 C6
East Chaldon 16 C1
East Challow 46 A1
East Chiltington 21 A6
East Chinnock 29 D4
East Chisenbury 45 D5
Eastchurch 52 B1
East Clandon 34 A3
East Claydon 66 A2
East Clyne 274 D2
East Coker 29 D5
Eastcombe 63 C4
East Combe 27 B6
East Common 149 D5
East Compton 29 A6
Eastcote
  London 48 A4
  Northants 82 B3
  W Mid 97 D4
Eastcott
  Corn 24 D3
  Wilts 44 D4
East Cottingwith . . .149 C6
Eastcourt
  Wilts 45 C6
  Wilts 63 D5
East Cowes 18 B4
East Cowton 157 A7
East Cramlington . . .179 B4
East Cranmore 29 A6
East Creech 16 C3
East Croachy 252 D2
East Croftmore 242 A2
East Curthwaite 164 A1
East Dean
  E Sus 22 C3
  Hants 31 C6

East Dean continued
  W Sus 20 A2
East Down 25 A7
East Drayton 132 B2
East Ella 142 A2
East End
  Dorset 16 B3
  E Yorks 143 A4
  Hants 18 B2
  Hants 33 C5
  Hants 46 C2
  Herts 69 A4
  Kent 37 C6
  N Som 42 B3
  Oxon 65 B4
Easter Ardross 264 C2
Easter Balmoral 243 C5
Easter Boleskine . . .251 D7
Easter Compton 43 A4
Easter Cringate 207 B5
Easter Davoch 244 B1
Easter Earshaig 184 B3
Easter Fearn 264 B2
Easter Galcantray . .253 B4
Eastergate 20 B2
Easterhouse 207 D4
Easter Howgate 209 D5
Easter Howlaws 197 B6
Easter Kinkell 252 A1
Easter Lednathie . . .232 B1
Easter Milton 253 A5
Easter Moniack 252 B1
Eastern Green 97 C5
Easter Ord 245 B5
Easter Quarff 285 K6
Easter Rhynd 219 C6
Easter Row 207 A5
Easter Silverford . . .268 C2
Easter Skeld 285 J5
Easterton 44 D4
Eastertown 42 D2
Eastertown of
  Auchleuchries . . .257 C5
Easter Whyntie 267 C7
East Farleigh 37 A5
East Farndon 99 C4
East Ferry 141 D6
Eastfield
  N Lanark 208 D1
  N Yorks 160 C4
Eastfield Hall 189 C5
East Fortune 210 C2
East Garston 46 B1
Eastgate
  Durham 166 B2
  Norf 120 C3
East Ginge 46 A2
East Goscote 115 D4
East Grafton 45 C6
East Grimstead 31 C6
East Grinstead 36 C1
East Guldeford 38 C1
East Haddon 82 A3
East Hagbourne 46 A3
East Halton 142 B3
Eastham 126 A3
East Ham 50 A1
Eastham Ferry 126 A3
Easthampstead 47 C6
East Hanney 65 D5
East Hanningfield . . .70 C1
East Hardwick 140 B2
East Harling 103 C5
East Harlsey 158 B3
East Harnham 31 C5
East Harptree 43 D4
East Hartford 179 B4
East Harting 33 D6
East Hatley 85 B4
East Hauxwell 157 B5
East Haven 221 A5
Eastheath 47 C6
East Heckington 117 A4
East Hedleyhope . . .167 A4
East Hendred 46 A2
East Herrington 179 D5
East Heslerton 160 D3
East Hoathly 22 A3
Easthope 94 B3
Easthorpe
  Essex 70 A3
  Leics 115 B6
  Notts 132 D2
East Horrington 29 A5
East Horsley 34 A3
East Horton 198 C4
Easthouses 209 D6
East Huntspill 28 A3
East Hyde 67 B6
East Ilkerton 26 A2

East Ilsley 46 A2
Eastington
Devon 12 A2
Glos 62 C3
Glos 64 B2
East Keal 134 C3
East Kennett 45 C5
East Keswick 148 C2
East Kilbride 205 C6
East Kirkby 134 C3
East Knapton 160 D2
East Knighton 16 C2
East Knoyle 30 B2
East Kyloe 199 C4
East Lambrook 28 D4
East Lamington 264 C3
East Langdon 39 A5
East Langton 99 B4
East Langwell 273 D5
East Lavant 20 B1
East Lavington 20 A2
East Layton 157 A5
Eastleach Martin 64 C3
Eastleach Turville 64 C2
East Leake 114 C3
East Learmouth 198 C2
Eastleigh
Devon 25 C5
Hants 32 D3
East Leigh 12 A1
East Lexham 119 D5
East Lilburn 188 A3
Eastling 51 D6
East Linton 210 C2
East Liss 33 C6
East Looe 6 B1
East Lound 141 D5
East Lulworth 16 C2
East Lutton 150 A2
East Lydford 29 B5
East Mains 244 C3
East Malling 37 A5
East March 220 A4
East Marden 33 D7
East Markham 132 B2
East Marton 146 B3
East Meon 33 C5
East Mere 27 D4
East Mersea 71 B4
East Mey 281 A5
East Molesey 49 C4
Eastmoor
Derbys 130 B3
Norf 102 A3
East Morden 16 B3
East Morton 147 C4
East Ness 159 D5
East Newton 151 D5
Eastney 19 B5
Eastnor 79 D5
East Norton 99 A4
East Nynehead 27 C6
East Oakley 46 D3
Eastoft 141 B6
East Ogwell 12 D3
Eastoke 19 B6
Easton
Cambs 100 D3
Cumb 175 C5
Cumb 176 B2
Devon 12 C2
Dorset 15 D6
Hants 32 B4
Lincs 116 C2
Norf 120 D3
Som 29 A5
Suff 88 B3
Wilts 44 B2
Easton Grey 44 A2
Easton-in-Gordano 43 B4
Easton Maudit 83 B5
Easton on the Hill 100 A2
Easton Royal 45 C6
East Orchard 30 D2
East Ord 198 A3
East Panson 11 B4
Eastpark 174 B3
East Peckham 37 B4
East Pennard 29 B5
East Perry 84 A3
East Portlemouth 7 D6
East Prawle 8 D1
East Preston 20 B3
East Putford 25 D4
East Quantoxhead 27 A6
East Rainton 167 A6
East Ravendale 143 D4
East Raynham 119 C5
Eastrea 101 B4
East Rhidorroch Lodge 262 A4
Eastriggs 175 B5
East Rigton 148 C2
Eastrington 141 A5
East Rounton 158 A3
East Row 169 D6
East Rudham 119 C5
East Runton 120 A3
East Ruston 121 C5
Eastry 53 D5
East Saltoun 210 D1
East Sleekburn 179 A4
East Somerton 121 D6
East Stockwith 141 D5
East Stoke
Dorset 16 C2
Notts 115 A5
East Stour 30 C2
East Stourmouth 53 C4
East Stowford 26 C1
East Stratton 32 B4
East Studdal 39 A5
East Suisnish 248 C2
East Taphouse 5 A6
East-the-Water 25 C5
East Thirston 189 D4
East Tilbury 50 B3
East Tisted 33 B6
East Torrington 133 A6
East Tuddenham 120 D2
East Tytherley 32 C1
East Tytherton 44 B3
East Village 12 A3
Eastville
Bristol 43 B5
Lincs 135 D4
East Wall 94 B3
East Walton 119 D4
Eastwell 115 C5
East Wellow 32 C2
East Wemyss 209 A6
East Whitburn 208 D2
Eastwick
Herts 68 B4
Shetland 284 F5
East Williamston 55 D6
East Winch 118 D3
East Winterslow 31 B6
East Wittering 19 B6
East Witton 157 C5
Eastwood
Notts 114 A2
Southend 51 A5
W Yorks 138 A2
East Woodburn 177 A7
East Woodhay 46 C2
East Worldham 33 B6
East Worlington 26 D2
East Worthing 21 B4
Eathorpe 81 A6
Eaton
Ches E 128 C3
Ches W 127 C5
Leics 115 C5
Norf 104 A3
Notts 132 B2
Oxon 65 C5
Shrops 94 C1
Shrops 94 C3
Eaton Bishop 78 D2
Eaton Bray 67 A4
Eaton Constantine 94 A3
Eaton Green 67 A4
Eaton Hastings 64 D3
Eaton on Tern 111 C5
Eaton Socon 84 B3
Eavestone 147 A6
Ebberston 160 C2
Ebbesbourne Wake 30 C3
Ebbw Vale
= *Glyn Ebwy* 60 C3
Ebchester 178 D3
Ebford 13 C4
Ebley 63 C4
Ebnal 110 A3
Ebrington 81 D4
Ecchinswell 46 D2
Ecclaw 211 D4
Ecclefechan 175 A4
Eccles
Borders 197 B6
Gtr Man 137 D6
Kent 51 C4
Ecclesall 130 A3
Ecclesfield 139 D6
Ecclesgreig 233 B5
Eccleshall 112 C2
Eccleshill 147 D5
Ecclesmachan 208 C3
Eccles on Sea 121 C6
Eccles Road 103 B6
Eccleston
Ches W 127 C4
Lancs 136 B4
Mers 136 D3
Eccleston Park 136 D3
Eccup 148 C1
Echt 245 B4
Eckford 187 A6
Eckington
Derbys 131 B4
Worcs 80 C2
Ecton 83 A5
Edale 129 A6
Edburton 21 A5
Edderside 174 D3
Edderton 264 B3
Eddistone 24 C3
Eddleston 196 B1
Edenbridge 36 B2
Edenfield 137 B6
Edenhall 164 B3
Edenham 116 C3
Eden Park 49 C6
Edensor 130 C2
Edentaggart 215 C6
Edenthorpe 140 C4
Edentown 175 C6
Ederline 214 B1
Edern 106 C2
Edgarley 29 B5
Edgbaston 96 C3
Edgcott
Bucks 66 A1
Som 26 B3
Edge 94 A1
Edgebolton 111 C4
Edge End 62 B1
Edgefield 120 B2
Edgefield Street 120 B2
Edge Green 127 D4
Edge Hill 136 D2
Edgeside 138 A1
Edgeworth 63 C5
Edgmond 111 D6
Edgmond Marsh 111 C6
Edgton 94 C1
Edgware 68 D1
Edgworth 137 B6
Edinample 217 B5
Edinbane 258 C3
Edinburgh 209 C5
Edingale 113 D6
Edingight House 267 D6
Edingley 131 D6
Edingthorpe 121 B5
Edingthorpe Green 121 B5
Edington
Som 28 B3
Wilts 44 D3
Edintore 255 B5
Edithmead 28 A3
Edith Weston 99 A6
Edlesborough 67 B4
Edlingham 189 C4
Edlington 134 B2
Edmondsham 31 D4
Edmondsley 167 A5
Edmondthorpe 115 D6
Edmonstone 282 E6
Edmonton 68 D3
Edmundbyers 178 D2
Ednam 197 C6
Ednaston 113 A6
Edradynate 230 C2
Edrom 198 A2
Edstaston 111 B4
Edstone 81 A4
Edvin Loach 79 B4
Edwalton 114 B3
Edwardstone 87 C5
Edwinsford 58 B3
Edwinstowe 131 C6
Edworth 84 C4
Edwyn Ralph 79 B4
Edzell 232 B3
Efail Isaf 41 C5
Efailnewydd 106 C3
Efailwen 72 D4
Efenechtyd 125 D6
Effingham 35 A4
Effirth 285 H5
Efford 12 A3
Egdon 80 B2
Egerton
Gtr Man 137 B6
Kent 37 B7
Egerton Forstal 37 B6
Eggborough 140 A3
Eggbuckland 7 B4
Eggington 67 A4
Egginton 113 C6
Egglescliffe 168 D2
Eggleston 166 C2
Egham 48 B3
Egleton 99 A5
Eglingham 189 B4
Egloshayle 9 D5
Egloskerry 10 C3
Eglwysbach 124 B3
Eglwys-Brewis 41 E5
Eglwys Cross 110 A3
Eglwys Fach 91 C4
Eglwyswen 73 C4
Eglwyswrw 72 C4
Egmanton 132 C2
Egremont
Cumb 162 C3
Mers 136 D2
Egton 159 A7
Egton Bridge 159 A7
Eight Ash Green 70 A3
Eignaig 226 B2
Eil 241 A6
Eilanreach 238 A2
Eileanach Lodge 264 D1
Eilean Darach 262 B3
Einacleite 288 E2
Eisgean 288 F4
Eisingrug 107 C6
Elan Village 76 A3
Elberton 43 A5
Elburton 7 B4
Elcho 219 B6
Elcombe 45 A5
Eldernell 101 B5
Eldersfield 79 D6
Elderslie 205 B4
Eldon 167 C5
Eldrick 181 C4
Eldroth 146 A1
Eldwick 147 C5
Elfhowe 154 B3
Elford
Northumb 199 C5
Staffs 113 D5
Elgin 266 C3
Elgol 247 C4
Elham 38 A3
Elie 221 D4
Elim 122 B3
Eling 32 D2
Elishader 259 B5
Elishaw 188 D1
Elkesley 132 B1
Elkstone 63 B5
Ellan 253 D4
Elland 139 A4
Ellary 202 A2
Ellastone 113 A5
Ellemford 211 D4
Ellenbrook 152 D3
Ellenhall 112 C2
Ellen's Green 34 C3
Ellerbeck 158 B3
Ellerburn 160 C2
Ellerby 169 D5
Ellerdine Heath 111 C5
Ellerhayes 13 A4
Elleric 227 B5
Ellerker 141 A7
Ellerton
E Yorks 149 D6
Shrops 111 C6
Ellesborough 66 C3
Ellesmere 110 B3
Ellesmere Port 127 B4
Ellingham
Norf 105 B4
Northumb 189 A4
Ellingstring 157 C5
Ellington
Cambs 100 D3
Northumb 189 D5
Elliot 221 A6
Ellisfield 33 A5
Ellistown 114 D2
Ellon 257 C4
Ellonby 164 B2
Ellough 105 C5
Elloughton 142 A1
Ellwood 62 C1
Elm 101 A6
Elmbridge 80 A2
Elmdon
Essex 85 D6
W Mid 97 C4
Elmdon Heath 97 C4
Elmers End 49 C6
Elmesthorpe 98 B1
Elmfield 19 B5
Elm Hill 30 C2
Elmhurst 113 D5
Elmley Castle 80 C2
Elmley Lovett 79 A6
Elmore 62 B3
Elmore Back 62 B3
Elm Park 50 A2
Elmscott 24 C3
Elmsett 87 C6
Elmstead Market 71 A4
Elmsted 38 A3
Elmstone 53 C4
Elmstone Hardwicke 63 A5
Elmswell
E Yorks 150 B2
Suff 87 A5
Elmton 131 B5
Elphin 271 C5
Elphinstone 209 C6
Elrick 245 B5
Elrig 171 C5
Elsdon 188 D2
Elsecar 140 C1
Elsenham 69 A5
Elsfield 65 B6
Elsham 142 B2
Elsing 120 D2
Elslack 146 C3
Elson 110 B2
Elsrickle 195 B5
Elstead 34 B2
Elsted 33 D7
Elsthorpe 116 C3
Elstob 167 C6
Elston
Notts 115 A5
Wilts 31 A4
Elstone 26 D1
Elstow 84 C2
Elstree 68 D1
Elstronwick 151 D5
Elswick 144 D4
Elsworth 85 A5
Elterwater 154 A2
Eltham 50 B1
Eltisley 85 B4
Elton
Cambs 100 B2
Ches W 127 B4
Derbys 130 C2
Glos 62 B3
Hereford 94 D2
Notts 115 B5
Stockton 168 D2
Elton Green 127 B4
Elvanfoot 184 A2
Elvaston 114 B2
Elveden 103 D4
Elvingston 210 C1
Elvington
Kent 53 D4
York 149 C5
Elwick
Hrtlpl 168 B2
Northumb 199 C5
Elworth 128 C2
Elworthy 27 B5
Ely
Cambs 102 C1
Cardiff 41 D6
Emberton 83 C5
Embleton
Cumb 163 A4
Northumb 189 A5
Embo 265 A4
Emborough 43 D5
Embo Street 265 A4
Embsay 147 B4
Emersons Green 43 B5
Emery Down 18 A1
Emley 139 B5
Emmbrook 47 C5
Emmer Green 47 B5
Emmington 66 C2
Emneth 101 A6
Emneth Hungate 101 A7
Empingham 99 A6
Empshott 33 B6
Emstrey 111 D4
Emsworth 19 A6
Enborne 46 C2
Enchmarsh 94 B3
Enderby 98 B2
Endmoor 154 C4
Endon 129 D4
Endon Bank 129 D4
Enfield 68 D3
Enfield Wash 68 D3
Enford 45 D5
Engamoor 285 H4
Engine Common 43 A5
Englefield 47 B4
Englefield Green 48 B2
Englesea-brook 128 D2
English Bicknor 62 B1
Englishcombe 43 C6
English Frankton 110 C3
Enham Alamein 32 A2
Enmore 28 B2
Ennerdale Bridge 162 C3
Enoch 183 B6
Enochdhu 231 B4
Ensay 224 B2
Ensbury 17 B4
Ensdon 110 D3
Ensis 25 C6
Enstone 65 A4
Enterkinfoot 183 B6
Enterpen 158 A3
Enville 95 C6
Eolaigearraidh 286 F3
Eorabus 224 D2
Eòropaidh 288 A6
Epperstone 115 A4
Epping 69 C4
Epping Green
Essex 68 C4
Herts 68 C2
Epping Upland 68 C4
Eppleby 167 D4
Eppleworth 150 D3
Epsom 49 C5
Epwell 81 C6
Epworth 141 C5
Epworth Turbary 141 C5
Erbistock 110 A2
Erbusaig 249 D4
Erchless Castle 251 B6
Erdington 96 B4
Eredine 214 B2
Eriboll 277 C5
Ericstane 184 A3
Eridge Green 36 C3
Erines 202 A3
Eriswell 102 D3
Erith 50 B2
Erlestoke 44 D3
Ermine 133 B4
Ermington 7 B5
Erpingham 120 B3
Errogie 252 D1
Errol 220 B2
Erskine 205 A4
Erskine Bridge 205 A4
Ervie 170 A2
Erwarton 88 D3
Erwood 77 C4
Eryholme 157 A7
Eryrys 126 D2
Escomb 167 C4
Escrick 149 C5
Esgairdawe 58 A3
Esgairgeiliog 91 B5
Esh 167 A4
Esher 48 C4
Esholt 147 C5
Eshott 189 D5
Eshton 146 B3
Esh Winning 167 A4
Eskadale 251 C6
Eskbank 209 D6
Eskdale Green 163 D4
Eskdalemuir 185 C5
Eske 150 C3
Eskham 143 D5
Esk Valley 159 A7
Esprick 144 D4
Essendine 116 D3
Essendon 68 C2
Essich 252 C2
Essington 96 A2
Esslemont 257 D4
Eston 168 D3
Eswick 285 H6
Etal 198 C3
Etchilhampton 44 C4
Etchingham 37 D5
Etchinghill
Kent 38 B3
Staffs 112 D4
Ethie Castle 233 D4
Ethie Mains 233 D4
Etling Green 120 D2
Eton 48 B2
Eton Wick 48 B2
Etteridge 241 C4

Ettersgill 166 C1
Ettingshall 96 B2
Ettington 81 C5
Etton
　E Yorks 150 C2
　Pboro 100 A3
Ettrick 185 A5
Ettrickbridge 186 A2
Ettrickhill 185 A5
Etwall 113 B6
Euston 103 D4
Euximoor Drove 101 B6
Euxton 137 B4
Evanstown 41 C4
Evanton 264 D2
Evedon 116 A3
Evelix 264 A3
Evenjobb 77 A6
Evenley 82 D2
Evenlode 64 A3
Evenwood 167 C4
Evenwood Gate 167 C4
Everbay 282 E7
Evercreech 29 B6
Everdon 82 B2
Everingham 149 C7
Everleigh 45 D6
Everley 160 C3
Eversholt 84 D1
Evershot 15 A5
Eversley 47 C5
Eversley Cross 47 C5
Everthorpe 150 D2
Everton
　C Beds 84 B4
　Hants 18 B1
　Mers 136 D2
　Notts 141 D4
Evertown 175 A6
Evesbatch 79 C4
Evesham 80 C3
Evington 98 A3
Ewden Village 139 D5
Ewell 49 C5
Ewell Minnis 39 A4
Ewelme 66 D1
Ewen 63 D6
Ewenny 40 D4
Ewerby 116 A4
Ewerby Thorpe 116 A4
Ewes 185 C6
Ewesley 188 D3
Ewhurst 34 B3
Ewhurst Green
　E Sus 37 D5
　Sur 34 C3
Ewloe 126 C3
Ewloe Green 126 C2
Ewood 137 A5
Eworthy 11 B5
Ewshot 33 A7
Ewyas Harold 61 A5
Exbourne 11 A7
Exbridge 27 C4
Exbury 18 B3
Exebridge 27 C4
Exelby 157 C6
Exeter 13 B4
Exford 26 B3
Exhall 80 B4
Exley Head 147 D4
Exminster 13 C4
Exmouth 13 C5
Exnaboe 285 M5
Exning 86 A2
Exton
　Devon 13 C4
　Hants 33 C5
　Rutland 116 D2
　Som. 27 B4
Exwick 13 B4
Eyam 130 B2
Eydon 82 B2
Eye
　Hereford 78 A2
　Pboro 100 A4
　Suff 104 D2
Eye Green 100 A4
Eyemouth 211 D6
Eyeworth 85 C4
Eyhorne Street 37 A6
Eyke 88 B4
Eynesbury 84 B3
Eynort 246 B2
Eynsford 50 C2
Eynsham 65 C5
Eype 14 B4
Eyre
　Highld 248 C2

Eyre continued
　Highld 259 C4
Eythorne 39 A4
Eyton
　Hereford 78 A2
　Shrops 94 C1
　Wrex 110 A2
Eyton upon the Weald
　Moors 111 D5

F

Faccombe 46 D1
Faceby 158 A3
Facit 138 B1
Faddiley 127 D5
Fadmoor 159 C5
Faerdre 40 A1
Failand 43 B4
Failford 193 C4
Failsworth 138 C1
Fain 262 C3
Fairbourne 90 A4
Fairburn 140 A2
Fairfield
　Derbys 129 B5
　Stockton 168 D2
　Worcs 80 C3
　Worcs 96 C3
Fairford 64 C2
Fair Green 118 D3
Fairhaven 136 A2
Fair Hill 164 B3
Fairlie 204 C2
Fairlight 23 A6
Fairlight Cove 23 A6
Fairmile 13 B5
Fairmilehead 209 D5
Fairoak 111 B6
Fair Oak 32 D3
Fair Oak Green 47 C4
Fairseat 50 C3
Fairstead
　Essex 70 B1
　Norf 118 D3
Fairwarp 36 D2
Fairy Cottage 152 C4
Fairy Cross 25 C5
Fakenham 119 C6
Fakenham Magna . . 103 D5
Fala 210 D1
Fala Dam 210 D1
Falahill 196 A2
Falcon 79 D4
Faldingworth 133 A5
Falfield 62 D2
Falkenham 88 D3
Falkirk 208 C1
Falkland 220 D2
Falla 187 B6
Fallgate 130 C3
Fallin 207 A6
Fallowfield 138 D1
Fallsidehill 197 B5
Falmer 21 B6
Falmouth 4 D3
Falsgrave 160 C4
Falstone 177 A5
Fanagmore 276 D2
Fangdale Beck 159 B4
Fangfoss 149 B6
Fankerton 207 B5
Fanmore 224 B3
Fannich Lodge 262 D4
Fans 197 B5
Far Bank 140 B4
Far Bletchley 83 D5
Farcet 100 B4
Far Cotton 83 B4
Farden 94 D3
Fareham 19 A4
Farewell 113 D4
Far Forest 95 D5
Farforth 134 B3
Faringdon 64 D3
Farington 136 A4
Farlam 176 D3
Farlary 273 D5
Far Laund 114 A1
Farleigh
　N Som 42 C3
　Sur 49 C6
Farleigh
　Hungerford 44 D2
Farleigh Wallop 33 A5
Farlesthorpe 135 B4
Farleton
　Cumb 154 C4
　Lancs 145 A5

Farley
　Shrops 94 A1
　Staffs 113 A4
　Wilts 31 C6
Farley Green 34 B3
Farley Hill
　Luton 67 A5
　Wokingham 47 C5
Farleys End 62 B3
Farlington 149 A5
Farlow 95 C4
Farmborough 43 C5
Farmcote
　Glos 63 A6
　Shrops 95 B5
Farmington 64 B2
Farmoor 65 C5
Farmtown 267 D6
Farnborough
　Hants 34 A1
　London 50 C1
　Warks 82 C1
　W Berks 46 A2
Farnborough
　Green 34 A1
Farncombe 34 B2
Farndish 83 A6
Farndon
　Ches W 127 D4
　Notts 132 D2
Farnell 233 C4
Farnham
　Dorset 30 D3
　Essex 69 A4
　N Yorks 148 A3
　Suff 89 A4
　Sur 34 B1
Farnham Common . . 48 A2
Farnham Green 69 A4
Farnham Royal 48 A2
Farnhill 147 C4
Farningham 50 C2
Farnley
　N Yorks 147 C6
　W Yorks 147 D6
Farnley Tyas 139 B4
Farnsfield 131 D6
Farnworth
　Gtr Man 137 C6
　Halton 127 A5
Farr
　Highld 241 B6
　Highld 252 C2
　Highld 278 B3
Farr House 252 C2
Farringdon 13 B5
Farrington Gurney . . 43 D5
Far Sawrey 154 B2
Farsley 147 D6
Farthinghoe 82 D2
Farthingloe 39 A4
Farthingstone 82 B3
Fartown 139 B4
Farway 14 B1
Fasag 249 A5
Fascadale 235 C4
Faslane Port 215 D5
Fasnacloich 227 B5
Fasnakyle Ho 251 D5
Fassfern 237 B4
Fatfield 179 D5
Fattahead 268 D1
Faugh 176 D3
Fauldhouse 208 D2
Faulkbourne 70 B1
Faulkland 43 D6
Fauls 111 B4
Faversham 52 C2
Favillar 254 C3
Fawdington 158 D3
Fawfieldhead 129 C5
Fawkham Green 50 C2
Fawler 65 B4
Fawley
　Bucks 47 A5
　Hants 18 A3
　W Berks 46 A1
Fawley Chapel 62 A1
Faxfleet 141 A6
Faygate 35 C5
Fazakerley 136 D2
Fazeley 97 A5
Fearby 157 C5
Fearn 265 C4
Fearnan 229 D6
Fearnbeg 249 A4
Fearnhead 137 D5
Fearn Lodge 264 B2
Fearnmore 261 D4
Fearn Station 265 C4

Featherstone
　Staffs 96 A2
　W Yorks 140 A2
Featherwood 187 C7
Feckenham 80 A3
Feering 70 A2
Feetham 156 B3
Feizor 146 A1
Felbridge 35 C6
Felbrigg 120 B4
Felcourt 36 B1
Felden 67 C5
Felin-Crai 59 C5
Felindre
　Carms 58 B3
　Carms 58 C2
　Carms 59 C4
　Carms 73 C6
　Ceredig 75 C4
　Powys 93 C5
　Swansea 57 B6
Felindre Farchog . . . 72 C4
Felinfach
　Ceredig 75 C4
　Powys 77 D4
Felinfoel 57 B5
Felingwm isaf 58 C2
Felingwm uchaf 58 C2
Felinwynt 73 A5
Felixkirk 158 C3
Felixstowe 88 D3
Felixstowe Ferry 88 D4
Felkington 198 B3
Felkirk 140 B1
Felling 179 C4
Fell Side 163 A6
Felmersham 84 B1
Felmingham 120 C4
Felpham 20 C2
Felsham 87 B5
Felsted 69 A6
Feltham 48 B4
Felthorpe 120 D3
Felton
　Hereford 78 C3
　Northumb 189 C4
　N Som 43 C4
Felton Butler 110 D2
Feltwell 102 B3
Fenay Bridge 139 B4
Fence 146 D2
Fence Houses 179 D5
Fen Ditton 85 A6
Fen Drayton 85 A5
Fen End 97 D5
Fengate
　Norf 120 C3
　Pboro 100 B4
Fenham 199 B4
Fenhouses 117 A5
Feniscliffe 137 A5
Feniscowles 137 A5
Feniton 13 B6
Fenlake 84 C2
Fenny Bentley 130 D1
Fenny Bridges 13 B6
Fenny Compton 81 B7
Fenny Drayton 97 B6
Fenny Stratford 83 D5
Fenrother 189 D4
Fen Side 134 D3
Fenstanton 85 A5
Fenton
　Cambs 101 D5
　Lincs 132 B3
　Lincs 132 D3
　Stoke 112 A6
Fenton Barns 210 B2
Fenton Town 198 C3
Fenwick
　E Ayrs 205 D4
　Northumb 178 B2
　Northumb 199 B4
　S Yorks 140 B3
Feochaig 190 D3
Feock 4 D3
Feolin Ferry 201 B4
Ferindonald 247 D5
Feriniquarrie 258 C1
Ferlochan 226 B4
Fern 232 B2
Ferndale 41 B5
Ferndown 17 A4
Ferness 253 B5
Ferney Green 154 B3
Fernham 64 D3
Fernhill Heath 79 B6
Fernhurst 34 D1
Fernie 220 C3
Ferniegair 194 A2

Fernilea 246 A2
Fernilee 129 B5
Ferrensby 148 A2
Ferring 20 B3
Ferrybridge 140 A2
Ferryden 233 C5
Ferryhill
　Aberdeen 245 B6
　Durham 167 B5
Ferry Hill 101 C5
Ferryhill Station 167 B6
Ferry Point 264 B3
Ferryside 56 A3
Fersfield 103 C6
Fersit 228 A2
Ferwig 73 B4
Feshiebridge 241 B6
Fetcham 35 A4
Fetterangus 269 D4
Fettercairn 233 A4
Fettes 252 A1
Fewcott 65 A6
Fewston 147 B5
Ffairfach 58 C3
Ffair-Rhos 75 B6
Ffaldybrenin 58 A3
Ffarmers 58 A3
Ffawyddog 60 B4
Fforest 57 B5
Fforest-fâch 57 C6
Ffostrasol 73 B6
Ffos-y-ffin 74 B3
Ffridd-Uchaf 107 A5
Ffrith 126 D2
Ffrwd 107 A4
Ffynnon ddrain 73 D7
Ffynnongroyw 125 A6
Ffynnon-oer 75 C4
Fidden 224 D2
Fiddes 245 D5
Fiddington
　Glos 80 D2
　Som 28 A2
Fiddleford 30 D2
Fiddlers Hamlet 69 C4
Field 112 B4
Field Broughton 154 C2
Field Dalling 120 B2
Field Head 98 A1
Fifehead Magdalen . 30 C1
Fifehead Neville 30 D1
Fifield
　Oxon 64 B3
　Wilts 45 D5
　Windsor 48 B2
Fifield Bavant 31 C4
Figheldean 31 A5
Filands 44 A3
Filby 121 D6
Filey 161 C5
Filgrave 83 C5
Filkins 64 C3
Filleigh
　Devon 26 C1
　Devon 26 D2
Fillingham 133 A4
Fillongley 97 C5
Filton 43 B5
Fimber 150 A1
Finavon 232 C2
Finchairn 214 B2
Fincham 102 A2
Finchampstead 47 C5
Finchdean 33 D6
Finchingfield 86 D2
Finchley 68 D2
Findern 113 B7
Findhorn 265 D6
Findhorn Bridge 253 D4
Findochty 267 C5
Findo Gask 219 B5
Findon
　Aberds 245 C6
　W Sus 21 B4
Findon Mains 264 D2
Findrack House 244 B3
Finedon 99 D6
Fingal Street 88 A3
Fingask 256 D2
Fingerpost 95 D5
Fingest 66 D2
Finghall 157 C5
Fingland
　Cumb 175 C5
　Dumfries 183 A5
Finglesham 53 D5
Fingringhoe 71 A4
Finlarig 217 A5
Finmere 82 D3
Finnart 229 C4

Finningham 87 A6
Finningley 141 D4
Finnygaud 267 D6
Finsbury 49 A6
Finstall 80 A2
Finsthwaite 154 C2
Finstock 65 B4
Finstown 282 F4
Fintry
　Aberds 268 D2
　Dundee 220 A4
　Stirling 207 B4
Finzean 244 C3
Fionnphort 224 D2
Fionnsbhagh 287 F5
Firbeck 131 A5
Firby
　N Yorks 149 A6
　N Yorks 157 C6
Firgrove 138 B2
Firsby 135 C4
Firsdown 31 B6
First Coast 261 A6
Fir Tree 166 B4
Firby
Fishbourne
　IoW 19 B4
　W Sus 20 B1
Fishburn 167 B6
Fishcross 208 A2
Fisherford 256 C1
Fisher Place 163 C6
Fisher's Pond 32 C5
Fisherstreet 34 C2
Fisherton
　Highld 252 A3
　S Ayrs 192 D2
Fishguard
　= Abergwaun 72 C2
Fishlake 141 B4
Fishleigh Barton 25 C6
Fishponds 43 B5
Fishpool 62 A2
Fishtoft 117 A6
Fishtoft Drove 117 A6
Fishtown of Usan . . . 233 C5
Fishwick 198 A3
Fiskavaig 246 A2
Fiskerton
　Lincs 133 B5
　Notts 132 D2
Fitling 151 D5
Fittleton 31 A5
Fittleworth 20 A3
Fitton End 118 D1
Fitz 110 D3
Fitzhead 27 C6
Fitzwilliam 140 B2
Fiunary 225 B5
Five Acres 62 B1
Five Ashes 36 D3
Fivecrosses 127 B5
Fivehead 28 C3
Five Oak Green 36 B4
Five Oaks
　Jersey 6
　W Sus 34 D3
Five Roads 57 B4
Flack's Green 70 B1
Flackwell Heath 48 A1
Fladbury 80 C2
Fladdabister 285 K6
Flagg 129 C6
Flamborough 161 D6
Flamstead 67 B5
Flamstead End 68 C3
Flansham 20 B2
Flanshaw 139 A6
Flasby 146 B3
Flash 129 C5
Flashader 258 C3
Flask Inn 160 A3
Flaunden 67 C5
Flawborough 115 A5
Flawith 148 A3
Flax Bourton 43 C4
Flaxby 148 B2
Flaxholme 114 A1
Flaxley 62 B2
Flaxpool 27 B6
Flaxton 149 A5
Fleckney 98 B3
Flecknoe 82 A2
Fledborough 132 B3
Fleet
　Hants 19 A6
　Hants 47 D6
　Lincs 117 C6
Fleetham 189 A4
Fleet Hargate 117 C6
Fleetlands 19 A4

Fleetville....67 C6
Fleetwood....144 C3
Flemingston....41 D5
Flemington....205 C6
Flempton....87 A4
Fleoideabhagh....287 F5
Fletchertown....175 D5
Fletching....36 D2
Flexbury....10 A3
Flexford....34 B2
Flimby....162 A3
Flimwell....37 C5
Flint = Y Fflint....126 B2
Flintham....115 A5
Flint Mountain....126 B2
Flinton....151 D5
Flintsham....77 B7
Flitcham....119 C4
Flitton....84 D2
Flitwick....84 D2
Flixborough....141 B6
Flixborough Stather....141 B6
Flixton
  Gtr Man....137 D6
  N Yorks....160 D4
  Suff....104 C4
Flockton....139 B5
Flodaigh....286 A4
Flodden....198 C3
Flodigarry....259 A4
Flood's Ferry....101 B5
Flookburgh....154 D2
Florden....104 B2
Flore....82 A3
Flotterton....188 C2
Flowton....88 C1
Flush House....139 C4
Flushing
  Aberds....257 B5
  Corn....4 D3
Flyford Flavell....80 B2
Foals Green....104 D3
Fobbing....51 A4
Fochabers....266 D4
Fochriw....60 C3
Fockerby....141 B6
Fodderletter....254 D2
Fodderty....251 A7
Foel....109 D4
Foel-gastell....57 A5
Foffarty....232 D2
Foggathorpe....149 D6
Fogo....197 B6
Fogorig....198 B1
Foindle....276 D2
Folda....231 B5
Fole....112 B4
Foleshill....97 C6
Folke....29 D6
Folkestone....39 B4
Folkingham....116 B3
Folkington....22 B3
Folksworth....100 C3
Folkton....161 D4
Folla Rule....256 C2
Follifoot....148 B2
Folly Gate....11 B6
Fonthill Bishop....30 B3
Fonthill Gifford....30 B3
Fontmell Magna....30 D2
Fontwell....20 B2
Foolow....130 B1
Foots Cray....50 B1
Forbestown....243 A6
Force Mills....154 B2
Forcett....167 D4
Ford
  Argyll....214 B1
  Bucks....66 C2
  Devon....25 C5
  Glos....64 A1
  Northumb....198 C3
  Shrops....110 D3
  Staffs....129 D5
  Wilts....44 B2
  W Sus....20 B2
Fordcombe....36 B3
Fordell....209 B4
Forden....93 A6
Ford End....69 B6
Forder Green....8 A1
Fordham
  Cambs....102 D2
  Essex....70 A3
  Norf....102 B2
Fordhouses....96 A2
Fordingbridge....31 D5
Fordon....160 D4
Fordoun....233 A5

Ford's Green....87 A6
Fordstreet....70 A3
Ford Street....27 D6
Fordwells....64 B4
Fordwich....52 D3
Fordyce....267 C6
Forebridge....112 C3
Forest....165 B6
Forest Becks....146 B1
Forestburn Gate....188 D3
Foresterseat....266 D2
Forest Gate....49 A7
Forest Green....35 B4
Forest Hall....154 A4
Forest Head....176 D3
Forest Hill....65 C6
Forest Lane Head....148 B2
Forest Lodge
  Argyll....228 D1
  Highld....242 A3
  Perth....230 A3
Forest Mill....208 A2
Forest Row....36 C2
Forestside....33 D6
Forest Town....131 C5
Forfar....232 C2
Forgandenny....219 C5
Forge....91 C5
Forge Side....60 C4
Forgewood....194 A2
Forgie....267 D4
Forglen House....268 D1
Formby....136 C2
Forncett End....104 B2
Forncett St Mary....104 B2
Forncett St Peter....104 B2
Forneth....231 D4
Fornham All Saints....87 A4
Fornham St Martin....87 A4
Forres....253 A6
Forrestfield....207 D6
Forrest Lodge....182 D3
Forsbrook....112 A3
Forse....275 A6
Forse House....275 A6
Forsinain....279 D5
Forsinard....279 D4
Forsinard Station....279 D4
Forston....15 B6
Fort Augustus....240 B1
Forteviot....219 C5
Fort George
  Guern....6
  Highld....252 A3
Forth....194 A4
Forthampton....79 D6
Forth Road Bridge....208 C4
Fortingall....229 D6
Forton
  Hants....32 A3
  Lancs....145 B4
  Shrops....110 D3
  Som....14 A3
  Staffs....111 C6
Forton Heath....110 D3
Fortrie....256 B1
Fortrose....252 A3
Fortuneswell....15 D6
Fort William....237 B5
Forty Green....67 D4
Forty Hill....68 D3
Forward Green....88 B1
Fosbury....45 D7
Fosdyke....117 B6
Foss....230 C1
Foss Cross....63 C6
Fossebridge....64 B1
Fosterhouses....141 B4
Foster Street....69 C4
Foston
  Derbys....113 B5
  Lincs....115 A4
  N Yorks....149 A5
Foston on the Wolds....151 B4
Fotherby....143 D5
Fotheringhay....100 B2
Foubister....283 G6
Foulby....140 B1
Foulden
  Borders....198 A3
  Norf....102 B3
Foulis Castle....264 D1
Foul Mile....22 A4
Foulridge....146 C2
Foulsham....120 C2
Fountainhall....196 B3
Four Ashes
  Staffs....95 C6
  Suff....103 D6

Four Crosses
  Powys....93 A4
  Powys....110 D1
  Wrex....126 D2
Four Elms....36 B2
Four Forks....28 B2
Four Gotes....118 D1
Fourlane Ends....130 D3
Four Lane Ends....127 C5
Four Lanes....3 B4
Four Marks....33 B5
Four Mile Bridge....122 C2
Four Oaks
  E Sus....37 D6
  W Mid....96 B4
  W Mid....97 C5
Fourpenny....265 A4
Four Roads
  Carms....57 B4
  IoM....152 E2
Fourstones....177 C6
Four Throws....37 D5
Fovant....31 C4
Foveran....257 D4
Fowey....5 B6
Fowley Common....137 D5
Fowlis....220 A3
Fowlis Wester....218 B4
Fowlmere....85 C6
Fownhope....78 D3
Foxbar....205 B4
Foxcombe Hill....65 C5
Fox Corner....34 A2
Foxdale....152 D2
Foxearth....87 C4
Foxfield....153 B3
Foxham....44 B3
Foxhole
  Corn....5 B4
  Swansea....57 C6
Foxholes....160 D4
Foxhunt Green....22 A3
Fox Lane....34 A1
Foxley
  Norf....120 C2
  Wilts....44 A2
Fox Street....71 A4
Foxt....112 A4
Foxton
  Cambs....85 C6
  Durham....167 C6
  Leics....99 B4
Foxup....156 D2
Foxwist Green....127 C6
Foxwood....95 D4
Foy....62 A1
Foyers....251 D6
Fraddam....2 B3
Fraddon....4 B4
Fradley....113 D5
Fradswell....112 B3
Fraisthorpe....151 A4
Framfield....36 D2
Framingham Earl....104 A3
Framingham Pigot....104 A3
Framlingham....88 A3
Frampton
  Dorset....15 B6
  Lincs....117 B6
Frampton Cotterell....43 A5
Frampton Mansell....63 C5
Frampton on Severn....62 C3
Frampton West End....117 A5
Framsden....88 B2
Framwellgate Moor....167 A5
Franche....95 D5
Frankby....126 A2
Frankley....96 C2
Frank's Bridge....77 B5
Frankton....98 D1
Frant....36 C3
Fraserburgh....269 C4
Frating Green....71 A4
Fratton....19 B5
Freathy....6 B3
Freckenham....102 D2
Freckleton....136 A3
Freeby....115 C6
Freehay....112 A4
Freeland....65 B5
Freester....285 H6
Freethorpe....105 A5
Freiston....117 A6
Fremington
  Devon....25 B6
  N Yorks....156 B4
Frenchay....43 B5

Frenchbeer....12 C1
Frenich....216 D4
Frensham....34 B1
Fresgoe....279 B5
Freshfield....136 C1
Freshford....44 C1
Freshwater....18 C2
Freshwater Bay....18 C2
Freshwater East....55 E6
Fressingfield....104 D3
Freston....88 D2
Freswick....281 B5
Fretherne....62 C3
Frettenham....120 D4
Freuchie....220 D2
Freuchies....231 B6
Freystrop....55 C5
Friar's Gate....36 C2
Friarton....219 B6
Friday Bridge....101 A6
Friday Street....22 B4
Fridaythorpe....150 B1
Friern Barnet....68 D2
Friesland....223 B4
Friesthorpe....133 A5
Frieston....116 A2
Frieth....66 D2
Frilford....65 D5
Frilsham....46 B3
Frimley....34 A1
Frimley Green....34 A1
Frindsbury....51 B4
Fring....119 B4
Fringford....65 A7
Frinsted....37 A6
Frinton-on-Sea....71 A6
Friockheim....232 D3
Friog....90 A4
Frisby on the Wreake....115 D4
Friskney....135 D4
Friskney Eaudike....135 D4
Friskney Tofts....135 D4
Friston
  E Sus....22 C3
  Suff....89 A5
Fritchley....130 D3
Fritham....31 D6
Frith Bank....117 A6
Frith Common....79 A4
Frithelstock....25 D5
Frithelstock Stone....25 D5
Frithville....134 D3
Frittenden....37 B6
Frittiscombe....8 C2
Fritton
  Norf....104 B3
  Norf....105 A5
Fritwell....65 A6
Frizinghall....147 D5
Frizington....162 C3
Frocester....62 C3
Frodesley....94 A3
Frodingham....141 B6
Frodsham....127 B5
Frogden....187 A6
Froggatt....130 B2
Froghall....112 A4
Frogmore
  Devon....7 C6
  Hants....34 A1
Frognall....117 D4
Frogshail....121 B4
Frolesworth....98 B2
Frome....30 A1
Frome St Quintin....15 A5
Fromes Hill....79 C4
Fron
  Denb....125 C5
  Gwyn....106 C3
  Gwyn....107 A5
  Powys....77 A4
  Powys....93 A6
  Powys....93 B5
Froncysyllte....110 A1
Frongoch....108 B4
Frostenden....105 C5
Frosterley....166 B3
Frotoft....282 E5
Froxfield....45 C6
Froxfield Green....33 C6
Froyle....33 A6
Fryerning....69 C6
Fryton....159 D5
Fulbeck....133 D4
Fulbourn....85 B7
Fulbrook....64 B3
Fulford
  Som....28 C2
  N Yorks....156 B4
  Staffs....112 B3

Fulford continued
  York....149 C5
Fulham....49 B5
Fulking....21 A5
Fullarton
  Glasgow....205 B6
  N Ayrs....192 B3
Fuller's Moor....127 D4
Fuller Street....70 B1
Fullerton....32 B2
Fulletby....134 B2
Full Sutton....149 B6
Fullwood....205 C4
Fulmer....48 A2
Fulmodestone....120 B1
Fulnetby....133 B5
Fulstow....143 D5
Fulwell....179 D5
Fulwood
  Lancs....145 D5
  S Yorks....130 A3
Fundenhall....104 B2
Fundenhall Street....104 B2
Funtington....19 A6
Funtley....19 A4
Funtullich....218 B2
Funzie....284 D8
Furley....14 A2
Furnace
  Argyll....214 B3
  Carms....57 B5
Furnace End....97 B5
Furneaux Pelham....68 A4
Furness Vale....129 A5
Furzehill....26 A2
Furze Platt....48 A1
Fyfett....28 D2
Fyfield
  Essex....69 C5
  Glos....64 C3
  Hants....32 A1
  Oxon....65 D5
  Wilts....45 C5
Fylingthorpe....160 A3
Fyvie....256 C2

G

Gabhsann bho Dheas....288 B5
Gabhsann bho Thuath....288 B5
Gablon....264 A3
Gabroc Hill....205 C4
Gaddesby....115 D4
Gadebridge....67 C5
Gaer....60 A3
Gaerllwyd....61 D6
Gaerwen....123 C4
Gagingwell....65 A5
Gaick Lodge....241 D5
Gailey....112 D3
Gainford....167 D4
Gainsborough
  Lincs....141 D6
  Suff....88 C2
Gainsford End....86 D3
Gairloch....261 C5
Gairlochy....239 D5
Gairney Bank....208 A4
Gairnshiel Lodge....243 B5
Gaisgill....155 A5
Gaitsgill....164 A1
Galashiels....196 C3
Galgate....145 B4
Galhampton....29 C6
Gallaberry....184 D2
Gallachoille....213 D5
Gallanach
  Argyll....223 A5
  Argyll....226 D3
Gallantry Bank....127 D5
Gallatown....209 A5
Galley Common....97 B6
Galleyend....69 C7
Galley Hill....85 A5
Galleywood....69 C7
Gallin....229 D4
Gallowfauld....232 D2
Gallows Green....113 A4
Galltair....249 D5
Galmisdale....234 B3
Galmpton
  Devon....7 C5
  Torbay....8 B2
Galphay....157 D6
Galston....193 B5
Galtrigill....258 C1
Gamblesby....165 B4

Gamesley....138 D3
Gamlingay....84 B4
Gammersgill....157 C4
Gamston....132 B2
Ganarew....62 B1
Ganavan....226 C3
Gang....6 A2
Ganllwyd....108 C2
Gannochy
  Angus....232 A3
  Perth....219 B6
Gansclet....281 D5
Ganstead....151 D4
Ganthorpe....159 D5
Ganton....160 D3
Garbat....263 D6
Garbhallt....214 C3
Garboldisham....103 C6
Garden City....126 C3
Gardenstown....268 C2
Garden Village
  Wrex....126 D3
  W Yorks....148 D3
Garderhouse....285 J5
Gardham....150 C2
Gardin....284 G6
Gare Hill....30 A1
Garelochhead....215 C5
Garford....65 D5
Garforth....148 D3
Gargrave....146 B3
Gargunnock....207 A5
Garlic Street....104 C3
Garlieston....171 C6
Garlinge Green....52 D3
Garlogie....245 B4
Garmond....268 D3
Garmony....225 B5
Garmouth....266 C4
Garnant....58 D3
Garndiffaith....61 C4
Garndolbenmaen....107 B4
Garnedd....124 D2
Garnett Bridge....154 B4
Garnfadryn....106 C2
Garnkirk....207 D4
Garnlydan....60 B3
Garnswllt....57 B6
Garn-yr-erw....60 B4
Garrabost....288 D6
Garraron....213 B6
Garras....3 C5
Garreg....107 B6
Garrick....218 C3
Garrigill....165 A5
Garriston....157 B5
Garroch....182 D3
Garrogie Lodge....240 A3
Garros....259 B4
Garrow....230 D2
Garryhorn....182 C3
Garsdale....155 C6
Garsdale Head....155 B6
Garsdon....44 A3
Garshall Green....112 B3
Garsington....65 C6
Garstang....145 C4
Garston....127 A4
Garswood....137 D4
Gartcosh....207 D4
Garth
  Bridgend....40 B3
  Gwyn....123 C5
  Powys....76 C3
  Shetland....285 H4
  Wrex....110 A1
Garthamlock....205 B6
Garthbrengy....76 D4
Garthdee....245 B6
Gartheli....75 C4
Garthmyl....93 B5
Garthorpe
  Leics....115 C6
  N Lincs....141 B6
Garth Row....154 B4
Gartly....255 C6
Gartmore....206 A3
Gartnagrenach....202 C2
Gartness
  N Lanark....207 D5
  Stirling....206 B3
Gartocharn....206 B2
Garton....151 D5
Garton-on-the-Wolds....150 B2
Gartsherrie....207 D5
Gartymore....274 C4
Garvald....210 C2

Garvamore 240 C3
Garvard 212 C1
Garvault Hotel 273 A5
Garve 263 D5
Garvestone 103 A6
Garvock
  Aberds 233 A5
  Invclyd 204 A2
Garway 61 A6
Garway Hill 61 A6
Gaskan 236 B1
Gastard 44 C2
Gasthorpe 103 C5
Gatcombe 18 C3
Gateacre 127 A4
Gatebeck 154 C4
Gate Burton 132 A3
Gateford 131 A5
Gateforth 140 A3
Gatehead 192 B3
Gate Helmsley 149 B5
Gatehouse 177 A5
Gatehouse of Fleet . .172 C4
Gatelawbridge 183 C7
Gateley 119 C6
Gatenby 158 C2
Gateshead 179 C4
Gatesheath 127 C4
Gateside
  Aberds 244 A3
  Angus 232 D2
  E Renf 205 C4
  Fife 219 D6
  N Ayrs 204 C3
Gathurst 136 C4
Gatley 128 A3
Gattonside 197 C4
Gatwick Airport 35 B5
Gaufron 76 A3
Gaulby 98 A3
Gauldry 220 B3
Gaunt's Common . . .17 A4
Gautby 134 B1
Gavinton 197 A6
Gawber 139 C6
Gawcott 82 D3
Gawsworth 128 C3
Gawthorpe 139 A5
Gawthrop 155 C5
Gawthwaite 153 B3
Gaydon 81 B6
Gayfield 282 B5
Gayhurst 83 C5
Gayle 156 C2
Gayles 157 A5
Gay Street 34 D3
Gayton
  Mers 126 A2
  Norf 119 D4
  Northants 83 B4
  Staffs 112 C3
Gayton le Marsh 135 A4
Gayton le Wold 134 A2
Gayton Thorpe 119 D4
Gaywood 118 C3
Gazeley 86 A3
Geanies House 265 C4
Gearraidh
  Bhailteas 286 D3
Gearraidh Bhaird . .288 E4
Gearraidh na h-
  Aibhne 288 D3
Gearraidh na
  Monadh 286 E3
Geary 258 B2
Geddes House 253 A4
Gedding 87 B5
Geddington 99 C5
Gedintailor 247 A4
Gedling 115 A4
Gedney 117 C7
Gedney Broadgate .117 C7
Gedney Drove End .118 C1
Gedney Dyke 117 C7
Gedney Hill 117 D6
Gee Cross 138 D2
Geilston 206 C1
Geirinis 286 B3
Geise 280 B3
Geisiadar 288 D2
Geldeston 105 B4
Gell 124 C2
Gelli
  Pembs. 55 C6
  Rhondda 41 B4
Gellideg 60 C2
Gellifor 125 C6
Gelligaer 41 B6

Gellilydan 107 C6
Gellinudd 40 A2
Gellyburn 219 A5
Gellywen 73 D5
Gelston
  Dumfries 173 C5
  Lincs 116 A2
Gembling 151 B4
Gentleshaw 113 D4
Geocrab 288 H2
Georgefield 185 C5
George Green 48 A3
Georgeham 25 B5
George Nympton . . .26 C2
Georgetown 60 C3
Gerlan 123 D6
Germansweek 11 B5
Germoe 2 C3
Gerrans 4 D3
Gerrards Cross 48 A3
Gestingthorpe 87 D4
Geuffordd 109 D7
Gibbet Hill 98 C2
Gibbshill 173 A5
Gib Hill 127 B6
Gidea Park 50 A2
Gidleigh 12 C1
Giffnock 205 C5
Gifford 210 D2
Giffordland 204 D2
Giffordtown 220 C2
Giggleswick 146 A2
Gilberdyke 141 A6
Gilchriston 210 D1
Gilcrux 163 A4
Gildersome 139 A5
Gildingwells 131 A5
Gileston 41 E5
Gilfach 41 B6
Gilfach Goch 41 C4
Gilfachrheda 73 A7
Gillamoor 159 C5
Gillar's Green 136 D3
Gillen 258 C2
Gilling East 159 D5
Gillingham
  Dorset 30 C2
  Medway 51 C4
  Norf 105 B5
Gilling West 157 A5
Gillock 280 C4
Gillow Heath 128 D3
Gills 281 A5
Gill's Green 37 C5
Gilmanscleuch 196 D2
Gilmerton
  Edin. 209 D5
  Perth. 218 B3
Gilmonby 166 D2
Gilmorton 98 C2
Gilmourton 205 D6
Gilsland 176 C4
Gilsland Spa 176 C4
Gilston
  Borders 196 A3
  Herts. 68 B4
Gilwern 60 B4
Gimingham 121 B4
Giosla 288 E2
Gipping 87 A6
Gipsey Bridge 117 A3
Girdle Toll 204 D3
Girlsta 285 H6
Girsby 158 A2
Girtford 84 B3
Girthon 172 C4
Girton
  Cambs. 85 A6
  Notts. 132 C3
Girvan 180 B3
Gisburn 146 C2
Gisleham 105 C6
Gislingham 104 D1
Gissing 104 C2
Gittisham 13 B6
Gladestry 77 B6
Gladsmuir 210 C1
Glais 40 A2
Glaisdale 159 A6
Glame 248 B2
Glamis 232 D1
Glan Adda 123 C5
Glanaman 57 A6
Glan Conwy 124 B3
Glandford 120 A2
Glan-Duar 58 A2
Glandwr 73 D4
Glan-Dwyfach 107 B4
Glandy Cross 72 D4
Glandyfi 91 C5

Glan Gors 123 C4
Glangrwyney 60 B4
Glanmule 93 B5
Glanrafon 90 D4
Glanrhyd
  Gwyn. 106 C2
  Pembs. 72 B4
Glan-rhyd 107 A4
Glanton 188 B3
Glanton Pike 188 B3
Glan-traeth 122 C2
Glanvilles Wootton . .15 A6
Glan-y-don 125 B6
Glan-y-nant 92 C3
Glan-yr-afon
  Anglesey 123 B6
  Gwyn. 108 A4
  Gwyn. 109 A5
Glan-y-wern 107 C6
Glapthorn 100 B2
Glapwell 131 C4
Glas-allt Shiel 243 D5
Glasbury 77 D5
Glaschoil 253 C6
Glascoed
  Denb 125 B4
  Mon 61 C5
  Powys 109 D6
Glascorrie 243 C6
Glascote 97 A5
Glascwm 77 B5
Glasdrum 227 B5
Glasfryn 125 D4
Glasgow 205 B5
Glashvin 259 B4
Glasinfryn 123 D5
Glasnacardoch 235 A5
Glasnakille 247 C4
Glasphein 258 D1
Glaspwll 91 C5
Glassburn 251 C5
Glasserton 171 D6
Glassford 194 B2
Glasshouse Hill 62 A3
Glasshouses 147 A5
Glasslie 220 D2
Glasson
  Cumb 175 B5
  Lancs 144 B4
Glassonby 164 B3
Glasterlaw 232 C3
Glaston 99 A5
Glastonbury 29 B5
Glatton 100 C3
Glazebrook 137 D5
Glazebury 137 D5
Glazeley 95 C5
Gleadless 130 A3
Gleadsmoss 128 C3
Gleann
  Tholàstaidh 288 C6
Gleaston 153 C3
Gleiniant 92 B3
Glemsford 87 C4
Glen
  Dumfries 172 C3
  Dumfries 173 A4
Glenamachrie 226 D4
Glen Auldyn 152 B4
Glenbarr 190 B2
Glenbeg
  Highld 235 D4
  Highld 253 D6
Glen Bernisdale . . .259 D4
Glenbervie 245 D4
Glenboig 207 D5
Glenborrodale 235 D5
Glenbranter 215 C4
Glenbreck 195 D5
Glenbrein Lodge . . .240 A2
Glenbrittle House . .246 B3
Glenbuchat Lodge . .243 A6
Glenbuck 194 D2
Glenburn 205 B4
Glencalvie Lodge . .263 B6
Glencanisp Lodge . .270 B4
Glencaple 174 B2
Glencarron Lodge . .250 A2
Glencarse 219 B6
Glencassley Castle .272 D2
Glenceitlein 227 B6
Glencoe 237 D4
Glencraig 209 A4
Glencripesdale 225 A5
Glencrosh 183 D5
Glendavan House . .244 B1
Glendevon 219 D4
Glendoebeg 240 B2
Glendoe Lodge 240 B2
Glendoick 220 B2

Glendoll Lodge 231 A6
Glendoune 180 B3
Glenduckie 220 C2
Glendye Lodge 244 D3
Gleneagles Hotel . .218 C4
Gleneagles House . .218 D4
Glenegedale 200 C3
Glenelg 238 A2
Glenernie 253 B6
Glenfarg 219 C6
Glenfarquhar
  Lodge 245 D4
Glenferness House .253 B5
Glenfeshie Lodge . .241 C6
Glenfield 98 A2
Glenfinnan 238 D3
Glenfoot 219 C6
Glenfyne Lodge 215 A5
Glengap 173 C4
Glengarnock 204 C3
Glengorm Castle . . .224 A3
Glengrasco 259 D4
Glenhead Farm 231 B6
Glen Ho 196 C1
Glenhoul 182 D4
Glenhurich 236 C2
Glenkerry 185 A5
Glenkiln 173 A6
Glenkindie 244 A1
Glenlatterach 266 D2
Glenlee 182 D4
Glenlichorn 218 C2
Glenlivet 254 D2
Glenlochsie 231 A4
Glenloig 191 B5
Glenluce 171 B4
Glenmallan 215 C5
Glenmarksie 251 A5
Glenmassan 215 D4
Glenmavis 207 D5
Glenmaye 152 D2
Glenmidge 183 D6
Glen Mona 152 C4
Glenmore
  Argyll 213 A6
  Highld 259 D4
Glenmore Lodge . . .242 B2
Glenmoy 232 B2
Glen Nevis House . .237 B5
Glenogil 232 B2
Glen Parva 98 B2
Glenprosen Lodge . .231 B6
Glenprosen Village .232 B1
Glenquiech 232 B2
Glenreasdell Mains .202 C3
Glenree 191 C5
Glenridding 164 D1
Glenrossal 272 D2
Glenrothes 220 D2
Glensanda 226 B3
Glensaugh 233 A4
Glenshero Lodge . . .240 C3
Glen Sluain 214 C3
Glenstockadale 170 A2
Glenstriven 203 A5
Glentaggart 194 D3
Glen Tanar House . .244 C1
Glentham 142 D2
Glentirranmuir 207 A4
Glenton 256 D1
Glentress 196 C1
Glentromie Lodge . .241 C5
Glen Trool Lodge . .181 C6
Glentrool Village . . .181 D5
Glentruan 152 A4
Glentruim House . . .241 C4
Glentworth 133 A4
Glenuig 235 C5
Glenurquhart 264 D3
Glen Village 208 C1
Glen Vine 152 D3
Glespin 194 D3
Gletness 285 H6
Glewstone 62 A1
Glinton 100 A3
Glooston 99 B4
Glororum 199 C5
Glossop 138 D3
Gloster Hill 189 C5
Gloucester 63 B4
Gloup 284 C7
Glusburn 147 C4
Glutt Lodge 274 A3
Glutton Bridge 129 C5
Glympton 65 A5
Glynarthen 73 B6
Glynbrochan 92 C3
Glyn-Ceiriog 109 B7
Glyncoch 41 B5
Glyncorrwg 40 B3

Glyn-cywarch 107 C6
Glynde 22 B2
Glyndebourne 22 A2
Glyndyfrdwy 109 A6
Glyn Ebwy
  =Ebbw Vale 60 C3
Glynedd
  =Glyn-neath 59 E5
Glyn-neath
  =Glynedd 59 E5
Glynogwr 41 C4
Glyntaff 41 C5
Glyntawe 59 D5
Gnosall 112 C2
Gnosall Heath 112 C2
Goadby 99 B4
Goadby Marwood . .115 C5
Goatacre 44 B4
Goathill 29 C6
Goathland 160 A2
Goathurst 28 B2
Goat Lees 38 A2
Gobernuisgach
  Lodge 277 D5
Gobhaig 287 D5
Gobowen 110 B2
Godalming 34 B2
Godley 138 D2
Godmanchester 100 D4
Godmanstone 15 B6
Godmersham 52 D2
Godney 29 A4
Godolphin Cross . . . 3 B4
Godre'r-graig 59 E4
Godshill
  Hants 31 D5
  IoW. 18 C4
Godstone 35 A6
Godwinscroft 17 B5
Goetre 61 C5
Goferydd 122 B2
Goff's Oak 68 C3
Gogar 209 C4
Goginan 91 D4
Golan 107 B5
Golant 5 B6
Golberdon 10 D4
Golborne 137 D5
Golcar 139 B4
Goldcliff 42 A2
Golden Cross 22 A3
Golden Green 36 B4
Golden Grove 57 A5
Goldenhill 128 D3
Golden Hill 17 B6
Golden Pot 33 A6
Golden Valley 63 A5
Golders Green 49 A5
Goldhanger 70 C3
Gold Hill 102 B1
Golding 94 A3
Goldington 84 B2
Goldsborough
  N Yorks 148 B2
  N Yorks 169 D6
Goldsithney 2 B3
Goldsworthy 25 C4
Goldthorpe 140 C2
Gollanfield 253 A4
Golspie 274 D2
Golval 279 B4
Gomeldon 31 B5
Gomersal 139 A5
Gomshall 34 B3
Gonalston 115 A4
Gonfirth 285 G5
Good Easter 69 B6
Gooderstone 102 A3
Goodleigh 25 B7
Goodmanham 150 C1
Goodnestone
  Kent 52 C2
  Kent 53 D4
Goodrich 62 B1
Goodrington 8 B2
Goodshaw 137 A7
Goodwick =Wdig . . .72 C2
Goodworth Clatford . .32 A2
Goole 141 A5
Goonbell 4 C2
Goonhavern 4 B2
Goose Eye 147 C4
Goose Green
  Gtr Man 137 C4
  Norf 104 C2
  W Sus 21 A4
Gooseham 24 D3
Goosey 65 D4
Goosnargh 145 D5
Goostrey 128 B2

Gorcott Hill 80 A3
Gord 285 L6
Gordon 197 B5
Gordonbush 274 D2
Gordonsburgh 267 C5
Gordonstoun 266 C2
Gordonstown
  Aberds 256 C2
  Aberds 267 D7
Gore 53 D5
Gorebridge 209 D6
Gore Cross 44 D4
Gorefield 117 D7
Gore Pit 70 B2
Gorey 6
Gorgie 209 C5
Goring 47 A4
Goring-by-Sea 21 B4
Goring Heath 47 B4
Gorleston-on-Sea . .105 A6
Gornalwood 96 B2
Gorrachie 268 D2
Gorran Churchtown . .5 C4
Gorran Haven 5 C5
Gorrenberry 186 D3
Gors 75 A5
Gorsedd 125 B6
Gorse Hill 45 A5
Gorseinon 57 C5
Gorseness 282 F5
Gorsgoch 74 C3
Gorslas 57 A5
Gorsley 62 A2
Gorstan 263 D5
Gorstanvorran 236 B2
Gorsteyhill 128 D2
Gorsty Hill 113 C5
Gortantaoid 200 A3
Gorton 138 D1
Gosbeck 88 B2
Gosberton 117 B5
Gosberton Clough . .117 C4
Gosfield 70 A1
Gosford 78 A3
Gosforth
  Cumb 162 D3
  T&W 179 C4
Gosmore 68 A1
Gosport 19 B5
Gossabrough 284 E7
Gossington 62 C3
Goswick 199 B4
Gotham 114 B3
Gotherington 63 A5
Gott 285 J6
Goudhurst 37 C5
Goulceby 134 B2
Gourdas 256 B2
Gourdon 233 A6
Gourock 204 A2
Govan 205 B5
Govanhill 205 B5
Goveton 7 C6
Govilon 61 B4
Gowanhill 269 C5
Gowdall 140 A4
Gowerton 57 C5
Gowkhall 208 B3
Gowthorpe 149 B6
Goxhill
  E Yorks 151 C4
  N Lincs 142 A3
Goxhill Haven 142 A3
Goytre 40 C2
Grabhair 288 F4
Graby 116 C3
Grade 3 D5
Graffham 20 A2
Grafham
  Cambs. 84 A3
  Sur 34 B3
Grafton
  Hereford 78 D2
  N Yorks 148 A3
  Oxon 64 C3
  Shrops 110 D3
  Worcs 78 A3
Grafton Flyford 80 B2
Grafton Regis 83 C4
Grafton Underwood .99 C6
Grafty Green 37 B6
Graianrhyd 126 D2
Graig
  Conwy 124 B3
  Denb 125 B5
Graig-fechan 125 D6
Grain 51 B5
Grainsby 143 D4
Grainthorpe 143 D5
Grampound 4 C4

Grampound Road 4 B4
Gramsdal. 286 A4
Granborough 66 A2
Granby. 115 B5
Grandborough. 82 A1
Grandtully. 230 C3
Grange
Cumb 163 C5
E Ayrs 193 B4
Medway 51 C4
Mers. 126 A2
Perth. 220 B2
Grange Crossroads.267 D5
Grange Hall 265 D6
Grange Hill. 68 D4
Grangemill 130 D2
Grange Moor 139 B5
Grangemouth. 208 B2
Grange of Lindores.220 C2
Grange-over-
Sands 154 D3
Grangepans 208 B3
Grangetown
Cardiff. 41 D6
Redcar 168 C3
Grange Villa 179 D4
Granish 242 A2
Gransmoor 151 B4
Granston 55 A4
Grantchester 85 B6
Grantham 116 B2
Grantley. 147 A6
Grantlodge 245 A4
Granton
Dumfries. 184 B3
Edin. 209 C5
Grantown-on-
Spey 253 D6
Grantshouse. 211 D5
Grappenhall 127 A6
Grasby 142 C2
Grasmere 154 A2
Grasscroft. 138 C2
Grassendale 126 A3
Grassholme 166 C2
Grassington 147 A4
Grassmoor 131 C4
Grassthorpe 132 C2
Grateley. 32 A1
Gratwich 112 B4
Graveley
Cambs. 84 A4
Herts. 68 A2
Gravelly Hill 96 B4
Gravels 94 A1
Graven 284 F6
Graveney 52 C2
Gravesend
Herts. 68 A4
Kent 50 B3
Grayingham 142 D1
Grayrigg 155 B4
Grays 50 B3
Grayshott 34 C1
Grayswood 34 C2
Graythorp 168 C3
Grazeley 47 C4
Greasbrough 140 D2
Greasby 126 A2
Great Abington 86 C1
Great Addington 99 D6
Great Alne. 80 B4
Great Altcar 136 C2
Great Amwell. 68 B3
Great Asby 165 D4
Great Ashfield 87 A5
Great Ayton. 168 D3
Great Baddow 70 C1
Great Bardfield 86 D2
Great Barford. 84 B3
Great Barr. 96 B3
Great Barrington. . . . 64 B3
Great Barrow 127 C4
Great Barton. 87 A4
Great Barugh 159 D6
Great Bavington . . .178 A1
Great Bealings. 88 C3
Great Bedwyn 45 C6
Great Bentley 71 A5
Great Billing. 83 A5
Great Bircham 119 B4
Great Blakenham . . . 88 B2
Great Blencow. 164 B2
Great Bolas. 111 C5
Great Bookham 35 A4
Great Bourton 82 C1
Great Bowden 99 C4
Great Bradley. 86 B2
Great Braxted. 70 B2
Great Bricett. 87 B6
Great Brickhill 83 D6
Great Bridge. 96 B2
Great Bridgeford. . .112 C2
Great Brington. 82 A3
Great Bromley 71 A4
Great Broughton
Cumb 162 A3
N Yorks 158 A4
Great Budworth. . . .127 B6
Great Burdon 167 D6
Great Burgh 35 A5
Great Burstead 69 D6
Great Busby 158 A4
Great Canfield 69 B5
Great Carlton 135 A4
Great Casterton. . . .100 A2
Great Chart. 38 A1
Great Chatwell. 112 D1
Great Chesterford . . . 85 C7
Great Cheverell 44 D3
Great Chishill 85 D6
Great Clacton. 71 B5
Great Cliff 139 B6
Great Clifton. 162 B3
Great Coates 143 C4
Great Comberton . . . 80 C2
Great Corby 176 D2
Great Cornard 87 C4
Great Cowden 151 C5
Great Coxwell. 64 D3
Great Crakehall 157 B6
Great Cransley. 99 D5
Great Cressingham.103 A4
Great Crosby 136 D2
Great Cubley. 113 B5
Great Dalby. 115 D5
Great Denham 84 C2
Great Doddington. . . 83 A5
Great Dunham 119 D5
Great Dunmow. 69 A6
Great Durnford 31 B5
Great Easton
Essex 69 A6
Leics. 99 B5
Great Eccleston. . . .144 C4
Great Edstone 159 C6
Great Ellingham . . .103 B6
Great Elm 30 A1
Greater Doward. 62 B1
Great Eversden 85 B5
Great Fencote 157 B6
Great Finborough . . . 87 B6
Greatford 116 D3
Great Fransham. . . .119 D5
Great Gaddesden . . . 67 B5
Greatgate 113 A4
Great Gidding. 100 C3
Great Givendale. . . .149 B7
Great Glemham 88 A4
Great Glen. 98 B3
Great Gonerby 116 B1
Great Gransden 85 B4
Great Green
Norf 104 C3
Suff. 87 B5
Great Habton 159 D6
Great Hale. 116 A4
Great Hallingbury . . . 69 B5
Greatham
Hants 33 B6
Hrtlpl 168 C2
W Sus. 20 A3
Great Hampden. 66 C3
Great Harrowden . . . 99 D5
Great Harwood 146 D1
Great Haseley. 66 C1
Great Hatfield 151 C4
Great Haywood 112 C3
Great Heath 97 C6
Great Heck 140 A3
Great Henny 87 D4
Great Hinton. 44 D3
Great Hockham 103 B5
Great Holland. 71 B6
Great Horkesley. 87 D5
Great Hormead 68 A3
Great Horton 147 D5
Great Horwood 83 D4
Great Houghton
Northants 83 B4
S Yorks 140 C2
Great Hucklow. 130 B1
Great Kelk. 151 B4
Great Kimble 66 C3
Great Kingshill. 66 D3
Great Langton 157 B6
Great Leighs. 70 B1
Great Lever. 137 C6
Great Limber 142 C3
Great Linford 83 C5
Great Livermere . . .103 D4
Great Longstone . . .130 B2
Great Lumley 167 A5
Great Lyth 94 A2
Great Malvern 79 C5
Great Maplestead . . . 87 D4
Great Marton 144 D3
Great Massingham .119 C4
Great Melton 104 A2
Great Milton. 66 C1
Great Missenden. . . . 66 C3
Great Mitton. 145 D7
Great Mongeham . . . 53 D5
Great Moulton 104 B2
Great Munden 68 A3
Great Musgrave. . . .165 D5
Great Ness 110 D2
Great Notley 70 A1
Great Oakley
Essex 71 A5
Northants 99 C5
Great Offley 67 A6
Great Ormside 165 D5
Great Orton. 175 C6
Great Ouseburn. . . .148 A3
Great Oxendon. 99 C4
Great Oxney Green . . 69 C6
Great Palgrave. 119 D5
Great Parndon 68 C4
Great Paxton 84 A4
Great Plumpton. . . .144 D3
Great Plumstead . . .121 D5
Great Ponton 116 B2
Great Preston. 140 A2
Great Raveley. 101 C4
Great Rissington 64 B2
Great Rollright. 81 D6
Great Ryburgh 119 C6
Great Ryle 188 B3
Great Ryton 94 A2
Great Saling 69 A7
Great Salkeld 164 B3
Great Sampford. 86 D2
Great Sankey 127 A5
Great Saxham 86 A3
Great Shefford. 46 B1
Great Shelford 85 B6
Great Smeaton. 158 A2
Great Snoring 119 B6
Great Somerford. . . . 44 A3
Great Stainton 167 C6
Great Stambridge . . . 70 D2
Great Staughton 84 A3
Great Steeping 135 C4
Great Stonar. 53 D5
Greatstone on Sea . . 38 C2
Great Strickland . . .164 C3
Great Stukeley 100 D4
Great Sturton 134 B2
Great Sutton
Ches W 126 B3
Shrops 94 C3
Great Swinburne. . .178 B1
Great Tew 65 A4
Great Tey 70 A2
Great Thurkleby. . . .158 D3
Great Thurlow 86 B2
Great Torrington 25 D5
Great Tosson. 188 C3
Great Totham
Essex 70 B2
Essex 70 B2
Great Tows 143 D4
Great Urswick 153 C3
Great Wakering 51 A6
Great Waldingfield . . 87 C5
Great Walsingham .119 B6
Great Waltham. 69 B6
Great Warley 69 D5
Great Washbourne . . 80 D2
Great Weldon. 99 C6
Great Welnetham . . . 87 B4
Great Wenham. 87 D6
Great Whittington. .178 B2
Great Wigborough . . 70 B3
Great Wilbraham. . . . 86 B1
Great Wishford 31 B4
Great Witcombe 63 B5
Great Witley 79 A5
Great Wolford 81 D5
Greatworth. 82 C2
Great Wratting. 86 C2
Great Wymondley . . . 68 A2
Great Wyrley 96 A2
Great Wytheford . . .111 D4
Great Yarmouth 105 A6
Great Yeldham 86 D3
Greave 138 A1
Greeba. 152 C3
Green. 125 C5
Greenbank 284 C7
Greenburn 208 D2
Greendikes 188 A3
Green End. 84 B3
Greenfield
C Beds 84 D2
Flint 126 B1
Gtr Man 138 C2
Highld. 239 B6
Oxon 66 D2
Greenford 48 A4
Greengairs 207 C5
Greenham. 46 C2
Green Hammerton . 148 B3
Greenhaugh 177 A5
Greenhead 177 C4
Greenhill
Falk. 207 C6
Kent 52 C3
Leics 114 D2
London 49 A4
Greenhills. 204 C3
Greenhithe 50 B2
Greenholm 193 B5
Greenholme 155 A4
Greenhouse 187 A4
Greenhow Hill 147 A5
Greenigoe. 283 G5
Greenland. 280 B4
Greenlands. 47 A5
Green Lane. 93 B5
Greenlaw
Aberds 268 D1
Borders. 197 B6
Greenlea 174 A3
Greenloaning. 218 D3
Greenmount. 137 B6
Greenmow 285 L6
Greenock 204 A2
Greenock West 204 A2
Greenodd 154 C2
Green Ore 43 D4
Greenrow 174 C4
Green St Green 50 C1
Greenside 178 C3
Greensidehill 188 B2
Greens Norton. 82 C3
Greenstead Green. . . 70 A2
Greensted 69 C5
Green Street. 68 D1
Greenwich 49 B6
Greet 80 D3
Greete 94 D3
Greetham
Lincs 134 B3
Rutland. 116 D2
Greetland 138 A3
Gregg Hall. 154 B3
Gregson Lane. 137 A4
Greinetobht 287 G3
Greinton 28 B4
Gremista 285 J6
Grenaby. 152 D2
Grendon
Northants 83 A5
Warks. 97 A5
Grendon Common . . . 97 B5
Grendon Green 78 B3
Grendon
Underwood. 66 A1
Grenofen. 11 D5
Grenoside 139 D6
Greosabhagh 288 H2
Gresford 126 D3
Gresham 120 B3
Greshornish 258 C3
Gressenhall 119 D6
Gressingham 145 A5
Gresty Green 128 D2
Greta Bridge. 166 D3
Gretna 175 B6
Gretna Green 175 B6
Gretton
Glos 80 D3
Northants 99 B5
Shrops 94 B3
Grewelthorpe. 157 D6
Greygarth 157 D5
Grey Green 141 C5
Greynor 57 B5
Greysouthen. 162 B3
Greystoke 164 B2
Greystone
Angus 232 D3
Dumfries. 174 A2
Greywell 47 D5
Griais 288 C5
Grianan 288 D5
Gribthorpe 149 D6
Gridley Corner 11 B4
Griff 97 C6
Griffithstown 61 D4
Grimbister 282 F4
Grimblethorpe. 134 A2
Grimeford Village . .137 B5
Grimethorpe 140 C2
Griminis. 286 A3
Grimister. 284 D6
Grimley 79 A6
Grimness. 283 H5
Grimoldby. 134 A3
Grimpo 110 C2
Grimsargh. 145 D5
Grimsbury. 82 C1
Grimsby. 143 B4
Grimscote. 82 B3
Grimscott 10 A3
Grimsthorpe. 116 C3
Grimston
E Yorks 151 D5
Leics 115 C4
Norf 119 C4
York 149 B5
Grimstone. 15 B6
Grinacombe Moor . . 11 B5
Grindale 161 D5
Grindigar. 283 G6
Grindiscol 285 K6
Grindle. 95 A5
Grindleford. 130 B2
Grindleton 146 C1
Grindley. 112 C4
Grindley Brook. 111 A4
Grindlow 130 B1
Grindon
Northumb 198 B3
Staffs 129 D5
Grindonmoor Gate .129 D5
Gringley on the
Hill 141 D5
Grinsdale 175 C6
Grinshill. 111 C4
Grinton 156 B4
Griomsidar. 288 E4
Grishipoll 223 B4
Grisling Common . . . 36 D2
Gristhorpe 161 C4
Griston. 103 B5
Gritley 283 G6
Grittenham. 44 A4
Grittleton 44 A2
Grizebeck 153 B3
Grizedale. 154 B2
Grobister. 282 E7
Groby 98 A2
Groes
Conwy. 125 C5
Neath 40 C2
Groes-faen. 41 C5
Groesffordd Marli . .125 B5
Groeslon
Gwyn. 107 A4
Gwyn. 123 D5
Groes-lwyd. 109 D7
Grogport 202 D3
Gromford 89 B4
Gronant. 125 A5
Groombridge 36 C3
Grosmont
Mon. 61 A6
N Yorks 160 A2
Groton 87 C5
Grougfoot 208 C3
Grouville 6
Grove
Dorset. 15 D7
Kent 53 C4
Notts. 132 B2
Oxon 65 D5
Grove Park 49 B7
Grovesend. 57 B5
Grove Vale. 96 B3
Grudie 263 D5
Gruids 272 D3
Gruinard House. . . .261 A6
Grula 246 B2
Gruline. 225 B4
Grunasound 285 K5
Grundisburgh. 88 B3
Grunsagill. 146 B1
Gruting 285 J4
Grutness 285 N6
Gualachulain 227 B6
Gualin House 276 C4
Guardbridge. 221 C4
Guarlford. 79 C6
Guay. 230 D4
Guestling Green 23 A6
Guestling Thorn. 23 A6
Guestwick 120 C2
Guestwick Green. . .120 C2
Guide 137 A6
Guide Post 179 A4
Guilden Morden 85 C4
Guilden Sutton 127 C4
Guildford. 34 B2
Guildtown. 219 A6
Guilsborough. 98 D3
Guilsfield. 109 D7
Guilton. 53 D4
Guineaford 25 B6
Guisborough 168 D4
Guiseley. 147 C5
Guist. 120 C1
Guith 282 D6
Guiting Power 64 A1
Gulberwick. 285 K6
Gullane 210 B1
Gulval. 2 B2
Gulworthy. 11 D5
Gumfreston 55 D7
Gumley 98 B3
Gummow's Shop. 4 B3
Gunby
E Yorks 149 D6
Lincs. 116 C2
Gundleton. 33 B5
Gun Hill 22 A3
Gunn. 26 B1
Gunnerside. 156 B3
Gunnerton 177 B7
Gunness 141 B6
Gunnislake 11 D5
Gunnista 285 J7
Gunthorpe
Norf 120 B2
Notts. 115 A4
Pboro 100 A3
Gunville. 18 C3
Gunwalloe 3 C4
Gurnard. 18 B3
Gurnett 129 B4
Gurney Slade 29 A6
Gurnos. 59 E4
Gussage All Saints . . 31 D4
Gussage St Michael . 30 D3
Guston 39 A5
Gutcher 284 D7
Guthrie 232 C3
Guyhirn 101 A5
Guyhirn Gull 101 A5
Guy's Head 118 C1
Guy's Marsh 30 C2
Guyzance 189 C5
Gwaenysgor 125 A5
Gwalchmai 122 C3
Gwaun-Cae-
Gurwen 59 D4
Gwaun-Leision 59 D4
Gwbert. 73 B4
Gweek 3 C5
Gwehelog 61 C5
Gwenddwr 77 C4
Gwennap. 4 D2
Gwenter. 3 D5
Gwernaffield 126 C2
Gwernesney 61 C6
Gwernogle 58 B2
Gwernymynydd 126 C2
Gwersyllt. 126 D3
Gwespyr 125 A6
Gwithian 2 A3
Gwredog 123 B4
Gwyddelwern. 109 A5
Gwyddgrug. 58 B1
Gwydyr Uchaf. 124 C2
Gwynfryn. 126 D2
Gwystre 77 A4
Gwytherin 124 C3
Gyfelia 110 A2
Gyffin 124 B2
Gyre 283 G4
Gyrn-goch 107 B4

H

Habberley. 94 A1
Habergham. 146 D2
Habrough 142 B3
Haceby. 116 B3
Hacheston 88 B4
Hackbridge. 49 C5
Hackenthorpe 131 A4
Hackford 103 A6
Hackforth 157 B6
Hackland. 282 E4
Hackleton 83 B5

Hackness
N Yorks 160 B3
Orkney 283 H4
Hackney 49 A6
Hackthorn 133 A4
Hackthorpe 164 C3
Haconby 116 C4
Hacton 50 A2
Hadden 198 C1
Haddenham
Bucks 66 C2
Cambs 101 D6
Haddington
E Loth 210 C2
Lincs 133 C4
Haddiscoe 105 B5
Haddon
Cambs 100 B3
Ches E 129 C4
Hade Edge 139 C4
Hademore 97 A4
Hadfield 138 D3
Hadham Cross 68 B4
Hadham Ford 68 A4
Hadleigh
Essex 51 A5
Suff 87 C6
Hadley 111 D5
Hadley End 113 C5
Hadlow 36 B4
Hadlow Down 36 D3
Hadnall 111 D4
Hadstock 86 C1
Hady 130 B3
Hadzor 80 A2
Haffenden Quarter 37 B6
Hafod-Dinbych 124 D3
Hafod-Iom 124 B3
Haggate 146 D2
Haggbeck 176 B2
Haggerston 198 B4
Haggrister 284 F5
Hagley
Hereford 78 C3
Worcs 96 C2
Hagworthingham 134 C3
Haigh
Gtr Man 137 C5
S Yorks 139 B5
Haigh Moor 139 A5
Haighton Green 145 D5
Haile 162 D3
Hailes 80 D3
Hailey
Herts 68 B3
Oxon 65 B4
Hailsham 22 B3
Hail Weston 84 A3
Haimer 280 B3
Hainault 69 D4
Hainford 120 D4
Hainton 134 A1
Hairmyres 205 C6
Haisthorpe 151 A4
Hakin 55 D4
Halam 132 D1
Halbeath 208 B4
Halberton 27 D5
Halcro 280 B4
Hale
Gtr Man 128 A2
Halton 127 A4
Hants 31 D5
Hale Bank 127 A4
Halebarns 128 A2
Hales
Norf 105 B4
Staffs 111 B6
Halesfield 95 A5
Halesgate 117 C6
Halesowen 96 C2
Hales Place 52 D3
Hale Street 37 B4
Halesworth 105 D4
Halewood 127 A4
Halford
Shrops 94 C2
Warks 81 C5
Halfpenny Furze 56 A2
Halfpenny Green 95 B6
Halfway
Carms 58 B3
Carms 59 B5
W Berks 46 C2
Halfway Bridge 34 D2
Halfway House 110 D2
Halfway Houses 51 B6
Halifax 138 A3
Halket 205 C4
Halkirk 280 C3
Halkyn 126 B2
Halland 22 A2
Hallaton 99 B4
Hallatrow 43 D5
Hallbankgate 176 D3
Hall Dunnerdale 153 A3
Hallen 43 A4
Hall Green
W Mid 96 C4
W Yorks 139 B6
Hall Grove 68 B2
Halliburton 197 B5
Hallin 258 C2
Halling 51 C4
Hallington
Lincs 134 A3
Northumb 178 B1
Halliwell 137 B6
Hall of Tankerness 283 G6
Hall of the Forest 93 C6
Halloughton 132 D1
Hallow 79 B6
Hallrule 187 B4
Halls 210 C3
Hallsands 8 D2
Hall's Green 68 A2
Hallthwaites 153 B2
Hallworthy 10 C2
Hallyburton House 220 A2
Hallyne 195 B6
Halmer End 112 A1
Halmore 62 C2
Halmyre Mains 195 B6
Halnaker 20 B2
Halsall 136 B2
Halse
Northants 82 C2
Som 27 C6
Halsetown 2 B3
Halsham 143 A4
Halsinger 25 B6
Halstead
Essex 87 D4
Kent 50 C1
Leics 99 A4
Halstock 15 A5
Haltham 134 C2
Haltoft End 117 A6
Halton
Bucks 66 B3
Halton 127 A5
Lancs 145 A5
Northumb 178 C1
Wrex 110 B2
W Yorks 148 D2
Halton East 147 B4
Halton Gill 156 D2
Halton Holegate 135 C4
Halton Lea Gate 176 D4
Halton West 146 B2
Haltwhistle 177 C5
Halvergate 105 A5
Halwell 8 B1
Halwill 11 B5
Halwill Junction 11 A5
Ham
Devon 14 A2
Glos 62 D2
Highld 280 A4
Kent 53 D5
London 49 B4
Shetland 285 K1
Wilts 46 C1
Hambleden 47 A5
Hambledon
Hants 33 D5
Sur 34 C2
Hamble-le-Rice 18 A3
Hambleton
Lancs 144 C3
N Yorks 149 D4
Hambridge 28 C3
Hambrook
S Glos 43 B5
W Sus 19 A6
Ham Common 30 C2
Hameringham 134 C3
Hamerton 100 D3
Hametoun 285 K1
Ham Green
Hereford 79 C5
Kent 37 D6
Kent 51 C5
N Som 43 B4
Worcs 80 A3
Hamilton 194 A2
Hammer 34 C1
Hammerpot 20 B3
Hammersmith 49 B5
Hammerwich 96 A3
Hammerwood 36 C2
Hammond Street 68 C3
Hammoon 30 D2
Hamnavoe
Shetland 284 E4
Shetland 284 E6
Shetland 284 F6
Shetland 285 K5
Hampden Park 22 B4
Hamperden End 86 D1
Hampnett 64 B1
Hampole 140 B3
Hampreston 17 B4
Hampstead 49 A5
Hampstead Norreys 46 B3
Hampsthwaite 147 B6
Hampton
London 48 C4
Shrops 95 C5
Worcs 80 C3
Hampton Bishop 78 D3
Hampton Heath 110 A3
Hampton in Arden 97 C5
Hampton Loade 95 C5
Hampton Lovett 80 A1
Hampton Lucy 81 B5
Hampton on the Hill 81 A5
Hampton Poyle 65 B6
Hamrow 119 C6
Hamsey 22 A2
Hamsey Green 35 A6
Hamstall Ridware 113 D5
Hamstead
IoW 18 B3
W Mid 96 B3
Hamstead Marshall 46 C2
Hamsterley
Durham 166 B4
Durham 178 D3
Hamstreet 38 B2
Ham Street 29 B5
Hamworthy 16 B3
Hanbury
Staffs 113 C5
Worcs 80 A2
Hanbury Woodend 113 C5
Hanby 116 B3
Hanchurch 112 A2
Handbridge 127 C4
Handcross 35 D5
Handforth 128 A3
Handley 127 D4
Handsacre 113 D4
Handsworth
S Yorks 131 A4
W Mid 96 B3
Handy Cross 25 C5
Hanford 112 A2
Hanging Langford 31 B4
Hangleton 20 B3
Hanham 43 B5
Hankelow 111 A5
Hankerton 63 D5
Hankham 22 B4
Hanley 112 A2
Hanley Castle 79 C6
Hanley Child 79 A4
Hanley Swan 79 C6
Hanley William 79 A4
Hanlith 146 A3
Hanmer 110 B3
Hannah 135 B5
Hannington
Hants 46 D3
Northants 99 D5
Swindon 64 D2
Hannington Wick 64 D2
Hansel Village 192 B3
Hanslope 83 C5
Hanthorpe 116 C3
Hanwell
London 49 A4
Oxon 82 C1
Hanwood 94 A2
Hanworth
London 48 B4
Norf 120 B3
Happendon 194 C3
Happisburgh 121 B5
Happisburgh Common 121 C5
Hapsford 127 B4
Hapton
Lancs 146 D1
Norf 104 B2
Harberton 8 B1
Harbertonford 8 B1
Harbledown 52 D3
Harborne 96 C3
Harborough Magna 98 D1
Harbottle 188 C2
Harbury 81 B6
Harby
Leics 115 B5
Notts 132 B3
Harcombe 13 B6
Harden
W Mid 96 A3
W Yorks 147 D4
Hardenhuish 44 B3
Hardgate 245 B4
Hardham 20 A3
Hardingham 103 A6
Hardingstone 83 B4
Hardington 43 D6
Hardington Mandeville 29 D5
Hardington Marsh 15 A5
Hardley 18 A3
Hardley Street 105 A4
Hardmead 83 C6
Hardrow 156 B2
Hardstoft 131 C4
Hardway
Hants 19 A5
Som 29 B7
Hardwick
Bucks 66 B3
Cambs 85 B5
Norf 104 C3
Norf 118 D3
Northants 83 A5
Notts 131 B6
Oxon 65 A6
Oxon 65 C4
W Mid 96 B3
Hardwicke
Glos 62 B3
Glos 63 A5
Hereford 77 C6
Hardy's Green 70 A3
Hareby 134 C3
Hareden 145 B6
Harefield 67 D5
Hare Green 71 A4
Hare Hatch 47 B6
Harehills 148 D2
Harehope 188 A3
Haresceugh 165 A4
Harescombe 63 B4
Haresfield 63 B4
Hareshaw 207 D6
Hareshaw Head 177 A6
Hare Street 68 A3
Harewood 148 C2
Harewood End 62 A1
Harford
Carms 58 A3
Devon 7 B5
Hargate 104 B2
Hargatewall 129 B6
Hargrave
Ches W 127 C4
Northants 100 D2
Suff 86 B3
Harker 175 B6
Harkland 284 E6
Harkstead 88 D2
Harlaston 113 D6
Harlaw House 256 D2
Harlaxton 116 B1
Harlech 107 C5
Harlequin 115 B4
Harlescott 111 D4
Harlesden 49 A5
Harleston
Devon 8 C1
Norf 104 C3
Suff 87 B6
Harlestone 83 A4
Harle Syke 146 D2
Harley
Shrops 94 A3
S Yorks 139 D6
Harleyholm 194 C4
Harlington
C Beds 84 D2
London 48 B3
S Yorks 140 C2
Harlosh 258 D2
Harlow 69 B4
Harlow Hill
Northumb 178 C2
N Yorks 148 B1
Harlthorpe 149 D6
Harlton 85 B5
Harman's Cross 16 C3
Harmby 157 C5
Harmer Green 68 B2
Harmer Hill 110 C3
Harmondsworth 48 B3
Harmston 133 C4
Harnham 178 B2
Harnhill 63 C6
Harold Hill 69 D5
Haroldston West 55 C4
Haroldswick 284 B8
Harold Wood 69 D5
Harome 159 C5
Harpenden 67 B6
Harpford 13 B5
Harpham 150 A3
Harpley
Norf 119 C4
Worcs 79 A4
Harpole 82 A3
Harpsdale 280 C3
Harpsden 47 A5
Harpswell 133 A4
Harpurhey 138 C1
Harpur Hill 129 B5
Harraby 175 C7
Harrapool 247 B5
Harrier 285 J1
Harrietfield 219 B4
Harrietsham 37 A6
Harrington
Cumb 162 B2
Lincs 134 B3
Northants 99 C4
Harringworth 99 B6
Harris 234 A2
Harrogate 148 B2
Harrold 83 B6
Harrow 49 A4
Harrowbarrow 6 A2
Harrowden 84 C2
Harrowgate Hill 167 D5
Harrow on the Hill 49 A4
Harrow Street 87 D5
Harrow Weald 67 D6
Harston
Cambs 85 B6
Leics 115 B6
Harswell 150 C1
Hart 168 B2
Hartburn
Northumb 178 A2
Stockton 168 D2
Hart Common 137 C5
Hartest 87 B4
Hartfield 36 C2
Hartford
Cambs 101 D4
Ches W 127 B6
Hartfordbridge 47 D5
Hartford End 69 B6
Hartforth 157 A5
Harthill
Ches W 127 D5
N Lanark 208 D2
S Yorks 131 A4
Hart Hill 67 A6
Hartington 129 C6
Hartland 24 C3
Hartlebury 95 D6
Hartlepool 168 B3
Hartley
Cumb 155 A6
Kent 37 C5
Kent 50 C3
Northumb 179 B5
Hartley Westpall 47 D4
Hartley Wintney 47 D5
Hartlip 51 C5
Hartoft End 159 B6
Harton
N Yorks 149 A6
Shrops 94 C2
T&W 179 C5
Hartpury 62 A3
Hartshead 139 A4
Hartshill 97 B6
Hartshorne 113 C7
Hartsop 164 D2
Hart Station 168 B2
Hartwell 83 B4
Hartwood 194 A3
Harvieston 206 B3
Harvington 80 C3
Harvington Cross 80 C3
Harwell 46 A2
Harwich 88 D3
Harwood
Durham 165 B6
Gtr Man 137 B6
Harwood Dale 160 B3
Harworth 140 D4
Hasbury 96 C2
Hascombe 34 B2
Haselbech 99 D4
Haselbury Plucknett 29 D4
Haseley 81 A5
Haselor 80 B4
Hasfield 63 A4
Hasguard 55 D4
Haskayne 136 C2
Hasketon 88 B3
Hasland 130 C3
Haslemere 34 C2
Haslingden 137 A6
Haslingfield 85 B6
Haslington 128 D2
Hassall 128 D2
Hassall Green 128 D2
Hassell Street 38 A2
Hassendean 186 A4
Hassingham 105 A4
Hassocks 21 A5
Hassop 130 B2
Hastigrow 281 B4
Hastingleigh 38 A2
Hastings 23 B6
Hastingwood 69 C4
Hastoe 67 C4
Haswell 167 A6
Haswell Plough 167 A6
Hatch
C Beds 84 C3
Hants 47 D4
Wilts 30 C3
Hatch Beauchamp 28 C3
Hatch End 67 D6
Hatchet Gate 18 A2
Hatch Green 28 D3
Hatching Green 67 B6
Hatchmere 127 B5
Hatcliffe 143 C4
Hatfield
Hereford 78 B3
Herts 68 C2
S Yorks 141 C4
Worcs 80 B1
Hatfield Broad Oak 69 B5
Hatfield Garden Village 68 C2
Hatfield Heath 69 B5
Hatfield Hyde 68 B2
Hatfield Peverel 70 B1
Hatfield Woodhouse 141 C4
Hatford 64 D4
Hatherden 46 D1
Hatherleigh 11 A6
Hathern 114 C2
Hatherop 64 C2
Hathersage 130 A2
Hathershaw 138 C2
Hatherton
Ches E 111 A5
Staffs 112 D3
Hatley St George 85 B4
Hatt 6 A2
Hattingley 33 B5
Hatton
Aberds 257 C5
Derbys 113 C6
Lincs 134 B1
Shrops 94 B2
Warks 81 A5
Warr 127 A5
Hatton Castle 256 B2
Hattoncrook 256 D3
Hatton Heath 127 C4
Hatton of Fintray 245 A5
Haugh
E Ayrs 193 C4
Gtr Man 138 B2
Lincs 135 B4
Haugham 134 A3
Haugh Head 188 A3
Haughley 87 A6
Haughley Green 87 A6
Haugh of Glass 255 C5
Haugh of Urr 173 B6
Haughs of Clinterty 245 A5
Haughton
Notts 132 B1
Shrops 95 A5
Shrops 95 B4
Shrops 110 C2
Shrops 111 D4
Staffs 112 C2
Haughton Castle 177 B7
Haughton Green 138 D2
Haughton Moss 127 D5
Haultwick 68 A3

Haunn
Argyll 224 B2
W Isles 286 E3
Haunton 113 D6
Hauxley 189 C5
Hauxton 85 B6
Havant 19 A6
Haven 78 B2
Haven Bank 134 D2
Haven Side 142 A3
Havenstreet 19 B4
Havercroft 140 B1
Haverfordwest
=Hwlffordd 55 C5
Haverhill 86 C2
Haverigg 153 C2
Havering-atte-Bower 69 D5
Haveringland 120 C3
Haversham 83 C5
Haverthwaite 154 C2
Haverton Hill 168 C2
Hawarden
=Penarlâg 126 C3
Hawcoat 153 C3
Hawen 73 B6
Hawes 156 C2
Hawes' Green 104 B3
Hawes Side 144 D3
Hawford 79 A6
Hawick 186 B4
Hawkchurch 14 A3
Hawkedon 86 B3
Hawkenbury
Kent 36 C3
Kent 37 B6
Hawkeridge 44 D2
Hawkerland 13 C5
Hawkesbury
S Glos 43 A6
Warks 97 C6
Hawkesbury Upton 44 A1
Hawkes End 97 C6
Hawk Green 129 A4
Hawkhill 189 B5
Hawkhurst 37 C5
Hawkinge 39 B4
Hawkley 33 C6
Hawkridge 26 B3
Hawkshead 154 B2
Hawkshead Hill 154 B2
Hawksland 194 C3
Hawkswick 156 D3
Hawksworth
Notts 115 A5
W Yorks 147 C5
W Yorks 147 D6
Hawkwell 70 D2
Hawley
Hants 34 A1
Kent 50 B2
Hawling 63 A6
Hawnby 158 C4
Haworth 147 D4
Hawstead 87 B4
Hawthorn
Durham 168 A2
Rhondda 41 C6
Wilts 44 C2
Hawthorn Hill
Brack 48 B1
Lincs 134 D2
Hawthorpe 116 C3
Hawton 132 D2
Haxby 149 B5
Haxey 141 C5
Haydock 137 D4
Haydon 29 D6
Haydon Bridge 177 C6
Haydon Wick 45 A5
Haye 6 A2
Hayes
London 48 A4
London 49 C7
Hayfield
Derbys 129 A5
Fife 209 A5
Hay Green 118 D2
Hayhill 182 A2
Hayhillock 232 D3
Hayle 2 B3
Haynes 84 C2
Haynes Church End 84 C2
Hay-on-Wye
=Y Gelli Gandryll 77 C6
Hayscastle 55 B4
Hayscastle Cross 55 B5
Hayshead 233 D4
Hay Street 68 A3
Hayton
Aberdeen 245 B6
Cumb 174 D4
Cumb 176 D3
E Yorks 149 C7
Notts 132 A2
Hayton's Bent 94 C3
Haytor Vale 12 D2
Haywards Heath 35 D6
Haywood 140 B3
Haywood Oaks 131 D6
Hazelbank 194 B3
Hazelbury Bryan 16 A1
Hazeley 47 D5
Hazel Grove 129 A4
Hazelhurst 138 C2
Hazelslade 112 D4
Hazel Street 37 C4
Hazelton 64 B1
Hazelton Walls 220 B3
Hazelwood 114 A1
Hazlemere 66 D3
Hazlerigg 179 B4
Hazlewood 147 B4
Hazon 189 C4
Heacham 118 B3
Headbourne Worthy 32 B3
Headbrook 77 B7
Headcorn 37 B6
Headingley 148 D1
Headington 65 C6
Headlam 167 D4
Headless Cross 80 A3
Headley
Hants 33 B7
Hants 46 C3
Sur 35 A5
Head of Muir 207 B6
Headon 132 B2
Heads 194 B2
Heads Nook 176 D2
Heage 130 D3
Healaugh
N Yorks 148 C3
N Yorks 156 B4
Heald Green 128 A3
Heale
Devon 26 A1
Som 29 A6
Healey
Gtr Man 138 B1
Northumb 178 D2
N Yorks 157 C5
Healing 143 B4
Heamoor 2 B2
Heanish 222 C3
Heanor 114 A2
Heanton Punchardon 25 B6
Heapham 132 A3
Hearthstane 195 D6
Heasley Mill 26 B2
Heast 247 C5
Heath
Cardiff 41 D6
Derbys 131 C4
Heath and Reach 67 A4
Heathcote 129 C6
Heath End
Hants 46 C3
Sur 34 B1
Warks 81 A5
Heather 114 D1
Heatherfield 259 D4
Heathfield
Devon 12 D3
E Sus 36 D3
Som 27 C6
Heathhall 174 A2
Heath Hayes 112 D4
Heath Hill 111 D6
Heath House 28 A4
Heathrow Airport 48 B3
Heathstock 14 A2
Heathton 95 B6
Heath Town 96 B2
Heatley 128 A2
Heaton
Lancs 144 A4
Staffs 129 C4
T&W 179 C4
W Yorks 147 D5
Heaton Moor 138 D1
Heaverham 36 A3
Heaviley 129 A3
Heavitree 13 B4
Hebburn 179 C5
Hebden 147 A4
Hebden Bridge 138 A2
Hebron
Anglesey 123 B4
Carms 73 D4
Northumb 178 A3
Heck 184 D3
Heckfield 47 C5
Heckfield Green 104 D2
Heckfordbridge 70 A3
Heckington 116 A4
Heckmondwike 139 A5
Heddington 44 C3
Heddle 282 F4
Heddon-on-the-Wall 178 C3
Hedenham 104 B4
Hedge End 32 D3
Hedgerley 48 A2
Hedging 28 C3
Hedley on the Hill 178 D2
Hednesford 112 D3
Hedon 142 A3
Hedsor 48 A2
Hedworth 179 C5
Hegdon Hill 78 B3
Heggerscales 165 D6
Heglibister 285 H5
Heighington
Darl 167 C5
Lincs 133 C5
Heights of Brae 263 D7
Heights of Kinlochewe 262 D2
Heilam 277 B5
Heiton 197 C6
Hele
Devon 13 A4
Devon 25 A6
Helensburgh 215 D5
Helford 3 C5
Helford Passage 3 C5
Helhoughton 119 C5
Helions Bumpstead 86 C2
Hellaby 140 D3
Helland 10 D1
Hellesdon 120 D4
Hellidon 82 B2
Hellifield 146 B2
Hellingly 22 A3
Hellington 104 A4
Hellister 285 J5
Helm 189 D4
Helmdon 82 C2
Helmingham 88 B2
Helmington Row 167 B4
Helmsdale 274 C4
Helmshore 137 A6
Helmsley 159 C5
Helperby 148 A3
Helperthorpe 160 D3
Helpringham 116 A4
Helpston 100 A3
Helsby 127 B4
Helsey 135 B5
Helston 3 C4
Helstone 10 C1
Helton 164 C3
Helwith Bridge 146 A2
Hemblington 121 D5
Hemel Hempstead 67 C5
Hemingbrough 149 D5
Hemingby 134 B2
Hemingford Abbots 101 D4
Hemingford Grey 101 D4
Hemingstone 88 B2
Hemington
Leics 114 C2
Northants 100 C2
Som 43 D6
Hemley 88 C3
Hemlington 168 D3
Hemp Green 89 A4
Hempholme 150 B3
Hempnall 104 B3
Hempnall Green 104 B3
Hempriggs House 281 D5
Hempstead
Essex 86 D2
Medway 51 C4
Norf 120 B3
Norf 121 C6
Hempsted 63 B4
Hempton
Norf 119 C6
Oxon 82 D1
Hemsby 121 D6
Hemswell 142 D1
Hemswell Cliff 133 A4
Hemsworth 140 B2
Hemyock 27 D6
Henbury
Bristol 43 B4
Ches E 128 B3
Hendon
London 49 A5
T&W 179 D6
Hendre 126 C1
Hendre-ddu 124 C3
Hendreforgan 41 C4
Hendy 57 B5
Heneglwys 123 C4
Hen-feddau fawr 73 C5
Henfield 21 A5
Henford 11 B4
Henghurst 38 B1
Hengoed
Caerph 41 B6
Powys 77 B6
Shrops 110 B1
Hengrave 87 A4
Henham 69 A5
Heniarth 93 A5
Henlade 28 C2
Henley
Shrops 94 D3
Som 28 B4
Suff 88 B2
W Sus 34 D1
Henley-in-Arden 81 A4
Henley-on-Thames 47 A5
Henley's Down 23 A5
Henllan
Ceredig 73 B6
Denb 125 C5
Henllan Amgoed 73 D4
Henllys 61 D4
Henlow 84 D3
Hennock 12 C3
Henny Street 87 D4
Henryd 124 B2
Henry's Moat 55 B6
Hensall 140 A3
Henshaw 177 C5
Hensingham 162 C2
Henstead 105 C5
Henstridge 30 D1
Henstridge Ash 29 C7
Henstridge Marsh 30 C1
Henton
Oxon 66 C2
Som 29 A4
Henwood 10 D3
Heogan 285 J6
Heol-las 40 B1
Heol Senni 59 C6
Heol-y-Cyw 40 C4
Hepburn 188 A3
Hepple 188 C2
Hepscott 179 A4
Heptonstall 138 A2
Hepworth
Suff 103 D5
W Yorks 139 C4
Herbrandston 55 D4
Hereford 78 C3
Heriot 196 A2
Hermiston 209 C4
Hermitage
Borders 186 D4
Dorset 15 A6
W Berks 46 B3
W Sus 19 A6
Hermon
Anglesey 122 D3
Carms 58 C3
Carms 73 C6
Pembs 73 C5
Herne 52 C3
Herne Bay 52 C3
Herner 25 C6
Hernhill 52 C2
Herodsfoot 5 A7
Herongate 69 D6
Heronsford 180 C3
Herriard 33 A5
Herringfleet 105 B5
Herringswell 102 D3
Hersden 53 C4
Hersham
Corn 10 A3
Sur 48 C4
Herstmonceux 22 A4
Herston 283 H5
Hertford 68 B3
Hertford Heath 68 B3
Hertingfordbury 68 B3
Hesketh Bank 136 A3
Hesketh Lane 145 C6
Hesket Newmarket 163 A6
Heskin Green 136 B4
Hesleden 168 B2
Hesleyside 177 A6
Heslington 149 B5
Hessay 148 B4
Hessenford 6 B2
Hessett 87 A5
Hessle 142 A2
Hest Bank 145 A4
Heston 48 B4
Hestwall 282 F3
Heswall 126 A2
Hethe 65 A6
Hethersett 104 A2
Hethersgill 176 C2
Hethpool 188 A1
Hett 167 B5
Hetton 146 B3
Hetton-le-Hole 167 A6
Hetton Steads 198 C4
Heugh 178 B2
Heugh-head 243 A6
Heveningham 104 D4
Hever 36 B2
Heversham 154 C3
Hevingham 120 C3
Hewas Water 5 C4
Hewelsfield 62 C1
Hewish
N Som 42 C3
Som 14 A4
Heworth 149 B5
Hexham 178 C1
Hextable 50 B2
Hexton 84 D3
Hexworthy 12 D1
Hey 146 C2
Heybridge
Essex 69 D6
Essex 70 C2
Heybridge Basin 70 C2
Heybrook Bay 7 C4
Heydon
Cambs 85 C6
Norf 120 C3
Heydour 116 B3
Heylipol 222 C2
Heylor 284 E4
Heysham 144 A4
Heyshott 20 A1
Heyside 138 C2
Heytesbury 30 A3
Heythrop 64 A4
Heywood
Gtr Man 138 B1
Wilts 44 D2
Hibaldstow 142 C1
Hickleton 140 C2
Hickling
Norf 121 C6
Notts 115 C4
Hickling Green 121 C6
Hickling Heath 121 C6
Hickstead 35 D5
Hidcote Boyce 81 C4
High Ackworth 140 B2
Higham
Derbys 130 D3
Kent 51 B4
Lancs 146 D2
Suff 86 A3
Suff 87 D6
Higham Dykes 178 B3
Higham Ferrers 83 A6
Higham Gobion 84 D3
Higham on the Hill 97 B6
Highampton 11 A5
Higham Wood 36 B3
High Angerton 178 A2
High Bankhill 164 A3
High Barnes 179 D5
High Beach 68 D4
High Bentham 145 A6
High Bickington 25 C7
High Birkwith 155 D6
High Blantyre 194 A1
High Bonnybridge 207 C6
High Bradfield 139 D5
High Bray 26 B1
Highbridge
Highld 239 D5
Som 28 A3
Highbrook 35 C6
High Brooms 36 B3
High Bullen 25 C6
Highburton 139 B4
Highbury 29 A6
High Buston 189 C5
High Callerton 178 B3
High Catton 149 B6
Highclere 46 C2
Highcliffe 17 B6
High Cogges 65 C4
High Coniscliffe 167 D5
High Cross
Hants 33 C6
Herts 68 B3
High Easter 69 B6
High Eggborough 140 A3
High Ellington 157 C5
Higher Ansty 16 A1
Higher Ashton 12 C3
Higher Ballam 144 D3
Higher Bartle 145 D5
Higher Boscaswell 2 B1
Higher Burwardsley 127 D5
High Ercall 111 D4
Higher Clovelly 24 C4
Higher End 136 C4
Higher Kinnerton 126 C3
Higher Penwortham 136 A4
Higher Town Scilly P02 E4
Higher Walreddon 11 D5
Higher Walton
Lancs 137 A4
Warr 127 A5
Higher Wheelton 137 A5
Higher Whitley 127 A6
Higher Wincham 128 B1
Higher Wych 110 A3
High Etherley 167 C4
Highfield
E Yorks 149 D6
Gtr Man 137 C6
N Ayrs 204 C3
Oxon 65 A6
S Yorks 130 A3
T&W 178 D3
Highfields
Cambs 85 B5
Northumb 198 A3
High Garrett 70 A1
Highgate 49 A5
High Grange 167 B4
High Green
Norf 104 A2
S Yorks 139 D6
Worcs 80 C1
High Halden 37 C6
High Halstow 51 B4
High Ham 28 B4
High Harrington 162 B3
High Hatton 111 C5
High Hawsker 160 A3
High Hesket 164 A2
High Hesleden 168 B2
High Hoyland 139 B5
High Hunsley 150 D2
High Hurstwood 36 D2
High Hutton 149 A6
High Ireby 163 A5
High Kelling 120 A3
High Kilburn 158 D4
High Lands 166 C4
Highlane
Ches E 128 C3
Derbys 131 A4
High Lane
Gtr Man 129 A4
Worcs 79 A4
High Laver 69 C5
Highlaws 174 D4
Highleadon 62 A3
High Legh 128 A2
Highleigh 20 C1
High Leven 168 D2
Highley 95 C5
High Littleton 43 D5
High Lorton 163 B4
High Marishes 159 D7
High Marnham 132 B3
High Melton 140 C3
High Mickley 178 C2
High Mindork 171 B5
Highmoor Cross 47 A5
Highmoor Hill 42 A3
Highnam 62 B3
Highnam Green 62 A3
High Newton 154 C3
High Newton-by-the-Sea 189 A5
High Nibthwaite 154 C1
High Offley 112 C1
High Ongar 69 C5
High Onn 112 D2
High Roding 69 B6
High Row 163 A6

High Salvington 21 B4
High Sellafield 162 D3
High Shaw 156 B2
High Spen 178 D3
Highsted 51 C6
High Stoop 166 A4
High Street
  Corn 5 B4
  Kent 37 C5
  Suff 87 C4
  Suff 89 B5
  Suff 105 D5
Highstreet Green 86 B3
High Street Green . . . 87 B6
Hightae 174 A3
Hightown
  Ches E. 128 C3
  Mers 136 C2
Hightown Green . . . 87 B5
High Toynton 134 C2
High Trewhitt 188 C3
High Valleyfield 208 B3
Highway 44 B4
Highweek 12 C5
High Westwood 178 D3
Highworth 64 D3
High Wray 154 B2
High Wych 69 B4
High Wycombe 66 D3
Hilborough 103 A4
Hilcote 131 D4
Hilcott 45 D5
Hildenborough . . . 36 B3
Hilden Park 36 B3
Hildersham 86 C1
Hilderstone 112 B3
Hilderthorpe 151 A4
Hilfield 15 A6
Hilgay 102 B2
Hill
  Pembs 55 D7
  S Glos 62 D2
  W Mid 96 B4
Hillam 140 A3
Hillbeck 165 D5
Hillborough 53 C4
Hillbrae
  Aberds 255 B7
  Aberds 256 D2
Hill Brow 33 C6
Hillbutts 16 A3
Hillclifflane 113 A6
Hillcommon 27 C6
Hill Dale 136 B3
Hill Dyke 117 A6
Hilland 208 B4
Hill End
  Durham 166 B3
  Fife 208 A3
  N Yorks 147 B4
Hillerton 12 B2
Hillesden 66 A1
Hillesley 43 A6
Hillfarance 27 C6
Hillhead
  Aberds 255 C6
  Devon 8 B3
  S Ayrs 182 A2
Hill Head
  Hants 18 A4
  Northumb 178 C1
Hillhead of
  Auchentumb 269 D4
Hillhead of
  Cocklaw 257 B5
Hillhouse 197 A4
Hilliclay 280 B3
Hillingdon 48 A3
Hillington
  Glasgow 205 B5
  Norf 119 C4
Hillmorton 98 D2
Hill Mountain 55 D5
Hillockhead
  Aberds 243 B6
  Aberds 244 A1
Hill of Beath 209 A4
Hill of Fearn 265 C4
Hill of Mountblairy .268 D1
Hill Ridware 113 D4
Hillside
  Aberds 245 C6
  Angus 233 B5
  Mers 136 B2
  Orkney 283 H5
  Shetland 285 G6
Hillswick 284 F4

Hill Top
  Durham 166 C2
  Hants 18 A3
  W Mid 96 B2
  W Yorks 139 B6
Hill View 16 B3
Hillway 19 C5
Hillwell 285 M5
Hilmarton 44 B4
Hilperton 44 D2
Hilsea 19 A5
Hilston 151 D5
Hilton
  Aberds 257 C4
  Cambs 85 A4
  Cumb 165 C5
  Derbys 113 B6
  Dorset 16 A1
  Durham 167 C4
  Highld 264 B3
  Shrops 95 B5
  Stockton 168 D2
Hilton of Cadboll . . .265 C4
Himbleton 80 B2
Himley 96 B1
Hincaster 154 C4
Hinckley 98 B1
Hinderclay 103 D6
Hinderton 126 B3
Hinderwell 169 D5
Hindford 110 B2
Hindhead 34 C1
Hindley 137 C5
Hindley Green 137 C5
Hindlip 80 B1
Hindolveston 120 C2
Hindon 30 B3
Hindringham 120 B1
Hingham 103 A6
Hinstock 111 C5
Hintlesham 88 C1
Hinton
  Hants 17 B6
  Hereford 78 D1
  Northants 82 B2
  S Glos 43 B6
  Shrops 94 A2
Hinton Ampner 33 C4
Hinton Blewett 43 D4
Hinton
  Charterhouse 43 D6
Hinton-in-the-
  Hedges 82 D2
Hinton Martell 17 A4
Hinton on the Green . 80 C3
Hinton Parva 45 A6
Hinton St George . . . 28 D4
Hinton St Mary 30 D1
Hinton Waldrist 65 D4
Hints
  Shrops 95 D4
  Staffs 97 A4
Hinwick 83 A6
Hinxhill 38 A2
Hinxton 85 C6
Hinxworth 84 C4
Hipperholme 139 A4
Hipswell 157 B5
Hirael 123 C5
Hiraeth 73 D4
Hirn 245 B4
Hirnant 109 C5
Hirst
  N Lanark 207 D6
  Northumb 179 A4
Hirst Courtney 140 A4
Hirwaen 125 C6
Hirwaun 59 E6
Hiscott 25 C6
Histon 85 A6
Hitcham 87 B5
Hitchin 68 A1
Hither Green 49 B6
Hittisleigh 12 B2
Hive 149 D7
Hixon 112 C4
Hoaden 53 D4
Hoaldalbert 61 A5
Hoar Cross 113 C5
Hoarwithy 62 A1
Hoath 53 C4
Hobarris 93 D7
Hobbister 283 G4
Hobkirk 187 B4
Hobson 178 D3
Hoby 115 D4
Hockering 120 D2
Hockerton 132 D2
Hockley 70 D2
Hockley Heath 97 D4

Hockliffe 67 A4
Hockwold cum
  Wilton 102 C3
Hockworthy 27 D5
Hoddesdon 68 C3
Hoddlesden 137 A6
Hoddomcross 175 A4
Hoddom Mains 175 A4
Hodgeston 55 E6
Hodley 93 B5
Hodnet 111 C5
Hodthorpe 131 B5
Hoe
  Hants 33 D4
  Norf 120 D1
Hoe Gate 33 D5
Hoff 165 D4
Hoggard's Green 87 B4
Hoggeston 66 A3
Hogha Gearraidh .287 G2
Hoghton 137 A5
Hognaston 130 D2
Hog Patch 34 B1
Hogsthorpe 135 B5
Holbeach 117 C6
Holbeach Bank 117 C6
Holbeach Clough 117 C6
Holbeach Drove 117 D6
Holbeach Hurn 117 C6
Holbeach St Johns . . .117 D6
Holbeach St Marks . . .117 B6
Holbeach
  St Matthew 117 B7
Holbeck
  Notts 131 B5
  W Yorks 148 D1
Holbeck
  Woodhouse 131 B5
Holberrow Green . . . 80 B3
Holbeton 7 B5
Holborn 49 A6
Holbrook
  Derbys 114 A1
  Suff 88 D2
  S Yorks 131 A4
Holburn 198 C4
Holbury 18 A3
Holcombe
  Devon 13 D4
  Som 29 A6
Holcombe Rogus . . . 27 D5
Holcot 83 A4
Holden 146 C1
Holdenby 82 A3
Holdenhurst 17 B5
Holdgate 94 C3
Holdingham 116 A3
Holditch 14 A3
Holefield 198 C2
Holehouses 128 B2
Hole-in-the-Wall . . . 62 A2
Holemoor 11 A5
Holestane 183 C6
Holford 27 A6
Holgate 149 B4
Holker 154 D2
Holkham 119 A5
Hollacombe 11 A4
Holland
  Orkney 282 B5
  Orkney 282 E7
Holland Fen 117 A5
Holland-on-Sea 71 B6
Hollandstoun 282 B8
Hollee 175 B5
Hollesley 89 C4
Hollicombe 8 A2
Hollingbourne 37 A6
Hollington
  Derbys 113 B6
  E Sus 23 A5
  Staffs 113 B4
Hollington Grove . . .113 B6
Hollingworth 138 D3
Hollins 137 C7
Hollinsclough 129 C5
Hollins Green 137 D5
Hollins Lane 145 B4
Hollinwood
  Gtr Man 138 C2
  Shrops 111 B4
Hollocombe 26 D1
Holloway 130 D3
Hollowell 98 D3
Hollow Meadows . . .130 A2
Hollybush
  Caerph 41 A6
  E Ayrs 182 A1
  Worcs 79 D5
Holly End 101 A6

Holly Green 79 C6
Hollym 143 A5
Hollywood 96 D3
Holmbridge 139 C4
Holmbury St Mary . . 35 B4
Holmbush 5 B5
Holmcroft 112 C3
Holme
  Cambs 100 C3
  Cumb 154 D4
  Notts 132 D3
  N Yorks 158 C2
  W Yorks 139 C4
Holme Chapel 138 A1
Holme Green 149 C4
Holme Hale 103 A4
Holme Lacy 78 D3
Holme Marsh 78 B1
Holme next the
  Sea 119 A4
Holme-on-Spalding-
  Moor 149 D7
Holme on the
  Wolds 150 C2
Holme Pierrepont . . .115 B4
Holmer 78 C3
Holmer Green 67 D4
Holme St Cuthbert .174 D4
Holmes Chapel 128 C2
Holmesfield 130 B3
Holmeswood 136 B3
Holmewood 131 C4
Holme Wood 147 D5
Holmfirth 139 C4
Holmhead
  Dumfries 183 D5
  E Ayrs 193 C5
Holmisdale 258 D1
Holmpton 143 A5
Holmrook 153 A1
Holmsgarth 285 J6
Holmwrangle 164 A3
Holne 7 A6
Holnest 15 A6
Holsworthy 10 A4
Holsworthy Beacon . 11 A4
Holt
  Dorset 17 A4
  Norf 120 B2
  Wilts 44 C2
  Worcs 79 A6
  Wrex 127 D4
Holtby 149 B5
Holt End
  Hants 33 B5
  Worcs 80 A3
Holt Fleet 79 A6
Holt Heath 79 A6
Holton
  Oxon 65 C7
  Som 29 C6
  Suff 105 D4
Holton cum
  Beckering 133 A6
Holton Heath 16 B3
Holton le Clay 143 C4
Holton le Moor 142 D2
Holton St Mary 87 D6
Holt Park 147 C6
Holwell
  Dorset 29 D7
  Herts 84 D3
  Leics 115 C5
  Oxon 64 C3
Holwick 166 C2
Holworth 16 C1
Holybourne 33 A6
Holy Cross 96 D2
Holyhead
  = Caergybi 122 B2
Holy Island 199 B5
Holymoorside 130 C3
Holyport 48 B1
Holystone 188 C2
Holytown 207 D5
Holywell
  Cambs 101 D5
  Corn 4 B2
  Dorset 15 A5
  E Sus 22 C3
  Northumb 179 B5
Holywell
  = Treffynnon 126 B1
Holywell Green 138 B3
Holywell Lake 27 C6
Holywell Row 102 D3
Holywood 184 D2
Homer 95 A4
Homersfield 104 C3
Hom Green 62 A1

Homington 31 C5
Honeyborough 55 D5
Honeybourne 80 C4
Honeychurch 12 A1
Honey Hill 52 C3
Honey Street 45 C5
Honey Tye 87 D5
Honiley 97 D5
Honing 121 C5
Honingham 120 D3
Honington
  Lincs 116 A2
  Suff 103 D5
  Warks 81 C5
Honiton 13 A6
Honley 139 B4
Hood Green 139 C6
Hooe
  E Sus 23 B4
  Plym 7 B4
Hooe Common 23 A4
Hoo Green 128 A2
Hook
  E Yorks 141 A5
  Hants 47 D5
  London 49 C4
  Pembs 55 C5
  Wilts 45 A4
Hooke 15 B5
Hookgate 111 B6
Hook Green
  Kent 37 C4
  Kent 50 C3
Hook Norton 81 D6
Hookway 12 B3
Hookwood 35 B5
Hoole 127 C4
Hooley 35 A5
Hoop 61 C7
Hoo St Werburgh . . . 51 B4
Hooton 126 B3
Hooton Levitt 140 D3
Hooton Pagnell 140 C2
Hooton Roberts 140 D2
Hope
  Derbys 129 A6
  Devon 7 D5
  Highld 277 C5
  Powys 93 A6
  Shrops 94 A1
  Staffs 129 D6
Hope = Yr Hôb 126 D3
Hope Bagot 94 D3
Hope Bowdler 94 B2
Hope End Green 69 A5
Hope Green 129 A4
Hopeman 266 C2
Hope Mansell 62 B2
Hopesay 94 C1
Hope's Green 51 A4
Hope under
  Dinmore 78 B3
Hopley's Green 78 B1
Hopperton 148 B3
Hop Pole 117 D4
Hopstone 95 B5
Hopton
  Shrops 110 C2
  Shrops 111 C4
  Staffs 112 C3
  Suff 105 D4
Hopton Cangeford . . 94 C3
Hopton Castle 94 D1
Hoptonheath 94 D1
Hopton on Sea 105 A6
Hopton Wafers 95 D4
Hopwas 97 A4
Hopwood
  Gtr Man 138 C1
  Worcs 96 D3
Horam 22 A3
Horbling 116 B4
Horbury 139 B5
Horcott 64 C2
Horden 168 A2
Horderley 94 C2
Hordle 17 B6
Hordley 110 B2
Horeb
  Carms 57 B4
  Carms 58 C2
  Ceredig 73 B6
Horfield 43 B5
Horham 104 D3
Horkesley Heath . . . 70 A3
Horkstow 142 B1
Horley
  Oxon 81 C7
  Sur 35 B5
Hornblotton Green . . 29 B5

Hornby
  Lancs 145 A5
  N Yorks 157 B6
  N Yorks 158 A2
Horncastle 134 C2
Hornchurch 50 A2
Horncliffe 198 B3
Horndean
  Borders 198 B3
  Hants 33 D6
Horndon 11 D6
Horndon on the Hill . 50 A3
Horne 35 B5
Horniehaugh 232 B2
Horning 121 D5
Horninghold 99 B5
Horninglow 113 C6
Horningsea 85 A6
Horningsham 30 A2
Horningtoft 119 C6
Hornsby 176 D3
Horns Corner 37 D5
Horns Cross
  Devon 25 C4
  E Sus 37 D6
Hornsea 151 C5
Hornsea Bridge 151 C5
Hornsey 49 A6
Hornton 81 C6
Horrabridge 7 A4
Horringer 87 A4
Horringford 18 C4
Horsebridge
  Devon 11 D5
  Hants 32 B2
Horse Bridge 129 D4
Horsebrook 112 D2
Horsehay 95 A4
Horseheath 86 C2
Horsehouse 156 C4
Horsell 34 A2
Horseman's Green . .110 A3
Horseway 101 C6
Horsey 121 C6
Horsford 120 D3
Horsforth 147 D6
Horsham
  Worcs 79 B5
  W Sus 35 C4
Horsham St Faith . .120 D4
Horsington
  Lincs 134 C1
  Som 29 C7
Horsley
  Derbys 114 A1
  Glos 63 D4
  Northumb 178 C2
  Northumb 188 D1
Horsley Cross 71 A5
Horsleycross Street . 71 A5
Horsleyhill 186 B4
Horsleyhope 166 A3
Horsley
  Woodhouse 114 A1
Horsmonden 37 B4
Horspath 65 C6
Horstead 121 D4
Horsted Keynes 36 D1
Horton
  Bucks 67 B4
  Dorset 17 A4
  Lancs 146 B2
  Northants 83 B5
  S Glos 43 A6
  Shrops 110 C3
  Som 28 D3
  Staffs 129 D4
  Swansea 57 D4
  Wilts 45 C4
  Windsor 48 B3
Horton-cum-
  Studley 65 B6
Horton Green 110 A3
Horton Heath 32 D3
Horton in
  Ribblesdale 155 D7
Horton Kirby 50 C2
Hortonlane 110 D3
Horwich 137 B5
Horwich End 129 A5
Horwood 25 C6
Hose 115 C5
Hoselaw 198 C2
Hoses 153 A3
Hosh 218 B3
Hosta 287 G2
Hoswick 285 L6
Hotham 150 D1
Hothfield 38 A1
Hoton 114 C3

Houbie 284 D8
Houdston 181 B3
Hough
  Ches E. 128 B3
  Ches E. 128 D2
Hougham 116 A1
Hough Green 127 A4
Hough-on-the-Hill 116 A2
Houghton
  Cambs. 101 D4
  Cumb 175 C7
  Hants 32 B2
  Pembs. 55 D5
  W Sus 20 A3
Houghton Conquest . 84 C2
Houghton Green
  E Sus 37 D7
  Warr 137 D5
Houghton-le-Side . 167 C5
Houghton-Le-
  Spring 167 A6
Houghton on the
  Hill 98 A3
Houghton Regis 67 A5
Houghton St Giles . 119 B6
Houlland
  Shetland 284 F7
  Shetland 285 H5
Houlsyke 159 A6
Hound 18 A3
Hound Green 47 D5
Houndslow 197 B5
Houndwood 211 D5
Hounslow 48 B4
Hounslow Green . . . 69 B6
Housay 284 F8
House of Daviot . . . 252 B3
House of
  Glenmuick 243 C6
Housetter 284 E5
Houss 285 K5
Houston 205 B4
Houstry 275 A5
Houton 283 G4
Hove 21 B5
Hoveringham 115 A4
Hoveton 121 D5
Hovingham 159 D5
How 176 D3
Howbrook 139 D6
How Caple 79 D4
Howden
  Borders 187 A5
  E Yorks 141 A5
Howden-le-Wear . . 167 B4
Howe
  Highld 281 B5
  Norf 104 A3
  N Yorks 158 C2
Howe Bridge 137 C5
Howe Green 70 C1
Howell 116 A4
How End 84 C2
Howe of Teuchar . . 256 B2
Howe Street
  Essex 69 B6
  Essex 86 D2
Howey 77 B4
Howgate 196 A1
How Green 36 B2
Howick 189 B5
Howle
  Durham 166 C3
  Telford 111 C5
Howlett End 86 D1
Howley 14 A2
Hownam 187 B6
Hownam Mains 187 A6
Howpasley 185 B6
Howsham
  N Lincs 142 C2
  N Yorks 149 A6
Howslack 184 B3
Howtel 198 C2
Howton 61 A6
Howtown 164 D2
Howwood 204 B3
Hoxne 104 D2
Hoy 283 G3
Hoylake 126 A2
Hoyland 139 C6
Hoylandswaine . . . 139 C5
Hubberholme 156 D3
Hubbert's Bridge . . 117 A5
Huby
  N Yorks 147 C6
  N Yorks 149 A4
Hucclecote 63 B4
Hucking 37 A6
Hucknall 114 A3

Huddersfield 139 B4
Huddington 80 B2
Hudswell 157 A5
Huggate 150 B1
Hugglescote 114 D2
Hughenden Valley . 66 D3
Hughley 94 B3
Hugh Town Scilly . . . 2 E4
Huish
  Devon 25 D6
  Wilts 45 C5
Huish Champflower . 27 C5
Huish Episcopi 28 C4
Hulcott 66 B3
Hulland 113 A6
Hulland Ward 113 A6
Hullavington 44 A2
Hullbridge 70 D2
Hulme 138 D1
Hulme End 129 D6
Hulme Walfield . . . 128 C3
Hulverstone 18 C2
Hulver Street 105 C5
Humber 78 B3
Humber Bridge . . . 142 A2
Humberston 143 C5
Humbie 210 D1
Humbleton
  E Yorks 151 D5
  Northumb 188 A2
Humby 116 B3
Hume 197 B6
Humshaugh 177 B7
Huna 281 A5
Huncoat 146 D1
Huncote 98 B2
Hundalee 187 B5
Hunderthwaite . . . 166 C2
Hundleby 134 C3
Hundle Houses . . . 134 D2
Hundleton 55 D5
Hundon 86 C3
Hundred Acres 33 D4
Hundred End 136 A3
Hundred House 77 B5
Hungarton 98 A3
Hungerford
  Hants 31 D5
  W Berks 46 C1
Hungerford
  Newtown 46 B1
Hungerton 116 C1
Hungladder 258 A3
Hunmanby 161 D4
Hunmanby Moor . . 161 D5
Hunningham 81 A6
Hunny Hill 18 C3
Hunsdon 68 B4
Hunsingore 148 B3
Hunslet 148 D2
Hunsonby 164 B3
Hunspow 280 A4
Hunstanton 118 A3
Hunstanworth . . . 166 A2
Hunsterson 111 A5
Hunston
  Suff 87 A4
  W Sus 20 B1
Hunstrete 43 C5
Hunt End 80 A3
Hunter's Quay 203 A6
Hunthill Lodge . . . 232 A2
Huntingdon 100 D4
Huntingfield 104 D4
Huntingford 30 B2
Huntington
  E Loth 210 C1
  Hereford 77 B6
  Staffs 112 D3
  York 149 B5
Huntingtower 219 B5
Huntley 62 B3
Huntly 255 C6
Huntlywood 197 B5
Hunton
  Kent 37 B5
  N Yorks 157 B5
Hunt's Corner 103 C6
Hunt's Cross 127 A4
Huntsham 27 C5
Huntspill 28 A3
Huntworth 28 B3
Hunwick 167 B4
Hunworth 120 B2
Hurdsfield 129 B4
Hurley
  Warks 97 B5
  Windsor 47 A6
Hurlford 193 B4

Hurliness 283 J3
Hurn 17 B5
Hurn's End 118 A1
Hursley 32 C3
Hurst
  N Yorks 156 A4
  Som. 29 D4
  Wokingham 47 B5
Hurstbourne Priors . 32 A3
Hurstbourne
  Tarrant 46 D1
Hurst Green
  E Sus. 37 D5
  Lancs 145 D6
Hurstpierpoint 21 A5
Hurst Wickham . . . 21 A5
Hurstwood 146 D2
Hurtmore 34 B2
Hurworth Place . . . 157 A6
Hury 166 D2
Husabost 258 C2
Husbands Bosworth . 98 C3
Husborne Crawley . 83 D6
Husthwaite 158 D4
Hutchwns 40 D3
Huthwaite 131 D4
Huttoft 135 B5
Hutton
  Borders 198 A3
  Cumb 164 C2
  Essex 69 D6
  E Yorks 150 B3
  Lancs 136 A3
  N Som 42 D2
Hutton Buscel 160 C3
Hutton Conyers . . 158 D2
Hutton Cranswick . 150 B3
Hutton End 164 B2
Hutton Gate 168 D3
Hutton Henry 168 B2
Hutton-le-Hole . . . 159 B6
Hutton Magna 166 D4
Hutton Roof
  Cumb 155 D4
  Cumb 163 A6
Hutton Rudby 158 A3
Hutton Sessay . . . 158 D3
Hutton Village . . . 168 D3
Hutton Wandesley . 148 B4
Huxley 127 C5
Huxter
  Shetland 285 G7
  Shetland 285 H5
Huxton 211 D5
Huyton 136 D3
Hwlffordd
  = Haverfordwest . . . 55 C5
Hycemoor 153 B1
Hyde
  Glos 63 C4
  Gtr Man 138 D2
  Hants 31 D5
Hyde Heath 67 C4
Hyde Park 140 C3
Hydestile 34 B2
Hylton Castle 179 D5
Hyndford Bridge . . 194 B4
Hynish 222 D2
Hyssington 93 B7
Hythe
  Hants 18 A3
  Kent 38 B3
Hythe End 48 B3
Hythie 269 D5

I

Ibberton 16 A1
Ible 130 D2
Ibsley 17 A5
Ibstock 114 D2
Ibstone 66 D2
Ibthorpe 46 D1
Ibworth 46 D3
Ichrachan 227 C5
Ickburgh 103 B4
Ickenham 48 A3
Ickford 66 C1
Ickham 53 D4
Ickleford 84 D3
Icklesham 23 A6
Ickleton 85 C6
Icklingham 102 D3
Ickwell Green 84 C3
Icomb 64 A3
Idbury 64 B3
Iddesleigh 11 A6
Ide 12 B3
Ideford 12 D3

Ide Hill 36 A2
Iden 37 D7
Iden Green
  Kent 37 C5
  Kent 37 C6
Idle 147 D5
Idlicote 81 C5
Idmiston 31 B5
Idole 57 A4
Idridgehay 113 A6
Idrigill 258 B3
Idstone 45 A6
Idvies 232 D3
Iffley 65 C6
Ifield 35 C5
Ifold 34 C3
Iford 22 B2
Ifton Heath 110 B2
Ightfield 111 B4
Ightham 36 A3
Iken 89 B5
Ilam 129 D6
Ilchester 29 C5
Ilderton 188 A3
Ilford 50 A1
Ilfracombe 25 A6
Ilkeston 114 A2
Ilketshall
  St Andrew 105 C4
Ilketshall
  St Lawrence 105 C4
Ilketshall
  St Margaret 104 C4
Ilkley 147 C5
Illey 96 C2
Illingworth 138 A3
Illogan 3 A4
Illston on the Hill . . 99 B4
Ilmer 66 C2
Ilmington 81 C5
Ilminster 28 D3
Ilsington 12 D2
Ilston 57 C5
Ilton
  N Yorks 157 D5
  Som. 28 D3
Imachar 202 D3
Imeraval 200 D3
Immingham 142 B3
Impington 85 A6
Ince 127 B4
Ince Blundell 136 C2
Ince in Makerfield . 137 C4
Inchbare 233 B4
Inchberry 266 D4
Inchbraoch 233 C5
Incheril 262 D2
Inchgrundle 232 A2
Inchina 261 A6
Inchinnan 205 B4
Inchkinloch 277 D6
Inchlaggan 239 B5
Inchlumpie 264 C1
Inchmore 251 B5
Inchnacardoch
  Hotel 240 A1
Inchnadamph 271 B5
Inch of Arnhall . . . 233 A4
Inchree 237 C4
Inchture 220 B2
Inchyra 219 B6
Indian Queens 4 B4
Inerval 200 D3
Ingatestone 69 C6
Ingbirchworth . . . 139 C5
Ingestre 112 C3
Ingham
  Lincs 133 A4
  Norf 121 C5
  Suff 103 D4
Ingham Corner . . . 121 C5
Ingleborough 118 D1
Ingleby
  Derbys 114 C1
  Lincs 132 B3
Ingleby Arncliffe . . 158 A3
Ingleby Barwick . . 168 D2
Ingleby Greenhow . 159 A4
Inglesbatch 43 C6
Inglesham 64 D3
Ingleton
  Durham 167 C4
  N Yorks 155 D5
Inglewhite 145 C5
Ingliston 208 C4
Ingoe 178 B2
Ingol 145 D5
Ingoldisthorpe . . . 118 B3
Ingoldmells 135 C5

Ingoldsby 116 B3
Ingon 81 B5
Ingram 188 B3
Ingrow 147 D4
Ings 154 B3
Ingst 43 A4
Ingworth 120 C3
Inham's End 101 B4
Inkberrow 80 B3
Inkpen 46 C1
Inkstack 281 A4
Inn 154 A2
Innellan 203 A6
Innerleithen 196 C2
Innerleven 220 D3
Innermessan 170 A2
Innerwick
  E Loth 211 C4
  Perth 229 D4
Innis Chonain 227 D6
Insch 256 D1
Insh 241 B6
Inshore 276 B4
Inskip 145 D4
Instoneville 140 B3
Instow 25 B5
Intake 140 C3
Inver
  Aberds 243 C5
  Highld 265 B4
  Perth 230 D3
Inverailort 235 B6
Inveraldie 220 A4
Inveralligin 249 A5
Inverallochy 269 C5
Inveran 264 A1
Inveraray 214 B3
Inverarish 248 C2
Inverarity 232 D2
Inverarnan 215 A6
Inverasdale 261 B5
Inverbeg 206 A1
Inverbervie 233 A6
Inverboyndie 268 C1
Inverbroom 262 B3
Invercassley 272 D2
Invercauld House . 243 C4
Inverchaolain 203 A5
Invercharnan 227 B6
Inverchoran 251 A4
Invercreran 227 B5
Inverdruie 242 A2
Inverebrie 257 C4
Invereck 215 D4
Inverernan House . 243 A6
Invereshie House . 241 B6
Inveresk 209 C6
Inverey 242 D3
Inverfarigaig 251 D7
Invergarry 239 B7
Invergelder 243 C5
Invergeldie 218 B2
Invergordon 264 D3
Invergowrie 220 A3
Inverguseran 247 D6
Inverhadden 229 C5
Inverharroch 255 C4
Inverherive 216 B3
Inverie 247 E6
Inverinan 214 A2
Inverinate 249 D5
Inverkeilor 233 D4
Inverkeithing 208 B4
Inverkeithny 256 B1
Inverkip 204 A2
Inverkirkaig 270 C3
Inverlael 262 B3
Inverlochlarig . . . 216 C4
Inverlochy
  Argyll 227 D6
  Highld 237 B5
Inverlussa 213 D4
Inver Mallie 239 D5
Invermark Lodge . . 244 D1
Invermoidart 235 C5
Invermoriston . . . 240 A2
Invernaver 278 B3
Inverneill 213 D6
Inverness 252 B2
Invernettie 257 B6
Invernoaden 215 C4
Inveroran Hotel . . 228 D1
Inverpolly Lodge . 270 C3
Inverquharity 232 C2
Inverquhomery . . . 257 B5
Inverroy 239 D6
Inversanda 236 D3
Invershiel 238 A3
Invershin 264 A1
Inversnaid Hotel . . 215 B6

Inverugie 257 B6
Inveruglas 215 B6
Inveruglass 241 B6
Inverurie 256 D2
Invervar 229 D5
Inverythan 256 B2
Inwardleigh 11 B6
Inworth 70 B2
Iochdar 286 B3
Iping 34 D1
Ipplepen 8 A2
Ipsden 47 A4
Ipsley 80 A3
Ipstones 129 D5
Ipswich 88 C2
Irby 126 A2
Irby in the Marsh . 135 C4
Irby upon Humber . 142 C3
Irchester 83 A6
Ireby
  Cumb 163 A5
  Lancs 155 D5
Ireland
  Orkney 283 G4
  Shetland 285 L5
Ireland's Cross . . . 111 A6
Ireleth 153 C3
Ireshopeburn 165 B6
Irlam 137 D6
Irnham 116 C3
Iron Acton 43 A5
Ironbridge 95 A4
Iron Cross 80 B3
Irongray 173 A7
Ironmacannie 173 A4
Ironside 268 D3
Ironville 131 D4
Irstead 121 C5
Irthington 176 C2
Irthlingborough . . . 99 D6
Irton 160 C4
Irvine 192 B3
Isauld 279 B5
Isbister
  Orkney 282 E3
  Orkney 282 F4
  Shetland 284 E5
  Shetland 285 G7
Isfield 22 A2
Isham 99 D5
Isle Abbotts 28 C3
Isle Brewers 28 C3
Isleham 102 D2
Isle of Whithorn . . 171 D6
Isleornsay 247 C6
Islesburgh 284 G5
Islesteps 174 A2
Isleworth 49 B4
Isley Walton 114 C2
Islibhig 287 B4
Islington 49 A6
Islip
  Northants 100 D1
  Oxon 65 B6
Istead Rise 50 C2
Isycoed 127 D4
Itchen 32 D3
Itchen Abbas 32 B4
Itchen Stoke 33 B4
Itchingfield 35 D4
Itchington 43 A5
Itteringham 120 B3
Itton 12 B1
Itton Common . . . 61 D6
Ivegill 164 A2
Iver 48 A3
Iver Heath 48 A3
Iveston 178 D3
Ivinghoe 67 B4
Ivinghoe Aston . . . 67 B4
Ivington 78 B2
Ivington Green . . . 78 B2
Ivybridge 7 B5
Ivy Chimneys 68 C4
Ivychurch 38 C2
Ivy Cross 30 C2
Ivy Hatch 36 A3
Iwade 51 C6
Iwerne Courtney or
  Shroton 30 D2
Iwerne Minster . . . 30 D2
Ixworth 103 D5
Ixworth Thorpe . . . 103 D5

J

Jack Hill 147 B6
Jack in the Green 13 B5
Jacksdale 131 D4
Jackstown 256 C2
Jacobstow 10 B2
Jacobstowe 11 A6
Jameston 55 E6
Jamestown
Dumfries 185 C6
Highld 251 A6
W Dunb 206 B1
Jarrow 179 C5
Jarvis Brook 36 D3
Jasper's Green 69 A7
Java 225 C6
Jawcraig 207 C6
Jaywick 71 B5
Jealott's Hill 47 B6
Jedburgh 187 A5
Jeffreyston 55 D6
Jellyhill 205 A6
Jemimaville 264 D3
Jersey Farm 67 C6
Jesmond 179 C4
Jevington 22 B3
Jockey End 67 B5
Johnby 164 B2
John o' Groats 281 A5
John's Cross 37 D5
Johnshaven 233 B5
Johnston 55 C5
Johnstone 205 B4
Johnstonebridge 184 C3
Johnstown
Carms 57 A4
Wrex 110 A2
Joppa
Edin 209 C6
S Ayrs 182 A2
Jordans 67 D4
Jordanthorpe 130 A3
Jump 140 C1
Jumpers Green 17 B5
Juniper Green 209 D4
Jurby East 152 B3
Jurby West 152 B3

K

Kaber 165 D5
Kaimend 195 B4
Kaimes 209 D5
Kalemouth 187 A6
Kames
Argyll 203 A4
Argyll 213 A6
E Ayrs 194 D1
Kea 4 C3
Keadby 141 B6
Keal Cotes 134 C3
Kearsley 137 C6
Kearstwick 155 C5
Kearton 156 B3
Kearvaig 276 A3
Keasden 145 A7
Keckwick 127 A5
Keddington 134 A3
Kedington 86 C3
Kedleston 113 A7
Keelby 142 B3
Keele 112 A2
Keeley Green 84 C2
Keeston 55 C5
Keevil 44 D3
Kegworth 114 C2
Kehelland 3 A4
Keig 244 A3
Keighley 147 C4
Keil 236 D3
Keilarsbrae 208 A1
Keilhill 268 D2
Keillmore 213 D4
Keillor 231 D6
Keillour 219 B4
Keills 201 B4
Keils 201 B5
Keinton Mandeville 29 B5
Keir Mill 183 C6
Keisby 116 C3
Keiss 281 B5
Keith 267 D5
Keith Inch 257 B6
Keithock 233 B4
Kelbrook 146 C3
Kelby 116 A3
Keld
Cumb 164 D3
N Yorks 156 A2
Keldholme 159 C6
Kelfield
N Lincs 141 C6
N Yorks 149 D4
Kelham 132 D2
Kellan 225 B4
Kellas
Angus 221 A4
Moray 266 D2
Kellaton 8 D2
Kelleth 155 A5
Kelleythorpe 150 B2
Kelling 120 A2
Kellingley 140 A3
Kellington 140 A3
Kelloe 167 B6
Kelloholm 183 A5
Kelly 11 C4
Kelly Bray 11 D4
Kelmarsh 99 D4
Kelmscot 64 D3
Kelsale 89 A4
Kelsall 127 C5
Kelsall Hill 127 C5
Kelshall 85 D5
Kelsick 175 C4
Kelso 197 C6
Kelstedge 130 C3
Kelstern 143 D4
Kelston 43 C6
Keltneyburn 229 D6
Kelton 174 A2
Kelty 208 A4
Kelvedon 70 B2
Kelvedon Hatch 69 D5
Kelvin 205 C6
Kelvinside 205 B5
Kelynack 2 B1
Kemback 220 C4
Kemberton 95 A5
Kemble 63 D5
Kemerton 80 D2
Kemeys Commander 61 C5
Kemnay 245 A4
Kempley 62 A2
Kempsey 79 C6
Kempsford 64 D2
Kemps Green 96 D4
Kempshott 47 D4
Kempston 84 C2
Kempston Hardwick 84 C2
Kempton 94 C1
Kemp Town 21 B6
Kemsing 36 A3
Kemsley 51 C6
Kenardington 38 B1
Kenchester 78 C2
Kencot 64 C3
Kendal 154 B4
Kendoon 182 D4
Kendray 139 C6
Kenfig 40 C3
Kenfig Hill 40 C3
Kenilworth 97 D5
Kenknock 217 A4
Kenley
London 35 A6
Shrops 94 A3
Kenmore
Highld 249 A4
Perth 230 D1
Kenn
Devon 13 C4
N Som 42 C3
Kennacley 288 H2
Kennacraig 202 B3
Kennerleigh 12 A3
Kennet 208 A2
Kennethmont 255 D6
Kennett 86 A2
Kennford 13 C4
Kenninghall 103 C6
Kenninghall Heath 103 C6
Kennington
Kent 38 A2
Oxon 65 C6
Kennoway 220 D3
Kenny Hill 102 D2
Kennythorpe 149 A6
Kenovay 222 C2
Kensaleyre 259 C4
Kensington 49 B5
Kensworth 67 B5
Kensworth Common 67 B5
Kentallen 237 D4
Kentchurch 61 A6
Kentford 86 A3
Kentisbeare 13 A5
Kentisbury 25 A7
Kentisbury Ford 25 A7
Kentmere 154 A3
Kenton
Devon 13 C4
Suff 88 A2
T&W 179 C4
Kenton Bankfoot 179 C4
Kentra 235 D5
Kents Bank 154 D2
Kent's Green 62 A3
Kent's Oak 32 C2
Kent Street
E Sus 23 A5
Kent 37 A4
W Sus 35 D5
Kenwick 110 B3
Kenwyn 4 C3
Keoldale 277 B4
Keppanach 237 C4
Keppoch 249 D6
Keprigan 190 D2
Kepwick 158 B3
Kerchesters 197 C6
Keresley 97 C6
Kernborough 8 C1
Kerne Bridge 62 B1
Kerris 2 C2
Kerry 93 C5
Kerrycroy 203 B6
Kerrysdale 261 C5
Kerry's Gate 78 D1
Kersall 132 C2
Kersey 87 C6
Kershopefoot 176 A2
Kersoe 80 D2
Kerswell 13 A5
Kerswell Green 79 C6
Kesgrave 88 C3
Kessingland 105 C6
Kessingland Beach 105 C6
Kessington 205 A5
Kestle 5 C4
Kestle Mill 4 B3
Keston 49 C7
Keswick
Cumb 163 B5
Norf 104 A3
Norf 121 B5
Ketley 111 D5
Ketley Bank 111 D5
Ketsby 134 B3
Kettering 99 D5
Ketteringham 104 A2
Kettins 220 A2
Kettlebaston 87 B5
Kettlebridge 220 D3
Kettleburgh 88 A3
Kettlehill 220 D3
Kettleholm 174 A4
Kettleness 169 D6
Kettleshume 129 B4
Kettlesing Bottom 147 B6
Kettlesing Head 147 B6
Kettlestone 119 B6
Kettlethorpe 132 B3
Kettletoft 282 D7
Kettlewell 156 D3
Ketton 100 A1
Kew 49 B4
Kew Bridge 49 B4
Kewstoke 42 C2
Kexbrough 139 C6
Kexby
Lincs 132 A3
York 149 B6
Key Green 128 C3
Keyham 98 A3
Keyhaven 18 B2
Keyingham 143 A4
Keymer 21 A6
Keynsham 43 C5
Keysoe 84 A2
Keysoe Row 84 A2
Keyston 100 D2
Keyworth 115 B4
Kibblesworth 179 D4
Kibworth
Beauchamp 98 B3
Kibworth Harcourt 98 B3
Kidbrooke 49 B7
Kiddemore Green 95 A6
Kidderminster 95 D6
Kiddington 65 A5
Kidlington 65 B5
Kidmore End 47 B4
Kidsgrove 128 D3
Kidstones 156 C3
Kidwelly = *Cydweli* 57 B4
Kiel Crofts 226 C4
Kielder 187 D5
Kierfiold Ho 282 F3
Kilbagie 208 B2
Kilbarchan 205 B4
Kilbeg 247 D5
Kilberry 202 B2
Kilbirnie 204 C3
Kilbride
Argyll 226 D3
Argyll 226 D4
Highld 247 B4
Kilburn
Angus 232 B1
Derbys 114 A1
London 49 A5
N Yorks 158 D4
Kilby 98 B3
Kilchamaig 202 B3
Kilchattan 212 C1
Kilchattan Bay 203 C6
Kilchenzie 190 C2
Kilcheran 226 C3
Kilchiaran 200 B2
Kilchoan
Argyll 213 A5
Highld 234 D3
Kilchoman 200 B2
Kilchrenan 227 D5
Kilconquhar 221 D4
Kilcot 62 A2
Kilcoy 252 A1
Kilcreggan 215 D5
Kildale 159 A5
Kildalloig 190 D3
Kildary 264 C3
Kildermorie Lodge 263 C7
Kildonan 191 C6
Kildonan Lodge 274 B3
Kildonnan 234 B3
Kildrummy 244 A1
Kildwick 147 C4
Kilfinan 203 A4
Kilfinnan 239 C6
Kilgetty 56 B1
Kilgwrrwg
Common 61 D6
Kilham
E Yorks 150 A3
Northumb 198 C2
Kilkenneth 222 C2
Kilkerran 190 D3
Kilkhampton 24 D3
Killamarsh 131 A4
Killay 57 C6
Killbeg 225 B5
Killean 202 D1
Killearn 206 B3
Killen 252 A2
Killerby 167 D4
Killichonan 229 C4
Killiechonate 239 D6
Killiechronan 225 B4
Killiecrankie 230 B3
Killiemor 224 C3
Killiemore House 224 D3
Killilan 249 C6
Killimster 281 C5
Killin 217 A5
Killinallan 200 A3
Killinghall 148 B1
Killington 155 C5
Killingworth 179 B4
Killin Lodge 240 B3
Killmahumaig 213 C5
Killochyett 196 B3
Killocraw 190 B2
Killundine 225 B4
Kilmacolm 204 B3
Kilmaha 214 B2
Kilmahog 217 D6
Kilmalieu 236 D2
Kilmaluag 259 A4
Kilmany 220 B3
Kilmarie 247 C4
Kilmarnock 193 B4
Kilmaron Castle 220 C3
Kilmartin 213 C6
Kilmaurs 205 D4
Kilmelford 213 A6
Kilmeny 200 B3
Kilmersdon 43 D5
Kilmeston 33 C4
Kilmichael 190 C2
Kilmichael
Glassary 214 C1
Kilmichael of
Inverlussa 213 D5
Kilmington
Devon 14 B2
Wilts 30 B1
Kilmonivaig 239 D5
Kilmorack 251 B6
Kilmore
Argyll 226 D3
Highld 247 D5
Kilmory
Argyll 202 A2
Highld 235 C4
Highld 246 D2
N Ayrs 191 C5
Kilmuir
Highld 252 B2
Highld 258 A3
Highld 258 D2
Highld 264 C3
Kilmun
Argyll 214 A2
Argyll 215 D4
Kilncadzow 194 B3
Kilndown 37 C5
Kilnhurst 140 D2
Kilninian 224 B2
Kilninver 226 D3
Kiln Pit Hill 178 D2
Kilnsea 143 B6
Kilnsey 146 A3
Kilnwick 150 C2
Kilnwick Percy 149 B7
Kiloran 212 C1
Kilpatrick 191 C5
Kilpeck 78 D2
Kilphedir 274 C3
Kilpin 141 A5
Kilpin Pike 141 A5
Kilrenny 221 D5
Kilsby 98 D2
Kilspindie 220 B2
Kilsyth 207 C5
Kiltarlity 251 B7
Kilton
Notts 131 B5
Som 27 A6
Kilton Thorpe 169 D4
Kilvaxter 258 B3
Kilve 27 A6
Kilvington 115 A5
Kilwinning 204 D3
Kimberley
Norf 103 A6
Notts 114 A3
Kimber worth 140 D2
Kimblesworth 167 A5
Kimble Wick 66 C3
Kimbolton
Cambs 84 A2
Hereford 78 A3
Kimcote 98 C2
Kimmeridge 16 D3
Kimmerston 198 C3
Kimpton
Hants 32 A1
Herts 68 B1
Kinbrace 274 A2
Kinbuck 218 D2
Kincaple 221 C4
Kincardine
Fife 208 B2
Highld 264 B2
Kincardine Bridge 208 B2
Kincardine O'Neil 244 C2
Kinclaven 219 A6
Kincorth 245 B6
Kincorth House 265 D6
Kincraig 241 B6
Kincraigie 230 D3
Kindallachan 230 D3
Kineton
Glos 64 A1
Warks 81 B6
Kinfauns 219 B6
Kingairloch 236 D2
Kingarth 203 C5
Kingcoed 61 C6
King Edward 268 D2
Kingerby 142 D2
Kingham 64 A3
Kingholm Quay 174 A2
Kinghorn 209 B5
Kingie 239 B5
Kinglassie 209 A5
Kingoodie 220 B3
King's Acre 78 C2
Kingsand 6 B3
Kingsbarns 221 C5
Kingsbridge
Devon 7 C6
Som 27 B4
King's Bromley 113 D5
Kingsburgh 258 C3
Kingsbury
London 49 A5
Warks 97 B5
Kingsbury Episcopi 28 C4
King's Caple 62 A1
Kingsclere 46 D3
King's Cliffe 100 B2
Kingscote 63 D4
Kingscott 25 D6
King's Coughton 80 B3
Kingscross 191 C6
Kingsdon 29 C5
Kingsdown 39 A5
Kingseat 208 A4
Kingsey 66 C2
Kingsfold 35 C4
Kingsford
E Ayrs 205 D4
Worcs 95 C6
Kingsforth 142 B2
Kingsgate 53 B5
Kingsheanton 25 B6
King's Heath 96 C3
Kings Hedges 85 A6
King's Hill 37 A4
Kingshouse Hotel 237 D6
Kingside Hill 175 C4
Kingskerswell 8 A2
Kingskettle 220 D3
Kingsland
Anglesey 122 B2
Hereford 78 A2
Kings Langley 67 C5
Kingsley
Ches W 127 B5
Hants 33 B6
Staffs 112 A4
Kingsley Green 34 C1
Kingsley Holt 112 A4
Kingsley Park 83 A4
King's Lynn 118 C3
King's Meaburn 165 C4
King's Mills 110 A2
Kingsmuir
Angus 232 D2
Fife 221 D5
Kings Muir 196 C1
King's Newnham 98 D1
King's Newton 114 C1
Kingsnorth 38 B2
King's Norton
Leics 98 A3
W Mid 96 D3
King's Nympton 26 D1
King's Pyon 78 B2
King's Ripton 101 D4
King's Somborne 32 B2
King's Stag 30 D1
King's Stanley 63 C4
King's Sutton 82 D1
Kingstanding 96 B3
Kingsteignton 12 D3
King Sterndale 129 B5
King's Thorn 78 D3
Kingsthorpe 83 A4
Kingston
Cambs 85 B5
Devon 7 C5
Dorset 16 A1
Dorset 16 D3
E Loth 210 B2
Hants 17 A5
IoW 18 C3
Kent 52 D3
Moray 266 C4
Kingston Bagpuize 65 D5
Kingston Blount 66 D2
Kingston by Sea 21 B5
Kingston Deverill 30 B2
Kingstone
Hereford 78 D2
Som 28 D3
Staffs 113 C4
Kingston Gorse 20 B3
Kingston Lisle 45 A7
Kingston Maurward 15 B7
Kingston near
Lewes 22 B1
Kingston on Soar 114 C3
Kingston Russell 15 B5
Kingston St Mary 28 C2
Kingston Seymour 42 C3
Kingston Upon
Hull 142 A2
Kingston upon
Thames 49 C4
Kingston Vale 49 B5
Kingstown 175 C6

Langford continued
Essex ... 70 C2
Notts ... 132 D3
Oxon ... 64 C3
Langford Budville ... 27 C6
Langham
Essex ... 87 D6
Norf ... 120 A2
Rutland ... 115 D6
Suff ... 103 E5
Langhaugh ... 195 C7
Langho ... 145 D7
Langholm ... 185 D6
Langleeford ... 188 A2
Langley
Ches E ... 129 B4
Hants ... 18 A3
Herts ... 68 A2
Kent ... 37 A6
Northumb ... 177 C6
Slough ... 48 B3
Warks ... 81 A4
W Sus ... 33 C7
Langley Burrell ... 44 B3
Langley Common ... 113 B6
Langley Heath ... 37 A6
Langley Lower
Green ... 85 D6
Langley Marsh ... 27 C5
Langley Park ... 167 A5
Langley Street ... 105 A4
Langley Upper
Green ... 85 D6
Langney ... 22 B4
Langold ... 131 A5
Langore ... 10 C4
Langport ... 28 C4
Langrick ... 117 A5
Langridge ... 43 C6
Langridge Ford ... 25 C6
Langrigg ... 175 D4
Langrish ... 33 C6
Langsett ... 139 C5
Langshaw ... 197 C4
Langside ... 218 C2
Langskaill ... 282 C5
Langstone
Hants ... 19 A6
Newport ... 61 D5
Langthorne ... 157 B6
Langthorpe ... 148 A2
Langthwaite ... 156 A4
Langtoft
E Yorks ... 150 A3
Lincs ... 116 D4
Langton
Durham ... 167 D4
Lincs ... 134 B3
Lincs ... 134 C2
N Yorks ... 149 A6
Langton by Wragby 133 B6
Langton Green
Kent ... 36 C3
Suff ... 104 D2
Langton Herring ... 15 C6
Langton Matravers ... 17 D4
Langtree ... 25 D5
Langwathby ... 164 B3
Langwell House ... 275 B5
Langwell Lodge ... 271 D4
Langwith ... 131 C5
Langwith Junction 131 C5
Langworth ... 133 B5
Lanivet ... 5 A5
Lanlivery ... 5 B5
Lanner ... 4 D2
Lanreath ... 5 B6
Lansallos ... 5 B6
Lansdown ... 63 A5
Lanteglos Highway ... 5 B6
Lanton
Borders ... 187 A5
Northumb ... 198 C3
Lapford ... 12 A2
Laphroaig ... 200 D3
La Planque ... 6
Lapley ... 112 D2
Lapworth ... 97 D4
Larachbeg ... 225 B5
Larbert ... 207 B6
Larden Green ... 127 D5
Largie ... 255 C7
Largiemore ... 214 D2
Largoward ... 221 D4
Largs ... 204 C2
Largybeg ... 191 C6
Largymore ... 191 C6
Larkfield ... 204 A2

Larkhall ... 194 A2
Larkhill ... 31 A5
Larling ... 103 C5
Larriston ... 186 D4
Lartington ... 166 D3
Lary ... 243 B6
Lasham ... 33 A5
Lashenden ... 37 B6
Lassington ... 62 A3
Lassodie ... 208 A4
Lastingham ... 159 B6
Latcham ... 29 A4
Latchford
Herts ... 68 A3
Warr ... 127 A6
Latchingdon ... 70 C2
Latchley ... 11 D5
Lately Common ... 137 D5
Lathbury ... 83 C5
Latheron ... 275 A5
Latheronwheel ... 275 A5
Latheronwheel
House ... 275 A5
Lathones ... 221 D4
Latimer ... 67 D5
Latteridge ... 43 A5
Lattiford ... 29 C6
Latton ... 64 D1
Latton Bush ... 69 C4
Lauchintilly ... 245 A4
Lauder ... 197 B4
Laugharne ... 56 A3
Laughterton ... 132 B3
Laughton
E Sus ... 22 A3
Leics ... 98 C3
Lincs ... 116 B3
Lincs ... 141 B3
Laughton Common 131 A5
Laughton en le
Morthen ... 131 A5
Launcells ... 10 A3
Launceston ... 10 C4
Launton ... 65 A7
Laurencekirk ... 233 A5
Laurieston
Dumfries ... 173 B4
Falk ... 208 C2
Lavendon ... 83 B6
Lavenham ... 87 C5
Laverhay ... 185 C4
Laversdale ... 176 C2
Laverstock ... 31 B5
Laverstoke ... 32 A3
Laverton
Glos ... 80 D3
N Yorks ... 157 D6
Som ... 44 D1
Lavister ... 126 D3
Law ... 194 A3
Lawers
Perth ... 217 A6
Perth ... 218 B2
Lawford ... 88 D1
Lawhitton ... 11 C4
Lawkland ... 146 A1
Lawley ... 95 A4
Lawnhead ... 112 C2
Lawrenny ... 55 D6
Lawshall ... 87 B4
Lawton ... 78 B2
Laxey ... 152 C4
Laxfield ... 104 D3
Laxfirth
Shetland ... 285 H6
Shetland ... 285 J6
Laxford Bridge ... 276 D3
Laxo ... 285 G6
Laxobigging ... 284 F6
Laxton
E Yorks ... 141 A5
Northants ... 99 B6
Notts ... 132 C2
Laycock ... 147 C4
Layer Breton ... 70 B3
Layer de la Haye ... 70 B3
Layer Marney ... 70 B3
Layham ... 87 C6
Laylands Green ... 46 C1
Laytham ... 149 D6
Layton ... 144 D3
Lazenby ... 168 C3
Lazonby ... 164 B3
Lea
Derbys ... 130 D3
Hereford ... 62 A2
Lincs ... 132 A3
Shrops ... 94 A2
Shrops ... 94 C1
Wilts ... 44 A3

Leabrooks ... 131 D4
Leac a Li ... 288 H2
Leachkin ... 252 B2
Leadburn ... 196 A1
Leadenham ... 133 D4
Leaden Roding ... 69 B5
Leadgate
Cumb ... 165 A5
Durham ... 178 D3
T&W ... 178 D3
Leadhills ... 183 A6
Leafield ... 64 B4
Leagrave ... 67 A5
Leake ... 158 B3
Leake
Commonside ... 134 D3
Lealholm ... 159 A6
Lealt
Argyll ... 213 C4
Highld ... 259 B5
Lea Marston ... 97 B5
Leamington
Hastings ... 82 A1
Leamonsley ... 96 A4
Leamside ... 167 A6
Leanaig ... 252 A1
Leargybreck ... 201 A5
Leasgill ... 154 C3
Leasingham ... 116 A3
Leasingthorne ... 167 C5
Leasowe ... 136 D1
Leatherhead ... 35 A4
Leatherhead
Common ... 35 A4
Leathley ... 147 C6
Leaton ... 110 D3
Lea Town ... 145 D4
Leaveland ... 52 D2
Leavening ... 149 A6
Leaves Green ... 49 C7
Leazes ... 178 D3
Lebberston ... 161 C4
Lechlade-on-
Thames ... 64 D3
Leck ... 155 D5
Leckford ... 32 B2
Leckfurin ... 278 C3
Leckgruinart ... 200 B2
Leckhampstead
Bucks ... 83 D4
W Berks ... 46 B2
Leckhampstead
Thicket ... 46 B2
Leckhampton ... 63 B5
Leckie ... 262 D2
Leckmelm ... 262 A3
Leckwith ... 41 D6
Leconfield ... 150 C3
Ledaig ... 226 C4
Ledburn ... 67 A4
Ledbury ... 79 D5
Ledcharrie ... 217 B5
Ledgemoor ... 78 B2
Ledicot ... 78 A2
Ledmore ... 271 C5
Lednagullin ... 278 B3
Ledsham
Ches W ... 126 B3
W Yorks ... 140 A2
Ledston ... 140 A2
Ledston Luck ... 148 D3
Ledwell ... 65 A5
Lee
Argyll ... 224 D3
Devon ... 25 A5
Hants ... 32 D2
Lancs ... 145 B5
Shrops ... 110 B3
Leeans ... 285 J5
Leebotten ... 285 L6
Leebotwood ... 94 B2
Lee Brockhurst ... 111 C4
Leece ... 153 D3
Leechpool ... 55 C5
Lee Clump ... 67 C4
Leeds
Kent ... 37 A6
W Yorks ... 148 D1
Leedstown ... 3 B4
Leek ... 129 D4
Leekbrook ... 129 D4
Leek Wootton ... 81 A5
Lee Mill ... 7 B5
Leeming ... 157 C6
Leeming Bar ... 157 B6
Lee Moor ... 7 A4
Lee-on-the-Solent 19 A4
Lees
Derbys ... 113 B6
Gtr Man ... 138 C2

Lees continued
W Yorks ... 147 D4
Leeswood ... 126 C2
Legbourne ... 134 A3
Legerwood ... 197 B4
Legsby ... 133 A6
Leicester ... 98 A2
Leicester Forest
East ... 98 A2
Leigh
Dorset ... 15 A6
Glos ... 63 A4
Gtr Man ... 137 C5
Kent ... 36 B3
Shrops ... 94 A1
Sur ... 35 B5
Wilts ... 63 D6
Worcs ... 79 B5
Leigh Beck ... 51 A5
Leigh Common ... 30 C1
Leigh Delamere ... 44 B2
Leigh Green ... 37 C7
Leigh on Sea ... 51 A5
Leigh Park ... 19 A6
Leigh Sinton ... 79 B5
Leighswood ... 96 A3
Leighterton ... 63 D7
Leighton
N Yorks ... 157 D5
Powys ... 93 A6
Shrops ... 95 A4
Som ... 29 A7
Leighton
Bromswold ... 100 D3
Leighton Buzzard ... 67 A4
Leigh upon Mendip 29 A6
Leigh Woods ... 43 B4
Leinthall Earls ... 78 A2
Leinthall Starkes ... 78 A2
Leintwardine ... 94 D2
Leire ... 98 B2
Leirinmore ... 277 B5
Leiston ... 89 A5
Leitfie ... 231 D6
Leith ... 209 C5
Leitholm ... 198 B1
Lelant ... 2 B3
Lelley ... 151 D5
Lem Hill ... 95 D5
Lemmington Hall ... 189 B4
Lempitlaw ... 198 C1
Lenchwick ... 80 C3
Lendalfoot ... 180 C3
Lendrick Lodge ... 217 D5
Lenham ... 37 A6
Lenham Heath ... 37 B7
Lennel ... 198 B2
Lennoxtown ... 205 A6
Lenton
Lincs ... 116 B3
Nottingham ... 114 B3
Lentran ... 252 B1
Lenwade ... 120 D2
Leny House ... 217 D5
Lenzie ... 205 A6
Leoch ... 220 A3
Leochel-Cushnie ... 244 A2
Leominster ... 78 B2
Leonard Stanley ... 63 C4
Leorin ... 200 D3
Lepe ... 18 B3
Lephin ... 258 D1
Lephinchapel ... 214 C2
Lephinmore ... 214 C2
Le Planel ... 6
Leppington ... 149 A6
Lepton ... 139 B5
Lerryn ... 5 B6
Lerwick ... 285 J6
Lesbury ... 189 B5
Le Skerne
Haughton ... 167 D6
Leslie
Aberds ... 255 D6
Fife ... 220 D2
Lesmahagow ... 194 C3
Lesnewth ... 10 B2
Lessendrum ... 255 B6
Lessingham ... 121 C5
Lessonhall ... 175 C5
Leswalt ... 170 A2
Letchmore Heath ... 67 D6
Letchworth ... 84 D4
Letcombe Bassett ... 46 A1
Letcombe Regis ... 46 A1
Letham
Angus ... 232 D3
Falk ... 208 B1
Fife ... 220 C3
Perth ... 219 B5

Letham Grange ... 233 D4
Lethenty ... 256 B3
Letheringham ... 88 B3
Letheringsett ... 120 B2
Lettaford ... 12 C2
Lettan ... 282 C8
Letterewe ... 261 C6
Letterfearn ... 249 D5
Letterfinlay ... 239 C6
Lettermorar ... 235 B6
Lettermore ... 224 B3
Letters ... 262 B5
Letterston ... 55 B5
Lettoch
Highld ... 242 A1
Highld ... 254 C1
Letton
Hereford ... 78 C1
Hereford ... 94 D1
Letton Green ... 103 A5
Letty Green ... 68 B2
Letwell ... 131 A5
Leuchars ... 221 B5
Leuchars House ... 266 C3
Leumrabhagh ... 288 F4
Levan ... 204 A2
Levaneap ... 285 G6
Levedale ... 112 D2
Leven
E Yorks ... 151 C4
Fife ... 220 D3
Levencorroch ... 191 C6
Levens ... 154 C3
Levens Green ... 68 A3
Levenshulme ... 138 D1
Levenwick ... 285 L6
Leverburgh
= An t-Ob ... 287 F5
Leverington ... 118 D1
Leverton ... 117 A7
Leverton Highgate ... 117 A7
Leverton
Lucasgate ... 117 A7
Leverton Outgate ... 117 A7
Le Villocq ... 6
Levington ... 88 D3
Levisham ... 160 B2
Levishie ... 240 A2
Lew ... 64 C4
Lewannick ... 10 C3
Lewdown ... 11 C5
Lewes ... 22 A2
Leweston ... 55 B5
Lewisham ... 49 B6
Lewiston ... 251 D7
Lewistown ... 40 C4
Lewknor ... 66 D2
Leworthy
Devon ... 10 A4
Devon ... 26 B1
Lewtrenchard ... 11 C5
Lexden ... 70 A3
Ley
Aberds ... 244 A2
Corn ... 5 A6
Leybourne ... 37 A4
Leyburn ... 157 B5
Leyfields ... 97 A5
Leyhill ... 67 C4
Leyland ... 136 A4
Leylodge ... 245 A4
Leymoor ... 139 B4
Leys
Aberds ... 269 D5
Perth ... 220 A2
Leys Castle ... 252 B2
Leysdown-on-Sea ... 52 B2
Leysmill ... 233 D4
Leys of Cossans ... 232 D1
Leysters Pole ... 78 A3
Leyton ... 49 A6
Leytonstone ... 49 A6
Lezant ... 10 D4
Leziate ... 118 D3
Lhanbryde ... 266 C3
Liatrie ... 250 C4
Libanus ... 60 A1
Libberton ... 195 B4
Liberton ... 209 D5
Liceasto ... 288 H2
Lichfield ... 96 A4
Lickey ... 96 D2
Lickey End ... 96 D2
Lickfold ... 34 D2
Liddel ... 283 J5
Liddesdale ... 236 D1
Liddington ... 45 A6
Lidgate ... 86 B3
Lidget ... 141 C4
Lidget Green ... 147 D5

Lidgett ... 131 C6
Lidlington ... 84 D1
Lidstone ... 65 A4
Lieurary ... 279 B6
Liff ... 220 A3
Lifton ... 11 C4
Liftondown ... 11 C4
Lighthorne ... 81 B6
Lightwater ... 48 C2
Lightwood ... 112 A3
Lightwood Green
Ches E ... 111 A5
Wrex ... 110 A2
Lilbourne ... 98 D2
Lilburn Tower ... 188 A3
Lilleshall ... 111 D6
Lilley
Herts ... 67 A6
W Berks ... 46 B2
Lilliesleaf ... 186 A4
Lillingstone
Dayrell ... 83 D4
Lillingstone Lovell ... 83 C4
Lillington
Dorset ... 29 D6
Warks ... 81 A6
Lilliput ... 17 B4
Lilstock ... 27 A6
Lilyhurst ... 111 D6
Limbury ... 67 A5
Limebrook ... 78 A1
Limefield ... 137 B7
Limekilnburn ... 194 A2
Limekilns ... 208 B3
Limerigg ... 207 C6
Limerstone ... 18 C3
Limington ... 29 C5
Limpenhoe ... 105 A4
Limpley Stoke ... 44 C1
Limpsfield ... 36 A2
Limpsfield Chart ... 36 A2
Linby ... 131 D5
Linchmere ... 34 C1
Lincluden ... 174 A2
Lincoln ... 133 B4
Lincomb ... 79 A6
Lincombe ... 7 B6
Lindale ... 154 C3
Lindal in Furness ... 153 C3
Lindean ... 196 C3
Lindfield ... 35 D6
Lindford ... 33 B7
Lindifferon ... 220 C3
Lindley ... 139 B4
Lindley Green ... 147 C6
Lindores ... 220 C2
Lindridge ... 79 A4
Lindsell ... 69 A6
Lindsey ... 87 C5
Linford
Hants ... 17 A5
Thurrock ... 50 B3
Lingague ... 152 D2
Lingards Wood ... 138 B3
Lingbob ... 147 D4
Lingdale ... 169 D4
Lingen ... 78 A1
Lingfield ... 36 B1
Lingreabhagh ... 287 F5
Lingwood ... 105 A4
Linicro ... 258 B3
Linkenholt ... 46 D1
Linkhill ... 37 D6
Linkinhorne ... 10 D4
Linklater ... 283 J5
Linksness ... 283 G3
Linktown ... 209 A5
Linley ... 94 B1
Linley Green ... 79 B4
Linlithgow ... 208 C3
Linlithgow Bridge ... 208 C2
Linshiels ... 188 C1
Linsiadar ... 288 D3
Linsidemore ... 264 A1
Linslade ... 67 A4
Linstead Parva ... 104 D4
Linstock ... 176 D2
Linthwaite ... 139 B4
Lintlaw ... 198 A2
Lintmill ... 267 C6
Linton
Borders ... 187 A6
Cambs ... 86 C1
Derbys ... 113 D6
Hereford ... 62 A2
Kent ... 37 B5
Northumb ... 189 D5
N Yorks ... 146 A3
W Yorks ... 148 C2
Linton-on-Ouse ... 148 A3

Linwood
Hants 17 A5
Lincs 133 A6
Renfs 205 B4
Lionacleit 286 B3
Lional 288 A6
Liphook 34 C1
Liscard 136 D2
Liscombe 26 B3
Liskeard 6 A1
L'Islet 6
Liss 33 C6
Lissett 151 B4
Liss Forest 33 C6
Lissington 133 A6
Lisvane 41 C6
Liswerry 42 A2
Litcham 119 D5
Litchborough 82 B3
Litchfield 46 D2
Litherland 136 D2
Litlington
Cambs 85 C5
E Sus 22 B3
Little Abington 86 C1
Little Addington 99 D6
Little Alne 80 A4
Little Altcar 136 C2
Little Asby 155 A5
Little Assynt 271 B4
Little Aston 96 A3
Little Atherfield 18 C3
Little Ayre 283 H4
Little-ayre 285 G5
Little Ayton 168 D3
Little Baddow 70 C1
Little Badminton 44 A2
Little Ballinluig 230 C3
Little Bampton 175 C5
Little Bardfield 86 D2
Little Barford 84 B3
Little Barningham . . . 120 B3
Little Barrington 64 B3
Little Barrow 127 B4
Little Barugh 159 D6
Little Bavington 178 B1
Little Bealings 88 C3
Littlebeck 160 A2
Little Bedwyn 45 C6
Little Bentley 71 A5
Little Berkhamsted . . 68 C2
Little Billing 83 A5
Little Birch 78 D3
Little Blakenham 88 C2
Little Blencow 164 B2
Little Bollington 128 A2
Little Bookham 35 A4
Littleborough
Gtr Man 138 B2
Notts 132 A3
Littlebourne 53 D4
Little Bowden 99 C4
Little Bradley 86 B2
Little Brampton 94 C1
Little Brechin 232 B3
Littlebredy 15 C5
Little Brickhill 83 D6
Little Brington 82 A3
Little Bromley 71 A4
Little Broughton 162 A3
Little Budworth 127 C6
Little Burstead 69 D6
Littlebury 85 D7
Littlebury Green 85 D6
Little Bytham 116 D3
Little Carlton
Lincs 134 A3
Notts 132 D2
Little Casterton 100 A2
Little Cawthorpe . . . 134 A3
Little Chalfont 67 D4
Little Chart 38 A1
Little Chesterford . . . 85 C7
Little Cheverell 44 D3
Little Chishill 85 D6
Little Clacton 71 B5
Little Clifton 162 B3
Little Colp 256 B2
Little Comberton 80 C2
Little Common 23 B6
Little Compton 81 D5
Little Cornard 87 D4
Little Cowarne 79 B4
Little Coxwell 64 D3
Little Crakehall 157 B6
Little Cressingham . . 103 B4
Little Crosby 136 C2
Little Dalby 115 D5
Little Dawley 95 A4
Littledean 62 B2

Little Dens 257 B5
Little Dewchurch 78 D3
Little Downham 101 C7
Little Driffield 150 B3
Little Dunham 119 D5
Little Dunkeld 230 D4
Little Dunmow 69 A6
Little Easton 69 A6
Little Eaton 114 A1
Little Eccleston 144 C4
Little Ellingham 103 B6
Little End 69 C5
Little Eversden 85 B5
Little Faringdon 64 C3
Little Fencote 157 B6
Little Fenton 148 D4
Littleferry 265 A4
Little Finborough 87 B6
Little Fransham 119 D6
Little Gaddesden 67 B4
Little Gidding 100 C3
Little Glemham 88 B4
Little Glenshee 219 A4
Little Gransden 85 B4
Little Green 29 A7
Little Grimsby 143 D5
Little Gruinard 261 B6
Little Habton 159 D6
Little Hadham 68 A4
Little Hale 116 A4
Little Hallingbury . . . 69 B4
Littleham
Devon 13 C5
Devon 25 C5
Little Hampden 66 C3
Littlehampton 20 B3
Little Harrowden 99 D5
Little Haseley 66 C1
Little Hatfield 151 B4
Little Hautbois 121 C4
Little Haven 55 C5
Little Hay 96 A4
Little Hayfield 129 A5
Little Haywood 112 C4
Little Heath 97 C6
Littlehempston 8 A2
Little Hereford 78 A3
Little Horkesley 87 D5
Little Horsted 22 A2
Little Horton 147 D5
Little Horwood 83 D4
Littlehoughton 189 B5
Little Houghton
Northants 83 B5
S Yorks 140 C2
Little Hucklow 129 B6
Little Hulton 137 C6
Little Humber 142 A3
Little Hungerford . . . 46 B3
Little Irchester 83 A6
Little Kimble 66 C3
Little Kineton 81 B6
Little Kingshill 66 D3
Little Langdale 154 A2
Little Langford 31 B4
Little Laver 69 C5
Little Leigh 127 B6
Little Leighs 69 B7
Little Lever 137 C6
Little London
Bucks 66 B1
E Sus 22 A3
Hants 32 A2
Hants 47 D4
Lincs 117 C5
Lincs 118 C1
Norf 120 C3
Powys 92 C4
Little Longstone . . . 130 B1
Little Lynturk 244 A2
Little Malvern 79 C5
Little Maplestead . . . 87 D4
Little Marcle 79 D4
Little Marlow 47 A6
Little Marsden 146 D2
Little Massingham . . 119 C4
Little Melton 104 A2
Littlemill
Aberds 243 C6
E Ayrs 182 A3
Highld 253 A5
Northumb 189 B5
Little Mill 61 C5
Little Milton 65 C7
Little Missenden 67 D4
Littlemoor 15 C6
Littlemore 65 C6
Little Musgrave 165 D5
Little Ness 110 D3
Little Neston 126 B2

Little Newcastle 55 B5
Little Newsham . . . 166 D4
Little Oakley
Essex 71 A6
Northants 99 C5
Little Orton 175 C6
Little Ouseburn 148 A3
Littleover 114 B1
Little Paxton 84 A3
Little Petherick 9 D5
Little Pitlurg 255 B5
Little Plumpton 144 D3
Little Plumstead . . . 121 D5
Little Ponton 116 B2
Littleport 102 C1
Little Raveley 101 D4
Little Reedness 141 A6
Little Ribston 148 B2
Little Rissington 64 B2
Little Ryburgh 119 C6
Little Ryle 188 B3
Little Salkeld 164 B3
Little Sampford 86 D2
Little Sandhurst 47 C6
Little Saxham 86 A3
Little Scatwell 251 A5
Little Sessay 158 D3
Little Shelford 85 B6
Little Singleton 144 D3
Little Skillymarno . . 269 D4
Little Smeaton 140 B3
Little Snoring 119 B6
Little Sodbury 43 A6
Little Somborne 32 B2
Little Somerford . . . 44 A3
Little Stainforth . . . 146 A2
Little Stainton 167 C6
Little Stanney 127 B4
Little Staughton 84 A3
Little Steeping 135 C4
Little Stoke 112 B3
Littlestone on Sea . . 38 C2
Little Stonham 88 A2
Little Stretton
Leics 98 A3
Shrops 94 B2
Little Strickland . . . 164 D3
Little Stukeley 100 D4
Little Sutton 126 B3
Little Tew 65 A4
Little Thetford 102 D1
Little Thirkleby 158 D3
Littlethorpe
Leics 98 B2
N Yorks 148 A2
Little Thurlow 86 B2
Little Thurrock 50 B3
Littleton
Ches W 127 C4
Hants 32 B3
Perth 220 A2
Som 29 B4
Sur 34 B2
Sur 48 C3
Littleton Drew 44 A2
Littleton-on-Severn 43 A4
Littleton Pannell . . . 44 D4
Little Torboll 264 A3
Little Torrington . . . 25 D5
Little Totham 70 B2
Little Toux 267 D6
Littletown 167 A6
Little Town
Cumb 163 C5
Lancs 145 D6
Little Urswick 153 C3
Little Wakering 51 A6
Little Walden 86 C1
Little Waldingfield . . 87 C5
Little Walsingham . . 119 B6
Little Waltham 69 B7
Little Warley 69 D6
Little Weighton 150 D2
Little Weldon 99 C6
Little Welnetham . . . 87 A4
Little Wenlock 95 A4
Little Whittingham
Green 104 D3
Littlewick Green . . . 47 B6
Little Wilbraham . . . 86 B1
Little Wishford 31 B4
Little Witley 79 A5
Little Wittenham . . . 65 D6
Little Wolford 81 D5
Littleworth
Bedford 84 C2
Glos 63 C4
Oxon 64 D4
Staffs 112 D4
Worcs 80 B1

Little Wratting 86 C2
Little Wymington . . . 83 A6
Little Wymondley . . . 68 A2
Little Wyrley 96 A3
Little Wyrdham 86 D3
Litton
Derbys 129 B6
N Yorks 156 D3
Som 43 D4
Litton Cheney 15 B5
Liurbost 288 E4
Liverpool 136 D2
Liverpool Airport . . 127 A4
Liversedge 139 A5
Liverton
Devon 12 D3
Redcar 169 D5
Livingston 208 D3
Livingston Village . . 208 D3
Lixwm 125 B6
Lizard 3 D5
Llaingoch 122 B2
Llaithddu 93 C4
Llan 91 B6
Llanaber 90 A4
Llanaelhaearn 106 B3
Llanafan 75 A5
Llanafan-fawr 76 B3
Llanallgo 123 B4
Llanandras
= Presteigne 77 A7
Llanarmon 107 C4
Llanarmon Dyffryn
Ceiriog 109 B6
Llanarmon-yn-Ial . . 126 D1
Llanarth
Ceredig 73 A7
Mon 61 B5
Llanarthne 58 C2
Llanasa 125 A6
Llanbabo 122 B3
Llanbadarn Fawr . . . 90 D4
Llanbadarn Fynydd . 93 D5
Llanbadarn-y-
Garreg 77 C5
Llanbadoc 61 C5
Llanbadrig 122 A3
Llanbeder 61 D5
Llanbedr
Gwyn 107 D5
Powys 60 A4
Powys 77 C5
Llanbedr-Dyffryn-
Clwyd 125 D6
Llanbedrgoch 123 B5
Llanbedrog 106 C3
Llanbedr Pont Steffan
= Lampeter 75 D4
Llanbedr-y-cennin . 124 C2
Llanberis 123 D5
Llanbethêry 41 E5
Llanbister 93 D5
Llanblethian 41 D4
Llanboidy 73 D5
Llanbradach 41 B6
Llanbrynmair 91 B6
Llancarfan 41 D5
Llancayo 61 C5
Llancloudy 61 A6
Llancynfelyn 90 C4
Llandaff 41 D6
Llandanwg 107 D5
Llandarcy 40 B2
Llandawke 56 A2
Llanddaniel Fab . . . 123 C4
Llanddarog 57 A5
Llanddeiniol 75 A4
Llanddeiniolen 123 D5
Llandderfel 109 B5
Llanddeusant
Anglesey 122 B3
Carms 59 C4
Llanddew 77 D4
Llanddewi 57 D4
Llanddewi-Brefi 75 C5
Llanddewi'r Cwm . . 76 C4
Llanddewi
Rhydderch 61 B5
Llanddewi Velfrey . . 56 A1
Llanddoged 124 C3
Llanddona 123 C5
Llanddowror 56 A2
Llanddulas 125 B4
Llanddwywe 107 D5
Llanddyfynan 123 C5
Llandefaelog Fach . . 76 D4
Llandefaelog-tre'r-
graig 77 E5
Llandefalle 77 D5
Llandegai 123 C5

Llandegfan 123 C5
Llandegla 126 D1
Llandegley 77 A5
Llandegveth 61 D5
Llandegwning 106 C2
Llandeilo 58 C3
Llandeilo Graban . . . 77 C4
Llandeilo'r Fan 59 B5
Llandeloy 55 B4
Llandenny 61 C6
Llandevenny 42 A3
Llandewednock 3 D5
Llandewi
Ystradenny 77 A5
Llandinabo 61 A7
Llandinam 92 C4
Llandissilio 55 B7
Llandogo 62 C1
Llandough
V Glam 41 D4
V Glam 41 D6
Llandovery
= Llanymddyfri . . . 59 B4
Llandow 40 D4
Llandre
Carms 58 A3
Ceredig 90 D4
Llandrillo 109 B5
Llandrillo-
yn-Rhos 124 A3
Llandrindod
= Llandrindod Wells . 77 A4
Llandrindod Wells
= Llandrindod 77 A4
Llandrinio 110 D1
Llandudno 124 A2
Llandudno Junction
= Cyffordd
Llandudno 124 B2
Llandwrog 107 A4
Llandybie 57 A6
Llandyfaelog 57 A4
Llandyfan 57 A6
Llandyfriog 73 B6
Llandyfrydog 123 B4
Llandygwydd 73 B5
Llandynan 109 A6
Llandyrnog 125 C6
Llandysilio 110 D1
Llandyssil 93 B5
Llandysul 73 B7
Llanedeyrn 41 C7
Llanedi 57 B5
Llaneglwys 77 D4
Llanegryn 90 B3
Llanegwad 58 C2
Llaneilian 123 A4
Llanelian-yn-Rhos 124 B3
Llanelidan 125 D6
Llanelieu 77 D5
Llanellen 61 B5
Llanelli 57 C5
Llanelltyd 91 A5
Llanelly 60 B4
Llanelly Hill 60 B4
Llanelwedd 76 B4
Llanelwy = St Asaph 125 B5
Llanenddwyn 107 D5
Llanengan 106 D2
Llanerchymedd . . . 123 B4
Llanerfyl 92 A4
Llanfachraeth 122 B3
Llanfachreth 108 C2
Llanfaelog 122 C3
Llanfaelrhys 106 D2
Llanfaenor 61 B6
Llanfaes
Anglesey 123 C6
Powys 60 A2
Llanfaethlu 122 B3
Llanfaglan 123 D4
Llanfair 107 D5
Llanfair-ar-y-bryn . . 59 B5
Llanfair Caereinion . 93 A5
Llanfair Clydogau . . 75 C5
Llanfair-Dyffryn-
Clwyd 125 D6
Llanfairfechan 124 B1
Llanfair Kilgheddin . 61 C5
Llanfair-
Nant-Gwyn 73 C4
Llanfairpwll-
gwyngyll 123 C5
Llanfair Talhaiarn . 125 B4
Llanfair Waterdine . 93 D6
Llanfair-ym-Muallt
= Builth Wells 76 B4
Llanfairyneubwll . . 122 C3
Llanfairynghornwy 122 A3
Llanfallteg 56 A1

Llanfaredd 77 B4
Llanfarian 75 A4
Llanfechain 109 C6
Llanfechan 76 B3
Llanfechell 122 A3
Llanfendigaid 90 B3
Llanferres 126 C1
Llan Ffestiniog 108 A2
Llanfflewyn 122 B3
Llanfihangel-ar-arth 58 B1
Llanfihangel-
Crucorney 61 A5
Llanfihangel Glyn
Myfyr 109 A4
Llanfihangel Nant
Bran 59 B6
Llanfihangel-nant-
Melan 77 B5
Llanfihangel
Rhydithon 77 A5
Llanfihangel Rogiet . 42 A3
Llanfihangel Tal-y-
llyn 60 A3
Llanfihangel-uwch-
Gwili 58 C1
Llanfihangel-y-
Creuddyn 75 A5
Llanfihangel-yn-
Ngwynfa 109 D5
Llanfihangel yn
Nhowyn 122 C3
Llanfihangel-y-pennant
Gwyn 91 B4
Gwyn 107 B5
Llanfihangel-y-
traethau 107 C5
Llanfilo 77 D5
Llanfoist 61 B4
Llanfor 108 B4
Llanfrechfa 61 D5
Llanfrothen 107 B6
Llanfrynach 60 A2
Llanfwrog
Anglesey 122 B3
Denb 125 D6
Llanfyllin 109 D6
Llanfynydd
Carms 58 C2
Flint 126 D2
Llanfyrnach 73 C5
Llangadfan 109 D5
Llangadog 59 C4
Llangadwaladr
Anglesey 122 D3
Powys 109 B6
Llangaffo 123 D4
Llangain 56 A3
Llangammarch
Wells 76 C3
Llangan 41 D4
Llangarron 62 A1
Llangasty Talyllyn . . 60 A3
Llangathen 58 C2
Llangattock 60 B4
Llangattock Lingoed 61 A5
Llangattock nigh
Usk 61 C5
Llangattock-Vibon-
Avel 61 B6
Llangedwyn 109 C6
Llangefni 123 C4
Llangeinor 40 C4
Llangeitho 75 C5
Llangeler 73 C6
Llangelynin 90 B3
Llangendeirne 57 A4
Llangennech 57 B5
Llangennith 57 C4
Llangenny 60 B4
Llangernyw 124 C3
Llangian 106 D2
Llanglydwen 73 D4
Llangoed 123 C6
Llangoedmor 73 B4
Llangollen 109 A7
Llangolman 55 B7
Llangors 60 A3
Llangovan 61 C6
Llangower 108 B4
Llangranog 73 A6
Llangristiolus 123 C4
Llangrove 62 B1
Llangua 61 A5
Llangunllo 93 D6
Llangunnor 57 A4
Llangurig 92 D3
Llangwm
Conwy 109 A4

Llangwm *continued*
Mon 61 C6
Pembs 55 D5
Llangwnnadl 106 C2
Llangwyfan 125 C6
Llangwyfan-isaf 122 D3
Llangwyllog 123 C4
Llangwyryfon 75 A4
Llangybi
Ceredig 75 C5
Gwyn 107 B4
Mon 61 D5
Llangyfelach 57 C6
Llangynhafal 125 C6
Llangynidr 60 B3
Llangynin 56 A2
Llangynog
Carms 56 A3
Powys 109 C5
Llangynwyd 40 C3
Llanhamlach 60 A2
Llanharan 41 C5
Llanharry 41 C5
Llanhennock 61 D5
Llanhiledd
=Llanhilleth 41 A7
Llanhilleth
=Llanhiledd 41 A7
Llanidloes 92 C3
Llaniestyn 106 C2
Llanifyny 91 D6
Llanigon 77 D6
Llanilar 75 A5
Llanilid 41 C4
Llanilltud Fawr
=Llantwit Major 41 E4
Llanishen
Cardiff 41 C6
Mon 61 C6
Llanllawddog 58 C1
Llanllechid 123 D6
Llanllowell 61 D5
Llanllugan 93 A4
Llanllwch 56 A3
Llanllwchaiarn 93 B5
Llanllwni 58 B1
Llanllyfni 107 A4
Llanmadoc 57 C4
Llanmaes 41 E4
Llanmartin 42 A2
Llanmihangel 41 D4
Llanmorlais 57 C5
Llannefydd 125 B4
Llannon 57 B5
Llannor 106 C3
Llanon 75 B4
Llanover 61 C5
Llanpumsaint 73 D7
Llanreithan 55 B4
Llanrhaeadr 125 C5
Llanrhaeadr-ym-Mochnant 109 C6
Llanrhian 54 A4
Llanrhidian 57 C4
Llanrhos 124 A2
Llanrhyddlad 122 B3
Llanrhystud 75 B4
Llanrosser 77 D6
Llanrothal 61 B6
Llanrug 123 D5
Llanrumney 41 C7
Llanrwst 124 C3
Llansadurnen 56 A2
Llansadwrn
Anglesey 123 C5
Carms 58 B3
Llansaint 56 B3
Llansamlet 40 B1
Llansannan 125 C4
Llansannor 41 D4
Llansantffraed
Ceredig 75 B4
Powys 60 A3
Llansantffraed Cwmdeuddwr 76 A3
Llansantffraed-in-Elvel 77 B4
Llansantffraid-ym-Mechain 109 C7
Llansawel 58 B3
Llansilin 109 C7
Llansoy 61 C6
Llanspyddid 60 A2
Llanstadwell 55 D5
Llansteffan 56 A3
Llanstephan 77 C5
Llantarnam 61 D5
Llanteg 56 A1
Llanthony 61 A4
Llantilio Crossenny 61 B5
Llantilio Pertholey 61 B5
Llantood 73 B4
Llantrisant
Anglesey 122 B3
Mon 61 D5
Rhondda 41 C5
Llantrithyd 41 D5
Llantwit Fardre 41 C5
Llantwit Major
=Llanilltud Fawr 41 E4
Llanuwchllyn 108 B3
Llanvaches 61 D6
Llanvair Discoed 61 D6
Llanvapley 61 B5
Llanvetherine 61 B5
Llanveynoe 77 D7
Llanvihangel Gobion 61 C5
Llanvihangel-Ystern-Llewern 61 B6
Llanwarne 61 A7
Llanwddyn 109 D5
Llanwenog 74 D3
Llanwern 42 A2
Llanwinio 73 D5
Llanwnda
Gwyn 107 A4
Pembs 72 C2
Llanwnnen 75 D4
Llanwnog 92 B4
Llanwrda 59 B4
Llanwrin 91 B5
Llanwrthwl 76 A3
Llanwrtud
=Llanwrtyd Wells 76 C2
Llanwrtyd 76 C2
Llanwrtyd Wells
=Llanwrtud 76 C2
Llanwyddelan 93 A4
Llanyblodwel 110 C1
Llanybri 56 A3
Llanybydder 58 A2
Llanycefn 55 B6
Llanychaer 72 C2
Llanycil 108 B4
Llanycrwys 75 D5
Llanymawddwy 91 A7
Llanymddyfri
=Llandovery 59 B4
Llanymynech 110 C1
Llanynghenedl 122 B3
Llanynys 125 C6
Llan-y-pwll 126 D3
Llanyre 76 A4
Llanystumdwy 107 C4
Llanywern 60 A3
Llawhaden 55 C6
Llawnt 110 B1
Llawr Dref 106 D2
Llawryglyn 92 B3
Llay 126 D3
Llechcynfarwy 122 B3
Llecheiddior 107 B4
Llechfaen 60 A2
Llechryd
Caerph 60 C3
Ceredig 73 B5
Llechrydau 110 B1
Lledrod 75 A5
Llenmerewig 93 B5
Llethrid 57 C5
Llidiad Nenog 58 B2
Llidiardau 108 B3
Llidiart-y-parc 109 A6
Llithfaen 106 B3
Llong 126 C2
Llowes 77 C5
Llundain-fach 75 C4
Llwydcoed 41 A4
Llwyn 93 C6
Llwyncelyn 74 C3
Llwyndafydd 73 A6
Llwynderw 93 A6
Llwyn-du 61 B4
Llwyndyrys 106 B3
Llwyngwril 90 B3
Llwyn-hendy 57 C5
Llwynmawr 110 B1
Llwyn-têg 57 B5
Llwyn-y-brain 56 A1
Llwyn-y-groes 75 C4
Llwynypia 41 B4
Llynclys 110 C1
Llynfaes 123 C4
Llysfaen 124 B3
Llyswen 77 D5
Llysworney 41 D4
Llys-y-frân 55 B6
Llywel 59 B5
Loan 208 C2
Loanend 198 A3
Loanhead 209 D5
Loans 192 B3
Loans of Tullich 265 C4
Lobb 25 B5
Loch a Charnain 286 B4
Loch a' Ghainmhich 288 E3
Lochailort 235 B6
Lochaline 225 B5
Lochanhully 253 D5
Lochans 170 B2
Locharbriggs 184 D2
Lochassynt Lodge 271 B4
Lochavich Ho 214 A2
Lochawe 227 D6
Loch Baghasdail
=Lochboisdale 286 E3
Lochboisdale
=Loch Baghasdail 286 E3
Lochbuie 225 D5
Lochcarron 249 C5
Loch Choire Lodge 273 A4
Lochdhu 279 D6
Lochdochart House 216 B4
Lochdon 225 C6
Lochdrum 263 C4
Lochead 202 A2
Lochearnhead 217 B5
Lochee 220 A3
Lochend
Highld 252 C1
Highld 281 B4
Locherben 184 C2
Loch Euphoirt 287 H3
Lochfoot 173 A6
Lochgair 214 C2
Lochgarthside 240 A3
Lochgelly 209 A4
Lochgilphead 214 D1
Lochgoilhead 215 B5
Loch Head 171 C5
Lochhill 266 C3
Lochindorb Lodge 253 C5
Lochinver 270 B3
Lochlane 218 B3
Loch Loyal Lodge 277 D7
Lochluichart 263 D5
Lochmaben 184 D3
Lochmaddy *=Loch nam Madadh* 287 H4
Lochmore Cottage 280 D2
Lochmore Lodge 271 A5
Loch nam Madadh
=Lochmaddy 287 H4
Lochore 209 A4
Lochportain 287 G4
Lochranza 203 C4
Lochs Crofts 266 C4
Loch Sgioport 286 C4
Lochside
Aberds 233 B5
Highld 253 A4
Highld 274 A2
Highld 277 C5
Lochslin 265 B4
Lochstack Lodge 276 D3
Lochton 245 C4
Lochty
Angus 232 B3
Fife 221 D5
Perth 219 B5
Lochuisge 236 D1
Lochurr 183 D5
Lochwinnoch 204 C3
Lochwood 184 C3
Lochyside 237 B5
Lockengate 5 A5
Lockerbie 185 D4
Lockeridge 45 C5
Lockerley 32 C1
Locking 42 D2
Lockinge 46 A2
Lockington
E Yorks 150 C2
Leics 114 C2
Lockleywood 111 C5
Locks Heath 18 A4
Lockton 160 B2
Lockwood 139 B4
Loddington
Leics 99 A4
Northants 99 D5
Loddiswell 7 C6
Loddon 105 B4
Lode 86 A1
Loders 15 B4
Lodsworth 34 D2
Lofthouse
N Yorks 157 D5
W Yorks 139 A6
Loftus 169 D5
Logan 193 C5
Loganlea 208 D2
Logan Mains 170 C2
Loggerheads 111 B6
Logie
Angus 233 B4
Fife 220 B4
Moray 253 A6
Logiealmond Lodge 219 A4
Logie Coldstone 244 B1
Logie Hill 264 C3
Logie Newton 256 C1
Logie Pert 233 B4
Logierait 230 C3
Login 73 D4
Lolworth 85 A5
Lonbain 248 A3
Londesborough 150 C1
London Colney 68 C1
Londonderry 157 C7
Londonthorpe 116 B2
Londubh 261 B5
Lonemore 264 B3
Long Ashton 43 B4
Longbar 204 C3
Long Bennington 115 A6
Longbenton 179 C4
Longborough 64 A2
Long Bredy 15 B5
Longbridge
Warks 81 A5
W Mid 96 D3
Longbridge Deverill 30 A2
Long Buckby 82 A3
Longburton 29 D6
Long Clawson 115 C5
Longcliffe 130 D2
Long Common 32 D4
Long Compton
Staffs 112 C2
Warks 81 D5
Longcot 64 D3
Long Crendon 66 C1
Long Crichel 30 D3
Longcroft 207 C5
Longden 94 A2
Long Ditton 49 C4
Longdon
Staffs 113 D4
Worcs 79 D6
Longdon Green 113 D4
Longdon on Tern 111 D5
Longdown 12 B3
Longdowns 4 D2
Long Drax 141 A4
Long Duckmanton 131 B4
Long Eaton 114 B2
Longfield
Kent 50 C3
Shetland 285 M5
Longford
Derbys 113 B6
Glos 63 A4
London 48 B3
Shrops 111 B5
Telford 111 D6
W Mid 97 C6
Longfordlane 113 B6
Longforgan 220 B3
Longformacus 197 A5
Longframlington 189 C4
Long Green 79 D6
Longham
Dorset 17 B4
Norf 119 D6
Long Hanborough 65 B5
Longhaven 257 C6
Longhill 269 D4
Longhirst 179 A4
Longhope
Glos 62 B2
Orkney 283 H4
Longhorsley 189 D4
Longhoughton 189 B5
Long Itchington 81 A7
Longlane
Derbys 113 B6
W Berks 46 B2
Long Lawford 98 D1
Longlevens 63 A4
Longley 139 C4
Longley Green 79 B5
Long Load 29 C4
Longmanhill 268 C2
Long Marston
Herts 66 B3
N Yorks 148 B4
Warks 81 C4
Long Marton 165 C4
Long Melford 87 C4
Longmoor Camp 33 B6
Longmorn 266 D3
Long Newnton 63 D5
Longnewton
Borders 187 A4
Stockton 167 D6
Long Newton 210 D2
Longney 62 B3
Longniddry 210 C1
Longnor
Shrops 94 A2
Staffs 129 C5
Longparish 32 A3
Longport 112 A2
Long Preston 146 B2
Longridge
Lancs 145 D6
Staffs 112 D3
W Loth 208 D2
Longriggend 207 C6
Long Riston 151 C4
Longsdon 129 D4
Longshaw 136 C4
Longside 257 B5
Long Sight 138 C2
Longstanton 85 A5
Longstock 32 B2
Longstone 56 B1
Longstowe 85 B5
Long Stratton 104 B2
Long Street 83 C4
Long Sutton
Hants 33 A6
Lincs 118 C1
Som 29 C4
Longthorpe 100 B3
Long Thurlow 87 A6
Longthwaite 164 C2
Longton
Lancs 136 A3
Stoke 112 A3
Longtown
Cumb 175 B6
Hereford 61 A5
Longview 136 D3
Longville in the Dale 94 B3
Long Whatton 114 C2
Longwick 66 C2
Long Wittenham 65 D6
Longwitton 178 A2
Longwood 95 A4
Longworth 65 D4
Longyester 210 D2
Lonmay 269 D5
Lonmore 258 D2
Looe 6 B1
Loose 37 A5
Loosley Row 66 C3
Lopcombe Corner 31 B6
Lopen 28 D4
Loppington 110 C3
Lopwell 6 A3
Lorbottle 188 C3
Lorbottle Hall 188 C3
Lornty 231 D5
Loscoe 114 A2
Losgaintir 287 E5
Lossiemouth 266 B3
Lossit 200 C1
Lostford 111 B5
Lostock Gralam 128 B1
Lostock Green 128 B1
Lostock Hall 136 A4
Lostock Junction 137 C5
Lostwithiel 5 B6
Loth 282 D7
Lothbeg 274 C3
Lothersdale 146 C3
Lothmore 274 C3
Loudwater 67 D4
Loughborough 114 D3
Loughor 57 C5
Loughton
Essex 68 D4
M Keynes 83 D5
Shrops 95 C4
Lound
Lincs 116 D3
Notts 132 A1
Suff 105 B6
Lount 114 D1
Louth 134 A3
Love Clough 137 A7
Lovedean 33 D5
Lover 31 C6
Loversall 140 D3
Loves Green 69 C6
Lovesome Hill 158 B2
Loveston 55 D6
Lovington 29 B5
Low Ackworth 140 B2
Low Barlings 133 B5
Low Bentham 145 A6
Low Bradfield 139 D5
Low Bradley 147 C4
Low Braithwaite 164 A2
Lowbridge House 154 A4
Low Brunton 177 B7
Low Burnham 141 C5
Low Burton 157 C6
Low Buston 189 C5
Lowca 162 B2
Low Catton 149 B6
Low Clanyard 170 C3
Low Coniscliffe 167 D5
Low Crosby 176 D2
Low Dalby 160 C2
Lowdham 115 A4
Low Dinsdale 167 D6
Lowe 111 B4
Lowe Hill 129 D4
Low Ellington 157 C6
Lower Aisholt 28 B2
Lower Arncott 65 B7
Lower Ashton 12 C3
Lower Assendon 47 A5
Lower Badcall 276 D2
Lower Bartle 145 D4
Lower Basildon 47 B4
Lower Beeding 35 D5
Lower Benefield 100 C1
Lower Boddington 82 B1
Lower Brailes 81 D6
Lower Breakish 247 B5
Lower Broadheath 79 B6
Lower Bullingham 78 D3
Lower Cam 62 C3
Lower Chapel 76 D4
Lower Chute 45 D7
Lower Cragabus 200 D3
Lower Crossings 129 A5
Lower Cumberworth 139 C5
Lower Darwen 137 A5
Lower Dean 84 A2
Lower Diabaig 261 D4
Lower Dicker 22 A3
Lower Dinchope 94 C2
Lower Down 94 C1
Lower Drift 2 C2
Lower Dunsforth 148 A3
Lower Egleton 79 C4
Lower Elkstone 129 D5
Lower End 67 A4
Lower Everleigh 45 D5
Lower Farringdon 33 B6
Lower Foxdale 152 D2
Lower Frankton 110 B2
Lower Froyle 33 A6
Lower Gledfield 264 A1
Lower Green 120 B1
Lower Hacheston 88 B4
Lower Halistra 258 C2
Lower Halstow 51 C5
Lower Hardres 52 D3
Lower Hawthwaite 153 B3
Lower Heath 128 C3
Lower Hempriggs 266 C2
Lower Hergest 77 B6
Lower Heyford 65 A5
Lower Higham 51 B4
Lower Holbrook 88 D2
Lower Hordley 110 C2
Lower Horsebridge 22 A3
Lower Killeyan 200 D2
Lower Kingswood 35 A5
Lower Kinnerton 126 C3
Lower Langford 42 C3
Lower Largo 220 D4
Lower Leigh 112 B4
Lower Lemington 81 D5
Lower Lenie 251 D7
Lower Lydbrook 62 B1
Lower Lye 78 A2
Lower Machen 42 A1
Lower Maes-coed 78 D1
Lower Mayland 70 C3
Lower Midway 113 C7
Lower Milovaig 258 C1
Lower Moor 80 C2
Lower Nazeing 68 C3
Lower Netchwood 95 B4
Lower Ollach 247 A4
Lower Penarth 41 D6

Lower Penn 95 B6
Lower Pennington 18 B2
Lower Peover 128 B2
Lower Pexhill 128 B3
Lower Place 138 B2
Lower Quinton 81 C4
Lower Rochford 79 A4
Lower Seagry 44 A3
Lower Shelton 84 C1
Lower Shiplake 47 B5
Lower Shuckburgh 82 A1
Lower Slaughter 64 A2
Lower Stanton St Quintin 44 A3
Lower Stoke 51 B5
Lower Stondon 84 D3
Lower Stow Bedon 103 B5
Lower Street
Norf 121 B4
Norf 121 D5
Lower Strensham 80 C2
Lower Stretton 127 A6
Lower Sundon 67 A5
Lower Swanwick 18 A3
Lower Swell 64 A2
Lower Tean 112 B4
Lower Thurlton 105 B5
Lower Tote 259 B5
Lower Town 72 C2
Lower Tysoe 81 C6
Lower Upham 32 D4
Lower Vexford 27 B6
Lower Weare 42 D3
Lower Welson 77 B6
Lower Whitley 127 B6
Lower Wield 33 A5
Lower Winchendon 66 B2
Lower Withington 128 C3
Lower Woodend 47 A6
Lower Woodford 31 B5
Lower Wyche 79 C5
Lowesby 99 A4
Lowestoft 105 B6
Loweswater 163 B4
Low Etherley 167 C4
Low Fell 179 D4
Lowford 32 D3
Low Fulney 117 C5
Low Garth 159 A6
Low Gate 177 C7
Lowgill
Cumb 155 B5
Lancs 145 A6
Low Grantley 157 D6
Low Habberley 95 D6
Low Ham 28 C4
Low Hesket 164 A2
Low Hesleyhurst 188 D3
Low Hutton 149 A6
Lowick
Northants 100 C1
Northumb 198 C4
Lowick Bridge 154 C1
Lowick Green 154 C1
Low Laithe 147 A5
Lowlands 61 D4
Low Leighton 129 A5
Low Lorton 163 B4
Low Marishes 159 D7
Low Marnham 132 C3
Low Mill 159 B5
Low Moor
Lancs 146 C1
W Yorks 139 A4
Lowmoor Row 165 C4
Low Moorsley 167 A6
Low Newton 154 C3
Low Newton-by-the-Sea 189 A5
Lownie Moor 232 D2
Low Row
Cumb 163 A6
Cumb 176 C3
N Yorks 156 B3
Low Salchrie 170 A2
Low Smerby 190 C3
Lowsonford 81 A4
Lowther 164 C3
Lowthorpe 150 A3
Lowton 137 D5
Lowton Common 137 D5
Low Torry 208 B3
Low Worsall 158 A2
Low Wray 154 A2
Loxbeare 27 D4
Loxhill 34 C3
Loxhore 25 B7
Loxley 81 B5
Loxton 42 D2
Loxwood 34 C3
Lubcroy 271 D6
Lubenham 99 C4
Luccombe 27 A4
Luccombe Village 19 D4
Lucker 199 C5
Luckett 11 D4
Luckington 44 A2
Lucklawhill 220 B4
Luckwell Bridge 27 B4
Lucton 78 A2
Ludag 286 E3
Ludborough 143 D4
Ludchurch 56 A1
Luddenden 138 A3
Luddenden Foot 138 A3
Luddesdown 50 C3
Luddington
N Lincs 141 B6
Warks 81 B4
Luddington in the Brook 100 C3
Lude House 230 B2
Ludford
Lincs 134 A2
Shrops 94 D3
Ludgershall
Bucks 66 B1
Wilts 45 D6
Ludgvan 2 B3
Ludham 121 D5
Ludlow 94 D3
Ludwell 30 C3
Ludworth 167 A6
Luffincott 10 B4
Lugar 193 C5
Luggate Burn 210 C3
Lugg Green 78 A2
Luggiebank 207 C5
Lugton 205 C4
Lugwardine 78 C3
Luib 247 B4
Lulham 78 C2
Lullenden 36 B2
Lullington
Derbys 113 D6
Som 44 D1
Lulsgate Bottom 43 C4
Lulsley 79 B5
Lumb 138 A3
Lumby 148 D3
Lumloch 205 B6
Lumphanan 244 B2
Lumphinnans 209 A4
Lumsdaine 211 D5
Lumsden 255 D5
Lunan 233 C4
Lunanhead 232 C2
Luncarty 219 B5
Lund
E Yorks 150 C2
N Yorks 149 D5
Shetland 284 C7
Lunderton 269 E6
Lundie
Angus 220 A2
Highld 239 A5
Lundin Links 220 D4
Lunga 213 B5
Lunna 284 G6
Lunning 284 G7
Lunnon 57 D5
Lunsford's Cross 23 A5
Lunt 136 C2
Luntley 78 B1
Luppitt 13 A6
Lupset 139 B6
Lupton 155 C4
Lurgashall 34 D2
Lusby 134 C3
Luson 7 C5
Luss 206 A1
Lussagiven 213 D4
Lusta 258 C2
Lustleigh 12 C2
Luston 78 A2
Luthermuir 233 B4
Luthrie 220 C3
Luton
Devon 13 D4
Luton 67 A5
Medway 51 C4
Lutterworth 98 C2
Lutton
Devon 7 B4
Lincs 118 C1
Northants 100 C3
Lutworthy 26 D2
Luxborough 27 B4
Luxulyan 5 B5
Lybster 275 A6
Lydbury North 94 C1
Lydcott 26 B1
Lydd 38 C2
Lydden 39 A4
Lyddington 99 B5
Lydd on Sea 38 C2
Lydeard St Lawrence 27 B6
Lyde Green 47 D5
Lydford 11 C6
Lydford-on-Fosse 29 B5
Lydgate 138 A2
Lydham 94 B1
Lydiard Green 45 A4
Lydiard Millicent 45 A4
Lydiate 136 C2
Lydlinch 30 D1
Lydney 62 C2
Lydstep 55 E6
Lye 96 C2
Lye Green
Bucks 67 C4
E Sus 36 C3
Lyford 65 D4
Lymbridge Green 38 A3
Lyme Regis 14 B3
Lyminge 38 A3
Lymington 18 B2
Lyminster 20 B3
Lymm 128 A1
Lymore 18 B1
Lympne 38 B3
Lympsham 42 D2
Lympstone 13 C4
Lynchat 241 B5
Lyndale House 258 C3
Lyndhurst 18 A2
Lyndon 99 A6
Lyne 48 C3
Lyneal 110 B3
Lyne Down 79 D4
Lyneham
Oxon 64 A3
Wilts 44 B4
Lynemore 253 D6
Lynemouth 189 D5
Lyne of Gorthleck 252 D1
Lyne of Skene 245 A4
Lyness 283 H4
Lyng
Norf 120 D2
Som 28 C3
Lynmouth 26 A2
Lynsted 51 C6
Lynton 26 A2
Lyon's Gate 15 A6
Lyonshall 78 B1
Lytchett Matravers 16 B3
Lytchett Minster 16 B3
Lyth 281 B4
Lytham 136 A2
Lytham St Anne's 136 A2
Lythe 169 D6
Lythes 283 J5

M

Mabe Burnthouse 4 D2
Mabie 174 A2
Mablethorpe 135 A5
Macclesfield 129 B4
Macclesfield Forest 129 B4
Macduff 268 C2
Mace Green 88 C2
Macharioch 190 E3
Machen 41 C7
Machrihanish 190 C2
Machynlleth 91 B5
Machynys 57 C5
Mackerel's Common 34 D3
Mackworth 113 B7
Macmerry 210 C1
Madderty 219 B4
Maddiston 208 C2
Madehurst 20 A2
Madeley
Staffs 111 A6
Telford 95 A4
Madeley Heath 112 A1
Madeley Park 112 A1
Madingley 85 A5
Madley 78 D2
Madresfield 79 C6
Madron 2 B2
Maenaddwyn 123 B4
Maenclochog 55 B6
Maendy 41 D5
Maentwrog 107 B6
Maen-y-groes 73 A6
Maer 112 B1
Maerdy
Conwy 109 A5
Rhondda 41 B4
Maesbrook 110 C1
Maesbury 110 C2
Maesbury Marsh 110 C2
Maesgwyn-Isaf 109 D6
Maesgwynne 73 D5
Maeshafn 126 C2
Maesllyn 73 B6
Maesmynis 76 C4
Maesteg 40 B3
Maestir 75 D4
Maes-Treylow 77 A6
Maesybont 57 A5
Maesycrugiau 58 A1
Maesy cwmmer 41 B6
Maesymeillion 73 B7
Magdalen Laver 69 C5
Maggieknockater 254 B4
Magham Down 22 A4
Maghull 136 C2
Magor 42 A3
Magpie Green 104 D1
Maiden Bradley 30 B2
Maidencombe 8 A3
Maidenhall 88 C2
Maidenhead 48 A1
Maiden Law 167 A4
Maiden Newton 15 B5
Maidens 192 E2
Maidensgrave 88 C3
Maiden's Green 48 B1
Maidenwell
Corn 10 D2
Lincs 134 B3
Maiden Wells 55 E5
Maidford 82 B3
Maids Moreton 83 D4
Maidstone 37 A5
Maidwell 99 D4
Mail 285 L6
Main 109 D6
Maindee 42 A2
Mainsforth 167 B6
Mains of Airies 170 A1
Mains of Allardice 233 A6
Mains of Annochie 257 B4
Mains of Ardestie 221 A5
Mains of Balhall 232 B3
Mains of Ballindarg 232 C2
Mains of Balnakettle 233 A4
Mains of Birness 257 C4
Mains of Burgie 266 D1
Mains of Clunas 253 B4
Mains of Crichie 257 B4
Mains of Dalvey 254 C2
Mains of Dellavaird 245 D4
Mains of Drum 245 C5
Mains of Edingight 267 D6
Mains of Fedderate 268 E3
Mains of Inkhorn 257 C4
Mains of Mayen 255 B6
Mains of Melgund 232 C3
Mains of Thornton 233 A4
Mains of Watten 281 C4
Mainsriddle 174 C2
Mainstone 93 C6
Maisemore 63 A4
Malacleit 287 G2
Malborough 7 D6
Malcoff 129 A5
Maldon 70 C2
Malham 146 A3
Maligar 259 B4
Mallaig 235 A5
Malleny Mills 209 D4
Malling 217 D5
Malltraeth 123 D4
Mallwyd 91 A6
Malmesbury 44 A3
Malmsmead 26 A2
Malpas
Ches W 110 A3
Corn 4 C3
Newport 61 D5
Malswick 62 A3
Maltby
Stockton 168 D2
S Yorks 140 D3
Maltby le Marsh 135 A4
Malting Green 70 A3
Maltman's Hill 37 B7
Malton 159 D6
Malvern Link 79 C5
Malvern Wells 79 C5
Mamble 95 D4
Manaccan 3 C5
Manafon 93 A5
Manar House 256 D2
Manaton 12 C2
Manby 134 A3
Mancetter 97 B6
Manchester 138 D1
Manchester Airport 128 A3
Mancot 126 C3
Mandally 239 B6
Manea 101 C6
Manfield 167 D5
Mangaster 284 F5
Mangotsfield 43 B5
Mangurstadh 287 A5
Mankinholes 138 A2
Manley 127 B5
Manmoel 41 A6
Mannal 222 C2
Mannerston 208 C3
Manningford Bohune 45 D5
Manningford Bruce 45 D5
Manningham 147 D5
Mannings Heath 35 D5
Mannington 17 A4
Manningtree 88 D1
Mannofield 245 B6
Manor 50 A1
Manorbier 55 E6
Manordeilo 58 C3
Manor Estate 130 A3
Manorhill 197 C5
Manorowen 72 C2
Manselfield 57 D5
Mansel Lacy 78 C2
Mansell Gamage 78 C1
Mansergh 155 C5
Mansfield
E Ayrs 182 A4
Notts 131 C5
Mansfield Woodhouse 131 C5
Mansriggs 154 C1
Manston
Dorset 30 D2
Kent 53 C5
W Yorks 148 D2
Manswood 16 A3
Manthorpe
Lincs 116 B2
Lincs 116 D3
Manton
N Lincs 142 C1
Notts 131 B5
Rutland 99 A5
Wilts 45 C5
Manuden 69 A4
Maperton 29 C6
Maplebeck 132 C2
Maple Cross 67 D5
Mapledurham 47 B4
Mapledurwell 47 D4
Maplehurst 35 D4
Maplescombe 50 C2
Mapleton 113 A5
Mapperley 114 A2
Mapperley Park 114 A3
Mapperton 15 B5
Mappleborough Green 80 A3
Mappleton 151 C5
Mappowder 16 A1
Maraig 288 G2
Marazanvose 4 B3
Marazion 2 B3
Marbhig 288 F5
Marbury 111 A4
March
Cambs 101 B6
S Lanark 184 A2
Marcham 65 D5
Marchamley 111 C4
Marchington 113 B5
Marchington Woodlands 113 C5
Marchroes 106 D3
Marchwiel 110 A2
Marchwood 32 D2
Marcross 40 E4
Marden
Hereford 78 C3
Kent 37 B5
T&W 179 B5
Wilts 45 D4
Marden Beech 37 B5
Marden Thorn 37 B5
Mardy 61 B5
Marefield 99 A4
Mareham le Fen 134 C2
Mareham on the Hill 134 C2
Marehay 114 A1
Marehill 20 A3
Maresfield 36 D2
Marfleet 142 A3
Marford 126 D3
Margam 40 C2
Margaret Marsh 30 D2
Margaret Roding 69 B5
Margaretting 69 C6
Margate 53 B5
Margnaheglish 191 B6
Margrove Park 169 D4
Marham 119 D4
Marhamchurch 10 A3
Marholm 100 A3
Mariandyrys 123 B6
Marianglas 123 B5
Mariansleigh 26 C2
Marionburgh 245 B4
Marishader 259 B4
Marjoriebanks 184 D3
Mark
Dumfries 170 B3
S Ayrs 180 D2
Som 28 A3
Markbeech 36 B2
Markby 135 B4
Mark Causeway 28 A3
Mark Cross
E Sus 22 A2
E Sus 36 C3
Market Bosworth 97 A7
Market Deeping 116 E4
Market Drayton 111 B5
Market Harborough 99 C4
Markethill 220 A2
Market Lavington 44 D4
Market Overton 116 D1
Market Rasen 133 A6
Market Stainton 134 B2
Market Warsop 131 C5
Market Weighton 150 C1
Market Weston 103 D5
Markfield 114 D2
Markham 41 A6
Markham Moor 132 B2
Markinch 220 D2
Markington 148 A1
Marksbury 43 C5
Marks Tey 70 A3
Markyate 67 B5
Marland 138 B1
Marlborough 45 C5
Marlbrook
Hereford 78 B3
Worcs 96 D2
Marlcliff 80 B3
Marldon 8 A2
Marlesford 88 B4
Marley Green 111 A4
Marley Hill 179 D4
Marley Mount 17 B6
Marlingford 104 A2
Mar Lodge 242 C3
Marloes 54 D3
Marlow
Bucks 47 A6
Hereford 94 D2
Marlow Bottom 47 A6
Marlpit Hill 36 B2
Marlpool 114 A2
Marnhull 30 D1
Marnoch 267 D6
Marnock 207 D5
Marple 129 A4
Marple Bridge 129 A4
Marr 140 C3
Marrel 274 C4
Marrick 157 B4
Marrister 285 G7
Marros 56 B2
Marsden
T&W 179 C5
W Yorks 138 B3
Marsett 156 C3
Marsh
Devon 28 D2
W Yorks 147 D4
Marshall's Heath 67 B6
Marshalsea 14 A3
Marshalswick 67 C6
Marsham 120 C3
Marshaw 145 B5

Marsh Baldon 65 D6
Marshborough 53 D5
Marshbrook 94 C2
Marshchapel 143 D5
Marshfield
Newport 42 A1
S Glos 44 B1
Marshgate 10 B2
Marsh Gibbon 66 A1
Marsh Green
Devon 13 B5
Kent 36 B2
Staffs 128 D3
Marshland St James 101 A7
Marsh Lane 131 B4
Marshside 136 B2
Marsh Street 27 A4
Marshwood 14 B3
Marske 157 A5
Marske-by-the-Sea 168 C4
Marston
Ches W 127 B6
Hereford 78 B1
Lincs 116 A1
Oxon 65 C6
Staffs 112 C3
Staffs 112 D2
Warks 97 B5
Wilts 44 D3
Marston Doles 82 B1
Marston Green 97 C4
Marston Magna 29 C5
Marston Meysey 64 D2
Marston Montgomery 113 B5
Marston Moretaine 84 C1
Marston on Dove 113 C6
Marston St Lawrence 82 C2
Marston Stannett 78 B3
Marston Trussell 98 C3
Marstow 62 B1
Marsworth 67 B4
Marten 45 D6
Marthall 128 B3
Martham 121 D6
Martin
Hants 31 D4
Kent 39 A5
Lincs 133 D6
Lincs 134 C2
Martin Dales 134 C1
Martin Drove End 31 C4
Martinhoe 26 A1
Martinhoe Cross 26 A1
Martin Hussingtree 80 A1
Martin Mill 39 A5
Martinscroft 127 A6
Martinstown 15 C6
Martlesham 88 C3
Martlesham Heath 88 C3
Martletwy 55 C6
Martley 79 A5
Martock 29 D4
Marton
Ches E 128 C3
E Yorks 151 D4
Lincs 132 A3
Mbro 168 D3
N Yorks 148 A3
N Yorks 159 C6
Shrops 93 A6
Shrops 110 C3
Warks 81 A7
Marton-le-Moor 158 D2
Martyr's Green 34 A3
Martyr Worthy 32 B4
Marwick 282 E3
Marwood 25 B6
Marybank 251 A6
Maryburgh 252 A1
Maryhill 205 B5
Marykirk 233 B4
Marylebone 137 C4
Marypark 254 C2
Maryport
Cumb 162 A3
Dumfries 170 D3
Mary Tavy 11 D6
Maryton 233 C4
Marywell
Aberds 244 C2
Aberds 245 C6
Angus 233 D4
Masham 157 C6
Mashbury 69 B6
Masongill 155 D5
Masonhill 192 C3
Mastin Moor 131 B4
Mastrick 245 B5
Matching 69 B5
Matching Green 69 B5
Matching Tye 69 B5
Matfen 178 B2
Matfield 37 B4
Mathern 62 D1
Mathon 79 C5
Mathry 55 A4
Matlaske 120 B3
Matlock 130 C2
Matlock Bath 130 D2
Matson 63 B4
Matterdale End 164 C1
Mattersey 132 A1
Mattersey Thorpe 132 A1
Mattingley 47 D5
Mattishall 120 D2
Mattishall Burgh 120 D2
Mauchline 193 C4
Maud 257 B4
Maugersbury 64 A3
Maughold 152 B4
Mauld 251 C6
Maulden 84 D2
Maulds Meaburn 165 D4
Maunby 158 C2
Maund Bryan 78 B3
Maundown 27 C5
Mautby 121 D6
Mavis Enderby 134 C3
Mawbray 174 D3
Mawdesley 136 B3
Mawdlam 40 C3
Mawgan 3 C5
Maw Green 128 D2
Mawla 4 C2
Mawnan 3 C5
Mawnan Smith 3 C5
Mawsley 99 D5
Maxey 100 A3
Maxstoke 97 C5
Maxton
Borders 197 C5
Kent 39 A5
Maxwellheugh 197 C6
Maxwelltown 174 A2
Maxworthy 10 B3
Mayals 57 C6
May Bank 112 A2
Maybole 192 E3
Mayfield
E Sus 36 D3
Midloth 209 D6
Staffs 113 A5
W Loth 208 D2
Mayford 34 A2
Mayland 70 C3
Maynard's Green 22 A3
Maypole
Mon 61 B6
Scilly 2 E4
Maypole Green
Essex 70 A3
Norf 105 B5
Suff 88 A3
Maywick 285 L5
Meadle 66 C3
Meadowtown 93 A7
Meaford 112 B2
Mealabost 288 D5
Mealabost Bhuirgh 288 B5
Meal Bank 154 B4
Mealsgate 175 D5
Meanwood 148 D1
Mearbeck 146 A2
Meare 29 A4
Meare Green 28 C3
Mears Ashby 83 A5
Measham 114 D1
Meath Green 35 B5
Meathop 154 C3
Meaux 150 D3
Meavy 7 A4
Medbourne 99 B4
Medburn 178 B3
Meddon 24 D3
Meden Vale 131 C5
Medlam 134 D3
Medmenham 47 A6
Medomsley 178 D3
Medstead 33 B5
Meerbrook 129 C4
Meer End 97 D5
Meers Bridge 135 A4
Meesden 85 D6
Meeth 11 A6
Meggethead 195 D6
Meidrim 73 D5
Meifod
Denb 125 D5
Powys 109 D6
Meigle
N Ayrs 204 B1
Perth 231 D6
Meikle Earnock 194 A2
Meikle Ferry 264 B3
Meikle Forter 231 B5
Meikle Gluich 264 B2
Meikleour 219 A6
Meikle Pinkerton 211 C4
Meikle Strath 233 A4
Meikle Tarty 257 D4
Meikle Wartle 256 C2
Meinciau 57 A4
Meir 112 A3
Meir Heath 112 A3
Melbourn 85 C5
Melbourne
Derbys 114 C1
E Yorks 149 C6
S Lanark 195 B5
Melbury Abbas 30 C2
Melbury Bubb 15 A5
Melbury Osmond 15 A5
Melbury Sampford 15 A5
Melby 285 H3
Melchbourne 84 A2
Melcombe Bingham 16 A1
Melcombe Regis 15 C6
Meldon
Devon 11 B6
Northumb 178 A3
Meldreth 85 C5
Meldrum House 256 D3
Melfort 213 A6
Melgarve 240 C2
Meliden 125 A5
Melinbyrhedyn 91 C6
Melincourt 40 A3
Melin-y-coed 124 C3
Melin-y-ddôl 93 A4
Melin-y-grug 93 A4
Melin-y-Wig 109 A5
Melkinthorpe 164 C3
Melkridge 177 C5
Melksham 44 C3
Melldalloch 203 A4
Melling
Lancs 155 D4
Mers 136 C2
Melling Mount 136 C3
Mellis 104 D2
Mellon Charles 261 A5
Mellon Udrigle 261 A5
Mellor
Gtr Man 129 A4
Lancs 145 D6
Mellor Brook 145 D6
Mells 30 A1
Melmerby
Cumb 165 B4
N Yorks 157 C4
N Yorks 158 D2
Melplash 15 B4
Melrose 197 C4
Melsetter 283 J3
Melsonby 157 A5
Meltham 138 B4
Melton 88 B3
Meltonby 149 B6
Melton Constable 120 B2
Melton Mowbray 115 D5
Melton Ross 142 B2
Melvaig 261 B4
Melverley 110 D2
Melverley Green 110 D2
Melvich 279 B4
Membury 14 A2
Memsie 269 C4
Memus 232 C2
Menabilly 5 B5
Menai Bridge
= *Porthaethwy* 123 C5
Mendham 104 C3
Mendlesham 88 A2
Mendlesham Green 88 A1
Menheniot 6 A1
Mennock 183 B6
Menston 147 C5
Menstrie 207 A6
Menthorpe 149 D5
Mentmore 67 B4
Meoble 238 D1
Meole Brace 110 D3
Meols 136 D1
Meonstoke 33 D5
Meopham 50 C3
Meopham Station 50 C3
Mepal 101 C6
Meppershall 84 D3
Merbach 77 C7
Mere
Ches E 128 A2
Wilts 30 B2
Mere Brow 136 B3
Mereclough 146 D2
Mere Green 96 B4
Mereside 144 D3
Mereworth 37 A4
Mergie 245 D4
Meriden 97 C5
Merkadale 246 A2
Merkland
Dumfries 173 A5
S Ayrs 181 B4
Merkland Lodge 271 B7
Merley 17 B4
Merlin's Bridge 55 C5
Merrington 110 C3
Merrion 55 E5
Merriott 28 D4
Merrivale 11 D6
Merrow 34 A3
Merrymeet 6 A1
Mersham 38 B2
Merstham 35 A5
Merston 20 B1
Merstone 18 C4
Merther 4 C3
Merthyr 73 D6
Merthyr Cynog 76 D3
Merthyr-Dyfan 41 E6
Merthyr Mawr 40 D3
Merthyr Tudful
= *Merthyr Tydfil* 60 C2
Merthyr Tydfil
= *Merthyr Tudful* 60 C2
Merthyr Vale 41 B5
Merton
Devon 25 D6
London 49 B5
Norf 103 B5
Oxon 65 B6
Mervinslaw 187 B5
Meshaw 26 D2
Messing 70 B2
Messingham 141 C6
Metfield 104 C3
Metheringham 133 C5
Methil 209 A6
Methlem 106 C1
Methley 140 A1
Methlick 256 C3
Methven 219 B5
Methwold 102 B3
Methwold Hythe 102 B3
Mettingham 105 C4
Mevagissey 5 C5
Mewith Head 145 A7
Mexborough 140 C2
Mey 281 A4
Meysey Hampton 64 D2
Miabhag
W Isles 287 D5
W Isles 288 H2
Miabhig 287 A5
Michaelchurch 61 A7
Michaelchurch Escley 77 D7
Michaelchurch on Arrow 77 B6
Michaelston-le-Pit 41 D6
Michaelston-y-Fedw 42 A1
Michaelstow 10 D1
Michealston-super-Ely 41 D6
Micheldever 32 B4
Michelmersh 32 C2
Mickfield 88 A2
Micklebring 140 D3
Mickleby 169 D6
Mickleham 35 A4
Mickleover 113 B7
Micklethwaite 147 C5
Mickleton
Durham 166 C2
Glos 81 C4
Mickletown 140 A1
Mickle Trafford 127 C4
Mickley 157 D6
Mickley Square 178 C2
Mid Ardlaw 269 C4
Mid Auchinlech 204 A3
Midbea 282 C5
Mid Beltie 244 B3
Mid Calder 208 D3
Mid Cloch Forbie 268 D2
Mid Clyth 275 A6
Middle Assendon 47 A5
Middle Aston 65 A5
Middle Barton 65 A5
Middlebie 175 A5
Middle Cairncake 256 B3
Middle Claydon 66 A2
Middle Drums 232 C3
Middleforth Green 136 A4
Middleham 157 C5
Middle Handley 131 B4
Middlehope 94 C2
Middle Littleton 80 C3
Middle Maes-coed 78 D1
Middlemarsh 15 A6
Middle Mill 54 B4
Middlemuir 257 D4
Middle Rasen 133 A5
Middle Rigg 219 D5
Middlesbrough 168 C2
Middleshaw
Cumb 155 C4
Dumfries 174 A4
Middlesmoor 157 D4
Middlestone 167 B5
Middlestone Moor 167 B5
Middlestown 139 B5
Middlethird 197 B5
Middleton
Aberds 245 A5
Argyll 222 C2
Cumb 155 C5
Derbys 130 C1
Derbys 130 D2
Essex 87 D4
Gtr Man 138 C1
Hants 32 A3
Hereford 78 A3
Lancs 144 B4
Midloth 196 A2
Norf 118 D3
Northants 99 C5
Northumb 178 A2
Northumb 199 C5
N Yorks 147 C5
N Yorks 159 C6
Perth 219 D6
Perth 231 D5
Shrops 93 B6
Shrops 94 D3
Shrops 110 C2
Suff 89 A5
Swansea 57 D4
Warks 97 B4
W Yorks 139 A5
Middleton Cheney 82 C1
Middleton Green 112 B3
Middleton Hall 188 A2
Middleton-in-Teesdale 166 C2
Middleton Moor 89 A5
Middleton One Row 167 D6
Middleton-on-Leven 158 A3
Middleton-on-Sea 20 B2
Middleton on the Hill 78 A3
Middleton-on-the-Wolds 150 C2
Middleton Priors 95 B4
Middleton Quernham 158 D2
Middleton St George 167 D6
Middleton Scriven 95 C4
Middleton Stoney 65 A6
Middleton Tyas 157 A6
Middletown
Cumb 162 D2
Powys 110 D2
Middle Tysoe 81 C6
Middle Wallop 32 B1
Middlewich 128 C1
Middle Winterslow 31 B6
Middle Woodford 31 B5
Middlewood Green 88 A1
Middlezoy 28 B3
Middridge 167 C5
Midfield 277 B6
Midge Hall 136 A4
Midgeholme 176 D4
Midgham 46 C3
Midgley
W Yorks 138 A3
W Yorks 139 B5
Midhopestones 139 D5
Midhurst 34 D1
Mid Lavant 20 B1
Midlem 186 A4
Mid Main 251 C6
Midmar 244 B3
Midsomer Norton 43 D5
Midton 204 A2
Midtown
Highld 261 B5
Highld 277 B6
Midtown of Buchromb 254 B4
Mid Urchany 253 B4
Midville 134 D3
Mid Walls 285 H4
Midway 129 A4
Mid Yell 284 D7
Migdale 264 A2
Migvie 244 B1
Milarrochy 206 A2
Milborne Port 29 D6
Milborne St Andrew 16 B2
Milborne Wick 29 C6
Milbourne 178 B3
Milburn 165 C4
Milbury Heath 62 D2
Milcombe 81 D7
Milden 87 C5
Mildenhall
Suff 102 D3
Wilts 45 C6
Milebrook 93 D7
Milebush 37 B5
Mile Cross 120 D4
Mile Elm 44 C3
Mile End
Essex 70 A3
Glos 62 B1
Mileham 119 D6
Mile Oak 21 B5
Milesmark 208 B3
Milfield 198 C3
Milford
Derbys 114 A1
Devon 24 C3
Powys 93 B4
Staffs 112 C3
Sur 34 B2
Wilts 31 C5
Milford Haven
= *Aberdaugleddau* 55 D5
Milford on Sea 18 B1
Milkwall 62 C1
Milkwell 30 C3
Milland 34 D1
Millarston 205 B4
Millbank
Aberds 257 B6
Highld 280 B3
Mill Bank 138 A3
Millbeck 163 B5
Millbounds 282 D6
Millbreck 257 B5
Millbridge 34 B1
Millbrook
C Beds 84 D2
Corn 6 B3
Soton 32 D2
Millburn 193 C4
Millcombe 8 C2
Mill Common 105 C5
Millcorner 37 D6
Milldale 129 D6
Millden Lodge 232 A3
Milldens 232 C3
Mill End
Bucks 47 A5
Herts 85 D5
Millerhill 209 D6
Miller's Dale 129 B6
Miller's Green 130 D2
Millgreen 111 C5
Mill Green
Essex 69 C6
Norf 104 C2
Suff 87 C5
Millhalf 77 C6
Millhayes 14 A2
Millhead 154 D3
Millheugh 194 A2
Mill Hill 68 D2
Millholme 155 B4
Millhouse
Argyll 203 A4
Cumb 163 A6
Millhousebridge 185 D4
Millhouse Green 139 C5
Millhouses 130 A3
Millikenpark 205 B4
Millin Cross 55 C5
Millington 150 B1

Mill Lane 47 D5
Millmeece 112 B2
Mill of Kingoodie . . 256 D3
Mill of Muiresk 256 B1
Mill of Sterin 243 C6
Mill of Uras 245 D5
Millom 153 B2
Millook 10 B2
Mill Place 142 C1
Millpool 10 D2
Millport 204 C1
Millquarter 182 C4
Mill Side 154 C3
Mill Street 120 D2
Millthorpe 116 B4
Millthrop 155 B5
Milltimber 245 B5
Milltown
　Corn 5 B6
　Derbys 130 C3
　Devon 25 B6
　Dumfries 175 A6
Milltown of
　Aberdalgie 219 B5
Milltown of
　Auchindoun . . . 255 B4
Milltown of
　Craigston 268 D2
Milltown of
　Edinvillie 254 B3
Milltown of
　Kildrummy 244 A1
Milltown of
　Rothiemay 255 B6
Milltown of Towie . 244 A1
Milnathort 219 D6
Milner's Heath 127 C4
Milngavie 205 A5
Milnrow 138 C2
Milnshaw 137 A6
Milnthorpe 154 C3
Milo 57 A5
Milson 95 D4
Milstead 37 A7
Milston 31 A5
Milton
　Angus 232 D1
　Cambs 85 A6
　Cumb 176 C3
　Derbys 113 C7
　Dumfries 171 B4
　Dumfries 173 A6
　Dumfries 183 D6
　Highld 251 A1
　Highld 251 C6
　Highld 252 B1
　Highld 264 C3
　Highld 281 D5
　Moray 267 C6
　Notts 132 B2
　N Som 42 C4
　Oxon 65 D5
　Oxon 82 D1
　Pembs 55 D6
　Perth 219 C4
　Ptsmth 19 B5
　Stirling 217 D5
　Stoke 129 D4
　W Dunb 205 A4
Milton Abbas 16 A2
Milton Abbot 11 D5
Milton Bridge 209 D5
Milton Bryan 83 D6
Milton Clevedon . . . 29 B6
Milton Coldwells . . 257 C4
Milton Combe 6 A3
Milton Damerel . . . 25 D4
Miltonduff 266 C2
Milton End 64 C2
Milton Ernest 84 B2
Milton Green 127 D4
Miltonhill 266 C2
Milton Hill 65 D5
Miltonise 180 D3
Milton Keynes 83 D5
Milton Keynes
　Village 83 D5
Milton Lilbourne . . . 45 C5
Milton Malsor 83 B4
Milton Morenish . . 217 A6
Milton of
　Auchinhove . . . 244 B2
Milton of Balgonie . 220 D3
Milton of
　Buchanan 206 A2
Milton of
　Campfield 244 B3
Milton of Campsie . 205 A6
Milton of
　Corsindae 244 B3

Milton of Cushnie . . 244 A2
Milton of Dalcapon . 230 C3
Milton of Edradour . 230 C3
Milton of
　Gollanfield . . . 252 A3
Milton of Lesmore . 255 D5
Milton of Logie . . . 244 B1
Milton of Murtle . . 245 B5
Milton of Noth . . . 255 D6
Milton of Tullich . . 243 C6
Milton on Stour . . . 30 C1
Milton Regis 51 C6
Milton under
　Wychwood 64 B3
Milverton
　Som 27 C6
　Warks 81 A6
Milwich 112 B3
Minard 214 C2
Minchinhampton . . . 63 C4
Mindrum 198 C2
Minehead 27 A4
Minera 126 D2
Minety 63 D6
Minffordd
　Gwyn 91 A5
　Gwyn 107 C5
　Gwyn 123 C5
Miningsby 134 C3
Minions 10 D3
Minishant 192 D3
Minllyn 91 A6
Minnes 257 D4
Minngearraidh 286 D3
Minnigaff 171 A6
Minnonie 268 C2
Minskip 148 A2
Minstead 32 D1
Minsted 34 D1
Minster
　Kent 51 B6
　Kent 53 C5
Minsterley 94 A1
Minster Lovell 64 B4
Minsterworth 62 B3
Minterne Magna . . . 15 A6
Minting 134 B1
Mintlaw 257 B5
Minto 187 A4
Minton 94 B2
Minwear 55 C6
Minworth 97 B4
Mirbister 282 E4
Mirehouse 162 C2
Mireland 281 B5
Mirfield 139 B5
Miserden 63 C5
Miskin 41 C5
Misson 141 D4
Misterton
　Leics 98 C2
　Notts 141 D5
　Som 15 A4
Mistley 88 D2
Mitcham 49 C5
Mitcheldean 62 B2
Mitchell 4 B3
Mitchel Troy 61 B6
Mitcheltroy
　Common 61 C6
Mitford 178 A3
Mithian 4 B2
Mitton 112 D2
Mixbury 82 D3
Moat 175 A4
Moats Tye 87 B6
Mobberley
　Ches E 128 B2
　Staffs 112 A4
Moccas 78 C1
Mochdre
　Conwy 124 B3
　Powys 93 C4
Mochrum 171 C5
Mockbeggar 17 A5
Mockerkin 162 B3
Modbury 7 B5
Moddershall 112 B3
Moelfre
　Anglesey 123 B5
　Powys 109 C6
Moffat 184 B3
Moggerhanger 84 C3
Moira 113 D7
Molash 52 D2
Mol-chlach 246 C3
Mold
　= Yr Wyddgrug . 126 C2
Moldgreen 139 B4
Molehill Green 69 A5

Molescroft 150 C3
Molesden 178 A3
Molesworth 100 D2
Moll 247 A4
Molland 26 C3
Mollington
　Ches W 126 B3
　Oxon 82 C1
Mollinsburn 207 C5
Monachty 75 B4
Monachylemore . . 217 C4
Monar Lodge 250 B4
Monaughty 77 A6
Monboddo House . . 233 A5
Mondynes 233 A5
Monevechadan . . . 215 B4
Monewden 88 B3
Moneydie 219 B5
Moniaive 183 C5
Monifieth 221 A4
Monikie 221 A4
Monimail 220 C2
Monington 72 B4
Monk Bretton 139 C6
Monken Hadley 68 D2
Monk Fryston 140 A3
Monkhopton 95 B4
Monkland 78 B2
Monkleigh 25 C5
Monknash 40 D4
Monkokehampton . 11 A6
Monkseaton 179 B5
Monks Eleigh 87 C5
Monk's Gate 35 D5
Monks Heath 128 B3
Monk Sherborne . . . 47 D4
Monkshill 256 B2
Monksilver 27 B5
Monks Kirby 98 C1
Monk Soham 88 A3
Monkspath 96 D4
Monks Risborough . 66 C3
Monk Street 69 A6
Monkswood 61 C5
Monkton
　Devon 14 A1
　Kent 53 C4
　Pembs 55 D5
　S Ayrs 192 C3
Monkton Combe . . . 44 C1
Monkton Deverill . . 30 B2
Monkton Farleigh . . 44 C2
Monkton Heathfield . 28 C2
Monkton Up
　Wimborne 31 D4
Monkwearmouth . . 179 D5
Monkwood 33 B5
Monmouth
　= Trefynwy 61 B7
Monmouth Cap 61 A5
Monnington on Wye . 78 C1
Monreith 171 C5
Monreith Mains . . . 171 C5
Montacute 29 D4
Montcoffer House . 268 C1
Montford
　Argyll 203 B6
　Shrops 110 D3
Montford Bridge . . 110 D3
Montgarrie 244 A2
Montgomery
　= Trefaldwyn . . . 93 B6
Montrave 220 D3
Montrose 233 C5
Mont Saint 6
Montsale 71 D4
Monxton 32 A2
Monyash 129 C6
Monymusk 244 A3
Monzie 218 B3
Monzie Castle 218 B3
Moodiesburn 207 C4
Moonzie 220 C3
Moor Allerton 148 D1
Moorby 134 C2
Moor Crichel 16 A3
Moordown 17 B4
Moore 127 A5
Moorend 62 C3
Moor End
　E Yorks 149 D7
　York 149 B5
Moorends 141 B4
Moorgate 140 D2
Moorgreen 114 A2
Moorhall 130 B3
Moorhampton 78 C1
Moorhead 147 D5
Moorhouse
　Cumb 175 C6

Moorhouse continued
　Notts 132 C2
Moorlinch 28 B3
Moor Monkton . . . 148 B4
Moor of Granary . . 253 A6
Moor of
　Ravenstone . . . 171 C5
Moor Row 162 C3
Moorsholm 169 D4
Moorside 138 C2
Moor Street 51 C5
Moorthorpe 140 B2
Moortown
　Hants 17 A5
　IoW 18 C3
　Lincs 142 D2
Morangie 264 B3
Morar 235 A5
Morborne 100 B3
Morchard Bishop . . 12 A2
Morcombelake 14 B4
Morcott 99 A6
Morda 110 C1
Morden
　Dorset 16 B3
　London 49 C5
Mordiford 78 D3
Mordon 167 C6
More 94 B1
Morebath 27 C4
Morebattle 187 A6
Morecambe 144 A4
Morefield 262 A3
Moreleigh 7 B6
Morenish 217 A5
Moresby 162 B2
Moresby Parks . . . 162 C2
Morestead 32 C4
Moreton
　Dorset 16 C2
　Essex 69 C5
　Mers 136 D1
　Oxon 66 C1
　Staffs 112 D1
Moreton Corbet . . . 111 C4
Moretonhampstead . 12 C2
Moreton-in-Marsh . 81 D5
Moreton Jeffries . . . 79 C4
Moreton Morrell . . . 81 B6
Moreton on Lugg . . 78 C3
Moreton Pinkney . . 82 C2
Moreton Say 111 B5
Moreton Valence . . . 62 C3
Morfa
　Carms 57 A5
　Carms 57 C5
Morfa Bach 56 A3
Morfa Bychan 107 C5
Morfa Dinlle 107 A4
Morfa Glas 59 E5
Morfa Nefyn 106 B2
Morfydd 109 A6
Morgan's Vale 31 C5
Moriah 75 A5
Morland 164 C3
Morley
　Derbys 114 A1
　Durham 166 C4
　W Yorks 139 A5
Morley Green 128 A3
Morley St Botolph . 104 B1
Morningside
　Edin 209 C5
　N Lanark 194 A3
Morningthorpe . . . 104 B3
Morpeth 179 A4
Morphie 233 B5
Morrey 113 D5
Morris Green 86 D3
Morriston 57 C6
Morston 120 A2
Mortehoe 25 A5
Mortimer 47 C4
Mortimer's Cross . . 78 A2
Mortimer West End . 47 C4
Mortlake 49 B5
Morton
　Cumb 175 C6
　Derbys 131 C4
　Lincs 116 C3
　Lincs 132 C3
　Lincs 141 D6
　Norf 120 D3
　Notts 132 D2
　S Glos 62 D2
　Shrops 110 C1
Morton Bagot 80 A4
Morton-on-Swale . 157 B7
Morvah 2 B2
Morval 6 B1

Morvich
　Highld 249 D6
　Highld 273 D5
Morville 95 B4
Morville Heath 95 B4
Morwenstow 24 D3
Mosborough 131 A4
Moscow 205 D4
Mosedale 163 A6
Moseley
　W Mid 96 B3
　W Mid 96 C3
　Worcs 79 B6
Moss
　Argyll 222 C2
　Highld 235 D5
　S Yorks 140 B3
　Wrex 126 D3
Mossat 244 A1
Mossbank 284 F6
Moss Bank 136 D4
Mossbay 162 B2
Mossblown 193 C4
Mossbrow 128 A2
Mossburnford 187 B5
Mossdale 173 A4
Moss Edge 144 C4
Mossend 207 D5
Moss End 47 B6
Mosser 163 B4
Mossfield 264 C2
Mossgiel 193 C4
Mosside 232 C2
Mossley
　Ches E 128 C3
　Gtr Man 138 C2
Mossley Hill 126 A3
Moss of
　Barmuckity . . . 266 C3
Moss Pit 112 C3
Moss-side 253 A4
Moss Side 144 D3
Mosstodloch 266 D4
Mosston 232 D3
Mossy Lea 136 B4
Mosterton 15 A4
Moston
　Gtr Man 138 C1
　Shrops 111 C4
Moston Green 128 C2
Mostyn 125 A6
Mostyn Quay 125 A6
Motcombe 30 C2
Mothecombe 7 C5
Motherby 164 C2
Motherwell 194 A2
Mottingham 49 B7
Mottisfont 32 C2
Mottistone 18 C3
Mottistone 18 C3
Mottram in
　Longdendale . . 138 D2
Mottram
　St Andrew 128 B3
Mouilpied 6
Mouldsworth 127 B5
Moulin 230 C3
Moulsecoomb 21 B6
Moulsford 46 A3
Moulsoe 83 C6
Moulton
　Ches W 127 C6
　Lincs 117 C6
　Northants 83 A4
　N Yorks 157 A6
　Suff 86 A2
　V Glam 41 D5
Moulton Chapel . . 117 D5
Moulton Eaugate . . 117 C6
Moulton St Mary . . 105 A4
Moulton
　Seas End 117 C6
Mounie Castle 256 D2
Mount
　Corn 4 B2
　Corn 5 A6
　Highld 253 B5
Mountain 147 D4
Mountain Ash
　= Aberpennar . . . 41 B5
Mountain Cross . . . 195 B6
Mountain Water . . . 55 B5
Mountbenger 196 D2
Mount Bures 87 D5
Mount Canisp 264 C3
Mountfield 37 D5
Mountgerald 264 D1
Mount Hawke 4 C2
Mountjoy 4 A3
Mountnessing 69 D6
Mounton 61 D7

Mount Pleasant
　Ches E 128 D3
　Derbys 113 D6
　Derbys 114 A1
　Flint 126 B2
　Hants 18 B1
　W Yorks 139 A5
Mountsorrel 114 D3
Mount Sorrel 31 C4
Mount Tabor 138 A3
Mousehole 2 C3
Mousen 199 C5
Mouswald 174 A3
Mow Cop 128 D3
Mowhaugh 187 A7
Mowsley 98 C3
Moxley 96 B2
Moy
　Highld 240 D2
　Highld 252 C3
Moy Hall 252 C3
Moy House 265 D6
Moyles Court 17 A5
Moylgrove 72 B4
Moy Lodge 240 D2
Muasdale 202 D1
Muchalls 245 C6
Much Birch 78 D3
Much Cowarne 79 C4
Much Dewchurch . . 78 D2
Muchelney 28 C4
Much Hadham 68 B4
Much Hoole 136 A3
Muchlarnick 5 B7
Much Marcle 79 D4
Muchrachd 251 C4
Much Wenlock 95 A4
Muckernich 252 A1
Mucking 50 A3
Muckleford 15 B6
Mucklestone 111 B6
Muckleton 111 C4
Muckletown 255 D6
Muckley Corner . . . 96 A3
Muckton 134 A3
Mudale 272 A3
Muddiford 25 B6
Mudeford 17 B5
Mudford 29 D5
Mudgley 28 A4
Mugdock 205 A5
Mugeary 246 A3
Mugginton 113 A6
Muggleswick 166 A3
Muie 273 D4
Muir 242 D3
Muirden 268 D2
Muirdrum 221 A5
Muirhead
　Angus 220 A3
　Fife 220 D2
　N Lanark 207 D4
　S Ayrs 192 B3
Muirhouselaw 187 A5
Muirhouses 208 B3
Muirkirk 194 D1
Muirmill 207 B5
Muir of Fairburn . . 251 A6
Muir of Fowlis 244 A2
Muir of Ord 252 A1
Muir of Pert 220 A4
Muirshearlich 239 D5
Muirskie 245 C5
Muirtack 257 C4
Muirton
　Highld 264 D3
　Perth 218 C4
　Perth 219 B6
Muirton Mains . . . 251 A6
Muirton of
　Ardblair 231 D5
Muirton of
　Ballochy 233 B4
Muiryfold 268 D2
Muker 156 B3
Mulbarton 104 A2
Mulben 267 D4
Mulindry 200 C3
Mullardoch House . 250 C4
Mullion 3 D4
Mullion Cove 3 D4
Mumby 135 B5
Munderfield Row . . 79 B4
Munderfield Stocks . 79 B4
Mundesley 121 B5
Mundford 103 B3
Mundham 104 B4
Mundon 70 C2

Mundurno 245 A6
Munerigie 239 B6
Muness 284 C8
Mungasdale 261 A6
Mungrisdale 163 A6
Munlochy 252 A2
Munsley 79 C4
Munslow 94 C3
Murchington 12 C1
Murcott 65 B6
Murkle 280 B3
Murlaggan
  Highld 238 C4
  Highld 239 D7
Murra 283 G3
Murrayfield 209 C5
Murrow 101 A5
Mursley 66 A3
Murthill 232 C2
Murthly 219 A5
Murton
  Cumb 165 C5
  Durham 167 A6
  Northumb 198 B3
  York 149 B5
Musbury 14 B2
Muscoates 159 C5
Musdale 226 D4
Musselburgh 209 C6
Muston
  Leics 115 B6
  N Yorks 161 D4
Mustow Green 95 D6
Mutehill 173 D4
Mutford 105 C5
Muthill 218 C3
Mutterton 13 A5
Muxton 111 D6
Mybster 280 C4
Myddfai 59 C4
Myddle 110 C3
Mydroilyn 74 C3
Myerscough 145 D4
Mylor Bridge 4 D3
Mynachlog-ddu . . 72 C4
Myndtown 94 C1
Mynydd Bach 75 A6
Mynydd-bach 61 D6
Mynydd Bodafon . . 123 B4
Mynydd Isa 126 C2
Mynyddygarreg 57 B4
Mynytho 106 C3
Myrebird 245 C4
Myrelandhorn 281 C4
Myreside 220 B2
Myrtle Hill 59 B4
Mytchett 34 A1
Mytholm 138 A2
Mytholmroyd 138 A3
Myton-on-Swale . . 148 A3
Mytton 110 D3

N

Naast 261 B5
Naburn 149 C4
Nackington 52 D3
Nacton 88 C3
Nafferton 150 B3
Na Gearrannan 288 C2
Nailbridge 62 B2
Nailsbourne 28 C2
Nailsea 42 B3
Nailstone 97 A7
Nailsworth 63 D4
Nairn 253 A4
Nalderswood 35 B5
Nancegollan 3 B4
Nancledra 2 B2
Nanhoron 106 C2
Nannau 108 C2
Nannerch 125 C6
Nanpantan 114 D3
Nanpean 5 B4
Nanstallon 5 A5
Nant-ddu 60 B2
Nanternis 73 A6
Nantgaredig 58 C1
Nantgarw 41 C6
Nant-glas 76 A3
Nantglyn 125 C5
Nantgwyn 92 D3
Nantlle 107 A5
Nantmawr 110 C1
Nantmel 76 A4
Nantmor 107 B6
Nant Peris 107 A6

Nant Uchaf 125 D5
Nantwich 127 D6
Nant-y-Bai 59 A4
Nant-y-cafn 59 E5
Nantycaws 57 A4
Nant-y-derry 61 C5
Nant-y-ffin 58 B2
Nantyffyllon 40 B3
Nantyglo 60 B3
Nant-y-moel 40 B4
Nant-y-pandy 124 B1
Naphill 66 D3
Nappa 146 B2
Napton on the Hill . . 82 A1
Narberth = Arberth . . 55 C7
Narborough
  Leics 98 B2
  Norf 119 D4
Nasareth 107 A4
Naseby 98 D3
Nash
  Bucks 83 D4
  Hereford 77 A7
  Newport 42 A2
  Shrops 95 D4
Nash Lee 66 C3
Nassington 100 B2
Nasty 68 A3
Nateby
  Cumb 155 A6
  Lancs 145 C4
Natland 154 C4
Naughton 87 C6
Naunton
  Glos 64 A2
  Worcs 80 D1
Naunton
  Beauchamp . . 80 B2
Navenby 133 D4
Navestock Heath . . . 69 D5
Navestock Side 69 D5
Navidale 274 C4
Nawton 159 C5
Nayland 87 D5
Nazeing 68 C4
Neacroft 17 B5
Neal's Green 97 C6
Neap 285 H7
Near Sawrey 154 B2
Neasham 167 D6
Neath = Castell-Nedd . 40 B2
Neath Abbey 40 B2
Neatishead 121 C5
Nebo
  Anglesey 123 A4
  Ceredig 75 B4
  Conwy 124 D3
  Gwyn 107 A4
Necton 103 A4
Nedd 270 A4
Nedderton 179 A4
Nedging Tye 87 C6
Needham 104 C3
Needham Market . . 88 B1
Needingworth 101 D5
Needwood 113 C5
Neen Savage 95 D4
Neen Sollars 95 D4
Neenton 95 C4
Nefyn 106 B3
Neilston 205 C4
Neinthirion 92 A3
Neithrop 82 C1
Nelly Andrews
  Green 93 A6
Nelson
  Caerph 41 B6
  Lancs 146 D2
Nelson Village 179 B4
Nemphlar 194 B3
Nempnett
  Thrubwell 43 C4
Nene Terrace 101 A4
Nenthall 165 A5
Nenthead 165 A5
Nenthorn 197 C5
Nerabus 200 C2
Nercwys 126 C2
Nerston 205 C6
Nesbit 198 C3
Ness 126 B3
Nesscliffe 110 D2
Neston
  Ches W 126 B2
  Wilts 44 C2
Nether Alderley 128 B3
Netheravon 31 A5
Nether Blainslie 197 B4
Nether Booth 129 A6
Netherbrae 268 D2

Netherbrough 282 F4
Nether Broughton . . . 115 C4
Netherburn 194 B3
Nether Burrow 155 D5
Netherbury 15 B4
Netherby
  Cumb 175 A6
  N Yorks 148 C2
Nether Cerne 15 B6
Nether Compton . . . 29 D5
Nethercote 82 A2
Nethercott 25 B5
Nether Crimond 256 D3
Nether Dalgliesh 185 B5
Nether Dallachy 267 C4
Netherend 62 C1
Nether Exe 13 A4
Netherfield 23 A5
Nether Glasslaw 268 D3
Netherhampton 31 C5
Nether Handwick . . 232 D1
Nether Haugh 140 D2
Nether Heage 130 D3
Nether Heyford 82 B3
Nether Hindhope . . . 187 B6
Nether
  Howecleuch 184 A3
Nether Kellet 145 A5
Nether Kinmundy . . . 257 B5
Nether Langwith 131 B5
Netherlaw 173 D5
Nether Leask 257 C5
Nether Lenshie 256 B1
Netherley
  Aberds 245 C5
  Mers 127 A4
Nethermill 184 D3
Nether Monynut 211 D4
Nethermuir 257 B4
Nether Padley 130 B2
Nether Park 269 D5
Netherplace 205 C5
Nether Poppleton . . . 149 B4
Netherseal 113 D6
Nether Silton 158 B3
Nether Stowey 28 B1
Netherthird 182 A3
Netherthong 139 C4
Netherthorpe 131 A5
Netherton
  Angus 232 C3
  Devon 12 D3
  Hants 46 D1
  Mers 136 C2
  Northumb 188 C2
  Oxon 65 D5
  Perth 231 C5
  Stirling 205 A5
  W Mid 96 C2
  Worcs 80 C2
  W Yorks 139 B4
  W Yorks 139 B5
Nethertown
  Cumb 162 D2
  Highld 281 A5
Nether Urquhart 219 D6
Nether Wallop 32 B2
Nether Wasdale 163 D4
Nether Whitacre 97 B5
Netherwitton 189 D4
Netherwood 193 C6
Nether Worton 82 D1
Nethy Bridge 253 D6
Netley 18 A3
Netley Marsh 32 D2
Netteswell 69 B4
Nettlebed 47 A5
Nettlebridge 29 A6
Nettlecombe 15 B5
Nettleden 67 B5
Nettleham 133 B5
Nettlestead 37 A4
Nettlestead Green . . . 37 A4
Nettlestone 19 B5
Nettlesworth 167 A5
Nettleton
  Lincs 142 C3
  Wilts 44 B2
Neuadd 58 C3
Nevendon 70 D1
Nevern 72 B3
New Abbey 174 B2
New Aberdour 268 C3
New Addington 49 C6
Newall 147 C5
New Alresford 33 B4
New Alyth 231 D6
Newark
  Orkney 282 C8
  Pboro 100 A4

Newark-on-Trent . . 132 D2
New Arley 97 C5
Newarthill 194 A2
New Ash Green 50 C3
New Barn 50 C3
New Barnetby 142 B2
Newbarns 153 C3
New Barton 83 A5
Newbattle 209 D6
New Bewick 188 A3
Newbiggin
  Cumb 153 A1
  Cumb 153 D3
  Cumb 164 A3
  Cumb 164 C2
  Cumb 165 C4
  Durham 166 C2
  N Yorks 156 B3
  N Yorks 156 C3
Newbiggin-by-the-
  Sea 179 A5
Newbigging
  Angus 220 A4
  Angus 221 A4
  Angus 231 D6
  S Lanark 195 B5
Newbiggin-on-
  Lune 155 A6
New Bilton 98 D1
Newbold
  Derbys 130 B3
  Leics 114 D2
Newbold on Avon . . 98 D1
Newbold on Stour . . 81 C5
Newbold Pacey 81 B5
Newbold Verdon . . . 98 A1
New Bolingbroke . . . 134 D3
Newborough
  Anglesey 123 D4
  Pboro 100 A4
  Staffs 113 C5
Newbottle
  Northants 82 D2
  T&W 179 D5
New Boultham 133 B4
Newbourne 88 C3
New Bradwell 83 C5
New Brancepeth . . . 167 A5
Newbridge
  Caerph 41 B7
  Ceredig 75 C4
  Corn 2 B2
  Corn 6 A2
  Dumfries 174 A2
  Edin 208 C4
  Hants 32 D1
  IoW 18 C3
  Pembs 55 A5
New Bridge 110 A1
Newbridge Green . . . 79 D6
Newbridge-on-Usk . 61 D5
Newbridge on Wye . . 76 B4
New Brighton
  Flint 126 C2
  Mers 136 D2
New Brinsley 131 D4
Newbrough 177 C6
New Broughton 126 D3
New Buckenham . . . 104 B1
Newbuildings 12 A2
Newburgh
  Aberds 257 D4
  Aberds 269 D4
  Borders 185 A6
  Fife 220 C2
  Lancs 136 B3
Newburn 178 C3
Newbury 46 C2
Newbury Park 50 A1
Newby
  Cumb 164 C3
  Lancs 146 C2
  N Yorks 155 D6
  N Yorks 160 B4
  N Yorks 168 D3
Newby Bridge 154 C2
Newby East 176 D2
New Byth 268 D3
Newby West 175 C6
Newby Wiske 158 C2
Newcastle
  Mon 61 B6
  Shrops 93 C6
Newcastle Emlyn
  = Castell Newydd
  Emlyn 73 B6
Newcastleton or
  Copshaw Holm . . . 176 A2
Newcastle-under-
  Lyme 112 A2

Newcastle Upon
  Tyne 179 C4
New Catton 120 D4
Newchapel
  Pembs 73 C5
  Powys 92 C3
  Staffs 128 D3
  Sur 35 B6
New Cheriton 33 C4
Newchurch
  Carms 73 D6
  IoW 19 C4
  Kent 38 B2
  Lancs 146 D2
  Mon 61 D6
  Powys 77 B6
  Staffs 113 C5
New Costessey 120 D3
Newcott 14 A2
New Cowper 174 D4
Newcraighall 209 C6
New Cross
  Ceredig 75 A5
  London 49 B6
New Cumnock 182 A4
New Deer 256 B3
New Delaval 179 B4
Newdigate 35 B4
New Duston 83 A4
New Earswick 149 B5
New Edlington 140 D3
New Elgin 266 C3
New Ellerby 151 D4
Newell Green 48 B1
New Eltham 50 B1
New End 80 B3
Newenden 37 D6
Newent 62 A3
Newerne 62 C2
New Farnley 147 D6
New Ferry 126 A3
Newfield
  Durham 167 B5
  Highld 264 C3
Newford Scilly 2 E4
Newfound 46 D3
New Fryston 140 A2
Newgale 54 B4
New Galloway 172 A4
Newgate 120 A2
Newgate Street 68 C3
New Gilston 220 D4
New Grimsby Scilly . . 2 E3
New Hainford 120 D4
Newhall
  Ches E 111 A5
  Derbys 113 C6
Newhall House 264 D2
Newhall Point 264 D3
Newham 189 A4
Newham Hall 189 A4
New Hartley 179 B5
Newhaven
  Derbys 129 D6
  Edin 209 C5
  E Sus 22 B2
New Haw 48 C3
New Hedges 56 B1
New Herrington 179 D5
Newhey 138 B2
New Hinksey 65 C6
New Holkham 119 B5
New Holland 142 A2
Newholm 169 D6
New Houghton
  Derbys 131 C4
  Norf 119 C4
Newhouse 207 D5
New Houses 155 D7
New Humberstone . . 98 A3
New Hutton 155 B4
New Hythe 37 A5
Newick 36 D2
Newingreen 38 B3
Newington
  Kent 38 B3
  Kent 51 C5
  Kent 53 C5
  Notts 141 D4
  Oxon 65 D7
  Shrops 94 C2
New Inn
  Carms 58 B1
  Mon 61 C6
  Pembs 55 A6
  Torf 61 D5
New Invention
  Shrops 93 D6
  W Mid 96 A2
New Kelso 249 B6

New Kingston 114 C3
New Lanark 194 B3
Newland
  Glos 62 C1
  Hull 150 D3
  N Yorks 141 A4
  Worcs 79 C5
Newlandrig 209 D6
Newlands
  Borders 186 D4
  Highld 252 B3
  Moray 266 D4
  Northumb 178 D2
Newland's Corner . . 34 B3
Newlandsmuir 205 C6
Newlands of Geise . . 280 B2
Newlands of Tynet . . 267 C4
Newlands Park 122 B2
New Lane 136 B3
New Lane End 137 D5
New Leake 135 D4
New Leeds 269 D4
New Longton 136 A4
Newlot 282 F6
New Luce 170 A4
Newlyn 2 C2
Newmachar 245 A5
Newmains 194 A3
New Malden 49 C5
Newmarket
  Suff 86 A2
  W Isles 288 D5
New Marske 168 C4
New Marton 110 B2
New Micklefield 148 D3
Newmill
  Borders 186 B3
  Corn 2 B2
  Moray 267 D5
New Mill
  Aberds 245 D4
  Herts 67 B4
  Wilts 45 C5
  W Yorks 139 C4
Newmill of
  Inshewan 232 B2
New Mills
  Ches E 128 A2
  Corn 4 B3
  Derbys 129 A4
  Powys 93 A4
Newmills of Boyne . 267 D6
Newmiln 219 A6
Newmilns 193 B5
New Milton 17 B6
New Moat 55 B6
Newnham
  Cambs 85 B6
  Glos 62 B2
  Hants 47 D5
  Herts 84 D4
  Kent 51 D6
  Northants 82 B2
Newnham Bridge . . . 79 A4
New Ollerton 131 C6
New Oscott 96 B3
Newpark 221 C4
New Park 148 B1
New Pitsligo 268 D3
New Polzeath 9 D5
Newport
  Devon 25 B6
  Essex 85 D7
  E Yorks 150 D1
  Highld 275 B5
  IoW 18 C4
  Norf 121 D7
  Telford 111 D6
Newport
  = Casnewydd 42 A2
Newport
  = Trefdraeth 72 C2
Newport-on-Tay . . . 220 B4
Newport Pagnell . . . 83 C5
Newpound Common 34 D3
Newquay 4 A3
New Quay
  = Ceinewydd 73 A6
New Rackheath 121 D4
New Radnor 77 A6
New Rent 164 B2
New Ridley 178 C2
New Road Side 146 C3
New Romney 38 C2
New Rossington 140 D4
New Row
  Ceredig 75 A6
  Lancs 145 D6
  N Yorks 168 D4
New Sarum 31 B5

Newsbank 128 C3
Newseat
Aberds 256 C2
Aberds 257 B5
Newsham
Northumb 179 B5
N Yorks 158 C2
N Yorks 166 D4
Newsholme
E Yorks 141 A5
Lancs 146 B2
New Silksworth 179 D5
Newsome 139 B4
Newstead
Borders 197 C4
Northumb 189 A4
Notts 131 D5
New Stevenston 194 A2
New Street 129 D5
New Street Lane 111 B5
New Swanage 17 C4
Newthorpe 148 D3
Newton
Argyll 214 C3
Borders 187 B2
Bridgend 40 D3
Cambs 85 C6
Cambs 118 D1
Cardiff 42 B1
Ches W 127 B5
Ches W 127 C4
Ches W 127 D5
Cumb 153 C3
Derbys 131 D4
Dorset 30 D1
Dumfries 175 A5
Dumfries 185 C4
Gtr Man 138 D2
Hereford 78 B3
Hereford 78 D1
Highld 252 B3
Highld 264 D3
Highld 271 A5
Highld 281 D5
Lancs 144 D4
Lancs 145 B6
Lancs 155 D4
Lincs 116 B3
Moray 266 C2
Norf 119 D5
Northants 99 C5
Northumb 178 C2
Notts 115 A4
Perth 218 A3
S Lanark 194 C4
S Lanark 205 B6
Staffs 112 C4
Suff 87 C5
Swansea 57 D6
S Yorks 140 C3
Warks 98 D2
Wilts 31 C6
W Loth 208 C3
Newton Abbot 12 D3
Newtonairds 183 D6
Newton Arlosh 175 C4
Newton Aycliffe 167 C5
Newton Bewley 168 C2
Newton Blossomville 83 B6
Newton Bromswold 84 A1
Newton Burgoland 97 A6
Newton by Toft 133 A5
Newton Ferrers 7 C4
Newton Flotman 104 B3
Newtongrange 209 D6
Newton Hall 178 C2
Newton Harcourt 98 B3
Newton Heath 138 C1
Newtonhill
Aberds 245 C6
Highld 252 B1
Newton House 256 D1
Newton Kyme 148 C3
Newton-le-Willows
Mers 137 D4
N Yorks 157 C6
Newton Longville 83 D5
Newton Mearns 205 C5
Newtonmill 233 B4
Newtonmore 241 C5
Newton Morrell 157 A6
Newton Mulgrave 169 D5
Newton of Ardtoe 235 C5
Newton of Balcanquhal 219 C6
Newton of Falkland 220 D2
Newton on Ayr 192 C3
Newton on Ouse 148 B4
Newton-on-Rawcliffe 159 B7
Newton-on-the-Moor 189 C4
Newton on Trent 132 B3
Newton Park 203 B6
Newton Poppleford 13 C5
Newton Purcell 82 D3
Newton Regis 97 A5
Newton Reigny 164 B2
Newton St Cyres 12 B3
Newton St Faith 120 D4
Newton St Loe 43 C6
Newton St Petrock 25 D5
Newton Solney 113 C6
Newton Stacey 32 A3
Newton Stewart 171 A6
Newton Tony 31 A6
Newton Tracey 25 C6
Newton under Roseberry 168 D3
Newton upon Derwent 149 C6
Newton Valence 33 B6
New Totley 130 B3
Newtown
Argyll 214 B3
BCP 17 B4
Ches W 127 B5
Corn 3 C5
Cumb 174 D3
Cumb 176 C3
Derbys 129 A4
Devon 26 C2
Glos 62 C2
Glos 80 D2
Hants 18 A3
Hants 31 D6
Hants 32 C2
Hants 32 D4
Hants 33 D5
Hants 46 C2
Hereford 79 C4
Highld 240 B1
IoM 152 D3
IoW 18 B3
Northumb 188 A3
Northumb 188 C3
Northumb 198 C3
Shrops 110 B3
Staffs 129 C4
Staffs 129 C5
Wilts 30 C3
New Town 210 C1
Newtown
= *Y Drenewydd* 93 B5
Newtown Linford 98 A2
Newtown St Boswells 197 C4
Newtown Unthank 98 A1
New Tredegar
= *Tredegar Newydd* 41 A6
New Trows 194 C3
Newtyle 231 D6
New Ulva 213 D5
New Walsoken 101 A6
New Waltham 143 C4
New Whittington 130 B3
New Wimpole 85 C5
New Winton 210 C1
New Yatt 65 B4
New York
Lincs 134 D2
N Yorks 147 A5
Neyland 55 D5
Niarbyl 152 D2
Nibley 43 A5
Nibley Green 62 D3
Nibon 284 F5
Nicholashayne 27 D6
Nicholaston 57 D5
Nidd 148 A2
Nigg
Aberdeen 245 B6
Highld 265 C4
Nigg Ferry 264 D3
Nightcott 26 C3
Nilig 125 D5
Nine Ashes 69 C5
Ninebanks 177 D5
Nine Mile Burn 195 A6
Nine Wells 54 B3
Ninfield 23 A5
Ningwood 18 C2
Nisbet 187 A5
Nisthouse
Orkney 282 F4
Shetland 285 G7
Niton 18 D4
Nitshill 205 B5
Noak Hill 69 D5
Noblethorpe 139 C5
Nobottle 82 A3
Nocton 133 C5
Noke 65 B6
Nolton 55 C4
Nolton Haven 55 C4
No Man's Heath
Ches W 111 A4
Warks 97 A5
Nomansland
Devon 26 D3
Wilts 31 D6
Noneley 110 C3
Nonikiln 264 C2
Nonington 53 D4
Noonsbrough 285 H4
Norbreck 144 C3
Norbridge 79 C5
Norbury
Ches E 111 A4
Derbys 113 A5
Shrops 94 B1
Staffs 112 C1
Nordelph 102 A1
Norden 138 B1
Norden Heath 16 C3
Nordley 95 B4
Norham 198 B3
Norley 127 B5
Norleywood 18 B2
Normanby
N Lincs 141 B6
N Yorks 159 C6
Redcar 168 D3
Normanby-by-Spital 133 A5
Normanby by Stow 132 A3
Normanby le Wold 142 D3
Norman Cross 100 B3
Normandy 34 A2
Norman's Bay 23 B4
Norman's Green 13 A5
Normanstone 105 B6
Normanton
Derby 114 B1
Leics 115 A6
Lincs 116 A2
Notts 132 D2
Rutland 99 A6
W Yorks 140 A1
Normanton le Heath 114 D1
Normanton on Soar 114 C3
Normanton-on-the-Wolds 115 B4
Normanton on Trent 132 C2
Normoss 144 D3
Norney 34 B2
Norrington Common 44 C2
Norris Green 136 D2
Norris Hill 114 D1
Northacre 103 B5
Northallerton 158 B2
Northam
Devon 25 C5
Soton 32 D3
Northampton 83 A4
North Anston 131 A5
North Aston 65 A5
Northaw 68 C2
North Baddesley 32 D2
North Ballachulish 237 C4
North Barrow 29 C6
North Barsham 119 B6
Northbeck 116 A3
North Benfleet 51 A4
North Bersted 20 B2
North Berwick 210 B2
North Boarhunt 33 D5
Northborough 100 A3
Northbourne 53 D5
North Bovey 12 C2
North Bradley 44 D2
North Brentor 11 C5
North Brewham 29 B7
Northbridge Street 37 D5
North Buckland 25 A5
North Burlingham 121 D5
North Cadbury 29 C6
North Cairn 180 D1
North Carlton 133 B4
North Carrine 190 E2
North Cave 150 D1
North Cerney 63 C6
Northchapel 34 D2
North Charford 31 D5
North Charlton 189 A4
North Cheriton 29 C6
Northchurch 67 C4
North Cliff 151 C5
North Cliffe 150 D1
North Clifton 132 B3
North Cockerington 143 D5
North Coker 29 D5
North Collafirth 284 E5
North Common 36 D1
North Connel 226 C4
North Cornelly 40 C3
North Cotes 143 C5
Northcott 10 B4
North Cove 105 C5
North Cowton 157 A6
North Crawley 83 C6
North Cray 50 B1
North Creake 119 B5
North Curry 28 C3
North Dalton 150 B2
North Dawn 283 G5
North Deighton 148 B2
Northdown 53 B5
North Duffield 149 D5
Northdyke 282 E3
North Elkington 143 D4
North Elmham 120 C1
North Elmshall 140 B2
Northend
Bath 44 C1
Bucks 66 D2
Warks 81 B6
North End
Bucks 66 A3
Essex 69 B6
E Yorks 151 D5
Hants 46 C2
Lincs 117 A5
N Som 42 C3
Ptsmth 19 A5
Som 28 C2
W Sus 21 B4
Northenden 137 D7
North Erradale 261 B4
North Fambridge 70 D2
North Fearns 248 C2
North Featherstone 140 A2
North Ferriby 142 A1
Northfield
Aberdeen 245 B6
Borders 211 D6
E Yorks 142 A2
W Mid 96 D3
Northfields 100 A2
Northfleet 50 B3
North Frodingham 151 B4
Northgate 117 C4
North Gluss 284 F5
North Gorley 31 D5
North Green
Norf 104 C3
Suff 89 A4
North Greetwell 133 B5
North Grimston 150 A1
North Halley 283 G6
North Halling 51 C4
North Hayling 19 A6
North Hazelrigg 199 C4
North Heasley 26 B2
North Heath 34 D3
North Hill
Cambs 101 D6
Corn 10 D3
North Hinksey 65 C5
North Holmwood 35 B4
Northhouse 186 C3
North Howden 149 D6
North Huish 7 B6
North Hykeham 133 C4
Northiam 37 D6
Northill 84 C3
Northington 33 B4
North Johnston 55 C5
North Kelsey 142 C2
North Kelsey Moor 142 C2
North Kessock 252 B2
North Killingholme 142 B3
North Kilvington 158 C3
North Kilworth 98 C3
North Kirkton 269 D6
North Kiscadale 191 C6
North Kyme 133 D6
North Lancing 21 B4
Northlands 134 D3
Northlea 179 D6
Northleach 64 B2
North Lee 66 C3
Northleigh 14 B1
North Leigh 65 B4
North Leverton with Habblesthorpe 132 A2
Northlew 11 B6
North Littleton 80 C3
North Lopham 103 C6
North Luffenham 99 A6
North Marden 33 D7
North Marston 66 A2
North Middleton
Midloth 196 A2
Northumb 188 A3
North Molton 26 C2
Northmoor 65 C5
Northmoor Green or Moorland 28 B3
North Moreton 46 A3
Northmuir 232 C1
North Mundham 20 B1
North Muskham 132 D2
North Newbald 150 D2
North Newington 81 D7
North Newnton 45 D5
North Newton 28 B2
Northney 19 A6
North Nibley 62 D3
North Oakley 46 D3
North Ockendon 50 A2
Northolt 48 A4
Northop 126 C2
Northop Hall 126 C2
North Ormesby 168 C3
North Ormsby 143 D4
Northorpe
Lincs 116 D3
Lincs 117 B5
Lincs 141 D6
North Otterington 158 C2
Northover
Som 29 B4
Som 29 C5
North Owersby 142 D2
Northowram 139 A4
North Perrott 15 A4
North Petherton 28 B2
North Petherwin 10 C3
North Pickenham 103 A4
North Piddle 80 B2
North Poorton 15 B5
Northport 16 C3
North Port 227 D5
Northpunds 285 L6
North Queensferry 208 B4
North Radworthy 26 B2
North Rauceby 116 A3
Northrepps 120 B4
North Reston 134 A3
North Rigton 148 C1
North Rode 128 C3
North Roe 284 E5
North Runcton 118 D3
North Sandwick 284 D7
North Scale 153 D2
North Scarle 132 C3
North Seaton 179 A4
North Shian 226 B4
North Shields 179 C5
North Shoebury 51 A6
North Shore 144 D3
North Side
Cumb 162 B3
Pboro 101 B4
North Skelton 169 D4
North Somercotes 143 D6
North Stainley 157 D6
North Stainmore 165 D6
North Stifford 50 A3
North Stoke
Bath 43 C6
Oxon 47 A4
W Sus 20 A3
North Street
Hants 33 B5
Kent 52 D2
Medway 51 B5
W Berks 47 B4
North Sunderland 199 C6
North Tamerton 10 B4
North Tawton 12 A1
North Thoresby 143 D4
North Tidworth 31 A6
North Togston 189 C5
Northtown 283 H5
North Tuddenham 120 D2
North Walbottle 178 C3
North Walsham 121 B4
North Waltham 33 A4
North Warnborough 47 D5
North Water Bridge 233 B4
North Watten 280 C4
Northway 80 D2
North Weald Bassett 69 C4
North Wheatley 132 A2
North Whilborough 8 A2
Northwich 127 B6
Northwick 43 A4
North Wick 43 C4
North Willingham 133 A6
North Wingfield 131 C4
North Witham 116 C2
Northwold 102 B3
Northwood
Derbys 130 C2
IoW 18 B3
Kent 53 C5
London 67 D5
Shrops 110 B3
Northwood Green 62 B3
North Woolwich 50 B1
North Wootton
Dorset 29 D6
Norf 118 C3
Som 29 A5
North Wraxall 44 B2
North Wroughton 45 A5
Norton
E Sus 22 B2
Glos 63 A4
Halton 127 A5
Herts 84 D4
IoW 18 C2
Mon 61 B6
Northants 82 A3
Notts 131 B5
Powys 77 A7
Shrops 94 A3
Shrops 94 C2
Shrops 95 A5
Stockton 168 C2
Suff 87 A5
S Yorks 140 B3
Wilts 44 A2
Worcs 80 B1
Worcs 80 C3
W Sus 20 B2
W Sus 20 C1
Norton Bavant 30 A3
Norton Bridge 112 B2
Norton Canes 96 A3
Norton Canon 78 C1
Norton Corner 120 C2
Norton Disney 132 D3
Norton East 96 A3
Norton Ferris 30 B1
Norton Fitzwarren 28 C1
Norton Green 18 C2
Norton Hawkfield 43 C4
Norton Heath 69 C6
Norton in Hales 111 B6
Norton-in-the-Moors 128 D3
Norton-Juxta-Twycross 97 A6
Norton-le-Clay 158 D3
Norton Lindsey 81 A5
Norton Malreward 43 C5
Norton Mandeville 69 C5
Norton-on-Derwent 159 D6
Norton St Philip 43 D6
Norton sub Hamdon 29 D4
Norton Woodseats 130 A3
Norwell 132 C2
Norwell Woodhouse 132 C2
Norwich 104 A3
Norwick 284 B8
Norwood 131 A4
Norwood Hill 35 B5
Norwoodside 101 B6
Noseley 99 B4
Noss 285 M5
Noss Mayo 7 C4
Nosterfield 157 C6
Nostie 249 D5
Notgrove 64 A2
Nottage 40 D3
Nottingham 114 B3
Nottington 15 C6
Notton
Wilts 44 C3
W Yorks 139 B6
Nounsley 70 B1
Noutard's Green 79 A5
Novar House 264 D2

Nox 110 D3
Nuffield 47 A4
Nunburnholme 150 C1
Nuncargate 131 D5
Nuneaton 97 B6
Nuneham Courtenay 65 D6
Nun Hills 138 A1
Nun Monkton 148 B4
Nunney 30 A1
Nunnington 159 D5
Nunnykirk 188 D3
Nunsthorpe 143 C4
Nunthorpe
  Mbro 168 D3
  York 149 B5
Nunton 31 C5
Nunwick 157 D7
Nupend 62 C3
Nursling 32 D2
Nursted 33 C6
Nutbourne
  W Sus 19 A6
  W Sus 20 A3
Nutfield 35 A6
Nuthall 114 A3
Nuthampstead 85 D6
Nuthurst 35 D4
Nutley
  E Sus 36 D2
  Hants 33 A5
Nutwell 140 C4
Nybster 281 B5
Nyetimber 20 C1
Nyewood 33 C7
Nymet Rowland 12 A2
Nymet Tracey 12 A2
Nympsfield 63 C4
Nynehead 27 C6
Nyton 20 B2

O

Oadby 98 A3
Oad Street 51 C5
Oakamoor 113 A4
Oakbank 208 D3
Oak Cross 11 B6
Oakdale 41 B6
Oake 27 C6
Oaken 95 A6
Oakenclough 145 C5
Oakengates 111 D6
Oakenholt 126 B2
Oakenshaw
  Durham 167 B5
  W Yorks 139 A4
Oakerthorpe 130 D3
Oakes 139 B4
Oakfield 61 D5
Oakford
  Ceredig 74 C3
  Devon 27 C4
Oakfordbridge 27 C4
Oakgrove 129 C4
Oakham 99 A5
Oakhanger 33 B6
Oakhill 29 A6
Oakhurst 36 A3
Oakington 85 A6
Oaklands
  Herts 68 B2
  Powys 76 B4
Oakle Street 62 B3
Oakley
  BCP 17 B4
  Bedford 84 B2
  Bucks 66 B1
  Fife 208 B3
  Hants 46 D3
  Oxon 66 C2
  Suff 104 D2
Oakley Green 48 B2
Oakley Park 92 C3
Oakmere 127 C5
Oakridge
  Glos 63 C5
  Hants 47 D4
Oaks 94 A2
Oaksey 63 D5
Oaks Green 113 B5
Oakthorpe 113 D7
Oakwoodhill 35 C4
Oakworth 147 D4
Oape 272 D2
Oare
  Kent 52 C2
  Som 26 A3

Oare *continued*
  W Berks 46 B3
  Wilts 45 C5
Oasby 116 B3
Oathlaw 232 C2
Oatlands 148 B2
Oban
  Argyll 226 D3
  Highld 238 D2
Oborne 29 D6
Obthorpe 116 D3
Occlestone Green . . 128 C1
Occold 104 D2
Ochiltree 193 C5
Ochtermuthill 218 C3
Ochtertyre 218 B3
Ockbrook 114 B2
Ockham 34 A3
Ockle 235 C4
Ockley 35 C4
Ocle Pychard 78 C3
Octon 150 A3
Octon Cross Roads . 150 A3
Odcombe 29 D5
Odd Down 43 C6
Oddendale 164 D3
Odder 133 B4
Oddingley 80 B2
Oddington
  Glos 64 A3
  Oxon 65 B6
Odell 83 B6
Odie 282 E7
Odiham 47 D5
Odstock 31 C5
Odstone 97 A6
Offchurch 81 A6
Offenham 80 C3
Offham
  E Sus 22 A1
  Kent 37 A4
  W Sus 20 B3
Offord Cluny 84 A4
Offord Darcy 84 A4
Offton 87 C6
Offwell 14 B1
Ogbourne Maizey . . . 45 B5
Ogbourne
  St Andrew 45 B5
Ogbourne St George 45 B6
Ogil 232 B2
Ogle 178 B3
Ogmore 40 D3
Ogmore-by-Sea 40 D3
Ogmore Vale 40 B4
Okeford Fitzpaine . . 30 D2
Okehampton 11 B6
Okehampton Camp . 11 B6
Okraquoy 285 K6
Old 99 D4
Old Aberdeen 245 B6
Old Alresford 33 B4
Oldany 270 A4
Old Arley 97 B5
Old Basford 114 A3
Old Basing 47 D4
Oldberrow 80 A4
Old Bewick 188 A3
Old Bolingbroke . . . 134 C3
Oldborough 12 A2
Old Bramhope 147 C6
Old Brampton 130 B3
Old Bridge of Tilt . . 230 B2
Old Bridge of Urr . . 173 B5
Old Buckenham 103 B6
Old Burghclere 46 D2
Oldbury
  Shrops 95 B5
  Warks 97 B6
  W Mid 96 C2
Oldbury-on-Severn . . 62 D2
Oldbury on the Hill . . 44 A2
Old Byland 159 C4
Old Cassop 167 B6
Oldcastle
  Bridgend 40 D4
  Mon 61 A5
Old Castleton 186 D4
Old Catton 120 D4
Old Clee 143 C4
Old Cleeve 27 A5
Old Clipstone 131 C6
Old Colwyn 124 B3
Oldcotes 131 A5
Old Coulsdon 35 A6
Old Crombie 267 D6
Old Dailly 181 B4
Old Dalby 115 C4
Old Deer 257 B4
Old Denaby 140 D2

Old Edlington 140 D3
Old Eldon 167 C5
Old Ellerby 151 D4
Oldfallow 112 D3
Old Felixstowe 88 D4
Oldfield 79 A6
Old Fletton 100 B3
Oldford 44 D1
Old Glossop 138 D3
Old Goole 141 A5
Old Hall 91 D7
Oldham 138 C2
Oldhamstocks 211 C4
Old Heath 71 A4
Old Heathfield 36 D3
Old Hill 96 C2
Old Hunstanton . . . 118 A3
Old Hurst 101 D4
Old Hutton 155 C4
Old Kea 4 C3
Old Kilpatrick 205 A4
Old Kinnernie 245 B4
Old Knebworth 68 A2
Oldland 43 B5
Old Langho 145 D7
Old Laxey 152 C4
Old Leake 135 D4
Old Malton 159 D6
Oldmeldrum 256 D3
Old Micklefield 148 D3
Old Milton 17 B6
Old Milverton 81 A5
Old Monkland 207 D5
Old Netley 18 A3
Old Philpstoun 208 C3
Old Quarrington . . . 167 B6
Old Radnor 77 B6
Old Rattray 269 D5
Old Rayne 256 D1
Old Romney 38 C2
Oldshore Beg 276 C2
Oldshoremore 276 C3
Old Sodbury 43 A6
Old Somerby 116 B2
Oldstead 158 C4
Old Stratford 83 C4
Old Thirsk 158 C3
Oldtown 255 D6
Old Town
  Cumb 155 C4
  Cumb 164 A2
  Northumb 188 D1
  Scilly 2 E4
Oldtown of Ord 267 D7
Old Trafford 137 D7
Old Tupton 130 C3
Old Warden 84 C3
Oldway 57 D5
Oldways End 26 C3
Old Weston 100 D2
Oldwhat 268 D3
Old Whittington . . . 130 B3
Old Wick 281 C5
Old Windsor 48 B2
Old Wives Lees 52 D2
Old Woking 34 A3
Old Woodhall 134 C2
Olgrinmore 280 C2
Oliver's Battery 32 C3
Ollaberry 284 E5
Ollerton
  Ches E 128 B2
  Notts 131 C6
  Shrops 111 C5
Olmarch 75 C5
Olney 83 B5
Olton 96 C4
Olveston 43 A5
Olwen 75 D4
Ombersley 79 A6
Ompton 132 C1
Onchan 152 D3
Onecote 129 D5
Onen 61 B6
Ongar Hill 118 C2
Ongar Street 78 A1
Onibury 94 D2
Onich 237 C4
Onllwyn 59 D5
Onneley 111 A6
Onslow Village 34 B2
Onthank 205 D4
Openwoodgate 114 A1
Opinan
  Highld 261 A5
  Highld 261 C4
Orange Lane 198 B1
Orange Row 118 C2
Orasaigh 288 F4

Orbliston 266 D4
Orbost 258 D2
Orby 135 C4
Orchard Hill 25 C5
Orchard Portman . . . 28 C2
Orcheston 31 A4
Orcop 61 A6
Orcop Hill 61 A6
Ord 247 C5
Ordhead 244 A3
Ordie 244 B1
Ordiequish 266 D4
Ordsall 132 A1
Ore 23 A6
Oreton 95 C4
Orford
  Suff 89 C5
  Warr 137 D5
Orgreave 113 D5
Orlestone 38 B1
Orleton
  Hereford 78 A2
  Worcs 79 A4
Orlingbury 99 D5
Ormesby 168 D3
Ormesby
  St Margaret 121 D6
Ormesby
  St Michael 121 D6
Ormiclate Castle . . . 286 C3
Ormiscaig 261 A5
Ormiston 209 D7
Ormsaigbeg 234 D3
Ormsaigmore 234 D3
Ormsary 202 A2
Ormsgill 153 C2
Ormskirk 136 C3
Orpington 50 C1
Orrell
  Gtr Man 136 C4
  Mers 136 D2
Orrisdale 152 B3
Orroland 173 D5
Orsett 50 A3
Orslow 112 D2
Orston 115 A5
Orthwaite 163 A5
Ortner 145 B5
Orton
  Cumb 155 A5
  Northants 99 D5
Orton Longueville . . 100 B3
Orton-on-the-Hill . . 97 A6
Orton Waterville . . . 100 B3
Orwell 85 B5
Osbaldeston 145 D6
Osbaldwick 149 B5
Osbaston 110 C2
Osbournby 116 B3
Oscroft 127 C5
Ose 258 D2
Osgathorpe 114 D2
Osgodby
  Lincs 142 D2
  N Yorks 149 D5
  N Yorks 161 C4
Oskaig 248 C2
Oskamull 224 B3
Osmaston
  Derby 114 B1
  Derbys 113 A6
Osmington 16 C1
Osmington Mills 16 C1
Osmotherley 158 B3
Ospisdale 264 B3
Ospringe 52 C2
Ossett 139 A5
Ossington 132 C2
Ostend 70 D3
Oswaldkirk 159 D5
Oswaldtwistle 137 A6
Oswestry 110 C1
Otford 36 A3
Otham 37 A5
Othery 28 B3
Otley
  Suff 88 B3
  W Yorks 147 C6
Otterbourne 32 C3
Otterburn
  Northumb 188 D1
  N Yorks 146 B2
Otterburn Camp . . . 188 D1
Otter Ferry 214 D2
Otterham 10 B2
Otterhampton 28 A2
Ottershaw 48 C3
Otterswick 284 E7
Otterton 13 C5
Ottery St Mary 13 B6

Ottinge 38 A3
Ottringham 143 A4
Oughterby 175 C5
Oughtershaw 156 C2
Oughterside 174 D4
Oughtibridge 139 D6
Oughtrington 128 A1
Oulston 158 D4
Oulton
  Cumb 175 C5
  Norf 120 C3
  Staffs 112 B3
  Suff 105 B6
  W Yorks 139 A6
Oulton Broad 105 B6
Oulton Street 120 C3
Oundle 100 C2
Ousby 165 B4
Ousdale 275 B4
Ousden 86 B3
Ousefleet 141 A6
Ouston
  Durham 179 D4
  Northumb 178 B2
Outertown 282 F3
Outgate 154 B2
Outhgill 155 A6
Outlane 138 B3
Out Newton 143 A5
Out Rawcliffe 144 C4
Outwell 101 A7
Outwick 31 D5
Outwood
  Sur 35 B6
  W Yorks 139 A6
Outwoods 112 D1
Ovenden 138 A3
Ovenscloss 196 C3
Over
  Cambs 101 D5
  Ches W 127 C6
  S Glos 43 A4
Overbister 282 C7
Overbury 80 D2
Overcombe 15 C6
Over Compton 29 D5
Overgreen 130 B3
Over Green 97 B4
Over Haddon 130 C2
Over Hulton 137 C5
Over Kellet 154 D4
Over Kiddington . . . 65 A5
Over Knutsford 128 B2
Overleigh 29 B4
Overley Green 80 B3
Over Monnow 61 B7
Over Norton 64 A4
Over Peover 128 B2
Overpool 126 B3
Overscaig Hotel . . . 271 B7
Overseal 113 D6
Over Silton 158 B3
Oversland 52 D2
Overstone 83 A5
Over Stowey 28 B1
Overstrand 120 A4
Over Stratton 28 D4
Over Tabley 128 A2
Overthorpe 82 C1
Overton
  Aberdeen 245 A5
  Ches W 127 B5
  Dumfries 174 B2
  Hants 32 A4
  Lancs 144 B4
  N Yorks 149 B4
  Shrops 94 D3
  Swansea 57 D4
  W Yorks 139 B5
Overton =Owrtyn . . 110 A2
Overton Bridge 110 A2
Overtown 194 A3
Over Wallop 32 B1
Over Whitacre 97 B5
Over Worton 65 A5
Oving
  Bucks 66 A2
  W Sus 20 B2
Ovingdean 21 B6
Ovingham 178 C2
Ovington
  Durham 166 D4
  Essex 86 C3
  Hants 33 B4
  Norf 103 A5
  Northumb 178 C2
Ower 32 D2
Owermoigne 16 C1
Owlbury 93 B7
Owler Bar 130 B2

Owlerton 130 A3
Owl's Green 88 A3
Owlswick 66 C2
Owmby 142 C2
Owmby-by-Spital . . 133 C5
Owrtyn =Overton . . 110 A2
Owslebury 32 C4
Owston
  Leics 99 A4
  S Yorks 140 B3
Owston Ferry 141 C6
Owstwick 151 D5
Owthorne 143 A5
Owthorpe 115 B4
Oxborough 102 A3
Oxcombe 134 B3
Oxenholme 154 C4
Oxenhope 147 D4
Oxen Park 154 C2
Oxenton 80 D2
Oxenwood 45 D7
Oxford 65 C6
Oxhey 67 D6
Oxhill 81 C6
Oxley 96 A2
Oxley Green 70 B3
Oxley's Green 37 D4
Oxnam 187 B2
Oxshott 48 C4
Oxspring 139 C5
Oxted 36 A1
Oxton
  Borders 196 A3
  Notts 131 D6
Oxwich 57 D4
Oxwick 119 C6
Oykel Bridge 271 D6
Oyne 256 D1

P

Pabail Iarach 288 D6
Pabail Uarach 288 D6
Pace Gate 147 B5
Packington 114 D1
Padanaram 232 C2
Padbury 83 D4
Paddington 49 A5
Paddlesworth 38 B3
Paddockhaugh 266 D3
Paddockhole 185 D5
Paddock Wood 37 B4
Padfield 138 D3
Padiham 146 D1
Padog 124 D3
Padside 147 B5
Padstow 9 D5
Padworth 47 C4
Page Bank 167 B5
Pagham 20 C1
Paglesham
  Churchend 70 D3
Paglesham Eastend . 70 D3
Paibeil 287 H2
Paible 287 E5
Paignton 8 A2
Pailton 98 C1
Painscastle 77 C5
Painshawfield 178 C2
Painsthorpe 149 B7
Painswick 63 C4
Pairc Shiaboist 288 C3
Paisley 205 B4
Pakefield 105 B6
Pakenham 87 A5
Pale 109 B4
Palestine 31 A6
Paley Street 47 B6
Palfrey 96 B3
Palgowan 181 C5
Palgrave 104 D2
Pallion 179 D5
Palmarsh 38 B3
Palnackie 173 C6
Palnure 171 A6
Palterton 131 C4
Pamber End 47 D4
Pamber Green 47 D4
Pamber Heath 47 C4
Pamphill 16 A3
Pampisford 85 C6
Pan 283 H4
Panbride 221 A5
Pancrasweek 10 A3
Pandy
  Gwyn 90 B4
  Mon 61 A4
  Powys 91 B7
  Wrex 109 B6

Pandy Tudur 124 C3
Panfield 70 A1
Pangbourne 47 B4
Pannal 148 B2
Panshanger 68 B2
Pant 110 C1
Pant-glas
Carms 58 C2
Gwyn 107 B4
Pant-glâs 91 C5
Pant-glas 110 B1
Pantgwyn
Carms 58 C2
Ceredig 73 B5
Pant-lasau 57 C6
Pant Mawr 91 D6
Panton 134 B1
Pantperthog 91 B5
Pant-teg 58 C1
Pant-y-Caws 73 D4
Pant-y-dwr 92 D3
Pant-y-ffridd 93 A5
Pantyffynnon 57 A6
Pantymwyn 126 C1
Pant-yr-awel 40 C4
Pant-y-Wacco 125 B6
Panxworth 121 D5
Papcastle 163 A4
Papigoe 281 C5
Papil 285 K5
Papley 283 H5
Papple 210 C2
Papplewick 131 D5
Papworth Everard 85 A4
Papworth St Agnes 85 A4
Par 5 B5
Parbold 136 B3
Parbrook
Som 29 B5
W Sus 34 D3
Parc 108 B3
Parcllyn 73 A5
Parc-Seymour 61 D6
Parc-y-rhôs 75 D4
Pardshaw 162 B3
Parham 88 A4
Park 183 C7
Park Corner
Oxon 47 A4
Windsor 47 A6
Parkend 62 C2
Park End
Mbro 168 D3
Northumb 177 B6
Parkeston 88 D3
Parkgate
Ches W 126 B2
Dumfries 184 D3
Kent 37 C6
Sur 35 B5
Park Gate 18 A4
Parkham 25 C4
Parkham Ash 25 C4
Park Hill
Notts 132 D1
N Yorks 148 A2
Parkhill House 245 A5
Parkhouse 61 C6
Parkhouse Green 131 C4
Parkhurst 18 B3
Parkmill 57 D5
Parkneuk 233 A5
Parkstone 17 B4
Park Street 35 C4
Parley Cross 17 B4
Parracombe 26 A1
Parrog 72 C3
Parsley Hay 129 C6
Parsonage Green 69 C7
Parsonby 163 A4
Parson Cross 139 D6
Parson Drove 101 A5
Parson's Heath 71 A4
Partick 205 B5
Partington 137 D6
Partney 135 C4
Parton
Cumb 162 B2
Dumfries 173 A4
Glos 63 A4
Partridge Green 21 A4
Parwich 130 D1
Passenham 83 D4
Paston 121 B5
Patchacott 11 B5
Patcham 21 B6
Patching 20 B3
Patchole 25 A7
Patchway 43 A4
Pateley Bridge 147 A5
Paternoster Heath 70 B3
Pathe 28 B3
Pathhead
Aberds 233 B5
E Ayrs 182 A4
Fife 209 A5
Midloth 209 D6
Path of Condie 219 C5
Pathstruie 219 C5
Patna 182 A2
Patney 45 D4
Patrick 152 C2
Patrick Brompton 157 B6
Patrington 143 A5
Patrixbourne 52 D3
Patterdale 164 D1
Pattingham 95 B6
Pattishall 82 B3
Pattiswick Green 70 A2
Patton Bridge 155 B4
Paul 2 C2
Paulerspury 83 C4
Paull 142 A3
Paulton 43 D5
Pavenham 84 B1
Pawlett 28 A3
Pawston 198 C2
Paxford 81 D4
Paxton 198 A3
Payhembury 13 A5
Paythorne 146 B2
Peacehaven 22 B2
Peak Dale 129 B5
Peak Forest 129 B6
Peakirk 100 A3
Pearsie 232 C1
Peasedown St John 43 D6
Peasemore 46 B2
Peasenhall 89 A4
Pease Pottage 35 C5
Peaslake 34 B3
Peasley Cross 136 D4
Peasmarsh 37 D6
Peaston 210 D1
Peastonbank 210 D1
Peathill 269 C4
Peat Inn 221 D4
Peatling Magna 98 B2
Peatling Parva 98 C2
Peaton 94 C3
Peats Corner 88 A2
Pebmarsh 87 D4
Pebworth 80 C4
Pecket Well 138 A2
Peckforton 127 D5
Peckham 49 B6
Peckleton 98 A1
Pedlinge 38 B3
Pedmore 96 C2
Pedwell 28 B4
Peebles 196 B1
Peel 152 C2
Peel Common 19 A4
Peel Park 205 C6
Peening Quarter 37 D6
Pegsdon 84 D3
Pegswood 179 A4
Pegwell 53 C5
Peinchorran 247 A4
Peinlich 259 C4
Pelaw 179 C4
Pelcomb Bridge 55 C5
Pelcomb Cross 55 C5
Peldon 70 B3
Pellon 138 A3
Pelsall 96 A3
Pelton 179 D4
Pelutho 174 D4
Pelynt 5 B7
Pemberton 137 C4
Pembrey 57 B4
Pembridge 78 B1
Pembroke = *Penfro* 55 D5
Pembroke Dock
= *Doc Penfro* 55 D5
Pembury 36 B4
Penallt 61 B7
Penally 55 E7
Penalt 62 A1
Penare 5 C4
Penarlâg
= *Hawarden* 126 C3
Penarth 41 D6
Pen-bont
Rhydybeddau 91 D4
Penbryn 73 A5
Pencader 58 B1
Pencaenewydd 107 B4
Pencaitland 210 D1
Pencarnisiog 122 C3
Pencarreg 75 D4
Pencelli 60 A2
Pen-clawdd 57 C5
Pencoed 41 C4
Pencombe 78 B3
Pencoyd 61 A7
Pencraig
Hereford 62 A1
Powys 109 C5
Pendeen 2 B1
Penderyn 59 E6
Pendine 56 B2
Pendlebury 137 C6
Pendleton 146 D1
Pendock 79 D5
Pendoggett 9 D6
Pendomer 29 D5
Pendoylan 41 D5
Pendre 40 C4
Penegoes 91 B5
Pen-ffordd 55 B6
Penfro = *Pembroke* 55 D5
Pengam 41 B6
Penge 49 B6
Pengenffordd 77 D5
Pengorffwysfa 123 A4
Pengover Green 6 A1
Pen-groes-oped 61 C5
Penhale
Corn 3 D4
Corn 4 B4
Penhalvaen 4 D2
Penhill 45 A5
Penhow 61 D6
Penhurst 23 A4
Peniarth 90 B4
Penicuik 209 D5
Peniel
Carms 58 C1
Denb 125 C5
Penifiler 259 D4
Peninver 190 C3
Penisarwaun 123 D5
Penistone 139 C5
Penjerrick 4 D2
Penketh 127 A5
Penkill 181 B4
Penkridge 112 D3
Penley 110 B3
Penllergaer 57 C6
Penllyn 41 D4
Pen-llyn 122 B3
Pen-lon 123 D4
Penmachno 124 D2
Penmaen 57 D5
Penmaenan 124 B2
Penmaenmawr 124 B2
Penmaenpool 91 A4
Penmark 41 E5
Penmarth 4 D2
Penmon 123 B6
Penmore Mill 224 A3
Penmorfa
Ceredig 73 A6
Gwyn 107 B5
Penmynydd 123 C5
Penn
Bucks 67 D4
W Mid 96 B1
Pennal 91 B5
Pennan 268 C3
Pennant
Ceredig 75 B4
Denb 109 B5
Denb 125 D5
Powys 91 C6
Pennant
Melangell 109 C5
Pennar 55 D5
Pennard 57 D5
Pennerley 94 B1
Pennington
Cumb 153 C3
Gtr Man 137 D5
Hants 18 B2
Penn Street 67 D4
Penny Bridge 154 C2
Pennycross 225 D4
Pennygate 121 C5
Pennygown 225 B4
Pennymoor 26 D3
Pennywell 179 D5
Penparc
Ceredig 73 B5
Pembs 55 A4
Penparcau 90 D3
Penperlleni 61 C5
Penpillick 5 B5
Penpol 4 D3
Penpoll 5 B6
Penpont
Dumfries 183 C6
Powys 59 C6
Penrherber 73 C5
Penrhiwceiber 41 B5
Penrhiw goch 57 A5
Penrhiw-llan 73 B6
Penrhiw-pâl 73 B6
Penrhos 106 C3
Penrhôs 61 B6
Penrhos 59 D4
Penrhosfeilw 122 B2
Penrhyn Bay 124 A3
Penrhyn-coch 90 D4
Penrhyndeudraeth 107 C6
Penrhynside 124 A3
Penrice 57 D4
Penrith 164 B3
Penrose 9 D4
Penruddock 164 C2
Penryn 4 D2
Pensarn
Carms 57 A4
Conwy 125 B4
Pen-sarn
Gwyn 107 B4
Gwyn 107 D5
Pensax 79 A5
Pensby 126 A2
Penselwood 30 B1
Pensford 43 C5
Penshaw 179 D5
Penshurst 36 B3
Pensilva 6 A1
Penston 210 C1
Pentewan 5 C5
Pentir 123 D5
Pentire 4 A2
Pentlow 87 C4
Pentney 119 D4
Penton Mewsey 32 A2
Pentraeth 123 C5
Pentre
Carms 57 A5
Powys 93 B6
Powys 93 C4
Rhondda 41 B4
Shrops 110 D2
Wrex 109 B6
Wrex 110 A1
Pentrebach
M Tydf 41 A5
Swansea 57 B6
Pentre-bâch 75 D4
Pentre-bach 59 B6
Pentrebeirdd 109 D6
Pentre Berw 123 C4
Pentre-bont 124 D2
Pentrecagal 73 B6
Pentre-celyn
Denb 125 D6
Powys 91 B6
Pentre-chwyth 57 C6
Pentre-cwrt 73 C6
Pentre Dolau-
Honddu 76 C3
Pentredwr 109 A6
Pentre-dwr 40 B1
Pentrefelin
Carms 58 C2
Ceredig 75 D5
Conwy 124 B3
Gwyn 107 C5
Pentrefoelas 124 D3
Pentre-galar 73 C4
Pentregat 73 A6
Pentre-Gwenlais 57 A6
Pentre Gwynfryn 107 D5
Pentre Halkyn 126 B2
Pentreheyling 93 B6
Pentre-Isaf 124 C3
Pentre Llanrhaeadr 125 C5
Pentre-llwyn-ll yd 76 B3
Pentre-llyn 75 A5
Pentre-llyn
cymmer 125 D4
Pentre Meyrick 41 D4
Pentre-poeth 42 A1
Pentre'r Felin 124 C3
Pentre'r-felin 59 B6
Pentre-rhew 75 C5
Pentre-tafarn-y-
fedw 124 C3
Pentre-ty-gwyn 59 B5
Pentrich 130 D3
Pentridge 31 D4
Pen-twyn 61 C7
Pentyrch 41 C6
Penuchadre 40 D3
Penuwch 75 B4
Penwithick 5 B5
Penwyllt 59 D5
Penybanc 57 A6
Pen-y-banc 58 C3
Penybont 77 A5
Pen-y-bont
Carms 73 D6
Gwyn 91 B5
Gwyn 107 D6
Powys 109 C7
Pen-y-bont ar Ogwr
= *Bridgend*
Bridgend 40 D4
Bridgend 40 D4
Penybontfawr 109 C5
Pen-y-bryn
Gwyn 91 A4
Pembs 73 B4
Penycae 110 A1
Pen-y-cae 59 D5
Pen-y-cae-mawr 61 D6
Pen-y-cefn 125 B6
Pen-y-clawdd 61 C6
Pen-y-coedcae 41 C5
Penycwm 54 B4
Pen-y-fai 40 C3
Penyffordd 126 C3
Penyffridd 107 A5
Pen-y-garn
Carms 58 B2
Ceredig 90 D4
Penygarnedd 109 C6
Pen-y-garnedd 123 C5
Pen-y-gop 108 A4
Penygraig 41 B4
Pen-y-graig 106 C1
Penygroes
Gwyn 107 A4
Pembs 73 C4
Pen-y-groes 57 A5
Pen-y-groeslon 106 C2
Pen-y-Gwryd
Hotel 107 A6
Penyrheol 41 C6
Pen-yr-heol 61 B6
Pen-yr-Heolgerrig 60 C2
Penysarn 123 A4
Pen-y-stryt 126 D1
Penywaun 41 A4
Penzance 2 B2
Peopleton 80 B2
Peover Heath 128 B2
Peper Harow 34 B2
Perceton 204 D3
Percie 244 C2
Percyhorner 269 C4
Periton 27 A4
Perivale 49 A4
Perkinsville 179 D4
Perlethorpe 131 B6
Perranarworthal 4 D2
Perranporth 4 B2
Perranuthnoe 2 C3
Perranzabuloe 4 B2
Perry Barr 96 B3
Perryfoot 129 A6
Perry Green
Herts 68 B4
Wilts 44 A3
Perry Street 50 B3
Pershall 112 B2
Pershore 80 C2
Pert 233 B4
Pertenhall 84 A2
Perth 219 B6
Perthy 110 B2
Perton 95 B6
Pertwood 30 B2
Peterborough 100 B3
Peterburn 261 B4
Peterchurch 78 D1
Peterculter 245 B5
Peterhead 257 B6
Peterlee 168 A2
Petersfield 33 C6
Peter's Green 67 B6
Peters Marland 25 D5
Peterstone
Wentlooge 42 A1
Peterston super-Ely 41 D5
Peterstow 62 A1
Peter Tavy 11 D6
Petertown 283 G4
Petham 52 D3
Petrockstow 11 A6
Pett 23 A6
Pettaugh 88 B2
Petteridge 37 B4
Pettinain 195 B4
Pettistree 88 B3
Petton
Devon 27 C5
Shrops 110 C3
Petts Wood 50 C1
Petty 256 C2
Pettycur 209 B5
Pettymuick 257 D4
Petworth 34 D2
Pevensey 22 B4
Pevensey Bay 23 B4
Pewsey 45 C5
Philham 24 C3
Philiphaugh 186 A3
Phillack 2 B3
Philleigh 4 D3
Philpstoun 208 C3
Phocle Green 62 A2
Phoenix Green 47 D5
Pica 162 B3
Piccotts End 67 C5
Pickering 159 C6
Picket Piece 32 A2
Picket Post 17 A5
Pickhill 158 C2
Picklescott 94 B2
Pickletillem 220 B4
Pickmere 128 B1
Pickney 28 C1
Pickstock 111 C6
Pickwell
Devon 25 A5
Leics 115 D5
Pickworth
Lincs 116 B3
Rutland 116 D2
Picton
Ches W 127 B4
Flint 125 A6
N Yorks 158 A3
Piddinghoe 22 B2
Piddington
Northants 83 B5
Oxon 66 B1
Piddlehinton 15 B7
Piddletrenthide 15 B7
Pidley 101 D5
Piercebridge 167 D5
Pierowall 282 C5
Pigdon 178 A3
Pikehall 130 D1
Pilgrims Hatch 69 D5
Pilham 141 D6
Pill 43 B4
Pillaton 6 A2
Pillerton Hersey 81 C6
Pillerton Priors 81 C5
Pilleth 77 A6
Pilley
Hants 18 B2
S Yorks 139 C6
Pilling 144 C4
Pilling Lane 144 C3
Pillowell 62 C2
Pillwell 30 D1
Pilning 43 A4
Pilsbury 129 C6
Pilsdon 14 B4
Pilsgate 100 A2
Pilsley
Derbys 130 B2
Derbys 131 C4
Pilton
Devon 25 B6
Northants 100 C2
Rutland 99 A6
Som 29 A5
Pilton Green 57 D4
Pimperne 16 A3
Pinchbeck 117 C5
Pinchbeck Bars 117 C4
Pinchbeck West 117 C5
Pincheon Green 141 B4
Pinehurst 45 A5
Pinfold 136 B2
Pinged 57 B4
Pinhoe 13 B4
Pinkneys Green 47 A6
Pinley 97 D6
Pin Mill 88 D3
Pinminnoch 180 B3
Pinmore 181 B4
Pinmore Mains 181 B4
Pinner 48 A4
Pinvin 80 C2
Pinwherry 180 C3
Pinxton 131 D4
Pipe and Lyde 78 C3
Pipe Gate 111 A6

Piperhill 253 A4
Piper's Pool 10 C3
Pipewell 99 C5
Pippacott 25 B6
Pipton 77 D5
Pirbright 34 A2
Pirnmill 202 D3
Pirton
Herts 84 D3
Worcs 80 C1
Pisgah
Ceredig 75 A5
Stirling 218 D2
Pishill 47 A5
Pistyll 106 B3
Pitagowan 230 B2
Pitblae 269 C4
Pitcairngreen 219 B5
Pitcalnie 265 C4
Pitcaple 256 D2
Pitchcombe 63 C4
Pitchcott 66 A2
Pitchford 94 A3
Pitch Green 66 C2
Pitch Place 34 A2
Pitcombe 29 B6
Pitcorthie 221 D5
Pitcox 210 C3
Pitcur 220 A2
Pitfichie 244 A3
Pitforthie 233 A6
Pitgrudy 264 A3
Pitkennedy 232 C3
Pitkevy 220 D2
Pitkierie 221 D5
Pitlessie 220 D3
Pitlochry 230 C3
Pitmachie 256 D1
Pitmain 241 B5
Pitmedden 256 D3
Pitminster 28 D2
Pitmuies 232 D3
Pitmunie 244 A3
Pitney 29 C4
Pitscottie 220 C4
Pitsea 51 A4
Pitsford 83 A4
Pitsmoor 130 A3
Pitstone 67 B4
Pitstone Green 67 B4
Pittendreich 266 C2
Pittentrail 273 D5
Pittenweem 221 D5
Pittington 167 A6
Pittodrie 256 D1
Pitton 31 B6
Pittswood 36 B4
Pittulie 269 C4
Pityme 9 D5
Pity Me 167 A5
Pityoulish 242 A2
Pixey Green 104 D3
Pixham 35 A4
Pixley 79 D4
Place Newton 160 D2
Plaidy 268 D2
Plains 207 D5
Plaish 94 B3
Plaistow 34 C3
Plaitford 32 D1
Plank Lane 137 D5
Plas-canol 90 A3
Plas Gogerddan 90 D4
Plas Llwyngwern 91 B5
Plas Nantyr 109 B6
Plastow Green 46 C3
Plas-yn-Cefn 125 B5
Platt 36 A4
Platt Bridge 137 C5
Platts Common 139 C6
Plawsworth 167 A5
Plaxtol 36 A4
Playden 37 D7
Playford 88 C3
Play Hatch 47 B5
Playing Place 4 C3
Playley Green 79 D5
Plealey 94 A2
Plean 207 B6
Pleasington 137 A5
Pleasley 131 C5
Pleckgate 145 D6
Plenmeller 177 C5
Pleshey 69 B6
Plockton 249 C5
Plocrapol 288 H2
Ploughfield 78 C1
Plowden 94 C1
Ploxgreen 94 A1
Pluckley 38 A1
Pluckley Thorne 37 B7
Plumbland 163 A4
Plumley 128 B2
Plumpton
Cumb 164 B2
E Sus 21 A6
Plumpton Green 21 A6
Plumpton Head 164 B3
Plumstead
London 50 B1
Norf 120 B3
Plumtree 115 B4
Plungar 115 B5
Plush 15 A7
Plwmp 73 A6
Plymouth 6 B3
Plympton 7 B4
Plymstock 7 B4
Plymtree 13 A5
Pockley 159 C5
Pocklington 149 C7
Pode Hole 117 C5
Podimore 29 C5
Podington 83 A6
Podmore 112 B1
Point Clear 71 B4
Pointon 116 B4
Pokesdown 17 B5
Pol a Charra 286 E3
Polbae 181 D4
Polbain 270 C2
Polbathic 6 B2
Polbeth 208 D3
Polchar 242 B1
Polebrook 100 C2
Pole Elm 79 C6
Polegate 22 B3
Poles 264 A3
Polesworth 97 A5
Polgigga 2 C1
Polglass 270 D3
Polgooth 5 B4
Poling 20 B3
Polkerris 5 B5
Polla 277 C4
Pollington 140 B4
Polloch 236 C1
Pollok 205 B5
Pollokshields 205 B5
Polmassick 5 C4
Polmont 208 C2
Polnessan 182 A2
Polnish 235 B6
Polperro 5 B7
Polruan 5 B6
Polsham 29 A5
Polstead 87 D5
Poltalloch 213 C6
Poltimore 13 B4
Polton 209 D5
Polwarth 197 A6
Polyphant 10 C3
Polzeath 9 D5
Pondersbridge 101 B4
Ponders End 68 D3
Pondtail 34 A1
Ponsanooth 4 D2
Ponsworthy 12 D2
Pont Aber 59 C4
Pont Aber-Geirw 108 C2
Pontamman 57 A6
Pontantwn 57 A4
Pontardawe 40 A2
Pontarddulais 57 B5
Pont-ar-gothi 58 C2
Pont ar Hydfer 59 C5
Pont-ar-llechau 59 C4
Pontarsais 58 C1
Pontblyddyn 126 C2
Pontbren Araeth 58 C3
Pontbren Llwyd 59 E6
Pont Cwm Pydew 109 B5
Pont Cyfyng 124 D2
Pont Cysyllte 110 A1
Pont Dolydd Prysor 108 B2
Pontefract 140 A2
Ponteland 178 B3
Ponterwyd 91 D5
Pontesbury 94 A1
Pontfadog 110 B1
Pontfaen 55 A6
Pont-faen 76 D3
Pont Fronwydd 108 C3
Pont-gareg 72 B4
Pontgarreg 73 A6
Pont-Henri 57 B4
Ponthir 61 D5
Ponthirwaun 73 B5
Pontllanfraith 41 B6
Pontlliw 57 B6
Pont-Llogel 109 D5
Pontllyfni 107 A4
Pontlottyn 60 C3
Pontneddfechan 59 E6
Pontnewydd 61 D4
Pont Pen-y-benglog 123 D6
Pontrhydfendigaid 75 B6
Pont Rhyd-goch 124 C1
Pont-Rhyd-sarn 108 C3
Pont Rhyd-y-cyff 40 C3
Pontrhydyfen 40 B2
Pont-rhyd-y-groes 75 A6
Pontrilas 61 A5
Pontrobert 109 D6
Pont-rug 123 D5
Pont Senni
=Sennybridge 59 C6
Ponts Green 23 A4
Pontshill 62 A2
Pont-siân 74 D3
Pontsticill 60 B2
Pontwgan 124 B2
Pontyates 57 B4
Pontyberem 57 A5
Pontyclun 41 C5
Pontycymer 40 B4
Pontyglasier 72 C4
Pont-y-gwaith 41 B5
Pont-y-pant 124 D2
Pont y Pennant 108 C4
Pontypool
=Pont-Y-Pŵl 61 C4
Pontypridd 41 C5
Pont-Y-Pŵl
=Pontypool 61 C4
Pont yr Afon-Gam 108 A2
Pont-yr-hafod 55 B5
Pontywaun 41 B7
Pooksgreen 32 D2
Pool
Corn 3 A4
W Yorks 147 C6
Poole 17 B4
Poole Keynes 63 D5
Poolend 129 D4
Poolewe 261 B5
Pooley Bridge 164 C2
Poolfold 128 D3
Poolhill 62 A3
Pool o' Muckhart 219 D5
Pool Quay 110 D1
Poolsbrook 131 B4
Pootings 36 B2
Pope Hill 55 C5
Popeswood 47 C6
Popham 33 A4
Poplar 49 A6
Popley 47 D4
Porchester 114 A3
Porchfield 18 B3
Porin 251 A5
Poringland 104 A3
Porkellis 3 B4
Porlock 26 A3
Porlock Weir 26 A3
Portachoillan 202 C2
Port Ann 214 D2
Port Appin 226 B4
Port Arthur 285 K5
Port Askaig 201 B4
Portavadie 203 B4
Port Bannatyne 203 B5
Portbury 43 B4
Port Carlisle 175 B5
Port Charlotte 200 C2
Portchester 19 A5
Portclair 240 A2
Port Clarence 168 C2
Port Driseach 203 A4
Port Ellen 200 D3
Port Elphinstone 256 E2
Portencalzie 180 D2
Portencross 204 D1
Port Erin 152 E1
Port Erroll 257 C5
Portesham 15 C6
Portessie 267 C5
Port e Vullen 152 B4
Port-Eynon 57 D4
Portfield Gate 55 C5
Portgate 11 C5
Port Gaverne 9 C6
Port Glasgow 204 A3
Portgordon 267 C4
Portgower 274 C4
Porth
Corn 4 A3
Porth *continued*
Rhondda 41 B5
Porthaethwy
=Menai Bridge 123 C5
Porthallow
Corn 3 C5
Corn 6 B1
Porthcawl 40 D3
Porthcothan 9 D4
Porthcurno 2 C1
Port Henderson 261 C4
Porthgain 54 A4
Porthill 110 D3
Porthkerry 41 E5
Porthleven 3 C4
Porthllechog 123 A4
Porthmadog 107 C5
Porthmeor 2 B2
Porth Navas 3 C5
Portholland 5 C4
Porthoustock 3 C6
Porthpean 5 B5
Porthtowan 3 A4
Porth Tywyn
=Burry Port 57 B4
Porthyrhyd
Carms 57 A5
Carms 59 B4
Porth-y-waen 110 C1
Portincaple 215 C5
Portington 149 D6
Portinnisherrich 214 A2
Portinscale 163 B5
Port Isaac 9 C5
Portishead 42 B3
Portkil 215 D5
Portknockie 267 C5
Port Lamont 203 A5
Portlethen 245 C6
Portling 173 C6
Port Lion 55 D5
Portloe 4 D4
Port Logan 170 C2
Portmahomack 265 B5
Portmeirion 107 C5
Portmellon 5 C5
Port Mholair 288 D6
Port Mor 234 C3
Portmore 18 B2
Port Mulgrave 169 D5
Portnacroish 226 B4
Portnahaven 200 C1
Portnalong 246 A2
Portnaluchaig 235 B5
Portnancon 277 B5
Port Nan Giùran 288 D6
Port nan Long 287 G3
Portnellan 216 B4
Port Nis 288 A6
Portobello 209 C6
Port of Menteith 217 D5
Porton 31 B5
Portpatrick 170 B2
Port Quin 9 C5
Port Ramsay 226 B3
Portreath 3 A4
Portree 259 D4
Port St Mary 152 E2
Portscatho 4 D3
Portsea 19 A5
Portskerra 279 B4
Portskewett 43 A4
Portslade 21 B5
Portslade-by-Sea 21 B5
Portsmouth
Ptsmth 19 A5
W Yorks 138 A2
Portsonachan 227 D5
Portsoy 267 C6
Port Sunlight 126 A3
Portswood 32 D3
Port Talbot 40 B2
Porttanachy 267 C4
Port Tennant 57 C6
Portuairk 234 D3
Portway
Hereford 78 D2
Worcs 96 D3
Port Wemyss 200 C1
Port William 171 C5
Portwrinkle 6 B2
Poslingford 86 C3
Postbridge 12 D1
Postcombe 66 D2
Postling 38 B3
Postwick 104 A3
Potholm 185 D6
Potsgrove 67 A4
Potten End 67 C5
Potter Brompton 160 D3
Potterhanworth 133 C5
Potterhanworth Booths 133 C5
Potter Heigham 121 D6
Potterne 44 D3
Potterne Wick 44 D4
Potternewton 148 D2
Potters Bar 68 C2
Potter's Cross 95 C6
Potterspury 83 C4
Potter Street 69 C4
Potterton
Aberds 245 A6
W Yorks 148 D3
Potto 158 A3
Potton 84 C4
Pott Row 119 C4
Pott Shrigley 129 B4
Poughill
Corn 10 A3
Devon 12 A3
Poulshot 44 D3
Poulton
Glos 64 C2
Mers 136 D2
Poulton-le-Fylde 144 D3
Pound Bank 95 D5
Poundfield 36 C3
Pound Green
E Sus 36 D3
IoW 18 C2
Worcs 95 D5
Pound Hill 35 C5
Poundland 180 C3
Poundon 66 A1
Poundsgate 12 D2
Poundstock 10 B3
Powburn 188 B3
Powderham 13 C4
Powerstock 15 B5
Powfoot 174 B4
Powick 79 B6
Powmill 208 A3
Poxwell 16 C1
Poyle 48 B3
Poynings 21 A5
Poyntington 29 D6
Poynton 129 A4
Poynton Green 111 D4
Poystreet Green 87 B5
Praa Sands 2 C3
Pratt's Bottom 50 C1
Praze 2 B3
Praze-an-Beeble 3 B4
Predannack Wollas 3 D4
Prees 111 B4
Preesall 144 C3
Prees Green 111 B4
Preesgweene 110 B1
Prees Heath 111 B4
Prees Higher Heath 111 B4
Prees Lower Heath 111 B4
Prenderguest 198 A3
Prendwick 188 B3
Prengwyn 73 B7
Prenteg 107 B5
Prenton 126 A3
Prescot 136 D3
Prescott 110 C3
Pressen 198 C2
Prestatyn 125 A5
Prestbury
Ches E 129 B4
Glos 63 A5
Presteigne
=Llanandras 77 A7
Presthope 94 B3
Prestleigh 29 A6
Preston
Borders 198 A1
Brighton 21 B6
Devon 12 D3
Dorset 15 C7
E Loth 210 C2
E Yorks 151 D4
Glos 63 C6
Glos 79 D4
Herts 68 A1
Kent 52 C2
Kent 53 C4
Lancs 136 A4
Northumb 189 A4
Rutland 99 A5
Shrops 111 D4
Wilts 44 B4
Wilts 45 B6
Preston Bagot 81 A4
Preston Bissett 66 A1
Preston Bowyer 27 C6
Preston Brockhurst 111 C4
Preston Brook 127 A5
Preston Candover 33 A5
Preston Capes 82 B2
Preston Crowmarsh 65 D7
Preston Gubbals 110 D3
Prestonmill 174 C2
Preston on Stour 81 C5
Preston on the Hill 127 A5
Preston on Wye 78 C1
Prestonpans 209 C6
Preston Plucknett 29 D5
Preston St Mary 87 B5
Preston-under-Scar 157 B4
Preston upon the Weald Moors 111 D5
Preston Wynne 78 C3
Prestwich 137 C7
Prestwick
Northumb 178 B3
S Ayrs 192 C3
Prestwood 66 C3
Price Town 40 B4
Prickwillow 102 C1
Priddy 43 D4
Priesthaugh 186 C3
Priest Hutton 154 D4
Priest Weston 93 B6
Primethorpe 98 B2
Primrose Green 120 D2
Primrosehill 67 C5
Primrose Valley 161 D5
Princes Gate 56 A1
Princes Risborough 66 C3
Princethorpe 97 D7
Princetown
Caerph 60 B3
Devon 11 D6
Prion 125 C5
Prior Muir 221 C5
Prior Park 198 A3
Priors Frome 78 D3
Priors Hardwick 82 B1
Priorslee 111 D6
Priors Marston 82 B1
Priory Wood 77 C6
Priston 43 C5
Pristow Green 104 C2
Prittlewell 51 A5
Privett 33 C5
Prixford 25 B6
Probus 4 C3
Proncy 264 A3
Prospect 174 D4
Prudhoe 178 C2
Ptarmigan Lodge 215 B6
Pubil 228 D3
Puckeridge 68 A3
Puckington 28 D3
Pucklechurch 43 B5
Pucknall 32 C2
Puckrup 80 D1
Puddinglake 128 C2
Puddington
Ches W 126 B3
Devon 26 D3
Puddledock 103 B6
Puddletown 16 B1
Pudleston 78 B3
Pudsey 147 D6
Pulborough 20 A3
Puleston 111 C6
Pulford 126 D3
Pulham 15 A7
Pulham Market 104 C2
Pulham St Mary 104 C3
Pulloxhill 84 D2
Pumpherston 208 D3
Pumsaint 58 A3
Puncheston 55 B6
Puncknowle 15 C5
Punnett's Town 36 D4
Purbrook 19 A5
Purewell 17 B5
Purfleet 50 B2
Puriton 28 A3
Purleigh 70 C2
Purley
London 49 C6
W Berks 47 B4
Purlogue 93 D6
Purls Bridge 101 C6
Purse Caundle 29 D6
Purslow 94 C1
Purston Jaglin 140 B2
Purton
Glos 62 C2
Glos 62 C2

Purton *continued*
Wilts 45 A4
Purton Stoke 64 D1
Pury End 83 C4
Pusey 65 D4
Putley 79 D4
Putney 49 B5
Putsborough 25 A5
Puttenham
Herts 66 B3
Sur 34 B2
Puxton 42 C3
Pwll 57 B4
Pwllcrochan 55 D5
Pwll-glas 125 D6
Pwllgloyw 76 D4
Pwllheli 106 C3
Pwllmeyric 61 D7
Pwll-trap 56 A2
Pwll-y-glaw 40 B2
Pyecombe 21 A5
Pye Corner 42 A2
Pye Green 112 D3
Pyewipe 143 B4
Pyle 18 D3
Pyle = *Y Pîl* 40 C3
Pylle 29 B6
Pymoor 101 C6
Pyrford 34 A3
Pyrton 66 D1
Pytchley 99 D5
Pyworthy 10 A4

Q

Quabbs 93 C6
Quadring 117 B5
Quainton 66 B2
Quarley 31 A6
Quarndon 114 A1
Quarrier's Homes 204 B3
Quarrington 116 A3
Quarrington Hill 167 B6
Quarry Bank 96 C2
Quarryford 210 D2
Quarryhill 264 B3
Quarrywood 266 C2
Quarter 194 A2
Quatford 95 B5
Quatt 95 C5
Quebec 167 A4
Quedgeley 63 B4
Queen Adelaide 102 C1
Queenborough 51 B6
Queen Camel 29 C5
Queen Charlton 43 C5
Queen Dart 26 D3
Queenhill 79 D6
Queen Oak 30 B1
Queensbury 147 D5
Queensferry
Edin 208 C4
Flint 126 C3
Queensferry Crossing 208 C4
Queen's Head 110 C2
Queen's Park
Bedford 84 C2
Northants 83 A4
Queenstown 144 D3
Queen Street
Kent 37 B4
Wilts 44 A4
Queenzieburn 207 C4
Quemerford 44 C4
Quendale 285 M5
Quendon 85 D7
Queniborough 115 D4
Quenington 64 C2
Quernmore 145 B5
Quethiock 6 A2
Quholm 282 F3
Quicks Green 46 B3
Quidenham 103 C6
Quidhampton
Hants 46 D3
Wilts 31 B5
Quilquox 257 C4
Quina Brook 111 B4
Quindry 283 H5
Quinton
Northants 83 B4
W Mid 96 C2
Quintrell Downs 4 A3
Quixhill 113 A5
Quoditch 11 B5
Quoig 218 B3
Quorndon 114 D3
Quothquan 195 C4
Quoyloo 282 E3
Quoyness 283 G3
Quoys
Shetland 284 B8
Shetland 285 G6

R

Raasay House 248 C2
Rabbit's Cross 37 B5
Raby 126 B3
Rachan Mill 195 C6
Rachub 123 D6
Rackenford 26 D3
Rackham 20 A3
Rackheath 121 D4
Racks 174 A3
Rackwick
Orkney 282 C5
Orkney 283 H3
Radbourne 113 B6
Radcliffe
Gtr Man 137 C6
Northumb 189 C5
Radcliffe on Trent 115 B4
Radclive 82 D3
Radcot 64 D3
Raddery 252 A3
Radernie 221 D4
Radford Semele 81 A6
Radipole 15 C6
Radlett 67 D6
Radley 65 D6
Radmanthwaite 131 C5
Radmoor 111 C5
Radmore Green 127 D5
Radnage 66 D2
Radstock 43 D5
Radstone 82 C2
Radway 81 C6
Radway Green 128 D2
Radwell
Bedford 84 B2
Herts 84 D4
Radwinter 86 D2
Radyr 41 C6
Rafford 253 A6
Ragdale 115 D4
Raglan 61 C6
Ragnall 132 B3
Rahane 215 D5
Rainford 136 C3
Rainford Junction 136 C3
Rainham
London 50 A2
Medway 51 C5
Rainhill 136 D3
Rainhill Stoops 136 D4
Rainow 129 B4
Rainton 158 D2
Rainworth 131 D5
Raisbeck 155 A5
Raise 165 A5
Rait 220 B2
Raithby
Lincs 134 A3
Lincs 134 C3
Rake 33 C7
Rakewood 138 B2
Ram 75 D4
Ramasaig 258 D1
Rame
Corn 4 D2
Corn 6 C3
Rameldry Mill Bank 220 D3
Ram Lane 38 A1
Ramnageo 284 C8
Rampisham 15 A5
Rampside 153 D3
Rampton
Cambs 85 A6
Notts 132 B2
Ramsbottom 137 B6
Ramsbury 45 B6
Ramscraigs 275 B5
Ramsdean 33 C6
Ramsdell 46 D3
Ramsden 65 B4
Ramsden Bellhouse 69 D7
Ramsden Heath 69 D7
Ramsey
Cambs 101 C4
Essex 88 D3
IoM 152 B4
Ramseycleuch 185 A5
Ramsey Forty Foot 101 C5
Ramsey Heights 101 C4
Ramsey Island 70 C3
Ramsey Mereside 101 C4
Ramsey St Mary's 101 C4
Ramsgate 53 C5
Ramsgill 157 D5
Ramshorn 113 A4
Ramsnest Common 34 C2
Ranais 288 E5
Ranby
Lincs 134 B2
Notts 131 A6
Rand 133 B6
Randwick 63 C4
Ranfurly 204 B3
Rangag 280 D3
Rangemore 113 C5
Rangeworthy 43 A5
Rankinston 182 A2
Ranmoor 130 A3
Ranmore Common 35 A4
Rannerdale 163 C4
Rannoch Station 228 C3
Ranochan 238 D2
Ranskill 131 A6
Ranton 112 C2
Ranworth 121 D5
Raploch 207 A5
Rapness 282 C6
Rascal Moor 149 D7
Rascarrel 173 D5
Rashiereive 257 D4
Raskelf 158 D3
Rassau 60 B3
Rastrick 139 A4
Ratagan 238 A3
Ratby 98 A2
Ratcliffe Culey 97 B6
Ratcliffe on Soar 114 C2
Ratcliffe on the Wreake 115 D4
Rathen 269 C5
Rathillet 220 B3
Rathmell 146 B2
Ratho 208 C4
Ratho Station 208 C4
Rathven 267 C5
Ratley 81 C6
Ratlinghope 94 B2
Rattar 281 A4
Ratten Row 144 C4
Rattery 7 A6
Rattlesden 87 B5
Rattray 231 D5
Raughton Head 164 A1
Raunds 100 D1
Ravenfield 140 D2
Ravenglass 153 A1
Raveningham 105 B4
Ravenscar 160 A3
Ravenscraig 204 A2
Ravensdale 152 B3
Ravensden 84 B2
Ravenseat 156 A2
Ravenshead 131 D5
Ravensmoor 127 D6
Ravensthorpe
Northants 98 D3
W Yorks 139 A5
Ravenstone
Leics 114 D2
M Keynes 83 B5
Ravenstonedale 155 A6
Ravenstown 154 D2
Ravenstruther 194 B4
Ravensworth 157 A5
Raw 160 A3
Rawcliffe
E Yorks 141 A4
York 149 B4
Rawcliffe Bridge 141 A4
Rawdon 147 D6
Rawmarsh 140 D2
Rawreth 70 D1
Rawridge 14 A2
Rawtenstall 137 A7
Raxton 256 C3
Raydon 87 D6
Raylees 188 D2
Rayleigh 70 D2
Rayne 70 A1
Rayners Lane 48 A4
Raynes Park 49 C5
Reach 86 A1
Read 146 D1
Reading 47 B5
Reading Street 37 C7
Reagill 165 D4
Rearquhar 264 A3
Rearsby 115 D4
Reaster 281 B4
Reawick 285 J5
Reay 279 B5
Rechullin 249 A5
Reculver 53 C4
Redberth 55 D6
Redbourn 67 B6
Redbourne 142 D1
Redbrook
Mon 62 B1
Wrex 111 A4
Redburn
Highld 253 B5
Highld 264 D1
Northumb 177 C5
Redcar 168 C4
Redcastle
Angus 233 C4
Highld 252 B1
Redcliff Bay 42 B3
Red Dial 175 D5
Redding 208 C2
Reddingmuirhead 208 C2
Reddish 138 D1
Redditch 80 A3
Rede 87 B4
Redenhall 104 C3
Redesdale Camp 187 D7
Redesmouth 177 A6
Redford
Aberds 233 A5
Angus 232 D3
Durham 166 B3
Redfordgreen 185 A6
Redgorton 219 B5
Redgrave 103 D6
Redhill
Aberds 245 B4
Aberds 256 C1
N Som 42 C3
Sur 35 A5
Red Hill 79 B6
Redhouse 202 B3
Redhouses 200 B3
Red Houses 6
Redisham 105 C5
Redland
Bristol 43 B4
Orkney 282 E4
Redlingfield 104 D2
Red Lodge 102 D2
Redlynch
Som 29 B7
Wilts 31 C6
Redmarley D'Abitot 79 D5
Redmarshall 167 C6
Redmile 115 B5
Redmire 156 B4
Redmoor 5 A5
Rednal 110 C2
Redpath 197 C4
Redpoint 261 D4
Red Rail 62 A1
Red Rock 137 C4
Red Roses 56 A2
Red Row 189 D5
Redruth 3 A4
Red Street 128 D3
Redvales 137 C7
Red Wharf Bay 123 B5
Redwick
Newport 42 A3
S Glos 43 A4
Redworth 167 C5
Reed 85 D5
Reedham 105 A5
Reedness 141 A5
Reeds Beck 134 C2
Reepham
Lincs 133 B5
Norf 120 C2
Reeth 156 B4
Regaby 152 B4
Regoul 253 A4
Reiff 270 C2
Reigate 35 A5
Reighton 161 D5
Reighton Gap 161 D5
Reinigeadal 288 G3
Reiss 281 C5
Rejerrah 4 B2
Releath 3 B4
Relubbus 2 B3
Relugas 253 B5
Remenham 47 A5
Remenham Hill 47 A5
Remony 229 D6
Rempstone 114 C3
Rendcomb 63 C6
Rendham 88 A4
Rendlesham 88 B4
Renfrew 205 B5
Renhold 84 B2
Renishaw 131 B4
Rennington 189 B5
Renton 206 C1
Renwick 164 A3
Repps 121 D6
Repton 113 C7
Reraig 249 D5
Rescobie 232 C3
Resipole 235 D6
Resolis 264 D2
Resolven 40 A3
Reston 211 D5
Reswallie 232 C3
Retew 4 B4
Retford 132 A2
Rettendon 70 D1
Rettendon Place 70 D1
Revesby 134 C2
Revesby Bridge 134 C3
Rewe 13 B4
Rew Street 18 B3
Reydon 105 D5
Reydon Smear 105 D5
Reymerston 103 A6
Reynalton 55 D6
Reynoldston 57 C4
Rezare 11 D4
Rhaeadr Gwy = *Rhayader* 76 A3
Rhandirmwyn 59 A4
Rhayader = *Rhaeadr Gwy* 76 A3
Rhyd-y-foel 125 B4
Rhedyn 106 C2
Rhemore 225 A4
Rhencullen 152 B3
Rhes-y-cae 126 B1
Rhewl
Denb 109 A6
Denb 125 C6
Rhian 272 C3
Rhicarn 270 B3
Rhiconich 276 C3
Rhicullen 264 C2
Rhidorroch House 262 A3
Rhifail 278 D3
Rhigos 59 E6
Rhilochan 273 D5
Rhiroy 262 B3
Rhisga = *Risca* 60 D4
Rhiw 106 D2
Rhiwabon = *Ruabon* 110 A2
Rhiwbina 41 C6
Rhiwbryfdir 107 B6
Rhiwderin 42 A1
Rhiwlas
Gwyn 108 B4
Gwyn 123 D5
Powys 109 B6
Rhodes 138 C1
Rhodesia 131 B5
Rhodes Minnis 38 A3
Rhodiad 54 B3
Rhondda 41 B4
Rhonehouse or Kelton Hill 173 C5
Rhoose = *Y Rhws* 41 E5
Rhôs
Carms 73 C6
Neath 40 A2
Rhosaman 59 D4
Rhosbeirio 122 A3
Rhoscefnhir 123 C5
Rhoscolyn 122 C2
Rhoscrowther 55 D5
Rhosesmor 126 C2
Rhos-fawr 106 C3
Rhosgadfan 107 A5
Rhosgoch 123 B4
Rhos-goch 77 C5
Rhos-hill 73 B4
Rhoshirwaun 106 D1
Rhoslan 107 B4
Rhoslefain 90 B3
Rhosllanerchrugog 110 A1
Rhosmaen 58 C3
Rhosmeirch 123 C4
Rhosneigr 122 C3
Rhosnesni 126 D3
Rhos-on-Sea 124 A3
Rhosrobin 126 D3
Rhossili 57 D4
Rhosson 54 B3
Rhostryfan 107 A4
Rhostyllen 110 A2
Rhosybol 123 B4
Rhos-y-brithdir 109 C6
Rhos-y-garth 75 A5
Rhos-y-gwaliau 108 B4
Rhos-y-llan 106 C2
Rhos-y-Madoc 110 A2
Rhos-y-meirch 77 A6
Rhu
Argyll 202 B3
Argyll 215 D5
Rhuallt 125 B5
Rhuddall Heath 127 C5
Rhuddlan
Ceredig 58 A1
Denb 125 B5
Rhue 262 A2
Rhulen 77 B5
Rhunahaorine 202 D2
Rhuthun = *Ruthin* 125 D6
Rhyd
Gwyn 107 B6
Powys 92 A3
Rhydaman = *Ammanford* 57 A6
Rhydargaeau 58 C1
Rhydcymerau 58 B2
Rhydd 79 C6
Rhyd-Ddu 107 A5
Rhydding 40 B2
Rhydfudr 75 B4
Rhydlewis 73 B6
Rhydlios 106 C1
Rhydlydan 124 D3
Rhyd-moel-ddu 93 D4
Rhydness 77 C5
Rhydowen 74 D3
Rhyd-Rosser 75 B4
Rhydspence 77 C6
Rhydtalog 126 D2
Rhyd-uchaf 108 B4
Rhyd-wen 91 A5
Rhydwyn 122 B3
Rhyd-y-clafdy 106 C3
Rhydycroesau 110 B1
Rhydyfelin
Ceredig 75 A4
Rhondda 41 C5
Rhyd-y-fro 59 E4
Rhyd-y-gwin 57 B6
Rhydymain 108 C3
Rhyd-y-meirch 61 C5
Rhyd-y-meudwy 125 D6
Rhydymwyn 126 C2
Rhyd-y-pandy 57 B6
Rhyd-yr-onen 90 B4
Rhyd-y-sarn 107 B6
Rhyl = *Y Rhyl* 125 A5
Rhymney = *Rhymni* 60 C3
Rhymni = *Rhymney* 60 C3
Rhynd
Fife 221 B4
Perth 219 B6
Rhynie
Aberds 255 D5
Highld 265 C4
Ribbesford 95 D5
Ribblehead 155 D6
Ribbleton 145 D5
Ribchester 145 D6
Ribigill 277 C6
Riby 142 C3
Riby Cross Roads 142 C3
Riccall 149 D5
Riccarton 193 B4
Richards Castle 78 A2
Richings Park 48 B3
Richmond
London 49 B4
N Yorks 157 A5
Rickarton 245 D5
Rickinghall 103 D6
Rickleton 179 D4
Rickling 85 D6
Rickmansworth 67 D5
Riddings
Cumb 175 A7
Derbys 131 D4
Riddlecombe 25 D7
Riddlesden 147 C4
Riddrie 205 B6
Ridge
Dorset 16 C3
Hants 32 D2
Wilts 30 B3
Ridgebourne 77 A4
Ridge Green 35 B6
Ridgehill 43 C4
Ridge Lane 97 B5
Ridgeway Cross 79 C5
Ridgewell 86 C3
Ridgewood 22 A2

Ridgmont 84 D1
Riding Mill 178 C2
Ridleywood 127 D4
Ridlington
Norf 121 B5
Rutland 99 A5
Ridsdale 177 A7
Riechip 231 D4
Riemore 230 D4
Rienachait 270 A3
Rievaulx 159 C4
Rift House 168 B2
Rigg 175 B5
Riggend 207 C5
Rigsby 135 B4
Rigside 194 C3
Riley Green 137 A5
Rileyhill 113 D5
Rilla Mill 10 D3
Rillington 160 D2
Rimington 146 C2
Rimpton 29 C6
Rimswell 143 A5
Rinaston 55 B5
Ringasta 285 M5
Ringford 173 C4
Ringinglow 130 A2
Ringland 120 D3
Ringles Cross 36 D2
Ringmer 22 A2
Ringmore 7 C5
Ringorm 254 B3
Ring's End 101 A5
Ringsfield 105 C5
Ringsfield Corner 105 C5
Ringshall
Herts 67 B4
Suff 87 B6
Ringshall Stocks 87 B6
Ringstead
Norf 119 A4
Northants 100 D1
Ringwood 17 A5
Ringwould 39 A5
Rinmore 243 A7
Rinnigill 283 H4
Rinsey 2 C3
Riof 288 D2
Ripe 22 A3
Ripley
Derbys 130 D3
Hants 17 B5
N Yorks 148 A1
Sur 34 A3
Riplingham 150 D2
Ripon 157 D7
Rippingale 116 C3
Ripple
Kent 39 A5
Worcs 79 D6
Ripponden 138 B3
Rireavach 262 A2
Risabus 200 D3
Risbury 78 B3
Risby 86 A3
Risca =*Rhisga* 60 D4
Rise 151 C4
Riseden 36 C4
Risegate 117 C5
Riseholme 133 B4
Riseley
Bedford 84 A2
Wokingham 47 C5
Rishangles 88 A2
Rishton 146 D1
Rishworth 138 B3
Rising Bridge 137 A6
Risley
Derbys 114 B2
Warr 137 D5
Risplith 147 A6
Rispond 277 B5
Rivar 45 C7
Rivenhall End 70 B2
River Bank 86 A1
Riverhead 36 A3
Rivington 137 B5
Roachill 26 C3
Roade 83 B4
Road Green 104 B3
Roadhead 176 B3
Roadmeetings 194 B3
Roadside 280 B3
Roadside of Catterline 233 A6
Roadside of Kinneff 233 A6
Roadwater 27 B5
Roag 258 D2
Roa Island 153 D3
Roath 41 D6
Roberton
Borders 186 B3
S Lanark 194 D4
Robertsbridge 37 D5
Roberttown 139 A4
Robeston Cross 55 D4
Robeston Wathen 55 C6
Robin Hood 139 A6
Robin Hood's Bay 160 A3
Roborough
Devon 7 A4
Devon 25 D6
Roby 136 D3
Roby Mill 136 C4
Rocester 113 B5
Roch 55 B4
Rochdale 138 B1
Roche 5 A4
Rochester
Medway 51 C4
Northumb 188 D1
Rochford 70 D2
Roch Gate 55 B4
Rock
Corn 9 D5
Northumb 189 A5
Worcs 95 D5
W Sus 21 A4
Rockbeare 13 B5
Rockbourne 31 D5
Rockcliffe
Cumb 175 B6
Dumfries 173 C6
Rock Ferry 126 A3
Rockfield
Highld 265 B5
Mon 61 B6
Rockford 17 A5
Rockhampton 62 D2
Rockingham 99 B5
Rockland All Saints 103 B5
Rockland St Mary 104 A4
Rockland St Peter 103 B5
Rockley 45 B5
Rockwell End 47 A5
Rockwell Green 27 C6
Rodborough 63 C4
Rodbourne
Swindon 45 A5
Wilts 44 A3
Rodbourne Cheney 45 A5
Rodd 77 A7
Roddam 188 A3
Rodden 15 C6
Rode 44 D2
Rodeheath 128 C3
Rode Heath 128 D3
Roden 111 D4
Rodhuish 27 B5
Rodington 111 D4
Rodley
Glos 62 B3
W Yorks 147 D6
Rodmarton 63 D5
Rodmell 22 B2
Rodmersham 51 C6
Rodney Stoke 42 D3
Rodsley 113 A6
Rodway 28 B2
Rodwell 15 D6
Roecliffe 148 A2
Roe Green 85 D5
Roehampton 49 B5
Roesound 284 G5
Roffey 35 C4
Rogart 273 D5
Rogart Station 273 D5
Rogate 33 C7
Rogerstone 42 A1
Roghadal 287 F5
Rogiet 42 A3
Rogue's Alley 101 A5
Roke 66 D1
Roker 179 D6
Rollesby 121 D6
Rolleston
Leics 99 A4
Notts 132 D2
Rolleston-on-Dove 113 C6
Rolston 151 C5
Rolvenden 37 C6
Rolvenden Layne 37 C6
Romaldkirk 166 C2
Romanby 158 B2
Romannobridge 195 B6
Romansleigh 26 C2
Romford 50 A2
Romiley 138 D2
Romsey 32 C2
Romsey Town 85 B6
Romsley
Shrops 95 C5
Worcs 96 D2
Ronague 152 D2
Rookhope 166 A2
Rookley 18 C4
Rooks Bridge 42 D2
Roos 151 D5
Roosebeck 153 D3
Rootham's Green 84 B3
Rootpark 195 A4
Ropley 33 B5
Ropley Dean 33 B5
Ropsley 116 B2
Rora 269 D5
Rorandle 244 A3
Rorrington 93 A7
Roscroggan 3 A4
Rose 4 B2
Roseacre
Kent 37 A5
Lancs 144 D4
Rose Ash 26 C2
Rosebank 194 B3
Rosebrough 189 A4
Rosebush 55 B6
Rosecare 10 B2
Rosedale Abbey 159 B6
Roseden 188 A3
Rosefield 253 A4
Rose Green 20 C2
Rose Grove 146 D2
Rosehall 272 D2
Rosehaugh Mains 252 A2
Rosehearty 269 C4
Rosehill 111 B5
Rose Hill
E Sus 22 A2
Lancs 146 D2
Suff 88 C2
Roseisle 266 C2
Roselands 22 B4
Rosemarket 55 D5
Rosemarkie 252 A3
Rosemary Lane 27 D6
Rosemount 231 D5
Rosenannon 5 A4
Rosewell 209 D5
Roseworth 168 C2
Roseworthy 3 B4
Rosgill 164 D3
Roshven 235 C6
Roskhill 258 D2
Roskill House 252 A2
Rosley 175 D6
Roslin 209 D5
Rosliston 113 D6
Rosneath 215 D5
Ross
Dumfries 172 D4
Northumb 199 C5
Perth 218 B2
Rossett 126 D3
Rossett Green 148 B2
Rossie Ochill 219 C5
Rossie Priory 220 A2
Rossington 140 D4
Rosskeen 264 D2
Rossland 205 A4
Ross-on-Wye 62 A2
Roster 281 E4
Rostherne 128 A2
Rosthwaite 163 C5
Roston 113 A5
Rosyth 208 B4
Rothbury 188 C3
Rotherby 115 D4
Rotherfield 36 D3
Rotherfield Greys 47 A5
Rotherfield Peppard 47 A5
Rotherham 140 D2
Rothersthorpe 83 B4
Rotherwick 47 D5
Rothes 254 B3
Rothesay 203 B5
Rothiebrisbane 256 C2
Rothienorman 256 C2
Rothiesholm 282 E7
Rothley
Leics 114 D3
Northumb 178 A2
Rothley Shield East 188 D3
Rothmaise 256 C1
Rothwell
Lincs 142 D3
Northants 99 C5
W Yorks 139 A6
Rothwell Haigh 139 A6
Rotsea 150 B3
Rottal 232 B1
Rotten End 89 A4
Rottingdean 21 B6
Rottington 162 C2
Roud 18 C4
Rougham
Norf 119 C5
Suff 87 A5
Rougham Green 87 A5
Roughburn 240 D1
Rough Close 112 B3
Rough Common 52 D3
Roughlee 146 C2
Roughley 96 B4
Roughsike 176 B3
Roughton
Lincs 134 C2
Norf 120 B4
Shrops 95 B5
Roughton Moor 134 C2
Roundhay 148 D2
Roundstonefoot 185 B4
Roundstreet Common 34 D3
Roundway 44 C4
Rousdon 14 B2
Rous Lench 80 B3
Routenburn 204 B1
Routh 150 C3
Row
Corn 10 D1
Cumb 154 C3
Rowanburn 175 A7
Rowardennan 206 A1
Rowde 44 C3
Rowen 124 B2
Rowfoot 177 C4
Row Heath 71 B5
Rowhedge 71 A4
Rowhook 35 C4
Rowington 81 A5
Rowland 130 B2
Rowlands Castle 33 D6
Rowlands Gill 178 D3
Rowledge 33 A7
Rowlestone 61 A5
Rowley
E Yorks 150 D2
Shrops 93 A7
Rowley Hill 139 B4
Rowley Regis 96 C2
Rowly 34 B3
Rowney Green 96 D3
Rownhams 32 D2
Rowrah 162 C3
Rowsham 66 B3
Rowsley 130 C2
Rowstock 46 A2
Rowston 133 D5
Rowton
Ches W 127 C4
Shrops 110 D2
Telford 111 D5
Roxburgh 197 C6
Roxby
N Lincs 141 B7
N Yorks 169 D5
Roxton 84 B3
Roxwell 69 C6
Royal Leamington Spa 81 A6
Royal Oak
Darl 167 C5
Lancs 136 C3
Royal Tunbridge Wells 36 C3
Royal Wootton Bassett 45 A4
Roybridge 239 D6
Roydhouse 139 B5
Roydon
Essex 68 C4
Norf 104 C1
Norf 119 C4
Roydon Hamlet 68 C4
Royston
Herts 85 C5
S Yorks 139 B6
Royton 138 C2
Rozel 6
Ruabon =*Rhiwabon* 110 A2
Ruaig 222 C3
Ruan Lanihorne 4 C3
Ruan Minor 3 D5
Ruarach 249 D6
Ruardean 62 B2
Ruardean Woodside 62 B2
Rubery 96 D2
Ruckcroft 164 A3
Ruckhall 78 D2
Ruckinge 38 B2
Ruckland 134 B3
Ruckley 94 A3
Rudbaxton 55 B5
Rudby 158 A3
Ruddington 114 B3
Rudford 62 A3
Rudge
Shrops 95 B6
Som 44 D2
Rudgeway 43 A5
Rudgwick 34 C3
Rudhall 62 A2
Rudheath 128 B1
Rudley Green 70 C2
Rudry 41 C6
Rudston 150 A3
Rudyard 129 D4
Rufford 136 B3
Rufforth 148 B4
Rugby 98 D2
Rugeley 112 D4
Ruglen 181 A4
Ruilick 251 B7
Ruishton 28 C2
Ruisigearraidh 287 F4
Ruislip 48 A3
Ruislip Common 48 A3
Rumbling Bridge 208 A3
Rumburgh 104 C4
Rumford 9 D4
Rumney 41 D7
Runcorn 127 A5
Runcton 20 B1
Runcton Holme 102 A2
Rundlestone 11 D6
Runfold 34 B1
Runhall 103 A6
Runham
Norf 105 A6
Norf 121 D6
Runnington 27 C6
Runsell Green 70 C1
Runswick Bay 169 D6
Runwell 70 D1
Ruscombe 47 B5
Rushall
Hereford 79 D4
Norf 104 C2
Wilts 45 D5
W Mid 96 A3
Rushbrooke 87 A4
Rushbury 94 B3
Rushden
Herts 85 D5
Northants 83 A6
Rushenden 51 B6
Rushford 103 C5
Rush Green 50 A2
Rush-head 256 B3
Rushlake Green 22 A4
Rushmere 105 C5
Rushmere St Andrew 88 C3
Rushmoor 34 B1
Rushock 96 D1
Rusholme 138 D1
Rushton
Ches W 127 C5
Northants 99 C5
Shrops 95 A4
Rushton Spencer 129 C4
Rushwick 79 B6
Rushyford 167 C5
Ruskie 217 D6
Ruskington 133 D5
Rusland 154 C2
Rusper 35 C5
Ruspidge 62 B2
Russell's Water 47 A5
Russel's Green 104 D3
Rusthall 36 C3
Rustington 20 B3
Ruston 160 C3
Ruston Parva 150 A3
Ruswarp 160 A2
Rutherford 197 C5
Rutherglen 205 B6
Ruthernbridge 5 A5
Ruthin =*Rhuthun* 125 D6
Ruthrieston 245 B6
Ruthven
Aberds 255 B6
Angus 231 D6
Highld 241 C5
Highld 253 C4
Ruthven House 231 D7
Ruthvoes 4 A4
Ruthwell 174 B3
Ruyton-XI-Towns 110 C2
Ryal 178 B2
Ryal Fold 137 A5
Ryall 14 B4
Ryarsh 37 A4
Rydal 154 A2
Ryde 19 B4
Rye 37 D7
Ryecroft Gate 129 C4
Rye Foreign 37 D6
Rye Harbour 38 D1
Ryehill 143 A4
Rye Park 68 B3
Rye Street 79 D5
Ryhall 116 D3
Ryhill 140 B1
Ryhope 179 D6
Rylstone 146 B3
Ryme Intrinseca 29 D5
Ryther 149 D4
Ryton
Glos 79 D5
N Yorks 159 D6
Shrops 95 A5
T&W 178 C3
Ryton-on-Dunsmore 97 D6

S

Sabden 146 D1
Sacombe 68 B3
Sacriston 167 A5
Sadberge 167 D6
Saddell 190 B3
Saddington 98 B3
Saddle Bow 118 D3
Saddlescombe 21 A5
Sadgill 154 A3
Saffron Walden 86 D1
Sageston 55 D6
Saham Hills 103 A5
Saham Toney 103 A5
Saighdinis 287 H3
Saighton 127 C4
St Abbs 211 D6
St Abb's Haven 211 D6
St Agnes
Corn 4 B2
Scilly 2 F3
St Albans 67 C6
St Allen 4 B3
St Andrews 221 C5
St Andrew's Major 41 D6
St Anne 7
St Annes 136 A2
St Ann's 184 C3
St Ann's Chapel
Corn 11 D5
Devon 7 C5
St Anthony-in-Meneage 3 C5
St Anthony's Hill 22 B4
St Arvans 61 D7
St Asaph =*Llanelwy* 125 B5
St Athan 41 E5
St Aubin 6
St Austell 5 B5
St Bees 162 C2
St Blazey 5 B5
St Boswells 197 C4
St Brelade 6
St Breock 9 D5
St Breward 10 D1
St Briavels 62 C1
St Bride's 54 C4
St Brides Major 40 D3
St Bride's Netherwent 42 A3
St Brides super Ely 41 D5
St Brides Wentlooge 42 A1
St Budeaux 6 B3
Saintbury 80 D4
St Buryan 2 C2
St Catherine 44 B1
St Catherine's 215 B4
St Clears =*Sanclêr* 56 A2
St Cleer 6 A1
St Clement 4 C3
St Clements 6
St Clether 10 C3
St Colmac 203 B5
St Columb Major 4 A4
St Columb Minor 4 A3
St Columb Road 4 B4
St Combs 269 C5

St Cross South Elmham 104 C3
St Cyrus 233 B5
St David's 218 B4
St David's = *Tyddewi* 54 B3
St Day 4 C2
St Dennis 4 B4
St Devereux 78 D2
St Dogmaels 73 B4
St Dogwells 55 B5
St Dominick 6 A3
St Donat's 40 E4
St Edith's 44 C3
St Endellion 9 D5
St Enoder 4 B3
St Erme 4 B3
St Erney 6 B2
St Erth 2 B3
St Ervan 9 D4
St Eval 4 A3
St Ewe 5 C4
St Fagans 41 D6
St Fergus 269 D5
St Fillans 217 B6
St Florence 55 D6
St Genny's 10 B2
St George 125 B4
St George's 41 D5
St Germans 6 B2
St Giles 133 B4
St Giles in the Wood 25 D6
St Giles on the Heath 11 B4
St Harmon 92 D3
St Helena 97 A5
St Helen Auckland 167 C4
St Helens
IoW 19 C5
Mers 136 D4
St Helen's 23 A6
St Helier
Jersey 6
London 49 C5
St Hilary
Corn 2 B3
V Glam 41 D5
Saint Hill 36 C1
St Illtyd 41 A7
St Ippollytts 68 A1
St Ishmael's 54 D4
St Issey 9 D5
St Ive 6 A2
St Ives
Cambs 101 D5
Corn 2 A3
Dorset 17 A5
St James South Elmham 104 C4
St Jidgey 9 E5
St John 6 B3
St John's
IoM 152 C2
Jersey 6
Sur 34 A2
Worcs 79 B6
St John's Chapel 166 B1
St John's Fen End 118 D2
St John's Highway 118 D2
St John's Town of Dalry 182 D4
St Judes 152 B3
St Just 2 B1
St Just in Roseland 4 D3
St Katherine's 256 C2
St Keverne 3 C5
St Kew 9 D6
St Kew Highway 9 D6
St Keyne 6 A1
St Lawrence
Corn 5 A5
Essex 70 C3
IoW 18 D4
St Leonards
Dorset 17 A5
E Sus 23 B5
St Leonard's 67 C4
Saint Leonards 205 C6
St Levan 2 C1
St Lythans 41 D6
St Mabyn 9 D6
St Madoes 219 B6
St Margarets 68 B3
St Margaret's 78 D1
St Margaret's at Cliffe 39 A5
St Margaret's Hope 283 H5
St Margaret South Elmham 104 C4
St Mark's 152 D2
St Martin 6 B1
St Martins
Corn 3 C5
Perth 219 A6
St Martin's
Jersey 6
Shrops 110 B2
St Mary Bourne 46 D2
St Mary Church 41 D5
St Mary Cray 50 C1
St Mary Hill 41 D4
St Mary Hoo 51 B5
St Mary in the Marsh 38 C2
St Mary's
Jersey 6
Orkney 283 G5
St Mary's Bay 38 C2
St Maughans 61 B6
St Mawes 4 D3
St Mawgan 4 A3
St Mellion 6 A2
St Mellons 42 A1
St Merryn 9 D4
St Mewan 5 B4
St Michael Caerhays 5 C4
St Michael Penkevil 4 C3
St Michaels 78 A3
St Michael's 37 C6
St Michael's on Wyre 145 C4
St Michael South Elmham 104 C4
St Minver 9 D5
St Monans 221 D5
St Neot 5 A6
St Neots 84 A3
St Newlyn East 4 B3
St Nicholas
Pembs 72 C1
V Glam 41 D5
St Nicholas at Wade 53 C4
St Ninians 207 A5
St Osyth 71 B5
St Osyth Heath 71 B5
St Ouens 6
St Owens Cross 62 A1
St Paul's Cray 50 C1
St Paul's Walden 68 A1
St Peter Port 6
St Peter's
Jersey 6
Kent 53 C5
St Petrox 55 E5
St Pinnock 5 A7
St Quivox 192 C3
St Ruan 3 D5
St Sampson 6
St Stephen 4 B4
St Stephens
Corn 6 B3
Herts 67 C6
St Stephen's 10 C4
St Teath 9 C6
St Thomas 13 B4
St Tudy 9 D6
St Twynnells 55 E5
St Veep 5 B6
St Vigeans 233 D4
St Wenn 5 A4
St Weonards 61 A6
Salcombe 7 D6
Salcombe Regis 13 C6
Salcott 70 B3
Sale 137 D6
Saleby 135 B4
Sale Green 80 B2
Salehurst 37 D5
Salem
Carms 58 C3
Ceredig 91 D4
Salen
Argyll 225 B4
Highld 235 D5
Salesbury 145 D6
Salford
C Beds 83 D6
Gtr Man 137 D7
Oxon 64 A3
Salford Priors 80 B3
Salfords 35 B5
Salhouse 121 D5
Saline 208 A3
Salisbury 31 C5
Sallachan 236 C3
Sallachy
Highld 249 C6
Highld 272 D3
Salle 120 C3
Salmonby 134 B3
Salmond's Muir 221 A5
Salperton 64 A1
Salph End 84 B2
Salsburgh 207 D6
Salt 112 C3
Saltaire 147 D5
Saltash 6 B3
Saltburn 264 D3
Saltburn-by-the-Sea 169 C4
Saltby 115 C6
Saltcoats
Cumb 153 A1
N Ayrs 204 D2
Saltdean 22 B1
Salt End 142 A3
Salter 145 A6
Salterforth 146 C2
Salterswall 127 C6
Saltfleet 143 D6
Saltfleetby All Saints 143 D6
Saltfleetby St Clements 143 D6
Saltfleetby St Peter 135 A4
Saltford 43 C5
Salthouse 120 A2
Saltmarshe 141 A5
Saltney 126 C3
Salton 159 D6
Saltwick 178 B3
Saltwood 38 B3
Salum 222 C3
Salvington 21 B4
Salwarpe 80 A1
Salwayash 15 B4
Sambourne 80 A3
Sambrook 111 C6
Samhla 287 H2
Samlesbury 145 D5
Samlesbury Bottoms 137 A5
Sampford Arundel 27 D6
Sampford Brett 27 A5
Sampford Courtenay 12 A1
Sampford Peverell 27 D5
Sampford Spiney 11 D6
Sampool Bridge 154 C3
Samuelston 210 C1
Sanachan 249 B5
Sanaigmore 200 A2
Sanclêr = *St Clears* 56 A2
Sancreed 2 C2
Sancton 150 D2
Sand
Highld 261 A6
Shetland 285 J5
Sandaig 247 D6
Sandale 175 D5
Sandal Magna 139 B6
Sandbach 128 C2
Sandbank 215 D4
Sandbanks 17 C4
Sandend 267 C6
Sanderstead 49 C6
Sandfields 63 A5
Sandford
Cumb 165 D5
Devon 12 A3
Dorset 16 C3
IoW 18 C4
N Som 42 D3
Shrops 111 B4
S Lanark 194 B2
Sandfordhill 257 B6
Sandford on Thames 65 C6
Sandford Orcas 29 C6
Sandford St Martin 65 A5
Sandgate 38 B3
Sandgreen 172 C3
Sandhaven 269 C4
Sandhead 170 C2
Sandhills 34 C2
Sandhoe 178 C1
Sand Hole 149 D7
Sandholme
E Yorks 150 D1
Lincs 117 B6
Sandhurst
Brack 47 C6
Glos 63 A4
Kent 37 D5
Sandhurst Cross 37 D5
Sandhutton 158 C2
Sand Hutton 149 B5
Sandiacre 114 B2
Sandilands
Lincs 135 A5
S Lanark 194 C3
Sandiway 127 B6
Sandleheath 31 D5
Sandling 37 A5
Sandlow Green 128 C2
Sandness 285 H3
Sandon
Essex 70 C1
Herts 85 D5
Staffs 112 B3
Sandown 19 C4
Sandplace 6 B1
Sandridge
Herts 67 B6
Wilts 44 C3
Sandringham 118 C3
Sandsend 169 D6
Sandside House 279 B5
Sandsound 285 J5
Sandtoft 141 C5
Sandway 37 A6
Sandwell 96 C3
Sandwich 53 D5
Sandwick
Cumb 164 D2
Orkney 283 J5
Shetland 285 L6
Sandwith 162 C2
Sandy
Carms 57 B4
C Beds 84 C3
Sandy Bank 134 D2
Sandycroft 126 C3
Sandyford
Dumfries 185 C5
Stoke 128 D3
Sandygate 152 B3
Sandy Haven 55 D4
Sandyhills 173 C6
Sandylands 144 A4
Sandy Lane
Wilts 44 C3
Wrex 110 A2
Sandypark 12 C2
Sandysike 175 B6
Sangobeg 277 B5
Sangomore 277 B5
Sanna 234 D3
Sanndabhaig
W Isles 286 B4
W Isles 288 D5
Sannox 203 D5
Sanquhar 183 B5
Santon 142 B1
Santon Bridge 163 D4
Santon Downham 103 C4
Sapcote 98 B1
Sapey Common 79 A5
Sapiston 103 D5
Sapley 100 D4
Sapperton
Glos 63 C5
Lincs 116 B3
Saracen's Head 117 C6
Sarclet 281 D5
Sardis 57 B5
Sarn
Bridgend 40 C4
Powys 93 B6
Sarnau
Carms 56 A3
Ceredig 73 A6
Gwyn 109 B4
Powys 76 D4
Powys 110 D1
Sarn Bach 106 D3
Sarnesfield 78 B1
Sarn Meyllteyrn 106 C2
Saron
Carms 57 A6
Carms 73 C6
Denb 125 C5
Gwyn 107 A4
Gwyn 123 D5
Sarratt 67 D5
Sarre 53 C4
Sarsden 64 A3
Sarsgrum 277 B4
Satley 166 A4
Satron 156 B3
Satterleigh 26 C1
Satterthwaite 154 B2
Satwell 47 A5
Sauchen 244 A3
Saucher 219 A6
Sauchie 208 A1
Sauchieburn 233 B4
Saughall 126 B3
Saughtree 187 D4
Saul 62 C3
Saundby 132 A2
Saundersfoot 56 B1
Saunderton 66 C2
Saunton 25 B5
Sausthorpe 134 C3
Saval 272 D3
Savary 225 B5
Savile Park 138 A3
Sawbridge 82 A2
Sawbridgeworth 69 B4
Sawdon 160 C3
Sawley
Derbys 114 B2
Lancs 146 C1
N Yorks 147 A6
Sawston 85 C6
Sawtry 100 C3
Saxby
Leics 115 D6
Lincs 133 A5
Saxby All Saints 142 B1
Saxelbye 115 C5
Saxham Street 88 A1
Saxilby 132 B3
Saxlingham 120 B2
Saxlingham Green 104 B3
Saxlingham Nethergate 104 B3
Saxlingham Thorpe 104 B3
Saxmundham 89 A4
Saxondale 115 B4
Saxon Street 86 B2
Saxtead 88 A3
Saxtead Green 88 A3
Saxthorpe 120 B3
Saxton 148 D3
Sayers Common 21 A5
Scackleton 159 D5
Scadabhagh 288 H2
Scaftworth 141 D4
Scagglethorpe 160 D2
Scaitcliffe 137 A6
Scalasaig 212 C1
Scalby
E Yorks 141 A6
N Yorks 160 B4
Scaldwell 99 D4
Scaleby 176 C2
Scaleby Hill 176 C2
Scale Houses 164 A3
Scales
Cumb 153 C3
Cumb 163 B6
Lancs 145 D4
Scalford 115 C5
Scaling 169 D5
Scallastle 225 C5
Scalloway 285 K6
Scalpay 288 H3
Scalpay House 247 B5
Scalpsie 203 C5
Scamadale 235 A6
Scamblesby 134 B2
Scamodale 236 B2
Scampston 160 D2
Scampton 133 B4
Scapa 283 G5
Scapegoat Hill 138 B3
Scar 282 C7
Scarborough 160 C4
Scarcliffe 131 C4
Scarcroft 148 C2
Scarcroft Hill 148 C2
Scardroy 250 A4
Scarff 284 E4
Scarfskerry 281 A4
Scargill 166 D3
Scarinish 222 C3
Scarisbrick 136 B2
Scarning 119 D6
Scarrington 115 A5
Scartho 143 C4
Scarwell 282 E3
Scatness 285 M5
Scatraig 252 C3
Scawby 142 C1
Scawsby 140 C3
Scawton 158 C4
Scayne's Hill 35 D6
Scethrog 60 A3
Scholar Green 128 D3
Scholes
W Yorks 139 A4
W Yorks 139 C4
W Yorks 148 D2
School Green 127 C6
Scleddau 55 A5
Scofton 131 A6
Scole 104 D2
Scolpaig 287 G2
Scone 219 B6
Sconser 247 A4
Scoonie 220 D3
Scoor 224 E3
Scopwick 133 D5
Scoraig 262 A2
Scorborough 150 C3
Scorrier 4 C2
Scorton
Lancs 145 C5
N Yorks 157 A6
Sco Ruston 121 C4
Scotbheinn 286 A4
Scotby 176 D2
Scotch Corner 157 A6
Scotforth 145 B4
Scothern 133 B5
Scotland Gate 179 A4
Scotlandwell 219 D6
Scotsburn 264 C3
Scotscalder Station 280 C2
Scotscraig 220 B4
Scots' Gap 178 A2
Scotston
Aberds 233 A5
Perth 230 D3
Scotstoun 205 B5
Scotstown 236 C2
Scotswood 178 C3
Scottas 247 D6
Scotter 141 C6
Scotterthorpe 141 C6
Scottlethorpe 116 C3
Scotton
Lincs 141 D6
N Yorks 148 B2
N Yorks 157 B5
Scottow 121 C4
Scoughall 210 B3
Scoulag 203 C6
Scoulton 103 A5
Scourie 276 D2
Scourie More 276 D2
Scousburgh 285 M5
Scrabster 280 B2
Scrafield 134 C3
Scrainwood 188 C2
Scrane End 117 A6
Scraptoft 98 A3
Scratby 121 D7
Scrayingham 149 A6
Scredington 116 A3
Scremby 135 C4
Scremerston 198 B4
Screveton 115 A5
Scrivelsby 134 C2
Scriven 148 B2
Scrooby 141 D4
Scropton 113 B5
Scrub Hill 134 D2
Scruton 157 B6
Sculcoates 150 D3
Sculthorpe 119 B5
Scunthorpe 141 B6
Scurlage 57 D4
Seaborough 14 A4
Seacombe 136 D2
Seacroft
Lincs 135 C5
W Yorks 148 D2
Seadyke 117 B6
Seafield
S Ayrs 192 C3
W Loth 208 D3
Seaford 22 C2
Seaforth 136 D2
Seagrave 115 D4
Seaham 168 A2
Seahouses 199 C6
Seal 36 A3
Sealand 126 C3
Seale 34 B1
Seamer
N Yorks 160 C4
N Yorks 168 D2
Seamill 204 D2
Sea Palling 121 C6
Searby 142 C2
Seasalter 52 C2
Seascale 162 D3
Seathorne 135 C5
Seathwaite
Cumb 153 A3
Cumb 163 C5
Seatoller 163 C5
Seaton
Corn 6 B2
Cumb 162 A3

Seaton continued
Devon 14 B2
Durham 179 D5
E Yorks 151 C4
Northumb 179 B5
Rutland 99 B6
Seaton Burn 179 B4
Seaton Carew 168 C3
Seaton Delaval 179 B5
Seaton Ross 149 C6
Seaton Sluice 179 B5
Seatown
Aberds 267 C6
Dorset 14 B4
Seave Green 159 A4
Seaview 19 B5
Seaville 175 C4
Seavington St Mary . 28 D3
Seavington
St Michael 28 D4
Sebergham 164 A1
Seckington 97 A5
Second Coast 261 A6
Sedbergh 155 B5
Sedbury 62 D1
Sedbusk 156 B2
Sedgeberrow 80 D3
Sedgebrook 115 B6
Sedgefield 167 C6
Sedgeford 119 B4
Sedgehill 30 C2
Sedgley 96 B2
Sedgwick 154 C4
Sedlescombe 23 A5
Sedlescombe Street . 23 A5
Seend 44 C3
Seend Cleeve 44 C3
Seer Green 67 D4
Seething 104 B4
Sefton 136 C2
Seghill 179 B4
Seifton 94 C2
Seighford 112 C2
Seilebost 287 E5
Seion 123 D5
Seisdon 95 B6
Seisiadar 288 D6
Selattyn 110 B1
Selborne 33 B6
Selby 149 D5
Selham 34 D2
Selhurst 49 C6
Selkirk 186 A3
Sellack 62 A1
Sellafirth 284 D7
Sellibister 282 C8
Sellindge 38 B2
Sellindge Lees 38 B3
Selling 52 D2
Sells Green 44 C3
Selly Oak 96 C3
Selmeston 22 B3
Selsdon 49 C6
Selsey 20 C1
Selsfield Common . . 35 C6
Selsted 39 A4
Selston 131 D4
Selworthy 27 A4
Semblister 285 H5
Semer 87 C5
Semington 44 C2
Semley 30 C2
Send 34 A3
Send Marsh 34 A3
Senghenydd 41 B6
Sennen 2 C1
Sennen Cove 2 C1
Sennybridge
=Pont Senni 59 C6
Serlby 131 A6
Sessay 158 D3
Setchey 118 D3
Setley 18 A2
Setter
Shetland 284 E6
Shetland 285 H5
Shetland 285 J7
Settiscarth 282 F4
Settle 146 A2
Settrington 160 D2
Sevenhampton 63 A6
Seven Kings 50 A1
Sevenoaks 36 A3
Sevenoaks Weald . . . 36 A3
Seven Sisters 59 E5
Severn Beach 43 A4
Severnhampton 64 D3
Severn Stoke 79 C6

Sevington 38 A2
Sewards End 86 D1
Sewardstone 68 D3
Sewardstonebury . . . 68 D3
Sewerby 151 A4
Seworgan 4 D2
Sewstern 116 C1
Sezincote 81 D4
Sgarasta Mhor 287 E5
Sgiogarstaigh 288 A6
Shabbington 66 C1
Shackerstone 97 A6
Shackleford 34 B2
Shade 138 A2
Shadforth 167 A6
Shadingfield 105 C5
Shadoxhurst 38 B1
Shadsworth 137 A6
Shadwell
Norf 103 C5
W Yorks 148 D2
Shaftesbury 30 C2
Shafton 140 B1
Shalbourne 45 C7
Shalcombe 18 C2
Shalden 33 A5
Shaldon 13 D4
Shalfleet 18 C3
Shalford
Essex 69 A7
Sur 34 B3
Shalford Green 69 A7
Shallowford 26 A2
Shalmsford Street . . . 52 D2
Shalstone 82 D3
Shamley Green 34 B3
Shandon 215 D5
Shandwick 265 C4
Shangton 99 B4
Shankhouse 179 B4
Shanklin 19 C4
Shanquhar 255 C6
Shanzie 231 C6
Shap 164 D3
Shapwick
Dorset 16 A3
Som 28 B4
Shardlow 114 B2
Shareshill 96 A2
Sharlston 140 B1
Sharlston Common . 140 B1
Sharnbrook 84 B1
Sharnford 98 B1
Sharoe Green 145 D5
Sharow 158 D2
Sharpenhoe 84 D2
Sharperton 188 C2
Sharpness 62 C2
Sharp Street 121 C5
Sharpthorne 35 C6
Sharrington 120 B2
Shatterford 95 C5
Shaugh Prior 7 A4
Shavington 128 D2
Shaw
Gtr Man 138 C2
W Berks 46 C2
Wilts 44 C2
Shawbury 111 C4
Shawdon Hall 188 B3
Shawell 98 C2
Shawford 32 C3
Shawforth 138 A1
Shaw Green 136 B4
Shawhead 173 A6
Shawhill 175 B5
Shaw Mills 147 A6
Shawton 194 B1
Shawtonhill 194 B1
Shear Cross 30 A2
Shearington 174 B3
Shearsby 98 B3
Shebbear 11 A5
Shebdon 111 C6
Shebster 279 B6
Sheddens 205 C5
Shedfield 33 D4
Sheen 129 C6
Sheepscar 148 D2
Sheepscombe 63 B4
Sheepstor 7 A4
Sheepwash 11 A5
Sheepway 42 B3
Sheepy Magna 97 A6
Sheepy Parva 97 A6
Sheering 69 B5
Sheerness 51 B6
Sheet 33 C6
Sheffield 130 A3
Sheffield Bottom . . . 47 C4

Sheffield Green 36 D2
Shefford 84 D3
Shefford Woodlands 46 B1
Sheigra 276 B2
Sheinton 95 A4
Shelderton 94 D2
Sheldon
Derbys 129 C6
Devon 13 A6
W Mid 97 C4
Sheldwich 52 D2
Shelf 139 A4
Shelfanger 104 C2
Shelfield
Warks 80 A4
W Mid 96 A3
Shelford 115 A4
Shellacres 198 B2
Shelley
Essex 69 C5
Suff 87 D6
W Yorks 139 B5
Shellingford 64 D4
Shellow Bowells 69 C6
Shelsley Beauchamp 79 A5
Shelsley Walsh 79 A5
Shelthorpe 114 D3
Shelton
Bedford 84 A2
Norf 104 B3
Notts 115 A5
Shrops 110 D3
Shelton Green 104 B3
Shelve 94 B1
Shelwick 78 C3
Shenfield 69 D6
Shenington 81 C6
Shenley 68 C1
Shenley Brook End . . 83 D5
Shenleybury 68 C1
Shenley Church End . 83 D5
Shenmore 78 D1
Shennanton 171 A5
Shenstone
Staffs 96 A4
Worcs 95 D6
Shenton 97 A6
Shenval
Highld 251 D6
Moray 254 D3
Shepeau Stow 117 D6
Shephall 68 A2
Shepherd's Green . . . 47 A5
Shepherd's Port . . . 118 B3
Shepherdswell 39 A4
Shepley 139 C4
Shepperdine 62 D2
Shepperton 48 C3
Shepreth 85 C5
Shepshed 114 D2
Shepton
Beauchamp 28 D4
Shepton Mallet 29 A6
Shepton Montague . . 29 B6
Shepway 37 A5
Sheraton 168 B2
Sherborne
Dorset 29 D6
Glos 64 B2
Sherborne St John . . 47 D4
Sherbourne 81 A5
Sherburn
Durham 167 A6
N Yorks 160 D3
Sherburn Hill 167 A6
Sherburn in Elmet . . 148 D3
Shere 34 B3
Shereford 119 C5
Sherfield English . . . 32 C1
Sherfield on Loddon . 47 D4
Sherford 8 C1
Sheriffhales 111 D6
Sheriff Hutton 149 A5
Sheringham 120 A3
Sherington 83 C5
Shernal Green 80 A2
Shernborne 119 B4
Sherrington 30 B3
Sherston 44 A2
Sherwood Green . . . 25 C6
Shettleston 205 B6
Shevington 136 C4
Shevington Moor . . . 136 B4
Shevington Vale 136 C4
Sheviock 6 B2
Shide 18 C3
Shiel Bridge 238 A3
Shieldaig
Highld 249 A5
Highld 261 C5

Shieldhill
Dumfries 184 D3
Falk 208 C1
S Lanark 195 B5
Shielfoot 235 D5
Shielhill
Angus 232 C2
Invclyd 204 A2
Shifford 65 C4
Shifnal 95 A5
Shilbottle 189 C4
Shildon 167 C5
Shillingford
Devon 27 C4
Oxon 65 D6
Shillingford
St George 13 C4
Shillingstone 30 D2
Shillington 84 D3
Shillmoor 188 C1
Shilton
Oxon 64 C3
Warks 97 C7
Shilvington 178 A3
Shimpling
Norf 104 C2
Suff 87 B4
Shimpling Street . . . 87 B4
Shincliffe 167 A5
Shiney Row 179 D5
Shinfield 47 C5
Shingham 102 A3
Shingle Street 89 C4
Shinner's Bridge 8 A1
Shinness 272 C3
Shipbourne 36 A3
Shipdham 103 A5
Shipham 42 D3
Shiphay 8 A2
Shiplake 47 B5
Shipley
Derbys 114 A2
Northumb 189 B4
Shrops 95 B6
W Sus 35 D4
W Yorks 147 D5
Shipley Shiels 187 D6
Shipmeadow 105 C4
Shippea Hill
Station 102 C2
Shippon 65 D5
Shipston-on-Stour . . 81 C5
Shipton
Glos 63 B6
N Yorks 149 B4
Shrops 94 B3
Shipton Bellinger . . . 31 A6
Shipton Gorge 15 B4
Shipton Green 19 A7
Shipton Moyne 44 A2
Shipton on Cherwell 65 B5
Shipton Solers 63 B6
Shiptonthorpe 150 C1
Shipton-under-
Wychwood 64 B3
Shirburn 66 D1
Shirdley Hill 136 B2
Shirebrook 131 C5
Shiregreen 139 D6
Shirehampton 43 B4
Shiremoor 179 B5
Shirenewton 61 D6
Shireoaks 131 A5
Shirkoak 38 B1
Shirland 130 D3
Shirley
Derbys 113 A6
London 49 C6
Soton 32 D3
W Mid 96 D4
Shirl Heath 78 B2
Shirrell Heath 33 D4
Shirwell 25 B6
Shirwell Cross 25 B6
Shiskine 191 C5
Shobdon 78 A2
Shobnall 113 C6
Shobrooke 12 A3
Shoby 115 D4
Shocklach 110 A3
Shoeburyness 51 A6
Sholden 53 D5
Sholing 32 D3
Shoot Hill 110 D3
Shop
Corn 9 D4
Corn 24 D3
Shop Corner 88 D3
Shoreditch 49 A6
Shoreham 50 C2

Shoreham-By-Sea . . 21 B5
Shore Mill 264 D3
Shoresdean 198 B3
Shoreswood 198 B3
Shoreton 264 D2
Shorncote 63 D6
Shorne 50 B3
Shortacombe 11 C6
Shortgate 22 A2
Short Heath 96 A2
Shortlanesend 4 C3
Shortlees 193 B4
Shortstown 84 C2
Shorwell 18 C3
Shoscombe 43 D6
Shotatton 110 C2
Shotesham 104 B3
Shotgate 70 D1
Shotley 88 D3
Shotley Bridge 178 D2
Shotleyfield 178 D2
Shotley Gate 88 D3
Shottenden 52 D2
Shottermill 34 C1
Shottery 81 B4
Shotteswell 81 C7
Shottisham 88 C4
Shottle 113 A7
Shottlegate 113 A7
Shotton
Durham 168 B2
Flint 126 C3
Northumb 198 C2
Shotton Colliery . . . 167 A6
Shotts 207 D6
Shotwick 126 B3
Shouldham 102 A2
Shouldham Thorpe . 102 A2
Shoulton 79 B6
Shover's Green 37 C4
Shrawardine 110 D3
Shrawley 79 A6
Shrewley Common . . 81 A5
Shrewsbury 110 D3
Shrewton 31 A4
Shripney 20 B2
Shrivenham 45 A6
Shropham 103 B5
Shrub End 70 A3
Shucknall 78 C3
Shudy Camps 86 C2
Shulishadermor . . . 259 D4
Shurdington 63 B5
Shurlock Row 47 B6
Shurrery 279 C6
Shurrery Lodge 279 C6
Shurton 28 A2
Shustoke 97 B5
Shute
Devon 12 A3
Devon 14 B2
Shutford 81 C6
Shuthonger 80 D1
Shutlanger 83 B4
Shuttington 97 A5
Shuttlewood 131 B4
Siabost bho Dheas . 288 C3
Siabost bho
Thuath 288 C3
Siadar 288 B4
Siadar Iarach 288 B4
Siadar Uarach 288 B4
Sibbaldbie 185 D4
Sibbertoft 98 C3
Sibdon Carwood 94 C2
Sibford Ferris 81 D6
Sibford Gower 81 D6
Sible Hedingham . . . 86 D3
Sibsey 134 D3
Sibson
Cambs 100 B2
Leics 97 A6
Sibthorpe 115 A5
Sibton 89 A4
Sibton Green 105 D4
Sicklesmere 87 A4
Sicklinghall 148 C2
Sid 13 C6
Sidbury
Devon 13 B6
Shrops 95 C4
Sidcot 42 D3
Sidcup 50 B1
Siddick 162 A3
Siddington
Ches E 128 B3
Glos 63 D6
Sidemoor 96 D2
Sidestrand 121 B4
Sidford 13 B6

Sidlesham 20 C1
Sidley 23 B5
Sidlow 35 B5
Sidmouth 13 C6
Sigford 12 D2
Sigglesthorne 151 C4
Sighthill 209 C4
Sigingstone 41 D4
Signet 64 B3
Silchester 47 C4
Sildinis 288 F3
Sileby 114 D3
Silecroft 153 B2
Silfield 104 B2
Silian 75 C4
Silkstone 139 C5
Silkstone Common . 139 C5
Silk Willoughby . . . 116 A3
Silloth 174 C4
Sills 188 C1
Sillyearn 267 D6
Siloh 59 B4
Silpho 160 B3
Silsden 147 C5
Silsoe 84 D2
Silverburn 209 D5
Silverdale
Lancs 154 D3
Staffs 112 A2
Silver End 70 B2
Silvergate 120 C3
Silverhill 23 A5
Silverley's Green . . . 104 D3
Silverstone 82 C3
Silverton 13 A4
Silvington 95 D4
Silwick 285 J4
Simmondley 138 D3
Simonburn 177 B6
Simonsbath 26 B2
Simonstone 146 D1
Simprim 198 B2
Simpson 83 D5
Simpson Cross 55 C4
Sinclair's Hill 198 A2
Sinclairston 182 A2
Sinderby 158 C2
Sinderhope 177 D6
Sindlesham 47 C5
Singdean 187 C4
Singleborough 83 D4
Singleton
Lancs 144 D3
W Sus 20 A1
Singlewell 50 B3
Sinkhurst Green 37 B6
Sinnahard 244 A1
Sinnington 159 C6
Sinton Green 79 A6
Sipson 48 B3
Sirhowy 60 B3
Sisland 104 B4
Sissinghurst 37 C5
Sisterpath 197 B6
Siston 43 B5
Sithney 3 C4
Sittingbourne 51 C5
Six Ashes 95 C5
Sixhills 133 A6
Six Hills 115 C4
Six Mile Bottom 86 B1
Sixpenny Handley . . . 30 D3
Sizewell 89 A5
Skail 278 D3
Skaill
Orkney 282 D5
Orkney 282 F3
Orkney 283 G6
Skares 182 A3
Skateraw 211 C4
Skaw 284 G7
Skeabost 259 D4
Skeabrae 282 E3
Skeeby 157 A6
Skeffington 99 A4
Skeffling 143 B5
Skegby 131 C4
Skegness 135 C5
Skelberry 285 M5
Skelbo 264 A3
Skelbrooke 140 B3
Skeldyke 117 B6
Skellingthorpe 133 B4
Skellister 285 H6
Skellow 140 B3
Skelmanthorpe 139 B5
Skelmersdale 136 C3
Skelmonae 256 C3
Skelmorlie 204 B1
Skelmuir 257 B4

Skelpick 278 C3
Skelton
  Cumb 164 B2
  E Yorks 141 A5
  N Yorks 157 A4
  Redcar 169 D4
  York 149 B4
Skelton-on-Ure. . . . 148 A2
Skelwick 282 C5
Skelwith Bridge. . . . 154 A2
Skendleby 135 C4
Skene House 245 B4
Skenfrith 61 A6
Skerne 150 B3
Skeroblingarry. 190 C3
Skerray 278 B2
Skerton 145 A4
Sketchley 98 B1
Sketty 57 C6
Skewen 40 B2
Skewsby 159 D5
Skeyton 120 C4
Skiag Bridge. 271 B5
Skibo Castle 264 B3
Skidbrooke 143 D6
Skidbrooke North
  End 143 D6
Skidby 150 D3
Skilgate 27 C4
Skillington 116 C1
Skinburness 174 C4
Skinflats 208 B2
Skinidin 258 D2
Skinnet 277 B6
Skinningrove 169 C5
Skipness 202 C3
Skippool 144 C3
Skipsea 151 B4
Skipsea Brough . . . 151 B4
Skipton 146 B3
Skipton-on-Swale .158 C2
Skipwith 149 D5
Skirbeck 117 A6
Skirbeck Quarter. . . 117 A6
Skirlaugh 151 D4
Skirling 195 C5
Skirmett 47 A5
Skirpenbeck 149 B6
Skirwith 165 B4
Skirza 281 B5
Skulamus 247 B5
Skullomie 277 B7
Skyborry Green 93 D6
Skye of Curr 253 D5
Skyreholme 147 A4
Slackhall 129 A5
Slackhead 267 C5
Slad 63 C4
Slade
  Devon 25 A6
  Pembs. 55 C5
Slade Green 50 B2
Slaggyford 177 D4
Slaidburn 145 B7
Slaithwaite 138 B3
Slaley 178 D1
Slamannan 207 C6
Slapton
  Bucks 67 A4
  Devon 8 C2
  Northants 82 C3
Slatepit Dale 130 C3
Slattocks 138 C1
Slaugham 35 D5
Slaughterford 44 B2
Slawston 99 B4
Sleaford
  Hants 33 B7
  Lincs 116 A3
Sleagill 164 D3
Sleapford 111 D5
Sledge Green 79 D6
Sledmere 150 A2
Sleightholme 166 D2
Sleights 160 A2
Slepe 16 B3
Slickly 281 B4
Sliddery 191 C5
Sligachan Hotel . . 246 B3
Slimbridge 62 C3
Slindon
  Staffs 112 B2
  W Sus 20 B2
Slinfold 35 C4
Sling 123 D6
Slingsby 159 D5
Slioch 255 C6
Slip End
  C Beds 67 B5
  Herts. 85 D4

Slipton 99 D6
Slitting Mill 112 D4
Slochd 253 D4
Slockavullin 213 C6
Sloley 121 C5
Sloothby 135 B4
Slough 48 B2
Slough Green 35 D5
Sluggan 253 D5
Slumbay 249 C5
Slyfield. 34 A2
Slyne 145 A4
Smailholm 197 C5
Smallbridge 138 B2
Smallburgh 121 C5
Smallburn
  Aberds 257 B5
  E Ayrs 194 D1
Small Dole 21 A5
Smalley 114 A2
Smallfield 35 B6
Small Hythe 37 C6
Smallridge 14 A3
Smannell 32 A2
Smardale 155 A6
Smarden 37 B6
Smarden Bell 37 B6
Smeatharpe 28 D1
Smeeth 38 B2
Smeeton Westerby . . 98 B3
Smercleit 286 E3
Smerral 275 A5
Smethwick 96 C3
Smirisary 235 C5
Smisby 114 D1
Smithfield 176 C2
Smith Green 145 B4
Smithincott 27 D5
Smith's Green 69 A5
Smithstown 261 C4
Smithton 252 B3
Smithy Green 128 B2
Smockington 98 C1
Smoogro 283 G4
Smythe's Green . . . 70 B3
Snaigow House . . . 231 D4
Snailbeach 94 A1
Snailwell 86 A2
Snainton 160 C3
Snaith 140 A4
Snape
  N Yorks 157 C6
  Suff 89 B4
Snape Green. 136 B2
Snarestone 97 A6
Snarford 133 A5
Snargate 38 C1
Snave 38 C2
Snead 93 B7
Sneath Common . . . 104 C2
Sneaton 160 A2
Sneatonthorpe 160 A3
Snelland 133 A5
Snelston 113 A5
Snettisham 118 B3
Sniseabhal 286 B3
Snitter 188 C3
Snitterby 142 D1
Snitterfield 81 B5
Snitton 94 D3
Snodhill 77 C7
Snodland 51 C3
Snowden Hill 139 C5
Snowdown 53 D4
Snowshill 80 D3
Snydale 140 B2
Soar
  Anglesey 122 C3
  Carms 58 C3
  Devon 7 D6
Soar-y-Mynydd 76 B1
Soberton 33 D5
Soberton Heath 33 D5
Sockbridge 164 C3
Sockburn 158 A2
Soham 102 D1
Soham Cotes 102 D1
Solas 287 G3
Soldon Cross 24 D4
Soldridge 33 B5
Sole Street
  Kent 38 A2
  Kent 50 C3
Solihull 97 D4
Sollers Dilwyn 78 B2
Sollers Hope 79 D4
Sollom 136 B3
Solva 54 B3
Somerby
  Leics 115 D5

Somerby continued
  Lincs 142 C2
Somercotes 131 D4
Somerford 17 B5
Somerford Keynes . . 63 D6
Somerley 19 B7
Somerleyton 105 B5
Somersal Herbert . . 113 B5
Somersby 134 B3
Somersham
  Cambs. 101 D5
  Suff 88 C1
Somerton
  Oxon 65 A5
  Som. 29 C4
Sompting 21 B4
Sonning 47 B5
Sonning Common . . 47 A5
Sonning Eye 47 B5
Sontley 110 A2
Sopley 17 B5
Sopwell 67 C6
Sopworth 44 A2
Sorbie 171 C6
Sordale 280 B3
Sorisdale 223 A5
Sorn 193 C5
Sornhill 193 B5
Sortat 281 B4
Sotby 134 B2
Sots Hole 133 C6
Sotterley 105 C5
Soudley 111 C6
Soughton 126 C2
Soulbury 66 A3
Soulby 165 D5
Souldern 82 D2
Souldrop 84 A1
Sound
  Ches E. 111 A5
  Shetland 285 H5
  Shetland 285 J6
Sound Heath 111 A5
Soundwell 43 B5
Sourhope 188 A1
Sourin 282 D5
Sourton 11 B6
Soutergate 153 B3
South Acre 119 D5
Southall 48 A4
South Allington 8 D1
South Alloa 208 A1
Southam
  Glos 63 A5
  Warks 81 A7
South Ambersham . 34 D2
Southampton 32 D3
South Anston 131 A5
South Ascot 48 C2
South Ballachulish . 237 D4
South Balloch 181 B5
South Bank 168 C3
South Barrow 29 C6
South Beach 106 C3
South Benfleet 51 A4
South Bersted 20 B2
Southborough 36 B3
Southbourne
  BCP. 17 B5
  W Sus 19 A6
South Brent 7 A5
South Brewham. . . . 29 B7
South Broomhill . . . 189 D5
Southburgh 103 A5
South Burlingham . 105 A4
Southburn. 150 B2
South Cadbury 29 C6
South Cairn 170 A1
South Carlton. 133 B4
South Cave 150 D2
South Cerney 63 D6
South Chard 14 A3
South Charlton . . . 189 A4
South Cheriton 29 C6
Southchurch 51 A6
South Cliffe 150 D1
South Clifton 132 B3
South
  Cockerington . . . 134 A3
South Cornelly 40 C3
Southcott 45 D5
Southcourt 66 C3
South Cove 105 C5
South Creagan . . . 227 B4
South Creake 119 C5
South Croxton 115 D4
South Croydon 49 C6
South Dalton 150 C2
South Darenth 50 C2
Southdean 187 C5

Southdene 136 D3
South Duffield 149 D5
Southease 22 B2
South Elkington. . . . 134 A3
South Elmsall 140 B2
Southend
  Argyll 190 E2
  W Berks 46 B3
  Wilts 45 B5
South End
  Bucks 66 A3
  Cumb 153 D3
  N Lincs 142 A3
Southend-on-Sea . . 51 A5
Southernden 37 B6
Southerndown 40 D3
Southerness. 174 C2
South Erradale. . . . 261 C4
Southery 102 B2
South Fambridge . . 70 D2
South Fawley 46 A1
South Ferriby 142 A1
Southfield 179 B4
Southfleet. 50 B3
South Garth 284 D7
South Garvan 236 B3
Southgate
  Ceredig. 75 A4
  London 68 D2
  Norf 120 C3
  Swansea 57 D5
South Glendale . . . 286 E3
South Godstone . . . 35 B6
South Gorley 31 D5
South Green
  Essex 69 D6
  Kent 51 C5
South-haa 284 E5
South Ham 47 D4
South Hanningfield . 70 D1
South Harting 33 D6
South Hatfield 68 C2
South Hayling 19 B6
South Hazelrigg . . . 199 C4
South Heath 67 C4
South Heighton 22 B2
South Hetton 167 A6
South Hiendley . . . 140 B1
South Hill 10 D4
South Hinksey 65 C6
South Hole 24 C3
South Holme 159 D5
South Holmwood . . 35 B4
South Hornchurch . . 50 A2
South Hykeham . . . 133 C4
South Hylton 179 D5
Southill 84 C3
South Kelsey. 142 D2
South Kessock . . . 252 B2
South Killingholme . 142 B3
South Kilvington . . 158 C3
South Kilworth. 98 C3
South Kirkby 140 B2
South Kirkton 245 B4
South Kiscadale . . 191 C6
South Kyme 117 A4
South Lancing 21 B4
Southleigh 14 B2
South Leigh 65 C4
South Leverton . . . 132 A2
South Littleton 80 C3
South Lopham 103 C6
South Luffenham . . 99 A6
South Malling 22 A2
South Marston. 45 A5
South Middleton . . 188 A2
South Milford 148 D3
South Millbrex . . . 256 B3
South Milton 7 C6
South Mimms 68 C2
Southminster 70 D3
South Molton 26 C2
Southmoor 65 D4
South Moreton 46 A3
South Mundham . . . 20 B1
South Muskham . . 132 D2
South Newbald . . . 150 D2
South Newington . . 81 D7
South Newton 31 B4
South Normanton . 131 D4
South Norwood 49 C6
South Nutfield 35 B6
South Ockendon . . . 50 A2
Southoe 84 A3
Southolt 88 A2
South Ormsby 134 B3
Southorpe 100 A2
South Otterington. . 158 C2
South Owersby . . . 142 D2
Southowram 139 A4

South Oxhey 67 D6
South Perrott. 15 A4
South Petherton . . . 28 D4
South Petherwin . . . 10 C4
South Pickenham . . 103 A4
South Pool 7 C6
Southport 136 B2
South Port 227 D5
Southpunds 285 L6
South Radworthy . . 26 B2
South Rauceby . . . 116 A3
South Raynham . . . 119 C5
Southrepps 121 B4
South Reston 135 A4
Southrey 133 C6
Southrop 64 C2
Southrope. 33 A5
South Runcton . . . 102 A2
South Scarle 132 C3
Southsea 19 B5
South Shian 226 B4
South Shields 179 C5
South Shore 144 D3
South Somercotes .143 D6
South Stainley 148 A2
South Stainmore . . 165 D6
South Stifford 50 B3
South Stoke
  Oxon 46 A3
  W Sus 20 B3
South Street
  E Sus. 22 A1
  Kent 52 C3
  Kent 52 D2
  London 36 A2
South Tawton 12 B1
South Thoresby . . . 135 B4
South Tidworth 31 A6
Southtown
  Norf 105 A6
  Orkney 283 H5
South Town 33 B5
South View 47 D4
Southwaite 164 A2
South Walsham . . . 121 D5
South Warnborough. 33 A6
Southwater 35 D4
Southwater Street . . 35 D4
Southway 29 A5
South Weald 69 D5
Southwell
  Dorset. 15 D6
  Notts. 132 D1
South Weston 66 D2
South Wheatley
  Corn 10 B3
  Notts. 132 A2
South Whiteness . . 285 J5
Southwick
  Hants 19 A5
  Northants 100 B2
  T&W 179 D5
  Wilts 44 D2
  W Sus 21 B5
South Widcombe . . 43 D4
South Wigston 98 B2
South Willingham . 134 A1
South Wingfield . . . 130 D3
South Witham 116 D2
Southwold 105 D6
South Wonston 32 B3
Southwood
  Norf 105 A4
  Som. 29 B5
South Woodham
  Ferrers 70 D2
South Wootton . . . 118 C3
South Wraxall 44 C2
South Zeal 12 B1
Soval Lodge 288 E4
Sowber Gate. 158 C2
Sowerby
  N Yorks 158 C3
  W Yorks 138 A3
Sowerby Bridge. . . 138 A3
Sowerby Row 164 B1
Sowood 138 B3
Sowton 13 B4
Soyal 264 A1
Spacey Houses. . . 148 B2
Spa Common 121 B4
Spadeadam Farm . 176 B3
Spalding 117 C5
Spaldington 149 D6
Spaldwick 100 D3
Spalford. 132 C3
Spanby 116 B3
Sparham 120 D3

Spark Bridge 154 C2
Sparkford 29 C6
Sparkhill 96 C3
Sparkwell 7 B4
Sparrow Green . . . 119 D6
Sparrowpit 129 A5
Sparsholt
  Hants 32 B3
  Oxon 46 A1
Spartylea 165 A6
Spaunton 159 C6
Spaxton 28 B2
Spean Bridge 239 D6
Spear Hill 21 A4
Speen
  Bucks 66 D3
  W Berks 46 C2
Speeton 161 D5
Speke 127 A4
Speldhurst 36 B3
Spellbrook 69 B4
Spelsbury 64 A4
Spelter 40 B3
Spencers Wood . . . 47 C5
Spennithorne 157 C5
Spennymoor 167 B5
Spetchley 80 B1
Spetisbury 16 A3
Spexhall 105 C4
Spey Bay 267 C4
Speybridge 253 D6
Speyview 254 B3
Spilsby 135 C4
Spindlestone 199 C5
Spinkhill 131 B4
Spinningdale 264 B2
Spirthill 44 B3
Spital Hill 140 D4
Spital in the Street .133 D4
Spithurst 22 A2
Spittal
  Dumfries. 171 B5
  E Loth 210 C1
  Highld 280 C3
  Northumb 198 A4
  Pembs. 55 B5
  Stirling 206 B3
Spittalfield 231 D5
Spittal of
  Glenmuick. 243 D6
Spittal of Glenshee .231 A5
Spixworth 120 D4
Splayne's Green . . . 36 D2
Spofforth 148 B2
Spondon 114 B2
Spon End 97 D6
Spon Green 126 C2
Spooner Row 104 B1
Sporle 119 D5
Spott 210 C3
Spratton 99 D4
Spreakley 34 A1
Spreyton 12 B1
Spridlington 133 A5
Springburn 205 B6
Springfield
  Dumfries. 175 B6
  Essex 69 C7
  Fife 220 C3
  Moray 253 A6
  W Mid 96 C3
Springhill 96 A2
Springholm 173 B6
Springkell 175 A5
Springside 192 B3
Springthorpe 132 A3
Spring Vale 139 C5
Spring Valley. 152 D3
Springwell 179 D4
Sproatley 151 D4
Sproston Green . . . 128 C2
Sprotbrough. 140 C3
Sproughton 88 C2
Sprouston 197 C6
Sprowston 120 D4
Sproxton
  Leics 115 C6
  N Yorks 159 C5
Spurstow 127 D5
Spynie 266 C3
Squires Gate. 144 D3
Srannda 287 F5
Sronphadruig
  Lodge 229 A6
Stableford
  Shrops 95 B5
  Staffs 112 B2
Stacey Bank 139 D5

Stackhouse 146 A2
Stackpole 55 E5
Staddiscombe 7 B4
Staddlethorpe 141 A6
Stadhampton 65 D7
Stadhlaigearraidh 286 C3
Staffield 164 A3
Staffin 259 B4
Stafford 112 C3
Stagsden 84 C1
Stainburn
Cumb 162 B3
N Yorks 147 C6
Stainby 116 C2
Staincross 139 B6
Staindrop 166 C4
Staines-upon-Thames 48 B3
Stainfield
Lincs 116 C3
Lincs 133 B6
Stainforth
N Yorks 146 A2
S Yorks 140 B4
Staining 144 D3
Stainland 138 B3
Stainsacre 160 A3
Stainsby 131 C4
Stainton
Cumb 154 C4
Cumb 164 C2
Durham 166 D3
Mbro 168 D2
N Yorks 157 B5
S Yorks 140 D3
Stainton by Langworth 133 B5
Staintondale 160 B3
Stainton le Vale 142 D3
Stainton with Adgarley 153 C3
Stair
Cumb 163 B5
E Ayrs 193 C4
Stairhaven 171 B4
Staithes 169 D5
Stakeford 179 A4
Stake Pool 144 C4
Stalbridge 30 D1
Stalbridge Weston 29 D7
Stalham 121 C5
Stalham Green 121 C5
Stalisfield Green 51 D6
Stallingborough 142 B3
Stalling Busk 156 C3
Stalmine 144 C3
Stalybridge 138 D2
Stambourne 86 D3
Stambourne Green 86 D3
Stamford 100 A2
Stamford Bridge
Ches W 127 C4
E Yorks 149 B6
Stamfordham 178 B2
Stanah 163 C6
Stanborough 68 B2
Stanbridge
C Beds 67 A4
Dorset 17 A4
Stanbrook 79 C6
Stanbury 147 D4
Stand
Gtr Man 137 C6
N Lanark 207 D5
Standburn 208 C2
Standeford 96 A2
Standen 37 B6
Standford 33 B7
Standingstone 162 A3
Standish 137 B4
Standlake 65 C4
Standon
Hants 32 C3
Herts 68 A3
Staffs 112 B2
Stane 194 A3
Stanfield 119 C6
Stanford
C Beds 84 C3
Kent 38 B3
Stanford Bishop 79 B4
Stanford Bridge 79 A5
Stanford Dingley 46 B3
Stanford in the Vale 64 D4
Stanford-le-Hope 50 A3
Stanford on Avon 98 D2
Stanford on Soar 114 C3
Stanford on Teme 79 A5
Stanford Rivers 69 C5
Stanfree 131 B4
Stanghow 169 D4
Stanground 100 B4
Stanhoe 119 B5
Stanhope
Borders 195 D6
Durham 166 B2
Stanion 99 C6
Stanley
Derbys 114 A2
Durham 178 D3
Lancs 136 C3
Perth 219 A6
Staffs 129 D4
W Yorks 139 A6
Stanley Common 114 A2
Stanley Gate 136 C3
Stanley Hill 79 C4
Stanlow 127 B4
Stanmer 21 B6
Stanmore
Hants 32 C3
London 67 D6
W Berks 46 B2
Stannergate 220 A4
Stanningley 147 D6
Stannington
Northumb 179 B4
S Yorks 130 A3
Stansbatch 78 A1
Stansfield 86 B3
Stanstead 87 C4
Stanstead Abbotts 68 B3
Stansted 50 C3
Stansted Airport 69 A5
Stansted Mountfitchet 69 A5
Stanton
Glos 80 D3
Mon 61 A5
Northumb 178 A3
Staffs 113 A5
Suff 103 D5
Stanton by Bridge 114 C1
Stanton-by-Dale 114 B2
Stanton Drew 43 C4
Stanton Fitzwarren 64 D2
Stanton Harcourt 65 C5
Stanton Hill 131 C4
Stanton in Peak 130 C2
Stanton Lacy 94 D2
Stanton Long 94 B3
Stanton-on-the-Wolds 115 B4
Stanton Prior 43 C5
Stanton St Bernard 45 C4
Stanton St John 65 C6
Stanton St Quintin 44 B3
Stanton Street 87 A5
Stanton under Bardon 114 D2
Stanton upon Hine Heath 111 C4
Stanton Wick 43 C5
Stanwardine in the Fields 110 C3
Stanwardine in the Wood 110 C3
Stanway
Essex 70 A3
Glos 80 D3
Stanway Green 104 D3
Stanwell 48 B3
Stanwell Moor 48 B3
Stanwick 100 D1
Stanwick-St-John 167 D4
Stanwix 175 C7
Stanydale 285 H4
Staoinebrig 286 C3
Stape 159 B6
Stapehill 17 A4
Stapeley 111 A5
Stapenhill 113 C6
Staple
Kent 53 D4
Som 27 A6
Staple Cross 37 D5
Staplefield 35 D5
Staple Fitzpaine 28 D2
Stapleford
Cambs 85 B6
Herts 68 B3
Leics 115 D6
Lincs 132 D3
Notts 114 B2
Wilts 31 B4
Stapleford Abbotts 69 D5
Stapleford Tawney 69 D5
Staplegrove 28 C2
Staplehay 28 C2
Staplehurst 37 B5
Staplers 18 C4
Stapleton
Bristol 43 B5
Cumb 176 B3
Hereford 78 A1
Leics 98 B1
N Yorks 167 D5
Shrops 94 A2
Som 29 C4
Stapley 28 D1
Staploe 84 A3
Staplow 79 C4
Star
Fife 220 D3
Pembs 73 C5
Som 42 D3
Stara 282 E3
Starbeck 148 B2
Starbotton 156 D3
Starcross 13 C4
Stareton 97 D6
Starkholmes 130 D3
Starlings Green 85 D6
Starston 104 C3
Startforth 166 D3
Startley 44 A3
Stathe 28 C3
Stathern 115 B5
Station Town 168 B2
Staughton Green 84 A3
Staughton Highway 84 A3
Staunton
Glos 62 A3
Glos 62 B1
Staunton in the Vale 115 A6
Staunton on Arrow 78 A1
Staunton on Wye 78 C1
Staveley
Cumb 154 B3
Cumb 154 C2
Derbys 131 B4
N Yorks 148 A2
Staverton
Devon 8 A1
Glos 63 A4
Northants 82 A2
Wilts 44 C2
Staverton Bridge 63 A4
Stawell 28 B3
Staxigoe 281 C5
Staxton 160 D4
Staylittle 91 C6
Staynall 144 C3
Staythorpe 132 D2
Stean 157 D4
Stearsby 159 D5
Steart 28 A2
Stebbing 69 A6
Stebbing Green 69 A6
Stedham 34 D1
Steele Road 186 D4
Steen's Bridge 78 B3
Steep 33 C6
Steeple
Dorset 16 C3
Essex 70 C3
Steeple Ashton 44 D3
Steeple Aston 65 A5
Steeple Barton 65 A5
Steeple Bumpstead 86 C2
Steeple Claydon 66 A1
Steeple Gidding 100 C3
Steeple Langford 31 B4
Steeple Morden 85 C4
Steep Marsh 33 C6
Steeton 147 C4
Stein 258 C2
Steinmanhill 256 B2
Stelling Minnis 38 A3
Stemster 280 B3
Stemster House 280 B3
Stenalees 5 B5
Stenhousemuir 207 B6
Stenigot 134 A2
Stenness 284 F4
Stenscholl 259 B4
Stenso 282 E4
Stenson 114 C1
Stenton
E Loth 210 C3
Fife 209 A5
Stenwith 115 B6
Stepaside 56 B1
Stepping Hill 129 A4
Steppingley 84 D2
Stepps 205 B6
Sterndale Moor 129 C6
Sternfield 89 A4
Sterridge 25 A6
Stert 44 D4
Stetchworth 86 B2
Stevenage 68 A2
Stevenston 204 D2
Steventon
Hants 32 A4
Oxon 65 D5
Stevington 84 B1
Stewartby 84 C2
Stewarton
Argyll 190 D2
E Ayrs 205 D4
Stewkley 66 A3
Stewton 134 A3
Steyne Cross 19 C5
Steyning 21 A4
Steynton 55 D5
Stibb 24 D3
Stibbard 120 C1
Stibb Cross 25 D5
Stibb Green 45 C6
Stibbington 100 B2
Stichill 197 C6
Sticker 5 B4
Stickford 134 D3
Sticklepath 12 B1
Stickney 134 D3
Stiffkey 119 A6
Stifford's Bridge 79 C5
Stillingfleet 149 C4
Stillington
N Yorks 149 A4
Stockton 167 C6
Stilton 100 C3
Stinchcombe 62 D3
Stinsford 15 B7
Stirchley 95 A5
Stirkoke House 281 C5
Stirling
Aberds 257 B6
Stirling 207 A5
Stisted 70 A1
Stithians 4 D2
Stittenham 264 C2
Stivichall 97 D6
Stixwould 134 C1
Stoak 127 B4
Stobieside 193 B6
Stobo 195 C6
Stoborough 16 C3
Stoborough Green 16 C3
Stobshiel 210 D1
Stobswood 189 D5
Stock 69 D6
Stockbridge 32 B2
Stockbury 51 C5
Stockcross 46 C2
Stockdalewath 164 A1
Stockerston 99 B5
Stock Green 80 B2
Stockheath 19 A6
Stockiemuir 206 B3
Stockingford 97 B6
Stocking Pelham 69 A4
Stockland 14 A2
Stockland Bristol 28 A2
Stockleigh English 12 A3
Stockleigh Pomeroy 12 A3
Stockley 44 C4
Stocklinch 28 D3
Stockport 138 D1
Stocksbridge 139 D5
Stocksfield 178 C2
Stockton
Hereford 78 A3
Norf 105 B4
Shrops 93 A6
Shrops 95 B5
Warks 82 A1
Wilts 30 B3
Stockton Heath 127 A6
Stockton-on-Tees 168 D2
Stockton on Teme 79 A5
Stockton on the Forest 149 B5
Stock Wood 80 B3
Stodmarsh 53 C4
Stody 120 B2
Stoer 270 B3
Stoford
Som 29 D5
Wilts 31 B4
Stogumber 27 B5
Stogursey 28 A2
Stoke
Devon 24 C3
Hants 19 A6
Hants 46 D2
Stoke *continued*
Medway 51 B5
Suff 88 C2
Stoke Abbott 15 A4
Stoke Albany 99 C5
Stoke Ash 104 D2
Stoke Bardolph 115 A4
Stoke Bliss 79 A4
Stoke Bruerne 83 C4
Stoke by Clare 86 C3
Stoke-by-Nayland 87 D5
Stoke Canon 13 B4
Stoke Charity 32 B3
Stoke Climsland 11 D4
Stoke D'Abernon 35 A4
Stoke Doyle 100 C2
Stoke Dry 99 B5
Stoke Farthing 31 C4
Stoke Ferry 102 B3
Stoke Fleming 8 C2
Stokeford 16 C2
Stoke Gabriel 8 B2
Stoke Gifford 43 B5
Stoke Golding 97 B6
Stoke Goldington 83 C5
Stoke Green 48 A2
Stokeham 132 B2
Stoke Hammond 66 A3
Stoke Heath 111 C5
Stoke Holy Cross 104 A3
Stokeinteignhead 13 D4
Stoke Lacy 79 C4
Stoke Lyne 65 A6
Stoke Mandeville 66 B3
Stokenchurch 66 D2
Stoke Newington 49 A6
Stokenham 8 C2
Stoke on Tern 111 C5
Stoke-on-Trent 112 A2
Stoke Orchard 63 A5
Stoke Poges 48 A2
Stoke Prior
Hereford 78 B3
Worcs 80 A2
Stoke Rivers 26 B1
Stoke Rochford 116 C2
Stoke Row 47 A4
Stoke St Gregory 28 C3
Stoke St Mary 28 C2
Stoke St Michael 29 A6
Stoke St Milborough 94 C3
Stokesay 94 C2
Stokesby 121 D6
Stokesley 158 A4
Stoke sub Hamdon 29 D4
Stoke Talmage 66 D1
Stoke Trister 30 C1
Stoke Wake 16 A1
Stolford 28 A2
Stondon Massey 69 C5
Stone
Bucks 66 B2
Glos 62 D2
Kent 38 C1
Kent 50 B2
Staffs 112 B3
S Yorks 131 A5
Worcs 95 D6
Stone Allerton 42 D3
Ston Easton 43 D5
Stone Bridge Corner 101 A4
Stonebroom 131 D4
Stone Chair 139 A4
Stone Cross
E Sus 22 B4
Kent 53 D5
Stone-edge Batch 42 B3
Stoneferry 151 D4
Stonefield 194 A1
Stonegate
E Sus 37 D4
N Yorks 159 A6
Stonegrave 159 D5
Stonehaugh 177 B5
Stonehaven 245 D5
Stonehouse
Glos 63 C4
Northumb 177 D4
S Lanark 194 B2
Stone House 155 C6
Stoneleigh 97 D6
Stonely 84 A3
Stoner Hill 33 C6
Stonesby 115 C6
Stonesfield 65 B4
Stone's Green 71 A5
Stone Street
Kent 36 A3
Suff 87 D5
Stone Street *continued*
Suff 105 C4
Stonethwaite 163 C5
Stoneybreck 285 R4
Stoneyburn 208 D2
Stoney Cross 31 D6
Stoneygate
Aberds 257 C5
Leicester 98 A3
Stoneyhills 70 D3
Stoneykirk 170 B2
Stoney Middleton 130 B2
Stoney Stanton 98 B1
Stoney Stoke 29 B7
Stoney Stratton 29 B6
Stoney Stretton 94 A1
Stoneywood
Aberdeen 245 A5
Falk 207 B5
Stonganess 284 C7
Stonham Aspal 88 B2
Stonnall 96 A3
Stonor 47 A5
Stonton Wyville 99 B4
Stony Cross 79 C5
Stonyfield 264 C2
Stony Stratford 83 C4
Stoodleigh 27 D4
Stopes 130 A2
Stopham 20 A3
Stopsley 67 A6
Stores Corner 89 C4
Storeton 126 A3
Stornoway 288 D5
Storridge 79 C5
Storrington 20 A3
Storrs 154 B2
Storth 154 C3
Storwood 149 C6
Stotfield 266 B3
Stotfold 84 D4
Stottesdon 95 C4
Stoughton
Leics 98 A3
Sur 34 A2
W Sus 33 D7
Stoul 235 A6
Stoulton 80 C2
Stourbridge 96 C2
Stourpaine 16 A2
Stourport on Severn 95 D6
Stour Provost 30 C1
Stour Row 30 C2
Stourton
Staffs 95 C6
Warks 81 D5
Wilts 30 B1
Stourton Caundle 29 D7
Stove
Orkney 282 D7
Shetland 285 L6
Stoven 105 C5
Stow
Borders 196 B3
Lincs 116 B3
Lincs 132 A3
Stow Bardolph 102 A2
Stow Bedon 103 B5
Stowbridge 102 A2
Stow cum Quy 85 A7
Stowe 93 D7
Stowe-by-Chartley 112 C4
Stowe Green 62 C1
Stowell 29 C6
Stowford 11 C5
Stowlangtoft 87 A5
Stow Longa 100 D3
Stow Maries 70 D2
Stowmarket 87 B6
Stow-on-the-Wold 64 A2
Stowting 38 A3
Stowupland 87 B6
Straad 203 B5
Strachan 244 C3
Stradbroke 104 D3
Stradishall 86 B3
Stradsett 102 A2
Stragglethorpe 133 D4
Straid 180 B3
Straith 183 D6
Straiton
Edin 209 D5
S Ayrs 181 A5
Straloch
Aberds 256 D3
Perth 230 B4
Stramshall 113 B4
Strang 152 D3
Stranraer 170 A2
Stratfield Mortimer 47 C4

Stratfield Saye 47 C4
Stratfield Turgis 47 D4
Stratford 49 A6
Stratford St Andrew 89 A4
Stratford St Mary 87 D6
Stratford Sub Castle 31 B5
Stratford Tony 31 C4
Stratford-upon-Avon 81 B4
Strath
Highld 261 C4
Highld 281 C4
Strathan
Highld 238 C3
Highld 270 B3
Highld 277 B6
Strathaven 194 B2
Strathblane 205 A5
Strathcanaird 271 D4
Strathcarron 249 B6
Strathcoil 225 C5
Strathdon 243 A6
Strathellie 269 C5
Strathkinness 221 C4
Strathmashie House 240 C3
Strathmiglo 220 C2
Strathmore Lodge 280 D3
Strathpeffer 251 A6
Strathrannoch 263 C5
Strathtay 230 C3
Strathvaich Lodge 263 C5
Strathwhillan 191 B6
Strathy 279 B4
Strathyre 217 C5
Stratton
Corn 10 A3
Dorset 15 B6
Glos 63 C6
Stratton Audley 65 A7
Stratton on the Fosse 43 D5
Stratton St Margaret 45 A5
Stratton St Michael 104 B3
Stratton Strawless 120 C4
Stravithie 221 C5
Streat 21 A6
Streatham 49 B6
Streatley
C Beds 67 A5
W Berks 46 A3
Street
Lancs 145 B5
N Yorks 159 A6
Som 29 B4
Street Dinas 110 B2
Street End
Kent 52 D3
W Sus 20 C1
Street Gate 179 D4
Streethay 113 D5
Streetlam 157 B7
Streetly 96 B3
Street Lydan 110 B3
Streetly End 86 C2
Strefford 94 C2
Strelley 114 A3
Strensall 149 A5
Stretcholt 28 A2
Strete 8 C2
Stretford 137 D7
Strethall 85 D6
Stretham 101 D7
Strettington 20 B1
Stretton
Ches W 127 D4
Derbys 130 C3
Rutland 116 D2
Staffs 112 D2
Staffs 113 C6
Warr 127 A6
Stretton Grandison 79 C4
Stretton-on-Dunsmore 97 D7
Stretton-on-Fosse 81 D5
Stretton Sugwas 78 C2
Stretton under Fosse 98 C1
Stretton Westwood 94 B3
Strichen 269 D4
Strines 129 A4
Stringston 28 A1
Strixton 83 A6
Stroat 62 D1
Stromeferry 249 C5
Stromemore 249 C5
Stromness 283 G3
Stronaba 239 D6
Stronachlachar 216 C4
Stronchreggan 237 B4
Stronchrubie 271 C5
Strone
Argyll 215 D4
Highld 239 D5
Highld 252 D1
Invclyd 204 A2
Stronmilchan 227 D6
Strontian 236 C2
Strood 51 C4
Strood Green
Sur 35 B5
W Sus 34 D3
W Sus 35 C4
Stroud
Glos 63 C4
Hants 33 C6
Stroud Green 70 D2
Stroxton 116 B2
Struan
Highld 246 A2
Perth 230 B2
Strubby 135 A4
Strumpshaw 104 A4
Strutherhill 194 B2
Struy 251 C5
Stryt-issa 110 A1
Stuartfield 257 B4
Stubbington 19 A4
Stubbins 137 B6
Stubbs Cross 38 B1
Stubbs Green 105 B4
Stubb's Green 104 B3
Stubhampton 30 D3
Stub Place 153 A1
Stubton 115 A6
Stuckgowan 215 B6
Stuckton 31 D5
Stud Green 48 B1
Studham 67 B5
Studland 17 C4
Studley
Warks 80 A3
Wilts 44 B3
Studley Roger 157 D6
Stump Cross 85 C7
Stuntney 102 D1
Sturbridge 112 B2
Sturmer 86 C2
Sturminster Marshall 16 A3
Sturminster Newton 30 D1
Sturry 52 C3
Sturton 142 C1
Sturton by Stow 132 A3
Sturton le Steeple 132 A2
Stuston 104 D2
Stutton
N Yorks 148 C3
Suff 88 D2
Styal 128 A3
Styrrup 140 D4
Suainebost 288 A6
Suardail 288 D5
Succoth
Aberds 255 C5
Argyll 215 B5
Suckley 79 B5
Suckquoy 283 J5
Sudborough 99 C6
Sudbourne 89 B5
Sudbrook
Lincs 116 A2
Mon 43 A4
Sudbrooke 133 B5
Sudbury
Derbys 113 B5
London 49 A4
Suff 87 C4
Suddie 252 A2
Sudgrove 63 C5
Suffield
Norf 120 B4
N Yorks 160 B3
Sugnall 112 B1
Suladale 258 C3
Sulaisiadar 288 D6
Sulby 152 B3
Sulgrave 82 C2
Sulham 47 B4
Sulhamstead 47 C4
Sulland 282 C6
Sullington 20 A3
Sullom 284 F5
Sullom Voe Oil Terminal 284 F5
Sully 41 E6
Sumburgh 285 N6
Summer Bridge 147 A6
Summercourt 4 B3
Summerfield 119 B4
Summergangs 151 D4
Summer-house 167 D5
Summerleaze 42 A3
Summersdale 20 B1
Summerseat 137 B6
Summertown 65 C6
Summit 138 C2
Sunbury-on-Thames 48 C4
Sundaywell 183 D6
Sunderland
Argyll 200 B2
Cumb 163 A4
T&W 179 D5
Sunderland Bridge 167 B5
Sundhope 196 D2
Sundon Park 67 A5
Sundridge 36 A2
Sunipol 224 A2
Sunk Island 143 B4
Sunningdale 48 C2
Sunninghill 48 C2
Sunningwell 65 C5
Sunniside
Durham 166 B4
T&W 179 D4
Sunnyhurst 137 A5
Sunnylaw 207 A5
Sunnyside 36 C1
Sunton 45 D6
Surbiton 49 C4
Surby 152 D2
Surfleet 117 C5
Surfleet Seas End 117 C5
Surlingham 104 A4
Sustead 120 B3
Susworth 141 C6
Sutcombe 24 D4
Suton 104 B1
Sutors of Cromarty 265 D4
Sutterby 134 B3
Sutterton 117 B5
Sutton
Cambs 101 D6
C Beds 84 C4
Kent 39 A5
London 49 C5
Mers 136 D4
Norf 121 C5
Notts 115 B5
Notts 132 A1
N Yorks 140 A2
Oxon 65 C5
Pboro 100 B2
Shrops 95 C5
Shrops 111 B5
Som 29 B6
Staffs 111 C6
Suff 88 C4
Sur 34 B4
S Yorks 140 B3
W Sus 20 A2
Sutton at Hone 50 B2
Sutton Bassett 99 B4
Sutton Benger 44 B3
Sutton Bonington 114 C3
Sutton Bridge 118 C1
Sutton Cheney 97 A7
Sutton Coldfield 96 B4
Sutton Courtenay 65 D6
Sutton Crosses 118 C1
Sutton Grange 157 D6
Sutton Green 34 A3
Sutton Howgrave 157 D7
Sutton In Ashfield 131 D4
Sutton-in-Craven 147 C4
Sutton Ings 151 D4
Sutton in the Elms 98 B2
Sutton Lane Ends 129 B4
Sutton Leach 136 D4
Sutton Maddock 95 A5
Sutton Mallet 28 B3
Sutton Mandeville 30 C3
Sutton Manor 136 D4
Sutton Montis 29 C6
Sutton on Hull 151 D4
Sutton on Sea 135 A5
Sutton-on-the-Forest 149 A4
Sutton on the Hill 113 B6
Sutton on Trent 132 C2
Sutton St Edmund 117 D6
Sutton St James 117 D6
Sutton St Nicholas 78 C3
Sutton Scarsdale 131 C4
Sutton Scotney 32 B3
Sutton under Brailes 81 D6
Sutton-under-Whitestonecliffe 158 C3
Sutton upon Derwent 149 C6
Sutton Valence 37 B6
Sutton Veny 30 A2
Sutton Waldron 30 D2
Sutton Weaver 127 B5
Sutton Wick 43 D4
Swaby 134 B3
Swadlincote 113 D7
Swaffham 103 A4
Swaffham Bulbeck 86 A1
Swaffham Prior 86 A1
Swafield 121 B4
Swainby 158 A3
Swainshill 78 C2
Swainsthorpe 104 A3
Swainswick 43 C6
Swalcliffe 81 D6
Swalecliffe 52 C3
Swallow 142 C3
Swallowcliffe 30 C3
Swallowfield 47 C5
Swallownest 131 A4
Swallows Cross 69 D6
Swanage 17 D4
Swanbister 283 G4
Swanbourne 66 A3
Swan Green
Ches W 128 B2
Suff 104 D3
Swanland 142 A1
Swanley 50 C2
Swanley Village 50 C2
Swanmore 33 D4
Swannington
Leics 114 D2
Norf 120 D3
Swanscombe 50 B3
Swansea = Abertawe 57 C6
Swanton Abbott 121 C4
Swanton Morley 120 D2
Swanton Novers 120 B2
Swanton Street 37 A6
Swanwick
Derbys 131 D4
Hants 18 A4
Swarby 116 A3
Swardeston 104 A3
Swarister 284 E7
Swarkestone 114 C1
Swarland 189 C4
Swarland Estate 189 C4
Swarthmoor 153 C3
Swathwick 130 C3
Swaton 116 B4
Swavesey 85 A5
Sway 18 B1
Swayfield 116 C2
Swaythling 32 D3
Sweet Green 79 A4
Sweetham 12 B3
Sweethouse 5 A5
Sweffling 88 A4
Swepstone 114 D1
Swerford 81 D6
Swettenham 128 C3
Swetton 157 D5
Swffryd 60 D4
Swiftsden 37 D5
Swilland 88 B2
Swillington 148 D2
Swimbridge 25 C7
Swimbridge Newland 25 B7
Swinbrook 64 B3
Swinderby 132 C3
Swindon
Glos 63 A5
Staffs 95 B6
Swindon 45 A5
Swine 151 D4
Swinefleet 141 A5
Swineshead
Bedford 84 A2
Lincs 117 A5
Swineshead Bridge 117 A5
Swiney 275 A6
Swinford
Leics 98 D2
Oxon 65 C5
Swingate 114 A3
Swingfield Minnis 39 A4
Swingfield Street 39 A4
Swinhoe 189 A5
Swinhope 143 D4
Swining 284 G6
Swinithwaite 156 C4
Swinnow Moor 147 D6
Swinscoe 113 A5
Swinside Hall 187 B6
Swinstead 116 C3
Swinton
Borders 198 B2
Gtr Man 137 C6
N Yorks 157 D6
N Yorks 159 D6
S Yorks 140 D2
Swintonmill 198 B2
Swithland 114 D3
Swordale 264 D1
Swordland 238 C1
Swordly 278 B3
Sworton Heath 128 A1
Swyddffynnon 75 B5
Swynnerton 112 B2
Swyre 15 C5
Sychtyn 92 A3
Syde 63 B5
Sydenham
London 49 B6
Oxon 66 C2
Sydenham Damerel 11 D5
Syderstone 119 B5
Sydling St Nicholas 15 B6
Sydmonton 46 D2
Syerston 115 A5
Syke 138 B1
Sykehouse 140 B4
Sykes 145 B6
Syleham 104 D3
Sylen 57 B5
Symbister 285 G7
Symington
S Ayrs 192 B3
S Lanark 195 C4
Symondsbury 14 B4
Symonds Yat 62 B1
Synod Inn 73 A7
Syre 278 D2
Syreford 63 A6
Syresham 82 C3
Syston
Leics 115 D4
Lincs 116 A2
Sytchampton 79 A6
Sywell 83 A5

T

Taagan 262 D2
Tàbost 288 A6
Tabost 288 F4
Tackley 65 A5
Tacleit 288 D2
Tacolneston 104 B2
Tadcaster 148 C3
Taddington 129 B6
Taddiport 25 D5
Tadley 47 C4
Tadlow 85 C4
Tadmarton 81 D6
Tadworth 35 A5
Tafarnau-bach 60 B3
Tafarn-y-gelyn 126 C1
Taff's Well 41 C6
Tafolwern 91 B6
Tai 124 C2
Taibach 40 C2
Tai-bach 109 C6
Taigh a Ghearraidh 287 G2
Tai-mawr 109 A4
Tain
Highld 264 B3
Highld 280 B4
Tainant 110 A1
Tainlon 107 A4
Tairbeart = Tarbert 288 G2
Tai'r-Bull 60 A1
Tairgwaith 59 D4
Tai-Ucha 125 D5
Takeley 69 A5
Takeley Street 69 A5
Talachddu 77 D4
Talacre 125 A6
Talardd 108 C3
Talaton 13 B5
Talbenny 54 C4
Talbot Green 41 C5
Talbot Village 17 B4
Tale 13 A5
Talerddig 92 A3
Talgarreg 74 C3
Talgarth 77 D5
Talisker 246 A2
Talke 128 D3
Talkin 176 D3
Talladale 261 C6
Talla Linnfoots 195 D6
Tallarn Green 110 A3
Tallentire 163 A4
Talley 58 B3
Tallington 100 A2
Talmine 277 B6
Talog 73 D6
Talsarn 59 C4
Tal-sarn 75 C4
Talsarnau 107 C6
Talskiddy 4 A4
Talwrn
Anglesey 123 C4
Wrex 110 A1
Tal-y-bont
Ceredig 91 D4
Conwy 124 C2
Gwyn 107 D5
Gwyn 123 C6
Talybont-on-Usk 60 A3
Tal-y-cafn 124 B2
Talygarn 41 C5
Talyllyn 60 A3
Tal-y-llyn 91 B5
Talysarn 107 A4
Talywain 61 C4
Tal-y-wern 91 B6
Tame Bridge 158 A4
Tamerton Foliot 6 A3
Tamworth 97 A5
Tandem 139 B4
Tanden 37 C7
Tandridge 35 A6
Tanerdy 73 D7
Tanfield 178 D3
Tanfield Lea 178 D3
Tangasdal 286 G2
Tangiers 55 C5
Tangley 46 D1
Tanglwst 73 C6
Tangmere 20 B2
Tangwick 284 F4
Tan Hinon 91 D6
Tankersley 139 C6
Tankerton 52 C3
Tan-lan
Conwy 124 C2
Gwyn 107 B6
Tannach 281 D5
Tannachie 245 D4
Tannadice 232 C2
Tannington 88 A3
Tansley 130 D3
Tansley Knoll 130 C3
Tansor 100 B2
Tantobie 178 D3
Tanton 168 D3
Tanworth-in-Arden 96 D4
Tan-y-bwlch 107 B6
Tan-y-fron 125 C4
Tan-y-graig
Anglesey 123 C5
Gwyn 106 C3
Tanygrisiau 107 B6
Tan-y-groes 73 B5
Tan-y-pistyll 109 C5
Tan-yr-allt 107 A4
Tanyrhydiau 75 B6
Taobh a Chaolais 286 E3
Taobh a' Ghlinne 288 F4
Taobh a Thuath Loch Aineort 286 D3
Taobh a Tuath Loch Baghasdail 286 D3
Taobh Tuath 287 F4
Taplow 48 A2
Tapton 130 B3
Tarbat House 264 C3
Tarbert
Argyll 202 B3
Argyll 202 C1
Argyll 213 D4
Tarbert = Tairbeart 288 G2
Tarbet
Argyll 215 B6
Highld 238 C1
Highld 276 D2
Tarbock Green 127 A4
Tarbolton 193 C4
Tarbrax 195 A5
Tardebigge 80 A3
Tarfside 232 A2
Tarland 244 B1
Tarleton 136 A3
Tarlogie 264 B3
Tarlscough 136 B3
Tarlton 63 D5

Tarnbrook.........145 B5
Tarporley.........127 C5
Tarr..............27 B6
Tarrant Crawford....16 A3
Tarrant Gunville.....30 D3
Tarrant Hinton......30 D3
Tarrant Keyneston...16 A3
Tarrant Launceston..16 A3
Tarrant Monkton....16 A3
Tarrant Rawston....16 A3
Tarrant Rushton....16 A3
Tarrel............265 B4
Tarring Neville.....22 B2
Tarrington.........79 C4
Tarsappie.........219 B6
Tarskavaig........247 D4
Tarves............256 C3
Tarvie
  Highld...........251 A6
  Perth............230 B4
Tarvin............127 C4
Tasburgh..........104 B3
Tasley............95 B4
Taston............65 A4
Tatenhill..........113 C6
Tathall End........83 C5
Tatham............145 A6
Tathwell..........134 A3
Tatling End........48 A3
Tatsfield..........36 A2
Tattenhall.........127 D4
Tattenhoe.........83 D5
Tatterford.........119 C5
Tattersett.........119 B5
Tattershall........134 D2
Tattershall Bridge..134 D1
Tattershall Thorpe..134 D2
Tattingstone.......88 D2
Tatworth..........14 A3
Taunton...........28 C2
Taverham..........120 D3
Tavernspite........56 A1
Tavistock..........11 D5
Taw Green.........12 B1
Tawstock..........25 C6
Taxal.............129 B5
Tay Bridge........220 B4
Tayinloan.........202 D1
Taymouth Castle...230 D1
Taynish...........213 D5
Taynton
  Glos.............62 A3
  Oxon............64 B3
Taynuilt...........227 C5
Tayport...........221 B4
Tayvallich.........213 D5
Tealby............142 D3
Tealing...........220 A4
Teangue...........247 D5
Teanna Mhachair..287 H2
Tebay............155 A5
Tebworth..........67 A4
Tedburn St Mary....12 B3
Teddington
  Glos.............80 D2
  London...........49 B4
Tedstone Delamere..79 B4
Tedstone Wafre.....79 B4
Teeton............98 D3
Teffont Evias......30 B3
Teffont Magna......30 B3
Tegryn............73 C5
Teigh.............115 D6
Teigncombe........12 C1
Teigngrace........12 D3
Teignmouth........13 D4
Telford............95 A4
Telham............23 A5
Tellisford.........44 D2
Telscombe.........22 B2
Telscombe Cliffs...22 B1
Templand.........184 D3
Temple
  Corn............10 D2
  Glasgow.........205 B5
  Midloth.........196 A2
Temple Balsall.....97 D5
Temple Bar
  Carms...........57 A5
  Ceredig.........75 C4
Temple Cloud.......43 D5
Temple Combe......29 C7
Temple Ewell......39 A4
Temple Grafton.....80 B4
Temple Guiting.....64 A1
Templehall........209 A5
Temple Herdewyke..81 B6
Temple Hirst......140 A4

Temple
  Normanton.......131 C4
Temple Sowerby....165 C4
Templeton
  Devon...........26 D3
  Pembs...........55 C7
Templeton Bridge...26 D3
Templetown.......178 D3
Tempsford.........84 B3
Tenbury Wells.....78 A3
Tenby =
  Dinbych-y-Pysgod...56 B1
Tendring..........71 A5
Tendring Green.....71 A5
Ten Mile Bank.....102 B2
Tenston...........282 F3
Tenterden.........37 C6
Terling...........70 B1
Ternhill..........111 B5
Terregles Banks....174 A2
Terrick...........66 C3
Terrington........159 D5
Terrington
  St Clement......118 D2
Terrington St John..118 D2
Teston............37 A5
Testwood..........32 D2
Tetbury...........63 D4
Tetbury Upton.....63 D4
Tetchill..........110 B2
Tetcott...........10 B4
Tetford...........134 B3
Tetney...........143 C5
Tetney Lock.......143 C5
Tetsworth.........66 C1
Tettenhall.........96 B1
Teuchan..........257 C5
Teversal..........131 C4
Teversham.........85 B6
Teviothead........186 C3
Tewel............245 D5
Tewin............68 B2
Tewkesbury........80 D1
Teynham..........51 C6
Thackthwaite......163 B4
Thainston.........233 A4
Thakeham.........21 A4
Thame............66 C2
Thames Ditton.....49 C4
Thames Haven.....51 A4
Thamesmead.......50 A1
Thanington........52 D3
Thankerton.......195 C4
Tharston..........104 B2
Thatcham.........46 C3
Thatto Heath......136 D4
Thaxted...........86 D2
The Aird..........259 C4
Theakston........157 C7
Thealby..........141 B6
Theale
  Som.............29 A4
  W Berks.........47 B4
The Arms.........103 B4
Thearne..........150 D3
The Bage.........77 C6
The Balloch......218 C3
The Barony.......282 E3
Theberton.........89 A5
The Bog...........94 B1
The Bourne.......33 A7
The Braes........247 A4
The Broad........78 A2
The Butts.........30 A1
The Camp
  Glos.............63 C5
  Herts...........67 C6
The Chequer......110 A3
The City..........66 D2
The Common.......31 B6
The Craigs........263 A6
The Cronk........152 B3
Theddingworth....98 C3
Theddlethorpe All
  Saints..........135 A4
Theddlethorpe
  St Helen........135 A4
The Dell.........105 B5
The Den..........204 C3
The Eals.........177 A5
The Eaves........62 C2
The Flatt.........176 B3
The Four Alls.....111 B5
The Garths.......284 B8
The Green
  Cumb...........153 B2
  Wilts...........30 B2
The Grove........174 A2
The Hall.........284 D8
The Haven........34 C3

The Heath
  Norf............120 C3
  Suff............88 D2
The Hill.........153 B2
The Howe
  Cumb...........154 C3
  IoM............152 E1
The Hundred......78 A3
Thelbridge Barton..26 D2
The Lee...........67 C4
The Lhen.........152 A3
Thelnetham.......103 D6
Thelveton.........104 C2
Thelwall.........127 A6
The Marsh
  Powys...........93 B7
  Wilts...........45 A4
Themelthorpe.....120 C2
The Middles......179 D4
The Moor..........37 D5
The Mumbles
  = Y Mwmbwls....57 D6
The Murray.......205 C6
The Neuk.........245 C4
Thenford..........82 C2
The Oval..........43 C6
The Pole of Itlaw..268 D1
The Quarry........62 D3
Therfield.........85 D5
The Rhos..........55 C6
The Rock..........95 A4
The Ryde..........68 C2
The Sands.........34 B1
The Stocks........37 D7
Thetford
  Lincs...........116 D4
  Norf............103 C4
The Throat........47 C6
The Vauld.........78 C3
The Wyke.........95 A5
Theydon Bois......68 D4
Thickwood.........44 B2
Thimbleby
  Lincs...........134 C2
  N Yorks.........158 B3
Thingwall........126 A3
Thirdpart.........204 D1
Thirlby..........158 C3
Thirlestane.......197 B4
Thirn............157 C5
Thirsk...........158 C3
Thirtleby.........151 D4
Thistleton
  Lancs...........144 D4
  Rutland........116 D2
Thistley Green.....102 D2
Thixendale.......150 A1
Thockrington.....178 B1
Tholomas Drove...101 A5
Tholthorpe.......148 A3
Thomas Chapel....55 D7
Thomas Close.....164 A2
Thomastown......255 C6
Thompson.........103 B4
Thomshill........266 D3
Thong............50 B3
Thongsbridge.....139 C4
Thoralby.........156 C4
Thoresway........142 D3
Thorganby
  Lincs...........143 D4
  N Yorks.........149 C5
Thorgill.........159 B6
Thorington.......105 D5
Thorington Street..87 D4
Thorlby..........146 B3
Thorley..........69 B4
Thorley Street
  Herts...........69 B4
  IoW............18 C2
Thormanby.......158 D3
Thornaby-on-Tees.168 D2
Thornage.........120 B2
Thornborough
  Bucks...........83 D4
  N Yorks.........157 D6
Thornbury
  Devon...........11 A5
  Hereford........79 B4
  S Glos..........62 D2
  W Yorks........147 D5
Thornby..........98 D3
Thorncliffe......129 D5
Thorncombe
  Dorset..........14 A3
  Dorset..........16 A2
Thorncombe Street.34 B3
Thorncote Green...84 C3
Thorncross........18 C3
Thorndon.........88 A2

Thorndon Cross.....11 B6
Thorne...........141 B4
Thorner..........148 C2
Thorne St Margaret..27 C5
Thorney
  Notts...........132 B3
  Pboro..........101 A4
Thorney Crofts....143 A4
Thorney Green.....87 A6
Thorney Hill......17 B5
Thorney Toll......101 A5
Thornfalcon.......28 C2
Thornford.........29 D6
Thorngumbald....143 A4
Thornham.........119 A4
Thornham Magna..104 D2
Thornham Parva..104 D2
Thornhaugh......100 A2
Thornhill
  Cardiff..........41 C6
  Cumb...........162 D3
  Derbys.........130 A1
  Dumfries........183 C6
  Soton...........32 D3
  Stirling.........207 A4
  W Yorks.........139 B5
Thornhill Edge....139 B5
Thornhill Lees....139 B5
Thornholme......151 A4
Thornley
  Durham.........166 B4
  Durham.........167 B6
Thornliebank.....205 C5
Thorns...........86 B3
Thornsett........129 A5
Thorns Green.....128 A2
Thornthwaite
  Cumb...........163 B5
  N Yorks.........147 B5
Thornton
  Angus..........232 D1
  Bucks...........83 D4
  E Yorks.........149 C6
  Fife............209 A5
  Lancs...........144 C3
  Leics...........98 A1
  Lincs...........134 C2
  Mbro...........168 D2
  Mers...........136 C2
  Northumb.......198 B3
  Pembs..........55 D5
  W Yorks.........147 D5
Thornton Curtis...142 B2
Thorntonhall.....205 C5
Thornton Heath....49 C6
Thornton Hough...126 A3
Thornton in Craven 146 C3
Thornton-le-Beans 158 B2
Thornton-le-Clay..149 A5
Thornton-le-Dale..160 C2
Thornton le Moor..142 D2
Thornton-le-Moor.158 C2
Thornton-le-
  Moors..........127 B4
Thornton-le-
  Street..........158 C3
Thorntonloch.....211 C4
Thorntonpark.....198 B3
Thornton Rust....156 C3
Thornton Steward.157 C5
Thornton Watlass..157 C6
Thornwood
  Common.........69 C4
Thornydykes.....197 B5
Thoroton........115 A5
Thorp Arch.......148 C3
Thorpe
  Derbys.........129 D6
  E Yorks.........150 C2
  Lincs...........135 A4
  Norf............105 B5
  Notts...........115 A5
  N Yorks.........147 A4
  Sur............48 C3
Thorpe Abbotts...104 D2
Thorpe Acre......114 C3
Thorpe Arnold....115 C5
Thorpe Audlin....140 B2
Thorpe Bassett...160 D2
Thorpe Bay.......51 A6
Thorpe by Water...99 B5
Thorpe Common....88 D2
Thorpe Constantine.97 A5
Thorpe Culvert...135 C4
Thorpe End.......121 D4
Thorpe Fendykes..135 C4
Thorpe Green
  Essex...........71 A5
  Suff............87 B5
Thorpe Hesley....140 D1

Thorpe in Balne...140 B3
Thorpe in the
  Fallows.........133 A4
Thorpe Langton....99 B4
Thorpe Larches...167 C6
Thorpe-le-Soken...71 A5
Thorpe le Street..150 C1
Thorpe Malsor.....99 D5
Thorpe Mandeville.82 C2
Thorpe Market....120 B4
Thorpe Marriot...120 D3
Thorpe Morieux....87 B5
Thorpeness.......89 B5
Thorpe on the Hill.133 C4
Thorpe St Andrew..104 A3
Thorpe St Peter...135 C4
Thorpe Salvin....131 A5
Thorpe Satchville..115 D5
Thorpe Thewles...168 C2
Thorpe Tilney....133 D6
Thorpe Underwood 148 B3
Thorpe Waterville.100 C2
Thorpe Willoughby.149 D5
Thorrington.......71 A4
Thorverton........13 A4
Thrandeston......104 D2
Thrapston........100 D1
Thrashbush.......207 D5
Threapland
  Cumb...........163 A4
  N Yorks.........146 A3
Threapwood
  Ches W.........110 A3
  Staffs..........112 A4
Three Ashes.......61 A7
Three Bridges.....35 C5
Three Burrows.....4 C2
Three Chimneys...37 C6
Three Cocks.......77 D5
Three Crosses.....57 C5
Three Cups Corner.36 D4
Threehammer
  Common.........121 D5
Three Holes......101 A7
Threekingham....116 B3
Three Leg Cross...37 C4
Three Legged Cross.17 A4
Threemile Cross...47 C5
Threemilestone....4 C2
Threemiletown....208 C3
Three Oaks.......23 A6
Threlkeld.........163 B6
Threshfield......146 A3
Thrigby..........121 D6
Thringarth.......166 C2
Thringstone......114 D2
Thrintoft.........157 B7
Thriplow..........85 C6
Throckenholt....101 A5
Throcking.........85 D5
Throckley........178 C3
Throckmorton.....80 C2
Throphill........178 A3
Thropton........188 C3
Throsk...........207 A6
Throwleigh........12 B1
Throwley.........52 D1
Thrumpton.......114 B3
Thrumster........281 D5
Thrunton........188 B3
Thrupp
  Glos............63 C4
  Oxon...........65 B5
Thrushelton......11 C5
Thrussington.....115 D4
Thruxton
  Hants...........32 A1
  Hereford........78 D2
Thrybergh.......140 D2
Thulston........114 B2
Thundergay......202 D3
Thundersley.....51 A4
Thundridge......68 B3
Thurcaston......114 D3
Thurcroft.......131 A4
Thurgarton
  Norf............120 B3
  Notts...........115 A4
Thurgoland.......139 C5
Thurlaston
  Leics...........98 B2
  Warks..........98 D1
Thurlbear........28 C2
Thurlby
  Lincs...........116 D4
  Lincs...........133 D4
Thurleigh........84 B2
Thurlestone.......7 C5
Thurloxton.......28 B2
Thurlstone......139 C5

Thurlton.........105 B5
Thurlwood.......128 D3
Thurmaston.......98 A3
Thurnby..........98 A3
Thurne..........121 D6
Thurnham
  Kent............37 A6
  Lancs..........145 B4
Thurning
  Norf............120 C2
  Northants.......100 C2
Thurnscoe.......140 C2
Thurnscoe East...140 C2
Thursby.........175 C5
Thursford.......120 B1
Thursley.........34 C2
Thurso..........280 B3
Thurso East......280 B3
Thurstaston.....126 A2
Thurston........87 A5
Thurstonfield....175 C5
Thurstonland....139 B4
Thurton.........104 A4
Thurvaston......113 B6
Thuxton.........103 A6
Thwaite
  N Yorks.........156 B2
  Suff............88 A2
Thwaites........147 C5
Thwaite St Mary..104 B4
Thwaites Brow...147 C4
Thwing..........160 D3
Tibbermore......219 B5
Tibberton
  Glos............62 A3
  Telford.........111 C5
  Worcs..........80 B2
Tibenham........104 C2
Tibshelf........131 C4
Tibthorpe.......150 B2
Ticehurst........37 C4
Tichborne.......33 B4
Tickencote......100 A1
Tickenham.......42 B3
Tickhill.........140 D3
Ticklerton.......94 B2
Ticknall.........114 C1
Tickton.........150 C3
Tidcombe........45 C6
Tiddington
  Oxon...........66 C1
  Warks..........81 B5
Tidebrook........36 C4
Tideford..........6 B2
Tideford Cross....6 A2
Tidenham........62 D1
Tideswell.......129 B6
Tidmarsh........47 B4
Tidmington......81 D5
Tidpit...........31 D4
Tidworth........31 A6
Tiers Cross......55 C5
Tiffield.........82 B3
Tifty...........256 B2
Tigerton........232 B3
Tigh-na-Blair....218 C2
Tighnabruaich...203 A4
Tighnafiline.....261 B5
Tigley...........7 A6
Tilbrook.........84 A2
Tilbury..........50 B3
Tilbury Juxta Clare.86 C3
Tile Cross.......97 C4
Tile Hill........97 D5
Tilehurst........47 B4
Tilford.........34 B1
Tilgate.........35 C5
Tilgate Forest Row.35 C5
Tillathrowie.....255 C5
Tilley..........111 C4
Tillicoultry.....208 A2
Tillingham.......70 C3
Tillington
  Hereford........78 C2
  W Sus..........34 D2
Tillington Common.78 C2
Tillyarblet......232 B3
Tillybirloch.....244 B3
Tillycorthie.....257 C4
Tillydrine.......244 C3
Tillyfour........244 A2
Tillyfourie......244 A3
Tillygarmond....244 C3
Tillygreig.......256 D3
Tillykerrie......256 D3
Tilmanstone.....53 D5
Tilney All Saints..118 D2
Tilney High End..118 D2
Tilney St Lawrence.118 D2
Tilshead.........31 A4

Tilstock....111 B4
Tilston....127 D4
Tilstone Fearnall...127 C5
Tilsworth....67 A4
Tilton on the Hill....99 A4
Timberland....133 D6
Timbersbrook....128 C3
Timberscombe....27 A4
Timble....147 B5
Timperley....128 A2
Timsbury
  Bath....43 D5
  Hants....32 C2
Timsgearraidh....287 A5
Timworth Green....87 A4
Tincleton....16 B1
Tindale....176 D4
Tingewick....82 D3
Tingley....139 A5
Tingrith....84 D2
Tingwall....282 E4
Tinhay....11 C4
Tinshill....147 D6
Tinsley....140 D2
Tintagel....9 C6
Tintern Parva....62 C1
Tintinhull....29 D5
Tintwistle....138 D3
Tinwald....184 D3
Tinwell....100 A2
Tipperty....257 D4
Tipsend....101 B7
Tipton....96 B2
Tipton St John....13 B5
Tiptree....70 B2
Tirabad....59 A5
Tiraghoil....224 D2
Tirley....63 A4
Tirphil....41 A6
Tirril....164 C3
Tir-y-dail....57 A6
Tisbury....30 C3
Tisman's Common....34 C3
Tissington....130 D1
Titchberry....24 C3
Titchfield....18 A4
Titchmarsh....100 D2
Titchwell....119 A4
Tithby....115 B4
Titley....78 A1
Titlington....189 B4
Titsey....36 A2
Tittensor....112 B2
Tittleshall....119 C5
Tiverton
  Ches W....127 C5
  Devon....27 D4
Tivetshall
  St Margaret....104 C2
Tivetshall St Mary....104 C2
Tividale....96 B2
Tivy Dale....139 C5
Tixall....112 C3
Tixover....99 A6
Toab
  Orkney....283 G6
  Shetland....285 M5
Toadmoor....130 D3
Tobermory....225 A4
Toberonochy....213 B5
Tobha Mor....286 C3
Tobhtarol....288 D2
Tobson....288 D2
Tocher....256 C1
Tockenham....44 B4
Tockenham Wick....44 A4
Tockholes....137 A5
Tockington....43 A5
Tockwith....148 B3
Todber....30 C2
Todding....94 D2
Toddington
  C Beds....67 A5
  Glos....80 D3
Todenham....81 D5
Todhills....175 B6
Todlachie....244 A3
Todmorden....138 A2
Todrig....186 B3
Todwick....131 A4
Toft
  Cambs....85 B5
  Lincs....116 D3
Toft Hill
  Durham....167 C4
  Lincs....134 C2
Toft Monks....105 B6
Toft next Newton...133 A5
Toftrees....119 C5
Tofts....281 B5

Toftwood....120 D1
Togston....189 C5
Tokavaig....247 C5
Tokers Green....47 B5
Tolastadh a
  Chaolais....288 D2
Tolastadh bho
  Thuath....288 C6
Tolland....27 B6
Tollard Royal....30 D3
Toll Bar....140 C3
Tollbar End....97 D6
Toll End....96 B2
Toller Fratrum....15 B5
Toller Porcorum....15 B5
Tollerton
  Notts....115 B4
  N Yorks....148 A4
Tollesbury....70 B3
Tolleshunt D'Arcy....70 B3
Tolleshunt Major...70 B3
Toll of Birness....257 C5
Tolm....288 D5
Tolpuddle....16 B1
Tolvah....241 C6
Tolworth....49 C4
Tomatin....253 D4
Tombreck....252 C2
Tomchrasky....239 A6
Tomdoun....239 B5
Tomich
  Highld....251 D5
  Highld....264 C2
Tomich House....252 B1
Tomintoul
  Aberds....242 C4
  Moray....243 A4
Tomnaven....255 C5
Tomnavoulin....254 D3
Tonbridge....36 B3
Tondu....40 C3
Tonfanau....90 B3
Tong
  Shrops....95 A5
  W Yorks....147 D6
Tonge....114 C2
Tongham....34 B1
Tongland....173 C4
Tong Norton....95 A5
Tongue....277 C6
Tongue End....117 D4
Tongwynlais....41 C6
Tonna....40 B2
Ton-Pentre....41 B4
Tonwell....68 B3
Tonypandy....41 B4
Tonyrefail....41 C5
Toot Baldon....65 C6
Toothill....32 D2
Toot Hill....69 C5
Topcliffe....158 D3
Topcroft....104 B3
Topcroft Street....104 B3
Top of Hebers....138 C1
Toppesfield....86 D3
Toppings....137 B6
Topsham....13 C4
Torbay....8 B3
Torbeg....191 C5
Torboll Farm....264 A3
Torbrex....207 A5
Torbryan....8 A2
Torcross....8 C2
Tore....252 A2
Torinturk....202 B3
Torksey....132 B3
Torlum....286 A3
Torlundy....237 B5
Tormarton....43 B6
Tormisdale....200 C1
Tormitchell....181 B4
Tormore....191 B4
Tornagrain....252 B3
Tornahaish....243 B5
Tornaveen....244 B3
Torness....252 D1
Toronto....167 B4
Torpenhow....163 A5
Torphichen....208 C2
Torphins....244 B3
Torpoint....6 B3
Torquay....8 A3
Torquhan....196 B3
Torran
  Argyll....214 B1
  Highld....248 B2
  Highld....264 C3
Torrance....205 A6
Torrans....224 D3
Torranyard....204 D3

Torre....8 A3
Torridon....249 A6
Torridon House....249 A5
Torrin....247 B4
Torrisdale....278 B2
Torrisdale-Square .190 B3
Torrish....274 C3
Torrisholme....145 A4
Torroble....272 D3
Torry
  Aberdeen....245 B6
  Aberds....255 C5
Torryburn....208 B3
Torterston....257 B5
Torthorwald....174 A3
Tortington....20 B3
Tortworth....62 D3
Torvaig....259 D4
Torver....154 B1
Torwood....207 B6
Torworth....131 A6
Tosberry....24 C3
Toscaig....249 C4
Toseland....84 A4
Tosside....146 B1
Tostock....87 A5
Totaig
  Highld....249 D5
  Highld....258 C2
Tote....259 D4
Totegan....279 B4
Tothill....135 A4
Totland....18 C2
Totnes....8 A2
Toton....114 B3
Totronald....223 B4
Totscore....258 B3
Tottenham....68 D3
Tottenhill....118 D3
Tottenhill Row....118 D3
Totteridge....68 D2
Totternhoe....67 A4
Tottington....137 B6
Totton....32 D2
Touchen End....48 B1
Tournaig....261 B5
Toux....269 D4
Tovil....37 A5
Toward....203 B6
Towcester....82 C3
Towednack....2 B2
Tower End....118 D3
Towersey....66 C2
Towie
  Aberds....244 A1
  Aberds....268 C3
Towiemore....255 B4
Tow Law....166 B4
Townend....205 A4
Town End
  Cambs....101 B6
  Cumb....154 C3
Towngate....116 D4
Townhead
  Cumb....164 B3
  Dumfries....173 D4
  S Ayrs....181 A4
  S Yorks....139 C4
Townhead of
  Greenlaw....173 B5
Townhill....208 B4
Town Row....36 C3
Townsend
  Bucks....66 C2
  Herts....67 C6
Townshend....2 B3
Town Yetholm....187 A7
Towthorpe....149 B5
Towton....148 D3
Towyn....125 B4
Toxteth....126 A3
Toynton All Saints.134 C3
Toynton Fen Side..134 C3
Toynton St Peter...135 C4
Toy's Hill....36 A2
Trabboch....193 C4
Traboe....3 C5
Tradespark
  Highld....253 A4
  Orkney....283 G5
Trafford Park....137 D6
Trallong....59 C6
Tranent....209 C7
Tranmere....126 A3
Trantlebeg....279 C4
Trantlemore....279 C4
Tranwell....178 A3
Trapp....57 A6
Traprain....210 C2
Traquair....196 C2

Trawden....146 D3
Trawsfynydd....108 B2
Trealaw....41 B5
Treales....144 D4
Trearddur....122 C2
Treaslane....258 C3
Trebanog....41 B5
Trebanos....40 A2
Trebartha....10 D3
Trebarwith....9 C6
Trebetherick....9 D5
Treborough....27 B5
Trebudannon....4 A3
Trebullett....10 D4
Treburley....10 D4
Trebyan....5 A5
Trecastle....59 C5
Trecenydd....41 C6
Trecwn....55 A5
Trecynon....41 A4
Tredavoe....2 C2
Treddiog....55 B4
Tredegar....60 C3
Tredegar Newydd
  =New Tredegar....41 A6
Tredington
  Glos....63 A5
  Warks....81 C5
Tredinnick....9 D5
Tredomen....77 D5
Tredunnock....61 D5
Tredustan....77 D5
Treen....2 C1
Treeton....131 A4
Trefaldwyn
  =Montgomery....93 B6
Trefasser....72 C1
Trefdraeth....123 C4
Trefdraeth
  =Newport....72 C3
Trefecca....77 D5
Trefechan....90 D3
Trefeglwys....92 B3
Trefenter....75 B5
Treffgarne....55 B5
Treffynnon....54 B4
Treffynnon
  =Holywell....126 B1
Trefgarn Owen....55 B4
Trefil....60 B3
Trefilan....75 C4
Trefin....54 A4
Treflach....110 C1
Trefnanney....109 D7
Trefnant....125 B5
Trefonen....110 C1
Trefor
  Anglesey....122 B3
  Gwyn....106 B3
Treforest....41 C5
Trefriw....124 C2
Tref-y-Clawdd
  =Knighton
Trefynwy
  =Monmouth....61 B7
Tregadillett....10 C3
Tregaian....123 C4
Tregare....61 B6
Tregaron....75 C5
Tregarth....123 D6
Tregeare....10 C3
Tregeiriog....109 B6
Tregele....122 A3
Tre-Gibbon....60 C1
Tregidden....3 C5
Treglemais....54 B4
Tregole....10 B2
Tregonetha....5 A4
Tregony....4 C4
Tregoss....5 A4
Tregoyd....77 D6
Tregroes....73 B7
Tregurrian....4 A3
Tregynon....93 B4
Trehafod....41 B5
Treharris....41 B5
Treherbert....40 B4
Trekenner....10 D4
Treknow....9 C6
Trelan....3 D5
Trelash....10 B2
Trelassick....4 B3
Trelawnyd....125 B5
Trelech....73 C5
Treleddyd-fawr....54 B3
Trelewis....41 B6
Treligga....9 C6
Trelights....9 D5

Trelill....9 D6
Trelissick....4 D3
Trellech....61 C7
Trelleck Grange....61 C6
Trelogan....125 A6
Trelystan....93 A6
Tremadog....107 B5
Tremail....10 C2
Tremain....73 B5
Tremaine....10 C3
Tremar....6 A1
Trematon....6 B2
Tremeirchion....125 B5
Trenance....4 A3
Trenarren....5 C5
Trench....111 D5
Treneglos....10 C3
Trenewan....5 B6
Trent....29 D5
Trentham....112 A2
Trentishoe....26 A1
Trent Vale....112 A2
Treoes....40 D4
Treorchy =Treorci...41 B4
Treorci =Treorchy..41 B4
Tre'r-ddôl....91 C4
Trerulefoot....6 B2
Tresaith....73 A5
Tresawle....4 C3
Trescott....95 B6
Trescowe....2 B3
Tresham....62 D3
Tresillian....4 C3
Tresinwen....72 B1
Treskinnick Cross...10 B3
Tresmeer....10 C3
Tresparrett....10 B2
Tresparrett Posts...10 B2
Tressait....230 B2
Tresta
  Shetland....284 D8
  Shetland....285 H5
Treswell....132 B2
Tre-Taliesin....91 C4
Trethosa....4 B4
Trethurgy....5 B5
Tretio....54 B3
Tretire....62 A1
Tretower....60 A3
Treuddyn....126 D2
Trevalga....10 C1
Trevalyn....126 D3
Trevanson....9 D5
Trevarren....4 A4
Trevarrian....4 A3
Trevarrick....5 C4
Tre-vaughan....73 D7
Trevaughan....56 A1
Treveighan....9 D6
Trevellas....4 B2
Treverva....4 D2
Trevethin....61 C4
Trevigro....6 A2
Treviscoe....4 B4
Trevone....9 D4
Trewarmett....9 C6
Trewassa....10 C2
Trewellard....2 B1
Trewen....10 C3
Trewennack....3 C4
Trewern....110 D1
Trewethern....9 D6
Trewidland....6 B1
Trewint
  Corn....10 B2
  Corn....10 C3
Trewithian....4 D3
Trewoofe....2 C2
Trewoon....5 B4
Treworga....4 C3
Treworlas....4 D3
Tre-wyn....61 A5
Treyarnon....9 D4
Treyford
  W Sus....20 A1
  W Sus....33 D7
Trezaise....5 B4
Ty'r-felin-isaf....124 C3
Triangle....138 A3
Triffleton....55 B5
Trimdon....167 B6
Trimdon Colliery....167 B6
Trimdon Grange....167 B6
Trimingham....121 B4
Trimley Lower
  Street....88 D3
Trimley St Martin..88 D3
Trimley St Mary....88 D3
Trimpley....95 D5
Trimsaran....57 B4

Trimstone....25 A5
Trinafour....229 B6
Trinant....41 A7
Tring....67 B4
Tring Wharf....67 B4
Trinity
  Angus....233 B4
  Jersey....6
Trisant....75 A6
Trislaig....237 B4
Trispen....4 B3
Tritlington....189 D5
Trochry....230 D3
Trodigal....190 C2
Troed-rhiwdalar....76 B3
Troedyraur....73 B6
Troedyrhiw....41 A5
Tromode....152 D3
Trondavoe....284 F5
Troon
  Corn....3 B4
  S Ayrs....192 B3
Trosaraidh....286 E3
Trossachs Hotel....217 D5
Troston....103 D4
Trottiscliffe....50 C3
Trotton....34 D1
Troutbeck
  Cumb....154 A3
  Cumb....164 C1
Troutbeck Bridge...154 A3
Trowbridge....44 D2
Trowell....114 B2
Trow Green....62 C1
Trowle Common....44 D2
Trowley Bottom....67 B5
Trows....197 C5
Trowse Newton....104 A3
Trudoxhill....30 A1
Trull....28 C2
Trumaisgear-
  raidh....287 G3
Trumpan....258 B2
Trumpet....79 D4
Trumpington....85 B6
Trunch....121 B4
Trunnah....144 C3
Truro....4 C3
Trusham....12 C3
Trusley....113 B6
Trusthorpe....135 A5
Trysull....95 B6
Tubney....65 D5
Tuckenhay....8 B2
Tuckhill....95 C5
Tuckingmill....3 A4
Tuddenham
  St Martin....88 C2
Tuddenham....88 C2
Tudeley....36 B4
Tudhoe....167 B5
Tudorville....62 A1
Tudweiliog....106 C2
Tuesley....34 B2
Tuffley....63 B4
Tufton
  Hants....32 A3
  Pembs....55 B6
Tugby....99 A4
Tugford....94 C3
Tullibardine....218 C4
Tullibody....207 A6
Tullich
  Argyll....214 A3
  Highld....252 D2
Tullich Muir....264 C3
Tulliemet....230 C3
Tulloch
  Aberds....233 A5
  Aberds....256 C3
  Perth....219 B5
Tulloch Castle....264 D1
Tullochgorm....214 C2
Tulloes....232 D3
Tullybannocher....218 B2
Tullybelton....219 A5
Tullyfergus....231 D6
Tullymurdoch....231 C5
Tullynessle....244 A2
Tumble....57 A5
Tumby Woodside...134 D2
Tummel Bridge....229 C6
Tunga....288 D5
Tunstall
  E Yorks....151 D6
  Kent....51 C5
  Lancs....155 D5
  Norf....105 A5

Tunstall *continued*
N Yorks 157 B6
Stoke 128 D3
Suff 89 B4
T&W 179 D5
Tunstead
Derbys 129 B6
Gtr Man 138 C3
Norf 121 C4
Tunworth 33 A5
Tupsley 78 C3
Tupton 130 C3
Turgis Green 47 D4
Turin 232 C3
Turkdean 64 B2
Tur Langton 99 B4
Turleigh 44 C2
Turn 137 B7
Turnastone 78 D1
Turnberry 192 E2
Turnditch 113 A6
Turners Hill 35 C6
Turners Puddle 16 B2
Turnford 68 C3
Turnhouse 209 C4
Turnworth 16 A2
Turriff 268 D2
Turton Bottoms 137 B6
Turves 101 B5
Turvey 83 B6
Turville 66 D2
Turville Heath 66 D2
Turweston 82 D3
Tushielaw 185 A6
Tutbury 113 C6
Tutnall 96 D2
Tutshill 62 D1
Tuttington 120 C4
Tutts Clump 46 B3
Tuxford 132 B2
Twatt
Orkney 282 E3
Shetland 285 H5
Twechar 207 C4
Tweedmouth 198 A3
Tweedsmuir 195 D5
Twelve Heads 4 C2
Twemlow Green 128 C2
Twenty 117 C4
Twerton 43 C6
Twickenham 49 B4
Twigworth 63 A4
Twineham 21 A5
Twinhoe 43 D6
Twinstead 87 D4
Twinstead Green 87 D4
Twiss Green 137 D5
Twiston 146 C2
Twitchen
Devon 26 B2
Shrops 94 D1
Two Bridges 11 D7
Two Dales 130 C2
Two Mills 126 B3
Twycross 97 A6
Twyford
Bucks 66 A1
Derbys 114 C1
Hants 32 C3
Leics 115 D5
Lincs 116 C2
Norf 120 C2
Wokingham 47 B5
Twyford Common 78 D3
Twynholm 173 C4
Twyning 80 D1
Twyning Green 80 D2
Twynllanan 59 C4
Twynmynydd 57 A6
Twyn-y-Sheriff 61 C6
Twywell 99 D6
Tyberton 78 D1
Tyburn 96 B4
Tycroes 57 A6
Tycrwyn 109 D6
Tyddewi = *St David's* 54 B3
Tydd Gote 118 D1
Tydd St Giles 118 D1
Tydd St Mary 118 D1
Tyddyn-mawr 107 B5
Ty-draw 124 D3
Tye Green
Essex 69 C4
Essex 70 A1
Essex 86 D1
Ty-hen
Carms 73 D6
Gwyn 106 C1
Tyldesley 137 C5
Tyler Hill 52 C3
Tylers Green 67 D4
Tylorstown 41 B5
Tylwch 92 C3
Ty-mawr 123 B4
Ty Mawr 58 A2
Ty Mawr Cwm 108 A4
Ty-nant
Conwy 109 A4
Gwyn 108 C4
Tyncelyn 75 B5
Tyndrum 216 A3
Tyneham 16 C2
Tynehead 196 A2
Tynemouth 179 C5
Tyne Tunnel 179 C5
Tynewydd 40 B4
Tyninghame 210 C3
Tynron 183 C6
Tyn-y-celyn 109 B6
Tyn-y-coed 110 C1
Tyn-y-fedwen 109 B6
Tyn-y-ffridd 109 B6
Tynygongl 123 B5
Tynygraig 75 B5
Tyn-y-graig 76 B4
Ty'n-y-groes 124 B2
Ty'n-y-maes 123 D6
Tyn-y-pwll 123 B4
Ty'n-yr-eithin 75 B5
Tyrie 269 C4
Tyringham 83 C5
Tythecott 25 D5
Tythegston 40 D3
Tytherington
Ches E 129 B4
S Glos 43 A5
Som 30 A1
Wilts 30 A3
Tytherleigh 14 A3
Ty-uchaf 109 C5
Tywardreath 5 B5
Tywyn
Conwy 124 B2
Gwyn 90 B3

U

Uachdar 286 A3
Uags 249 C4
Ubbeston Green 104 D4
Ubley 43 D4
Uckerby 157 A6
Uckfield 36 D2
Uckington 63 A5
Uddingston 207 D4
Uddington 194 C3
Udimore 23 A6
Udny Green 256 D3
Udny Station 257 D4
Udston 194 A1
Udstonhead 194 B2
Uffcott 45 B5
Uffculme 27 D5
Uffington
Lincs 100 A2
Oxon 45 A7
Shrops 111 D4
Ufford
Pboro 100 A2
Suff 88 B3
Ufton 81 A6
Ufton Nervet 47 C4
Ugadale 190 C3
Ugborough 7 B5
Uggeshall 105 C5
Ugglebarnby 160 A2
Ughill 139 D5
Ugley 69 A5
Ugley Green 69 A5
Ugthorpe 169 D5
Uidh 286 G2
Uig
Argyll 215 D4
Highld 258 B3
Highld 258 C1
Uigen 287 A5
Uigshader 259 D4
Uisken 224 E2
Ulbster 281 D5
Ulceby
Lincs 135 B4
N Lincs 142 B3
Ulceby Skitter 142 B3
Ulcombe 37 B6
Uldale 163 A5
Uley 62 D3
Ulgham 189 D5
Ullapool 262 A3
Ullenhall 80 A4
Ullenwood 63 B5
Ulleskelf 148 C4
Ullesthorpe 98 C2
Ulley 131 A4
Ullingswick 78 C3
Ullinish 246 A2
Ullock 162 B3
Ulnes Walton 136 B4
Ulpha 153 A2
Ulrome 151 B4
Ulsta 284 E6
Ulva House 224 C3
Ulverston 154 D1
Ulwell 17 C4
Umberleigh 25 C7
Unapool 271 A5
Unasary 286 D3
Underbarrow 154 B3
Undercliffe 147 D5
Underhoull 284 C7
Underriver 36 A3
Underwood 131 D4
Undy 42 A3
Unifirth 285 H4
Union Cottage 245 C5
Union Mills 152 D3
Union Street 37 C5
Unstone 130 B3
Unstone Green 130 B3
Unthank
Cumb 164 B2
Cumb 165 A4
Unthank End 164 B2
Upavon 45 D5
Up Cerne 15 A6
Upchurch 51 C5
Upcott 78 B1
Upend 86 B2
Up Exe 13 A4
Upgate 120 D3
Uphall 208 C3
Uphall Station 208 C3
Upham
Devon 12 A3
Hants 32 C4
Uphampton 79 A6
Up Hatherley 63 A5
Uphill 42 D2
Up Holland 136 C4
Uplawmoor 205 C4
Upleadon 62 A3
Upleatham 168 D4
Uplees 52 C1
Uploders 15 B5
Uplowman 27 D5
Uplyme 14 B3
Up Marden 33 D6
Upminster 50 A2
Up Nately 47 D4
Upnor 51 B4
Upottery 14 A2
Upper Affcot 94 C2
Upper Ardchronie 264 B2
Upper Arley 95 C5
Upper Arncott 65 B7
Upper Astrop 82 D2
Upper Badcall 276 D2
Upper Basildon 46 B3
Upper Beeding 21 A4
Upper Benefield 100 C1
Upper Bighouse 279 C4
Upper Boddington 82 B1
Upper Borth 90 D4
Upper Boyndlie 269 C4
Upper Brailes 81 D6
Upper Breakish 247 B5
Upper Breinton 78 C2
Upper Broadheath 79 B6
Upper Broughton 115 C4
Upper Bucklebury 46 C3
Upper Burnhaugh 245 C5
Upperby 175 C7
Upper Caldecote 84 C3
Upper Catesby 82 B2
Upper Chapel 76 C4
Upper Church
Village 41 C5
Upper Chute 45 D6
Upper Clatford 32 A2
Upper Clynnog 107 B4
Upper
Cumberworth 139 C5
Upper Cwmbran 61 D4
Upper Dallachy 267 C4
Upper Dean 84 A2
Upper Denby 139 C5
Upper Denton 176 C4
Upper Derraid 253 C6
Upper Dicker 22 B3
Upper Dovercourt 88 D3
Upper Druimfin 225 A4
Upper Dunsforth 148 A3
Upper Eathie 264 D3
Upper Elkstone 129 D5
Upper End 129 B5
Upper Farringdon 33 B6
Upper Framilode 62 B3
Upper Glenfintaig 239 D6
Upper Gornal 96 B2
Upper Gravenhurst 84 D3
Upper Green
Mon 61 B5
W Berks 46 C1
Upper Grove
Common 62 A1
Upper Hackney 130 C2
Upper Hale 34 B1
Upper Halistra 258 C2
Upper Halling 50 C3
Upper Hambleton 99 A5
Upper Hardres
Court 52 D3
Upper Hartfield 36 C2
Upper Haugh 140 D2
Upper Heath 94 C3
Upper Hellesdon 120 D4
Upper Helmsley 149 B5
Upper Hergest 77 B6
Upper Heyford
Northants 82 B3
Oxon 65 A5
Upper Hill 78 B2
Upper Hopton 139 B4
Upper Horsebridge 22 A3
Upper Hulme 129 C5
Upper Inglesham 64 D3
Upper Inverbrough 253 C4
Upper Killay 57 C5
Upper Knockando 254 B2
Upper Lambourn 45 A7
Upper Leigh 112 B4
Upper Lenie 251 D7
Upper Lochton 244 C3
Upper Longdon 113 D4
Upper Lybster 275 A6
Upper Lydbrook 62 B2
Upper Maes-coed 78 D1
Upper Midway 113 C6
Uppermill 138 C2
Upper Milovaig 258 D1
Upper Minety 63 D6
Upper Mitton 95 D6
Upper North Dean 66 D3
Upper Obney 219 A5
Upper Ollach 247 A4
Upper Padley 130 B2
Upper Pollicott 66 B2
Upper Poppleton 149 B4
Upper Quinton 81 C4
Upper Ratley 32 C2
Upper Rissington 64 B3
Upper Rochford 79 A4
Upper Sandaig 238 A1
Upper Sanday 283 G6
Upper Sapey 79 A4
Upper Saxondale 115 B4
Upper Seagry 44 A3
Upper Shelton 84 C1
Upper Sheringham 120 A3
Upper Skelmorlie 204 B2
Upper Slaughter 64 A2
Upper Soudley 62 B2
Uppersound 285 J6
Upper Stondon 84 D3
Upper Stowe 82 B3
Upper Stratton 45 A5
Upper Street
Hants 31 D5
Norf 121 D5
Norf 121 D5
Suff 88 D2
Upper Strensham 80 D2
Upper Sundon 67 A5
Upper Swell 64 A2
Upper Tean 112 B4
Upperthong 139 C4
Upperthorpe 141 C5
Upper Tillyrie 219 D6
Upperton 34 D2
Upper Tooting 49 B5
Upper Tote 259 C5
Uppertown
Derbys 130 C3
Highld 281 A5
Orkney 283 H5
Upper Town 43 C4
Upper Treverward 93 D6
Upper Tysoe 81 C6
Upper Upham 45 B6
Upper Wardington 82 C1
Upper Weald 83 D4
Upper Weedon 82 B3
Upper Wield 33 B5
Upper Winchendon 66 B2
Upper Witton 96 B3
Upper Woodend 244 A3
Upper Woodford 31 B5
Upper Wootton 46 D3
Upper Wyche 79 C5
Uppingham 99 B5
Uppington 95 A4
Upsall 158 C3
Upshire 68 C4
Up Somborne 32 B2
Upstreet 53 C4
Up Sydling 15 A6
Upthorpe 103 D5
Upton
Cambs 100 D3
Ches W 127 C4
Corn 10 A3
Dorset 16 B3
Dorset 16 C1
Hants 32 D2
Hants 46 D1
Leics 97 B6
Lincs 132 A3
Mers 126 A2
Norf 121 D5
Northants 83 A4
Notts 132 B2
Notts 132 D2
Oxon 46 A3
Pboro 100 A3
Slough 48 B2
Som 27 C4
W Yorks 140 B2
Upton Bishop 62 A2
Upton Cheyney 43 C5
Upton Cressett 95 B4
Upton Cross 10 D3
Upton Grey 33 A5
Upton Hellions 12 A3
Upton Lovell 30 A3
Upton Magna 111 D4
Upton Noble 29 B7
Upton Pyne 13 B4
Upton St Leonard's 63 B4
Upton Scudamore 30 A2
Upton Snodsbury 80 B2
Upton upon Severn 79 C6
Upton Warren 80 A2
Upwaltham 20 A2
Upware 102 D1
Upwell 101 A6
Upwey 15 C6
Upwood 101 C4
Uradale 285 K6
Urafirth 284 F5
Urchfont 44 D4
Urdimarsh 78 C3
Ure 284 F4
Ure Bank 157 D7
Urgha 288 H2
Urishay Common 77 D7
Urlay Nook 167 D6
Urmston 137 D6
Urpeth 179 D4
Urquhart
Highld 252 A1
Moray 266 C3
Urra 159 A4
Urray 251 A7
Ushaw Moor 167 A5
Usk = *Brynbuga* 61 C5
Usselby 142 D2
Usworth 179 D5
Utkinton 127 C5
Utley 147 C4
Uton 12 B3
Utterby 143 D5
Uttoxeter 113 B4
Uwchmynydd 106 D1
Uxbridge 48 A3
Uyeasound 284 C7
Uzmaston 55 C5

V

Valley 122 C2
Valleyfield 173 C4
Valley Truckle 10 C1
Valsgarth 284 B8
Valtos 259 B5
Van 92 C3
Vange 51 A4
Varteg 61 C4
Vatten 258 D2
Vaul 222 C3
Vaynor 60 B2
Veensgarth 285 J6
Velindre 77 D5
Vellow 27 B5
Veness 282 E6
Venn Green 25 D4
Vennington 94 A1
Venn Ottery 13 B5
Venny Tedburn 12 B3
Ventnor 19 D4
Vernham Dean 46 D1
Vernham Street 46 D1
Vernolds Common 94 C2
Verwood 17 A4
Veryan 4 D4
Vicarage 14 C2
Vickerstown 153 D2
Victoria
Corn 5 A4
S Yorks 139 C4
Vidlin 284 G6
Viewpark 207 D5
Vigo Village 50 C3
Vinehall Street 37 D5
Vine's Cross 22 A3
Viney Hill 62 C2
Virginia Water 48 C2
Virginstow 11 B4
Vobster 29 A7
Voe
Shetland 284 E5
Shetland 285 G6
Vowchurch 78 D1
Voxter 284 F5
Voy 282 F3

W

Wackerfield 167 C4
Wacton 104 B2
Wadbister 285 J6
Wadborough 80 C2
Waddesdon 66 B2
Waddingham 142 D1
Waddington
Lancs 146 C1
Lincs 133 C4
Wadebridge 9 D5
Wadeford 28 D3
Wadenhoe 100 C2
Wadesmill 68 B3
Wadhurst 36 C4
Wadshelf 130 B3
Wadsley 139 D6
Wadsley Bridge 139 D6
Wadworth 140 D3
Waen
Denb 125 C4
Denb 125 C6
Waen Fach 109 D7
Waen Goleugoed 125 B5
Wag 274 B4
Wainfleet All
Saints 135 D4
Wainfleet Bank 135 D4
Wainfleet St Mary 135 D5
Wainfleet Tofts 135 D4
Wainhouse Corner 10 B2
Wainscott 51 B4
Wainstalls 138 A3
Waitby 155 A6
Waithe 143 C4
Wakefield 139 A6
Wake Lady Green 159 B5
Wakerley 99 B6
Wakes Colne 70 A2
Walberswick 105 D5
Walberton 20 B2
Walbottle 178 C3
Walcot
Lincs 116 B3
N Lincs 141 A6
Shrops 94 C1
Swindon 45 A5
Telford 111 D4
Walcote
Leics 98 C2
Warks 80 B4
Walcot Green 104 C2
Walcott
Lincs 133 D6
Norf 121 B5
Walden 156 C4
Walden Head 156 C3
Walden Stubbs 140 B3
Waldersey 101 A6
Walderslade 51 C4

Walderton 33 D6
Walditch 15 B4
Waldley 113 B5
Waldridge 179 D4
Waldringfield 88 C3
Waldringfield Heath . 88 C3
Waldron 22 A3
Wales 131 A4
Walesby
 Lincs 142 D3
 Notts 132 B1
Walford
 Hereford 62 A1
 Hereford 94 D1
 Shrops 110 C3
Walford Heath 110 D3
Walgherton 111 A5
Walgrave 99 D5
Walhampton 18 B2
Walkden 137 C6
Walker 179 C4
Walker Barn 129 B4
Walkerburn 196 C2
Walker Fold 145 C6
Walkeringham 141 D5
Walkerith 141 D5
Walkern 68 A2
Walker's Green 78 C3
Walkerville 157 B6
Walkford 17 B6
Walkhampton 7 A4
Walkington 150 D2
Walkley 130 A3
Walk Mill 146 D2
Wall
 Northumb 177 C7
 Staffs 96 A4
Wallaceton 183 D6
Wallacetown
 S Ayrs 181 A4
 S Ayrs 192 C3
Wallands Park 22 A2
Wallasey 136 D2
Wall Bank 94 B3
Wallcrouch 37 C4
Wall Heath 96 C1
Wallingford 47 A4
Wallington
 Hants 19 A4
 Herts 85 D4
 London 49 C5
Wallis 55 B6
Walliswood 35 C4
Walls 285 J4
Wallsend 179 C4
Wallston 41 D6
Wall under
 Heywood 94 B3
Wallyford 209 C6
Walmer 53 D5
Walmer Bridge 136 A3
Walmersley 137 B7
Walmley 96 B4
Walpole 105 D4
Walpole Cross
 Keys 118 D2
Walpole Highway . . 118 D2
Walpole Marsh 118 D1
Walpole St Andrew . 118 D2
Walpole St Peter . . 118 D2
Walsall 96 B3
Walsall Wood 96 A3
Walsden 138 A2
Walsgrave on Sowe . 97 C6
Walsham le
 Willows 103 D5
Walshaw 137 B6
Walshford 148 B3
Walsoken 118 D1
Walston 195 B5
Walsworth 84 D4
Walters Ash 66 D3
Walterston 41 D5
Walterstone 61 A5
Waltham
 Kent 38 A3
 NE Lincs 143 C4
Waltham Abbey 68 C3
Waltham Chase 33 D4
Waltham Cross 68 C3
Waltham on the
 Wolds 115 C6
Waltham
 St Lawrence 47 B6
Walthamstow 49 A6
Walton
 Cumb 176 C3
 Derbys 130 C3
 Leics 98 C2
 Mers 136 D2

Walton continued
 M Keynes 83 D5
 Pboro 100 A3
 Powys 77 B6
 Som 29 B4
 Staffs 112 B2
 Suff 88 D3
 Telford 111 D4
 Warks 81 B5
 W Yorks 139 B6
 W Yorks 148 C3
Walton Cardiff 80 D2
Walton East 55 B6
Walton-in-Gordano . 42 B3
Walton-le-Dale . . . 137 A4
Walton-on-the-
 Naze 71 A6
Walton on the
 Wolds 114 D3
Walton-on-Trent . . 113 D6
Walton West 55 C4
Walwen 126 B2
Walwick 177 B7
Walworth 167 D5
Walworth Gate . . . 167 C5
Walwyn's Castle . . . 55 C4
Wambrook 14 A2
Wanborough
 Sur 34 B2
 Swindon 45 A6
Wandsworth 49 B5
Wangford 105 D5
Wanlockhead 183 A6
Wansford
 E Yorks 150 B3
 Pboro 100 B2
Wanstead 49 A7
Wanstrow 29 A7
Wanswell 62 C2
Wantage 46 A1
Wapley 43 B6
Wappenbury 81 A6
Wappenham 82 C3
Warbleton 22 A4
Warblington 19 A6
Warborough 65 D6
Warboys 101 C5
Warbreck 144 D3
Warbstow 10 B3
Warburton 128 A2
Warcop 165 D5
Warden
 Kent 52 B2
 Northumb 177 C7
Ward End 96 C4
Ward Green 87 A6
Wardhill 282 E7
Wardington 82 C1
Wardlaw 185 A5
Wardle
 Ches E 127 D6
 Gtr Man 138 B2
Wardley 99 A5
Wardlow 130 B1
Wardy Hill 101 C6
Ware
 Herts 68 B3
 Kent 53 C4
Wareham 16 C3
Warehorne 38 B1
Warenford 189 A4
Waren Mill 199 C5
Warenton 199 C5
Wareside 68 B3
Waresley
 Cambs 84 B4
 Worcs 95 D6
Warfield 48 B1
Warfleet 8 B2
Wargrave 47 B5
Warham 119 A6
Warhill 138 D2
Wark
 Northumb 177 B6
 Northumb 198 C2
Warkleigh 26 C1
Warkton 99 D5
Warkworth
 Northants 82 C1
 Northumb 189 C5
Warlaby 158 B2
Warland 138 A2
Warleggan 5 A6
Warlingham 35 A6
Warmfield 140 A1
Warmingham 128 C2

Warmington
 Northants 100 B2
 Warks 81 C7
Warminster 30 A2
Warmlake 37 A6
Warmley 43 B5
Warmley Tower 43 B5
Warmonds Hill 83 A6
Warmsworth 140 C3
Warmwell 16 C1
Warndon 80 B1
Warnford 33 C5
Warnham 35 C4
Warninglid 35 D5
Warren
 Ches E 128 B3
 Pembs 55 E5
Warren Heath 88 C3
Warren Row 47 A6
Warren Street 51 D6
Warrington
 M Keynes 83 B5
 Warr 127 A6
Warsash 18 A3
Warslow 129 D5
Warter 150 B1
Warthermarske . . . 157 D6
Warthill 149 B5
Wartling 23 B4
Wartnaby 115 C5
Warton
 Lancs 136 A3
 Lancs 154 D3
 Northumb 188 C3
 Warks 97 A5
Warwick 81 A5
Warwick Bridge . . . 176 D2
Warwick on Eden . . 176 D2
Wasbister 282 D4
Wasdale Head 163 D4
Washaway 5 A5
Washbourne 8 B1
Wash Common 46 C2
Washfield 27 D4
Washfold 157 A4
Washford 27 A5
Washford Pyne 26 D3
Washingborough . . 133 B5
Washington
 T&W 179 D5
 W Sus 21 A4
Wasing 46 C3
Waskerley 166 A3
Wasperton 81 B5
Wasps Nest 133 C5
Wass 159 D4
Watchet 27 A5
Watchfield
 Oxon 64 D3
 Som 28 A3
Watchgate 154 B4
Watchhill 175 D4
Watcombe 8 A3
Watendlath 163 C5
Water
 Devon 12 C2
 Lancs 138 A1
Waterbeach 85 A6
Waterbeck 175 A5
Waterden 119 B5
Water End
 E Yorks 149 D6
 Herts 67 B5
 Herts 68 C2
Waterfall 129 D5
Waterfoot
 E Renf 205 C5
 Lancs 138 A1
Waterford
 Hants 18 B2
 Herts 68 B3
Waterhead
 Cumb 154 A2
 Dumfries 185 C4
Waterheads 196 A1
Waterhouses
 Durham 167 A4
 Staffs 129 D5
Wateringbury 37 A4
Waterloo
 BCP 17 B4
 Gtr Man 138 C2
 Highld 247 B5
 Mers 136 D2
 N Lanark 194 A3
 Norf 120 D4
 Perth 219 A5
 Shrops 111 B4
Waterloo Port 123 D4
Waterlooville 19 A5

Watermeetings 184 A2
Watermillock 164 C2
Water Newton 100 B3
Water Orton 97 B4
Waterperry 66 C1
Waterrow 27 C5
Watersfield 20 A3
Waterside
 Aberds 257 D5
 Blackburn 137 A6
 Cumb 175 D5
 E Ayrs 182 B2
 E Ayrs 205 D4
 E Dunb 207 C4
 E Renf 205 C5
Water's Nook 137 C5
Waterstock 66 C1
Waterston 55 D5
Water Stratford 82 D3
Waters Upton 111 D5
Water Yeat 154 C1
Watford
 Herts 67 D6
 Northants 82 A3
Watford Gap 96 A4
Wath
 N Yorks 147 A5
 N Yorks 157 D7
 N Yorks 159 D5
Wath Brow 162 C3
Wath upon Dearne . 140 C2
Watley's End 43 A5
Watlington
 Norf 118 D3
 Oxon 66 D1
Watnall 114 A3
Watten 280 C4
Wattisfield 103 D6
Wattisham 87 B6
Wattlesborough
 Heath 110 D2
Watton
 E Yorks 150 B3
 Norf 103 A5
Watton at Stone . . . 68 B3
Wattston 207 C5
Wattstown 41 B5
Wauchan 238 D3
Waulkmill Lodge . . 283 G4
Waun 91 B6
Waunarlwydd 57 C6
Waunclunda 58 B3
Waunfawr 107 A5
Waungron 57 B5
Waunlwyd 60 C3
Waun-y-clyn 57 B4
Wavendon 83 D6
Waverbridge 175 D5
Waverton
 Ches W 127 C4
 Cumb 175 D5
Wavertree 126 A3
Wawne 150 D3
Waxham 121 C6
Waxholme 143 A5
Way 53 C5
Wayfield 51 C4
Wayford 14 A4
Waymills 111 A4
Wayne Green 61 B6
Way Village 26 D3
Wdig =Goodwick . . 72 C2
Weachyburn 268 D1
Weald 64 C4
Wealdstone 49 A4
Weardley 148 C1
Weare 42 D3
Weare Giffard 25 C5
Wearhead 165 B6
Weasdale 155 A5
Weasenham All
 Saints 119 C5
Weasenham
 St Peter 119 C5
Weatherhill 35 B6
Weaverham 127 B6
Weaverthorpe 160 D3
Webheath 80 A3
Wedderlairs 256 C3
Wedderlie 197 A5
Weddington 97 B6
Wedhampton 45 D4
Wedmore 28 A4
Wednesbury 96 B2
Wednesfield 96 A2
Weedon 66 B3
Weedon Bec 82 B3
Weedon Lois 82 C3
Weeford 96 A4
Week 26 D2

Weeke 32 B3
Weekley 99 C5
Week St Mary 10 B3
Weel 150 D3
Weeley 71 A5
Weeley Heath 71 A5
Weem 230 D2
Weeping Cross 112 C3
Weethley Gate 80 B3
Weeting 102 C3
Weeton
 E Yorks 143 A5
 Lancs 144 D3
 N Yorks 148 C1
Weetwood Hall . . . 188 A3
Weir 138 A1
Weir Quay 6 A3
Welborne 120 E2
Welbourn 133 D4
Welburn
 N Yorks 149 A6
 N Yorks 159 C5
Welbury 158 A2
Welby 116 B2
Welches Dam 101 C6
Welcombe 24 D3
Weld Bank 137 B4
Weldon 189 D4
Welford
 Northants 98 C3
 W Berks 46 B2
Welford-on-Avon . . 81 B4
Welham
 Leics 99 B4
 Notts 132 A2
Welham Green 68 C2
Well
 Hants 33 A6
 Lincs 135 B4
 N Yorks 157 C5
Welland 79 C5
Wellbank 221 A4
Welldale 175 B4
Well End 48 A1
Wellesbourne 81 B5
Well Heads 147 D4
Well Hill 50 C1
Welling 50 B1
Wellingborough . . . 83 A5
Wellingham 119 C5
Wellingore 133 D4
Wellington
 Cumb 162 D3
 Hereford 78 C2
 Som 27 C6
 Telford 111 D5
Wellington Heath . . 79 C5
Wellington Hill . . . 148 D2
Wellow
 Bath 43 D6
 IoW 18 C2
 Notts 131 C6
Wellpond Green . . . 68 A4
Wells 29 A5
Wellsborough 97 A6
Wells Green 128 D1
Wells-Next-The-
 Sea 119 A6
Wellswood 8 A3
Well Town 13 A4
Wellwood 208 B3
Welney 102 B1
Welshampton 110 B3
Welsh Bicknor 62 B1
Welsh End 111 B4
Welsh Frankton . . . 110 B2
Welsh Hook 55 B5
Welsh Newton 61 B6
Welshpool
 = Y Trallwng 93 A6
Welsh St Donats . . . 41 D5
Welton
 Cumb 164 A1
 E Yorks 142 A1
 Lincs 133 B5
 Northants 82 A2
Welton Hill 133 B5
Welton le Marsh . . 135 C4
Welton le Wold . . . 134 A2
Welwick 143 A5
Welwyn 68 B2
Welwyn Garden City . 68 B2
Wem 111 C4
Wembdon 28 B2
Wembley 49 A4
Wembury 7 C4
Wembworthy 12 A1
Wemyss Bay 204 B1
Wenallt
 Ceredig 75 A5

Wenallt continued
 Gwyn 109 A4
Wendens Ambo . . . 85 D7
Wendlebury 65 B6
Wendling 119 D6
Wendover 66 C3
Wendron 3 B4
Wendy 85 C5
Wenfordbridge 10 D1
Wenhaston 105 D5
Wennington
 Cambs 100 D4
 Lancs 155 D5
 London 50 A2
Wensley
 Derbys 130 C2
 N Yorks 157 C4
Wentbridge 140 B2
Wentnor 94 B1
Wentworth
 Cambs 101 D6
 S Yorks 140 D1
Wenvoe 41 D6
Weobley 78 B2
Weobley Marsh 78 B2
Wereham 102 A2
Wergs 95 A6
Wern
 Powys 109 D4
 Powys 110 D1
Wernffrwd 57 C5
Wernyrheolydd 61 B5
Werrington
 Corn 10 C4
 Pboro 100 A3
 Staffs 112 A3
Wervin 127 B4
Wesham 144 D4
Wessington 130 D3
Westacott 25 B6
West Acre 119 D4
West Adderbury . . . 82 D1
West Allerdean . . . 198 B3
West Alvington 7 C6
West Amesbury . . . 31 A5
West Anstey 26 C3
West Ashby 134 B2
West Ashling 19 A7
West Ashton 44 D2
West Auckland . . . 167 C4
West Ayton 160 C3
West Bagborough . . 27 B6
West Barkwith . . . 133 A6
West Barnby 169 D6
West Barns 210 C3
West Barsham 119 B6
West Bay 15 B4
West Beckham 120 B3
West Bedfont 48 B3
West Benhar 208 D1
Westbere 52 C3
West Bergholt 70 A3
West Bexington . . . 15 C5
West Bilney 119 D4
West Blatchington . 21 B5
Westborough 115 A6
Westbourne
 BCP 17 B4
 Suff 88 C2
 W Sus 19 A6
West Bowling 147 D5
West Bradford 146 C1
West Bradley 29 B5
West Bretton 139 B5
West Bridgford . . . 114 B3
West Bromwich . . . 96 B3
Westbrook 46 B2
West Buckland
 Devon 26 B1
 Som 28 C1
West Burrafirth . . . 285 H4
West Burton
 N Yorks 156 C4
 W Sus 20 A2
Westbury
 Bucks 82 D3
 Shrops 94 A1
 Wilts 44 D2
Westbury Leigh . . . 44 D2
Westbury-on-
 Severn 62 B3
Westbury on Trym . 43 B4
Westbury-sub-
 Mendip 29 A5
West Butterwick . . 141 C6
Westby 144 D3
West Byfleet 48 C3
West Caister 121 D7

West Calder......208 D3
West Camel.......29 C5
West Challow.....46 A1
West Chelborough...15 A5
West Chevington...189 D5
West Chiltington...20 A3
West Chiltington Common...20 A3
West Chinnock....29 D4
West Chisenbury...45 C5
West Clandon....34 A3
West Cliffe.....39 A5
Westcliff-on-Sea...51 A4
West Clyne.....274 D2
West Clyth.....275 A6
West Coker.....29 D5
Westcombe.....29 B6
West Compton
  Dorset.....15 B5
  Som.....29 A5
Westcote.....64 A3
Westcott
  Bucks.....66 B2
  Devon.....13 A5
  Sur.....35 B4
Westcott Barton...65 A5
West Cowick.....140 A4
West Cranmore....29 A6
West Cross.....57 D6
West Cullery.....245 B4
West Curry.....10 B3
West Curthwaite...175 D6
West Darlochan...190 C2
Westdean.....22 C3
West Dean
  Wilts.....31 C6
  W Sus.....20 A1
West Deeping.....100 A3
Westdene.....21 B5
West Derby.....136 D2
West Dereham....102 A2
West Didsbury....138 D1
West Ditchburn...189 A4
West Down.....25 A6
West Drayton
  London.....48 B3
  Notts.....132 B2
West Ella.....142 A2
West End
  Bedford.....84 B1
  E Yorks.....150 D2
  E Yorks.....151 D4
  Hants.....32 D3
  Lancs.....137 A6
  Norf.....103 A5
  Norf.....121 D7
  N Som.....42 C3
  N Yorks.....147 B5
  Oxon.....65 C5
  S Lanark.....195 B4
  Suff.....105 C5
  Sur.....48 C2
  S Yorks.....141 C4
  Wilts.....30 C3
  Wilts.....44 B3
  W Sus.....21 A5
West End Green.....47 C4
Wester Aberchalder.....252 D1
Wester Balgedie...219 D6
Wester Culbeuchly.268 C1
Westerdale
  Highld.....280 C3
  N Yorks.....159 A5
Wester Dechmont.208 D3
Wester Denoon...232 D1
Westerfield
  Shetland.....285 H5
  Suff.....88 C2
Wester Fintray...245 A5
Westergate.....20 B2
Wester Gruinards.263 A7
Westerham.....36 A2
Westerhope.....178 C3
Wester Lealty....264 C2
Westerleigh.....43 B6
Wester Milton....253 A6
Wester Newburn..220 D4
Wester Quarff....285 K6
Wester Skeld....285 J4
Westerton
  Angus.....233 C4
  Durham.....167 B5
  W Sus.....20 B1
Westerwick.....285 J4
West Farleigh....37 A5
West Felton.....110 C2
West Fenton.....210 B1

West Ferry.....221 A4
Westfield
  Cumb.....162 B2
  E Sus.....23 A6
  Hereford.....79 C5
  Highld.....279 B6
  N Lanark.....207 C5
  Norf.....103 A5
  W Loth.....208 C2
Westfields.....15 A7
Westfields of Rattray.....231 D5
West Firle.....22 B2
Westgate
  Durham.....166 B2
  N Lincs.....141 C5
  Norf.....119 A5
  Norf.....119 A6
Westgate on Sea...53 B5
West Ginge.....46 A2
West Grafton.....45 C6
West Green.....47 D5
West Greenskares.268 C2
West Grimstead...31 C6
West Grinstead....35 D4
West Haddlesey..140 A3
West Haddon.....98 D3
West Hagbourne...46 A3
West Hagley.....96 C2
Westhall
  Aberds.....256 D1
  Suff.....105 C5
West Hall.....176 C3
West Hallam.....114 A4
West Halton.....141 A7
Westham
  Dorset.....15 D6
  E Sus.....22 B4
  Som.....28 A4
West Ham.....49 A7
Westhampnett.....20 B1
West Handley.....130 B3
West Hanney.....65 D5
West Hanningfield..70 D1
West Hardwick...140 B2
West Harnham...31 C5
West Harptree.....43 D4
West Hatch.....28 C2
Westhay.....28 A4
Westhead.....136 C3
West Head.....102 A1
West Heath
  Ches E.....128 C3
  Hants.....34 A1
  Hants.....46 D3
West Helmsdale..274 C4
West Hendred....46 A2
West Heslerton..160 D3
Westhide.....78 C3
Westhill
  Aberds.....245 B5
  Highld.....252 B3
West Hill
  Devon.....13 B5
  E Yorks.....151 A4
  N Som.....42 B3
West Hoathly.....35 C6
West Holme.....16 C2
Westhope
  Hereford.....78 B2
  Shrops.....94 C2
West Horndon....50 A3
Westhorpe
  Lincs.....117 B5
  Suff.....87 A6
West Horrington...29 A5
West Horsley.....34 A3
West Horton....198 C4
West Hougham....39 A4
Westhoughton...137 C5
West Houlland..285 H4
Westhouse.....155 D5
Westhouses.....131 D4
Westhumble.....35 A4
West Huntington.149 B5
West Hythe.....38 B3
West Ilsley.....46 A2
Westing.....284 C7
West Itchenor...19 A6
West Keal.....134 C3
West Kennett.....45 C5
West Kilbride...204 D2
West Kingsdown...50 C2
West Kington....44 B2
West Kinharrachie.257 C4
West Kirby.....126 A2
West Knapton...160 D2
West Knighton...16 C1
West Knoyle.....30 B2
West Kyloe.....199 B4

Westlake.....7 B5
West Lambrook....28 D4
West Langdon....39 A5
West Langwell...273 D4
West Lavington
  Wilts.....44 D4
  W Sus.....34 D1
West Layton....157 A5
West Lea.....168 A2
West Leake.....114 C3
West Learmouth..198 C2
Westleigh
  Devon.....25 C5
  Devon.....27 D5
  Gtr Man.....137 C5
West Leigh.....12 A1
Westleton.....89 A5
West Lexham....119 D5
Westley
  Shrops.....94 A1
  Suff.....87 A4
Westley Waterless..86 B2
West Lilling.....149 A5
Westlington.....66 B2
West Linton....175 B6
West Liss.....33 C6
West Littleton...43 B6
West Looe.....6 B1
West Luccombe...26 A3
West Lulworth...16 C2
West Lutton....150 A2
West Lydford....29 B5
West Lyng.....28 C3
West Lynn.....118 C3
West Malling.....37 A4
West Malvern....79 C5
West Marden....33 D6
West Marina....23 B5
West Markham...132 B2
Westmarsh.....53 C4
West Marsh.....143 B4
West Marton....146 B2
West Meon.....33 C5
West Mersea.....71 B4
Westmeston.....21 A6
Westmill.....68 A3
West Milton.....15 B5
Westminster.....49 B6
West Minster....51 B6
West Molesey....48 C4
West Monkton...28 C2
West Moors.....17 A4
West Morriston..197 B5
Westmuir.....232 C1
West Muir.....232 B3
Westness.....282 E4
West Ness.....159 D5
West Newham...178 B2
Westnewton
  Cumb.....174 D4
  Northumb.....198 C3
West Newton
  E Yorks.....151 D4
  Norf.....118 C3
West Norwood....49 B6
Westoe.....179 C5
West Ogwell.....12 D3
Weston
  Bath.....43 C6
  Ches E.....128 D2
  Devon.....13 C6
  Dorset.....15 D6
  Halton.....127 A5
  Hants.....33 C6
  Herts.....85 D4
  Lincs.....117 C5
  Northants.....82 C2
  Notts.....132 C2
  N Yorks.....147 C5
  Shrops.....94 B3
  Shrops.....111 C4
  Staffs.....112 C3
  W Berks.....46 B1
Weston Beggard...78 C3
Westonbirt.....44 A2
Weston by Welland..99 B4
Weston Colville...86 B2
Westoncommon..110 C3
Weston Coyney...112 A3
Weston Favell...83 A4
Weston Green
  Cambs.....86 B2
  Norf.....120 D3
Weston Heath...112 D1
Weston Hills....117 C5
Westoning.....84 D2
Weston-in-Gordano 42 B3
Weston Jones...111 C6
Weston Longville..120 D3

Weston Lullingfields.....110 C3
Weston-on-the-Green.....65 B6
Weston-on-Trent..114 C2
Weston Patrick....33 A5
Weston Rhyn....110 B1
Weston-Sub-Edge..80 C4
Weston-super-Mare 42 C2
Weston Turville...66 B3
Weston under Lizard.....112 D2
Weston under Penyard.....62 A2
Weston under Wetherley.....81 A6
Weston Underwood
  Derbys.....113 A6
  M Keynes.....83 B5
Westonzoyland...28 B3
West Orchard....30 D2
West Overton....45 C5
Westow.....149 A6
West Park.....168 B2
West Parley.....17 B4
West Peckham...36 A4
West Pelton....179 D4
West Pennard....29 B5
West Pentire.....4 A2
West Perry.....84 A3
Westport
  Argyll.....190 C2
  Som.....28 D3
West Putford....25 D4
West Quantoxhead..27 A6
West Rainton...167 A6
West Rasen....133 A5
West Raynham...119 C5
West Retford...132 A1
Westrigg.....208 D2
West Rounton...158 A3
West Row.....102 D2
West Rudham...119 C5
West Runton....120 A3
Westruther.....197 B5
Westry.....101 B5
West Saltoun...210 D1
West Sandwick..284 E6
West Scrafton...157 C4
West Sleekburn..179 A4
West Somerton..121 D6
West Stafford....16 C1
West Stockwith..141 D5
West Stoke.....20 B1
West Stonesdale.156 A2
West Stoughton...28 A4
West Stour.....30 C1
West Stourmouth..53 C4
West Stow.....103 D4
West Stowell....45 C5
West Strathan...277 B6
West Stratton....32 A4
West Street.....37 A7
West Tanfield...157 D6
West Taphouse....5 A6
West Tarbert....202 B3
West Thirston...189 D4
West Thorney...19 A6
West Thurrock...50 B2
West Tilbury.....50 B3
West Tisted.....33 C5
West Tofts
  Norf.....103 B4
  Perth.....219 A6
West Torrington..133 A6
West Town
  Hants.....19 B6
  N Som.....42 C3
West Tytherley...32 C1
West Tytherton...44 B3
Westville.....114 A3
West Walton....118 D1
West Walton Highway.....118 D1
Westward.....175 D5
Westward Ho!....25 C5
Westwell
  Kent.....38 A1
  Oxon.....64 C3
Westwell Leacon...38 A1
West Wellow....32 D1
West Wemyss....209 A6
Westwick
  Cambs.....85 A6
  Durham.....166 D3
  Norf.....121 C4
West Wick.....42 C2
West Wickham
  Cambs.....86 C2
  London.....49 C6

West Williamston...55 D6
West Willoughby..116 A2
West Winch.....118 D3
West Winterslow...31 B6
West Wittering...19 B6
West Witton....157 C4
Westwood
  Devon.....13 B5
  Wilts.....44 D2
West Woodburn..177 A6
West Woodhay....46 C1
West Woodlands..30 A1
Westwoodside...141 D5
West Worldham...33 B6
West Worlington..26 D2
West Worthing...21 B4
West Wratting...86 B2
West Wycombe...66 D3
West Wylam....178 C3
West Yell.....284 E6
Wetheral.....176 D2
Wetherby.....148 C3
Wetherden.....87 A6
Wetheringsett...88 A2
Wethersfield....86 D3
Wethersta.....284 G5
Wetherup Street...88 A2
Wetley Rocks....112 A3
Wettenhall.....127 C6
Wetton.....129 D6
Wetwang.....150 B2
Wetwood.....111 B6
Wexcombe.....45 D6
Wexham Street...48 A2
Weybourne.....120 A3
Weybread.....104 C3
Weybridge.....48 C3
Weycroft.....14 B3
Weydale.....280 B3
Weyhill.....32 A2
Weymouth.....15 D6
Whaddon
  Bucks.....83 D5
  Cambs.....85 C5
  Glos.....63 B4
  Wilts.....31 C5
Whale.....164 C3
Whaley.....131 B5
Whaley Bridge...129 A5
Whaley Thorns..131 B5
Whaligoe.....281 D5
Whalley.....146 D1
Whalton.....178 A3
Wham.....146 A1
Whaplode.....117 C6
Whaplode Drove..117 D6
Whaplode St Catherine.....117 C6
Wharfe.....146 A1
Wharles.....144 D4
Wharncliffe Side..139 D5
Wharram le Street.150 A1
Wharton.....127 C6
Wharton Green...127 C6
Whashton.....157 A5
Whatcombe.....16 A2
Whatcote.....81 C6
Whatfield.....87 C6
Whatley
  Som.....14 A3
  Som.....30 A1
Whatlington...23 A5
Whatstandwell..130 D3
Whatton.....115 B5
Whauphill.....171 C6
Whaw.....156 A3
Wheatacre.....105 B5
Wheatcroft.....130 D3
Wheathampstead..68 B1
Wheathill.....95 C4
Wheatley
  Devon.....13 B4
  Hants.....33 A6
  Oxon.....65 C6
  S Yorks.....140 C3
  W Yorks.....138 A3
Wheatley Hill....167 B6
Wheaton Aston..112 D2
Wheddon Cross...27 B4
Wheedlemont...255 D5
Wheelerstreet...34 B2
Wheelock.....128 D2
Wheelock Heath..128 D2
Wheelton.....137 A5
Wheen.....232 A1
Wheldrake.....149 C5
Whelford.....64 D2
Whelpley Hill....67 C4
Whempstead.....68 A3
Whenby.....149 A5

Whepstead.....87 B4
Wherstead.....88 C2
Wherwell.....32 A2
Wheston.....129 B6
Whetsted.....37 B4
Whetstone.....98 B2
Whicham.....153 B2
Whichford.....81 D6
Whickham.....179 C4
Whiddon Down...12 B1
Whigstreet.....232 D2
Whilton.....82 A3
Whimble.....11 A4
Whim Farm.....195 A7
Whimple.....13 B5
Whimpwell Green..121 C5
Whinburgh.....103 A6
Whinnieliggate..173 C5
Whinnyfold.....257 C5
Whippingham....18 B4
Whipsnade.....67 B5
Whipton.....13 B4
Whirlow.....130 A3
Whisby.....133 C4
Whissendine....115 D6
Whissonsett....119 C6
Whistlefield
  Argyll.....215 C4
  Argyll.....215 C5
Whistley Green...47 B5
Whiston
  Mers.....136 D3
  Northants.....83 A5
  Staffs.....112 A4
  Staffs.....112 D2
  S Yorks.....131 A4
Whitbeck.....153 B2
Whitbourne.....79 B5
Whitburn
  T&W.....179 C6
  W Loth.....208 D2
Whitburn Colliery.179 C6
Whitby
  Ches W.....126 B3
  N Yorks.....169 D6
Whitbyheath.....126 B3
Whitchurch
  Bath.....43 C5
  Bucks.....66 A2
  Cardiff.....41 C6
  Devon.....11 D5
  Hants.....32 A3
  Hereford.....62 B1
  Oxon.....47 B4
  Pembs.....54 B3
  Shrops.....111 A4
Whitchurch Canonicorum.....14 B3
Whitchurch Hill...47 B4
Whitcombe.....15 C7
Whitcott Keysett..93 C6
Whiteacen.....254 B3
Whiteacre Heath...97 B5
Whitebridge.....240 A2
Whitebrook.....62 C1
Whiteburn.....197 B4
Whitecairn.....171 B4
Whitecairns.....245 A6
Whitecastle.....195 B5
Whitechapel.....145 C5
Whitecleat.....283 G6
White Coppice...137 B5
Whitecraig.....209 C6
Whitecroft.....62 C2
Whitecross
  Corn.....9 D5
  Falk.....208 C2
  Staffs.....112 C2
Whiteface.....264 B3
Whitefarland.....202 D3
Whitefaulds.....192 E2
Whitefield
  Gtr Man.....137 C7
  Perth.....219 A6
Whiteford.....256 D2
Whitegate.....127 C6
Whitehall
  Blackburn.....137 A5
  W Sus.....35 D4
Whitehall Village..282 E7
Whitehaven.....162 C2
Whitehill.....33 B6
Whitehills
  Aberds.....268 C1
  S Lanark.....205 C6
Whitehough.....129 A5
Whitehouse
  Aberds.....244 A3
  Argyll.....202 B3
Whiteinch.....205 B5

Whitekirk 210 B2
White Lackington . . 15 B7
White Ladies Aston . . 80 B2
Whitelaw 205 B6
Whiteleas 179 C5
Whiteley Bank 19 C4
Whiteley Green 129 B4
Whiteley Village . . . 48 C3
White Lund 144 A4
Whitemans Green . . 35 D6
White Mill 58 C1
Whitemire 253 A5
Whitemoor 5 B4
Whitemore 128 C3
Whitenap 32 C2
White Ness 285 J5
White Notley 70 B1
Whiteoak Green . . . 64 B4
Whiteparish 31 C6
White Pit 134 B3
White Post 131 D6
Whiterashes 256 D3
White Rocks 61 A6
White Roding 69 B5
Whiterow 281 D5
Whiteshill 63 C4
Whiteside
  Northumb 177 C5
  W Loth 208 D2
Whitesmith 22 A3
Whitestaunton 28 D2
Whitestone
  Devon 12 B3
  Devon 25 A5
  Warks 97 C6
Whitestones 268 D3
Whitestreet Green . . 87 D5
Whitewall Corner . . 159 D6
White Waltham . . . 47 B6
Whiteway
  Glos 63 B5
  Glos 63 D4
Whitewell
  Aberds 269 C4
  Lancs 145 C6
Whitewell Bottom . 138 A1
Whiteworks 11 D7
Whitfield
  Kent 39 A5
  Northants 82 D3
  Northumb 177 D5
  S Glos 62 D2
Whitford
  Devon 14 B2
  Flint 125 B6
Whitgift 141 A6
Whitgreave 112 C2
Whithorn 171 C6
Whiting Bay 191 C6
Whitkirk 148 D2
Whitland 56 A1
Whitletts 192 C3
Whitley
  N Yorks 140 A3
  Reading 47 B5
  Wilts 44 C2
Whitley Bay 179 B5
Whitley Chapel . . . 178 D1
Whitley Lower 139 B5
Whitley Row 36 A2
Whitlock's End 96 D4
Whitminster 62 C3
Whitmore 112 A2
Whitnage 27 D5
Whitnash 81 A6
Whitney-on-Wye . . 77 C6
Whitrigg
  Cumb 163 A5
  Cumb 175 C5
Whitsbury 31 D5
Whitsome 198 A2
Whitson 42 A2
Whitstable 52 C3
Whitstone 10 B3
Whittingham 188 B3
Whittingslow 94 C2
Whittington
  Glos 63 A6
  Lancs 155 D5
  Norf 102 B3
  Shrops 110 B2
  Staffs 95 C6
  Staffs 97 A4
  Worcs 80 B1
Whittlebury 82 C3
Whittle-le-Woods . 137 A4
Whittlesey 101 B4
Whittlesford 85 C6
Whittlestone
  Head 137 B6

Whitton
  Borders 187 A6
  N Lincs 141 A7
  Northumb 188 C3
  Powys 77 A6
  Shrops 94 D3
  Stockton 167 C6
  Suff 88 C2
Whittonditch 45 B6
Whittonstall 178 D2
Whitway 46 D2
Whitwell
  Derbys 131 B5
  Herts 68 A1
  IoW 18 D4
  N Yorks 157 B6
  Rutland 99 A6
Whitwell-on-the-
  Hill 149 A6
Whitwell Street . . . 120 C3
Whitwick 114 D2
Whitwood 140 A2
Whitworth 138 B1
Whixall 111 B4
Whixley 148 B3
Whoberley 97 D6
Whorlton
  Durham 166 D4
  N Yorks 158 A3
Whygate 177 B5
Whyle 78 A3
Whyteleafe 35 A6
Wibdon 62 D1
Wibsey 147 D5
Wibtoft 98 C1
Wichenford 79 A5
Wichling 37 A7
Wick
  BCP 17 B5
  Devon 13 A6
  Highld 281 C5
  S Glos 43 B6
  Shetland 285 K6
  V Glam 40 D4
  Wilts 31 C5
  Worcs 80 C2
  W Sus 20 B3
Wicken
  Cambs 102 D1
  Northants 83 D4
Wicken Bonhunt . . . 85 D6
Wickenby 133 A5
Wicken Green
  Village 119 B5
Wickersley 140 D2
Wickford 70 D1
Wickham
  Hants 33 D4
  W Berks 46 B1
Wickham Bishops . . 70 B2
Wickhambreux 53 D4
Wickhambrook 86 B3
Wickhamford 80 C3
Wickham Market . . 88 B4
Wickhampton 105 A5
Wickham St Paul . . 87 D4
Wickham Skeith . . . 88 A1
Wickham Street
  Suff 86 B3
  Suff 88 A1
Wick Hill 47 C5
Wicklewood 104 A1
Wickmere 120 B3
Wick St Lawrence . . 42 C2
Wickwar 43 A6
Widdington 86 D1
Widdrington 189 D5
Widdrington
  Station 189 D5
Widecombe in the
  Moor 12 D2
Widegates 6 B1
Widemouth Bay . . . 10 A3
Wide Open 179 B4
Widewall 283 H5
Widford
  Essex 69 C6
  Herts 68 B4
Widham 45 A4
Widmer End 66 D3
Widmerpool 115 C4
Widnes 127 A4
Wigan 137 C4
Wiggaton 13 B6
Wiggenhall
  St Germans 118 D2
Wiggenhall St Mary
  Magdalen 118 D2
Wiggenhall St Mary the
  Virgin 118 D2

Wigginton
  Herts 67 B4
  Oxon 81 D6
  Staffs 97 A5
  York 149 B4
Wigglesworth 146 B2
Wiggonby 175 C5
Wiggonholt 20 A3
Wighill 148 C3
Wighton 119 B6
Wigley 32 D2
Wigmore
  Hereford 78 A2
  Medway 51 C5
Wigsley 132 B3
Wigsthorpe 100 C2
Wigston 98 B3
Wigthorpe 131 A5
Wigtoft 117 B5
Wigton 175 D5
Wigtown 171 B6
Wigtwizzle 139 D5
Wike 148 C2
Wike Well End 141 B4
Wilbarston 99 C5
Wilberfoss 149 B6
Wilberlee 138 B3
Wilburton 101 D6
Wilby
  Norf 103 C6
  Northants 83 A5
  Suff 104 D3
Wilcot 45 C5
Wilcott 110 D2
Wilcrick 42 A3
Wilday Green 130 B3
Wildboarclough . . 129 C4
Wilden
  Bedford 84 B2
  Worcs 95 D6
Wildhern 46 D1
Wildhill 68 C2
Wildmoor 96 D2
Wildsworth 141 D6
Wilford 114 B3
Wilkesley 111 A5
Wilkhaven 265 B5
Wilkieston 208 D4
Willand 27 D5
Willaston
  Ches E 128 D1
  Ches W 126 B3
Willen 83 C5
Willenhall
  W Mid 96 B2
  W Mid 97 D6
Willerby
  E Yorks 150 D3
  N Yorks 160 D4
Willersey 80 D4
Willersley 77 C7
Willesborough 38 A2
Willesborough
  Lees 38 A2
Willesden 49 A5
Willett 27 B6
Willey
  Shrops 95 B4
  Warks 98 C1
Willey Green 34 A2
Williamscott 82 C1
Willian 84 D4
Willingale 69 C5
Willingdon 22 B3
Willingham 101 D6
Willingham by
  Stow 132 A3
Willington
  Bedford 84 C3
  Derbys 113 C6
  Durham 167 B4
  T&W 179 C5
  Warks 81 D5
Willington Corner . 127 C5
Willisham Tye 87 B6
Willitoft 149 D6
Williton 27 A5
Willoughbridge . . . 111 A6
Willoughby
  Lincs 135 B4
  Warks 82 A2
Willoughby-on-
  the-Wolds 115 C4
Willoughby
  Waterleys 98 B2
Willoughton 142 D1
Willows Green 69 B7
Willsbridge 43 B5
Willsworthy 11 C6
Wilmcote 81 B4

Wilmington
  Devon 14 B2
  E Sus 22 B3
  Kent 50 B2
Wilminstone 11 D5
Wilmslow 128 A3
Wilnecote 97 A5
Wilpshire 145 D6
Wilsden 147 D4
Wilsford
  Lincs 116 A3
  Wilts 31 B5
  Wilts 45 D5
Wilsill 147 A5
Wilsley Pound 37 C5
Wilsom 33 B6
Wilson 114 C2
Wilsontown 195 A4
Wilstead 84 C2
Wilsthorpe 116 D3
Wilstone 67 B4
Wilton
  Borders 186 B3
  Cumb 162 C3
  N Yorks 160 C2
  Redcar 168 D3
  Wilts 31 B4
  Wilts 45 C6
Wimbish 86 D1
Wimbish Green 86 D2
Wimblebury 112 D4
Wimbledon 49 B5
Wimblington 101 B6
Wimborne Minster . 17 B4
Wimborne St Giles . 31 D4
Wimbotsham 102 A2
Wimpson 32 D2
Wimpstone 81 C5
Wincanton 29 C7
Wincham 128 B1
Winchburgh 208 C3
Winchcombe 63 A6
Winchelsea 23 A7
Winchelsea Beach . . 23 A7
Winchester 32 C3
Winchet Hill 37 B5
Winchfield 47 D5
Winchmore Hill
  Bucks 67 D4
  London 68 D3
Wincle 129 C4
Wincobank 140 D1
Windermere 154 B3
Winderton 81 C6
Windhill 252 B1
Windhouse 284 D6
Windlehurst 129 A4
Windlesham 48 C2
Windley 113 A7
Windmill Hill
  E Sus 22 A4
  Som 28 D3
Windrush 64 B2
Windsor
  N Lincs 141 B5
  Windsor 48 B2
Windsoredge 63 C4
Windygates 220 D3
Windyknowe 208 D2
Windywalls 197 C6
Wineham 35 D5
Winestead 143 A4
Winewall 146 C3
Winfarthing 104 C2
Winford
  IoW 19 C4
  N Som 43 C4
Winforton 77 C6
Winfrith Newburgh . 16 C2
Wing
  Bucks 66 A3
  Rutland 99 A5
Wingate 168 B2
Wingates
  Gtr Man 137 C5
  Northumb 189 D4
Wingerworth 130 C3
Wingfield
  C Beds 67 A4
  Suff 104 D3
  Wilts 44 D2
Wingham 53 D4
Wingmore 38 A3
Wingrave 66 B3
Winkburn 132 D2
Winkfield 48 B2
Winkfield Row 48 B1
Winkhill 129 D5
Winklebury 47 D4
Winkleigh 12 A1

Winksley 157 D6
Winkton 17 B5
Winlaton 178 C3
Winless 281 C5
Winmarleigh 145 C4
Winnal 78 D2
Winnall 32 C3
Winnersh 47 B5
Winscales 162 B3
Winscombe 42 D3
Winsford
  Ches W 127 C6
  Som 27 B4
Winsham 14 A3
Winshill 113 C6
Winskill 164 B3
Winslade 33 A5
Winsley 44 C2
Winslow 66 A2
Winson 64 C1
Winson Green 96 C3
Winsor 32 D2
Winster
  Cumb 154 B3
  Derbys 130 C2
Winston
  Durham 166 D4
  Suff 88 A2
Winstone 63 C5
Winston Green 88 A2
Winswell 25 D5
Winterborne
  Clenston 16 A2
Winterborne
  Herringston 15 C6
Winterborne
  Houghton 16 A2
Winterborne
  Kingston 16 B2
Winterborne
  Monkton 15 C6
Winterborne
  Stickland 16 A2
Winterborne
  Whitechurch . . . 16 A2
Winterborne Zelston 16 B2
Winterbourne
  S Glos 43 A5
  W Berks 46 B2
Winterbourne
  Abbas 15 B6
Winterbourne
  Bassett 45 B5
Winterbourne
  Dauntsey 31 B5
Winterbourne Down 43 B5
Winterbourne Earls . 31 B5
Winterbourne
  Gunner 31 B5
Winterbourne
  Monkton 45 B5
Winterbourne
  Steepleton 15 C6
Winterbourne Stoke . 31 A4
Winterburn 146 B3
Winter Gardens . . . 51 A4
Winteringham 142 A1
Winterley 128 C2
Wintersett 140 B1
Wintershill 32 D4
Winterton 142 B1
Winterton-on-Sea . 121 D6
Winthorpe
  Lincs 135 C5
  Notts 132 D2
Winton
  BCP 17 B4
  Cumb 165 D5
  N Yorks 158 B3
Wintringham 160 D2
Winwick
  Cambs 100 C3
  Northants 98 D3
  Warr 137 D5
Wirksworth 130 D2
Wirksworth Moor . 130 D3
Wirswall 111 A4
Wisbech 101 A6
Wisbech St Mary . . 101 A6
Wisborough Green . 34 D3
Wiseton 132 A2
Wishaw
  N Lanark 194 A2
  Warks 97 B4
Wisley 34 A3
Wispington 134 B2
Wissenden 37 B7
Wissett 105 D4
Wistanstow 94 C2
Wistanswick 111 C5
Wistaston 128 D1

Wistaston Green . . 128 D1
Wiston
  Pembs 55 C6
  S Lanark 195 C4
  W Sus 21 A4
Wistow
  Cambs 101 C4
  N Yorks 149 D4
Wiswell 146 D1
Witcham 101 C6
Witchampton 16 A3
Witchford 101 D7
Witham 70 B2
Witham Friary 30 A1
Witham on the Hill . 116 D3
Withcall 134 A2
Withdean 21 B6
Witherenden Hill . . 36 D4
Witheridge 26 D3
Witherley 97 B6
Withern 135 A4
Withernsea 143 A5
Withernwick 151 C4
Withersdale Street . 104 C3
Withersfield 86 C2
Witherslack 154 C3
Withiel 5 A4
Withiel Florey 27 B4
Withington
  Glos 63 B6
  Gtr Man 138 D1
  Hereford 78 C3
  Shrops 111 D4
  Staffs 112 B4
Withington Green . 128 B3
Withleigh 27 D4
Withnell 137 A5
Withybrook 98 C1
Withycombe 27 A5
Withycombe Raleigh 13 C5
Withyham 36 C2
Withypool 26 B3
Witley 34 C2
Witnesham 88 B2
Witney 65 B4
Wittering 100 A2
Wittersham 37 D6
Witton
  Angus 232 A3
  Worcs 80 A1
Witton Bridge 121 B5
Witton Gilbert 167 A5
Witton-le-Wear . . 166 B4
Witton Park 167 B4
Wiveliscombe 27 C5
Wivelrod 33 B5
Wivelsfield 35 D6
Wivelsfield Green . . 35 D6
Wivenhoe 71 A4
Wivenhoe Cross . . . 71 A4
Wiveton 120 A2
Wix 71 A5
Wixford 80 B3
Wixhill 111 C4
Wixoe 86 C3
Woburn 83 D6
Woburn Sands 83 D6
Wokefield Park 47 C4
Woking 34 A3
Wokingham 47 C6
Wolborough 12 D3
Woldingham 35 A6
Wold Newton
  E Yorks 160 D4
  NE Lincs 143 D4
Wolfclyde 195 C5
Wolferton 118 C3
Wolfhill 219 A6
Wolf's Castle 55 B5
Wolfsdale 55 B5
Woll 186 A3
Wollaston
  Northants 83 A6
  Shrops 110 D2
Wollaton 114 B3
Wollerton 111 B5
Wollescote 96 C2
Wolsingham 166 B3
Wolstanton 112 A2
Wolston 97 D7
Wolvercote 65 C5
Wolverhampton . . . 96 B2
Wolverley
  Shrops 110 B3
  Worcs 95 D6
Wolverton
  Hants 46 D3
  M Keynes 83 C5

Wolverton continued
Warks....81 A5
Wolverton Common.46 D3
Wolvesnewton....61 D6
Wolvey....98 C1
Wolviston....168 C2
Wombleton....159 C5
Wombourne....95 B6
Wombwell....140 C1
Womenswold....53 D4
Womersley....140 B3
Wonastow....61 B6
Wonersh....34 B3
Wonson....12 C1
Wonston....32 B3
Wooburn....48 A2
Wooburn Green....48 A2
Woodacott....11 A4
Woodale....156 D4
Woodbank....190 D2
Woodbastwick....121 D5
Woodbeck....132 B2
Woodborough
Notts....115 A4
Wilts....45 D5
Woodbridge
Dorset....29 D7
Suff....88 C3
Woodbury....13 C5
Woodbury Salterton.13 C5
Woodchester....63 C4
Woodchurch
Kent....38 B1
Mers....126 A2
Woodcombe....27 A4
Woodcote....47 A4
Woodcott....46 D2
Woodcroft....62 D1
Woodcutts....30 D3
Wood Dalling....120 C2
Woodditton....86 B2
Woodeaton....65 B6
Woodend
Cumb....153 A2
Northants....82 C3
W Sus....19 A7
Wood End
Herts....68 A3
Warks....96 D4
Warks....97 B5
Wood Enderby....134 C2
Woodend Green....82 C3
Woodfalls....31 C5
Woodfield
Oxon....65 A6
S Ayrs....192 C3
Wood Field....35 A4
Woodford
Corn....24 D3
Devon....8 B1
Glos....62 D2
Gtr Man....128 A3
London....68 D4
Northants....99 D6
Woodford Bridge....68 D4
Woodford Halse....82 B2
Woodgate
Norf....120 D2
W Mid....96 C2
Worcs....80 A2
W Sus....20 B2
Woodgreen....31 D5
Wood Green....68 D3
Woodhall
Herts....68 B2
Invclyd....204 A3
N Yorks....156 B3
Woodhall Spa....134 C1
Woodham....48 C3
Woodham Ferrers....70 D1
Woodham Mortimer.70 C2
Woodham Walter....70 C2
Woodhaven....220 B4
Wood Hayes....96 A2
Woodhead....256 C2
Woodhey....137 B6
Woodhill....95 C5
Woodhorn....179 A4
Woodhouse
Leics....114 D3
N Lincs....141 C5
S Yorks....131 A4
W Yorks....140 A1
W Yorks....148 D1
Woodhouse Eaves.114 D3
Woodhouselee..209 D5
Woodhouselees...175 A6
Woodhouse Park..128 A3

Woodhouses....113 D5
Woodhurst....101 D5
Woodingdean....21 B6
Woodkirk....139 A5
Woodland
Devon....8 A1
Durham....166 C3
Woodlands
Aberds....245 C4
Dorset....17 A4
Hants....32 D2
Highld....264 D1
N Yorks....148 B2
S Yorks....140 C3
Woodlands Park....47 B6
Woodlands St Mary.46 B1
Woodlane....113 C5
Wood Lanes....129 A4
Woodleigh....7 C6
Woodlesford....139 A6
Woodley
Gtr Man....138 D2
Wokingham....47 B5
Woodmancote
Glos....62 D3
Glos....63 A5
Glos....63 C6
W Sus....19 A6
W Sus....21 A5
Woodmancott....33 A4
Woodmansey....150 D3
Woodmansterne....35 A5
Woodminton....31 C4
Woodnesborough....53 D5
Woodnewton....100 B2
Wood Norton....120 C2
Woodplumpton....145 D5
Woodrising....103 A5
Woodseaves
Shrops....111 B5
Staffs....112 C1
Woodsend....45 B6
Woodsetts....131 A5
Woodsford....16 B1
Wood's Green....36 C4
Woodside
Aberdeen....245 B6
Aberds....257 B5
Brack....48 B2
Fife....220 D4
Hants....18 B1
Herts....68 C2
Perth....220 A2
**Woodside of
Arbeadie**....245 C4
Woodstock
Oxon....65 B5
Pembs....55 B6
Wood Street
Norf....121 C5
Sur....34 A2
Woodthorpe
Derbys....131 B4
Leics....114 D3
Lincs....135 A4
York....149 C4
Woodton....104 B3
Woodtown
Devon....25 C5
Devon....25 C5
Woodvale....136 B2
Woodville....113 D7
Woodyates....31 D4
Woofferton....78 A3
Wookey....29 A5
Wookey Hole....29 A5
Wool....16 C2
Woolacombe....25 A5
Woolage Green....39 A4
Woolaston....62 D1
Woolavington....28 A3
Woolbeding....34 D1
Wooldale....139 C4
Wooler....188 A2
Woolfardisworthy
Devon....12 A3
Devon....24 C4
**Woolfords
Cottages**....195 A5
Woolhampton....46 C3
Woolhope....79 D4
**Woolhope
Cockshoot**....79 D4
Woolland....16 A1
Woollaton....25 D5
Woolley
Bath....43 C6
Cambs....100 D3
Corn....24 D3

Woolley continued
Derbys....130 C3
W Yorks....139 B6
Woolmere Green....80 A2
Woolmer Green....68 B2
Woolpit....87 A5
Woolscott....82 A1
Woolsington....178 C3
Woolstanwood....128 D1
Woolstaston....94 B2
Woolsthorpe
Lincs....115 B6
Lincs....116 C2
Woolston
Devon....7 C6
Shrops....94 C2
Shrops....110 C2
Soton....32 D3
Warr....127 A6
Woolstone
M Keynes....83 D5
Oxon....45 A6
Woolton....127 A4
Woolton Hill....46 C2
Woolverstone....88 D2
Woolverton....44 D1
Woolwich....50 B1
Woolwich Ferry....50 B1
Woonton....78 B1
Wooperton....188 A3
Woore....111 A6
Wootten Green....104 D3
Wootton
Bedford....84 C2
Hants....17 B6
Hereford....78 B1
Kent....39 A4
N Lincs....142 B2
Northants....83 B4
Oxon....65 B5
Oxon....65 C5
Shrops....94 C2
Shrops....110 C2
Staffs....112 C2
Staffs....113 A5
Wootton Bridge....18 B4
Wootton Common....18 B4
Wootton Courtenay.27 A4
Wootton Fitzpaine.14 B3
Wootton Rivers....45 C5
**Wootton
St Lawrence**....46 D3
Wootton Wawen....81 A4
Worcester....79 B6
Worcester Park....49 C5
Wordsley....96 C1
Worfield....95 B5
Work....282 F5
Workington....162 B2
Worksop....131 B5
Worlaby....142 B2
World's End....46 B2
Worle....42 C2
Worleston....127 D6
Worlingham....105 C5
Worlington....102 D2
Worlingworth....88 A3
Wormald Green....148 A2
Wormbridge....78 D2
Wormegay....118 D3
Wormelow Tump....78 D2
Wormhill....129 B6
Wormingford....87 D5
Worminghall....66 C1
Wormington....80 D3
Worminster....29 A5
Wormit....220 B3
Wormleighton....82 B1
Wormley
Herts....68 C3
Sur....34 C2
Wormley West End....68 C3
Wormshill....37 A6
Wormsley....78 C2
Worplesdon....34 A2
Worrall....139 D6
Worsbrough....139 C6
**Worsbrough
Common**....139 C6
Worsley....137 C6
Worstead....121 C5
Worsthorne....146 D2
Worston....146 C1
Worswell....7 C4
Worth
Kent....53 D5
W Sus....35 C6
Wortham....104 D1
Worthen....94 A1
Worthenbury....110 A3

Worthing
Norf....120 D1
W Sus....21 B4
Worthington....114 C2
Worth Matravers....16 D3
Worting....47 D4
Wortley
S Yorks....139 D6
W Yorks....147 D6
Worton
N Yorks....156 B3
Wilts....44 D3
Wortwell....104 C3
Wotherton....93 A6
Wotter....7 A4
Wotton....35 B4
Wotton-under-Edge 62 D3
Wotton Underwood.66 B1
**Woughton on the
Green**....83 D5
Wouldham....51 C4
Wrabness....88 D2
Wrafton....25 B5
Wragby
Lincs....133 B6
W Yorks....140 B2
Wragholme....143 D5
Wramplingham....104 A2
Wrangbrook....140 B2
Wrangham....256 C1
Wrangle....135 D4
Wrangle Bank....135 D4
Wrangle Lowgate....135 D4
Wrangway....27 D6
Wrantage....28 C3
Wrawby....142 C2
Wraxall
Dorset....15 A5
N Som....42 B3
Som....29 B6
Wray....145 A6
Wraysbury....48 B3
Wrayton....155 D5
Wrea Green....144 D3
Wreay
Cumb....164 A2
Cumb....164 C2
Wrecclesham....34 B1
Wrecsam
=Wrexham....126 D3
Wrekenton....179 D4
Wrelton....159 C6
Wrenbury....111 A4
Wrench Green....160 C3
Wreningham....104 B2
Wrentham....105 C5
Wrenthorpe....139 A6
Wrentnall....94 A2
Wressle
E Yorks....149 D6
N Lincs....142 C1
Wrestlingworth....85 C4
Wretham....103 C5
Wretton....102 B2
Wrexham
=Wrecsam....126 D3
**Wrexham Industrial
Estate**....110 A2
Wribbenhall....95 D5
Wrightington Bar....136 B4
Wrinehill....111 A6
Wrington....42 C3
Writhlington....43 D6
Writtle....69 C6
Wrockwardine....111 D5
Wroot....141 C5
Wrotham....36 A4
Wrotham Heath....36 A4
Wroughton....45 A5
Wroxall
IoW....19 D4
Warks....97 D5
Wroxeter....94 A3
Wroxham....121 D5
Wroxton....81 C7
Wyaston....113 A5
Wyberton....117 A6
Wyboston....84 B3
Wybunbury....111 A6
Wychbold....80 A2
Wych Cross....36 C2
Wyck....33 B6
Wyck Rissington....64 A2
Wycoller....146 D3
Wycomb....115 C5
Wycombe Marsh....66 D3
Wyddial....85 D5
Wye....38 A2
Wyesham....61 B7
Wyfordby....115 D5

Wyke
Dorset....30 C1
Shrops....95 A4
Sur....34 A2
W Yorks....139 A4
Wykeham
N Yorks....159 D7
N Yorks....160 C3
Wyken....97 C6
Wyke Regis....15 D6
Wykey....110 C2
Wylam....178 C3
Wylde Green....96 B4
Wyllie....41 B6
Wylye....31 B4
Wymering....19 A5
Wymeswold....115 C4
Wymington....83 A6
Wymondham
Leics....115 D6
Norf....104 A2
Wyndham....40 B4
Wynford Eagle....15 B5
Wyng....283 H4
Wynyard Village....168 C2
Wyre Piddle....80 C2
Wysall....115 C4
Wythall....96 D3
Wytham....65 C5
Wythburn....163 C6
Wythenshawe....128 A3
Wythop Mill....163 B6
Wyton....101 D4
Wyverstone....87 A6
Wyverstone Street....87 A6
Wyville....116 C1
Wyvis Lodge....263 C6

Y

Yaddlethorpe....141 C6
Yafford....18 C3
Yafforth....158 B2
Yalding....37 A4
Yanworth....63 B6
Yapham....149 B6
Yapton....20 B2
Yarburgh....143 D5
Yarcombe....14 A2
Yard....27 B5
Yardley....96 C4
Yardley Gobion....83 C4
Yardley Hastings....83 B5
Yardro....77 B6
Yarkhill....79 C4
Yarlet....112 C3
Yarlington....29 C6
Yarlside....153 D3
Yarm....168 D2
Yarmouth....18 C2
Yarnbrook....44 D2
Yarnfield....112 B2
Yarnscombe....25 C6
Yarnton....65 B5
Yarpole....78 A2
Yarrow....196 D2
Yarrow Feus....196 D2
Yarsop....78 C2
Yarwell....100 B2
Yate....43 A6
Yateley....47 C6
Yatesbury....45 B4
Yattendon....46 B3
Yatton
Hereford....78 A2
N Som....42 C3
Yatton Keynell....44 B2
Yaverland....19 C5
Yaxham....120 D2
Yaxley
Cambs....100 B3
Suff....104 D2
Yazor....78 C2
Y Bala =Bala....108 B4
Y Barri =Barry....41 E6
**Y Bont-Faen
=Cowbridge**....41 D4
**Y Drenewydd
=Newtown**....93 B5
Yeading....48 A4
Yeadon....147 C6
Yealand Conyers....154 D4
Yealand Redmayne.154 D4
Yealmpton....7 B4
Yearby....168 C4
Yearsley....159 D4
Yeaton....110 D3
Yeaveley....113 A5
Yedingham....160 D2

Yeldon....84 A2
Yelford....65 C4
Yelland....25 B5
Yelling....85 A4
Yelvertoft....98 D2
Yelverton
Devon....7 A4
Norf....104 A3
Yenston....29 C7
Yeoford....12 B2
Yeolmbridge....10 C4
Yeo Mill....26 C3
Yeovil....29 D5
Yeovil Marsh....29 D5
Yeovilton....29 C5
Yerbeston....55 D6
Yesnaby....282 F3
Yetlington....188 C3
Yetminster....29 D5
Yettington....13 C5
Yetts o' Muckhart....219 D5
Y Felinheli....123 D5
**Y Fenni
=Abergavenny**....61 B4
Y Fflint =Flint....126 B2
Y Ffôr....106 C3
Y-Ffrith....125 A5
**Y Gelli Gandryll
=Hay-on-Wye**....77 C6
Yieldshields....194 A3
Yiewsley....48 A3
**Y Mwmbwls
=The Mumbles**....57 D6
Ynysboeth....41 B5
Ynysddu....41 B6
Ynysgyfflog....90 A4
Ynyshir....41 B5
Ynyslas....90 C4
Ynys-meudwy....59 E4
Ynystawe....40 A1
Ynysybwl....41 B5
Yockenthwaite....156 D3
Yockleton....110 D2
Yokefleet....141 A6
Yoker....205 B5
Yonder Bognie....255 B6
York....149 B4
Yorkletts....52 C2
Yorkley....62 C2
York Town....47 C6
Yorton....111 C4
Youlgreave....130 C2
Youlstone....24 D3
Youlthorpe....149 B6
Youlton....148 A3
Young's End....70 B1
Young Wood....133 B6
Yoxall....113 D5
Yoxford....89 A4
Y Pîl =Pyle....40 C3
Yr Hôb =Hope....126 D3
Y Rhws =Rhoose....41 E5
Y Rhyl =Rhyl....125 A5
**Yr Wyddgrug
=Mold**....126 C2
Ysbyty-Cynfyn....75 A6
Ysbyty Ifan....108 A3
Ysbyty Ystwyth....75 A6
Ysceifiog....125 B6
Yspitty....57 C5
Ystalyfera....59 E4
Ystrad....41 B4
Ystrad Aeron....75 C4
Ystradfellte....59 D6
Ystradffin....76 C1
Ystradgynlais....59 D4
Ystradmeurig....75 B6
Ystrad-mynach....41 B6
Ystradowen
Carms....59 D4
V Glam....41 D5
Ystumtuen....75 A6
Ythanbank....257 C4
Ythanwells....256 C1
Ythsie....256 C3
**Y Trallwng
=Welshpool**....93 A6
Y Waun =Chirk....110 B1

Z

Zeal Monachorum....12 A2
Zeals....30 B1
Zelah....4 B3
Zennor....2 B2